기출 프리미엄

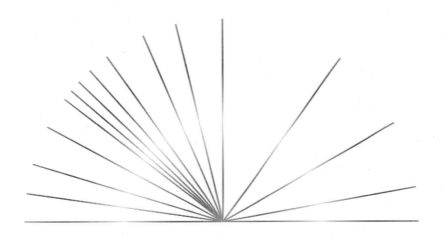

Premium

저자

김기훈 現 ㈜ 쎄듀 대표이사
現 메가스터디 영어영역 대표강사
前 서울특별시 교육청 외국어 교육정책자문위원회 위원
저서 천일문 / 천일문 Training Book / 천일문 GRAMMAR
첫단추 BASIC / 쎄듀 본영어 / 어휘끝 / 어법끝 / 문법의 골든룰 101
절대평가 PLAN A / 리딩 플랫폼 / ALL씀 서술형
Reading Relay / The 리딩플레이어 / 빈칸백서 / 오답백서
첫단추 / 파워업 / 수능영어 절대유형 / 수능실감 등

쎄듀 영어교육연구센터
쎄듀 영어교육센터는 영어 콘텐츠에 대한 전문지식과 경험을 바탕으로
최고의 교육 콘텐츠를 만들고자 최선의 노력을 다하는 전문가 집단입니다.
오혜정 센터장 · **장정문** 선임연구원 · **김진경** 전임연구원 · **오승은** 연구원 · **남현화** 연구원

마케팅 콘텐츠 마케팅 사업본부
영업 문병구
제작 정승호
인디자인 편집 올댓에디팅
디자인 윤혜영·정지은

Preface

이 책을 내며

대수능 영어는 18학년도 절대평가 전환, 22학년도 간접연계 100% 전환, 24학년도 '킬러문항' 배제 등 적지 않은 변동을 겪고 있다. 이중 가장 큰 변화는 간접연계 100% 전환이다. 간접연계는 사실상 비연계와 다름이 없으므로, 학생들은 EBS 연계교재에서 보지 못했던 지문들로만 구성된 수능 영어를 치르게 된다. 과거 EBS 직접연계 시행 시절의 비정상적인 학습 행태로는 더 이상 효과를 보기 힘들어졌고, 진정한 영어 실력의 향상만이 1등급을 향할 수 있는 근본 대책이 되었다. 이는 현재 킬러문항 배제 시대에도 마찬가지이다.

진정한 영어 실력을 갖추기 위해서는 정확한 문장 해석력과 어휘력, 더 나아가 문제 해결력이 필요하다. 하루아침에 이루어지기는 힘들지만, 절대평가이기 때문에 다른 수험생들의 실력과 상관없이 오로지 나의 실력만 키우면 원하는 등급을 보장받는다. 꾸준히 올바른 방향으로만 하면 된다는 생각으로, 자신감과 신념을 가지고 학습해 나가도록 하자.

문장 해석력과 어휘력을 갖추는 것은 기본적으로 해야 할 일이고, 킬러문항 배제 이후의 모평과 수능에서 요구하는 문제 해결력은 다양한 능력을 포함한다.

❶ 지문의 많은 정보 중 핵심에 해당하는 것을 정확히 잡아내면서 읽을 수 있어야 한다. 핵심을 오판하거나 핵심이 아닌 부분에 휘둘리면 시간을 낭비하게 되고 오답으로 이끌릴 확률이 높아진다.

❷ 지문의 핵심을 이해했다고 해도, 저절로 정답이 보이는 시험이 아니다. 매력적인 오답을 소거하면서 매력 없는 정답을 골라낼 수 있는 논리 사고력이 필요하다.

위의 내용이 구체적으로 어떤 의미인지를 가장 잘 이해할 수 있는 것은 기출이다. 모두가 기출을 풀지만, 기출에서 얻어야 할 많은 것을 놓치고 있다는 생각이 든다. 기출에서 반복 출제되고 있는 함정에 매년 빠지는 것만 봐도 알 수 있다. 25학년도 수능을 치를 수험생들은 더더군다나 24학년도 수능을 비롯하여 역대 기출에 대한 면밀한 분석과 철저한 준비가 필요하다. 방향이 옳으면 속도는 문제가 되지 않는다고 했다. 이 책으로 역대 기출이 우리에게 주는 모든 메시지를 제대로, 정확히 이해하도록 하자. 이를 방향타로 삼아, 여러분의 앞날에 찬란한 미래가 함께 하기를 간절히 기원한다.

저자

ABOUT THIS BOOK

1 PART 1과 2의 단계적 학습

Part 1은 유형별로 해법을 집중 정리한다. 3문제씩 이틀 간 학습하며, DAY 1st로는 전략을 집중해서 익히고 DAY 2nd로는 학습한 전략을 적용해볼 수 있게 하였다. 이를 바탕으로, Part 2는 주요 유형을 고루 접하면서 학습할 수 있다. 또한 문제 순서는 가장 최신 것부터 수록하였으므로, 24학년도 수능을 가장 먼저 접할 수 있다.

PART 1 + **DAY 1st** 전략 익히기 + **DAY 2nd** 전략 적용하기

PART 2 + 주요 유형을 고루 접하면서 학습

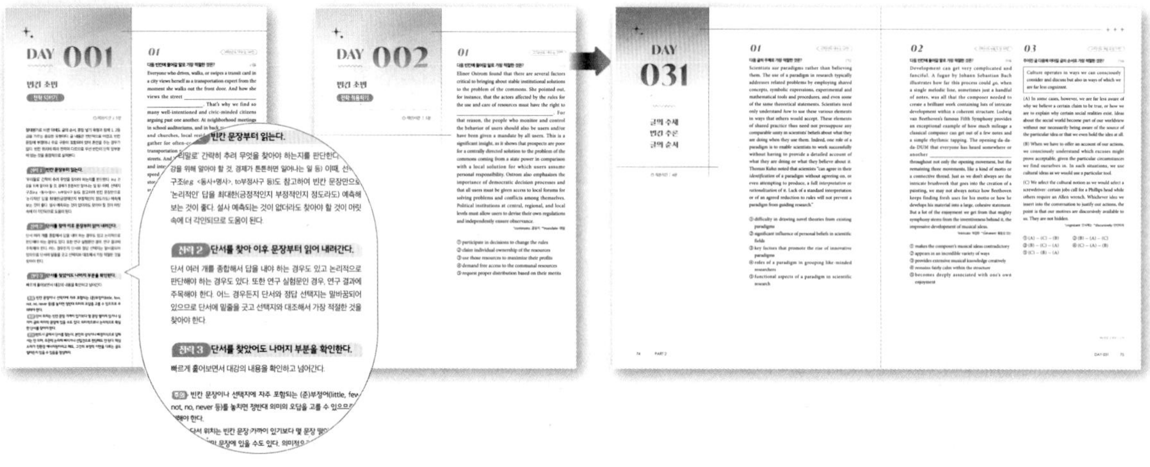

2 빈칸, 순서, 문장 넣기 등 주요 문제 집중 수록

아래 표에서 볼 수 있듯이, 매년 오답률 상위를 차지하는 빈칸, 순서, 문장 넣기를 집중 수록하였다. 따라서, 충분한 양의 주요 문제를 학습할 수 있다.

유형	총 수록 문항 수	유형	총 수록 문항 수
빈칸 추론	92문항	글의 제목	16문항
글의 순서	39문항	무관 문장	16문항
문장 넣기	39문항	요약문	16문항
함의 추론	17문항	복합 유형	24문항
필자 주장	8문항	밑줄 어법	11문항
글의 요지	8문항	낱말 쓰임	11문항
글의 주제	16문항		

3 부록: 역대 킬러 문항 수록

킬러 문항으로 발표된 것들과 그 기준에 합당하는 역대 킬러 문항 13문항을 부록으로 수록하였다. 참고로 하기 바란다.

4 자세하고 친절한 해설

❶ 구문 분석 & 직독직해
❷ 글의 소재
❸ 해석 및 어휘
❹ 도입/주제문/세부 사항 구분 및 내용 요약
❺ 의미 이해를 돕는 추가 설명
❻ 주요 문법 설명
❼ 정답 단서 표시
❽ 글의 이해를 돕는 유용한 배경지식

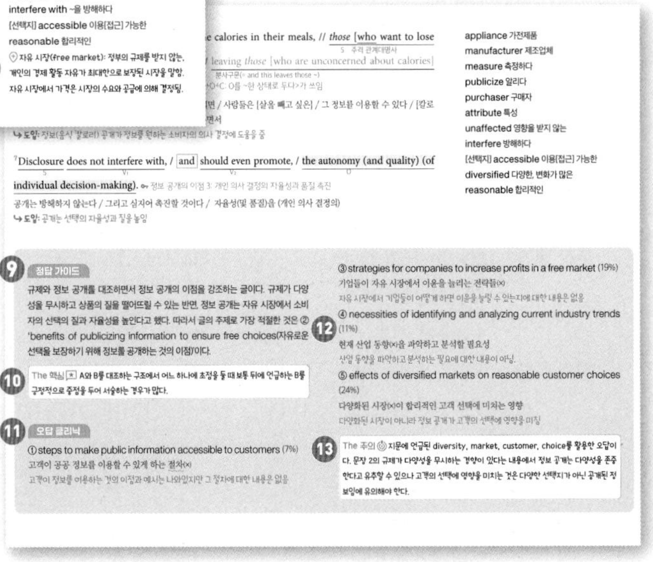

❾ 정답 도출 과정을 자세히 설명한 정답 가이드
❿ 유사 문제에 대한 실전 적용력을 길러주는 The 핵심
⓫ 오답 이유를 명쾌하게 설명한 오답 클리닉
⓬ 오답률 표시
⓭ 재발 방지를 위한 선택률 높은 오답 분석 The 주의

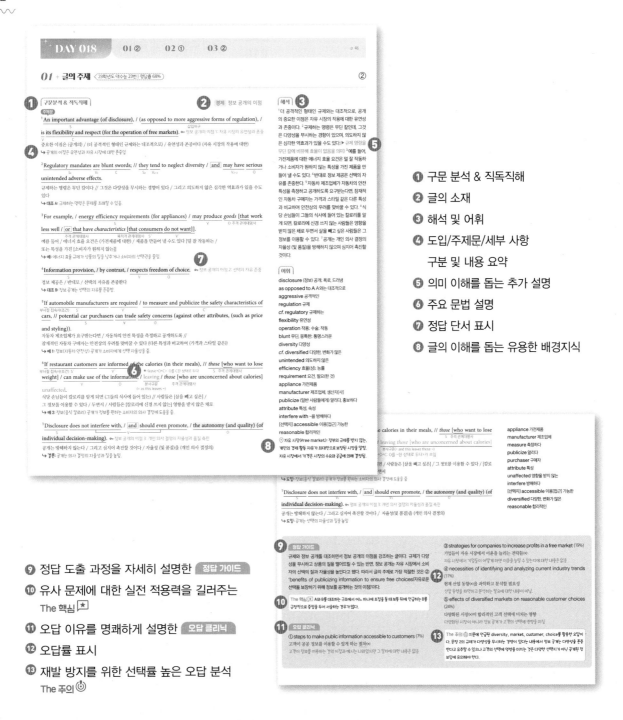

CONTENTS

PART 1 유형별 집중 학습

DAY			정오체크	문제	정답
DAY 031	글의 주제	수능 22년 23번	□	74	120
	빈칸 추론	모평 23년 6월 34번	□		
	글의 순서	모평 23년 9월 37번	□		
DAY 032	글의 제목	수능 22년 24번	□	76	124
	빈칸 추론	모평 23년 6월 33번	□		
	문장 넣기	수능 23년 38번	□		
DAY 033	함의 추론	모평 22년 9월 21번	□	78	128
	빈칸 추론	모평 23년 6월 32번	□		
	무관 문장	수능 22년 35번	□		
DAY 034	글의 요지	수능 23년 22번	□	80	132
	빈칸 추론	모평 22년 9월 32번	□		
	글의 순서	모평 23년 9월 36번	□		
DAY 035	필자 주장	수능 23년 20번	□	82	136
	빈칸 추론	모평 22년 9월 33번	□		
	문장 넣기	모평 23년 9월 39번	□		
DAY 036	요약문	수능 22년 40번	□	84	140
	복합 유형	모평 24년 6월 41~42번	□		
DAY 037	빈칸 추론	모평 22년 9월 31번	□	86	144
	글의 순서	모평 23년 6월 37번	□		
	문장 넣기	모평 23년 9월 38번	□		
DAY 038	글의 주제	모평 22년 9월 23번	□	88	148
	빈칸 추론	모평 22년 6월 32번	□		
	글의 순서	모평 23년 6월 36번	□		
DAY 039	글의 제목	모평 22년 9월 24번	□	90	152
	빈칸 추론	수능 21년 34번	□		
	문장 넣기	모평 23년 6월 39번	□		
DAY 040	함의 추론	모평 22년 6월 21번	□	92	156
	빈칸 추론	수능 21년 33번	□		
	무관 문장	모평 22년 9월 35번	□		
DAY 041	글의 요지	모평 23년 9월 22번	□	94	160
	빈칸 추론	수능 21년 32번	□		
	글의 순서	수능 22년 37번	□		
DAY 042	필자 주장	모평 23년 9월 20번	□	96	164
	빈칸 추론	수능 21년 31번	□		
	문장 넣기	모평 23년 6월 38번	□		
DAY 043	요약문	모평 22년 9월 40번	□	98	168
	복합 유형	수능 23년 41~42번	□		
DAY 044	빈칸 추론	모평 21년 9월 34번	□	100	171
	글의 순서	수능 22년 36번	□		
	문장 넣기	수능 22년 39번	□		
DAY 045	글의 주제	모평 22년 6월 23번	□	102	175
	빈칸 추론	모평 21년 9월 33번	□		
	글의 순서	모평 22년 9월 37번	□		

DAY			정오체크	문제	정답
DAY 046	글의 제목	모평 22년 6월 24번	□	104	179
	빈칸 추론	모평 21년 9월 32번	□		
	문장 넣기	모평 22년 9월 38번	□		
DAY 047	함의 추론	수능 21년 21번	□	106	183
	빈칸 추론	모평 21년 9월 31번	□		
	무관 문장	모평 22년 6월 35번	□		
DAY 048	글의 요지	모평 23년 6월 22번	□	108	187
	빈칸 추론	모평 21년 6월 34번	□		
	글의 순서	모평 22년 9월 36번	□		
DAY 049	필자 주장	모평 23년 6월 20번	□	110	191
	빈칸 추론	모평 21년 6월 33번	□		
	문장 넣기	모평 22년 6월 39번	□		
DAY 050	요약문	모평 22년 6월 40번	□	112	195
	복합 유형	모평 23년 9월 41~42번	□		
DAY 051	빈칸 추론	모평 21년 6월 32번	□	114	198
	글의 순서	모평 22년 6월 37번	□		
	문장 넣기	모평 22년 6월 38번	□		
DAY 052	글의 주제	수능 21년 23번	□	116	202
	빈칸 추론	모평 21년 6월 31번	□		
	글의 순서	수능 21년 37번	□		
DAY 053	글의 제목	수능 21년 24번	□	118	206
	빈칸 추론	수능 20년 34번	□		
	문장 넣기	수능 21년 39번	□		
DAY 054	함의 추론	모평 21년 9월 21번	□	120	210
	빈칸 추론	수능 20년 33번	□		
	무관 문장	수능 21년 35번	□		
DAY 055	글의 요지	수능 22년 22번	□	122	214
	빈칸 추론	수능 20년 32번	□		
	글의 순서	수능 21년 36번	□		
DAY 056	필자 주장	수능 22년 20번	□	124	218
	빈칸 추론	수능 20년 31번	□		
	문장 넣기	수능 21년 38번	□		
DAY 057	요약문	수능 21년 40번	□	126	222
	복합 유형	모평 23년 6월 41~42번	□		
DAY 058	빈칸 추론	모평 20년 9월 34번	□	128	226
	글의 순서	모평 21년 9월 37번	□		
	문장 넣기	모평 21년 9월 39번	□		
DAY 059	글의 주제	모평 21년 9월 23번	□	130	230
	빈칸 추론	모평 20년 9월 33번	□		
	글의 순서	모평 21년 9월 36번	□		
DAY 060	글의 제목	모평 21년 9월 24번	□	132	234
	빈칸 추론	모평 20년 9월 32번	□		
	문장 넣기	모평 21년 9월 38번	□		

DAY	유형	출처	정오체크	문제	정답
DAY 061	함의 추론	모평 21년 6월 21번	☐	134	238
	빈칸 추론	모평 20년 9월 31번	☐		
	무관 문장	모평 21년 9월 35번	☐		
DAY 062	글의 요지	모평 22년 9월 22번	☐	136	242
	빈칸 추론	모평 20년 6월 33번	☐		
	글의 순서	모평 21년 6월 37번	☐		
DAY 063	필자 주장	모평 22년 9월 20번	☐	138	246
	빈칸 추론	모평 20년 6월 32번	☐		
	문장 넣기	모평 21년 6월 39번	☐		
DAY 064	요약문	모평 21년 9월 40번	☐	140	250
	복합 유형	수능 22년 41~42번	☐		
			☐		
DAY 065	빈칸 추론	모평 20년 6월 31번	☐	142	253
	글의 순서	모평 21년 6월 36번	☐		
	문장 넣기	모평 21년 6월 38번	☐		
DAY 066	글의 주제	모평 21년 6월 23번	☐	144	257
	빈칸 추론	수능 19년 33번	☐		
	글의 순서	수능 20년 37번	☐		
DAY 067	글의 제목	모평 21년 6월 24번	☐	146	261
	빈칸 추론	수능 19년 32번	☐		
	문장 넣기	수능 20년 39번	☐		
DAY 068	함의 추론	수능 20년 21번	☐	148	265
	빈칸 추론	수능 19년 31번	☐		
	무관 문장	모평 21년 6월 35번	☐		
DAY 069	밑줄 어법	수능 22년 29번	☐	150	269
	빈칸 추론	모평 19년 9월 34번	☐		
	글의 순서	수능 20년 36번	☐		
DAY 070	낱말 쓰임	수능 22년 30번	☐	152	273
	빈칸 추론	모평 19년 9월 33번	☐		
	문장 넣기	수능 20년 38번	☐		
DAY 071	요약문	모평 21년 6월 40번	☐	154	277
	복합 유형	모평 22년 9월 41~42번	☐		
			☐		
DAY 072	빈칸 추론	모평 19년 9월 32번	☐	156	280
	글의 순서	모평 20년 9월 37번	☐		
	문장 넣기	모평 20년 9월 39번	☐		
DAY 073	글의 주제	수능 20년 23번	☐	158	284
	빈칸 추론	모평 19년 9월 31번	☐		
	글의 순서	모평 20년 9월 36번	☐		
DAY 074	글의 제목	수능 20년 24번	☐	160	288
	빈칸 추론	모평 19년 6월 33번	☐		
	문장 넣기	모평 20년 9월 38번	☐		
DAY 075	함의 추론	모평 20년 9월 21번	☐	162	292
	빈칸 추론	모평 19년 6월 32번	☐		
	무관 문장	수능 20년 35번	☐		

DAY	유형	출처	정오체크	문제	정답
DAY 076	밑줄 어법	모평 22년 9월 29번	☐	164	296
	빈칸 추론	모평 19년 6월 31번	☐		
	글의 순서	모평 20년 6월 37번	☐		
DAY 077	낱말 쓰임	모평 22년 9월 30번	☐	166	300
	빈칸 추론	수능 18년 34번	☐		
	문장 넣기	모평 20년 6월 39번	☐		
DAY 078	요약문	수능 20년 40번	☐	168	304
	복합 유형	모평 22년 6월 41~42번	☐		
			☐		
DAY 079	빈칸 추론	수능 18년 33번	☐	170	307
	글의 순서	모평 20년 6월 36번	☐		
	문장 넣기	모평 20년 6월 38번	☐		
DAY 080	글의 주제	모평 20년 9월 23번	☐	172	311
	빈칸 추론	수능 18년 32번	☐		
	글의 순서	수능 19년 37번	☐		
DAY 081	글의 제목	모평 20년 9월 24번	☐	174	315
	빈칸 추론	수능 18년 31번	☐		
	문장 넣기	수능 19년 39번	☐		
DAY 082	함의 추론	모평 20년 6월 21번	☐	176	319
	빈칸 추론	모평 18년 9월 34번	☐		
	무관 문장	모평 20년 9월 35번	☐		
DAY 083	밑줄 어법	모평 22년 6월 29번	☐	178	323
	빈칸 추론	모평 18년 9월 33번	☐		
	글의 순서	수능 19년 36번	☐		
DAY 084	낱말 쓰임	모평 22년 6월 30번	☐	180	327
	빈칸 추론	모평 18년 9월 32번	☐		
	문장 넣기	수능 19년 38번	☐		
DAY 085	요약문	모평 20년 9월 40번	☐	182	331
	복합 유형	수능 21년 41~42번	☐		
			☐		
DAY 086	빈칸 추론	모평 18년 9월 31번	☐	184	334
	글의 순서	모평 19년 9월 37번	☐		
	문장 넣기	모평 19년 9월 39번	☐		
DAY 087	글의 주제	모평 20년 6월 23번	☐	186	338
	빈칸 추론	모평 18년 6월 34번	☐		
	글의 순서	모평 19년 9월 36번	☐		
DAY 088	글의 제목	모평 20년 6월 24번	☐	188	342
	빈칸 추론	모평 18년 6월 33번	☐		
	문장 넣기	모평 19년 9월 38번	☐		
DAY 089	함의 추론	수능 19년 21번	☐	190	346
	빈칸 추론	모평 18년 6월 32번	☐		
	무관 문장	모평 20년 6월 35번	☐		
DAY 090	밑줄 어법	수능 21년 29번	☐	192	350
	빈칸 추론	모평 18년 6월 31번	☐		
	글의 순서	모평 19년 6월 37번	☐		

			정오체크	문제	정답
DAY 091	낱말 쓰임	수능 21년 30번	☐	194	354
	빈칸 추론	수능 17년 34번	☐		
	문장 넣기	모평 19년 6월 39번	☐		
DAY 092	요약문	모평 20년 6월 40번	☐	196	358
	복합 유형	모평 21년 9월 41~42번	☐ ☐		
DAY 093	빈칸 추론	수능 17년 33번	☐	198	361
	글의 순서	모평 19년 6월 36번	☐		
	문장 넣기	모평 19년 6월 38번	☐		
DAY 094	글의 주제	수능 19년 23번	☐	200	365
	빈칸 추론	수능 17년 32번	☐		
	글의 순서	수능 18년 37번	☐		
DAY 095	글의 제목	수능 19년 24번	☐	202	369
	빈칸 추론	수능 17년 31번	☐		
	문장 넣기	수능 18년 39번	☐		
DAY 096	함의 추론	모평 19년 9월 21번	☐	204	373
	빈칸 추론	모평 17년 9월 34번	☐		
	무관 문장	수능 19년 35번	☐		
DAY 097	밑줄 어법	모평 21년 9월 29번	☐	206	377
	빈칸 추론	모평 17년 6월 34번	☐		
	글의 순서	수능 18년 36번	☐		
DAY 098	낱말 쓰임	모평 21년 9월 30번	☐	208	381
	빈칸 추론	모평 17년 6월 33번	☐		
	문장 넣기	수능 18년 38번	☐		
DAY 099	요약문	수능 19년 40번	☐	210	385
	복합 유형	모평 21년 6월 41~42번	☐ ☐		
DAY 100	빈칸 추론	모평 17년 6월 32번	☐	212	388
	글의 순서	모평 18년 9월 37번	☐		
	문장 넣기	모평 18년 9월 39번	☐		

부록 초고난도 킬러 문항

		정오체크	문제	정답
함의 추론	수능 22년 21번	☐	216	392
빈칸 추론	모평 24년 6월 33번	☐		
빈칸 추론	모평 24년 6월 34번	☐		
빈칸 추론	수능 23년 34번	☐		
빈칸 추론	수능 22년 34번	☐		
빈칸 추론	모평 22년 6월 31번	☐		
빈칸 추론	모평 20년 6월 34번	☐		
빈칸 추론	수능 19년 34번	☐		
빈칸 추론	모평 19년 6월 34번	☐		
글의 순서	수능 23년 37번	☐		
글의 순서	모평 22년 6월 36번	☐		
문장 넣기	수능 22년 38번	☐		
문장 넣기	모평 22년 9월 39번	☐		

PART 1

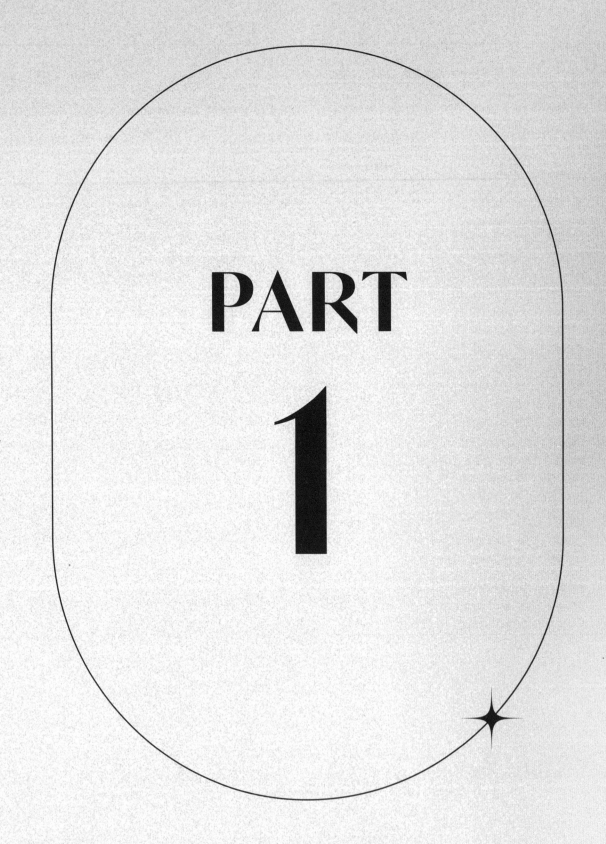

DAY 001~030

유형별 집중 학습

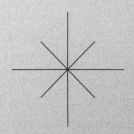

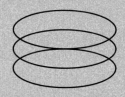

Part 1에서는 수능과 모의고사에 출제되는
주요 유형 13가지의 해결 전략을 집중해서 알아봅니다.
학습한 전략은 기출 문제에 바로 적용해보며 익혀보세요.
본격적인 문제풀이는 Part 2에서 이어집니다.

DAY 001

빈칸 초반

전략 익히기

⏱ 제한시간 | 5분

절대평가로 바뀐 뒤에도 글의 순서, 문장 넣기 유형과 함께 1, 2등급을 가르는 중요한 유형이다. 글 내용은 전반적으로 어렵고, 빈칸 문장에 부정어나 주요 구문이 포함되어 있어 혼란을 주는 경우가 많다. 빈칸 위치에 따라 전략이 다르므로 우선 빈칸이 단락 앞부분에 있는 것을 중점적으로 살펴본다.

전략 1 빈칸 문장부터 읽는다.

'우리말로' 간략히 추려 무엇을 찾아야 하는지를 판단한다. (*e.g.* 건강을 위해 알아야 할 것, 경제가 튼튼하면 일어나는 일 등) 이때, 선택지 구조(*e.g.* <동사+명사>, to부정사구 등)도 참고하여 빈칸 문장만으로 '논리적인' 답을 최대한(긍정적인지 부정적인지 정도라도) 예측해 보는 것이 좋다. 설사 예측되는 것이 없더라도 찾아야 할 것이 머릿속에 더 각인되므로 도움이 된다.

전략 2 단서를 찾아 이후 문장부터 읽어 내려간다.

단서 여러 개를 종합해서 답을 내야 하는 경우도 있고 논리적으로 판단해야 하는 경우도 있다. 또한 연구 실험문인 경우, 연구 결과에 주목해야 한다. 어느 경우든지 단서와 정답 선택지는 말바꿈되어 있으므로 단서에 밑줄을 긋고 선택지와 대조해서 가장 적절한 것을 찾아야 한다.

전략 3 단서를 찾았어도 나머지 부분을 확인한다.

빠르게 훑어보면서 대강의 내용을 확인하고 넘어간다.

주의 빈칸 문장이나 선택지에 자주 포함되는 (준)부정어(little, few, not, no, never 등)를 놓치면 정반대 의미의 오답을 고를 수 있으므로 주의해야 한다.

주의 단서 위치는 빈칸 문장 가까이 있기보다 몇 문장 떨어져 있거나 심지어 글의 마지막 문장에 있을 수도 있다. 의미적으로나 논리적으로 확실한 단서를 찾아야 한다.

주의 반드시 글에서 단서를 찾는다. 본인의 상식이나 배경지식으로 답해서는 안 되며, 주관적 논리에 빠지거나 선입견으로 판단해도 안 된다. 핵심 소재가 친환경 에너지원이라고 해도, 그것의 부정적 이면을 다루는 글도 얼마든지 있을 수 있음을 명심하자.

01

〈24학년도 대수능 34번〉

다음 빈칸에 들어갈 말로 가장 적절한 것은? [3점]

Everyone who drives, walks, or swipes a transit card in a city views herself as a transportation expert from the moment she walks out the front door. And how she views the street ________________________________. That's why we find so many well-intentioned and civic-minded citizens arguing past one another. At neighborhood meetings in school auditoriums, and in back rooms at libraries and churches, local residents across the nation gather for often-contentious discussions about transportation proposals that would change a city's streets. And like all politics, all transportation is local and intensely personal. A transit project that could speed travel for tens of thousands of people can be stopped by objections to the loss of a few parking spaces or by the simple fear that the project won't work. It's not a challenge of the data or the traffic engineering or the planning. Public debates about streets are typically rooted in emotional assumptions about how a change will affect a person's commute, ability to park, belief about what is safe and what isn't, or the bottom line of a local business.

*swipe: 판독기에 통과시키다 **contentious: 논쟁적인 ***commute: 통근

① relies heavily on how others see her city's streets
② updates itself with each new public transit policy
③ arises independently of the streets she travels on
④ tracks pretty closely with how she gets around
⑤ ties firmly in with how her city operates

02

24학년도 9월 모평 34번

다음 빈칸에 들어갈 말로 가장 적절한 것은? [3점]

Prior to photography, ______________________________. While painters have always lifted particular places out of their 'dwelling' and transported them elsewhere, paintings were time-consuming to produce, relatively difficult to transport and one-of-a-kind. The multiplication of photographs especially took place with the introduction of the half-tone plate in the 1880s that made possible the mechanical reproduction of photographs in newspapers, periodicals, books and advertisements. Photography became coupled to consumer capitalism and the globe was now offered 'in limitless quantities, figures, landscapes, events which had not previously been utilised either at all, or only as pictures for one customer'. With capitalism's arrangement of the world as a 'department store', 'the proliferation and circulation of representations ... achieved a spectacular and virtually inescapable global magnitude'. Gradually photographs became cheap mass-produced objects that made the world visible, aesthetic and desirable. Experiences were 'democratised' by translating them into cheap images. Light, small and mass-produced photographs became dynamic vehicles for the spatiotemporal circulation of places.

*proliferation: 확산 **magnitude: (큰) 규모 ***aesthetic: 미적인

① paintings alone connected with nature
② painting was the major form of art
③ art held up a mirror to the world
④ desire for travel was not strong
⑤ places did not travel well

03

23학년도 대수능 33번

다음 빈칸에 들어갈 말로 가장 적절한 것은? [3점]

The entrance to a honeybee colony, often referred to as the dancefloor, is a market place for information about the state of the colony and the environment outside the hive. Studying interactions on the dancefloor provides us with a number of illustrative examples of how individuals changing their own behavior in response to local information ______________________________. For example, upon returning to their hive honeybees that have collected water search out a receiver bee to unload their water to within the hive. If this search time is short then the returning bee is more likely to perform a waggle dance to recruit others to the water source. Conversely, if this search time is long then the bee is more likely to give up collecting water. Since receiver bees will only accept water if they require it, either for themselves or to pass on to other bees and brood, this unloading time is correlated with the colony's overall need of water. Thus the individual water forager's response to unloading time (up or down) regulates water collection in response to the colony's need.

*brood: 애벌레 **forager: 조달자

① allow the colony to regulate its workforce
② search for water sources by measuring distance
③ decrease the colony's workload when necessary
④ divide tasks according to their respective talents
⑤ train workers to acquire basic communication patterns

정답 및 해설 p. 2

DAY 002

빈칸 초반

전략 적용하기

⏱ 제한시간 | 5분

01

22학년도 대수능 33번

다음 빈칸에 들어갈 말로 가장 적절한 것은? [3점]

Elinor Ostrom found that there are several factors critical to bringing about stable institutional solutions to the problem of the commons. She pointed out, for instance, that the actors affected by the rules for the use and care of resources must have the right to ______________________________. For that reason, the people who monitor and control the behavior of users should also be users and/or have been given a mandate by all users. This is a significant insight, as it shows that prospects are poor for a centrally directed solution to the problem of the commons coming from a state power in comparison with a local solution for which users assume personal responsibility. Ostrom also emphasizes the importance of democratic decision processes and that all users must be given access to local forums for solving problems and conflicts among themselves. Political institutions at central, regional, and local levels must allow users to devise their own regulations and independently ensure observance.

*commons: 공유지 **mandate: 위임

① participate in decisions to change the rules
② claim individual ownership of the resources
③ use those resources to maximize their profits
④ demand free access to the communal resources
⑤ request proper distribution based on their merits

02

22학년도 대수능 32번

다음 빈칸에 들어갈 말로 가장 적절한 것은?

News, especially in its televised form, is constituted not only by its choice of topics and stories but by its ________________________________. Presentational styles have been subject to a tension between an informational-educational purpose and the need to engage us entertainingly. While current affairs programmes are often 'serious' in tone sticking to the 'rules' of balance, more popular programmes adopt a friendly, lighter, idiom in which we are invited to consider the impact of particular news items from the perspective of the 'average person in the street'. Indeed, contemporary news construction has come to rely on an increased use of faster editing tempos and 'flashier' presentational styles including the use of logos, sound-bites, rapid visual cuts and the 'star quality' of news readers. Popular formats can be said to enhance understanding by engaging an audience unwilling to endure the longer verbal orientation of older news formats. However, they arguably work to reduce understanding by failing to provide the structural contexts for news events.

① coordination with traditional display techniques
② prompt and full coverage of the latest issues
③ educational media contents favoured by producers
④ commitment to long-lasting news standards
⑤ verbal and visual idioms or modes of address

03

22학년도 9월 모평 34번

다음 빈칸에 들어갈 말로 가장 적절한 것은? [3점]

Enabling animals to ____________________________ ________________ is an almost universal function of learning. Most animals innately avoid objects they have not previously encountered. Unfamiliar objects may be dangerous; treating them with caution has survival value. If persisted in, however, such careful behavior could interfere with feeding and other necessary activities to the extent that the benefit of caution would be lost. A turtle that withdraws into its shell at every puff of wind or whenever a cloud casts a shadow would never win races, not even with a lazy rabbit. To overcome this problem, almost all animals habituate to safe stimuli that occur frequently. Confronted by a strange object, an inexperienced animal may freeze or attempt to hide, but if nothing unpleasant happens, sooner or later it will continue its activity. The possibility also exists that an unfamiliar object may be useful, so if it poses no immediate threat, a closer inspection may be worthwhile.

*innately: 선천적으로

① weigh the benefits of treating familiar things with care
② plan escape routes after predicting possible attacks
③ overcome repeated feeding failures for survival
④ operate in the presence of harmless stimuli
⑤ monitor the surrounding area regularly

정답 및 해설 p. 6

DAY 003

빈칸 중반

전략 익히기

⏱ 제한시간 | 5분

빈칸이 중반에 있는 경우, 글의 구조는 보통 아래와 같다.

1. 다소 긴 도입(Introduction)-빈칸 문장(주제문)-세부 사항/결론
   이때 단서는 빈칸 문장 이후의 세부 사항에 있다.
2. 도입-주제문-빈칸 문장(세부 사항)
   단서는 앞의 주제문에 있다.

전략 1 빈칸 문장부터 읽는다.

빈칸에 들어갈 어구를 논리적으로 최대한 예측해보는 것도 잊지 않는다. 빈칸 문장 이후에 주목하여 단서를 찾는다.

전략 2 빈칸 문장의 연결어를 이용한다.

특히 빈칸 문장이 중반에 있을 때 연결어가 이끄는 경우가 많다. 예를 들어, 빈칸 문장이 세부 사항임을 나타내는 연결어가 있으면 빈칸 문장의 앞부분에 있을 주제문에 주목해야 한다

주의 빈칸 문장에 대명사 등 의미가 확실하지 않은 어구가 포함된 경우, 앞 내용을 통해 지칭하는 것을 정확히 파악해야 한다.

주의 빈칸 문장이나 선택지에 포함된 (준)부정어 little, few, not, no, never 등을 놓치지 말아야 한다.

주의 반드시 지문에서 단서를 찾는다. 본인의 상식이나 배경지식으로 답해서는 안 된다.

01

24학년도 대수능 33번

다음 빈칸에 들어갈 말로 가장 적절한 것은? [3점]

There have been psychological studies in which subjects were shown photographs of people's faces and asked to identify the expression or state of mind evinced. The results are invariably very mixed. In the 17th century the French painter and theorist Charles Le Brun drew a series of faces illustrating the various emotions that painters could be called upon to represent. What is striking about them is that __________________________________. What is missing in all this is any setting or context to make the emotion determinate. We must know who this person is, who these other people are, what their relationship is, what is at stake in the scene, and the like. In real life as well as in painting we do not come across just faces; we encounter people in particular situations and our understanding of people cannot somehow be precipitated and held isolated from the social and human circumstances in which they, and we, live and breathe and have our being.

*evince: (감정 따위를) 분명히 나타내다 **precipitate: 촉발하다

① all of them could be matched consistently with their intended emotions
② every one of them was illustrated with photographic precision
③ each of them definitively displayed its own social narrative
④ most of them would be seen as representing unique characteristics
⑤ any number of them could be substituted for one another without loss

02

(24학년도 9월 모평 32번)

다음 빈칸에 들어갈 말로 가장 적절한 것은?

Many people create and share pictures and videos on the Internet. The difficulty is finding what you want. Typically, people want to search using words (rather than, say, example sketches). Because most pictures don't come with words attached, it is natural to try and build tagging systems that tag images with relevant words. The underlying machinery is straightforward — we apply image classification and object detection methods and tag the image with the output words. But tags aren't ______________________________. It matters who is doing what, and tags don't capture this. For example, tagging a picture of a cat in the street with the object categories "cat", "street", "trash can" and "fish bones" leaves out the information that the cat is pulling the fish bones out of an open trash can on the street.

① a set of words that allow users to identify an individual object
② a comprehensive description of what is happening in an image
③ a reliable resource for categorizing information by pictures
④ a primary means of organizing a sequential order of words
⑤ a useful filter for sorting similar but not identical images

03

(24학년도 9월 모평 31번)

다음 빈칸에 들어갈 말로 가장 적절한 것은?

In the post-World War II years after 1945, unparalleled economic growth fueled a building boom and a massive migration from the central cities to the new suburban areas. The suburbs were far more dependent on the automobile, signaling the shift from primary dependence on public transportation to private cars. Soon this led to the construction of better highways and freeways and the decline and even loss of public transportation. With all of these changes came a ______________ of leisure. As more people owned their own homes, with more space inside and lovely yards outside, their recreation and leisure time was increasingly centered around the home or, at most, the neighborhood. One major activity of this home-based leisure was watching television. No longer did one have to ride the trolly to the theater to watch a movie; similar entertainment was available for free and more conveniently from television.

*unparalleled: 유례없는

① downfall
② uniformity
③ restoration
④ privatization
⑤ customization

정답 및 해설 p. 10

DAY 004

빈칸 중반

전략 적용하기

제한시간 | 5분

01

24학년도 6월 모평 32번

다음 빈칸에 들어갈 말로 가장 적절한 것은?

In labor-sharing groups, people contribute labor to other people on a regular basis (for seasonal agricultural work such as harvesting) or on an irregular basis (in the event of a crisis such as the need to rebuild a barn damaged by fire). Labor sharing groups are part of what has been called a "moral economy" since no one keeps formal records on how much any family puts in or takes out. Instead, accounting is ____________________. The group has a sense of moral community based on years of trust and sharing. In a certain community of North America, labor sharing is a major economic factor of social cohesion. When a family needs a new barn or faces repair work that requires group labor, a barn-raising party is called. Many families show up to help. Adult men provide manual labor, and adult women provide food for the event. Later, when another family needs help, they call on the same people.

*cohesion: 응집성

① legally established
② regularly reported
③ socially regulated
④ manually calculated
⑤ carefully documented

02

24학년도 6월 모평 31번

다음 빈칸에 들어갈 말로 가장 적절한 것은?

People have always needed to eat, and they always will. Rising emphasis on self-expression values does not put an end to material desires. But prevailing economic orientations are gradually being reshaped. People who work in the knowledge sector continue to seek high salaries, but they place equal or greater emphasis on doing stimulating work and being able to follow their own time schedules. Consumption is becoming progressively less determined by the need for sustenance and the practical use of the goods consumed. People still eat, but a growing component of food's value is determined by its ____________ aspects. People pay a premium to eat exotic cuisines that provide an interesting experience or that symbolize a distinctive life-style. The publics of postindustrial societies place growing emphasis on "political consumerism," such as boycotting goods whose production violates ecological or ethical standards. Consumption is less and less a matter of sustenance and more and more a question of life-style — and choice.

*prevail: 우세하다 **cuisine: 요리

① quantitative
② nonmaterial
③ nutritional
④ invariable
⑤ economic

03

23학년도 9월 모평 32번

다음 빈칸에 들어갈 말로 가장 적절한 것은?

Fans feel for feeling's own sake. They make meanings beyond what seems to be on offer. They build identities and experiences, and make artistic creations of their own to share with others. A person can be an individual fan, feeling an "idealized connection with a star, strong feelings of memory and nostalgia," and engaging in activities like "collecting to develop a sense of self." But, more often, individual experiences are embedded in social contexts where other people with shared attachments socialize around the object of their affections. Much of the pleasure of fandom ______________________________. In their diaries, Bostonians of the 1800s described being part of the crowds at concerts as part of the pleasure of attendance. A compelling argument can be made that what fans love is less the object of their fandom than the attachments to (and differentiations from) one another that those affections afford.

*embed: 끼워 넣다 **compelling: 강력한

① is enhanced by collaborations between global stars
② results from frequent personal contact with a star
③ deepens as fans age together with their idols
④ comes from being connected to other fans
⑤ is heightened by stars' media appearances

정답 및 해설 p. 14

DAY 005

빈칸 후반

전략 익히기

⏱ 제한시간 | 5분

빈칸 문장 뒤에 문장이 한두 개 더 있는 경우이다. 단서 위치가 빈칸 문장 앞, 글의 앞부분, 마지막 문장, 심지어 빈칸 문장 자체 등 가장 다양하게 나타나는 유형이다.

전략 1 빈칸 문장부터 읽는다.

빈칸 문장이 초중반에 있을 때와 마찬가지로, 빈칸 문장부터 먼저 읽고 찾아야 할 것을 우리말로 간략히 추린 후 빈칸에 들어갈 어구를 예측해본다. 빈칸 문장의 연결어나 어구 등을 통해 단서 위치를 추측할 수도 있다.

전략 2 빈칸 문장 뒤 마지막 문장(들)을 읽는다.

빈칸 문장과 한 묶음으로 먼저 읽기를 권한다. 빈칸에 들어갈 어구를 객관적·논리적으로 추론할 수 있는 경우도 있다.

주의 빈칸 문장의 주어가 대명사일 때는 앞 문장을 통해 지칭하는 것을 파악해야 한다.

주의 빈칸 문장이나 선택지에 포함된 (준)부정어 little, few, not, no, never 등을 놓치지 말아야 한다.

주의 반드시 지문에서 단서를 찾는다. 본인의 상식이나 배경지식으로 답해서는 안 된다.

01

24학년도 대수능 32번

다음 빈칸에 들어갈 말로 가장 적절한 것은?

A musical score within any film can add an additional layer to the film text, which goes beyond simply imitating the action viewed. In films that tell of futuristic worlds, composers, much like sound designers, have added freedom to create a world that is unknown and new to the viewer. However, unlike sound designers, composers often shy away from creating unique pieces that reflect these new worlds and often present musical scores that possess familiar structures and cadences. While it is possible that this may interfere with creativity and a sense of space and time, it in fact ____________________. Through recognizable scores, visions of the future or a galaxy far, far away can be placed within a recognizable context. Such familiarity allows the viewer to be placed in a comfortable space so that the film may then lead the viewer to what is an unfamiliar, but acceptable vision of a world different from their own.

*score: 악보 **cadence: (율동적인) 박자

① frees the plot of its familiarity
② aids in viewer access to the film
③ adds to an exotic musical experience
④ orients audiences to the film's theme
⑤ inspires viewers to think more deeply

02

24학년도 대수능 31번

다음 빈칸에 들어갈 말로 가장 적절한 것은?

Over the last decade the attention given to how children learn to read has foregrounded the nature of *textuality*, and of the different, interrelated ways in which readers of all ages make texts mean. 'Reading' now applies to a greater number of representational forms than at any time in the past: pictures, maps, screens, design graphics and photographs are all regarded as text. In addition to the innovations made possible in picture books by new printing processes, design features also predominate in other kinds, such as books of poetry and information texts. Thus, reading becomes a more complicated kind of interpretation than it was when children's attention was focused on the printed text, with sketches or pictures as an adjunct. Children now learn from a picture book that words and illustrations complement and enhance each other. Reading is not simply ____________________. Even in the easiest texts, what a sentence 'says' is often not what it means.

*adjunct: 부속물

① knowledge acquisition
② word recognition
③ imaginative play
④ subjective interpretation
⑤ image mapping

03

24학년도 9월 모평 33번

다음 빈칸에 들어갈 말로 가장 적절한 것은? [3점]

An invention or discovery that is too far ahead of its time is worthless; no one can follow. Ideally, an innovation opens up only the next step from what is known and invites the culture to move forward one hop. An overly futuristic, unconventional, or visionary invention can fail initially (it may lack essential not-yet-invented materials or a critical market or proper understanding) yet succeed later, when the ecology of supporting ideas catches up. Gregor Mendel's 1865 theories of genetic heredity were correct but ignored for 35 years. His sharp insights were not accepted because they did not explain the problems biologists had at the time, nor did his explanation operate by known mechanisms, so his discoveries were out of reach even for the early adopters. Decades later science faced the urgent questions that Mendel's discoveries could answer. Now his insights ____________________. Within a few years of one another, three different scientists each independently rediscovered Mendel's forgotten work, which of course had been there all along.

*ecology: 생태 환경 **heredity: 유전

① caught up to modern problems
② raised even more questions
③ addressed past and current topics alike
④ were only one step away
⑤ regained acceptance of the public

정답 및 해설 p. 18

DAY 006

빈칸 후반

전략 적용하기

제한시간 | 5분

01

23학년도 대수능 32번

다음 빈칸에 들어갈 말로 가장 적절한 것은?

People have always wanted to be around other people and to learn from them. Cities have long been dynamos of social possibility, foundries of art, music, and fashion. Slang, or, if you prefer, "lexical innovation," has always started in cities — an outgrowth of all those different people so frequently exposed to one another. It spreads outward, in a manner not unlike transmissible disease, which itself typically "takes off" in cities. If, as the noted linguist Leonard Bloomfield argued, the way a person talks is a "composite result of what he has heard before," then language innovation would happen where the most people heard and talked to the most other people. Cities drive taste change because they ______________________, who not surprisingly are often the creative people cities seem to attract. Media, ever more global, ever more far-reaching, spread language faster to more people.

*foundry: 주물 공장 **lexical: 어휘의

① provide rich source materials for artists
② offer the greatest exposure to other people
③ cause cultural conflicts among users of slang
④ present ideal research environments to linguists
⑤ reduce the social mobility of ambitious outsiders

02

23학년도 9월 모평 31번

다음 빈칸에 들어갈 말로 가장 적절한 것은?

More than just *having* territories, animals also *partition* them. And this insight turned out to be particularly useful for zoo husbandry. An animal's territory has an internal arrangement that Heini Hediger compared to the inside of a person's house. Most of us assign separate functions to separate rooms, but even if you look at a one-room house you will find the same internal specialization. In a cabin or a mud hut, or even a Mesolithic cave from 30,000 years ago, this part is for cooking, that part is for sleeping; this part is for making tools and weaving, that part is for waste. We keep ________________________. To a varying extent, other animals do the same. A part of an animal's territory is for eating, a part for sleeping, a part for swimming or wallowing, a part may be set aside for waste, depending on the species of animal.

*husbandry: 관리

① an interest in close neighbors
② a neat functional organization
③ a stock of emergency supplies
④ a distance from potential rivals
⑤ a strictly observed daily routine

03

22학년도 6월 모평 33번

다음 빈칸에 들어갈 말로 가장 적절한 것은? [3점]

Concepts of nature are always cultural statements. This may not strike Europeans as much of an insight, for Europe's landscape is so much of a blend. But in the new worlds — 'new' at least to Europeans — the distinction appeared much clearer not only to European settlers and visitors but also to their descendants. For that reason, they had the fond conceit of primeval nature uncontrolled by human associations which could later find expression in an admiration for wilderness. Ecological relationships certainly have their own logic and in this sense 'nature' can be seen to have a self-regulating but not necessarily stable dynamic independent of human intervention. But the context for ecological interactions ________________________. We may not determine how or what a lion eats but we certainly can regulate where the lion feeds.

*conceit: 생각 **primeval: 원시(시대)의 ***ecological: 생태학의

① has supported new environment-friendly policies
② has increasingly been set by humanity
③ inspires creative cultural practices
④ changes too frequently to be regulated
⑤ has been affected by various natural conditions

정답 및 해설 p. 22

DAY 007

빈칸 마지막

전략 익히기

⏲ 제한시간 | 5분

빈칸이 마지막 문장에 있는 경우이다.

전략 1 역시 빈칸 문장부터 읽어야 한다.

무엇을 찾아 읽어야 할지를 파악하고, 빈칸 어구와 단서 위치도 논리적으로 최대한 예측해 본다. 빈칸 후반에서 마지막 문장을 한 묶음으로 읽었듯이 여기서도 직전 문장과 함께 읽기를 권한다. 직전 문장에 단서가 있을 경우 이를 빨리 발견할 수 있을 것이다.

전략 2 글의 첫 부분에 주목한다.

양괄식의 경우, 글의 첫 부분에 주제문이 있고 빈칸 문장은 이를 재서술하는 것이다. 따라서, 첫 부분을 주목해서 단서를 찾아야 한다. 주제문이 워낙 추상적이어서 이해가 어려울 경우, 세부 사항에 구체적으로 서술된 것들을 통해 판단한다.

주의 빈칸 문장의 주어가 대명사일 때는 앞 문장을 통해 지칭하는 것을 파악해야 한다.

주의 빈칸 문장이나 선택지에 포함된 (준)부정어 little, few, not, no, never 등을 놓치지 말아야 한다.

주의 반드시 지문에서 단서를 찾는다. 본인의 상식이나 배경지식으로 답해서는 안 된다.

01

23학년도 대수능 31번

다음 빈칸에 들어갈 말로 가장 적절한 것은?

There is something deeply paradoxical about the professional status of sports journalism, especially in the medium of print. In discharging their usual responsibilities of description and commentary, reporters' accounts of sports events are eagerly consulted by sports fans, while in their broader journalistic role of covering sport in its many forms, sports journalists are among the most visible of all contemporary writers. The ruminations of the elite class of 'celebrity' sports journalists are much sought after by the major newspapers, their lucrative contracts being the envy of colleagues in other 'disciplines' of journalism. Yet sports journalists do not have a standing in their profession that corresponds to the size of their readerships or of their pay packets, with the old saying (now reaching the status of cliché) that sport is the 'toy department of the news media' still readily to hand as a dismissal of the worth of what sports journalists do. This reluctance to take sports journalism seriously produces the paradoxical outcome that sports newspaper writers are much read but little ______________.

*discharge: 이행하다 **rumination: 생각 ***lucrative: 돈을 많이 버는

① paid
② admired
③ censored
④ challenged
⑤ discussed

02

〈 23학년도 9월 모평 34번 〉

다음 빈칸에 들어갈 말로 가장 적절한 것은? [3점]

In trying to explain how different disciplines attempt to understand autobiographical memory the literary critic Daniel Albright said, "Psychology is a garden, literature is a wilderness." He meant, I believe, that psychology seeks to make patterns, find regularity, and ultimately impose order on human experience and behavior. Writers, by contrast, dive into the unruly, untamed depths of human experiences. What he said about understanding memory can be extended to our questions about young children's minds. If we psychologists are too bent on identifying the orderly pattern, the regularities of children's minds, we may miss an essential and pervasive characteristic of our topic: the child's more unruly and imaginative ways of talking and thinking. It is not only the developed writer or literary scholar who seems drawn toward a somewhat wild and idiosyncratic way of thinking; young children are as well. The psychologist interested in young children may have to ______________________________ in order to get a good picture of how children think.

*unruly: 제멋대로 구는 **pervasive: 널리 퍼져 있는 ***idiosyncratic: 색다른

① venture a little more often into the wilderness
② help them recall their most precious memories
③ better understand the challenges of parental duty
④ disregard the key characteristics of children's fiction
⑤ standardize the paths of their psychological development

03

〈 23학년도 9월 모평 33번 〉

다음 빈칸에 들어갈 말로 가장 적절한 것은? [3점]

There was nothing modern about the idea of men making women's clothes — we saw them doing it for centuries in the past. In the old days, however, the client was always primary and her tailor was an obscure craftsman, perhaps talented but perhaps not. She had her own ideas like any patron, there were no fashion plates, and the tailor was simply at her service, perhaps with helpful suggestions about what others were wearing. Beginning in the late nineteenth century, with the hugely successful rise of the artistic male couturier, it was the designer who became celebrated, and the client elevated by his inspired attention. In a climate of admiration for male artists and their female creations, the dress-designer first flourished as the same sort of creator. Instead of the old rule that dressmaking is a craft, ______________________________ was invented that had not been there before.

*obscure: 무명의 **patron: 후원자 ***couturier: 고급 여성복 디자이너

① a profitable industry driving fast fashion
② a widespread respect for marketing skills
③ a public institution preserving traditional designs
④ a modern connection between dress-design and art
⑤ an efficient system for producing affordable clothing

정답 및 해설 p. 26

DAY 008

빈칸 마지막

전략 적용하기

제한시간 | 5분

01

23학년도 6월 모평 31번

다음 빈칸에 들어갈 말로 가장 적절한 것은?

Young contemporary artists who employ digital technologies in their practice rarely make reference to computers. For example, Wade Guyton, an abstractionist who uses a word processing program and inkjet printers, does not call himself a computer artist. Moreover, some critics, who admire his work, are little concerned about his extensive use of computers in the art-making process. This is a marked contrast from three decades ago when artists who utilized computers were labeled by critics — often disapprovingly — as computer artists. For the present generation of artists, the computer, or more appropriately, the laptop, is one in a collection of integrated, portable digital technologies that link their social and working life. With tablets and cell phones surpassing personal computers in Internet usage, and as slim digital devices resemble nothing like the room-sized mainframes and bulky desktop computers of previous decades, it now appears that the computer artist is finally ______________.

① awake　　② influential
③ distinct　　④ troublesome
⑤ extinct

02

22학년도 대수능 31번

다음 빈칸에 들어갈 말로 가장 적절한 것은?

Humour involves not just practical disengagement but cognitive disengagement. As long as something is funny, we are for the moment not concerned with whether it is real or fictional, true or false. This is why we give considerable leeway to people telling funny stories. If they are getting extra laughs by exaggerating the silliness of a situation or even by making up a few details, we are happy to grant them comic licence, a kind of poetic licence. Indeed, someone listening to a funny story who tries to correct the teller — 'No, he didn't spill the spaghetti on the keyboard and the monitor, just on the keyboard' — will probably be told by the other listeners to stop interrupting. The creator of humour is putting ideas into people's heads for the pleasure those ideas will bring, not to provide ______________ information.

*cognitive: 인식의 **leeway: 여지

① accurate
② detailed
③ useful
④ additional
⑤ alternative

03

22학년도 6월 모평 34번

다음 빈칸에 들어갈 말로 가장 적절한 것은? [3점]

Emma Brindley has investigated the responses of European robins to the songs of neighbors and strangers. Despite the large and complex song repertoire of European robins, they were able to discriminate between the songs of neighbors and strangers. When they heard a tape recording of a stranger, they began to sing sooner, sang more songs, and overlapped their songs with the playback more often than they did on hearing a neighbor's song. As Brindley suggests, the overlapping of song may be an aggressive response. However, this difference in responding to neighbor versus stranger occurred only when the neighbor's song was played by a loudspeaker placed at the boundary between that neighbor's territory and the territory of the bird being tested. If the same neighbor's song was played at another boundary, one separating the territory of the test subject from another neighbor, it was treated as the call of a stranger. Not only does this result demonstrate that ______________________________, but it also shows that the choice of songs used in playback experiments is highly important.

*robin: 울새 **territory: 영역

① variety and complexity characterize the robins' songs
② song volume affects the robins' aggressive behavior
③ the robins' poor territorial sense is a key to survival
④ the robins associate locality with familiar songs
⑤ the robins are less responsive to recorded songs

정답 및 해설 p. 30

DAY 009

글의 순서

전략 익히기

⏱ 제한시간 | 5분

절대평가 이후 난이도가 높아졌고, 두 문제 중 하나는 3점짜리로 출제된다. 2점짜리도 종종 오답률 상위에 랭크된다.

전략 1 주어진 글을 우리말로 간략히 정리한다.

글의 핵심어나 대의를 판단하고 앞으로 전개될 내용을 최대한 예측해본다.

전략 2 연결어, 대명사, 관사 등으로 의미적, 문법적 관계를 판단한다.

글의 선후관계를 확실히 규정짓는 연결어, 대명사, 관사(a(n) ~ → the ~)가 큰 역할을 할 수밖에 없다. 따라서 이들에 주목하여 순서를 판단하는 것이 기본이다. 이들이 보이지 않을 때는 아래와 같은 논리 관계, 최대한 자연스러운 의미 흐름에 따라 순서를 판단한다.

1. 일반적/추상적 진술 → 세부적/구체적 진술
2. 시간 순 *e.g.* 1800s → 1900s → 21C
단계별 과정(process)을 설명하는 글도 문맥상 시간 순으로 맨 처음으로 이뤄져야 할 단계와 그 이후 단계들의 순서를 판단한다.
3. 질문 → 해답
4. 생소한 개념어 제시 → 정의(definition) → 예시 등의 부연 설명

전략 3 두 글의 순서가 확실할 경우 선택지 소거법을 적극 이용한다.

B-A가 확실하면 A-B 순서 선택지를 모두 소거하고, C-B-A 또는 B-A-C를 놓고 정답을 판단한다.

주의 주어진 글의 마지막 문장에 등장한 어구로 시작하는 글이 있는 경우, 오답을 유도하는 함정일 수 있으므로 그 어구가 다른 글에도 있지 않은지 살펴보고 판단해야 한다.

주의 대명사 단서가 등장하더라도 문법적으로 가능한 지칭 대상이 두 개 이상인 경우가 있으므로, 무엇을 지칭하는지 문맥을 정확히 판단해야 한다. they는 사람, 사물에 다 쓸 수 있음을 잊지 말자.

주의 연결어는 오로지 두 글을 논리적으로 연결할 뿐이므로 글의 위치까지 선입견을 가지고 판단해서는 안 된다. 즉 결과[결론]를 의미하는 연결어(Thus, Therefore 등)는 글 후반에 등장할 가능성이 크긴 하지만, 주어진 글 뒤에 이어지는 것도 얼마든지 가능하다.

01

〈24학년도 대수능 36번〉

주어진 글 다음에 이어질 글의 순서로 가장 적절한 것은?

> Negotiation can be defined as an attempt to explore and reconcile conflicting positions in order to reach an acceptable outcome.

(A) Areas of difference can and do frequently remain, and will perhaps be the subject of future negotiations, or indeed remain irreconcilable. In those instances in which the parties have highly antagonistic or polarised relations, the process is likely to be dominated by the exposition, very often in public, of the areas of conflict.

(B) In these and sometimes other forms of negotiation, negotiation serves functions other than reconciling conflicting interests. These will include delay, publicity, diverting attention or seeking intelligence about the other party and its negotiating position.

(C) Whatever the nature of the outcome, which may actually favour one party more than another, the purpose of negotiation is the identification of areas of common interest and conflict. In this sense, depending on the intentions of the parties, the areas of common interest may be clarified, refined and given negotiated form and substance.

*reconcile: 화해시키다 **antagonistic: 적대적인 ***exposition: 설명

① (A) – (C) – (B)
② (B) – (A) – (C)
③ (B) – (C) – (A)
④ (C) – (A) – (B)
⑤ (C) – (B) – (A)

02

24학년도 9월 모평 37번

주어진 글 다음에 이어질 글의 순서로 가장 적절한 것은? [3점]

> Norms emerge in groups as a result of people conforming to the behavior of others. Thus, the start of a norm occurs when one person acts in a particular manner in a particular situation because she thinks she ought to.

(A) Thus, she may prescribe the behavior to them by uttering the norm statement in a prescriptive manner. Alternately, she may communicate that conformity is desired in other ways, such as by gesturing. In addition, she may threaten to sanction them for not behaving as she wishes. This will cause some to conform to her wishes and act as she acts.

(B) But some others will not need to have the behavior prescribed to them. They will observe the regularity of behavior and decide on their own that they ought to conform. They may do so for either rational or moral reasons.

(C) Others may then conform to this behavior for a number of reasons. The person who performed the initial action may think that others ought to behave as she behaves in situations of this sort.

*sanction: 제재를 가하다

① (A) – (C) – (B)　② (B) – (A) – (C)
③ (B) – (C) – (A)　④ (C) – (A) – (B)
⑤ (C) – (B) – (A)

03

24학년도 9월 모평 36번

주어진 글 다음에 이어질 글의 순서로 가장 적절한 것은?

> The intuitive ability to classify and generalize is undoubtedly a useful feature of life and research, but it carries a high cost, such as in our tendency to stereotype generalizations about people and situations.

(A) Intuitively and quickly, we mentally sort things into groups based on what we perceive the differences between them to be, and that is the basis for stereotyping. Only afterwards do we examine (or not examine) more evidence of how things are differentiated, and the degree and significance of the variations.

(B) Our brain performs these tasks efficiently and automatically, usually without our awareness. The real danger of stereotypes is not their inaccuracy, but their lack of flexibility and their tendency to be preserved, even when we have enough time to stop and consider.

(C) For most people, the word stereotype arouses negative connotations: it implies a negative bias. But, in fact, stereotypes do not differ in principle from all other generalizations; generalizations about groups of people are not necessarily always negative.

*intuitive: 직관적인 **connotation: 함축

① (A) – (C) – (B)　② (B) – (A) – (C)
③ (B) – (C) – (A)　④ (C) – (A) – (B)
⑤ (C) – (B) – (A)

정답 및 해설 p. 34

DAY 010

글의 순서

전략 적용하기

제한시간 | 5분

01

〈24학년도 9월 모평 37번〉

주어진 글 다음에 이어질 글의 순서로 가장 적절한 것은? [3점]

Plants show finely tuned adaptive responses when nutrients are limiting. Gardeners may recognize yellow leaves as a sign of poor nutrition and the need for fertilizer.

(A) In contrast, plants with a history of nutrient abundance are risk averse and save energy. At all developmental stages, plants respond to environmental changes or unevenness so as to be able to use their energy for growth, survival, and reproduction, while limiting damage and nonproductive uses of their valuable energy.

(B) Research in this area has shown that plants are constantly aware of their position in the environment, in terms of both space and time. Plants that have experienced variable nutrient availability in the past tend to exhibit risk-taking behaviors, such as spending energy on root lengthening instead of leaf production.

(C) But if a plant does not have a caretaker to provide supplemental minerals, it can proliferate or lengthen its roots and develop root hairs to allow foraging in more distant soil patches. Plants can also use their memory to respond to histories of temporal or spatial variation in nutrient or resource availability.

*nutrient: 영양소 **fertilizer: 비료 ***forage: 구하러 다니다

① (A) – (C) – (B)　② (B) – (A) – (C)
③ (B) – (C) – (A)　④ (C) – (A) – (B)
⑤ (C) – (B) – (A)

02

〈24학년도 6월 모평 36번〉

주어진 글 다음에 이어질 글의 순서로 가장 적절한 것은?

> The growing complexity of computer software has direct implications for our global safety and security, particularly as the physical objects upon which we depend — things like cars, airplanes, bridges, tunnels, and implantable medical devices — transform themselves into computer code.

(A) As all this code grows in size and complexity, so too does the number of errors and software bugs. According to a study by Carnegie Mellon University, commercial software typically has twenty to thirty bugs for every thousand lines of code — 50 million lines of code means 1 million to 1.5 million potential errors to be exploited.

(B) This is the basis for all malware attacks that take advantage of these computer bugs to get the code to do something it was not originally intended to do. As computer code grows more elaborate, software bugs flourish and security suffers, with increasing consequences for society at large.

(C) Physical things are increasingly becoming information technologies. Cars are "computers we ride in," and airplanes are nothing more than "flying Solaris boxes attached to bucketfuls of industrial control systems."

*exploit: 활용하다

① (A) – (C) – (B)　② (B) – (A) – (C)
③ (B) – (C) – (A)　④ (C) – (A) – (B)
⑤ (C) – (B) – (A)

03

〈24학년도 6월 모평 37번〉

주어진 글 다음에 이어질 글의 순서로 가장 적절한 것은? [3점]

> Darwin saw blushing as uniquely human, representing an involuntary physical reaction caused by embarrassment and self-consciousness in a social environment.

(A) Maybe our brief loss of face benefits the long-term cohesion of the group. Interestingly, if someone blushes after making a social mistake, they are viewed in a more favourable light than those who don't blush.

(B) If we feel awkward, embarrassed or ashamed when we are alone, we don't blush; it seems to be caused by our concern about what others are thinking of us. Studies have confirmed that simply being told you are blushing brings it on. We feel as though others can see through our skin and into our mind.

(C) However, while we sometimes want to disappear when we involuntarily go bright red, psychologists argue that blushing actually serves a positive social purpose. When we blush, it's a signal to others that we recognize that a social norm has been broken; it is an apology for a faux pas.

*faux pas: 실수

① (A) – (C) – (B)　② (B) – (A) – (C)
③ (B) – (C) – (A)　④ (C) – (A) – (B)
⑤ (C) – (B) – (A)

정답 및 해설 p. 38

DAY 011

문장 넣기

전략 익히기

⏱ 제한시간 | 5분

빈칸 추론, 글의 순서 유형처럼 고난도 유형에 속한다. 글의 순서 유형과 마찬가지로, 연결어, 대명사, 관사 단서가 중요하다. 단서가 없으면 문장 간의 논리적 의미 관계로 판단해야 한다.

전략 1 주어진 문장부터 읽고 우리말로 간략히 내용을 추린다.

앞뒤 내용이나 글이 다루는 내용 등 예측할 수 있는 것이 있는지 확인한다. 선택지 번호가 시작되기 전의 초반 내용은 예측에 도움이 될 수 있다.

전략 2 글을 읽으면서 흐름이 부자연스럽게 이어지는 부분을 찾는다. 또는 논리적 의미 관계를 판단해본다.

흐름이 부자연스러운 부분이 딱히 보이지 않을 때는, 글의 구조를 따져봐야 한다. 세부 사항이 <주 세부 사항(a)-부 세부 사항(a′) / 주 세부 사항(b)-부 세부 사항(b′)>으로 연결되는 구조를 예로 들어보자. a, b는 주제문을 뒷받침하는 서로 다른 내용이므로, 부 세부 사항을 어떤 주 세부 사항 뒤에 넣어야 할지를 판단해야 한다. 즉, a′는 a 뒤에, b′는 b 뒤에 넣어야 한다.

전략 3 정답 앞뒤 선택지가 확실한 오답인지를 반드시 확인한다.

정답 앞뒤의 오답 선택지를 선택하여 틀리는 경우가 매우 많기 때문에, 흐름이 자연스러운지를 반드시 확인해야 한다.

주의 정답 앞뒤 문장을 선택하는 비율이 높다. 그만큼 함정이나 매력적인 요소가 있으므로, 정답을 선택하기 전에 글 전체 흐름을 반드시 파악해야 한다.

주의 주어진 문장에 등장한 어구가 보이면 그 앞이나 뒤를 정답으로 선택하는 경우가 많다. 함정일 가능성이 있으므로 주의한다.

01

24학년도 대수능 38번

글의 흐름으로 보아, 주어진 문장이 들어가기에 가장 적절한 곳은?

> Yes, some contests are seen as world class, such as identification of the Higgs particle or the development of high temperature superconductors.

Science is sometimes described as a winner-take-all contest, meaning that there are no rewards for being second or third. This is an extreme view of the nature of scientific contests. (①) Even those who describe scientific contests in such a way note that it is a somewhat inaccurate description, given that replication and verification have social value and are common in science. (②) It is also inaccurate to the extent that it suggests that only a handful of contests exist. (③) But many other contests have multiple parts, and the number of such contests may be increasing. (④) By way of example, for many years it was thought that there would be "one" cure for cancer, but it is now realized that cancer takes multiple forms and that multiple approaches are needed to provide a cure. (⑤) There won't be one winner — there will be many.

*replication: 반복 **verification: 입증

02

24학년도 대수능 39번

글의 흐름으로 보아, 주어진 문장이 들어가기에 가장 적절한 곳은? [3점]

> At the next step in the argument, however, the analogy breaks down.

Misprints in a book or in any written message usually have a negative impact on the content, sometimes (literally) fatally. (①) The displacement of a comma, for instance, may be a matter of life and death. (②) Similarly most mutations have harmful consequences for the organism in which they occur, meaning that they reduce its reproductive fitness. (③) Occasionally, however, a mutation may occur that increases the fitness of the organism, just as an accidental failure to reproduce the text of the first edition might provide more accurate or updated information. (④) A favorable mutation is going to be more heavily represented in the next generation, since the organism in which it occurred will have more offspring and mutations are transmitted to the offspring. (⑤) By contrast, there is no mechanism by which a book that accidentally corrects the mistakes of the first edition will tend to sell better.

*analogy: 유사 **mutation: 돌연변이

03

24학년도 9월 모평 38번

글의 흐름으로 보아, 주어진 문장이 들어가기에 가장 적절한 곳은?

> Because the manipulation of digitally converted sounds meant the reprogramming of binary information, editing operations could be performed with millisecond precision.

The shift from analog to digital technology significantly influenced how music was produced. First and foremost, the digitization of sounds — that is, their conversion into numbers — enabled music makers to undo what was done. (①) One could, in other words, twist and bend sounds toward something new without sacrificing the original version. (②) This "undo" ability made mistakes considerably less momentous, sparking the creative process and encouraging a generally more experimental mindset. (③) In addition, digitally converted sounds could be manipulated simply by programming digital messages rather than using physical tools, simplifying the editing process significantly. (④) For example, while editing once involved razor blades to physically cut and splice audiotapes, it now involved the cursor and mouse-click of the computer-based sequencer program, which was obviously less time consuming. (⑤) This microlevel access at once made it easier to conceal any traces of manipulations (such as joining tracks in silent spots) and introduced new possibilities for manipulating sounds in audible and experimental ways.

*binary: 2진법의 **splice: 합쳐 잇다

정답 및 해설 p. 42

DAY 012

문장 넣기

전략 적용하기

⏱ 제한시간 | 5분

01

24학년도 9월 모평 39번

글의 흐름으로 보아, 주어진 문장이 들어가기에 가장 적절한 곳은? [3점]

> In the case of specialists such as art critics, a deeper familiarity with materials and techniques is often useful in reaching an informed judgement about a work.

Acknowledging the making of artworks does not require a detailed, technical knowledge of, say, how painters mix different kinds of paint, or how an image editing tool works. (①) All that is required is a general sense of a significant difference between working with paints and working with an imaging application. (②) This sense might involve a basic familiarity with paints and paintbrushes as well as a basic familiarity with how we use computers, perhaps including how we use consumer imaging apps. (③) This is because every kind of artistic material or tool comes with its own challenges and affordances for artistic creation. (④) Critics are often interested in the ways artists exploit different kinds of materials and tools for particular artistic effect. (⑤) They are also interested in the success of an artist's attempt — embodied in the artwork itself — to push the limits of what can be achieved with certain materials and tools.

*affordance: 행위유발성 **exploit: 활용하다

02

(24학년도 6월 모평 38번)

글의 흐름으로 보아, 주어진 문장이 들어가기에 가장 적절한 곳은?

> Instead, much like the young child learning how to play 'nicely', the apprentice scientist gains his or her understanding of the moral values inherent in the role by absorption from their colleagues — socialization.

As particular practices are repeated over time and become more widely shared, the values that they embody are reinforced and reproduced and we speak of them as becoming 'institutionalized'. (①) In some cases, this institutionalization has a formal face to it, with rules and protocols written down, and specialized roles created to ensure that procedures are followed correctly. (②) The main institutions of state — parliament, courts, police and so on — along with certain of the professions, exhibit this formal character. (③) Other social institutions, perhaps the majority, are not like this; science is an example. (④) Although scientists are trained in the substantive content of their discipline, they are not formally instructed in 'how to be a good scientist'. (⑤) We think that these values, along with the values that inform many of the professions, are under threat, just as the value of the professions themselves is under threat.

*apprentice: 도제, 견습 **inherent: 내재된

03

(24학년도 6월 모평 39번)

글의 흐름으로 보아, 주어진 문장이 들어가기에 가장 적절한 곳은? [3점]

> As a result, they are fit and grow better, but they aren't particularly long-lived.

When trees grow together, nutrients and water can be optimally divided among them all so that each tree can grow into the best tree it can be. If you "help" individual trees by getting rid of their supposed competition, the remaining trees are bereft. They send messages out to their neighbors unsuccessfully, because nothing remains but stumps. Every tree now grows on its own, giving rise to great differences in productivity. (①) Some individuals photosynthesize like mad until sugar positively bubbles along their trunk. (②) This is because a tree can be only as strong as the forest that surrounds it. (③) And there are now a lot of losers in the forest. (④) Weaker members, who would once have been supported by the stronger ones, suddenly fall behind. (⑤) Whether the reason for their decline is their location and lack of nutrients, a passing sickness, or genetic makeup, they now fall prey to insects and fungi.

*bereft: 잃은 **stump: 그루터기 ***photosynthesize: 광합성하다

정답 및 해설 p. 46

DAY 013

함의 추론

전략 익히기

제한시간 | 4분

밑줄 친 어구가 나타내는 글자 그대로의 의미(사전적 의미)가 아니라 '문맥상 새롭게 만들어진' 의미(함축적 의미)를 묻는다. 보통, 비유적·상징적 표현이 밑줄 대상이다. 이들 표현은 읽는 이의 주의를 끌어 기억하게 만드는 효과가 있으므로 글의 대의와 관계가 깊다.

전략 1 밑줄 친 어구가 있는 문장 전체를 이해한다.

빈칸 유형을 풀 때 빈칸 문장부터 읽고 무엇을 묻는지를 판단하는 것과 마찬가지이다.

e.g. • 밑줄 어구 문장: Individuals are only "a link in a chain, a phase in a process."

함축적 의미라고 해도 어느 정도는 사전적 의미에 기초하므로, '개인은 단지 사슬의 한 고리, 과정의 한 단계일 뿐'이라는 의미임을 이해한다.

전략 2 밑줄 문장과 '공통 속성'을 가진 어구에 주목한다.

비유나 상징 표현은 나타내려는 의미와 공통 속성을 가진다. 저녁형 인간을 a night owl로 표현하는 것은 올빼미가 야행성이라는 공통 속성이 있기 때문이다. 따라서, 글에서 밑줄 어구와 '공통 속성'을 가진 어구를 파악해야 한다. 중간중간 모호하고 관념적인 말이 있을 수 있으나, 이에 휘둘리지 말고 정확히 문제에서 요구하는 것을 짚어내도록 한다.

• 단서 문장: Creativity results from a complex interaction between a person and his or her environment or culture.
(a person ≒ a link, a phase / his or her environment or culture ≒ a chain, a process)

• 정답: Individual creativity emerges only in its necessary conditions. [19학년도 9월 모평 21번]

주의 지문에 반복적으로 사용되는 어구로 연상되는 그럴듯한 오답에 주의한다.

01

24학년도 대수능 21번

밑줄 친 a nonstick frying pan이 다음 글에서 의미하는 바로 가장 적절한 것은? [3점]

How you focus your attention plays a critical role in how you deal with stress. Scattered attention harms your ability to let go of stress, because even though your attention is scattered, it is narrowly focused, for you are able to fixate only on the stressful parts of your experience. When your attentional spotlight is widened, you can more easily let go of stress. You can put in perspective many more aspects of any situation and not get locked into one part that ties you down to superficial and anxiety-provoking levels of attention. A narrow focus heightens the stress level of each experience, but a widened focus turns down the stress level because you're better able to put each situation into a broader perspective. One anxiety-provoking detail is less important than the bigger picture. It's like transforming yourself into a nonstick frying pan. You can still fry an egg, but the egg won't stick to the pan.

*provoke: 유발시키다

① never being confronted with any stressful experiences in daily life
② broadening one's perspective to identify the cause of stress
③ rarely confining one's attention to positive aspects of an experience
④ having a larger view of an experience beyond its stressful aspects
⑤ taking stress into account as the source of developing a wide view

02

24학년도 9월 모평 21번

밑줄 친 "The best is the enemy of the good."이 다음 글에서 의미하는 바로 가장 적절한 것은? [3점]

Gold plating in the project means needlessly enhancing the expected results, namely, adding characteristics that are costly, not required, and that have low added value with respect to the targets — in other words, giving more with no real justification other than to demonstrate one's own talent. Gold plating is especially interesting for project team members, as it is typical of projects with a marked professional component — in other words, projects that involve specialists with proven experience and extensive professional autonomy. In these environments specialists often see the project as an opportunity to test and enrich their skill sets. There is therefore a strong temptation, in all good faith, to engage in gold plating, namely, to achieve more or higher-quality work that gratifies the professional but does not add value to the client's requests, and at the same time removes valuable resources from the project. As the saying goes, "The best is the enemy of the good."

*autonomy: 자율성 **gratify: 만족시키다

① Pursuing perfection at work causes conflicts among team members.
② Raising work quality only to prove oneself is not desirable.
③ Inviting overqualified specialists to a project leads to bad ends.
④ Responding to the changing needs of clients is unnecessary.
⑤ Acquiring a range of skills for a project does not ensure success.

03

24학년도 6월 모평 21번

밑줄 친 a stick in the bundle가 다음 글에서 의미하는 바로 가장 적절한 것은? [3점]

Lawyers sometimes describe ownership as a bundle of sticks. This metaphor was introduced about a century ago, and it has dramatically transformed the teaching and practice of law. The metaphor is useful because it helps us see ownership as a grouping of interpersonal rights that can be separated and put back together. When you say *It's mine* in reference to a resource, often that means you own a lot of the sticks that make up the full bundle: the sell stick, the rent stick, the right to mortgage, license, give away, even destroy the thing. Often, though, we split the sticks up, as for a piece of land: there may be a landowner, a bank with a mortgage, a tenant with a lease, a plumber with a license to enter the land, an oil company with mineral rights. Each of these parties owns a stick in the bundle.

*mortgage: 저당잡히다 **tenant: 임차인

① a legal obligation to develop the resource
② a priority to legally claim the real estate
③ a right to use one aspect of the property
④ a building to be shared equally by tenants
⑤ a piece of land nobody can claim as their own

정답 및 해설 p. 50

DAY 014

함의 추론

전략 적용하기

제한시간 | 5분

01

23학년도 대수능 21번

밑줄 친 make oneself public to oneself가 다음 글에서 의미하는 바로 가장 적절한 것은? [3점]

Coming of age in the 18th and 19th centuries, the personal diary became a centerpiece in the construction of a modern subjectivity, at the heart of which is the application of reason and critique to the understanding of world and self, which allowed the creation of a new kind of knowledge. Diaries were central media through which enlightened and free subjects could be constructed. They provided a space where one could write daily about her whereabouts, feelings, and thoughts. Over time and with rereading, disparate entries, events, and happenstances could be rendered into insights and narratives about the self, and allowed for the formation of subjectivity. It is in that context that the idea of "the self [as] both made and explored with words" emerges. Diaries were personal and private; one would write for oneself, or, in Habermas's formulation, one would make oneself public to oneself. By making the self public in a private sphere, the self also became an object for self-inspection and self-critique.

*disparate: 이질적인 **render: 만들다

① use writing as a means of reflecting on oneself
② build one's identity by reading others' diaries
③ exchange feedback in the process of writing
④ create an alternate ego to present to others
⑤ develop topics for writing about selfhood

02

(23학년도 9월 모평 21번)

밑줄 친 send us off into different far corners of the library가 다음 글에서 의미하는 바로 가장 적절한 것은? [3점]

You may feel there is something scary about an algorithm deciding what you might like. Could it mean that, if computers conclude you won't like something, you will never get the chance to see it? Personally, I really enjoy being directed toward new music that I might not have found by myself. I can quickly get stuck in a rut where I put on the same songs over and over. That's why I've always enjoyed the radio. But the algorithms that are now pushing and pulling me through the music library are perfectly suited to finding gems that I'll like. My worry originally about such algorithms was that they might drive everyone into certain parts of the library, leaving others lacking listeners. Would they cause a convergence of tastes? But thanks to the nonlinear and chaotic mathematics usually behind them, this doesn't happen. A small divergence in my likes compared to yours can send us off into different far corners of the library.

*rut: 관습, 틀 **gem: 보석 ***divergence: 갈라짐

① lead us to music selected to suit our respective tastes
② enable us to build connections with other listeners
③ encourage us to request frequent updates for algorithms
④ motivate us to search for talented but unknown musicians
⑤ make us ignore our preferences for particular music genres

03

(23학년도 6월 모평 21번)

밑줄 친 "view from nowhere"가 다음 글에서 의미하는 바로 가장 적절한 것은? [3점]

Our view of the world is not given to us from the outside in a pure, objective form; it is shaped by our mental abilities, our shared cultural perspectives and our unique values and beliefs. This is not to say that there is no reality outside our minds or that the world is just an illusion. It is to say that our version of reality is precisely that: *our* version, not *the* version. There is no single, universal or authoritative version that makes sense, other than as a theoretical construct. We can see the world only as it appears to us, not "as it truly is," because there is no "as it truly is" without a perspective to give it form. Philosopher Thomas Nagel argued that there is no "view from nowhere," since we cannot see the world except from a particular perspective, and that perspective influences what we see. We can experience the world only through the human lenses that make it intelligible to us.

*illusion: 환영

① perception of reality affected by subjective views
② valuable perspective most people have in mind
③ particular view adopted by very few people
④ critical insight that defeats our prejudices
⑤ unbiased and objective view of the world

정답 및 해설 p. 54

DAY 015

주장과 요지

전략 익히기

⏱ 제한시간 | 4분

필자의 주장은 학생, 일반인, 특정 집단(기업, 부모, 대학 등)을 대상으로 '조언'해주는 것이다. 이에 비해 요지는 핵심 소재에 대해 글쓴이가 하고자 하는 말을 의미한다. 두 가지 모두 주제문으로 표현된다.

전략 1 필자의 주장: 주장 표현이 담긴 주제문을 찾는다. 글의 구성 및 흐름에 주목한다.

주장 표현: must, should, have to, need to, 명령문, 부정 명령문, A is B 등의 단정적 표현 / important, crucial, necessary, essential, key, imperative 등의 표현

대부분 아래와 같은 구성 요소로 나눌 수 있으며, 차례대로 전개되는 것이 보통이다.

문제점/비판	대부분 부정 의미의 표현을 담고 있다. (e.g. ~하지 않는다, ~하는 것은 좋지 않다)
해결책/주장(조언)	주제문 (e.g. ~해야 한다)
부연 설명	논거 (주장의 근거: ~이기 때문에 (~해야 하는 것이다))

전략2 요지: 주제문을 찾는다.

글에서 가장 전체적, 포괄적, 추상적인 문장이며 세부 사항으로 부연 설명되는 것이어야 한다. may, can 등을 사용한 약한 주장도 세부 사항 논거에 의해 뒷받침되면 주제문이 될 수 있다. 주제문이 명시되어 있지 않으면 세부 사항으로 유추해야 한다.

주제문의 핵심 소재는 글에 반복적으로 제시되며, 선택지에 반복되는 어구일 가능성이 크다.

① 미디어 환경의 변화로 **음악 비평**이 대중의 영향을 받게 되었다. (정답)
② 인터넷의 발달로 다양한 장르의 음악을 접하는 것이 가능해졌다.
③ 비평가의 **음악 비평**은 자신의 주관적인 경험을 기반으로 한다.
④ 오늘날 새로운 음악은 대중의 기호를 확인한 후에 공개된다.
⑤ 온라인 환경의 대두로 **음악 비평**의 질이 전반적으로 상승하였다.

[21학년도 대수능 22번]

주의 '필자'의 주장, '글'의 요지를 선택해야 한다. 일반적으로 알려진 상식과는 다를 수도 있음을 유념한다.

주의 지문의 일부 어구를 이용하여 그럴듯하게 만들어 낸 선택지에 주의한다.

01

24학년도 대수능 20번

다음 글에서 필자가 주장하는 바로 가장 적절한 것은?

Values alone do not create and build culture. Living your values only some of the time does not contribute to the creation and maintenance of culture. Changing values into behaviors is only half the battle. Certainly, this is a step in the right direction, but those behaviors must then be shared and distributed widely throughout the organization, along with a clear and concise description of what is expected. It is not enough to simply talk about it. It is critical to have a visual representation of the specific behaviors that leaders and all people managers can use to coach their people. Just like a sports team has a playbook with specific plays designed to help them perform well and win, your company should have a playbook with the key shifts needed to transform your culture into action and turn your values into winning behaviors.

① 조직 문화 혁신을 위해서 모든 구성원이 공유할 핵심 가치를 정립해야 한다.
② 조직 구성원의 행동을 변화시키려면 지도자는 명확한 가치관을 가져야 한다.
③ 조직 내 문화가 공유되기 위해서 구성원의 자발적 행동이 뒷받침되어야 한다.
④ 조직의 핵심 가치 실현을 위해 구성원 간의 지속적인 의사소통이 필수적이다.
⑤ 조직의 문화 형성에는 가치를 반영한 행동의 공유를 위한 명시적 지침이 필요하다.

02

〈 24학년도 9월 모평 20번 〉

다음 글에서 필자가 주장하는 바로 가장 적절한 것은?

Confident is not the same as comfortable. One of the biggest misconceptions about becoming self-confident is that it means living fearlessly. The key to building confidence is quite the opposite. It means we are willing to let fear be present as we do the things that matter to us. When we establish some self-confidence in something, it feels good. We want to stay there and hold on to it. But if we only go where we feel confident, then confidence never expands beyond that. If we only do the things we know we can do well, fear of the new and unknown tends to grow. Building confidence inevitably demands that we make friends with vulnerability because it is the only way to be without confidence for a while. But the only way confidence can grow is when we are willing to be without it. When we can step into fear and sit with the unknown, it is the courage of doing so that builds confidence from the ground up.

*vulnerability: 취약성

① 적성을 파악하기 위해서는 자신 있는 일을 다양하게 시도해야 한다.

② 자신감을 키우기 위해 낯설고 두려운 일에 도전하는 용기를 가져야 한다.

③ 어려운 일을 자신 있게 수행하기 위해 사전에 계획을 철저히 세워야 한다.

④ 과도한 자신감을 갖기보다는 자신의 약점을 객관적으로 분석해야 한다.

⑤ 자신의 경험과 지식을 바탕으로 당면한 문제에 자신 있게 대처해야 한다.

03

〈 24학년도 대수능 22번 〉

다음 글의 요지로 가장 적절한 것은?

Being able to prioritize your responses allows you to connect more deeply with individual customers, be it a one-off interaction around a particularly delightful or upsetting experience, or the development of a longer-term relationship with a significantly influential individual within your customer base. If you've ever posted a favorable comment — or any comment, for that matter — about a brand, product or service, think about what it would feel like if you were personally acknowledged by the brand manager, for example, as a result. In general, people post because they have something to say — and because they want to be recognized for having said it. In particular, when people post positive comments they are expressions of appreciation for the experience that led to the post. While a compliment to the person standing next to you is typically answered with a response like "Thank You," the sad fact is that most brand compliments go unanswered. These are lost opportunities to understand what drove the compliments and create a solid fan based on them.

*compliment: 칭찬

① 고객과의 관계 증진을 위해 고객의 브랜드 칭찬에 응답하는 것은 중요하다.

② 고객의 피드백을 면밀히 분석함으로써 브랜드의 성공 가능성을 높일 수 있다.

③ 신속한 고객 응대를 통해서 고객의 긍정적인 반응을 이끌어 낼 수 있다.

④ 브랜드 매니저에게는 고객의 부정적인 의견을 수용하는 태도가 요구된다.

⑤ 고객의 의견을 경청하는 것은 브랜드의 새로운 이미지 창출에 도움이 된다.

정답 및 해설 p. 58

DAY 016

주장과 요지

전략 적용하기

제한시간 | 4분

01

24학년도 6월 모평 20번

다음 글에서 필자가 주장하는 바로 가장 적절한 것은?

Certain hindrances to multifaceted creative activity may lie in premature specialization, i.e., having to choose the direction of education or to focus on developing one ability too early in life. However, development of creative ability in one domain may enhance effectiveness in other domains that require similar skills, and flexible switching between generality and specificity is helpful to productivity in many domains. Excessive specificity may result in information from outside the domain being underestimated and unavailable, which leads to fixedness of thinking, whereas excessive generality causes chaos, vagueness, and shallowness. Both tendencies pose a threat to the transfer of knowledge and skills between domains. What should therefore be optimal for the development of cross-domain creativity is support for young people in taking up creative challenges in a specific domain and coupling it with encouragement to apply knowledge and skills in, as well as from, other domains, disciplines, and tasks.

① 창의성을 개발하기 위해서는 도전과 실패를 두려워하지 말아야 한다.
② 전문 지식과 기술을 전수하려면 집중적인 투자가 선행되어야 한다.
③ 창의적인 인재를 육성하기 위해 다양한 교육 과정을 준비해야 한다.
④ 특정 영역에서 개발된 창의성이 영역 간 활용되도록 장려해야 한다.
⑤ 조기 교육을 통해 특정 분야의 전문가를 지속적으로 양성해야 한다.

02

24학년도 9월 모평 22번

다음 글의 요지로 가장 적절한 것은?

The need to assimilate values and lifestyle of the host culture has become a growing conflict. Multiculturalists suggest that there should be a model of partial assimilation in which immigrants retain some of their customs, beliefs, and language. There is pressure to conform rather than to maintain their cultural identities, however, and these conflicts are greatly determined by the community to which one migrates. These experiences are not new; many Europeans experienced exclusion and poverty during the first two waves of immigration in the 19th and 20th centuries. Eventually, these immigrants transformed this country with significant changes that included enlightenment and acceptance of diversity. People of color, however, continue to struggle for acceptance. Once again, the challenge is to recognize that other cultures think and act differently and that they have the right to do so. Perhaps, in the not too distant future, immigrants will no longer be strangers among us.

① 이민자 고유의 정체성을 유지할 권리에 대한 공동체의 인식이 필요하다.
② 이민자의 적응을 돕기 위해 그들의 요구를 반영한 정책 수립이 중요하다.
③ 이민자는 미래 사회의 긍정적 변화에 핵심적 역할을 수행할 수 있다.
④ 다문화 사회의 안정을 위해서는 국제적 차원의 지속적인 협력이 요구된다.
⑤ 문화적 동화는 장기적이고 체계적인 과정을 통해 점진적으로 이루어진다.

03

24학년도 6월 모평 22번

다음 글의 요지로 가장 적절한 것은?

When it comes to the Internet, it just pays to be a little paranoid (but not a lot). Given the level of anonymity with all that resides on the Internet, it's sensible to question the validity of any data that you may receive. Typically it's to our natural instinct when we meet someone coming down a sidewalk to place yourself in some manner of protective position, especially when they introduce themselves as having known you, much to your surprise. By design, we set up challenges in which the individual must validate how they know us by presenting scenarios, names or acquaintances, or evidence by which to validate (that is, photographs). Once we have received that information and it has gone through a cognitive validation, we accept that person as more trustworthy. All this happens in a matter of minutes but is a natural defense mechanism that we perform in the real world. However, in the virtual world, we have a tendency to be less defensive, as there appears to be no physical threat to our well-being.

*paranoid: 편집성의 **anonymity: 익명

① 가상 세계 특유의 익명성 때문에 표현의 자유가 남용되기도 한다.
② 인터넷 정보의 신뢰도를 검증하는 기술은 점진적으로 향상되고 있다.
③ 가상 세계에서는 현실 세계와 달리 자유로운 정보 공유가 가능하다.
④ 안전한 인터넷 환경 구축을 위해 보안 프로그램을 설치하는 것이 좋다.
⑤ 방어 기제가 덜 작동하는 가상 세계에서는 신중한 정보 검증이 중요하다.

정답 및 해설 p. 62

DAY 017

글의 주제

전략 익히기

⏱ 제한시간 | 4분

주제문을 요약한 어구 또는 글의 핵심 소재를 말한다.

전략 1 주제문을 찾는다.

주요 세부 사항들에 의해 뒷받침되거나 구체적으로 부연 설명되고 있는 것을 종합적, 포괄적, 추상적으로 표현한 1~2문장이다. 주요 세부 사항들이 어떤 주장을 뒷받침하는 구체적인 논거일 경우는 그 주장이 주제문이다. 주장은 강하게 표현될 수도 있지만, may, can 등의 여러 표현으로 다소 약하게 표현될 수도 있다.

그 외, 아래와 같은 구조의 지문에 주의한다.

1. A와 B를 대조하는 글: 긍정적으로 서술하는 것
오로지 A와 B가 다르다는 것을 말하기 위한 글도 있지만 수능에서는 드물다. 보통 A, B 중 뒤에 나오는 B를 긍정적으로 서술하여 내용상 강조한다. 이때는 B가 곧 주제이다.

2. 원인/결과 구조: 뒤에 서술하는 것
즉, 원인→결과 구조는 '결과'가, 결과→원인 구조는 '원인'이 주제이다.

3. Myth-Truth 구조
Truth가 주제이며, Problem-Solution 구조에서는 Solution이 주제이다.

4. 실험 연구문
연구 결과 또는 시사점을 간략히 표현한 것이 주제이다.

전략 2 주제문이 명시되어 있지 않을 경우, 주요 세부 사항으로 추론한다.

주의 보이는 표현만으로 주제문을 섣불리 판단해서는 안 된다. 역접 접속사나 주장 표현이 있지만 세부 사항인 문장이나, 바로 뒤에 예가 따르지만 도입에 불과한 문장에 주의해야 한다. 주제문은 주요 세부 사항에 의해 뒷받침되어야 한다는 것을 항상 기억해야 한다.

주의 오답 선택지는 흔히 지문에 자주 반복되는 단어나 쉽게 연상되는 어구를 포함한다. 특히 긴 세부 사항에서 반복되는 단어를 글의 핵심어로 판단하지 않도록 해야 한다.

01

24학년도 대수능 23번

다음 글의 주제로 가장 적절한 것은?

Managers of natural resources typically face market incentives that provide financial rewards for exploitation. For example, owners of forest lands have a market incentive to cut down trees rather than manage the forest for carbon capture, wildlife habitat, flood protection, and other ecosystem services. These services provide the owner with no financial benefits, and thus are unlikely to influence management decisions. But the economic benefits provided by these services, based on their non-market values, may exceed the economic value of the timber. For example, a United Nations initiative has estimated that the economic benefits of ecosystem services provided by tropical forests, including climate regulation, water purification, and erosion prevention, are over three times greater per hectare than the market benefits. Thus cutting down the trees is economically inefficient, and markets are not sending the correct "signal" to favor ecosystem services over extractive uses.

*exploitation: 이용 **timber: 목재

① necessity of calculating the market values of ecosystem services
② significance of weighing forest resources' non-market values
③ impact of using forest resources to maximize financial benefits
④ merits of balancing forests' market and non-market values
⑤ ways of increasing the efficiency of managing natural resources

02

24학년도 9월 모평 23번

다음 글의 주제로 가장 적절한 것은?

The primary purpose of commercial music radio broadcasting is to deliver an audience to a group of advertisers and sponsors. To achieve commercial success, that audience must be as large as possible. More than any other characteristics (such as demographic or psychographic profile, purchasing power, level of interest, degree of satisfaction, quality of attention or emotional state), the quantity of an audience aggregated as a mass is the most significant metric for broadcasters seeking to make music radio for profitable ends. As a result, broadcasters attempt to maximise their audience size by playing music that is popular, or — at the very least — music that can be relied upon not to cause audiences to switch off their radio or change the station. Audience retention is a key value (if not the key value) for many music programmers and for radio station management. In consequence, a high degree of risk aversion frequently marks out the 'successful' radio music programmer. Playlists are restricted, and often very small.

*aggregate: 모으다 **aversion: 싫어함

① features of music playlists appealing to international audiences
② influence of advertisers on radio audiences' musical preferences
③ difficulties of increasing audience size in radio music programmes
④ necessity of satisfying listeners' diverse needs in the radio business
⑤ outcome of music radio businesses' attempts to attract large audiences

03

24학년도 6월 모평 23번

다음 글의 주제로 가장 적절한 것은? [3점]

There are pressures *within* the museum that cause it to emphasise what happens in the galleries over the activities that take place in its unseen zones. In an era when museums are forced to increase their earnings, they often focus their energies on modernising their galleries or mounting temporary exhibitions to bring more and more audiences through the door. In other words, as museums struggle to survive in a competitive economy, their budgets often prioritise those parts of themselves that are consumable: infotainment in the galleries, goods and services in the cafes and the shops. The unlit, unglamorous storerooms, if they are ever discussed, are at best presented as service areas that process objects for the exhibition halls. And at worst, as museums pour more and more resources into their publicly visible faces, the spaces of storage may even suffer, their modernisation being kept on hold or being given less and less space to house the expanding collections and serve their complex conservation needs.

① importance of prioritising museums' exhibition spaces
② benefits of diverse activities in museums for audiences
③ necessity of expanding storerooms for displaying objects
④ consequences of profit-oriented management of museums
⑤ ways to increase museums' commitment to the public good

정답 및 해설 p. 66

DAY 018

글의 주제

전략 적용하기

⏱ 제한시간 | 4분

01

〈23학년도 대수능 23번〉

다음 글의 주제로 가장 적절한 것은? [3점]

An important advantage of disclosure, as opposed to more aggressive forms of regulation, is its flexibility and respect for the operation of free markets. Regulatory mandates are blunt swords; they tend to neglect diversity and may have serious unintended adverse effects. For example, energy efficiency requirements for appliances may produce goods that work less well or that have characteristics that consumers do not want. Information provision, by contrast, respects freedom of choice. If automobile manufacturers are required to measure and publicize the safety characteristics of cars, potential car purchasers can trade safety concerns against other attributes, such as price and styling. If restaurant customers are informed of the calories in their meals, those who want to lose weight can make use of the information, leaving those who are unconcerned about calories unaffected. Disclosure does not interfere with, and should even promote, the autonomy (and quality) of individual decision-making.

*mandate: 명령 **adverse: 거스르는 ***autonomy: 자율성

① steps to make public information accessible to customers
② benefits of publicizing information to ensure free choices
③ strategies for companies to increase profits in a free market
④ necessities of identifying and analyzing current industry trends
⑤ effects of diversified markets on reasonable customer choices

02

〈23학년도 9월 모평 23번〉

다음 글의 주제로 가장 적절한 것은? [3점]

Environmental learning occurs when farmers base decisions on observations of "payoff" information. They may observe their own or neighbors' farms, but it is the empirical results they are using as a guide, not the neighbors themselves. They are looking at farming activities as experiments and assessing such factors as relative advantage, compatibility with existing resources, difficulty of use, and "trialability" — how well can it be experimented with. But that criterion of "trialability" turns out to be a real problem; it's true that farmers are always experimenting, but working farms are very flawed laboratories. Farmers cannot set up the controlled conditions of professional test plots in research facilities. Farmers also often confront complex and difficult-to-observe phenomena that would be hard to manage even if they could run controlled experiments. Moreover farmers can rarely acquire payoff information on more than a few of the production methods they might use, which makes the criterion of "relative advantage" hard to measure.

*empirical: 경험적인 **compatibility: 양립성 ***criterion: 기준

① limitations of using empirical observations in farming
② challenges in modernizing traditional farming equipment
③ necessity of prioritizing trialability in agricultural innovation
④ importance of making instinctive decisions in agriculture
⑤ ways to control unpredictable agricultural phenomena

03

〈23학년도 6월 모평 23번〉

다음 글의 주제로 가장 적절한 것은? [3점]

Considerable work by cultural psychologists and anthropologists has shown that there are indeed large and sometimes surprising differences in the words and concepts that different cultures have for describing emotions, as well as in the social circumstances that draw out the expression of particular emotions. However, those data do not actually show that different cultures have different emotions, if we think of emotions as central, neurally implemented states. As for, say, color vision, they just say that, despite the same internal processing architecture, how we interpret, categorize, and name emotions varies according to culture and that we learn in a particular culture the social context in which it is appropriate to express emotions. However, the emotional states themselves are likely to be quite invariant across cultures. In a sense, we can think of a basic, culturally universal emotion set that is shaped by evolution and implemented in the brain, but the links between such emotional states and stimuli, behavior, and other cognitive states are plastic and can be modified by learning in a specific cultural context.

*anthropologist: 인류학자 **stimuli: 자극 ***cognitive: 인지적인

① essential links between emotions and behaviors
② culturally constructed representation of emotions
③ falsely described emotions through global languages
④ universally defined emotions across academic disciplines
⑤ wider influence of cognition on learning cultural contexts

정답 및 해설 p. 70

DAY 019

글의 제목

전략 익히기

⌚ 제한시간 | 4분

주제 유형에서처럼 주제문을 찾아 해결한다.

전략 1 주제문을 찾는다.

전략 2 선택지 특성을 미리 이해한다.

선택지들은 '제목' 본연의 기능(독자로 하여금 글을 읽고 싶게 하는)에 맞추어 '멋있게 포장'된 느낌을 준다. 주제와 별다른 차이가 없는 선택지도 있을 수 있지만, 대부분은 아래와 같은 기법들을 이용하여 제목 특유의 느낌이 드러난다.

비유	e.g. 긍정적 면과 부정적 면을 다 가지고 있는 것: double-edged sword(양날의 검)
A: B	콜론 앞뒤는 다른 것을 풀어서 설명하거나 수식한다. A≒B로 이해하면 쉽다.
의문문	1. 글의 핵심을 질문 형식으로 표현한 것이다. 2. 핵심 소재에 대한 부정적 견해를 수사의문문으로 표현할 수 있다.
명령문	필자 주장이 주제문인 경우, 이를 명령문으로 표현할 수 있다.
생략	대명사, be동사, 전치사, 관사 등은 자주 생략하여 간결하고 임팩트 있게 표현한다.

주의 정답 선택지는 주제문의 핵심을 명확히 담지 않을 수도 있다. 5개의 선택지 중 '가장 적절한 것'을 선택하는 것임을 잊지 말자.

예1. 'A의 주요 역할은 B'라는 글이 있을 때, 제목은 B를 빼고 '무엇이 A의 주요 역할인가'로 표현될 수 있다. B가 주제문의 핵심인데도 제외하고 표현할 수 있다. 이는 독자의 호기심을 자아내기 때문에 대표적인 제목 기법 중의 하나이다.
예2. 'A가 아니라 B'라는 글은 B를 주장하고 있는 것임에도 제목은 'A인가 B인가'로 표현될 수 있다.

01

24학년도 대수능 24번

다음 글의 제목으로 가장 적절한 것은? [3점]

The concept of overtourism rests on a particular assumption about people and places common in tourism studies and the social sciences in general. Both are seen as clearly defined and demarcated. People are framed as bounded social actors either playing the role of hosts or guests. Places, in a similar way, are treated as stable containers with clear boundaries. Hence, places can be full of tourists and thus suffer from overtourism. But what does it mean for a place to be full of people? Indeed, there are examples of particular attractions that have limited capacity and where there is actually no room for more visitors. This is not least the case with some man-made constructions such as the Eiffel Tower. However, with places such as cities, regions or even whole countries being promoted as destinations and described as victims of overtourism, things become more complex. What is excessive or out of proportion is highly relative and might be more related to other aspects than physical capacity, such as natural degradation and economic leakages (not to mention politics and local power dynamics).

*demarcate: 경계를 정하다

① The Solutions to Overtourism: From Complex to Simple
② What Makes Popular Destinations Attractive to Visitors?
③ Are Tourist Attractions Winners or Losers of Overtourism?
④ The Severity of Overtourism: Much Worse than Imagined
⑤ Overtourism: Not Simply a Matter of People and Places

02

(24학년도 9월 모평 24번)

다음 글의 제목으로 가장 적절한 것은? [3점]

Before the web, newspaper archives were largely the musty domain of professional researchers and journalism students. Journalism was, by definition, current. The general accessibility of archives has greatly extended the shelf life of journalism, with older stories now regularly cited to provide context for more current ones. With regard to how meaning is made of complex issues encountered in the news, this departure can be understood as a readiness by online news consumers to engage with the underlying issues and contexts of the news that was not apparent in, or even possible for, print consumers. One of the emergent qualities of online news, determined in part by the depth of readily accessible online archives, seems to be the possibility of understanding news stories as the manifest outcomes of larger economic, social and cultural issues rather than short-lived and unconnected media spectacles.

*archive: 기록 보관소 **musty: 곰팡내 나는 ***manifest: 분명한

① Web-based Journalism: Lasting Longer and Contextually Wider
② With the Latest Content, Online News Beats Daily Newspapers!
③ How Online Media Journalists Reveal Hidden Stories Behind News
④ Let's Begin a Journey to the Past with Printed Newspapers!
⑤ Present and Future of Journalism in the Web World

03

(24학년도 6월 모평 24번)

다음 글의 제목으로 가장 적절한 것은?

Hyper-mobility — the notion that more travel at faster speeds covering longer distances generates greater economic success — seems to be a distinguishing feature of urban areas, where more than half of the world's population currently reside. By 2005, approximately 7.5 billion trips were made each day in cities worldwide. In 2050, there may be three to four times as many passenger-kilometres travelled as in the year 2000, infrastructure and energy prices permitting. Freight movement could also rise more than threefold during the same period. Mobility flows have become a key dynamic of urbanization, with the associated infrastructure invariably constituting the backbone of urban form. Yet, despite the increasing level of urban mobility worldwide, access to places, activities and services has become increasingly difficult. Not only is it less convenient — in terms of time, cost and comfort — to access locations in cities, but the very process of moving around in cities generates a number of negative externalities. Accordingly, many of the world's cities face an unprecedented accessibility crisis, and are characterized by unsustainable mobility systems.

*freight: 화물

① Is Hyper-mobility Always Good for Cities?
② Accessibility: A Guide to a Web of Urban Areas
③ A Long and Winding Road to Economic Success
④ Inevitable Regional Conflicts from Hyper-mobility
⑤ Infrastructure: An Essential Element of Hyper-mobility

정답 및 해설 p. 74

DAY 020

글의 제목

전략 적용하기

제한시간 | 4분

01

23학년도 대수능 24번

다음 글의 제목으로 가장 적절한 것은?

Different parts of the brain's visual system get information on a need-to-know basis. Cells that help your hand muscles reach out to an object need to know the size and location of the object, but they don't need to know about color. They need to know a little about shape, but not in great detail. Cells that help you recognize people's faces need to be extremely sensitive to details of shape, but they can pay less attention to location. It is natural to assume that anyone who sees an object sees everything about it — the shape, color, location, and movement. However, one part of your brain sees its shape, another sees color, another detects location, and another perceives movement. Consequently, after localized brain damage, it is possible to see certain aspects of an object and not others. Centuries ago, people found it difficult to imagine how someone could see an object without seeing what color it is. Even today, you might find it surprising to learn about people who see an object without seeing where it is, or see it without seeing whether it is moving.

① Visual Systems Never Betray Our Trust!
② Secret Missions of Color-Sensitive Brain Cells
③ Blind Spots: What Is Still Unknown About the Brain
④ Why Brain Cells Exemplify Nature's Recovery Process
⑤ Separate and Independent: Brain Cells' Visual Perceptions

02

23학년도 9월 모평 24번

다음 글의 제목으로 가장 적절한 것은?

Not only musicians and psychologists, but also committed music enthusiasts and experts often voice the opinion that the beauty of music lies in an expressive deviation from the exactly defined score. Concert performances become interesting and gain in attraction from the fact that they go far beyond the information printed in the score. In his early studies on musical performance, Carl Seashore discovered that musicians only rarely play two equal notes in exactly the same way. Within the same metric structure, there is a wide potential of variations in tempo, volume, tonal quality and intonation. Such variation is based on the composition but diverges from it individually. We generally call this 'expressivity'. This explains why we do not lose interest when we hear different artists perform the same piece of music. It also explains why it is worthwhile for following generations to repeat the same repertoire. New, inspiring interpretations help us to expand our understanding, which serves to enrich and animate the music scene.

*deviation: 벗어남

① How to Build a Successful Career in Music Criticism
② Never the Same: The Value of Variation in Music Performance
③ The Importance of Personal Expression in Music Therapy
④ Keep Your Cool: Overcoming Stage Fright When Playing Music
⑤ What's New in the Classical Music Industry?

03

23학년도 6월 모평 24번

다음 글의 제목으로 가장 적절한 것은?

The approach, *joint cognitive systems*, treats a robot as part of a human-machine team where the intelligence is synergistic, arising from the contributions of each agent. The team consists of at least one robot and one human and is often called a *mixed team* because it is a mixture of human and robot agents. Self-driving cars, where a person turns on and off the driving, is an example of a joint cognitive system. Entertainment robots are examples of mixed teams as are robots for telecommuting. The design process concentrates on how the agents will cooperate and coordinate with each other to accomplish the team goals. Rather than treating robots as peer agents with their own completely independent agenda, joint cognitive systems approaches treat robots as helpers such as service animals or sheep dogs. In joint cognitive system designs, artificial intelligence is used along with human-robot interaction principles to create robots that can be intelligent enough to be good team members.

① Better Together: Human and Machine Collaboration
② Can Robots Join Forces to Outperform Human Teams?
③ Loss of Humanity in the Human and Machine Conflict
④ Power Off: When and How to Say No to Robot Partners
⑤ Shifting from Service Animals to Robot Assistants of Humans

정답 및 해설 p. 78

DAY 021

무관 문장

전략 익히기

⏱ 제한시간 | 4분

대부분 선택지 번호가 없는 글 초반에 주제문이 있다. 이후 선택지 번호가 매겨진 문장들은 이를 구체적으로 설명하거나 뒷받침하는 세부 사항들이다.

전략 1 선택지 번호가 없는 초반 부분을 보고 글의 대의를 확인한다.

구체적인 설명이 뒷받침되어야 할 주장이나 핵심 어구가 무엇인지를 판단한다.

전략 2 정답의 속성을 알아둔다.

글의 대의를 반대로 뒷받침하거나, 핵심어를 담되 다른 방향으로 서술한다. 예를 들어 A의 긍정적 효과를 말하는 글에서, A의 부정적 효과를 말하는 문장이나 A의 전파 과정을 서술하는 문장이 정답이다.

주의 대부분의 정답 문장은 아래와 같은 속성을 포함하여 글의 전체 흐름과 유관하게 보이는 동시에 특히 앞 문장과 강하게 연결된 듯이 보이도록 연출하므로 주의해야 한다.

1. 글에서 자주 반복되는 핵심어를 포함한다.
2. This is why, therefore, however 등의 연결어를 사용한다.
3. 바로 앞 문장의 어구와 같은 어구를 사용한다.

주의 주로, 정답의 앞뒤 문장을 오답으로 선택하는 확률이 높으므로 선택한 정답의 앞뒤 문장이 확실한 오답인지 확인하는 것이 좋다. 정답 선택지를 제외하고 앞뒤 문장이 자연스럽게 연결되는지도 확인한다.

01

〈24학년도 대수능 35번〉

다음 글에서 전체 흐름과 관계 없는 문장은?

Speaking fast is a high-risk proposition. It's nearly impossible to maintain the ideal conditions to be persuasive, well-spoken, and effective when the mouth is traveling well over the speed limit. ① Although we'd like to think that our minds are sharp enough to always make good decisions with the greatest efficiency, they just aren't. ② In rcality, the brain arrives at an intersection of four or five possible things to say and sits idling for a couple of seconds, considering the options. ③ Making a good decision helps you speak faster because it provides you with more time to come up with your responses. ④ When the brain stops sending navigational instructions back to the mouth and the mouth is moving too fast to pause, that's when you get a verbal fender bender, otherwise known as filler. ⑤ *Um*, *ah*, *you know*, and *like* are what your mouth does when it has nowhere to go.

02

24학년도 9월 모평 35번

다음 글에서 전체 흐름과 관계 없는 문장은?

Although organizations are offering telecommuting programs in greater numbers than ever before, acceptance and use of these programs are still limited by a number of factors. ① These factors include manager reliance on face-to-face management practices, lack of telecommuting training within an organization, misperceptions of and discomfort with flexible workplace programs, and a lack of information about the effects of telecommuting on an organization's bottom line. ② Despite these limitations, at the beginning of the 21st century, a new "anytime, anywhere" work culture is emerging. ③ Care must be taken to select employees whose personal and working characteristics are best suited for telecommuting. ④ Continuing advances in information technology, the expansion of a global workforce, and increased desire to balance work and family are only three of the many factors that will gradually reduce the current barriers to telecommuting as a dominant workforce development. ⑤ With implications for organizational cost savings, especially with regard to lower facility costs, increased employee flexibility, and productivity, telecommuting is increasingly of interest to many organizations.

*telecommute: (컴퓨터로) 집에서 근무하다

03

24학년도 6월 모평 35번

다음 글에서 전체 흐름과 관계 없는 문장은?

Interestingly, experts do not suffer as much as beginners when performing complex tasks or combining multiple tasks. Because experts have extensive practice within a limited domain, the key component skills in their domain tend to be highly practiced and more automated. ① Each of these highly practiced skills then demands relatively few cognitive resources, effectively lowering the total cognitive load that experts experience. ② Thus, experts can perform complex tasks and combine multiple tasks relatively easily. ③ Furthermore, beginners are excellent at processing the tasks when the tasks are divided and isolated. ④ This is not because they necessarily have more cognitive resources than beginners; rather, because of the high level of fluency they have achieved in performing key skills, they can do more with what they have. ⑤ Beginners, on the other hand, have not achieved the same degree of fluency and automaticity in each of the component skills, and thus they struggle to combine skills that experts combine with relative ease and efficiency.

정답 및 해설 p. 82

DAY 022

무관 문장

전략 적용하기

제한시간 | 4분

01

23학년도 대수능 35번

다음 글에서 전체 흐름과 관계 없는 문장은?

Actors, singers, politicians and countless others recognise the power of the human voice as a means of communication beyond the simple decoding of the words that are used. Learning to control your voice and use it for different purposes is, therefore, one of the most important skills to develop as an early career teacher. ① The more confidently you give instructions, the higher the chance of a positive class response. ② There are times when being able to project your voice loudly will be very useful when working in school, and knowing that you can cut through a noisy classroom, dinner hall or playground is a great skill to have. ③ In order to address serious noise issues in school, students, parents and teachers should search for a solution together. ④ However, I would always advise that you use your loudest voice incredibly sparingly and avoid shouting as much as possible. ⑤ A quiet, authoritative and measured tone has so much more impact than slightly panicked shouting.

02

23학년도 9월 모평 35번

다음 글에서 전체 흐름과 관계 없는 문장은?

Because plants tend to recover from disasters more quickly than animals, they are essential to the revitalization of damaged environments. Why do plants have this preferential ability to recover from disaster? It is largely because, unlike animals, they can generate new organs and tissues throughout their life cycle. ① This ability is due to the activity of plant meristems — regions of undifferentiated tissue in roots and shoots that can, in response to specific cues, differentiate into new tissues and organs. ② If meristems are not damaged during disasters, plants can recover and ultimately transform the destroyed or barren environment. ③ You can see this phenomenon on a smaller scale when a tree struck by lightning forms new branches that grow from the old scar. ④ In the form of forests and grasslands, plants regulate the cycling of water and adjust the chemical composition of the atmosphere. ⑤ In addition to regeneration or resprouting of plants, disturbed areas can also recover through reseeding.

*revitalization: 소생

03

23학년도 6월 모평 35번

다음 글에서 전체 흐름과 관계 없는 문장은?

The animal in a conflict between attacking a rival and fleeing may initially not have sufficient information to enable it to make a decision straight away. ① If the rival is likely to win the fight, then the optimal decision would be to give up immediately and not risk getting injured. ② But if the rival is weak and easily defeatable, then there could be considerable benefit in going ahead and obtaining the territory, females, food or whatever is at stake. ③ Animals under normal circumstances maintain a very constant body weight and they eat and drink enough for their needs at regular intervals. ④ By taking a little extra time to collect information about the opponent, the animal is more likely to reach a decision that maximizes its chances of winning than if it takes a decision without such information. ⑤ Many signals are now seen as having this information gathering or 'assessment' function, directly contributing to the mechanism of the decision-making process by supplying vital information about the likely outcomes of the various options.

정답 및 해설 p. 86

DAY 023

요약문

전략 익히기

ⓛ 제한시간 | 4분

주어진 요약문은 글의 중요 내용을 담고 있으며, 서로 다른 두 개의 핵심어 빈칸을 포함한다. 빈칸 하나를 정확히 추론했다고 해서 나머지 하나를 자동적으로 알 수 있지는 않으므로 각각 판단해야 한다.

전략 1 요약문부터 읽는다.

요약문은 빈칸을 제외하더라도 중요 정보가 많이 들어있으므로 완전히 숙지해야 한다. 찾아야 할 것이 무엇인지도 분명히 파악한다.

전략 2 선택지를 빈칸에 대입해보고 단서를 찾아 글을 읽는다.

각 (A), (B)의 빈칸 선택지는 같은 단어를 중복 제시하여 3개 또는 모두 다른 5개 단어씩으로 구성된다. 크게 긍정적-부정적 두 가지 어감으로 좁힐 수도 있다. 아래처럼 빈칸에 선택지를 대입해보는 과정이 중요하다.

> In vertical transfer, lower level knowledge is ____(A)____ before one proceeds to a higher level; however, in the case of lateral transfer, ____(B)____ knowledge can be helpful, but it is not required.

(A)		(B)	(A)		(B)
① essential	……	prior	② practical	……	detailed
③ useless	……	relevant	④ practical	……	independent
⑤ essential	……	unbiased			

→ 요약문은 vertical transfer와 lateral transfer를 대조하여 각 지식이 어떠하다는 내용이다.

i) vertical transfer에서는 낮은 레벨의 지식이 어떤(필수적/실용적/소용없는) 것일지?

ii) lateral transfer에서는 어떤(선험적/자세한/유관한/독립적/편견 없는) 지식이 도움이 될지?

주의 요약문의 부정 표현(not, no, never, little, few 등)이나 의미상 혼동을 주는 구문에 주의한다.

주의 반드시 지문 속의 단서를 근거로 정답을 선택해야 한다. 정답을 주관적 논리로 추론하는 것은 어떤 유형에서도 금물이다.

01

24학년도 대수능 40번

다음 글의 내용을 한 문장으로 요약하고자 한다. 빈칸 (A), (B)에 들어갈 말로 가장 적절한 것은?

Even those with average talent can produce notable work in the various sciences, so long as they do not try to embrace all of them at once. Instead, they should concentrate attention on one subject after another (that is, in different periods of time), although later work will weaken earlier attainments in the other spheres. This amounts to saying that the brain adapts to universal science in *time* but not in *space*. In fact, even those with great abilities proceed in this way. Thus, when we are astonished by someone with publications in different scientific fields, realize that each topic was explored during a specific period of time. Knowledge gained earlier certainly will not have disappeared from the mind of the author, but it will have become simplified by condensing into formulas or greatly abbreviated symbols. Thus, sufficient space remains for the perception and learning of new images on the cerebral blackboard.

*condense: 응축하다 **cerebral: 대뇌의

↓

> Exploring one scientific subject after another ____(A)____ remarkable work across the sciences, as the previously gained knowledge is retained in simplified forms within the brain, which ____(B)____ room for new learning.

	(A)		(B)
①	enables	……	leaves
②	challenges	……	spares
③	delays	……	creates
④	requires	……	removes
⑤	invites	……	diminishes

02

〈24학년도 9월 모평 40번〉

다음 글의 내용을 한 문장으로 요약하고자 한다. 빈칸 (A), (B)에 들어 갈 말로 가장 적절한 것은?

Research for historical fiction may focus on under-documented ordinary people, events, or sites. Fiction helps portray everyday situations, feelings, and atmosphere that recreate the historical context. Historical fiction adds "flesh to the bare bones that historians are able to uncover and by doing so provides an account that while not necessarily true provides a clearer indication of past events, circumstances and cultures." Fiction adds color, sound, drama to the past, as much as it invents parts of the past. And Robert Rosenstone argues that invention is not the weakness of films, it is their strength. Fiction can allow users to see parts of the past that have never — for lack of archives — been represented. In fact, Gilden Seavey explains that if producers of historical fiction had strongly held the strict academic standards, many historical subjects would remain unexplored for lack of appropriate evidence. Historical fiction should, therefore, not be seen as the opposite of professional history, but rather as a challenging representation of the past from which both public historians and popular audiences may learn.

↓

> While historical fiction reconstructs the past using ____(A)____ evidence, it provides an inviting description, which may ____(B)____ people's understanding of historical events.

(A)		(B)
① insignificant	……	delay
② insufficient	……	enrich
③ concrete	……	enhance
④ outdated	……	improve
⑤ limited	……	disturb

03

〈24학년도 6월 모평 40번〉

다음 글의 내용을 한 문장으로 요약하고자 한다. 빈칸 (A), (B)에 들어 갈 말로 가장 적절한 것은?

The evolutionary process works on the genetic variation that is available. It follows that natural selection is unlikely to lead to the evolution of perfect, 'maximally fit' individuals. Rather, organisms come to match their environments by being 'the fittest available' or 'the fittest yet': they are not 'the best imaginable'. Part of the lack of fit arises because the present properties of an organism have not all originated in an environment similar in every respect to the one in which it now lives. Over the course of its evolutionary history, an organism's remote ancestors may have evolved a set of characteristics — evolutionary 'baggage' — that subsequently constrain future evolution. For many millions of years, the evolution of vertebrates has been limited to what can be achieved by organisms with a vertebral column. Moreover, much of what we now see as precise matches between an organism and its environment may equally be seen as constraints: koala bears live successfully on *Eucalyptus* foliage, but, from another perspective, koala bears cannot live without *Eucalyptus* foliage.

*vertebrate: 척추동물

↓

> The survival characteristics that an organism currently carries may act as a(n) ____(A)____ to its adaptability when the organism finds itself coping with changes that arise in its ____(B)____.

(A)		(B)
① improvement	……	diet
② obstacle	……	surroundings
③ advantage	……	genes
④ regulator	……	mechanisms
⑤ guide	……	traits

정답 및 해설 p. 90

DAY 024

요약문

전략 적용하기

⏱ 제한시간 | 4분

01

〈23학년도 대수능 40번〉

다음 글의 내용을 한 문장으로 요약하고자 한다. 빈칸 (A), (B)에 들어갈 말로 가장 적절한 것은?

"Craftsmanship" may suggest a way of life that declined with the arrival of industrial society — but this is misleading. Craftsmanship names an enduring, basic human impulse, the desire to do a job well for its own sake. Craftsmanship cuts a far wider swath than skilled manual labor; it serves the computer programmer, the doctor, and the artist; parenting improves when it is practiced as a skilled craft, as does citizenship. In all these domains, craftsmanship focuses on objective standards, on the thing in itself. Social and economic conditions, however, often stand in the way of the craftsman's discipline and commitment: schools may fail to provide the tools to do good work, and workplaces may not truly value the aspiration for quality. And though craftsmanship can reward an individual with a sense of pride in work, this reward is not simple. The craftsman often faces conflicting objective standards of excellence; the desire to do something well for its own sake can be weakened by competitive pressure, by frustration, or by obsession.

*swath: 구획

↓

Craftsmanship, a human desire that has ____(A)____ over time in diverse contexts, often encounters factors that ____(B)____ its full development.

	(A)		(B)
①	persisted	……	limit
②	persisted	……	cultivate
③	evolved	……	accelerate
④	diminished	……	shape
⑤	diminished	……	restrict

02

(23학년도 9월 모평 40번)

다음 글의 내용을 한 문장으로 요약하고자 한다. 빈칸 (A), (B)에 들어갈 말로 가장 적절한 것은?

A striving to demonstrate individual personality through designs should not be surprising. Most designers are educated to work as individuals, and design literature contains countless references to 'the designer'. Personal flair is without doubt an absolute necessity in some product categories, particularly relatively small objects, with a low degree of technological complexity, such as furniture, lighting, small appliances, and housewares. In larger-scale projects, however, even where a strong personality exercises powerful influence, the fact that substantial numbers of designers are employed in implementing a concept can easily be overlooked. The emphasis on individuality is therefore problematic — rather than actually designing, many successful designer 'personalities' function more as creative managers. A distinction needs to be made between designers working truly alone and those working in a group. In the latter case, management organization and processes can be equally as relevant as designers' creativity.

*strive: 애쓰다 **flair: 재능

↓

> Depending on the ____(A)____ of a project, the capacity of designers to ____(B)____ team-based working environments can be just as important as their personal qualities.

(A)		(B)
① size	……	coordinate
② cost	……	systematize
③ size	……	identify
④ cost	……	innovate
⑤ goal	……	investigate

03

(23학년도 6월 모평 40번)

다음 글의 내용을 한 문장으로 요약하고자 한다. 빈칸 (A), (B)에 들어갈 말로 가장 적절한 것은?

Mobilities in transit offer a broad field to be explored by different disciplines in all faculties, in addition to the humanities. In spite of increasing acceleration, for example in travelling through geographical or virtual space, our body becomes more and more a passive non-moving container, which is transported by artefacts or loaded up with inner feelings of being mobile in the so-called information society. Technical mobilities turn human beings into some kind of terminal creatures, who spend most of their time at rest and who need to participate in sports in order to balance their daily disproportion of motion and rest. Have we come closer to Aristotle's image of God as the immobile mover, when elites exercise their power to move money, things and people, while they themselves do not need to move at all? Others, at the bottom of this power, are victims of mobility-structured social exclusion. They cannot decide how and where to move, but are just moved around or locked out or even locked in without either the right to move or the right to stay.

↓

> In a technology and information society, human beings, whose bodily movement is less ____(A)____, appear to have gained increased mobility and power, and such a mobility-related human condition raises the issue of social ____(B)____.

(A)		(B)
① necessary	……	inequality
② necessary	……	growth
③ limited	……	consciousness
④ desirable	……	service
⑤ desirable	……	divide

정답 및 해설 p. 94

DAY 025

글의 순서 | 복합 유형

전략 익히기

⏱ 제한시간 | 4분

보통 하나의 긴 단락으로 출제된다. '(도입)-주제문-주요 세부 사항'의 구성 요소를 판단하면서 긴 호흡으로 읽어야 한다. 이전에는 주로 제목과 빈칸 문제였으나 절대평가 이후로는 제목과 문맥상 낱말 쓰임을 묻는 문제가 출제되고 있다. 앞서 살펴본 글의 제목, 낱말 쓰임 유형의 전략에 따라 해결하되, 한 지문에 풀어야 할 문제가 두 개이므로 아래 전략에 유념한다.

전략 1 문맥상 낱말 쓰임 문제부터 해결하고 제목 문제를 푼다.

낱말 쓰임이 올바른지에 주목하다 보면 풀다 보면 글의 대의를 자연스럽게 알 수 있다. 두 문제이기 때문에 글을 두 번 읽겠다고 생각하지 말고, 한번 읽고 두 문제를 동시에 푸는 방식이 좋다. 낱말 문제는 낱말 쓰임 유형에서 정리한 전략(→ p. 68), 제목 문제는 앞서 글의 제목 유형에서 정리한 전략(→ p. 48)과 동일하다.

전략 2 가장 적절한 제목을 찾는 것은 복합 유형도 마찬가지이다.

단락이 두 개인 경우 두 단락을 모두 아우른 제목이 없으면 두 번째 단락의 제목을 찾는다. 첫 단락이 두 번째 단락을 말하기 위한 도입이라면 제목에 그 내용을 포함하지 않아도 상관없다.

01

23학년도 대수능 36번

주어진 글 다음에 이어질 글의 순서로 가장 적절한 것은?

> A fascinating species of water flea exhibits a kind of flexibility that evolutionary biologists call *adaptive plasticity*.

(A) That's a clever trick, because producing spines and a helmet is costly, in terms of energy, and conserving energy is essential for an organism's ability to survive and reproduce. The water flea only expends the energy needed to produce spines and a helmet when it needs to.

(B) If the baby water flea is developing into an adult in water that includes the chemical signatures of creatures that prey on water fleas, it develops a helmet and spines to defend itself against predators. If the water around it doesn't include the chemical signatures of predators, the water flea doesn't develop these protective devices.

(C) So it may well be that this plasticity is an adaptation: a trait that came to exist in a species because it contributed to reproductive fitness. There are many cases, across many species, of adaptive plasticity. Plasticity is conducive to fitness if there is sufficient variation in the environment.

*spine: 가시 돌기 **conducive: 도움 되는

① (A) – (C) – (B)　② (B) – (A) – (C)
③ (B) – (C) – (A)　④ (C) – (A) – (B)
⑤ (C) – (B) – (A)

02~03

24학년도 대수능 모평 41~42번

다음 글을 읽고, 물음에 답하시오.

One way to avoid contributing to overhyping a story would be to say nothing. However, that is not a realistic option for scientists who feel a strong sense of responsibility to inform the public and policymakers and/or to offer suggestions. Speaking with members of the media has (a) advantages in getting a message out and perhaps receiving favorable recognition, but it runs the risk of misinterpretations, the need for repeated clarifications, and entanglement in never-ending controversy. Hence, the decision of whether to speak with the media tends to be highly individualized. Decades ago, it was (b) unusual for Earth scientists to have results that were of interest to the media, and consequently few media contacts were expected or encouraged. In the 1970s, the few scientists who spoke frequently with the media were often (c) criticized by their fellow scientists for having done so. The situation now is quite different, as many scientists feel a responsibility to speak out because of the importance of global warming and related issues, and many reporters share these feelings. In addition, many scientists are finding that they (d) enjoy the media attention and the public recognition that comes with it. At the same time, other scientists continue to resist speaking with reporters, thereby preserving more time for their science and (e) running the risk of being misquoted and the other unpleasantries associated with media coverage.

*overhype: 과대광고하다 **entanglement: 얽힘

02

윗글의 제목으로 가장 적절한 것은?

① The Troubling Relationship Between Scientists and the Media
② A Scientist's Choice: To Be Exposed to the Media or Not?
③ Scientists! Be Cautious When Talking to the Media
④ The Dilemma over Scientific Truth and Media Attention
⑤ Who Are Responsible for Climate Issues, Scientists or the Media?

03

밑줄 친 (a)~(e) 중에서 문맥상 낱말의 쓰임이 적절하지 않은 것은?

① (a) ② (b) ③ (c) ④ (d) ⑤ (e)

정답 및 해설 p. 98

DAY 026

문장 넣기 | 복합 유형

전략 적용하기

제한시간 | 4분

01

23학년도 대수능 39번

글의 흐름으로 보아, 주어진 문장이 들어가기에 가장 적절한 곳은? [3점]

> It may be easier to reach an agreement when settlement terms don't have to be implemented until months in the future.

Negotiators should try to find ways to slice a large issue into smaller pieces, known as using *salami tactics*. (①) Issues that can be expressed in quantitative, measurable units are easy to slice. (②) For example, compensation demands can be divided into cents-per-hour increments or lease rates can be quoted as dollars per square foot. (③) When working to fractionate issues of principle or precedent, parties may use the time horizon (when the principle goes into effect or how long it will last) as a way to fractionate the issue. (④) Another approach is to vary the number of ways that the principle may be applied. (⑤) For example, a company may devise a family emergency leave plan that allows employees the opportunity to be away from the company for a period of no longer than three hours, and no more than once a month, for illness in the employee's immediate family.

*increment: 증가 **fractionate: 세분하다

02~03

24학년도 9월 모평 41~42번

다음 글을 읽고, 물음에 답하시오.

One reason we think we forget most of what we learned in school is that we underestimate what we actually remember. Other times, we know we remember something, but we don't recognize that we learned it in school. Knowing where and when you learned something is usually called *context information*, and context is handled by (a) different memory processes than memory for the content. Thus, it's quite possible to retain content without remembering the context.

For example, if someone mentions a movie and you think to yourself that you heard it was terrible but can't remember (b) where you heard that, you're recalling the content, but you've lost the context. Context information is frequently (c) easier to forget than content, and it's the source of a variety of memory illusions. For instance, people are (d) unconvinced by a persuasive argument if it's written by someone who is not very credible (e.g., someone with a clear financial interest in the topic). But in time, readers' attitudes, on average, change in the direction of the persuasive argument. Why? Because readers are likely to remember the content of the argument but forget the source — someone who is not credible. If remembering the source of knowledge is difficult, you can see how it would be (e) challenging to conclude you don't remember much from school.

*illusion: 착각

02

윗글의 제목으로 가장 적절한 것은?

① Learned Nothing in School?: How Memory Tricks You
② Why We Forget Selectively: Credibility of Content
③ The Constant Battle Between Content and Context
④ How Students Can Learn More and Better in School
⑤ Shift Your Focus from Who to What for Memory Building

03

밑줄 친 (a)~(e) 중에서 문맥상 낱말의 쓰임이 적절하지 않은 것은?

① (a) ② (b) ③ (c) ④ (d) ⑤ (e)

정답 및 해설 p. 101

DAY 027

밑줄 어법

전략 익히기

⏱ 제한시간 | 4분

세세한 포인트가 골고루 다양하게 출제되기보다는 주요 포인트들이 반복 출제된다.

전략 1 반복 출제되는 포인트를 알아둔다.

1. 정동사 vs. 준동사: 절에는 동사가 반드시 필요하다. 동사 이외에는 준동사로 표현된다.
2. 관계대명사 vs. 접속사: 절이 완전한 구조인지 아닌지에 따라 판단한다. 1, 2문형(SV, SVC)에 주의한다.
3. 병렬 구조: and, but, or 뒤에 밑줄이 있으며, 연결하는 것을 찾아 문법적으로 대등한지를 판단한다.
4. 능동(v-ing) vs. 수동(p.p.): (의미상) 주어나 수식 받는 명사가 동작을 하면 v-ing, 받으면 p.p.이다.
5. 수일치: 주어를 찾아 동사에 수일치시킨다. 준동사 주어는 단수동사로 받는다.
6. 분사구문: 의미상 분사구문 자리인지 확인한다. 의미상 주어인 주절의 주어가 분사의 동작을 행하는지 받는지로 분사 형태를 판단한다.
7. 형용사 vs. 부사: 형용사는 명사 앞뒤에서 수식하거나 보어 역할을 한다. 그 외는 부사 자리이다.
8. 대동사: <be동사+ ~>는 be동사, <일반동사+ ~>는 do동사를 사용하되, 시제, 수일치에 주의한다.
9. 대명사 vs. 재귀대명사: 주어와 목적어가 동일 대상일 경우 대명사 대신 재귀대명사를 쓴다.
10. 목적격보어(준동사): 동사에 따라, 또는 목적어와 의미 관계에 따라 적절한 형태를 판단한다.

전략 2 정확한 해석 및 구조분석을 토대로 규칙을 적용해야 한다.

문맥과 어법 규칙의 통합적 이해를 묻기 때문에 정확한 해석 없이 규칙을 기계적으로 적용하면 함정에 빠질 수 있다.

e.g. She made a substantial donation to help protect endangered species in their natural habitats.

여기서 made는 <사역동사 make+O+C(v)>가 아닌 '(기부)했다'의 의미이므로 목적을 뜻하는 부사적 용법의 to help는 적절하다.

주의 오판을 유도하는 함정에 주의해야 한다. 정답이 아닐 경우 해설과 대조하여 미처 생각하지 못한 부분을 확실히 익혀야 한다.

01

24학년도 대수능 29번

다음 글의 밑줄 친 부분 중, 어법상 틀린 것은?

A number of studies provide substantial evidence of an innate human disposition to respond differentially to social stimuli. From birth, infants will orient preferentially towards the human face and voice, ① seeming to know that such stimuli are particularly meaningful for them. Moreover, they register this connection actively, imitating a variety of facial gestures that are presented to them — tongue protrusions, lip tightenings, mouth openings. They will even try to match gestures ② which they have some difficulty, experimenting with their own faces until they succeed. When they ③ do succeed, they show pleasure by a brightening of their eyes; when they fail, they show distress. In other words, they not only have an innate capacity for matching their own kinaesthetically experienced bodily movements with ④ those of others that are visually perceived; they have an innate drive to do so. That is, they seem to have an innate drive to imitate others whom they judge ⑤ to be 'like me'.

*innate: 타고난 **disposition: 성향 ***kinaesthetically: 운동감각적으로

02

(24학년도 9월 모평 29번)

다음 글의 밑줄 친 부분 중, 어법상 틀린 것은?

Viewing the stress response as a resource can transform the physiology of fear into the biology of courage. It can turn a threat into a challenge and can help you ① do your best under pressure. Even when the stress doesn't feel helpful — as in the case of anxiety — welcoming it can transform ② it into something that is helpful: more energy, more confidence, and a greater willingness to take action. You can apply this strategy in your own life anytime you notice signs of stress. When you feel your heart beating or your breath quickening, ③ realizing that it is your body's way of trying to give you more energy. If you notice tension in your body, remind yourself ④ that the stress response gives you access to your strength. Sweaty palms? Remember what it felt like ⑤ to go on your first date — palms sweat when you're close to something you want.

*physiology: 생리 기능

03

(24학년도 6월 모평 29번)

다음 글의 밑줄 친 부분 중, 어법상 틀린 것은?

Consider *The Wizard of Oz* as a psychological study of motivation. Dorothy and her three friends work hard to get to the Emerald City, overcoming barriers, persisting against all adversaries. They do so because they expect the Wizard to give ① them what they are missing. Instead, the wonderful (and wise) Wizard makes them aware that they, not he, always had the power ② to fulfill their wishes. For Dorothy, *home* is not a place but a feeling of security, of comfort with people she loves; it is wherever her heart is. The courage the Lion wants, the intelligence the Scarecrow longs for, and the emotions the Tin Man dreams of ③ being attributes they already possess. They need to think about these attributes not as internal conditions but as positive ways ④ in which they are already relating to others. After all, didn't they demonstrate those qualities on the journey to Oz, a journey ⑤ motivated by little more than an *expectation*, an idea about the future likelihood of getting something they wanted?

*adversary: 적(상대)

정답 및 해설 p. 104

DAY 028

밑줄 어법

전략 적용하기

⏱ 제한시간 | 4분

01

23학년도 대수능 29번

다음 글의 밑줄 친 부분 중, 어법상 틀린 것은?

Trends constantly suggest new opportunities for individuals to restage themselves, representing occasions for change. To understand how trends can ultimately give individuals power and freedom, one must first discuss fashion's importance as a basis for change. The most common explanation offered by my informants as to why fashion is so appealing is ① that it constitutes a kind of theatrical costumery. Clothes are part of how people present ② them to the world, and fashion locates them in the present, relative to what is happening in society and to fashion's own history. As a form of expression, fashion contains a host of ambiguities, enabling individuals to recreate the meanings ③ associated with specific pieces of clothing. Fashion is among the simplest and cheapest methods of self-expression: clothes can be ④ inexpensively purchased while making it easy to convey notions of wealth, intellectual stature, relaxation or environmental consciousness, even if none of these is true. Fashion can also strengthen agency in various ways, ⑤ opening up space for action.

*stature: 능력

02

〈23학년도 9월 모평 29번〉

다음 글의 밑줄 친 부분 중, 어법상 틀린 것은?

Recognizing ethical issues is the most important step in understanding business ethics. An ethical issue is an identifiable problem, situation, or opportunity that requires a person to choose from among several actions that may ① be evaluated as right or wrong, ethical or unethical. ② Learn how to choose from alternatives and make a decision requires not only good personal values, but also knowledge competence in the business area of concern. Employees also need to know when to rely on their organizations' policies and codes of ethics or ③ have discussions with co-workers or managers on appropriate conduct. Ethical decision making is not always easy because there are always gray areas ④ that create dilemmas, no matter how decisions are made. For instance, should an employee report on a co-worker engaging in time theft? Should a salesperson leave out facts about a product's poor safety record in his presentation to a customer? Such questions require the decision maker to evaluate the ethics of his or her choice and decide ⑤ whether to ask for guidance.

03

〈23학년도 6월 모평 29번〉

다음 글의 밑줄 친 부분 중, 어법상 틀린 것은? [3점]

Ecosystems differ in composition and extent. They can be defined as ranging from the communities and interactions of organisms in your mouth or ① those in the canopy of a rain forest to all those in Earth's oceans. The processes ② governing them differ in complexity and speed. There are systems that turn over in minutes, and there are others ③ which rhythmic time extends to hundreds of years. Some ecosystems are extensive ('biomes', such as the African savanna); some cover regions (river basins); many involve clusters of villages (micro-watersheds); others are confined to the level of a single village (the village pond). In each example there is an element of indivisibility. Divide an ecosystem into parts by creating barriers, and the sum of the productivity of the parts will typically be found to be lower than the productivity of the whole, other things ④ being equal. The mobility of biological populations is a reason. Safe passages, for example, enable migratory species ⑤ to survive.

*canopy: 덮개 **basin: 유역

정답 및 해설 p. 108

DAY 029

낱말 쓰임

전략 익히기

⏱ 제한시간 | 4분

두 가지 유형(네모 안에서 고르기, 밑줄 어휘 중에서 고르기) 중 주로 밑줄 어휘가 출제된다. 주제문과 세부 사항의 내용이 대의를 일관되게 서술하는지를 묻는다. 밑줄 어휘로는 중간 난도 어휘들이 대세를 이루므로, 어휘 자체의 의미를 모르는 것이 있더라도 당황하지 말고 나머지 선택지들을 잘 고려해서 답을 선택하면 된다.

전략 1 **밑줄 문장을 포함해서 앞뒤 문장에 단서가 있다.**

대부분 밑줄 문장을 포함하여 주변 문장의 밑줄 없는 부분에 단서가 있으므로 바로 정오답 판단이 가능하다. 즉, 한참 뒤에 판단 근거가 나오거나 다시 역으로 거슬러 올라가야 단서가 있는 것은 출제되지 않는다.

전략 2 **글의 대의를 반대로 뒷받침하는 것을 고른다.**

밑줄은 정오 판단이 가능한 어디에나 있을 수 있지만, 대부분의 정답은 대의를 반대 의미로 뒷받침하는 주요 세부 사항에 있다. 따라서 반대 의미로 바꿨을 때 글의 흐름이 자연스러운지를 확인한다.

전략 3 **네모 안의 어휘를 고르는 유형은 소거법을 적극 이용한다.**

세 쌍의 네모가 주어지므로, 정확히 아니라고 판단되는 것들을 소거하면서 푼다.

01

24학년도 대수능 30번

다음 글의 밑줄 친 부분 중, 문맥상 낱말의 쓰임이 적절하지 않은 것은? [3점]

Bazaar economies feature an apparently flexible price-setting mechanism that sits atop more enduring ties of shared culture. Both the buyer and seller are aware of each other's ① restrictions. In Delhi's bazaars, buyers and sellers can ② assess to a large extent the financial constraints that other actors have in their everyday life. Each actor belonging to a specific economic class understands what the other sees as a necessity and a luxury. In the case of electronic products like video games, they are not a ③ necessity at the same level as other household purchases such as food items. So, the seller in Delhi's bazaars is careful not to directly ask for very ④ low prices for video games because at no point will the buyer see possession of them as an absolute necessity. Access to this type of knowledge establishes a price consensus by relating to each other's preferences and limitations of belonging to a ⑤ similar cultural and economic universe.

*constraint: 압박 **consensus: 일치

02

(24학년도 9월 모평 30번)

다음 글의 밑줄 친 부분 중, 문맥상 낱말의 쓰임이 적절하지 않은 것은? [3점]

Why is the value of place so important? From a historical perspective, until the 1700s textile production was a hand process using the fibers available within a ① particular geographic region, for example, cotton, wool, silk, and flax. Trade among regions ② increased the availability of these fibers and associated textiles made from the fibers. The First Industrial Revolution and subsequent technological advancements in manufactured fibers ③ added to the fact that fibers and textiles were no longer "place-bound." Fashion companies created and consumers could acquire textiles and products made from textiles with little or no connection to where, how, or by whom the products were made. This ④ countered a disconnect between consumers and the products they use on a daily basis, a loss of understanding and appreciation in the skills and resources necessary to create these products, and an associated disregard for the human and natural resources necessary for the products' creation. Therefore, renewing a value on place ⑤ reconnects the company and the consumer with the people, geography, and culture of a particular location.

*textile: 직물

03

(24학년도 6월 모평 30번)

(A), (B), (C)의 각 네모 안에서 문맥에 맞는 낱말로 가장 적절한 것은? [3점]

To the extent that an agent relies on the prior knowledge of its designer rather than on its own percepts, we say that the agent lacks autonomy. A rational agent should be autonomous — it should learn what it can to (A) [compensate / prepare] for partial or incorrect prior knowledge. For example, a vacuum-cleaning agent that learns to foresee where and when additional dirt will appear will do better than one that does not. As a practical matter, one seldom requires complete autonomy from the start: when the agent has had little or no experience, it would have to act (B) [purposefully / randomly] unless the designer gave some assistance. So, just as evolution provides animals with enough built-in reflexes to survive long enough to learn for themselves, it would be reasonable to provide an artificial intelligent agent with some initial knowledge as well as an ability to learn. After sufficient experience of its environment, the behavior of a rational agent can become effectively (C) [independent / protective] of its prior knowledge. Hence, the incorporation of learning allows one to design a single rational agent that will succeed in a vast variety of environments.

	(A)		(B)		(C)
①	compensate	……	randomly	……	protective
②	compensate	……	purposefully	……	protective
③	prepare	……	randomly	……	protective
④	compensate	……	randomly	……	independent
⑤	prepare	……	purposefully	……	independent

정답 및 해설 p. 112

DAY 030

낱말 쓰임

전략 적용하기

제한시간 | 4분

01

23학년도 대수능 30번

다음 글의 밑줄 친 부분 중, 문맥상 낱말의 쓰임이 적절하지 <u>않은</u> 것은? [3점]

Everywhere we turn we hear about almighty "cyberspace"! The hype promises that we will leave our boring lives, put on goggles and body suits, and enter some metallic, three-dimensional, multimedia otherworld. When the Industrial Revolution arrived with its great innovation, the motor, we didn't leave our world to go to some ① <u>remote</u> motorspace! On the contrary, we brought the motors into our lives, as automobiles, refrigerators, drill presses, and pencil sharpeners. This ② <u>absorption</u> has been so complete that we refer to all these tools with names that declare their usage, not their "motorness." These innovations led to a major socioeconomic movement precisely because they entered and ③ <u>affected</u> profoundly our everyday lives. People have not changed fundamentally in thousands of years. Technology changes constantly. It's the one that must ④ <u>adapt</u> to us. That's exactly what will happen with information technology and its devices under human-centric computing. The longer we continue to believe that computers will take us to a magical new world, the longer we will ⑤ <u>maintain</u> their natural fusion with our lives, the hallmark of every major movement that aspires to be called a socioeconomic revolution.

*hype: 과대광고 **hallmark: 특징

02

〈23학년도 9월 모평 30번〉

다음 글의 밑줄 친 부분 중, 문맥상 낱말의 쓰임이 적절하지 않은 것은?

Although the wonders of modern technology have provided people with opportunities beyond the wildest dreams of our ancestors, the good, as usual, is weakened by a downside. One of those downsides is that anyone who so chooses can pick up the virtual megaphone that is the Internet and put in their two cents on any of an infinite number of topics, regardless of their ① qualifications. After all, on the Internet, there are no regulations ② preventing a kindergarten teacher from offering medical advice or a physician from suggesting ways to safely make structural changes to your home. As a result, misinformation gets disseminated as information, and it is not always easy to ③ differentiate the two. This can be particularly frustrating for scientists, who spend their lives learning how to understand the intricacies of the world around them, only to have their work summarily ④ challenged by people whose experience with the topic can be measured in minutes. This frustration is then ⑤ diminished by the fact that, to the general public, both the scientist and the challenger are awarded equal credibility.

*put in one's two cents: 의견을 말하다 **disseminate: 퍼뜨리다
***intricacy: 복잡성

03

〈23학년도 6월 모평 30번〉

다음 글의 밑줄 친 부분 중, 문맥상 낱말의 쓰임이 적절하지 않은 것은?

In recent years urban transport professionals globally have largely acquiesced to the view that automobile demand in cities needs to be managed rather than accommodated. Rising incomes inevitably lead to increases in motorization. Even without the imperative of climate change, the physical constraints of densely inhabited cities and the corresponding demands of accessibility, mobility, safety, air pollution, and urban livability all ① limit the option of expanding road networks purely to accommodate this rising demand. As a result, as cities develop and their residents become more prosperous, ② persuading people to choose *not* to use cars becomes an increasingly key focus of city managers and planners. Improving the quality of ③ alternative options, such as walking, cycling, and public transport, is a central element of this strategy. However, the most direct approach to ④ accommodating automobile demand is making motorized travel more expensive or restricting it with administrative rules. The contribution of motorized travel to climate change ⑤ reinforces this imperative.

*acquiesce: 따르다 **imperative: 불가피한 것 ***constraint: 압박

정답 및 해설 p. 116

PART 2

DAY 031~100

전략의 적용

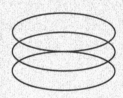

Part 1에서 배운 해결 전략을 적용해서 기출 문제를 풀어보세요.
수능과 모의고사에서 1등급을 결정짓는 주요 유형을
DAY별로 3가지씩 골고루 담았습니다.
문제에서 잘 모르는 부분은 해설지를 참고해 꼭 해결하고 넘어가세요.

DAY 031

글의 주제
빈칸 추론
글의 순서

제한시간 | 4분

01

22학년도 대수능 23번

다음 글의 주제로 가장 적절한 것은? [3점]

Scientists *use* paradigms rather than believing them. The use of a paradigm in research typically addresses related problems by employing shared concepts, symbolic expressions, experimental and mathematical tools and procedures, and even some of the same theoretical statements. Scientists need only understand *how* to use these various elements in ways that others would accept. These elements of shared practice thus need not presuppose any comparable unity in scientists' beliefs about what they are doing when they use them. Indeed, one role of a paradigm is to enable scientists to work successfully without having to provide a detailed account of what they are doing or what they believe about it. Thomas Kuhn noted that scientists "can agree in their *identification* of a paradigm without agreeing on, or even attempting to produce, a full *interpretation* or *rationalization* of it. Lack of a standard interpretation or of an agreed reduction to rules will not prevent a paradigm from guiding research."

① difficulty in drawing novel theories from existing paradigms
② significant influence of personal beliefs in scientific fields
③ key factors that promote the rise of innovative paradigms
④ roles of a paradigm in grouping like-minded researchers
⑤ functional aspects of a paradigm in scientific research

02

23학년도 6월 모평 34번

다음 빈칸에 들어갈 말로 가장 적절한 것은? [3점]

Development can get very complicated and fanciful. A fugue by Johann Sebastian Bach illustrates how far this process could go, when a single melodic line, sometimes just a handful of notes, was all that the composer needed to create a brilliant work containing lots of intricate development within a coherent structure. Ludwig van Beethoven's famous Fifth Symphony provides an exceptional example of how much mileage a classical composer can get out of a few notes and a simple rhythmic tapping. The opening da-da-da-DUM that everyone has heard somewhere or another ______________________ throughout not only the opening movement, but the remaining three movements, like a kind of motto or a connective thread. Just as we don't always see the intricate brushwork that goes into the creation of a painting, we may not always notice how Beethoven keeps finding fresh uses for his motto or how he develops his material into a large, cohesive statement. But a lot of the enjoyment we get from that mighty symphony stems from the inventiveness behind it, the impressive development of musical ideas.

*intricate: 복잡한 **coherent: 통일성 있는

① makes the composer's musical ideas contradictory
② appears in an incredible variety of ways
③ provides extensive musical knowledge creatively
④ remains fairly calm within the structure
⑤ becomes deeply associated with one's own enjoyment

03

23학년도 9월 모평 37번

주어진 글 다음에 이어질 글의 순서로 가장 적절한 것은? [3점]

Culture operates in ways we can consciously consider and discuss but also in ways of which we are far less cognizant.

(A) In some cases, however, we are far less aware of why we believe a certain claim to be true, or how we are to explain why certain social realities exist. Ideas about the social world become part of our worldview without our necessarily being aware of the source of the particular idea or that we even hold the idea at all.

(B) When we have to offer an account of our actions, we consciously understand which excuses might prove acceptable, given the particular circumstances we find ourselves in. In such situations, we use cultural ideas as we would use a particular tool.

(C) We select the cultural notion as we would select a screwdriver: certain jobs call for a Phillips head while others require an Allen wrench. Whichever idea we insert into the conversation to justify our actions, the point is that our motives are discursively available to us. They are not hidden.

*cognizant: 인식하는 **discursively: 만연하게

① (A) – (C) – (B)
② (B) – (A) – (C)
③ (B) – (C) – (A)
④ (C) – (A) – (B)
⑤ (C) – (B) – (A)

정답 및 해설 p. 120

DAY 032

글의 제목
빈칸 추론
문장 넣기

제한시간 | 4분

01

22학년도 대수능 24번

다음 글의 제목으로 가장 적절한 것은?

Mending and restoring objects often require even more creativity than original production. The preindustrial blacksmith made things to order for people in his immediate community; customizing the product, modifying or transforming it according to the user, was routine. Customers would bring things back if something went wrong; repair was thus an extension of fabrication. With industrialization and eventually with mass production, making things became the province of machine tenders with limited knowledge. But repair continued to require a larger grasp of design and materials, an understanding of the whole and a comprehension of the designer's intentions. "Manufacturers all work by machinery or by vast subdivision of labour and not, so to speak, by hand," an 1896 *Manual of Mending and Repairing* explained. "But all repairing *must* be done by hand. We can make every detail of a watch or of a gun by machinery, but the machine cannot mend it when broken, much less a clock or a pistol!"

① Still Left to the Modern Blacksmith: The Art of Repair
② A Historical Survey of How Repairing Skills Evolved
③ How to Be a Creative Repairperson: Tips and Ideas
④ A Process of Repair: Create, Modify, Transform!
⑤ Can Industrialization Mend Our Broken Past?

02

23학년도 6월 모평 33번

다음 빈칸에 들어갈 말로 가장 적절한 것은? [3점]

Manufacturers design their innovation processes around the way they think the process works. The vast majority of manufacturers still think that product development and service development are always done by manufacturers, and that their job is always to find a need and fill it rather than to sometimes find and commercialize an innovation that ______________________________. Accordingly, manufacturers have set up market-research departments to explore the needs of users in the target market, product-development groups to think up suitable products to address those needs, and so forth. The needs and prototype solutions of lead users — if encountered at all — are typically rejected as outliers of no interest. Indeed, when lead users' innovations do enter a firm's product line — and they have been shown to be the actual source of many major innovations for many firms — they typically arrive with a lag and by an unusual and unsystematic route.

*lag: 지연

① lead users tended to overlook
② lead users have already developed
③ lead users encountered in the market
④ other firms frequently put into use
⑤ both users and firms have valued

03

23학년도 대수능 38번

글의 흐름으로 보아, 주어진 문장이 들어가기에 가장 적절한 곳은?

There's a reason for that: traditionally, park designers attempted to create such a feeling by planting tall trees at park boundaries, building stone walls, and constructing other means of partition.

Parks take the shape demanded by the cultural concerns of their time. Once parks are in place, they are no inert stage — their purposes and meanings are made and remade by planners and by park users. Moments of park creation are particularly telling, however, for they reveal and actualize ideas about nature and its relationship to urban society. (①) Indeed, what distinguishes a park from the broader category of public space is the representation of nature that parks are meant to embody. (②) Public spaces include parks, concrete plazas, sidewalks, even indoor atriums. (③) Parks typically have trees, grass, and other plants as their central features. (④) When entering a city park, people often imagine a sharp separation from streets, cars, and buildings. (⑤) What's behind this idea is not only landscape architects' desire to design aesthetically suggestive park spaces, but a much longer history of Western thought that envisions cities and nature as antithetical spaces and oppositional forces.

*aesthetically: 미적으로 **antithetical: 대조적인

정답 및 해설 p. 124

DAY 033

함의 추론
빈칸 추론
무관 문장

⏲ 제한시간 | 4분

01

22학년도 9월 모평 21번

밑줄 친 Flicking the collaboration light switch가 다음 글에서 의미하는 바로 가장 적절한 것은? [3점]

Flicking the collaboration light switch is something that leaders are uniquely positioned to do, because several obstacles stand in the way of people voluntarily working alone. For one thing, the fear of being left out of the loop can keep them glued to their enterprise social media. Individuals don't want to be — or appear to be — isolated. For another, knowing what their teammates are doing provides a sense of comfort and security, because people can adjust their own behavior to be in harmony with the group. It's risky to go off on their own to try something new that will probably not be successful right from the start. But even though it feels reassuring for individuals to be hyper-connected, it's better for the organization if they periodically go off and think for themselves and generate diverse — if not quite mature — ideas. Thus, it becomes the leader's job to create conditions that are good for the whole by enforcing intermittent interaction even when people wouldn't choose it for themselves, without making it seem like a punishment.

*intermittent: 간헐적인

① breaking physical barriers and group norms that prohibit cooperation
② having people stop working together and start working individually
③ encouraging people to devote more time to online collaboration
④ shaping environments where higher productivity is required
⑤ requiring workers to focus their attention on group projects

02

23학년도 6월 모평 32번

다음 빈칸에 들어갈 말로 가장 적절한 것은?

The critic who wants to write about literature from a formalist perspective must first be a close and careful reader who examines all the elements of a text individually and questions how they come together to create a work of art. Such a reader, who respects the autonomy of a work, achieves an understanding of it by ________________________________. Instead of examining historical periods, author biographies, or literary styles, for example, he or she will approach a text with the assumption that it is a self-contained entity and that he or she is looking for the governing principles that allow the text to reveal itself. For example, the correspondences between the characters in James Joyce's short story "Araby" and the people he knew personally may be interesting, but for the formalist they are less relevant to understanding how the story creates meaning than are other kinds of information that the story contains within itself.

*entity: 실체

① putting himself or herself both inside and outside it
② finding a middle ground between it and the world
③ searching for historical realities revealed within it
④ looking inside it, not outside it or beyond it
⑤ exploring its characters' cultural relevance

03

22학년도 대수능 35번

다음 글에서 전체 흐름과 관계 없는 문장은?

Since their introduction, information systems have substantially changed the way business is conducted. ① This is particularly true for business in the shape and form of cooperation between firms that involves an integration of value chains across multiple units. ② The resulting networks do not only cover the business units of a single firm but typically also include multiple units from different firms. ③ As a consequence, firms do not only need to consider their internal organization in order to ensure sustainable business performance; they also need to take into account the entire ecosystem of units surrounding them. ④ Many major companies are fundamentally changing their business models by focusing on profitable units and cutting off less profitable ones. ⑤ In order to allow these different units to cooperate successfully, the existence of a common platform is crucial.

정답 및 해설 p. 128

DAY

034

글의 요지
빈칸 추론
글의 순서

제한시간 | 4분

01

23학년도 대수능 22번

다음 글의 요지로 가장 적절한 것은?

Urban delivery vehicles can be adapted to better suit the density of urban distribution, which often involves smaller vehicles such as vans, including bicycles. The latter have the potential to become a preferred 'last-mile' vehicle, particularly in high-density and congested areas. In locations where bicycle use is high, such as the Netherlands, delivery bicycles are also used to carry personal cargo (e.g. groceries). Due to their low acquisition and maintenance costs, cargo bicycles convey much potential in developed and developing countries alike, such as the *becak* (a three-wheeled bicycle) in Indonesia. Services using electrically assisted delivery tricycles have been successfully implemented in France and are gradually being adopted across Europe for services as varied as parcel and catering deliveries. Using bicycles as cargo vehicles is particularly encouraged when combined with policies that restrict motor vehicle access to specific areas of a city, such as downtown or commercial districts, or with the extension of dedicated bike lanes.

① 도시에서 자전거는 효율적인 배송 수단으로 사용될 수 있다.
② 자전거는 출퇴근 시간을 줄이기 위한 대안으로 선호되고 있다.
③ 자전거는 배송 수단으로의 경제적 장단점을 모두 가질 수 있다.
④ 수요자의 요구에 부합하는 다양한 용도의 자전거가 개발되고 있다.
⑤ 세계 각국에서는 전기 자전거 사용을 장려하는 정책을 추진하고 있다.

02

22학년도 9월 모평 32번

다음 빈칸에 들어갈 말로 가장 적절한 것은?

Even as mundane a behavior as watching TV may be a way for some people to ____________________ ____________________. To test this idea, Sophia Moskalenko and Steven Heine gave participants false feedback about their test performance, and then seated each one in front of a TV set to watch a video as the next part of the study. When the video came on, showing nature scenes with a musical soundtrack, the experimenter exclaimed that this was the wrong video and went supposedly to get the correct one, leaving the participant alone as the video played. The participants who had received failure feedback watched the video much longer than those who thought they had succeeded. The researchers concluded that distraction through television viewing can effectively relieve the discomfort associated with painful failures or mismatches between the self and self-guides. In contrast, successful participants had little wish to be distracted from their self-related thoughts!

*mundane: 보통의

① ignore uncomfortable comments from their close peers
② escape painful self-awareness through distraction
③ receive constructive feedback from the media
④ refocus their divided attention to a given task
⑤ engage themselves in intense self-reflection

03

23학년도 9월 모평 36번

주어진 글 다음에 이어질 글의 순서로 가장 적절한 것은?

> When two natural bodies of water stand at different levels, building a canal between them presents a complicated engineering problem.

(A) Then the upper gates open and the ship passes through. For downstream passage, the process works the opposite way. The ship enters the lock from the upper level, and water is pumped from the lock until the ship is in line with the lower level.

(B) When a vessel is going upstream, the upper gates stay closed as the ship enters the lock at the lower water level. The downstream gates are then closed and more water is pumped into the basin. The rising water lifts the vessel to the level of the upper body of water.

(C) To make up for the difference in level, engineers build one or more water "steps," called locks, that carry ships or boats up or down between the two levels. A lock is an artificial water basin. It has a long rectangular shape with concrete walls and a pair of gates at each end.

*rectangular: 직사각형의

① (A) – (C) – (B)
② (B) – (A) – (C)
③ (B) – (C) – (A)
④ (C) – (A) – (B)
⑤ (C) – (B) – (A)

정답 및 해설 p. 132

DAY 035

필자 주장
빈칸 추론
문장 넣기

제한시간 | 4분

01

23학년도 대수능 20번

다음 글에서 필자가 주장하는 바로 가장 적절한 것은?

At every step in our journey through life we encounter junctions with many different pathways leading into the distance. Each choice involves uncertainty about which path will get you to your destination. Trusting our intuition to make the choice often ends up with us making a suboptimal choice. Turning the uncertainty into numbers has proved a potent way of analyzing the paths and finding the shortcut to your destination. The mathematical theory of probability hasn't eliminated risk, but it allows us to manage that risk more effectively. The strategy is to analyze all the possible scenarios that the future holds and then to see what proportion of them lead to success or failure. This gives you a much better map of the future on which to base your decisions about which path to choose.

*junction: 분기점 **suboptimal: 차선의

① 성공적인 삶을 위해 미래에 대한 구체적인 계획을 세워야 한다.
② 중요한 결정을 내릴 때에는 자신의 직관에 따라 판단해야 한다.
③ 더 나은 선택을 위해 성공 가능성을 확률적으로 분석해야 한다.
④ 빠른 목표 달성을 위해 지름길로 가고자 할 때 신중해야 한다.
⑤ 인생의 여정에서 선택에 따른 결과를 스스로 책임져야 한다.

02

22학년도 9월 모평 33번

다음 빈칸에 들어갈 말로 가장 적절한 것은? [3점]

It is important to recognise the interdependence between individual, culturally formed actions and the state of cultural integration. People work within the forms provided by the cultural patterns that they have internalised, however contradictory these may be. Ideas are worked out as logical implications or consequences of other accepted ideas, and it is in this way that cultural innovations and discoveries are possible. New ideas are discovered through logical reasoning, but such discoveries are inherent in and integral to the conceptual system and are made possible only because of the acceptance of its premises. For example, the discoveries of new prime numbers are 'real' consequences of the particular number system employed. Thus, cultural ideas show 'advances' and 'developments' because they ______________________________________. The cumulative work of many individuals produces a corpus of knowledge within which certain 'discoveries' become possible or more likely. Such discoveries are 'ripe' and could not have occurred earlier and are also likely to be made simultaneously by numbers of individuals.

*corpus: 집적(集積) **simultaneously: 동시에

① are outgrowths of previous ideas
② stem from abstract reasoning ability
③ form the basis of cultural universalism
④ emerge between people of the same age
⑤ promote individuals' innovative thinking

03

23학년도 9월 모평 39번

글의 흐름으로 보아, 주어진 문장이 들어가기에 가장 적절한 곳은? [3점]

> On top of the hurdles introduced in accessing his or her money, if a suspected fraud is detected, the account holder has to deal with the phone call asking if he or she made the suspicious transactions.

Each new wave of technology is intended to enhance user convenience, as well as improve security, but sometimes these do not necessarily go hand-in-hand. For example, the transition from magnetic stripe to embedded chip slightly slowed down transactions, sometimes frustrating customers in a hurry. (①) Make a service too burdensome, and the potential customer will go elsewhere. (②) This obstacle applies at several levels. (③) Passwords, double-key identification, and biometrics such as fingerprint-, iris-, and voice recognition are all ways of keeping the account details hidden from potential fraudsters, of keeping your data dark. (④) But they all inevitably add a burden to the use of the account. (⑤) This is all useful at some level — indeed, it can be reassuring knowing that your bank is keeping alert to protect you — but it becomes tiresome if too many such calls are received.

*fraud: 사기

정답 및 해설 p. 136

DAY 036

요약문 복합 유형

⏱ 제한시간 | 5분

01

22학년도 대수능 40번

다음 글의 내용을 한 문장으로 요약하고자 한다. 빈칸 (A), (B)에 들어갈 말로 가장 적절한 것은?

Philip Kitcher and Wesley Salmon have suggested that there are two possible alternatives among philosophical theories of explanation. One is the view that scientific explanation consists in the *unification* of broad bodies of phenomena under a minimal number of generalizations. According to this view, the (or perhaps, a) goal of science is to construct an economical framework of laws or generalizations that are capable of subsuming all observable phenomena. Scientific explanations organize and systematize our knowledge of the empirical world; the more economical the systematization, the deeper our understanding of what is explained. The other view is the *causal/mechanical* approach. According to it, a scientific explanation of a phenomenon consists of uncovering the mechanisms that produced the phenomenon of interest. This view sees the explanation of individual events as primary, with the explanation of generalizations flowing from them. That is, the explanation of scientific generalizations comes from the causal mechanisms that produce the regularities.

*subsume: 포섭(포함)하다 **empirical: 경험적인

↓

Scientific explanations can be made either by seeking the ___(A)___ number of principles covering all observations or by finding general ___(B)___ drawn from individual phenomena.

	(A)		(B)
①	least	……	patterns
②	fixed	……	features
③	limited	……	functions
④	fixed	……	rules
⑤	least	……	assumptions

02~03

24학년도 6월 모평 41~42번

다음 글을 읽고, 물음에 답하시오.

Many negotiators assume that all negotiations involve a fixed pie. Negotiators often approach integrative negotiation opportunities as zero-sum situations or win-lose exchanges. Those who believe in the mythical fixed pie assume that parties' interests stand in opposition, with no possibility for integrative settlements and mutually beneficial trade-offs, so they (a) suppress efforts to search for them. In a hiring negotiation, a job applicant who assumes that salary is the only issue may insist on $75,000 when the employer is offering $70,000. Only when the two parties discuss the possibilities further do they discover that moving expenses and starting date can also be negotiated, which may (b) block resolution of the salary issue.

The tendency to see negotiation in fixed-pie terms (c) varies depending on how people view the nature of a given conflict situation. This was shown in a clever experiment by Harinck, de Dreu, and Van Vianen involving a simulated negotiation between prosecutors and defense lawyers over jail sentences. Some participants were told to view their goals in terms of personal gain (e.g., arranging a particular jail sentence will help your career), others were told to view their goals in terms of effectiveness (a particular sentence is most likely to prevent recidivism), and still others were told to focus on values (a particular jail sentence is fair and just). Negotiators focusing on personal gain were most likely to come under the influence of fixed-pie beliefs and approach the situation (d) competitively. Negotiators focusing on values were least likely to see the problem in fixed-pie terms and more inclined to approach the situation cooperatively. Stressful conditions such as time constraints contribute to this common misperception, which in turn may lead to (e) less integrative agreements.

*prosecutor: 검사 **recidivism: 상습적 범행

02

윗글의 제목으로 가장 적절한 것은?

① Fixed Pie: A Key to Success in a Zero-sum Game
② Fixed Pie Tells You How to Get the Biggest Salary
③ Negotiators, Wake Up from the Myth of the Fixed Pie!
④ Want a Fairer Jail Sentence? Stick to the Fixed Pie
⑤ What Alternatives Maximize Fixed-pie Effects?

03

밑줄 친 (a)~(e) 중에서 문맥상 낱말의 쓰임이 적절하지 않은 것은?

① (a) ② (b) ③ (c) ④ (d) ⑤ (e)

정답 및 해설 p. 140

DAY 037

빈칸 추론
글의 순서
문장 넣기

제한시간 | 5분

01

22학년도 9월 모평 31번

다음 빈칸에 들어갈 말로 가장 적절한 것은?

When examining the archaeological record of human culture, one has to consider that it is vastly ______________. Many aspects of human culture have what archaeologists describe as low archaeological visibility, meaning they are difficult to identify archaeologically. Archaeologists tend to focus on tangible (or material) aspects of culture: things that can be handled and photographed, such as tools, food, and structures. Reconstructing intangible aspects of culture is more difficult, requiring that one draw more inferences from the tangible. It is relatively easy, for example, for archaeologists to identify and draw inferences about technology and diet from stone tools and food remains. Using the same kinds of physical remains to draw inferences about social systems and what people were thinking about is more difficult. Archaeologists do it, but there are necessarily more inferences involved in getting from physical remains recognized as trash to making interpretations about belief systems.

*archaeological: 고고학의

① outdated
② factual
③ incomplete
④ organized
⑤ detailed

02

23학년도 6월 모평 37번

주어진 글 다음에 이어질 글의 순서로 가장 적절한 것은? [3점]

> In economics, there is a principle known as the *sunk cost fallacy*. The idea is that when you are invested and have ownership in something, you overvalue that thing.

(A) Sometimes, the smartest thing a person can do is quit. Although this is true, it has also become a tired and played-out argument. Sunk cost doesn't always have to be a bad thing.

(B) This leads people to continue on paths or pursuits that should clearly be abandoned. For example, people often remain in terrible relationships simply because they've invested a great deal of themselves into them. Or someone may continue pouring money into a business that is clearly a bad idea in the market.

(C) Actually, you can leverage this human tendency to your benefit. Like someone invests a great deal of money in a personal trainer to ensure they follow through on their commitment, you, too, can invest a great deal up front to ensure you stay on the path you want to be on.

*leverage: 이용하다

① (A) – (C) – (B)
② (B) – (A) – (C)
③ (B) – (C) – (A)
④ (C) – (A) – (B)
⑤ (C) – (B) – (A)

03

23학년도 9월 모평 38번

글의 흐름으로 보아, 주어진 문장이 들어가기에 가장 적절한 곳은?

> In particular, they define a group as two or more people who interact with, and exert mutual influences on, each other.

In everyday life, we tend to see any collection of people as a group. (①) However, social psychologists use this term more precisely. (②) It is this sense of mutual interaction or inter-dependence for a common purpose which distinguishes the members of a group from a mere aggregation of individuals. (③) For example, as Kenneth Hodge observed, a collection of people who happen to go for a swim after work on the same day each week does not, strictly speaking, constitute a group because these swimmers do not interact with each other in a structured manner. (④) By contrast, a squad of young competitive swimmers who train every morning before going to school *is* a group because they not only share a common objective (training for competition) but also interact with each other in formal ways (e.g., by warming up together beforehand). (⑤) It is this sense of people coming together to achieve a common objective that defines a "team".

*exert: 발휘하다 **aggregation: 집합

정답 및 해설 p. 144

DAY 038

글의 주제
빈칸 추론
글의 순서

제한시간 | 4분

01

22학년도 9월 모평 23번

다음 글의 주제로 가장 적절한 것은? [3점]

In Kant's view, geometrical shapes are too perfect to induce an aesthetic experience. Insofar as they agree with the underlying concept or idea — thus possessing the *precision* that the ancient Greeks sought and celebrated — geometrical shapes can be grasped, but they do not give rise to emotion, and, most importantly, they do not move the imagination to free and new (mental) lengths. Forms or phenomena, on the contrary, that possess a degree of immeasurability, or that do not appear constrained, stimulate the human imagination — hence their ability to induce a sublime aesthetic experience. The pleasure associated with experiencing immeasurable objects — indefinable or formless objects — can be defined as enjoying one's own emotional and mental activity. Namely, the pleasure consists of being challenged and struggling to understand and decode the phenomenon present to view. Furthermore, part of the pleasure comes from having one's comfort zone (momentarily) violated.

*geometrical: 기하학의 **aesthetic: 심미적인 ***sublime: 숭고한

① diversity of aesthetic experiences in different eras
② inherent beauty in geometrically perfect shapes
③ concepts of imperfection in modern aesthetics
④ natural inclination towards aesthetic precision
⑤ aesthetic pleasure from things unconstrained

02

22학년도 6월 모평 32번

다음 빈칸에 들어갈 말로 가장 적절한 것은?

Some of the most insightful work on information seeking emphasizes "strategic self-ignorance," understood as "the use of ignorance as an excuse to engage excessively in pleasurable activities that may be harmful to one's future self." The idea here is that if people are present-biased, they might avoid information that would ____________________ — perhaps because it would produce guilt or shame, perhaps because it would suggest an aggregate trade-off that would counsel against engaging in such activities. St. Augustine famously said, "God give me chastity — tomorrow." Present-biased agents think: "Please let me know the risks — tomorrow." Whenever people are thinking about engaging in an activity with short-term benefits but long-term costs, they might prefer to delay receipt of important information. The same point might hold about information that could make people sad or mad: "Please tell me what I need to know — tomorrow."

*aggregate: 합계의 **chastity: 정결

① highlight the value of preferred activities
② make current activities less attractive
③ cut their attachment to past activities
④ enable them to enjoy more activities
⑤ potentially become known to others

03

23학년도 6월 모평 36번

주어진 글 다음에 이어질 글의 순서로 가장 적절한 것은?

The fossil record provides evidence of evolution. The story the fossils tell is one of change. Creatures existed in the past that are no longer with us. Sequential changes are found in many fossils showing the change of certain features over time from a common ancestor, as in the case of the horse.

(A) If multicelled organisms were indeed found to have evolved before single-celled organisms, then the theory of evolution would be rejected. A good scientific theory always allows for the possibility of rejection. The fact that we have not found such a case in countless examinations of the fossil record strengthens the case for evolutionary theory.

(B) The fossil record supports this prediction — multicelled organisms are found in layers of earth millions of years after the first appearance of single-celled organisms. Note that the possibility always remains that the opposite could be found.

(C) Apart from demonstrating that evolution did occur, the fossil record also provides tests of the predictions made from evolutionary theory. For example, the theory predicts that single-celled organisms evolved before multicelled organisms.

① (A) – (C) – (B)　② (B) – (A) – (C)
③ (B) – (C) – (A)　④ (C) – (A) – (B)
⑤ (C) – (B) – (A)

정답 및 해설 p. 148

DAY

039

글의 제목
빈칸 추론
문장 넣기

제한시간 | 4분

01

22학년도 9월 모평 24번

다음 글의 제목으로 가장 적절한 것은?

The world has become a nation of laws and governance that has introduced a system of public administration and management to keep order. With this administrative management system, urban institutions of government have evolved to offer increasing levels of services to their citizenry, provided through a taxation process and/or fee for services (e.g., police and fire, street maintenance, utilities, waste management, etc.). Frequently this has displaced citizen involvement. Money for services is not a replacement for citizen responsibility and public participation. Responsibility of the citizen is slowly being supplanted by government being the substitute provider. Consequentially, there is a philosophical and social change in attitude and sense of responsibility of our urban-based society to become involved. The sense of community and associated responsibility of all citizens to be active participants is therefore diminishing. Governmental substitution for citizen duty and involvement can have serious implications. This impedes the nations of the world to be responsive to natural and man-made disasters as part of global preparedness.

*supplant: 대신하다 **impede: 방해하다

① A Sound Citizen Responsibility in a Sound Government
② Always Better than Nothing: The Roles of Modern Government
③ Decreased Citizen Involvement: A Cost of Governmental Services
④ Why Does Global Citizenship Matter in Contemporary Society?
⑤ How to Maximize Public Benefits of Urban-Based Society

02

21학년도 대수능 34번

다음 빈칸에 들어갈 말로 가장 적절한 것은? [3점]

Successful integration of an educational technology is marked by that technology being regarded by users as an unobtrusive facilitator of learning, instruction, or performance. When the focus shifts from the technology being used to the educational purpose that technology serves, then that technology is becoming a comfortable and trusted element, and can be regarded as being successfully integrated. Few people give a second thought to the use of a ball-point pen although the mechanisms involved vary — some use a twist mechanism and some use a push button on top, and there are other variations as well. Personal computers have reached a similar level of familiarity for a great many users, but certainly not for all. New and emerging technologies often introduce both fascination and frustration with users. As long as ______________________ in promoting learning, instruction, or performance, then one ought not to conclude that the technology has been successfully integrated — at least for that user.

*unobtrusive: 눈에 띄지 않는

① the user successfully achieves familiarity with the technology
② the user's focus is on the technology itself rather than its use
③ the user continues to employ outdated educational techniques
④ the user involuntarily gets used to the misuse of the technology
⑤ the user's preference for interaction with other users persists

03

23학년도 6월 모평 39번

글의 흐름으로 보아, 주어진 문장이 들어가기에 가장 적절한 곳은? [3점]

> This makes sense from the perspective of information reliability.

The dynamics of collective detection have an interesting feature. Which cue(s) do individuals use as evidence of predator attack? In some cases, when an individual detects a predator, its best response is to seek shelter. (①) Departure from the group may signal danger to nonvigilant animals and cause what appears to be a coordinated flushing of prey from the area. (②) Studies on dark-eyed juncos (a type of bird) support the view that nonvigilant animals attend to departures of individual group mates but that the departure of multiple individuals causes a greater escape response in the nonvigilant individuals. (③) If one group member departs, it might have done so for a number of reasons that have little to do with predation threat. (④) If nonvigilant animals escaped each time a single member left the group, they would frequently respond when there was no predator (a false alarm). (⑤) On the other hand, when several individuals depart the group at the same time, a true threat is much more likely to be present.

*predator: 포식자 **vigilant: 경계하는 ***flushing: 날아오름

정답 및 해설 p. 152

DAY 040

함의 추론
빈칸 추론
무관 문장

제한시간 | 4분

01

22학년도 6월 모평 21번

밑줄 친 an empty inbox가 다음 글에서 의미하는 바로 가장 적절한 것은? [3점]

The single most important change you can make in your working habits is to switch to creative work first, reactive work second. This means blocking off a large chunk of time every day for creative work on your own priorities, with the phone and e-mail off. I used to be a frustrated writer. Making this switch turned me into a productive writer. Yet there wasn't a single day when I sat down to write an article, blog post, or book chapter without a string of people waiting for me to get back to them. It wasn't easy, and it still isn't, particularly when I get phone messages beginning "I sent you an e-mail *two hours ago*...!" By definition, this approach goes against the grain of others' expectations and the pressures they put on you. It takes willpower to switch off the world, even for an hour. It feels uncomfortable, and sometimes people get upset. But it's better to disappoint a few people over small things, than to abandon your dreams for an empty inbox. Otherwise, you're sacrificing your potential for the illusion of professionalism.

① following an innovative course of action
② attempting to satisfy other people's demands
③ completing challenging work without mistakes
④ removing social ties to maintain a mental balance
⑤ securing enough opportunities for social networking

02

< 21학년도 대수능 33번

다음 빈칸에 들어갈 말로 가장 적절한 것은? [3점]

Thanks to newly developed neuroimaging technology, we now have access to the specific brain changes that occur during learning. Even though all of our brains contain the same basic structures, our neural networks are as unique as our fingerprints. The latest developmental neuroscience research has shown that the brain is much more malleable throughout life than previously assumed; it develops in response to its own processes, to its immediate and distant "environments," and to its past and current situations. The brain seeks to create meaning through establishing or refining existing neural networks. When we learn a new fact or skill, our neurons communicate to form networks of connected information. Using this knowledge or skill results in structural changes to allow similar future impulses to travel more quickly and efficiently than others. High-activity synaptic connections are stabilized and strengthened, while connections with relatively low use are weakened and eventually pruned. In this way, our brains are ______________________.

*malleable: 순응성이 있는 **prune: 잘라 내다

① sculpted by our own history of experiences
② designed to maintain their initial structures
③ geared toward strengthening recent memories
④ twinned with the development of other organs
⑤ portrayed as the seat of logical and creative thinking

03

< 22학년도 9월 모평 35번

다음 글에서 전체 흐름과 관계 없는 문장은?

A variety of theoretical perspectives provide insight into immigration. Economics, which assumes that actors engage in utility maximization, represents one framework. ① From this perspective, it is assumed that individuals are rational actors, i.e., that they make migration decisions based on their assessment of the costs as well as benefits of remaining in a given area versus the costs and benefits of leaving. ② Benefits may include but are not limited to short-term and long-term monetary gains, safety, and greater freedom of cultural expression. ③ People with greater financial benefits tend to use their money to show off their social status by purchasing luxurious items. ④ Individual costs include but are not limited to the expense of travel, uncertainty of living in a foreign land, difficulty of adapting to a different language, uncertainty about a different culture, and the great concern about living in a new land. ⑤ Psychic costs associated with separation from family, friends, and the fear of the unknown also should be taken into account in cost-benefit assessments.

*psychic: 심적인

정답 및 해설 p. 156

DAY

041

글의 요지
빈칸 추론
글의 순서

⏲ 제한시간 | 4분

01

23학년도 9월 모평 22번

다음 글의 요지로 가장 적절한 것은?

Historically, drafters of tax legislation are attentive to questions of economics and history, and less attentive to moral questions. Questions of morality are often pushed to the side in legislative debate, labeled too controversial, too difficult to answer, or, worst of all, irrelevant to the project. But, in fact, the moral questions of taxation are at the very heart of the creation of tax laws. Rather than irrelevant, moral questions are fundamental to the imposition of tax. Tax is the application of a society's theories of distributive justice. Economics can go a long way towards helping a legislature determine whether or not a particular tax law will help achieve a particular goal, but economics cannot, in a vacuum, identify the goal. Creating tax policy requires identifying a moral goal, which is a task that must involve ethics and moral analysis.

*legislation: 입법 **imposition: 부과

① 분배 정의를 실현하려면 시민 단체의 역할이 필요하다.
② 사회적 합의는 민주적인 정책 수립의 선행 조건이다.
③ 성실한 납세는 안정적인 정부 예산 확보의 기반이 된다.
④ 경제학은 세법을 개정할 때 이론적 근거를 제공한다.
⑤ 세법을 만들 때 도덕적 목표를 설정하는 것이 중요하다.

02

21학년도 대수능 32번

다음 빈칸에 들어갈 말로 가장 적절한 것은?

Choosing similar friends can have a rationale. Assessing the survivability of an environment can be risky (if an environment turns out to be deadly, for instance, it might be too late by the time you found out), so humans have evolved the desire to associate with similar individuals as a way to perform this function efficiently. This is especially useful to a species that lives in so many different sorts of environments. However, the carrying capacity of a given environment ____________________. If resources are very limited, the individuals who live in a particular place cannot all do the exact same thing (for example, if there are few trees, people cannot all live in tree houses, or if mangoes are in short supply, people cannot all live solely on a diet of mangoes). A rational strategy would therefore sometimes be to *avoid* similar members of one's species.

① exceeds the expected demands of a community
② is decreased by diverse means of survival
③ places a limit on this strategy
④ makes the world suitable for individuals
⑤ prevents social ties to dissimilar members

03

22학년도 대수능 37번

주어진 글 다음에 이어질 글의 순서로 가장 적절한 것은? [3점]

In spite of the likeness between the fictional and real world, the fictional world deviates from the real one in one important respect.

(A) The author has selected the content according to his own worldview and his own conception of relevance, in an attempt to be neutral and objective or convey a subjective view on the world. Whatever the motives, the author's subjective conception of the world stands between the reader and the original, untouched world on which the story is based.

(B) Because of the inner qualities with which the individual is endowed through heritage and environment, the mind functions as a filter; every outside impression that passes through it is filtered and interpreted. However, the world the reader encounters in literature is already processed and filtered by another consciousness.

(C) The existing world faced by the individual is in principle an infinite chaos of events and details before it is organized by a human mind. This chaos only gets processed and modified when perceived by a human mind.

*deviate: 벗어나다 **endow: 부여하다 ***heritage: 유산

① (A) – (C) – (B)
② (B) – (A) – (C)
③ (B) – (C) – (A)
④ (C) – (A) – (B)
⑤ (C) – (B) – (A)

정답 및 해설 p. 160

DAY

042

필자 주장
빈칸 추론
문장 넣기

제한시간 | 4분

01

23학년도 9월 모평 20번

다음 글에서 필자가 주장하는 바로 가장 적절한 것은?

Becoming competent in another culture means looking beyond behavior to see if we can understand the attitudes, beliefs, and values that motivate what we observe. By looking only at the visible aspects of culture — customs, clothing, food, and language — we develop a short-sighted view of intercultural understanding — just the tip of the iceberg, really. If we are to be successful in our business interactions with people who have different values and beliefs about how the world is ordered, then we must go below the surface of what it means to understand culture and attempt to see what Edward Hall calls the "hidden dimensions." Those hidden aspects are the very foundation of culture and are the reason why culture is actually more than meets the eye. We tend not to notice those cultural norms until they violate what we consider to be common sense, good judgment, or the nature of things.

① 타 문화 사람들과 교류를 잘하려면 그 문화의 이면을 알아야 한다.
② 문화 배경이 다른 직원과 협업할 때 공정하게 업무를 나눠야 한다.
③ 여러 문화에 대한 이해를 통해 공동체 의식을 길러야 한다.
④ 원만한 대인 관계를 위해서는 서로의 공통점을 우선 파악해야 한다.
⑤ 문화적 갈등을 줄이려면 구성원 간의 소통을 활성화해야 한다.

02

21학년도 대수능 31번

다음 빈칸에 들어갈 말로 가장 적절한 것은?

In the classic model of the Sumerian economy, the temple functioned as an administrative authority governing commodity production, collection, and redistribution. The discovery of administrative tablets from the temple complexes at Uruk suggests that token use and consequently writing evolved as a tool of centralized economic governance. Given the lack of archaeological evidence from Uruk-period domestic sites, it is not clear whether individuals also used the system for ____________________. For that matter, it is not clear how widespread literacy was at its beginnings. The use of identifiable symbols and pictograms on the early tablets is consistent with administrators needing a lexicon that was mutually intelligible by literate and nonliterate parties. As cuneiform script became more abstract, literacy must have become increasingly important to ensure one understood what he or she had agreed to.

*archaeological: 고고학적인 **lexicon: 어휘 목록
***cuneiform script: 쐐기 문자

① religious events
② personal agreements
③ communal responsibilities
④ historical records
⑤ power shifts

03

23학년도 6월 모평 38번

글의 흐름으로 보아, 주어진 문장이 들어가기에 가장 적절한 곳은?

> Also, it has become difficult for companies to develop new pesticides, even those that can have major beneficial effects and few negative effects.

Simply maintaining yields at current levels often requires new cultivars and management methods, since pests and diseases continue to evolve, and aspects of the chemical, physical, and social environment can change over several decades. (①) In the 1960s, many people considered pesticides to be mainly beneficial to mankind. (②) Developing new, broadly effective, and persistent pesticides often was considered to be the best way to control pests on crop plants. (③) Since that time, it has become apparent that broadly effective pesticides can have harmful effects on beneficial insects, which can negate their effects in controlling pests, and that persistent pesticides can damage non-target organisms in the ecosystem, such as birds and people. (④) Very high costs are involved in following all of the procedures needed to gain government approval for new pesticides. (⑤) Consequently, more consideration is being given to other ways to manage pests, such as incorporating greater resistance to pests into cultivars by breeding and using other biological control methods.

*pesticide: 살충제 **cultivar: 품종 ***breed: 개량하다

정답 및 해설 p. 164

DAY 043

요약문 복합 유형

◷ 제한시간 | 5분

01

22학년도 9월 모평 40번

다음 글의 내용을 한 문장으로 요약하고자 한다. 빈칸 (A), (B)에 들어갈 말로 가장 적절한 것은?

The computer has, to a considerable extent, solved the problem of acquiring, preserving, and retrieving information. Data can be stored in effectively unlimited quantities and in manageable form. The computer makes available a range of data unattainable in the age of books. It packages it effectively; style is no longer needed to make it accessible, nor is memorization. In dealing with a single decision separated from its context, the computer supplies tools unimaginable even a decade ago. But it also diminishes perspective. Because information is so accessible and communication instantaneous, there is a diminution of focus on its significance, or even on the definition of what is significant. This dynamic may encourage policymakers to wait for an issue to arise rather than anticipate it, and to regard moments of decision as a series of isolated events rather than part of a historical continuum. When this happens, manipulation of information replaces reflection as the principal policy tool.

*retrieve: (정보를) 추출하다 **diminution: 감소

↓

> Although the computer is clearly ____(A)____ at handling information in a decontextualized way, it interferes with our making ____(B)____ judgments related to the broader context, as can be seen in policymaking processes.

	(A)		(B)
①	competent	......	comprehensive
②	dominant	......	biased
③	imperfect	......	informed
④	impressive	......	legal
⑤	inefficient	......	timely

02~03

23학년도 대수능 41~42번

다음 글을 읽고, 물음에 답하시오.

There is evidence that even very simple algorithms can outperform expert judgement on simple prediction problems. For example, algorithms have proved more (a) accurate than humans in predicting whether a prisoner released on parole will go on to commit another crime, or in predicting whether a potential candidate will perform well in a job in future. In over 100 studies across many different domains, half of all cases show simple formulas make (b) better significant predictions than human experts, and the remainder (except a very small handful), show a tie between the two. When there are a lot of different factors involved and a situation is very uncertain, simple formulas can win out by focusing on the most important factors and being consistent, while human judgement is too easily influenced by particularly salient and perhaps (c) irrelevant considerations. A similar idea is supported by further evidence that 'checklists' can improve the quality of expert decisions in a range of domains by ensuring that important steps or considerations aren't missed when people are feeling (d) relaxed. For example, treating patients in intensive care can require hundreds of small actions per day, and one small error could cost a life. Using checklists to ensure that no crucial steps are missed has proved to be remarkably (e) effective in a range of medical contexts, from preventing live infections to reducing pneumonia.

*parole: 가석방 **salient: 두드러진 ***pneumonia: 폐렴

02

윗글의 제목으로 가장 적절한 것은?

① The Power of Simple Formulas in Decision Making
② Always Prioritise: Tips for Managing Big Data
③ Algorithms' Mistakes: The Myth of Simplicity
④ Be Prepared! Make a Checklist Just in Case
⑤ How Human Judgement Beats Algorithms

03

밑줄 친 (a)~(e) 중에서 문맥상 낱말의 쓰임이 적절하지 않은 것은?

① (a) ② (b) ③ (c) ④ (d) ⑤ (e)

정답 및 해설 p. 168

DAY

044

빈칸 추론
글의 순서
문장 넣기

제한시간 | 5분

01

21학년도 9월 모평 34번

다음 빈칸에 들어갈 말로 가장 적절한 것은? [3점]

Protopia is a state of becoming, rather than a destination. It is a process. In the protopian mode, things are better today than they were yesterday, although only a little better. It is incremental improvement or mild progress. The "pro" in protopian stems from the notions of process and progress. This subtle progress is not dramatic, not exciting. It is easy to miss because a protopia generates almost as many new problems as new benefits. The problems of today were caused by yesterday's technological successes, and the technological solutions to today's problems will cause the problems of tomorrow. This circular expansion of both problems and solutions ________________________. Ever since the Enlightenment and the invention of science, we've managed to create a tiny bit more than we've destroyed each year. But that few percent positive difference is compounded over decades into what we might call civilization. Its benefits never star in movies.

*incremental: 증가의 **compound: 조합하다

① conceals the limits of innovations at the present time
② makes it difficult to predict the future with confidence
③ motivates us to quickly achieve a protopian civilization
④ hides a steady accumulation of small net benefits over time
⑤ produces a considerable change in technological successes

02

22학년도 대수능 36번

주어진 글 다음에 이어질 글의 순서로 가장 적절한 것은?

According to the market response model, it is increasing prices that drive providers to search for new sources, innovators to substitute, consumers to conserve, and alternatives to emerge.

(A) Many examples of such "green taxes" exist. Facing landfill costs, labor expenses, and related costs in the provision of garbage disposal, for example, some cities have required households to dispose of all waste in special trash bags, purchased by consumers themselves, and often costing a dollar or more each.

(B) Taxing certain goods or services, and so increasing prices, should result in either decreased use of these resources or creative innovation of new sources or options. The money raised through the tax can be used directly by the government either to supply services or to search for alternatives.

(C) The results have been greatly increased recycling and more careful attention by consumers to packaging and waste. By internalizing the costs of trash to consumers, there has been an observed decrease in the flow of garbage from households.

① (A) – (C) – (B)
② (B) – (A) – (C)
③ (B) – (C) – (A)
④ (C) – (A) – (B)
⑤ (C) – (B) – (A)

03

22학년도 대수능 39번

글의 흐름으로 보아, 주어진 문장이 들어가기에 가장 적절한 곳은? [3점]

As long as the irrealism of the silent black and white film predominated, one could not take filmic fantasies for representations of reality.

Cinema is valuable not for its ability to make visible the hidden outlines of our reality, but for its ability to reveal what reality itself veils — the dimension of fantasy. (①) This is why, to a person, the first great theorists of film decried the introduction of sound and other technical innovations (such as color) that pushed film in the direction of realism. (②) Since cinema was an entirely fantasmatic art, these innovations were completely unnecessary. (③) And what's worse, they could do nothing but turn filmmakers and audiences away from the fantasmatic dimension of cinema, potentially transforming film into a mere delivery device for representations of reality. (④) But sound and color threatened to create just such an illusion, thereby destroying the very essence of film art. (⑤) As Rudolf Arnheim puts it, "The creative power of the artist can only come into play where reality and the medium of representation do not coincide."

*decry: 공공연히 비난하다 **fantasmatic: 환상의

정답 및 해설 p. 171

DAY 045

글의 주제
빈칸 추론
글의 순서

제한시간 | 4분

01

22학년도 6월 모평 23번

다음 글의 주제로 가장 적절한 것은? [3점]

Children can move effortlessly between play and absorption in a story, as if both are forms of the same activity. The taking of roles in a narratively structured game of pirates is not very different than the taking of roles in identifying with characters as one watches a movie. It might be thought that, as they grow towards adolescence, people give up childhood play, but this is not so. Instead, the bases and interests of this activity change and develop to playing and watching sports, to the fiction of plays, novels, and movies, and nowadays to video games. In fiction, one can enter possible worlds. When we experience emotions in such worlds, this is not a sign that we are being incoherent or regressed. It derives from trying out metaphorical transformations of our selves in new ways, in new worlds, in ways that can be moving and important to us.

*pirate: 해적 **incoherent: 일관되지 않은

① relationship between play types and emotional stability
② reasons for identifying with imaginary characters in childhood
③ ways of helping adolescents develop good reading habits
④ continued engagement in altered forms of play after childhood
⑤ effects of narrative structures on readers' imaginations

02

〈21학년도 9월 모평 33번〉

다음 빈칸에 들어갈 말로 가장 적절한 것은? [3점]

Since human beings are at once both similar and different, they should be treated equally because of both. Such a view, which grounds equality not in human uniformity but in the interplay of uniformity and difference, builds difference into the very concept of equality, breaks the traditional equation of equality with similarity, and is immune to monist distortion. Once the basis of equality changes so does its content. Equality involves equal freedom or opportunity to be different, and treating human beings equally requires us to take into account both their similarities and differences. When the latter are not relevant, equality entails uniform or identical treatment; when they are, it requires differential treatment. Equal rights do not mean identical rights, for individuals with different cultural backgrounds and needs might ______________________________ in respect of whatever happens to be the content of their rights. Equality involves not just rejection of irrelevant differences as is commonly argued, but also full recognition of legitimate and relevant ones.

*monist: 일원론의 **entail: 내포하다

① require different rights to enjoy equality
② abandon their own freedom for equality
③ welcome the identical perception of inequality
④ accept their place in the social structure more easily
⑤ reject relevant differences to gain full understanding

03

〈22학년도 9월 모평 37번〉

주어진 글 다음에 이어질 글의 순서로 가장 적절한 것은? [3점]

> Recently, a number of commercial ventures have been launched that offer social robots as personal home assistants, perhaps eventually to rival existing smart-home assistants.

(A) They might be motorized and can track the user around the room, giving the impression of being aware of the people in the environment. Although personal robotic assistants provide services similar to those of smart-home assistants, their social presence offers an opportunity that is unique to social robots.

(B) Personal robotic assistants are devices that have no physical manipulation or locomotion capabilities. Instead, they have a distinct social presence and have visual features suggestive of their ability to interact socially, such as eyes, ears, or a mouth.

(C) For instance, in addition to playing music, a social personal assistant robot would express its engagement with the music so that users would feel like they are listening to the music together with the robot. These robots can be used as surveillance devices, act as communicative intermediates, engage in richer games, tell stories, or be used to provide encouragement or incentives.

*locomotion: 이동 **surveillance: 감시

① (A) – (C) – (B)
② (B) – (A) – (C)
③ (B) – (C) – (A)
④ (C) – (A) – (B)
⑤ (C) – (B) – (A)

정답 및 해설 p. 175

DAY 046

글의 제목
빈칸 추론
문장 넣기

제한시간 | 4분

01

22학년도 6월 모평 24번

다음 글의 제목으로 가장 적절한 것은?

Although cognitive and neuropsychological approaches emphasize the losses with age that might impair social perception, motivational theories indicate that there may be some gains or qualitative changes. Charles and Carstensen review a considerable body of evidence indicating that, as people get older, they tend to prioritize close social relationships, focus more on achieving emotional well-being, and attend more to positive emotional information while ignoring negative information. These changing motivational goals in old age have implications for attention to and processing of social cues from the environment. Of particular importance in considering emotional changes in old age is the presence of a positivity bias: that is, a tendency to notice, attend to, and remember more positive compared to negative information. The role of life experience in social skills also indicates that older adults might show gains in some aspects of social perception.

*cognitive: 인식의 **impair: 해치다

① Social Perception in Old Age: It's Not All Bad News!
② Blocking Out the Negative Sharpens Social Skills
③ Lessons on Life-long Goals from Senior Achievers
④ Getting Old: A Road to Maturity and Objectivity
⑤ Positive Mind and Behavior: Tips for Reversing Aging

02

21학년도 9월 모평 32번

다음 빈칸에 들어갈 말로 가장 적절한 것은?

Genetic engineering followed by cloning to distribute many identical animals or plants is sometimes seen as a threat to the diversity of nature. However, humans have been replacing diverse natural habitats with artificial monoculture for millennia. Most natural habitats in the advanced nations have already been replaced with some form of artificial environment based on mass production or repetition. The real threat to biodiversity is surely the need to convert ever more of our planet into production zones to feed the ever-increasing human population. The cloning and transgenic alteration of domestic animals makes little difference to the overall situation. Conversely, the renewed interest in genetics has led to a growing awareness that there are many wild plants and animals with interesting or useful genetic properties that could be used for a variety of as-yet-unknown purposes. This has led in turn to a realization that ______________________ because they may harbor tomorrow's drugs against cancer, malaria, or obesity.

*monoculture: 단일 경작

① ecological systems are genetically programmed
② we should avoid destroying natural ecosystems
③ we need to stop creating genetically modified organisms
④ artificial organisms can survive in natural environments
⑤ living things adapt themselves to their physical environments

03

22학년도 9월 모평 38번

글의 흐름으로 보아, 주어진 문장이 들어가기에 가장 적절한 곳은?

It was not until relatively recent times that scientists came to understand the relationships between the structural elements of materials and their properties.

The earliest humans had access to only a very limited number of materials, those that occur naturally: stone, wood, clay, skins, and so on. (①) With time, they discovered techniques for producing materials that had properties superior to those of the natural ones; these new materials included pottery and various metals. (②) Furthermore, it was discovered that the properties of a material could be altered by heat treatments and by the addition of other substances. (③) At this point, materials utilization was totally a selection process that involved deciding from a given, rather limited set of materials, the one best suited for an application based on its characteristics. (④) This knowledge, acquired over approximately the past 100 years, has empowered them to fashion, to a large degree, the characteristics of materials. (⑤) Thus, tens of thousands of different materials have evolved with rather specialized characteristics that meet the needs of our modern and complex society, including metals, plastics, glasses, and fibers.

정답 및 해설 p. 179

DAY 047

함의 추론
빈칸 추론
무관 문장

⏱ 제한시간 | 4분

01

21학년도 대수능 21번

밑줄 친 the role of the 'lion's historians'가 다음 글에서 의미하는 바로 가장 적절한 것은?

There is an African proverb that says, 'Till the lions have their historians, tales of hunting will always glorify the hunter'. The proverb is about power, control and law making. Environmental journalists have to play the role of the 'lion's historians'. They have to put across the point of view of the environment to people who make the laws. They have to be the voice of wild India. The present rate of human consumption is completely unsustainable. Forest, wetlands, wastelands, coastal zones, eco-sensitive zones, they are all seen as disposable for the accelerating demands of human population. But to ask for any change in human behaviour — whether it be to cut down on consumption, alter lifestyles or decrease population growth — is seen as a violation of human rights. But at some point human rights become 'wrongs'. It's time we changed our thinking so that there is no difference between the rights of humans and the rights of the rest of the environment.

① uncovering the history of a species' biological evolution
② urging a shift to sustainable human behaviour for nature
③ fighting against widespread violations of human rights
④ rewriting history for more underrepresented people
⑤ restricting the power of environmental lawmakers

02

21학년도 9월 모평 31번

다음 빈칸에 들어갈 말로 가장 적절한 것은?

"What's in a name? That which we call a rose, by any other name would smell as sweet." This thought of Shakespeare's points up a difference between roses and, say, paintings. Natural objects, such as roses, are not ____________. They are not taken as vehicles of meanings and messages. They belong to no tradition, strictly speaking have no style, and are not understood within a framework of culture and convention. Rather, they are sensed and savored relatively directly, without intellectual mediation, and so what they are called, either individually or collectively, has little bearing on our experience of them. What a work of art is titled, on the other hand, has a significant effect on the aesthetic face it presents and on the qualities we correctly perceive in it. A painting of a rose, by a name other than the one it has, might very well smell different, aesthetically speaking. The painting titled *Rose of Summer* and an indiscernible painting titled *Vermillion Womanhood* are physically, but also semantically and aesthetically, distinct objects of art.

*savor: 음미하다 **indiscernible: 식별하기 어려운 ***semantically: 의미적으로

① changed ② classified ③ preserved
④ controlled ⑤ interpreted

03

22학년도 6월 모평 35번

다음 글에서 전체 흐름과 관계 없는 문장은?

Kinship ties continue to be important today. In modern societies such as the United States people frequently have family get-togethers, they telephone their relatives regularly, and they provide their kin with a wide variety of services. ① Eugene Litwak has referred to this pattern of behaviour as the 'modified extended family'. ② It is an extended family structure because multigenerational ties are maintained, but it is modified because it does not usually rest on co-residence between the generations and most extended families do not act as corporate groups. ③ Although modified extended family members often live close by, the modified extended family does not require geographical proximity and ties are maintained even when kin are separated by considerable distances. ④ The oldest member of the family makes the decisions on important issues, no matter how far away family members live from each other. ⑤ In contrast to the traditional extended family where kin always live in close proximity, the members of modified extended families may freely move away from kin to seek opportunities for occupational advancement.

*kin: 친족 **proximity: 근접

정답 및 해설 p. 183

DAY 048

글의 요지
빈칸 추론
글의 순서

제한시간 | 4분

01

23학년도 6월 모평 22번

다음 글의 요지로 가장 적절한 것은?

Often overlooked, but just as important a stakeholder, is the consumer who plays a large role in the notion of the privacy paradox. Consumer engagement levels in all manner of digital experiences and communities have simply exploded — and they show little or no signs of slowing. There is an awareness among consumers, not only that their personal data helps to drive the rich experiences that these companies provide, but also that sharing this data is the price you pay for these experiences, in whole or in part. Without a better understanding of the what, when, and why of data collection and use, the consumer is often left feeling vulnerable and conflicted. "I love this restaurant-finder app on my phone, but what happens to my data if I press 'ok' when asked if that app can use my current location?" Armed with tools that can provide them options, the consumer moves from passive bystander to active participant.

*stakeholder: 이해관계자 **vulnerable: 상처를 입기 쉬운

① 개인 정보 제공의 속성을 심층적으로 이해하면 주체적 소비자가 된다.
② 소비자는 디지털 시대에 유용한 앱을 적극 활용하는 자세가 필요하다.
③ 현명한 소비자가 되려면 다양한 디지털 데이터를 활용해야 한다.
④ 기업의 디지털 서비스를 이용하면 상응하는 대가가 뒤따른다.
⑤ 타인과의 정보 공유로 인해 개인 정보가 유출되기도 한다.

02

21학년도 6월 모평 34번

다음 빈칸에 들어갈 말로 가장 적절한 것은? [3점]

A large part of what we see is what we expect to see. This explains why we "see" faces and figures in a flickering campfire, or in moving clouds. This is why Leonardo da Vinci advised artists to discover their motifs by staring at patches on a blank wall. A fire provides a constant flickering change in visual information that never integrates into anything solid and thereby allows the brain to engage in a play of hypotheses. On the other hand, the wall does not present us with very much in the way of visual clues, and so the brain begins to make more and more hypotheses and desperately searches for confirmation. A crack in the wall looks a little like the profile of a nose and suddenly a whole face appears, or a leaping horse, or a dancing figure. In cases like these the brain's visual strategies are ______________________.

*flicker: 흔들리다

① ignoring distracting information unrelated to visual clues
② projecting images from within the mind out onto the world
③ categorizing objects into groups either real or imagined
④ strengthening connections between objects in the real world
⑤ removing the broken or missing parts of an original image

03

22학년도 9월 모평 36번

주어진 글 다음에 이어질 글의 순서로 가장 적절한 것은?

> Green products involve, in many cases, higher ingredient costs than those of mainstream products.

(A) They'd rather put money and time into known, profitable, high-volume products that serve populous customer segments than into risky, less-profitable, low-volume products that may serve current noncustomers. Given that choice, these companies may choose to leave the green segment of the market to small niche competitors.

(B) Even if the green product succeeds, it may cannibalize the company's higher-profit mainstream offerings. Given such downsides, companies serving mainstream consumers with successful mainstream products face what seems like an obvious investment decision.

(C) Furthermore, the restrictive ingredient lists and design criteria that are typical of such products may make green products inferior to mainstream products on core performance dimensions (e.g., less effective cleansers). In turn, the higher costs and lower performance of some products attract only a small portion of the customer base, leading to lower economies of scale in procurement, manufacturing, and distribution.

*segment: 조각 **cannibalize: 잡아먹다 ***procurement: 조달

① (A) – (C) – (B)
② (B) – (A) – (C)
③ (B) – (C) – (A)
④ (C) – (A) – (B)
⑤ (C) – (B) – (A)

정답 및 해설 p. 187

DAY 049

필자 주장
빈칸 추론
문장 넣기

제한시간 | 4분

01

23학년도 6월 모평 20번

다음 글에서 필자가 주장하는 바로 가장 적절한 것은?

Consider two athletes who both want to play in college. One says she has to work very hard and the other uses goal setting to create a plan to stay on track and work on specific skills where she is lacking. Both are working hard but only the latter is working smart. It can be frustrating for athletes to work extremely hard but not make the progress they wanted. What can make the difference is drive — utilizing the mental gear to maximize gains made in the technical and physical areas. Drive provides direction (goals), sustains effort (motivation), and creates a training mindset that goes beyond simply working hard. Drive applies direct force on your physical and technical gears, strengthening and polishing them so they can spin with vigor and purpose. While desire might make you spin those gears faster and harder as you work out or practice, drive is what built them in the first place.

*vigor: 활력, 활기

① 선수들의 훈련 방식은 장점을 극대화하는 방향으로 이루어져야 한다.
② 선수들은 최고의 성과를 얻기 위해 정신적 추진력을 잘 활용해야 한다.
③ 선수들은 단기적 훈련 성과보다 장기적 목표 달성에 힘써야 한다.
④ 선수들은 육체적 훈련과 정신적 훈련을 균형 있게 병행해야 한다.
⑤ 선수들은 수립한 계획을 실행하면서 꾸준히 수정하여야 한다.

02

21학년도 6월 모평 33번

다음 빈칸에 들어갈 말로 가장 적절한 것은? [3점]

Even when we do something as apparently simple as picking up a screwdriver, our brain automatically ______________________________. We can literally feel things with the end of the screwdriver. When we extend a hand, holding the screwdriver, we automatically take the length of the latter into account. We can probe difficult-to-reach places with its extended end, and comprehend what we are exploring. Furthermore, we instantly regard the screwdriver we are holding as "our" screwdriver, and get possessive about it. We do the same with the much more complex tools we use, in much more complex situations. The cars we pilot instantaneously and automatically become ourselves. Because of this, when someone bangs his fist on our car's hood after we have irritated him at a crosswalk, we take it personally. This is not always reasonable. Nonetheless, without the extension of self into machine, it would be impossible to drive.

*probe: 탐색하다

① recalls past experiences of utilizing the tool
② recognizes what it can do best without the tool
③ judges which part of our body can best be used
④ perceives what limits the tool's functional utility
⑤ adjusts what it considers body to include the tool

03

22학년도 6월 모평 39번

글의 흐름으로 보아, 주어진 문장이 들어가기에 가장 적절한 곳은? [3점]

> This is particularly true since one aspect of sleep is decreased responsiveness to the environment.

The role that sleep plays in evolution is still under study. (①) One possibility is that it is an advantageous adaptive state of decreased metabolism for an animal when there are no more pressing activities. (②) This seems true for deeper states of inactivity such as hibernation during the winter when there are few food supplies, and a high metabolic cost to maintaining adequate temperature. (③) It may be true in daily situations as well, for instance for a prey species to avoid predators after dark. (④) On the other hand, the apparent universality of sleep, and the observation that mammals such as cetaceans have developed such highly complex mechanisms to preserve sleep on at least one side of the brain at a time, suggests that sleep additionally provides some vital service(s) for the organism. (⑤) If sleep is universal even when this potential price must be paid, the implication may be that it has important functions that cannot be obtained just by quiet, wakeful resting.

*metabolism: 신진대사 **mammal: 포유동물

정답 및 해설 p. 191

DAY 050

요약문 복합 유형

제한시간 | 4분

01

22학년도 6월 모평 40번

다음 글의 내용을 한 문장으로 요약하고자 한다. 빈칸 (A), (B)에 들어갈 말로 가장 적절한 것은?

The idea that *planting* trees could have a social or political significance appears to have been invented by the English, though it has since spread widely. According to Keith Thomas's history *Man and the Natural World*, seventeenth- and eighteenth-century aristocrats began planting hardwood trees, usually in lines, to declare the extent of their property and the permanence of their claim to it. "What can be more pleasant," the editor of a magazine for gentlemen asked his readers, "than to have the bounds and limits of your own property preserved and continued from age to age by the testimony of such living and growing witnesses?" Planting trees had the additional advantage of being regarded as a patriotic act, for the Crown had declared a severe shortage of the hardwood on which the Royal Navy depended.

*aristocrat: 귀족 **patriotic: 애국적인

↓

For English aristocrats, planting trees served as statements to mark the ____(A)____ ownership of their land, and it was also considered to be a(n) ____(B)____ of their loyalty to the nation.

(A)		(B)
① unstable	……	confirmation
② unstable	……	exaggeration
③ lasting	……	exhibition
④ lasting	……	manipulation
⑤ official	……	justification

02~03

23학년도 9월 모평 41~42번

다음 글을 읽고, 물음에 답하시오.

Climate change experts and environmental humanists alike agree that the climate crisis is, at its core, a crisis of the imagination and much of the popular imagination is shaped by fiction. In his 2016 book *The Great Derangement*, anthropologist and novelist Amitav Ghosh takes on this relationship between imagination and environmental management, arguing that humans have failed to respond to climate change at least in part because fiction (a) fails to believably represent it. Ghosh explains that climate change is largely absent from contemporary fiction because the cyclones, floods, and other catastrophes it brings to mind simply seem too "improbable" to belong in stories about everyday life. But climate change does not only reveal itself as a series of (b) extraordinary events. In fact, as environmentalists and ecocritics from Rachel Carson to Rob Nixon have pointed out, environmental change can be "imperceptible"; it proceeds (c) rapidly, only occasionally producing "explosive and spectacular" events. Most climate change impacts cannot be observed day-to-day, but they become (d) visible when we are confronted with their accumulated impacts.
Climate change evades our imagination because it poses significant representational challenges. It cannot be observed in "human time," which is why documentary filmmaker Jeff Orlowski, who tracks climate change effects on glaciers and coral reefs, uses "before and after" photographs taken several months apart in the same place to (e) highlight changes that occurred gradually.

*anthropologist: 인류학자 **catastrophe: 큰 재해 ***evade: 피하다

02

윗글의 제목으로 가장 적절한 것은?

① Differing Attitudes Towards Current Climate Issues
② Slow but Significant: The History of Ecological Movements
③ The Silence of Imagination in Representing Climate Change
④ Vivid Threats: Climate Disasters Spreading in Local Areas
⑤ The Rise and Fall of Environmentalism and Ecocriticism

03

밑줄 친 (a)~(e) 중에서 문맥상 낱말의 쓰임이 적절하지 않은 것은? [3점]

① (a) ② (b) ③ (c) ④ (d) ⑤ (e)

정답 및 해설 p. 195

DAY

051

빈칸 추론
글의 순서
문장 넣기

제한시간 | 5분

01

21학년도 6월 모평 32번

다음 빈칸에 들어갈 말로 가장 적절한 것은?

One of the great risks of writing is that even the simplest of choices regarding wording or punctuation can sometimes ______________________________ in ways that may seem unfair. For example, look again at the old grammar rule forbidding the splitting of infinitives. After decades of telling students to never split an infinitive (something just done in this sentence), most composition experts now acknowledge that a split infinitive is *not* a grammar crime. Suppose you have written a position paper trying to convince your city council of the need to hire security personnel for the library, and half of the council members — the people you wish to convince — remember their eighth-grade grammar teacher's warning about splitting infinitives. How will they respond when you tell them, in your introduction, that librarians are compelled "to always accompany" visitors to the rare book room because of the threat of damage? How much of their attention have you suddenly lost because of their automatic recollection of what is now a nonrule? It is possible, in other words, to write correctly and still offend your readers' notions of your language competence.

*punctuation: 구두점 **infinitive: 부정사(不定詞)

① reveal your hidden intention
② distort the meaning of the sentence
③ prejudice your audience against you
④ test your audience's reading comprehension
⑤ create fierce debates about your writing topic

02

22학년도 6월 모평 37번

주어진 글 다음에 이어질 글의 순서로 가장 적절한 것은? [3점]

> A firm is deciding whether to invest in shipbuilding. If it can produce at sufficiently large scale, it knows the venture will be profitable.

(A) There is a "good" outcome, in which both types of investments are made, and both the shipyard and the steelmakers end up profitable and happy. Equilibrium is reached. Then there is a "bad" outcome, in which neither type of investment is made. This second outcome also is an equilibrium because the decisions not to invest reinforce each other.

(B) Assume that shipyards are the only potential customers of steel. Steel producers figure they'll make money if there's a shipyard to buy their steel, but not otherwise. Now we have two possible outcomes — what economists call "multiple equilibria."

(C) But one key input is low-cost steel, and it must be produced nearby. The company's decision boils down to this: if there is a steel factory close by, invest in shipbuilding; otherwise, don't invest. Now consider the thinking of potential steel investors in the region.

*equilibrium: 균형

① (A) – (C) – (B)
② (B) – (A) – (C)
③ (B) – (C) – (A)
④ (C) – (A) – (B)
⑤ (C) – (B) – (A)

03

22학년도 6월 모평 38번

글의 흐름으로 보아, 주어진 문장이 들어가기에 가장 적절한 곳은?

> A problem, however, is that supervisors often work in locations apart from their employees and therefore are not able to observe their subordinates' performance.

In most organizations, the employee's immediate supervisor evaluates the employee's performance. (①) This is because the supervisor is responsible for the employee's performance, providing supervision, handing out assignments, and developing the employee. (②) Should supervisors rate employees on performance dimensions they cannot observe? (③) To eliminate this dilemma, more and more organizations are implementing assessments referred to as *360-degree evaluations*. (④) Employees are rated not only by their supervisors but by coworkers, clients or citizens, professionals in other agencies with whom they work, and subordinates. (⑤) The reason for this approach is that often coworkers and clients or citizens have a greater opportunity to observe an employee's performance and are in a better position to evaluate many performance dimensions.

*subordinate: 부하 직원

정답 및 해설 p. 198

DAY

052

글의 주제
빈칸 추론
글의 순서

제한시간 | 4분

01

21학년도 대수능 23번

다음 글의 주제로 가장 적절한 것은? [3점]

Difficulties arise when we do not think of people and machines as collaborative systems, but assign whatever tasks can be automated to the machines and leave the rest to people. This ends up requiring people to behave in machine-like fashion, in ways that differ from human capabilities. We expect people to monitor machines, which means keeping alert for long periods, something we are bad at. We require people to do repeated operations with the extreme precision and accuracy required by machines, again something we are not good at. When we divide up the machine and human components of a task in this way, we fail to take advantage of human strengths and capabilities but instead rely upon areas where we are genetically, biologically unsuited. Yet, when people fail, they are blamed.

① difficulties of overcoming human weaknesses to avoid failure
② benefits of allowing machines and humans to work together
③ issues of allocating unfit tasks to humans in automated systems
④ reasons why humans continue to pursue machine automation
⑤ influences of human actions on a machine's performance

02

21학년도 6월 모평 31번

다음 빈칸에 들어갈 말로 가장 적절한 것은? [3점]

Research with human runners challenged conventional wisdom and found that the ground-reaction forces at the foot and the shock transmitted up the leg and through the body after impact with the ground ____________________ as runners moved from extremely compliant to extremely hard running surfaces. As a result, researchers gradually began to believe that runners are subconsciously able to adjust leg stiffness prior to foot strike based on their perceptions of the hardness or stiffness of the surface on which they are running. This view suggests that runners create soft legs that soak up impact forces when they are running on very hard surfaces and stiff legs when they are moving along on yielding terrain. As a result, impact forces passing through the legs are strikingly similar over a wide range of running surface types. Contrary to popular belief, running on concrete is not more damaging to the legs than running on soft sand.

*compliant: 말랑말랑한 *terrain: 지형

① varied little
② decreased a lot
③ suddenly peaked
④ gradually appeared
⑤ were hardly generated

03

21학년도 대수능 37번

주어진 글 다음에 이어질 글의 순서로 가장 적절한 것은? [3점]

Experts have identified a large number of measures that promote energy efficiency. Unfortunately many of them are not cost effective. This is a fundamental requirement for energy efficiency investment from an economic perspective.

(A) And this has direct repercussions at the individual level: households can reduce the cost of electricity and gas bills, and improve their health and comfort, while companies can increase their competitiveness and their productivity. Finally, the market for energy efficiency could contribute to the economy through job and firms creation.

(B) There are significant externalities to take into account and there are also macroeconomic effects. For instance, at the aggregate level, improving the level of national energy efficiency has positive effects on macroeconomic issues such as energy dependence, climate change, health, national competitiveness and reducing fuel poverty.

(C) However, the calculation of such cost effectiveness is not easy: it is not simply a case of looking at private costs and comparing them to the reductions achieved.

*repercussion: 반향, 영향 **aggregate: 집합의

① (A) – (C) – (B)
② (B) – (A) – (C)
③ (B) – (C) – (A)
④ (C) – (A) – (B)
⑤ (C) – (B) – (A)

정답 및 해설 p. 202

DAY

053

글의 제목
빈칸 추론
문장 넣기

제한시간 | 4분

01

21학년도 대수능 24번

다음 글의 제목으로 가장 적절한 것은?

People don't usually think of touch as a temporal phenomenon, but it is every bit as time-based as it is spatial. You can carry out an experiment to see for yourself. Ask a friend to cup his hand, palm face up, and close his eyes. Place a small ordinary object in his palm — a ring, an eraser, anything will do — and ask him to identify it without moving any part of his hand. He won't have a clue other than weight and maybe overall size. Then tell him to keep his eyes closed and move his fingers over the object. He'll most likely identify it at once. By allowing the fingers to move, you've added time to the sensory perception of touch. There's a direct analogy between the fovea at the center of your retina and your fingertips, both of which have high acuity. Your ability to make complex use of touch, such as buttoning your shirt or unlocking your front door in the dark, depends on continuous time-varying patterns of touch sensation.

*analogy: 유사 **fovea: (망막의) 중심와(窩) ***retina: 망막

① Touch and Movement: Two Major Elements of Humanity
② Time Does Matter: A Hidden Essence of Touch
③ How to Use the Five Senses in a Timely Manner
④ The Role of Touch in Forming the Concept of Time
⑤ The Surprising Function of Touch as a Booster of Knowledge

02

20학년도 대수능 34번

다음 빈칸에 들어갈 말로 가장 적절한 것은? [3점]

There have been many attempts to define what music is in terms of the specific attributes of musical sounds. The famous nineteenth-century critic Eduard Hanslick regarded 'the measurable tone' as 'the primary and essential condition of all music'. Musical sounds, he was saying, can be distinguished from those of nature by the fact that they involve the use of fixed pitches, whereas virtually all natural sounds consist of constantly fluctuating frequencies. And a number of twentieth-century writers have assumed, like Hanslick, that fixed pitches are among the defining features of music. Now it is true that in most of the world's musical cultures, pitches are ________________________. However, this is a generalization about music and not a definition of it, for it is easy to put forward counter-examples. Japanese *shakuhachi* music and the *sanjo* music of Korea, for instance, fluctuate constantly around the notional pitches in terms of which the music is organized.

① not so much artificially fixed as naturally fluctuating
② not only fixed, but organized into a series of discrete steps
③ hardly considered a primary compositional element of music
④ highly diverse and complicated, and thus are immeasurable
⑤ a vehicle for carrying unique and various cultural features

03

21학년도 대수능 39번

글의 흐름으로 보아, 주어진 문장이 들어가기에 가장 적절한 곳은? [3점]

> Note that copyright covers the expression of an idea and not the idea itself.

Designers draw on their experience of design when approaching a new project. This includes the use of previous designs that they know work — both designs that they have created themselves and those that others have created. (①) Others' creations often spark inspiration that also leads to new ideas and innovation. (②) This is well known and understood. (③) However, the expression of an idea is protected by copyright, and people who infringe on that copyright can be taken to court and prosecuted. (④) This means, for example, that while there are numerous smartphones all with similar functionality, this does not represent an infringement of copyright as the idea has been expressed in different ways and it is the expression that has been copyrighted. (⑤) Copyright is free and is automatically invested in the author, for instance, the writer of a book or a programmer who develops a program, unless they sign the copyright over to someone else.

*infringe: 침해하다 **prosecute: 기소하다

정답 및 해설 p. 206

DAY 054

함의 추론
빈칸 추론
무관 문장

제한시간 | 4분

01

21학년도 9월 모평 21번

밑줄 친 don't knock the box가 다음 글에서 의미하는 바로 가장 적절한 것은?

By expecting what's likely to happen next, you prepare for the few most likely scenarios so that you don't have to figure things out while they're happening. It's therefore not a surprise when a restaurant server offers you a menu. When she brings you a glass with a clear fluid in it, you don't have to ask if it's water. After you eat, you don't have to figure out why you aren't hungry anymore. All these things are expected and are therefore not problems to solve. Furthermore, imagine how demanding it would be to always consider all the possible uses for all the familiar objects with which you interact. *Should I use my hammer or my telephone to pound in that nail?* On a daily basis, functional fixedness is a relief, not a curse. That's why you shouldn't even attempt to consider all your options and possibilities. You can't. If you tried to, then you'd never get anything done. So don't knock the box. Ironically, although it limits your thinking, it also makes you smart. It helps you to stay one step ahead of reality.

① Deal with a matter based on your habitual expectations.
② Question what you expect from a familiar object.
③ Replace predetermined routines with fresh ones.
④ Think over all possible outcomes of a given situation.
⑤ Extend all the boundaries that guide your thinking to insight.

02

20학년도 대수능 33번

다음 빈칸에 들어갈 말로 가장 적절한 것은? [3점]

The future of our high-tech goods may lie not in the limitations of our minds, but in ________________________________. In previous eras, such as the Iron Age and the Bronze Age, the discovery of new elements brought forth seemingly unending numbers of new inventions. Now the combinations may truly be unending. We are now witnessing a fundamental shift in our resource demands. At no point in human history have we used *more* elements, in *more* combinations, and in increasingly refined amounts. Our ingenuity will soon outpace our material supplies. This situation comes at a defining moment when the world is struggling to reduce its reliance on fossil fuels. Fortunately, rare metals are key ingredients in green technologies such as electric cars, wind turbines, and solar panels. They help to convert free natural resources like the sun and wind into the power that fuels our lives. But without increasing today's limited supplies, we have no chance of developing the alternative green technologies we need to slow climate change.

*ingenuity: 창의력

① our ability to secure the ingredients to produce them
② our effort to make them as eco-friendly as possible
③ the wider distribution of innovative technologies
④ governmental policies not to limit resource supplies
⑤ the constant update and improvement of their functions

03

21학년도 대수능 35번

다음 글에서 전체 흐름과 관계 없는 문장은?

Workers are united by laughing at shared events, even ones that may initially spark anger or conflict. Humor reframes potentially divisive events into merely "laughable" ones which are put in perspective as subservient to unifying values held by organization members. Repeatedly recounting humorous incidents reinforces unity based on key organizational values. ① One team told repeated stories about a dumpster fire, something that does not seem funny on its face, but the reactions of workers motivated to preserve safety sparked laughter as the stories were shared multiple times by multiple parties in the workplace. ② Shared events that cause laughter can indicate a sense of belonging since "you had to be there" to see the humor in them, and non-members were not and do not. ③ Since humor can easily capture people's attention, commercials tend to contain humorous elements, such as funny faces and gestures. ④ Instances of humor serve to enact bonds among organization members. ⑤ Understanding the humor may even be required as an informal badge of membership in the organization.

*subservient: 도움이 되는

정답 및 해설 p. 210

DAY 055

글의 요지
빈칸 추론
글의 순서

제한시간 | 4분

01

22학년도 대수능 22번

다음 글의 요지로 가장 적절한 것은?

Environmental hazards include biological, physical, and chemical ones, along with the human behaviors that promote or allow exposure. Some environmental contaminants are difficult to avoid (the breathing of polluted air, the drinking of chemically contaminated public drinking water, noise in open public spaces); in these circumstances, exposure is largely involuntary. Reduction or elimination of these factors may require societal action, such as public awareness and public health measures. In many countries, the fact that some environmental hazards are difficult to avoid at the individual level is felt to be more morally egregious than those hazards that can be avoided. Having no choice but to drink water contaminated with very high levels of arsenic, or being forced to passively breathe in tobacco smoke in restaurants, outrages people more than the personal choice of whether an individual smokes tobacco. These factors are important when one considers how change (risk reduction) happens.

*contaminate: 오염시키다 **egregious: 매우 나쁜

① 개인이 피하기 어려운 유해 환경 요인에 대해서는 사회적 대응이 필요하다.
② 환경 오염으로 인한 피해자들에게 적절한 보상을 하는 것이 바람직하다.
③ 다수의 건강을 해치는 행위에 대해 도덕적 비난 이상의 조치가 요구된다.
④ 환경 오염 문제를 해결하기 위해서는 사후 대응보다 예방이 중요하다.
⑤ 대기 오염 문제는 인접 국가들과의 긴밀한 협력을 통해 해결할 수 있다.

02

20학년도 대수능 32번

다음 빈칸에 들어갈 말로 가장 적절한 것은?

The Swiss psychologist Jean Piaget frequently analyzed children's conception of time via their ability to compare or estimate the time taken by pairs of events. In a typical experiment, two toy cars were shown running synchronously on parallel tracks, ______________________. The children were then asked to judge whether the cars had run for the same time and to justify their judgment. Preschoolers and young school-age children confuse temporal and spatial dimensions: Starting times are judged by starting points, stopping times by stopping points and durations by distance, though each of these errors does not necessitate the others. Hence, a child may claim that the cars started and stopped running together (correct) and that the car which stopped further ahead, ran for more time (incorrect).

*synchronously: 같은 시간에

① one running faster and stopping further down the track
② both stopping at the same point further than expected
③ one keeping the same speed as the other to the end
④ both alternating their speed but arriving at the same end
⑤ both slowing their speed and reaching the identical spot

03

21학년도 대수능 36번

주어진 글 다음에 이어질 글의 순서로 가장 적절한 것은?

> The objective of battle, to "throw" the enemy and to make him defenseless, may temporarily blind commanders and even strategists to the larger purpose of war. War is never an isolated act, nor is it ever only one decision.

(A) To be political, a political entity or a representative of a political entity, whatever its constitutional form, has to have an intention, a will. That intention has to be clearly expressed.

(B) In the real world, war's larger purpose is always a political purpose. It transcends the use of force. This insight was famously captured by Clausewitz's most famous phrase, "War is a mere continuation of politics by other means."

(C) And one side's will has to be transmitted to the enemy at some point during the confrontation (it does not have to be publicly communicated). A violent act and its larger political intention must also be attributed to one side at some point during the confrontation. History does not know of acts of war without eventual attribution.

*entity: 실체 **transcend: 초월하다

① (A) – (C) – (B)
② (B) – (A) – (C)
③ (B) – (C) – (A)
④ (C) – (A) – (B)
⑤ (C) – (B) – (A)

정답 및 해설 p. 214

DAY 056

필자 주장
빈칸 추론
문장 넣기

제한시간 | 4분

01

22학년도 대수능 20번

다음 글에서 필자가 주장하는 바로 가장 적절한 것은?

One of the most common mistakes made by organizations when they first consider experimenting with social media is that they focus too much on social media tools and platforms and not enough on their business objectives. The reality of success in the social web for businesses is that creating a social media program begins not with insight into the latest social media tools and channels but with a thorough understanding of the organization's own goals and objectives. A social media program is not merely the fulfillment of a vague need to manage a "presence" on popular social networks because "everyone else is doing it." "Being in social media" serves no purpose in and of itself. In order to serve any purpose at all, a social media presence must either solve a problem for the organization and its customers or result in an improvement of some sort (preferably a measurable one). In all things, purpose drives success. The world of social media is no different.

① 기업 이미지에 부합하는 소셜 미디어를 직접 개발하여 운영해야 한다.
② 기업은 사회적 가치와 요구를 반영하여 사업 목표를 수립해야 한다.
③ 기업은 소셜 미디어를 활용할 때 사업 목표를 토대로 해야 한다.
④ 소셜 미디어로 제품을 홍보할 때는 구체적인 정보를 제공해야 한다.
⑤ 소비자의 의견을 수렴하기 위해 소셜 미디어를 적극 활용해야 한다.

02

20학년도 대수능 31번

다음 빈칸에 들어갈 말로 가장 적절한 것은?

The role of science can sometimes be overstated, with its advocates slipping into scientism. Scientism is the view that the scientific description of reality is the only truth there is. With the advance of science, there has been a tendency to slip into scientism, and assume that any factual claim can be authenticated if and only if the term 'scientific' can correctly be ascribed to it. The consequence is that non-scientific approaches to reality — and that can include all the arts, religion, and personal, emotional and value-laden ways of encountering the world — may become labelled as merely subjective, and therefore of little ____________ in terms of describing the way the world is. The philosophy of science seeks to avoid crude scientism and get a balanced view on what the scientific method can and cannot achieve.

*ascribe: 속하는 것으로 생각하다 **crude: 투박한

① question ② account ③ controversy
④ variation ⑤ bias

03

21학년도 대수능 38번

글의 흐름으로 보아, 주어진 문장이 들어가기에 가장 적절한 곳은?

I have still not exactly pinpointed Maddy's character since wickedness takes many forms.

Imagine I tell you that Maddy is bad. Perhaps you infer from my intonation, or the context in which we are talking, that I mean morally bad. Additionally, you will probably infer that I am disapproving of Maddy, or saying that I think you should disapprove of her, or similar, given typical linguistic conventions and assuming I am sincere. (①) However, you might not get a more detailed sense of the particular sorts of way in which Maddy is bad, her typical character traits, and the like, since people can be bad in many ways. (②) In contrast, if I say that Maddy is wicked, then you get more of a sense of her typical actions and attitudes to others. (③) The word 'wicked' is more specific than 'bad'. (④) But there is more detail nevertheless, perhaps a stronger connotation of the sort of person Maddy is. (⑤) In addition, and again assuming typical linguistic conventions, you should also get a sense that I am disapproving of Maddy, or saying that you should disapprove of her, or similar, assuming that we are still discussing her moral character.

*connotation: 함축

정답 및 해설 p. 218

DAY

057

요약문
복합 유형

제한시간 | 4분

01

21학년도 대수능 40번

다음 글의 내용을 한 문장으로 요약하고자 한다. 빈칸 (A), (B)에 들어갈 말로 가장 적절한 것은?

From a cross-cultural perspective the equation between public leadership and dominance is questionable. What does one mean by 'dominance'? Does it indicate coercion? Or control over 'the most valued'? 'Political' systems may be about both, either, or conceivably neither. The idea of 'control' would be a bothersome one for many peoples, as for instance among many native peoples of Amazonia where all members of a community are fond of their personal autonomy and notably allergic to any obvious expression of control or coercion. The conception of political power as a *coercive* force, while it may be a Western fixation, is not a universal. It is very unusual for an Amazonian leader to give an order. If many peoples do not view political power as a coercive force, *nor as the most valued domain*, then the leap from 'the political' to 'domination' (as coercion), *and from there* to 'domination of women', is a shaky one. As Marilyn Strathern has remarked, the notions of 'the political' and 'political personhood' are cultural obsessions of our own, a bias long reflected in anthropological constructs.

*coercion: 강제 **autonomy: 자율 ***anthropological: 인류학의

↓

> It is ____(A)____ to understand political power in other cultures through our own notion of it because ideas of political power are not ____(B)____ across cultures.

(A)		(B)
① rational	……	flexible
② appropriate	……	commonplace
③ misguided	……	uniform
④ unreasonable	……	varied
⑤ effective	……	objective

02~03

23학년도 6월 모평 41~42번

다음 글을 읽고, 물음에 답하시오.

Once an event is noticed, an onlooker must decide if it is truly an emergency. Emergencies are not always clearly (a) labeled as such; "smoke" pouring into a waiting room may be caused by fire, or it may merely indicate a leak in a steam pipe. Screams in the street may signal an attack or a family quarrel. A man lying in a doorway may be having a coronary — or he may simply be sleeping off a drunk.

A person trying to interpret a situation often looks at those around him to see how he should react. If everyone else is calm and indifferent, he will tend to remain so; if everyone else is reacting strongly, he is likely to become alert. This tendency is not merely blind conformity; ordinarily we derive much valuable information about new situations from how others around us behave. It's a (b) rare traveler who, in picking a roadside restaurant, chooses to stop at one where no other cars appear in the parking lot.

But occasionally the reactions of others provide (c) accurate information. The studied nonchalance of patients in a dentist's waiting room is a poor indication of their inner anxiety. It is considered embarrassing to "lose your cool" in public. In a potentially acute situation, then, everyone present will appear more (d) unconcerned than he is in fact. A crowd can thus force (e) inaction on its members by implying, through its passivity, that an event is not an emergency. Any individual in such a crowd fears that he may appear a fool if he behaves as though it were.

*coronary: 관상 동맥증 **nonchalance: 무관심, 냉담

02

윗글의 제목으로 가장 적절한 것은?

① Do We Judge Independently? The Effect of Crowds
② Winning Strategy: How Not to Be Fooled by Others
③ Do Emergencies Affect the Way of Our Thinking?
④ Stepping Towards Harmony with Your Neighbors
⑤ Ways of Helping Others in Emergent Situations

03

밑줄 친 (a)~(e) 중에서 문맥상 낱말의 쓰임이 적절하지 않은 것은?

① (a) ② (b) ③ (c) ④ (d) ⑤ (e)

정답 및 해설 p. 222

DAY

058

빈칸 추론
글의 순서
문장 넣기

제한시간 | 5분

01

20학년도 9월 모평 34번

다음 빈칸에 들어갈 말로 가장 적절한 것은? [3점]

The debates between social and cultural anthropologists concern not the differences between the concepts but the analytical priority: which should come first, the social chicken or the cultural egg? British anthropology emphasizes the social. It assumes that social institutions determine culture and that universal domains of society (such as kinship, economy, politics, and religion) are represented by specific institutions (such as the family, subsistence farming, the British Parliament, and the Church of England) which can be compared cross-culturally. American anthropology emphasizes the cultural. It assumes that culture shapes social institutions by providing the shared beliefs, the core values, the communicative tools, and so on that make social life possible. It does not assume that there are universal social domains, preferring instead to discover domains empirically as aspects of each society's own classificatory schemes — in other words, its culture. And it rejects the notion that any social institution can be understood ________________________.

*anthropology: 인류학 **subsistence farming: 자급 농업
***empirically: 경험적으로

① in relation to its cultural origin
② in isolation from its own context
③ regardless of personal preferences
④ without considering its economic roots
⑤ on the basis of British-American relations

02

21학년도 9월 모평 37번

주어진 글 다음에 이어질 글의 순서로 가장 적절한 것은? [3점]

> It can be difficult to decide the place of fine art, such as oil paintings, watercolours, sketches or sculptures, in an archival institution.

(A) The best archival decisions about art do not focus on territoriality (this object belongs in my institution even though I do not have the resources to care for it) or on questions of monetary value or prestige (this object raises the cultural standing of my institution). The best decisions focus on what evidential value exists and what is best for the item.

(B) But art can also carry aesthetic value, which elevates the job of evaluation into another realm. Aesthetic value and the notion of artistic beauty are important considerations, but they are not what motivates archival preservation in the first instance.

(C) Art can serve as documentary evidence, especially when the items were produced before photography became common. Sketches of soldiers on a battlefield, paintings of English country villages or portraits of Dutch townspeople can provide the only visual evidence of a long-ago place, person or time.

*archival: 기록(보관소)의 **prestige: 명성, 위신 ***realm: 영역

① (A) – (C) – (B)
② (B) – (A) – (C)
③ (B) – (C) – (A)
④ (C) – (A) – (B)
⑤ (C) – (B) – (A)

03

21학년도 9월 모평 39번

글의 흐름으로 보아, 주어진 문장이 들어가기에 가장 적절한 곳은? [3점]

> Rather, it evolved naturally as certain devices were found in practice to be both workable and useful.

Film has no grammar. (①) There are, however, some vaguely defined rules of usage in cinematic language, and the syntax of film — its systematic arrangement — orders these rules and indicates relationships among them. (②) As with written and spoken languages, it is important to remember that the syntax of film is a result of its usage, not a determinant of it. (③) There is nothing preordained about film syntax. (④) Like the syntax of written and spoken language, the syntax of film is an organic development, descriptive rather than prescriptive, and it has changed considerably over the years. (⑤) "Hollywood Grammar" may sound laughable now, but during the thirties, forties, and early fifties it was an accurate model of the way Hollywood films were constructed.

*preordained: 미리 정해진

정답 및 해설 p. 226

DAY 059

글의 주제
빈칸 추론
글의 순서

제한시간 | 4분

01

21학년도 9월 모평 23번

다음 글의 주제로 가장 적절한 것은? [3점]

Conventional wisdom in the West, influenced by philosophers from Plato to Descartes, credits individuals and especially geniuses with creativity and originality. Social and cultural influences and causes are minimized, ignored, or eliminated from consideration at all. Thoughts, original and conventional, are identified with individuals, and the special things that individuals are and do are traced to their genes and their brains. The "trick" here is to recognize that individual humans are social constructions themselves, embodying and reflecting the variety of social and cultural influences they have been exposed to during their lives. Our individuality is not denied, but it is viewed as a product of specific social and cultural experiences. The brain itself is a social thing, influenced structurally and at the level of its connectivities by social environments. The "individual" is a legal, religious, and political fiction just as the "I" is a grammatical illusion.

① recognition of the social nature inherent in individuality
② ways of filling the gap between individuality and collectivity
③ issues with separating original thoughts from conventional ones
④ acknowledgment of the true individuality embodied in human genes
⑤ necessity of shifting from individualism to interdependence

02

20학년도 9월 모평 33번

다음 빈칸에 들어갈 말로 가장 적절한 것은? [3점]

If one looks at the Oxford definition, one gets the sense that post-truth is not so much a claim that truth *does not exist* as that *facts are subordinate to our political point of view*. The Oxford definition focuses on "*what*" post-truth is: the idea that feelings sometimes matter more than facts. But just as important is the next question, which is *why* this ever occurs. Someone does not argue against an obvious or easily confirmable fact for no reason; he or she does so when it is to his or her advantage. When a person's beliefs are threatened by an "inconvenient fact," sometimes it is preferable to challenge the fact. This can happen at either a conscious or unconscious level (since sometimes the person we are seeking to convince is ourselves), but the point is that this sort of post-truth relationship to facts occurs only when we are seeking to assert something ______________________.

*subordinate: 종속하는

① to hold back our mixed feelings
② that balances our views on politics
③ that leads us to give way to others in need
④ to carry the constant value of absolute truth
⑤ that is more important to us than the truth itself

03

21학년도 9월 모평 36번

주어진 글 다음에 이어질 글의 순서로 가장 적절한 것은?

> In the fifth century *B.C.E.*, the Greek philosopher Protagoras pronounced, "Man is the measure of all things." In other words, we feel entitled to ask the world, "What good are you?"

(A) Abilities said to "make us human" — empathy, communication, grief, toolmaking, and so on — all exist to varying degrees among other minds sharing the world with us. Animals with backbones (fishes, amphibians, reptiles, birds, and mammals) all share the same basic skeleton, organs, nervous systems, hormones, and behaviors.

(B) We assume that we are the world's standard, that all things should be compared to us. Such an assumption makes us overlook a lot.

(C) Just as different models of automobiles each have an engine, drive train, four wheels, doors, and seats, we differ mainly in terms of our outside contours and a few internal tweaks. But like naive car buyers, most people see only animals' varied exteriors.

*contour: 윤곽, 외형 **tweak: 조정, 개조

① (A) – (C) – (B)
② (B) – (A) – (C)
③ (B) – (C) – (A)
④ (C) – (A) – (B)
⑤ (C) – (B) – (A)

정답 및 해설 p. 230

DAY 060

글의 제목 빈칸 추론 문장 넣기

제한시간 | 4분

01

21학년도 9월 모평 24번

다음 글의 제목으로 가장 적절한 것은?

The discovery that man's knowledge is not, *and never has been*, perfectly accurate has had a humbling and perhaps a calming effect upon the soul of modern man. The nineteenth century, as we have observed, was the last to believe that the world, as a whole as well as in its parts, could ever be perfectly known. We realize now that this is, and always was, impossible. We know within limits, not absolutely, even if the limits can usually be adjusted to satisfy our needs. Curiously, from this new level of uncertainty even greater goals emerge and appear to be attainable. Even if we cannot know the world with absolute precision, we can still control it. Even our inherently incomplete knowledge seems to work as powerfully as ever. In short, we may never know precisely how high is the highest mountain, but we continue to be certain that we can get to the top nevertheless.

① Summits Yet to Be Reached: An Onward Journey to Knowledge
② Over the Mountain: A Single But Giant Step to Success
③ Integrating Parts into a Whole: The Road to Perfection
④ How to Live Together in an Age of Uncertainty
⑤ The Two Faces of a Knowledge-Based Society

02

20학년도 9월 모평 32번

다음 빈칸에 들어갈 말로 가장 적절한 것은?

With population growth slowing, the strongest force increasing demand for more agricultural production will be *rising incomes*, which are desired by practically all governments and individuals. Although richer people spend smaller proportions of their income on food, in total they consume more food — and richer food, which contributes to various kinds of disease and debilitation. The changes in diet that usually accompany higher incomes will require relatively greater increases in the production of feed grains, rather than food grains, as foods of animal origin partly ______________________. It takes two to six times more grain to produce food value through animals than to get the equivalent value directly from plants. It is thus quite credible to estimate that in order to meet economic and social needs within the next three to five decades, the world should be producing more than twice as much grain and agricultural products as at present, but in ways that these are accessible to the food-insecure.

*debilitation: 건강 악화

① displace plant-based foods in people's diets
② demand eco-friendly processing systems
③ cause several nutritional imbalances
④ indicate the consumers' higher social status
⑤ play an important role in population growth

03

21학년도 9월 모평 38번

글의 흐름으로 보아, 주어진 문장이 들어가기에 가장 적절한 곳은?

As long as you do not run out of copies before completing this process, you will know that you have a sufficient number to go around.

We sometimes solve number problems almost without realizing it. (①) For example, suppose you are conducting a meeting and you want to ensure that everyone there has a copy of the agenda. (②) You can deal with this by labelling each copy of the handout in turn with the initials of each of those present. (③) You have then solved this problem without resorting to arithmetic and without explicit counting. (④) There are numbers at work for us here all the same and they allow precise comparison of one collection with another, even though the members that make up the collections could have entirely different characters, as is the case here, where one set is a collection of people, while the other consists of pieces of paper. (⑤) What numbers allow us to do is to compare the relative size of one set with another.

*arithmetic: 산수

정답 및 해설 p. 234

DAY

061

함의 추론
빈칸 추론
무관 문장

제한시간 | 4분

01

21학년도 6월 모평 21번

밑줄 친 journey edges가 다음 글에서 의미하는 바로 가장 적절한 것은? [3점]

Many ancillary businesses that today seem almost core at one time started out as journey edges. For example, retailers often boost sales with accompanying support such as assembly or installation services. Think of a home goods retailer selling an unassembled outdoor grill as a box of parts and leaving its customer's mission incomplete. When that retailer also sells assembly and delivery, it takes another step in the journey to the customer's true mission of cooking in his backyard. Another example is the business-to-business service contracts that are layered on top of software sales. Maintenance, installation, training, delivery, anything at all that turns do-it-yourself into a do-it-for-me solution originally resulted from exploring the edge of where core products intersect with customer journeys.

*ancillary: 보조의, 부차적인 **intersect: 교차하다

① requiring customers to purchase unnecessary goods
② decreasing customers' dependence on business services
③ focusing more on selling end products than components
④ adding a technological breakthrough to their core products
⑤ providing extra services beyond customers' primary purchase

02

20학년도 9월 모평 31번

다음 빈칸에 들어갈 말로 가장 적절한 것은?

When you begin to tell a story again that you have retold many times, what you retrieve from memory is the index to the story itself. That index can be embellished in a variety of ways. Over time, even the embellishments become standardized. An old man's story that he has told hundreds of times shows little variation, and any variation that does exist becomes part of the story itself, regardless of its origin. People add details to their stories that may or may not have occurred. They are recalling indexes and reconstructing details. If at some point they add a nice detail, not really certain of its validity, telling the story with that same detail a few more times will ensure its permanent place in the story index. In other words, the stories we tell time and again are ____________ to the memory we have of the events that the story relates.

*retrieve: 회수하다 **embellish: 윤색하다

① identical ② beneficial ③ alien
④ prior ⑤ neutral

03

21학년도 9월 모평 35번

다음 글에서 전체 흐름과 관계 없는 문장은?

In a highly commercialized setting such as the United States, it is not surprising that many landscapes are seen as commodities. In other words, they are valued because of their market potential. Residents develop an identity in part based on how the landscape can generate income for the community. ① This process involves more than the conversion of the natural elements into commodities. ② The landscape itself, including the people and their sense of self, takes on the form of a commodity. ③ Landscape protection in the US traditionally focuses on protecting areas of wilderness, typically in mountainous regions. ④ Over time, the landscape identity can evolve into a sort of "logo" that can be used to sell the stories of the landscape. ⑤ Thus, California's "Wine Country," Florida's "Sun Coast," or South Dakota's "Badlands" shape how both outsiders and residents perceive a place, and these labels build a set of expectations associated with the culture of those who live there.

정답 및 해설 p. 238

DAY 062

글의 요지
빈칸 추론
글의 순서

⏱ 제한시간 | 4분

01

22학년도 9월 모평 22번

다음 글의 요지로 가장 적절한 것은?

Historically, the professions and society have engaged in a negotiating process intended to define the terms of their relationship. At the heart of this process is the tension between the professions' pursuit of autonomy and the public's demand for accountability. Society's granting of power and privilege to the professions is premised on their willingness and ability to contribute to social well-being and to conduct their affairs in a manner consistent with broader social values. It has long been recognized that the expertise and privileged position of professionals confer authority and power that could readily be used to advance their own interests at the expense of those they serve. As Edmund Burke observed two centuries ago, "Men are qualified for civil liberty in exact proportion to their disposition to put moral chains upon their own appetites." Autonomy has never been a one-way street and is never granted absolutely and irreversibly.

*autonomy: 자율성 **privilege: 특권 ***premise: 전제로 말하다

① 전문직에 부여되는 자율성은 그에 상응하는 사회적 책임을 수반한다.
② 전문직의 권위는 해당 집단의 이익을 추구하는 데 이용되어 왔다.
③ 전문직의 사회적 책임을 규정할 수 있는 제도 정비가 필요하다.
④ 전문직이 되기 위한 자격 요건은 사회 경제적 요구에 따라 변화해 왔다.
⑤ 전문직의 업무 성과는 일정 수준의 자율성과 특권이 부여될 때 높아진다.

02

20학년도 6월 모평 33번

다음 빈칸에 들어갈 말로 가장 적절한 것은? [3점]

Digital technology accelerates dematerialization by hastening the migration from products to services. The liquid nature of services means they don't have to be bound to materials. But dematerialization is not just about digital goods. The reason even solid physical goods — like a soda can — can deliver more benefits while inhabiting less material is because their heavy atoms are substituted by weightless bits. The tangible is replaced by intangibles — intangibles like better design, innovative processes, smart chips, and eventually online connectivity — that do the work that more aluminum atoms used to do. Soft things, like intelligence, are thus embedded into hard things, like aluminum, that make hard things behave more like software. Material goods infused with bits increasingly act as if ____________________. Nouns morph to verbs. Hardware behaves like software. In Silicon Valley they say it like this: "Software eats everything."

*morph: 변화하다

① they were intangible services
② they replaced all digital goods
③ hardware could survive software
④ digital services were not available
⑤ software conflicted with hardware

03

21학년도 6월 모평 37번

주어진 글 다음에 이어질 글의 순서로 가장 적절한 것은? [3점]

> The fruit ripening process brings about the softening of cell walls, sweetening and the production of chemicals that give colour and flavour. The process is induced by the production of a plant hormone called ethylene.

(A) If ripening could be slowed down by interfering with ethylene production or with the processes that respond to ethylene, fruit could be left on the plant until it was ripe and full of flavour but would still be in good condition when it arrived at the supermarket shelf.

(B) In some countries they are then sprayed with ethylene before sale to the consumer to induce ripening. However, fruit picked before it is ripe has less flavour than fruit picked ripe from the plant. Biotechnologists therefore saw an opportunity in delaying the ripening and softening process in fruit.

(C) The problem for growers and retailers is that ripening is followed sometimes quite rapidly by deterioration and decay and the product becomes worthless. Tomatoes and other fruits are, therefore, usually picked and transported when they are unripe.

*deterioration: (품질의) 저하

① (A) – (C) – (B)
② (B) – (A) – (C)
③ (B) – (C) – (A)
④ (C) – (A) – (B)
⑤ (C) – (B) – (A)

정답 및 해설 p. 242

DAY 063

필자 주장
빈칸 추론
문장 넣기

제한시간 | 4분

01

22학년도 9월 모평 20번

다음 글에서 필자가 주장하는 바로 가장 적절한 것은?

We live in a time when everyone seems to be looking for quick and sure solutions. Computer companies have even begun to advertise ways in which computers can replace parents. They are too late —television has already done that. Seriously, however, in every branch of education, including moral education, we make a mistake when we suppose that a particular batch of content or a particular teaching method or a particular configuration of students and space will accomplish our ends. The answer is both harder and simpler. We, parents and teachers, have to live with our children, talk to them, listen to them, enjoy their company, and show them by what we do and how we talk that it is possible to live appreciatively or, at least, nonviolently with most other people.

① 교육은 일상에서 아이들과의 상호 작용을 통해 이루어져야 한다.
② 도덕 교육을 강화하여 타인을 배려하는 공동체 의식을 높여야 한다.
③ 텔레비전의 부정적 영향을 줄이려는 사회적 노력이 있어야 한다.
④ 다양한 매체를 활용하여 학교와 가정 교육의 한계를 보완해야 한다.
⑤ 아이들의 온라인 예절 교육을 위해 적절한 콘텐츠를 개발해야 한다.

02

20학년도 6월 모평 32번

다음 빈칸에 들어갈 말로 가장 적절한 것은?

Through recent decades academic archaeologists have been urged to conduct their research and excavations according to hypothesis-testing procedures. It has been argued that we should construct our general theories, deduce testable propositions and prove or disprove them against the sampled data. In fact, the application of this 'scientific method' often ran into difficulties. The data have a tendency to lead to unexpected questions, problems and issues. Thus, archaeologists claiming to follow hypothesis-testing procedures found themselves having to create a fiction. In practice, their work and theoretical conclusions partly developed ____. In other words, they already knew the data when they decided upon an interpretation. But in presenting their work they rewrote the script, placing the theory first and claiming to have tested it against data which they discovered, as in an experiment under laboratory conditions.

*excavation: 발굴 **deduce: 추론하다

① from the data which they had discovered
② from comparisons of data in other fields
③ to explore more sites for their future studies
④ by supposing possible theoretical frameworks
⑤ by observing the hypothesis-testing procedures

03

21학년도 6월 모평 39번

글의 흐름으로 보아, 주어진 문장이 들어가기에 가장 적절한 곳은?

When the team painted fireflies' light organs dark, a new set of bats took twice as long to learn to avoid them.

Fireflies don't just light up their behinds to attract mates, they also glow to tell bats not to eat them. This twist in the tale of the trait that gives fireflies their name was discovered by Jesse Barber and his colleagues. The glow's warning role benefits both fireflies and bats, because these insects taste disgusting to the mammals. (①) When swallowed, chemicals released by fireflies cause bats to throw them back up. (②) The team placed eight bats in a dark room with three or four fireflies plus three times as many tasty insects, including beetles and moths, for four days. (③) During the first night, all the bats captured at least one firefly. (④) But by the fourth night, most bats had learned to avoid fireflies and catch all the other prey instead. (⑤) It had long been thought that firefly bioluminescence mainly acted as a mating signal, but the new finding explains why firefly larvae also glow despite being immature for mating.

*bioluminescence: 생물 발광(發光) **larvae: larva(애벌레)의 복수형

정답 및 해설 p. 246

DAY

064

요약문
복합 유형

제한시간 | 4분

01

21학년도 9월 모평 40번

다음 글의 내용을 한 문장으로 요약하고자 한다. 빈칸 (A), (B)에 들어갈 말로 가장 적절한 것은?

Research from the Harwood Institute for Public Innovation in the USA shows that people feel that 'materialism' somehow comes between them and the satisfaction of their social needs. A report entitled *Yearning for Balance*, based on a nationwide survey of Americans, concluded that they were 'deeply ambivalent about wealth and material gain'. A large majority of people wanted society to 'move away from greed and excess toward a way of life more centred on values, community, and family'. But they also felt that these priorities were not shared by most of their fellow Americans, who, they believed, had become 'increasingly atomized, selfish, and irresponsible'. As a result they often felt isolated. However, the report says, that when brought together in focus groups to discuss these issues, people were 'surprised and excited to find that others share[d] their views'. Rather than uniting us with others in a common cause, the unease we feel about the loss of social values and the way we are drawn into the pursuit of material gain is often experienced as if it were a purely private ambivalence which cuts us off from others.

*ambivalent: 양면 가치의

↓

Many Americans, believing that materialism keeps them from ____(A)____ social values, feel detached from most others, but this is actually a fairly ____(B)____ concern.

	(A)		(B)
①	pursuing	……	unnecessary
②	pursuing	……	common
③	holding	……	personal
④	denying	……	ethical
⑤	denying	……	primary

02~03

22학년도 대수능 41~42번

다음 글을 읽고, 물음에 답하시오.

Classifying things together into groups is something we do all the time, and it isn't hard to see why. Imagine trying to shop in a supermarket where the food was arranged in random order on the shelves: tomato soup next to the white bread in one aisle, chicken soup in the back next to the 60-watt light bulbs, one brand of cream cheese in front and another in aisle 8 near the cookies. The task of finding what you want would be (a) time-consuming and extremely difficult, if not impossible.

In the case of a supermarket, someone had to (b) design the system of classification. But there is also a ready-made system of classification embodied in our language. The word "dog," for example, groups together a certain class of animals and distinguishes them from other animals. Such a grouping may seem too (c) abstract to be called a classification, but this is only because you have already mastered the word. As a child learning to speak, you had to work hard to (d) learn the system of classification your parents were trying to teach you. Before you got the hang of it, you probably made mistakes, like calling the cat a dog. If you hadn't learned to speak, the whole world would seem like the (e) unorganized supermarket; you would be in the position of an infant, for whom every object is new and unfamiliar. In learning the principles of classification, therefore, we'll be learning about the structure that lies at the core of our language.

02

윗글의 제목으로 가장 적절한 것은?

① Similarities of Strategies in Sales and Language Learning
② Classification: An Inherent Characteristic of Language
③ Exploring Linguistic Issues Through Categorization
④ Is a Ready-Made Classification System Truly Better?
⑤ Dilemmas of Using Classification in Language Education

03

밑줄 친 (a)~(e) 중에서 문맥상 낱말의 쓰임이 적절하지 않은 것은?

① (a) ② (b) ③ (c) ④ (d) ⑤ (e)

정답 및 해설 p. 250

DAY 065

빈칸 추론
글의 순서
문장 넣기

제한시간 | 5분

01

20학년도 6월 모평 31번

다음 빈칸에 들어갈 말로 가장 적절한 것은?

Some people have defined wildlife damage management as the science and management of overabundant species, but this definition is too narrow. All wildlife species act in ways that harm human interests. Thus, all species cause wildlife damage, not just overabundant ones. One interesting example of this involves endangered peregrine falcons in California, which prey on another endangered species, the California least tern. Certainly, we would not consider peregrine falcons as being overabundant, but we wish that they would not feed on an endangered species. In this case, one of the negative values associated with a peregrine falcon population is that its predation reduces the population of another endangered species. The goal of wildlife damage management in this case would be to stop the falcons from eating the terns without ______________ the falcons.

*peregrine falcon: 송골매 **least tern: 작은 제비갈매기

① cloning ② harming ③ training
④ overfeeding ⑤ domesticating

02

21학년도 6월 모평 36번

주어진 글 다음에 이어질 글의 순서로 가장 적절한 것은?

> Studies of people struggling with major health problems show that the majority of respondents report they derived benefits from their adversity. Stressful events sometimes force people to develop new skills, reevaluate priorities, learn new insights, and acquire new strengths.

(A) High levels of adversity predicted poor mental health, as expected, but people who had faced intermediate levels of adversity were healthier than those who experienced little adversity, suggesting that moderate amounts of stress can foster resilience. A follow-up study found a similar link between the amount of lifetime adversity and subjects' responses to laboratory stressors.

(B) Intermediate levels of adversity were predictive of the greatest resilience. Thus, having to deal with a moderate amount of stress may build resilience in the face of future stress.

(C) In other words, the adaptation process initiated by stress can lead to personal changes for the better. One study that measured participants' exposure to thirty-seven major negative events found a curvilinear relationship between lifetime adversity and mental health.

*resilience: 회복력

① (A) – (C) – (B)
② (B) – (A) – (C)
③ (B) – (C) – (A)
④ (C) – (A) – (B)
⑤ (C) – (B) – (A)

03

21학년도 6월 모평 38번

글의 흐름으로 보아, 주어진 문장이 들어가기에 가장 적절한 곳은? [3점]

> Compounding the difficulty, now more than ever, is what ergonomists call information overload, where a leader is overrun with inputs — via e-mails, meetings, and phone calls — that only distract and confuse her thinking.

Clarity is often a difficult thing for a leader to obtain. Concerns of the present tend to seem larger than potentially greater concerns that lie farther away. (①) Some decisions by their nature present great complexity, whose many variables must come together a certain way for the leader to succeed. (②) Alternatively, the leader's information might be only fragmentary, which might cause her to fill in the gaps with assumptions — sometimes without recognizing them as such. (③) And the merits of a leader's most important decisions, by their nature, typically are not clear-cut. (④) Instead those decisions involve a process of assigning weights to competing interests, and then determining, based upon some criterion, which one predominates. (⑤) The result is one of judgment, of shades of gray; like saying that Beethoven is a better composer than Brahms.

*ergonomist: 인간 공학자 **fragmentary: 단편적인

정답 및 해설 p. 253

DAY 066

글의 주제
빈칸 추론
글의 순서

제한시간 | 4분

01

21학년도 6월 모평 23번

다음 글의 주제로 가장 적절한 것은?

Problem framing amounts to defining *what* problem you are proposing to solve. This is a critical activity because the frame you choose strongly influences your understanding of the problem, thereby conditioning your approach to solving it. For an illustration, consider Thibodeau and Broditsky's series of experiments in which they asked people for ways to reduce crime in a community. They found that the respondents' suggestions changed significantly depending on whether the metaphor used to describe crime was as a virus or as a beast. People presented with a metaphor comparing crime to a virus invading their city emphasized prevention and addressing the root causes of the problem, such as eliminating poverty and improving education. On the other hand, people presented with the beast metaphor focused on remediations: increasing the size of the police force and prisons.

① importance of asking the right questions for better solutions
② difficulty of using a metaphor to find solutions to a problem
③ reasons why problem framing prevents solutions from appearing
④ usefulness of preventive measures in reducing community crime
⑤ effect of problem framing on approaching and solving problems

02

〈19학년도 대수능 33번〉

다음 빈칸에 들어갈 말로 가장 적절한 것은? [3점]

Heritage is concerned with the ways in which very selective material artefacts, mythologies, memories and traditions become resources for the present. The contents, interpretations and representations of the resource are selected according to the demands of the present; an imagined past provides resources for a heritage that is to be passed onto an imagined future. It follows too that the meanings and functions of memory and tradition are defined in the present. Further, heritage is more concerned with meanings than material artefacts. It is the former that give value, either cultural or financial, to the latter and explain why they have been selected from the near infinity of the past. In turn, they may later be discarded as the demands of present societies change, or even, as is presently occurring in the former Eastern Europe, when pasts have to be reinvented to reflect new presents. Thus heritage is ______________________ ______________________.

① a collection of memories and traditions of a society
② as much about forgetting as remembering the past
③ neither concerned with the present nor the future
④ a mirror reflecting the artefacts of the past
⑤ about preserving universal cultural values

03

〈20학년도 대수능 37번〉

주어진 글 다음에 이어질 글의 순서로 가장 적절한 것은? [3점]

> Traditionally, Kuhn claims, the primary goal of historians of science was 'to clarify and deepen an understanding of *contemporary* scientific methods or concepts by displaying their evolution.'

(A) Some discoveries seem to entail numerous phases and discoverers, none of which can be identified as definitive. Furthermore, the evaluation of past discoveries and discoverers according to present-day standards does not allow us to see how significant they may have been in their own day.

(B) This entailed relating the progressive accumulation of breakthroughs and discoveries. Only that which survived in some form in the present was considered relevant. In the mid-1950s, however, a number of faults in this view of history became apparent. Closer analysis of scientific discoveries, for instance, led historians to ask whether the dates of discoveries and their discoverers can be identified precisely.

(C) Nor does the traditional view recognise the role that non-intellectual factors, especially institutional and socio-economic ones, play in scientific developments. Most importantly, however, the traditional historian of science seems blind to the fact that the concepts, questions and standards that they use to frame the past are themselves subject to historical change.

① (A) – (C) – (B)　　② (B) – (A) – (C)
③ (B) – (C) – (A)　　④ (C) – (A) – (B)
⑤ (C) – (B) – (A)

정답 및 해설 p. 257

DAY 067

글의 제목
빈칸 추론
문장 넣기

제한시간 | 4분

01

21학년도 6월 모평 24번

다음 글의 제목으로 가장 적절한 것은?

A common error in current Darwinian thinking is the assumption that "selfish genes" are the prime mover in evolution. In strict Darwinism the prime mover is environmental threat. In the absence of threat, natural selection tends to *resist* change. It is un-biological to "explain" behavioural change as *resulting from* genetic change or the *ex vacuo* emergence of domain-specific brain modules. Evolutionary psychologists surely know why brains evolved: as Cosmides and Tooby point out, brains are found only in animals that move. Brains are behavioural organs, and behavioural adaptation, being immediate and non-random, is vastly more efficient than genetic adaptation. So, in animals with brains, behavioural change is the usual first response to environmental threat. If the change is successful, genetic adaptation to the new behaviour will follow more gradually. Animals do not evolve carnivore teeth and then decide it might be a good idea to eat meat.

*ex vacuo: 무(無)에서의 **carnivore: 육식 동물

① Which Adapts First, Behaviour or Genes?
② The Brain Under Control of Selfish Genes
③ Why Animals Eat Meat: A Story of Survival
④ Genes Always Win the Battle Against Nature!
⑤ The Superior Efficiency of Genetic Adaptation

02

19학년도 대수능 32번

다음 빈칸에 들어갈 말로 가장 적절한 것은?

Minorities tend not to have much power or status and may even be dismissed as troublemakers, extremists or simply 'weirdos'. How, then, do they ever have any influence over the majority? The social psychologist Serge Moscovici claims that the answer lies in their *behavioural style*, i.e. the *way* ______________________. The crucial factor in the success of the suffragette movement was that its supporters were *consistent* in their views, and this created a considerable degree of social influence. Minorities that are active and organised, who support and defend their position *consistently*, can create social conflict, doubt and uncertainty among members of the majority, and ultimately this may lead to social change. Such change has often occurred because a minority has converted others to its point of view. Without the influence of minorities, we would have no innovation, no social change. Many of what we now regard as 'major' social movements (e.g. Christianity, trade unionism or feminism) were originally due to the influence of an outspoken minority.

*dismiss: 일축하다 **weirdo: 별난 사람 ***suffragette: 여성 참정권론자

① the minority gets its point across
② the minority tones down its voice
③ the majority cultivates the minority
④ the majority brings about social change
⑤ the minority cooperates with the majority

03

20학년도 대수능 39번

글의 흐름으로 보아, 주어진 문장이 들어가기에 가장 적절한 곳은? [3점]

> Still, it is arguable that advertisers worry rather too much about this problem, as advertising in other media has always been fragmented.

The fragmentation of television audiences during recent decades, which has happened throughout the globe as new channels have been launched everywhere, has caused advertisers much concern. (①) Advertisers look back nostalgically to the years when a single spot transmission would be seen by the majority of the population at one fell swoop. (②) This made the television advertising of mass consumer products relatively straightforward — not to say easy — whereas today it is necessary for advertisers to build up coverage of their target markets over time, by advertising on a host of channels with separate audiences. (③) Moreover, advertisers gain considerable benefits from the price competition between the numerous broadcasting stations. (④) And television remains much the fastest way to build up public awareness of a new brand or a new campaign. (⑤) Seldom does a new brand or new campaign that solely uses other media, without using television, reach high levels of public awareness very quickly.

*fragment: 조각내다 **at one fell swoop: 단번에, 일거에

정답 및 해설 p. 261

DAY 068

함의 추론
빈칸 추론
무관 문장

⏲ 제한시간 | 4분

01

20학년도 대수능 21번

밑줄 친 playing intellectual air guitar가 다음 글에서 의미하는 바로 가장 적절한 것은? [3점]

Any learning environment that deals with only the database instincts or only the improvisatory instincts ignores one half of our ability. It is bound to fail. It makes me think of jazz guitarists: They're not going to make it if they know a lot about music theory but don't know how to jam in a live concert. Some schools and workplaces emphasize a stable, rote-learned database. They ignore the improvisatory instincts drilled into us for millions of years. Creativity suffers. Others emphasize creative usage of a database, without installing a fund of knowledge in the first place. They ignore our need to obtain a deep understanding of a subject, which includes memorizing and storing a richly structured database. You get people who are great improvisers but don't have depth of knowledge. You may know someone like this where you work. They may look like jazz musicians and have the appearance of jamming, but in the end they know nothing. They're playing intellectual air guitar.

*rote-learned: 기계적으로 암기한

① acquiring necessary experience to enhance their creativity
② exhibiting artistic talent coupled with solid knowledge of music
③ posing as experts by demonstrating their in-depth knowledge
④ performing musical pieces to attract a highly educated audience
⑤ displaying seemingly creative ability not rooted in firm knowledge

02

19학년도 대수능 31번

다음 빈칸에 들어갈 말로 가장 적절한 것은?

Finkenauer and Rimé investigated the memory of the unexpected death of Belgium's King Baudouin in 1993 in a large sample of Belgian citizens. The data revealed that the news of the king's death had been widely socially shared. By talking about the event, people gradually constructed a social narrative and a collective memory of the emotional event. At the same time, they consolidated their own memory of the personal circumstances in which the event took place, an effect known as "flashbulb memory." The more an event is socially shared, the more it will be fixed in people's minds. Social sharing may in this way help to counteract some natural tendency people may have. Naturally, people should be driven to "forget" undesirable events. Thus, someone who just heard a piece of bad news often tends initially to deny what happened. The ________________ social sharing of the bad news contributes to realism.

*consolidate: 공고히 하다

① biased ② illegal ③ repetitive
④ temporary ⑤ rational

03

21학년도 6월 모평 35번

다음 글에서 전체 흐름과 관계 없는 문장은?

One of the most widespread, and sadly mistaken, environmental myths is that living "close to nature" out in the country or in a leafy suburb is the best "green" lifestyle. Cities, on the other hand, are often blamed as a major cause of ecological destruction — artificial, crowded places that suck up precious resources. Yet, when you look at the facts, nothing could be farther from the truth. ① The pattern of life in the country and most suburbs involves long hours in the automobile each week, burning fuel and pumping out exhaust to get to work, buy groceries, and take kids to school and activities. ② City dwellers, on the other hand, have the option of walking or taking transit to work, shops, and school. ③ The larger yards and houses found outside cities also create an environmental cost in terms of energy use, water use, and land use. ④ This illustrates the tendency that most city dwellers get tired of urban lives and decide to settle in the countryside. ⑤ It's clear that the future of the Earth depends on more people gathering together in compact communities.

*compact: 밀집한

정답 및 해설 p. 265

DAY 069

밑줄 어법
빈칸 추론
글의 순서

제한시간 | 4분

01

22학년도 대수능 29번

다음 글의 밑줄 친 부분 중, 어법상 틀린 것은? [3점]

Like whole individuals, cells have a life span. During their life cycle (cell cycle), cell size, shape, and metabolic activities can change dramatically. A cell is "born" as a twin when its mother cell divides, ① producing two daughter cells. Each daughter cell is smaller than the mother cell, and except for unusual cases, each grows until it becomes as large as the mother cell ② was. During this time, the cell absorbs water, sugars, amino acids, and other nutrients and assembles them into new, living protoplasm. After the cell has grown to the proper size, its metabolism shifts as it either prepares to divide or matures and ③ differentiates into a specialized cell. Both growth and development require a complex and dynamic set of interactions involving all cell parts. ④ What cell metabolism and structure should be complex would not be surprising, but actually, they are rather simple and logical. Even the most complex cell has only a small number of parts, each ⑤ responsible for a distinct, well-defined aspect of cell life.

*metabolic: 물질대사의 **protoplasm: 원형질

02

19학년도 9월 모평 34번

다음 빈칸에 들어갈 말로 가장 적절한 것은? [3점]

Modern psychological theory states that the process of understanding is a matter of construction, not reproduction, which means that the process of understanding takes the form of the interpretation of data coming from the outside and generated by our mind. For example, the perception of a moving object as a car is based on an interpretation of incoming data within the framework of our knowledge of the world. While the interpretation of simple objects is usually an uncontrolled process, the interpretation of more complex phenomena, such as interpersonal situations, usually requires active attention and thought. Psychological studies indicate that it is knowledge possessed by the individual that determines which stimuli become the focus of that individual's attention, what significance he or she assigns to these stimuli, and how they are combined into a larger whole. This subjective world, interpreted in a particular way, is for us the "objective" world; we cannot know any world other than ______________________.

① the reality placed upon us through social conventions
② the one we know as a result of our own interpretations
③ the world of images not filtered by our perceptual frame
④ the external world independent of our own interpretations
⑤ the physical universe our own interpretations fail to explain

03

20학년도 대수능 36번

주어진 글 다음에 이어질 글의 순서로 가장 적절한 것은?

Movies may be said to support the dominant culture and to serve as a means for its reproduction over time.

(A) The bad guys are usually punished; the romantic couple almost always find each other despite the obstacles and difficulties they encounter on the path to true love; and the way we wish the world to be is how, in the movies, it more often than not winds up being. No doubt it is this utopian aspect of movies that accounts for why we enjoy them so much.

(B) The simple answer to this question is that movies do more than present two-hour civics lessons or editorials on responsible behavior. They also tell stories that, in the end, we find satisfying.

(C) But one may ask why audiences would find such movies enjoyable if all they do is give cultural directives and prescriptions for proper living. Most of us would likely grow tired of such didactic movies and would probably come to see them as propaganda, similar to the cultural artwork that was common in the Soviet Union and other autocratic societies.

*didactic: 교훈적인 **autocratic: 독재적인

① (A) – (C) – (B)
② (B) – (A) – (C)
③ (B) – (C) – (A)
④ (C) – (A) – (B)
⑤ (C) – (B) – (A)

정답 및 해설 p. 269

DAY 070

낱말 쓰임
빈칸 추론
문장 넣기

제한시간 | 4분

01

22학년도 대수능 30번

다음 글의 밑줄 친 부분 중, 문맥상 낱말의 쓰임이 적절하지 않은 것은?

It has been suggested that "organic" methods, defined as those in which only natural products can be used as inputs, would be less damaging to the biosphere. Large-scale adoption of "organic" farming methods, however, would ① reduce yields and increase production costs for many major crops. Inorganic nitrogen supplies are ② essential for maintaining moderate to high levels of productivity for many of the non-leguminous crop species, because organic supplies of nitrogenous materials often are either limited or more expensive than inorganic nitrogen fertilizers. In addition, there are ③ benefits to the extensive use of either manure or legumes as "green manure" crops. In many cases, weed control can be very difficult or require much hand labor if chemicals cannot be used, and ④ fewer people are willing to do this work as societies become wealthier. Some methods used in "organic" farming, however, such as the sensible use of crop rotations and specific combinations of cropping and livestock enterprises, can make important ⑤ contributions to the sustainability of rural ecosystems.

*nitrogen fertilizer: 질소 비료 **manure: 거름 ***legume: 콩과(科) 식물

02

19학년도 9월 모평 33번

다음 빈칸에 들어갈 말로 가장 적절한 것은?

Food unites as well as distinguishes eaters because what and how one eats forms much of one's emotional tie to a group identity, be it a nation or an ethnicity. The famous twentieth-century Chinese poet and scholar Lin Yutang remarks, "Our love for fatherland is largely a matter of recollection of the keen sensual pleasure of our childhood. The loyalty to Uncle Sam is the loyalty to American doughnuts, and the loyalty to the *Vaterland* is the loyalty to *Pfannkuchen* and *Stollen*." Such keen connection between food and national or ethnic identification clearly indicates the truth that cuisine and table narrative occupy a significant place in the training grounds of a community and its civilization, and thus, eating, cooking, and talking about one's cuisine are vital to ______________________________. In other words, the destiny of a community depends on how well it nourishes its members.

*nourish: 기르다

① an individual's dietary choices
② one's diverse cultural experiences
③ one's unique personality and taste
④ a community's wholeness and continuation
⑤ a community's dominance over other cultures

03

20학년도 대수능 38번

글의 흐름으로 보아, 주어진 문장이 들어가기에 가장 적절한 곳은?

> Thus, individuals of many resident species, confronted with the fitness benefits of control over a productive breeding site, may be forced to balance costs in the form of lower nonbreeding survivorship by remaining in the specific habitat where highest breeding success occurs.

Resident-bird habitat selection is seemingly a straightforward process in which a young dispersing individual moves until it finds a place where it can compete successfully to satisfy its needs. (①) Initially, these needs include only food and shelter. (②) However, eventually, the young must locate, identify, and settle in a habitat that satisfies not only survivorship but reproductive needs as well. (③) In some cases, the habitat that provides the best opportunity for survival may not be the same habitat as the one that provides for highest reproductive capacity because of requirements specific to the reproductive period. (④) Migrants, however, are free to choose the optimal habitat for survival during the nonbreeding season and for reproduction during the breeding season. (⑤) Thus, habitat selection during these different periods can be quite different for migrants as opposed to residents, even among closely related species.

*disperse: 흩어지다 **optimal: 최적의

정답 및 해설 p. 273

DAY 071

요약문 복합 유형

⏱ 제한시간 | 4분

01

21학년도 6월 모평 40번

다음 글의 내용을 한 문장으로 요약하고자 한다. 빈칸 (A), (B)에 들어갈 말로 가장 적절한 것은?

Some environments are more likely to lead to fossilization and subsequent discovery than others. Thus, we cannot assume that more fossil evidence from a particular period or place means that more individuals were present at that time, or in that place. It may just be that the circumstances at one period of time, or at one location, were more favourable for fossilization than they were at other times, or in other places. Likewise, the absence of hominin fossil evidence at a particular time or place does not have the same implication as its presence. As the saying goes, 'absence of evidence is not evidence of absence'. Similar logic suggests that taxa are likely to have arisen before they first appear in the fossil record, and they are likely to have survived beyond the time of their most recent appearance in the fossil record. Thus, the first appearance datum, and the last appearance datum of taxa in the hominin fossil record are likely to be conservative statements about the times of origin and extinction of a taxon.

*subsequent: 다음의 **hominin fossil: 인류 화석
***taxa: taxon(분류군)의 복수형

↓

Since fossilization and fossil discovery are affected by ___(A)___ conditions, the fossil evidence of a taxon cannot definitely ___(B)___ its population size or the times of its appearance and extinction.

(A)		(B)
① experimental	……	confirm
② experimental	……	reveal
③ environmental	……	clarify
④ environmental	……	conceal
⑤ accidental	……	mask

02~03

22학년도 9월 모평 41~42번

다음 글을 읽고, 물음에 답하시오.

In studies examining the effectiveness of vitamin C, researchers typically divide the subjects into two groups. One group (the experimental group) receives a vitamin C supplement, and the other (the control group) does not. Researchers observe both groups to determine whether one group has fewer or shorter colds than the other. The following discussion describes some of the pitfalls inherent in an experiment of this kind and ways to (a) avoid them. In sorting subjects into two groups, researchers must ensure that each person has an (b) equal chance of being assigned to either the experimental group or the control group. This is accomplished by randomization; that is, the subjects are chosen randomly from the same population by flipping a coin or some other method involving chance. Randomization helps to ensure that results reflect the treatment and not factors that might influence the grouping of subjects. Importantly, the two groups of people must be similar and must have the same track record with respect to colds to (c) rule out the possibility that observed differences in the rate, severity, or duration of colds might have occurred anyway. If, for example, the control group would normally catch twice as many colds as the experimental group, then the findings prove (d) nothing. In experiments involving a nutrient, the diets of both groups must also be (e) different, especially with respect to the nutrient being studied. If those in the experimental group were receiving less vitamin C from their usual diet, then any effects of the supplement may not be apparent.

*pitfall: 함정

02

윗글의 제목으로 가장 적절한 것은?

① Perfect Planning and Faulty Results: A Sad Reality in Research
② Don't Let Irrelevant Factors Influence the Results!
③ Protect Human Subjects Involved in Experimental Research!
④ What Nutrients Could Better Defend Against Colds?
⑤ In-depth Analysis of Nutrition: A Key Player for Human Health

03

밑줄 친 (a)~(e) 중에서 문맥상 낱말의 쓰임이 적절하지 않은 것은?

① (a) ② (b) ③ (c) ④ (d) ⑤ (e)

정답 및 해설 p. 277

DAY 072

빈칸 추론
글의 순서
문장 넣기

제한시간 | 5분

01

19학년도 9월 모평 32번

다음 빈칸에 들어갈 말로 가장 적절한 것은? [3점]

Although most people, including Europe's Muslims, have numerous identities, few of these are politically salient at any moment. It is only when a political issue affects the welfare of those in a particular group that ______________________. For instance, when issues arise that touch on women's rights, women start to think of gender as their principal identity. Whether such women are American or Iranian or whether they are Catholic or Protestant matters less than the fact that they are women. Similarly, when famine and civil war threaten people in sub-Saharan Africa, many African-Americans are reminded of their kinship with the continent in which their ancestors originated centuries earlier, and they lobby their leaders to provide humanitarian relief. In other words, each issue calls forth somewhat different identities that help explain the political preferences people have regarding those issues.

*salient: 두드러진

① identity assumes importance
② religion precedes identity
③ society loses stability
④ society supports diversity
⑤ nationality bears significance

02

20학년도 9월 모평 37번

주어진 글 다음에 이어질 글의 순서로 가장 적절한 것은?

> Because a main goal of science is to discover lawful relationships, science assumes that what is being investigated is lawful. For example, the chemist assumes that chemical reactions are lawful, and the physicist assumes that the physical world is lawful.

(A) The determinist, then, assumes that everything that occurs is a function of a finite number of causes and that, if these causes were known, an event could be predicted with complete accuracy. However, knowing *all* causes of an event is not necessary; the determinist simply assumes that they exist and that as more causes are known, predictions become more accurate.

(B) The assumption that what is being studied can be understood in terms of causal laws is called determinism. Richard Taylor defined determinism as the philosophical doctrine that "states that for everything that ever happens there are conditions such that, given them, nothing else could happen."

(C) For example, almost everyone would agree that the weather is a function of a finite number of variables such as sunspots, high-altitude jet streams, and barometric pressure; yet weather forecasts are always probabilistic because many of these variables change constantly, and others are simply unknown.

*altitude: 고도(高度) **barometric: 기압의

① (A) – (C) – (B)
② (B) – (A) – (C)
③ (B) – (C) – (A)
④ (C) – (A) – (B)
⑤ (C) – (B) – (A)

03

20학년도 9월 모평 39번

글의 흐름으로 보아, 주어진 문장이 들어가기에 가장 적절한 곳은? [3점]

> So, there was a social pressure for art to come up with some vocation that both distinguished it from science and, at the same time, made it equal in stature to science.

Representational theories of art treat the work of the artist as similar to that of the scientist. Both, so to speak, are involved in describing the external world. (①) But by the nineteenth century, any comparison between the scientist and the artist was bound to make the artist look like a poor relation in terms of making discoveries about the world or holding a mirror up to nature. (②) Here, science clearly had the edge. (③) The notion that art specialized in the expression of the emotions was particularly attractive in this light. (④) It rendered unto science its own — the exploration of the objective world — while saving something comparably important for art to do — to explore the inner world of feeling. (⑤) If science held the mirror up to nature, art turned a mirror at the self and its experiences.

*vocation: 소명 **stature: 수준 ***render: 주다

정답 및 해설 p. 280

DAY 073

글의 주제
빈칸 추론
글의 순서

제한시간 | 4분

01

20학년도 대수능 23번

다음 글의 주제로 가장 적절한 것은?

Human beings do not enter the world as competent moral agents. Nor does everyone leave the world in that state. But somewhere in between, most people acquire a bit of decency that qualifies them for membership in the community of moral agents. Genes, development, and learning all contribute to the process of becoming a decent human being. The interaction between nature and nurture is, however, highly complex, and developmental biologists are only just beginning to grasp just how complex it is. Without the context provided by cells, organisms, social groups, and culture, DNA is inert. Anyone who says that people are "genetically programmed" to be moral has an oversimplified view of how genes work. Genes and environment interact in ways that make it nonsensical to think that the process of moral development in children, or any other developmental process, can be discussed in terms of nature *versus* nurture. Developmental biologists now know that it is really both, or nature *through* nurture. A complete scientific explanation of moral evolution and development in the human species is a very long way off.

*decency: 예의 **inert: 비활성의

① evolution of human morality from a cultural perspective
② difficulties in studying the evolutionary process of genes
③ increasing necessity of educating children as moral agents
④ nature versus nurture controversies in developmental biology
⑤ complicated gene-environment interplay in moral development

02

19학년도 9월 모평 31번

다음 빈칸에 들어갈 말로 가장 적절한 것은?

Among the most fascinating natural temperature-regulating behaviors are those of social insects such as bees and ants. These insects are able to maintain a nearly constant temperature in their hives or mounds throughout the year. The constancy of these microclimates depends not just on the location and insulation of the habitat, but on ______________________________. When the surrounding temperature increases, the activity in the hive decreases, which decreases the amount of heat generated by insect metabolism. In fact, many animals decrease their activity in the heat and increase it in the cold, and people who are allowed to choose levels of physical activity in hot or cold environments adjust their workload precisely to body temperature. This behavior serves to avoid both hypothermia and hyperthermia.

*insulation: 단열 **hypothermia: 저체온(증) ***hyperthermia: 고체온(증)

① the activity of the insects in the colony
② the interaction with other species
③ the change in colony population
④ the building materials of the habitat
⑤ the physical development of the inhabitants

03

20학년도 9월 모평 36번

주어진 글 다음에 이어질 글의 순서로 가장 적절한 것은? [3점]

A sovereign state is usually defined as one whose citizens are free to determine their own affairs without interference from any agency beyond its territorial borders.

(A) No citizen could be a full member of the community so long as she was tied to ancestral traditions with which the community might wish to break — the problem of Antigone in Sophocles' tragedy. Sovereignty and citizenship thus require not only borders in space, but also borders in time.

(B) Sovereignty and citizenship require freedom from the past at least as much as freedom from contemporary powers. No state could be sovereign if its inhabitants lacked the ability to change a course of action adopted by their forefathers in the past, or even one to which they once committed themselves.

(C) But freedom in space (and limits on its territorial extent) is merely one characteristic of sovereignty. Freedom in time (and limits on its temporal extent) is equally important and probably more fundamental.

*sovereign: 주권의 **territorial: 영토의

① (A) — (C) — (B)
② (B) — (A) — (C)
③ (B) — (C) — (A)
④ (C) — (A) — (B)
⑤ (C) — (B) — (A)

정답 및 해설 p. 284

DAY 074

글의 제목
빈칸 추론
문장 넣기

제한시간 | 4분

01

20학년도 대수능 24번

다음 글의 제목으로 가장 적절한 것은?

Invasions of natural communities by non-indigenous species are currently rated as one of the most important global-scale environmental problems. The loss of biodiversity has generated concern over the consequences for ecosystem functioning and thus understanding the relationship between both has become a major focus in ecological research during the last two decades. The "biodiversity-invasibility hypothesis" by Elton suggests that high diversity increases the competitive environment of communities and makes them more difficult to invade. Numerous biodiversity experiments have been conducted since Elton's time and several mechanisms have been proposed to explain the often observed negative relationship between diversity and invasibility. Beside the decreased chance of empty ecological niches but the increased probability of competitors that prevent invasion success, diverse communities are assumed to use resources more completely and, therefore, limit the ability of invaders to establish. Further, more diverse communities are believed to be more stable because they use a broader range of niches than species-poor communities.

*indigenous: 토착의 **niche: 생태적 지위

① Carve Out More Empty Ecological Spaces!
② Guardian of Ecology: Diversity Resists Invasion
③ Grasp All, Lose All: Necessity of Species-poor Ecology
④ Challenges in Testing Biodiversity-Invasibility Hypothesis
⑤ Diversity Dilemma: The More Competitive, the Less Secure

02

19학년도 6월 모평 33번

다음 빈칸에 들어갈 말로 가장 적절한 것은? [3점]

Theorists of the novel commonly define the genre as a biographical form that came to prominence in the late eighteenth and nineteenth centuries ________________ as a replacement for traditional sources of cultural authority. The novel, Georg Lukács argues, "seeks, by giving form, to uncover and construct the concealed totality of life" in the interiorized life story of its heroes. The typical plot of the novel is the protagonist's quest for authority within, therefore, when that authority can no longer be discovered outside. By this accounting, there are no objective goals in novels, only the subjective goal of seeking the law that is necessarily created by the individual. The distinctions between crime and heroism, therefore, or between madness and wisdom, become purely subjective ones in a novel, judged by the quality or complexity of the individual's consciousness.

① to establish the individual character
② to cast doubt on the identity of a criminal
③ to highlight the complex structure of social consciousness
④ to make the objective distinction between crime and heroism
⑤ to develop the inner self of a hero into a collective wisdom

03

20학년도 9월 모평 38번

글의 흐름으로 보아, 주어진 문장이 들어가기에 가장 적절한 곳은?

> The field of international politics is, however, dominated by states and other powerful actors (such as multinational corporations) that have priorities other than human rights.

There is obviously a wide gap between the promises of the Universal Declaration of Human Rights in 1948 and the real world of human-rights violations. In so far as we sympathize with the victims, we may criticize the UN and its member governments for failing to keep their promises. (①) However, we cannot understand the gap between human-rights ideals and the real world of human-rights violations by sympathy or by legal analysis. (②) Rather, it requires investigation by the various social sciences of the causes of social conflict and political oppression, and of the interaction between national and international politics. (③) The UN introduced the concept of human rights into international law and politics. (④) It is a leading feature of the human-rights field that the governments of the world proclaim human rights but have a highly variable record of implementing them. (⑤) We must understand why this is so.

*oppression: 억압

정답 및 해설 p. 288

DAY 075

함의 추론
빈칸 추론
무관 문장

제한시간 | 4분

01

20학년도 9월 모평 21번

밑줄 친 a cage model이 다음 글에서 의미하는 바로 가장 적절한 것은? [3점]

For a long time, tourism was seen as a huge monster invading the areas of indigenous peoples, introducing them to the evils of the modern world. However, research has shown that this is not the correct way to perceive it. In most places, tourists are welcome and indigenous people see tourism as a path to modernity and economic development. But such development is always a two-edged sword. Tourism can mean progress, but most often also means the loss of traditions and cultural uniqueness. And, of course, there are examples of 'cultural pollution', 'vulgarization' and 'phony-folk-cultures'. The background for such characteristics is often more or less romantic and the normative ideas of a former or prevailing authenticity. Ideally (to some) there should exist ancient cultures for modern consumers to gaze at, or even step into for a while, while travelling or on holiday. This is a cage model that is difficult to defend in a global world where we all, indigenous or not, are part of the same social fabric.

*indigenous: 토착의 **vulgarization: 상스럽게 함

① preserving a past culture in its original form for consumption
② restoring local cultural heritages that have long been neglected
③ limiting public access to prehistoric sites for conservation
④ confining tourism research to authentic cultural traditions
⑤ maintaining a budget for cultural policies and regulations

02

19학년도 6월 모평 32번

다음 빈칸에 들어갈 말로 가장 적절한 것은? [3점]

An individual characteristic that moderates the relationship with behavior is self-efficacy, or a judgment of one's capability to accomplish a certain level of performance. People who have a high sense of self-efficacy tend to pursue challenging goals that may be outside the reach of the average person. People with a strong sense of self-efficacy, therefore, may be more willing to step outside the culturally prescribed behaviors to attempt tasks or goals for which success is viewed as improbable by the majority of social actors in a setting. For these individuals, ______________________________. For example, Australians tend to endorse the "Tall Poppy Syndrome." This saying suggests that any "poppy" that outgrows the others in a field will get "cut down;" in other words, any overachiever will eventually fail. Interviews and observations suggest that it is the high self-efficacy Australians who step outside this culturally prescribed behavior to actually achieve beyond average.

*self-efficacy: 자기 효능감 **endorse: 지지하다

① self-efficacy is not easy to define
② culture will have little or no impact on behavior
③ setting a goal is important before starting a task
④ high self-efficacy is a typical quality of Australians
⑤ judging the reaction from the community will be hard

03

20학년도 대수능 35번

다음 글에서 전체 흐름과 관계 없는 문장은?

Although commonsense knowledge may have merit, it also has weaknesses, not the least of which is that it often contradicts itself. For example, we hear that people who are similar will like one another ("Birds of a feather flock together") but also that persons who are dissimilar will like each other ("Opposites attract"). ① We are told that groups are wiser and smarter than individuals ("Two heads are better than one") but also that group work inevitably produces poor results ("Too many cooks spoil the broth"). ② Each of these contradictory statements may hold true under particular conditions, but without a clear statement of when they apply and when they do not, aphorisms provide little insight into relations among people. ③ That is why we heavily depend on aphorisms whenever we face difficulties and challenges in the long journey of our lives. ④ They provide even less guidance in situations where we must make decisions. ⑤ For example, when facing a choice that entails risk, which guideline should we use — "Nothing ventured, nothing gained" or "Better safe than sorry"?

*aphorism: 격언, 경구(警句) **entail: 수반하다

정답 및 해설 p. 292

DAY 076

밑줄 어법
빈칸 추론
글의 순서

제한시간 | 4분

01

22학년도 9월 모평 29번

다음 글의 밑줄 친 부분 중, 어법상 틀린 것은?

Accepting whatever others are communicating only pays off if their interests correspond to ours — think cells in a body, bees in a beehive. As far as communication between humans is concerned, such commonality of interests ① is rarely achieved; even a pregnant mother has reasons to mistrust the chemical signals sent by her fetus. Fortunately, there are ways of making communication work even in the most adversarial of relationships. A prey can convince a predator not to chase ② it. But for such communication to occur, there must be strong guarantees ③ which those who receive the signal will be better off believing it. The messages have to be kept, on the whole, ④ honest. In the case of humans, honesty is maintained by a set of cognitive mechanisms that evaluate ⑤ communicated information. These mechanisms allow us to accept most beneficial messages — to be open — while rejecting most harmful messages — to be vigilant.

*fetus: 태아 **adversarial: 반대자의 ***vigilant: 경계하는

02

19학년도 6월 모평 31번

다음 빈칸에 들어갈 말로 가장 적절한 것은? [3점]

Although prices in most retail outlets are set by the retailer, this does not mean that these prices ______________________. On any particular day we find that all products have a specific price ticket on them. However, this price may be different from day to day or week to week. The price that the farmer gets from the wholesaler is much more flexible from day to day than the price that the retailer charges consumers. If, for example, bad weather leads to a poor potato crop, then the price that supermarkets have to pay to their wholesalers for potatoes will go up and this will be reflected in the prices they mark on potatoes in their stores. Thus, these prices do reflect the interaction of demand and supply in the wider marketplace for potatoes. Although they do not change in the supermarket from hour to hour to reflect local variations in demand and supply, they do change over time to reflect the underlying conditions of the overall production of and demand for the goods in question.

① reflect the principle of demand and supply
② may not change from hour to hour
③ go up due to bad weather
④ do not adjust to market forces over time
⑤ can be changed by the farmer's active role

03

20학년도 6월 모평 37번

주어진 글 다음에 이어질 글의 순서로 가장 적절한 것은? [3점]

Marshall McLuhan, among others, noted that clothes are people's extended skin, wheels extended feet, camera and telescopes extended eyes. Our technological creations are great extrapolations of the bodies that our genes build.

(A) The blueprints for our shells spring from our minds, which may spontaneously create something none of our ancestors ever made or even imagined. If technology is an extension of humans, it is not an extension of our genes but of our minds. Technology is therefore the extended body for ideas.

(B) In this way, we can think of technology as our extended body. During the industrial age it was easy to see the world this way. Steam-powered shovels, locomotives, television, and the levers and gears of engineers were a fabulous exoskeleton that turned man into superman.

(C) A closer look reveals the flaw in this analogy: The extended costume of animals is the result of their genes. They inherit the basic blueprints of what they make. Humans don't.

*extrapolation: 연장(延長) **exoskeleton: 외골격 ***flaw: 결함

① (A) – (C) – (B)
② (B) – (A) – (C)
③ (B) – (C) – (A)
④ (C) – (A) – (B)
⑤ (C) – (B) – (A)

정답 및 해설 p. 296

DAY 077

낱말 쓰임
빈칸 추론
문장 넣기

제한시간 | 4분

01

22학년도 9월 모평 30번

다음 글의 밑줄 친 부분 중, 문맥상 낱말의 쓰임이 적절하지 않은 것은? [3점]

In economic systems what takes place in one sector has impacts on another; demand for a good or service in one sector is derived from another. For instance, a consumer buying a good in a store will likely trigger the replacement of this product, which will generate ① demands for activities such as manufacturing, resource extraction and, of course, transport. What is different about transport is that it cannot exist alone and a movement cannot be ② stored. An unsold product can remain on the shelf of a store until bought (often with discount incentives), but an unsold seat on a flight or unused cargo capacity in the same flight remains unsold and cannot be brought back as additional capacity ③ later. In this case an opportunity has been ④ seized, since the amount of transport being offered has exceeded the demand for it. The derived demand of transportation is often very difficult to reconcile with an equivalent supply, and actually transport companies would prefer to have some additional capacity to accommodate ⑤ unforeseen demand (often at much higher prices).

*reconcile: 조화시키다

02

18학년도 대수능 34번

다음 빈칸에 들어갈 말로 가장 적절한 것은? [3점]

Over the past 60 years, as mechanical processes have replicated behaviors and talents we thought were unique to humans, we've had to change our minds about what sets us apart. As we invent more species of AI, we will be forced to surrender more of what is supposedly unique about humans. Each step of surrender — we are not the only mind that can play chess, fly a plane, make music, or invent a mathematical law — will be painful and sad. We'll spend the next three decades — indeed, perhaps the next century — in a permanent identity crisis, continually asking ourselves what humans are good for. If we aren't unique toolmakers, or artists, or moral ethicists, then what, if anything, makes us special? In the grandest irony of all, the greatest benefit of an everyday, utilitarian AI will not be increased productivity or an economics of abundance or a new way of doing science — although all those will happen. The greatest benefit of the arrival of artificial intelligence is that ______________________.

*replicate: 복제하다

① AIs will help define humanity
② humans could also be like AIs
③ humans will be liberated from hard labor
④ AIs could lead us in resolving moral dilemmas
⑤ AIs could compensate for a decline in human intelligence

03

20학년도 6월 모평 39번

글의 흐름으로 보아, 주어진 문장이 들어가기에 가장 적절한 곳은? [3점]

> That puts you each near a focus, a special point at which the sound of your voice gets focused as it reflects off the passageway's curved walls and ceiling.

Whispering galleries are remarkable acoustic spaces found beneath certain domes or curved ceilings. A famous one is located outside a well-known restaurant in New York City's Grand Central Station. (①) It's a fun place to take a date: the two of you can exchange romantic words while you're forty feet apart and separated by a busy passageway. (②) You'll hear each other clearly, but the passersby won't hear a word you're saying. (③) To produce this effect, the two of you should stand at diagonally opposite corners of the space, facing the wall. (④) Ordinarily, the sound waves you produce travel in all directions and bounce off the walls at different times and places, scrambling them so much that they are inaudible when they arrive at the ear of a listener forty feet away. (⑤) But when you whisper at a *focus*, the reflected waves all arrive at the *same* time at the other focus, thus reinforcing one another and allowing your words to be heard.

*acoustic: 음향의 **diagonally: 대각선으로

정답 및 해설 p. 300

DAY

078

요약문
복합 유형

◷ 제한시간 | 4분

01

20학년도 대수능 40번

다음 글의 내용을 한 문장으로 요약하고자 한다. 빈칸 (A), (B)에 들어갈 말로 가장 적절한 것은?

Because elephant groups break up and reunite very frequently — for instance, in response to variation in food availability — reunions are more important in elephant society than among primates. And the species has evolved elaborate greeting behaviors, the form of which reflects the strength of the social bond between the individuals (much like how you might merely shake hands with a long-standing acquaintance but hug a close friend you have not seen in a while, and maybe even tear up). Elephants may greet each other simply by reaching their trunks into each other's mouths, possibly equivalent to a human peck on the cheek. However, after long absences, members of family and bond groups greet one another with incredibly theatrical displays. The fact that the intensity reflects the duration of the separation as well as the level of intimacy suggests that elephants have a sense of time as well. To human eyes, these greetings strike a familiar chord. I'm reminded of the joyous reunions so visible in the arrivals area of an international airport terminal.

*acquaintance: 지인 **peck: 가벼운 입맞춤

↓

> The evolved greeting behaviors of elephants can serve as an indicator of how much they are socially ___(A)___ and how long they have been ___(B)___.

(A)		(B)
① competitive	······	disconnected
② tied	······	endangered
③ responsible	······	isolated
④ competitive	······	united
⑤ tied	······	parted

02~03

22학년도 6월 모평 41~42번

다음 글을 읽고, 물음에 답하시오.

The right to privacy may extend only to the point where it does not restrict someone else's right to freedom of expression or right to information. The scope of the right to privacy is (a) <u>similarly</u> restricted by the general interest in preventing crime or in promoting public health. However, when we move away from the property-based notion of a right (where the right to privacy would protect, for example, images and personality), to modern notions of private and family life, we find it (b) <u>easier</u> to establish the limits of the right. This is, of course, the strength of the notion of privacy, in that it can adapt to meet changing expectations and technological advances.

In sum, *what* is privacy today? The concept includes a claim that we should be unobserved, and that certain information and images about us should not be (c) <u>circulated</u> without our permission. *Why* did these privacy claims arise? They arose because powerful people took offence at such observation. Furthermore, privacy incorporated the need to protect the family, home, and correspondence from arbitrary (d) <u>interference</u> and, in addition, there has been a determination to protect honour and reputation. *How* is privacy protected? Historically, privacy was protected by restricting circulation of the damaging material. But if the concept of privacy first became interesting legally as a response to reproductions of images through photography and newspapers, more recent technological advances, such as data storage, digital images, and the Internet, (e) <u>pose</u> new threats to privacy. The right to privacy is now being reinterpreted to meet those challenges.

*arbitrary: 임의의

02

윗글의 제목으로 가장 적절한 것은?

① Side Effects of Privacy Protection Technologies
② The Legal Domain of Privacy Claims and Conflicts
③ The Right to Privacy: Evolving Concepts and Practices
④ Who Really Benefits from Looser Privacy Regulations?
⑤ Less Is More: Reduce State Intervention in Privacy!

03

밑줄 친 (a)~(e) 중에서 문맥상 낱말의 쓰임이 적절하지 <u>않은</u> 것은? [3점]

① (a) ② (b) ③ (c) ④ (d) ⑤ (e)

정답 및 해설 p. 304

DAY 079

빈칸 추론
글의 순서
문장 넣기

제한시간 | 5분

01

18학년도 대수능 33번

다음 빈칸에 들어갈 말로 가장 적절한 것은? [3점]

In the less developed world, the percentage of the population involved in agriculture is declining, but at the same time, those remaining in agriculture are not benefiting from technological advances. The typical scenario in the less developed world is one in which a very few commercial agriculturalists are technologically advanced while the vast majority are incapable of competing. Indeed, this vast majority ______________________ because of larger global causes. As an example, in Kenya, farmers are actively encouraged to grow export crops such as tea and coffee at the expense of basic food production. The result is that a staple crop, such as maize, is not being produced in a sufficient amount. The essential argument here is that the capitalist mode of production is affecting peasant production in the less developed world in such a way as to limit the production of staple foods, thus causing a food problem.

*staple: 주요한 **maize: 옥수수 ***peasant: 소농(小農)

① have lost control over their own production
② have turned to technology for food production
③ have challenged the capitalist mode of production
④ have reduced their involvement in growing cash crops
⑤ have regained their competitiveness in the world market

02

20학년도 6월 모평 36번

주어진 글 다음에 이어질 글의 순서로 가장 적절한 것은?

> Notation was more than a practical method for preserving an expanding repertoire of music.

(A) Written notes freeze the music rather than allowing it to develop in the hands of individuals, and it discourages improvisation. Partly because of notation, modern classical performance lacks the depth of nuance that is part of aural tradition. Before notation arrived, in all history music was largely carried on as an aural tradition.

(B) It changed the nature of the art itself. To write something down means that people far away in space and time can re-create it. At the same time, there are downsides.

(C) Most world music is still basically aural, including sophisticated musical traditions such as Indian and Balinese. Most jazz musicians can read music but often don't bother, and their art is much involved with improvisation. Many modern pop musicians, one example being Paul McCartney, can't read music at all.

*improvisation: 즉흥 연주 **aural: 청각의

① (A) – (C) – (B)
② (B) – (A) – (C)
③ (B) – (C) – (A)
④ (C) – (A) – (B)
⑤ (C) – (B) – (A)

03

20학년도 6월 모평 38번

글의 흐름으로 보아, 주어진 문장이 들어가기에 가장 적절한 곳은?

> Rather, happiness is often found in those moments we are most vulnerable, alone or in pain.

We seek out feel-good experiences, always on the lookout for the next holiday, purchase or culinary experience. This approach to happiness is relatively recent; it depends on our capacity both to pad our lives with material pleasures and to feel that we can control our suffering. (①) Painkillers, as we know them today, are a relatively recent invention and access to material comfort is now within reach of a much larger proportion of the world's population. (②) These technological and economic advances have had significant cultural implications, leading us to see our negative experiences as a problem and maximizing our positive experiences as the answer. (③) Yet, through this we have forgotten that being happy in life is not just about pleasure. (④) Comfort, contentment and satisfaction have never been the elixir of happiness. (⑤) Happiness is there, on the edges of these experiences, and when we get a glimpse of *that* kind of happiness it is powerful, transcendent and compelling.

*culinary: 요리의 **elixir: 특효약 ***transcendent: 뛰어난

정답 및 해설 p. 307

DAY 080

글의 주제
빈칸 추론
글의 순서

제한시간 | 4분

01

20학년도 9월 모평 23번

다음 글의 주제로 가장 적절한 것은?

Libraries are becoming increasingly interested in the services they are providing for their users. This is an important focus — especially as more and more information becomes available electronically. However, the traditional strengths of libraries have always been their collections. This is true still today — especially in research libraries. Also, collection makeup is the hardest thing to change quickly. For example, if a library has a long tradition of heavily collecting materials published in Mexico, then even if that library stops purchasing all Mexican imprints, its Mexican collection will still be large and impressive for several years to come unless they start withdrawing books. Likewise, if a library has not collected much in a subject, and then decides to start collecting heavily in that area it will take several years for the collection to be large enough and rich enough to be considered an important research tool.

① lasting significance of library collections even in the digital age
② changing roles of local libraries and their effects on society
③ growing needs for analyzing a large volume of library data
④ online services as a key to the success of research libraries
⑤ rare book collectors' contributions to a library's reputation

02

18학년도 대수능 32번

다음 빈칸에 들어갈 말로 가장 적절한 것은? [3점]

How many of the lunches that you ate over the last week can you recall? Do you remember what you ate today? I hope so. Yesterday? I bet it takes a moment's effort. And what about the day before yesterday? What about a week ago? It's not so much that your memory of last week's lunch has disappeared; if provided with the right cue, like where you ate it, or whom you ate it with, you would likely recall what had been on your plate. Rather, it's difficult to remember last week's lunch because your brain has filed it away with all the other lunches you've ever eaten as *just another lunch*. When we try to recall something from a category that includes as many instances as "lunch" or "wine," many memories compete for our attention. The memory of last Wednesday's lunch isn't necessarily gone; it's that you lack ________________________________. But a wine that talks: That's unique. It's a memory without rivals.

① the channel to let it flow into the pool of ordinary memories
② the right hook to pull it out of a sea of lunchtime memories
③ the glue to attach it to just another lunch memory
④ the memory capacity to keep a box of sleeping memories
⑤ the sufficient number of competitors in a battle for attention

03

19학년도 대수능 37번

주어진 글 다음에 이어질 글의 순서로 가장 적절한 것은? [3점]

Clearly, schematic knowledge helps you — guiding your understanding and enabling you to reconstruct things you cannot remember.

(A) Likewise, if there are things you can't recall, your schemata will fill in the gaps with knowledge about what's typical in that situation. As a result, a reliance on schemata will inevitably make the world seem more "normal" than it really is and will make the past seem more "regular" than it actually was.

(B) Any reliance on schematic knowledge, therefore, will be shaped by this information about what's "normal." Thus, if there are things you don't notice while viewing a situation or event, your schemata will lead you to fill in these "gaps" with knowledge about what's normally in place in that setting.

(C) But schematic knowledge can also hurt you, promoting errors in perception and memory. Moreover, the *types* of errors produced by schemata are quite predictable: Bear in mind that schemata summarize the broad pattern of your experience, and so they tell you, in essence, what's typical or ordinary in a given situation.

① (A) – (C) – (B)　　② (B) – (A) – (C)
③ (B) – (C) – (A)　　④ (C) – (A) – (B)
⑤ (C) – (B) – (A)

정답 및 해설 p. 311

DAY 081

글의 제목
빈칸 추론
문장 넣기

제한시간 | 4분

01

20학년도 9월 모평 24번

다음 글의 제목으로 가장 적절한 것은?

From the late nineteenth century on, the dullness found in the senile, their isolation and withdrawal, their clinging to the past and lack of interest in worldly affairs were characteristically represented as the *symptoms* of senility — the social shame of the inevitable deterioration of the brain. Following World War II, academic discourse on aging typically represented these as the *causes* of senility. The location of senile mental deterioration was no longer the aging brain but a society that, through involuntary retirement, social isolation, and the loosening of traditional family ties, stripped the elderly of the roles that had sustained meaning in their lives. When elderly people were deprived of these meaningful social roles, when they became increasingly isolated and were cut off from the interests and activities that had earlier occupied them, not surprisingly their mental functioning deteriorated. The elderly did not so much lose their minds as lose their place.

*senile: 노쇠한 **deterioration: 노화

① Aged Mind in Concert with Aged Body: An Unfailing Truth

② No Change from Past to Present: Social Images of Old Age

③ No Country for Old Men: Age Discrimination Intensified

④ What Makes the Elderly Decline: Being Left Out Socially

⑤ Not Disabled But Differently Abled: New Faces of Old Age

02

18학년도 대수능 31번

다음 빈칸에 들어갈 말로 가장 적절한 것은? [3점]

Apocalypse Now, a film produced and directed by Francis Ford Coppola, gained widespread popularity, and for good reason. The film is an adaptation of Joseph Conrad's novel *Heart of Darkness*, which is set in the African Congo at the end of the 19th century. Unlike the original novel, *Apocalypse Now* is set in Vietnam and Cambodia during the Vietnam War. The setting, time period, dialogue and other incidental details are changed but the fundamental narrative and themes of *Apocalypse Now* are the same as those of *Heart of Darkness*. Both describe a physical journey, reflecting the central character's mental and spiritual journey, down a river to confront the deranged Kurtz character, who represents the worst aspects of civilisation. By giving *Apocalypse Now* a setting that was contemporary at the time of its release, audiences were able to experience and identify with its themes more easily than they would have if the film had been ______________________________.

*deranged: 제정신이 아닌

① a literal adaptation of the novel
② a source of inspiration for the novel
③ a faithful depiction of the Vietnam War
④ a vivid dramatisation of a psychological journey
⑤ a critical interpretation of contemporary civilisation

03

19학년도 대수능 39번

글의 흐름으로 보아, 주어진 문장이 들어가기에 가장 적절한 곳은? [3점]

> A round hill rising above a plain, therefore, would appear on the map as a set of concentric circles, the largest at the base and the smallest near the top.

A major challenge for map-makers is the depiction of hills and valleys, slopes and flatlands collectively called the *topography*. This can be done in various ways. One is to create an image of sunlight and shadow so that wrinkles of the topography are alternately lit and shaded, creating a visual representation of the shape of the land. (①) Another, technically more accurate way is to draw contour lines. (②) A contour line connects all points that lie at the same elevation. (③) When the contour lines are positioned closely together, the hill's slope is steep; if they lie farther apart, the slope is gentler. (④) Contour lines can represent scarps, hollows, and valleys of the local topography. (⑤) At a glance, they reveal whether the relief in the mapped area is great or small: a "busy" contour map means lots of high relief.

*concentric: 중심이 같은 **scarp: 가파른 비탈 ***relief: (토지의) 고저, 기복

정답 및 해설 p. 315

DAY 082

함의 추론
빈칸 추론
무관 문장

제한시간 | 4분

01

20학년도 6월 모평 21번

밑줄 친 "Garbage in, garbage out"이 다음 글에서 의미하는 바로 가장 적절한 것은?

Many companies confuse activities and results. As a consequence, they make the mistake of designing a process that sets out milestones in the form of activities that must be carried out during the sales cycle. Salespeople have a genius for doing what's compensated rather than what's effective. If your process has an activity such as "submit proposal" or "make cold call," then that's just what your people will do. No matter that the calls were to the wrong customer or went nowhere. No matter that the proposal wasn't submitted at the right point in the buying decision or contained inappropriate information. The process asked for activity, and activity was what it got. Salespeople have done what was asked for. "Garbage in, garbage out" they will delight in telling you. "It's not our problem, it's this dumb process."

① In seeking results, compensation is the key to quality.
② Salespeople should join in a decision-making process.
③ Shared understanding does not always result in success.
④ Activities drawn from false information produce failure.
⑤ Processes focused on activities end up being ineffective.

02

18학년도 9월 모평 34번

다음 빈칸에 들어갈 말로 가장 적절한 것은? [3점]

The narratives that people create to understand their landscapes come to be viewed as marketable entities and a source of income for residents. Landscapes with a strong place identity have an advantage in marketing to tourists, as it is relatively easy to compartmentalize and market their narratives. Such places may have disadvantages as well, however. If place identity is tied to a particular industry, local residents may feel strongly attached to the definitions of place that stem from involvement in that industry, and they may ______________________ in favor of one based on a tourism industry. People rooted in landscape may feel strong connections to other community members and may resent the invasion of outsiders who they believe are different and challenge their common identity. Finally, local residents may feel that this process reduces their identities to mere commercial transactions, and they may believe they sacrifice what is unique and special about their place.

*entity: 실재 **compartmentalize: 구획하다 ***transaction: 거래

① resist losing that identity
② stop persisting with the old tie
③ tolerate the shift of that industry
④ alienate themselves from that place
⑤ refuse the advantage of that industry

03

20학년도 9월 모평 35번

다음 글에서 전체 흐름과 관계 없는 문장은?

Much of what we do each day is automatic and guided by habit, requiring little conscious awareness, and that's not a bad thing. As Duhigg explains, our habits are necessary mental energy savers. ① We need to relieve our conscious minds so we can solve new problems as they come up. ② Once we've solved the puzzle of how to ballroom dance, for example, we can do it by habit, and so be mentally freed to focus on a conversation while dancing instead. ③ But try to talk when first learning to dance the tango, and it's a disaster — we need our conscious attention to focus on the steps. ④ Tango musicians bring different genres of music together to attract a more diverse audience from varying backgrounds. ⑤ Imagine how little we'd accomplish if we had to focus consciously on every behavior — e.g., on where to place our feet for each step we take.

정답 및 해설 p. 319

DAY 083

밑줄 어법
빈칸 추론
글의 순서

제한시간 | 4분

01

22학년도 6월 모평 29번

다음 글의 밑줄 친 부분 중, 어법상 틀린 것은?

Most historians of science point to the need for a reliable calendar to regulate agricultural activity as the motivation for learning about what we now call astronomy, the study of stars and planets. Early astronomy provided information about when to plant crops and gave humans ① their first formal method of recording the passage of time. Stonehenge, the 4,000-year-old ring of stones in southern Britain, ② is perhaps the best-known monument to the discovery of regularity and predictability in the world we inhabit. The great markers of Stonehenge point to the spots on the horizon ③ where the sun rises at the solstices and equinoxes — the dates we still use to mark the beginnings of the seasons. The stones may even have ④ been used to predict eclipses. The existence of Stonehenge, built by people without writing, bears silent testimony both to the regularity of nature and to the ability of the human mind to see behind immediate appearances and ⑤ discovers deeper meanings in events.

*monument: 기념비 **eclipse: (해·달의) 식(蝕) ***testimony: 증언

02

18학년도 9월 모평 33번

다음 빈칸에 들어갈 말로 가장 적절한 것은? [3점]

Externalization is the foundation from which many narrative conversations are built. This requires a particular shift in the use of language. Often externalizing conversations involve tracing the influence of the problem in a child's life over time and how the problem has disempowered the child by limiting his ability to see things in a different light. The counsellor helps the child to change by deconstructing old stories and reconstructing preferred stories about himself and his life. To help the child to develop a new story, the counsellor and child search for times when the problem has not influenced the child or the child's life and focus on the different ways the child thought, felt and behaved. These ________________________ help the child create a new and preferred story. As a new and preferred story begins to emerge, it is important to assist the child to hold on to, or stay connected to, the new story.

① exceptions to the problem story
② distances from the alternative story
③ problems that originate from the counsellor
④ efforts to combine old and new experiences
⑤ methods of linking the child's stories to another's

03

19학년도 대수능 36번

주어진 글 다음에 이어질 글의 순서로 가장 적절한 것은?

> Researchers in psychology follow the scientific method to perform studies that help explain and may predict human behavior. This is a much more challenging task than studying snails or sound waves.

(A) But for all of these difficulties for psychology, the payoff of the scientific method is that the findings are replicable; that is, if you run the same study again following the same procedures, you will be very likely to get the same results.

(B) It often requires compromises, such as testing behavior within laboratories rather than natural settings, and asking those readily available (such as introduction to psychology students) to participate rather than collecting data from a true cross-section of the population. It often requires great cleverness to conceive of measures that tap into what people are thinking without altering their thinking, called reactivity.

(C) Simply knowing they are being observed may cause people to behave differently (such as more politely!). People may give answers that they feel are more socially desirable than their true feelings.

*replicable: 반복 가능한

① (A) – (C) – (B)
② (B) – (A) – (C)
③ (B) – (C) – (A)
④ (C) – (A) – (B)
⑤ (C) – (B) – (A)

정답 및 해설 p. 323

DAY

084

낱말 쓰임
빈칸 추론
문장 넣기

제한시간 | 4분

01

22학년도 6월 모평 30번

다음 글의 밑줄 친 부분 중, 문맥상 낱말의 쓰임이 적절하지 않은 것은?

Sport can trigger an emotional response in its consumers of the kind rarely brought forth by other products. Imagine bank customers buying memorabilia to show loyalty to their bank, or consumers ① identifying so strongly with their car insurance company that they get a tattoo with its logo. We know that some sport followers are so ② passionate about players, teams and the sport itself that their interest borders on obsession. This addiction provides the emotional glue that binds fans to teams, and maintains loyalty even in the face of on-field ③ failure. While most managers can only dream of having customers that are as passionate about their products as sport fans, the emotion triggered by sport can also have a negative impact. Sport's emotional intensity can mean that organisations have strong attachments to the past through nostalgia and club tradition. As a result, they may ④ increase efficiency, productivity and the need to respond quickly to changing market conditions. For example, a proposal to change club colours in order to project a more attractive image may be ⑤ defeated because it breaks a link with tradition.

*memorabilia: 기념품 **obsession: 집착

02

18학년도 9월 모평 32번

다음 빈칸에 들어갈 말로 가장 적절한 것은? [3점]

Let me spend a moment on the idea of adjusting to another person's mental orientation. What I mean is this. At any moment, a person has a ______________________________. The person notices this rather than that, and she has feelings and makes judgements about one rather than another aspect of events. If she is hungry, for example, she may notice that a shop is selling groceries; her friend may notice only that it sells newspapers. If she is short of money, she may resent that the fruit is overpriced; meanwhile her friend may feel tempted by some juicy peaches. In one sense the two friends are experiencing the same shop and its contents, but they are having quite different experiences of that shop. A more extreme case arises when one person comprehends things in a peculiar and individual way, for instance, in mistaking the shop for a cinema.

① desire to make better choices
② point of view similar to that of others
③ personal preference on where to shop
④ particular take on what is happening
⑤ tendency to stick to traditions

03

19학년도 대수능 38번

글의 흐름으로 보아, 주어진 문장이 들어가기에 가장 적절한 곳은?

> The advent of literacy and the creation of handwritten scrolls and, eventually, handwritten books strengthened the ability of large and complex ideas to spread with high fidelity.

The printing press boosted the power of ideas to copy themselves. Prior to low-cost printing, ideas could and did spread by word of mouth. While this was tremendously powerful, it limited the complexity of the ideas that could be propagated to those that a single person could remember. (①) It also added a certain amount of guaranteed error. (②) The spread of ideas by word of mouth was equivalent to a game of telephone on a global scale. (③) But the incredible amount of time required to copy a scroll or book by hand limited the speed with which information could spread this way. (④) A well-trained monk could transcribe around four pages of text per day. (⑤) A printing press could copy information thousands of times faster, allowing knowledge to spread far more quickly, with full fidelity, than ever before.

*fidelity: 충실 **propagate: 전파하다

정답 및 해설 p. 327

DAY 085

요약문 복합 유형

⏲ 제한시간 | 4분

01

20학년도 9월 모평 40번

다음 글의 내용을 한 문장으로 요약하고자 한다. 빈칸 (A), (B)에 들어갈 말로 가장 적절한 것은?

Over the past few decades, architecture as an idea and practice has increasingly limited its definition of itself. In the foreseeable future, the instrumentality of architecture in effecting actual change — that is, change that challenges the dominance of commercial institutions, their aims, and values — will diminish. While the present day seems to be a time of unparalleled innovation and freedom of choice, the reality is that architectural styles and forms are often the attractive packaging and repackaging of the same proven, marketable concepts. The speed with which "radical" designs by celebrity architects achieve acceptance and popularity demonstrates that formal innovation has itself become an important commodity. However, beneath the cloak of radicalism, the conventions of existing building typologies and programs, with all their comforting familiarity, still rule — and sell. What is needed desperately today are approaches to architecture that can free its potential to transform our ways of thinking and acting.

*cloak: 망토 **typology: 유형학

↓

Seemingly innovative, architecture has actually become ____(A)____ in its own convention and commercialized environment, so efforts should be made to ____(B)____ its power to change us.

	(A)		(B)
①	fixed	……	share
②	trapped	……	activate
③	standardized	……	control
④	localized	……	share
⑤	underestimated	……	activate

02~03

21학년도 대수능 41~42번

다음 글을 읽고, 물음에 답하시오.

Our irresistible tendency to see things in human terms — that we are often mistaken in attributing complex human motives and processing abilities to other species — does not mean that an animal's behavior is not, in fact, complex. Rather, it means that the complexity of the animal's behavior is not purely a (a) <u>product</u> of its internal complexity. Herbert Simon's "parable of the ant" makes this point very clearly. Imagine an ant walking along a beach, and (b) <u>visualize</u> tracking the trajectory of the ant as it moves. The trajectory would show a lot of twists and turns, and would be very irregular and complicated. One could then suppose that the ant had equally complicated (c) <u>internal</u> navigational abilities, and work out what these were likely to be by analyzing the trajectory to infer the rules and mechanisms that could produce such a complex navigational path. The complexity of the trajectory, however, "is really a complexity in the surface of the beach, not a complexity in the ant." In reality, the ant may be using a set of very (d) <u>complex</u> rules: it is the interaction of these rules with the environment that actually produces the complex trajectory, not the ant alone. Put more generally, the parable of the ant illustrates that there is no necessary correlation between the complexity of an (e) <u>observed</u> behavior and the complexity of the mechanism that produces it.

*parable: 우화 **trajectory: 이동 경로

02

윗글의 제목으로 가장 적절한 것은?

① Open the Mysterious Door to Environmental Complexity!
② Peaceful Coexistence of Human Beings and Animals
③ What Makes the Complexity of Animal Behavior?
④ Animals' Dilemma: Finding Their Way in a Human World
⑤ Environmental Influences on Human Behavior Complexity

03

밑줄 친 (a)~(e) 중에서 문맥상 낱말의 쓰임이 적절하지 <u>않은</u> 것은? [3점]

① (a) ② (b) ③ (c) ④ (d) ⑤ (e)

정답 및 해설 p. 331

DAY 086

빈칸 추론
글의 순서
문장 넣기

제한시간 | 5분

01

18학년도 9월 모평 31번

다음 빈칸에 들어갈 말로 가장 적절한 것은?

One unspoken truth about creativity — it isn't about wild talent so much as it is about ______________. To find a few ideas that work, you need to try a lot that don't. It's a pure numbers game. Geniuses don't necessarily have a higher success rate than other creators; they simply do more — and they do a range of different things. They have more successes *and* more failures. That goes for teams and companies too. It's impossible to generate a lot of good ideas without also generating a lot of bad ideas. The thing about creativity is that at the outset, you can't tell which ideas will succeed and which will fail. So the only thing you can do is try to fail faster so that you can move onto the next idea.

*at the outset: 처음에

① sensitivity
② superiority
③ imagination
④ productivity
⑤ achievement

02

19학년도 9월 모평 37번

주어진 글 다음에 이어질 글의 순서로 가장 적절한 것은?

> Ever since the first scientific opinion polls revealed that most Americans are at best poorly informed about politics, analysts have asked whether citizens are equipped to play the role democracy assigns them.

(A) Such factors, however, can explain only the misinformation that has always been with us. The sharp rise in misinformation in recent years has a different source: our media. "They are making us dumb," says one observer. When fact bends to fiction, the predictable result is political distrust and polarization.

(B) It's the difference between ignorance and irrationality. Whatever else one might conclude about self-government, it's at risk when citizens don't know what they're talking about. Our misinformation owes partly to psychological factors, including our tendency to see the world in ways that suit our desires.

(C) However, there is something worse than an inadequately informed public, and that's a misinformed public. It's one thing when citizens don't know something, and realize it, which has always been a problem. It's another thing when citizens don't know something, but think they know it, which is the new problem.

*poll: 여론 조사

① (A) – (C) – (B)
② (B) – (A) – (C)
③ (B) – (C) – (A)
④ (C) – (A) – (B)
⑤ (C) – (B) – (A)

03

19학년도 9월 모평 39번

글의 흐름으로 보아, 주어진 문장이 들어가기에 가장 적절한 곳은? [3점]

> We become entrusted to teach culturally appropriate behaviors, values, attitudes, skills, and information about the world.

Erikson believes that when we reach the adult years, several physical, social, and psychological stimuli trigger a sense of *generativity*. A central component of this attitude is the desire to care for others. (①) For the majority of people, parenthood is perhaps the most obvious and convenient opportunity to fulfill this desire. (②) Erikson believes that another distinguishing feature of adulthood is the emergence of an inborn desire to teach. (③) We become aware of this desire when the event of being physically capable of reproducing is joined with the events of participating in a committed relationship, the establishment of an adult pattern of living, and the assumption of job responsibilities. (④) According to Erikson, by becoming parents we learn that we have the need to be needed by others who depend on our knowledge, protection, and guidance. (⑤) By assuming the responsibilities of being primary caregivers to children through their long years of physical and social growth, we concretely express what Erikson believes to be an inborn desire to teach.

정답 및 해설 p. 334

DAY 087

글의 주제
빈칸 추론
글의 순서

제한시간 | 4분

01

20학년도 6월 모평 23번

다음 글의 주제로 가장 적절한 것은?

In the twelfth to thirteenth centuries there appeared the first manuals teaching "table manners" to the offspring of aristocrats. It was a genre that subsequently had a great success in the early modern period with *The Courtier* by Baldassare Castiglione, *The Galateo* by Monsignor Della Casa, and many others produced in different European countries. In a variety of ways and meanings, these are all instruments intended to define or distinguish who is *in* from who is *out*, separating the participants from the ostracized. It is for this reason that manuals of "good manners" addressed to the aristocracy always have a negative reference to the peasant who behaves badly, who "doesn't know" what the rules are, and for this reason is excluded from the lordly table. Food etiquette had become a sign of social barriers and of the impossibility of breaking them down.

*aristocrat: 귀족 **ostracize: 추방하다

① table manners as a marker for class distinction
② publications to bring about equality between classes
③ unintended effects of distinguishing insiders from outsiders
④ attempts to elaborate food etiquette for educational purposes
⑤ roles of manners in uniting people from different backgrounds

02

18학년도 6월 모평 34번

다음 빈칸에 들어갈 말로 가장 적절한 것은? [3점]

Since life began in the oceans, most life, including freshwater life, has a chemical composition more like the ocean than fresh water. It appears that most freshwater life did not originate in fresh water, but is secondarily adapted, having passed from ocean to land and then back again to fresh water. As improbable as this may seem, the bodily fluids of aquatic animals show a strong similarity to oceans, and indeed, most studies of ion balance in freshwater physiology document the complex regulatory mechanisms by which fish, amphibians and invertebrates attempt to ______________________________. It is these sorts of unexpected complexities and apparent contradictions that make ecology so interesting. The idea of a fish in a freshwater lake struggling to accumulate salts inside its body to mimic the ocean reminds one of the other great contradiction of the biosphere: plants are bathed in an atmosphere composed of roughly three-quarters nitrogen, yet their growth is frequently restricted by lack of nitrogen.

*amphibian: 양서류 **invertebrate: 무척추동물

① maintain an inner ocean in spite of surrounding fresh water
② attain ion balance by removing salts from inside their body
③ return to the ocean to escape from their natural enemies
④ rebuild their external environment to obtain resources
⑤ change their physiology in accord with their surroundings

03

19학년도 9월 모평 36번

주어진 글 다음에 이어질 글의 순서로 가장 적절한 것은? [3점]

> Most of us have a general, rational sense of what to eat and when — there is no shortage of information on the subject.

(A) *Emotional eating* is a popular term used to describe eating that is influenced by emotions, both positive and negative. Feelings may affect various aspects of your eating, including your motivation to eat, your food choices, where and with whom you eat, and the speed at which you eat. Most overeating is prompted by feelings rather than physical hunger.

(B) Yet there is often a disconnect between what we know and what we do. We may have the facts, but decisions also involve our feelings. Many people who struggle with difficult emotions also struggle with eating problems.

(C) Individuals who struggle with obesity tend to eat in response to emotions. However, people who eat for emotional reasons are not necessarily overweight. People of any size may try to escape an emotional experience by preoccupying themselves with eating or by obsessing over their shape and weight.

*obsess: 강박감을 갖다

① (A) – (C) – (B)
② (B) – (A) – (C)
③ (B) – (C) – (A)
④ (C) – (A) – (B)
⑤ (C) – (B) – (A)

정답 및 해설 p. 338

DAY 088

글의 제목
빈칸 추론
문장 넣기

제한시간 | 4분

01

20학년도 6월 모평 24번

다음 글의 제목으로 가장 적절한 것은? [3점]

Racial and ethnic relations in the United States are better today than in the past, but many changes are needed before sports are a model of inclusion and fairness. The challenges today are different from the ones faced twenty years ago, and experience shows that when current challenges are met, a new social situation is created in which new challenges emerge. For example, once racial and ethnic segregation is eliminated and people come together, they must learn to live, work, and play with each other despite diverse experiences and cultural perspectives. Meeting this challenge requires a commitment to equal treatment, *plus* learning about the perspectives of others, understanding how they define and give meaning to the world, and then determining how to form and maintain relationships while respecting differences, making compromises, and supporting one another in the pursuit of goals that may not always be shared. None of this is easy, and challenges are never met once and for all time.

*segregation: 분리

① Ongoing Challenges in Sports: Racial and Ethnic Issues
② Racial and Ethnic Injustice in Sports: Cause and Effect
③ The History of Racial and Ethnic Diversity in Sports
④ All for One, One for All: The Power of Team Sports
⑤ Cooperation Lies at the Heart of Sportsmanship

02

18학년도 6월 모평 33번

다음 빈칸에 들어갈 말로 가장 적절한 것은? [3점]

To make plans for the future, the brain must have an ability to take certain elements of prior experiences and reconfigure them in a way that does not copy any actual past experience or present reality exactly. To accomplish that, the organism must go beyond the mere ability to form internal representations, the models of the world outside. It must acquire the ability to ______________________. We can argue that tool-making, one of the fundamental distinguishing features of primate cognition, depends on this ability, since a tool does not exist in a ready-made form in the natural environment and has to be imagined in order to be made. The neural machinery for creating and holding 'images of the future' was a necessary prerequisite for tool-making, and thus for launching human civilization.

① mirror accurate images of the world outside
② manipulate and transform these models
③ visualize the present reality as it is
④ bring the models back from memory
⑤ identify and reproduce past experiences faithfully

03

19학년도 9월 모평 38번

글의 흐름으로 보아, 주어진 문장이 들어가기에 가장 적절한 곳은?

> Moreover, more than half of Americans age 18 and older derive benefits from various transfer programs, while paying little or no personal income tax.

Both the budget deficit and federal debt have soared during the recent financial crisis and recession. (①) During 2009—2010, nearly 40 percent of federal expenditures were financed by borrowing. (②) The huge recent federal deficits have pushed the federal debt to levels not seen since the years immediately following World War II. (③) The rapid growth of baby-boomer retirees in the decade immediately ahead will mean higher spending levels and larger and larger deficits for both Social Security and Medicare. (④) All of these factors are going to make it extremely difficult to slow the growth of federal spending and keep the debt from ballooning out of control. (⑤) Projections indicate that the net federal debt will rise to 90 percent of GDP by 2019, and many believe it will be even higher unless constructive action is taken soon.

*deficit: 부족, 결손 **federal: 연방의 ***soar: 급등하다, 치솟다

정답 및 해설 p. 342

DAY 089

함의 추론
빈칸 추론
무관 문장

제한시간 | 4분

01

19학년도 대수능 21번

밑줄 친 refining ignorance가 다음 글에서 의미하는 바로 가장 적절한 것은?

Although not the explicit goal, the best science can really be seen as refining ignorance. Scientists, especially young ones, can get too obsessed with results. Society helps them along in this mad chase. Big discoveries are covered in the press, show up on the university's home page, help get grants, and make the case for promotions. But it's wrong. Great scientists, the pioneers that we admire, are not concerned with results but with the next questions. The highly respected physicist Enrico Fermi told his students that an experiment that successfully proves a hypothesis is a measurement; one that doesn't is a discovery. A discovery, an uncovering — of new ignorance. The Nobel Prize, the pinnacle of scientific accomplishment, is awarded, not for a lifetime of scientific achievement, but for a single discovery, a result. Even the Nobel committee realizes in some way that this is not really in the scientific spirit, and their award citations commonly honor the discovery for having "opened a field up," "transformed a field," or "taken a field in new and unexpected directions."

*pinnacle: 정점

① looking beyond what is known towards what is left unknown
② offering an ultimate account of what has been discovered
③ analyzing existing knowledge with an objective mindset
④ inspiring scientists to publicize significant discoveries
⑤ informing students of a new field of science

02

18학년도 6월 모평 32번

다음 빈칸에 들어갈 말로 가장 적절한 것은? [3점]

Politics cannot be suppressed, whichever policy process is employed and however sensitive and respectful of differences it might be. In other words, there is no end to politics. It is wrong to think that proper institutions, knowledge, methods of consultation, or participatory mechanisms can make disagreement go away. Theories of all sorts promote the view that there are ways by which disagreement can be processed or managed so as to make it disappear. The assumption behind those theories is that disagreement is wrong and consensus is the desirable state of things. In fact, consensus rarely comes without some forms of subtle coercion and the absence of fear in expressing a disagreement is a source of genuine freedom. Debates cause disagreements to evolve, often for the better, but a positively evolving debate does not have to equal a reduction in disagreement. The suppression of disagreement should never be made into a goal in political deliberation. A defense is required against any suggestion that ________________________.

*consensus: 합의 **coercion: 강압

① political development results from the freedom of speech
② political disagreement is not the normal state of things
③ politics should not restrict any form of difference
④ freedom could be achieved only through tolerance
⑤ suppression could never be a desirable tool in politics

03

20학년도 6월 모평 35번

다음 글에서 전체 흐름과 관계 없는 문장은?

When a dog is trained to detect drugs, explosives, contraband, or other items, the trainer doesn't actually teach the dog how to smell; the dog already knows how to discriminate one scent from another. Rather, the dog is trained to become emotionally aroused by one smell versus another. ① In the step-by-step training process, the trainer attaches an "emotional charge" to a particular scent so that the dog is drawn to it above all others. ② And then the dog is trained to search out the desired item on cue, so that the trainer can control or release the behavior. ③ This emotional arousal is also why playing tug with a dog is a more powerful emotional reward in a training regime than just giving a dog a food treat, since the trainer invests more emotion into a game of tug. ④ As long as the trainer gives the dog a food reward regularly, the dog can understand its "good" behavior results in rewards. ⑤ From a dog's point of view, the tug toy is compelling because the trainer is "upset" by the toy.

*contraband: 밀수품 **tug: 잡아당김

정답 및 해설 p. 346

DAY 090

밑줄 어법
빈칸 추론
글의 순서

제한시간 | 4분

01

21학년도 대수능 29번

다음 글의 밑줄 친 부분 중, 어법상 틀린 것은? [3점]

Regulations covering scientific experiments on human subjects are strict. Subjects must give their informed, written consent, and experimenters must submit their proposed experiments to thorough examination by overseeing bodies. Scientists who experiment on themselves can, functionally if not legally, avoid the restrictions ① associated with experimenting on other people. They can also sidestep most of the ethical issues involved: nobody, presumably, is more aware of an experiment's potential hazards than the scientist who devised ② it. Nonetheless, experimenting on oneself remains ③ deeply problematic. One obvious drawback is the danger involved; knowing that it exists ④ does nothing to reduce it. A less obvious drawback is the limited range of data that the experiment can generate. Human anatomy and physiology vary, in small but significant ways, according to gender, age, lifestyle, and other factors. Experimental results derived from a single subject are, therefore, of limited value; there is no way to know ⑤ what the subject's responses are typical or atypical of the response of humans as a group.

*consent: 동의 **anatomy: (해부학적) 구조 ***physiology: 생리적 현상

02

18학년도 6월 모평 31번

다음 빈칸에 들어갈 말로 가장 적절한 것은?

Interest in extremely long periods of time sets geology and astronomy apart from other sciences. Geologists think in terms of billions of years for the age of Earth and its oldest rocks — numbers that, like the national debt, are not easily comprehended. Nevertheless, the ________________________ are important for environmental geologists because they provide a way to measure human impacts on the natural world. For example, we would like to know the rate of natural soil formation from solid rock to determine whether topsoil erosion from agriculture is too great. Likewise, understanding how climate has changed over millions of years is vital to properly assess current global warming trends. Clues to past environmental change are well preserved in many different kinds of rocks.

① time scales of geological activity
② global patterns in species diversity
③ regional differences in time perception
④ statistical methods for climate projections
⑤ criticisms of geological period classifications

03

19학년도 6월 모평 37번

주어진 글 다음에 이어질 글의 순서로 가장 적절한 것은? [3점]

Promoting attractive images of one's country is not new, but the conditions for trying to create soft power have changed dramatically in recent years. For one thing, nearly half the countries in the world are now democracies.

(A) Technological advances have led to a dramatic reduction in the cost of processing and transmitting information. The result is an explosion of information, and that has produced a "paradox of plenty." Plentiful information leads to scarcity of attention.

(B) In such circumstances, diplomacy aimed at public opinion can become as important to outcomes as traditional classified diplomatic communications among leaders. Information creates power, and today a much larger part of the world's population has access to that power.

(C) When people are overwhelmed with the volume of information confronting them, they have difficulty knowing what to focus on. Attention, rather than information, becomes the scarce resource, and those who can distinguish valuable information from background clutter gain power.

*clutter: 혼란

① (A) – (C) – (B)
② (B) – (A) – (C)
③ (B) – (C) – (A)
④ (C) – (A) – (B)
⑤ (C) – (B) – (A)

정답 및 해설 p. 350

DAY 091

낱말 쓰임
빈칸 추론
문장 넣기

제한시간 | 4분

01

21학년도 대수능 30번

다음 글의 밑줄 친 부분 중, 문맥상 낱말의 쓰임이 적절하지 <u>않은</u> 것은?

How the bandwagon effect occurs is demonstrated by the history of measurements of the speed of light. Because this speed is the basis of the theory of relativity, it's one of the most frequently and carefully measured ① <u>quantities</u> in science. As far as we know, the speed hasn't changed over time. However, from 1870 to 1900, all the experiments found speeds that were too high. Then, from 1900 to 1950, the ② <u>opposite</u> happened — all the experiments found speeds that were too low! This kind of error, where results are always on one side of the real value, is called "bias." It probably happened because over time, experimenters subconsciously adjusted their results to ③ <u>match</u> what they expected to find. If a result fit what they expected, they kept it. If a result didn't fit, they threw it out. They weren't being intentionally dishonest, just ④ <u>influenced</u> by the conventional wisdom. The pattern only changed when someone ⑤ <u>lacked</u> the courage to report what was actually measured instead of what was expected.

*bandwagon effect: 편승 효과

02

17학년도 대수능 34번

다음 빈칸에 들어갈 말로 가장 적절한 것은? [3점]

Over a period of time the buildings which housed social, legal, religious, and other rituals evolved into forms that we subsequently have come ______________________________. This is a two-way process; the building provides the physical environment and setting for a particular social ritual such as traveling by train or going to the theater, as well as the symbolic setting. The meaning of buildings evolves and becomes established by experience and we in turn read our experience into buildings. Buildings arouse an empathetic reaction in us through these projected experiences, and the strength of these reactions is determined by our culture, our beliefs, and our expectations. They tell stories, for their form and spatial organization give us hints about how they should be used. Their physical layout encourages some uses and inhibits others; we do not go backstage in a theater unless especially invited. Inside a law court the precise location of those involved in the legal process is an integral part of the design and an essential part of ensuring that the law is upheld.

*empathetic: 공감할 수 있는

① to identify and relate to a new architectural trend
② to recognize and associate with those buildings' function
③ to define and refine by reflecting cross-cultural interactions
④ to use and change into an integral part of our environment
⑤ to alter and develop for the elimination of their meanings

03

19학년도 6월 모평 39번

글의 흐름으로 보아, 주어진 문장이 들어가기에 가장 적절한 곳은?

There are also clinical cases that show the flip side of this coin.

Humans can tell lies with their faces. Although some are specifically trained to detect lies from facial expressions, the average person is often misled into believing false and manipulated facial emotions. One reason for this is that we are "two-faced." By this I mean that we have two different neural systems that manipulate our facial muscles. (①) One neural system is under voluntary control and the other works under involuntary control. (②) There are reported cases of individuals who have damaged the neural system that controls voluntary expressions. (③) They still have facial expressions, but are incapable of producing deceitful ones. (④) The emotion that you see is the emotion they are feeling, since they have lost the needed voluntary control to produce false facial expressions. (⑤) These people have injured the system that controls their involuntary expressions, so that the only changes in their demeanor you will see are actually willed expressions.

*demeanor: 태도, 표정

정답 및 해설 p. 354

DAY 092

요약문 복합 유형

제한시간 | 4분

01

20학년도 6월 모평 40번

다음 글의 내용을 한 문장으로 요약하고자 한다. 빈칸 (A), (B)에 들어갈 말로 가장 적절한 것은?

After the United Nations environmental conference in Rio de Janeiro in 1992 made the term "sustainability" widely known around the world, the word became a popular buzzword by those who wanted to be seen as pro-environmental but who did not really intend to change their behavior. It became a public relations term, an attempt to be seen as abreast with the latest thinking of what we must do to save our planet from widespread harm. But then, in a decade or so, some governments, industries, educational institutions, and organizations started to use the term in a serious manner. In the United States a number of large corporations appointed a vice president for sustainability. Not only were these officials interested in how their companies could profit by producing "green" products, but they were often given the task of making the company more efficient by reducing wastes and pollution and by reducing its carbon emissions.

*buzzword: 유행어 **abreast: 나란히

↓

While the term "sustainability," in the initial phase, was popular among those who ____(A)____ to be eco-conscious, it later came to be used by those who would ____(B)____ their pro-environmental thoughts.

	(A)		(B)
①	pretended	……	actualize
②	pretended	……	disregard
③	refused	……	realize
④	refused	……	idealize
⑤	attempted	……	mask

02~03

21학년도 9월 모평 41~42번

다음 글을 읽고, 물음에 답하시오.

To the extent that sufficient context has been provided, the reader can come to a well-crafted text with no expert knowledge and come away with a good approximation of what has been intended by the author. The text has become a public document and the reader can read it with a (a) minimum of effort and struggle; his experience comes close to what Freud has described as the deployment of "evenly-hovering attention." He puts himself in the author's hands (some have had this experience with great novelists such as Dickens or Tolstoy) and he (b) follows where the author leads. The real world has vanished and the fictive world has taken its place. Now consider the other extreme. When we come to a badly crafted text in which context and content are not happily joined, we must struggle to understand, and our sense of what the author intended probably bears (c) close correspondence to his original intention. An out-of-date translation will give us this experience; as we read, we must bring the language up to date, and understanding comes only at the price of a fairly intense struggle with the text. Badly presented content with no frame of reference can provide (d) the same experience; we see the words but have no sense of how they are to be taken. The author who fails to provide the context has (e) mistakenly assumed that his picture of the world is shared by all his readers and fails to realize that supplying the right frame of reference is a critical part of the task of writing.

*deployment: (전략적) 배치
**evenly-hovering attention: 고르게 주의를 기울이는 것

02

윗글의 제목으로 가장 적절한 것은?

① Building a Wall Between Reality and the Fictive World
② Creative Reading: Going Beyond the Writer's Intentions
③ Usefulness of Readers' Experiences for Effective Writing
④ Context in Writing: A Lighthouse for Understanding Texts
⑤ Trapped in Their Own Words: The Narrow Outlook of Authors

03

밑줄 친 (a)~(e) 중에서 문맥상 낱말의 쓰임이 적절하지 않은 것은? [3점]

① (a) ② (b) ③ (c) ④ (d) ⑤ (e)

정답 및 해설 p. 358

DAY 093

빈칸 추론
글의 순서
문장 넣기

제한시간 | 5분

01

17학년도 대수능 33번

다음 빈칸에 들어갈 말로 가장 적절한 것은? [3점]

Grief is unpleasant. Would one not then be better off without it altogether? Why accept it even when the loss is real? Perhaps we should say of it what Spinoza said of regret: that whoever feels it is "twice unhappy or twice helpless." Laurence Thomas has suggested that the utility of "negative sentiments" (emotions like grief, guilt, resentment, and anger, which there is seemingly a reason to believe we might be better off without) lies in their providing a kind of guarantee of authenticity for such dispositional sentiments as love and respect. No occurrent feelings of love and respect need to be present throughout the period in which it is true that one loves or respects. One might therefore sometimes suspect, in the absence of the positive occurrent feelings, that ______________________________. At such times, negative emotions like grief offer a kind of testimonial to the authenticity of love or respect.

*dispositional: 성향적인 **testimonial: 증거

① one no longer loves
② one is much happier
③ an emotional loss can never be real
④ respect for oneself can be guaranteed
⑤ negative sentiments do not hold any longer

02

19학년도 6월 모평 36번

주어진 글 다음에 이어질 글의 순서로 가장 적절한 것은?

A carbon sink is a natural feature that absorbs or stores more carbon than it releases.

(A) Carbon sinks have been able to absorb about half of this excess CO_2, and the world's oceans have done the major part of that job. They absorb about one-fourth of humans' industrial carbon emissions, doing half the work of all Earth's carbon sinks combined.

(B) Its mass of plants and other organic material absorb and store tons of carbon. However, the planet's major carbon sink is its oceans. Since the Industrial Revolution began in the eighteenth century, CO_2 released during industrial processes has greatly increased the proportion of carbon in the atmosphere.

(C) The value of carbon sinks is that they can help create equilibrium in the atmosphere by removing excess CO_2. One example of a carbon sink is a large forest.

*equilibrium: 평형 상태

① (A) – (C) – (B)
② (B) – (A) – (C)
③ (B) – (C) – (A)
④ (C) – (A) – (B)
⑤ (C) – (B) – (A)

03

19학년도 6월 모평 38번

글의 흐름으로 보아, 주어진 문장이 들어가기에 가장 적절한 곳은?

There is a considerable difference as to whether people watch a film about the Himalayas on television and become excited by the 'untouched nature' of the majestic mountain peaks, or whether they get up and go on a trek to Nepal.

Tourism takes place simultaneously in the realm of the imagination and that of the physical world. In contrast to literature or film, it leads to 'real', tangible worlds, while nevertheless remaining tied to the sphere of fantasies, dreams, wishes — and myth. It thereby allows the ritual enactment of mythological ideas. (①) Even in the latter case, they remain, at least partly, in an imaginary world. (②) They experience moments that they have already seen at home in books, brochures and films. (③) Their notions of untouched nature and friendly, innocent indigenous people will probably be confirmed. (④) But now this confirmation is anchored in a physical experience. (⑤) The myth is thus transmitted in a much more powerful way than by television, movies or books.

*indigenous: 토착의

정답 및 해설 p. 361

DAY

094

글의 주제
빈칸 추론
글의 순서

제한시간 | 4분

01

19학년도 대수능 23번

다음 글의 주제로 가장 적절한 것은? [3점]

We argue that the ethical principles of justice provide an essential foundation for policies to protect unborn generations and the poorest countries from climate change. Related issues arise in connection with current and persistently inadequate aid for these nations, in the face of growing threats to agriculture and water supply, and the rules of international trade that mainly benefit rich countries. Increasing aid for the world's poorest peoples can be an essential part of effective mitigation. With 20 percent of carbon emissions from (mostly tropical) deforestation, carbon credits for forest preservation would combine aid to poorer countries with one of the most cost-effective forms of abatement. Perhaps the most cost-effective but politically complicated policy reform would be the removal of several hundred billions of dollars of direct annual subsidies from the two biggest recipients in the OECD — destructive industrial agriculture and fossil fuels. Even a small amount of this money would accelerate the already rapid rate of technical progress and investment in renewable energy in many areas, as well as encourage the essential switch to conservation agriculture.

*mitigation: 완화 **abatement: 감소 ***subsidy: 보조금

① reforming diplomatic policies in poor countries
② increasing global awareness of the environmental crisis
③ reasons for restoring economic equality in poor countries
④ coping with climate change by reforming aid and policies
⑤ roles of the OECD in solving international conflicts

02

17학년도 대수능 32번

다음 빈칸에 들어갈 말로 가장 적절한 것은? [3점]

Temporal resolution is particularly interesting in the context of satellite remote sensing. The temporal density of remotely sensed imagery is large, impressive, and growing. Satellites are collecting a great deal of imagery as you read this sentence. However, most applications in geography and environmental studies do not require extremely fine-grained temporal resolution. Meteorologists may require visible, infrared, and radar information at sub-hourly temporal resolution; urban planners might require imagery at monthly or annual resolution; and transportation planners may not need any time series information at all for some applications. Again, the temporal resolution of imagery used should ____________________. Sometimes researchers have to search archives of aerial photographs to get information from that past that pre-date the collection of satellite imagery.

*meteorologist: 기상학자 **infrared: 적외선의

① be selected for general purposes
② meet the requirements of your inquiry
③ be as high as possible for any occasion
④ be applied to new technology by experts
⑤ rely exclusively upon satellite information

03

18학년도 대수능 37번

주어진 글 다음에 이어질 글의 순서로 가장 적절한 것은? [3점]

To modern man disease is a biological phenomenon that concerns him only as an individual and has no moral implications. When he contracts influenza, he never attributes this event to his behavior toward the tax collector or his mother-in-law.

(A) Sometimes they may not strike the guilty person himself, but rather one of his relatives or tribesmen, to whom responsibility is extended. Disease, action that might produce disease, and recovery from disease are, therefore, of vital concern to the whole primitive community.

(B) Disease, as a sanction against social misbehavior, becomes one of the most important pillars of order in such societies. It takes over, in many cases, the role played by policemen, judges, and priests in modern society.

(C) Among primitives, because of their supernaturalistic theories, the prevailing moral point of view gives a deeper meaning to disease. The gods who send disease are usually angered by the moral offences of the individual.

*sanction: 제재

① (A) – (C) – (B)
② (B) – (A) – (C)
③ (B) – (C) – (A)
④ (C) – (A) – (B)
⑤ (C) – (B) – (A)

정답 및 해설 p. 365

DAY

095

글의 제목
빈칸 추론
문장 넣기

제한시간 | 4분

01

19학년도 대수능 24번

다음 글의 제목으로 가장 적절한 것은?

A defining element of catastrophes is the magnitude of their harmful consequences. To help societies prevent or reduce damage from catastrophes, a huge amount of effort and technological sophistication are often employed to assess and communicate the size and scope of potential or actual losses. This effort assumes that people can understand the resulting numbers and act on them appropriately. However, recent behavioral research casts doubt on this fundamental assumption. Many people do not understand large numbers. Indeed, large numbers have been found to lack meaning and to be underestimated in decisions unless they convey affect (feeling). This creates a paradox that rational models of decision making fail to represent. On the one hand, we respond strongly to aid a single individual in need. On the other hand, we often fail to prevent mass tragedies or take appropriate measures to reduce potential losses from natural disasters.

*catastrophe: 큰 재해

① Insensitivity to Mass Tragedy: We Are Lost in Large Numbers
② Power of Numbers: A Way of Classifying Natural Disasters
③ How to Reach Out a Hand to People in Desperate Need
④ Preventing Potential Losses Through Technology
⑤ Be Careful, Numbers Magnify Feelings!

02

17학년도 대수능 31번

다음 빈칸에 들어갈 말로 가장 적절한 것은? [3점]

The creativity that children possess needs to be cultivated throughout their development. Research suggests that overstructuring the child's environment may actually limit creative and academic development. This is a central problem with much of science instruction. The exercises or activities are devised to eliminate different options and to focus on predetermined results. The answers are structured to fit the course assessments, and the wonder of science is lost along with cognitive intrigue. We define cognitive intrigue as the wonder that stimulates and intrinsically motivates an individual to voluntarily engage in an activity. The loss of cognitive intrigue may be initiated by the sole use of play items with predetermined conclusions and reinforced by rote instruction in school. This is exemplified by toys, games, and lessons that are a(n) ______________ in and of themselves and require little of the individual other than to master the planned objective.

*rote: 기계적인 암기

① end ② input ③ puzzle
④ interest ⑤ alternative

03

18학년도 대수능 39번

글의 흐름으로 보아, 주어진 문장이 들어가기에 가장 적절한 곳은?

> It is postulated that such contamination may result from airborne transport from remote power plants or municipal incinerators.

An incident in Japan in the 1950s alerted the world to the potential problems of organic mercury in fish. Factories were discharging mercury into the waters of Minamata Bay, which also harbored a commercial fishing industry. Mercury was being bioaccumulated in the fish tissue and severe mercury poisoning occurred in many people who consumed the fish. (①) The disabling neurological symptoms were subsequently called Minamata disease. (②) Control over direct discharge of mercury from industrial operations is clearly needed for prevention. (③) However, it is now recognized that traces of mercury can appear in lakes far removed from any such industrial discharge. (④) Strictly controlled emission standards for such sources are needed to minimize this problem. (⑤) Fish advisories have been issued for many lakes in the United States; these recommend limits on the number of times per month particular species of fish should be consumed.

*postulate: 가정하다 **incinerator: 소각로

정답 및 해설 p. 369

DAY

096

함의 추론
빈칸 추론
무관 문장

제한시간 | 4분

01

19학년도 9월 모평 21번

밑줄 친 "a link in a chain, a phase in a process"가 다음 글에서 의미하는 바로 가장 적절한 것은? [3점]

Psychologist Mihaly Csikszentmihalyi suggests that the common idea of a creative individual coming up with great insights, discoveries, works, or inventions in isolation is wrong. Creativity results from a complex interaction between a person and his or her environment or culture, and also depends on timing. For instance, if the great Renaissance artists like Ghiberti or Michelangelo had been born only 50 years before they were, the culture of artistic patronage would not have been in place to fund or shape their great achievements. Consider also individual astronomers: Their discoveries could not have happened unless centuries of technological development of the telescope and evolving knowledge of the universe had come before them. Csikszentmihalyi's point is that we should devote as much attention to the development of a domain as we do to the people working within it, as only this can properly explain how advances are made. Individuals are only "a link in a chain, a phase in a process," he notes.

*patronage: 보호, 후원, 찬조

① Individuals' creativity results only from good fortune.
② Discoveries can be made only due to existing knowledge.
③ One's genius is a key element of a series of breakthroughs.
④ Individuals receive no credit for their creative achievements.
⑤ Individual creativity emerges only in its necessary conditions.

02

17학년도 9월 모평 34번

다음 빈칸에 들어갈 말로 가장 적절한 것은? [3점]

Even if it is correct to say that we *express* and *represent* our thoughts in language, it may be a big mistake to suppose that there are structural similarities between what is doing the representing and what is represented. Robert Stalnaker, in his book *Inquiry*, suggests an analogy with the representation of *numbers*: The number 9 can be *represented* as '12 — 3' but it does not follow that 12, 3, or *subtraction* are *constituents* of the number 9. We could compare a thought and its verbal expression with toothpaste and its 'expression' from a tube. That the result of expressing toothpaste is a long, thin, cylinder does not entail that toothpaste itself is long, thin, or cylindrical. Similarly, a thought might get expressed out loud in a statement with a particular linguistic structure. It does not follow that ______________________________ ______________________. Suppose, for example, that I look at a fruit bowl, and think that there is an apple and an orange in that bowl. The objects in front of my eyes include some pieces of fruit and a bowl, but no object corresponding to the word 'and' exists either in the world or in my visual image.

*subtraction: 빼기 **entail: 의미[함의]하다

① the thought itself has such a structure
② linguistic analysis of a thought is unlikely
③ the language in mind lacks a logical structure
④ a thought and its verbal expression are distinct
⑤ the sentence structurally differs from the thought

03

19학년도 대수능 35번

다음 글에서 전체 흐름과 관계 없는 문장은?

When photography came along in the nineteenth century, painting was put in crisis. The photograph, it seemed, did the work of imitating nature better than the painter ever could. ① Some painters made practical use of the invention. ② There were Impressionist painters who used a photograph in place of the model or landscape they were painting. ③ But by and large, the photograph was a challenge to painting and was one cause of painting's moving away from direct representation and reproduction to the abstract painting of the twentieth century. ④ Therefore, the painters of that century put more focus on expressing nature, people, and cities as they were in reality. ⑤ Since photographs did such a good job of representing things as they existed in the world, painters were freed to look inward and represent things as they were in their imagination, rendering emotion in the color, volume, line, and spatial configurations native to the painter's art.

*render: 표현하다 **configuration: 배치

정답 및 해설 p. 373

DAY

097

밑줄 어법
빈칸 추론
글의 순서

제한시간 | 4분

01

21학년도 9월 모평 29번

다음 글의 밑줄 친 부분 중, 어법상 틀린 것은? [3점]

Competitive activities can be more than just performance showcases ① which the best is recognized and the rest are overlooked. The provision of timely, constructive feedback to participants on performance ② is an asset that some competitions and contests offer. In a sense, all competitions give feedback. For many, this is restricted to information about whether the participant is an award- or prizewinner. The provision of that type of feedback can be interpreted as shifting the emphasis to demonstrating superior performance but not ③ necessarily excellence. The best competitions promote excellence, not just winning or "beating" others. The emphasis on superiority is what we typically see as ④ fostering a detrimental effect of competition. Performance feedback requires that the program go beyond the "win, place, or show" level of feedback. Information about performance can be very helpful, not only to the participant who does not win or place but also to those who ⑤ do.

*foster: 조장하다 **detrimental: 유해한

02

17학년도 6월 모평 34번

다음 빈칸에 들어갈 말로 가장 적절한 것은? [3점]

One remarkable aspect of aboriginal culture is the concept of "totemism," where the tribal member at birth assumes the soul and identity of a part of nature. This view of the earth and its riches as an intrinsic part of oneself clearly rules out mistreatment of the environment because this would only constitute a destruction of self. Totems are more than objects. They include spiritual rituals, oral histories, and the organization of ceremonial lodges where records of the past travel routes of the soul can be exchanged with others and converted to mythology. The primary motivation is the preservation of tribal myths and a consolidation and sharing of every individual's origins in nature. The aborigines see ______________________________, through a hierarchy of totems that connect to their ancestral origins, a cosmology that places them at one with the earth, and behavior patterns that respect ecological balance.

*aboriginal: 원주민의 **consolidation: 병합, 강화

① themselves as incompatible with nature and her riches
② their mythology as a primary motive toward individualism
③ their identity as being self-contained from surrounding nature
④ their relationship to the environment as a single harmonious continuum
⑤ their communal rituals as a gateway to distancing themselves from their origins

03

18학년도 대수능 36번

주어진 글 다음에 이어질 글의 순서로 가장 적절한 것은?

> Most consumer magazines depend on subscriptions and advertising. Subscriptions account for almost 90 percent of total magazine circulation. Single-copy, or newsstand, sales account for the rest.

(A) For example, the *Columbia Journalism Review* is marketed toward professional journalists and its few advertisements are news organizations, book publishers, and others. A few magazines, like *Consumer Reports*, work toward objectivity and therefore contain no advertising.

(B) However, single-copy sales are important: they bring in more revenue per magazine, because subscription prices are typically at least 50 percent less than the price of buying single issues.

(C) Further, potential readers explore a new magazine by buying a single issue; all those insert cards with subscription offers are included in magazines to encourage you to subscribe. Some magazines are distributed only by subscription. Professional or trade magazines are specialized magazines and are often published by professional associations. They usually feature highly targeted advertising.

*revenue: 수입

① (A) – (C) – (B)　② (B) – (A) – (C)
③ (B) – (C) – (A)　④ (C) – (A) – (B)
⑤ (C) – (B) – (A)

정답 및 해설 p. 377

DAY 098

낱말 쓰임
빈칸 추론
문장 넣기

ⓒ 제한시간 | 4분

01

21학년도 9월 모평 30번

다음 글의 밑줄 친 부분 중, 문맥상 낱말의 쓰임이 적절하지 <u>않은</u> 것은?

If I say to you, 'Don't think of a white bear', you will find it difficult not to think of a white bear. In this way, 'thought suppression can actually increase the thoughts one wishes to suppress instead of calming them'. One common example of this is that people on a diet who try not to think about food often begin to think much ① <u>more</u> about food. This process is therefore also known as the *rebound effect*. The ② <u>ironic</u> effect seems to be caused by the interplay of two related cognitive processes. This dual-process system involves, first, an intentional operating process, which consciously attempts to locate thoughts ③ <u>unrelated</u> to the suppressed ones. Second, and simultaneously, an unconscious monitoring process tests whether the operating system is functioning effectively. If the monitoring system encounters thoughts inconsistent with the intended ones, it prompts the intentional operating process to ensure that these are replaced by ④ <u>inappropriate</u> thoughts. However, it is argued, the intentional operating system can fail due to increased cognitive load caused by fatigue, stress and emotional factors, and so the monitoring process filters the inappropriate thoughts into consciousness, making them highly ⑤ <u>accessible</u>.

02

17학년도 6월 모평 33번

다음 빈칸에 들어갈 말로 가장 적절한 것은? [3점]

It is not hard to see that a strong economy, where opportunities are plentiful and jobs go begging, ______________________. Biased employers may still dislike hiring members of one group or another, but when nobody else is available, discrimination most often gives way to the basic need to get the work done. The same goes for employees with prejudices about whom they do and do not like working alongside. In the American construction boom of the late 1990s, for example, even the carpenters' union — long known as a "traditional bastion of white men, a world where a coveted union card was handed down from father to son" — began openly encouraging women, blacks, and Hispanics to join its internship program. At least in the workplace, jobs chasing people obviously does more to promote a fluid society than people chasing jobs.

*bastion: 요새 **coveted: 부러움을 사는

① allows employees to earn more income
② helps break down social barriers
③ simplifies the hiring process
④ increases wage discrimination
⑤ improves the productivity of a company

03

18학년도 대수능 38번

글의 흐름으로 보아, 주어진 문장이 들어가기에 가장 적절한 곳은?

Experiments show that rats display an immediate liking for salt the first time they experience a salt deficiency.

Both humans and rats have evolved taste preferences for *sweet* foods, which provide rich sources of calories. A study of food preferences among the Hadza hunter-gatherers of Tanzania found that honey was the most highly preferred food item, an item that has the highest caloric value. (①) Human newborn infants also show a strong preference for sweet liquids. (②) Both humans and rats dislike *bitter* and *sour* foods, which tend to contain toxins. (③) They also adaptively adjust their eating behavior in response to deficits in water, calories, and salt. (④) They likewise increase their intake of sweets and water when their energy and fluids become depleted. (⑤) These appear to be specific evolved mechanisms, designed to deal with the adaptive problem of food selection, and coordinate consumption patterns with physical needs.

*deficiency: 결핍 **deplete: 고갈시키다

정답 및 해설 p. 381

DAY 099

요약문
복합 유형

제한시간 | 4분

01

19학년도 대수능 40번

다음 글의 내용을 한 문장으로 요약하고자 한다. 빈칸 (A), (B)에 들어갈 말로 가장 적절한 것은?

Biological organisms, including human societies both with and without market systems, discount distant outputs over those available at the present time based on risks associated with an uncertain future. As the timing of inputs and outputs varies greatly depending on the type of energy, there is a strong case to incorporate time when assessing energy alternatives. For example, the energy output from solar panels or wind power engines, where most investment happens before they begin producing, may need to be assessed differently when compared to most fossil fuel extraction technologies, where a large proportion of the energy output comes much sooner, and a larger (relative) proportion of inputs is applied during the extraction process, and not upfront. Thus fossil fuels, particularly oil and natural gas, in addition to having energy quality advantages (cost, storability, transportability, etc.) over many renewable technologies, also have a "temporal advantage" after accounting for human behavioral preference for current consumption/return.

*upfront: 선행 투자의

↓

Due to the fact that people tend to favor more ___(A)___ outputs, fossil fuels are more ___(B)___ than renewable energy alternatives in regards to the distance between inputs and outputs.

	(A)		(B)
①	immediate	……	competitive
②	available	……	expensive
③	delayed	……	competitive
④	convenient	……	expensive
⑤	abundant	……	competitive

02~03

21학년도 6월 모평 41~42번

다음 글을 읽고, 물음에 답하시오.

In many mountain regions, rights of access to water are associated with the possession of land — until recently in the Andes, for example, land and water rights were (a) combined so water rights were transferred with the land. However, through state land reforms and the development of additional sources of supply, water rights have become separated from land, and may be sold at auction. This therefore (b) favours those who can pay, rather than ensuring access to all in the community. The situation arises, therefore, where individuals may hold land with no water. In Peru, the government grants water to communities separately from land, and it is up to the community to allocate it. Likewise in Yemen, the traditional allocation was one measure (*tasah*) of water to one hundred '*libnah*' of land. This applied only to traditional irrigation supplies — from runoff, wells, etc., where a supply was (c) guaranteed. Water derived from the capture of flash floods is not subject to Islamic law as this constitutes an uncertain source, and is therefore free for those able to collect and use it. However, this traditional allocation per unit of land has been bypassed, partly by the development of new supplies, but also by the (d) decrease in cultivation of a crop of substantial economic importance. This crop is harvested throughout the year and thus requires more than its fair share of water. The economic status of the crop (e) ensures that water rights can be bought or bribed away from subsistence crops.

*irrigation: 관개(灌漑) **bribe: 매수하다
***subsistence crop: 생계용 작물

02

윗글의 제목으로 가장 적절한 것은?

① Water Rights No Longer Tied to Land
② Strategies for Trading Water Rights
③ Water Storage Methods: Mountain vs. Desert
④ Water Supplies Not Stable in Mountain Regions
⑤ Unending Debates: Which Crop We Should Grow

03

밑줄 친 (a)~(e) 중에서 문맥상 낱말의 쓰임이 적절하지 않은 것은? [3점]

① (a) ② (b) ③ (c) ④ (d) ⑤ (e)

정답 및 해설 p. 385

DAY 100

빈칸 추론
글의 순서
문장 넣기

제한시간 | 5분

01

17학년도 6월 모평 32번

다음 빈칸에 들어갈 말로 가장 적절한 것은? [3점]

What story could be harsher than that of the Great Auk, the large black-and-white seabird that in northern oceans took the ecological place of a penguin? Its tale rises and falls like a Greek tragedy, with island populations savagely destroyed by humans until almost all were gone. Then the very last colony found safety on a special island, one protected from the destruction of humankind by vicious and unpredictable ocean currents. These waters presented no problem to perfectly adapted seagoing birds, but they prevented humans from making any kind of safe landing. After enjoying a few years of comparative safety, disaster of a different kind struck the Great Auk. Volcanic activity caused the island refuge to sink completely beneath the waves, and surviving individuals were forced to find shelter elsewhere. The new island home they chose ______________________ in one terrible way. Humans could access it with comparative ease, and they did! Within just a few years the last of this once-plentiful species was entirely eliminated.

*savagely: 잔혹하게

① lacked the benefits of the old
② denied other colonies easy access
③ faced unexpected natural disasters
④ caused conflicts among the refugees
⑤ had a similar disadvantage to the last island

02

18학년도 9월 모평 37번

주어진 글 다음에 이어질 글의 순서로 가장 적절한 것은? [3점]

> Today the term artist is used to refer to a broad range of creative individuals across the globe from both past and present. This rather general usage erroneously suggests that the concept or word "artist" existed in original contexts.

(A) Inventions, ideas, and discoveries have been credited to the persons who originated them. This view is also at the core of the definition of an "artist." Artists are perceived to establish a strong bond with their art to the point of combining into one "entity."

(B) In contrast to the diversity it is applied to, the meaning of this term continues to be mostly based on Western views and values. Since the fifteenth century, this tradition has been concerned with recognizing individual achievements.

(C) Art history has reinforced this oneness: A painting by Pablo Picasso is called "a Picasso." This union between artists and their work has determined the essential qualities of an artist: originality, authorship, and authenticity.

*authenticity: 진정함, 확실성

① (A) – (C) – (B)
② (B) – (A) – (C)
③ (B) – (C) – (A)
④ (C) – (A) – (B)
⑤ (C) – (B) – (A)

03

18학년도 9월 모평 39번

글의 흐름으로 보아, 주어진 문장이 들어가기에 가장 적절한 곳은? [3점]

> But it is no light matter to quickly and correctly pen a long and complicated composition.

There are many instances of rapid work on the part of the great composers; and their facility and quickness of composition causes great wonder and admiration. (①) But our admiration is often misdirected. (②) When we hear of some of the speedy writing of great works by Mozart or Mendelssohn, we might think that this speed was of the composing power as well as of pen, but, in fact, such was seldom the case. (③) These great musicians generally did their composition mentally without reference to pen or piano, and simply postponed the unpleasant manual labor of committing their music to paper until it became absolutely necessary. (④) Then they got credit for incredible rapidity of composition. (⑤) One has only to copy a piece of music or to try to put into notes some piece of music previously memorized, to realize this.

정답 및 해설 p. 388

부록

초고난도 킬러 문항

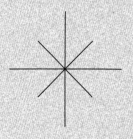

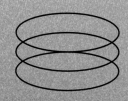

교육부 지정 킬러 문항과 정답률 30% 이하 문항을
초고난도 문항으로 묶어 수록했습니다.
역대 기출에서 어려웠던 문항들을 풀어보며
최고난도의 어려움의 정도도 함께 경험해보세요.

초고난도 킬러 문항

01

22학년도 대수능 21번

밑줄 친 whether to make ready for the morning commute or not 이 다음 글에서 의미하는 바로 가장 적절한 것은? [3점]

Scientists have no special purchase on moral or ethical decisions; a climate scientist is no more qualified to comment on health care reform than a physicist is to judge the causes of bee colony collapse. The very features that create expertise in a specialized domain lead to ignorance in many others. In some cases lay people — farmers, fishermen, patients, native peoples — may have relevant experiences that scientists can learn from. Indeed, in recent years, scientists have begun to recognize this: the Arctic Climate Impact Assessment includes observations gathered from local native groups. So our trust needs to be limited, and focused. It needs to be very *particular*. Blind trust will get us into at least as much trouble as no trust at all. But without some degree of trust in our designated experts — the men and women who have devoted their lives to sorting out tough questions about the natural world we live in — we are paralyzed, in effect not knowing whether to make ready for the morning commute or not.

*lay: 전문가가 아닌 **paralyze: 마비시키다 ***commute: 통근

① questionable facts that have been popularized by non-experts
② readily applicable information offered by specialized experts
③ common knowledge that hardly influences crucial decisions
④ practical information produced by both specialists and lay people
⑤ biased knowledge that is widespread in the local community

02

24학년도 6월 모평 33번

다음 빈칸에 들어갈 말로 가장 적절한 것은? [3점]

Whatever their differences, scientists and artists begin with the same question: *can you and I see the same thing the same way? If so, how?* The scientific thinker looks for features of the thing that can be stripped of subjectivity — ideally, those aspects that can be quantified and whose values will thus never change from one observer to the next. In this way, he arrives at a reality independent of all observers. The artist, on the other hand, relies on the strength of her artistry to effect a marriage between her own subjectivity and that of her readers. To a scientific thinker, this must sound like magical thinking: *you're saying you will imagine something so hard it'll pop into someone else's head exactly the way you envision it?* The artist has sought the opposite of the scientist's observer-independent reality. She creates a reality dependent upon observers, indeed a reality in which ______________________ in order for it to exist at all.

① human beings must participate
② objectivity should be maintained
③ science and art need to harmonize
④ readers remain distanced from the arts
⑤ she is disengaged from her own subjectivity

03

24학년도 6월 모평 34번

다음 빈칸에 들어갈 말로 가장 적절한 것은? [3점]

One of the common themes of the Western philosophical tradition is the distinction between sensual perceptions and rational knowledge. Since Plato, the supremacy of rational reason is based on the assertion that it is able to extract true knowledge from experience. As the discussion in the *Republic* helps to explain, perceptions are inherently unreliable and misleading because the senses are subject to errors and illusions. Only the rational discourse has the tools to overcome illusions and to point towards true knowledge. For instance, perception suggests that a figure in the distance is smaller than it really is. Yet, the application of logical reasoning will reveal that the figure only appears small because it obeys the laws of geometrical perspective. Nevertheless, even after the perspectival correction is applied and reason concludes that perception is misleading, the figure still *appears* small, and the truth of the matter is revealed ____________________.

*discourse: 담화 **geometrical: 기하학의

① as the outcome of blindly following sensual experience
② by moving away from the idea of perfect representation
③ beyond the limit of where rational knowledge can approach
④ through a variety of experiences rather than logical reasoning
⑤ not in the perception of the figure but in its rational representation

04

23학년도 대수능 34번

다음 빈칸에 들어갈 말로 가장 적절한 것은? [3점]

We understand that the segregation of our consciousness into present, past, and future is both a fiction and an oddly self-referential framework; your present was part of your mother's future, and your children's past will be in part your present. Nothing is generally wrong with structuring our consciousness of time in this conventional manner, and it often works well enough. In the case of climate change, however, the sharp division of time into past, present, and future has been desperately misleading and has, most importantly, hidden from view the extent of the responsibility of those of us alive now. The narrowing of our consciousness of time smooths the way to divorcing ourselves from responsibility for developments in the past and the future with which our lives are in fact deeply intertwined. In the climate case, it is not that ____________________________________. It is that the realities are obscured from view by the partitioning of time, and so questions of responsibility toward the past and future do not arise naturally.

*segregation: 분리 **intertwine: 뒤얽히게 하다 ***obscure: 흐릿하게 하다

① all our efforts prove to be effective and are thus encouraged
② sufficient scientific evidence has been provided to us
③ future concerns are more urgent than present needs
④ our ancestors maintained a different frame of time
⑤ we face the facts but then deny our responsibility

정답 및 해설 p. 392

05

22학년도 대수능 34번

다음 빈칸에 들어갈 말로 가장 적절한 것은? [3점]

Precision and determinacy are a necessary requirement for all meaningful scientific debate, and progress in the sciences is, to a large extent, the ongoing process of achieving ever greater precision. But historical representation puts a premium on a proliferation of representations, hence not on the refinement of one representation but on the production of an ever more varied set of representations. Historical insight is not a matter of a continuous "narrowing down" of previous options, not of an approximation of the truth, but, on the contrary, is an "explosion" of possible points of view. It therefore aims at the unmasking of previous illusions of determinacy and precision by the production of new and alternative representations, rather than at achieving truth by a careful analysis of what was right and wrong in those previous representations. And from this perspective, the development of historical insight may indeed be regarded by the outsider as a process of creating ever more confusion, a continuous questioning of ____________________, rather than, as in the sciences, an ever greater approximation to the truth.

*proliferation: 증식

① criteria for evaluating historical representations
② certainty and precision seemingly achieved already
③ possibilities of alternative interpretations of an event
④ coexistence of multiple viewpoints in historical writing
⑤ correctness and reliability of historical evidence collected

06

22학년도 6월 모평 31번

다음 빈칸에 들어갈 말로 가장 적절한 것은?

The growth of academic disciplines and sub-disciplines, such as art history or palaeontology, and of particular figures such as the art critic, helped produce principles and practices for selecting and organizing what was worthy of keeping, though it remained a struggle. Moreover, as museums and universities drew further apart toward the end of the nineteenth century, and as the idea of objects as a highly valued route to knowing the world went into decline, collecting began to lose its status as a worthy intellectual pursuit, especially in the sciences. The really interesting and important aspects of science were increasingly those invisible to the naked eye, and the classification of things collected no longer promised to produce cutting-edge knowledge. The term "butterfly collecting" could come to be used with the adjective "mere" to indicate a pursuit of ____________ academic status.

*palaeontology: 고생물학 **adjective: 형용사

① competitive
② novel
③ secondary
④ reliable
⑤ unconditional

07

20학년도 6월 모평 34번

다음 빈칸에 들어갈 말로 가장 적절한 것은? [3점]

Not all Golden Rules are alike; two kinds emerged over time. The negative version instructs restraint; the positive encourages intervention. One sets a baseline of at least not causing harm; the other points toward aspirational or idealized beneficent behavior. While examples of these rules abound, too many to list exhaustively, let these versions suffice for our purpose here: "What is hateful to you do not do to another" and "Love another as yourself." Both versions insist on caring for others, whether through acts of omission, such as not injuring, or through acts of commission, by actively intervening. Yet while these Golden Rules encourage an agent to care for an other, they ______________________________. The purposeful displacement of concern away from the ego nonetheless remains partly self-referential. Both the negative and the positive versions invoke the ego as the fundamental measure against which behaviors are to be evaluated.

*an other: 타자(他者)

① do not lead the self to act on concerns for others
② reveal inner contradiction between the two versions
③ fail to serve as a guide when faced with a moral dilemma
④ do not require abandoning self-concern altogether
⑤ hardly consider the benefits of social interactions

08

19학년도 대수능 34번

다음 빈칸에 들어갈 말로 가장 적절한 것은? [3점]

The human species is unique in its ability to expand its functionality by inventing new cultural tools. Writing, arithmetic, science — all are recent inventions. Our brains did not have enough time to evolve for them, but I reason that they were made possible because ______________________________. When we learn to read, we recycle a specific region of our visual system known as the visual word-form area, enabling us to recognize strings of letters and connect them to language areas. Likewise, when we learn Arabic numerals we build a circuit to quickly convert those shapes into quantities — a fast connection from bilateral visual areas to the parietal quantity area. Even an invention as elementary as finger-counting changes our cognitive abilities dramatically. Amazonian people who have not invented counting are unable to make exact calculations as simple as, say, 6–2. This "cultural recycling" implies that the functional architecture of the human brain results from a complex mixture of biological and cultural constraints.

*bilateral: 양측의 **parietal: 정수리(부분)의 ***constraint: 제약

① our brains put a limit on cultural diversity
② we can mobilize our old areas in novel ways
③ cultural tools stabilize our brain functionality
④ our brain regions operate in an isolated manner
⑤ we cannot adapt ourselves to natural challenges

정답 및 해설 p. 397

09

19학년도 6월 모평 34번

다음 빈칸에 들어갈 말로 가장 적절한 것은? [3점]

Rules can be thought of as formal types of game cues. They tell us the structure of the test, that is, what should be accomplished and how we should accomplish it. In this sense, ____. Only within the rules of the game of, say, basketball or baseball do the activities of jump shooting and fielding ground balls make sense and take on value. It is precisely the artificiality created by the rules, the distinctive problem to be solved, that gives sport its special meaning. That is why getting a basketball through a hoop while not using a ladder or pitching a baseball across home plate while standing a certain distance away becomes an important human project. It appears that respecting the rules not only preserves sport but also makes room for the creation of excellence and the emergence of meaning. Engaging in acts that would be considered inconsequential in ordinary life also liberates us a bit, making it possible to explore our capabilities in a protected environment.

*inconsequential: 중요하지 않은

① rules prevent sports from developing a special meaning
② rules create a problem that is artificial yet intelligible
③ game structures can apply to other areas
④ sports become similar to real life due to rules
⑤ game cues are provided by player and spectator interaction

10

23학년도 대수능 37번

주어진 글 다음에 이어질 글의 순서로 가장 적절한 것은? [3점]

> The most commonly known form of results-based pricing is a practice called *contingency pricing*, used by lawyers.

(A) Therefore, only an outcome in the client's favor is compensated. From the client's point of view, the pricing makes sense in part because most clients in these cases are unfamiliar with and possibly intimidated by law firms. Their biggest fears are high fees for a case that may take years to settle.

(B) By using contingency pricing, clients are ensured that they pay no fees until they receive a settlement. In these and other instances of contingency pricing, the economic value of the service is hard to determine before the service, and providers develop a price that allows them to share the risks and rewards of delivering value to the buyer.

(C) Contingency pricing is the major way that personal injury and certain consumer cases are billed. In this approach, lawyers do not receive fees or payment until the case is settled, when they are paid a percentage of the money that the client receives.

*intimidate: 위협하다

① (A) – (C) – (B)
② (B) – (A) – (C)
③ (B) – (C) – (A)
④ (C) – (A) – (B)
⑤ (C) – (B) – (A)

11

22학년도 6월 모평 36번

주어진 글 다음에 이어질 글의 순서로 가장 적절한 것은?

> Spatial reference points are larger than themselves. This isn't really a paradox: landmarks are themselves, but they also define neighborhoods around themselves.

(A) In a paradigm that has been repeated on many campuses, researchers first collect a list of campus landmarks from students. Then they ask another group of students to estimate the distances between pairs of locations, some to landmarks, some to ordinary buildings on campus.

(B) This asymmetry of distance estimates violates the most elementary principles of Euclidean distance, that the distance from A to B must be the same as the distance from B to A. Judgments of distance, then, are not necessarily coherent.

(C) The remarkable finding is that distances from an ordinary location to a landmark are judged shorter than distances from a landmark to an ordinary location. So, people would judge the distance from Pierre's house to the Eiffel Tower to be shorter than the distance from the Eiffel Tower to Pierre's house. Like black holes, landmarks seem to pull ordinary locations toward themselves, but ordinary places do not.

*asymmetry: 비대칭

① (A) – (C) – (B)
② (B) – (A) – (C)
③ (B) – (C) – (A)
④ (C) – (A) – (B)
⑤ (C) – (B) – (A)

12

22학년도 대수능 38번

글의 흐름으로 보아, 주어진 문장이 들어가기에 가장 적절한 곳은?

> Retraining current employees for new positions within the company will also greatly reduce their fear of being laid off.

Introduction of robots into factories, while employment of human workers is being reduced, creates worry and fear. (①) It is the responsibility of management to prevent or, at least, to ease these fears. (②) For example, robots could be introduced only in new plants rather than replacing humans in existing assembly lines. (③) Workers should be included in the planning for new factories or the introduction of robots into existing plants, so they can participate in the process. (④) It may be that robots are needed to reduce manufacturing costs so that the company remains competitive, but planning for such cost reductions should be done jointly by labor and management. (⑤) Since robots are particularly good at highly repetitive simple motions, the replaced human workers should be moved to positions where judgment and decisions beyond the abilities of robots are required.

정답 및 해설 p. 402

13

22학년도 9월 모평 39번

글의 흐름으로 보아, 주어진 문장이 들어가기에 가장 적절한 곳은? [3점]

Personal stories connect with larger narratives to generate new identities.

The growing complexity of the social dynamics determining food choices makes the job of marketers and advertisers increasingly more difficult. (①) In the past, mass production allowed for accessibility and affordability of products, as well as their wide distribution, and was accepted as a sign of progress. (②) Nowadays it is increasingly replaced by the fragmentation of consumers among smaller and smaller segments that are supposed to ref lect personal preferences. (③) Everybody feels different and special and expects products serving his or her inclinations. (④) In reality, these supposedly individual preferences end up overlapping with emerging, temporary, always changing, almost tribal formations solidifying around cultural sensibilities, social identifications, political sensibilities, and dietary and health concerns. (⑤) These consumer communities go beyond national boundaries, feeding on global and widely shared repositories of ideas, images, and practices.

*fragmentation: 파편화 **repository: 저장소

정답 및 해설 p. 407

ANSWERS

DAY 001	01 ④	02 ⑤	03 ①
DAY 002	01 ①	02 ⑤	03 ④
DAY 003	01 ⑤	02 ②	03 ④
DAY 004	01 ③	02 ②	03 ④
DAY 005	01 ②	02 ②	03 ④
DAY 006	01 ②	02 ②	03 ②
DAY 007	01 ②	02 ①	03 ④
DAY 008	01 ⑤	02 ①	03 ④
DAY 009	01 ④	02 ④	03 ④
DAY 010	01 ⑤	02 ④	03 ③
DAY 011	01 ③	02 ④	03 ⑤
DAY 012	01 ③	02 ⑤	03 ②
DAY 013	01 ④	02 ②	03 ③
DAY 014	01 ①	02 ①	03 ⑤
DAY 015	01 ⑤	02 ②	03 ①
DAY 016	01 ④	02 ①	03 ⑤
DAY 017	01 ②	02 ⑤	03 ④
DAY 018	01 ②	02 ①	03 ②
DAY 019	01 ⑤	02 ①	03 ①
DAY 020	01 ⑤	02 ②	03 ①
DAY 021	01 ③	02 ③	03 ③
DAY 022	01 ③	02 ④	03 ③
DAY 023	01 ①	02 ②	03 ②
DAY 024	01 ①	02 ①	03 ①
DAY 025	01 ②	02 ②	03 ⑤
DAY 026	01 ④	02 ①	03 ⑤
DAY 027	01 ②	02 ③	03 ③
DAY 028	01 ②	02 ②	03 ③
DAY 029	01 ④	02 ④	03 ④
DAY 030	01 ⑤	02 ⑤	03 ④
DAY 031	01 ⑤	02 ②	03 ③
DAY 032	01 ①	02 ②	03 ⑤
DAY 033	01 ②	02 ④	03 ④
DAY 034	01 ①	02 ②	03 ⑤
DAY 035	01 ③	02 ①	03 ⑤
DAY 036	01 ①	02 ③	03 ②
DAY 037	01 ③	02 ②	03 ②
DAY 038	01 ⑤	02 ②	03 ⑤
DAY 039	01 ③	02 ②	03 ③
DAY 040	01 ②	02 ①	03 ③
DAY 041	01 ⑤	02 ③	03 ⑤
DAY 042	01 ①	02 ②	03 ④
DAY 043	01 ①	02 ①	03 ④
DAY 044	01 ④	02 ②	03 ④
DAY 045	01 ④	02 ①	03 ②
DAY 046	01 ①	02 ②	03 ④
DAY 047	01 ②	02 ⑤	03 ④
DAY 048	01 ①	02 ②	03 ⑤
DAY 049	01 ②	02 ⑤	03 ⑤
DAY 050	01 ③	02 ③	03 ③
DAY 051	01 ③	02 ⑤	03 ②
DAY 052	01 ③	02 ①	03 ⑤
DAY 053	01 ②	02 ②	03 ④
DAY 054	01 ①	02 ①	03 ③
DAY 055	01 ①	02 ①	03 ②
DAY 056	01 ③	02 ②	03 ④
DAY 057	01 ③	02 ①	03 ③
DAY 058	01 ②	02 ⑤	03 ④
DAY 059	01 ①	02 ⑤	03 ②
DAY 060	01 ①	02 ①	03 ③
DAY 061	01 ⑤	02 ①	03 ③
DAY 062	01 ①	02 ①	03 ⑤
DAY 063	01 ①	02 ①	03 ⑤
DAY 064	01 ②	02 ②	03 ③
DAY 065	01 ②	02 ④	03 ②
DAY 066	01 ⑤	02 ②	03 ②
DAY 067	01 ①	02 ①	03 ③
DAY 068	01 ⑤	02 ③	03 ④
DAY 069	01 ④	02 ②	03 ⑤
DAY 070	01 ③	02 ④	03 ④
DAY 071	01 ③	02 ②	03 ⑤
DAY 072	01 ①	02 ②	03 ③
DAY 073	01 ⑤	02 ①	03 ⑤
DAY 074	01 ②	02 ①	03 ④
DAY 075	01 ①	02 ②	03 ③
DAY 076	01 ③	02 ④	03 ③
DAY 077	01 ④	02 ①	03 ④
DAY 078	01 ⑤	02 ③	03 ②
DAY 079	01 ①	02 ②	03 ⑤
DAY 080	01 ①	02 ②	03 ⑤
DAY 081	01 ④	02 ①	03 ③
DAY 082	01 ⑤	02 ①	03 ④
DAY 083	01 ⑤	02 ①	03 ③
DAY 084	01 ④	02 ④	03 ③
DAY 085	01 ②	02 ③	03 ④
DAY 086	01 ④	02 ⑤	03 ⑤
DAY 087	01 ①	02 ①	03 ②
DAY 088	01 ①	02 ②	03 ④
DAY 089	01 ①	02 ②	03 ④
DAY 090	01 ⑤	02 ①	03 ②
DAY 091	01 ⑤	02 ②	03 ⑤
DAY 092	01 ①	02 ④	03 ③
DAY 093	01 ①	02 ⑤	03 ①
DAY 094	01 ④	02 ②	03 ④
DAY 095	01 ①	02 ①	03 ④
DAY 096	01 ⑤	02 ①	03 ④
DAY 097	01 ①	02 ④	03 ③
DAY 098	01 ④	02 ②	03 ④
DAY 099	01 ①	02 ①	03 ④
DAY 100	01 ①	02 ②	03 ⑤
부록: 초고난도 킬러 문항	01 ②	02 ①	03 ⑤
	04 ⑤	05 ②	06 ③
	07 ④	08 ②	09 ②
	10 ④	11 ①	12 ⑤
	13 ⑤		

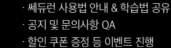

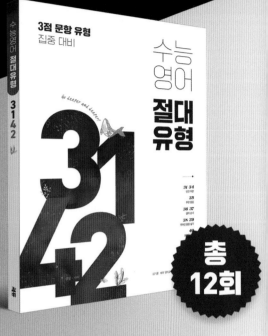

쎄듀 초·중등 커리큘럼

예비초 / 초1 / 초2 / 초3 / 초4 / 초5 / 초6

구문
- 신간 천일문 365 일력 | 초1-3 | 교육부 지정 초등 필수 영어 문장
- 초등코치 천일문 SENTENCE 1001개 통문장 암기로 완성하는 초등 영어의 기초

문법
- 초등코치 천일문 GRAMMAR 1001개 예문으로 배우는 초등 영문법
- 왓츠 Grammar Start (초등 기초 영문법) / Plus (초등 영문법 마무리)

독해
- 왓츠 리딩 70 / 80 / 90 / 100 A / B 쉽고 재미있게 완성되는 영어 독해력

어휘
- 초등코치 천일문 VOCA&STORY 1001개의 초등 필수 어휘와 짧은 스토리
- 패턴으로 말하는 초등 필수 영단어 1 / 2 문장 패턴으로 완성하는 초등 필수 영단어

ELT
- Oh! My PHONICS 1 / 2 / 3 / 4 유·초등학생을 위한 첫 영어 파닉스
- Oh! My SPEAKING 1 / 2 / 3 / 4 / 5 / 6 핵심 문장 패턴으로 더욱 쉬운 영어 말하기
- Oh! My GRAMMAR 1 / 2 / 3 쓰기로 완성하는 첫 초등 영문법

예비중 / 중1 / 중2 / 중3

구문
- 천일문 STARTER 1 / 2 중등 필수 구문 & 문법 총정리

문법
- 천일문 GRAMMAR LEVEL 1 / 2 / 3 예문 중심 문법 기본서
- GRAMMAR Q Starter 1, 2 / Intermediate 1, 2 / Advanced 1, 2 학기별 문법 기본서
- 잘 풀리는 영문법 1 / 2 / 3 문제 중심 문법 적용서
- GRAMMAR PIC 1 / 2 / 3 / 4 이해가 쉬운 도식화된 문법서
- 1센치 영문법 1권으로 핵심 문법 정리

문법+어법
- 첫단추 BASIC 문법·어법편 1 / 2 문법·어법의 기초

문법+쓰기
- EGU 영단어&품사 / 문장 형식 / 동사 써먹기 / 문법 써먹기 / 구문 써먹기 서술형 기초 세우기와 문법 다지기
- 올씀 1 기본 문장 PATTERN 내신 서술형 기본 문장 학습

쓰기
- 거침없이 Writing LEVEL 1 / 2 / 3 중등 교과서 내신 기출 서술형
- 중학 영어 쓰작 1 / 2 / 3 중등 교과서 패턴 드릴 서술형

어휘
- 신간 천일문 VOCA 중등 스타트/필수/마스터 2800개 중등 3개년 필수 어휘
- 어휘끝 중학 필수편 중학 필수어휘 1000개
- 어휘끝 중학 마스터편 고난도 중학어휘 +고등기초 어휘 1000개

독해
- Reading Relay Starter 1, 2 / Challenger 1, 2 / Master 1, 2 타교과 연계 배경 지식 독해
- READING Q Starter 1, 2 / Intermediate 1, 2 / Advanced 1, 2 예측/추론/요약 사고력 독해

독해전략
- 리딩 플랫폼 1 / 2 / 3 논픽션 지문 독해

독해유형
- Reading 16 LEVEL 1 / 2 / 3 수능 유형 맛보기 + 내신 대비
- 첫단추 BASIC 독해편 1 / 2 수능 유형 독해 입문

듣기
- Listening Q 유형편 / 1 / 2 / 3 유형별 듣기 전략 및 실전 대비
- 쎄듀 빠르게 중학영어듣기 모의고사 1 / 2 / 3 교육청 듣기평가 대비

기출 프리미엄

Premium

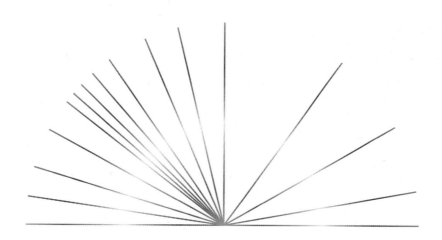

정답 및 해설

01 빈칸 초반 (24학년도 대수능 34번 | 정답률 24%) ④

구문분석 & 직독직해

교통 교통을 바라보는 개인적인 방식

도로를 이용하는 모두가 자신을 교통 전문가라 여김. *<view A as B>: A를 B로 여기다

[1] *Everyone* [who drives, walks, or swipes a transit card / in a city] / views herself / as a transportation expert / from *the moment* [(when) she walks out the front door].

(S 주격 관계대명사 V O 전치사(~로(서)) 관계부사 생략 S′ V′)

모든 사람은 [운전하거나 걷거나 교통 카드를 단말기에 대는 / 도시에서] / 자신을 여긴다 / 교통 전문가로 / 순간부터 [현관문을 나서는]

↳ **도입:** 운전하거나 걷거나 대중교통을 이용하는 모든 사람은 자신을 교통 전문가로 여김.

주제문

[2] And how she views the street **tracks pretty closely / with how she gets around.**

(S(명사절) V with의 O(명사절))

그리고 그 사람이 도로를 바라보는 방식은 매우 밀접하게 일치한다 / 그 사람이 돌아다니는 방식과

↳ **원인:** 사람은 개인의 이동 방식에 따라 도로를 바라봄 → 교통에 대해 서로 의견이 다름.

[3] That's // (the reason) why we find so many well-intentioned and civic-minded citizens / arguing past one another.

(That (= 앞 문장) S V 선행사 생략 is의 C(명사절) 관계부사 S′ V′ O′ C′(현재분사구))

그것이 ~이다 // 우리가 선의의 공중도덕심이 있는 매우 많은 시민들이 (~하는 것을) 보는 이유 / 서로 다른 목적으로 언쟁하는 것을

[4] At neighborhood meetings (in school auditoriums), / and in back rooms (at libraries and churches), / local residents (across the nation) / gather / for often-contentious discussions (about *transportation proposals* [that would change a city's streets]).

(전치사구 병렬 S(복수) V(복수) 주격 관계대명사)

주민 회의에서 (학교 강당에서 열리는) / 그리고 밀실에서 (도서관과 교회의) /

지역 주민들이 (전국의) / 모인다 / 흔히 논쟁적인 토론을 위해 (교통 계획에 대하여 [도시의 도로를 바꿀])

↳ **부연 설명(결과):** 선량한 시민들도 교통에 대해서는 언쟁하며, 전국의 지역 주민들은 모여 교통 계획에 대해 논쟁적인 토론을 함.

[5] And like all politics, / all transportation is local and intensely personal. 교통은 지역적이고 개인적인 문제임.

(전치사(~와 마찬가지로) S V C)

그리고 모든 정치와 마찬가지로 / 모든 교통은 지역적이고 몹시 개인적이다

↳ **세부 사항:** 교통은 지역적이고 몹시 개인적인 문제임.

[6] *A transit project* [that could speed travel (for tens of thousands of people)] / can be stopped / by objections (to the loss of a few parking spaces) / or by the simple fear // that the project won't work.

(S 주격 관계대명사 V 전치사구 병렬 =)

교통 프로젝트는 [이동 속도를 높일 수 있는 (수만 명의)] / 중단될 수 있다 /

반대에 의해 (몇 개의 주차 공간 상실에 대한) / 또는 단순한 두려움에 의해 // 프로젝트가 효과가 없을 것이라는

↳ **논거:** 다수에게 이득이 되는 교통 프로젝트도 일부의 반대에 의해 중단될 수 있음.

[7] It's not a challenge (of the data or the traffic engineering or the planning).

(It (= A transit project) S V C)

그것(교통 프로젝트)은 문제가 아니다 (데이터나 교통 공학 또는 계획의)

[8] Public debates (about streets) / are typically rooted / in emotional assumptions (about how a change will affect / a person's commute, ability to park, belief about what is safe and what isn't (safe), or the bottom line of a local business).

(S V about의 O(명사절) 의문사 S′ V′ O′₁ O′₂ O′₃ O′₄)

도로에 대한 토론은 개인의 감정적인 추정에 뿌리를 둠.

공개 토론은 (도로에 대한) / 보통 뿌리 내려져 있다 / 감정적인 추정에

(변화가 어떤 영향을 미칠지에 대한 / 개인의 통근, 주차 능력, 안전한 것과 안전하지 않은 것에 대한 생각, 또는 지역 산업의 순익에)

↳ **부연 설명:** 도로에 대한 공개 토론은 변화가 개인과 지역의 편익에 미치는 영향에 대한 감정적인 추정에 기반함.

해석

[1]도시에서 운전하거나 걷거나 교통 카드를 단말기에 대는 모든 사람은 현관문을 나서는 순간부터 자신을 교통 전문가로 여긴다. [2]그리고 그 사람이 도로를 바라보는 방식은 그 사람이 돌아다니는 방식과 매우 밀접하게 일치한다.(▶ 사람들은 자신이 교통을 이용하는 개인적인 방식으로 교통을 생각한다는 의미) [3]그것이 우리가 선의의 공중도덕심이 있는 매우 많은 시민들이 서로 다른 목적으로 언쟁하는 것을 보는 이유이다. [4]학교 강당에서 열리는 주민 회의에서, 그리고 도서관과 교회의 밀실에서, 전국의 지역 주민들이 도시의 도로를 바꿀 교통 계획에 대하여 흔히 논쟁적인 토론을 위해 모인다. [5]그리고 모든 정치와 마찬가지로, 모든 교통은 지역적이고 몹시 개인적이다. [6]수만 명의 이동 속도를 높일 수 있는 교통 프로젝트는 몇 개의 주차 공간 상실에 대한 반대나 프로젝트가 효과가 없을 것이라는 단순한 두려움에 의해 중단될 수 있다. [7]그것(교통 프로젝트)은 데이터나 교통 공학 또는 계획의 문제가 아니다. [8]도로에 대한 공개 토론은 보통 변화가 개인의 통근, 주차 능력, 안전한 것과 안전하지 않은 것에 대한 생각, 또는 지역 산업의 순익에 어떤 영향을 미칠지에 대한 감정적인 추정에 뿌리 내려져 있다.

어휘

- transit 교통 (체계); 운송
- track with ~와 일치하다
- get around 돌아다니다
- well-intentioned 선의의
- civic-minded 공중도덕심이 있는, 공공시민의 의식이 있는
- auditorium 강당; 객석, 청중석
- proposal 계획; 제안; 신청
- intensely 몹시, 극도로; 열심히
- objection 반대; 이의
- engineering 공학 (기술)
- debate 토론(하다); 논쟁
- assumption 추정, 가정; 인수
- bottom line 순익; 핵심
- [선택지] rely on ~에 의존하다
- heavily 크게, 몹시; 무겁게
- policy 정책
- arise 발생하다, 생기다
- independently of ~와 관계없이
- tie in with ~와 결부되다
- firmly 단단히, 굳게; 단호하게

정답 가이드

빈칸 문장으로 보아 그녀(도로 이용자)가 도로를 바라보는 방식이 어떠하다는 것인지를 추론해야 한다. 앞에서 도로를 이용하는 모든 사람들은 자신을 교통 전문가로 여긴다고 했고 이들이 하는 논쟁은 지역적이고 개인적이며 감정적인 추정에 뿌리를 내리고 있다고 했다. 이를 통해 사람들이 교통을 자신을 중심으로 생각한다는 것을 알 수 있으므로, 빈칸에 들어갈 말로 가장 적절한 것은 ④ 'tracks pretty closely with how she gets around(그 사람이 돌아다니는 방식과 매우 밀접하게 일치한다)'이다.

The 핵심 ★ how she gets around가 '개인적인 방식'을 의미함을 파악할 수 있어야 한다.

오답 클리닉

① relies heavily on how others see her city's streets (19%)
다른 사람이 그 사람의 도시 도로를 어떻게 보느냐에 크게 의존한다
교통에 관한 생각은 개인적이고 감정적이라고 했으므로 다른 사람이 어떻게 보느냐에 의존하는 것이 아님.

② updates itself with each new public transit policy (27%)
각각의 새로운 대중교통 정책에 맞춰 자체를 업데이트한다
대중교통 정책에 따르는 것이 아니고 개인의 편익에 따라 논쟁한다고 했으므로 틀림.

③ arises independently of the streets she travels on (7%)
그 사람이 이동하는 도로와 관계없이 발생한다
도로를 이용하는 모든 사람들이 자신을 교통 전문가로 여긴다고 했으므로 개인이 이용하는 도로와 밀접하게 관련될 것임.

⑤ ties firmly in with how her city operates (23%)
그 사람의 도시가 작동하는 방식과 단단히 결부되어 있다
도시가 작동하는 방식은 언급되지 않은 내용임.

02 + 빈칸 초반 〈24학년도 9월 모평 34번 | 정답률 24%〉 ⑤

구문분석 & 직독직해

예술 사진의 대량 생산이 가져온 변화

[1]Prior to photography, / **places did not travel well**.
~이전에 / S / V
사진이 나오기 전에 / 장소들은 잘 이동하지 않았다

⊶ 사진이 나오기 전에 그림으로 장소를 옮기는 것은 어려웠음.

[2]While painters have always lifted particular places / out of their 'dwelling' / [and] (have) transported them elsewhere, //
부사절 접속사(~하지만) / V'₁ / O'₁ / V'₂ / O'₂ ↳ (= particular places)
화가들이 항상 특정한 장소를 들어 올려왔지만 / 그것의 '거주지'에서 / 그리고 그것(특정한 장소)을 다른 곳으로 옮겨 (왔지만) //

paintings were time-consuming to produce, / relatively difficult to transport / [and] one-of-a-kind.
S / V / C₁ 형용사 time-consuming 수식 / C₂ 형용사 difficult 수식 / C₃
그림은 제작하는 데 많은 시간이 걸렸다 / 상대적으로 운반하기 어려웠다 / 그리고 유일무이했다

↳ **도입(사진이 나오기 전):** 그림으로 특정한 장소를 옮기는 데에는 제약이 있었음.

[3]The multiplication (of photographs) / especially took place / with the introduction of *the half-tone plate* (in the 1880s)
S / V
증가는 (사진의) / 특히 일어났다 / 망판의 도입으로 (1880년대)

[that made possible the mechanical reproduction (of photographs) / in newspapers, periodicals, books and advertisements].
주격 관계대명사 V' / C' / O' / ★<make+O+C>에서 목적어와 보어가 도치된 구조
[기계적인 복제를 가능하게 한 (사진의) / 신문, 정기 간행물, 책 그리고 광고에서]

↳ **세부 사항(사진이 나온 후):** 사진의 복제를 가능하게 하는 망판의 도입으로 사진이 증가함.

★<offer+IO+DO(IO에게 DO를 제공하다)>의 수동형

[4]Photography became coupled / to consumer capitalism // [and] the globe was now offered / 'in limitless quantities, / *figures, landscapes, events* [which had not previously been utilised [either] at all, / [or] only as pictures for one customer]'.
S₁ / V₁ / C / S₂(←IO) / V₂ / O(←DO) / 주격 관계대명사 / ★<(not) at all>: 전혀 ~ 않다
사진은 결합하게 되었다 / 소비 자본주의와 // 그리고 이제 세계는 제공받았다 / '무제한의 양으로 / 인물, 풍경, 사건들을 [이전에는 전혀 이용되지 않았거나 / 오직 한 명의 고객을 위한 그림으로만 이용되었던]'

[5]With capitalism's arrangement of the world / as a 'department store', / 'the proliferation and circulation (of representations) ... / achieved a spectacular and virtually inescapable global magnitude'.
S / (= photographs) / V / O
자본주의가 세계를 배열함에 따라 / '백화점'으로 / '확산과 유통은 (표현물(사진)의) / 극적이고 사실상 피할 수 없는 세계적 규모를 달성했다'

↳ **부연 설명:** 자본주의와 함께 사진이 세계적 규모로 확산되고 유통됨.

해석

[1]사진이 나오기 전에 장소들은 잘 이동하지 않았다. [2]화가들이 항상 특정한 장소를 그것의 '거주지'에서 들어 올려 다른 곳으로 옮겨왔지만, 그림은 제작하는 데 많은 시간이 걸렸고, 상대적으로 운반하기 어려웠고, 유일무이했다. [3]사진의 증가는 특히 신문, 정기 간행물, 책 그리고 광고에서 사진의 기계적인 복제를 가능하게 한 1880년대 망판의 도입으로 일어났다. [4]사진은 소비 자본주의와 결합하게 되었고 이제 세계는 '이전에는 전혀 이용되지 않았거나 오직 한 명의 고객을 위한 그림으로만 이용되었던 인물, 풍경, 사건들을 무제한의 양으로' 제공받았다. [5]자본주의가 세계를 '백화점'으로 배열함에 따라, '표현물(사진)의 확산과 유통은 ... 극적이고 사실상 피할 수 없는 세계적 규모를 달성했다'. [6]점차 사진은 세계를 가시적이고, 미적이며, 얻고 싶게 만드는 값싼 대량 생산품이 되었다.(▶ 세계를 백화점으로 여기는 자본주의 환경에서 물건을 사고파는 데 사진이 더 널리 쓰였다는 의미) [7]경험은 그것을 저렴한 이미지로 바꿈으로써 '대중화'되었다. [8]가볍고 작고 대량생산된 사진은 장소의 시공간적 이동을 위한 역동적인 수단이 되었다.

어휘

dwelling 거주(지), 사는 집
time-consuming (많은) 시간이 걸리는
one-of-a-kind 유일한; 특별한
multiplication 증가, 증식
half-tone plate 망판(網版) ((신문의 사진과 같이 미세한 점으로 사진을 나타내는 인쇄용 판))
reproduction 복제; 생식, 번식
periodical 정기 간행물
couple 결합[연결]하다; 두 사람[개]
capitalism 자본주의
utilise[utilize] 이용[활용]하다

[6]Gradually / photographs became *cheap mass-produced objects* [that made the world visible, aesthetic and desirable].

S V C 주격 관계대명사 V′ O′ C′

점차 / 사진은 값싼 대량 생산품이 되었다 [세계를 가시적이고, 미적이며, 얻고 싶게 만드는]

[7]Experiences were 'democratised' / by translating them / into cheap images.

S V <by v-ing>: v함으로써 (= experiences)

경험은 '대중화'되었다 / 그것(경험)을 바꿈으로써 / 저렴한 이미지로

[8]Light, small and mass-produced photographs / became dynamic vehicles (for the spatiotemporal circulation (of places)). 사진의 확산으로 장소의 시공간적 이동이 쉬워짐.

S V C

가볍고 작고 대량생산된 사진은 / 역동적인 수단이 되었다 (시공간적 이동을 위한 (장소의))

↳ **결과:** 사진을 통한 경험이 대중화되고 사진은 장소의 시공간적 이동의 수단이 됨.

arrangement 배열, 정리; 준비; 합의
circulation 유통; 이동; 순환
representation 표현[묘사](한 것); 대표
spectacular 극적인; 장관을 이루는
virtually 사실상; 가상으로
democratise[democratize] 대중화하다; 민주화하다
dynamic 역동적인; 역학
vehicle 수단; 차량, 탈것
spatiotemporal 시공간적인
[선택지] hold up a mirror to A A를 여실히 보여주다, A를 그대로 반영하다

정답 가이드

빈칸 문장과 선택지로 보아, 사진이 나오기 전인 과거에는 '무엇이 어떠했는지'를 찾아야 한다. 바로 뒤에 나오는 문장은 화가들과 그림을 서술하므로, 사진이 나오기 전인 과거는 '그림을 그리던 시대'를 말하는 것임을 알 수 있다. 즉 화가들은 특정 장소를 그림에 담을 수는 있었지만 시간이 많이 걸리고 운반도 (사진에 비해) 어려웠으며, 그림은 하나밖에 존재할 수 없는 것이었다. 이어서 사진에는 그림의 이 같은 제약이 없었음을 설명하는 내용이 전개된다. 따라서, 빈칸에는 '그림'과 관련하여 글에서 서술된 두 번째 문장에 해당하는 내용이 들어가야 하며, 제작, 운반 등의 이유로 특정한 장소를 많은 사람들에게 보여주기 힘들었다는 내용을 나타내는 ⑤ 'places did not travel well(장소들이 잘 이동하지 않았다)'이 가장 적절하다. travel은 '여행하다'란 의미 외에 '이동하다'라는 의미로도 많이 쓰이며, 여기서는 '그림에 담겨 다른 곳으로 이동하다'를 의미한다.

오답 클리닉

① paintings alone connected with nature (18%)
그림만이 자연과 연관되었다
자연과의 연관성에 관한 내용이 아님.

② painting was the major form of art (23%)
그림은 예술의 주요한 형식이었다
그림이 예술의 주요한 형식이었는지는 언급되지 않음.

③ art held up a mirror to the world (22%)
예술이 세상을 여실히 보여주었다
세상을 보여준 것은 그림과 사진 둘 다에 해당하는데, 그림에는 제약이 따랐다고 했으므로 정답이 될 수 없음.

④ desire for travel was not strong (12%)
이동에 대한 욕구가 강하지 않았다
이동의 욕구가 강했는지는 언급되지 않음.

03 + 빈칸 초반 〈23학년도 대수능 33번 | 정답률 47%〉 ①

구문분석 & 직독직해

생물 꿀벌의 상호 작용을 통한 노동력 조절

★<refer to A as B(A를 B라고 부르다)>의 수동형

[1]The entrance (to a honeybee colony), / often referred to as the dancefloor, / is a market place (for information (about the state of the colony and the environment outside the hive)).

S 분사구문(= and it is often referred ~) V C

입구는 (꿀벌 군집의) / 흔히 댄스 플로어라고 불리는 / 시장이다 (정보를 얻기 위한 (군집의 상태와 벌집 밖의 환경에 관한))

↳ **도입:** 벌집 입구(댄스 플로어)에서 정보가 교환됨.

주제문

★<provide A with B>: A에게 B를 제공하다

[2]Studying interactions on the dancefloor provides us / with a number of illustrative examples (of how *individuals* (changing their own behavior / in response to local information) / allow the colony to regulate its workforce).

S(동명사구) V(단수) O ★<allow+O+to-v>: O가 v하게 하다

의문사 S′ (= the colony's) 현재분사구 V′ O′ C′

댄스 플로어에서의 상호 작용을 연구하는 것은 우리에게 제공한다 / 많은 예증이 되는 예들을
(어떻게 개체들이 (자신들의 행동을 바꾸는 / 지엽적인 정보에 반응하여) / 군집이 그것(군집)의 노동력을 조절하게 하는지에 대한)

↳ 벌들은 지엽적인 정보에 따라 행동을 달리해 군집의 노동력을 조절함.

[3]For example, / upon returning to their hive / *honeybees* [that have collected water] / search out a receiver bee / to unload their water / to within the hive.

<(up)on v-ing>: v하자마자 S(복수) 주격 관계대명사

V(복수) O 목적(~하기 위해)

예를 들어 / 자신들의 벌집으로 돌아오자마자 / 꿀벌들은 [물을 가져온] /
(물을) 받을 벌을 찾아낸다 / 자신들의 물을 내리기 위해 / 벌집 안으로

해석

[1]흔히 댄스 플로어라고 불리는 꿀벌 군집의 입구는 군집의 상태와 벌집 밖의 환경에 관한 정보를 얻기 위한 시장이다. [2]댄스 플로어에서의 상호 작용을 연구하는 것은 지엽적인 정보에 반응하여 자신들의 행동을 바꾸는 개체들이 어떻게 군집이 군집의 노동력을 조절하게 하는지에 대한 많은 예증이 되는 예들을 우리에게 제공한다. [3]예를 들어 자신들의 벌집으로 돌아오자마자 물을 가져온 꿀벌들은 자신들의 물을 벌집 안으로 내리기 위해 (물을) 받을 벌을 찾아낸다. [4]만약 이 찾는 시간이 짧으면, 그 돌아오는 벌은 수원지로 (데려갈) 다른 벌들을 모집하기 위해 8자 춤을 출 가능성이 더 크다. [5]반대로 이 찾는 시간이 길면, 그 벌은 물을 가져오는 것을 그만둘 가능성이 더 크다. [6](물을) 받는 벌들은 자신들을 위해서든 다른 벌들과 애벌레들에게 전해주기 위해서든 그들이 물을 필요로 하는 경우에 물을 받을 것이기 때문에, 이러한 물을 내리는 시간은 군집의 전반적인 물에 대한 수요와 상관관계가 있다. [7]따라서 (시간이 늘어나든 혹은 줄어들든 간에) 물을 내리는 시간에 대한 개별적인 물 조달자의 반응은 군집의 수요에 반응하여 물 수집(량)을 조절한다.

*<be more likely to-v>: v할 가능성이 더 크다

[4]If this search time is short // then the returning bee is more likely to perform a waggle dance / to recruit others / to the water source. 🔑 물을 받을 벌을 빨리 찾으면(수요↑) 물을 가지러 갈 다른 벌들을 모집할 것임.

부사절 접속사(조건) / S / V / C / 목적(~하기 위해)

만약 이 찾는 시간이 짧으면 // 그러면 그 돌아오는 벌은 8자 춤을 출 가능성이 더 크다 / (데려갈) 다른 벌들을 모집하기 위해 / 수원지로

🔑 물을 받을 벌을 늦게 찾으면(수요↓) 물을 가지러 가는 것을 그만둘 것임.

[5]Conversely, / if this search time is long // then the bee is more likely to give up / collecting water.

부사절 접속사(조건) / S / V / C / to give up의 O(동명사구)

반대로 / 이 찾는 시간이 길면 // 그러면 그 벌은 그만둘 가능성이 더 크다 / 물을 가져오는 것을

↳ **예:** 가져온 물을 받을 벌을 탐색하는 시간의 길이에 따라 물을 더 가져오려고 하거나 그만둘 것임.

[6]Since receiver bees will only accept water // if they require it, / either for themselves or to pass on to other bees and brood, //

부사절 접속사(~ 때문에) S′ / V′ / O′ / 부사절 접속사(조건) / (= water) / <either A or B>: A든지 B든지

(물을) 받는 벌들은 오직 물을 받을 것이기 때문에 // 그들이 그것(물)을 필요로 하는 경우에 / 자신들을 위해서든 다른 벌들과 애벌레들에게 전해주기 위해서든 //

this unloading time is correlated / with the colony's overall need of water.

S / V

이러한 물을 내리는 시간은 상관관계가 있다 / 군집의 전반적인 물에 대한 수요와

↳ **물 내리는 시간과 물 수요의 상관관계:** 수요가 많으면 물을 빨리 받을 것이고 아니면 늦게 받을 것임.

[7]Thus / the individual water forager's response (to unloading time (up or down)) / regulates water collection / in response to the colony's need. 🔑 꿀벌은 군집의 물 수요에 따라 물 수집량, 즉 물 조달자의 수를 조절함.

S / V / O

따라서 / 개별적인 물 조달자의 반응은 (물을 내리는 시간에 대한 (늘어나든 혹은 줄어들든 간에)) / 물 수집(량)을 조절한다 / 군집의 수요에 반응하여

↳ **결론:** 물을 가져오는 벌은 군집의 물 수요에 따라 반응을 달리해 수집량을 조절함.

어휘

entrance 입구; 입장
colony 군집; 식민지
dancefloor 댄스 플로어, 무도장
hive 벌집
illustrative 예증이 되는
in response to A A에 반응하여
regulate 조절하다; 규제하다
workforce 노동력
unload (짐을) 내리다
waggle dance (8자의) 춤 ((꿀벌이 꽃 등의 방향과 거리를 동료에게 알리는 동작))
recruit 모집하다
conversely 반대로, 역으로
pass on to A A에게 전하다
correlate 상관관계[연관성]가 있다
overall 전반적인
[선택지] workload 작업량
respective 각자의
acquire 습득하다; 획득하다

정답 가이드

빈칸 문장을 요약하면 지엽적인 정보에 따라 행동을 바꾸는 개체들이 어떻게 '~하는지'를 추론해야 한다. 빈칸 문장 뒤에 이어지는 예에서 물을 가져온 꿀벌이 물을 받을 벌을 찾아내는 시간의 길이(지엽적인 정보)로 군집의 물 수요를 파악해 물을 가져올 다른 벌을 모집하거나 물을 가져오기를 그만둔다고 했다. 이는 꿀벌이 상호 작용을 통해 얻는 정보로 '물을 가져올 조달자의 수를 조절하는' 예로 볼 수 있으므로 빈칸에 들어갈 말로 가장 적절한 것은 ① 'allow the colony to regulate its workforce(군집이 군집의 노동력을 조절하게 한다)'이다.

오답 클리닉

② search for water sources by measuring distance (24%)
거리를 측정하여 수원지를 찾는다
water source를 이용한 오답. 거리를 측정한다는 내용은 없음.

③ decrease the colony's workload when necessary (16%)
필요할 때 군집의 작업량을 줄인다
물을 전달하는 시간의 길이에 따라 작업량을 늘리기도 줄이기도 한다고 했으므로 줄이는 것만 언급한 것은 적절치 않음.

④ divide tasks according to their respective talents (8%)
자신들 각자의 재능에 따라 일을 나눈다
재능에 따라서 일을 나눈다는 내용은 없음.

⑤ train workers to acquire basic communication patterns (5%)
기본적인 의사소통 패턴을 습득하도록 일벌들을 훈련시킨다
꿀벌에게 의사소통 패턴을 훈련시킨다는 내용은 없음.

01 빈칸 초반 〈22학년도 대수능 33번 | 정답률 51%〉 ①

구문분석 & 직독직해

사회 공유지 문제의 해결 방안

주제문

[1]Elinor Ostrom found // that there are *several factors* (critical to bringing about stable institutional solutions / to the problem of the commons).

(found의 O(명사절) / S V 명사절 접속사 V′ S′)

Elinor Ostrom은 알게 되었다 // 몇몇 요인이 있다는 것을 (안정적인 제도적 해결책을 가져오는 데 중대한 / 공유지 문제에 대한)

[2]She pointed out, / for instance, // that *the actors* (affected by the rules (for the use and care of resources)) / must have the right (to **participate in decisions (to change the rules)**).

(pointed out의 O(명사절) / S V 명사절 접속사 S′ V′ O′)

그녀는 지적했다 / 예를 들어 // 행위자들이 (규칙의 영향을 받는 (자원의 이용 및 관리에 대한)) / 권리를 가져야 한다고 (결정에 참여할 (규칙을 변경하는))

↳ **세부 사항 1:** 공유지 문제를 해결하려면 이용 당사자들이 규칙을 변경하는 결정에 참여해야 함.

공유지 이용자의 감시 및 통제는 이용자 또는 모든 이용자에게 위임받은 사람에 의한 것이어야 함 → 이용자의 결정 권한을 중시함.

[3]For that reason, / *the people* [who monitor and control the behavior of users] / should also be users / and/or (should) have been given a mandate / by all users.

(S 주격 관계대명사 V₁ C V₂ DO)

그러한 이유로 / 사람들은 [이용자들의 행동을 감시하고 통제하는] / 또한 이용자들이어야 한다 / 그리고/또는 위임을 받았어야 한다 / 모든 이용자들에 의해

↳ **부연 설명:** 공유지 이용자를 감시하고 통제하는 사람은 이용 당사자들이거나 모든 이용자들에게 위임을 받은 사람이어야 함.

[4]This is a significant insight, // as it shows // that prospects are poor (for *a centrally directed solution* (to the problem of the commons) (coming from a state power)) / in comparison with *a local solution* [for which users assume personal responsibility].

((= 앞 문장) S V C 부사절 접속사(~ 때문에) shows의 O(명사절) 명사절 접속사 S″ V″ C″ 현재분사구 전치사+관계대명사 S′ V′ O′)

이것은 중요한 통찰이다 // 그것이 보여주기 때문이다 // 전망이 좋지 않다는 것을 (중앙 통제된 해결책의 (공유지 문제에 대한) (국가 권력에서 나오는)) / 지역적인 해결책에 비해서 [이용자들이 개인적인 책임을 지는]

↳ 공유지 문제에 대해서는 국가에 의한 중앙 통제적 해결책보다 이용자 개인이 책임을 지는 지역적 해결책이 더 나음.

민주적 의사 결정 과정은 모든 이용자들의 참여를 중시함.

[5]Ostrom also emphasizes / the importance (of democratic decision processes) / and that all users must be given access / to local forums (for solving problems and conflicts (among themselves)).

(S V O₁(명사구) O₂(명사절))

Ostrom은 또한 강조한다 / 중요성을 (민주적 의사 결정 과정의) / 그리고 모든 이용자에게 참가할 권리가 주어져야 한다는 것을 / 지역 포럼에 (문제와 갈등을 해결하기 위한 (그들 사이의))

↳ **세부 사항 2:** 민주적 의사 결정 과정이 중요함.

이용자가 자신들이 준수해야 할 규칙을 직접 만듦.

[6]Political institutions (at central, regional, and local levels) / must allow users / to devise their own regulations / and (to) independently ensure observance.

(S V O C₁ C₂ ★<allow+O+to-v>: O가 v하도록 하다)

정치 기관들은 (중앙, 지방 및 지역 차원의) / 이용자들이 (~하도록) 해야 한다 / 자체 규정을 고안하도록 / 그리고 독립적으로 준수할 수 있도록

↳ **부연 설명:** 이용자가 자체 규칙을 고안하고 준수할 수 있도록 해야 함.

해석

[1]Elinor Ostrom은 공유지 문제에 대한 안정적인 제도적 해결책을 가져오는 데 중대한 몇몇 요인이 있다는 것을 알게 되었다. [2]예를 들어, 그녀는 자원의 이용 및 관리에 대한 규칙의 영향을 받는 행위자들이 규칙을 변경하는 결정에 참여할 권리를 가져야 한다고 지적했다. [3]그러한 이유로 이용자들의 행동을 감시하고 통제하는 사람들은 또한 이용자들이고/이용자이거나 모든 이용자들에 의해 위임을 받았어야 한다. [4]이것은 중요한 통찰인데, 이용자들이 개인적인 책임을 지는 지역적인 해결책에 비해 국가 권력에서 나오는 공유지 문제에 대한 중앙 통제된 해결책의 전망이 좋지 않다는 것을 그것이 보여주기 때문이다. [5]Ostrom은 또한 민주적 의사 결정 과정의 중요성과 모든 이용자에게 그들 사이의 문제와 갈등을 해결하기 위한 지역 포럼에 참가할 권리가 주어져야 한다는 것을 강조한다. [6]중앙, 지방 및 지역 차원의 정치 기관들은 이용자들이 자체 규정을 고안하고 독립적으로 준수할 수 있도록 해야 한다.

어휘

critical 중대한, 결정적인; 비판적인
bring about ~을 가져오다[초래하다]
stable 안정적인; 마구간
institutional 제도적인
cf. institution 기관, 협회
point out ~을 지적하다
monitor 감시하다; 관찰하다
insight 통찰(력)
prospect 전망; 가망, 가능성
directed 통제된, 규제된
in comparison with ~에 비해서
assume (책임 등을) 지다; 추정하다
democratic 민주적인
access 참가[이용]할 권리; 접근 (방법)
regional 지방[지역]의
devise 고안하다, 발명하다
regulation 규정, 규칙; 규제, 단속
observance (법률·관례의) 준수; 관찰
[선택지] ownership 소유(권)
maximize 최대화하다
communal 공동의
merit 공로; 장점; 가치

⊕ 공유지(commons): 특정한 개인의 소유가 아닌, 국가 또는 공공단체에 의하여 소유되는 토지. 여기서는 바다 속 물고기, 문화재, 공동 목초지 등의 공유 자원을 뜻하며, 사람들의 남용으로 쉽게 고갈되는 문제점을 '공유지의 비극'이라고 함.

정답 가이드

예시 문장에 빈칸이 있으므로 빈칸의 내용은 주제문을 잘 뒷받침하는 것이어야 한다. 첫 문장과 빈칸 문장의 내용은 공유지 문제에 대한 제도적 해결책을 세울 때 중요한 몇 가지 요소의 한 예로 자원(공유지)의 사용 규칙에 영향받는 행위자들이 '어떤' 권리를 가져야 한다고 주장하는 것이다. 이어지는 내용은 이용자들이 직접 감시·통제하는 것, 민주적 의사 결정, 지역 포럼에 참가할 권리, 자체 규정을 고안하고 준수할 수 있게 해야 한다는 것들이므로 이들을 종합하면, 공유지 이용자들이 가져야 할 권리로 가장 적절한 것은 ① 'participate in decisions to change the rules(규칙을 변경하는 결정에 참여하다)'이다.

오답 클리닉

② claim individual ownership of the resources (27%)
자원에 대한 개인의 소유권을 주장하다
이용자들이 공유지를 개인적으로 소유할 권리에 대한 내용이 아님.

③ use those resources to maximize their profits (5%)
자신의 이익을 최대화하기 위해 그 자원을 이용하다
개인의 이익을 추구하기 위해 자원을 이용한다는 내용은 없음.

④ demand free access to the communal resources (11%)
공동 자원에 대한 자유로운 접근권을 요구하다
이용자들이 규칙을 만들고 준수하도록 해야 한다고 했으므로 자유로운 접근권은 적절하지 않음.

⑤ request proper distribution based on their merits (6%)
자신의 공로를 바탕으로 적당한 분배를 요청하다
공유지의 분배 기준에 관한 내용이 아님.

02 + 빈칸 초반 (22학년도 대수능 32번 | 정답률 48%) ⑤

구문분석 & 직독직해

미디어 현대 뉴스의 대중적인 구성 방식과 장단점

주제문

★<not only A but (also) B>: A뿐만 아니라 B도

[1]News, / (especially in its televised form), / is constituted / [not only] by its choice of topics and stories / [but] by its **verbal and visual idioms or modes of address.**

(S / 전치사구 삽입 / V / 전치사구 병렬 / 전치사구 병렬)

뉴스는 / (특히 텔레비전으로 방송되는 형태) / 구성된다 / 그것의 주제와 이야기 선정에 의해서 뿐만 아니라 / 그것의 언어적, 시각적 표현 양식이나 보도 방식에 의해서도

↳ 텔레비전으로 방송되는 뉴스는 내용뿐만 아니라 언어적, 시각적 표현 양식 및 보도 방식에 의해서도 구성됨.

★<be subject to A>: A의 영향을 받다

[2]Presentational styles have been subject to a tension ([between] an informational-educational purpose [and] the need (to engage us entertainingly)).

(S / V / C)

(뉴스) 표현 방식은 긴장 상태의 영향을 받아 왔다 (정보 제공 및 교육적인 목적과 필요성 사이의 (재미있게 우리의 주의를 끌))

↳ **세부 사항:** 뉴스 보도 방식은 정보 제공/교육과 재미 추구 사이 긴장 상태의 영향을 받음.

[3]While current affairs programmes are often 'serious' in tone / sticking to the 'rules' of balance, //

(부사절 접속사(~인 반면에) S′ V′ C′ / 분사구문(= and they stick ~))

시사 프로그램들은 흔히 어조가 '진지'한 반면에 / 균형이라는 '규칙'을 고수하며 //

more popular programmes adopt / *a friendly, lighter, idiom* [in which we are invited to consider the impact (of particular news items) / from the perspective of the 'average person in the street'].

(S / V / O / 전치사+관계대명사 S′ V′ C′)

더 대중적인 프로그램들은 채택한다 / 친근하고 더 가벼운 표현 양식을 / [우리가 영향을 고려하게 하는 (특정 뉴스 기사의) / '길거리의 보통 사람'의 관점에서]

↳ **예:** 시사 프로그램은 진지한 어조인 반면, 대중적인 프로그램은 친근하고 가벼운 표현 양식을 사용함.

🔑 현대 뉴스는 다양한 언어적, 시각적 표현 방식을 사용함.

[4]Indeed, / contemporary news construction has come to rely / on an increased use (of faster editing tempos / [and] 'flashier' presentational styles (including the use (of logos, sound-bites, rapid visual cuts and the 'star quality' of news readers))).

(S / V / on의 O(명사구) / 전치사(~을 포함하여))

실제로 / 현대의 뉴스 구성은 의존하게 되었다 / 증가된 사용에 (더 빠른 편집 속도의 / 그리고 '더 현란한' 표현 방식의 (이용을 포함하여 (로고, 짧은 어록, 빠른 시각적 컷(장면), 그리고 뉴스 프로 진행자의 '스타 기질'의)))

↳ **부연 설명:** 현대 뉴스는 다양한 언어적, 시각적 표현 방식 사용에 의존함.

해석

[1]뉴스, 특히 텔레비전으로 방송되는 형태는 그것의 주제와 이야기 선정뿐만 아니라 그것의 언어적, 시각적 표현 양식이나 보도 방식에 의해서도 구성된다. [2](뉴스) 표현 방식은 정보 제공 및 교육적인 목적과 재미있게 우리의 주의를 끌 필요성 사이의 긴장 상태의 영향을 받아 왔다. [3]시사 프로그램들은 균형이라는 '규칙'을 고수하며 흔히 어조가 '진지'한 반면에, 더 대중적인 프로그램들은 우리가 '길거리의 보통 사람'의 관점에서 특정 뉴스 기사의 영향을 고려하게 하는 친근하고 더 가벼운 표현 양식을 채택한다. [4]실제로, 현대의 뉴스 구성은 로고, 짧은 어록, 빠른 시각적 컷(장면), 그리고 뉴스 프로 진행자의 '스타 기질'의 이용을 포함하여 더 빠른 편집 속도와 '더 현란한' 표현 방식의 증가된 사용에 의존하게 되었다. [5]대중적인 구성은 더 오래된 뉴스 구성의 더 긴 언어적 지향을 견디기를 꺼리는 시청자를 끎으로써 이해를 높인다고 할 수 있다. [6]하지만 그것은 뉴스 사건에 관한 구조적 맥락을 제공하지 못함으로써 아마 틀림없이 이해를 감소시키는 효과가 있다.

어휘

constitute 구성하다; (법률을) 제정하다
idiom 표현 양식; 관용구, 숙어
address 보도, 전달; 연설
engage (주의를) 끌다; 관여하다
current affairs (정치·사회 등의) 시사
stick to A A를 고수하다
contemporary 현대의, 당대의; 동시대의
construction 구성; 건설, 건축
flashy 현란한; 호화스러운

★<unwilling to-v>: v하기를 꺼리는

[5]Popular formats can be said to enhance understanding / by engaging *an audience* (unwilling to endure the longer verbal orientation (of older news formats)).

S V <by v-ing>: v함으로써 형용사구

대중적인 구성은 이해를 높인다고 할 수 있다 / 시청자를 끎으로써 (더 긴 언어적 지향을 견디기를 꺼리는 (더 오래된 뉴스 구성의))

↳ **대중적인 구성의 장점:** 장황함을 싫어하는 대중의 주의를 끌어 뉴스 이해를 높임.

[6]However, / they arguably work to reduce understanding / by failing to provide the structural contexts (for news events).

S(= popular formats) V <by v-ing>: v함으로써

하지만 / 그것(대중적인 구성)은 아마 틀림없이 이해를 감소시키는 효과가 있다 / 구조적 맥락을 제공하지 못함으로써 (뉴스 사건에 관한)

↳ **대중적인 구성의 단점:** 사건의 맥락을 전달하지 못해 이해를 감소시킴.

sound-bite (방송용으로 발췌한) 짧은 어록
enhance 높이다, 강화하다
endure 견디다, 인내하다
orientation 지향, 방향성; 경향
arguably 아마 틀림없이
[선택지] coordination 조화; 합동
display 표현; 전시, 진열
prompt 신속한
coverage (뉴스의) 보도, 취재 범위

정답 가이드

TV 뉴스는 주제 선정 외에 '무엇'으로도 구성되는지를 추론해야 한다. 이어지는 내용에서 뉴스 표현 방식이 정보, 교육, 재미를 제공하는 목적에 영향을 받는다고 하며, 그에 따른 최근 프로그램들의 어조, 현대 뉴스의 빠른 속도와 현란함 등을 설명하고 있으므로, 빈칸에 들어갈 뉴스의 구성 요소로 가장 적절한 것은 ⑤ 'verbal and visual idioms or modes of address(언어적, 시각적 표현 양식이나 보도 방식)'가 가장 적절하다.

오답 클리닉

① coordination with traditional display techniques (19%)
전통적인 표현 기법과의 조화
문장 5에서 현대의 뉴스는 더 오래된 뉴스 구성인 긴 언어적 지향을 꺼린다고 했으므로, 전통적인 표현 기법과 조화를 이룬다는 내용은 틀림.

② prompt and full coverage of the latest issues (21%)
최신 이슈에 대한 신속하고도 완전한 보도
뉴스가 최신 이슈를 신속하게 보도한다는 내용이 아님.

③ educational media contents favoured by producers (6%)
제작자에 의해 선호되는 교육용 미디어 콘텐츠
교육용 콘텐츠에 관한 내용이 아님.

④ commitment to long-lasting news standards (7%)
오래 지속되는 뉴스 기준에 대한 전념
뉴스 기준이 무엇인지에 대한 언급은 없음.

03 + 빈칸 초반 〈22학년도 9월 모평 34번 | 정답률 42%〉 ④

구문분석 & 직독직해 동물 동물의 안전 자극 학습과 활동

주제문

★<enable+O+to-v>: O가 v할 수 있게 하다

[1]Enabling animals to operate / **in the presence of harmless stimuli** / is an almost universal function (of learning).

S(동명사구) V(단수) C

동물이 움직일 수 있게 하는 것은 / 무해한 자극이 있을 때 / 거의 보편적인 기능이다 (학습의)

↳ 무해한 자극이 있을 때 움직이는 것은 동물의 학습 결과임.

[2]Most animals innately avoid / *objects* [(which[that]) they have not previously encountered].

S V O 목적격 관계대명사 생략

대부분의 동물은 선천적으로 피한다 / 대상을 [그것들이 이전에 마주친 적이 없는]

(= unfamiliar objects)

[3]Unfamiliar objects may be dangerous; // treating them with caution / has survival value.

S_1 V_1 C_1 S_2(동명사구) V_2 O_2

익숙하지 않은 대상들은 위험할 수도 있다 // 그것들을 조심해서 다루는 것은 / 생존가를 갖는다

↳ **동물의 습성:** 선천적으로 익숙지 않은 대상을 피함.

조심스러운 행동이 지속되면 필수 생존 활동을 제대로 할 수 없음.

[4]If persisted in, / however, // such careful behavior could interfere with / feeding and other necessary activities / to *the extent* [that the benefit of caution would be lost].

접속사를 생략하지 않은 분사구문(= If it is persisted in ~) S V O 관계부사

만약 지속된다면 / 그러나 // 그러한 조심스러운 행동은 (~을) 방해할 수도 있다 / 먹이 섭취와 다른 필요한 활동을 / 정도까지 [조심해서 얻는 이익이 없어질]

↳ **문제점:** 동물의 너무 조심스런 행동은 오히려 생존을 방해할 수 있음.

해석

[1]동물이 무해한 자극이 있을 때 움직일 수 있게 하는 것은 학습의 거의 보편적인 기능이다. [2]대부분의 동물은 그것들이 이전에 마주친 적이 없는 대상을 선천적으로 피한다. [3]익숙하지 않은 대상들은 위험할 수도 있으므로, 그것들을 조심해서 다루는 것은 생존가(生存價)를 갖는다. [4]그러나 만약 지속된다면, 그러한 조심스러운 행동은 조심해서 얻는 이익이 없어질 정도까지 먹이 섭취와 다른 필요한 활동을 방해할 수도 있다. [5]바람이 한 번 불 때마다, 또는 구름이 그림자를 드리울 때마다 등딱지 속으로 움츠리는 거북은 게으른 토끼와 하더라도 경주에서 결코 이기지 못할 것이다. [6]이 문제를 극복하기 위해, 거의 모든 동물은 자주 발생하는 안전한 자극에 습관화된다. [7]낯선 대상에 직면하면, 경험이 없는 동물은 얼어붙거나 숨으려고 할 수도 있지만, 불쾌한 일이 일어나지 않으면 그것은 머잖아 활동을 계속할 것이다. [8]익숙하지 않은 대상이 유용할지도 모르는 가능성도 있으므로, 그것이 즉각적인 위협을 제기하지 않는다면, 더 면밀한 조사가 가치 있을 수도 있다.

*whenever(~할 때마다)는 부사절을 이끄는 접속사이자 부사절에서 부사 역할도 하는 복합관계부사임.

[5] *A turtle* [that withdraws into its shell / at every puff of wind // or whenever a cloud casts a shadow] / would never win races, / not even with a lazy rabbit.

S 주격 관계대명사 / 부사절 접속사 S′ V′ / O′ V O

거북은 [그것의 등딱지 속으로 움츠리는 / 바람이 한 번 불 때마다 // 또는 구름이 그림자를 드리울 때마다] / 경주에서 결코 이기지 못할 것이다 / 게으른 토끼와 하더라도

↳ **예(겁 많은 거북):** 조심스러우면 아무것도 할 수 없음.

🗝 문장 1의 harmless stimuli가 safe stimuli로 말바꿈 됨.

[6] To overcome this problem, / almost all animals habituate / to *safe stimuli* [that occur frequently].

목적(~하기 위해) S V 주격 관계대명사

이 문제를 극복하기 위해 / 거의 모든 동물은 습관화된다 / 안전한 자극에 [자주 발생하는]

↳ **해결책:** 동물은 자주 발생하는 안전한 자극에 익숙해짐.

[7] Confronted by a strange object, / an inexperienced animal may freeze or (may) attempt to hide, // but if nothing unpleasant happens, // sooner or later it will continue its activity.

분사구문(= When it is confronted ~) S₁ V₁ (= the inexperienced animal)

부사절 접속사(조건) S′ V′ S₂ V₂ O₂

낯선 대상에 직면하면 / 경험이 없는 동물은 얼어붙거나 숨으려고 할 수도 있다 // 그러나 불쾌한 일이 일어나지 않으면 // 그것(경험이 없는 동물)은 머잖아 활동을 계속할 것이다

🗝 낯선 대상을 마주쳐도 해롭지 않으면 그 자극에 적응해 활동을 계속함.

↳ **예:** 동물은 낯선 대상을 만나도 그 자극이 안전하면 익숙해져서 계속 활동함.

[8] The possibility also exists // that an unfamiliar object may be useful, // so if it poses no immediate threat, // a closer inspection may be worthwhile.

S₁ V₁ 동격 접속사 = (= the unfamiliar object)

부사절 접속사(조건) S₂ V₂ C₂

가능성도 있다 // 익숙하지 않은 대상이 유용할지도 모르는 // 그래서 그것이 즉각적인 위협을 제기하지 않는다면 // 더 면밀한 조사가 가치 있을 수도 있다

↳ **부연 설명:** 낯선 대상이 유용할 수도 있으므로 위협이 없는 한 활동하는 것이 더 나음.

어휘

operate 움직이다; 작동되다
in the presence of ~이 있을 때; ~이 있는 데서
stimulus (*pl.* stimuli) 자극
universal 보편적인; 전 세계의
previously 이전에; 미리
encounter 마주치다, (우연히) 만나다; 맞닥뜨리다
persist in ~을 지속하다
interfere with ~을 방해하다
to the extent that ~할 정도까지
withdraw 움츠리다, 뒤로 빼다; 취소[철회]하다
shell (거북 등의) 등딱지, 껍데기
puff (바람·연기 등의) 한 번 불기
cast (그림자를) 드리우다; 던지다
overcome 극복하다, 이겨내다
habituate (행동 따위가) 습관화 되다
confront 직면하다, 맞서다
inexperienced 경험이 없는, 미숙한
sooner or later 머잖아, 조만간
pose (위협·문제 등을) 제기하다; 포즈를 취하다
inspection 조사, 검사
worthwhile 가치 있는
[선택지] weigh 따져 보다, 저울질하다; 무게를 달다
escape route 탈출로
surrounding 주변의

⊕ 생존가(survival value): 생물의 특징(행동, 형태, 색체 등)이 그 생물의 생존 및 번식에 미치는 영향

정답 가이드

동물이 '무슨 일'을 할 수 있게 하는 것이 '학습'의 보편적 기능인지를 찾아야 한다. 바로 이어지는 문장에서 동물은 '선천적'으로는 익숙하지 않은 대상을 피하고 조심한다고 했으므로, 후천적으로, 즉 '학습'을 통해서는 반대의 상황이 된다는 설명이 이어질 것임을 예측할 수 있다. 이후 설명과 예를 보면, 익숙하지 않은 대상에 계속해서 조심하고 숨는 선천적 행동은 다른 필요한 활동을 못하게 하는데, 이를 극복하기 위해 자주 발생하는 안전한 자극에 습관화되어(학습하여) 활동을 계속한다는 것이다. 따라서, 빈칸에 들어갈 말로 가장 적절한 것은 ④ 'operate in the presence of harmless stimuli(무해한 자극이 있을 때 움직이다)'이다.

오답 클리닉

① weigh the benefits of treating familiar things with care (20%)
익숙한 것을 조심해서 다루는 것의 이점을 따져 보다
익숙한 것이 아니라 익숙하지 않은 것을 조심하는 동물의 행동이 지속되면 생존에 해가 될 수 있다고 했음.

② plan escape routes after predicting possible attacks (16%)
가능성 있는 공격을 예측한 이후에 탈출로를 계획하다
위협이 될 수 있는 낯선 대상에게 잡혀 탈출을 모색하는 내용이 아님.

③ overcome repeated feeding failures for survival (14%)
생존을 위해 반복되는 먹이 섭취의 실패를 극복하다
먹이 섭취는 조심스러운 행동이 계속될 때 해를 입을 수 있는 필수 생존 활동의 예로 언급된 것임.

⑤ monitor the surrounding area regularly (9%)
주변 지역을 정기적으로 관찰하다
주변 지역을 정기적으로 관찰한다는 내용은 없음.

01 빈칸 중반 (24학년도 대수능 33번 | 정답률 18%) ⑤

구문분석 & 직독직해

인지 맥락 없이 사람을 이해하는 것의 어려움

[1] There have been *psychological studies* [in which subjects were shown photographs of people's faces and (were) asked to identify *the expression or state of mind* (evinced)].

(V / S / 전치사+관계대명사 / S′ / V′₁ / O′ / V′₂ / C′ / 과거분사)

심리학 연구가 있어 왔다 [피실험자들이 사람들의 얼굴 사진을 보는 / 그리고 표정이나 마음 상태를 식별하도록 요청받은 (분명히 나타나는)]

주제문

[2] The results are invariably very mixed. (S / V / C) 같은 얼굴 사진이어도 다르게 해석될 수 있음.

그 결과는 언제나 매우 엇갈린다

↳ 사람의 얼굴 사진을 보고 분명히 나타나는 표정이나 마음 상태를 알아내도록 한 실험의 결과는 매우 엇갈림.

[3] In the 17th century / the French painter and theorist Charles Le Brun drew / *a series of faces* (illustrating *the various emotions* [that painters could be called upon to represent]).

(S / V / O / 현재분사구 / 목적격 관계대명사)

17세기에 / 프랑스의 화가이자 이론가인 Charles Le Brun은 그렸다 / 일련의 얼굴을 (다양한 감정을 분명히 보여주는 [화가가 표현해 달라고 요청받을 수 있는])

↳ **세부 사항(예):** 화가가 다양한 감정을 분명히 보여주는 얼굴을 그렸음.

[4] What is striking about them is // that **any number of them could be substituted / for one another / without loss.**

(S(명사절) / (= faces) / V / 명사절 접속사 / S′ / V′ / → is의 C(명사절))

그것들(얼굴 그림)에 관해 놀라운 점은 ~이다 // 그것들(얼굴 그림)이 얼마든지 대체될 수 있었다는 것 / 서로 / 손실 없이

↳ **결과:** 얼굴 그림은 서로 별 차이 없이 대체될 수 있었음.

얼굴 그림에는 감정을 확실하게 알게 해주는 배경과 맥락이 빠져 있음.

[5] What is missing in all this / is *any setting or context* (to make the emotion determinate).

(S(명사절) / V / C / ★<make+O+C>: O를 C로 만들다)

이 모든 것에서 빠진 것은 / 어떤 배경이나 맥락이다 (감정을 확실하게 만들어 주는)

[6] We must know // who this person is, / who these other people are, / what their relationship is, / what is at stake in the scene, / and the like.

(S / V / O_1(명사절) / O_2(명사절) / O_3(명사절) / O_4(명사절) / O_5)

우리는 알아야 한다 // 이 사람이 누구인지를 / 이 다른 사람들이 누구인지를 / 그들의 관계가 무엇인지를 / 그 장면에서 성패가 달려 있는 것이 무엇인지를 / 그리고 기타 등등을

↳ **원인:** 얼굴 그림의 감정을 확실히 알려면 배경과 맥락을 알아야 하는데 이것이 빠져 있었음.

★<A as well as B>: B뿐만 아니라 A도 ★세미콜론(;)이 <not A but B>의 but를 대신함.

[7] In real life as well as in painting / we do not come across just faces; // we encounter people / in particular situations // and our understanding (of people) / cannot somehow be precipitated / and (cannot be) held / isolated from *the social and human circumstances* [in which they, and we, live and breathe and have our being].

(전치사구 병렬 / S_1 / V_1 / O_1 / S_2 / V_2 / O_2 / S_3 / V_{3-1} / V_{3-2} / 분사구문(= while it is isolated ~) / 전치사+관계대명사)

그림에서뿐만 아니라 실생활에서도 / 우리는 단지 얼굴만 우연히 마주치는 것이 아니다 //

우리는 사람들을 마주친다 / 특정한 상황에서 // 그리고 우리의 이해는 (사람들에 대한) / 어떻게든 촉발될 수 없다 / 그리고 유지(될 수는 없다) /

사회적, 인간적 상황으로부터 고립된 채로 [그들과 우리가 살아 숨 쉬고 우리 존재를 지니는]

↳ **결론:** 사회적, 인간적 상황을 알아야 사람을 이해할 수 있음.

해석

[1]피실험자들이 사람들의 얼굴 사진을 보고 분명히 나타나는 표정이나 마음 상태를 식별하도록 요청받은 심리학 연구가 있어 왔다. [2]그 결과는 언제나 매우 엇갈린다. [3]17세기에 프랑스의 화가이자 이론가인 Charles Le Brun은 화가가 표현해 달라고 요청받을 수 있는 다양한 감정을 분명히 보여주는 일련의 얼굴을 그렸다. [4]그것들(다양한 감정을 보여주는 얼굴 그림)에 관해 놀라운 점은 그것들(얼굴 그림)이 얼마든지 손실 없이 서로 대체될 수 있었다는 것이다.(▶ 여러 분명한 감정을 나타내는 얼굴 그림이 서로 비슷하게 보였다는 의미) [5]이 모든 것에서 빠진 것은 감정을 확실하게 만들어 주는 어떤 배경이나 맥락이다. [6]우리는 이 사람이 누구인지, 이 다른 사람들이 누구인지, 그들의 관계가 무엇인지, 그 장면에서 성패가 달려 있는 것이 무엇인지, 그리고 기타 등등을 알아야 한다. [7]그림에서뿐만 아니라 실생활에서도 우리는 단지 얼굴만 우연히 마주치는 것이 아니라, 우리는 특정한 상황에서 사람들을 마주치고, 사람들에 대한 우리의 이해는 그들과 우리가 살아 숨 쉬고 우리 존재를 지니는 사회적, 인간적 상황으로부터 고립된 채로 어떻게든 촉발되어 유지될 수는 없다.

어휘

- psychological 심리학의; 심리[정신]적인
- subject 피실험자; 주제; 학과, 과목
- identify 식별하다; 확인하다; 동일시하다
- invariably 언제나, 변함없이
- mixed (의견·생각 등이) 엇갈리는; 혼합된
- illustrate 분명히 보여주다
- call (up)on ~에게 요청하다, 부탁하다
- striking 놀라운, 두드러진, 눈에 띄는
- any number of 얼마든지, 많은
- substitute 대체[대신]하다; 대신하는 사람[것]
- determinate 확실한, 확정적인
- at stake 성패가 달려 있는
- come across ~을 우연히 마주치다[발견하다]
- encounter 마주치다; 맞닥뜨리다; 만남, 접촉
- somehow 어떻게든, 어쨌든; 어쩐지
- circumstance 상황, 환경
- [선택지] consistently 일관되게; 끊임없이
- intended 의도된, 계획된
- precision 정밀(성); 정확(성)
- definitively 명확하게; 결정적으로
- narrative 이야기; 서술
- characteristic 특징; 특유의

정답 가이드

빈칸 문장과 앞 문장으로 보아, 그것들(다양한 감정을 보여주는 얼굴 그림)에 관해 놀라운 점이 '무엇'인지를 추론해야 한다. 앞에서 피실험자들에게 얼굴 사진을 보고 마음 상태를 알아내도록 한 실험의 결과가 언제나 매우 엇갈린다고 한 것에서 피실험자들은 얼굴 사진을 보고 마음 상태를 정확하게 파악할 수 없었다는 것을 알 수 있다. 이어지는 또 다른 실험 내용에서는 다양한 감정을 보여주는 얼굴 그림이 어떠한 놀라운 결과를 나타냈는데, 그 모든 것(첫 번째 실험의 얼굴 사진과 두 번째 실험의 얼굴 그림)에는 감정을 확실히 알 수 있게 만들어주는 배경이나 맥락이 빠져있었다는 것이다. 따라서 두 번째 실험의 결과 역시 사람들이 얼굴 그림으로 감정을 정확하게 파악할 수 없었다는 내용이 되어야 하므로, 빈칸에 들어갈 말로 가장 적절한 것은 ⑤ 'any number of them could be substituted for one another without loss(그것들이 얼마든지 손실 없이 서로 대체될 수 있었다)'이다.

The 핵심 ★ 손실 없이 서로 대체될 수 있었다는 것은 그림의 얼굴이 나타내는 감정이 확실하게 분간되지 않았기 때문에 가능한 것이다.

오답 클리닉

① all of them could be matched consistently with their intended emotions (24%)
그것들 모두가 의도된 감정과 일관되게 일치할 수 있었다
배경과 맥락이 빠져 있는 얼굴 그림을 보고 의도된 감정을 맞출 수 없다는 내용이므로 글의 내용과 반대됨.

② every one of them was illustrated with photographic precision (24%) 모든 얼굴 그림들이 사진과 같이 정밀하게 그려졌다
얼굴 그림이 사진과 같이 정밀했는지는 언급되지 않음.

③ each of them definitively displayed its own social narrative (19%)
그것들 각각이 자체의 사회적 이야기를 명확하게 보여주었다
배경과 맥락이 빠져있는 얼굴 그림들은 사회적 이야기를 보여주지 못할 것이므로 틀림.

④ most of them would be seen as representing unique characteristics (14%) 그것들 대부분이 고유한 특징을 나타내는 것으로 여겨질 것이다
얼굴 그림들이 고유한 특징을 나타냈다면 감정을 정확하게 식별할 수 있었을 것이므로 틀림.

02 + 빈칸 중반 〈24학년도 9월 모평 32번 | 정답률 54%〉 ②

구문분석 & 직독직해

기술 인터넷 태그 시스템과 그 한계

[1]Many people create [and] share pictures and videos / on the Internet.
(S: Many people / V: create and share / O: pictures and videos)
많은 사람이 사진과 비디오를 만들고 공유한다 / 인터넷에서
↳ **도입(태그 시스템 설명):** 사람들은 인터넷에서 사진과 비디오를 만들어 공유함.

[2]The difficulty is finding what you want.
(S: The difficulty / V: is / C: finding what you want / 동명사 finding의 O(명사절): what you want)
어려운 점은 여러분이 원하는 것을 찾는 것이다

[3]Typically, / people want to search / using words (rather than, say, example sketches).
(S: people / V: want / O: to search / 분사구문(= as they use ~): using words)
일반적으로 / 사람들은 검색하기를 원한다 / 단어를 사용하여 (이를테면, 예시 스케치 대신)
↳ 인터넷에서 원하는 것을 찾기 쉽지 않고, 사람들은 검색을 단어로 하고 싶어함.

[4]Because most pictures don't come / with words attached, // it is natural / to try and (to) build *tagging systems* [that tag images / with relevant words].
(부사절 접속사(이유): Because / ★<with+O'+p.p.>: O'가 ~되어[~된 채로] / 수동 관계: words attached / 가주어: it / 진주어: to try and (to) build ~ / 주격 관계대명사: that)
대부분의 사진은 나오지 않기 때문에 / 단어가 첨부되어 // (~은) 당연하다 / 태그 시스템을 시도하고 만드는 것은 [이미지를 태그하는 / 관련 있는 단어로]
↳ 단어가 첨부되어 있지 않은 이미지를 검색하기 위해 이미지를 관련 있는 단어로 태그하는 시스템을 만듦.

[5]The underlying machinery is straightforward — // we apply image classification and object detection methods / [and] tag the image / with the output words.
(S: The underlying machinery / V: is / C: straightforward / S: we / V_1: apply / O_1: image classification and object detection methods / V_2: tag / O_2: the image)
기저에 있는 기제는 간단하다 // 우리는 이미지 분류와 객체 감지 방법을 적용한다 / 그리고 이미지를 태그한다 / 출력 단어로
↳ 태그 시스템은 이미지를 분류하고 객체를 감지해서 이미지에 관련 단어를 태그하는 것임.

주제문
[6]But / tags aren't **a comprehensive description (of what is happening / in an image)**.
(S: tags / V: aren't / C: a comprehensive description ~ / of의 O(명사절): what is happening)
하지만 / 태그는 포괄적인 설명이 아니다 (일어나고 있는 일에 대한 / 이미지에서)
↳ 그러나 태그는 이미지를 포괄적으로 설명하지 못함.

[7]It matters // who is doing what, // [and] tags don't capture this.
(가주어: It / V_1: matters / 진주어(명사절): who is doing what / S_2: tags / V_2: don't capture / O_2: this / who is doing what = this)
(~가) 중요하다 // 누가 무엇을 하고 있는지가 // 그리고 태그는 이것(누가 무엇을 하고 있는지)을 포착하지 못한다
🔑 태그는 이미지에서 누가 무엇을 하고 있는지에 대한 정보를 포착하지 못함.
↳ **부연 설명(한계점):** 태그는 이미지에서 누가 무엇을 하고 있는지를 담지 못함.

해석

[1]인터넷에서 많은 사람이 사진과 비디오를 만들고 공유한다. [2]어려운 점은 여러분이 원하는 것을 찾는 것이다. [3]일반적으로 사람들은 (이를테면, 예시 스케치 대신) 단어를 사용하여 검색하기를 원한다. [4]대부분의 사진은 단어가 첨부되어 나오지 않기 때문에 이미지를 관련 있는 단어로 태그하는 태그 시스템을 시도하고 만드는 것은 당연하다. [5]기저에 있는 체계는 간단한데, 우리는 이미지 분류와 객체 감지 방법을 적용하여 출력 단어로 이미지를 태그한다. [6]하지만 태그는 이미지에서 일어나고 있는 일에 대한 포괄적인 설명이 아니다. [7]누가 무엇을 하고 있는지가 중요한데, 태그는 이것을 포착하지 못한다. [8]예를 들어, 거리에 있는 고양이의 사진을 '고양이', '거리', '쓰레기통', '생선 뼈'의 객체 범주로 태그하는 것은 그 고양이가 거리에 있는 뚜껑이 없는 쓰레기통에서 생선 뼈를 빼내고 있다는 정보를 빠뜨린다.

어휘

typically 일반적으로; 전형적으로
attach 첨부하다, 붙이다
natural 당연한; 자연의; 타고난
relevant 관련 있는, 적절한
underlying 기저에 있는, 근본적인
machinery 기제, 조직; 기계(류)
straightforward 간단한; 솔직한
classification 분류; 유형, 범주
detection 감지, 발견
output 출력(하다); 생산[산출](량)
comprehensive 포괄적인, 종합적인
category 범주
cf. categorize 분류하다

8For example, / tagging a picture (of a cat (in the street)) / with the object categories "cat", "street", "trash can" and "fish bones" /
S(동명사구)

예를 들어 / 사진을 태그하는 것은 (고양이의 (거리에 있는)) / '고양이', '거리', '쓰레기통', 그리고 '생선 뼈'의 객체 범주로 /

leaves out the information // that the cat is pulling the fish bones / out of an open trash can (on the street). 객체 정보는 포함하지만 고양이가 무엇을 하고 있는지에 대한 정보는 빠뜨림.
V(단수) O = 동격 접속사

정보를 빠뜨린다 // 그 고양이가 생선 뼈를 빼내고 있다는 / 뚜껑이 없는 쓰레기통에서 (거리에 있는)

↳ 예: 거리에 있는 고양이 사진을 관련 단어로 태그하는 것은 그 고양이가 무엇을 하고 있는지에 대한 정보를 빠뜨림.

leave out ~을 빠뜨리다, 빼다
[선택지] sequential 순차적인
identical 동일한
⊕태그(를 붙이다)(tag): 어떤 정보를 검색할 때 사용하기 위해 부여하는 단어 혹은 키워드. 소셜 네트워크에 관심 있는 글을 검색하거나 관심사를 공유하는 등 태그의 활용이 높아지고 있음.

정답 가이드

빈칸 문장은 역접 연결어 But이 이끌어 태그들은 '무엇'이 아니라는 내용이다. 우선 태그를 이해하기 위해 앞 내용을 보면, 이미지가 검색되도록 태그 시스템을 이용해서 출력된 단어로 이미지를 태그한다는 내용이 나온다. 즉 여기서 태그는 검색용으로 자동 출력된 '단어'를 뜻한다. 빈칸 문장 뒤의 설명은 누가 무엇을 하고 있는지가 중요한데 태그들은 이를 포착하지 못한다는 것이다. 이어지는 예에서도 개별 단어들로 태그하는 것은 '누가 어디에서 무엇을 하고 있다'라는 중요한 정보를 빠뜨린다고 했다. 따라서 이 개별 단어 태그들은 이미지에서 일어나는 일을 포괄적으로 설명하지 못한다는 것을 알 수 있으므로, 빈칸에 들어갈 말로 가장 적절한 것은 ② 'a comprehensive description of what is happening in an image(이미지에서 일어나고 있는 일에 대한 포괄적인 설명)'이다.

오답 클리닉

① a set of words that allow users to identify an individual object (16%)
사용자가 개별 객체를 식별할 수 있게 하는 단어의 집합
태그로 사용자는 개별 객체를 식별할 수 있으므로 틀림.

③ a reliable resource for categorizing information by pictures (13%)
사진으로 정보를 분류하는 신뢰할 만한 자원
태그가 믿을 만한 자원이 아니라는 언급은 없음.

④ a primary means of organizing a sequential order of words (9%)
단어의 순차적 순서를 구성하는 주요 수단
단어의 순차적인 순서를 구성하는 수단이 아니라는 언급은 없음.

⑤ a useful filter for sorting similar but not identical images (8%)
유사하지만 동일하지 않은 이미지를 분류하는 유용한 필터
태그 시스템이 유사한 이미지를 분류하는 데 유용하지 않다는 언급은 없음.

03 + 빈칸 중반 (24학년도 9월 모평 31번 | 정답률 58%) ④

구문분석 & 직독직해 사회 제2차 세계대전 이후 사회적 변화

1In the post-World War II years after 1945, / unparalleled economic growth fueled / a building boom / and a massive migration (from the central cities to the new suburban areas).
S V O1 O2 <from A to B>: A에서 B로

1945년 이후 제2차 세계 대전 다음 시기에 / 유례없는 경제 성장은 부채질했다 / 건축 붐을 / 그리고 대규모 이주를 (중심 도시에서 새로운 교외 지역으로의)

*far는 비교급 수식 부사로 '훨씬'을 뜻함.

2The suburbs were far more dependent on the automobile, / signaling the shift (from primary dependence on public transportation to private cars).
S V C 분사구문(= and it signalled ~)

교외는 자동차에 훨씬 더 많이 의존했다 / 그리고 이는 전환을 시사했다 (대중교통에의 주된 의존에서 자가용으로의)

3Soon / this led / to the construction (of better highways and freeways) / and the decline and even loss (of public transportation).
(= 앞 문장) S V to의 O(명사구 병렬)

곧 / 이것은 이어졌다 / 건설로 (더 나은 고속도로와 초고속도로의) / 그리고 감소, 심지어 상실로까지 (대중교통의)

↳ 도입: 제2차 세계 대전 이후에 여러 변화가 일어남.

주제문

4With all of these changes / came a **privatization** (of leisure). *부사구(With ~ changes)가 문장 앞에 나와 <동사+주어> 어순으로 도치됨.
부사구 V S

이러한 모든 변화와 함께 / 사유화가 이루어졌다 (여가의)

↳ 여가의 사유화가 이루어짐.

해석

1 1945년 이후 제2차 세계 대전 다음 시기에 유례없는 경제 성장은 건축 붐과 중심 도시에서 새로운 교외 지역으로의 대규모 이주를 부채질했다. 2 교외는 자동차에 훨씬 더 많이 의존했고, 이는 대중교통에의 주된 의존에서 자가용으로의 전환을 시사했다. 3 곧 이것은 더 나은 고속도로와 초고속도로의 건설과 대중교통의 감소, 심지어 상실로까지 이어졌다. 4 이러한 모든 변화와 함께 여가의 사유화가 이루어졌다. 5 더 많은 사람이 내부에는 더 많은 공간이 있고 외부에는 아름다운 마당이 있는 자신의 집을 소유함에 따라 그들의 휴양과 여가 시간은 점점 더 집이나 기껏해야 이웃에 집중되었다. 6 이러한 가정에 기반한 여가의 한 가지 주요 활동은 텔레비전을 시청하는 것이었다. 7 더 이상 사람들은 영화를 보기 위해 전차를 타고 극장까지 갈 필요가 없었고, 텔레비전에서 유사한 오락물이 무료로 그리고 더 편리하게 이용 가능했다.

[5] As more people owned their own homes, / (with more space inside and lovely yards outside), //
부사절 접속사(~함에 따라) 전치사구 삽입
더 많은 사람이 자신의 집을 소유함에 따라 / (내부에는 더 많은 공간이 있고 외부에는 아름다운 마당이 있는) //

their recreation and leisure time was increasingly centered / around the home or, at most, the neighborhood. 🔑 휴양과 여가 시간이 집이나 이웃을 중심으로 함.
S V
그들의 휴양과 여가 시간은 점점 더 집중되었다 / 집이나 기껏해야 이웃에

↳ **부연 설명:** 공간이 넓은 자신의 집을 소유하게 되면서 휴양과 여가 시간이 집이나 이웃에게 집중됨.

🔑 가정에 기반한 여가는 집에서 이루어지는 여가 활동을 의미함.

[6] One major activity (of this home-based leisure) / was watching television.
S V C
한 가지 주요 활동은 (이러한 가정에 기반한 여가의) / 텔레비전을 시청하는 것이었다

*부정어 포함 어구(No longer)가 문장 앞에 나와 <조동사+주어+동사> 어순으로 도치됨.

[7] No longer did one have to ride the trolly to the theater / to watch a movie; //
부정어 포함 어구 조동사 S_1 V_1 O 목적(~하기 위해)
더 이상 사람들은 전차를 타고 극장까지 갈 필요가 없었다 / 영화를 보기 위해 //

similar entertainment was available / for free and more conveniently / from television.
S_2 V_2 C
유사한 오락물이 이용 가능했다 / 무료로 그리고 더 편리하게 / 텔레비전에서

↳ **예:** 집에서 텔레비전을 통해 영화와 같은 오락물을 즐길 수 있어짐.

어휘

fuel 부채질하다; 연료(를 공급하다)
massive 대규모의; 거대한
migration 이주, 이동
suburban 교외의
cf. suburb 교외
signal 시사[암시]하다; 신호(를 보내다)
primary 주된, 주요한
construction 건설; 구성
freeway 초고속도로 ((교차, 건널목 그 밖의 장애물이 없는 고속 자동차 도로))
privatization 사유화
leisure 여가
recreation 휴양, 오락
center around ~에 집중하다
at (the) most 기껏해야
trolly 전차; 손수레
entertainment 오락(물)
conveniently 편리하게

정답 가이드

빈칸 문장은 문장 앞의 With all of these changes로 보아, 앞부분에 어떤 변화들이 언급되고, 빈칸을 포함하는 '여가의 '무엇'이 이루어졌다'라는 어구는 뒤에서 구체적으로 설명될 것임을 알 수 있다. 이어지는 설명을 보면, 많은 사람이 자신의 집을 소유하게 되면서 휴양과 여가 시간이 점점 더 집이나 이웃에 집중되었다고 했다. 가정에 기반한 주요 여가 활동은 텔레비전 시청이었으며, (다른 사람들과 함께 약속된 시간에 봐야 하는) 영화를 보기 위해 (다른 많은 사람들이 이용하는) 전차를 타고 극장에 갈 필요가 없게 되었다고 했다. 즉, 다른 많은 대중들과 상관없이 개인적으로 자신의 집에서 여가를 즐길 수 있게 되었다는 것이므로, 빈칸에 들어갈 말로 가장 적절한 것은 ④ 'privatization(사유화)'이다.

오답 클리닉

① downfall (10%) 몰락
여가가 몰락했다는 내용이 아님.

② uniformity (16%) 획일성
여가가 획일적으로 이루어졌다는 내용은 없음. 텔레비전 시청은 집을 기반으로 한 여가 활동의 한 예로 언급된 것으로, 그것으로 여가가 획일화되었다는 내용이 아님.

③ restoration (6%) 부활
여가가 없어졌다가 다시 생겼다는 내용이 아님.

⑤ customization (9%) 맞춤화
개인의 취향에 맞춘 여가 생활이 이루어졌다는 내용이 아님.

01 + 빈칸 중반 〈24학년도 6월 모평 32번 | 정답률 56%〉 ③

구문분석 & 직독직해

사회 '도덕 경제'로서의 노동 공유 집단

[1]In labor-sharing groups, / people contribute labor / to other people /
S V O ★<contribute A to B>: A를 B에 제공하다[주다]
노동 공유 집단에서 / 사람들은 노동을 제공한다 / 다른 사람들에게

on a regular basis (for seasonal agricultural work (such as harvesting)) / or on an irregular basis
전치사구 병렬
(in the event of a crisis (such as *the need* (to rebuild *a barn* (damaged by fire)))).
과거분사구
정기적으로 (계절에 따른 농사일을 위해 (수확과 같은)) / 혹은 비정기적으로
(위기가 발생할 경우 (필요성과 같은 (헛간을 다시 지을 (화재로 손상된))))
↳ **도입:** 노동 공유 집단은 정기적 또는 비정기적으로 다른 사람들에게 노동력을 제공함.

주제문
★<call+O+C(O를 C라고 부르다)>의 수동형
[2]Labor sharing groups are part (of what has been called a "moral economy") //
S V C of의 O(명사절)
노동 공유 집단은 일부이다 ('도덕 경제'라고 불려온 것의) //
부사절 접속사(~ 때문에)
since no one keeps formal records (on how much any family puts in or takes out).
S′ V′ O′ on의 O(명사절)
아무도 공식적인 기록을 해두지 않기 때문에 (어떤 가족이 얼마나 많은 것을 들이고 얼마나 많은 것을 가져갔는지에 대한)
🔑 공식적으로 기록해 노동을 주고받지 않음.

[3]Instead, / accounting is **socially regulated**.
S V
대신에 / 계산은 사회적으로 규제된다
↳ 주고받는 도움을 공식적으로 기록해 두지 않기 때문에 '도덕 경제'로 불리며 대신 계산은 사회적으로 규제됨.

[4]The group has / *a sense of moral community* (based on years of trust and sharing).
S V O 과거분사구
그 집단은 가지고 있다 / 도덕적 공동체 의식을 (다년간의 신뢰와 나눔에 기반한)
🔑 노동 공유 집단은 신뢰와 나눔을 기반으로 함.
↳ **세부 사항:** 노동 공유 집단은 신뢰와 나눔을 기반으로 한 공동체 의식을 가지고 있음.

[5]In a certain community (of North America), / labor sharing is a major economic factor (of social cohesion).
S V C
특정 지역 사회에서 (북미의) / 노동 공유는 주요 경제적 요소이다 (사회적 응집성의)

[6]When a family needs a new barn / or faces *repair work* [that requires group labor], //
부사절 접속사(시간) S′ V′1 O′1 V′2 O′2 주격 관계대명사
a barn-raising party is called.
S V
한 가족이 새 헛간을 필요로 할 때 / 또는 수리 작업에 직면할 때 [집단 노동을 필요로 하는] //
헛간을 세우는 모임이 소집된다

[7]Many families show up / to help.
S V 목적(~하기 위해)
여러 가족이 나온다 / 돕기 위해

[8]Adult men provide manual labor, // and adult women provide food (for the event).
S1 V1 O1 S2 V2 O2
성인 남성은 육체노동을 제공한다 // 그리고 성인 여성은 음식을 제공한다 (행사를 위한)

[9]Later, / when another family needs help, // they call on the same people.
부사절 접속사(시간) S′ V′ O′ S V O
나중에 / 다른 가족이 도움을 필요로 할 때 // 그들은 같은 사람들에게 요청한다
↳ **예(북미 특정 지역):** 노동력 공유는 사회를 결속시키는 주요 경제적 요소로, 사람들은 집단 노동이 필요할 때 서로 도움을 주고받음.

해석

[1]노동 공유 집단에서 사람들은 정기적으로 (수확과 같은 계절에 따른 농사일을 위해) 혹은 비정기적으로 (화재로 손상된 헛간을 다시 지을 필요성과 같은 위기가 발생할 경우) 다른 사람들에게 노동을 제공한다. [2]아무도 어떤 가족이 얼마나 많은 것을 들이고 얼마나 많은 것을 가져갔는지에 대한 공식적인 기록을 해두지 않기 때문에, 노동 공유 집단은 '도덕 경제'라고 불려온 것의 일부이다. [3]대신에, 계산은 사회적으로 규제된다. [4]그 집단은 다년간의 신뢰와 나눔에 기반한 도덕적 공동체 의식을 가지고 있다. [5]북미의 특정 지역 사회에서 노동 공유는 사회적 응집성의 주요 경제적 요소이다. [6]한 가족이 새 헛간을 필요로 하거나 집단 노동을 필요로 하는 수리 작업에 직면할 때, 헛간을 세우는 모임이 소집된다. [7]여러 가족이 돕기 위해 나온다. [8]성인 남성은 육체노동을 제공하고, 성인 여성은 행사를 위한 음식을 제공한다. [9]나중에, 다른 가족이 도움을 필요로 할 때, 그들은 같은 사람들에게 요청한다.

어휘

on a regular basis 정기적으로
seasonal 계절에 따른, 계절의
agricultural 농사[농업]의
in the event of ~할 경우, 만약 ~하면
barn 헛간; 외양간
call ~라고 부르다[칭하다]; 소집하다
moral 도덕(상)의; 도덕적인
put in (시간·노력 등을) 들이다[쏟다]
accounting 계산; 회계
regulate 규제하다; 조절하다
manual 육체를 쓰는; 수동의; 손의, 손을 쓰는
cf. manually 수동으로; 손으로
call on ~에게 요청[요구]하다
[선택지] legally 법률적[합법적]으로
document 기록하다; 서류, 문서

정답 가이드

빈칸 문장과 앞 문장으로 보아, '도덕 경제'로 불려온 노동 공유 집단에서 노동에 대한 계산이 공식적으로 기록되는 대신 '어떻게' 이루어지는지를 추론해야 한다. 빈칸 문장 뒤에 이어지는 설명에서 노동 공유 집단이 신뢰와 나눔을 기반으로 한 도덕적 공동체 의식을 가지고 있으며, 어떤 가족을 도우면 나중에 그 사람들에게 도움을 요청한다고 했다. 즉, 노동 공유에 대한 계산은 공식적인 기록이 아니라, ③ 'socially regulated(사회적으로 규제된다)'가 가장 적절하다.

오답 클리닉

① legally established (7%) 법률적으로 확립된다
노동 공유에 대한 계산이 법적으로 정해진다는 내용은 없음.
② regularly reported (18%) 정기적으로 보고된다
공유한 노동을 정기적으로 보고한다는 내용은 언급되지 않음.
④ manually calculated (14%) 수동으로 계산된다
주고받은 노동을 수동으로 직접 계산한다는 내용은 언급되지 않음.
⑤ carefully documented (5%) 신중하게 기록된다
공유한 노동에 대해 아무도 공식적인 기록을 해두지 않는다고 했으므로 틀림.

02 + 빈칸 중반 (24학년도 6월 모평 31번 | 정답률 52%) ②

구문분석 & 직독직해

사회 생존보다 생활 방식과 선택의 문제인 소비

[1]People have always needed to eat, // and they always will (need to eat).
S1 V1 O S2 V2 반복어구 생략
사람들은 항상 먹을 필요가 있었다 // 그리고 그들은 항상 그럴 것이다

*<put an end to A>: A를 끝내다
[2]Rising emphasis (on self-expression values) / does not put an end to material desires.
S(단수) V(단수) O
커지는 강조가 (자기표현 가치에 관한) / 물질적 욕구를 끝내지는 않는다
↳ **도입:** 사람은 항상 먹을 필요가 있는데, 자기표현의 가치가 커진다고 해서 물질적 욕구가 없어지는 것은 아님.

주제문
[3]But / prevailing economic orientations are gradually being reshaped.
S V
하지만 / 우세한 경제적 방향성들이 차츰 다시 형성되고 있다
↳ 우세한 경제적 방향성들이 재형성되고 있음.

[4]*People* [who work in the knowledge sector] / continue to seek high salaries, //
S1 주격 관계대명사 V1 O1
사람들은 [지식 분야에서 일하는] / 계속 높은 임금을 추구한다 //
but they place equal or greater emphasis / on doing stimulating work / and being able to follow their own time schedules.
S2 V2 O2 on의 O(동명사구 병렬)
하지만 그들은 동등한 또는 더 큰 중점을 둔다 / 자극이 되는 일을 하는 것에 / 그리고 그들 자신의 시간 일정을 따를 수 있는 것에
↳ **세부 사항 1:** 높은 임금만큼 또는 그보다 일이 자극이 되는지와 자신의 일정에 따라 일할 수 있는지를 중시함.

[5]Consumption is becoming progressively less determined / by the need (for sustenance) / and the practical use (of *the goods* (consumed)).
S V C by의 O(명사구 병렬) 과거분사
소비는 점차 덜 결정된다 / 필요에 의해 (생명을 유지하는 것의) / 그리고 실질적인 사용에 의해 (상품의 (소비되는))
↳ **세부 사항 2:** 소비는 생존이나 실질적 사용에 의해 덜 결정됨.

[6]People still eat, // but a growing component (of food's value) / is determined / by its **nonmaterial** aspects.
S1 V1 S2 V2
사람들은 여전히 먹는다 // 하지만 증가하는 구성 요소가 (음식 가치의) / 결정된다 / 그것의 비물질적인 측면에 의해
↳ **예 1:** 비물질적인 측면이 소비하는 음식의 가치를 결정함.

⊶ 흥미로운 경험을 제공하고 독특한 생활 방식을 상징하는 음식을 먹으려고 할증료를 냄.
[7]People pay a premium / to eat *exotic cuisines* [that provide an interesting experience / or that symbolize a distinctive life-style].
S V O 목적(~하기 위해) 주격 관계대명사 주격 관계대명사
*선행사 exotic cuisines를 수식하는 두 개의 관계사절이 or로 연결됨.
사람들은 할증료를 낸다 / 이국적인 요리를 먹기 위해 [흥미로운 경험을 제공하는 / 또는 독특한 생활 방식을 상징하는]
↳ **예 1의 부연 설명:** 사람들은 돈을 더 내고 흥미로운 경험을 제공하거나 독특한 생활 방식을 상징하는 음식을 먹음.

해석

[1]사람들은 항상 먹을 필요가 있었고, 항상 그럴 것이다. [2]자기표현 가치에 관한 커지는 강조가 물질적 욕구를 끝내지는 않는다. [3]하지만 우세한 경제적 방향성들이 차츰 다시 형성되고 있다. [4]지식 분야에서 일하는 사람들은 계속 높은 임금을 추구하지만, 그들은 자극이 되는 일을 하는 것과 그들 자신의 시간 일정을 따를 수 있는 것에 동등한 또는 더 큰 중점을 둔다. [5]소비는 생명을 유지하는 것의 필요와 소비되는 상품의 실질적인 사용에 의해 점차 덜 결정된다. [6]사람들은 여전히 먹지만, 음식 가치의 증가하는 구성 요소가 그것의 비물질적인 측면에 의해 결정된다. [7]사람들은 흥미로운 경험을 제공하거나 독특한 생활 방식을 상징하는 이국적인 요리를 먹기 위해 할증료를 낸다. [8]후기 산업 사회의 대중은 생산이 생태학적 또는 윤리적 기준을 위반하는 상품의 구매를 거부하는 것과 같은 '정치적 소비주의'에 점점 더 많은 중점을 둔다. [9]소비는 점점 덜 생명을 유지하는 것의 문제이며 점점 더 생활 방식, 그리고 선택의 문제이다.

어휘

emphasis 강조, 중점
self-expression 자기표현
material 물질적인; 재료(↔ nonmaterial 비물질적인)
orientation 방향(성), 지향; 예비 교육
sector 분야[부문]
stimulating 자극이 되는, 고무적인
consumption 소비; 소비량[액]
cf. consume 소비하다; 먹다
cf. consumerism 소비주의
progressively 점차, 서서히; 계속해서
sustenance 생명을 유지하는 것; 생계
component (구성) 요소; 부품
premium 할증료; 아주 높은, 고급의
exotic 이국적인; 외국의
distinctive 독특한; 뚜렷이 구별되는

[8]The publics (of postindustrial societies) / place growing emphasis / on "political consumerism," /
S V O
대중은 (후기 산업 사회의) / 점점 더 많은 중점을 둔다 / '정치적 소비주의'에 /
(such as boycotting *goods* [whose production violates ecological or ethical standards]).
소유격 관계대명사
(상품의 구매를 거부하는 것과 같은 [생산이 생태학적 또는 윤리적 기준을 위반하는])
↳ **예 2:** 정치적 소비주의에 중점을 두어 생태학적 또는 윤리적 측면을 고려함.

★<비교급 and 비교급>: 점점 ~한
🔑 소비는 생활 방식 그리고 선택의 문제임.
[9]Consumption is less and less a matter (of sustenance) / and more and more a question (of life-style — and choice).
S V C
소비는 점점 덜 문제이다 (생명을 유지하는 것의) / 그리고 점점 더 문제이다 (생활 방식 그리고 선택의)
↳ **세부 사항 2의 재진술:** 소비는 점점 생존보다 생활 방식과 선택에 관한 것임.

postindustrial 후기 산업의, 탈공업화의
boycott 구매를 거부하다; 불매 운동
ecological 생태학의; 환경의
ethical 윤리적인
[선택지] quantitative 양적인
invariable 불변의

정답 가이드

빈칸 문장은 사람들이 먹는 음식의 가치를 구성하는 요소가 '어떤' 측면에 의해 결정된다고 했는데, 뒤이은 문장의 예에서는 사람들이 흥미로운 경험을 제공하고 독특한 생활 방식을 상징하는 이국적인 요리를 먹기 위해 할증료를 낸다고 했다. 이를 설명하는 단어로 가장 적절한 것은 ② 'nonmaterial(비물질적인)' 밖에 없으므로 일차적으로 정답을 판단할 수 있다. 앞선 내용을 좀 더 살펴보면, 물질적 욕구는 끝나지 않지만 우세한 경제적 방향성들이 다시 형성되고 있다(비물질적 욕구가 형성되고 있음을 의미)고 했다. 구체적으로 높은 임금만큼 또는 그보다 자극이 되는 일과 자신의 일정에 중점을 둔다고 했고, 소비도 변화한다고 하며 그 예로 빈칸 문장이 등장한 것이다. 따라서 사람들이 흥미로운 경험을 제공하는 이국적 요리에 돈을 지불하는 것은 음식의 가치를 구성하는 요소가 'nonmaterial(비물질적인)' 측면에 의해 결정되기 때문임을 확인할 수 있다.

오답 클리닉

① quantitative (10%) 양적인
음식의 양에 대한 언급은 없음.
③ nutritional (9%) 영양의
음식의 영양에 따라 가치가 결정된다는 내용이 아님.
④ invariable (9%) 불변의
음식 가치의 변하지 않는 측면은 언급되지 않음.
⑤ economic (21%) 경제적인
사람들이 이국적인 요리를 먹기 위해 할증료를 낸다는 것은 경제적인 측면에 의해 음식의 가치를 구성하는 요소가 결정되지 않음을 의미함.

03 + 빈칸 중반 〈23학년도 9월 모평 32번 | 정답률 65%〉 ④

구문분석 & 직독직해

사회 팬 서로 간의 관계에서 오는 팬덤의 즐거움

[1]Fans feel / for feeling's own sake.
팬은 느낀다 / 감정 그 자체를

→ (= Fans)
[2]They make meanings / beyond what seems to be on offer.
S V O 전치사(~이상) beyond의 O(명사절)
그들은 의미를 만든다 / 제공되는 것으로 보이는 것 이상의
↳ 팬은 감정 자체를 느끼며, 제공되는 것 이상의 의미를 만듦.

[3]They build identities and experiences, / and make artistic creations (of their own) / to share with others.
S V₁ O₁ V₂ O₂ 목적(~하기 위해)
그들은 정체성과 경험을 형성한다 / 그리고 예술적 창작물을 만든다 (그들 자신의) / 다른 사람들과 공유하기 위해
↳ 팬은 정체성 및 경험을 형성하고 공유할 창작물을 만듦.

★현재분사 feeling과 engaging은 and로 연결되어 동시동작을 나타내는 분사구문을 이끎.
[4]A person can be an individual fan, / feeling / an "idealized connection with a star, / strong feelings (of memory and nostalgia)," / and engaging in activities (like "*collecting* (to develop a sense of self))."
S V C 분사구문(= as she/he feels ~ and engages ~) feeling의 O 전치사(~ 같은)
한 사람은 개인적인 팬이 될 수 있다 / 느끼며 / '어떤 스타와 이상화된 관계를 / 강한 감정을 (추억과 향수(鄕愁)의)' / 그리고 활동에 참여하며 ('수집하기'와 같은 (자아감을 발달시키는))
↳ 개인적인 감정과 활동으로 스타의 팬이 되어감.

해석

[1]팬은 감정 그 자체를 느낀다. [2]그들은 제공되는 것으로 보이는 것 이상의 의미를 만든다. [3]그들은 정체성과 경험을 형성하고, 다른 사람들과 공유하기 위해 그들 자신의 예술적 창작물을 만든다. [4]한 사람은 '어떤 스타와 이상화된 관계, 추억과 향수(鄕愁)의 강한 감정'을 느끼며, '자아감을 발달시키는 수집하기'와 같은 활동에 참여하며 개인적인 팬이 될 수 있다. [5]그러나 더 흔히 개인적인 경험은 공유된 애착을 가진 다른 사람들이 그들 애정의 대상을 중심으로 어울리는 사회적인 상황에 깊이 새겨진다. [6]팬덤의 많은 즐거움은 다른 팬들과 연결되는 데서 온다. [7]1800년대의 보스턴 사람들은 그들의 일기에서 콘서트에서 군중의 일부가 되는 것을 참석의 즐거움의 일부로 묘사했다. [8]팬이 사랑하는 것은 그들 팬덤의 대상이라기보다는 그 애정이 제공하는 서로에 대한 애착이라는 (그리고 서로 간의 차이라는) 강력한 주장이 제기될 수 있다.

주제문

🔑 개인적인 경험은 같은 스타를 좋아하는 타인과 어울리는 사회적 상황에서 형성됨.

[5]But, more often, / individual experiences (S) are embedded (V) / in *social contexts* [where (관계부사) other people (S′) (with shared attachments) / socialize (V′) / around the object (of their affections)].

그러나 더 흔히 / 개인적인 경험은 깊이 새겨진다 / 사회적인 상황에 [다른 사람들이 (공유된 애착을 가진) / 어울리는 / 대상을 중심으로 (그들 애정의)]

↳ 개인적인 경험은 타인과 어울리는 사회적 상황에서 새겨짐.

[6]Much of the pleasure (S) (of fandom) / **comes from** (V) **being connected to other fans.** (O(동명사구))

많은 즐거움은 (팬덤의) / 다른 팬들과 연결되는 데서 온다

↳ **세부 사항:** 팬덤의 즐거움은 다른 팬들과 관계를 맺을 때 나옴.

*<describe A as B>: A를 B로 묘사하다

[7]In their (= Bostonians') diaries, / Bostonians (S) (of the 1800s) / described (V) / being part of the crowds / at concerts (O(동명사구)) / as (전치사(~로(서))) part of the pleasure (of attendance).

그들의 일기에서 / 보스턴 사람들은 (1800년대의) / 묘사했다 / 군중의 일부가 되는 것을 / 콘서트에서 / 즐거움의 일부로 (참석의)

↳ **예:** 콘서트에 모인 군중의 일부가 되는 것이 팬들의 즐거움임.

🔑 팬들은 '스타'보다 '팬들 간의 애착과 차이'를 더 사랑함.

[8]A compelling argument (S) can be made (V) // that (= 동격 접속사) what fans love (S′(명사절)) is (V′) less the object (of their fandom) / than *the attachments* to (and differentiations from) one another [that (목적격 관계대명사) those affections afford]. (<less A than B>: A라기보다는 B)

강력한 주장이 제기될 수 있다 // 팬이 사랑하는 것은 대상이라기보다는 (그들 팬덤의) / 서로에 대한 애착이라는 (그리고 서로 간의 차이라는) [그 애정이 제공하는]

↳ **결론:** 팬들이 사랑하는 것은 팬덤의 대상이라기보다는 팬들 간의 애착과 차이임.

어휘

for one's own sake ~ 자체가 목적으로, ~ 자체를 위해
on offer 제공되는
identity 정체(성)
idealize 이상화하다
nostalgia 향수(鄕愁)
engage in ~에 참여하다
context 상황; 문맥
attachment 애착; 붙이기
socialize 어울리다, 교제하다; 사회화하다
affection 애정
fandom 팬덤 ((유명인이나 특정 분야를 열성적으로 좋아하는 사람이나 그 무리))
attendance 참석, 출석
differentiation 차이
afford 제공하다; ~할 여유가 되다, ~할 수 있다
[선택지] enhance 향상시키다
collaboration 협업
result from ~에서 기인하다
deepen 깊어지다
heighten 고조시키다
appearance 출연, 등장; (겉)모습

정답 가이드

팬덤의 많은 즐거움이 '어떠하다'는 것인지를 추론해야 한다. 이어지는 구체적인 예에서 콘서트에 모인 '군중의 일부가 되는 것'이 즐거움의 일부이고, 팬이 사랑하는 것은 '서로에 대한 애착이나 서로 간의 차이'라고 주장할 수 있다고 했으므로, 팬덤의 많은 즐거움은 ④ 'comes from being connected to other fans(다른 팬들과 연결되는 데서 온다)'라고 볼 수 있다.

오답 클리닉

① is enhanced by collaborations between global stars (10%)
세계적인 스타들 간의 협업으로 향상된다
팬덤의 대상인 스타들로부터 즐거움을 얻는다는 내용이 아님.

② results from frequent personal contact with a star (15%)
스타와 잦은 개인적인 연락을 나누는 데서 기인한다
팬들과 스타가 서로 개인적인 연락을 나눈다는 내용은 없음.

③ deepens as fans age together with their idols (6%)
팬이 그들의 우상과 함께 나이 들어갈수록 깊어진다
나이에 비례하여 더 즐거워진다는 내용은 없음.

⑤ is heightened by stars' media appearances (3%)
스타가 미디어에 출연함으로써 고조된다
스타가 미디어에 나와서 즐거움이 커진다는 내용은 없음.

01 + 빈칸 후반 (24학년도 대수능 32번 | 정답률 45%) ②

구문분석 & 직독직해

영화 친숙한 영화 음악의 효과

주제문

[1]A musical score / within any film / can add an additional layer / to the film text, //
S V O
음악은 / 어떤 영화 속에서든 / 추가적인 층을 더할 수 있다 / 영화 텍스트에 //

which goes beyond simply imitating / *the action* (viewed).
관계대명사(앞 절 보충 설명) 과거분사
그리고 그것은 단순히 모방하는 것을 넘어선다 / 연기를 (보이는)

↳ 영화 속 음악은 연기를 모방하는 것 이상의 역할을 함.

[2]In *films* [that tell of futuristic worlds], / composers, / (much like sound designers), / have added *freedom* (to create *a world* [that is unknown and new / to the viewer]).
주격 관계대명사 S 전치사구 삽입 V O 주격 관계대명사
영화에서 [미래 세계에 관해 말하는] / 작곡가는 / (사운드 디자이너와 아주 마찬가지로) / 자유를 더해 왔다 (세계를 창조할 수 있는 [알려지지 않은 새로운 / 관객에게])

[3]However, / unlike sound designers, / composers often shy away from / creating *unique pieces* [that reflect these new worlds] /
전치사(~와 달리) S V_1 O_1(동명사구) 주격 관계대명사
그러나 / 사운드 디자이너와 달리 / 작곡가는 흔히 (~을) 피한다 / 독특한 곡을 만들어 내는 것을 [이러한 새로운 세계를 반영하는] /

and often present *musical scores* [that possess familiar structures and cadences].
V_2 O_2 주격 관계대명사
그리고 음악을 흔히 제시한다 [친숙한 구조와 박자를 가진]

↳ **세부 사항(예):** 미래를 배경으로 하는 영화에서 작곡가는 독특한 곡 대신 친숙한 곡을 제시함.

→ 부사절 접속사(~하지만) → (= presenting musical scores ~ cadences)
[4]While it is possible // that this may interfere with creativity and a sense of space and time, //
가주어 V C 진주어(명사절)
it in fact **aids / in viewer access to the film.**
S V
가능하긴 하지만 // 이것(친숙한 구조와 박자를 가진 음악을 제시하는 것)이 창의성과 시공간의 감각을 방해하는 것이 //
사실 그것은 도움이 된다 / 관객이 영화에 접근하는 데

↳ **결과:** 익숙한 곡은 영화의 창의성과 시공간 감각을 방해할 수도 있으나, 실제로는 관객이 영화에 접근하는 데 도움이 됨.

쉽게 알아볼 수 있는 음악을 통해 영화의 상상은 쉽게 알 수 있는 맥락에 놓이게 됨.
[5]Through recognizable scores, / visions (of the future or *a galaxy* (far, far away)) / can be placed / within a recognizable context.
전치사(~을 통해) S 형용사구 V
쉽게 알아볼 수 있는 음악을 통해 / 상상은 (미래나 은하계에 대한 (멀고 먼)) / 놓일 수 있다 / 쉽게 알아볼 수 있는 맥락 안에

[6]Such familiarity allows the viewer to be placed / in a comfortable space //
S V O C
그러한 친숙함이 관객을 놓이게 한다 / 편안한 공간에 //
음악의 친숙함은 관객이 낯선 배경의 영화를 받아들이도록 함.

so that the film may then lead the viewer / to what is an unfamiliar, but acceptable vision (of *a world* (different from their own)).
결과(그래서) S′ V′ O′ to의 O(명사절) 형용사구
그래서 영화는 관객을 인도할 수 있다 / 낯설지만 받아들일 수 있는 영상으로 (세계에 관한 (그들 자신의 것과 다른))

↳ **부연 설명:** 음악의 친숙함을 통해 관객은 낯선 배경의 영화를 받아들이게 됨.

해석

[1]어떤 영화 속에서든 음악은 영화 텍스트에 추가적인 층을 추가할 수 있는데, 그것은 보이는 연기를 단순히 모방하는 것을 넘어선다. [2]미래 세계에 관해 말하는 영화에서, 작곡가는 사운드 디자이너와 아주 마찬가지로, 관객에게 알려지지 않은 새로운 세계를 창조할 수 있는 자유를 더해 왔다. [3]그러나 사운드 디자이너와 달리, 작곡가는 흔히 이러한 새로운 세계를 반영하는 독특한 곡을 만들어 내는 것을 피하고, 친숙한 구조와 박자를 가진 음악을 흔히 제시한다. [4]이것이 창의성과 시공간 감각을 방해할 수 있긴 하지만, 사실 그것은 관객이 영화에 접근하는 데 도움이 된다. [5]쉽게 알아볼 수 있는 음악을 통해 미래나 멀고 먼 은하계에 대한 상상은 쉽게 알아볼 수 있는 맥락 안에 놓일 수 있다. [6]그러한 친숙함이 관객을 편안한 공간에 놓이게 하고, 그래서 영화는 관객을 그들 자신의 것과 다른 세계에 관한 낯설지만 받아들일 수 있는 영상으로 인도할 수 있다.(▶ 영화 음악이 친숙하면 관객은 낯선 배경의 영화를 받아들일 수 있게 된다는 의미)

어휘

layer 층, 겹
go beyond ~을 넘어서다
futuristic 미래의; 초현대적인
composer 작곡가
shy away from ~을 피하다
piece (짧은) 악곡; 조각; 부분
reflect 반영하다; 반사하다; 깊이 생각하다
familiar 친숙한, 익숙한
cf. familiarity 친숙함, 익숙함
interfere with ~을 방해하다
aid 도움(이 되다); 지원
recognizable (쉽게) 알아볼 수 있는
vision 상상, 환상; (영화 스크린의) 영상; 시력
acceptable 받아들일 수 있는
[선택지] free A of B A에서 B를 제거하다
plot 줄거리[구성]; 음모[모의]하다
exotic 이국적인, 외국의
orient ~로 향하게 하다; (특정 목적에) 맞추다
inspire 고취하다; 고무[격려]하다; 영감을 주다

정답 가이드

빈칸 문장에 양보의 부사절이 있고 주절이 앞 내용과 반대되는 내용을 이끌 수 있는 in fact로 이어지고 있다. 이 부사절은 '부정적' 내용이므로 빈칸에는 이와 대조되는 '긍정적' 내용이 들어가야 함을 추론할 수 있다. 부사절의 this와 주절의 it은 모두 앞 문장의 '친숙한 구조와 박자를 가진 음악을 제시하는 것'을 지칭하는데, 부사절에서는 그것이 창의성과 공간 감각을 방해할 수 있다고 하고, 빈칸 문장 뒤에 이어지는 내용에서는 그것이 상상을 쉽게 하고, 낯선 다른 세계에 관해 받아들일 수 있게 인도한다고 했다. 따라서 친숙한 구조와 박자를 가진 음악을 제시하는 것은 사실 ② 'aids in viewer access to the film(관객이 영화에 접근하는 데 도움이 된다)'고 할 수 있다.

오답 클리닉

① frees the plot of its familiarity (25%)
줄거리에서 그것의 친숙함을 제거한다
친숙한 곡을 통해 맥락을 쉽게 알아볼 수 있게 된다고 했으므로 글의 내용과 반대됨.

③ adds to an exotic musical experience (8%)
이국적인 음악 경험을 더한다
친숙한 구조와 박자를 가진 음악을 제시하는 것이므로 이국적인 음악은 적절하지 않음.

④ orients audiences to the film's theme (10%)
관객이 영화의 주제로 향하게 하다
관객을 영화의 주제가 아닌 영화 속 새로운 세계로 향하게 하는 것임.

⑤ inspires viewers to think more deeply (13%)
관객이 더 깊이 생각할 수 있도록 고취한다
영화의 친숙한 곡이 관객을 더 깊이 생각하도록 고취한다는 내용은 없음.

02 + 빈칸 후반 (24학년도 대수능 31번 | 정답률 77%) ②

구문분석 & 직독직해 교육 다양한 표현 형식으로 확장된 읽기

[1]Over the last decade / *the attention* (given to how children learn to read) / has foregrounded /
(S, 과거분사구, V)
지난 10년 동안 / 관심은 (어린이가 읽는 법을 배우는 방법에 주어졌던) / 특히 중시했다 /

the nature (of *textuality*), / and (the nature) (of *the different, interrelated ways* [in which readers of all ages make texts mean]).
(O_1 ★<사역동사 make+O+원형부정사(v)>: O가 v하게 하다[만들다], O_2, 전치사+관계대명사, S′, V′, O′, C′)
본질을 ('텍스트성'의) / 그리고 (본질을) (여러 가지의 서로 밀접하게 연관된 방식의 [모든 연령의 독자가 텍스트를 의미하게 하는])

↳ **대조 A(과거):** 아이들의 읽기 학습에 대한 관심은 텍스트와 의미 이해를 중시함.

주제문
[2]'Reading' now applies / to a greater number of representational forms / than at any time in the past: //
(S_1, V_1)
이제 '읽기'는 적용된다 / 훨씬 더 많은 표현 형식에 / 과거 어느 때보다 //

🔑 글 이외의 다양한 표현 형식들도 텍스트로 여겨짐.
pictures, maps, screens, design graphics and photographs are all regarded / as text.
(S_2, V_2)
그림, 지도, 화면, 디자인 그래픽, 사진이 모두 여겨진다 / 텍스트로 ★<regard A as B(A를 B로 여기다)>의 수동형

↳ **대조 B(현재):** 글 이외의 여러 표현 형식이 텍스트로 여겨지고 '읽기'가 적용됨.

[3]In addition to *the innovations* (made possible in picture books / by new printing processes), /
(~에 더해, 과거분사구)
혁신에 더해 (그림책에서 가능해진 / 새로운 인쇄 공정에 의해) /

design features also predominate / in other kinds, / such as books of poetry and information texts.
(S, V)
디자인적 특징이 또한 두드러진다 / 다른 종류에서도 / 시집이나 정보 텍스트와 같은

↳ **부연 설명:** 그림책에서 가능해진 혁신에 더해 디자인적 특징도 다른 종류의 텍스트에서 두드러짐.

🔑 텍스트에만 집중하던 때보다 해석이 복잡해짐.
[4]Thus, / reading becomes a more complicated kind of interpretation // than it was // when children's attention was focused / on the printed text, / with sketches or pictures as an adjunct.
(S, V, C, 접속사, S′ (= reading), V′, 부사절 접속사(시간), S″, V″, 전치사(~로(서)))
그러므로 / 읽기는 더 복잡한 종류의 해석이 된다 // 그것(읽기)이 그랬던 것보다 // 어린이들의 주의가 집중되었을 때 / 인쇄된 텍스트에 / 스케치나 그림이 부속물이었던

[5]Children now learn / from a picture book // that words and illustrations complement and enhance each other.
(S, V, learn의 O(명사절), 명사절 접속사, S′, V′, O′)
이제 어린이들은 알게 된다 / 그림책으로부터 // 글과 삽화가 서로를 보완하여 향상시킨다는 것을

↳ **결과:** 텍스트에만 집중하던 때에 비해 읽기는 복잡한 해석이 되었으며 아이들은 글과 삽화가 상호 보완적임을 앎.

해석

[1]지난 10년 동안 어린이가 읽는 법을 배우는 방법에 주어졌던 관심은 '텍스트성'의 본질과 모든 연령의 독자가 텍스트를 의미하게 하는 여러 가지의 서로 밀접하게 연관된 방식의 본질을 특히 중시했다. [2]이제 '읽기'는 과거 어느 때보다 훨씬 더 많은 표현 형식에 적용되는데, 그림, 지도, 화면, 디자인 그래픽, 사진이 모두 텍스트로 여겨진다. [3]새로운 인쇄 공정에 의해 그림책에서 가능해진 혁신에 더해, 시집이나 정보 텍스트와 같은 다른 종류에서도 디자인적 특징이 또한 두드러진다. [4]그러므로, 읽기는 어린이들의 주의가 인쇄된 텍스트에 집중되고 스케치나 그림이 부속물이었던 때 그랬던 것보다 더 복잡한 종류의 해석이 된다. [5]이제 어린이들은 그림책으로부터 글과 삽화가 서로를 보완하여 향상시킨다는 것을 알게 된다. [6]읽기는 단순히 단어 인식이 아니다. [7]가장 쉬운 텍스트에서조차도 문장이 '말하는 것'이 흔히 그 문장이 의미하는 것은 아니다.

어휘

attention 관심; 주의, 주목
foreground 특히 중시하다; (그림·사진 등의) 전경
nature 본질; 자연; 천성, 본성
textuality 텍스트성
interrelated 서로 밀접하게 연관된
apply 적용되다[하다]; 신청하다; (약 등을) 바르다
representational (있는 그대로) 표현의, 재현적인
innovation 혁신; 획기적인 것
predominate 두드러지다; 우위를 차지하다
interpretation 해석, 이해, 설명
illustration 삽화; 실례
complement 보완[보충]하다
enhance 향상시키다[높이다]
recognition 인식; 인정
[선택지] acquisition 습득, 획득
subjective 주관적인

[6]Reading is not simply **word recognition**.
S V C
읽기는 단순히 단어 인식이 아니다

🔑 문장이 '말하는 것'이 의미하는 것과 다를 수 있음.
[7]Even in the easiest texts, / what a sentence 'says' / is often not what it means.
S(명사절) V C(명사절)
가장 쉬운 텍스트에서조차도 / 문장이 '말하는 것'이 / 흔히 그 문장이 의미하는 것은 아니다
↳ **결론:** 어떤 문장이 말하는 것과 의미하는 것은 다를 수 있으므로 읽기는 단순한 단어 인식이 아님.

정답 가이드

빈칸 문장으로 보아 읽기가 단순히 '무엇'이 아닌지를 추론해야 한다. 마지막 문장은 아무리 쉬운 텍스트라도 문장의 의미가 글자 그대로가 아닐 수 있음을 설명한다. 따라서, 읽기가 단순한 ② 'word recognition(단어 인식)'이 아니라는 것을 알 수 있다. 정답을 확신하기 위해 글을 처음부터 읽어보면, 과거에 텍스트를 중심으로 의미를 파악했던 것과 달리 이제는 그림, 지도, 사진 등도 텍스트로 여겨져 읽기가 다양한 표현 형식에 적용된다고 했다. 그 결과 읽기는 해석하기 복잡한 것이 되었고 어린이들은 글과 삽화가 서로를 보완하여 의미를 향상시킨다는 것을 알게 된다고 했다. 즉 문장을 이해하려면 삽화와 함께 이해해야 한다는 것이므로 읽기는 단순히 ② 'word recognition(단어 인식)'이 아님을 뒷받침한다.

오답 클리닉

① knowledge acquisition (9%) 지식 습득
지식 습득을 위해 읽기를 한다는 내용은 언급되지 않음.
③ imaginative play (3%) 상상 놀이
읽기는 상상이 아닌 텍스트에 집중되어 있었음.
④ subjective interpretation (5%) 주관적인 해석
읽기가 더 복잡한 해석이 되고 나서는 표면적인 의미를 이해하는 단순한 해석이 아니게 되었을 것임.
⑤ image mapping (6%) 이미지 매핑
이미지 매핑은 텍스트 외의 표현 형식에 해당하므로 틀림.

03 + 빈칸 후반 〈24학년도 9월 모평 33번 | 정답률 21%〉 ④

구문분석 & 직독직해 과학 시대를 앞서간 발명과 발견의 수용

[1]*An invention or discovery* [that is too far ahead of its time] / is worthless; // no one can follow.
S1 주격 관계대명사 V1 C S2 V2
발명이나 발견은 [그 시대보다 너무 앞선] / 가치가 없다 // 누구도 따라갈 수 없기 때문이다
↳ **도입:** 시대보다 앞선 발명이나 발견은 따라갈 수 없기 때문에 가치가 없음.

🔑 이상적인 혁신은 알려진 것에서 한 단계만 나아가게 함.
[2]Ideally, / an innovation opens up only the next step / from what is known /
S V1 O1 from의 O(명사절)
and invites the culture to move forward one hop. ★<invite+O+to-v>: O에게 v할 것을 청하다[권하다]
V2 O2 C
이상적으로 / 혁신은 단지 다음 단계만을 가능하게 한다 / 알려진 것으로부터 /
그리고 그 문화에게 한 걸음 앞으로 나아갈 것을 청한다
↳ **부연 설명:** 혁신은 기존의 발견에서 딱 한 걸음만 나아간 것임.

주제문
[3]An overly futuristic, unconventional, or visionary invention / can fail initially / (it may lack essential not-yet-invented materials or a critical market or proper understanding) /
S1 V1
지나치게 시대를 앞서거나 관습에 얽매이지 않는, 혹은 비현실적인 발명은 / 처음에는 실패할 수도 있다 / (그것은 아직 발명되지 않은 필수적인 물질이나 결정적인 시장 또는 적절한 이해가 부족할 수 있다) /
yet (can) succeed *later*, // when the ecology (of supporting ideas) / catches up.
V2 관계부사(보충 설명) 🔑 시대를 앞서간 발명은 나중에 생태 환경이 아이디어를 따라잡을 때 성공할 수도 있음.
그러나 나중에 성공할 수도 있다 // 생태 환경이 (아이디어를 뒷받침하는) / 따라잡을 때
↳ 지나치게 앞서간 발명은 처음에 실패할 수 있지만 아이디어를 뒷받침하는 생태 환경이 따라잡을 때 성공할 수도 있음.

[4]Gregor Mendel's 1865 theories of genetic heredity / were correct but ignored / for 35 years.
S(복수) V(복수) C1 C2
Gregor Mendel의 1865년 유전자 유전 이론은 / 옳았지만 무시되었다 / 35년 동안
↳ **예:** Gregor Mendel의 유전자 유전 이론은 옳았지만 35년간 무시됨.

★<nor+V+S>: S도 그렇지 않다 ((nor은 접속사로 앞의 not, no, never를 포함한 절 뒤에서 부정문의 연속을 나타냄.))
[5]His sharp insights were not accepted // because they did not explain / *the problems* [(which[that]) biologists had at the time], // nor did his explanation operate / by known mechanisms, //
S1 V1 부사절 접속사(이유) S′ V′ O′ 목적격 관계대명사 생략 조동사 S2 V2
그의 날카로운 통찰력은 받아들여지지 않았다 // 그것(그의 날카로운 통찰력)이 설명하지 않았기 때문에 / 문제들을 [생물학자들이 그 당시에 가졌던] // 그의 설명 역시 작동되지 않았다 / 알려진 메커니즘에 의해 //

해석

[1]그 시대보다 너무 앞선 발명이나 발견은 가치가 없는데, 누구도 따라갈 수 없기 때문이다. [2]이상적으로, 혁신은 알려진 것으로부터 단지 다음 단계만을 가능하게 하고, 그 문화에게 한 걸음 앞으로 나아갈 것을 청한다. [3]지나치게 시대를 앞서거나 관습에 얽매이지 않는, 혹은 비현실적인 발명은 처음에는 실패할 수도 있지만 (그것은 아직 발명되지 않은 필수적인 물질이나 결정적인 시장 또는 적절한 이해가 부족할 수 있다) 아이디어를 뒷받침하는 생태 환경이 따라잡을 때 나중에 성공할 수도 있다. [4]Gregor Mendel의 1865년 유전자 유전 이론은 옳았지만 35년 동안 무시되었다. [5]그의 날카로운 통찰력은 생물학자들이 그 당시에 가졌던 문제들을 설명하지 않았기 때문에 받아들여지지 않았고, 그의 설명 역시 알려진 메커니즘에 의해 작동되지 않았는데, 그래서 그의 발견은 얼리어댑터들에게도 이해 범위 밖에 있었다. [6]수십 년 후 과학은 Mendel의 발견이 답할 수 있는 긴급한 질문에 직면했다. [7]이제 그의 통찰력은 단 한 걸음만 떨어져 있었다. [8]서로 몇 년 이내로, 세 명의 다른 과학자들이 각각 따로 Mendel의 잊힌 연구를 재발견했는데, 물론 그 연구는 내내 그곳에 있었다.

어휘

worthless 가치 없는
ideally 이상적으로
open up ~을 가능하게 하다; ~을 열다
overly 지나치게
futuristic 시대를 앞서는; 미래의

↳ 부사절 접속사(결과)

so his discoveries were out of reach / even for the early adopters.

S′ V′ C′

그래서 그의 발견은 이해 범위 밖에 있었다 / 얼리어댑터들에게도

↳ 부연 설명(발견 초기): 시대를 앞서간 Mendel의 이론은 이해 범위 밖에 있었음.

6 Decades later / science faced *the urgent questions* [that Mendel's discoveries could answer].

S V O 목적격 관계대명사

수십 년 후 / 과학은 긴급한 질문에 직면했다 [Mendel의 발견이 답할 수 있는]

🔑 Mendel의 발견이 답할 수 있는 질문에 직면함 → 받아들여짐.

7 Now / his insights **were only one step away**.

S V C

이제 / 그의 통찰력은 단 한 걸음만 떨어져 있었다

8 Within a few years of one another, / three different scientists each independently rediscovered *Mendel's forgotten work*, // which of course had been there all along.

S V O 관계대명사(보충 설명)

서로 몇 년 이내로 / 세 명의 다른 과학자들이 각각 따로 Mendel의 잊힌 연구를 재발견했다 // 그리고 물론 그 연구는 내내 그곳에 있었다

↳ 부연 설명(수십 년 후): 유전 이론으로 답할 수 있는 질문에 봉착하고서야 다른 과학자들이 이를 재발견하고 받아들이게 됨.

unconventional 관습에 얽매이지 않는
visionary 비현실적인, 공상적인
critical 결정적인, 중대한; 비판적인
catch up (~을) 따라잡다
genetic 유전자의; 유전(학)의
sharp 날카로운, 예리한; 급격한
biologist 생물학자
operate 작동되다; 수술하다
reach (이해) 범위, 능력; 이르다, 닿다
early adopter 얼리어댑터 ((남들보다 먼저 신제품을 구매하는 소비자))
all along 내내, 줄곧
[선택지] raise (질문·문제를) 제기하다; 올리다; 기르다
address 다루다; 주소(를 쓰다); 연설(하다)
alike 동등하게, 똑같이
regain 되찾다

정답 가이드

빈칸 문장과 그 앞 문장을 함께 보면, (어떤 일이 있은 지) 수십 년 후에 과학은 Mendel의 발견이 답할 수 있는 문제에 직면했으며, 이제 Mendel의 통찰력이 '어떠했다'는 것인지를 추론해야 한다. 빈칸 뒤 문장은 Mendel의 연구가 재발견된 것임을 서술한다. 빈칸 문장과 앞뒤 문장을 요약하면 Mendel의 발견을 수십 년 후 재발견하여 질문에 답할 수 있게 된 상황이므로, 빈칸에는 그의 통찰력에 대해 '긍정적'인 내용이 와야 할 것임을 알 수 있다. 앞에서부터 읽어보면, 시대를 너무 앞선 발명이나 발견은 가치가 없으며, 혁신이란 한 걸음만 앞으로 나아가야 함을 서술한다. 이어서 시대를 너무 앞선 예로 Mendel의 유전자 유전 이론이 제시되었고, Mendel이 발견한 지 수십 년 후 그 발견으로 답할 수 있는 시대가 됐을 때에는 그의 통찰력은 단지 다음 단계를 가능하게 하는 것, 즉 한 걸음만 앞으로 나아간 것이 된다. 따라서 빈칸에 들어갈 말로 가장 적절한 것은 ④ 'were only one step away(단 한 걸음만 떨어져 있었다)'이다.

오답 클리닉

① caught up to modern problems (29%)
현대의 문제를 따라잡았다
현대 문제에 관한 언급은 없음. 시대를 앞서간 Mendel의 이론을 과학이 따라잡는 것임.

② raised even more questions (17%)
훨씬 더 많은 질문을 제기했다
Mendel의 이론이 과학이 직면한 질문에 답할 수 있었다고 했으므로 틀림.

③ addressed past and current topics alike (10%)
과거와 현재의 주제를 동등하게 다루었다
Mendel의 이론이 과거와 현재의 주제를 다루었다는 언급은 없음.

⑤ regained acceptance of the public (23%)
대중의 수용을 되찾았다
Mendel의 이론은 이전에 수용된 적이 없으므로 되찾았다는 것은 틀림.

01 빈칸 후반 (23학년도 대수능 32번 | 정답률 68%) ②

구문분석 & 직독직해 언어 언어 혁신을 이끄는 도시

[1] People have always wanted / to be around other people and to learn from them.
S V O(to-v구 병렬)
사람들은 항상 원해 왔다 / 다른 사람들 주위에 머무르며 그들로부터 배우기를

[2] Cities have long been dynamos (of social possibility), / foundries (of art, music, and fashion).
S V C =
도시는 오랫동안 발전기였다 (사회적 가능성의) / 즉 주물 공장 (예술, 음악, 패션의)
↳ 도입: 사람들의 접촉이 활발한 도시를 중심으로 여러 사회적 가능성들이 발전해 왔음.

도시에서 시작된 속어는 사람들이 서로에게 빈번히 노출된 결과물임.
[3] Slang, / or, (if you prefer), / "lexical innovation," / has always started in cities — / an outgrowth (of *all those different people* (so frequently exposed / to one another)).
S 삽입절 V 과거분사구
속어 / 또는 (여러분이 선호한다면) / '어휘의 혁신'은 / 항상 도시에서 시작되었다 / 결과물 (그 모든 각양각색의 사람들의 (매우 빈번히 노출된 / 서로에게))
↳ 세부 사항 1: 속어는 사람들 간의 소통이 빈번한 도시에서 시작됨.

(= Slang) *이중부정은 긍정을 의미함. 강조(생략 가능)
[4] It spreads outward, / in a manner (not unlike *transmissible disease*), // which itself typically "takes off" in cities.
S V 관계대명사(보충 설명) V'
그것(속어)은 밖으로 퍼져나간다 / 방식으로 (전염성 질병과 다르지 않은) // 그리고 그것(전염성 질병) 자체는 보통 도시에서 '시작한다'

[5] If, / (as the noted linguist Leonard Bloomfield argued), // *the way* [(that) a person talks] / is a "composite result (of what he has heard before)," //
부사절 접속사(조건) 삽입절 S' 관계부사 생략 V' C' of의 O(명사절)
만약에 ~라면 / (저명한 언어학자 Leonard Bloomfield가 주장하듯) // 방식이 [한 사람이 말하는] / '합성 결과물'이(라면) (그가 전에 들었던 것의) //

언어 혁신은 많은 사람들이 소통하는 곳(도시)에서 일어남.
then language innovation would happen // where the most people / heard and talked to the most other people.
S V 장소의 부사절 heard와 talked to의 공통 O
그렇다면 언어 혁신은 일어날 것이다 // 가장 많은 사람들이 (~한) 곳에서 / 가장 많은 다른 사람들이 하는 말을 듣고 가장 많은 다른 사람들에게 말한
↳ 세부 사항 2: 전염성 질병이 퍼져나가듯이 언어 혁신도 많은 사람들이 소통하는 도시에서 일어남.

주제문
(= cities)
[6] Cities drive taste change // because they **offer** / **the greatest exposure** (**to *other people***), //
S V O 부사절 접속사 S' V' O'
도시는 취향 변화를 이끈다 // 그곳이 제공하기 때문에 / 가장 많은 노출을 (다른 사람들에 대한) //
who not surprisingly are often *the creative people* [(who(m)[that]) cities seem to attract].
관계대명사(보충 설명) V' C' 목적격 관계대명사 생략
그리고 그들(다른 사람들)은 놀랄 것도 없이 흔히 창의적인 사람들이다 [도시가 끌어들이는 듯 보이는]
↳ 사람들 간의 접촉이 가장 많은 도시에서 취향 변화가 일어남.

[7] *Media*, / (ever more global, ever more far-reaching), / spread language faster / to more people.
S 형용사구 삽입 V O
미디어는 / (그 어느 때보다 더 세계적이고, 그 어느 때보다 더 멀리까지 미치는) / 언어를 더 빨리 퍼뜨린다 / 더 많은 사람에게
↳ 부연 설명: 미디어를 통해 언어 변화는 더 빨리 전파됨.

해석

[1]사람들은 항상 다른 사람들 주위에 머무르며 그들로부터 배우기를 원해 왔다. [2]도시는 오랫동안 사회적 가능성의 발전기, 즉 예술, 음악, 패션의 주물 공장이었다. [3]속어, 또는 여러분이 선호한다면 '어휘의 혁신'은 항상 도시에서 시작되었는데, 서로에게 매우 빈번히 노출된 그 모든 각양각색의 사람들의 결과물이다. [4]그것(속어)은 전염성 질병과 다르지 않은 방식으로 밖으로 퍼져나가는데, 그것(전염성 질병) 자체는 보통 도시에서 '시작한다.' [5]저명한 언어학자 Leonard Bloomfield가 주장하듯, 만약에 한 사람이 말하는 방식이 '그가 전에 들었던 것의 합성 결과물'이라면, 언어 혁신은 가장 많은 사람들이 가장 많은 다른 사람들이 하는 말을 듣고 가장 많은 다른 사람들에게 말한 곳에서 일어날 것이다. [6]도시는 그곳이 다른 사람들에 대한 가장 많은 노출을 제공하기 때문에 취향 변화를 이끄는데, 그들(다른 사람들)은 놀랄 것도 없이 흔히 도시가 끌어들이는 듯 보이는 창의적인 사람들이다. [7]그 어느 때보다 더 세계적이고, 그 어느 때보다 더 멀리까지 미치는 미디어는 언어를 더 빨리 더 많은 사람에게 퍼뜨린다.

어휘

dynamo 발전기
slang 속어, 은어
innovation 혁신; 획기적인 것
outgrowth 결과물; ~에서 자라난 것
frequently 빈번히, 종종
expose 노출시키다, 드러내다
cf. exposure 노출; 폭로
spread 퍼지다; 퍼뜨리다; 확산
transmissible 전염성의; 보낼[전할] 수 있는
take off 시작[출발]하다; 이륙하다
noted 저명한, 유명한
linguist 언어학자
composite 합성의; 합성물
drive 이끌다, 추진하다; (차를) 몰다
far-reaching (영향이) 멀리까지 미치는
[선택지] ideal 이상적인
social mobility 사회 이동
ambitious 야심 있는

정답 가이드

빈칸 문장으로 보아 도시가 '무엇' 때문에 취향을 변화시키는지를 추론해야 한다. 이어지는 설명은 '그들이 도시가 끌어들이는 창의적인 사람들이고 미디어가 언어를 더 빨리 퍼뜨린다'는 내용이므로 '그들'이라는 창의적인 사람들 때문에 취향이 변화된다는 것으로 이해된다. 앞부터 설명을 읽어보면, 도시는 사회 발전기이며 '서로에게 매우 빈번히 노출된 각양각색의 사람들'의 결과물인 속어와 같은 어휘 혁신이 도시에서 시작된다고 했다. 사람은 전에 들었던 것을 합성해 말하므로, 언어 혁신은 많은 사람들이 모인 곳에서 일어날 것이다. 즉, 취향을 변화시키는 것은 도시의 이러한 특성 때문일 것이므로 빈칸에 들어갈 말로 가장 적절한 것은 도시가 ② 'offer the greatest exposure to other people(다른 사람들에 대한 많은 노출을 제공한다)'이다.

오답 클리닉

① provide rich source materials for artists (17%)
예술가들에게 풍부한 원재료를 공급한다
art와 creative people을 활용한 오답. 원재료를 공급한다는 내용은 없음.

③ cause cultural conflicts among users of slang (6%)
속어 사용자들 사이에서 문화 갈등을 초래한다
문화 갈등으로 언어 취향의 변화가 생긴다는 내용은 없음.

④ present ideal research environments to linguists (6%)
언어학자들에게 이상적인 연구 환경을 제공한다
언어학자의 말을 인용한 것을 활용한 오답.

⑤ reduce the social mobility of ambitious outsiders (3%)
야심 있는 외부인의 사회 이동을 줄인다
외부인의 사회 이동에 관한 언급은 없음.

02 ✦ 빈칸 후반 〈23학년도 9월 모평 31번 | 정답률 74%〉 ②

구문분석 & 직독직해 동물 인간과 비슷한 동물의 영역 분할

1 More than just *having* territories, / animals also *partition* them.
(animals: S, partition: V, them: O(= territories))
그저 영역을 '갖는 것'을 넘어서 / 동물은 또한 그것들(영역)을 '분할한다'

2 And / this insight turned out / to be particularly useful / for zoo husbandry.
(this insight: S, turned out: V, to be particularly useful: C)
그리고 / 이러한 통찰은 밝혀졌다 / 특히 유용하다고 / 동물원 관리에
↳ **도입:** 동물들은 자신의 영역을 분할함.

주제문
3 An animal's territory has / *an internal arrangement* [that Heini Hediger compared / to the inside of a person's house].
(An animal's territory: S, has: V, an internal arrangement: O, that: 목적격 관계대명사)
동물의 영역은 갖는다 / 내부 배치를 [Heini Hediger가 비유한 / 사람의 집 내부에]
↳ 인간이 집 내부를 나누듯이 동물도 영역을 나눔.

4 Most of us assign separate functions / to separate rooms, // ⊶ 인간은 방에 따라 다른 기능을 할당함.
(S_1: Most of us, V_1: assign, O_1: separate functions)
우리 대부분은 서로 다른 기능을 할당한다 / 서로 다른 방에 //
★조건의 부사절에서는 현재시제가 미래를 대신함.
but even if you look at a one-room house // you will find the same internal specialization.
(even if: 부사절 접속사(조건, 양보), S_2: you, V_2: will find, O_2: the same internal specialization)
하지만 여러분이 원룸 주택을 살펴봐도 // 여러분은 같은 내부의 특수화를 발견할 것이다
↳ **세부 사항 1(인간의 영역 구분):** 방에 따라 기능을 나눔.

5 In a cabin or a mud hut, / or even a Mesolithic cave (from 30,000 years ago), /
오두막이나 진흙 오두막 안 / 혹은 심지어 중석기 시대의 동굴 안에도 (3만 년 전의) /
this part is for cooking, // that part is for sleeping; // this part is for making tools and weaving, // that part is for waste.
⊶ 공간별 다른 기능 할당을 예를 들어 보여줌.
이 부분은 요리를 위한 것이다 // 저 부분은 잠을 자기 위한 것이다 // 이 부분은 도구 제작과 옷감 짜기를 위한 것이다 // 저 부분은 폐기물을 위한 것이다
↳ **예:** 요리 공간, 자는 공간, 작업 공간, 폐기물을 두는 공간을 분리함.

6 We keep **a neat functional organization.**
(We: S, keep: V, a neat functional organization: O)
우리는 정돈된 기능적 구조를 유지한다
↳ **결론:** 인간은 기능에 따라 공간을 나눔.

7 To a varying extent, / other animals do the same.
(other animals: S, do: V, the same: O)
다양한 정도로 / 다른 동물들도 똑같은 것을 한다

해석

1 그저 영역을 '갖는 것'을 넘어서, 동물은 또한 영역을 '분할한다'. 2 그리고 이러한 통찰은 동물원 관리에 특히 유용하다고 밝혀졌다. 3 동물의 영역은 Heini Hediger가 사람의 집 내부에 비유한 내부 배치를 갖는다. 4 우리 대부분은 서로 다른 방에 서로 다른 기능을 할당하지만, 여러분이 원룸 주택을 살펴봐도 여러분은 같은 내부의 특수화를 발견할 것이다. 5 오두막이나 진흙 오두막 안, 혹은 심지어 3만 년 전의 중석기 시대의 동굴 안에도, 이 부분은 요리를 위한 것이고, 저 부분은 잠을 자기 위한 것이며, 이 부분은 도구 제작과 옷감 짜기를 위한 것이고, 저 부분은 폐기물을 위한 것이다. 6 우리는 정돈된 기능적 구조를 유지한다. 7 다양한 정도로, 다른 동물들도 똑같은 것을 한다. 8 동물의 종에 따라, 동물의 영역 중 일부는 먹기 위한 것이고, 일부는 잠을 자기 위한 것이며, 일부는 헤엄치거나 뒹굴기 위한 것이고, 일부는 폐기물을 위해 남겨질 수도 있다.

어휘

territory 영역; 지역, 영토
partition 분할(하다); 칸막이
insight 통찰(력)
internal 내부의; 내재적인
arrangement 배치; 준비; 정돈
assign 할당하다, 배정하다; 선임하다
separate 서로 다른, 별개의; 분리된; 분리하다
specialization 특수[전문]화
cabin (보통 나무로 된) 오두막; (비행기) 객실
Mesolithic 중석기 시대의
weave (옷감 등을) 짜다
neat 정돈된, 단정한; 깔끔한
organization 구조, 구성; 조직, 기구
extent 정도, 규모
wallow 뒹굴다

🗝 동물도 기능에 따라 영역을 구분함.

[8]A part of an animal's territory is for eating, / a part (is) for sleeping, / a part (is) for swimming or wallowing, // a part may be set aside for waste, / depending on the species of animal.

*a part와 for 사이에는 반복되는 is가 생략됨.

동물의 영역 중 일부는 먹기 위한 것이다 / 일부는 잠을 자기 위한 것이다 / 일부는 헤엄치거나 뒹굴기 위한 것이다 // 일부는 폐기물을 위해 따로 남겨질 수도 있다 / 동물의 종에 따라

↳ **세부 사항 2(동물의 영역 구분):** 먹는 공간, 자는 공간, 활동하는 공간, 폐기물을 두는 공간 등을 나눔.

set aside ~을 따로 남겨 두다
[선택지] stock 비축, 저장; 재고품
supply 용품, 비품; 공급(하다)
observe (규칙 등을) 지키다, 준수하다; (관찰에 의해) 알다, 보다

정답 가이드

빈칸 문장으로 보아 우리가 '무엇을' 유지하는지를 추론해야 한다. 이어지는 설명에서 다른 동물도 똑같은 것을 하며, 종에 따라 영역 중 일부는 먹기 위한 것, 일부는 잠을 자기 위한 것 등으로 구분되어 있음을 설명했다. 이는 우리가 기능에 따라 영역을 구분한다는 내용이므로, 빈칸에 들어갈 말로 가장 적절한 것은 ② 'a neat functional organization(정돈된 기능적 구조)'이다. 글의 나머지 부분을 통해 확인하면, 우리가 서로 다른 방에 서로 다른 기능을 할당한다거나 오래 전 동굴 안에도 부분마다 서로 다른 기능이 있었다는 것과도 의미 연결이 자연스럽다.

오답 클리닉

① an interest in close neighbors (8%) 가까운 이웃에 대한 관심
이웃에 관한 내용은 언급되지 않음.

③ a stock of emergency supplies (4%) 비상 용품의 비축
비상 용품의 비축에 관한 내용이 아님.

④ a distance from potential rivals (6%) 잠재적 경쟁자로부터의 거리
잠재적 경쟁자에 대한 언급은 없음.

⑤ a strictly observed daily routine (8%) 엄격하게 지켜지는 일상
일상을 지키는 것에 관한 내용이 아님.

03 + 빈칸 후반 〈22학년도 6월 모평 33번 | 정답률 44%〉 ②

구문분석 & 직독직해

환경 인간의 통제를 배제할 수 없는 자연

[1]Concepts (of nature) / are always cultural statements.
S(복수) V(복수) C

개념은 (자연의) / 항상 문화적 진술이다

↳ **도입:** 자연은 문화적으로 정의됨.

*much of a(n): ((부정문에서)) 대단한; 심한, 지독한

[2]This may not strike Europeans / as much of an insight, // for Europe's landscape is so much of a blend.
S V O 부사절 접속사(이유) S′ V′ C′

이것은 유럽인들에게 인상을 주지 않을지도 모른다 / 대단한 통찰이라는 // 왜냐하면 유럽의 풍경은 아주 많은 혼합이기 때문이다

[3]But / in the new worlds — / 'new' at least to Europeans — / the distinction appeared much clearer / not only to European settlers and visitors / but also to their descendants.
S V (↱ 비교급 강조 부사) C

*<not only A but also B>: A뿐만 아니라 B도 / 전치사구 병렬

그러나 / 신세계(아메리카 대륙)에서 / 적어도 유럽인들에게는 '새로운' / 그 차이는 훨씬 더 분명해 보였다 / 유럽 정착민과 방문객에게뿐만 아니라 / 그들의 후손에게도

↳ 유럽인들은 문화적 자연 개념에 익숙하지만, 새로운 세계에서는 차이를 구분하게 됨.

[4]For that reason, / they had *the fond conceit* (of *primeval nature* (uncontrolled / by human associations))
S V O 과거분사구

그런 이유 때문에 / 그들은 허황된 생각을 가졌다 (원시 자연에 관해 (통제되지 않는 / 인간과의 연관에 의해))

[which could later find expression / in an admiration for wilderness].
주격 관계대명사

[후에 표현을 찾을 수 있었던 / 황야에 대한 감탄에서]

↳ **결과:** 인간의 손이 닿지 않은 원시 자연에 대해 생각하게 됨.

🗝 자연은 인간의 개입을 받지 않는 자율적인 역동성이 있다고 보일 수 있음.

[5]Ecological relationships certainly have their own logic // and in this sense / 'nature' can be seen / to have a self-regulating but not necessarily stable *dynamic* (independent of human intervention).
S_1 V_1 O S_2 V_2 C 형용사구

*<not necessarily>: ((부분 부정)) 반드시 ~은 아닌

생태학적 관계는 확실히 그것 나름의 논리를 가지고 있었다 // 그리고 이런 의미에서 / '자연'은 보일 수 있다 / 자율적이지만 반드시 안정적이지는 않은 역동성을 가지고 있는 것으로 (인간의 개입과 무관한)

↳ **부연 설명:** (원시) 자연은 인간의 개입과 무관한 역동성을 지니는 것으로 보일 수 있음.

해석

[1]자연의 개념은 항상 문화적 진술이다.(▶ 자연의 개념은 문화의 영향을 받는다는 의미) [2]이것은 유럽인들에게 대단한 통찰이라는 인상을 주지 않을지도 모르는데, 왜냐하면 유럽의 풍경(자연)은 아주 많은 혼합(▶ 많은 문화의 영향을 받았다는 의미)이기 때문이다. [3]그러나 적어도 유럽인들에게는 '새로운' 신세계(아메리카 대륙)에서 그 차이(▶ 유럽의 자연과 달리 문화의 영향을 받지 않은 신세계 자연이 주는 차이)는 유럽 정착민과 방문객뿐만 아니라 그들의 후손에게도 훨씬 더 분명해 보였다. [4]그런 이유 때문에, 그들은 인간과의 연관에 의해 통제되지 않는 원시 자연에 관해 후에 황야에 대한 감탄에서 표현을 찾을 수 있었던 허황된 생각을 가졌다. [5]생태학적 관계는 확실히 그것 나름의 논리를 가지고 있었고, 이런 의미에서 '자연'은 자율적이지만 반드시 안정적이지는 않은 인간의 개입과 무관한 역동성을 가지고 있는 것으로 보일 수 있다. [6]그러나 생태학적 상호 작용의 환경은 점점 더 인류에 의해 설정되어 왔다. [7]우리는 사자가 어떻게 또는 무엇을 먹는지를 정하지 못할 수도 있지만, 사자가 어디에서 먹이를 먹을지를 확실히 통제할 수 있다.

어휘

statement 진술, 성명
strike A as B A에게 B라는 인상[느낌]을 주다
landscape 풍경
blend 혼합(물); 섞다
distinction 차이, 구별
settler 정착민
descendant 후손, 자손

주제문

[6]But / the context (for ecological interactions) / **has increasingly been set** / **by humanity.**
S(단수) V
그러나 / 환경은 (생태학적 상호 작용의) / 점점 더 설정되어 왔다 / 인류에 의해
↳ **역접:** 자연은 인간의 개입으로 만들어짐.

인간은 사실 자연을 통제할 수 있음.
[7]We may not determine / how or what a lion eats // but we certainly can regulate / where the lion feeds.
S₁ V₁ O₁(명사절) S₂ V₂ O₂(명사절)
우리는 정하지 못할 수도 있다 / 사자가 어떻게 또는 무엇을 먹는지를 // 하지만 우리는 확실히 통제할 수 있다 / 사자가 어디에서 먹이를 먹을지를
↳ **부연 설명:** 인간은 부분적으로 자연을 통제함.

fond 허황된; 애정 어린
association 연관(성); 연상; 연합
admiration 감탄, 존경
wilderness 황야, 황무지
self-regulating 자율적인
dynamic 역동성, 역학
independent 무관한, 별개의; 독립적인
intervention 개입; 중재
[선택지] practice 관행, 관례; 실행(하다)

정답 가이드

빈칸이 있는 문장이 역접 연결어 But으로 이어지므로, 앞 내용과 상반되는 내용임을 알 수 있다. 이어지는 문장에서 구체적으로 사자를 예로 들어서, 우리는 사자가 먹이를 먹을 곳을 통제할 수 있다고 했으므로, 생태학적 상호 작용 환경은 '인간이 통제할 수 있다'는 내용이 되어야 적절하다. 이를 확인하기 위해 앞에서부터 읽어보면, 유럽들이 신대륙에 와서 인간에 의해 통제되지 않는 원시 자연에 대해 감탄했다고 하며, '자연'은 인간의 개입과 무관한 역동성을 갖는 것으로 보일 수 있다고 했다. 이와 역접 내용이 되려면 인간이 개입하는 내용이 들어가야 하므로 빈칸에 들어갈 말로 가장 적절한 것은 ② 'has increasingly been set by humanity(점점 더 인류에 의해 설정되어 왔다)'이다.

오답 클리닉

① has supported new environment-friendly policies (16%)
새로운 친환경적인 정책을 지지해 왔다
친환경적인 정책은 언급되지 않음.

③ inspires creative cultural practices (10%)
창의적인 문화적 관행을 고무한다
창의적인 문화적 관행은 언급되지 않음.

④ changes too frequently to be regulated (14%)
너무 자주 바뀌어 통제될 수 없다
환경이 자주 바뀐다는 언급은 없으며, 인간의 통제를 받는다고 했으므로 틀림.

⑤ has been affected by various natural conditions (16%)
다양한 자연 조건의 영향을 받아 왔다
자연 조건의 영향이 아니라 인간의 통제를 받는 것이므로 틀림.

01 + 빈칸 마지막 〈23학년도 대수능 31번 | 정답률 47%〉 ②

구문분석 & 직독직해 사회 스포츠 저널리즘의 역설적 지위

주제문

[1]There is *something* deeply paradoxical (about the professional status of sports journalism), / especially in the medium of print.
V S
몹시 역설적인 것이 있다 (스포츠 저널리즘의 직업적 지위에 관해) / 특히 인쇄 매체에서
↳ 스포츠 저널리즘의 직업적 위상에 대한 역설이 있음.

[2]In discharging their usual responsibilities (of description and commentary), / reporters' accounts of sports events are eagerly consulted / by sports fans, //
= S V
그들(기자)의 일상적인 책무를 이행함에 있어서 (설명과 해설인) /
기자들의 스포츠 경기에 관한 설명은 열심히 찾아진다 / 스포츠 팬들에 의해 //

while in their broader journalistic role (of covering sport in its many forms), / sports journalists are among the most visible (of all contemporary writers).
부사절 접속사(~ 한편) = S′ V′ C′ ★<the+형용사>: ~인[한] 사람들
한편 그들의 더 폭넓은 기자의 역할에서 (여러 형식으로 스포츠를 취재하는) / 스포츠 기자들은 가장 눈에 띄는 사람들 중 하나이다 (모든 현대의 저술가들 중에서)
↳ **스포츠 기자 직업의 긍정적 측면 1:** 영향력 있고 돋보임.

[3]The ruminations (of the elite class of 'celebrity' sports journalists) / are much sought after / by the major newspapers, /
S V
숙고는 ('유명 인사' 스포츠 기자들로 이루어진 엘리트 등급의) / 많이 찾아진다 / 주요 신문사에 의해 /
★분사구문의 의미상의 주어(their lucrative contracts)와 문장의 주어(The ruminations)가 일치하지 않아 분사 앞에 의미상의 주어를 남김.
their lucrative contracts being the envy (of colleagues (in other 'disciplines' of journalism)).
분사구문(= and their lucrative contracts are ~)
그들('유명 인사' 엘리트급의 스포츠 기자들)의 수익성이 좋은 계약은 부러움의 대상이다 (동료들의 (저널리즘의 다른 '분야'에 있는))
↳ **스포츠 기자 직업의 긍정적 측면 2:** 좋은 금전적 대우를 받음.

🔑 앞의 긍정적 측면과 대비되는 부정적 측면이 제시됨: 직업적 위상이 없음.
[4]Yet sports journalists do not have *a standing* in their profession [that corresponds to the size (of their readerships [or] of their pay packets)], /
주격 관계대명사 전치사구 병렬
하지만 스포츠 기자들은 자신들의 직업에서 지위를 갖지 않는다 [크기와 일치하는 (그들의 독자 수나 급여 액수의)]

with *the old saying* (now reaching the status of cliché) // that sport is the 'toy department of the news media' / still (being) readily to hand / as a dismissal of the worth (of what sports journalists do).
★<with+O'+v-ing>: O'가 ~한 채로[~하면서] 현재분사구 동격 접속사 전치사(~로(서)) of의 O(명사절)
옛말이 ~한 채로 (이제는 상투적인 문구의 지위에 도달한) // 스포츠는 '뉴스 매체의 장난감 부서'라는 /
여전히 손쉽게 접할 수 있는 / 가치에 대한 묵살로서 (스포츠 기자들이 하는 일의)
↳ **스포츠 기자 직업의 부정적 측면:** 하는 일이 평가절하됨.

동격 접속사
[5]This reluctance / to take sports journalism seriously / produces the paradoxical outcome // that sports newspaper writers are much read [but] little **admired**.
S V O = 거의 ~않는(준부정어)
이러한 꺼림은 / 스포츠 저널리즘을 진지하게 받아들이는 데 대한 / 역설적인 결과를 만들어 낸다 // 스포츠 신문 기자들이 많이 읽히지만 거의 존경받지 못하는
↳ **결과:** 사람들이 스포츠 기사를 많이 봐도(긍정적 측면) 스포츠 기자는 존경하지 않음(부정적 측면).

해석

[1]특히 인쇄 매체에서 스포츠 저널리즘의 직업적 지위에 관해 몹시 역설적인 것이 있다. [2]기자들의 일상적인 책무인 설명과 해설을 이행함에 있어서 기자들의 스포츠 경기에 관한 설명은 스포츠 팬들에 의해 열심히 찾아지는 한편, 여러 형식으로 스포츠를 취재하는 그들의 더 폭넓은 기자의 역할에서 스포츠 기자들은 모든 현대의 저술가들 중에서 가장 눈에 띄는 사람들 중 하나이다. [3]'유명 인사' 스포츠 기자들로 이루어진 엘리트 등급의 숙고는 주요 신문사에 의해 많이 찾아지며, 그들의 수익성이 좋은 계약은 저널리즘의 다른 '분야'에 있는 동료들의 부러움의 대상이다. [4]하지만 스포츠 기자들은 자신들의 직업에서 그들의 독자 수나 급여 액수의 크기와 일치하는 지위를 갖지 않으며, 스포츠 기자들이 하는 일의 가치에 대한 묵살로서 (이제는 상투적인 문구의 지위에 도달한) 스포츠는 '뉴스 매체의 장난감 부서'라는 옛말을 여전히 손쉽게 접할 수 있다. (▶정치, 경제 분야의 뉴스와 달리 스포츠 뉴스는 오락으로 치부되어 진지하게 여겨지지 않는다는 의미) [5]스포츠 저널리즘을 진지하게 받아들이는 데 대한 이러한 꺼림은 스포츠 신문 기자들이 많이 읽히지만 거의 존경받지 못하는 역설적인 결과를 만들어 낸다.

어휘

paradoxical 역설적인
status 지위, 신분; 상황
medium (*pl.* media) 매체, 수단; 중간의
description 설명, 서술
commentary (스포츠·텔레비전의) 해설, 실황 방송
account 설명, 기술; (예금) 계좌
eagerly 열심히; 열망하여
consult 찾아보다, 참고하다; 상담하다
cover 취재하다; 덮다, 가리다
visible 눈에 띄는, 두드러진; 눈에 보이는
contemporary 현대의, 동시대의
celebrity 유명 인사
sought after 많이 찾아지는, 수요가 많은
discipline 분야, 부문; 규율, 훈육; 학문
standing 지위, 평판
correspond to A A와 일치하다
readership 독자 수[층]
pay packet 급여 액수
cliché 상투적인 문구[생각]
readily 손쉽게; 선뜻
to hand (쉽게) 접할[사용할] 수 있는
dismissal 묵살, 일축; 해고
reluctance 꺼림, 마지못해 함
take A seriously A를 진지하게 받아들이다
[선택지] censor 검열하다; 검열관

정답 가이드

스포츠 저널리즘을 진지하게 받아들이지 않는 것은 스포츠 신문 기자들이 쓴 것을 많이 읽지만 동시에 '무엇'하지 못하는 역설이 있는지를 추론해야 한다. 지문 초반에서 스포츠 기자는 영향력 있고 수익성이 좋다는 장점을 언급했지만, 역접 연결어 Yet(하지만) 이후에서는 스포츠 기자의 일은 가치가 묵살된다는 부정적 측면이 제시되었다. 따라서 빈칸에 들어갈 말로 가장 적절한 것은 ② 'admired(존경받는)'이다.

The 주의 앞에 준부정어 little(거의 ~ 않는)이 있어 빈칸을 부정하는 의미가 됨에 주의한다.

오답 클리닉

① paid (32%) 돈을 받는
문장 3에서 유명 스포츠 기자들은 수익성이 좋다고 했으므로 글의 내용과 반대됨.

The 주의 마지막 문장에서 little은 역접 연결어 but으로 much read와 연결되었다. 독자가 기사를 많이 찾아본다는 긍정적 측면이 much read로 표현된 것이고 but 뒤에는 부정적인 내용을 담아야 앞과 반대되는 역설 관계가 완성될 수 있다.

③ censored (8%) 검열되는
news와 연관된 어휘이지만 검열에 관한 내용은 없음.

④ challenged (8%) 도전받는
스포츠 기자라는 직업은 오히려 직업적 위상이 높지 않다고 했으므로 글의 내용과 반대됨.

⑤ discussed (6%) 논의되는
스포츠 기자라는 직업에 대한 논의가 없다는 내용은 없고, 오히려 눈에 띈다고 했음.

02 + 빈칸 마지막 (23학년도 9월 모평 34번 | 정답률 55%) ①

구문분석 & 직독직해

학문 아동 연구 심리학에 필요한 문학적 접근법

[1] In trying to explain // how different disciplines attempt to understand autobiographical memory / the literary critic Daniel Albright said, // "Psychology is a garden, // literature is a wilderness."
(in의 O(동명사구); to explain의 O(명사절); S; V)
설명하려고 할 때 // 서로 다른 학문이 자전적 기억을 어떻게 이해하려고 시도하는지를 / 문학평론가 Daniel Albright는 말했다 // '심리학은 정원이다 // 문학은 황무지이다'
↳ 심리학과 문학은 인간의 자전적 기억을 이해하는 방식이 서로 다름.

[2] He meant, // (I believe), // that psychology seeks / to make patterns, / (to) find regularity, / and ultimately (to) impose order / on human experience and behavior.
(S; V; 삽입절; 명사절 접속사; S'; V'; O'1; O'2; O'3; → meant의 O(명사절); *<seek to-v>: v하려고 하다)
그는 (~의) 뜻으로 말했다 // (내가 생각하기에) // 심리학이 (~하려고) 한다는 / 패턴을 만들려고 / 규칙성을 발견하려고 / 그리고 궁극적으로 질서를 부과하려고 / 인간의 경험과 행동에
↳ 대조 A(심리학): 경험의 패턴과 규칙성, 질서에 초점을 둠.

[3] Writers, / by contrast, / dive into the unruly, untamed depths (of human experiences).
(S; V; O(명사구))
작가는 / 반면에 / 제멋대로 굴고, 길들여지지 않은 깊이에 몰두한다 (인간 경험의)
↳ 대조 B(문학): 경험의 제멋대로인, 길들여지지 않은 측면에 초점을 둠.

[4] What he said about understanding memory / can be extended / to our questions (about young children's minds).
(S(명사절); V)
기억을 이해하는 것에 관해 그가 말한 것은 / 확장될 수 있다 / 우리의 질문으로 (어린아이의 마음에 관한)
↳ 예: 아동의 마음을 이해하는 경우

[5] If we psychologists are too bent / on identifying the orderly pattern, / the regularities of children's minds, // we may miss / an essential and pervasive characteristic (of our topic): // the child's more unruly and imaginative ways (of talking and thinking).
(부사절 접속사(조건); the orderly pattern = the regularities of children's minds; S; V; O; characteristic = the child's more unruly ... ways)
만약 우리 심리학자들이 너무 열심이라면 / 질서 있는 패턴을 찾는 데 / 즉 아이 마음의 규칙성 //
⊶ 심리학자들의 접근법은 아이들의 근본적이고 만연한 특성을 놓칠 수 있음.
우리는 놓칠 수도 있다 / 근본적이고 만연한 특성을 (우리 주제의) // 즉 아이의 더욱 제멋대로이고 상상력이 풍부한 방식 (대화와 사고의)
↳ 대조 A(심리학): 심리학의 방식은 아동의 자유분방함이라는 근본적인 특성을 놓칠 수 있음.

해석

[1] 서로 다른 학문이 자전적 기억을 어떻게 이해하려고 시도하는지를 설명하려고 할 때, 문학평론가 Daniel Albright는 '심리학은 정원이고, 문학은 황무지이다'라고 말했다.(▶ 심리학의 접근법이 정원을 잘 정돈하는 것, 문학의 접근법이 거친 자연 그대로의 것을 받아들이라는 것과 같음을 함축한 표현) [2] 내가 생각하기에, 그는 심리학이 패턴을 만들고, 규칙성을 발견하고, 궁극적으로 인간의 경험과 행동에 질서를 부과하려고 한다는 뜻으로 말했다. [3] 반면에, 작가는 인간 경험의 제멋대로 굴고, 길들여지지 않은 깊이에 몰두한다. [4] 기억을 이해하는 것에 관해 그가 말한 것은 어린아이의 마음에 관한 우리의 질문으로 확장될 수 있다. [5] 만약 우리 심리학자들이 질서 있는 패턴, 즉 아이 마음의 규칙성을 찾는 데 너무 열심이라면, 우리는 우리 주제의 근본적이고 만연한 특성, 즉 아이의 더욱 제멋대로이고 상상력이 풍부한 대화와 사고의 방식을 놓칠 수도 있다. [6] 다소 제멋대로이고 색다른 사고방식에 끌리는 것처럼 보이는 사람은 재능이 발달한 작가나 문학 학자뿐만이 아니라, 어린아이도 또한 그러하다. [7] 어린아이에게 관심이 있는 심리학자는 아이가 어떻게 생각하는지를 잘 이해하기 위해 조금 더 자주 위험을 무릅쓰고 황무지로 들어가야 할지도 모른다.

어휘

autobiographical 자전적인, 자서전체의
wilderness 황무지, 황야
regularity 규칙성
ultimately 궁극적으로, 결국
impose A on B A를 B에 부과하다
order 질서; 순서; 명령, 지시; 주문
cf. orderly 질서 있는; 정돈된
dive into ~에 몰두하다; ~에 뛰어들다

아이들의 제멋대로이고 색다른 사고방식은 문학이 초점을 두는 부분과 같음.

⁶It is not only the developed writer or literary scholar // who seems drawn / toward a somewhat wild and idiosyncratic way of thinking; // young children are as well.

강조구문(…한 사람[것]은 바로 ~이다) *are은 대동사로 뒤에 drawn ~ thinking이 생략됨. S₂ V₂(대동사)

재능이 발달한 작가나 문학 학자뿐만이 아니다 // 끌리는 것처럼 보이는 사람은 / 다소 제멋대로이고 색다른 사고방식에 // 어린아이도 또한 그러하다

↳ **대조 B(문학):** 아동의 자유분방함에 대한 이해는 문학적 접근법이 더 잘 맞음.

주제문

⁷*The psychologist* (interested in young children) / may have to **venture a little more often into the wilderness** / in order to get a good picture (of how children think).

S 과거분사구 V O 목적(~하기 위해) of의 O(명사절)

심리학자는 (어린아이에게 관심이 있는) / 조금 더 자주 위험을 무릅쓰고 황무지로 들어가야 할지도 모른다 / 잘 이해하기 위해 (아이가 어떻게 생각하는지를)

↳ **심리학자에게 필요한 자세:** 아동의 사고방식을 이해하기 위해 문학적 접근법을 취할 필요가 있음.

untamed 길들여지지 않은
extend 확장[확대]하다
bent on ~에 열심인
identify 찾다, 발견하다; 알아보다
venture into 위험을 무릅쓰고 ~으로 들어가다
wilderness 황무지
[선택지] recall 생각해 내다; 회수[리콜]하다
precious 소중한; 귀중한
disregard 무시[경시](하다)
standardize 표준화하다

정답 가이드

빈칸 문장으로 보아, 심리학자가 아이의 생각을 이해하기 위해 '무엇을 해야' 할지도 모른다는 것인지를 추론해야 한다. Daniel Albright는 자전적 기억을 이해하는 데 있어 심리학은 정원, 문학은 황무지라고 했다. 이는 심리학이 인간의 경험과 행동에 정원 같은 질서를 부과하는 반면 문학은 황무지처럼 제멋대로의 길들여지지 않은 인간 경험에 몰두한다는 것이다. 기억을 이해하는 것은 어린아이의 마음에 대한 질문으로 확장되는데, 심리학자들이 아이 마음에서 질서를 찾는 데 열중하면, 아이의 근본적인 특성인 제멋대로이고 상상력이 풍부한 대화와 사고방식 등을 놓칠 수 있다고 했다. 즉 심리학자가 아이의 생각을 이해하기 위해서는 문학의 접근법을 이용할 필요가 있는 것이다. 따라서 빈칸에 들어갈 말로 가장 적절한 것은 ① 'venture a little more often into the wilderness(조금 더 자주 위험을 무릅쓰고 황무지로 들어간다)'이다.

오답 클리닉

② help them recall their most precious memories (16%)
그들이 자신의 가장 소중한 기억을 생각해 내도록 돕다
기억의 상기가 아닌 자전적 기억 이해에 관한 내용임.

③ better understand the challenges of parental duty (7%)
부모의 의무라는 과제를 더 잘 이해한다
부모의 의무는 언급되지 않은 내용임.

④ disregard the key characteristics of children's fiction (13%)
아동 소설의 핵심적인 특징을 무시한다
아동 소설에 관한 내용이 아님.

⑤ standardize the paths of their psychological development (9%)
그들의 심리적 발달의 경로를 표준화한다
표준화하는 것은 패턴과 규칙성에 초점을 두는 심리학의 접근법으로 볼 수 있으므로 아이의 마음을 연구하는 적절한 방법으로 볼 수 없음.

03 + 빈칸 마지막 〈23학년도 9월 모평 33번 | 정답률 48%〉 ④

구문분석 & 직독직해

예술 예술가로 격상된 의상 디자이너의 위상

*men은 동명사 making의 의미상 주어임.

¹There was *nothing* modern / about the idea / of men making women's clothes — // we saw them doing it / for centuries / in the past.

V₁ S₁ S₂ V₂ O(= men) C ↳ (= making women's clothes)

현대적인 것이 전혀 없었다 / 생각에는 / 남자가 여자 옷을 만든다는 // 즉 우리는 그들이 그것(여자 옷을 만드는 것)을 하는 것을 보았다 / 여러 세기 동안 / 과거에

↳ **도입:** 남자 재단사는 옛날부터 있었음.

²In the old days, / however, / the client was always primary // and her tailor was *an obscure craftsman*, (perhaps talented but perhaps not).

S₁ V₁ C₁ S₂ V₂ C₂

옛날에는 / 하지만 / 고객이 항상 가장 중요했다 // 그리고 그녀의 재단사는 무명의 장인이었다 (아마도 재능이 있었을지도 모르지만 아마도 없었을지도 모르는)

³She had her own ideas / like any patron, // there were no fashion plates, // and the tailor was simply at her service, / perhaps with helpful suggestions (about what others were wearing).

S₁ V₁ O V₂ S₂ S₃ V₃ C about의 O(명사절)

그녀는 자기 자신의 생각이 있었다 / 여느 고객처럼 // 패션 플레이트(유행복 그림판)는 없었다 // 그리고 재단사는 그저 그녀(고객)의 요구를 따랐다 / 아마도 도움이 되는 제안을 가지고 (다른 사람들이 무엇을 입고 있는지에 관한)

↳ **대조 A(과거):** 의상 제작은 재단사보다는 고객 의견 위주로 이루어졌음.

해석

¹남자가 여자 옷을 만든다는 생각에는 현대적인 것이 전혀 없었다. 즉 우리는 그들이 그것(여자 옷을 만드는 것)을 하는 것을 과거에 여러 세기 동안 보았다. ²하지만 옛날에는 고객이 항상 가장 중요했고 그녀의 재단사는 아마도 재능이 있었을지도 모르지만 아마도 없었을지도 모르는 무명의 장인이었다. ³그녀(고객)는 여느 고객처럼 자기 자신의 생각이 있었고, 패션 플레이트(유행복 그림판)는 없었으며, 재단사는 아마도 다른 사람들이 무엇을 입고 있는지에 관한 도움이 되는 제안을 가지고 그저 그녀(고객)의 요구를 따랐다.(▶ 재단사가 아니라 고객이 원하는 옷이 만들어졌다는 의미) ⁴예술적인 남성 고급 여성복 디자이너의 매우 성공적인 부상과 함께 19세기 후반에 시작하여, 유명해진 사람은 바로 디자이너였고, 고객은 그의 영감 어린 관심에 의해 (격이) 높아졌다. ⁵남성 예술가와 그들의 여성을 위한 창작물(여성복)에 대한 감탄의 분위기 속에서, 의상 디자이너는 처음으로 같은 종류의 창작자로서 성공했다. ⁶의상 제작은 기술이라는

[4]Beginning in the late nineteenth century, / with the hugely successful rise (of the artistic male couturier), /
19세기 후반에 시작하여 / 매우 성공적인 부상과 함께 (예술적인 남성 고급 여성복 디자이너의) /

it was the designer who became celebrated, // and the client (became) elevated / by his inspired attention.
(it was … who: 강조구문(…한 사람[것]은 바로 ~이다) / the client: S_2 / (became): V_2 / elevated: C_2)
유명해진 사람은 바로 디자이너였다 // 그리고 고객은 (격이) 높아졌다 / 그의 영감 어린 관심에 의해
↳ **대조 B(19세기 후반 이후):** 고급 여성복을 만드는 남성 디자이너가 성공하고 유명해짐.

[5]In a climate of admiration (for male artists and their female creations), / the dress-designer first flourished / as the same sort of creator. 의상 디자이너가 창작자로 성공함.
(the dress-designer: S / flourished: V)
감탄의 분위기 속에서 (남성 예술가와 그들의 여성을 위한 창작물(여성복)에 대한) / 의상 디자이너는 처음으로 성공했다 / 같은 종류의 창작자로서
↳ **대조 B의 부연 설명:** 의상 디자이너가 창작자로 인정받고 성공함.

주제문
[6]Instead of the old rule // that dressmaking is a craft, / ***a modern connection* (between dress-design and art)** / was invented [that had not been there before].
(the old rule = that …: 동격 접속사 / a modern connection: S / was invented: V / that: 주격 관계대명사)
옛 규칙 대신에 // 의상 제작은 기술이라는 / 현대적 연결이 (의상 디자인과 예술 사이의) / 만들어졌다 [이전에는 없었던]
↳ **결과:** 의상 제작을 기술이 아닌 예술과 연결하게 됨.

옛 규칙 대신에, 이전에는 없었던 의상 디자인과 예술 사이의 현대적 연결이 만들어졌다.

어휘

primary 가장 중요한, 주된; 기본적인; 최초의
tailor 재단사
craftsman 장인; 공예가
cf. craft 기술; (수)공예
talented 재능이 있는
fashion plate 패션 플레이트 (패션 디자인의 유행을 전달하는 용도로 쓰인 복식 도판)
at one's service ~의 요구를 따르는
hugely 매우, 엄청나게; 크게
celebrated 유명한, 저명한
elevated (지위 등이) 높아진, 높은
inspired 영감을 받은
climate 분위기; 기후
admiration 감탄, 존경
flourish 성공하다; 번영[번창]하다
[선택지] profitable 수익성이 있는
preserve 보존하다; 지키다
affordable (가격이) 알맞은, 감당할 수 있는

정답 가이드

빈칸 문장으로 보아, 의상 제작에 있어서 기술은 예전의 규칙이고 지금은 이전에 없었던 '무엇'이 만들어졌다는 것인지를 추론해야 한다. 과거에 고객의 요구에 따라 옷을 만들었던 재단사와 달리, 19세기 후반부터 예술적인 남성 디자이너가 성공적으로 부상하게 되면서 창작자로 성공하게 되었다고 했다. 따라서 의상 제작은 옛날처럼 재단사의 기술이 아니라 이전에 없었던 '예술적 창작'으로 본다는 내용이 되어야 하므로, 빈칸에 들어갈 말로 가장 적절한 것은 ④ 'a modern connection between dress-design and art(의상 디자인과 예술 사이의 현대적 연결)'이다.

오답 클리닉

① a profitable industry driving fast fashion (17%)
패스트 패션을 추진시키는 수익성 있는 산업
패스트 패션이나 수익성에 대한 내용은 없음.
② a widespread respect for marketing skills (12%)
마케팅 기술에 대한 광범위한 존중
마케팅에 대한 언급은 없음.
③ a public institution preserving traditional designs (8%)
전통 디자인을 보존하는 공공기관
의상 디자이너가 전통 디자인을 보존하는 공공기관의 역할을 했다는 내용이 아님.
⑤ an efficient system for producing affordable clothing (14%)
가격이 알맞은 의류를 생산하기 위한 효율적인 체계
가격이나 의류 생산에 초점을 둔 글이 아님.

01 빈칸 마지막 (23학년도 6월 모평 31번 | 정답률 36%) ⑤

구문분석 & 직독직해 예술 현대에 사라진 컴퓨터 예술가

주제문 🔑 디지털 기술을 사용하는 현대 예술가는 컴퓨터를 언급하지 않음.

[1] *Young contemporary artists* [who employ digital technologies / in their practice] / rarely make reference to computers.
S 주격 관계대명사 V O
젊은 현대 예술가들은 [디지털 기술을 이용하는 / 자신들의 작업에] / 컴퓨터를 거의 언급하지 않는다
↳ 디지털 기술을 이용하는 현대 예술가들은 컴퓨터를 사용한 것을 언급하지 않음.

[2] For example, / Wade Guyton, / *an abstractionist* [who uses a word processing program and inkjet printers], / does not call himself a computer artist. 🔑 예술가는 자신을 컴퓨터 예술가라고 부르지 않음.
S = 주격 관계대명사 V O(= Wade Guyton) C ★<call+O+C>: O를 C라고 부르다
예를 들어 / Wade Guyton은 / 추상파 화가인 [워드 프로세싱 프로그램과 잉크젯식 프린터를 사용하는] / 스스로를 컴퓨터 예술가라고 부르지 않는다

🔑 비평가들은 예술가의 컴퓨터 사용을 신경 쓰지 않음.

[3] Moreover, / *some critics*, // who admire his work, / are little concerned / about his extensive use of computers / in the art-making process.
S 주격 관계대명사(보충 설명) V C
게다가 / 몇몇 비평가들은 // 그의 작품을 높이 평가하는 / 거의 신경 쓰지 않는다 / 그의 폭넓은 컴퓨터 사용에 관해 / 예술 창작 과정에서
↳ **예:** 예술가와 비평가는 창작 과정에서의 컴퓨터 사용을 언급하지도 신경 쓰지도 않음.

→ (= 앞 문장)
[4] This is a marked contrast / from *three decades ago* [when *artists* [who utilized computers] / were labeled by critics — / often disapprovingly — / as computer artists].
S V C 관계부사 S' 주격 관계대명사 V' ★<label A as B(A에 B라는 꼬리표를 붙이다, A를 B라고 부르다)>의 수동형
이것은 눈에 띄는 차이이다 / 30년 전과 [예술가들이 [컴퓨터를 활용한] / 비평가들에 의해 꼬리표가 붙여진 / 자주 탐탁지 않게 / 컴퓨터 예술가라고]
↳ **과거:** 비평가들이 컴퓨터를 활용하는 예술가를 '컴퓨터 예술가'로 분류함.

[5] For the present generation of artists, / the computer, or more appropriately, the laptop, /
S
현세대의 예술가들에게 / 컴퓨터, 혹은 더 적절히는 휴대용 컴퓨터는 /
is one (in a collection of *integrated, portable digital technologies* [that link their social and working life]).
V C 주격 관계대명사
하나이다 (통합된, 휴대용 디지털 기술의 모음 중 [그들의 사회생활과 직업 생활을 연결하는])
↳ **현재:** 컴퓨터는 예술가의 사회생활과 직업 생활을 연결하는 역할을 함.

★<with+O'+v-ing>: O'가 ~하면서[~한 채로]
[6] With tablets and cell phones surpassing personal computers / in Internet usage, /
능동관계
태블릿 컴퓨터와 휴대 전화가 개인용 컴퓨터를 능가하면서 / 인터넷 사용에서 /
and / as slim digital devices resemble nothing / like the room-sized mainframes and bulky desktop computers (of previous decades), // 🔑 오늘날의 디지털 기기들은 수십 년 전의 컴퓨터와 다름.
부사절 접속사(~ 때문에) S' V' O' 전치사구
그리고 / 얇은 디지털 기기들이 전혀 닮지 않았기 때문에 / 방 크기의 중앙 컴퓨터 그리고 부피가 큰 탁상용 컴퓨터와 (수십 년 전의) //
it now appears // that the computer artist is finally **extinct**.
가주어 V 진주어(명사절)
현재로는 ~으로 보인다 // 컴퓨터 예술가가 결국 사라진 것
↳ 오늘날 사용하는 디지털 기기는 옛날의 컴퓨터와는 달라 컴퓨터 예술가는 사라진 것으로 보임.

해석

[1]자신들의 작업에 디지털 기술을 이용하는 젊은 현대 예술가들은 컴퓨터를 거의 언급하지 않는다. [2]예를 들어, 워드 프로세싱 프로그램과 잉크젯식 프린터를 사용하는 추상파 화가인 Wade Guyton은 스스로를 컴퓨터 예술가라고 부르지 않는다. [3]게다가, 그의 작품을 높이 평가하는 몇몇 비평가들은 예술 창작 과정에서 그의 폭넓은 컴퓨터 사용에 관해 거의 신경 쓰지 않는다. [4]이것은 컴퓨터를 활용한 예술가들이 비평가들에 의해 자주 탐탁지 않게 컴퓨터 예술가라고 꼬리표가 붙여진 30년 전과 눈에 띄는 차이이다. [5]현세대의 예술가들에게 컴퓨터, 혹은 더 적절히는 휴대용 컴퓨터는, 그들의 사회생활과 직업 생활을 연결하는 통합된, 휴대용 디지털 기술의 모음 중 하나이다. [6]인터넷 사용에서 태블릿 컴퓨터와 휴대 전화가 개인용 컴퓨터를 능가하면서, 그리고 얇은 디지털 기기들이 수십 년 전의 방 크기의 중앙 컴퓨터 그리고 부피가 큰 탁상용 컴퓨터와 전혀 닮지 않았기 때문에 현재로는 컴퓨터 예술가가 결국 사라진 것으로 보인다.

어휘

contemporary 현대의; 동시대의
employ 이용하다; 고용하다
make reference to A A를 언급하다
abstractionist 추상파 화가
critic 비평가, 평론가
admire 높이 평가하다; 존경하다; 감탄하다
extensive 폭넓은, 광범위한
marked 눈에 띄는, 두드러진
contrast 차이; 대조(적인 것[사람]); 대조하다
decade 10년
utilize 활용하다, 이용하다
disapprovingly 탐탁지 않게
generation 세대 ((비슷한 연령층))
integrate 통합하다, 전체로 합치다
portable 휴대용의, 들고 다닐 수 있는
surpass 능가하다, 뛰어넘다
device 기기, 장치
resemble 닮다, 비슷[유사]하다
mainframe 중앙 컴퓨터
bulky 부피가 큰
previous 이전의
extinct 사라진; (동식물 등이) 멸종된

정답 가이드

빈칸 문장이 길므로 빈칸을 중심으로 추론 대상을 살펴보면, 현재에는 컴퓨터 예술가가 결국 '어떻게' 되었다는 것이다. 이 컴퓨터 예술가에 대한 서술에 집중하여 읽어보면, 과거에 컴퓨터를 활용하는 예술가들을 '컴퓨터 예술가'라고 했다는 부분이 나온다. 반면, 현대 예술가들에게는 휴대용 컴퓨터가 사회생활과 직업 생활을 연결하며, 태블릿 컴퓨터와 휴대전화가 개인용 컴퓨터를 능가하고 이들은 예전의 중앙 컴퓨터, 탁상용 컴퓨터와는 전혀 다르다고 했다. 따라서 과거의 '컴퓨터 예술가'는 이제 ⑤ 'extinct(사라진)' 것을 추론할 수 있다.

오답 클리닉

① awake (20%) 깨어 있는
'컴퓨터 예술가'라고 꼬리표가 붙었던 과거와 달리 컴퓨터 사용을 언급하지도 신경 쓰지도 않는다고 했으므로 컴퓨터 예술가가 깨어난다고 볼 수 없음.
② influential (28%) 영향력 있는
컴퓨터 예술가가 없어진다는 내용이므로 영향력이 있는 것과는 반대됨.
③ distinct (12%) 뚜렷이 다른
오늘날 비평가들은 예술가의 컴퓨터 사용을 대수롭지 않게 여긴다고 했으므로 틀림.
④ troublesome (4%) 골칫거리의
과거에는 컴퓨터를 사용하는 예술가를 부정적으로 여겼지만 현재에는 신경 쓰지 않는다고 했으므로 틀림.

02 + 빈칸 추론 (22학년도 대수능 31번 | 정답률 67%)

①

구문분석 & 직독직해

생활 재미를 위한 유머의 희극적 허용

<not just A but (also) B>: A뿐만 아니라 B도

[1]Humour involves not just practical disengagement but cognitive disengagement.

S V O₁ O₂

유머는 실질적인 이탈뿐만 아니라 인식의 이탈도 포함한다

↳ 유머는 우리 인식에서 벗어나 있음.

주제문

*명사절을 이끄는 whether는 '~인지(아닌지)'의 의미.

[2]As long as something is funny, // we are for the moment not concerned / with whether it is real or fictional, true or false. ⊶ 유머의 사실 여부에 신경 쓰지 않음.

부사절 접속사(~하기만 하면) S V with의 O(명사절)

어떤 것이 재미있기만 하면 // 우리는 당장은 관심을 갖지 않는다 / 그것이 진짜인지 꾸며낸 것인지, 진실인지 거짓인지에 관해

(= 앞 문장) *선행사와 관계부사가 the reason why일 때 선행사나 관계부사 중 하나를 생략하는 경우가 많음.

[3]This is // (the reason) why we give considerable leeway / to *people* (telling funny stories).

S V 선행사 생략 C 현재분사구

이것이 ~이다 // 우리가 상당한 여지를 주는 이유 / 사람들에게 (재미있는 이야기를 하는)

↳ 이야기가 재미를 주면 그것의 사실 여부에 관심을 두지 않음.

(= people telling funny stories)

[4]If they are getting extra laughs / by exaggerating the silliness (of a situation) / or even by making up a few details, //

부사절 접속사(조건) 전치사구 병렬

만약 그들이 추가 웃음을 자아내고 있다면 / 우스꽝스러움을 과장함으로써 (상황의) / 혹은 심지어 몇 가지 세부 사항을 지어냄으로써 //

*<grant+IO+DO>: IO에게 DO를 허락[승인]하다

we are happy to grant them comic licence, / a kind of poetic licence. ⊶ 재미를 위해서 희극적 자유를 허용함.

<be happy to-v>: 기꺼이 v하다 =

우리는 그들에게 기꺼이 희극적 자유를 허락한다 / 즉 일종의 시적 자유

↳ 우리는 재미있으면 과장하거나 없는 사실을 지어내더라도 허용함.

[5]Indeed, / *someone* (listening to a funny story) [who tries to correct the teller — / 'No, he didn't spill the spaghetti on the keyboard and the monitor, just on the keyboard'] — / will probably be told / by the other listeners / to stop interrupting.

S 현재분사구 주격 관계대명사 V <stop v-ing>: v하는 것을 멈추다

실제로 / 누군가는 (재미있는 이야기를 듣고 있는) [이야기하는 사람을 바로잡으려고 하는 / '아니야, 그는 스파게티를 키보드와 모니터에 흘린 것이 아니라 키보드에만 흘렸어.'라고] / 아마 들을 것이다 / 다른 청자들로부터 / 방해하는 것을 멈추라고

↳ 예: 재미있는 이야기의 정확한 사실 여부를 따지는 것은 방해로 취급됨.

[6]The creator of humour is putting ideas / into people's heads / for *the pleasure* [(which[that]) those ideas will bring], / not to provide **accurate** information.

S V O 목적격 관계대명사 생략 목적(~하기 위해)

유머를 만드는 사람은 생각을 집어넣고 있는 것이다 / 사람들의 머릿속에 / 즐거움을 위해서 [그 생각이 가져올] / 정확한 정보를 제공하기 위해서가 아니라

↳ 유머는 정확한 정보 제공이 아니라 재미를 위한 것임.

해석

[1]유머는 실질적인 이탈뿐만 아니라 인식의 이탈도 포함한다. [2]어떤 것이 재미있기만 하면, 우리는 당장은 그것이 진짜인지 꾸며낸 것인지, 진실인지 거짓인지에 관해 관심을 갖지 않는다. [3]이것이 우리가 재미있는 이야기를 하는 사람들에게 상당한 여지를 주는 이유이다. [4]만약 그들이 상황의 우스꽝스러움을 과장함으로써 혹은 심지어 몇 가지 세부 사항을 지어냄으로써 추가 웃음을 자아내고 있다면, 우리는 그들에게 기꺼이 희극적 자유, 즉 일종의 시적 자유를 허락한다. [5]실제로, 재미있는 이야기를 듣다가 '아니야, 그는 스파게티를 키보드와 모니터에 흘린 것이 아니라 키보드에만 흘렸어.'라고 이야기하는 사람을 바로잡으려고 하는 누군가는 아마 다른 청자들로부터 방해하는 것을 멈추라고 들을 것이다. [6]유머를 만드는 사람은 정확한 정보를 제공하기 위해서가 아니라, 그 생각이 가져올 즐거움을 위해서 사람들의 머릿속에 생각을 집어넣고 있는 것이다.

어휘

practical 실질[현실]적인; 실용적인
disengagement 이탈; 해방
for the moment 당장은, 우선은
fictional 꾸며낸, 허구의
considerable 상당한, 많은
get a laugh 웃음을 자아내다
exaggerate 과장하다
silliness 우스꽝스러움; 어리석음
make up ~을 지어[만들어]내다; ~을 이루다[형성하다]
grant 허락[승인]하다; 주다, 수여하다
licence 자유[허용]; 면허[자격](증)
poetic 시적인, 시의
spill 흘리다, 쏟다
interrupt 방해하다, 훼방 놓다; 가로막다

정답 가이드

빈칸 문장으로 보아, 유머를 만드는 것이 '어떤' 정보를 제공하기 위해서가 아닌지를 추론해야 한다. 앞부터 내용을 살펴보면, 어떤 것이 재미있기만 하면 우리는 그것의 사실 여부에 관심을 두지 않으며 재미를 위해 과장하거나 꾸며내는 것을 허용한다고 했다. 만약 이런 유머의 내용을 바로잡으려 한다면 방해하지 말라는 말을 듣게 될 것이라고 했으므로, 유머는 사실 전달이 아닌 즐거움을 위한 것임을 알 수 있다. 따라서 빈칸에 들어갈 말로 가장 적절한 것은 ① 'accurate(정확한)'이다.

오답 클리닉

② detailed (20%) 상세한
details를 활용한 오답. 유머를 듣는 사람들이 신경 쓰지 않는 것은 정보의 사실 여부이지 상세함의 정도가 아님.
③ useful (6%) 유용한
정보의 유용성에 대해서는 언급되지 않음.
④ additional (4%) 부가적인
유머가 추가 정보를 제공하는지 여부는 언급되지 않음.
⑤ alternative (3%) 대안적인
유머에 기존의 것을 대신하는 정보가 없다는 내용이 아님.

03 + 빈칸 추론 (22학년도 6월 모평 34번 | 정답률 34%) ④

구문분석 & 직독직해

동물 장소와 노래를 연관 짓는 유럽울새

[1]Emma Brindley(S) has investigated(V) the responses(O) (of European robins) / to the songs (of neighbors and strangers).
Emma Brindley는 반응을 조사해왔다 (유럽울새의) / 노래에 대한 (이웃 새와 낯선 새의)
↳ 유럽울새가 다른 새의 노래에 보이는 반응을 연구함.

[2]Despite(전치사(~에도 불구하고)) the large and complex song repertoire of European robins(despite의 O(명사구)), / they(S) (→ = European robins) were(V) able to discriminate(C) / between the songs of neighbors and strangers.
유럽울새의 광범위하고 복잡한 노래 목록에도 불구하고 / 그것들(유럽울새)은 구별할 수 있었다 / 이웃 새와 낯선 새의 노래를
↳ **연구 결과:** 유럽울새는 이웃 새와 낯선 새의 노래를 구별함.

[3]When(부사절 접속사(시간)) they heard a tape recording (of a stranger), //
그것들(유럽울새)은 테이프 녹음을 들었을 때 (낯선 새의) //
they(S) began(V_1) to sing(O_1) sooner, / sang(V_2) more songs(O_2), / [and] overlapped(V_3) their songs(O_3) with the playback / more often //
더 일찍 노래하기 시작했다 / 더 많이 노래했다 / 그리고 자신들의 노래를 재생된 소리와 겹치게 했다 / 더 자주 //
than they did(V'(대동사)) / on hearing(<on v-ing>: v할 때) a neighbor's song.
*did는 대동사로 began ~ more often을 대신함.
그것들이 그랬던 것보다 / 이웃 새의 노래를 들었을 때

[4]As(부사절 접속사(~처럼)) Brindley suggests, // the overlapping of song(S) may be(V) an aggressive response(C).
Brindley가 말한 것처럼 // 노래를 겹치게 하는 것은 공격적인 반응일 수도 있다
↳ **낯선 새의 노래에 대한 반응:** 더 일찍, 더 많이, 소리가 더 겹치게(공격적인 반응) 노래함.

[5]However, / this difference (in responding to neighbor versus stranger)(S) / occurred(V) //
그러나 / 이러한 차이는 (낯선 새와 비교해 이웃 새에 대한 반응에서의) / 발생했다 //
only when(부사절 접속사(시간)) the neighbor's song(S') was played(V') / by *a loudspeaker* (placed(과거분사구) at the boundary ([between] that neighbor's territory [and] the territory of *the bird* (being tested(현재분사구)))).
🔑 이웃 새의 노래가 특정 경계에서 들릴 때만 이웃으로 구별함.
오직 이웃 새의 노래가 재생되었을 때만 / 확성기로 (경계에 놓인 (그 이웃 새의 영역과 새의 영역 사이의 (실험되고 있는)))
↳ **이웃 새와 낯선 새의 노래 구별:** 이웃 새의 영역과 자신의 영역 사이에서 들릴 때만 구별함.

[6]If(부사절 접속사(조건)) the same neighbor's song was played / at another boundary, / *one* (→ = boundary) (separating(현재분사구) / the territory (of the test subject) / from (the territory of) another neighbor), //
*<separate A from B>: A와 B를 분리하다
🔑 친숙한 소리여도 다른 영역 경계에서 들리면 낯선 새의 소리로 여김.
동일한 이웃 새의 노래가 재생된 경우에는 / 다른 경계에서 / 즉 경계 (분리하는 / 영역과 (실험 대상의) / 또 다른 이웃 새의 영역을) //

해석

[1]Emma Brindley는 이웃 새와 낯선 새의 노래에 대한 유럽울새의 반응을 조사해왔다. [2]유럽울새의 광범위하고 복잡한 노래 목록에도 불구하고, 그것들(유럽울새)은 이웃 새와 낯선 새의 노래를 구별할 수 있었다. [3]그것들(유럽울새)은 낯선 새의 테이프 녹음을 들었을 때, 이웃 새의 노래를 들었을 때 그랬던 것보다 더 일찍 노래하기 시작했고, 더 많이 노래했으며, 더 자주 자신들의 노래를 재생된 소리와 겹치게 했다. [4]Brindley가 말한 것처럼, 노래를 겹치게 하는 것은 공격적인 반응일 수도 있다. [5]그러나 낯선 새와 비교해 이웃 새에 대한 반응에서의 이러한 차이는 오직 이웃 새의 노래가 그 이웃 새의 영역과 실험되고 있는 새의 영역 사이의 경계에 놓인 확성기로 재생되었을 때만 발생했다. [6]동일한 이웃 새의 노래가 다른 경계, 즉 실험 대상의 영역과 또 다른 이웃 새의 영역을 분리하는 경계에서 재생된 경우에는, 그것(동일한 이웃 새의 노래)은 낯선 새의 소리로 여겨졌다. [7]이 결과는 울새가 장소를 친숙한 노래와 연관시킨다는 것을 입증할 뿐만 아니라, 재생 실험에 사용된 노래의 선택이 매우 중요하다는 것도 보여 준다.

어휘

investigate 조사[연구]하다; 수사하다
response 반응, 대응; 대답
cf. responsive 반응[대응]하는; 호응하는
repertoire (노래·연주) 목록, 레퍼토리
discriminate 구별[식별]하다; 차별하다
overlap 겹치게 하다; 겹치다
playback (녹음한 테이프 등의) 재생(된 내용)
aggressive 공격적인; 적극적인, 의욕적인
versus ~와 비교하여; (경기에서) ~ 대(對)
loudspeaker 확성기, 스피커
boundary 경계(선); 한계
subject 실험[연구] 대상; 주제; 학과, 과목
treat 여기다, 간주하다; 대하다; 치료하다
demonstrate 입증하다; 보여주다[설명하다]

(= the same neighbor's song)
it was treated / as the call of a stranger.
S V 전치사(~로(서))
그것(동일한 이웃 새의 노래)은 여겨졌다 / 낯선 새의 소리로
↳ 같은 이웃 새의 노래가 다른 새의 영역(장소)에서 들리면 낯선 새의 소리로 여김.

주제문

★부정어 not only가 문장의 맨 앞에 위치하면서 <조동사+V+S>로 도치가 일어남.

(demonstrate의 O(명사절))

[7] Not only does this result demonstrate // that **the robins associate locality with familiar songs**, //
조동사 S_1 V_1 명사절 접속사 S′ V′ O′
이 결과는 입증할 뿐만 아니라 // 울새가 장소를 친숙한 노래와 연관시킨다는 것을 //

(= this result) (shows의 O(명사절))
but it also shows // that the choice (of *songs* (used in playback experiments)) / is highly important.
S_2 V_2 명사절 접속사 S′(단수) 과거분사구 V′(단수) C′
~도 보여 준다 // 선택이 (노래의 (재생 실험에 사용된)) / 매우 중요하다는 것
↳ **시사점:** 울새는 노래가 들리는 장소와 연관시켜 이웃을 구분함.

associate A with B A를 B와 연관시키다
locality 장소, 소재
[선택지] characterize (~의) 특징이 되다
volume 음량; 크기; 부피, 양
sense 감각; 관념, 생각; 의미

정답 가이드

빈칸이 실험 결과가 나타내는 시사점에 있으므로, 실험 결과를 추론해야 한다. 실험에 의하면 유럽울새는 이웃 새와 낯선 새의 노래를 구별할 수 있어서 서로 다른 반응을 보이는데, 동일한 이웃 새의 노래라도 어느 영역의 경계에서 들리는지에 따라 낯선 새의 소리로 여기기도 한다고 했다. 이는 소리가 들리는 장소가 이웃 새와 낯선 새를 구별하는 데 중요하다는 의미이므로, 빈칸에 들어갈 말로 가장 적절한 것은 ④ 'the robins associate locality with familiar songs(울새가 장소를 친숙한 노래와 연관시킨다)'이다.

오답 클리닉

① variety and complexity characterize the robins' songs (20%)
다양성과 복잡성이 울새 노래의 특징이 된다
the large and complex song repertoire를 활용한 오답으로 울새 노래의 특징을 설명하는 내용이 아님.

② song volume affects the robins' aggressive behavior (24%)
노래 음량이 울새의 공격적 행동에 영향을 미친다
노래 음량이 아니라 어느 영역에서 노래가 들리는지가 울새의 행동에 영향을 미친다고 했음.

③ the robins' poor territorial sense is a key to survival (15%)
울새의 형편없는 영역 감각이 생존의 열쇠이다
울새는 소리가 들려오는 영역과 연관 지어 소리의 친숙함을 판단하므로 뛰어난 영역 감각을 가졌다고 볼 수 있음.

⑤ the robins are less responsive to recorded songs (6%)
울새는 녹음된 노래에 대해서는 더 적게 반응한다
녹음된 노래와 실제 노래에 대한 반응 차이를 비교하는 내용이 아님.

01 ✦ 글의 순서 〈24학년도 대수능 36번 | 정답률 38%〉 ④

구문분석 & 직독직해 사회 협상의 목적과 기능

★<define A as B(A를 B로 정의하다)>의 수동형
[1]Negotiation(S) can be defined(V) / as(전치사(~로(서))) an attempt (to explore and reconcile conflicting positions / in order to(목적(~하기 위해)) reach an acceptable outcome).
협상은 정의될 수 있다 / 시도로 (상충되는 입장을 탐색하고 조정하려는 / 받아들일 수 있는 어떤 결과에 도달하기 위해)
↳ **협상의 정의:** 협상은 모든 당사자가 받아들일 수 있는 결과를 얻기 위해 상충되는 입장을 탐색하고 조정하려는 시도임.

🔑 주어진 글의 an acceptable outcome을 가리킴.
(C) [2]Whatever(양보 부사절(= No matter what ~)) the nature (of *the outcome*) (is), // which(관계대명사(보충 설명)) may actually favour(V′) one party(O′) more than another, // ★whatever(무엇이 ~하더라도)는 부사절 접속사이면서 be동사의 보어 역할을 하는 복합관계대명사로 쓰임.
속성이 무엇이든 (그 결과의) // 실제로 다른 당사자보다 한쪽 당사자에게 더 유리할 수도 있는 //
the purpose (of negotiation)(S) / is(V) the identification (of areas (of common interest and conflict))(C).
목적은 (협상의) / 확인하는 것이다 (영역을 (공통의 이익과 갈등의))
↳ **협상의 목적:** 당사자들 공통의 이익과 갈등의 영역을 발견하는 것임.

[3]In this sense, / depending on(전치사(~에 따라)) the intentions (of the parties), / the areas of common interest(S) may be clarified(V₁), / (may be) refined(V₂) / and (may be) given(V₃) negotiated form and substance(O₃).
이러한 의미에서 / 의도에 따라 (당사자들의) / 공통의 이익 영역은 명확해질 수 있다 / 정제될 (수 있다) / 그리고 협상된 형식과 내용이 주어질 (수 있다)
↳ **공통의 이익 영역:** 협상으로 보다 구체화되고 협의가 이루어질 수 있음.

🔑 (A)의 공통의 이익 영역에 이어 의견 차이가 있는 공통의 갈등 영역을 설명함.
(A) [4]Areas of difference(S) can (remain)(V₁) and do(동사 강조) frequently remain(V₂), / and will perhaps be(V₃) the subject (of future negotiations)(C₃), / or (will) indeed remain(V₄) irreconcilable(C₄). ★<remain+C(형용사)>: C한 상태로 남다
의견 차이가 있는 영역은 남을 수 있고, 실제로 자주 남는다 / 그리고 아마도 주제가 될 것이다 (미래 협상의) / 또는 실제로 타협할 수 없는 상태로 남을 (것이다)
↳ **공통의 갈등 영역:** 협상으로 조정되지 않고 미해결된 채로 남을 수 있음.

[5]In *those instances* [in which(전치사+관계대명사) the parties have highly antagonistic or polarised relations], /
그런 경우에 [당사자들이 매우 적대적이거나 양극화된 관계를 맺고 있는] /
the process(S) is(V) likely(C) / to be dominated / by the exposition, / (very often in public)(형용사 likely 수식), / (of the areas of conflict).
그 과정은 가능성이 있다 / 지배될 / 설명에 의해 / (매우 자주 공개적으로) / (갈등 영역에 대한)
↳ **부연 설명:** 당사자들이 서로 적대적이고 양극화된 경우 협상 과정은 갈등 영역의 설명이 공개적으로 이루어질 수 있음.

🔑 (A)의 당사자들이 적대적이거나 양극화된 관계를 맺고 있는 경우를 지칭함.
(B) [6]In these and sometimes other forms of negotiation, / negotiation(S) serves(V) / functions(O) (other than(~ 외의) reconciling conflicting interests(other than의 O(동명사구))).
이러한 방식의 협상과 때로는 다른 방식의 협상에서 / 협상은 수행한다 / 기능을 (상충되는 이익을 조정하는 것 외의)

(= Functions other than ~ interests)
[7]These(S) will include(V) delay(O₁), publicity(O₂), diverting attention(O₃(동명사구)) / or seeking intelligence (about the other party and its negotiating position)(O₄(동명사구)).
이러한 것들(상충되는 이익을 조정시키는 것 외의 기능)은 지연, 홍보, 주의를 돌리는 것을 포함하기 마련이다 / 또는 정보를 구하는 것을 (상대방과 그쪽의 협상 입장에 관한)
↳ **협상의 기타 기능:** 지연, 홍보, 주의를 돌리는 것, 서로의 협상 입장에 관한 정보 얻기가 있음.

해석

[1]협상은 받아들일 수 있는 어떤 결과에 도달하기 위해 상충되는 입장을 탐색하고 조정하려는 시도로 정의될 수 있다. (C) [2]그 결과의 속성이 무엇이든, 그것(결과)은 실제로 다른 당사자보다 한쪽 당사자에게 더 유리할 수도 있는데, 협상의 목적은 공통의 이익과 갈등의 영역을 확인하는 것이다. [3]이러한 의미에서 당사자들의 의도에 따라 공통의 이익 영역은 명확해지고, 정제되며, 협상된 형식과 내용이 주어질 수 있다. (A) [4]의견 차이가 있는 영역은 남을 수 있고, 실제로 자주 남으며, 아마도 미래 협상의 주제가 되거나 실제로 타협할 수 없는 상태로 남을 것이다. [5]당사자들이 매우 적대적이거나 양극화된 관계를 맺고 있는 그런 경우에, 그 과정은 매우 자주 공개적으로 갈등 영역에 대한 설명에 의해 지배될 가능성이 있다.(▶ 당사자들이 격한 고성으로 입장을 설명하고 주장한다는 의미) (B) [6]이러한 방식의 협상과 때로는 다른 방식의 협상에서, 협상은 상충되는 이익을 조정하는 것 외의 기능을 수행한다. [7]이러한 것들은 지연(▶ 협상으로 결정을 미루고 시간을 벌 수 있음을 의미), 홍보(▶ 협상에서 본인들의 주장을 드러내어 더 많은 사람들에게 알릴 수 있음을 의미), 주의를 돌리거나 상대방과 그쪽의 협상 입장에 관한 정보를 구하는 것을 포함하기 마련이다.

어휘

negotiation 협상, 교섭
cf. negotiate 협상[교섭]하다
conflicting 상충[상반]되는
acceptable 받아들일 수 있는; 용인되는
outcome 결과
favo(u)r ~에게 유리하다; 선호하다
party (소송·계약 등의) 당사자; 정당; 파티
identification 확인, 감정; 빌견, 인지; 신분증
intention 의도; 목적
refine 정제하다
substance 내용; 물질; 실체
instance 경우, 사례
polarise[polarize] 양극화하다
dominate 지배하다; 우세하다
in public 공개적으로
publicity 홍보, 광고
divert (생각·관심을) 다른 데로 돌리다; 우회시키다
intelligence 정보; 지능

정답 가이드

협상은 받아들일 수 있는 어떤 결과에 도달하고자 상충되는 입장을 탐색하고 조정하는 것이라고 정의하는 주어진 글 다음에는 마지막에 언급한 an acceptable outcome을 the outcome으로 받아 그 결과의 속성이 무엇이든 협상의 목적은 공통의 이익과 갈등의 영역을 확인하는 것이라고 설명하는 (C)가 이어지는 것이 적절하다. 이 두 가지 협상의 목적 중에서 (C)는 공통의 이익 영역에 관한 부연 설명으로 끝나므로 그 뒤에는 갈등의 영역에 대해 부연 설명하는 (A)가 오고, 마지막으로 (A)에서 언급한 당사자들의 관계가 적대적이거나 양극화된 경우를 these (forms of negotiation)로 받아 이런 협상에서는 상충되는 이익을 조정하는 기능이 아닌 다른 다양한 기능을 포함하기 마련이라는 것을 설명하는 (B)가 오는 것이 자연스럽다.

오답 클리닉

① (A) - (C) - (B) (1%)
흐름상 (A)가 주어진 글 뒤에 이어질 수도 있으나 주어진 글의 an acceptable outcome을 the outcome으로 받아 설명하는 (C)가 이어지는 것이 더 적절하다.
② (B) - (A) - (C) (21%) / ③ (B) - (C) - (A) (14%)
주어진 글에는 (B)의 these (forms of negotiation)가 지칭할 협상의 형태들이 언급되지 않았으므로 (B)는 주어진 글 뒤에 올 수 없다.
⑤ (C) - (B) - (A) (26%)
(B)의 these (forms of negotiation)는 (A)의 those instances ~ relations를 받아 상충되는 이익을 조정하는 것 외의 협상의 기능을 추가 제시하므로 (A) 뒤에 와야 한다.

02 + 글의 순서 (24학년도 대수능 37번 | 정답률 37%) ④

구문분석 & 직독직해 사회 집단 내 규범의 발생 과정

주제문
[1]Norms emerge / in groups / as a result of people conforming / to the behavior (of others).
S V 동명사의 의미상 주어 of의 O(동명사구)
규범은 생긴다 / 집단에서 / 사람들이 순응하는 것의 결과로 / 행동에 (다른 사람들의)
↳ 규범은 집단에서 다른 사람들의 행동을 따르는 결과로 생김.

[2]Thus, / the start of a norm occurs // when one person acts / in a particular manner /
S V 부사절 접속사(시간) S′ V′
in a particular situation // because she thinks // (that) she ought to.
부사절 접속사 S″ V″ O″(명사절)
따라서 / 규범의 시작은 발생한다 // 한 사람이 행동할 때 / 특정 방식으로 /
특정 상황에서 // 그 사람이 생각하여 // 자신이 그래야 한다고
↳ 규범은 한 사람이 처음 당위성을 가지고 특정 상황에 특정 방식으로 행동할 때 발생함.

🔑 순응할 행동이 발생하고 난 다음에 이어져야 함.
(C) [3]Others may then conform / to this behavior / for a number of reasons.
S V
그런 다음 다른 사람들은 순응할 수도 있다 / 이 행동에 / 여러 가지 이유로
↳ 사람들이 그 행동에 순응하는 데는 여러 이유가 있음.

[4]*The person* [who performed the initial action] / may think //
S 주격 관계대명사 V
사람은 [최초의 행동을 한] / 생각할 수도 있다 //
↱ may think의 O(명사절) ↱ 부사절 접속사(~대로)
that others ought to behave // as she behaves / in situations of this sort.
명사절 접속사 S′ V′ S″ V″
다른 사람들이 행동해야 한다고 // 그 사람이 행동하는 대로 / 이러한 종류의 상황에서

🔑 (C)의 다른 사람들이 자신의 행동을 따라야 한다고 생각해서 행동을 지시하는 내용이 이어짐.
(A) [5]Thus, / she may prescribe the behavior / to them / by uttering the norm statement /
S V O (= others) <by v-ing>: v함으로써
in a prescriptive manner.
따라서 / 그 (최초의 행동을 한) 사람은 행동을 지시할 수도 있다 / 그들에게 / 규범 진술을 말함으로써 /
지시하는 방식으로

↱ may communicate의 O(명사절)
[6]Alternately, / she may communicate // that conformity is desired / in other ways, / such as by gesturing.
S V 명사절 접속사 S′ V′
다른 방식으로 / 그 사람은 전달할 수도 있다 // 순응이 요구된다는 것을 / 다른 방식으로 / 몸짓과 같은

↱ 부사절 접속사(~대로)
[7]In addition, / she may threaten to sanction them / for not behaving // as she wishes.
S V O 전치사(~에 대해) S′ V′
게다가 / 그 사람은 그들에게 제재를 가하겠다고 위협할 수도 있다 / 행동하지 않은 것에 대해 // 자신이 원하는 대로

↱ (= 앞 문장) ★<cause+O+to-v>: O가 v하게 하다
[8]This will cause some / to conform to her wishes / and (to) act // as she acts.
S V O C(to-v구 병렬) 부사절 접속사(~대로)
이것은 일부 사람들이 (~하게) 할 것이다 / 그 사람의 바람에 순응하게 / 그리고 행동하게 // 그 사람이 행동하는 대로
↳ **이유 1:** 처음 행동을 한 사람이 말, 몸짓, 위협으로 행동을 따를 것을 지시해서 일부는 순응함.

해석

[1]규범은 사람들이 다른 사람들의 행동에 순응하는 것의 결과로 집단에서 생긴다. [2]따라서 규범의 시작은 한 사람이 자신이 그래야 한다고 생각하여 특정 상황에서 특정 방식으로 행동할 때 발생한다. (C) [3]그런 다음 다른 사람들은 여러 가지 이유로 이 행동에 순응할 수도 있다. [4]최초의 행동을 한 사람은 다른 사람들이 이러한 종류의 상황에서 자신이 행동하는 대로 행동해야 한다고 생각할 수도 있다. (A) [5]따라서 그 사람은 지시하는 방식으로 규범 진술을 말함으로써 그들에게 행동을 지시할 수도 있다. [6]다른 방식으로, 그 사람은 몸짓과 같은 다른 방식으로 순응이 요구된다는 것을 전달할 수도 있다. [7]게다가 그 사람은 자신이 원하는 대로 행동하지 않은 것에 대해 그들에게 제재를 가하겠다고 위협할 수도 있다. [8]이것은 일부 사람들이 그 사람의 바람에 순응하고 그 사람이 행동하는 대로 행동하게 할 것이다. (B) [9]그러나 다른 일부 사람들은 그 행동이 자신에게 지시되게 할 필요가 없을 것이다. [10]그들은 행동의 규칙성을 관찰하고 자신이 순응해야 한다고 스스로 결정할 것이다. [11]그들은 합리적 또는 도덕적 이유로 그렇게 할 수도 있다.

어휘

norm 규범; 표준; 기준
emerge 생기다; 나오다, 나타나다
conform 순응하다[따르다]; 일치하다
cf. conformity 순응, 따름
manner 방식; 태도; 예절
initial 최초의, 처음의; 이름의 첫 글자
sort 종류, 유형; 분류[구분]하다
prescribe 지시하다; 규정하다; 처방을 내리다
cf. prescriptive 지시하는; 규범적인
utter 말하다, 발언하다; 완전한
statement 진술(서), 성명(서)
alternately 다른 방식으로; 번갈아
communicate 전달하다; 의사소통을 하다
desire 요구하다, 원하다; 욕구

🔑 (A)의 지시에 따라 순응하는 사람들과 반대의 경우가 역접으로 이어짐. ★<사역동사 have+O+p.p.>: O가 ~되게 하다

(B) [9]But / some others will not need / to have the behavior prescribed / to them.
S V O

그러나 / 다른 일부 사람들은 필요가 없을 것이다 / 그 행동이 지시되게 할 / 자신에게

[10]They will observe / the regularity (of behavior) / and (will) decide on their own // that they ought to conform.
S V₁ O₁ V₂ O₂(명사절)

그들은 관찰할 것이다 / 규칙성을 (행동의) / 그리고 스스로 결정할 것이다 // 자신이 순응해야 한다고

[11]They may do so / for either rational or moral reasons.
S V

그들은 그렇게 할 수도 있다 / 합리적 또는 도덕적 이유로

↳ **이유 2:** 다른 일부는 누군가의 지시 없이 합리적 또는 도덕적 이유로 행동을 따르는 것을 결정함.

threaten 위협[협박]하다
observe 관찰하다; 보다, 목격하다; 말하다
regularity 규칙성; 정기적임
rational 합리적인, 이성적인
moral 도덕적인; 도덕(상)의

정답 가이드

주어진 글에서 규범은 집단 내에서 사람들이 다른 사람들의 행동을 따라 하는 결과이며, 따라서 규범은 한 사람의 어떤 행동으로 시작된다고 했다. 바로 뒤에는 그런 다음(then) 다른 사람들이 그 사람의 행동을 여러 이유로 따라한다는 문장으로 시작하는 (C)가 오는 것이 적절하다. (C)에서 그 첫 번째 이유로, 최초로 행동한 사람이 다른 사람들도 그렇게 행동해야 한다고 생각할 수도 있다고 제시했으므로, 그들에게 행동을 말로 지시하거나 몸짓으로 전달하거나 또는 위협을 가할 수도 있다고 설명하는 (A)가 뒤따라야 한다. 마지막으로 역접 연결어 But으로 (A)의 지시에 순응하는 일부 사람들(some)과 대조되는, 지시 없이 스스로 순응을 결정하는 다른 일부 사람들(some others)에 대한 내용이 이어지는 것이 흐름상 적절하다.

오답 클리닉

① (A) - (C) - (B) (4%)
주어진 글에는 (A)의 them이 지칭할 대상이 없으므로 (A)는 주어진 글 뒤에 이어질 수 없다.

② (B) - (A) - (C) (15%) / ③ (B) - (C) - (A) (15%)
주어진 글에는 some others와 But으로 대조될 수 있는 대상이 없으므로 (B)는 주어진 글 뒤에 올 수 없다.

⑤ (C) - (B) - (A) (29%)
Thus로 이어지는 (A)는 (C)의 결과에 해당하며, 역접 연결어 But으로 (A)의 지시에 순응하는 일부 사람들(some)과 (B)의 스스로 순응을 결정하는 다른 일부 사람들(some others)이 대조되는 흐름이 자연스러우므로 (B)는 (A) 뒤에 이어져야 한다.

03 + 글의 순서 〈24학년도 9월 모평 36번 | 정답률 53%〉 ④

구문분석 & 직독직해

인지 나쁜 것만은 아닌 고정 관념

[1]The intuitive ability (to classify and generalize) / is undoubtedly a useful feature (of life and research), //
S₁ = V₁ C

직관적인 능력은 (분류하고 일반화하는) / 의심할 여지 없이 유용한 특징이다 (삶과 연구에 있어) //

(= the intuitive ability to classify and generalize)
but it carries a high cost, / such as in our tendency (to stereotype generalizations (about people and situations)).
S₂ V₂ O =

그러나 그것(분류하고 일반화하는 직관적인 능력)은 큰 대가를 수반한다 / 우리의 경향에 있어서와 같이 (일반화를 고정시키는 (사람과 상황에 대한))

↳ **도입:** 분류하고 일반화하는 직관적 능력은 유용하지만 일반화를 고정시키는 것과 같은 대가를 수반함.

🔑 주어진 글에서 일반화를 고정하는 것을 큰 대가라고 언급한 것과 관련해 부정적 의미를 설명함.

(C) [2]For most people, / the word stereotype arouses negative connotations: //
S₁ V₁ O₁

(= the word stereotype)
it implies a negative bias.
S₂ V₂ O₂

대부분 사람들에게 / 고정 관념이라는 단어는 부정적인 함축을 불러일으킨다 //
즉 그것(고정 관념이라는 단어)은 부정적인 편견을 의미한다

↳ **통념(Myth):** 고정 관념이라는 단어는 부정적인 편견을 의미함.

주제문

[3]But, in fact, / stereotypes do not differ / in principle / from all other generalizations; //
S₁ V₁

그러나 사실 / 고정 관념은 다르지 않다 / 원칙적으로 / 모든 다른 일반화와 //

★<not necessarily[always]>: ((부분 부정)) 반드시[항상] ~인 것은 아닌

generalizations (about groups of people) / are not necessarily always negative.
S₂ V₂ C

그리고 일반화가 (사람들의 집단에 대한) / 반드시 항상 부정적인 것은 아니다

↳ **사실(Truth):** 고정 관념은 다른 일반화와 다르지 않으며 항상 부정적인 것만은 아님.

해석

[1]분류하고 일반화하는 직관적인 능력은 의심할 여지 없이 삶과 연구에 있어 유용한 특징이지만, 그것은 사람과 상황에 대한 일반화를 고정시키는 우리의 경향에 있어서와 같이 큰 대가를 수반한다. (C) [2]대부분 사람들에게, 고정 관념이라는 단어는 부정적인 함축을 불러일으키는데, 즉 그것은 부정적인 편견을 의미한다. [3]그러나 사실 고정 관념은 원칙적으로 모든 다른 일반화와 다르지 않으며, 사람들의 집단에 대한 일반화가 반드시 항상 부정적인 것은 아니다. (A) [4]직관적이고 빠르게, 우리는 우리가 사물들 간의 차이라고 인식하는 것에 근거하여 마음속으로 사물들을 집단으로 분류하며, 그것이 고정관념의 근간이다. [5]그 후에야 우리는 사물이 어떻게 구별되는지에 대한, 그리고 그 차이의 정도와 중요성에 대한 더 많은 증거를 조사한다 (또는 조사하지 않는다). (B) [6]우리의 뇌는, 대개 우리의 자각 없이 이러한 일을 효율적이고 자동적으로 수행한다. [7]고정 관념의 진짜 위험은 그것들의 부정확성이 아니라, 그것들의 유연성 부족과 우리가 멈추어 생각할 충분한 시간이 있을 때조차도 유지되려는 경향이다.

🗝 일반화가 항상 부정적인 것은 아니라는 (C)의 마지막 문장을 부연 설명함. ★ <perceive A (to be) B>: A를 B라고 인식하다

(A) [4]Intuitively and quickly, / we mentally sort things / into groups / based on what we perceive the differences between them to be, // and that is the basis (for stereotyping).

(S_1 we, V_1 sort, O things, ~에 근거하여 based on, based on의 O(명사절), (= things) them, S_2 that, V_2 is, C the basis)

직관적이고 빠르게 / 우리는 마음속으로 사물들을 분류한다 / 집단으로 / 우리가 그것들(사물) 간의 차이라고 인식하는 것에 근거하여 // 그리고 그것이 근간이다 (고정 관념의)

★준부정어(only) 포함 어구가 문두에 와서 <조동사+주어+동사> 어순으로 도치가 일어남.

[5]Only afterwards / do we examine (or not examine) / more evidence (of how things are differentiated, / and the degree and significance (of the variations)).

(준부정어 포함 어구 Only afterwards, 조동사 do, S we, V examine, O more evidence, of의 O_1(명사절), of의 O_2(명사구))

그 후에야 / 우리는 조사한다 (또는 조사하지 않는다) / 더 많은 증거를 (사물이 어떻게 구별되는지에 대한 / 그리고 정도와 중요성에 대한 (그 차이의))

↳ **부연 설명:** 직관적이고 빠르게 사물들 간의 차이를 인식한 것에 근거해 사물들을 분류한 다음 차이에 대한 증거를 조사함.

🗝 these tasks는 (A)에서 언급한 사물을 분류하고 증거를 조사하는 일을 의미함.

(B) [6]Our brain performs these tasks efficiently and automatically, / usually without our awareness.

(S Our brain, V performs, O these tasks)

우리의 뇌는 이러한 일을 효율적이고 자동적으로 수행한다 / 대개 우리의 자각 없이

★<not A but B>: A가 아니라 B

[7]The real danger (of stereotypes) / is not their inaccuracy, / but their lack of flexibility and their tendency (to be preserved), // even when we have *enough time* (to stop and consider).

(S(단수) The real danger, V(단수) is, C_1 their inaccuracy, C_2 their lack of flexibility and their tendency, 부사절 접속사(시간) even when, S′ we, V′ have, O′ enough time)

진짜 위험은 (고정 관념의) / 그것들의 부정확성이 아니라 / 그것들의 융통성 부족과 경향이다 (유지되려는) // 우리가 충분한 시간이 있을 때조차도 (멈추어 생각할)

↳ **결론:** 고정 관념은 사물을 분류하고 조사하는 데 효율적이며, 진짜 위험은 융통성 부족과 생각을 유지하려는 경향임.

어휘

classify 분류하다
generalize 일반화하다
cf. generalization 일반화
undoubtedly 의심할 여지 없이, 틀림없이
feature 특징(으로 삼다); 특집 (기사)
carry 수반하다; 나르다
stereotype 고정시키다; 고정 관념
arouse 불러일으키다; 자극하다
imply 의미하다; 암시[시사]하다
bias 편견, 편향
in principle 원칙적으로, 이론상으로는
mentally 마음속으로, 정신적으로
sort A into B A를 B로 분류하다
basis 근간, 이유; 기초
examine 조사하다; 검사하다
differentiate 구별[차별]하다
significance 중요성; 의미
variation 차이; 변화
awareness 자각, 인식; 의식
inaccuracy 부정확(성)
flexibility 융통성, 유연성
preserve 유지[지속]하다; 보호하다

정답 가이드

주어진 글은 분류하고 일반화하는 우리의 직관적인 능력은 유용하지만 일반화를 고정시키는 우리의 경향(고정관념을 가지는 경향)은 큰 대가를 수반한다는 내용이다. 그 다음에는 먼저 고정 관념에 대한 부정적인 함축 의미를 설명하는 (C)가 이어져야 한다. (C)의 마지막 문장에서 고정 관념은 반드시 항상 부정적인 것은 아니라는 내용의 긍정적 서술로 전환이 일어나고, 그 뒤에는 고정 관념의 긍정적인 작용(직관적이고 빠르게 사물들 간의 차이를 인식하고 분류함)을 구체적으로 설명하는 (A)가 와야 한다. 마지막으로 (A)에서 언급한 긍정적인 작용을 these tasks로 받아 설명하는 (B)가 오는 것이 흐름상 자연스럽다.

오답 클리닉

① (A) - (C) - (B) (2%)
분류하고 일반화하는 직관적인 능력이 유용하지만 대가를 수반한다는 주어진 글 뒤에 대가에 대한 부정적인 내용이 아닌 빠르게 사물을 분류하는 효율성에 관해 설명하는 (A)가 이어지는 것은 부적절하다.

② (B) - (A) - (C) (13%) / ③ (B) - (C) - (A) (15%)
주어진 글에는 (B)의 these tasks가 가리킬 수 있는 내용이 없으므로 주어진 글 바로 뒤에 (B)는 올 수 없다.

⑤ (C) - (B) - (A) (16%)
(B)의 these tasks는 (A)에서 언급한 긍정적인 작용을 가리키므로 (A) 뒤에 와야 한다.

01 + 글의 순서 〈24학년도 9월 모평 37번 | 정답률 41%〉 ⑤

구문분석 & 직독직해

생물 식물의 조정된 적응 반응

[1] Plants show finely tuned adaptive responses // when nutrients are limiting.
S V O 부사절 접속사(시간) S′ V′ C′
식물은 미세하게 조정된 적응 반응을 보인다 // 영양분이 제한적일 때
↳ **세부 사항 1:** 식물은 제한적인 영양분에 대해 조정된 적응 반응을 보임.

★<recognize A as B>: A를 B로 인식하다
[2] Gardeners may recognize yellow leaves / as a sign (of poor nutrition and the need for fertilizer).
S V O =
정원사는 노란 잎을 인식할 수도 있다 / 신호로 (부족한 영양과 비료 필요의)
↳ **예 1:** 정원사에게 노란 잎은 영양 부족과 비료 필요의 신호가 됨.

관리인이 있는 경우와 없는 경우 식물의 적응 반응이 But으로 대조됨.
(C) [3] But / if a plant does not have / *a caretaker* (to provide supplemental minerals), //
부사절 접속사(조건) S′ V′ O′
그러나 / 식물에 없다면 / 관리인이 (추가 미네랄을 공급해 줄) //
↳ (= the plant)
it can proliferate or lengthen its roots / and (can) develop root hairs / to allow foraging / in more distant soil patches.
S V₁ O₁ V₂ O₂ 목적(~하도록)
그것(식물)은 그것의 뿌리를 증식하거나 늘일 수 있다 / 그리고 뿌리털을 발달시킬 수 있다 / (미네랄을) 구하러 다니도록 / 더 먼 토양에서
↳ **예 2:** 관리인이 없는 경우 식물은 뿌리털을 발달시켜 스스로 미네랄을 보충함.

[4] Plants can also use their memory / to respond to histories (of temporal or spatial variation (in nutrient or resource availability)).
S V O 목적(~하기 위해)
식물은 또한 자신의 기억을 이용할 수 있다 / 역사에 대응하기 위해 (시간적 또는 공간적 변화의 (영양분 혹은 자원 이용 가능성에 있어))
↳ **세부 사항 2:** 식물은 기억을 이용해 영양분 혹은 자원 이용 가능성에 관한 시공간 변화에 대응함.

this area는 (C)의 마지막에 언급된 식물의 기억에 관한 연구 분야를 의미함.
↳ has shown의 O(명사절)
(B) [5] Research (in this area) / has shown // that plants are constantly aware / of their position (in the environment), / in terms of both space and time.
S V 명사절 접속사 S′ V′ C′ ~의 측면에서
(C)의 temporal or spatial variation이 space and time으로 연결됨.
연구는 (이 분야에서의) / 보여주었다 // 식물이 끊임없이 인식한다는 것을 / 자신의 위치를 (환경에서의) / 공간과 시간 모두의 측면에서
↳ **논거(연구 결과):** 식물은 공간 및 시간 측면에서 환경에서의 자신의 위치를 인식함.

[6] *Plants* [that have experienced variable nutrient availability / in the past] / tend to exhibit risk-taking behaviors, / (such as spending energy on root lengthening / instead of leaf production).
S 주격 관계대명사 ★<spend A on B>: B하는 데 A를 쓰다[들이다] V ~와 같은
식물은 [일정하지 않은 영양분 이용 가능성을 경험한 / 과거에] / 위험을 감수하는 행동을 보이는 경향이 있다 / (뿌리를 늘이는 데 에너지를 쓰는 것과 같은 / 잎 생산 대신)
↳ **예 1:** 영양분이 일정하지 않았던 식물은 뿌리를 늘이는 데 에너지를 쓰는 것과 같은 위험을 감수하는 행동을 보임.

(B)에 언급된 영양분 이용이 일정하지 않았던 식물과 반대로 영양분이 풍족했던 식물이 대조됨.
(A) [7] In contrast, / plants (with a history of nutrient abundance) / are risk averse / and save energy.
S(복수) V₁(복수) C V₂(복수) O
반대로 / 식물은 (영양분이 풍족했던 내력을 가진) / 위험을 회피하려 한다 / 그리고 에너지를 절약한다
↳ **예 2:** 영양분이 풍족했던 식물은 위험을 회피하며 에너지를 절약함.

주제문
[8] At all developmental stages, / plants respond / to environmental changes or unevenness /
S V
모든 발달 단계에서 / 식물은 반응한다 / 환경 변화나 불균형에 /
so as to be able to use their energy / for growth, survival, and reproduction, /
(= in order to) 목적(~하도록)
에너지를 사용할 수 있도록 / 성장, 생존, 번식에 /

해석

[1] 식물은 영양분이 제한적일 때 미세하게 조정된 적응 반응을 보인다. [2] 정원사는 노란 잎을 부족한 영양과 비료 필요의 신호로 인식할 수도 있다. (C) [3] 그러나 식물에 추가 미네랄을 공급해 줄 관리인이 없다면, 그것(식물)은 더 먼 토양에서 (미네랄을) 구하러 다니도록 뿌리를 증식하거나 늘이고 뿌리털을 발달시킬 수 있다. [4] 식물은 또한 영양분 혹은 자원 이용 가능성에 있어 시간적 또는 공간적 변화의 역사에 대응하기 위해 자신의 기억을 이용할 수 있다. (B) [5] 이 분야에서의 연구는 식물이 공간과 시간 모두의 측면에서 환경에서의 자신의 위치를 끊임없이 인식한다는 것을 보여주었다. [6] 과거에 일정하지 않은 영양분 이용 가능성을 경험한 식물은 잎 생산 대신 뿌리를 늘이는 데 에너지를 쓰는 것과 같은 위험을 감수하는 행동을 보이는 경향이 있다. (A) [7] 반대로, 영양분이 풍족했던 내력을 가진 식물은 위험을 회피하려 하고 에너지를 절약한다.(▶ 영양분을 스스로 찾을 필요가 없었기 때문에 뿌리를 늘이는 데 에너지를 쓰는 위험을 감수하지 않는다는 의미) [8] 모든 발달 단계에서 식물은 그것의 귀중한 에너지의 손상과 비생산적인 사용을 제한하는 동시에, 성장, 생존, 번식에 에너지를 사용할 수 있도록 환경 변화나 불균형에 반응한다.

어휘

finely 미세하게; 세밀하게
tune 조정하다; 조율하다; 곡(조)
adaptive 적응성의[이 있는]
limiting 제한[한정]적인
supplemental 추가[보충]의
proliferate 증식[번식]하다
lengthen 늘이다, 길게 하다
distant (거리가) 먼, 떨어져 있는
patch 좁은 땅; 밭
temporal 시간적인; 일시적인; 속세의
spatial 공간적인
variation 변화, 변동; (~의) 변형
cf. variable 일정하지 않은, 변화하기 쉬운
constantly 끊임없이, 계속
exhibit 보이다[드러내다]; 전시하다
risk-taking 위험을 감수하는
abundance 풍족, 풍부
risk averse 위험을 회피하려 하는
unevenness 불균형; 고르지 않음
reproduction 번식; 복제
nonproductive 비생산적인

while limiting / damage and nonproductive uses (of their valuable energy).
접속사를 생략하지 않은 분사구문(= while they limit ~)
제한하는 동시에 / 손상과 비생산적인 사용을 (그것의 귀중한 에너지의)
↳ 식물은 환경 변화나 불균형에 반응해 에너지를 조정하는 적응 반응을 보임.

정답 가이드

주어진 글은 식물이 영양분이 제한적일 때 조정된 적응 반응을 보이는 예로 정원사에게 노란 잎으로 영양이 부족하다는 신호를 보내는 것을 들고 있다. 그다음에는 역접 연결어 But이 이끌어, 정원사와 같은 관리인이 없는 경우에 보이는 식물의 적응 반응을 언급하는 (C)가 와야 한다. (B)와 (A)는 (C)의 마지막에 언급된 기억을 이용한 식물의 적응 반응에 대한 구체적인 서술이므로 (C) 뒤에 이어지는 것이 적절하다. (B)는 과거에 '일정하지 않은 영양분'의 이용 가능성을 경험한 식물의 적응 반응에 대한 것이고 (A)는 반대로(In contrast), '영양분이 풍족했던' 내력을 가진 식물의 적응 반응이므로 차례대로 (B) - (A)가 오는 것이 자연스럽다.

오답 클리닉

① (A) - (C) - (B) (2%) / ④ (C) - (A) - (B) (20%)
(A)에서 영양분이 풍족했던 식물의 대응이 In contrast로 연결되므로 그 앞에는 그와 대조되는, 즉 영양분이 풍족하지 않았던 식물의 대응에 관한 내용이 와야 한다. 따라서 (A)는 (B) 뒤에 와야 한다.
② (B) - (A) - (C) (18%) / ③ (B) - (C) - (A) (19%)
주어진 글에는 (B)의 this area가 지칭할 대상이 없으므로 (B)는 주어진 글 바로 뒤에 올 수 없다.

02 + 글의 순서 (24학년도 6월 모평 36번 | 정답률 58%)

④

구문분석 & 직독직해

기술 컴퓨터 코드 복잡성 증가에 따른 보안 악화

주제문

[1]The growing complexity (of computer software) / has direct implications / for our global safety and security, //
S / V / O
증가하는 복잡성은 (컴퓨터 소프트웨어의) / 직접적인 영향을 미친다 / 전 세계의 안전과 보안에 //
particularly as *the physical objects* [upon which we depend] — / things (like cars, airplanes, bridges, tunnels, and implantable medical devices) — / transform themselves into computer code.
부사절 접속사(~하면서) S′ 전치사+관계대명사 V′ O′
특히 물리적 사물이 ~하면서 [우리가 의존하는] / 즉 (~할) 것들 (자동차, 비행기, 교량, 터널, 이식할 수 있는 의료 기기와 같은) / 스스로를 컴퓨터 코드로 전환(하면서)
↳ 물리적 사물을 컴퓨터 코드로 전환하면서 컴퓨터 소프트웨어의 복잡성이 전 세계의 안전과 보안에 영향을 미침.

🔑 주어진 글에서 언급한 물리적 사물의 컴퓨터 코드로의 전환을 구체적으로 설명함.
(C) [2]Physical things are increasingly becoming information technologies.
S V C
물리적 사물들은 점점 더 정보 기술이 되어가고 있다

★<nothing more than ~>: ~에 불과한
[3]Cars are / "*computers* [(which[that]) we ride in]," // and airplanes are nothing more than "*flying Solaris boxes* (attached to bucketfuls of industrial control systems)"
S₁ V₁ C₁ 목적격 관계대명사 생략 S₂ V₂ C₂ 과거분사구
자동차는 ~이다 / '컴퓨터 [우리가 타는]' // 그리고 비행기는 '나는 솔라리스(미국 컴퓨터 회사에서 개발한 운영체제) 박스'에 불과하다 (수많은 산업 제어 시스템에 부착된)
↳ **부연 설명(예):** 자동차와 비행기 같은 사물들이 정보 기술화 되고 있음.

★<so+V+S(S도 또한 V하다)>의 도치구문으로 여기서 does는 grows를 의미함.
(A) [4]As all this code grows / in size and complexity, // so too does / the number (of errors and software bugs).
부사절 접속사(~함에 따라) S′ V′ V S
🔑 위에서 언급된 computer code[software]를 all this code로 받아 복잡성 증가로 인한 문제점을 설명함.
이 모든 코드가 증가함에 따라 / 크기와 복잡성에서 // 또한 증가한다 / 수도 (오류와 소프트웨어 버그의)
↳ **코드 증가의 문제점:** 코드가 크기와 복잡성에서 증가함에 따라 오류와 소프트웨어 버그도 증가함.

[5]According to a study by Carnegie Mellon University, / commercial software typically has twenty to thirty bugs / for every thousand lines of code — //
S₁ V₁ O₁
Carnegie Mellon 대학교의 연구에 따르면 / 상업용 소프트웨어에는 보통 20~30개의 버그가 있다 / 코드 1,000줄마다 //
★50 million lines of code는 한 줄 한 줄의 코드가 아닌 총체적인 개념으로 보아 단수 취급함.
50 million lines of code means / *1 million to 1.5 million potential errors* (to be exploited).
S₂ V₂ O₂
5천만 줄의 코드는 의미한다 / 1백만~150만 개의 잠재적 오류를 ((부적절하게) 활용될 수 있는)
↳ **부연 설명(예):** 코드가 많아질수록 부적절하게 활용될 수 있는 오류도 많아짐.

해석

[1]컴퓨터 소프트웨어의 증가하는 복잡성은 전 세계의 안전과 보안에 직접적인 영향을 미치는데, 우리가 의존하는 물리적 사물, 즉 자동차, 비행기, 교량, 터널, 이식할 수 있는 의료 기기와 같은 것들이 스스로를 컴퓨터 코드로 전환하면서 특히 그렇다. (C) [2]물리적 사물들은 점점 더 정보 기술이 되어가고 있다. [3]자동차는 '우리가 타는 컴퓨터'이고, 비행기는 '수많은 산업 제어 시스템에 부착된 '나는 솔라리스(미국 컴퓨터 회사에서 개발한 운영체제) 박스'에 불과하다. (A) [4]이 모든 코드가 크기와 복잡성에서 증가함에 따라, 오류와 소프트웨어 버그의 수도 또한 증가한다. [5]Carnegie Mellon 대학교의 연구에 따르면, 상업용 소프트웨어에는 보통 코드 1,000줄마다 20~30개의 버그가 있는데, 5천만 줄의 코드는 (부적절하게) 활용될 수 있는 1백만~150만 개의 잠재적 오류를 의미한다. (B) [6]이것이 코드가 원래 하도록 의도되지 않았던 것을 하도록 이 컴퓨터 버그를 이용하는 모든 악성 소프트웨어 공격의 근간이다. [7]컴퓨터 코드가 더 복잡해짐에 따라, 소프트웨어 버그는 난무하고 전반적인 사회에 대한 커지는 영향과 함께 보안은 악화된다.

어휘

implication 영향, 결과; 의미, 함의
implantable 이식할 수 있는
transform 전환하다, 바꾸다
attach A to B A를 B에 부착하다
bucketfuls of 수많은, 대량의
industrial 산업[공업]의
bug (컴퓨터 프로그래밍의) 버그, 오류; 작은 곤충
commercial 상업(용)의; 영리적인
potential 잠재적인; 잠재력
malware 악성 소프트웨어

🔑 This는 (A)에서 언급한 코드가 증가하면 오류와 버그도 증가한다는 내용을 가리킴.

(B) [6]This is the basis (for *all malware attacks* [that take advantage of these computer bugs / to get the code to do *something* [(that) it was not originally intended to do]]).

S V C ★<get+O+to-v>: O가 v하게 하다 / 주격 관계대명사 / 목적(~하도록) / 목적격 관계대명사 생략

이것이 근간이다 (모든 악성 소프트웨어 공격의 [이 컴퓨터 버그를 이용하는 / (~한) 것을 코드가 하도록 [그것이 원래 하도록 의도되지 않았던]])

↳ **결과:** 코드 증가에 따른 오류와 버그 증가는 컴퓨터 버그를 악용하는 악성 소프트웨어 공격의 근간이 됨.

[7]As computer code grows more elaborate, // software bugs flourish // and security suffers, / with increasing consequences (for society at large).

부사절 접속사(~함에 따라) / S_1 V_1 S_2 V_2

컴퓨터 코드가 더 복잡해짐에 따라 // 소프트웨어 버그가 난무한다 // 그리고 보안은 악화된다 / 커지는 영향과 함께 (전반적인 사회에 대한)

↳ **결론(주제문 재진술):** 컴퓨터 코드가 복잡해지면서 버그가 늘어나 보안이 악화됨.

take advantage of ~을 이용하다
intend 의도하다; 의미하다
elaborate 복잡한; 정교한
flourish 난무하다; 번창[번성]하다
suffer 악화되다; 고통받다; 겪다
consequence 영향(력); 결과
at large 전반적인, 대체적인

정답 가이드

주어진 글은 점점 더 복잡해지는 컴퓨터 소프트웨어가 전 세계의 안전과 보안에 직접적인 영향을 미친다는 내용이다. 그 뒤에는 주어진 글에서 언급한 물리적 사물의 컴퓨터 코드화를 자동차와 비행기를 예로 들어 부연 설명하는 (C)가 이어진 다음, 언급된 모든 computer code를 all this code로 받아 코드의 크기와 복잡성이 증가함에 따라 오류와 버그가 증가하는 문제를 설명하는 (A)가 와야 한다. (B)의 This는 (A)에서 언급한 '코드에 오류와 버그가 증가하는 문제'를 가리켜 그것이 악성 소프트웨어 공격의 근간이라고 밝히며 주제문을 재진술하여 글을 맺고 있으므로 마지막에 오는 것이 자연스럽다.

오답 클리닉

① (A) - (C) - (B) (3%)
흐름상 주어진 글 뒤에 (A)와 (C) 둘 다 바로 이어질 수는 있으나, 물리적 사물이 컴퓨터 코드로 전환된다는 주어진 글을 구체적으로 예를 들어 설명하는 (C)의 연결이 더 긴밀하므로 주어진 글 뒤에는 (C)가 먼저 와야 한다.

② (B) - (A) - (C) (11%) / ③ (B) - (C) - (A) (7%)
주어진 글에는 컴퓨터 버그에 관한 내용이 없으므로 (B)의 these computer bugs가 바로 연결될 수 없다.

⑤ (C) - (B) - (A) (21%)
(B)의 This는 코드가 증가하면 오류와 버그도 증가한다는 (A)의 첫 번째 문장의 내용을 가리키며, these computer bugs가 가리키는 대상이 (A)의 errors and software bugs이므로 (B)는 (A) 뒤에 와야 한다.

03 + 글의 순서 〈24학년도 6월 모평 37번 | 정답률 58%〉 ③

구문분석 & 직독직해 사회 얼굴 붉어짐의 긍정적인 사회적 기능

★<see A as B>: A를 B로 여기다[간주하다]

[1]Darwin saw blushing / as (being) uniquely human, / (as) representing *an involuntary physical reaction* (caused by embarrassment and self-consciousness / in a social environment).

S V O 동명사 being 생략 / 과거분사구

Darwin은 얼굴이 붉어지는 것을 여겼다 / 고유하게 인간적인 것으로 / 즉 비자발적인 신체 반응을 나타내는 것(으로) (당혹감과 자의식으로 야기된 / 사회적 환경에서)

↳ **도입:** Darwin은 얼굴 붉어짐을 사회적 환경에서 일어나는 비자발적인 신체 반응으로 여김.

🔑 얼굴 붉어짐이 사회적 환경에서 나타난다는 주어진 글의 내용을 구체적으로 설명함.

(B) [2]If we feel awkward, embarrassed or ashamed // when we are alone, // we don't blush; // it seems to be caused / by our concern (about what others are thinking of us).

부사절 접속사(양보) V' C'₁ C'₂ C'₃ 부사절 접속사(시간) S_1 V_1 / → (= blushing) / S_2 V_2 C / about의 O(명사절)

우리가 어색하거나 당혹스럽거나 부끄럽다고 느끼더라도 // 우리가 혼자 있을 때 // 우리는 얼굴이 붉어지지 않는다 // 그것(얼굴이 붉어지는 것)은 야기되는 것처럼 보인다 / 우리의 염려에 의해 (다른 사람들이 우리를 어떻게 생각하고 있는지에 대한)

↳ **얼굴 붉어짐의 원인:** 혼자 있을 때는 일어나지 않으며, 다른 사람들이 자신을 어떻게 생각할지 염려하는 것에 의해 일어남.

[3]Studies have confirmed // that simply being told // (that) you are blushing / brings it on.

S V → have confirmed의 O(명사절) / 명사절 접속사 / S'(동명사구) / V' / O'(= blushing)

연구는 확인했다 // 단지 듣는 것만으로도 // 얼굴이 붉어졌다고 / 그것(얼굴이 붉어지는 것)을 야기한다는 것을

[4]We feel // as though others can see / through our skin and into our mind.

S V 부사절 접속사(= as if) S' V' / 전치사구 병렬

우리는 느낀다 // 마치 다른 사람들이 볼 수 있는 것처럼 / 우리의 피부를 꿰뚫어 우리의 마음을 들여다

↳ **부연 설명:** 우리는 얼굴이 붉어졌다는 말만 들어도 그렇게 되며 다른 사람들이 자신을 꿰뚫어 본다고 느낌.

해석

[1]Darwin은 얼굴이 붉어지는 것을 고유하게 인간적인 것, 즉 사회적 환경에서 당혹감과 자의식으로 야기된 비자발적인 신체 반응을 나타내는 것으로 여겼다. (B) [2]우리가 혼자 있을 때 어색하거나 당혹스럽거나 부끄럽다고 느끼더라도 우리는 얼굴이 붉어지지 않는데, 그것(얼굴이 붉어지는 것)은 다른 사람들이 우리를 어떻게 생각하고 있는지에 대한 우리의 염려에 의해 야기되는 것처럼 보인다. [3]연구는 단지 얼굴이 붉어졌다고 듣는 것만으로도 그것(얼굴이 붉어지는 것)을 야기한다는 것을 확인했다. [4]우리는 마치 다른 사람들이 우리의 피부를 꿰뚫어 우리의 마음을 들여다볼 수 있는 것처럼 느낀다. (C) [5]그러나, 우리는 가끔 자신도 모르게 얼굴이 새빨개질 때 사라지고 싶어 하는 반면에, 심리학자들은 얼굴이 붉어지는 것이 실제로는 긍정적인 사회적 목적에 도움이 된다고 주장한다. [6]우리가 얼굴이 붉어질 때, 그것은 다른 사람들에게 우리가 사회적 규범이 어겨졌음을 인식한다는 신호이며, 실수에 대한 사과이다. (A) [7]어쩌면 우리가 잠시 체면을 잃는 것이 집단의 장기적인 결합에 도움이 될지도 모른다.(▶ 사회적 규범을 어기고도 얼굴이 붉어지지 않는 것은 규범을 어겼음을 인정하지 않는 것이

주제문 (B)의 얼굴 붉어짐과 관련한 부정적인 느낌과 상반되는 긍정적인 내용이 However로 이어짐.

(C) [5]However, / while we sometimes want to disappear // when we involuntarily go bright red, //
부사절 접속사(~인 반면에) V′ O′ 부사절 접속사(시간) S″ V″ C″
그러나 / 우리는 가끔 사라지고 싶어 하는 반면에 // 자신도 모르게 얼굴이 새빨개질 때 //

psychologists argue // that blushing actually serves a positive social purpose.
S V 명사절 접속사 S′ V′ O′ (argue의 O(명사절))
심리학자들은 주장한다 // 얼굴이 붉어지는 것이 실제로는 긍정적인 사회적 목적에 도움이 된다고
↳ 얼굴이 붉어지는 것은 긍정적인 사회적 목적에 도움이 됨.

[6]When we blush, // it's a signal to others // that we recognize // that a social norm has been broken;
부사절 접속사(시간) S_1 V_1 C_1 = 동격 접속사 S′ V′ O′(명사절) (it = blushing)
// it is an apology (for a faux pas).
S_2 V_2 C_2 (it = blushing)
우리가 얼굴이 붉어질 때 // 그것(얼굴이 붉어지는 것)은 다른 사람들에게 신호이다 // 우리가 인식한다는 // 사회적 규범이 어겨졌음을 // 그리고 그것(얼굴이 붉어지는 것)은 사과이다 (실수에 대한)
↳ **부연 설명:** 얼굴 붉어짐은 사회적 규범을 어겼음을 인정하는 신호이자 실수에 대한 사과임.

(C)에서 언급한 긍정적인 사회적 목적을 구체적으로 설명함.

(A) [7]Maybe / our brief loss of face benefits / the long-term cohesion (of the group).
S V O
어쩌면 / 우리가 잠시 체면을 잃는 것이 도움이 될지도 모른다 / 장기적인 결합에 (집단의)
↳ **세부 사항:** 얼굴이 붉어져 잠시 체면을 잃는 것이 장기적인 집단의 결합에 도움이 됨.

[8]Interestingly, / if someone blushes / after making a social mistake, //
부사절 접속사(조건) S′ V′
흥미롭게도 / 누군가가 얼굴이 붉어지면 / 사회적 실수를 저지른 후 //
they are viewed / in a more favourable light / than *those* [who don't blush].
S V 주격 관계대명사
그들은 바라봐진다 / 더 호의적인 관점에서 / 사람들보다 [얼굴이 붉어지지 않는]
↳ **부연 설명:** 사회적 실수를 저지른 후 얼굴이 붉어지는 사람이 그렇지 않은 사람보다 더 호의적으로 여겨짐.

며 이는 결국 집단의 결합을 해칠 것임) [8]흥미롭게도 누군가가 사회적 실수를 저지른 후 얼굴이 붉어지면, 그들은 얼굴이 붉어지지 않는 사람들보다 더 호의적인 관점에서 바라봐진다.

어휘

blush 얼굴이 붉어지다; 부끄러워하다
uniquely 고유하게, 독특하게
represent 나타내다; 대표[대신]하다
involuntary 비자발적인, 무의식적인
cf. involuntarily 자신도 모르게, 무의식중에
embarrassment 당혹(감); 어색함
cf. embarrassed 당혹스러운, 어색한
self-consciousness 자의식
awkward 어색한; 곤란한
ashamed 부끄러운, 창피한
concern 염려[걱정](하다); 관련되다
bring on ~을 야기하다[초래하다]
serve (목적에) 도움이 되다; 만족시키다, 채우다
norm 규범; 표준
face 체면, 면목
cohesion 결합, 단결
favourable 호의적인; (인상이) 좋은; 유리한
light 관점, 견지; 빛(을 비추다)

정답 가이드

주어진 글은 다윈이 얼굴이 붉어지는 것을 사회적 환경에서 일어나는 인간 고유의 비자발적인 신체 반응으로 여겼다는 내용이다. 이 다음에는 주어진 글의 '사회적 환경'과 관련해 얼굴 붉어짐이 일어나는 원인을 구체적으로 설명하는 (B)가 와야 한다. (B)의 마지막 문장은 얼굴이 붉어짐에 대해 우리가 느끼는 부정적인 느낌을 설명하는데, 그 뒤에는 역접 연결어 However로 얼굴이 붉어지는 것이 긍정적인 사회적 목적에 도움이 된다고 내용이 전환되는 (C)가 이어지는 것이 적절하다. (A)의 '잠시 체면을 잃는 것'은 얼굴이 붉어지는 것을 의미하며 그것이 집단의 장기적 결합에 도움이 된다고 했는데, 이는 사회적 실수를 저지른 후 얼굴이 붉어지는 사람을 호의적으로 바라보기 때문이라는 것이다. 즉, (C)에서 언급한 '긍정적인 사회적 목적에 도움이 된다'는 주장을 구체적으로 부연 설명한 것이므로, (A)가 마지막에 오는 것이 자연스럽다.

오답 클리닉

① (A) - (C) - (B) (2%) / ② (B) - (A) - (C) (23%)
(A)는 얼굴이 붉어지는 것이 긍정적인 사회적 목적에 도움이 된다는 (C)의 내용을 구체적으로 설명하는 세부 사항에 해당하므로 (C) 뒤에 와야 한다.
④ (C) - (A) - (B) (8%) / ⑤ (C) - (B) - (A) (8%)
얼굴이 붉어지는 것이 긍정적인 사회적 목적에 도움이 된다는 (C)가 역접 연결어 However로 이어진 것으로 보아 그 앞에는 얼굴 붉어짐과 관련한 부정적인 내용이 언급되어야 한다. 그러나 주어진 글에는 그러한 내용이 없으므로 (C)가 바로 뒤에 이어지는 것은 어색하다.

01 + 문장 넣기 〈24학년도 대수능 38번 | 정답률 45%〉 ③

구문분석 & 직독직해

과학 과학이 승자독식 경쟁이라는 부정확한 견해

[1]Science is sometimes described / as a winner-take-all contest, / meaning // that there are no rewards (for being second or third).

S V 전치사(~로(서)) 분사구문 (= and it means ~) 현재분사 meaning의 O(명사절)

과학은 때때로 묘사된다 / 승자독식 경쟁으로 / 그리고 이는 의미한다 // 보상이 없다는 것을 (2등이나 3등인 것에 대한)

(= 앞 문장)
[2]This is an extreme view (of the nature (of scientific contests)).

S V C

이는 극단적인 견해이다 (본질에 대한 (과학 경쟁의))

↳ **견해 1:** 과학을 승자독식 경쟁으로 묘사하는 것은 과학 경쟁의 본질에 대한 극단적인 견해임.

(①) [3]Even *those* [who describe scientific contests / in such a way] / note // that it is a somewhat inaccurate description, //

S 주격 관계대명사 V O(명사절)

사람들조차도 [과학 경쟁을 묘사하는 / 그런 식으로] / 말한다 // 그것(과학을 승자독식 경쟁으로 묘사하는 것)이 다소 부정확한 묘사라고 //

given that replication and verification have social value [and] are common in science.

~을 고려할 때 S′ V′₁ O′ V′₂ C′

반복과 입증이 사회적 가치를 지니고 있고 과학에서는 일반적이라는 것을 고려할 때

↳ **견해 1의 부연 설명:** 과학을 반복하고 입증하는 것이 사회적으로 가치 있으며 과학에서는 일반적임.

(②) [4]It is also inaccurate / to the extent that it suggests // that only a handful of contests exist.

S V C ~일 경우에 S′ V′ O′(명사절)

그것(과학을 승자독식 경쟁으로 묘사하는 것)은 또한 부정확하다 / 그것이 나타낼 경우에 // 단지 소수의 경쟁만 존재한다는 것을

↳ **견해 2:** 과학은 승자독식의 소수의 경쟁만 있는 것이 아님.

뒤에 other contests에 대한 내용이 언급되어야 함.

(③) [5]Yes, / some contests are seen / as world class, / such as identification of the Higgs particle [or] the development of high temperature superconductors.)

S V 전치사(~로(서)) ★<see A as B(A를 B로 여기다)>의 수동형 명사구 병렬

물론 / 몇몇 경쟁은 여겨진다 / 세계적인 수준으로 / 힉스 입자의 확인 또는 고온 초전도체 개발과 같은

[6]But / many other contests have multiple parts, // [and] the number (of such contests) / may be increasing.

S_1 V_1 O S_2 V_2

하지만 / 다른 많은 경쟁에는 다양한 부분이 있다 // 그리고 수는 (그런 경쟁의) / 증가하고 있을 것이다

↳ **견해 2의 부연 설명:** 일부 소수의 과학 경쟁은 세계적인 수준이지만, 다양한 부분을 포함한 다른 많은 경쟁 부분이 증가하고 있음.

(④) [7]By way of example, / for many years / it was thought // that there would be "one" cure (for cancer), //

가주어₁ V_1 진주어₁(명사절)

한 예로 / 여러 해 동안 / (~라고) 생각되었다 // '하나'의 치료법만 있다고 (암에 대해) //

[but] it is now realized // that cancer takes multiple forms // [and] that multiple approaches are needed / to provide a cure.

가주어₂ V_2 진주어₂(명사절 병렬) 목적(~하기 위해)

그러나 (~라고) 이제 인식된다 // 암은 다양한 형태를 띤다고 // 그리고 다양한 접근법이 필요하다고 / 치료를 제공하기 위해

↳ **예:** 하나의 치료법으로만 암을 치료할 수 있다는 초기 믿음은 다양한 형태의 암으로 인해 여러 접근법이 필요하다는 인식으로 발전함.

(⑤) [8]There won't be one winner — // there will be many (winners).

V_1 S_1 V_2 S_2

승자는 한 명이 아닐 것이다 // 즉 여러 명이 있을 것이다

↳ **견해 2의 맺음말:** 과학은 단 하나의 이론만이 승리하는 경쟁이 아님.

해석

[1]과학은 때때로 승자독식 경쟁으로 묘사되는데, 이는 2등이나 3등인 것에 대한 보상이 없다는 것을 의미한다. [2]이는 과학 경쟁의 본질에 대한 극단적인 견해이다. (①) [3]과학 경쟁을 그런 식으로 묘사하는 사람들조차도 그것(과학을 승자독식 경쟁으로 묘사하는 것)이 다소 부정확한 묘사라고 말하는데, 반복과 입증이 사회적 가치를 지니고 있고 과학에서는 일반적이라는 것을 고려할 때 그렇다. (②) [4]그것은 단지 소수의 경쟁만 존재한다는 것을 나타낼 경우에 또한 부정확하다. (③ [5]물론, 힉스 입자의 확인 또는 고온 초전도체 개발과 같은 몇몇 경쟁은 세계적인 수준으로 여겨진다.) [6]하지만 다른 많은 경쟁에는 다양한 부분이 있고, 그런 경쟁의 수는 증가하고 있을 것이다. (④) [7]한 예로, 여러 해 동안 암에 대해 '하나'의 치료법만 있다고 생각되었지만, 암은 다양한 형태를 띠고 치료를 제공하기 위해 다양한 접근법이 필요하다고 이제 인식된다. (⑤) [8]승자는 한 명이 아니라 여러 명이 있을 것이다.

어휘

describe 묘사하다, 말하다
cf. description 묘사[서술]
winner-take-all 승자독식의
contest 경쟁(을 벌이다); 대회
reward 보상(하다)
extreme 극단적인; 극심한
somewhat 다소, 약간
inaccurate 부정확한
common 일반적인, 흔한; 공통의
a handful of 소수의
identification 확인; 발견; 신분증
particle 입자; 작은 조각
superconductor 초전도체
multiple 다양한; 많은
cure 치료(법); 치료하다
approach 접근(법); 다가가다[오다]

정답 가이드

주어진 문장은 부정적인 내용에 대해 긍정의 내용을 이끄는 Yes로 시작하여 몇몇 경쟁(some contests)은 세계적 수준으로 여겨진다는 내용이다. 글을 처음부터 읽어보면, 과학 경쟁을 승자독식이라고 묘사하거나 소수의 경쟁만 존재한다고 하는 것은 부정확하다고 설명한다. 이어서 ③ 뒤에는 역접 연결어 But이 이끌어 다른 많은 경쟁(many other contests)에는 다양한 부분이 있다는 내용이 이어진다. 즉 ③의 앞과 뒤 문장은 모두 소수의 경쟁만 존재하는 것이 아니라는 내용이므로 But으로 연결될 수 없다. 주어진 문장을 ③에 넣어보면 소수의 경쟁만 존재한다는 것은 부정확하며, 물론(Yes) 몇몇 경쟁(some contests)은 세계적인 수준(소수의 경쟁)이지만, 다른 많은 경쟁(many other contests)은 그렇지 않다는 내용이 자연스럽게 이어진다.

오답 클리닉

① (3%) in such a way와 it은 앞부분의 과학을 승자독식 경쟁으로 묘사하는 것을 받아 그것이 극단적인 견해라고 주장하는 논거를 제시한다.

② (8%) 앞 문장에 이어 또 다른 견해가 also로 이어지는 것은 자연스럽다.

④ (34%) 암의 다양한 형태와 접근법을 예로 들어 과학 경쟁에는 다양한 부분이 있다는 앞 문장을 구체적으로 설명하는 내용이다.

The 주의 주어진 문장은 세계적인 수준으로 승자독식이 이루어지는 몇몇 소수의 경쟁에 대해 이야기하므로 뒤에 암의 치료에 대한 다양한 접근법에 관한 예가 이어지는 것은 어색하다.

⑤ (10%) 과학은 승자독식 경쟁이 아니라고 글을 맺고 있다.

02 + 문장 넣기 〈24학년도 대수능 39번 | 정답률 53%〉 ④

구문분석 & 직독직해 생물 돌연변이와 인쇄 오류의 유사점과 차이점

[1] Misprints (in a book [or] in any written message) / usually have a negative impact on the content, / sometimes (literally) fatally.
(S(복수): Misprints, 전치사구 병렬 / V(복수): have / O: a negative impact)
오자는 (책이나 어떤 서면 메시지 속의) / 보통 내용에 부정적인 영향을 미친다 / 때로는 (문자 그대로) 치명적이게

(①) [2] The displacement of a comma, / for instance, / may be a matter of life and death.
(S: The displacement of a comma / V: may be / C: a matter of life and death)
쉼표를 잘못된 곳에 배치한 것은 / 예를 들어 / 생사의 문제일 수 있다

🔑 인쇄 오류와 돌연변이의 유사점을 설명함.

(②) [3] Similarly / most mutations have harmful consequences / for *the organism* [in which they occur], / meaning // that they reduce its reproductive fitness.
(S: most mutations / V: have / O: harmful consequences / (= mutations) / 전치사+관계대명사: in which / 분사구문(= and it means ~) / 현재분사 meaning의 O(명사절))
마찬가지로 / 대부분의 돌연변이는 해로운 결과를 가져온다 / 유기체에 [그것들(돌연변이)이 발생하는] / 그리고 이는 뜻한다 // 그것들(돌연변이)이 그것(유기체)의 생식 적합성을 감소시킨다는 것을

↳ **유사점 1(단점):** 오자가 내용에 부정적인 영향을 미치듯이 돌연변이는 유기체에 생식 적합성 감소라는 해로운 영향을 미침.

★that이 이끄는 관계사절은 주어 a mutation을 수식함.

(③) [4] Occasionally, / however, / *a mutation* may occur [that increases the fitness of the organism], // just as an accidental failure / to reproduce the text of the first edition / might provide more accurate or updated information.
(S: a mutation / V: may occur / 주격 관계대명사: that / V′: increases / O′: the fitness of the organism / 부사절 접속사(꼭 ~처럼): just as / S′: an accidental failure / V′: might provide / O′: more accurate or updated information)
때때로 / 그러나 / 돌연변이가 발생할 수 있다 [유기체의 적합성을 향상시키는] // 꼭 우연한 실수가 ~처럼 / 초판본의 원문을 다시 만들어 내는 데 / 더 정확하거나 최신의 정보를 제공할 수도 있는 것(처럼)

↳ **유사점 2(장점):** 초판본의 원문을 다시 만들어 낼 때 우연한 실수로 내용이 향상되는 것처럼 유기체의 적합성을 향상시키는 돌연변이가 발생할 수 있음.

🔑 인쇄 오류와 돌연변이의 유사성이 깨진 내용이 이어져야 함.

(④ [5] At the next step in the argument, / however, / the analogy breaks down.)
(S: the analogy / V: breaks down)
논거의 다음 단계에서 / 그러나 / 그 유사성은 깨진다

↳ 인쇄 오류와 돌연변이 간의 유사점만 있는 것은 아님.

[6] A favorable mutation is going to be more heavily represented / in the next generation, // since *the organism* [in which it occurred] / will have more offspring // [and] mutations are transmitted to the offspring.
(S: A favorable mutation / V: is going to be ... represented / 부사절 접속사(~ 때문에): since / S′₁: the organism / 전치사+관계대명사: in which / it (= a favorable mutation) / V′₁: will have / O′₁: more offspring / S′₂: mutations / V′₂: are transmitted)
유리한 돌연변이는 더 많이 나타날 것이다 / 다음 세대에 // 유기체는 ~ 때문에 [그것(유리한 돌연변이)이 발생한] / 더 많은 자손을 낳을 것이기 (때문에) // 그리고 돌연변이가 자손에게 유전되기 (때문에)

해석

[1]책이나 어떤 서면 메시지 속의 오자는 보통 내용에 부정적인 영향을 미치며, 때로는 (문자 그대로) 치명적이게 그러하다. (①) [2]예를 들어, 쉼표를 잘못된 곳에 배치한 것은 생사의 문제일 수 있다. (②) [3]마찬가지로 대부분의 돌연변이는 그것들이 발생하는 유기체에 해로운 결과를 가져오는데, 이는 그것들(돌연변이)이 유기체의 생식 적합성을 감소시킨다는 것을 뜻한다. (③) [4]그러나 때때로 꼭 초판본의 원문을 다시 만들어 내는 데 우연한 실수(▶ 오류를 의도치않게 바로잡음)가 더 정확하거나 최신의 정보를 제공할 수도 있는 것처럼, 유기체의 적합성을 향상시키는 돌연변이가 발생할 수 있다. (④) [5]그러나 논거의 다음 단계에서 그 유사성은 깨진다.) [6]유리한 돌연변이는 다음 세대에 더 많이 나타날 것인데, 그것이 발생한 유기체는 더 많은 자손을 낳아 돌연변이가 자손에게 유전되기 때문이다. (⑤) [7]대조적으로, 우연히 초판의 오류를 바로잡은 책이 더 잘 팔리는 경향이 있는 메커니즘은 없다.

어휘

- misprint 오자; 잘못 인쇄하다
- impact 영향, 충격; 영향을 주다
- literally 문자[말] 그대로
- fatally 치명적으로; 숙명적으로
- displacement (제자리에서 쫓겨난) 이동
- consequence 결과
- organism 유기체, 생물(체)
- reproductive 생식[번식]의
- fitness 적합성; (신체적인) 건강
- accidental 우연한, 돌발적인
- failure 실수, 실패; 불이행, (~하지) 않는 것
- argument 논거, 주장; 논쟁
- favorable 유리한; 호의적인
- represent 나타내다, 표현하다; 대표하다

🔑 인쇄 오류와 돌연변이의 차이점이 대조됨.

(⑤) ⁷By contrast, / there is no *mechanism* [by which *a book* [that accidentally corrects the mistakes of the first edition] / will tend to sell better].

V S 전치사+관계대명사 S′ 주격 관계대명사 V′

대조적으로 / 메커니즘은 없다 [책이 [우연히 초판의 오류를 바로잡은] / 더 잘 팔리는 경향이 있는]

↳ **차이점:** 유리한 돌연변이는 유전되어 다음 세대에 더 많이 나타나는 반면에, 책은 우연히 오류를 바로잡아도 판매량이 오르지는 않음.

offspring 자손; 자식; (동물의) 새끼
transmit 유전시키다; 보내다; 전달하다
mechanism 메커니즘 ((어떤 대상의 작용 원리나 구조))
correct 바로잡다, 정정하다; 정확한; 올바른

정답 가이드

역접 연결어 however(하지만)를 포함한 주어진 문장은 논거의 다음 단계에서는 그 유사성(the analogy)이 깨진다는 내용이므로 앞에는 어떤 유사성이 서술되고 뒤에는 그 유사성이 깨진 것을 설명하는 내용이 이어질 것임을 알 수 있다. 글을 처음부터 읽어보면, 책의 오자나 유기체의 돌연변이는 둘 다 해로운 결과를 가져오지만 때때로 이 둘은 각각 더 정확한 정보를 제공하거나 유기체의 적합성을 향상시킬 수 있다고 했다. 즉 ④의 앞 문장은 인쇄 오류와 돌연변이 둘 간의 유사성을 서술한 것이다. 이어서 ④의 뒤 내용은 유리한 돌연변이는 다음 세대에 더 많이 나타나지만, 초판의 오류를 바로잡은 책이 더 잘 팔리지는 않는다고 했으므로 유사성이 깨진 것에 대한 설명에 해당한다. 따라서 주어진 문장이 들어가기에 가장 적절한 곳은 ④이다.

오답 클리닉

① (2%) 오자가 부정적인 영향을 미친다는 앞 문장의 예로 잘못된 곳에 배치된 쉼표를 든 것은 적절하다.
② (7%) 오자의 부정적 영향과 유사한 돌연변이의 해로운 영향이 Similarly(마찬가지로)로 이어지는 것은 자연스럽다.
③ (10%) 역접 연결어 however로 앞의 부정적인 돌연변이의 영향과 반대되는 긍정적인 내용이 자연스럽게 이어진다.
⑤ (29%) 역접 연결어 By contrast를 사용해 유리한 돌연변이의 증가와 우연히 오류를 바로잡은 책의 오르지 않는 판매량을 대조하여 설명하고 있다.

03 + 문장 넣기 (24학년도 9월 모평 38번 | 정답률 23%) ⑤

구문분석 & 직독직해

기술 디지털 기술이 음악 제작 방식에 미친 영향

주제문

¹The shift (from analog to digital technology) / significantly influenced // how music was produced.

S V O(명사절)

전환은 (아날로그 기술에서 디지털 기술로의) / 크게 영향을 미쳤다 // 음악이 제작되는 방식에

↳ 아날로그에서 디지털 기술로의 전환이 음악 제작 방식에 큰 영향을 미침.

²First and foremost, / the digitization (of sounds) — / that is, their conversion into numbers — / enabled music makers to undo what was done.

★<enable+O+to-v>: O가 v할 수 있게 하다 S = V O C to undo의 O(명사절)

다른 무엇보다도 / 디지털화 (소리의) / 즉 그것(소리)의 숫자로의 변환은 / 음악 제작자들이 이미 행해진 것을 무효로 만들 수 있게 해주었다

(①) ³One could, in other words, twist [and] bend sounds / toward something new / without sacrificing the original version.

S V O

<without v-ing>: v하지 않고

다시 말해 누구든 소리를 비틀고 구부릴 수 있었다 / 새로운 것을 얻기 위해 / 원본을 희생하지 않고

↳ **영향 1:** 음악 제작자들이 작업했던 것을 무효로 만들 수 있게 됨.

(②) ⁴This "undo" ability made mistakes considerably less momentous, / sparking the creative process / [and] encouraging a generally more experimental mindset.

S V O C

분사구문(= and it sparked ~ and encouraged ~)

이러한 '무효화' 기능은 실수를 상당히 덜 중대하게 만들었다 / 그리고 창작 과정을 촉발했다 / 그리고 대개 더 실험적인 사고방식을 장려했다

↳ **부연 설명:** 원본을 희생하지 않는 '무효화' 기능은 실수를 덜 중요하게 만들어 창작을 촉발하고 실험적 사고방식을 장려함.

(③) ⁵In addition, / digitally converted sounds could be manipulated / simply by programming digital messages / [rather than] using physical tools, / simplifying the editing process significantly.

★<A rather than B>: B라기보다는 A S V

by의 O(동명사구 병렬) 분사구문(= and they simplified ~)

게다가 / 디지털로 변환된 소리는 조작될 수 있었다 / 단순히 디지털 메시지를 프로그래밍함으로써 / 물리적인 도구를 사용하기보다는 / 그리고 편집 과정을 크게 간소화했다

↳ **영향 2:** 프로그래밍을 통한 조작으로 음악 편집 과정이 간소화됨.

해석

¹아날로그 기술에서 디지털 기술로의 전환은 음악이 제작되는 방식에 크게 영향을 미쳤다. ²다른 무엇보다도, 소리의 디지털화, 즉 그것(소리)의 숫자로의 변환은 음악 제작자들이 이미 행해진 것을 무효로 만들 수 있게 해주었다. (①) ³다시 말해, 누구든 원본을 희생하지 않고 새로운 것을 얻기 위해 소리를 비틀고 구부릴 수 있었다. (②) ⁴이러한 '무효화' 기능은 실수를 상당히 덜 중대하게 만들어, 창작 과정을 촉발하고 대개 더 실험적인 사고방식을 장려했다. (③) ⁵게다가, 디지털로 변환된 소리는 물리적인 도구를 사용하기보다는 단순히 디지털 메시지를 프로그래밍함으로써 조작될 수 있어서, 편집 과정을 크게 간소화했다. (④) ⁶예를 들어, 편집은 한때 음성 녹음 테이프를 물리적으로 자르고 합쳐 잇기 위해 면도날을 수반했지만, 이제 그것(편집)은 컴퓨터를 이용한 시퀀서 프로그램의 커서와 마우스 클릭을 수반했고, 그것은 확실히 시간이 덜 걸렸다. (⑤ ⁷디지털로 변환된 소리의 조작은 2진 정보의 재프로그래밍을 의미했으므로, 편집 작업은 1,000분의 1초의 정밀도로 수행될 수 있었다.) ⁸이러한 매우 작은 수준의 접근은 (소리 없는 지점에서 트랙을 결합하는 것과 같은) 조작의 흔적을 숨기는 것을 더 쉽게 만든 동시에, 들을 수 있는 실험적인 방식으로 소리를 조작할 새로운 가능성을 내놓았다.

어휘

analog 아날로그의 ((데이터나 물리량을 연속 변화하는 양으로 나타냄))

(④) [6]For example, / while editing once involved razor blades / to physically cut and splice audiotapes, //
부사절 접속사(~하지만) S′ V′ O′ 목적(~하기 위해)

예를 들어 / 편집은 한때 면도날을 수반했지만 / 음성 녹음 테이프를 물리적으로 자르고 합쳐 잇기 위해 //

(= editing)
it now involved the cursor and mouse-click (of the computer-based sequencer program), //
S V O
which was obviously less time consuming.
관계대명사(앞 절 보충 설명)

이제 그것(편집)은 커서와 마우스 클릭을 수반했다 (컴퓨터를 이용한 시퀀서 프로그램의) //
그리고 그것은 확실히 시간이 덜 걸렸다

↳ **예:** 한때 테이프를 자르고 이어 편집했던 것이 오늘날에는 컴퓨터 프로그램을 이용해 마우스 클릭으로 가능해짐.

(⑤ [7]Because the manipulation (of digitally converted sounds) / meant the reprogramming (of binary information), // editing operations could be performed / with millisecond precision.)
부사절 접속사(이유) S′ V′ O′ S V

조작은 ~하므로 (디지털로 변환된 소리의) / 재프로그래밍을 의미했(으므로) (2진 정보의) //
편집 작업은 수행될 수 있었다 / 1,000분의 1초의 정밀도로

↳ **영향 3:** 편집 작업이 매우 정밀해짐.

주어진 문장의 1,000분의 1초의 정밀한 편집 작업을 의미함.
[8]This microlevel access / at once / made it easier / to conceal any traces of manipulations (such as joining tracks / in silent spots) /
S V₁ 가목적어 C₁ 진목적어(to-v구)

이러한 매우 작은 수준의 접근은 / 동시에 / (~을) 더 쉽게 만들었다 / 조작의 흔적을 숨기는 것을 (트랙을 결합하는 것과 같은 / 소리 없는 지점에서) /

and introduced new possibilities (for manipulating sounds / in audible and experimental ways).
V₂ O₂

그리고 새로운 가능성을 내놓았다 (소리를 조작할 / 들을 수 있는 실험적인 방식으로)

↳ **부연 설명:** 소리의 조작 흔적을 더 쉽게 숨기고 실험적인 방식으로 소리를 조작할 수 있게 됨.

first and foremost 다른 무엇보다도
digitization 디지털화
conversion 변환, 전환; 개조
cf. convert 변환[전환]시키다; 개조하다
undo 무효로 만들다; (매듭을) 풀다
bend 구부리다; 굴복하다
sacrifice 희생(하다)
considerably 상당히, 많이
momentous 중대한
spark 촉발시키다, 유발하다; 불꽃(을 일으키다)
mindset 사고방식
manipulate 조작하다; 조종하다
simplify 간소화[단순화]하다
razor blade 면도날
sequencer 시퀀서, 순서기 ((악보를 음으로 바꿀 수 있는 전자 녹음 장비))
time consuming 시간이 걸리는
operation 작업; 수술
millisecond 1,000분의 1초
precision 정밀(도), 정확(성)
micro- 매우 작은
at once 동시에; 즉시
conceal 숨기다, 감추다
trace 흔적; 추적하다, 찾아내다
track 트랙 ((테이프나 디스크의 데이터 구획 단위)); 길; 자국
audible 들을 수 있는, 잘 들리는

정답 가이드

주어진 문장의 내용은 ⑤ 이전까지 서술된 컴퓨터를 사용한 편집상의 장점을 구체적으로 설명한 것이고, ⑤ 뒤에 나오는 This microlevel access는 주어진 문장의 디지털로 변환된 소리를 조작하는 편집 작업이 1,000분의 1초의 정밀도로 수행될 수 있다는 내용을 지칭함을 알 수 있다. 따라서 주어진 문장이 들어가기에 가장 적절한 곳은 ⑤이다.

The 핵심 이 글은 디지털 기술로의 전환이 음악 제작 방식에 미친 세 가지 영향을 설명하는 내용으로, 편집 작업이 정밀해졌다는 주어진 문장은 그 중 세 번째 영향에 해당한다.

오답 클리닉

① (2%) 소리의 디지털화로 음악 제작자들이 작업했던 것을 무효화하는 것이 가능해졌다는 앞 문장을 in other words로 상술하는 내용이다.
② (5%) 문장 2에서 언급한 undo를 This "undo" ability로 받아 부연 설명하는 것은 자연스럽다.
③ (19%) 첨가 연결어 In addition으로 또 다른 영향인 음악 편집 과정의 간소화를 제시하는 것은 자연스럽다.
④ (51%) 물리적 도구를 사용한 과거와 컴퓨터를 이용하는 오늘날의 편집을 비교하는 예를 들어 앞 문장을 구체적으로 설명하는 내용이다.

The 주의 ④의 앞 문장에 있는 programming이 주어진 문장의 reprogramming으로 연결된다고 섣부르게 판단하지 않도록 주의한다. 주어진 문장은 편집 작업이 정밀해졌다는 내용으로, 편집 과정이 간소화 되었다는 ④의 앞 문장의 부연 설명이 될 수 없다.

01 문장 넣기 〈24학년도 9월 모평 39번 | 정답률 42%〉 ③

구문분석 & 직독직해 예술 예술 전문가에게 유용한 재료와 기법의 깊은 이해

[1]Acknowledging the making of artworks does not require / a detailed, technical knowledge (of, (say), how painters mix different kinds of paint, / or how an image editing tool works).

S(동명사구) V(단수) O 삽입어 of의 O(명사절 병렬)

예술품의 제작을 인정하는 것은 필요로 하지 않는다 / 자세하고 기술적인 지식을 ((예를 들어), 화가가 다양한 종류의 물감을 섞는 방법에 관한 / 또는 이미지 편집 도구가 작동하는 방식에 관한)

↳ **대조 A(도입):** 예술품을 인정하는 것은 자세한 기술적인 지식을 필요로 하지 않음.

(①) [2]*All* [that is required] / is a general sense (of a significant difference (between working with paints / and working with an imaging application)).

S 주격 관계대명사 V(단수) C 동명사구 병렬

전부는 [필요한] / 일반적인 감각이다 (중요한 차이에 대한 (물감으로 작업하는 것과 / 이미징 응용 프로그램을 사용하는 것 사이의))

(= The general sense ~ an imaging application) 기본적인 숙지에 관한 내용임.

(②) [3]This sense might involve / a basic familiarity (with paints and paintbrushes) /

S V O₁

이러한 감각은 포함할 수도 있다 / 기본적인 숙지를 (물감과 그림붓에 대한) /

as well as a basic familiarity (with how we use computers, / perhaps including how we use consumer imaging apps).

O₂ with의 O(명사절) ~을 포함하여 including의 O(명사절) *<A as well as B>: B뿐만 아니라 A도

기본적인 숙지뿐만 아니라 (컴퓨터를 사용하는 방법에 대한 / 아마도 우리가 소비자 이미징 응용 프로그램을 사용하는 방법을 포함하여)

↳ **부연 설명:** 재료와 프로그램 사용에 대한 기본적인 숙지를 포함하여 서로 다른 작업 간의 차이를 알기만 하면 됨.

주제문 전문가의 경우에는 더 깊은 지식이 필요하다는 상반되는 내용이 이어짐.

(③ [4]In the case of specialists (such as art critics), / a deeper familiarity (with materials and techniques) / is often useful / in reaching an informed judgement (about a work).)

~의 경우에는 S(단수) V(단수) C

전문가의 경우에는 (예술 비평가와 같은) / 더 깊은 숙지가 (재료와 기법에 대한) / 흔히 유용하다 / 정보에 입각한 판단에 도달하는 데 (작품에 대한)

↳ **대조 B(주제문):** 전문가들이 정보에 입각한 판단을 하는 데는 예술 재료와 기법을 더 깊이 숙지하는 것이 유용함.

is의 C(명사절) This는 주어진 문장을 지칭함.

[5]This is // because every kind of artistic material or tool comes / with its own challenges and affordances (for artistic creation).

S V 명사절 접속사 S′(단수) V′(단수) * because는 명사절을 이끌어 문장의 주어나 보어로 쓰일 수 있음.

이것은 ~이다 // 모든 종류의 예술 재료나 도구가 함께 오기 때문 / 그것의 고유한 도전 그리고 행위유발성과 (예술 창작을 위한)

↳ **논거:** 예술 재료나 도구에는 고유한 도전 및 창작 행위 유발이 따르기 때문임.

(④) [6]Critics are often interested / in *the ways* [(that) artists exploit different kinds of materials and tools / for particular artistic effect].

S V 관계부사 생략 S′ V′ O′

비평가들은 흔히 관심이 있다 / 방식에 [예술가들이 다양한 종류의 재료와 도구를 활용하는 / 특정한 예술적 효과를 위해]

(= Critics) 과거분사구 삽입

(⑤) [7]They are also interested / in the success of *an artist's attempt* — / (embodied in the artwork itself) — / (to push the limits (of what can be achieved / with certain materials and tools)).

S V C of의 O(명사절)

그들(비평가들)은 또한 관심이 있다 / 예술가의 시도 성공에 / (예술품 그 자체로 구현된) / (한계를 밀어붙이려는 (달성될 수 있는 것의 / 특정 재료와 도구로))

↳ **결과:** 비평가들은 예술가들이 다양한 재료와 도구를 활용하는 방식과 달성할 수 있는 한계를 넘으려는 시도에 관심이 있음.

해석

[1]예술품의 제작을 인정하는 것은 예를 들어, 화가가 다양한 종류의 물감을 섞는 방법이나 이미지 편집 도구가 작동하는 방식에 관한 자세하고 기술적인 지식을 필요로 하지 않는다. (①) [2]필요한 전부는 물감으로 작업하는 것과 이미징 응용 프로그램을 사용하는 것 사이의 중요한 차이점에 대한 일반적인 감각이다. (②) [3]이러한 감각은 아마도 우리가 소비자 이미징 응용 프로그램을 사용하는 방법을 포함하여, 컴퓨터를 사용하는 방법에 대한 기본적인 숙지뿐만 아니라 물감과 그림붓에 대한 기본적인 숙지를 포함할 수도 있다. (③ [4]예술 비평가와 같은 전문가의 경우에는 재료와 기법에 대한 더 깊은 숙지가 작품에 대한 정보에 입각한 판단에 도달하는 데 흔히 유용하다.) [5]이것은 모든 종류의 예술 재료나 도구가 예술 창작을 위한 그것의 고유한 도전 그리고 행위유발성과 함께 오기 때문이다.(▶ 예를 들어 수채화 물감을 이용하는 것과 유화 물감을 이용하는 것에 따르는 도전과 유발되는 창작 행위는 다를 것임.) (④) [6]비평가들은 흔히 예술가들이 특정한 예술적 효과를 위해 다양한 종류의 재료와 도구를 활용하는 방식에 관심이 있다. (⑤) [7]그들(비평가)은 또한 예술품 그 자체로 구현된, 특정 재료와 도구로 달성될 수 있는 것의 한계를 밀어붙이려는 예술가의 시도 성공에 관심이 있다.

어휘

acknowledge 인정하다, 동의하다
artwork 예술[미술]품
detailed 자세한, 상세한
editing 편집
sense 감각,지각; 의미
significant 중요한; 상당한
imaging 이미징 ((시각적으로 인식할 수 있는 형태로 정보를 표현하는 것))
application 응용 프로그램(app); 지원(서); 적용
involve 포함[수반]하다; 참여시키다
familiarity 숙지, 잘 앎; 친숙(함)
specialist 전문가
critic 비평가
material 재료; 직물, 천; 자료
reach 도달하다; (목적지에) 이르다
informed 정보에 입각한
judgement 판단; 판결, 심판
attempt 시도(하다)
embody 구현하다

정답 가이드

주어진 문장은 예술 비평가와 같은 전문가의 경우에는 재료와 기법에 대한 더 깊은 숙지가 작품에 대한 판단에 도움이 된다는 내용이다. ③ 앞은 우리 일반인들은 컴퓨터 및 응용 프로그램, 예술 재료와 도구에 대한 기본적 숙지만 필요하다는 내용이고, 뒤에 이어지는 내용은 ③ 앞의 문장이 아니라 이와 대조되는 주어진 문장을 This로 받아 예술가는 더 깊은 숙지가 필요한 구체적 이유를 설명하는 문장으로 봐야 한다. 따라서, 주어진 문장이 들어가기에 가장 적절한 곳은 ③이다.

The 핵심 주어진 문장에 역접 연결어는 없지만 In the case of specialists가 글의 내용을 전환하는 역할을 한다.

오답 클리닉

① (2%) 예술품의 제작을 인정하는 데 자세한 기술적인 지식이 필요한 것은 아니라는 앞 문장에 이어 필요한 것은 서로 다른 작업 간의 차이를 아는 일반적인 감각이라는 내용이 오는 것은 자연스럽다.

② (8%) 앞에서 언급된 a general sense를 This sense로 받아 부연 설명하는 내용이다.

④ (33%) 앞에서 언급된 every kind of artistic material or tool이 different kinds of materials and tools로 연결되어 모든 예술 재료와 도구가 그 고유의 도전과 행위를 유발하므로 비평가는 그것의 활용 방식에 관심을 둔다는 결과가 연결되는 것은 자연스럽다.

The 주의 ④의 앞 문장은 예술 재료와 도구를 더 깊이 알아야 하는 이유에 해당하며 ③ 앞의 기본적 숙지를 포함할 수도 있다는 내용에 대한 이유로 볼 수 없으므로 주어진 문장이 나온 뒤에 와야 한다.

⑤ (15%) also로 앞 문장에 이어 비평가들의 관심사를 추가 제시하고 있다.

02 + 문장 넣기 〈24학년도 6월 모평 38번 | 정답률 54%〉 ⑤

구문분석 & 직독직해 사회 제도화되지 않은 직업이 받는 가치의 위협

[1]As particular practices are repeated over time / and become more widely shared, //
부사절 접속사(~함에 따라) V'1 V'2 C'2
특정 관행이 오랜 시간 동안 반복됨에 따라 / 그리고 더 널리 공유됨에 따라 //

the values [that they embody] / are reinforced and reproduced // and we speak of them /
S1 목적격 관계대명사 (= particular practices) V1 S2 V2 (= particular practices)

as becoming 'institutionalized'.
전치사(~로(서))
가치는 [그것(특정 관행)이 구현하는] / 강화되고 재생산된다 // 그리고 우리는 그것들(특정 관행)에 대해 말한다 / '제도화' 되는 것이라고

↳ **도입:** '제도화'되는 것은 특정 관행이 반복되고 널리 공유됨에 따라 그것이 구현하는 가치가 강화되고 재생산되는 것임.

(①) [2]In some cases, / this institutionalization has a formal face (to it), /
S V O (= this institutionalization)
어떤 경우에 / 이러한 제도화는 공식적인 면을 갖춘다 (그것에 대한) /

*<with+O'+p.p.>: O가 ~되면서, ~된 채로
with rules and protocols written down, / and (with) specialized roles created / to ensure //
수동 관계 수동 관계 목적(~하기 위해)

that procedures are followed correctly.
to ensure의 O(명사절)
규칙과 규약이 문서화되면서 / 그리고 전문화된 역할이 만들어지면서 / 확실히 하기 위해 // 절차가 올바르게 지켜지는 것을

↳ **대조 A(공식적 제도화):** 규칙과 규약이 문서화되고 절차를 지키도록 하는 전문 역할이 만들어지며 공식화됨.

(②) [3]The main institutions (of state) — / parliament, courts, police and so on — / along with
S(복수) = ~와 함께

certain of the professions, / exhibit this formal character.
V(복수) O
주요 기관들은 (국가의) / 의회, 법원, 경찰 등 / 일부 직업과 함께 / 이러한 공식적인 성격을 보여준다

↳ **예:** 국가의 주요 기관과 일부 직업이 공식적인 제도화의 성격을 보여줌.

(③) [4]Other social institutions, / perhaps the majority, / are not like this; // science is an example.
S1 V1 C1 S2 V2 C2
다른 사회 기관들은 / 아마도 대다수가 / 이와 같지 않다 // 과학이 한 예이다

↳ **대조 B(비공식적 사회화):** 과학과 같은 대다수의 다른 사회 기관은 공식적인 성격을 보이지 않음.

*<train A in B(A에게 B를 훈련시키다)>의 수동형
(④) [5]Although scientists are trained / in the substantive content (of their discipline), //
부사절 접속사(양보) S' V'
과학자들이 훈련을 받긴 하지만 / 실질적인 내용에 대해서 (자기 학문 분야의) //

they are not formally instructed / in 'how to be a good scientist'.
S V <how to-v>: v하는 방법
그들은 공식적으로 교육받지 않는다 / '좋은 과학자가 되는 방법'에 대해서는

해석

[1]특정 관행이 오랜 시간 동안 반복되고 더 널리 공유됨에 따라, 그것(특정 관행)이 구현하는 가치는 강화되고 재생산되며 우리는 그것들(특정 관행)에 대해 '제도화'되는 것이라고 말한다. (①) [2]어떤 경우에 이러한 제도화는 규칙과 규약이 문서화되고 절차가 올바르게 지켜지는 것을 확실히 하기 위해 전문화된 역할이 만들어지면서, 그것(제도화)에 대한 공식적인 면을 갖춘다. (②) [3]국가의 주요 기관들인 의회, 법원, 경찰 기구 등은 일부 직업과 함께 이러한 공식적인 성격을 보여준다. (③) [4]다른 사회 기관들은 아마도 대다수가 이와 같지 않을 것인데, 과학이 한 예이다. (④) [5]과학자들이 자기 학문 분야의 실질적인 내용에 대해서 훈련을 받긴 하지만, 그들은 '좋은 과학자가 되는 방법'(▶ 직업의 도덕적 가치를 의미)에 대해서는 공식적으로 교육받지 않는다. (⑤ [6]대신, 마치 '착하게' 노는 법을 배우는 어린아이처럼 초보 과학자는 동료들로부터의 흡수, 즉 사회화를 통해 그 역할에 내재한 도덕적 가치에 대한 자신의 이해를 얻는다.) [7]우리는 직업 자체의 가치가 위협받고 있는 것처럼, 이러한 가치가 직업에 관한 많은 것을 특징짓는 가치와 함께 위협받고 있다고 생각한다.

어휘

practice 관행, 관례
embody 구현하다, 구체화하다
reinforce 강화하다
institutionalize 제도화하다
cf. institutionalization 제도화
cf. institution 기관; 제도
protocol (통신) 규약; (조약) 원안
specialized 전문화된
procedure 절차; 순서

Instead로 대안이 이어지므로 앞에는 그와 대조되는 내용이 제시되어야 함.
(⑤ [6]Instead, / much like *the young child* (learning how to play 'nicely'), /
대신 / 마치 어린아이처럼 ('착하게' 노는 법을 배우는) / 현재분사구
the apprentice scientist gains his or her understanding (of *the moral values* (inherent in the role)) /
S V O 형용사구
by absorption (from their colleagues) — / socialization.)
초보 과학자는 자신의 이해를 얻는다 (도덕적 가치에 대한 (그 역할에 내재한)) / 흡수를 통해 (동료들로부터의) / 즉 사회화
↳ **부연 설명:** 과학자들은 학문에 대한 교육은 받지만 좋은 과학자가 되는 방법과 같은 도덕적 가치에 대한 이해는 사회화를 통해 얻음.

think의 O(명사절) 주어진 문장의 the moral values inherent in the role을 지칭함.
[7]We think // that these values, / along with *the values* [that inform many of the professions], / are under threat, //
S V 명사절 접속사 S'(복수) 주격 관계대명사 V'(복수) C'
우리는 생각한다 // 이러한 가치(그 역할에 내재한 도덕적 가치)가 / 가치와 함께 [직업에 관한 많은 것을 특징짓는] / 위협받고 있다고 //
부사절 접속사(~처럼)
just as the value (of the professions themselves) / is under threat.
S'(단수) 재귀대명사(강조) V'(단수) C'
가치가 ~인 것처럼 (직업 자체의) / 위협받고 있는 (것처럼)
↳ **결론:** 공식적인 성격을 가지지 않는 직업 자체의 가치가 위협받고 있는 것처럼 그것의 도덕적 가치도 위협받고 있음.

parliament 의회, 국회
court 법원; 재판; 왕궁
certain of 일부 ~
profession 직업; 전문직
exhibit 보이다, 드러내다; 전시(하다)
substantive 실질[본질]적인
discipline 학문 (분야); 훈련, 단련
instruct 교육하다; 지시[명령]하다; 알리다
moral 도덕적인; 도덕과 관련된
absorption 흡수, 통합; 동화
socialization 사회화
inform 특징짓다; 알리다
under threat 위협[협박]을 받는

정답 가이드

주어진 문장은 과학자가 역할에 내재한 도덕적 가치를 사회화를 통해 알게 된다는 내용인데, Instead로 시작하는 것으로 보아 그 앞에는 이와 대조되는 내용이 와야 한다. ⑤의 앞 문장은 과학자들이 '좋은 과학자가 되는 방법'에 대해서는 공식적인 교육을 받지 않는다는 내용으로, 사회화를 통해 도덕적 가치를 배운다는 내용의 주어진 문장과 대조된다. 따라서, 주어진 문장이 들어가기에 가장 적절한 곳은 ⑤이다. 그렇게 되면 주어진 문장의 the moral values inherent in the role이 ⑤의 뒤 문장에서 these values로 이어지는 연결도 자연스러워진다.

오답 클리닉

① (2%) 앞에서 언급된 제도화의 공식적인 면모를 설명하는 내용이다.
② (6%) 제도화의 공식적 성격을 보여주는 기관을 예를 들어 설명하는 내용이다.
③ (16%) The main institutions와 대조를 이루는 other social institutions의 예로 과학을 들고 있다.
④ (22%) 공식적인 성격이 없는 기관으로 과학을 예로 든 다음 '좋은 과학자가 되는 방법'에 대해 공식적으로 교육받지 않는다고 부연 설명한다.

03 + 문장 넣기 〈24학년도 6월 모평 39번 | 정답률 40%〉 ②

구문분석 & 직독직해

생물 나무가 함께 자라야 하는 이유

주제문
[1]When trees grow together, // nutrients and water can be optimally divided / among them all //
부사절 접속사(시간) S V
나무들이 함께 자랄 때 // 영양분과 물이 최적으로 분배될 수 있다 / 그것들 모두 사이에서 //
부사절 접속사(~하도록)
so that each tree can grow / into *the best tree* [(which[that]) it can be].
S' V' 관계대명사 생략
각 나무가 자랄 수 있도록 / 최고의 나무로 [그것이 될 수 있는]
↳ 나무는 함께 자랄 때 영양분과 물이 최적으로 분배되어 잘 자랄 수 있음.

[2]If you "help" individual trees / by getting rid of their supposed competition, // the remaining trees are bereft.
부사절 접속사(조건) <by v-ing>: v함으로써 S V C
만약 여러분이 개별 나무를 '도와주면' / 그것들의 경쟁 상대로 여겨지는 나무를 제거함으로써 // 남은 나무들은 잃게 된다

(= The remaining trees) O ★여기서 but은 '~외에(는)'를 뜻하는 전치사로 쓰임.
[3]They send messages out to their neighbors unsuccessfully, // because nothing remains / but stumps.
S V 부사절 접속사(이유) S' V'
그것들(남아 있는 나무들)은 이웃 나무들에게 메시지를 보내지만 성공하지 못한다 // 왜냐하면 아무것도 남아 있지 않기 때문이다 / 그루터기 외에는

★<give rise to A>: A를 낳다[일으키다]
[4]Every tree now grows on its own, / giving rise to great differences / in productivity.
S V 분사구문 (= and it gives ~)
이제 모든 나무가 독자적으로 자란다 / 그리고 이는 큰 차이를 낳는다 / 생산성에
↳ **세부 사항(가정):** 경쟁 나무를 잘라 개별 나무를 도우면 남은 나무들은 혼자 자라 생산성에 큰 차이를 낳음.

해석

[1]나무들이 함께 자랄 때 각 나무가 그것이 될 수 있는 최고의 나무로 자랄 수 있도록 영양분과 물이 그것들 모두 사이에서 최적으로 분배될 수 있다. [2]만약 여러분이 그것들의 경쟁 상대로 여겨지는 나무를 제거함으로써 개별 나무를 '도와주면' 남은 나무들은 잃게 된다. [3]그것들은 이웃 나무들에게 메시지를 보내지만 성공하지 못하는데, 왜냐하면 그루터기 외에는 아무것도 남아 있지 않기 때문이다. [4]이제 모든 나무가 독자적으로 자라고, 이는 생산성에 큰 차이를 낳는다. (①) [5]어떤 개체들은 당분이 나무줄기를 따라 확실히 흐를 때까지 맹렬히 광합성을 한다. (② [6]그 결과, 그것들은 건강하고 더 잘 자라지만 특별히 오래 살지는 않는다.) [7]이는 나무가 오직 그것을 둘러싸고 있는 숲만큼만 강할 수 있기 때문이다. (③) [8]그리고 이제 숲에는 많은 패자가 있다. (④) [9]한때는 더 강한 구성원들에 의해 지원받았을 더 약한 구성원들이 갑자기 뒤처진다. (⑤) [10]그것들의 쇠약의 원인이 위치와 영양분 부족이든, 일시적인 질병이든, 혹은 유전적 구성이든, 이제 그것들은 곤충과 균류의 먹이가 된다.

주어진 문장의 원인에 해당함.

(①) [5]Some individuals photosynthesize like mad // until sugar positively bubbles / along their trunk.

S V 부사절 접속사(시간) S′ V′

어떤 개체들은 맹렬히 광합성을 한다 // 당분이 확실히 흐를 때까지 / 그것들의 나무 줄기를 따라

(= some individuals) 개체들이 건강하고 더 잘 자랄 수 있다는 결과 앞에는 그 원인이 있어야 함.

(② [6]As a result, / they are fit and grow better, // but they aren't particularly long-lived.)

S1 V1-1 C1-1 V1-2 C1-2 S2 V2 C2

그 결과 / 그것들은 건강하고 더 잘 자란다 // 하지만 그것들은 특별히 오래 살지는 않는다

(= 앞 문장) is의 C(명사절) 주어진 문장을 This로 지칭하면서 잘 자라지만 오래 살지 못하는 원인을 설명함.

[7]This is // because a tree can be only as strong / as *the forest* [that surrounds it].

S V 명사절 접속사 S′ V′ C′ 주격 관계대명사 (= the tree)

*<A as 형용사/부사 as B>: A는 B만큼 ~한[하게]

이는 ~이다 // 나무가 오직 강할 수 있기 때문 / 숲만큼만 [그것(나무)을 둘러싸고 있는]

↳ 부연 설명: 함께 자라지 않는 나무들 중 일부 개체들은 맹렬히 광합성을 해서 잘 자라지만 나무는 자신을 둘러싼 숲만큼만 강할 수 있기 때문에 오래 살지는 못함.

(③) [8]And / there are now a lot of losers / in the forest.

V S

그리고 / 이제 많은 패자가 있다 / 숲에는

↳ 결과: 함께 자라는 나무가 없는 숲에는 많은 패자가 있음.

*<would have p.p.>: ~했었을 텐데

(④) [9]Weaker members, // who would once have been supported / by the stronger ones, / suddenly fall behind.

S 관계대명사(보충 설명) (= members) V

더 약한 구성원들이 // 한때는 지원받았을 / 더 강한 것들(구성원)에 의해 / 갑자기 뒤처진다

(= weaker members)

(⑤) [10]Whether the reason (for their decline) / is their location and lack of nutrients, a passing sickness, or genetic makeup, // they now fall prey to insects and fungi.

부사절 접속사(~이든) S′ V′ C′1 C′2 C′3 (= weaker members) S V C

*<fall prey to A>: A의 먹이가 되다

원인이 (그것들(더 약한 구성원들)의 쇠약의) / 위치와 영양분 부족이든, 일시적인 질병이든, 혹은 유전적 구성이든 // 이제 그것들(더 약한 구성원들)은 곤충과 균류의 먹이가 된다

↳ 부연 설명: 더 약한 나무들은 주변에 지원해줄 더 강한 나무들이 없어 쇠약해지고 결국 곤충과 균류의 먹이가 됨.

어휘

- nutrient 영양분, 영양소
- optimally 최적[최선]으로
- get rid of ~을 제거하다
- supposed ~이라고 여겨지는, 가정의
- remaining 남은, 남아 있는
- unsuccessfully 성공하지 못하고, 실패하여
- on one's own 혼자서, 단독으로
- productivity 생산성
- like mad 맹렬히; 미친 듯이
- positively 확실히, 분명히; 긍정적으로
- bubble (졸졸) 흐르다; 거품(이 일다)
- trunk (나무)줄기; 몸통; 여행용 큰 가방
- fit 건강한; 적합한, 알맞은
- fall behind 뒤처지다
- decline 쇠약; 거절하다; 감소(하다)
- passing 일시적인; 지나가는
- genetic 유전(학)적인
- makeup 구성, 구조
- fungus (*pl.* fungi) 균류, 곰팡이류

정답 가이드

주어진 문장은 그것들이 건강하고 더 잘 자라지만 특별히 오래 살지는 않는다는 내용인데, 결과를 나타내는 As a result와 대명사 they가 있는 것으로 보아 그 앞에는 나무가 건강하고 잘 자라는 원인과 they가 지칭하는 대상이 제시되어야 한다. ②의 앞 문장은 어떤 나무 개체들은 당분이 줄기를 따라 흐를 때까지 맹렬히 광합성을 한다는 내용으로, 주어진 문장이 뒤에 결과로 이어지는 흐름이 자연스러우며 they가 지칭하는 대상은 앞 문장의 some individuals가 된다. 또한 주어진 문장을 This로 받아 나무들이 특별히 오래 살지 못하는 이유를 설명하는 ②의 뒤 문장과의 연결도 자연스러워진다. 따라서 주어진 문장이 들어가기에 가장 적절한 곳은 ②이다.

오답 클리닉

① (4%) 혼자 자라는 나무가 생산성에 큰 차이를 낳는다는 앞 내용에 대해 일부 개체들이 맹렬히 광합성을 한다는 부연 설명이 이어진다.

③ (21%) 나무는 자신을 둘러싼 숲만큼만 강할 수 있다는 내용 뒤에 함께 자라는 나무가 없는 숲에는 많은 패자가 있다는 결과가 뒤따른다.

④ (16%) 앞 문장의 losers를 Weaker members로 받아 부연 설명한다.

⑤ (19%) 앞의 더 약한 구성원들이 뒤처진다는 내용을 their decline으로 받아 곤충과 균류의 먹이가 된다는 결과가 마지막에 이어진다.

01 + 함의 추론 〈24학년도 대수능 21번 | 정답률 61%〉 ④

구문분석 & 직독직해

인지 스트레스를 낮추는 넓은 초점

[1] How you focus your attention / plays a critical role / in how you deal with stress.
S(명사절) V O in의 O(명사절)
여러분이 여러분의 주의를 집중시키는 방식은 / 중요한 역할을 한다 / 여러분이 스트레스를 다루는 방식에
↳ **도입:** 주의 집중 방식이 스트레스 대응 방식에 중요한 역할을 함.

[2] Scattered attention harms your ability (to let go of stress), //
S V O =
흩어진 주의력은 여러분의 능력을 손상시킨다 (스트레스를 푸는) //

(= your attention)
because even though your attention is scattered, // it is narrowly focused, //
부사절 접속사(이유) 부사절(양보) S′ V′
왜냐하면 여러분의 주의력이 흩어지더라도 // 그것(여러분의 주의력)이 좁게 집중되기 때문이다 //

for you are able to fixate / only on the stressful parts (of your experience).
부사절 접속사(이유)
여러분은 집착할 수 있으므로 / 스트레스가 많은 부분에만 (여러분의 경험 중)
↳ **문제점:** 주의력이 흩어지면 스트레스가 많은 경험에만 집중하게 되므로 스트레스를 풀기 어려움.

주제문 🔑 주의의 초점이 넓어지면 스트레스를 쉽게 풀 수 있음.
[3] When your attentional spotlight is widened, // you can more easily let go of stress.
부사절 접속사(시간) S′ V′ S V O
여러분의 주의의 초점이 넓어지면 // 여러분은 스트레스를 더 쉽게 풀 수 있다
↳ **해결책:** 주의의 초점이 넓어지면 스트레스를 쉽게 풀 수 있음.

★<put A in(to) perspective>: A를 균형 잡힌 시각으로[넓게] 보다
[4] You can put in perspective many more aspects of any situation /
S V_1 O
여러분은 어떤 상황이라도 그 상황의 더 많은 측면을 균형 잡힌 시각으로 볼 수 있다 /

and (can) not get locked / into *one part* [that ties you down / to superficial and anxiety-provoking levels of attention].
V_2 C 주격 관계대명사 O′ V′ ★<tie A down (to B)>: A를 (B에) 옭아매다[구속하다]
그리고 갇히지 않을 수 있다 / 한 부분에 [여러분을 옭아매는 / 피상적이고 불안을 유발하는 주의력 수준에]
↳ **논거:** 상황을 균형 잡힌 시각으로 보고 문제가 되는 한 부분에 갇히지 않을 수 있음.

🔑 좁은 초점은 스트레스를 높이지만 넓은 초점은 스트레스를 낮춤.
[5] A narrow focus heightens the stress level (of each experience), // but a widened focus turns down the stress level // because you're better able to put each situation / into a broader perspective.
S_1 V_1 O_1 S_2 V_2 O_2 부사절 접속사(이유) S′ V′ C′
좁은 초점은 스트레스 수준을 높인다 (각 경험의) // 그러나 넓은 초점은 스트레스 수준을 낮춘다
// 여러분이 각 상황을 더 잘 볼 수 있기 때문에 / 더 넓은 시각으로
↳ **부연 설명:** 좁은 초점은 경험의 스트레스를 높이는 반면 넓은 초점은 상황을 더 넓은 시각으로 볼 수 있기 때문에 스트레스를 낮춤.

🔑 불안감을 유발하는 하나의 세부 사항보다 전체 상황을 보는 것이 중요함.
[6] One anxiety-provoking detail is less important / than the bigger picture.
S V C
불안감을 유발하는 하나의 세부 사항은 덜 중요하다 / 더 큰 전체적인 상황보다

(= 앞 문장) ★<transform A into B>: A를 B로 변형시키다[바꾸다]
[7] It's like transforming yourself / into **a nonstick frying pan**.
S V C like의 O(동명사구)
그것은 여러분 자신을 변형시키는 것과 같다 / 들러붙지 않는 프라이팬으로

[8] You can still fry an egg, // but the egg won't stick to the pan.
S_1 V_1 O S_2 V_2
여러분은 여전히 달걀을 부칠 수 있다 // 그러나 그 달걀은 팬에 들러붙지 않을 것이다
↳ **결론:** 스트레스를 주는 세부 사항에 집중하기보다 전체적인 상황을 넓게 봐야 스트레스를 떨쳐낼 수 있음.

해석

[1]여러분이 여러분의 주의를 집중시키는 방식은 여러분이 스트레스를 다루는 방식에 중요한 역할을 한다. [2]흩어진 주의력은 여러분의 스트레스를 푸는 능력을 손상시키는데, 왜냐하면 여러분의 주의력이 흩어지더라도, 여러분은 여러분의 경험 중 스트레스가 많은 부분에만 집착할 수 있으므로, 그것(여러분의 주의력)이 좁게 집중되기 때문이다. [3]여러분의 주의의 초점이 넓어지면, 여러분은 스트레스를 더 쉽게 풀 수 있다. [4]여러분은 어떤 상황이라도 그 상황의 더 많은 측면을 균형 잡힌 시각으로 볼 수 있으며, 피상적이고 불안을 유발하는 주의력 수준에 여러분을 옭아매는 한 부분에 갇히지 않을 수 있다. [5]좁은 초점은 각 경험의 스트레스 수준을 높이지만, 넓은 초점은 여러분이 각 상황을 더 넓은 시각으로 더 잘 볼 수 있기 때문에 스트레스 수준을 낮춘다. [6]불안감을 유발하는 하나의 세부 사항은 더 큰 전체적인 상황보다 덜 중요하다. [7]그것은 여러분 자신을 들러붙지 않는 프라이팬으로 변형시키는 것과 같다. [8]여러분은 여전히 달걀을 부칠 수 있지만, 그 달걀은 팬에 들러붙지 않을 것이다.(▶ 상황을 넓은 시각으로 바라봄으로써 스트레스를 주는 경험(달걀)에 집착하지 않게 됨을 의미)

어휘

attention 주의(력); 관심
cf. attentional 주의의
play a role 역할을 하다
critical 중요한; 비판적인; 위기의
deal with ~을 다루다; ~에 대처하다
scattered 흩어진, 산재한; 산만한
let go of ~을 풀다[놓아주다]
fixate 집착하다; 정착[고정]시키다
spotlight 초점; (세간이) 주목, 관심
superficial 피상[표면]적인; 깊이 없는, 얄팍한
heighten 높이다; 증가시키다
turn down ~을 낮추다; ~을 거절하다
nonstick 들러붙지 않는
cf. stick 들러붙다; 찌르다; 고정하다
[선택지] confront 직면하다
broaden 넓히다; 넓어지다
identify 찾다, 발견하다; 확인하다
rarely 좀처럼 ~하지 않는, 드물게
confine 국한시키다; 가두다
take A into account A를 고려하다, A를 계산에 넣다
source 원천, 근원; (자료의) 출처

정답 가이드

밑줄 문장과 마지막 문장으로 보아, 우리 자신을 달걀이 들러붙지 않는 프라이팬으로 변형시킨다는 것이 어떤 의미인지를 찾아야 한다. 첫 문장에서, 스트레스를 다룰 때 주의 집중 방식이 중요한 역할을 한다고 한 다음, 좁은 초점은 스트레스를 높이는 반면 넓은 초점은 스트레스를 낮춘다고 했다. 불안감, 즉 스트레스를 유발하는 하나의 세부 사항보다 더 큰 전체적인 상황을 보는 넓은 초점을 가져야 한다는 것으로 요약되는데, 이를 '(달걀, 즉 스트레스가) 들러붙지 않는 프라이팬'으로 변형시키는 것에 비유한 것이다. 따라서 밑줄 친 부분이 글에서 의미하는 바와 가장 가까운 것은 ④ 'having a larger view of an experience beyond its stressful aspects(스트레스를 주는 측면을 넘어 경험을 더 넓은 시각으로 바라보는 것)'이다.

오답 클리닉

① never being confronted with any stressful experiences in daily life (6%) 일상생활에서 스트레스가 많은 어떤 경험에도 결코 직면하지 않는 것(×)
스트레스가 많은 경험을 피하는 것에 관한 내용이 아님.

② broadening one's perspective to identify the cause of stress (13%)
스트레스의 원인을 찾기 위해(×) 시각을 넓히는 것
스트레스의 원인을 찾는 내용은 언급되지 않음.

③ rarely confining one's attention to positive aspects of an experience (6%)
경험의 긍정적인 측면(×)에 주의를 좀처럼 국한시키지 않는 것
경험의 부정적인 부분에 집중하지 말고 넓은 시각에서 전체적인 상황을 봐야 한다고 했음.

⑤ taking stress into account as the source of developing a wide view (13%)
넓은 시각을 기르는 원천(×)으로 스트레스를 고려하는 것
넓은 시각이 스트레스에서 비롯된다는 내용이 아니고, 넓은 시각을 가짐으로써 스트레스를 주는 부분에 얽매이지 않을 수 있다는 내용임.

02 함의 추론 〈24학년도 9월 모평 21번 | 정답률 39%〉 ②

구문분석 & 직독직해

비즈니스 결과를 불필요하게 향상시키는 금도금

🔑 금도금은 예상되는 결과를 불필요하게 향상시키는 것임.

[1]Gold plating (in the project) / means needlessly enhancing the expected results, /
(S: Gold plating / V: means / O(동명사구): needlessly enhancing the expected results)
금도금은 (프로젝트에서의) / 예상되는 결과를 불필요하게 향상시키는 것을 의미한다 /

namely, adding *characteristics* [that are costly, not required], / and [that have low added value / with respect to the targets] — /
(관계사절 병렬; that: 주격 관계대명사; with respect to: ~에 관하여)
*세 개의 동명사구(needlessly enhancing ~ results, adding ~ targets, giving ~ talent)가 동격으로 이어짐.
즉 특성을 추가하는 것 [값비싸지만 필요하지는 않은] / 그리고 [낮은 부가 가치를 갖는 / 목표에 관하여] /

in other words, / giving more / with no real justification / other than to demonstrate one's own talent.
🔑 실질적인 명분 없이 그저 자신의 기량을 보여주려고 더 많은 것을 제공함. (other than: ~ 외에)
다시 말해 / 더 많은 것을 제공하는 것 / 실질적인 명분 없이 / 자신의 기량을 보여주는 것 외에
↳ **도입(정의):** 금도금은 예상되는 결과를 불필요하게 향상시키는 것을 의미함.

[2]Gold plating is especially interesting / for project team members, // as it is typical / of projects (with a marked professional component) / —
(S: Gold plating / V: is / C: especially interesting; as: 부사절 접속사(~ 때문에); projects = with a marked professional component)
금도금은 특히 흥미롭다 / 프로젝트 팀원들에게 // 그것이 일반적이기 때문이다 / 프로젝트에서 (뚜렷한 전문 요소를 갖춘) /

in other words, / *projects* [that involve specialists (with proven experience and extensive professional autonomy)].
(that: 주격 관계대명사)
다시 말해 / 프로젝트 [전문가들을 수반하는 (입증된 경험과 폭넓은 전문적 자율성을 갖춘)]
↳ 금도금은 전문가들이 참여하는 프로젝트에서 일반적임.

*<see A as B>: A를 B로 여기다[간주하다]

[3]In these environments / specialists often see the project / as an opportunity (to test and (to) enrich their skill sets).
(S: specialists / V: see / O: the project / as: 전치사(~로(서)); to test and (to) enrich =)
이러한 환경에서 / 전문가들이 종종 프로젝트를 여긴다 / 기회로 (자신의 다양한 능력을 시험하고 향상시킬)
↳ **원인:** 전문가는 프로젝트를 자신의 다양한 능력을 시험하고 향상시킬 기회로 여김.

해석

[1]프로젝트에서의 금도금은 예상되는 결과를 불필요하게 향상시키는 것, 즉 값비싸지만 필요하지는 않으며 목표에 관하여 낮은 부가 가치를 갖는 특성을 추가하는 것으로, 다시 말해 자신의 기량을 보여주는 것 외에 실질적인 명분 없이 더 많은 것을 제공하는 것을 의미한다. [2]금도금은 특히 프로젝트 팀원들에게 흥미로운데, 그것이 뚜렷한 전문 요소를 갖춘 프로젝트, 다시 말해 입증된 경험과 폭넓은 전문적 자율성을 갖춘 전문가들을 수반하는 프로젝트에서 일반적이기 때문이다. [3]이러한 환경에서 전문가들은 종종 프로젝트를 자신의 다양한 능력을 시험하고 향상시킬 기회로 여긴다. [4]따라서 오로지 선의로 금도금을 하려는, 즉 전문가를 만족시키지만, 고객의 요구 사항에 가치를 더하지 않는 동시에 프로젝트에서 귀중한 자원을 없애는 더 많은 또는 더 높은 품질의 성과를 달성하려는 강한 유혹이 있다. [5]속담에도 이르듯이, '최고는 좋은 것의 적이다.'

어휘

plate (금·은으로) 도금하다; 접시, 그릇
needlessly 불필요하게
costly 값비싼; 대가[희생]가 큰
added value 부가 가치
justification 명분; 정당화
demonstrate 보여주다, 발휘하다; 입증하다

⁴There is therefore *a strong temptation*, / (in all good faith), / (to engage in gold plating), /
(→ 전치사구 삽입) V S
따라서 강한 유혹이 있다 / (오로지 선의로) / (금도금을 하려는) / ★to engage ~ plating과 to achieve ~ project가 a strong temptation을 수식함.

namely, (to achieve / more or higher-quality *work* [that gratifies the professional /
주격 관계대명사 V′₁ O′₁
but does not add value to the client's requests, / and at the same time removes valuable resources
V′₂ O′₂ V′₃ O′₃
/ from the project]). 고객의 요구에 가치를 더하지 않고 자원을 없애며 전문가만 만족시킬 뿐인 고품질을 달성하려 함.

즉 (달성하려는 / 더 많은 또는 더 높은 품질의 성과를 [전문가를 만족시키는 /
하지만 고객의 요구 사항에 가치를 더하지 않는 / 그리고 동시에 귀중한 자원을 없애는 / 프로젝트에서])
↳ **결과:** 불필요하게 고품질을 달성하려는 금도금을 하려는 강한 유혹이 생김.

⁵As the saying goes, // **"The best is the enemy (of the good)."**
부사절 접속사(~듯이) S V C
속담에도 이르듯이 // '최고는 적이다 (좋은 것의).'
↳ **결론(인용):** 최고를 달성하려다 오히려 좋은 것을 망칠 수 있음.

marked 뚜렷한, 두드러진
component (구성) 요소, 성분
specialist 전문가
extensive 폭넓은, 광범위한
enrich (질·가치 등을) 향상시키다; 풍요롭게 하다
skill set 다양한 능력[재주]
temptation 유혹(하는 것)
in good faith 선의로; 옳다고 믿고
valuable 귀중한, 소중한
resource 자원; 원천
saying 속담, 격언
[선택지] desirable 바람직한
overqualified 필요 이상의 자격[경력]을 갖춘
acquire 습득하다; 획득하다
ensure 보장하다

정답 가이드

금도금은 결과를 불필요하게 향상시키는 것을 의미하며 낮은 부가 가치를 갖는 특성을 추가하는 것으로, 실질적인 명분 없이 더 많은 것을 제공하는 것이라는 첫 문장의 정의에서, 금도금을 부정적으로 바라보고 있음을 알 수 있다. 이어지는 내용에서 전문가가 프로젝트를 자신의 능력을 시험하고 향상시킬 기회로 여겨 자신만 만족시킬 뿐인 고품질의 성과를 달성하려고 한다고 했다. 따라서 밑줄 친 부분이 의미하는 바로 가장 적절한 것은 ② 'Raising work quality only to prove oneself is not desirable.(오로지 자신을 증명하기 위해 성과의 질을 올리는 것은 바람직하지 않다.)'이다.

오답 클리닉

① Pursuing perfection at work causes conflicts among team members. (6%)
일에서 완벽을 추구하는 것은 팀원 간 갈등(×)을 유발한다.
팀원 간의 갈등에 관한 언급은 없음.

③ Inviting overqualified specialists to a project leads to bad ends. (29%) 프로젝트에 필요 이상의 자격을 갖춘 전문가를 초청하는 것은 나쁜 결과(×)로 이어진다.
프로젝트에 필요 이상의 자격을 갖춘 전문가를 포함하는 것 자체가 문제되는 것이 아니며, 전문가들이 불필요하게 성과의 질을 높이려 하는 것이 문제가 된다는 내용이므로 틀림.

④ Responding to the changing needs of clients is unnecessary. (12%)
고객의 변화하는 요구(×)에 대응하는 것은 불필요하다.
고객의 변화하는 요구에 대응하는 필요성은 언급되지 않음.

⑤ Acquiring a range of skills for a project does not ensure success. (14%) 프로젝트를 위한 다양한 기술을 습득하는 것(×)이 성공을 보장하지는 않는다.
전문가들이 프로젝트를 자신의 다양한 능력을 시험하고 향상시킬 기회로 여긴다는 내용은 있으나, 다양한 기술을 습득한다는 내용은 없음.

03 + 함의 추론 〈24학년도 6월 모평 21번 | 정답률 59%〉 ③

구문분석 & 직독직해

법 '막대 묶음'으로 비유되는 소유권의 의미

★<describe A as B>: A를 B로 묘사하다
¹Lawyers sometimes describe ownership / as a *bundle of sticks*. 소유권이 막대 묶음이므로, 그 중 하나의 막대는 소유권의 일부를 의미함.
S V O
변호사들은 때때로 소유권을 묘사한다 / '막대 묶음'으로

²This metaphor was introduced / about a century ago, // and it has dramatically transformed
S₁ V₁ S₂ (→ (= this metaphor)) V₂
the teaching and practice of law.
O
이 비유는 도입되었다 / 약 1세기 전에 // 그리고 이것(이 비유)은 법률 교육과 실무를 극적으로 변화시켰다
↳ **도입:** 소유권을 '막대 묶음'으로 묘사하는 것은 법률 교육과 실무를 극적으로 변화시킴.

소유권은 분리되거나 합쳐질 수 있는 개인 간의 권리 모음임.
³The metaphor is useful // because it helps us see ownership / as *a grouping of interpersonal rights*
S V C 부사절 접속사(이유) S′ V′ O′ C′ ★<see A as B>: A를 B로 간주하다
[that can be separated and (can be) put back together].
주격 관계대명사 V′₁ V′₂
그 비유는 유용하다 // 그것(그 비유)이 우리가 소유권을 간주하도록 돕기 때문에 / 개인 간의 권리들의 모음으로
[분리될 수 있고 다시 합쳐질 수 있는]
↳ **세부 사항:** '막대 묶음' 비유는 소유권을 분리되고 다시 합쳐질 수 있는 개인 간의 권리로 간주하게 함.

해석

¹변호사들은 때때로 소유권을 '막대 묶음'으로 묘사한다. ²이 비유는 약 1세기 전에 도입되었고, 이것은 법률 교육과 실무를 극적으로 변화시켰다. ³그 비유는 그것이 우리가 소유권을 분리될 수 있고 다시 합쳐질 수 있는, 개인 간의 권리들의 모음으로 간주하도록 돕기 때문에 유용하다. ⁴어떤 자원에 관해 '그것은 내 것이다.'라고 말할 때, 흔히 이는 여러분이 그 묶음 전체를 구성하는 많은 막대, 즉 판매 막대, 임대 막대, 그것(자원)을 저당잡히고, 허가하고, 증여하며, 심지어 파괴할 수 있는 권리를 소유한다는 것을 의미한다. ⁵그러나 흔히 우리는 토지 한 구획에 대해 그 막대들을 분할한다. 즉 토지 소유자, 저당권을 가진 은행, 임대차 계약을 맺은 세입자, 토지에 들어갈 허가를 받은 배관공, 채굴권이 있는 석

[4]When you say *It's mine* / in reference to a resource, // often that means //
부사절 접속사(시간) ~에 관하여 S V
'그것은 내 것이다.'라고 말할 때 / 어떤 자원에 관해 // 흔히 이는 의미한다 //
↱ means의 O(명사절) ↱ 주격 관계대명사
(that) you own / *a lot of the sticks* [that make up the full bundle]: / the sell stick, the rent stick,
접속사 생략 S′ V′ O′
the right (to mortgage, license, give away, even destroy the thing).
🔑 어떤 자원을 소유한다는 것은 그것에 대한 여러 막대(권리)를 갖는 것을 의미함.
여러분이 소유한다는 것을 / 많은 막대를 [그 묶음 전체를 구성하는] / 즉 판매 막대, 임대 막대,
권리 (그것(자원)을 저당잡히고, 허가하고, 증여하며, 심지어 파괴할 수 있는)
↳ 부연 설명 1: 소유권은 어떤 자원에 대한 여러 권리를 가짐을 의미함.

[5]Often, though, / we split the sticks up, / as for a piece of land: //
S₁ V₁ O ~에 대해(= regarding)
그러나 흔히 / 우리는 그 막대들을 분할한다 / 토지 한 구획에 대해 //
🔑 토지 한 구획에 대한 권리가 여러 당사자들에게 나뉘짐.
there may be / a landowner, / a bank (with a mortgage), / a tenant (with a lease), /
V₂ S₂(명사구 병렬)
a plumber (with *a license* (to enter the land)), / an oil company (with mineral rights).
즉 ~가 있을 수 있다 / 토지 소유자 / 은행 (저당권을 가진) / 세입자 (임대차 계약을 맺은) /
배관공 (허가를 받은 (토지에 들어갈)) / 석유 회사 (채굴권이 있는)

[6]Each (of these parties) / owns / **a stick (in the bundle)**.
S(단수) V(단수) O
각각은 (이러한 당사자들의) / 소유한다 / 막대 하나를 (그 묶음의)
↳ 부연 설명 2: 토지 소유권을 분할하여 여러 당사자들이 토지에 대한 권리 일부를 나눠 가짐.

유 회사가 있을 수 있다. [6]이러한 각 당사자는 그 묶음의 막대 하나를 소유한다.

어휘

ownership 소유(권)
bundle 묶음, 다발
metaphor 비유, 은유
dramatically 극적으로
practice 실무, 업무; 실행, 실천
interpersonal 개인 간의; 대인 관계의
make up ~을 구성하다; ~을 형성하다
license 허가(하다); 면허(증)
give away ~을 증여하다[거저 주다]
split up ~을 분할하다, 나누다
lease 임대차 계약; 임대하다
plumber 배관공
mineral rights 채굴권; 광업권
party 당사자; 정당
[선택지] legal 법률(상)의; 법적인; 합법의
obligation 의무, 책임
priority 우선(권); 우선 사항
claim 차지하다, 얻다; (권리를) 주장하다
real estate 부동산
property 재산, 소유물; 부동산

정답 가이드

첫 문장의 소유권을 '막대 묶음'에 비유한 것에서 밑줄 친 부분인 '그 묶음의 막대 하나'는 소유권의 일부를 의미함을 유추할 수 있다. 소유권은 개인 간의 권리들의 모음이라고 하면서 어떤 자원을 소유한다는 의미는 그것에 대한 여러 막대들, 즉 여러 권리를 가지는 것이고, 우리는 흔히 토지에 대해 이 권리들을 분할해 각각의 당사자들이 나눠 갖는다고 했다. 따라서 밑줄 친 부분이 의미하는 바로 가장 적절한 것은 ③ 'a right to use one aspect of the property(그 재산의 한 측면을 사용할 수 있는 권리)'이다.

오답 클리닉

① a legal obligation to develop the resource (6%)
그 자원을 개발할(×) 법률상의 의무
resource를 활용한 오답. 자원 개발이 아닌 소유에 관한 내용임.
② a priority to legally claim the real estate (10%)
법적으로 그 부동산을 차지할 우선권(×)
부동산 권리에 우선권이 있다는 언급은 없음.
④ a building to be shared equally by tenants (7%)
임차인들에 의해(×) 동등하게 공유되는(×) 건물
임차인에 한정된 내용이 아니며, 모두가 같은 권리를 공유하는 것이 아님.
⑤ a piece of land nobody can claim as their own (18%)
아무도 자신의 것으로 주장할 수 없는(×) 토지의 한 구획
토지 한 구획에 대한 여러 소유권을 당사자들이 나눠 갖는 것이므로 각자의 권리는 주장할 수 있음.

01 + 함의 추론 (23학년도 대수능 21번 | 정답률 68%) ①

구문분석 & 직독직해

철학 주체성 형성과 자아 성찰의 매개로서의 일기

[1]Coming of age in the 18th and 19th centuries, / the personal diary became a centerpiece (in *the construction of a modern subjectivity*), //
분사구문(= As it came of age ~) S V C
18세기와 19세기에 충분히 발달함에 따라 / 개인 일기는 중심이 되었다 (근대적 주체성 구축의) //
★여기서 which는 the construction ~ subjectivity를 보충 설명하며, 장소부사구가 앞으로 오면서 도치가 일어남.
at the heart of which is *the application* (of reason and critique) / to the understanding of world and self, // which allowed the creation (of a new kind of knowledge).
관계대명사(보충 설명) V′ S′ 관계대명사(보충 설명)
그것의 중심에는 적용이 있다 (이성과 비판의) / 세계와 자아에 대한 이해에 //
이는 창조를 가능하게 했다 (새로운 종류의 지식의)
↳ **도입:** 개인 일기를 통해 주체성을 확립하고 새로운 지식을 만들었음.

[2]Diaries were *central media* [through which enlightened and free subjects could be constructed].
전치사+관계대명사 S′ V′
일기는 중심 매체였다 [그것을 통해 계몽된 자유로운 주체가 만들어질 수 있는]

[3]They provided *a space* [where one could write daily / about her whereabouts, feelings, and thoughts].
(= Diaries) 관계부사
그것은 공간을 제공했다 [개인이 매일 쓸 수 있는 / 자신의 행방, 감정, 그리고 생각에 대해]
↳ **상술:** 일기는 주체를 형성하는 중심 매체로 자신에 대해 쓰는 공간을 제공함.

[4]Over time and with rereading, / disparate entries, events, and happenstances / could be rendered into insights and narratives (about the self), / and allowed for the formation (of subjectivity).
S V1 V2
시간이 지남에 따라 그리고 다시 읽음으로써 / 이질적인 내용, 사건 및 우연이 / 통찰과 이야기로 만들어질 수 있었다 (자신에 관한) / 그리고 형성을 가능하게 만들었다 (주체성의)

★<It is ~ that ...> 강조구문: …인 것은 바로 ~이다
[5]It is in that context // that the idea of "the self [as] both made and explored with words" emerges.
강조구문 S′ = V′
바로 그러한 맥락에서다 // '말로 만들어지고 탐구되는 (것으로서의) 자아'라는 개념이 나타나는 것은
↳ 일기를 다시 읽으면서 자신에 대한 통찰과 주체성이 형성됨 → 자아의 발생.

[6]Diaries were personal and private; // one would write for oneself, // or, in Habermas's formulation, / one would **make oneself public to oneself.** ★<make+O+C>: O를 C하게 만들다
S1 V1 C1 S2 V2 S3 V3 O3 C3
일기는 개인적이고 사적인 것이었다 // 사람은 자신을 위해 쓰곤 했다 // Habermas의 명확한 표현으로 다시 말하면 /
사람은 자신을 자신에게 공개적으로 만들곤 했다
↳ 자신(내면의 생각, 감정, 경험 등)을 일기에 써서 자신에게 공개함.

[7]By making the self public in a private sphere, / the self also became an object (for self-inspection and self-critique). 🔑 사적 영역, 즉 일기장에 쓰는 솔직한 글은 스스로를 되돌아보게 함.
<by v-ing>: v함으로써 S V O
자아를 사적 영역에서 공개함으로써 / 자아는 또한 대상이 되었다 (자기 점검과 자기비판의)
↳ 일기를 쓰면서 자기 점검과 자기비판을 함.

해석

[1]18세기와 19세기에 충분히 발달함에 따라(▶ 대중화되었다는 의미) 개인 일기는 근대적 주체성 구축의 중심이 되었는데 그것의 중심에는 세계와 자아에 대한 이해에 이성과 비판의 적용이 있고 이는 새로운 종류의 지식의 창조를 가능하게 했다. [2]일기는 그것을 통해 계몽된 자유로운 주체가 만들어질 수 있는 중심 매체였다. [3]그것은 개인이 자신의 행방, 감정, 그리고 생각에 대해 매일 쓸 수 있는 공간을 제공했다. [4]시간이 지남에 따라 그리고 다시 읽음으로써, 이질적인 내용, 사건 및 우연이 자신에 관한 통찰과 이야기로 만들어질 수 있었으며, 주체성의 형성을 가능하게 만들었다. [5]'말로 만들어지고 또한 탐구되는 (것으로서의) 자아'라는 개념이 나타나는 것은 바로 그러한 맥락에서다. [6]일기는 개인적이고 사적인 것으로 사람들은 자신을 위해 쓰곤 했는데, Habermas의 명확한 표현으로 다시 말하면, 사람은 자신을 자신에게 공개적으로 만들곤 했다. [7]자아를 사적 영역에서 공개함으로써 자아는 또한 자기 점검과 자기비판의 대상이 되었다.

어휘

come of age (무엇이) 충분히 발달한 상태가 되다
centerpiece 중심(적 존재); 중앙 장식물
construction 구축, 건설
subjectivity 주체성, 주관(성)
critique 비판; 평론
enlighten 계몽하다, 깨우치다
whereabouts 행방, 소재
entry (일기 등의 개별) 항목, 내용; 들어감[옴]
happenstance 우연
narrative 이야기; 서술 (기법)
emerge 나타나다, 떠오르다
formulation 명확한 표현
self-inspection 자기 점검
[선택지] as a means of ~의 수단으로서
alternate 대체[대리]의; 번갈아 일어나는
selfhood 자아, 개성

정답 가이드

개인의 주체성 형성과 자아 성찰의 수단으로서 일기의 기능을 설명하는 글이다. 밑줄 친 어구에서 일기가 자신을 자기 자신에게 공개하는 사적인 공간이라고 한 후, 이어지는 문장에서는 그렇게 함으로써 자신을 점검하고 비판의 대상으로 보게 된다고 했다. 따라서 밑줄 친 부분이 의미하는 바로 가장 적절한 것은 ① 'use writing as a means of reflecting on oneself(글을 자신을 되돌아보는 수단으로 사용하다)'이다.

오답 클리닉

② build one's identity by reading others' diaries (13%)
타인의 일기를 읽음으로써(×) 자신의 정체성을 확립하다
타인의 일기를 읽는 내용은 언급되지 않았음.

③ exchange feedback in the process of writing (4%)
글쓰기 과정에서 의견을 교환하다(×)
문장 6에서 일기는 개인적인 것이라고 했으므로 의견을 교환하는 것은 틀림.

④ create an alternate ego to present to others (9%)
다른 사람에게 제시하기 위한 대체 자아(×)를 창조하다
일기는 자신을 자기 자신에게만 드러내 보이는 곳이므로 타인에게 보이기 위한 것이 아니며 대체 자아도 언급되지 않음.

⑤ develop topics for writing about selfhood (7%)
자아에 관한 글을 쓰기 위한 주제를 개발하다(×)
일기가 자아에 관한 것은 맞으나, 일기를 쓰기 위해 주제를 개발한다는 내용은 없음.

02 + 함의 추론 〈23학년도 9월 모평 21번 | 정답률 55%〉 ①

구문분석 & 직독직해

기술 개인의 음악 취향을 존중하는 알고리즘

[1]You may feel // (that) there is something scary (about *an algorithm* (deciding what you might like)).
(S / V / 명사절 접속사 생략 / V′ / S′ / 현재분사구; (that) → feel의 O(명사절))
여러분은 느낄지도 모른다 // 무서운 것이 있다고 (알고리즘에 대해 (여러분이 좋아할지도 모르는 것을 결정하는))
↳ **도입:** 개인의 선호를 파악하는 알고리즘 기술은 무서울 정도임.

[2]Could it mean // that, if computers conclude // (that) you won't like something, // you will never get *the chance* (to see it)?
(V: Could ~ mean / S: it / that: 명사절 접속사 / if: 부사절 접속사 / S″ / V″ / 명사절 접속사 생략 / O″(명사절) / S′ / V′ / O′; that → could mean의 O(명사절); it = the thing that computers conclude you won't like)
그것은 의미하는가 // 컴퓨터가 결론을 내린다면 // 당신이 뭔가를 좋아하지 않을 것이라고 // 당신은 기회를 결코 얻지 못할 것을 (그것을 볼)
↳ **문제 제기:** 알고리즘이 우리가 좋아할 만한 정보만을 제공하여 결코 보지 못하는 정보가 있게 될 것인가에 대한 의문.

[3]Personally, / I really enjoy / being directed toward *new music* [that I might not have found by myself].
(S / V / O / 목적격 관계대명사; ★enjoy의 동명사 목적어가 수동형으로 쓰임.; by myself = alone)
개인적으로 / 나는 정말 좋아한다 / 새로운 음악 쪽으로 안내받는 것을 [내가 혼자서는 찾아내지 못했을]

[4]I can quickly get stuck / in *a rut* [where I put on the same songs over and over].
(where: 관계부사)
나는 빨리 갇힐 수가 있다 / 틀에 [내가 같은 노래들을 반복해서 재생하는]

[5]That's // (*the reason*) why I've always enjoyed the radio.
(S V / 선행사 생략 / 관계부사 / C(명사절))
그것이 ~이다 // 내가 항상 라디오를 즐기는 이유
↳ **필자의 사례:** 틀에 갇히지 않고 새로운 음악을 접할 수 있는 라디오를 듣는 것을 좋아함.

[6]But / *the algorithms* [that are now pushing and pulling me through the music library] / are perfectly suited / to finding *gems* [that I'll like].
(S / 주격 관계대명사 / V / 목적격 관계대명사; gems → (= new musics))
그러나 / 알고리즘은 [지금 음악 라이브러리의 끝에서 끝까지 나를 밀고 당기는] / 완벽하게 적합하다 / 보석(새로운 음악)을 찾는 일에 [내가 좋아할]
↳ 좋아할 만한 새 음악을 찾는 데 알고리즘이 안성맞춤임.

[7]My worry (originally about such algorithms) was // that they might drive everyone into certain parts (of the library), / leaving others lacking listeners.
(S / V / 명사절 접속사 / S′ / V′ / O′; that → was의 C(명사절); 분사구문(= and they might leave ~))
★분사구문의 의미상 주어는 they(= algorithms)이며 <leave+O+v-ing>는 'O가 (어떤 상태가) 되게 하다'의 뜻.
나의 걱정은 (원래 그런 알고리즘에 대한) ~이었다 // 그것이 모든 사람을 특정 부분으로 몰아넣을지도 모르는 것 (그 라이브러리의) / 다른 부분은 듣는 사람들이 없게 하면서
↳ **우려:** 알고리즘이 특정 음악으로 모든 사용자들을 이끌까 걱정함.

해석

[1]여러분은 여러분이 좋아할지도 모르는 것을 결정하는 알고리즘에 대해 무서운 것이 있다고 느낄지도 모른다. [2]그것은 당신이 뭔가를 좋아하지 않을 것이라고 컴퓨터가 결론을 내린다면 당신은 그것을 볼 기회를 결코 얻지 못할 것을 의미하는가? [3]개인적으로, 나는 내가 혼자서는 찾아내지 못했을 새로운 음악 쪽으로 안내받는 것을 정말 좋아한다. [4]나는 같은 노래를 반복해서 재생하는 틀에 빨리 갇힐 수가 있다. [5]그것이 내가 항상 라디오를 즐기는 이유이다. [6]그러나 지금 음악 라이브러리의 끝에서 끝까지 나를 밀고 당기는 알고리즘은 내가 좋아할 보석(새로운 음악)을 찾는 일에 완벽하게 적합하다. [7]원래 그런 알고리즘에 대한 나의 걱정은 그것이 모든 사람을 그 라이브러리의 특정 부분으로 몰아넣고 다른 부분은 듣는 사람들이 없게 할지도 모른다는 것이었다. [8]그것은 취향을 하나로 모이게 할 것인가? [9]그러나 보통 알고리즘의 배후에 있는 비선형적이고 불규칙적인 계산 덕분에 이것(취향을 하나로 모으는 것)은 발생하지 않는다. [10]여러분의 것과 비교하여 내가 선호하는 것들 중의 작은 갈라짐(차이)이 우리를 (음악) 라이브러리의 다른 멀리 떨어진 구석들로 보낼 수 있다.

어휘

conclude 결론을 내리다
direct 안내하다; ~로 향하다; 직접적인
by oneself 혼자서, 스스로
get stuck in ~에 갇히다
library 라이브러리 ((다양한 콘텐츠를 한데 모아 놓은 가상 폴더)); 도서관; 서재
be suited to A A에 적합하다
cf. suit 맞다, 적합하다; 어울리다
drive (어떤 방향으로) 몰다; 운전[조종]하다
certain 특정한; 확실한, 틀림없는
lacking (~이) 없는[부족한]
convergence 하나로 모이게 함, 수렴

(= algorithms)
[8]Would they cause a convergence of tastes?
그것(알고리즘)은 취향을 하나로 모이게 할 것인가?
↳ **질문:** 알고리즘이 취향의 다양성을 없애는가에 대한 의문.

주제문 — 알고리즘은 취향을 하나로 모으지 않음 → 다양성 존중.
[9]But / thanks to the nonlinear and chaotic mathematics usually behind them, / this doesn't happen.
(= a convergence of tastes)
그러나 / 보통 그것(알고리즘)의 배후에 있는 비선형적이고 불규칙적인 계산 덕분에 / 이것(취향을 하나로 모으는 것)은 발생하지 않는다
↳ **답변:** 알고리즘은 취향의 다양성을 없애지 않음.

[10]A small divergence in *my likes* (compared to yours) / can **send us off into different far corners (of the library)**.
S / 과거분사구 / V / O
내가 선호하는 것들 중의 작은 갈라짐(차이)이 (여러분의 것과 비교하여) / 우리를 다른 멀리 떨어진 구석들로 보낼 수 있다 ((음악) 라이브러리의)
↳ **부연 설명:** 알고리즘은 각기 다른 취향에 맞춘 노래를 듣게 할 수 있음.

taste 취향, 기호; 맛
thanks to A A 덕분에[때문에]
nonlinear 비선형적인, 직선이 아닌
chaotic 불규칙적인, 무질서한; 혼돈 상태인
mathematics 계산; 수학
[선택지] select 선택하다, 선발[선정]하다
respective 각각의, 각자의
frequent 잦은, 빈번한
motivate 동기를 주다; 이유가 되다
talented (타고난) 재능이 있는
preference 선호(도)

정답 가이드

사용자의 취향에 맞는 음악을 찾아 안내해주는 알고리즘이 역으로 특정 음악만을 추천해 모든 이들의 취향을 하나로 모이게 할 가능성에 대해 필자는 질문을 던지고 있다. 이에 대해 비선형적이고 불규칙적인 계산이 알고리즘에 쓰이기 때문에 사람들을 특정 부분으로 몰리게 하는 일은 발생하지 않는다고 답한다. 밑줄 친 부분이 있는 마지막 문장은 이를 부연 설명하는데, 사용자들의 작은 선호의 차이가 다른 음악을 안내하게 한다는 내용이 되어야 하므로 밑줄 친 부분이 의미하는 바로 가장 적절한 것은 ① 'lead us to music selected to suit our respective tastes(우리를 각각 자신의 취향에 맞게 선택된 음악으로 이끌다)'이다.

오답 클리닉

② enable us to build connections with other listeners (13%)
우리가 다른 청취자들과 관계를 맺을(×) 수 있게 하다
청취자들끼리 소통하거나 연결된다는 내용은 언급되지 않음.

③ encourage us to request frequent updates for algorithms (9%)
우리가 알고리즘을 위한 잦은 업데이트를 요구하도록(×) 장려하다
업데이트에 관한 내용은 언급되지 않음.

④ motivate us to search for talented but unknown musicians (10%)
우리에게 재능이 있지만 알려지지 않은 음악가들을 찾도록(×) 동기를 주다
우리가 재능 있지만 알려지지 않은 음악가를 찾는 것이 아니라 알고리즘이 사용자가 좋아할 만한 음악을 찾아주는 것임.

⑤ make us ignore our preferences for particular music genres (13%)
우리가 특별한 음악 장르에 대한 우리의 선호를 무시하도록(×) 만들다
알고리즘이 취향을 하나로 모으지 않고 개별 취향을 반영해준다고 했으므로 글의 요지와 반대됨.

03 + 함의 추론 (23학년도 6월 모평 21번 | 정답률 59%) ⑤

구문분석 & 직독직해 — 철학 주관적 관점으로 형성되는 인간의 세계관

주제문
[1]Our view of the world is not given to us from the outside / in a pure, objective form; //
S_1 V_1
우리의 세계관은 외부로부터 우리에게 주어지는 것이 아니다 / 순수하고 객관적인 형태로 //
(= our view of the world)
it is shaped / by our mental abilities, our shared cultural perspectives and our unique values and beliefs.
S_2 V_2 — 세계관은 특정한 관점으로 형성됨.
그것(우리의 세계관)은 형성된다 / 우리의 정신 능력, 우리의 공유된 문화적 관점, 그리고 우리의 독특한 가치관과 신념에 의해
↳ 세계관은 객관이 아닌 주관에 의해 형성됨.

(= 앞 문장)
[2]This is not to say // that there is no reality outside our minds / or that the world is just an illusion.
S V C — to say의 O(명사절 병렬)
이것은 말하는 것이 아니다 // 우리의 마음 외부에 현실이 없다고 / 또는 세계는 단지 환영일 뿐이라고

(to say의 O(명사절))
[3]It is to say // that our version of reality is precisely that: / *our* version, not *the* version.
명사절 접속사 S' V' C' =
그것은 말하는 것이다 // 현실에 대한 우리의 버전은 바로 그것이라고 / 즉 '우리의' 버전이지 (유일한) '그' 버전이 아닌
↳ **부연 설명:** 현실은 우리가 각자 만들어 내는 것이며 어떤 고유한 현실이 있는 것이 아님.

해석

[1]우리의 세계관은 순수하고 객관적인 형태로 외부로부터 우리에게 주어지는 것이 아니라, 그것은 우리의 정신 능력, 우리의 공유된 문화적 관점, 그리고 우리의 독특한 가치관과 신념에 의해 형성된다. [2]이것은 우리의 마음 외부에 현실이 없다거나 세계는 단지 환영일 뿐이라고 말하는 것이 아니다. [3]그것은 현실에 대한 우리의 버전은 바로 그것, 즉 '우리의' 버전이지 (유일한) '그' 버전이 아니라고 말하는 것이다. [4]이론적 구성 개념으로서가 아닌, 의미가 통하는 단일하거나 보편적이거나 권위 있는 버전은 없다. [5]우리는 세계를 '정말 있는 그대로'가 아니라, 그것이 우리에게 보이는 대로만 볼 수 있는데, 왜냐하면 세계에 형태를 부여하는 관점이 없다면 '정말 있는 그대로'는 없기 때문이다. [6]철학자 Thomas Nagel은 '아무것도 아닌 곳(특정 관점이 없는 곳)에서 나온 관점'은 없다고 주장했는데, 왜냐하면 우

[4]There is no *single, universal or authoritative version* [that makes sense], / other than as a theoretical construct.

V / S / 주격 관계대명사 / 전치사(~로서)

단일하거나 보편적이거나 권위 있는 버전은 없다 [의미가 통하는] / 이론적 구성 개념으로서가 아닌

↳ 단 하나의 객관적인 현실 세계란 존재하지 않음.

🔑 있는 그대로 존재하는 세계, 즉 객관적 세계는 없음.

[5]We can see the world // only as it appears to us, / not "as it truly is," // because there is no "as it truly is" / without *a perspective* (to give it form). *to give 뒤의 it은 간접목적어, form은 직접목적어임.

(= the world) 부사절 접속사(~대로) (= the world) 부사절 접속사(이유) (= the world) (= the world)

우리는 세계를 볼 수 있다 // 그것이 우리에게 보이는 대로만 / '그것이 정말 있는 대로'가 아니라 // 왜냐하면 '그것이 정말 있는 대로'는 없기 때문이다 / 관점이 없다면 (그것에 형태를 부여하는)

↳ 관점이 있어야 세계를 볼 수 있음.

[6]Philosopher Thomas Nagel argued // that there is no "**view from nowhere**," // since we cannot see the world / except from a particular perspective, // and that perspective influences what we see.

S / V / 명사절 접속사 (argued의 O(명사절)) / 부사절 접속사(~ 때문에) / S′₁ V′₁ O′₁ / S′₂ V′₂ O′₂

🔑 세계는 특정한 관점 없이는 볼 수 없음.

철학자 Thomas Nagel은 주장했다 // '아무것도 아닌 곳(특정 관점이 없는 곳)에서 나온 관점'은 없다고 // 왜냐하면 우리는 세계를 볼 수 없기 때문이다 / 특정 관점에서 보는 것 외에는 // 그리고 그 관점이 우리가 보는 것에 영향을 미치기 때문이다

↳ 주관적 관점 없이는 세계를 볼 수 없음.

🔑 인간의 렌즈 = 인간의 주관적인 시각 *<make+O+C>: O를 C하게 만들다

[7]We can experience the world / only through *the human lenses* [that make it intelligible to us].

주격 관계대명사 V′ O′ (= the world) C′

우리는 세계를 경험할 수 있다 / 인간의 렌즈를 통해서만 [우리가 그것(세계)을 이해할 수 있게 만드는]

↳ **결론:** 인간은 주관을 통해서만 세계를 경험함.

리는 특정 관점에서 보는 것 외에는 세계를 볼 수 없고, 그 관점이 우리가 보는 것에 영향을 미치기 때문이다. [7]우리가 세계를 이해할 수 있게 만드는 인간의 렌즈를 통해서만 우리는 세계를 경험할 수 있다.

어휘

objective 객관적인(↔ subjective 주관적인)
perspective 관점, 시각
values 가치관
precisely 바로, 정확하게
universal 보편적인; 전 세계의
authoritative 권위 있는, 권위적인
make sense 의미가 통하다; 타당하다
other than ~이 아닌; ~외에
theoretical 이론적인
construct 구성 개념; 구성하다
intelligible (쉽게) 이해할 수 있는
[선택지] perception 인식, 지각
have A in mind A를 염두에 두다
adopt 채택하다; 입양하다
insight 통찰(력)
defeat 물리치다, 패배시키다
prejudice 편견
unbiased 편견 없는

정답 가이드

세계관이 우리의 주관적인 관점으로 형성된다는 주제문의 내용을 일관되게 설명하는 글이다. 철학자 Thomas Nagel의 말은 이 주제문을 뒷받침하므로 'view from nowhere'가 없다는 것은 '우리의 주관적 관점'과 대비되는 '객관적 관점'이란 없음을 뜻한다. 따라서 밑줄 친 부분이 의미하는 바로 가장 적절한 것은 ⑤ 'unbiased and objective view of the world(편견 없고 객관적인 세계관)'이다.

오답 클리닉

① perception of reality affected by subjective views (21%)
주관적인 견해에 영향받은(×) 현실 인식
주관적인 관점이 세계관을 형성한다는 글의 주제와 일치하지만, 밑줄 친 부분 앞에 부정어 no가 있어 의미가 정반대됨.

The 주의 밑줄 친 부분을 포함한 문장에 부정어가 있는 경우 글의 주제와 반대 내용을 의미할 수 있기 때문에 해석에 주의한다.

② valuable perspective most people have in mind (10%)
대부분의 사람이 염두에 두고 있는 가치 있는 관점(×)
우리가 특정한 관점으로 세계를 바라본다고 했지만 그 관점의 가치에 대해서는 언급되지 않음.

③ particular view adopted by very few people (6%)
극소수의 사람에 의해 채택된(×) 특정한 견해
사람마다 독특한 관점으로 세계관이 형성된다고 했으므로 극소수의 사람에 의해 채택된 것으로 볼 수 없음.

④ critical insight that defeats our prejudices (4%)
우리의 편견(×)을 물리치는 비판적 통찰(×)
비판적 통찰을 통해 편견을 물리칠 수 있다는 내용은 언급되지 않음.

01 + 필자 주장 (24학년도 대수능 20번 | 정답률 76%) ⑤

구문분석 & 직독직해 경영 조직 문화 형성을 위한 명확한 행동 지침의 필요성

[1] Values alone do not create [and] (do not) build culture.
S / V / O
가치관은 홀로 문화를 창조하고 형성하지는 않는다

[2] Living your values only some of the time / does not contribute / to the creation and maintenance (of culture).
S(동명사구) / V(단수) / to의 O(명사구)
약간의 시간에만 가치관에 따라 사는 것은 / 기여하지 않는다 / 창조와 유지에 (문화의)

[3] Changing values into behaviors / is only half the battle.
S(동명사구) / V(단수) / C
가치관을 행동으로 바꾸는 것은 / 전투의 절반에 불과하다
↳ **도입:** 가치 정립만으로는 문화를 창조하고 형성할 수 없으며 가치관을 행동으로 바꾸는 것도 충분치 않음.

주제문
(this = changing values into behaviors)
[4] Certainly, / this is a step (in the right direction), // [but] those behaviors must then be shared and distributed widely / throughout the organization, /
S1 V1 C / S2 V2
물론 / 이것(가치관을 행동으로 바꾸는 것)은 단계이다 (올바른 방향으로 나아가는) // 그러나 그러한 행동은 그 후에 널리 공유되고 배포되어야 한다 / 조직 전체에 /
along with a clear and concise description (of what is expected). 🔑 가치관이 반영된 행동은 명확한 설명과 함께 조직 전체에 공유·배포되어야 함.
~와 함께 / of의 O(명사절)
명확하고 간결한 설명과 함께 (기대되는 것에 대한)
↳ 가치관을 반영한 행동은 명확한 설명과 함께 조직 전체에 공유되고 배포되어야 함.

(it = what is expected)
[5] It is not enough / to simply talk about it.
가주어 V C / 진주어(to-v구)
(~은) 충분하지 않다 / 단순히 그것(기대되는 것)에 관해 이야기하는 것은

🔑 설명은 특정 행동을 시각적으로 표현해야 함.
[6] It is critical / to have a visual representation (of *the specific behaviors* [that leaders and all people managers can use / to coach their people]).
가주어 V C / 진주어(to-v구) / 목적격 관계대명사 / 목적(~하기 위해)
(~이) 중요하다 / 시각적 표현을 갖는 것이 (특정 행동에 대한 [리더와 모든 인력 관리자가 사용할 수 있는 / 자신의 팀을 지도하기 위해])
↳ **부연 설명:** 단지 말로만 설명하는 것이 아닌 특정 행동을 시각적으로 명확하게 표현하는 것이 중요함.

[7] Just like a sports team has a playbook (with *specific plays* (designed to help them perform well [and] win)), //
부사절 접속사(~처럼) S′ V′ O′ / 과거분사구
*<help+O+(to-)v>에서 목적격보어로 쓰인 원형부정사 perform과 win이 and로 연결됨.
마치 스포츠 팀이 플레이 북을 가지고 있는 것처럼 (특정 플레이를 담은 (그들이 잘 경기하고 승리하는 데 도움이 되도록 고안된)) //
🔑 회사는 핵심적인 변화를 담은 플레이 북을 가지고 있어야 함. *<transform[turn] A into B>: A를 B로 바꾸다
your company should have / a playbook (with *the key shifts* (needed to transform your culture into action / [and] (to) turn your values into winning behaviors)).
S V O / 과거분사구
여러분의 회사는 가지고 있어야 한다 / 플레이 북을 (핵심적인 변화를 담은 (여러분의 문화를 행동으로 바꾸는 데 필요로 되는 / 그리고 여러분의 가치관을 승리하는 행동으로 바꾸는 데 (필요로 되는)))
↳ **예(비유):** 스포츠 팀의 플레이 북처럼 문화를 행동으로 바꾸는 핵심 변화를 담은 플레이 북이 회사에도 필요함.

해석

[1]가치관은 홀로 문화를 창조하고 형성하지는 않는다. [2]약간의 시간에만 가치관에 따라 사는 것은 문화의 창조와 유지에 기여하지 않는다. [3]가치관을 행동으로 바꾸는 것은 전투의 절반에 불과하다. [4]물론, 이것(가치관을 행동으로 바꾸는 것)은 올바른 방향으로 나아가는 단계이지만, 그러한 행동은 그 후에 기대되는 것에 대한 명확하고 간결한 설명과 함께 조직 전체에 널리 공유되고 배포되어야 한다. [5]단순히 그것에 관해 이야기하는 것은 충분하지 않다. [6]리더와 모든 인력 관리자가 자신의 팀을 지도하기 위해 사용할 수 있는 특정 행동에 대한 시각적 표현을 갖는 것이 중요하다. [7]마치 스포츠 팀이 그들이 잘 경기하고 승리하는 데 도움이 되도록 고안된 특정 플레이를 담은 플레이 북을 가지고 있는 것처럼, 여러분의 회사는 여러분의 문화를 행동으로 바꾸고 여러분의 가치관을 승리하는 행동으로 바꾸는 데 필요로 되는 핵심적인 변화를 담은 플레이 북을 가지고 있어야 한다.

어휘

contribute to A A에 기여하다; A의 원인이 되다
maintenance 유지[지속]; 보수
direction 방향; 지시; 감독
distribute 배포하다; 분배하다
concise 간결한, 간명한
description 설명, 서술; 묘사
critical (대단히) 중요한; 비판적인
visual 시각적인
representation 표현, 묘사; 대표(자)
coach 지도하다; (경기의) 코치
playbook 플레이 북 ((팀의 공수 작전을 그림과 함께 기록한 책))
design 고안하다, 만들다; 설계하다
shift 변화, 전환; 이동하다; 바꾸다

정답 가이드

조직의 문화를 형성하고 유지하기 위해서는 가치관을 행동으로 바꾸는 것과 아울러 그 가치관이 반영된 행동을 명확한 설명과 함께 조직 전체에 공유해야 한다고 했다. 이 주제문 뒤에 이어지는 내용은 그 명확한 설명에 대해 부연 설명하는데, 특정 행동에 대한 시각적인 표현을 갖는 것이 중요하다고 하면서 스포츠 팀의 플레이 북과 같이 회사에도 핵심적인 변화를 담은 플레이 북이 있어야 한다고 했다. 따라서 필자가 주장하는 바로 가장 적절한 것은 ⑤ '조직의 문화 형성에는 가치를 반영한 행동의 공유를 위한 명시적 지침이 필요하다.'이다.

오답 클리닉

① 조직 문화 혁신(×)을 위해서 모든 구성원이 공유할 핵심 가치를 정립(×)해야 한다.
(8%) 조직 문화의 혁신이 아닌 형성과 유지에 관한 내용이며, 가치 정립만으로는 부족하다고 했으므로 틀림.
② 조직 구성원의 행동을 변화시키려면 지도자는 명확한 가치관(×)을 가져야 한다.
(9%) 명확한 가치관이 아닌 명확한 지침이 필요하다고 했으므로 틀림.
③ 조직 내 문화가 공유되기 위해서 구성원의 자발적 행동(×)이 뒷받침되어야 한다.
(5%) 구성원의 자발적인 행동이 필요하다는 내용은 언급되지 않음.
④ 조직의 핵심 가치 실현을 위해 구성원 간의 지속적인 의사소통(×)이 필수적이다.
(3%) 구성원 간의 의사소통에 관한 내용은 없음.

02 + 필자 주장 〈24학년도 9월 모평 20번 | 정답률 96%〉 ②

구문분석 & 직독직해

심리 자신감을 키우는 방법

[1]Confident is not the same / as comfortable.
S V C
자신감이 있는 것은 똑같지 않다 / 마음 편한 것과

★<mean v-ing>: ~을 의미하다
[2]One (of the biggest misconceptions (about becoming self-confident)) / is // that it means living fearlessly.
S V C(명사절)
하나는 (가장 큰 오해 중 (자신감 있게 되는 것에 관한)) / ~이다 // 그것이 두려움 없이 사는 것을 의미한다는 것
↳ **도입(Myth):** 자신감이 있다는 것은 마음이 편하거나 두려움 없이 사는 것이 아님.

[3]The key (to building confidence) / is quite the opposite.
S to의 O(동명사구) V C
핵심은 (자신감을 키우는 것의) / 완전히 그 반대이다

주제문
↱ means의 O(명사절) ★<let+O+C(v)>: O가 v하도록 놓아 두다 🔑 자신감을 키우려면 두려움이 존재하게 해야 함.
[4]It means // (that) we are willing to let fear be present // as we do *the things* [that matter to us].
S V 접속사 생략 S′ V′ C′ 부사절 접속사(~할 때) S″ V″ O″ 주격 관계대명사
그것은 의미한다 // 우리가 기꺼이 두려움이 존재하도록 놓아 두는 것을 // 우리가 일을 할 때 [우리에게 중요한]
↳ **사실(Truth):** 자신감을 키우는 것의 핵심은 두려움이 존재하도록 놔두는 것임.

[5]When we establish some self-confidence / in something, // it feels good.
부사절 접속사(시간) S V C
우리가 어느 정도의 자신감을 확립할 때 / 어떤 것에 대해 // 기분이 좋다

↱ (= self-confidence)
[6]We want to stay there / and (to) hold on to it.
S V O_1 O_2
우리는 거기에 머무르고 싶어 한다 / 그리고 그것(자신감)을 계속 유지하고 싶어 한다
↳ 우리는 자신감을 확립할 때 기분이 좋아서 그것을 유지하고 싶어함.

[7]But / if we only go // where we feel confident, // then confidence never expands / beyond that.
부사절 접속사(조건) V′ 부사절 접속사 S″ V″ C″ S V
하지만 / 우리가 오직 간다면 // 자신감을 느끼는 곳으로만 // 그렇다면 자신감은 절대 확장되지 않는다 / 그 이상으로

[8]If we only do *the things* [(which[that]) (we know) we can do well], // fear (of the new and unknown) / tends to grow.
부사절 접속사(조건) 목적격 관계대명사 생략 삽입절 S V
★<the+형용사>: ~한 것(추상명사)
우리가 일만 한다면 [(우리가 알기로) 우리가 잘할 수 있는] // 두려움은 (새롭고 미지의 것에 대한) / 커지는 경향이 있다
↳ **문제점:** 자신감을 느끼는 일만 하려고 하면 자신감은 확장되지 않고 새로운 것에 대한 두려움은 커짐.

[9]Building confidence inevitably demands // that we make friends / with vulnerability // because it is *the only way* (to be without confidence / for a while).
S(동명사구) V(단수) O(명사절) 부사절 접속사(이유)
자신감을 쌓는 것은 필연적으로 요구한다 // 우리가 친구가 되는 것을 / 취약성과 //
그것(우리가 취약성과 친구가 되는 것)이 유일한 방법이기 때문이다 (자신감 없이 있을 수 있는 / 한동안)

해석

[1]자신감 있는 것과 마음 편한 것은 똑같지 않다. [2]자신감 있게 되는 것에 관한 가장 큰 오해 중 하나는 그것이 두려움 없이 사는 것을 의미한다는 것이다. [3]자신감을 키우는 것의 핵심은 완전히 그 반대이다. [4]그것은 우리가 우리에게 중요한 일을 할 때 기꺼이 두려움이 존재하도록 놓아 두는 것을 의미한다. [5]우리가 어떤 것에 대해 어느 정도의 자신감을 확립할 때 기분이 좋다. [6]우리는 거기에 머무르고 그것(자신감)을 계속 유지하고 싶어 한다. [7]하지만 우리가 오직 자신감을 느끼는 곳으로만 간다면, 자신감은 절대 그 이상으로 확장되지 않는다. [8]우리가 알기로 우리가 잘할 수 있는 일만 한다면, 새롭고 미지의 것에 대한 두려움은 커지는 경향이 있다. [9]자신감을 쌓는 것은 필연적으로 우리가 취약성과 친구가 되는 것을 요구하는데, 그것이 한동안 자신감 없이 있을 수 있는 유일한 방법이기 때문이다. [10]하지만 자신감이 커질 수 있는 유일한 방법은 우리가 기꺼이 그것(자신감) 없이 있으려 할 때이다. [11]우리가 두려움 속으로 발을 내딛고 미지의 것과 한자리에 앉을 수 있을 때, 밑바닥에서부터 끝까지 자신감을 쌓아 올리는 것은 바로 그렇게 하는 용기이다.

어휘

confident 자신감 있는 (= self-confident)
cf. confidence 자신(감) (= self-confidence)
comfortable 마음 편한, 편안한
misconception 오해
fearlessly 두려움 없이, 대담하게
opposite 반대(의); 다른 편[쪽]의
be willing to-v 기꺼이 v하다
present 존재하는; 현재(의); 참석[출석]한; 제시하다
matter 중요하다; 문제
establish 확립하다; 설립하다
hold on to A A를 계속 유지하다[고수하다]
expand 확장[확대]되다
unknown 미지의, 알려지지 않은

🔑 자신감 없이 있으려 할 때 자신감이 커질 수 있음.

[10]But / *the only way* [(that) confidence can grow] / is // when we are willing to be / without it.
S 관계부사 생략 V C(명사절) (= confidence)
하지만 / 유일한 방법은 [자신감이 커질 수 있는] / ~이다 // 우리가 기꺼이 있으려 할 때 / 그것(자신감) 없이
↳ **해결책:** 취약성을 수용하고 기꺼이 자신감 없이 있으려 할 때 비로소 자신감을 키울 수 있음.

🔑 자신감을 키우는 것은 두려움 속으로 들어가 미지의 것과 함께 있게 하는 용기임.
[11]When we can step into fear / and (can) sit with the unknown, //
부사절 접속사(시간) V'1 V'2
우리가 두려움 속으로 발을 내디딜 수 있을 때 / 그리고 미지의 것과 한자리에 앉을 수 있을 때 //
it is the courage (of doing so) // that builds confidence / from the ground up.
<It is ~ that ...> 강조구문: …인 것은 바로 ~이다
바로 용기이다 (그렇게 하는) // 자신감을 쌓아 올리는 것은 / 밑바닥에서부터 끝까지
↳ **해결책 상술:** 두려움과 미지의 것에 마주할 수 있을 때 자신감을 키울 수 있음.

tend to-v v하는 경향이 있다
inevitably 필연적으로, 불가피하게
demand 요구(하다); 수요
courage 용기
from the ground up 밑바닥에서부터 끝까지

정답 가이드

자신감을 키우는 것의 핵심은 두려움이 존재하도록 놔두는 것이라고 했다. 이어지는 부연 설명에서 자신감이 커질 수 있는 유일한 방법은 두려움 속으로 발을 내딛고 미지의 것과 한 자리에 있을 수 있을 때 그렇게 하는 용기라고 설명한다. 따라서 필자가 주장하는 바로 가장 적절한 것은 ② '자신감을 키우기 위해 낯설고 두려운 일에 도전하는 용기를 가져야 한다'이다.

오답 클리닉

① 적성을 파악(×)하기 위해서는 자신 있는 일(×)을 다양하게 시도해야 한다. (1%)
적성을 파악하기 위해서가 아니라 자신감을 키우기 위해 자신 없는 일에 도전해야 한다는 내용임.

③ 어려운 일을 자신 있게 수행하기 위해 사전에 계획(×)을 철저히 세워야 한다. (1%) 어려운 일을 수행할 때 미리 계획을 세워야 한다는 내용이 아님.

④ 과도한 자신감을 갖기보다는 자신의 약점을 객관적으로 분석(×)해야 한다. (2%)
약점을 객관적으로 분석하는 내용은 언급되지 않음.

⑤ 자신의 경험과 지식을 바탕으로(×) 당면한 문제에 자신 있게(×) 대처해야 한다. (1%) 자신감을 키우기 위해 새롭고 우리가 모르는 미지의 것에 도전해야 한다고 했으므로 경험과 지식을 바탕으로 자신 있게 대처하는 것과 반대됨.

03 + 글의 요지 〈24학년도 대수능 22번 | 정답률 86%〉 ①

구문분석 & 직독직해

비즈니스 긍정적인 고객 의견에 응답하는 것의 중요성

주제문
🔑 응답에 우선순위를 매기는 것은 고객과 깊이 관계를 맺게 해줌.
[1]Being able to prioritize your responses / allows you to connect more deeply / with individual customers, //
S(동명사구) V(단수) O C
여러분의 응답에 우선순위를 매기는 것은 / 여러분이 더 깊이 관계를 맺을 수 있게 해준다 / 개별 고객들과 //
*<whether it be A or B>는 가정의 의미를 나타내는데, 접속사 whether가 생략되어 <동사+주어> 어순으로 도치됨.
be it a one-off interaction (around a particularly delightful or upsetting experience), /
명사구 병렬
그것이 단 한 번의 상호 작용이든 (특별히 즐겁거나 속상하게 하는 경험에 대한) /
or the development (of a longer-term relationship (with a significantly influential individual / within your customer base)).
명사구 병렬
또는 발전이든 (장기적 관계의 (상당히 영향력 있는 개인과의 / 여러분의 고객 층 내의))
↳ 응답에 우선 순위를 매기는 것이 고객과 깊은 관계를 맺을 수 있게 해줌.

부사절 접속사(조건)
[2]If you've ever posted a favorable comment — / or any comment, (for that matter) — /
S' V' O'1 O'2
(about a brand, product or service), //
a favorable comment 수식
만약 여러분이 호의적인 의견을 올려 본 적이 있다면 / 혹은 어떠한 의견이라도 (그 문제에 대한) /
(어떤 브랜드, 제품 또는 서비스에 관해) //
부사절 접속사(조건)
think about / what it would feel like // if you were personally acknowledged /
V(명령문) about의 O(명사절) S' V'
by the brand manager, / for example, / as a result.
*가정법 과거 <if+S'+동사의 과거형 ~, S+would 동사원형 ...>: 만약 ~라면, …할 텐데
생각해 보라 / 기분이 어떨지 // 여러분이 개인적으로 인정을 받는다면 /
그 브랜드 매니저에 의해 / 예를 들어 / 그 결과
↳ **세부 사항(예):** 브랜드에 대해 호의적인 의견을 올리고 그것에 대해 개인적으로 인정(응답)을 받으면 기분이 좋을 것임.

해석

[1]여러분의 응답에 우선순위를 매기는 것은 그것이 특별히 즐겁거나 속상하게 하는 경험에 대한 단 한 번의 상호 작용이든, 여러분의 고객 층 내의 상당히 영향력 있는 개인과의 장기적 관계의 발전이든, 여러분이 개별 고객들과 더 깊이 관계를 맺을 수 있게 해 준다. [2]만약 여러분이 어떤 브랜드, 제품 또는 서비스에 관해 호의적인 의견이나 혹은 그 문제에 대한 어떠한 의견이라도 올려 본 적이 있다면, 그 결과, 예를 들어, 그 브랜드 매니저에 의해 여러분이 개인적으로 답해진다면 기분이 어떨지 생각해 보라. [3]일반적으로, 사람들은 할 말이 있기 때문에, 그리고 그것을 말한 것에 대해 인정받고 싶어 하기 때문에 글을 올린다. [4]특히, 사람들이 긍정적인 의견을 올릴 때 그것들(긍정적인 의견)은 그 글을 올리게 된 경험에 대한 감사의 표현이다. [5]여러분 옆에 서 있는 사람에 대한 칭찬은 보통 '감사합니다'와 같은 대답으로 응답되는 반면에, 슬픈 사실은 대부분의 브랜드 칭찬은 응답받지 못한다는 것이다. [6]이것은 무엇이 칭찬을 이끌어 냈는지 이해하고 그것들(칭찬)을 바탕으로 하여 확고한 팬을 만들어 낼 수 있는 기회를 잃은 것이다.

[3]In general, / people post // because they have *something* (to say) — // and because they want to be recognized / for having said it. ★동명사의 완료형(having p.p.)을 사용해 부사절의 동사 want보다 이전의 일임을 나타냄.
일반적으로 / 사람들은 글을 올린다 // 말이 있기 때문에 (할) // 그리고 인정받고 싶어 하기 때문에 / 그것을 말한 것에 대해

[4]In particular, / when people post positive comments // they are expressions (of appreciation (for *the experience* [that led to the post])).
특히 / 사람들이 긍정적인 의견을 올릴 때 // 그것들(긍정적인 의견)은 표현이다 (감사의 (경험에 대한 [그 글을 올리게 된]))

[5]While a compliment (to *the person* (standing next to you)) / is typically answered / with a response (like "Thank You)," //
칭찬은 ~인 반면에 (사람에 대한 (여러분 옆에 서 있는)) / 보통 응답되는 (반면에) / 대답으로 ('감사합니다'와 같은) //
the sad fact is // that most brand compliments go unanswered. ★<go+C(형용사)>: ~한 상태가 되다
슬픈 사실은 ~이다 // 대부분의 브랜드 칭찬은 응답받지 못한다는 것

고객의 칭찬에 답함으로써 칭찬의 이유를 이해하고 고객과의 관계를 확고히 할 수 있음.
[6]These are lost opportunities (to understand // what drove the compliments / and (to) create a solid fan / based on them).
이것은 잃어버린 기회이다 (이해할 수 있는 // 무엇이 칭찬을 이끌어 냈는지를 / 그리고 확고한 팬을 만들어 낼 수 있는 / 그것들(칭찬)을 바탕으로 하여)

↳ 부연 설명: 사람들은 보통 자신이 올린 글에 대해 인정받고 싶어하므로 고객의 브랜드 칭찬에 응답하는 것은 칭찬의 이유를 이해하고 고객과의 관계를 확고히 할 기회가 됨.

어휘
prioritize 우선순위를 매기다
individual 개별의; 개인(의)
one-off 단 한 번의 (것), 1회성의 (일)
delightful 즐거운
upsetting 속상하게 하는
influential 영향력 있는
customer base 고객 층[기반]
favorable 호의적인; 유리한
comment 의견; 논평(하다)
acknowledge 인정하다
in general 일반적으로
recognize 인정하다; 알아보다
post (정보를) 올리다, 게시하다; 발송하다
appreciation 감사; 감상; 진가(를 인정함)
lead to A (결과적으로) A하게 되다, A에 이르다
solid 확고한; 단단한; 고체(의)

정답 가이드
첫 문장에서 응답에 우선순위를 매기는 것이 개별 고객들과 더 깊이 관계를 맺을 수 있게 한다고 한 다음 긍정적인 의견을 올린 것에 대해 브랜드 매니저로부터 응답받는 것을 예로 들었다. 이어지는 부연 설명에서 고객은 자신이 올린 글에 대해 인정받고 싶어 하므로 고객의 브랜드 칭찬에 응답하지 않는 것은 칭찬의 이유를 이해하고 고객과의 관계를 확고히 할 기회를 잃은 것이라고 설명한다. 따라서 글의 요지로 가장 적절한 것은 ① '고객과의 관계 증진을 위해 고객의 브랜드 칭찬에 응답하는 것은 중요하다.'이다.

오답 클리닉
② 고객의 피드백을 면밀히 분석함(×)으로써 브랜드의 성공 가능성을 높일 수 있다.
(4%) 고객의 긍정적인 의견에 응답해야 한다는 것이지 면밀히 분석해야 한다는 내용이 아님.
③ 신속한(×) 고객 응대를 통해서 고객의 긍정적인 반응을 이끌어(×) 낼 수 있다.
(4%) 고객의 긍정적인 반응을 이끌어내는 방법에 관한 내용이 아님.
④ 브랜드 매니저에게는 고객의 부정적인 의견을 수용하는 태도(×)가 요구된다.
(3%) 부정적 의견을 수용하라는 내용은 언급되지 않음.
⑤ 고객의 의견을 경청하는 것은 브랜드의 새로운 이미지 창출(×)에 도움이 된다.
(3%) 브랜드의 새로운 이미지 창출에 관한 언급은 없음.

01 + 필자 주장 (24학년도 6월 모평 20번 | 정답률 83%) ④

구문분석 & 직독직해 교육 영역 간 창의성 개발의 최선책

[1]Certain hindrances (to multifaceted creative activity) / may lie / in premature specialization, /
S V
어떤 방해 요인은 (다면적인 창의적 활동의) / 있을 수 있다 / 너무 이른 전문화에 /

i.e., having to choose the direction of education / or to focus on developing one ability / too early / in life.
(= that is) to-v구 병렬
즉 교육 방향을 선택해야 하는 것 / 또는 한 가지 능력을 개발하는 데 집중해야 하는 것 / 너무 일찍 / 인생에서

↳ **대조 A(이른 전문화의 단점):** 다면적인 창의적 활동을 방해함.

한 영역에서의 창의적 능력 개발이 다른 영역 개발에도 도움이 됨.

[2]However, / development (of creative ability (in one domain)) / may enhance effectiveness / in *other domains* [that require similar skills], //
S_1 V_1 O 주격 관계대명사
그러나 / 개발은 (창의적 능력의 (한 영역에서의)) / 효과성을 높일 수도 있다 / 다른 영역에서 [비슷한 기술을 필요로 하는] //

and flexible switching (between generality and specificity) / is helpful to productivity / in many domains.
S_2 A와 B 사이의 V_2 C
그리고 유연한 전환은 (일반성과 특수성 사이의) / 생산성에 도움이 된다 / 많은 영역에서

↳ **대조 B(이른 전문화의 장점):** 비슷한 기술을 필요로 하는 영역의 효과성을 높이고, 일반성과 특수성 간의 유연한 전환은 생산성에 도움이 됨.

[3]Excessive specificity may result in / information from outside the domain being underestimated and unavailable, // which leads to fixedness (of thinking), //
S V 동명사 being의 의미상 주어 may result in의 O(동명사구) 관계대명사(앞 절 보충 설명)
지나친 특수성은 ~을 야기할 수도 있다 / 그 영역 외부로부터의 정보가 과소평가되고 이용할 수 없게 되는 것 // 그리고 이는 고착으로 이어진다 (사고의) //

whereas excessive generality causes chaos, vagueness, and shallowness.
부사절 접속사(대조) S′ V′ O′
반면 지나친 일반성은 혼돈, 모호함, 얕음을 초래한다

(= Excessive specificity and generality)
[4]Both tendencies pose a threat / to the transfer of knowledge and skills (between domains).
S V O
두 가지 경향(지나친 특수성과 일반성) 모두 위협을 가한다 / 지식과 기술의 전이에 (영역 간)

↳ **문제점:** 지나친 특수성은 사고의 고착을, 지나친 일반성은 혼돈, 모호함, 얕음을 초래해 영역 간 지식과 기술의 전이를 어렵게 함.

주제문 특정 영역에서의 창의적 도전을 지원하고 다른 영역 간 지식과 기술을 적용하도록 장려해야 함.

[5]What should therefore be optimal / for the development (of cross-domain creativity) /
S(명사절)
그러므로 최선인 것은 / 개발을 위해 (영역 간 창의성의) /

is support for young people / in taking up creative challenges / in a specific domain /
V(단수) C_1
젊은이들에 대한 지원이다 / 창의적인 도전을 시작하는 데 있어 / 특정한 영역에서 /

★<couple A with B>: A와 B를 결합시키다 ★<A as well as B>: B뿐만 아니라 A도
and coupling it / with *encouragement* (to apply knowledge and skills / in, as well as from, other domains, disciplines, and tasks).
C_2 (= support) in과 from의 공통 O
그리고 그것(지원)을 결합하는 것 / 장려와 (지식과 기술을 적용하도록 하는 / 다른 영역, 학문 분야, 과업으로부터뿐만 아니라 다른 영역, 학문 분야, 과업에도)

↳ **결론:** 영역 간 창의성 개발을 위해 특정 영역에서 창의적 도전을 하도록 지원하고, 다른 영역 간 지식과 기술을 적용하도록 장려해야 함.

해석

[1]다면적인 창의적 활동의 어떤 방해 요인은 너무 이른 전문화, 즉 인생에서 너무 일찍 교육 방향을 선택해야 하거나 한 가지 능력을 개발하는 데 집중해야 하는 것에 있을 수 있다. [2]그러나 한 영역에서의 창의적 능력의 개발은 비슷한 기술을 필요로 하는 다른 영역에서 효과성을 높일 수도 있으며, 일반성과 특수성 사이의 유연한 전환은 많은 영역에서 생산성에 도움이 된다. [3]지나친 특수성은 그 영역 외부로부터의 정보가 과소평가되고 이용할 수 없게 되는 것을 야기할 수도 있는데, 이는 사고의 고착으로 이어지는 반면, 지나친 일반성은 혼돈, 모호함, 얕음을 초래한다. [4]두 가지 경향 모두 영역 간 지식과 기술의 전이에 위협을 가한다. [5]그러므로 영역 간 창의성의 개발을 위해 최선인 것은 특정한 영역에서 창의적인 도전을 시작하는 데 있어 젊은이들에 대한 지원, 그리고 그것(지원)을 다른 영역, 학문 분야, 과업으로부터뿐만 아니라 다른 영역, 학문 분야, 과업에도 지식과 기술을 적용하도록 하는 장려와 결합하는 것이다.

어휘

hindrance 방해 (요인)
multifaceted 다면적인
premature 너무 이른, 시기상조의
specialization 전문화
domain 영역, 분야; 영토
flexible 유연한, 잘 구부러지는
switch 전환되다, 바뀌다
generality 일반성, 보편성
specificity 특수성, 전문성
productivity 생산성
excessive 지나친, 과도한
underestimate 과소평가하다
fixedness 고착, 고정
vagueness 모호함, 애매함
shallowness 얕음
pose a threat to A A에 위협을 가하다
transfer 전이, 이동
optimal 최선의, 최적의
take up ~을 시작하다; (시간·공간을) 차지하다
encouragement 장려, 격려
discipline (학문) 분야; 규율

정답 가이드

한 영역에서의 창의적 능력 개발은 비슷한 기술을 필요로 하는 다른 영역에서 효과성을 높이고 일반적인 능력과 특수한 능력 간의 전환은 많은 영역에서 생산성에 도움이 되므로, 영역 간 창의성 개발을 위해서는 특정 영역에서 창의적 능력을 함양하도록 지원하는 것과 더불어 그 능력을 영역 간 적용하도록 장려해야 한다고 했다. 따라서 필자가 주장하는 바로 가장 적절한 것은 ④ '특정 영역에서 개발된 창의성이 영역 간 활용되도록 장려해야 한다'이다.

오답 클리닉

① 창의성을 개발하기 위해서는 도전과 실패를 두려워하지 말아야(×) 한다. (3%)
창의성 개발을 위해 도전과 실패를 두려워하지 말라는 언급은 없음.
② 전문 지식과 기술을 전수하려면 집중적인 투자(×)가 선행되어야 한다. (2%)
지식과 기술의 전수가 아닌 영역 간 창의성 개발에 관한 내용이며, 투자에 대한 언급도 없음.
③ 창의적인 인재를 육성하기 위해 다양한 교육 과정(×)을 준비해야 한다. (8%)
창의성 개발을 위해 다양한 교육 과정이 필요하다는 내용이 아님.
⑤ 조기 교육을 통해 특정 분야의 전문가(×)를 지속적으로 양성해야 한다. (4%)
전문가 양성에 관한 내용이 아님.

02 + 글의 요지 (24학년도 9월 모평 22번 | 정답률 71%) ①

구문분석 & 직독직해

사회 이민자 문화의 인정과 수용의 필요성

[1] *The need* (to assimilate values and lifestyle (of the host culture)) / has become a growing conflict.
S V C
필요성은 (가치와 생활방식에 동화해야 할 (주류 문화의)) / 커지는 갈등이 되었다
↳ **도입:** 주류 문화에 동화해야 한다는 필요성이 갈등을 키움.

🗝 이민자의 문화 일부를 유지하는 부분 동화 모델이 있어야 함.
[2] Multiculturalists suggest // that there should be *a model of partial assimilation* [in which immigrants retain some (of their customs, beliefs, and language)].
S V (suggest의 O(명사절)) 명사절 접속사 V′ S′ 전치사+관계대명사
다문화주의자들은 제안한다 // 부분 동화 모델이 있어야 한다고 [이민자들이 일부를 유지하는 (자신의 관습, 신념, 언어 중)]
↳ 다문화주의자들은 이민자들의 문화 일부를 유지하는 부분 동화 모델을 제안함.

[3] There is *pressure* (to conform / rather than to maintain their cultural identities), / however, // and these conflicts are greatly determined / by *the community* [to which one migrates].
V_1 S_1 S_2 V_2 전치사+관계대명사
*<A rather than B>: B라기보다는 A
압력이 있다 (순응해야 한다는 / 그들의 문화적 정체성을 유지하기보다는) / 그러나 //
그리고 이러한 갈등은 크게 결정된다 / 공동체에 의해 [이민자가 이주해 온]
↳ **문제점:** 이민자들은 문화적 정체성을 유지하기보다 주류 문화에 순응하라는 압력을 받음.

[4] These experiences are not new; // many Europeans experienced exclusion and poverty / during the first two waves of immigration / in the 19th and 20th centuries.
S_1 V_1 C S_2 V_2 O
이러한 경험은 새로운 것이 아니다 // 많은 유럽인이 배제와 빈곤을 겪었다 /
첫 두 차례의 이민 물결 동안 / 19세기와 20세기에

[5] Eventually, / these immigrants transformed this country / with *significant changes* [that included enlightenment and acceptance of diversity].
S V O 주격 관계대명사
결국 / 이 이민자들은 이 나라를 탈바꿈시켰다 / 상당한 변화로 [계몽과 다양성 수용을 포함하는]

[6] People of color, / however, / continue to struggle for acceptance.
S V O
유색 인종들은 / 그러나 / 계속 수용을 위해 애쓰고 있다
↳ **예:** 과거 유럽 이민자들이 배제와 빈곤을 겪다 마침내 계몽과 다양성 수용을 이뤘지만, 유색 인종들은 여전히 받아들여지지 않고 있음.

주제문 🗝 이민자들의 다른 문화와 권리를 인정하는 것이 필요함.
[7] Once again, / the challenge is to recognize // that other cultures think and act differently / and that they have *the right* (to do so).
S V C (to recognize의 O_1(명사절)) (to recognize의 O_2(명사절))
다시 말해 / 문제는 인정하는 것이다 // 다른 문화는 다르게 생각하고 행동한다는 것을 /
그리고 그들은 권리가 있다는 것을 (그렇게 할)
↳ **해결책:** 다르게 생각하고 행동하는 이민자들의 문화와 권리를 인정해야 함.

해석

[1]주류 문화의 가치와 생활방식에 동화해야 할 필요성은 커지는 갈등이 되었다. [2]다문화주의자들은 이민자들이 자신의 관습, 신념, 언어 중 일부를 유지하는 부분 동화 모델이 있어야 한다고 제안한다. [3]그러나 그들의 문화적 정체성을 유지하기보다는 순응해야 한다는 압력이 있으며, 이러한 갈등은 이민자가 이주해 온 공동체에 의해 크게 결정된다. [4]이러한 경험은 새로운 것이 아닌데, 많은 유럽인이 19세기와 20세기에 첫 두 차례의 이민 물결 동안 배제와 빈곤을 겪었다. [5]결국 이 이민자들은 계몽과 다양성 수용을 포함하는 상당한 변화로 이 나라를 탈바꿈시켰다. [6]그러나 유색 인종들은 계속 수용을 위해 애쓰고 있다. [7]다시 말해, 문제는 다른 문화는 다르게 생각하고 행동하며 그들은 그렇게 할 권리가 있다는 것을 인정하는 것이다. [8]아마도, 그리 머지않은 미래에 이민자들이 우리 사이에서 더는 이방인이 아닐 것이다.

어휘

assimilate 동화하다, 같게 하다
cf. assimilation 동화
host 다수, 무리; 주인
multiculturalist 다문화주의자
partial 부분의, 부분적인
immigrant 이민자, 이주민
cf. immigration 이민, 이주
retain 유지[보유]하다
custom 관습, 풍습
conform 순응하다, 따르다
identity 정체성; 신원; 동일함
migrate 이주[이동]하다
exclusion 배제, 제외
poverty 빈곤, 가난
transform 탈바꿈시키다; 변형시키다
enlightenment 계몽; 깨달음
acceptance 수용, 받아들임

[8]Perhaps, / in the not too distant future, / immigrants will no longer be strangers / among us.
S V C
아마도 / 그리 머지않은 미래에 / 이민자들이 더는 이방인이 아닐 것이다 / 우리 사이에서
↳ **결과:** 이민자의 문화를 인정하고 수용하는 사회가 만들어질 것임.

diversity 다양성
person of color 유색 인종
stranger 이방인, 외국인; 낯선 사람

정답 가이드

이민자들이 이민해 온 나라의 문화(주류 문화)에 동화해야 하느냐의 문제로 갈등이 커지는 것에 대한 글이다. 이민자들의 문화를 일부 유지하는 부분 동화 모델이 있긴 하지만, 정체성 유지보다 순응을 요구하는 압력이 있으며, 이주해 온 '공동체'에 의해 갈등이 결정된다고 했다. 즉, 공동체는 이민자들의 문화와 그들이 이를 유지할 권리를 인정해야 한다는 것이다. 따라서, 글의 요지로 가장 적절한 것은 ① '이민자 고유의 정체성을 유지할 권리에 대한 공동체의 인식이 필요하다'이다.

오답 클리닉

② 이민자의 적응을 돕기 위해 그들의 요구를 반영한 정책 수립(×)이 중요하다.
(3%) 정책에 이민자들의 요구를 반영해야 한다는 내용은 언급되지 않음.

③ 이민자는 미래 사회의 긍정적 변화에 핵심적 역할을 수행(×)할 수 있다. (14%)
이민자들의 문화를 인정하고 수용하는 미래 사회의 모습을 긍정적 변화로 볼 수 있으나, 이민자들이 이에 핵심적 역할을 수행하는 것은 아님.

The 주의 문장 5의 유럽 이민자들이 나라를 탈바꿈시켰다는 내용은 이민자가 어려움을 겪다가 마침내 사회에 포용된 긍정적인 과거의 사례로 제시된 것임에 주의한다.

④ 다문화 사회의 안정을 위해서는 국제적 차원의 지속적인 협력(×)이 요구된다.
(2%) 다문화 사회 안정을 위한 국제적 차원의 협력은 언급되지 않음.

⑤ 문화적 동화는 장기적이고 체계적인 과정(×)을 통해 점진적으로 이루어진다.
(10%) 문화적 동화가 이루어지는 과정에 관한 내용이 아님.

03 글의 요지 (24학년도 6월 모평 22번 | 정답률 86%) ⑤

구문분석 & 직독직해

정보 인터넷 정보를 받아들이는 자세

[1]When it comes to the Internet, / it just pays / to be a little paranoid (but not a lot).
~에 관한 한 가주어 V 진주어(to-v구)
인터넷에 관한 한 / (~이) 정말 이득이 된다 / 약간 편집증적으로 되는 것이 (많이는 아니고)
↳ **도입:** 인터넷에 관한 한 약간 편집증적인 것이 이득이 됨.

주제문
[2]Given the level of anonymity (with *all* [that resides on the Internet]), /
전치사(~을 고려해 볼 때) 주격 관계대명사
익명성 수준을 고려해 볼 때 (모든 것의 [인터넷에 있는]) /
it's sensible / to question the validity (of *any data* [that you may receive]).
가주어 진주어(to-v구) 목적격 관계대명사
(~이) 합리적이다 / 타당성에 의문을 갖는 것이 (모든 자료의 [여러분이 받을지도 모르는])
↳ 인터넷의 익명성을 고려해 볼 때 자료의 타당성에 의문을 갖는 약간의 편집성은 이득이 됨.

인터넷 자료가 타당한지 의문을 제기하는 것은 합리적임.

[3]Typically / it's to our natural instinct // when we meet *someone* (coming down a sidewalk) /
가주어 전치사구 부사절 접속사(시간) S′ V′ O′ 현재분사구
to place yourself / in some manner of protective position, //
진주어(to-v구)
일반적으로 / (~은) 우리의 자연스러운 본능에 부합한다 // 우리가 누군가를 만날 때 (인도를 따라 내려오는) /
스스로를 두는 것은 / 어떤 방식의 방어적인 태도에 //
*동명사의 완료형 <having p.p.>는 소개하는(introduce) 시점보다 앞선 때를 나타냄.
especially when they introduce themselves / as having known you, / much to your surprise.
부사절 접속사(시간) S′ V′ O′ 전치사(~라고)
특히 그들이 자신을 소개할 때 / 여러분을 알고 있었다고 / 매우 놀랍게도
↳ **대조 A(현실 세계):** 우연히 누군가를 마주칠 때 우리는 본능적으로 방어적인 태도를 취함.

[4]By design, / we set up / *challenges* [in which the individual must validate how they know us /
S V O 전치사+관계대명사 S′ V′ O′(명사절)
계획적으로 / 우리는 마련한다 / 과제를 [그 사람이 우리를 어떻게 아는지를 입증해야만 하는 /
by presenting / scenarios, names or acquaintances, or *evidence* [by which to validate] / (that is, photographs)].
<by v-ing>: v함으로써 전치사+관계대명사
*<전치사+관계대명사+to-v>는 <to-v+전치사>보다 격식적인 표현임.
제시함으로써 / 시나리오, 이름이나 지인, 혹은 증거를 [입증할] / (말하자면, 사진)]

[5]Once we have received that information / and it has gone through a cognitive validation, //
부사절 접속사(일단 ~하면) S′1 V′1 O′1 (= that information) S′2 V′2 O′2
we accept that person / as more trustworthy.
S V O
일단 우리가 그 정보를 받으면 / 그리고 그것(그 정보)이 인지적 확인을 거치면 //
우리는 그 사람을 받아들인다 / 더 신뢰할 수 있다고

해석

[1]인터넷에 관한 한, (많이는 아니고) 약간 편집증적으로 되는 것이 정말 이득이 된다. [2]인터넷에 있는 모든 것의 익명성 수준을 고려해 볼 때, 여러분이 받을지도 모르는 모든 자료의 타당성에 의문을 갖는 것이 합리적이다. [3]일반적으로 우리가 인도를 따라 내려오는 누군가를 만날 때, 특히 매우 놀랍게도 그들이 여러분을 알고 있었다고 자신을 소개할 때, 스스로를 어떤 방식의 방어적인 태도에 두는 것은 우리의 자연스러운 본능에 부합한다. [4]계획적으로 우리는 시나리오, 이름이나 지인, 혹은 입증할 증거(말하자면, 사진)를 제시함으로써 그 사람이 우리를 어떻게 아는지를 입증해야만 하는 과제를 마련한다. [5]일단 우리가 그 정보를 받고 그것이 인지적 확인을 거치면, 우리는 그 사람을 더 신뢰할 수 있다고 받아들인다. [6]이 모든 것이 불과 몇 분 안에 일어나지만, 우리가 현실 세계에서 행하는 자연스러운 방어 기제이다. [7]하지만, 가상 세계에서 우리의 안녕에 물리적인 위협이 없는 것처럼 보이기 때문에 우리는 덜 방어적인 경향이 있다.

어휘

pay 이득이 되다; 지불하다
reside 있다, 존재하다; 거주하다
sensible 합리적인, 분별 있는
validity 타당성; 유효함
cf. validate 입증하다; 인증하다
cf. validation 확인
instinct 본능; 직감
to one's surprise 놀랍게도
by design 계획적으로, 고의로
set up ~을 마련하다; ~을 설치하다
acquaintance 지인, 아는 사람
cognitive 인지적인

[6] All this happens / in a matter of minutes / [but] is *a natural defense mechanism* [that we perform / in the real world].

S V1 V2 C 목적격 관계대명사

이 모든 것이 일어난다 / 불과 몇 분 안에 / 그러나 자연스러운 방어 기제이다 [우리가 행하는 / 현실 세계에서]

↳ **부연 설명:** 상대에게 우리가 아는 사이임을 입증할 정보를 요구하고 그 정보의 확인을 거쳐 신뢰하는 것은 자연스러운 방어 기제임.

[7] However, / in the virtual world, / we have a tendency (to be less defensive), //

S V O =

하지만 / 가상 세계에서 / 우리는 경향이 있다 (덜 방어적인) //

↱ 부사절 접속사(~ 때문에)

as there appears to be no physical threat / to our well-being.

V' C'

물리적인 위협이 없는 것처럼 보이기 때문에 / 우리의 안녕에

↳ **대조 B(가상 세계):** 가상 세계는 물리적인 위협이 없어 보이기 때문에 우리는 덜 방어적인 경향이 있음.

🔑 가상 세계에서 우리는 덜 방어적인 경향이 있음.

trustworthy 신뢰할 수 있는
a matter of 불과 ~, 겨우 ~
defense 방어
cf. defensive 방어적인
mechanism 기제, 구조
virtual 가상의; 사실상의
well-being 안녕, 행복, 복지

정답 가이드

첫 문장에서 인터넷에 관한 한 약간 편집증적으로 되는 것이 이득이 된다고 했고, 두 번째 문장에서 인터넷의 익명성을 고려해 볼 때 자료의 타당성에 (편집증적으로) 의문을 갖는 것이 합리적이라고 주장했다. 뒤에 이어지는 문장들은 이 주장을 뒷받침하는 논거이므로 세부 사항에 해당한다. 즉, 현실 세계와 가상 세계에서의 우리의 태도를 대조하며, 현실 세계와 달리 물리적 위협이 없는 것처럼 보이는 가상 세계에서는 우리가 덜 방어적인 경향이 있다고 지적한다. 따라서, 글의 요지로 가장 적절한 것은 주제문인 두 번째 문장을 간략히 표현한 ⑤ '방어 기제가 덜 작동하는 가상 세계에서는 신중한 정보 검증이 중요하다'이다.

오답 클리닉

① 가상 세계 특유의 익명성 때문에 표현의 자유가 남용(×)되기도 한다. (5%)
익명성으로 인해 표현의 자유가 남용된다는 문제점을 지적하는 내용이 아님.

② 인터넷 정보의 신뢰도를 검증하는 기술(×)은 점진적으로 향상되고 있다. (2%)
인터넷 정보의 신뢰도를 검증하는 기술은 언급되지 않음.

③ 가상 세계에서는 현실 세계와 달리 자유로운 정보 공유(×)가 가능하다. (6%)
가상 세계와 현실 세계는 우리의 방어적인 태도를 대조하기 위한 예임.

④ 안전한 인터넷 환경 구축(×)을 위해 보안 프로그램(×)을 설치하는 것이 좋다. (2%) 인터넷 보안 프로그램에 관한 내용이 아님.

01 + 글의 주제 〈24학년도 대수능 23번 | 정답률 55%〉 ②

구문분석 & 직독직해

환경 산림 자원의 시장 가치를 능가하는 비시장적 가치

[1]Managers (of natural resources) / typically face / *market incentives* [that provide financial rewards / for exploitation].
(S / V / O / 주격 관계대명사)
*<provide A for B>: B에 A를 제공하다

관리자는 (천연자원의) / 보통 직면한다 / 시장 유인에 [재정적 보상을 제공하는 / (천연자원) 이용에]
↳ **도입:** 천연자원 관리자는 천연자원 이용에 재정적 보상을 제공하는 시장 유인에 직면함.

*두 개의 to-v구가 <A rather than B(B라기보다는 A)>로 연결됨.

[2]For example, / owners of forest lands have / *a market incentive* (to cut down trees / rather than (to) manage the forest / for carbon capture, wildlife habitat, flood protection, and other ecosystem services).
(S / V / O)

예를 들어 / 산림 지대의 소유자는 가지고 있다 / 시장 유인을 (나무를 베어내는 / 숲을 관리하기보다는 / 탄소 포집, 야생 동물 서식지, 홍수 방어, 그리고 다른 생태계 도움을 위해)

→ (= Carbon ~ services)
[3]These services provide the owner with no financial benefits, / and thus are unlikely to influence management decisions.
(S / V_1 / O / V_2 / C / 형용사 unlikely 수식)

이러한 도움은 소유자에게 어떠한 재정적 이익도 제공하지 않는다 / 그러므로 관리 결정에 영향을 미칠 것 같지 않다
↳ **예:** 산림 소유자는 숲을 관리하기보다는 이용하는 데 시장 유인을 가지며, 재정적 이익을 제공하지 않는 생태계 도움은 숲을 관리하는 결정에 영향을 미치지 않음.

주제문 — 생태계 도움의 비시장적 가치가 벌목으로 얻는 경제적 가치보다 클 수 있음.

[4]But / *the economic benefits* (provided by these services), / based on their non-market values, / may exceed the economic value (of the timber).
(S / 과거분사구 / V / O)

그러나 / 경제적 이익은 (이러한 도움에 의해 제공되는) / 그것의 비시장적 가치에 기반하여 / 경제적 가치를 넘을 수도 있다 (목재의)
↳ 산림을 관리해서 얻는 생태계 도움의 이익이 벌목으로 얻는 이익을 능가할 수 있음.

[5]For example, / a United Nations initiative has estimated //
(S / V)
예를 들어 / 유엔의 한 계획은 추정했다 //

→ has estimated의 O(명사절) — 생태계 도움의 경제적 이익이 시장 이익보다 큼.

that the economic benefits (of *ecosystem services* (provided by tropical forests)), / (including climate regulation, water purification, and erosion prevention), / are over three times greater per hectare / than the market benefits.
(명사절 접속사 / S′ / 과거분사구 / 전치사구 삽입(ecosystem services 부연 설명) / V′ / C′)

경제적 이익이 (생태계 도움의 (열대림에 의해 제공되는)) / (기후 조절, 수질 정화, 그리고 침식 예방을 포함하여) / 헥타르당 3배보다 더 크다고 / 시장 이익보다
↳ **세부 사항(예):** 열대림이 제공하는 생태계 도움의 경제적 이익이 그것을 파괴해서 얻는 시장 이익보다 3배 더 큼.

[6]Thus / cutting down the trees is economically inefficient, // and markets are not sending / *the correct "signal"* (to favor ecosystem services / over extractive uses).
(S_1(동명사구) / V_1(단수) / C / S_2 / V_2 / O)

따라서 / 나무를 베는 것은 경제적으로 비효율적이다 // 그런데 시장은 보내지 않고 있다 / 올바른 '신호'를 (생태계 도움을 선호하는 / 추출하는 이용보다)
↳ **결론:** 벌목은 경제적으로 비효율적인데도 시장은 나무를 벌목하는 것보다 자원을 관리함으로써 얻는 도움을 선호하지 않음.

해석

[1]천연자원의 관리자는 보통 (천연자원) 이용에 재정적 보상을 제공하는 시장 유인에 직면한다. [2]예를 들어, 산림 지대의 소유자는 탄소 포집, 야생 동물 서식지, 홍수 방어, 그리고 다른 생태계 도움을 위해 숲을 관리하기보다는 나무를 베어 내는 시장 유인을 가지고 있다. [3]이러한 도움은 소유자에게 어떠한 재정적 이익도 제공하지 않으므로, 관리 결정에 영향을 미칠 것 같지 않다.(▶ 숲을 관리해서 얻는 여러 생태계 도움은 경제적 이익이 아니므로 숲 소유자가 하는 결정에 유인을 제공하지 않는다는 의미) [4]그러나 비시장적 가치에 기반하여 이러한 도움에 의해 제공되는 경제적 이익은 목재의 경제적 가치를 넘을 수도 있다. [5]예를 들어, 유엔의 한 계획은 기후 조절, 수질 정화, 그리고 침식 예방을 포함하여 열대림에 의해 제공되는 생태계 도움의 경제적 이익이 시장 이익보다 헥타르당 3배보다 더 크다고 추정했다. [6]따라서 나무를 베는 것은 경제적으로 비효율적인데, 시장은 (삼림을) 추출하는 이용보다 생태계 도움을 지지하는 올바른 '신호'를 보내지 않고 있다.

어휘

natural resource 천연자원
incentive 유인(책), 동기
carbon capture 탄소 포집 ((화석연료 사용 시 발생하는 이산화탄소를 모으는 기술))
habitat 서식지
be unlikely to-v v할 것 같지 않다
exceed 넘다, 초과하다
initiative 계획; 진취성; 주도(권)
estimate 추정(하다); 평가(하다)
purification 정화, 청소
erosion 침식, 부식
favor 선호하다; 지지하다; 호의; 부탁
extractive 추출하는, 뽑아내는
[선택지] significance 중요성, 의의; 의미
weigh (결정을 내리기 전에) 따져 보다; 무게가 ~이다
maximize 극대화하다
merit 장점; 가치

정답 가이드

도입부에서 천연 자원의 관리자가 직면하는 시장 유인을 언급한 뒤, 이어지는 예에서 산림 자원의 생태계 도움은 재정적 이익을 제공하지 않아 소유자는 숲을 관리하기보다 나무를 베어내는 시장 유인을 갖는다고 했다. 그러나(But) 비시장적 가치에 근거한 생태계 도움의 경제적 이익은 목재로 얻는 경제적 가치를 넘을 수도 있다고 하면서 열대림을 예로 들어 산림 자원을 보호해서 얻는 이익이 시장 이익보다 더 크다고 설명한다. 따라서 글의 주제로 가장 적절한 것은 ② 'significance of weighing forest resources' non-market values(산림 자원의 비시장적 가치를 따져 보는 것의 중요성)'이다.

오답 클리닉

① necessity of calculating the market values of ecosystem services (14%) 생태계 도움의 시장 가치(×) 산출의 필요성
비시장적 가치에 근거한 생태계 도움의 이익에 관한 내용이므로 틀림.

③ impact of using forest resources to maximize financial benefits (11%) 재정적 이익을 극대화(×)하기 위한 산림 자원 이용의 영향(×)
산림 자원 이용으로 인한 영향은 언급되지 않음.

④ merits of balancing forests' market and non-market values (8%) 숲의 시장 가치와 비시장 가치의 균형을 맞추는 장점(×)
숲의 비시장 가치가 시장 가치보다 크므로 보존해야 한다는 내용임.

⑤ ways of increasing the efficiency of managing natural resources (13%) 천연자원 관리의 효율성을 높이는 방법(×)
천연자원 관리의 효율성을 높이는 방법은 언급되지 않음.

02 + 글의 주제 〈24학년도 9월 모평 23번 | 정답률 61%〉 ⑤

구문분석 & 직독직해

방송 음악 라디오 방송의 곡 목록이 한정되는 이유

[1]The primary purpose (of commercial music radio broadcasting) / is to deliver an audience / to a group of advertisers and sponsors.
S V C

주된 목적은 (민영 음악 라디오 방송의) / 청취자를 인도하는 것이다 / 광고주와 후원 업체에

↳ **도입:** 민영 음악 라디오 방송은 청취자를 광고주와 후원 업체로 끌어들이는 것을 목표로 함.

🔑 상업적 성공을 위해서는 청취자가 많아야 함.

[2]To achieve commercial success, / that audience must be as large as possible.
목적(~하기 위해) S V C ★<as ~ as possible>: 가능한 한 ~한/하게

상업적 성공을 달성하기 위해 / 그 청취자는 가능한 한 많아야 한다

[3]More than any other characteristics (such as demographic or psychographic profile, purchasing power, level of interest, degree of satisfaction, quality of attention or emotional state), /
<비교급 than any other ~>: 다른 어떤 ~보다도 더 …한

다른 어떤 특성보다도 (인구 통계학적 또는 심리 통계학적 개요, 구매력, 관심 수준, 만족도, 주의 집중의 질 또는 정서 상태와 같은) /

the quantity (of *an audience* (aggregated as a mass)) / is the most significant metric / for *broadcasters* (seeking to make music radio / for profitable ends).
S 과거분사구 V C
★<seek to-v>: v하려고 하다 현재분사구

양은 (청취자의 (집단으로 모인)) / 가장 중요한 측정 기준이다 / 방송 제작자에게 (음악 라디오를 만들려고 하는 / 수익 목적을 위해)

↳ **원인 1:** 상업적 성공을 달성하려면 청취자가 많아야 하므로 청취자 집단의 규모는 가장 중요함.

🔑 청취자를 늘리려고 인기 있거나 청취자가 이탈하지 않을 것 같은 음악을 틀어줌.

[4]As a result, / broadcasters attempt to maximise their audience size /
S V O

결과적으로 / 방송 제작자는 청취자의 규모를 극대화하려고 한다 /

by playing *music* [that is popular], / or — at the very least — / *music* [that can be relied upon / not to cause audiences to switch off their radio [or] (to) change the station].
<by v-ing>: v함으로써 주격 관계대명사 ★<cause+O+to-v>: O가 v하게 하다 주격 관계대명사
V' O' C'(to-v구 병렬)

음악을 틀어줌으로써 [인기 있는] / 또는 적어도 / 음악을 [믿어질 수 있는 / 청취자가 라디오를 끄거나 방송 주파수를 바꾸게 하지 않을 것이라고]

↳ **결과 1:** 인기 있거나 청취자가 이탈하지 않을 것 같은 음악만 틀어서 청취자를 늘리려 함.

★<if not>: ~까지는 아니더라도

[5]Audience retention is a key value / (if not the key value) / for many music programmers [and] for radio station management.
S V C 삽입절 전치사구 병렬

청취자 유지는 하나의 핵심 가치이다 / (유일한 핵심 가치까지는 아니더라도) / 많은 음악 프로 제작자와 라디오 방송국 경영진에게

↳ **원인 2:** 청취자를 유지하는 것이 하나의 핵심 가치임.

해석

[1]민영 음악 라디오 방송의 주된 목적은 청취자를 광고주와 후원 업체에 인도하는 것이다. [2]상업적 성공을 달성하기 위해, 그 청취자는 가능한 한 많아야 한다. [3](인구 통계학적 또는 심리 통계학적 개요, 구매력, 관심 수준, 만족도, 주의 집중의 질 또는 정서 상태와 같은) 다른 어떤 특성보다도, 집단으로 모인 청취자의 양은 수익 목적을 위해 음악 라디오를 만들려고 하는 방송 제작자에게 가장 중요한 측정 기준이다. [4]결과적으로 방송 제작자는 인기 있는 음악, 또는 적어도 청취자가 라디오를 끄거나 방송 주파수를 바꾸게 하지 않을 것이라고 믿어질 수 있는 음악을 틀어줌으로써 청취자의 규모를 극대화하려고 한다. [5]청취자 유지는 많은 음악 프로 제작자와 라디오 방송국 경영진에게 (유일한 핵심 가치까지는 아니더라도) 하나의 핵심 가치이다. [6]그 결과 위험을 싫어하는 것의 높은 정도는 흔히 '성공한' 라디오 음악 프로 제작자를 나타낸다. [7]곡 목록은 한정되고 흔히 매우 적다.

어휘

primary 주된, 주요한
commercial 민영의, 민간의; 상업적인
broadcasting (라디오·TV의) 방송
cf. broadcaster 방송 제작자, 방송사[국]
deliver 인도하다; 배달하다; (연설·강연 등을) 하다
sponsor 후원 업체[광고주]; 후원자
demographic 인구 통계학적인
profile 개요; (얼굴의) 옆모습
mass 집단; (큰) 덩어리; 대량의
metric 측정 기준; 미터(법)의
profitable 수익성이 있는; 유익한
at the (very) least 적어도, 최소한
rely upon ~을 믿다; ~에 의지하다
station 방송 주파수; 방송국; (철도의) 역

🗝 성공한 라디오 제작자는 위험을 싫어하는 특징이 있음.

[6]In consequence, / a high degree (of risk aversion) / frequently marks out the 'successful' radio music programmer.
S V O
그 결과 / 높은 정도는 (위험을 싫어하는 것의) / 흔히 '성공한' 라디오 음악 프로 제작자를 나타낸다

[7]Playlists are restricted, and often very small. 🗝 곡 목록이 한정되고 적어짐.
S V C1 C2
곡 목록은 한정되고 흔히 매우 적다

↳ **결과 2:** 청취자 유지를 위해 위험을 싫어하게 되고 곡 목록은 한정되고 적어짐.

retention 유지, 보유
in consequence 그 결과(로서)
mark out ~을 나타내다[표시하다]
restrict 한정[제한]하다
[선택지] feature 특징; 특별히 포함하다
appeal 관심을 끌다; 호소(하다)
outcome 결과

정답 가이드

민영 음악 라디오 방송이 상업적 성공을 달성하려면 가능한 한 많은 청취자를 끌어들여야 한다고 하면서 결과적으로(As a result) 청취자 규모를 극대화할 수 있는 음악만 튼다고 했다. 또한 확보한 청취자를 유지하는 것이 핵심 가치여서 그 결과(In consequence) 음악 프로 제작자는 위험을 싫어하게 되고 곡 목록은 한정된다고 했다. 따라서 글의 주제로 가장 적절한 것은 ⑤ 'outcome of music radio businesses' attempts to attract large audiences(음악 라디오 사업의 대규모 청취자를 끌어들이려는 시도의 결과)'이다.

오답 클리닉

① features of music playlists appealing to international audiences (4%) 국제적 청취자(×)의 관심을 끄는 곡 목록의 특징
국제적 청취자가 좋아하는 곡 목록에 대한 글이 아님.

② influence of advertisers on radio audiences' musical preferences (13%) 라디오 청취자의 음악적 선호에 광고주가 미치는 영향(×)
광고주가 라디오 청취자의 음악적 선호에 영향을 미친다는 내용이 아님. 청취자를 끌어들이기 위해 라디오 방송이 청취자가 좋아할 만한 음악만 튼다는 내용임.

③ difficulties of increasing audience size in radio music programmes (10%) 라디오 음악 프로그램에서 청취자 규모를 늘리는 것의 어려움(×)
라디오 청취자 규모를 늘리는 것이 어렵다는 언급은 없음.

④ necessity of satisfying listeners' diverse needs in the radio business (12%) 라디오 사업에서 청취자의 다양한 요구(×)를 충족시킬 필요성
청취자의 다양한 요구에 관한 내용이 아님. 대중적인 선호에 의해 오히려 곡 목록이 한정된다고 했음.

03 + 글의 주제 〈24학년도 6월 모평 23번 | 정답률 55%〉 ④

구문분석 & 직독직해

비즈니스 박물관의 이윤 지향에 따른 결과

[1]There are *pressures* (*within* the museum) [that cause it to emphasise // what happens in the galleries / over *the activities* [that take place / in its unseen zones]].
V S 주격 관계대명사 V′ O′(the museum =) C′ (to emphasise의 O(명사절)) 주격 관계대명사
압력이 있다 (박물관 '내부의') [그것(박물관)이 강조하게 하는 // 전시관에서 일어나는 일을 / 활동보다 [일어나는 / 그것의 보이지 않는 구역에서]]

↳ **문제점:** 박물관 내부에는 눈에 보이지 않는 공간보다 눈에 보이는 공간에서 일어나는 일을 강조하는 압력이 있음.

★<force+O+to-v(O가 v하도록 강요하다)>의 수동형

[2]In *an era* [when museums are forced to increase their earnings], /
관계부사 S′ V′ C′
시대에 [박물관이 수입을 늘리도록 강요당하는] /
🗝 수입을 늘리기 위해 전시관을 현대화하거나 임시 전시회를 여는 데 집중함.

they often focus their energies / on modernising their galleries / or mounting temporary exhibitions / to bring more and more audiences / through the door.
S(= museums) V O ★<비교급 and 비교급>: 점점 더 ~ on의 O(동명사구 병렬) 목적(~하기 위해)
그것들(박물관)은 흔히 자신들의 에너지를 집중시킨다 / 그것의 전시관을 현대화하는 데 / 또는 임시 전시회를 시작하는 데 / 점점 더 많은 관람객을 데려오기 위해 / 문을 통해

[3]In other words, / as museums struggle to survive / in a competitive economy, //
부사절 접속사(~할 때) S′ V′ 목적(~하려고)
다시 말해서 / 박물관이 살아남으려고 고군분투할 때 / 경쟁 경제에서 //

their budgets often prioritise / *those parts of themselves* [that are consumable]: / infotainment (in the galleries), / goods and services (in the cafes and the shops).
S V O 주격 관계대명사 =
그것의 예산은 종종 우선시한다 / 그것들 자체의 부분들을 [소비할 수 있는] / 즉 인포테인먼트 (전시관의) / 상품과 서비스 (카페와 상점의)

↳ **원인:** 박물관은 수입을 늘리기 위해 관람객이 둘러보고 소비하는 부분들에 에너지와 예산을 쏟음.

해석

[1]박물관의 보이지 않는 구역에서 일어나는 활동보다 전시관에서 일어나는 일을 강조하게 하는 박물관 '내부의' 압력이 있다.(▶ 관람객들이 둘러보는 전시 공간만 신경 쓴다는 의미) [2]박물관이 수입을 늘리도록 강요당하는 시대에, 그것들(박물관)은 점점 더 많은 관람객을 문을 통해 데려오기 위해 전시관을 현대화하거나 임시 전시회를 시작하는 데 흔히 자신들의 에너지를 집중시킨다. [3]다시 말해서, 박물관이 경쟁 경제에서 살아남으려고 고군분투할 때, 그것의 예산은 종종 소비할 수 있는 박물관 자체의 부분들, 즉 전시관의 인포테인먼트, 카페와 상점의 상품과 서비스를 우선시한다. [4]불이 켜져 있지 않고 매력이 없는 저장실(▶ 첫 문장에 언급된 '보이지 않는 구역'의 구체적인 예)은, 그것들이 논의된다고 해도, 기껏해야 전시장에 둘 물품을 처리하는 서비스 공간으로 제시된다. [5]그리고 최악의 경우 박물관이 공개적으로 보이는 겉면에 점점 더 많은 자원을 쏟을수록, 저장 공간의 현대화가 계속 보류되거나 확장되는 소장품을 보관하고 그것들의 복잡한 보존 요구를 충족시킬 공간이 점점 더 적게 주어짐으로 인해 저장 공간은 심지어 더 나빠질지도 모른다.

[4]The unlit, unglamorous storerooms, / (if they are ever discussed), / are at best presented /
S 부사절 삽입 V
as *service areas* [that process objects (for the exhibition halls)].
전치사(~로(서)) 주격 관계대명사
불이 켜져 있지 않고 매력이 없는 저장실은 / (그것들이 논의된다고 해도) / 기껏해야 제시된다 /
서비스 공간으로 [물품을 처리하는 (전시장에 둘)]
↳ **결과 1:** 저장실(눈에 보이지 않는 구역)은 전시품을 처리하는 공간 정도로만 활용됨.

[5]And at worst, / as museums pour more and more resources / into their publicly visible faces, //
부사절 접속사(~할수록) S' V' O'
the spaces (of storage) / may even suffer, / 저장실의 현대화가 보류되고 공간이 부족해지면서 저장 공간은 더 나빠짐.
S V
그리고 최악의 경우 / 박물관이 점점 더 많은 자원을 쏟을수록 / 공개적으로 보이는 겉면에 //
공간은 (저장의) / 심지어 더 나빠질지도 모른다 /
*첫 번째 분사의 의미상 주어는 문장의 주어(the spaces of storage)와 달라 분사 앞에 명시하였고, 두 번째 분사의 의미상 주어는 문장의 주어와 같아 생략됨.
their modernisation being kept on hold / [or] being given / less and less *space* (to house the expanding collections / [and] (to) serve their complex conservation needs).
분사구문(= because their modernisation is kept ~) (= because they are given ~)

그것들(저장 공간)의 현대화가 계속 보류됨으로 인해 / 또는 주어짐으로 인해 / 점점 더 적은 공간이 (확장되는 소장품을 보관할 / 그리고 그것들의 복잡한 보존 요구를 충족시킬)
↳ **결과 2:** 저장실의 현대화는 계속 보류되고, 늘어나는 소장품을 보관하고 보존할 공간은 줄어들어 저장 공간의 상황이 더 나빠질 수 있음.

어휘

emphasise[emphasize] 강조하다
earnings 수입, 소득
modernise[modernize] 현대화하다
cf. modernisation[modernization] 현대화
mount 시작하다; (산 등에) 오르다
prioritise[prioritize] 우선시하다; 우선 순위를 매기다
consumable 소비할 수 있는
unlit 불이 켜져 있지 않은
unglamorous 매력이 없는
at best 기껏해야, 잘해야 (↔ at worst 최악의 경우에)
publicly 공개적으로
cf. public 공공의
face 겉면, 표면
suffer 더 나빠지다; 시달리다, 고통받다
on hold 보류된[연기된]
house 보관하다
conservation 보존; 보호
[선택지] -oriented ~지향의
management 경영, 관리
commitment 헌신, 전념; 약속
⊕인포테인먼트(infotainment): 정보(information)와 오락(entertainment)의 합성어로, 정보와 오락을 함께 제공하는 프로그램을 지칭함.

정답 가이드

첫 문장에서 박물관이 보이지 않는 구역보다 보이는 구역인 전시관에서 일어나는 활동을 강조한다는 문제를 제기한 후, 수입을 늘리기 위해 관람객이 둘러보는 부분들(전시관, 임시 전시회)과 소비하는 부분들(인포테인먼트, 상품, 서비스)에 에너지와 예산을 쏟는 박물관의 행태를 설명한다. 그로 인해 눈에 보이지 않는 저장 공간의 현대화는 보류되고 공간도 줄어들어 저장 공간의 여건은 더 나빠질 수 있다는 결과를 서술하고 있으므로, 글의 주제로 가장 적절한 것은 ④ 'consequences of profit-oriented management of museums(박물관의 이윤 지향 경영의 결과)'이다. 주제문은 명시되어 있지 않지만, 이윤 지향 경영의 부정적인 결과를 서술하면서, '박물관의 이윤 지향적인 경영은 바람직하지 못하다'고 주장하고 있다.

오답 클리닉

① importance of prioritising museums' exhibition spaces (18%)
박물관 전시 공간을 우선시하는 것의 중요성(×)
이윤 추구를 위해 전시 공간에 에너지를 집중했다는 내용은 있지만, 그것을 바람직하게 여기는 내용이 아님.
② benefits of diverse activities in museums for audiences (7%)
관람객을 위한 박물관에서의 다양한 활동의 이점(×)
박물관에서의 다양한 활동의 이점을 설명하는 내용이 아님.
③ necessity of expanding storerooms for displaying objects (14%)
물품 전시를 위해 저장실을 확장할 필요성(×)
저장 공간이 점점 더 적게 주어진다는 결과를 언급했을 뿐, 그것을 확장해야 할 필요성에 대한 언급은 없음.
⑤ ways to increase museums' commitment to the public good (5%)
공공의 이익(×)에 대한 박물관의 헌신(×)을 늘리는 방법
박물관이 공공의 이익을 위해 헌신한다는 내용이 아님.

01 + 글의 주제 (23학년도 대수능 23번 | 정답률 68%) ②

구문분석 & 직독직해 경제 정보 공개의 이점

주제문

[1]An important advantage (of disclosure), / (as opposed to more aggressive forms of regulation), / is its flexibility and respect (for the operation of free markets). 정보 공개의 이점 1: 자유 시장의 유연성과 존중

S 삽입어구 V C

중요한 이점은 (공개의) / (더 공격적인 형태인 규제와는 대조적으로) / 유연성과 존중이다 (자유 시장의 작용에 대한)

↳ 공개의 이점은 유연성과 자유 시장에 대한 존중임

[2]Regulatory mandates are blunt swords; // they tend to neglect diversity / and may have serious unintended adverse effects.

S1 V1 C S2 V2-1 V2-2 O

규제하는 명령은 무딘 칼이다 // 그것은 다양성을 무시하는 경향이 있다 / 그리고 의도하지 않은 심각한 역효과가 있을 수도 있다

↳ **대조 A:** 규제하는 명령은 문제를 초래할 수 있음.

[3]For example, / energy efficiency requirements (for appliances) / may produce *goods* [that work less well / or that have *characteristics* [that consumers do not want]].

S V O 주격 관계대명사 주격 관계대명사 목적격 관계대명사 S′ V′

예를 들어 / 에너지 효율 요건은 (가전제품에 대한) / 제품을 만들어 낼 수도 있다 [덜 잘 작동하는 / 또는 특성을 가진 [소비자가 원하지 않는]]

↳ **예:** 에너지 효율 규제가 상품의 질을 낮추거나 소비자의 선택권을 줄임.

[4]Information provision, / by contrast, / respects freedom of choice. 정보 공개의 이점 2: 선택의 자유 존중

S V O

정보 제공은 / 반대로 / 선택의 자유를 존중한다

↳ **대조 B:** 정보 공개는 선택의 자유를 존중함.

[5]If automobile manufacturers are required / to measure and publicize the safety characteristics of cars, // potential car purchasers can trade safety concerns (against other attributes, (such as price and styling)).

부사절 접속사(조건) S′ V′ C′ S V O

자동차 제조업체가 요구받는다면 / 자동차의 안전 특성을 측정하고 공개하도록 //
잠재적인 자동차 구매자는 안전상의 우려를 맞바꿀 수 있다 (다른 특성과 비교하여 (가격과 스타일 같은))

↳ **예 1:** 정보(자동차 안전성) 공개가 소비자에게 선택 자율성을 줌.

[6]If restaurant customers are informed of the calories (in their meals), // *those* [who want to lose weight] / can make use of the information, / leaving / *those* [who are unconcerned about calories] unaffected.

부사절 접속사(조건) S′ V′ ★<leave+O+C>: O를 C한 상태로 두다 S 주격 관계대명사 V O 분사구문 (= as this leaves ~) 주격 관계대명사

식당 손님들이 칼로리를 알게 되면 (그들의 식사에 들어 있는) // 사람들은 [살을 빼고 싶은] /
그 정보를 이용할 수 있다 / 두면서 / 사람들은 [칼로리에 신경 쓰지 않는] 영향을 받지 않은 채로

↳ **예 2:** 정보(음식 칼로리) 공개가 정보를 원하는 소비자의 의사 결정에 도움을 줌.

[7]Disclosure does not interfere with, / and should even promote, / the autonomy (and quality) (of individual decision-making). 정보 공개의 이점 3: 개인 의사 결정의 자율성과 품질 촉진

S V O

공개는 방해하지 않는다 / 그리고 심지어 촉진할 것이다 / 자율성 (및 품질)을 (개인 의사 결정의)

↳ **결론:** 공개는 의사 결정의 자율성과 질을 높임.

해석

[1]더 공격적인 형태인 규제와는 대조적으로, 공개의 중요한 이점은 자유 시장의 작용에 대한 유연성과 존중이다. [2]규제하는 명령은 무딘 칼인데, 그것은 다양성을 무시하는 경향이 있으며, 의도하지 않은 심각한 역효과가 있을 수도 있다.(▶ 규제 명령을 무딘 칼에 비유해 효율이 없음을 의미) [3]예를 들어, 가전제품에 대한 에너지 효율 요건은 덜 잘 작동하거나 소비자가 원하지 않는 특성을 가진 제품을 만들어 낼 수도 있다. [4]반대로 정보 제공은 선택의 자유를 존중한다. [5]자동차 제조업체가 자동차의 안전 특성을 측정하고 공개하도록 요구받는다면, 잠재적인 자동차 구매자는 가격과 스타일 같은 다른 특성과 비교하여 안전상의 우려를 맞바꿀 수 있다. [6]식당 손님들이 그들의 식사에 들어 있는 칼로리를 알게 되면, 칼로리에 신경 쓰지 않는 사람들은 영향을 받지 않은 채로 두면서 살을 빼고 싶은 사람들은 그 정보를 이용할 수 있다. [7]공개는 개인 의사 결정의 자율성 (및 품질)을 방해하지 않으며 심지어 촉진할 것이다.

어휘

disclosure (정보) 공개; 폭로, 드러냄
as opposed to A A와는 대조적으로
aggressive 공격적인
regulation 규제
cf. regulatory 규제하는
flexibility 유연성
operation 작용; 수술; 작동
blunt 무딘, 뭉툭한; 퉁명스러운
diversity 다양성
cf. diversified 다양한, 변화가 많은
unintended 의도하지 않은
efficiency 효율(성); 능률
requirement 요건, 필요(한 것)
appliance 가전제품
manufacturer 제조업체, 생산자[사]
publicize (일반 사람들에게) 알리다, 홍보하다
attribute 특성, 속성
interfere with ~을 방해하다
[선택지] accessible 이용[접근] 가능한
reasonable 합리적인

⊕ 자유 시장(free market): 정부의 규제를 받지 않는, 개인의 경제 활동 자유가 최대한으로 보장된 시장을 말함. 자유 시장에서 가격은 시장의 수요와 공급에 의해 결정됨.

정답 가이드

규제와 반대로 공개가 이점이 있다고 한 뒤 이에 대한 부연 설명으로 규제와 정보 공개를 대조하는 글이다. 규제가 다양성을 무시하고 상품의 질을 떨어뜨릴 수 있는 반면, 정보 제공('공개(disclosure)'를 말바꿈한 표현)은 자유 시장에서 소비자의 선택의 질과 자율성을 높인다고 했다. 긍정적으로 서술하고 있는 '정보 제공', 즉 '공개'의 이점을 글의 주제로 보아야 하므로, 글의 주제로 가장 적절한 것은 ② 'benefits of publicizing information to ensure free choices(자유로운 선택을 보장하기 위해 정보를 알리는 것의 이점)'이다.

The 핵심 A와 B를 대조하는 구조에서 어느 하나에 초점을 둘 때 보통 뒤에 언급하는 B를 긍정적으로 중점을 두어 서술하는 경우가 많다.

오답 클리닉

① steps to make public information accessible to customers (6%)
고객이 공공 정보를 이용할 수 있게 하는 절차(x)
고객이 정보를 이용하는 것의 이점과 예시는 나와 있지만 그 절차에 대한 내용은 없음.

③ strategies for companies to increase profits in a free market (8%)
기업들이 자유 시장에서 이윤을 늘리는 전략들(x)
자유 시장에서 기업들이 어떻게 하면 이윤을 늘릴 수 있는지에 대한 내용은 없음.

④ necessities of identifying and analyzing current industry trends (4%) 현재 산업 동향(x)을 파악하고 분석할 필요성
산업 동향을 파악하고 분석하는 것이 필요하다는 내용이 아님.

⑤ effects of diversified markets on reasonable customer choices (13%) 다양화된 시장(x)이 합리적인 고객 선택에 미치는 영향
다양화된 시장이 아니라 정보 공개가 고객의 선택에 영향을 미침.

The 주의 지문에 언급된 diversity, market, customer, choice를 활용한 오답이다. 문장 2의 규제가 다양성을 무시하는 경향이 있다는 내용에서 정보 공개는 다양성을 존중한다고 유추할 수 있으나 고객의 선택에 영향을 미치는 것은 다양한 선택지가 아닌 공개된 정보임에 유의해야 한다.

02 + 글의 주제 (23학년도 9월 모평 23번 | 정답률 73%) ①

구문분석 & 직독직해

농업 농부가 사용하는 경험적 관찰의 한계

*<base A on B>: A의 근거를 B에 두다

[1]Environmental learning occurs // when farmers base decisions / on observations (of "payoff" information).
(S: Environmental learning / V: occurs / 부사절 접속사: when / S′: farmers / V′: base / O′: decisions)
환경적 학습이 일어난다 // 농부들이 결정의 근거를 둘 때 / 관찰에 ('이익이 되는' 정보에 관한)
↳ 도입: 농부들은 이익이 되는 정보를 관찰해서 결정함.

[2]They may observe their own or neighbors' farms, //
(S_1(= farmers) / V_1 / O)
그들(농부들)은 자신들의 혹은 이웃의 농장을 관찰할 수도 있다 //
*<It is ~ that ...> 강조구문에서 that이 생략되었으며, 목적어인 the empirical results가 강조됨.
but it is the empirical results // (that) they are using / as a guide, / not the neighbors themselves.
(강조구문 / S'_2 / V'_2 / 전치사(~로(서)))
하지만 바로 경험적 결과이다 // 그들이 사용하고 있는 것은 / 지침으로 / 이웃 자체가 아니라
↳ 방법: 농부들은 본인의 경험적 결과를 지침으로 활용함.

*<such A as B> = <A such as B(B와 같은 A)>
[3]They are looking at farming activities / as experiments / and assessing such factors (as relative advantage, compatibility with existing resources, difficulty of use, and "trialability") — // how well can it be experimented with.
(S / V_1 / O_1 / V_2 / O_2)
*trialability(시험 가능성)가 무엇인지 대시(—) 뒤에서 설명함.
그들은 농업 활동을 보고 있다 / 실험으로 / 그리고 요인을 평가하고 있다 (상대적 이점, 기존 자원과의 양립성, 사용의 어려움, 그리고 '시험 가능성'과 같은) // 즉 그것이 얼마나 잘 실험될 수 있는가를
↳ 경험적 결과의 부연 설명: 농부들은 농업 활동을 실험으로 보고 얼마나 잘 실험될 수 있는지 평가함.

주제문
[4]But / that criterion of "trialability" / turns out to be a real problem; //
(S_1 / V_1 / C_1)
하지만 / 그 '시험 가능성'의 기준이 / 정말 문제인 것으로 밝혀진다 //
↱ 명사절 접속사
it's true // that farmers are always experimenting, // but working farms are very flawed laboratories.
(가주어 V_2 C_2 / 진주어(명사절) / S_3 / V_3 / C_3)
⊶ 경험적 관찰 방식에 문제가 있음이 드러남.
(~은) 사실이다 // 농부들이 항상 실험하는 것은 // 하지만 작업을 하는 농장은 매우 결함이 있는 실험실이다
↳ 문제점: 작업하는 농장은 실험을 하기에 결함이 있음.

[5]Farmers cannot set up the controlled conditions (of professional test plots (in research facilities)).
(S / V / O)
농부들은 통제된 조건을 마련할 수 없다 (전문적인 실험용 토지의 (연구 시설에 있는))
↳ 결함 1: 통제된 실험이 아님.

해석

[1]농부들이 결정의 근거를 '이익이 되는' 정보에 관한 관찰에 둘 때 환경적 학습이 일어난다. [2]그들은 자신들의 혹은 이웃의 농장을 관찰할 수도 있지만, 그들이 지침으로 사용하고 있는 것은 이웃 자체가 아니라 바로 경험적 결과이다. [3]그들은 농업 활동을 실험으로 보고 상대적 이점, 기존 자원과의 양립성, 사용의 어려움, 그리고 '시험 가능성', 즉 그것이 얼마나 잘 실험될 수 있는가와 같은 요인을 평가하고 있다. [4]하지만 그 '시험 가능성'의 기준이 정말 문제인 것으로 밝혀지는데, 농부들이 항상 실험하는 것은 사실이지만, 작업을 하는 농장은 매우 결함이 있는 실험실이다. [5]농부들은 연구 시설에 있는 전문적인 실험용 토지의 통제된 조건을 마련할 수 없다. [6]또한 통제된 실험을 할 수 있다고 하더라도, 농부들은 관리하기 힘들 복잡하고 관찰하기 어려운 현상에 자주 직면한다. [7]게다가 농부들은 자신이 사용할 수 있는 몇 가지 생산 방법을 넘어서는 것에 대한 이익이 되는 정보를 거의 얻을 수 없고, 이는 '상대적 이점'의 기준을 측정하기 어렵게 만든다.

어휘

payoff 이익, 보상
assess 평가하다; 재다, 가늠하다
relative 상대적인; 친척
existing 기존의, 현재 사용되는
trialability 시험 가능성
turn out ~인 것으로 밝혀지다; 모습을 드러내다
flawed 결함이 있는, 흠이 있는
laboratory 실험실
plot 작은 토지, 터; 구성, 줄거리
facility 시설; 편의; 용이함
confront 직면하다; 맞서다

[6]Farmers also often confront / *complex and difficult-to-observe phenomena* [that would be hard to manage] // even if they could run controlled experiments.

S ↱ 형용사 hard 수식 / V / O / 주격 관계대명사 / 부사절 접속사(양보) S′ / V′ / O′

농부들은 또한 자주 직면한다 / 복잡하고 관찰하기 어려운 현상에 [관리하기 힘든] // 그들이 통제된 실험을 할 수 있다고 하더라도

↳ **결함 2:** 통제된 실험이라 하더라도 관리하기 힘든 현상들이 발생함.

[7]Moreover / farmers can rarely acquire / payoff information (on more than *a few of the production methods* [(which[that]) they might use]), //

S / V / O / 목적격 관계대명사 생략

게다가 / 농부들은 거의 얻을 수 없다 / 이익이 되는 정보를 (몇 가지 생산 방법을 넘어서는 것에 대한 [자신이 사용할 수 있는]) //

↱ 관계대명사(앞 절 보충 설명)

which makes the criterion of "relative advantage" hard to measure.

V′ / O′ / C′ 형용사 hard 수식

그리고 이것은 '상대적 이점'의 기준을 측정하기 어렵게 만든다

↳ **결함 3:** 농부가 얻을 수 있는 이익 정보가 한정적임.

phenomenon (*pl.* phenomena) 현상
rarely 거의 ~않는
[선택지] limitation 한계; 제한
modernize 현대화하다
equipment 장비, 용품
prioritize 우선시키다
agricultural 농업의
cf. agriculture 농업
innovation 혁신
instinctive 본능적인
unpredictable 예측할 수 없는

정답 가이드

농부는 관찰, 즉 경험적 결과를 통해 어떤 농업 활동이 이익을 가져다줄지를 학습하는데, 농부가 경험적 결과를 얻기 위해 농업 활동을 실험하는 농장은 매우 결함이 있는 실험실이어서 여러 한계(통제된 실험 조건을 마련할 수 없음, 관리하기 힘든 현상에 마주하게 됨, 얻을 수 있는 이익 정보가 한정적이어서 상대적 이점을 측정하기 어려움)가 있음을 서술하고 있다. 따라서 글의 주제로 가장 적절한 것은 ① 'limitations of using empirical observations in farming(농업에서 경험적 관찰을 사용하는 것의 한계)'이다.

오답 클리닉

② challenges in modernizing traditional farming equipment (4%)
기존 농업 장비를 현대화하는 데(×) 있어서의 난제
농업 장비의 현대화에 대한 언급은 없음.

③ necessity of prioritizing trialability in agricultural innovation (9%)
농업 혁신(×)에서 시험 가능성을 우선시켜(×)야 할 필요성
trialability를 활용한 오답. 농업 혁신에 대한 언급은 없으며 시험 가능성을 우선시키는 것이 아니라 그 기준에 문제가 있다는 내용임.

④ importance of making instinctive decisions in agriculture (8%)
농업에서 본능적 결정(×)을 하는 것의 중요성
본능적 결정이 아닌 경험적 관찰의 한계에 대한 내용임.

⑤ ways to control unpredictable agricultural phenomena (5%)
예측할 수 없는 농업 현상을 통제하는 방법(×)
controlled와 phenomena를 활용한 오답. 농부들이 통제된 조건을 마련할 수 없고 그럴 수 있다 하더라도 관리하기 힘든 복잡하고 관찰하기 어려운 현상에 자주 직면한다고 했으나 이를 통제하는 방법에 대한 내용은 없음.

03 + 글의 주제 〈23학년도 6월 모평 23번 | 정답률 63%〉 ②

구문분석 & 직독직해

문화 문화적으로 학습되는 감정 표현

주제문

[1]Considerable work (by cultural psychologists and anthropologists) / has shown //

S / V

많은 연구는 (문화 심리학자들과 인류학자들에 의한) / 보여주었다 //

↱ has shown의 O(명사절)

that there are indeed large and sometimes surprising differences / 🔑 연구 결과: 감정 표현이 문화마다 다름.

명사절 접속사 V′ / S′

정말로 크고 때로는 놀랄만한 차이가 있다는 것을 /

*<A as well as B(B뿐만 아니라 A도)>로 두 개의 전치사구가 병렬 연결됨.

in *the words and concepts* [that different cultures have / for describing emotions], / as well as in *the social circumstances* [that draw out the expression (of particular emotions)].

목적격 관계대명사 / 주격 관계대명사

어휘와 개념에도 [서로 다른 문화가 가지고 있는 / 감정을 묘사하기 위해] / 사회적 상황에서뿐만 아니라 [표현을 끌어내는 (특정한 감정의)]

↳ 감정을 묘사하는 어휘와 개념은 문화마다 많이 다름.

해석

[1]문화 심리학자들과 인류학자들에 의한 많은 연구는 특정한 감정의 표현을 끌어내는 사회적 상황에서뿐만 아니라, 감정을 묘사하기 위해 서로 다른 문화가 가지고 있는 어휘와 개념에도 정말로 크고 때로는 놀랄만한 차이가 있다는 것을 보여주었다. [2]하지만 그런 데이터가 서로 다른 문화가 서로 다른 감정을 갖는다는 것을 실제로 보여주는 것은 아닌데(▶ 문화가 달라도 감정은 같다는 의미), 만약 우리가 감정을 중추 신경의, 즉 신경계로 실행되는 상태라고 생각한다면 말이다. [3]이를테면, 색각(색을 식별하는 감각)에 관해서, 데이터들은 그저, 동일한 체내의 처리 구조에도 불구하고 우리가 감정을 해석하고, 범주화하고, 명명하는 방식은 문화에 따라 다

↱ do not show의 O(명사절)
[2] However, / those data do not actually show // that different cultures have different emotions, //
S V 명사절 접속사 S′ V′ O′
하지만 / 그런 데이터가 실제로 보여주는 것은 아니다 // 서로 다른 문화가 서로 다른 감정을 갖는다는 것을 //

↱ 부사절 접속사(조건)
if we think of emotions / as central, neurally implemented states.
S′ V′ O′ ★<think of A as B>: A를 B로 생각하다[여기다]
만약 우리가 감정을 생각한다면 / 중추 신경의, 즉 신경계로 실행되는 상태라고
↳ 문화마다 감정이 서로 다른 것은 아님.

★say는 예를 들 때 쓰는 표현으로 '이를테면, 말하자면'의 뜻임.
[3] As for, say, color vision, / they just say //
(= regarding) S(= those data) V
이를테면, 색각(색을 식별하는 감각)에 관해서 / 그것들(데이터)은 그저 말한다 //

that, / despite the same internal processing architecture, / how we interpret, categorize, and name
★접속사 that이 이끄는 두 개의 명사절이 and로 연결되어 동사 say의 목적어 역할을 함. S′₁ (명사절 주어)
emotions varies / according to culture /
V′₁
~라고 / 동일한 체내의 처리 구조에도 불구하고 / 우리가 감정을 해석하고, 범주화하고, 명명하는 방식은 다르다(고) /
문화에 따라 /
🔑 감정 자체는 동일해도 이해, 표현 방식은 문화에 따라 다를 수 있음.

and that we learn / in a particular culture / *the social context* [in which it is appropriate to express
S′₂ V′₂ O′₂ 전치사+관계대명사 가주어 진주어(to-v구)
emotions].
그리고 우리가 배운다고 / 특정 문화에서 / 사회적 맥락을 [감정을 표현하는 것이 적절한]
↳ **예(색각):** 체내 (신경계) 처리는 동일해도 감정에 대한 이해와 표현하는 사회적 맥락이 문화마다 다름.

[4] However, / the emotional states themselves / are likely to be quite invariant / across cultures.
S V C
하지만 / 감정 상태 그 자체는 / 절대로 변함없을 가능성이 있다 / 문화 전반에 걸쳐
↳ 감정 그 자체는 모든 문화에서 동일함.

[5] In a sense, / we can think of / *a basic, culturally universal emotion set* [that is shaped by evolution /
S₁ V₁ O 주격 관계대명사 V′₁
and (is) implemented in the brain], //
V′₂
어떤 의미에서 / 우리는 ~을 생각할 수 있다 / 기본적인, 문화적으로 보편적인 감정 모음 [진화에 의해 형성되는 /
그리고 두뇌에서 실행되는] //
🔑 문화적 상황에서의 학습에 의해 바뀔 수 있음.

but / the links (between such emotional states and stimuli, behavior, and other cognitive states) /
S₂
are plastic / and can be modified / by learning in a specific cultural context.
V₂₋₁ C V₂₋₂
그러나 / 연결은 (그런 감정 상태와 자극, 행동, 그리고 다른 인지 상태 간의) /
바꾸기 쉽다 / 그리고 수정될 수 있다 / 특정한 문화적 상황에서의 학습에 의해
↳ 감정 상태와 자극, 행동, 인지 상태 간의 연결은 문화적 학습에 따라 달라질 수 있음.

르며, 우리가 특정 문화에서 감정을 표현하는 것이 적절한 사회적 맥락을 배운다고 말한다. [4]하지만 감정 상태 그 자체는 문화 전반에 걸쳐 절대로 변함없을 가능성이 있다. [5]어떤 의미에서 우리는 진화에 의해 형성되어 두뇌에서 실행되는 기본적인, 문화적으로 보편적인 감정 모음을 생각할 수 있지만, 그런 감정 상태와 자극, 행동, 그리고 다른 인지 상태 간의 연결은 바꾸기 쉬워, 특정한 문화적 상황에서의 학습에 의해 수정될 수 있다.(▶ 감정은 보편적이지만 그것이 자극, 행동, 다른 인지 상태와 연결되는 것, 즉 나타나는 것은 문화적 학습에 따라 다를 수 있다는 의미)

어휘

considerable 많은; 상당한
central 《해부》 중추 신경의; 중심[중앙]의
neurally 신경(계)으로
implement 실행[시행]하다
state 상태; 국가, 나라
internal 체내의; 내부의
architecture 구조; 건축(술)
interpret 해석하다; 이해하다; 통역하다
categorize 범주화하다
vary 다르다, 차이가 있다
invariant 변함없는, 불변의
universal 보편적인; 일반적인; 전 세계의
cf. universally 보편적으로, 일반적으로
plastic 바꾸기 쉬운, 가소성이 좋은
modify 수정하다, 변경하다; 조정하다
[선택지] essential 근본적인; 필수적인
construct 구성하다; 건설하다
discipline (학문의) 분야; 훈육
cognition 인지, 인식

정답 가이드

첫 문장에서 감정을 묘사하는 어휘, 개념 등은 문화에 따라 다르다는 연구 결과를 제시했다. 이어지는 내용은 문화마다 감정 자체는 같지만, 감정이 자극, 행동 등으로 연결되는 것이 문화적 학습에 따라 쉽게 바뀌어서 달라진다는 것으로 첫 문장을 뒷받침한다. 따라서 글의 주제로 가장 적절한 것은 ② 'culturally constructed representation of emotions(문화적으로 구성되는 감정 표현)'이다.

오답 클리닉

① essential links between emotions and behaviors (9%)
감정과 행동(×) 간의 근본적 연관성
감정과 행동이 아닌 감정과 문화의 연관성에 관한 내용임.

③ falsely described emotions through global languages (5%)
세계 공용어(×)를 통해 잘못 묘사되는 감정
세계 공용어는 언급되지 않음.

④ universally defined emotions across academic disciplines (8%)
학문 분야(×) 전반에 걸쳐 보편적으로 정의되는(×) 감정
감정 상태 자체가 보편성을 가진다는 내용은 있으나 중심 내용은 아님.

⑤ wider influence of cognition on learning cultural contexts (15%)
문화적 상황을 학습하는 데 미치는 인지의 더 광범위한 영향(×)
문화적 상황에서의 학습으로 감정과 인지 상태와의 연결이 바뀔 수 있다고 했으나, 인지가 학습에 영향을 미친다는 내용은 없음.

The 주의 본문에서 언급된 어휘(cognitive)를 조합하여 매력적인 오답을 만드는 경우, 인과 관계에 오류가 없는지 특히 유의해야 한다.

01 + 글의 제목 (24학년도 대수능 24번 | 정답률 70%) ⑤

구문분석 & 직독직해

관광 과잉 관광의 개념의 복잡성

🔑 과잉 관광의 개념은 사람과 장소에 관한 특정한 가정에 기초함.

[1]The concept (of overtourism) / rests on *a particular assumption* (about people and places) / (common / in tourism studies and the social sciences in general).
S / V / O
형용사구(a particular assumption 수식)
개념은 (과잉 관광의) / 어떤 특정한 가정에 기초한다 (사람과 장소에 관한) / (흔한 / 관광학과 사회 과학 전반에서)
↳ **도입:** 과잉 관광의 개념은 사람과 장소에 관한 특정 가정에 기초함.

(= People and places) ★<see A as B(A를 B로 간주하다)>의 수동형
[2]Both are seen / as clearly defined [and] demarcated.
S / V / 전치사(~로(서)) / 과거분사구 병렬
둘(사람과 장소)은 모두 간주된다 / 명확하게 정의되고 경계가 정해진 것으로

<either A or B>: A이든 B이든 둘 중 하나
[3]People are framed / as *bounded social actors* ([either] playing the role of hosts [or] guests).
S / V / 전치사(~로(서)) / 현재분사구
사람들은 표현된다 / 경계가 있는 사회적 행위자로 (주인이나 손님의 역할을 하는)

★<treat A as B(A를 B로 취급하다)>의 수동형
[4]Places, / (in a similar way), / are treated / as stable containers (with clear boundaries).
S / 전치사구 삽입 / V / 전치사(~로(서))
장소는 / (비슷한 방식으로) / 취급된다 / 안정적인 용기로 (명확한 경계가 있는)

[5]Hence, / places can be full of tourists / [and] thus suffer from overtourism.
S / V_1 / C / V_2 / O
그러므로 / 장소는 관광객으로 가득 찰 수 있다 / 그리고 따라서 과잉 관광으로 고통받을 수 있다
↳ **도입부 부연 설명:** 사람과 장소는 경계가 명확하게 정해진 것으로 간주되므로 장소는 관광객으로 가득 차면 과잉 관광으로 고통받게 됨.

[6]But what does it mean / for a place to be full of people?
의문사(O) / V / 가주어 / to-v의 의미상 주어 / 진주어(to-v구)
하지만 (~은) 무엇을 의미하는가 / 어떤 장소가 사람으로 가득 차 있다는 것은
↳ **질문:** 어떤 장소가 사람으로 가득 차 있는 것(과잉 관광)의 의미는?

[7]Indeed, / there are examples (of *particular attractions* [that have limited capacity / [and] where there is actually no room (for more visitors)]).
V / S / 주격 관계대명사 V′ / O′ / 관계부사 / V′ / S′
사실 / 예가 있다 (특정 명소의 [한정된 수용력을 지니고 있는 / 그리고 공간이 사실상 없는 (더 많은 방문객을 수용할)])

[8]This is not least the case (with some man-made constructions (such as the Eiffel Tower)).
S / V (= in particular) / C
이것은 특히 경우이다 (일부 인공 건축물의 (에펠탑과 같은))
↳ **답변(예):** 수용력이 한정된 특정 명소(에펠탑)에 더 많은 방문객을 수용할 공간이 없는 것임 → 과잉 관광은 사람과 장소의 문제임.

주제문
🔑 범위가 확장된 장소의 경우 상황이 더 복잡해짐.

[9]However, / with places (such as *cities, regions or even whole countries* (being promoted as destinations / [and] (being) described as victims of overtourism)), / things become more complex.
현재분사구 병렬 / S / V / C
그러나 / 장소의 경우 (도시, 지역 또는 심지어 국가 전체와 같은 (목적지로 홍보되는 / 그리고 과잉 관광의 피해지로 묘사되는)) / 상황이 더 복잡해진다
↳ **답변 반박:** 장소의 범위가 넓어지면 상황이 더 복잡해짐.

🔑 물리적 수용력(사람과 장소의 문제)보다 더 관련된 다른 측면이 있을 수 있음.

[10]What is excessive or out of proportion / is highly relative / [and] might be more related to other aspects / than physical capacity, / such as natural degradation and economic leakages / (not to mention politics and local power dynamics).
S(명사절) / V_1 / C / V_2 / ~은 말할 것도 없이
과도하거나 균형이 안 맞는 것은 / 매우 상대적이다 / 그리고 다른 측면과 더 관련이 있을 수도 있다 / 물리적 수용력보다 / 자연의 (질적) 저하와 경제적 누출과 같은 / (정치 및 지방 권력 역학은 말할 것도 없이)
↳ **부연 설명:** 과도하다는 것은 매우 상대적이며, 물리적 수용력보다 더 관련된 다른 측면(정치, 경제, 환경)의 문제가 있을 수 있음.

해석

[1]과잉 관광의 개념은 사람과 장소에 관한, 관광학과 사회 과학 전반에서 흔한 어떤 특정한 가정에 기초한다. [2]둘(사람과 장소)은 모두 명확하게 정의되고 경계가 정해진 것으로 간주된다. [3]사람들은 주인이나 손님의 역할을 하는 경계가 있는 사회적 행위자로 표현된다. [4]장소는 비슷한 방식으로, 명확한 경계가 있는 안정적인 용기로 취급된다. [5]그러므로 장소는 관광객으로 가득 찰 수 있고, 따라서 과잉 관광으로 고통받을 수 있다. [6]하지만 어떤 장소가 사람으로 가득 차 있다는 것은 무엇을 의미하는가? [7]사실, 한정된 수용력을 지니고 있어서 더 많은 방문객을 수용할 공간이 사실상 없는 특정 명소의 예가 있다. [8]이것은 특히 에펠탑과 같은 일부 인공 건축물의 경우이다. [9]그러나 목적지로 홍보되고 과잉 관광의 피해지로 묘사되는 도시, 지역 또는 심지어 국가 전체와 같은 장소의 경우 상황이 더 복잡해진다. [10]과도하거나 균형이 안 맞는 것은 매우 상대적이며 물리적 수용력보다 (정치 및 지방 권력 역학은 말할 것도 없이) 자연의 (질적) 저하와 경제적 누출과 같은 다른 측면과 더 관련이 있을 수도 있다.

어휘

rest on ~에 기초하다; ~에 달려 있다[의지하다]
assumption 가정, 가설
frame 표현하다; 틀(에 넣다); 뼈대
bounded 경계가 있는
container 용기, 그릇; (화물 수송용) 컨테이너
boundary 경계(선)
suffer from ~로 고통받다
attraction 명소[명물]; 매력(적인 요소)
capacity 수용력; 용량; 능력
not least 특히
man-made 인공의, 사람이 만든
victim 피해자
excessive 과도한, 지나친
out of proportion 균형이 안 맞는
relative 상대적인; 친척; 동족
degradation (품격·질 등의) 저하; 쇠퇴
leakage 누출; (비밀 등의) 누설
dynamics 역학; 원동력, 힘
[선택지] severity 심각성; 엄격, 엄함
matter 문제; 중요하다

정답 가이드

도입부에서 과잉 관광의 개념은, 사람과 장소가 명확하게 정의되고 경계가 정해진 것으로 보는 가정에 기초하는데 장소가 사람으로 가득 찬다는 것, 즉 과잉 관광의 의미는 장소의 수용력이 한정적이어서 더 많은 방문객을 수용할 공간이 없는 것이라고 설명한다. 그러나 역접 연결어 However 이후에는 장소의 범위가 넓어지면 상황이 더 복잡해서 과잉 관광은 사람과 장소의 물리적 수용력만의 문제라기보다 정치, 경제, 환경 등의 다른 측면과 더 관련되어 있을 수 있다고 했다. 따라서 글의 제목으로 가장 적절한 것은 ⑤ 'Overtourism: Not Simply a Matter of People and Places(과잉 관광은 단순히 사람과 장소의 문제가 아니다)'이다.

오답 클리닉

① The Solutions to Overtourism: From Complex to Simple (6%)
과잉 관광의 해결책(×), 즉 복잡한 것에서 단순한 것으로
과잉 관광의 해결책을 제시하는 내용이 아님.

② What Makes Popular Destinations Attractive to Visitors? (7%)
무엇이(×) 인기 있는 목적지를 방문객에게 매력적으로 만드는가(×)?
관광 명소를 매력적으로 만드는 요소에 관한 내용이 아님.

③ Are Tourist Attractions Winners or Losers of Overtourism? (5%)
관광 명소는 과잉 관광의 승자인가 아니면 패자인가(×)?
관광 명소가 과잉 관광의 승자인지 패자인지를 따지는 내용이 아님.

④ The Severity of Overtourism: Much Worse than Imagined (13%)
상상했던 것보다 훨씬 더 나쁜 과잉 관광의 심각성(×)
과잉 관광으로 고통받을 수 있다고는 했으나 그것이 얼마나 더 심각한지에 대한 언급은 없음.

02 + 글의 제목 ‹24학년도 9월 모평 24번 | 정답률 53%› ①

구문분석 & 직독직해

방송 웹 이전과 이후 저널리즘의 차이

¹Before the web, / newspaper archives were largely the musty domain (of professional researchers and journalism students).
S / V / C
웹 이전에 / 신문 기록 보관소는 주로 곰팡내 나는 영역이었다 (전문 연구원과 언론학과 학생의)

²Journalism was, (by definition), current.
S / V / C
저널리즘은 (당연히) 최신에 관한 것이었다
↳ **도입:** 웹 이전에 신문 기록 보관소는 접근이 제한적이었고 저널리즘은 최신 사건에 관한 것이었음.

🔑 오래된 기사가 최신 기사의 맥락을 제공하기 위해 인용되며 저널리즘의 지속성이 늘어남.

³The general accessibility (of archives) / has greatly extended / the shelf life (of journalism), /
S(단수) / V(단수) / O
일반적 접근 가능성은 (기록 보관소의) / 크게 늘렸다 / 유통 기한을 (저널리즘의) /
★<with+O'+p.p.>: O'가 ~되면서[된 채로]
with older stories now regularly cited / to provide context (for more current ones).
수동 관계 / 목적(~하기 위해) / (= stories)
더 오래된 기사가 이제는 자주 인용되면서 / 맥락을 제공하기 위해 (더 최신의 것들(기사)에 관한)
↳ **세부 사항 1:** 접근성이 확장되고 최신 기사의 맥락을 제공하기 위해 과거 기사가 자주 인용되면서 저널리즘의 유통 기한이 길어짐.

⁴With regard to how meaning is made / of *complex issues* (encountered in the news), /
~와 관련하여 / to의 O(명사절) / 과거분사구
this departure can be understood /
S / V
어떻게 의미가 만들어지는지와 관련하여 / 복잡한 이슈로 (뉴스에서 마주친) /
이 새로운 시도(최신 기사의 맥락을 제공하기 위해 오래된 기사를 인용하는 것)는 이해될 수 있다 /
as *a readiness* (by online news consumers) (to engage with *the underlying issues and contexts* (of the news) [that was not apparent in, / or even possible for, / print consumers]).
전치사(~로(서)) / 주격 관계대명사 / 형용사구(보어) 병렬 / in과 for의 공통 O
준비로 (온라인 뉴스 소비자의) (기저에 있는 이슈와 맥락에 관여할 (뉴스의)
[명백하지 않았던 / 또는 심지어 가능하지 않았던 / 인쇄물 소비자에게는])
↳ **부연 설명:** 맥락을 제공하기 위해 오래된 기사를 인용하는 것은 온라인 뉴스 소비자들이 뉴스의 기저에 있는 이슈와 맥락을 알게 해줌.

해석

¹웹 이전에 신문 기록 보관소는 주로 전문 연구원과 언론학과 학생의 곰팡내 나는 영역이었다.(▶ 일반인의 접근은 용이하지 않았다는 의미) ²저널리즘은 당연히 최신에 관한 것이었다. ³(웹 등장 이후에) 기록 보관소의 일반적 접근 가능성은 더 오래된 기사가 이제는 자주 더 최신의 기사에 관한 맥락을 제공하기 위해 인용되면서, 저널리즘의 유통 기한을 크게 늘렸다. ⁴뉴스에서 마주친 복잡한 이슈로 의미가 어떻게 만들어지는지와 관련하여, 이 새로운 시도(최신 기사에 관한 맥락을 제공하기 위해 더 오래된 기사를 인용하는 것)는 인쇄물 소비자(▶ 예전의 신문 구독자를 의미)에게는 명백하지 않았던, 또는 심지어 가능하지 않았던, 뉴스의 기저에 있는 이슈와 맥락에 온라인 뉴스 소비자들이 관여할 준비로 이해될 수 있다. ⁵온라인 뉴스의 떠오르는 특성 중 하나는, 부분적으로는 쉽게 접근 가능한 온라인 기록 보관소의 깊이로 결정되는데, 뉴스 기사를 일시적이고 관련이 없는 미디어 구경거리라기보다는 더 큰 경제적, 사회적, 문화적 이슈의 분명한 결과로 이해할 가능성인 듯하다.(▶ 온라인 뉴스 소비자들은 더 큰 경제적, 사회적 문화적 배경과 연결하여 뉴스를 그 결과로 이해할 것이라는 의미)

어휘

domain 영역; 범위
journalism (대학의) 언론[신문]학과; 저널리즘 ((신문·방송·잡지의 기삿거리를 모으고 기사를 쓰는 일))

[5]One (of the emergent qualities of online news), / determined in part / by the depth (of readily accessible online archives), /
S(단수) 분사구문(= and it is determined ~)
하나는 (온라인 뉴스의 떠오르는 특성 중) / 부분적으로는 결정되는데 / 깊이로 (쉽게 접근 가능한 온라인 기록 보관소의) /
더 큰 이슈의 명백한 결과로 뉴스를 이해함.
seems to be the possibility (of understanding news stories / as the manifest outcomes (of larger economic, social and cultural issues / rather than short-lived and unconnected media spectacles)).
V(단수) C = *<A rather than B>: B라기보다는 A
가능성인 듯하다 (뉴스 기사를 이해할 / 분명한 결과로 (더 큰 경제적, 사회적, 문화적 이슈의 / 일시적이고 관련이 없는 미디어 구경거리라기보다는)
↳ **세부 사항 2:** 쉽게 접근 가능한 온라인 기록 보관소를 통해 뉴스가 더 큰 맥락 안에서 이해가 가능해짐.

by definition 당연히; 정의상
current 최신의; 현재의; 흐름
accessibility 접근 (가능성)
cf. accessible 접근 가능한
extend 늘리다, 연장하다; 확장하다
shelf life 유통 기한
cite 인용하다; (예를) 들다
context 맥락, 문맥
cf. contextually 문맥상
departure (새로운) 시도, 발전; 출발
readiness 준비(가 되어 있음)
engage with ~에 관여하다; ~을 다루다
underlying 기저에 있는, 근본적인
apparent 명백한, 분명한; 외견상의
emergent 떠오르는, 나타나는; 신흥의
readily 쉽게; 선뜻
outcome 결과
short-lived 일시적인; 단명하는
spectacle 구경거리; 광경
[선택지] beat 능가하다; 이기다

정답 가이드

접근이 제한적이고 최신의 것만 다루던 과거 웹 이전의 저널리즘과 달리, 지금의 저널리즘은 기록 보관소의 일반적인 접근이 가능해짐에 따라 유통 기한이 늘어나고, 더 큰 경제적, 사회적, 문화적 이슈의 결과로 이해할 수 있게 되었다고 했다. 따라서 글의 제목으로 가장 적절한 것은 ① 'Web-based Journalism: Lasting Longer and Contextually Wider(더 오래 지속되고 문맥상 더 넓은 웹 기반 저널리즘)'이다.

오답 클리닉

② With the Latest Content, Online News Beats Daily Newspapers! (17%) 최신 콘텐츠(×)로 온라인 뉴스가 일간 신문을 능가한다!
최신 콘텐츠를 다루는 것은 웹 이전 저널리즘의 특징임.

③ How Online Media Journalists Reveal Hidden Stories Behind News (13%)
온라인 미디어 저널리스트(×)가 뉴스 뒤에 숨겨진 이야기를 드러내는 방법
저널리스트가 숨겨진 이야기를 드러내는 방법에 관한 내용이 아님.

④ Let's Begin a Journey to the Past with Printed Newspapers! (8%)
인쇄된 신문으로 과거로의 여행(×)을 시작하자!
과거의 신문이 아니라 지금의 웹 기반 온라인 뉴스에 관한 내용임.

⑤ Present and Future of Journalism in the Web World (9%)
웹 세계에서 저널리즘의 현재와 미래(×)
웹 세계 저널리즘의 미래에 대한 언급은 없음.

03 + 글의 제목 〈24학년도 6월 모평 24번 | 정답률 72%〉 ①

구문분석 & 직독직해

교통 하이퍼 모빌리티로 인한 접근성의 위기

[1]Hyper-mobility — / the notion // that more travel at faster speeds (covering longer distances) / generates greater economic success — /
S = ↱동격 접속사 S′ 현재분사구 V′ O′
하이퍼 모빌리티는 / 개념인 // 더 빠른 속도로 더 많이 이동하는 것이 (더 먼 거리를 가는) / 더 큰 경제적 성공을 만들어 낸다는 /
seems to be a distinguishing feature (of *urban areas*), // where more than half of the world's population currently reside.
V C 관계부사(보충 설명)
구별되는 특징인 것으로 보인다 (도시 지역의) // 현재 세계 인구의 절반이 넘는 사람이 거주하는
↳ **도입:** 하이퍼 모빌리티는 도시 지역의 두드러진 특징임.

[2]By 2005, / approximately 7.5 billion trips were made / each day / in cities worldwide.
S V
2005년에는/ 약 75억 건의 이동이 이루어졌다 / 매일 / 전 세계 도시에서

해석

[1]더 먼 거리를 더 빠른 속도로, 더 많이 이동하는 것이 더 큰 경제적 성공을 만들어 낸다는 개념인 하이퍼 모빌리티는 현재 세계 인구의 절반이 넘는 사람이 거주하는 도시 지역의 구별되는 특징인 것으로 보인다. [2]2005년에는 전 세계 도시에서 매일 약 75억 건의 이동이 이루어졌다. [3]2050년에는 사회 기반 시설 및 에너지 가격이 허락한다면, 2000년의 서너 배만큼 많은 인킬로미터 이동이 있을지도 모른다. [4]화물 이동도 같은 기간 동안 세 배 넘게 증가할 수 있다. [5]이동성 흐름은 관련 사회 기반 시설이 변함없이 도시 형태의 중추를 구성하면서 도시화의 핵심 동력이 되었다. [6]그러나 전 세계적으로 증가하는 도시 이동성 수준에도 불구하고, 장소,

★<A 배수 as 원급 as B>: A는 B의 ~배만큼 …한[하게]

[3]In 2050, / there may be / three to four times as many passenger-kilometres (travelled) / as in the year 2000, / infrastructure and energy prices permitting. ★분사구문의 의미상 주어가 문장의 주어와 달라 생략하지 않음.

V S 과거분사 분사구문(= if infrastructure and energy prices permit)

2050년에는 / 있을지도 모른다 / 서너 배만큼 많은 인킬로미터가 (이동된) / 2000년의 / 사회 기반 시설 및 에너지 가격이 허락한다면

[4]Freight movement could also rise more than threefold / during the same period.

S V

화물 이동도 세 배 넘게 증가할 수 있다 / 같은 기간 동안

↳ **부연 설명:** 사회 기반 시설과 에너지 가격이 허락하는 한 도시에서 사람과 화물의 이동은 앞으로 더욱 증가할 것임.

🔑 이동성 흐름은 도시화의 핵심 동력임. ★<with+O'+v-ing>: O'가 ~하면서, ~한 채로

[5]Mobility flows have become / a key dynamic (of urbanization), / with the associated infrastructure invariably constituting the backbone (of urban form).

S V C 능동 관계

이동성 흐름은 되었다 / 핵심 동력이 (도시화의) / 관련 사회 기반 시설이 변함없이 중추를 구성하면서 (도시 형태의)

↳ **도입부의 결론:** 이동성의 흐름은 도시화의 핵심 동력임. (긍정적)

주제문

🔑 이동성의 증가에도 불구하고 장소, 활동 및 서비스에 대한 접근이 점점 더 어려워짐.

[6]Yet, / despite the increasing level of urban mobility worldwide, / access (to places, activities and services) / has become increasingly difficult.

전치사(~에도 불구하고) S(단수) V(단수) C

그러나 / 전 세계적으로 증가하는 도시 이동성 수준에도 불구하고 / 접근은 (장소, 활동 및 서비스에 대한) / 점점 더 어려워졌다

↳ **문제점:** 도시 이동성은 증가했지만 장소, 활동, 서비스에 대한 접근성은 나빠짐. (부정적)

★부정어 포함 어구(Not only)가 문장 앞에 오면서 주어(it)와 동사(is)가 도치됨.

[7]Not only is it less convenient — / in terms of time, cost and comfort — / to access locations in cities, //

부정어구 V_1 가주어 C ~의 측면에서 진주어(to-v구)

(~이) 덜 편리할 뿐만 아니라 / 시간, 비용 및 편안함의 측면에서 / 도시에서 장소에 접근하는 것이 //

but the very process (of moving around in cities) / generates a number of negative externalities.

S_2(단수) V_2(단수) O

바로 그 과정이 (도시에서 여기저기 이동하는) / 많은 부정적인 외부 효과를 발생시킨다

↳ **부연 설명:** 도시에서의 접근성은 덜 편리할 뿐 아니라 이동 과정은 부정적인 외부 효과를 발생시킴.

🔑 많은 세계 도시들은 전례 없는 접근성 위기에 직면해 있음.

[8]Accordingly, / many of the world's cities face / an unprecedented accessibility crisis, / and are characterized / by unsustainable mobility systems.

S V_1 O V_2

따라서 / 세계의 많은 도시는 직면한다 / 전례 없는 접근성 위기에 / 그리고 특징지어진다 / 지속 불가능한 이동성 체계로

↳ **결과:** 세계 도시들은 접근성 위기에 직면해 있으며 지속 불가능한 이동성 체계를 특징으로 함.

활동 및 서비스에 대한 접근은 점점 더 어려워졌다. [7]시간, 비용 및 편안함의 측면에서 도시에서 장소에 접근하는 것이 덜 편리할 뿐만 아니라, 도시에서 여기저기 이동하는 바로 그 과정이 많은 부정적인 외부 효과(▶ 이동이 늘어남에 따라 외부적으로는 교통 혼잡, 환경 오염 등의 부작용이 있음을 암시함)를 발생시킨다. [8]따라서 세계의 많은 도시는 전례 없는 접근성 위기에 직면하고 지속 불가능한 이동성 체계(▶ 현재의 이동 수단이나 방법 등이 장기적으로는 유지되기 어려울 것임을 의미)로 특징지어진다.

어휘

hyper- ((접두사)) 과도함, 초월을 의미
mobility 이동성; 유동성
cover 가다, 이동하다; 가리다; 덮다
distinguishing 구별되는, 특징적인
urban 도시의
cf. urbanization 도시화
reside 거주하다, 살다
infrastructure 사회[공공] 기반 시설
-fold ((접미사)) ~배, ~겹
dynamic (원)동력; 역동적인
invariably 변함없이, 언제나
constitute 구성하다
backbone 중추, 근간; 척추, 등뼈
externality 외부 효과
accordingly 따라서
unprecedented 전례 없는
characterize 특징짓다
unsustainable 지속 불가능한
[선택지] winding 구불구불한, 굽이진
inevitable 불가피한
regional 지역의

⊕ 인킬로미터(passenger-kilometre): 승객 수에 수송 거리를 곱한 값으로 교통 체계 및 이동 패턴을 분석하는 지표가 됨.

정답 가이드

도입부에서 하이퍼 모빌리티의 개념을 소개하고 증가하는 이동성이 도시화의 핵심 동력이라고 한 뒤, 역접 연결어 Yet 이후부터 이동성은 증가했음에도 불구하고 장소, 활동 및 서비스에 대한 접근이 점점 더 어려워졌다는 하이퍼 모빌리티 이면의 문제점에 관해 설명하고 있다. 따라서 글의 제목으로 가장 적절한 것은 ① 'Is Hyper-mobility Always Good for Cities?(하이퍼 모빌리티는 도시에 항상 이로운가?)'이다.

오답 클리닉

② Accessibility: A Guide to a Web of Urban Areas (6%)
도시 지역망의 안내서(×)로서의 접근성
접근성이 도시 지역망의 안내서라는 내용은 없음.

③ A Long and Winding Road to Economic Success (4%)
경제적 성공으로 가는(×) 길고 구불구불한 길
경제적 성공에 이르는 힘든 여정에 관한 내용이 아님.

④ Inevitable Regional Conflicts from Hyper-mobility (8%)
하이퍼 모빌리티로 인한 불가피한 지역 갈등(×)
지역 갈등에 관한 언급은 없음.

⑤ Infrastructure: An Essential Element of Hyper-mobility (10%)
하이퍼 모빌리티의 필수 요소(×)인 사회 기반 시설
사회 기반 시설은 도시를 구성하는 중추 요소로 언급되었으나 글의 중심 내용은 아님.

01 ✦ 글의 제목 〈23학년도 대수능 24번 | 정답률 78%〉 ⑤

구문분석 & 직독직해

생물 뇌의 시각 체계의 독립적인 정보 처리

주제문

🗝 뇌의 시각 체계는 모든 정보가 아닌 꼭 필요한 정보만 수집함.

[1]Different parts (of the brain's visual system) / get information / on a need-to-know basis.
S(복수) V(복수) O
다양한 부분들은 (뇌의 시각 체계의) / 정보를 얻는다 / 꼭 필요한 때 꼭 필요한 것만 알려주는 방식으로
↳ 뇌의 시각 체계는 알아야 할 정보만 취함.

★<help+O+(to-)v>: O가 v하도록 돕다

[2]*Cells* [that help your hand muscles reach out to an object] / need to know / the size and location (of the object), // but they don't need to know / about color.
S₁ 주격 관계대명사 V₁ S₂ V₂
세포들은 [여러분의 손 근육이 어떤 물체에 닿도록 돕는] / 알아야 한다 / 크기와 위치를 (그 물체의) // 하지만 그것들은 알 필요는 없다 / 색깔에 대해

[3]They need to know a little about shape, / but not in great detail.
(= Cells ~ an object)
그것들(그 세포들)은 모양에 대해 약간 알아야 한다 / 하지만 매우 자세히는 아니다
↳ **예 1:** 물체를 잡으려 할 때, 크기, 위치, 약간의 모양 정보만 알면 됨.

[4]*Cells* [that help you recognize people's faces] / need to be extremely sensitive / to details of shape, // but they can pay less attention to location.
S₁ 주격 관계대명사 V₁ S₂ V₂ O
세포는 [여러분이 사람들의 얼굴을 인식하도록 돕는] / 극도로 예민해야 할 필요가 있다 / 모양의 세부 사항에 // 하지만 그것들은 위치에는 덜 집중해도 된다
↳ **예 2:** 얼굴을 인식하려는 경우, 위치보다 모양을 자세히 봐야 함.

→ 진주어(to-v구) ★to assume의 목적어로 접속사 that이 이끄는 명사절이 옴.

[5]It is natural / to assume // that *anyone* [who sees an object] / sees everything (about it) — / the shape, color, location, and movement.
가주어 명사절 접속사 S′ V′ O′
(~은) 당연하다 / 추정하는 것은 // 사람은 누구든 [어떤 물체를 보는] / 모든 것을 보고 있다고 (그 물체에 관한) / 모양, 색깔, 위치, 움직임과 같은
↳ **통념(Myth):** 사람들은 물체의 전부를 보고 있다고 생각함.

🗝 각각의 뇌세포가 물체의 특징을 따로따로 인식함.

[6]However, / one part of your brain sees its shape, // another sees color, // another detects location, // and another perceives movement.
(= an object's)
하지만 / 여러분 뇌의 한 부분은 그것(물체)의 모양을 본다 // 또 한 부분은 색깔을 본다 // 또 한 부분은 위치를 감지한다 // 그리고 또 한 부분은 움직임을 인식한다
↳ **사실(Truth):** 각각의 뇌세포는 사물의 특징을 부분적으로 인식함.

[7]Consequently, / after localized brain damage, / it is possible / to see certain aspects of an object and not others.
가주어 진주어(to-v구)
따라서 / 국부적 뇌 손상 후에 / (~이) 가능하다 / 물체의 특정한 측면은 보면서 다른 측면은 보지 못하는 것이
↳ **부연 설명:** 부분적 뇌 손상이 일어나면 물체의 특징 일부를 인식하지 못할 수 있음.

[8]Centuries ago, / people found it difficult / to imagine // how someone could see an object / without seeing what color it is.
S V 가목적어 C 진목적어(to-v구) to imagine의 O(명사절)
수 세기 전 / 사람들은 (~을) 어려워했다 / 상상하는 것을 // 어떻게 누군가가 물체를 볼 수 있는지를 / 그것이 무슨 색깔인지는 보지 못하고

해석

[1]뇌의 시각 체계의 다양한 부분들은 꼭 필요한 때 꼭 필요한 것만 알려주는 방식으로 정보를 얻는다. [2]여러분의 손 근육이 어떤 물체에 닿도록 돕는 세포들은 그 물체의 크기와 위치를 알아야 하지만, 색깔에 대해 알 필요는 없다. [3]그것들(그 세포들)은 모양에 대해 약간 알아야 하지만, 매우 자세히는 아니다. [4]여러분이 사람들의 얼굴을 인식하도록 돕는 세포는 모양의 세부 사항에 극도로 예민해야 할 필요가 있지만, 위치에는 덜 집중해도 된다.(▶ 물체를 볼 때 필요한 정보만 알면 되기 때문에 모든 정보를 알 필요는 없다는 의미) [5]어떤 물체를 보는 사람은 누구든 모양, 색깔, 위치, 움직임과 같은 그 물체에 관한 모든 것을 보고 있다고 추정하는 것은 당연하다. [6]하지만 여러분 뇌의 한 부분은 그것(물체)의 모양을 보고, 또 한 부분은 색깔을 보며, 또 한 부분은 위치를 감지하고, 또 한 부분은 움직임을 인식한다. [7]따라서 국부적 뇌 손상 후에 물체의 특정한 측면은 보면서 다른 측면은 보지 못하는 것이 가능하다. [8]수 세기 전, 사람들은 어떻게 누군가가 물체가 무슨 색깔인지는 보지 못하고 그것을 볼 수 있는지를 상상하는 것을 어려워했다. [9]심지어 오늘날에도 여러분은 물체가 어디에 있는지 보지 못하고 그것을 보거나 물체가 움직이고 있는지 보지 못하고 그것을 보는 사람들에 대해 알게 되면 놀라워할 수도 있다. (▶ 뇌세포별로 인지하는 물체의 특징이 분리되어 있어서 한 세포가 본 것을 다른 세포는 보지 못할 수 있다는 의미)

어휘

visual 시각의, 시각적인
on a need-to-know basis 꼭 필요한 때 꼭 필요한 것만 알려주는 방식으로
extremely 극도로, 극단적으로; 매우
sensitive 예민한, 민감한; 세심한
assume 추정[가정]하다; (책임을) 지다
detect 감지하다, 발견하다
perceive 인식[인지]하다
cf. perception 인식; 자각
consequently 따라서, 그 결과
localized 국부적인
aspect 측면, 면; 양상
[선택지] betray 저버리다; 배신하다
blind spot 맹점, 약점; 사각지대
exemplify 전형적인 예가 되다; 예를 들다

[9]Even today, / you might find it surprising / to learn about *people* [who see an object / without seeing where it is, / or see it / without seeing whether it is moving].

V 가목적어 C 진목적어(to-v구) 주격 관계대명사

심지어 오늘날에도 / 여러분은 (~하면) 놀라워할 수도 있다 / 사람들에 대해 알게 되면 [물체를 보는 / 그것이 어디에 있는지 보지 못하고 / 또는 물체를 보는 / 그것이 움직이고 있는지 보지 못하고]

↳ **부연 설명:** 물체의 모든 정보를 파악하지 않고도 물체를 보는 것이 가능함.

정답 가이드

뇌의 시각 체계는 꼭 알아야 할 정보만 선별적으로 취하는데, 각각의 뇌세포가 인지하는 물체의 특징이 달라 한 뇌세포가 인지하는 특징을 다른 뇌세포는 인지하지 못할 수 있다는 내용의 글이다. 따라서 글의 제목으로 가장 적절한 것은 ⑤ 'Separate and Independent: Brain Cells' Visual Perceptions(분리되고 독립적인 것은 뇌세포의 시각적 인식)'이다.

오답 클리닉

① Visual Systems Never Betray Our Trust! (5%)
시각 체계는 결코 우리의 신뢰(×)를 저버리지 않는다!
우리가 시각 체계를 믿는다는 내용과 시각 체계가 우리의 믿음대로 작용한다는 내용은 언급되지 않음.

② Secret Missions of Color-Sensitive Brain Cells (9%)
색에 예민한(×) 뇌세포의 비밀 임무(×)
color와 sensitive를 활용한 오답. 색을 따로 인지하는 뇌의 부분이 있다고는 했으나 색인지에 국한된 내용이 아님.

③ Blind Spots: What Is Still Unknown About the Brain (6%)
맹점은 뇌에 관해 아직 알려지지 않은 것(×)
뇌의 미지의 영역에 대한 내용이 아니라 뇌의 시각 정보 처리 원리를 설명하는 글임.

④ Why Brain Cells Exemplify Nature's Recovery Process (3%)
뇌세포가 자연의 회복 과정(×)의 전형적인 예가 되는 이유
뇌세포에 대한 글은 맞지만 자연 회복 과정은 언급되지 않음.

02 + 글의 제목 〈23학년도 9월 모평 24번 | 정답률 86%〉 ②

구문분석 & 직독직해

예술 음악 연주에서 표현성의 가치

주제문 <not only A but also B>: A뿐만 아니라 B도

[1]Not only musicians and psychologists, but also committed music enthusiasts and experts / often voice the opinion // that the beauty of music lies / in an expressive deviation (from the exactly defined score). 🔑 음악의 아름다움은 악보에 정해진 표현을 벗어나는 것에 있음.

동격 접속사 S V O S′ V′

음악가와 심리학자뿐만 아니라, 열성적인 음악 애호가와 전문가도 / 흔히 의견을 말한다 //
음악의 아름다움은 있다고 / 표현상의 벗어남에 (정확히 정해진 악보로부터)

↳ 음악은 정해진 악보에서 표현상 벗어날 때 아름다움.

[2]Concert performances become interesting / and gain in attraction / from the fact // that they go far beyond *the information* (printed in the score).

동격 접속사 S V₁ C V₂ O (= concert performances) 과거분사구

콘서트 공연은 흥미로워진다 / 그리고 매력을 얻는다 / 사실에서 // 그것(콘서트 공연)이 정보를 훨씬 뛰어넘는다는 (악보에 인쇄된)

↳ **논거(예):** 악보 이상의 것을 보여준다는 점에서 콘서트 공연은 흥미롭고 매력적임.

[3]In his early studies (on musical performance), / Carl Seashore discovered // that musicians only rarely play two equal notes / in exactly the same way. 🔑 음악가는 같은 음을 동일하게 연주하지 않음.

discovered의 O(명사절) S V 명사절 접속사 S′ V′ O′

자신의 초기 연구에서 (음악 연주에 관한) / Carl Seashore는 발견했다 // 음악가들이 두 개의 같은 음을 좀처럼 연주하지 않는다는 것을 / 정확히 같은 방식으로

[4]Within the same metric structure, / there is a wide potential of variations (in tempo, volume, tonal quality and intonation).

V S

같은 운율 구조 내에서 / 광범위한 변화 가능성이 있다 (박자, 음량, 음색 및 인토네이션에 있어)

[5]Such variation is based on the composition / but diverges from it individually.

S V₁ C V₂ (= the composition)

이러한 변화는 작품에 기초한다 / 그러나 그것(작품)으로부터 개별적으로 갈라진다

해석

[1]음악가와 심리학자뿐만 아니라, 열성적인 음악 애호가와 전문가도 음악의 아름다움은 정확히 정해진 악보로부터 표현상의 벗어남에 있다고 흔히 의견을 말한다. [2]콘서트 공연은 악보에 인쇄된 정보를 훨씬 뛰어넘는다는 사실에서 흥미로워지고 매력을 얻는다. [3]음악 연주에 관한 자신의 초기 연구에서, Carl Seashore는 음악가들이 두 개의 같은 음을 좀처럼 정확히 같은 방식으로 연주하지 않는다는 것을 발견했다. [4]같은 운율 구조 내에서, 박자, 음량, 음색 및 인토네이션에 있어 광범위한 변화 가능성이 있다. [5]이러한 변화는 작품에 기초하지만, 그것(작품)으로부터 개별적으로 갈라진다. [6]우리는 일반적으로 이것을 '표현성'이라고 부른다. [7]이것(표현성)은 서로 다른 예술가가 같은 곡을 연주하는 것을 들을 때 왜 우리가 흥미를 잃지 않는지를 설명한다. [8]이것(표현성)은 또한 다음 세대가 같은 연주곡목을 반복하는 것이 왜 가치 있는지를 설명한다. [9]새롭고 영감을 주는 해석은 우리가 이해를 넓히는 데 도움을 주는데, 이는 음악계를 풍요롭게 하고 활기를 불어넣는 역할을 한다.

어휘

committed 열성적인, 헌신적인
enthusiast 애호가, 열렬한 지지자
score 악보, (음악) 작품; 득점(을 하다)
gain in ~을 얻다
go beyond ~을 뛰어넘다, 능가하다
metric 운율[운문]의; 미터법의

[6]We generally call this 'expressivity'. (= 앞 문장) 연주가 작품에서 달라지는 변화를 '표현성'이라 부름.
S V O C
우리는 일반적으로 이것을 '표현성'이라고 부른다
↳ **연구 내용:** 음악 연주가 달라지는 변화는 '표현성' 때문임.

(= Expressivity) 연주자의 표현성에 따라 같은 곡이라도 흥미로움. ★<지각동사 hear+O+v>: O가 v하는 것을 듣다
[7]This explains // why we do not lose interest // when we hear different artists perform the same piece of music.
S V O(명사절) 부사절 접속사 S′ V′ O′ C′
이것(표현성)은 설명한다 // 왜 우리가 흥미를 잃지 않는지를 // 우리가 서로 다른 예술가가 같은 곡을 연주하는 것을 들을 때
↳ **표현성의 장점 1:** 연주자마다 표현이 달라 같은 곡도 흥미로움.

explains의 O(명사절) 같은 곡을 반복해도 표현이 다르기 때문에 가치 있음.
[8]It also explains // why it is worthwhile for following generations to repeat the same repertoire.
(= Expressivity) V 가주어′ V′ C′ to-v의 의미상 주어 진주어′(to-v구)
이것은 또한 설명한다 // 다음 세대가 같은 연주곡목을 반복하는 것이 왜 가치 있는지를
↳ **표현성의 장점 2:** 다음 세대가 같은 곡을 반복해도 가치가 있음.

[8]New, inspiring interpretations help / us to expand our understanding, // which serves to enrich and animate the music scene.
S V O C 관계대명사(앞 절 보충설명)
새롭고 영감을 주는 해석은 도움을 준다 / 우리가 이해를 넓히는 데 // 그리고 이는 음악계를 풍요롭게 하고 활기를 불어넣는 역할을 한다
↳ **결론:** 새로운 곡 해석(표현성)이 이해를 넓혀 음악계를 풍요롭게 함.

variation 변화, 변동
tonal 음의, 음조의
intonation 인토네이션 ((음 높낮이의 정확도))
composition (음악의) 작품; 작곡; 구성
diverge 갈라지다, 나뉘다
worthwhile 가치 있는
repertoire 연주곡목, 레퍼토리
expand 넓히다, 확장하다
serve 역할을 하다; 도움이 되다
enrich 풍요롭게 하다; 질을 높이다
animate 활기[생기]를 불어넣다
music scene 음악계
[선택지] criticism 비평, 평론; 비판
overcome 극복하다
stage fright 무대 공포증

정답 가이드

음악의 아름다움은 악보의 정해진 표현을 벗어나는 것에 있다고 하며, 음악가의 연주가 변화하는 것을 '표현성'으로 설명한다. 같은 곡도 연주가에 따라 다르게 표현될 수 있기 때문에 우리는 음악에 대한 흥미를 유지하고, 같은 곡을 반복 연주하는 것이 가치 있게 되어 결과적으로 음악계가 풍요로워지고 활기를 띠게 된다고 했다. 따라서 글의 제목으로 가장 적절한 것은 ② 'Never the Same: The Value of Variation in Music Performance(절대 같지 않음, 즉 음악 연주에서 변화의 가치)'이다.

오답 클리닉

① How to Build a Successful Career in Music Criticism (2%)
음악 비평(×)에서 성공적인 이력을 쌓는 방법(×)
음악 비평이나 이력 쌓는 법 모두 언급되지 않음.

③ The Importance of Personal Expression in Music Therapy (8%)
음악 치료(×)에서 개인적 표현의 중요성
연주자의 표현성을 중시하는 글이지만 음악 치료에 대한 내용이 아님.

④ Keep Your Cool: Overcoming Stage Fright When Playing Music (2%) 냉정을 유지하라, 음악 연주 시 무대 공포증 극복하기(×)
연주가가 냉정을 유지해서 무대 공포증을 극복하는 내용이 아님.

⑤ What's New in the Classical Music Industry? (1%)
클래식 음악 산업(×)에서 새로운 것은 무엇인가?
클래식 음악 산업에 대한 내용이 아님.

03 + 글의 제목 (23학년도 6월 모평 24번 | 정답률 75%) ①

구문분석 & 직독직해 기술 인간과 로봇이 협동하는 합동 인지 시스템

주제문 ★<treat A as B>: A를 B로 여기다[간주하다] 인간과 로봇이 한 팀이 되면 시너지를 낼 수 있음.
[1]The approach, joint cognitive systems, / treats a robot / as part of a *human-machine team* [where the intelligence is synergistic, / arising from the contributions (of each agent)].
S = V O 전치사(~로(서)) 관계부사 S′ V′ C′ 분사구문(= and it arises ~)
'합동 인지 시스템' 접근법은 / 로봇을 여긴다 / 인간-기계 팀의 일부로 [지력이 상승 작용을 하는 / 기여로 발생하여 (각 행위자의)]
↳ **합동 인지 시스템:** 로봇을 시너지 효과를 내는 인간-기계 팀의 일부로 여김.

[2]The team consists of at least one robot and one human / and is often called a *mixed team* // because it is a mixture (of human and robot agents).
S V_1 O V_2 C 부사절 접속사 S′ V′ C′
그 팀은 적어도 한 로봇과 한 인간으로 구성된다 / 그리고 흔히 '혼합 팀'이라고 불린다 // 그 팀이 혼합체이기 때문에 (인간 행위자와 로봇 행위자의)
↳ 인간-기계 팀은 인간과 로봇으로 구성된 '혼합 팀'임.

해석
[1]'합동 인지 시스템' 접근법은 로봇을 각 행위자의 기여로 발생하여 지력이 상승 작용을 하는 인간-기계 팀의 일부로 여긴다. [2]그 팀은 적어도 한 로봇과 한 인간으로 구성되고 그 팀이 인간 행위자와 로봇 행위자의 혼합체이기 때문에 흔히 '혼합 팀'이라고 불린다. [3]사람이 주행을 켜고 끄는 자율 주행 차는 합동 인지 시스템의 한 예이다. [4]오락 로봇은 재택근무를 위한 로봇처럼 혼합 팀의 예이다. [5]설계 과정은 그 행위자들이 팀의 목표를 달성하기 위해 어떻게 서로 협력하고 조화를 이룰지에 집중한다. [6]합동 인지 시스템 접근법은 로봇을 그것들 자체의 완전히 독립적인 행동 지침을 가진 동등한 행위자로 여기기보다는 도우미 동물이나 양치기 개와 같은 조력자로 여긴다. [7]합동 인지 시스템 설계에서,

[3]*Self-driving cars*, // where a person turns on and off the driving, / is an example (of a joint cognitive system).

S 관계부사(보충 설명) S′ V′ O′ V C

자율 주행 차는 // 사람이 주행을 켜고 끄는 / 한 예이다 (합동 인지 시스템의)

↳ **합동 인지 시스템의 예:** 자율 주행 차

*as 이하에 앞에서 언급된 내용이 반복될 때, be동사/조동사로 대체하고 도치가 일어남.

[4]Entertainment robots are examples (of mixed teams) // as are robots (for telecommuting).

S V C 부사절 접속사(~처럼)

오락 로봇은 예이다 (혼합 팀의) // 로봇처럼 (재택근무를 위한)

↳ **혼합 팀의 예:** 오락용 로봇, 재택근무용 로봇

🔑 설계 시 인간과 로봇의 협동과 조화가 중시됨.

[5]The design process concentrates on / how the agents will cooperate and coordinate with each other / to accomplish the team goals.

S V O(명사절) 목적 (~하기 위해)

설계 과정은 ~에 집중한다 / 그 행위자들이 어떻게 서로 협력하고 조화를 이룰지(에) / 팀의 목표를 달성하기 위해

↳ **설계 과정의 특징:** 인간과 로봇의 협력과 조화에 중점을 둠.

[6]Rather than treating robots / as peer agents (with their own completely independent agenda), / joint cognitive systems approaches treat robots / as helpers (such as service animals or sheep dogs).

(= Instead of) 전치사(~로(서))

로봇을 여기기보다는 / 동등한 행위자로 (그것들 자체의 완전히 독립적인 행동 지침을 가진) /

S V O 🔑 로봇은 팀에 도움을 줌.

합동 인지 시스템 접근법은 로봇을 여긴다 / 조력자로 (도우미 동물이나 양치기 개와 같은)

↳ 합동 인지 시스템은 로봇을 동등한 행위자보다는 조력자로 여김.

[7]In joint cognitive system designs, / artificial intelligence is used / along with human-robot interaction principles / to create *robots* [that can be intelligent enough / to be good team members].

S V 목적(~하기 위해) 주격 관계대명사

합동 인지 시스템 설계에서 / 인공 지능이 사용된다 / 인간-로봇 상호 작용 원리와 함께 / 로봇을 만들기 위해 [충분히 똑똑할 수 있는 / 훌륭한 팀 구성원이 될 만큼]

↳ 설계 시 로봇이 좋은 팀원이 될 만큼 똑똑하도록 인간-로봇 상호 작용 원리와 인공 지능이 사용됨.

훌륭한 팀 구성원이 될 만큼 충분히 똑똑할 수 있는 로봇을 만들기 위해 인공 지능이 인간-로봇 상호 작용 원리와 함께 사용된다.

어휘

approach 접근법; 접근하다
joint 합동[공동]의; 관절
synergistic (효과 등이) 상승 작용을 하는, 함께 작용하는
arise 발생하다, 일어나다
contribution 기여, 공헌; 기부(금)
agent 행위자; 대리인, 대행자
consists of ~로 구성되다
mixed 혼합된, 뒤섞인
cf. mixture 혼합(체)
telecommuting 재택근무
coordinate 조화를 이루다
peer 동등한 것; 동료
agenda 행동 지침, 계획; 안건 (목록)
service animal 도우미 동물 ((장애인을 돕도록 훈련받은 동물))
sheep dog 양치기 개
artificial intelligence 인공 지능
principle 원리, 원칙
[선택지] join forces 힘을 합치다, 협력하다
outperform 능가하다, ~보다 뛰어나다
shift 변경하다, 바꾸다; 변화; 옮기다; 교대 근무
assistant 조수, 보조자

정답 가이드

로봇과 인간이 팀을 이루어 목표를 달성하기 위해 협력하고 조화를 이루는 합동 인지 시스템을 설명하는 글이므로 글의 제목으로 가장 적절한 것은 ① 'Better Together: Human and Machine Collaboration(함께 하는 것이 더 낫다, 즉 인간과 기계의 협동)'이다.

오답 클리닉

② Can Robots Join Forces to Outperform Human Teams? (13%)
로봇은 인간 팀을 능가하기(×) 위해 힘을 합칠 수 있을까(×)?
인간을 능가하기 위한 로봇들의 합동이 아닌 로봇과 인간의 합동에 관한 내용임.

③ Loss of Humanity in the Human and Machine Conflict (3%)
인간과 기계의 대립(×)에서 인간성의 상실(×)
인간과 기계는 협동 관계라고 했으며 인간성 상실은 언급되지 않음.

④ Power Off: When and How to Say No to Robot Partners (2%)
전원 끄기, 즉 로봇 파트너(×)에게 아니라고 말해야 할 시기와 방법(×)
로봇을 조력자로 여긴다고 했고, 저지하는 것과는 관련이 없음.

⑤ Shifting from Service Animals to Robot Assistants of Humans (7%)
도우미 동물에서 인간을 돕는 로봇 조수로의 변경(×)
로봇을 도우미 동물과 같은 조력자로 여긴다고 했으므로 역할이 바뀌는 것이 아님.

01 + 무관 문장 ⟨24학년도 대수능 35번 | 정답률 80%⟩ ③

구문분석 & 직독직해

언어 빨리 말하기의 위험성

주제문 빨리 말하는 것의 위험성에 관한 글임.

[1] Speaking fast is a high-risk proposition.
S(동명사구) V(단수) C
빨리 말하는 것은 위험성이 높은 일이다

[2] It's nearly impossible / to maintain the ideal conditions (to be persuasive, well-spoken, and effective) // when the mouth is traveling / well over the speed limit.
가주어 / V / C / 진주어(to-v구) / 부사절 접속사(시간) S′ V′
(~은) 거의 불가능하다 / 이상적인 상태를 유지하는 것은 (설득력 있고, 말을 잘하며, 효과적인) // 입이 움직이고 있을 때 / 제한 속도를 훨씬 초과하여
↳ 빨리 말할 때 이상적인 의사소통 상태를 유지하는 것은 불가능함.

*<형용사+enough+(for A)+to-v>: (A가) v할 (수 있을) 만큼 충분히 ~한

① [3] Although we'd like to think // that our minds are sharp enough / to always make good decisions / with the greatest efficiency, // they just aren't.
부사절 접속사(양보) S′ V′ O′ / (= our minds) / to think의 O(명사절) / S V
우리는 생각하고 싶겠지만 // 우리의 정신이 충분히 예리하다고 / 항상 좋은 결정을 내릴 수 있을 만큼 / 최고의 효율성으로 // 그것(우리의 정신)은 정말 그렇지 않다
↳ 세부 사항(논거): 우리의 정신은 최고의 효율성으로 항상 좋은 결정을 내릴 수 있을 만큼 예리하지 않음.

② [4] In reality, / the brain arrives at an intersection (of *four or five possible things* (to say)) / and sits idling / for a couple of seconds, / considering the options.
S V_1 O / V_2 C / 분사구문(= as it considers ~)
실제로 / 뇌는 교차 지점에 도달한다 (가능성이 있는 4~5가지의 것들의 (말할)) / 그리고 빈둥거린다 / 몇 초 동안 / 선택지를 고려하면서
↳ 부연 설명: 뇌는 말할 선택지를 고려하는 데 몇 초의 시간이 걸림.

좋은 결정을 내리는 것이 빨리 말하도록 돕는다는 내용임.

③ [5] Making a good decision / helps you speak faster // *<help+O+(to-)v>: O가 v하도록 돕다
because it provides you / with *more time* (to come up with your responses).
S(동명사구) V(단수) O C / 부사절 접속사(이유)
좋은 결정을 내리는 것은 / 여러분이 더 빨리 말하도록 돕는다 // 그것(좋은 결정을 내리는 것)이 여러분에게 제공하기 때문에 / 더 많은 시간을 (대답을 생각해 낼)
↳ 좋은 결정을 내리면 대답을 생각할 시간이 많아져서 더 빨리 말하게 됨.

④ [6] When the brain stops sending navigational instructions back / to the mouth // and the mouth is moving too fast to pause, // *<too ~ to-v>: 너무 ~해서 (그 결과) v할 수 없다
부사절 접속사(시간) S'_1 V'_1 O′(동명사구) / S'_2 V'_2
뇌가 주행 지시를 다시 보내는 것을 멈출 때 / 입에 // 그리고 입은 너무 빨리 움직여 멈출 수 없을 (때) //
that's // when you get a verbal fender bender, / otherwise known as filler.
S V C(명사절)
이때가 바로 ~이다 // 여러분이 가벼운 언어적 추돌 사고를 겪게 되는 때 / 또는 필러라고도 알려진
↳ 부연 설명: 뇌가 선택지를 고려하는 동안 입에 지시를 보내는 것을 멈출 때 언어적 추돌 사고를 겪게 됨.

⑤ [7] *Um, ah, you know,* and *like* are what your mouth does // when it has *nowhere* (to go).
S V C(명사절) 부사절 접속사(시간) (= your mouth)
'음, 아, 알다시피, 그러니까'는 여러분의 입이 하는 것이다 // 그것(여러분의 입)이 (~할) 곳이 없을 때 (갈)
↳ 예: 입이 갈 곳이 없을 때 '음, 아, 알다시피, 그러니까'라는 필러를 사용함.

해석

[1] 빨리 말하는 것은 위험성이 높은 일이다. [2] 입이 제한 속도를 훨씬 초과하여 움직이고 있을 때 설득력 있고, 말을 잘하며, 효과적인 이상적인 상태를 유지하는 것은 거의 불가능하다. ① [3] 우리는 우리의 정신이 항상 최고의 효율성으로 좋은 결정을 내릴 수 있을 만큼 충분히 예리하다고 생각하고 싶겠지만, 그것(우리의 정신)은 정말 그렇지 않다. ② [4] 실제로 뇌는 말할 가능성이 있는 4~5가지의 것들의 교차 지점에 도달하고서 선택지를 고려하며 몇 초 동안 빈둥거린다. (③ [5] 좋은 결정을 내리는 것은 대답을 생각해 낼 더 많은 시간을 여러분에게 제공하기 때문에, 여러분이 더 빨리 말하도록 돕는다.) ④ [6] 뇌가 입에 주행 지시를 다시 보내는 것을 멈추었는데 입은 너무 빨리 움직여 멈출 수 없을 때, 이때가 바로 여러분이 가벼운 언어적 추돌 사고, 또는 필러라고도 알려진 것을 겪게 되는 때이다. ⑤ [7] '음, 아, 알다시피, 그러니까'는 여러분의 입이 갈 곳이 없을 때 하는 것이다.

어휘

high-risk 위험성이 높은
proposition 일, 문제; (사업상) 제안; 명제
maintain 유지하다
ideal 이상(적인)
condition 상태; 상황, 사정; 조건
persuasive 설득력 있는
well-spoken 말을 잘하는
speed limit 제한 속도
sharp 예리한; (칼날 등이) 날카로운; 급격한
efficiency 효율(성)
intersection 교차 지점, 교차로
idle 빈둥거리다; 게으른
come up with ~을 생각해 내다
navigational 주행의; 항해의
instruction 지시; 설명; 교육
verbal 언어의; 구두의
fender bender (가벼운) 추돌 사고
filler 필러, (중요하지는 않고 시간 등을) 채우기 위한 것

정답 가이드

빨리 말하는 것의 위험성을 교통에 빗대어 설명하는 글이다. 우리의 뇌가 말할 내용을 정하느라 입에 지시를 보내는 것을 멈췄는데 우리의 입은 너무 빨리 움직여 멈출 수 없을 때 우리는 언어적 추돌 사고를 겪을 위험이 있다고 했다. 하지만 ③은 좋은 결정을 내리는 것이 우리가 더 빨리 말하도록 도움을 준다는 내용으로, 빨리 말하기의 언어적 위험성을 설명하는 글의 전체 흐름과 무관하다.

오답 클리닉

① (2%) 우리 정신이 항상 좋은 결정을 내릴 수 있을 만큼 예리하지 않기 때문에 말을 빨리 하는 것은 위험하다고 이야기한다.
② (4%) 우리의 정신이 예리하지 않다는 앞 내용에 대해 실제로 뇌가 선택지를 고려하면서 몇 초간 빈둥거린다고 부연 설명한다.
④ (11%) 뇌가 선택지를 고려하는 몇 초 동안 겪게 되는 일을 설명하고 있다.
⑤ (3%) 앞에서 언급한 필러의 예를 제시하는 내용이다.

02 + 무관 문장 〈24학년도 9월 모평 35번 | 정답률 68%〉 ③

구문분석 & 직독직해

기업 '언제 어디서나' 일할 수 있는 새로운 근무 문화

[1]Although organizations are offering / telecommuting programs (in greater numbers / than ever before), //
(Although: 부사절 접속사(양보), organizations: S′, are offering: V′, telecommuting programs: O′)
조직들이 제공하고 있긴 하지만 / 컴퓨터로 집에서 근무하는(재택근무) 프로그램을 (더 많은 수의 / 그 어느 때보다도) //
acceptance and use (of these programs) / are still limited / by a number of factors.
(acceptance and use: S, are ... limited: V, a number of (= many, several))
수용과 이용은 (이러한 프로그램의) / 여전히 제한된다 / 많은 요인에 의해

① [2]These factors include / manager reliance (on face-to-face management practices), / lack (of telecommuting training (within an organization)), /
(These factors: S, include: V, manager reliance: O_1, lack: O_2)
이러한 요인들은 포함한다 / 관리자의 의존을 (대면 관리 관행에 대한) / 부족을 (재택근무 교육의 (조직 내)) /
misperceptions of and discomfort with flexible workplace programs, / and a lack (of information (about the effects of telecommuting / on an organization's bottom line)).
(misperceptions of and discomfort with: O_3, flexible workplace programs: of와 with의 공통 O(명사구), a lack: O_4)
탄력적인 직장 프로그램에 대한 오해와 불편함을 / 그리고 부족을 (정보의 (재택근무가 미치는 영향에 대한 / 조직의 최종 결과에))
↳ **도입:** 재택근무는 많은 요인에 의해 여전히 수용과 이용이 제한됨.

② [3]Despite these limitations, / at the beginning of the 21st century, / a new "anytime, anywhere" work culture is emerging. 🔑 새롭게 떠오르는 '언제 어디서나' 일할 수 있는 근무 문화에 관한 글임.
(Despite: 전치사(~에도 불구하고), a new "anytime, anywhere" work culture: S, is emerging: V)
이러한 한계에도 불구하고 / 21세기 초에는 / 새로운 '언제 어디서나' 근무 문화가 떠오르고 있다
↳ **세부 사항:** '언제 어디서나' 일할 수 있는 새로운 근무 문화가 떠오르고 있음.

🔑 글의 소재인 재택근무가 언급되긴 했지만 직원 선발에 관한 내용임.

③ [4]Care must be taken / to select *employees* [whose personal and working characteristics are best suited / for telecommuting].
(Care: S, must be taken: V, to select: 목적(~하기 위해), whose: 소유격 관계대명사)
주의가 기울여져야 한다 / 직원을 선발하기 위해 [개인적 그리고 업무적 특성이 가장 적합한 / 재택근무에]
↳ 재택근무에 적합한 직원을 선발하는 데 주의를 기울여야 함.

④ [5]Continuing advances (in information technology), / the expansion (of a global workforce), / and increased desire (to balance work and family) /
(Continuing advances: S_1, the expansion: S_2, increased desire: S_3)
지속적인 발전은 (정보 기술에서의) / 확대는 (세계 노동력의) / 그리고 증가한 욕구는 (일과 가정의 균형을 이루려는) /
are only three (of *the many factors* [that will gradually reduce / the current barriers (to telecommuting / as a dominant workforce development)]).
(are: V(복수), three: C, that: 주격 관계대명사)
세 가지에 불과하다 (많은 요소 중 [서서히 낮출 / 현재의 장벽을 (재택근무에 대한 / 지배적인 노동력 개발로서)])
↳ **부연 설명 1:** 정보 기술의 발전, 세계 노동력의 확대, 일과 가정의 균형에 대한 욕구 증가는 재택근무의 장벽을 낮춰줄 것임.

해석

[1]조직들이 그 어느 때보다도 더 많은 수의 재택근무 프로그램을 제공하고 있지만, 이러한 프로그램의 수용과 이용은 여전히 많은 요인에 의해 제한된다. ① [2]이러한 요인들은 대면 관리 관행에 대한 관리자의 의존, 조직 내 재택근무 교육의 부족, 탄력적인 직장 프로그램에 대한 오해와 불편함, 그리고 재택근무가 조직의 최종 결과에 미치는 영향에 대한 정보의 부족을 포함한다. ② [3]이러한 한계에도 불구하고, 21세기 초에는, 새로운 '언제 어디서나' 근무 문화가 떠오르고 있다. ③ [4]개인적 그리고 업무적 특성이 재택근무에 가장 적합한 직원을 선발하기 위해 주의가 기울여져야 한다. ④ [5]정보 기술에서의 지속적인 발전, 세계 노동력의 확대, 일과 가정의 균형을 이루려는 증가한 욕구는 지배적인 노동력 개발로서 재택근무에 대한 현재의 장벽을 서서히 낮출 많은 요소 중 세 가지에 불과하다. ⑤ [6]특히 더 낮은 시설 비용, 증가된 직원 유연성, 그리고 생산성과 관련하여 조직 비용 절감에 대한 영향과 함께, 재택근무는 점점 더 많은 조직에게 관심사가 되고 있다.

어휘

acceptance 수용, 받아들임
reliance 의존, 의지
face-to-face 대면의, 마주보는
practice 관행; 실행(하다); 연습(하다)
misperception 오해, 오인
flexible 탄력적인, 유연한
cf. flexibility 유연성, 융통성
bottom line 최종 결과; 핵심, 요점
be suited for ~에 적합하다[맞다]
advance 발전, 진전
expansion 확대, 확장
workforce 노동력; 노동자
barrier 장벽, 장애물
dominant 지배적인, 우세한
implication 영향; 함축

⑤ [6]With implications (for organizational cost savings), / (especially with regard to lower facility costs, increased employee flexibility, and productivity), /
전치사구 삽입
영향과 함께 (조직 비용 절감에 대한) / (특히 더 낮은 시설 비용, 증가된 직원 유연성, 그리고 생산성과 관련하여) /
★<be of interest to A>: A에게 관심사가 되다
telecommuting is increasingly of interest / to many organizations.
S V C
재택근무는 점점 더 관심사가 되고 있다 / 많은 조직에게
↳ **부연 설명 2:** 조직의 비용을 절감해 주므로 재택근무는 많은 조직의 관심사가 되고 있음.

with regard to A A와 관련하여, A에 대하여
facility 시설, 기관
productivity 생산성

정답 가이드

도입 부분에서 많은 요인에 의해 재택근무가 여전히 제한적으로 수용되고 있다고 했으나, 이어지는 내용에서 최근에는 더 나아가 '언제 어디서나' 일할 수 있는 새로운 근무 문화가 떠오르고 있으며, 많은 요소들이 재택근무 장벽을 낮추고 점점 더 많은 조직의 관심사가 되고 있다고 했다. 즉 재택근무가 앞으로 더 확대될 가능성이 있음을 뒷받침하는 세부 내용이 전개되고 있는데, ③은 재택근무에 적합한 직원 선발에 관한 내용이므로 글의 흐름과 무관하다.

오답 클리닉

① (1%) 앞 문장의 a number of factors를 These factors로 받아 구체적으로 설명하는 내용이다.
② (9%) 앞에서 언급된 재택근무의 수용과 이용을 제한하는 요인들을 these limitations로 받아 그럼에도 '언제 어디서나' 일할 수 있는 새로운 근무 문화가 떠오르고 있다는 내용이 역접으로 연결되는 것은 자연스럽다.
④ (19%) 재택근무 문화가 떠오르도록 그 장벽을 낮춰주는 요소들을 설명하는 내용이다.
⑤ (3%) 장벽을 낮추는 요소로 비용 절감을 추가하며 재택근무가 많은 조직의 관심사라고 글을 끝맺고 있다.

03 ✦ 무관 문장 〈24학년도 6월 모평 35번 | 정답률 81%〉 ③

구문분석 & 직독직해 인지 전문가의 뛰어난 과제 수행 능력

주제문 ⊶ 전문가의 복잡하고 많은 과제를 수행하는 뛰어난 능력에 관한 내용임.
[1]Interestingly, / experts do not suffer as much as beginners //
S V
흥미롭게도 / 전문가는 초심자만큼 많이 고생하지 않는다 //
when performing complex tasks / or combining multiple tasks.
접속사를 생략하지 않은 분사구문(= when they perform ~ or combine ~)
복잡한 과제를 수행할 때 / 또는 많은 과제를 병행할 때
↳ 전문가는 초심자만큼 과제를 해결하는 데 고생하지 않음.

[2]Because experts have extensive practice / within a limited domain, // the key component skills (in their domain) / tend to be highly practiced and more automated.
부사절 접속사(이유) S(복수) V(복수) 과거분사구 병렬
전문가는 광범위한 훈련을 하기 때문에 / 제한된 영역 내에서 // 핵심 구성 기술은 (그들의 영역에서의) / 고도로 숙련되고 더 자동화되는 경향이 있다

★<few>: ((부정 표현)) (수가) 적은, 많지 않은
① [3]Each (of these highly practiced skills) / then / demands relatively few cognitive resources, /
S(단수) V(단수) O
각각은 (이 고도로 숙련된 기술의) / 그래서 / 비교적 적은 인지적 자원을 필요로 한다 /
effectively lowering *the total cognitive load* [that experts experience].
분사구문(= and it effectively lowers ~) 목적격 관계대명사
그리고 이는 총 인지 부하를 효과적으로 낮춘다 [전문가가 겪는]
↳ **논거:** 전문가의 고도로 숙련되고 자동화된 기술은 수행에 필요한 인지적 자원이 적어 인지 부하를 낮춰줌.

② [4]Thus, / experts can perform complex tasks / and (can) combine multiple tasks / relatively easily.
S V_1 O_1 V_2 O_2
따라서 / 전문가는 복잡한 과제를 수행할 수 있다 / 그리고 많은 과제를 병행할 수 있다 / 비교적 쉽게
↳ **결과(주제문 재진술):** 전문가는 복잡한 과제 수행이나 많은 과제의 병행을 비교적 쉽게 할 수 있음.

⊶ 전문가가 아닌 초심자의 탁월한 과제 처리 능력에 관한 내용임.
③ [5]Furthermore, / beginners are excellent at processing the tasks // when the tasks are divided and isolated.
S V C 부사절 접속사(시간)
게다가 / 초심자는 그 과제들을 처리하는 데 탁월하다 // 과제가 나눠지고 분리될 때
↳ 초심자는 과제가 작게 나눠지면 잘 처리함.

해석

[1]흥미롭게도, 전문가는 복잡한 과제를 수행하거나 많은 과제를 병행할 때 초심자만큼 많이 고생하지 않는다. [2]전문가는 제한된 영역 내에서 광범위한 훈련을 하기 때문에, 그들의 영역에서의 핵심 구성 기술은 고도로 숙련되고 더 자동화되는 경향이 있다. ① [3]그래서 이 고도로 숙련된 기술은 각각 비교적 적은 인지적 자원을 필요로 하며, 이는 전문가가 겪는 총 인지 부하를 효과적으로 낮춘다. ② [4]따라서 전문가는 비교적 쉽게 복잡한 과제를 수행하고 많은 과제를 병행할 수 있다. ③ [5]게다가, 초심자는 과제가 나눠지고 분리될 때 그 과제들을 처리하는 데 탁월하다. ④ [6]이것은 그들(전문가)이 반드시 초심자보다 더 많은 인지적 자원을 가지고 있기 때문인 것은 아니며, 오히려 그들이 핵심 기술을 수행하는 데 있어 달성한 높은 수준의 능숙도 때문에 그들은 자신들이 가지고 있는 것으로 더 많은 것을 할 수 있다. ⑤ [7]반면에, 초심자는 각각의 구성 기술에서 (전문가와) 동일한 정도의 능숙도와 자동성을 달성하지 못했으며, 따라서 그들(초심자)은 전문가가 비교적 쉽고 효율적으로 결합하는 기술을 결합하려고 애쓴다.

어휘

expert 전문가; 전문적인
suffer 고생하다; 악화되다
combine (두 가지 이상의 일을) 병행하다; 결합하다
extensive 광범위한; 넓은
domain 영역, 범위
component 구성하는; (구성) 요소, 부품
practiced 숙련된, 경험이 풍부한
automate 자동화하다

↱ (= 문장 4) ↱ is not의 C(명사절) 🔑 This는 문장 4를, they는 experts를 지칭함.

④ [6]This is not // because they necessarily have more cognitive resources / than beginners; //

S1 V1 명사절 접속사 S′(= experts) V′ O′

이것은 아니다 // 그들(전문가들)이 반드시 더 많은 인지적 자원을 가지고 있기 때문인 것은 / 초심자보다 //

rather, / because of *the high level of fluency* [(which[that]) they have achieved / in performing key skills], / they can do more / with what they have.

전치사(~ 때문에) 목적격 관계대명사 생략 S2 V2 O with의 O(명사절)

오히려 / 높은 수준의 능숙도 때문에 [그들이 달성한 / 핵심 기술을 수행하는 데 있어] / 그들은 더 많은 것을 할 수 있다 / 자신들이 가지고 있는 것으로

↳ 논거 추가: 전문가가 많은 것을 할 수 있는 이유는 핵심 기술을 수행하는 높은 능숙도 때문임.

⑤ [7]Beginners, / on the other hand, / have not achieved the same degree of fluency and automaticity / in each of the component skills, //

S1 V1 O1

초심자는 / 반면에 / (전문가와) 동일한 정도의 능숙도와 자동성을 달성하지 못했다 / 각각의 구성 기술에서 //

★ <with+추상명사=부사>로 with ease and efficiency는 easily and efficiently와 같음.

and thus / they struggle to combine / *skills* [that experts combine / with relative ease and efficiency].

S2 V2 목적(~하려고) 목적격 관계대명사

그리고 따라서 / 그들(초심자)은 결합하려고 애쓴다 / 기술을 [전문가가 결합하는 / 비교적 쉽고 효율적으로]

↳ 대조: 초심자는 전문가 만큼의 기술 능숙도와 자동성을 달성하지 못함.

cf. automaticity 자동성

relatively 비교적; 상대적으로

cf. relative 비교적인; 관계있는; 상대적인; 친척

cognitive load 인지 부하 ((인지적 처리 과정에서의 정신적 요구량 정도))

fluency (일의) 능숙도; (말의) 유창성

efficiency 효율(성)

정답 가이드

주제문인 첫 문장에서 전문가가 복잡한 과제를 수행하거나 많은 과제를 병행할 때 초심자만큼 많이 고생하지 않는다고 한 뒤, 그 이유가 전문가의 고도로 숙련되고 자동화된 기술과 높은 수준의 능숙도 때문이라고 설명하는 내용의 글이다. 그런데 내용을 첨가하는 연결어 furthermore(게다가)로 이어지는 ③은 전문가가 아닌 초보자의 탁월한 과제 처리 능력에 관한 내용이므로 글의 전체 흐름과 무관하다.

오답 클리닉

① (2%) these highly practiced skills는 앞 문장에서 언급한 고도로 숙련되고 자동화된 전문가의 핵심 기술을 의미하며, 이것이 적은 인지적 자원을 필요로 하여 총 인지 부하를 낮춰준다고 부연 설명한다.

② (5%) Thus로 앞 내용에 대한 결과가 연결되는 것은 자연스럽다.

④ (9%) This는 전문가가 비교적 쉽게 복잡한 과제를 수행하고 많은 과제를 병행할 수 있다는 문장 4의 내용을 의미하고, because가 이끄는 명사절의 they는 experts를 지칭하며 전문가의 높은 수준의 능숙도에 관한 내용이 이어진다.

⑤ (3%) 역접 연결어 on the other hand로 앞에서 설명한 전문가의 능숙도와 대조되는 초심자에 관한 내용이 자연스럽게 이어진다.

01 + 무관 문장 (23학년도 대수능 35번 | 정답률 82%) ③

구문분석 & 직독직해

교육 교사에게 중요한 목소리 제어 기술

[1]Actors, singers, politicians and countless others recognise / the power (of the human voice) / as a means of communication / beyond the simple decoding (of *the words* [that are used]).

(S: Actors ~ others / V: recognise / O: the power / as: 전치사(~로(서)) / that: 주격 관계대명사)

배우, 가수, 정치인, 그리고 무수한 다른 사람들은 안다 / 힘을 (인간 목소리의) / 의사소통의 수단으로서 / 단순한 해독을 넘어 (단어의 [사용된])

↳ **도입:** 의사소통 수단으로서 인간의 목소리는 영향력이 있음.

주제문 — 교사는 목소리를 잘 통제해서 사용할 줄 알아야 함.

[2]Learning to control your voice and (to) use it for different purposes is, therefore, / one (of *the most important skills* (to develop / as an early career teacher)).

(S(동명사구): Learning ~ purposes / V(단수): is / C: one)

따라서 여러분의 목소리를 제어하고 서로 다른 목적을 위해 그것을 사용하는 것을 배우는 것은 ~이다 / 하나 (가장 중요한 기술 중 (개발해야 할 / 경력 초기 교사로서))

↳ 경력 초기 교사는 목소리를 통제하고 목적에 맞게 사용하는 것을 배워야 함.

<the 비교급 ~, the 비교급 ...>: ~하면 할수록 더욱 …하다

① [3]The more confidently you give instructions, // the higher the chance (of a positive class response) (is).

(S_1: you / V_1: give / O: instructions / S_2: the chance ~ response / V_2: is)

여러분이 더 자신 있게 가르칠수록 // 가능성은 더욱 높다 (긍정적인 학급 반응의)

② [4]There are *times* [when being able to project your voice loudly will be very useful / when working in school], //

(V_1: are / S_1: times / when: 관계부사 / S′(동명사구): being able to project your voice loudly / V′: will be / C′: very useful / when working in school: 접속사를 생략하지 않은 분사구문(= when you work ~))

때가 있다 [여러분의 목소리를 크게 높일 수 있는 것이 아주 유용할 / 학교에서 근무할 때] //

and knowing // that you can cut through a noisy classroom, dinner hall or playground / is *a great skill* (to have).

(→ 동명사 knowing의 O(명사절) / S_2(동명사구): knowing ~ playground / V_2: is / C: a great skill)

그리고 아는 것은 // 여러분이 시끄러운 교실, 구내식당 또는 운동장을 꿰뚫을 수 있다는 것을 / 훌륭한 기술이다 (갖춰야 할)

↳ **세부 사항 1:** 자신 있고 큰 목소리가 학교 근무시 유용함.

교사의 목소리 사용과 무관한 학교의 소음 문제 해결책을 강구하는 것에 관한 내용임.

③ [5]In order to address serious noise issues in school, / students, parents and teachers should search for a solution together.

(목적(~하기 위해))

교내 심각한 소음 문제를 다루기 위해 / 학생, 학부모, 그리고 교사는 해결책을 함께 찾아야 한다

↳ 교내 소음 문제는 학생, 학부모, 교사가 해결책을 함께 찾아야 함.

④ [6]However, / I would always advise // that you use your loudest voice incredibly sparingly / and avoid shouting / as much as possible.

(S: I / V: would advise / that: 명사절 접속사 (→ would advise의 O(명사절)) / V'_1: use / O'_1: your loudest voice / V'_2: avoid / O'_2: shouting)

★주장·요구·제안·명령 등의 동사 뒤의 that절 내용이 '~해야 한다'라는 당위성을 의미할 때 목적어 that절의 동사는 <(should+)동사원형> 형태로 씀.

그러나 / 나는 항상 조언할 것이다 // 여러분의 가장 큰 목소리를 믿을 수 없을 정도로 드물게 사용해야 한다고 / 그리고 소리 지르는 것을 피해야 한다고 / 가능한 한 많이

↳ **세부 사항 2:** 그러나 큰 목소리는 아주 드물게 사용해야 함.

⑤ [7]A quiet, authoritative and measured tone has so much more impact / than slightly panicked shouting.

(S: A quiet, authoritative and measured tone / V: has / so much: 비교급 강조 부사 / O: more impact)

조용하고 권위 있으며 침착한 어조는 아주 훨씬 더 큰 영향력이 있다 / 조금 당황한 고함보다

↳ **부연 설명:** 큰 목소리보다 조용하고 침착한 어조가 더 영향력 있음.

해석

[1]배우, 가수, 정치인, 그리고 무수한 다른 사람들은 사용된 단어의 단순한 해독을 넘어 의사소통의 수단으로서 인간 목소리의 힘을 안다. [2]따라서 여러분의 목소리를 제어하고 서로 다른 목적을 위해 그것을 사용하는 것을 배우는 것은 경력 초기 교사로서 개발해야 할 가장 중요한 기술 중 하나이다. ① [3]여러분이 더 자신 있게 가르칠수록, 긍정적인 학급 반응의 가능성은 더욱 높다. ② [4]학교에서 근무할 때 여러분의 목소리를 크게 높일 수 있는 것이 아주 유용할 때가 있고, 여러분이 시끄러운 교실, 구내식당 또는 운동장을 꿰뚫을 수 있다는 것을 아는 것은 갖춰야 할 훌륭한 기술이다. ③ [5]교내 심각한 소음 문제를 다루기 위해 학생, 학부모, 그리고 교사는 해결책을 함께 찾아야 한다. ④ [6]그러나, 나는 여러분의 가장 큰 목소리를 믿을 수 없을 정도로 드물게 사용하고 소리 지르는 것을 가능한 한 많이 피해야 한다고 항상 조언할 것이다. ⑤ [7]조용하고 권위 있으며 침착한 어조는 조금 당황한 고함보다 아주 훨씬 더 큰 영향력이 있다.

어휘

countless 무수한, 셀 수 없이 많은
means 수단, 방법
decode (암호를) 해독하다
instruction 가르침, 지도; 지시
project (목소리를) 높이다; 계획하다; 발사하다
address (문제 등을) 다루다, 처리하다; 연설하다
incredibly 믿을 수 없을 정도로
sparingly 드물게; 절약하여
authoritative 권위 있는
measured 침착한, 신중한
tone 어조, 말투; 분위기
panicked 당황한, 허둥지둥한

정답 가이드

도입 부분에서 목적에 따라 목소리를 제어해서 사용하는 것을 배우는 것이 경력 초기 교사가 개발해야 할 중요한 기술이라고 했으므로, 이와 관련된 구체적인 내용이 전개되어야 한다. 이어지는 내용에서 교사의 자신 있는 큰 목소리의 역할과 유용성을 설명하고 있다. 하지만, ③은 교내 소음 문제 해결책을 학생, 학부모, 교사가 같이 찾아야 한다는 내용이므로, 교사의 목소리 사용 기술에 관한 글의 전체 흐름과 무관하다.

The 주의 ③의 serious noise issues in school은 ②의 a noisy classroom에 연결되는 것처럼 보이기 위한 함정이다. 일부 어구만 보고 정답을 판단하지 말아야 하며 글의 핵심 소재와 흐름을 봐야 한다.

오답 클리닉

① (3%) 교실에서 자신 있는 목소리 사용의 좋은 점을 설명한다.
② (2%) 학교에서 큰 목소리를 낼 수 있는 것이 유용하다는 내용이다.
④ (11%) 앞에서 유용하다고 했던 큰 목소리 사용을 반대로 자제하라고 조언하는 내용이 역접 연결어 However로 연결되는 것은 자연스럽다.
⑤ (3%) 앞의 조언에 이어 침착한 어조가 더 영향력이 있다고 근거를 덧붙인다.

02 + 무관 문장 (23학년도 9월 모평 35번 | 정답률 80%) ④

구문분석 & 직독직해

생물 환경을 소생시키는 식물의 회복 능력

주제문

[1]Because plants tend to recover / from disasters / more quickly than animals, //
(부사절 접속사(이유))
식물들은 회복하는 경향이 있기 때문에 / 재해로부터 / 동물보다 더 빨리 //

they are essential / to the revitalization (of damaged environments).
(they = plants; S V C)
그것들은 필수적이다 / 소생에 (손상된 환경의)

↳ 식물은 재해로부터의 빠른 회복력이 있어 손상된 환경을 소생하는 데 필수적임.

[2]Why do plants have this preferential ability (to recover from disaster)?
(의문사, V: do ~ have, S, O, =)
왜 식물은 이 특별한 능력이 있을까 (재해로부터 회복하는)

↳ **질문:** 식물이 재해로부터 회복하는 능력이 있는 이유는?

🔑 재해로부터 회복하는 식물의 능력에 관한 내용임.

*because는 보어 역할의 명사절을 이끄는 접속사로 쓰임.

[3]It is largely // because, (unlike animals), they can generate new organs and tissues / throughout their life cycle.
(S V, C, 전치사구 삽입, S′(= plants), V′, O′)
그것은 대체로 ~이다 // (동물과는 달리) 그것들(식물)이 새로운 기관과 조직을 만들어 낼 수 있기 때문(이다) / 그것들(식물)의 생애 주기 내내

↳ **답변:** 식물은 새로운 기관과 조직 생성이 가능함.

*대시(—) 이하가 plant meristems를 부연 설명함.

① [4]This ability is due to the activity (of plant meristems) — / regions (of undifferentiated tissue (in roots and shoots)) [that can, / (in response to specific cues), / differentiate into new tissues and organs].
(S V C(전치사구), 주격 관계대명사, 전치사구 삽입, V′)
이 능력은 활동 때문이다 (식물 분열 조직의) / 즉 부위 (미분화된 조직의 (뿌리와 싹에 있는))
[~할 수 있는 / (특정 신호에 대한 반응으로) / 새로운 조직과 기관으로 분화(할 수 있는)]

↳ **부연 설명:** 식물의 재생 능력은 새로운 조직과 기관으로 분화 가능한 식물 분열 조직의 활동 때문임.

② [5]If meristems are not damaged / during disasters, // plants can recover / and ultimately transform / the destroyed or barren environment.
(부사절 접속사(조건), V′, S, V_1, V_2, O)
분열 조직이 손상되지 않으면 / 재해 동안 // 식물은 회복할 수 있다 / 그리고 궁극적으로 변형시킬 수 있다 / 파괴되거나 척박한 환경을

↳ **부연 설명:** 분열 조직이 손상되지 않으면 식물은 재해에서 회복해 환경을 변화시킬 수 있음.

③ [6]You can see this phenomenon / on a smaller scale // when a tree (struck by lightning) / forms new branches [that grow from the old scar].
(S V O, 부사절 접속사, S′, 과거분사구, V′, O′, 주격 관계대명사)
여러분은 이 현상을 볼 수 있다 / 더 작은 규모로 // 나무가 ~할 때 (번개에 맞은) / 새 나뭇가지를 형성(할 때)
[오래된 상처에서 자라나는]

↳ **예:** 번개에 맞은 나무가 새 가지를 만들어냄.

해석

[1]식물들은 동물보다 더 빨리 재해로부터 회복하는 경향이 있기 때문에 그것들은 손상된 환경의 소생에 필수적이다. [2]왜 식물은 재해로부터 회복하는 이 특별한 능력이 있을까? [3]그것은 대체로 그것들(식물)이 동물과는 달리 그것들의 생애 주기 내내 새로운 기관과 조직을 만들어 낼 수 있기 때문이다. ① [4]이 능력은 식물 분열 조직, 즉 특정 신호에 대한 반응으로 새로운 조직과 기관으로 분화할 수 있는 뿌리와 싹에 있는 미분화된 조직 부위의 활동 때문이다. ② [5]재해 동안 분열 조직이 손상되지 않으면, 식물은 회복해서 파괴되거나 척박한 환경을 궁극적으로 변형시킬 수 있다. ③ [6]여러분은 번개에 맞은 나무가 오래된 상처에서 자라나는 새 나뭇가지를 형성할 때 더 작은 규모로 이 현상을 볼 수 있다. ④ [7]숲과 초원의 형태로 식물은 물의 순환을 조절하고 대기의 화학적 구성을 조정한다. ⑤ [8]식물의 재생이나 재발아 외에도, 교란된 지역은 다시 씨를 뿌리는 것을 통해 또한 회복할 수 있다.

어휘

preferential 특혜[우선권]를 주는
organ 기관, 장기
tissue (세포) 조직
due to A A 때문에
meristem ((식물)) 분열 조직
region 부위; 지역, 지방
undifferentiated 미분화된, 구분되지 않는
cf. differentiate 분화하다; 구별하다
shoot (새로 돋아난) 싹[순]; (총을) 쏘다
in response to A A에 대한 반응으로
cue 신호(를 주다)
barren 척박한, 황량한
phenomenon 현상
scale 규모, 범위; 등급
strike 치다, 때리다
grassland 초원, 풀밭
regulate 조정[조절]하다; 규제하다
adjust 조정[조절]하다

🔑 식물이라는 소재는 같지만 회복 능력과는 무관한 내용.

④ [7]In the form of forests and grasslands, / plants regulate the cycling (of water) / and adjust the chemical composition (of the atmosphere).

숲과 초원의 형태로 / 식물은 순환을 조절한다 (물의) / 그리고 화학적 구성을 조정한다 (대기의)
↳ 식물은 물의 순환을 조절하고 대기의 화학적 구성을 조정함.

composition 구성, 합성; 작문; 작곡
regeneration 재생; 재건, 부흥
resprout 재발아하다
disturbed 교란된, 흐트러진; 불안한
reseed 다시 씨를 뿌리다

⑤ [8]In addition to regeneration or resprouting of plants, / disturbed areas can also recover / through reseeding.

식물의 재생이나 재발아 외에도 / 교란된 지역은 또한 회복할 수 있다 / 다시 씨를 뿌리는 것을 통해
↳ **추가 사항:** 식물을 재파종하는 것으로도 환경 회복이 가능함.

정답 가이드

도입 부분에서 식물이 동물보다 더 빨리 재해로부터 회복하는 능력이 있다고 했으므로 이와 관련된 구체적 내용이 전개될 것임을 예측할 수 있다. 이어지는 내용에서 식물의 이러한 회복 능력이 무엇 때문인지와 재해가 있을 때 어떻게 이런 능력이 발휘되는지를 설명하고 있다. 하지만 ④는 식물이 물의 순환과 대기의 화학적 구성을 조정한다는 내용으로, 재해 시에 일어나는 식물의 회복 능력과는 무관하다.

오답 클리닉

① (1%) This ability는 앞 문장에서 언급된 식물이 생애 주기 내내 새로운 기관과 조직을 만들어 내는 것을 지칭하며 그 이유를 부연 설명한다.
② (4%) 앞에서 설명한 식물의 분열 조직이 할 수 있는 일을 보여준다.
③ (13%) 분열 조직이 손상되지 않은 식물이 회복할 수 있다는 앞 문장의 예로 번개에 맞은 나무에서 새 나뭇가지가 나는 것을 들고 있다.
⑤ (2%) 식물의 재생이나 재발아 외에도 다시 씨를 뿌리는 것을 통해 환경을 회복시킬 수 있다는 내용을 첨가한다.

03 + 무관 문장 (23학년도 6월 모평 35번 | 정답률 83%) ③

구문분석 & 직독직해

인지 동물의 의사 결정에서 정보 수집의 중요성

🔑 상대에 대한 충분한 정보가 없어 공격할지 도망갈지 갈등하는 동물에 관한 내용임.

[1]The animal (in a conflict (between attacking a rival and fleeing) / may initially not have / *sufficient information* (to enable it to make a decision / straight away).

S: The animal, (= the animal) ← it, A와 B 사이에서: between A and B, V: may initially not have, O: sufficient information
★<enable+O+to-v>: O가 v할 수 있게 하다

동물은 (갈등하는 (적수를 공격하는 것과 도망치는 것 사이에서)) / 처음에는 갖지 못할 수도 있다 / 충분한 정보를 (그것(동물)이 결정을 내릴 수 있게 하는 / 즉시)
↳ **도입:** 동물은 공격할지 도망갈지를 결정할 충분한 정보가 처음에 없을 수 있음.

① [2]If the rival is likely to win the fight, // then the optimal decision would be / to give up immediately / and not (to) risk getting injured.

부사절 접속사(조건): If, <be likely to-v>: v할 것 같다, v할 가능성이 있다, S: the optimal decision, V: would be, C_1: to give up immediately, C_2: not (to) risk getting injured

만약 적수가 싸움에서 이길 것 같다면 // 그렇다면 최적의 결정은 ~일 것이다 / 즉시 포기하는 것 / 그리고 부상당할 위험을 무릅쓰지 않는 것

② [3]But if the rival is weak and easily defeatable, // then there could be considerable benefit / in going ahead and obtaining / the territory, females, food or whatever is at stake.

부사절 접속사(조건): if, V: could be, S: considerable benefit, in의 O(동명사구 병렬): going ahead and obtaining, 복합관계대명사: whatever
★<whatever ~>: ~하는 것은 무엇이든지 (= anything that ~)

하지만 만약 적수가 약해서 쉽게 이길 만하다면 // 그렇다면 상당한 이익이 있을 수 있다 / 밀고 나가서 얻는 것에 / 영역, 암컷, 먹이 또는 걸려 있는 것은 무엇이든
↳ **예(대조):** 상대가 강하면 포기하는 것이 최적의 결정인 반면, 상대가 약하면 싸워 쟁취하는 것이 이득임.

🔑 동물이라는 소재만 같은 무관한 문장.

③ [4]Animals (under normal circumstances) / maintain a very constant body weight // and they eat and drink enough / for their needs / at regular intervals.

S_1: Animals, V_1: maintain, O: a very constant body weight, S_2: they, V_2: eat and drink

동물은 (보통의 상황에 있는) / 매우 일정한 체중을 유지한다 //
그리고 그들은 충분히 먹고 마신다 / 자신들에게 필요한 만큼 / 규칙적인 간격으로
↳ 동물은 일정한 체중을 유지하고 규칙적으로 먹이를 먹음.

해석

[1]적수를 공격하는 것과 도망치는 것 사이에서 갈등하는 동물은 처음에는 즉시 결정을 내릴 수 있게 하는 충분한 정보를 갖지 못할 수도 있다. ① [2]만약 적수가 싸움에서 이길 것 같다면, 그렇다면 최적의 결정은 즉시 포기하고 부상당할 위험을 무릅쓰지 않는 것일 것이다. ② [3]하지만 만약 적수가 약해서 쉽게 이길 만하다면, 그렇다면 밀고 나가서 영역, 암컷, 먹이 또는 걸려 있는 것은 무엇이든 얻는 것에 상당한 이익이 있을 수 있다. ③ [4]보통의 상황에 있는 동물은 매우 일정한 체중을 유지하며, 그들은 규칙적인 간격으로 자신들에게 필요한 만큼 충분히 먹고 마신다. ④ [5]상대에 대한 정보를 수집할 약간의 추가 시간을 들임으로써, 그 동물은 그러한 정보 없이 결정을 내리는 경우보다 자신의 이길 가능성을 최대화하는 결정에 도달할 가능성이 더 크다. ⑤ [6]많은 신호들이 이제 이러한 정보 수집 또는 '평가' 기능을 갖는 것으로 간주되며(▶ 예를 들어, 동물의 울부짖는 소리 또는 상대를 살피며 거리를 두고 거닐기와 같은 행동은 서로에 대한 정보를 수집하고 평가하는 것으로 볼 수 있음), 다양한 선택의 가능한 결과에 관한 매우 중대한 정보를 제공함으로써 의사 결정 과정의 메커니즘에 직접적으로 기여한다.

어휘

flee 도망치다, 달아나다
initially 처음에

주제문

④ [5]By taking *a little extra time* (to collect information about the opponent), /
<by v-ing>: v함으로써
약간의 추가 시간을 들임으로써 (상대에 대한 정보를 수집할) /

the animal is more likely to reach / *a decision* [that maximizes its chances of winning] / than if it takes a decision / without such information.
S V C 주격 관계대명사 (= the animal's) 부사절 접속사(조건)
그 동물은 도달할 가능성이 더 크다 / 결정에 [자신의 이길 가능성을 최대화하는] / 결정을 내리는 경우보다 / 그러한 정보 없이

↳ 상대에 대해 정보를 수집하면 이길 가능성을 최대화하는 결정을 할 가능성이 더 큼.

★<see A as B(A를 B로 간주하다[여기다])>의 수동형
⑤ [6]Many signals are now seen / as having this information gathering or 'assessment' function, /
S V 전치사(~로(서))
많은 신호들이 이제 간주되며 / 이러한 정보 수집 또는 '평가' 기능을 갖는 것으로 /

directly contributing to the mechanism (of the decision-making process) / by supplying vital information (about the likely outcomes (of the various options)).
분사구문(= and they directly contribute ~) <by v-ing>: v함으로써
메커니즘에 직접적으로 기여한다 (의사 결정 과정의) / 매우 중대한 정보를 제공함으로써 (가능한 결과에 관한 (다양한 선택의))

↳ **부연 설명:** 정보 수집 또는 평가 기능을 갖는 동물들이 내는 신호는 의사 결정을 하는 데 중요한 정보가 됨.

sufficient 충분한
optimal 최적의, 최선의
go ahead 밀고 나가다; 진행[추진]하다
obtain 얻다, 구하다
territory 영역, 영토
at stake (내기 등에) 걸려 있는; 성패가 달려 있는
constant 일정한, 변함없는
interval 간격; 사이
opponent 상대, 적수
maximize 최대화하다
assessment 평가
function 기능(하다)
contribute to A A에 기여하다
mechanism 메커니즘, 방법; 기계 장치
vital 매우 중대한; 생명의
outcome 결과

정답 가이드

첫 문장으로 보아, 적수를 만났을 때 동물이 어떤 행동을 할지에 대한 결정과 정보에 대한 내용이 전개될 것임을 알 수 있다. 이어지는 내용에서 의사 결정 과정에서 상대의 정보를 수집하는 것이 최적의 결정을 내릴 수 있게 해준다는 것을 구체적으로 설명하고 있다. 반면, ③은 동물이라는 소재만 같을 뿐 체중 유지와 규칙적인 먹이 섭취에 관한 내용이므로 글의 흐름과 무관하다.

오답 클리닉

① (1%) / ② (3%) 상대에 대한 정보가 충분하지 않아 동물이 공격할지 도망갈지 갈등한다는 앞 문장의 내용에 이어 상대가 강하면 포기하고, 상대가 약하면 싸우는 것이 최적의 결정임을 번갈아 보여주는 예이다.
④ (9%) 상대에 대한 정보를 수집하는 것이 이길 가능성을 최대화하는 결정을 할 수 있게 한다는 내용이 동물의 정보 수집과 의사 결정이라는 글의 핵심 내용을 담고 있다.
⑤ (4%) 정보를 수집하고 평가하는 동물들의 신호가 의사 결정에 있어 중요한 정보를 제공한다고 부연 설명하는 내용이다.

01 요약문 (24학년도 대수능 40번 | 정답률 58%) ①

구문분석 & 직독직해

과학 순차적으로 과학을 탐구해야 하는 이유

주제문

[1] Even those (with average talent) / can produce notable work / in the various sciences, //
S V O
사람들이라도 (보통의 재능을 가진) / 주목할 만한 성과를 낼 수 있다 / 다양한 과학 분야에서 //

(부사절 접속사(~하는 한))
so long as they do not try to embrace all of them / at once.
S′ V′ O′(to-v구) (= the various sciences)
그들이 그것들(다양한 과학 분야) 모두를 수용하려고 하지 않는 한 / 한 번에

(A) 다양한 과학 분야에서 주목할 만한 성과를 내려면 모든 분야를 한꺼번에 수용하지 말고 한 번에 하나씩 수용해야 함.

(= those with average talent)
[2] Instead, / they should concentrate attention / on one subject after another / (that is, in different periods of time), //
S V O 전치사(~다음에)
대신에 / 그들(보통의 재능을 가진 사람들)은 주의를 집중해야 한다 / 한 주제 다음에 다른 주제로 / (즉, 서로 다른 기간에) //

although later work will weaken / earlier attainments (in the other spheres).
부사절 접속사(양보) S′ V′ O′
비록 나중의 성과가 약화시킬지라도 / 더 이전의 성취를 (다른 영역에서의)

↳ 보통의 재능을 가진 사람들이 과학 분야에서 성과를 내기 위해서는 한 번에 하나의 주제에 집중해야 함.

[3] This amounts to saying // that the brain adapts / to universal science / in *time* but not in *space*.
S V O(동명사구) 동명사 saying의 O(명사절)
이것은 말하는 것과 마찬가지이다 // 뇌가 적응한다고 / 보편적 과학에 / '공간' 속에서가 아니라 '시간' 속에서

↳ **논거:** 뇌는 한 번에 여러 주제에 적응하지 않고 한 번에 하나의 주제에 적응함.

[4] In fact, / even those (with great abilities) / proceed / in this way.
S V
사실 / 사람들조차도 (뛰어난 능력을 가진) / 나아간다 / 이런 방식으로

↳ **부연 설명:** 뛰어난 능력을 가진 사람들도 마찬가지임.

(부사절 접속사(시간))
[5] Thus, / when we are astonished / by someone (with publications / in different scientific fields), //
realize의 O(명사절) S′ V′
realize // that each topic was explored / during a specific period of time.
V(명령문) 명사절 접속사 S′ V′
따라서 / 우리가 놀랄 때 / 누군가에게 (출판물을 가진 / 서로 다른 과학 분야의) //
깨달아라 // 각 주제가 탐구되었다는 것을 / 특정 기간 동안

↳ **결론:** 누군가의 여러 과학 분야에서의 성과는 서로 다른 시기에 이루어진 것임.

[6] *Knowledge* (gained earlier) / certainly will not have disappeared / from the mind of the author, //
S 과거분사구 V
지식은 (더 이전에 얻어진) / 분명 사라지지 않을 것이다 / 저자의 마음에서 //

(= knowledge gained earlier)
but it will have become simplified / by condensing into formulas or greatly abbreviated symbols.
S V C <by v-ing>: v함으로써 into의 O
그러나 그것(더 이전에 얻어진 지식)은 단순화될 것이다 / 공식 또는 크게 축약된 기호로 응축함으로써

(B) 이전에 얻은 지식은 단순화되어 뇌에는 새로운 학습을 위한 공간이 남게 됨.

[7] Thus, / sufficient space remains (for the perception and learning (of new images)) / on the cerebral blackboard.
S V
따라서 / 충분한 공간이 남는다 (인식과 학습을 위한 (새로운 이미지의)) / 대뇌의 칠판에

↳ **부연 설명(이유):** 과거에 얻은 지식은 사라지지 않고 단순화되므로 새로운 정보를 인식할 공간이 남게 됨.

↓

[8] Exploring one scientific subject after another / (A) **enables** remarkable work / across the sciences, //
S(동명사구) V(단수) O
하나의 과학 주제 다음에 다른 주제를 탐구하는 것은 / 주목할 만한 일을 (A) 가능하게 한다 / 과학 전반에 걸쳐 //

as the previously gained knowledge is retained / in simplified forms / within the brain, //
부사절 접속사(~ 때문에) S′ V′

which (B) **leaves** room (for new learning).
관계대명사(앞 절 보충 설명)
이전에 얻어진 지식은 보유되기 때문에 / 단순화된 형태로 / 뇌 안에서 //
그리고 이는 공간을 (B) 남겨둔다 (새로운 학습을 위한)

해석

[1] 보통의 재능을 가진 사람들이라도 다양한 과학 분야에서 주목할 만한 성과를 낼 수 있는데, 그들이 한 번에 그것들(다양한 과학 분야) 모두를 수용하려고 하지 않는 한 그렇다. [2] 대신에 그들(보통의 재능을 가진 사람들)은 한 주제 다음에 다른 주제로 (즉, 서로 다른 기간에) 주의를 집중해야 하는데, 비록 나중의 성과가 다른 영역에서의 더 이전의 성취를 약화시킬지라도 말이다. [3] 이것은 뇌가 '공간' 속에서가 아니라 '시간' 속에서 보편적 과학에 적응한다고 말하는 것과 마찬가지이다.(▶ 학습은 한꺼번에 여러 주제를 탐구하는 공간의 문제가 아닌 한 번에 하나의 주제를 탐구하는 시간의 문제라는 의미) [4] 사실, 뛰어난 능력을 가진 사람들조차도 이런 방식으로 나아간다. [5] 따라서, 우리가 서로 다른 과학 분야의 출판물을 가진 누군가에게 놀랄 때, 각 주제가 특정 기간 동안 탐구되었다는 것을 깨달아라. [6] 더 이전에 얻어진 지식은 분명 저자의 마음에서 사라지지 않을 것이지만, 그것은 공식이나 크게 축약된 기호로 응축함으로써 단순화될 것이다. [7] 따라서 대뇌의 칠판에 새로운 이미지의 인식과 학습을 위한 충분한 공간이 남는다.

↓

[8] 하나의 과학 주제 다음에 다른 주제를 탐구하는 것은 과학 전반에 걸쳐 주목할 만한 일을 (A) 가능하게 하는데, 이전에 얻어진 지식은 뇌 안에서 단순화된 형태로 보유되며, 이는 새로운 학습을 위한 공간을 (B) 남겨두기 때문이다.

어휘

average 보통(의); 평균(의)
notable 주목할 만한; 유명한
embrace 수용하다, 받아들이다; 포옹하다
attainment 성취, 달성
sphere 영역; 구(球)
amount to A A와 마찬가지이다; (합계가) A에 달하다
universal 보편적인; 일반적인
proceed 나아가다; (계속) 진행하다
astonish (깜짝) 놀라게 하다
publication 출판(물); 발표, 공표
simplify 단순화[간소화]하다
formula 공식, 식(式)
abbreviated 축약하다, 줄여 쓰다
sufficient 충분한
perception 인식; 지각
blackboard 칠판
[요약문] remarkable 주목할 만한, 놀라운
previously 이전에
retain 보유[유지]하다

정답 가이드

선택지로 보아 모두 요약문의 동사 부분에 빈칸이 있다. 빈칸 (A)가 있는 절은 하나의 과학 주제를 탐구한 뒤에 또 다른 것을 탐구하는 것이 주목할 만한 일을 '어떻게 한다'는 것이고, 그 뒤는 as가 이끌어 그렇게 되는 이유를 말한다. 즉 이전 지식이 뇌 속에 단순화되어 있어 새 학습을 위한 공간을 '어떻게 하기' 때문이라는 것이다. 뇌에 이전 지식이 단순화되어 있으면 새 학습을 위한 공간이 '있다'는 의미의 단어가 들어가는 것이 적절함을 요약문만으로도 추론할 수 있다. 글을 처음부터 읽어보면, 보통의 재능을 가진 사람들도 다양한 과학 분야를 한꺼번에 수용하지 않고 한 번에 하나의 주제에 집중하면 주목할 만한 성과를 '낼 수 있다'고 했고, 그것은 이전에 얻은 지식이 단순화됨으로써 새로운 인식과 학습을 위한 충분한 공간이 대뇌에 '남기' 때문이라고 설명한다. 따라서 요약문의 빈칸 (A)와 (B)에 각각 들어갈 말로 가장 적절한 것은 ① 'enables(가능하게 하다) - leaves(남겨두다)'이다.

오답 클리닉

(A) (B)

② challenges - spares (23%) 이의를 제기하다 - 떼어 두다
(A)는 틀리며, (B)는 맞음. challenge는 어떤 결과를 내기보다 문제를 제기하거나 맞서 도전한다는 의미이므로 적절하지 않음.

③ delays - creates (10%) 지연시키다 - 만들다
(A)는 틀리며, (B)는 맞음.

④ requires - removes (5%) 필요로 하다 - 없애다
(A)와 (B) 모두 틀림.

⑤ invites - diminishes (4%) 가져오다 - 감소시키다
(A)는 맞지만, (B)는 틀림.

02 + 요약문 (24학년도 9월 모평 40번 | 정답률 54%)

②

구문분석 & 직독직해

역사 과거에 대한 도전적인 표현인 역사적 허구

[1]Research (for historical fiction) / may focus / on under-documented ordinary people, events, or sites.
S: Research (for historical fiction), V: may focus
🔑 (A) 역사적 허구는 문서로 덜 기록된 것들에 초점을 맞춤.
연구는 (역사적 허구에 대한) / 초점을 맞출 수 있다 / 문서로 덜 기록된 평범한 사람, 사건, 또는 장소에
↳ **도입:** 역사적 허구에 대한 연구는 문서로 덜 기록된 대상에 초점을 둠.

★<help+(to-)v>: v하는 것에 도움이 되다
[2]Fiction helps portray / everyday situations, feelings, and atmosphere [that recreate the historical context].
S: Fiction, V: helps, O: everyday situations, feelings, and atmosphere, that: 주격 관계대명사
허구는 묘사하는 데 도움이 된다 / 일상적인 상황, 감정, 분위기를 [역사적인 맥락을 재창조하는]
↳ **세부 사항 1:** 허구는 역사적 맥락을 재창조하는 상황, 감정, 분위기를 묘사하는 데 도움이 됨.

[3]Historical fiction adds "flesh / to *the bare bones* [that historians are able to uncover] /
S: Historical fiction, V₁: adds, O₁: flesh, that: 목적격 관계대명사
역사적 허구는 "살을 붙인다 / 가장 기본적인 뼈대에 [역사가들이 발견할 수 있는] /
and by doing so / provides *an account* [that while (it is) not necessarily true // provides a clearer indication (of past events, circumstances and cultures)]."
V₂: provides, O₂: an account, that: 주격 관계대명사, while: 부사절 접속사(~하지만)
★<not necessarily ~>: ((부분 부정)) 반드시 ~인 것은 아닌
그리고 그렇게 함으로써 / 설명을 제공한다 [반드시 사실인 것은 아니지만 // 더 분명한 표현을 제공하는 (과거의 사건, 상황, 그리고 문화에 대한)]"

[4]Fiction adds color, sound, drama / to the past, // as much as it invents / parts (of the past).
S: Fiction, V: adds, O: color, sound, drama; S′: it (= fiction), V′: invents, O′: parts
허구는 색채, 소리, 극적 효과를 더한다 / 과거에 // 그것(허구)이 꾸며내는 것만큼이나 / 일부를 (과거의)
↳ **부연 설명:** 역사적 허구는 역사적 사실에 살을 붙여 과거에 대한 설명을 제공함.

[5]And / Robert Rosenstone argues // that invention is not the weakness (of films), // it is their strength.
S: Robert Rosenstone, V: argues, that: argues의 O(명사절), 명사절 접속사; S′₁: invention, V′₁: is not, C′₁: the weakness; S′₂: it (= invention), V′₂: is, C′₂: their strength
그리고 / Robert Rosenstone은 주장한다 // 꾸며낸 것은 약점이 아니라고 ((역사) 영화의) // 그것(꾸며낸 것)은 그것((역사) 영화)의 강점이라고
↳ **세부 사항 2:** 꾸며낸 것은 약점이 아닌 강점임.

🔑 (A), (B) 역사적 허구는 옛 기록이 부족해 표현되지 않았던 과거를 볼 수 있게 함.
[6]Fiction can allow users to see / *parts of the past* [that have never — (for lack of archives) — been represented].
S: Fiction, V: can allow, O: users, C: to see, that: 주격 관계대명사, (for lack of archives): 전치사구 삽입
허구는 이용자들이 보도록 해 준다 / 과거의 일부를 [(옛 기록의 부족으로) 한 번도 표현되지 않았던]
↳ **세부 사항 2의 논거:** 옛 기록의 부족으로 한 번도 표현되지 않았던 과거의 일부분을 볼 수 있음.

해석

[1]역사적 허구에 대한 연구는 문서로 덜 기록된 평범한 사람, 사건, 또는 장소에 초점을 맞출 수 있다. [2]허구는 역사적인 맥락을 재창조하는 일상적인 상황, 감정, 분위기를 묘사하는 데 도움이 된다. [3]역사적 허구는 "역사가들이 발견할 수 있는 가장 기본적인 뼈대에 살을 붙이고, 그렇게 함으로써 반드시 사실인 것은 아니지만 과거의 사건, 상황, 문화에 대한 더 분명한 표현을 제공하는 설명을 제공한다." [4]허구는 그것이 과거의 일부를 꾸며내는 것만큼이나, 과거에 색채, 소리, 극적 효과를 더한다. [5]그리고 Robert Rosenstone은 꾸며낸 것은 (역사) 영화의 약점이 아니라 강점이라고 주장한다. [6]허구는 옛 기록의 부족으로 한 번도 표현되지 않았던 과거의 일부를 이용자들이 보도록 해 준다. [7]실제로 Gilden Seavey는 역사적 허구의 제작자들이 강경하게 엄격한 학문 기준을 고수했다면, 많은 역사적 주제가 적절한 증거의 부족으로 탐구되지 않은 채 남아 있을 것이라고 설명한다. [8]따라서 역사적 허구는 전문적인 역사의 정반대의 것으로 여겨져서는 안 되며, 오히려 대중 역사학자와 대중 관객 모두가 배울 수도 있는 과거에 대한 도전적인 표현으로 여겨져야 한다.

↓

[9]역사적 허구는 (A) 불충분한 증거를 사용하여 과거를 재구성하지만, 그것은 매력적인 설명을 제공하는데, 그것이 역사적 사건에 대한 사람들의 이해를 (B) 풍부하게 할 수도 있다.

어휘

document 문서(에 기록하다)
ordinary 평범한; 보통의
portray 묘사하다, 그리다

[7]In fact, / Gilden Seavey explains // that if producers (of historical fiction) / had strongly held the strict academic standards, //

(→ explains의 O(명사절)) S V 명사절 접속사 S″ V″ O″

★혼합 가정문 <if+주어+had p.p. ~, 주어+would+동사원형 ...>: (과거에) ~했다면, (지금) …할 것이다

실제로 / Gilden Seavey는 설명한다 // 제작자들이 ~라면 (역사적 허구의) / 강경하게 엄격한 학문 기준을 고수했다(면) //

🔑 (A) 적절한 증거가 부족한 역사 주제를 탐구함.

many historical subjects would remain unexplored / for lack (of appropriate evidence).

S′ V′ C′

많은 역사적 주제가 탐구되지 않은 채 남아 있을 것이라고 / 부족으로 (적절한 증거의)

↳ **부연 설명:** 제작자들이 엄격한 학문 기준을 고수하지 않았기에 증거가 부족한 많은 역사적 주제가 탐구될 수 있었음.

주제문

★<see A as B(A를 B로 여기다)>의 수동형

[8]Historical fiction should, therefore, not be seen / as the opposite (of professional history), /

S V 전치사구 병렬

따라서 역사적 허구는 여겨져서는 안 된다 / 정반대의 것으로 (전문적인 역사의) /

🔑 (B) 역사적 허구는 대중들이 배울 수 있는 과거에 대한 도전적인 표현임.

but (should) rather (be seen) as *a challenging representation* (of the past) [from which both public historians and popular audiences may learn].

전치사구 병렬 전치사+관계대명사

오히려 도전적인 표현으로 여겨져야 한다 (과거에 대한) [대중 역사학자와 대중 관객 모두가 배울 수도 있는]

↳ **결론:** 역사적 허구는 역사의 정반대가 아닌 대중들이 배울 수도 있는 과거에 대한 도전적인 표현임.

↓

[9]While historical fiction reconstructs the past / using **(A) insufficient** evidence, //

부사절 접속사(~하지만) S′ V′ O′ 분사구문(= as it uses ~)

역사적 허구는 과거를 재구성하지만 / (A) 불충분한 증거를 이용하여 //

→ (= historical fiction)

it provides *an inviting description*, // which may **(B) enrich** people's understanding (of historical events).

S V O 관계대명사(보충 설명)

그것(역사적 허구)은 매력적인 설명을 제공한다 // 그리고 그것이 사람들의 이해를 (B) 풍부하게 할 수도 있다 (역사적 사건에 대한)

atmosphere 분위기; 대기; 공기
flesh 살; 육체
bare 가장 기본적인; 맨-, 벌거벗은
uncover 발견하다; 덮개를 벗기다; 폭로하다
account 설명(하다); 여기다; 계좌
indication 표현, 표시; 조짐, 암시
circumstance 상황; 사정
invent 지어내다; 발명하다
cf. invention 꾸며낸 것, 지어냄; 발명(품)
archive 옛 기록; 기록 보관소
represent 표현하다; 대표[대신]하다
cf. representation 표현; 대표, 대리
unexplored 탐구되지 않은
appropriate 적절한
opposite 정반대의 (것); 다른 편의
challenging 도전적인; 저항하는
[요약문] reconstruct 재구성하다; 재건[복원]하다
inviting 매력적인, 마음을 끄는
description 설명, 서술, 표현

정답 가이드

요약문으로 보아, 역사적 허구는 '어떤' 증거로 과거를 재구성하지만 매력적인 설명을 제공하며, 역사적 사건에 대한 이해를 '어떻게' 할 수 있는지를 찾아야 한다. 역사적 허구에 대해 긍정적인 서술을 하는 글임이 예측된다. 글을 읽어보면, 역사적 허구는 문서에 덜 기록된 대상에 초점을 맞추며 옛 기록이 '부족해' 표현되거나 탐구되지 않았던 부분을 볼 수 있게 해주므로 사람들이 '배울 수 있는' 과거에 대한 도전적인 표현으로 여겨져야 한다고 했다. 따라서 요약문의 빈칸 (A)와 (B)에 각각 들어갈 말로 적절한 것은 ② 'insufficient(불충분한) - enrich(풍부하게 하다)'이다.

오답 클리닉

(A) (B)
① insignificant - delay (12%) 중요하지 않은 - 미루다
(A)와 (B) 모두 틀림.
③ concrete - enhance (16%) 구체적인 - 높이다
(A)는 글의 내용과 반대되며, (B)는 맞음.
④ outdated - improve (12%) 시대에 뒤진 - 향상시키다
(A)는 틀리지만, (B)는 맞음.
⑤ limited - disturb (6%) 제한된 - 방해하다
(A)는 맞지만, (B)는 글의 내용과 반대됨.

03 + 요약문 〈24학년도 6월 모평 40번 | 정답률 53%〉 ②

구문분석 & 직독직해

생물 환경에 적응을 제한하는 진화의 짐

[1]The evolutionary process works / on *the genetic variation* [that is available].

S V 주격 관계대명사

진화 과정은 작용한다 / 유전 변이에 [존재하고 있는]

→ 진주어(명사절)

[2]It follows // that natural selection is unlikely to lead / to the evolution (of perfect, 'maximally fit' individuals).

가주어 V 명사절 접속사 S′ V′ C′

따라서 (~이다) // 자연 선택이 이어질 가능성은 낮다 / 진화로 (완벽하고 '최대로 적합한' 개체들의)

해석

[1]진화 과정은 (현재) 존재하고 있는 유전 변이에 작용한다. [2]따라서 자연 선택이 완벽하고 '최대로 적합한' 개체들의 진화로 이어질 가능성은 낮다. [3]오히려, 생물체는 '(이용) 가능한 가장 적합한' 혹은 '아직은 가장 적합한' 상태가 됨으로써 그들의 환경에 맞추게 되는데, 즉 그것들이 '상상할 수 있는 최상의' 상태는 아니다.(▶ 진화는 현재 환경에 적합한 상태가 되는 것이며 완벽하고 최상인 상태가 되는 것은 아니라는 의미) [4]어떤 생물체의 현재 특성은 그 생물체가 현재 살고 있는 환경과 모든 면에서 유사한 환경에서 전부 유래한 것이 아니기 때문에 적합성 결여의 일부가 발생한다.(▶ 생물체의 현재 특성은 현재

*<come to-v>: v하게 되다

3Rather, / organisms come to match their environments / by being 'the fittest available' or 'the fittest yet': // they are not 'the best imaginable'.

S V <by v-ing>: v함으로써 S V C

오히려 / 생물체는 그들의 환경에 맞추게 된다 / '(이용) 가능한 가장 적합한' 혹은 '아직은 가장 적합한' 상태가 됨으로써 // 즉 그것들이 '상상할 수 있는 최상의' 상태는 아니다

↳ **도입:** 진화는 가장 완벽한 개체로 진화하는 것이라기보다 생물체의 환경에 가능한 가장 적합한 상태로 적응하는 것임.

(A) 생물체의 특성에 적합성 결여가 발생함.

4Part (of the lack of fit) / arises // because the present properties (of an organism) / have not all originated /

S V 부사절 접속사(이유) S′(복수) V′(복수)

일부가 (적합성 결여의) / 발생한다 // 현재 특성은 (~하기) 때문에 (어떤 생물체의) / 전부 유래한 것은 아니기 (때문에) /

in *an environment* (similar in every respect / to *the one* [in which it now lives]).

(= environment) (= the organism) 형용사구 전치사+관계대명사

환경에서 (모든 면에서 유사한 / 환경과 [그것(그 생물체)이 현재 살고 있는])

↳ **문제점 1:** 생물체의 특성이 현재와 유사한 환경에서 전부 유래한 것이 아니기 때문에 일부 특성은 현재 환경에 적합하지 않음.

*<may have p.p.>: ((과거 추측)) ~했을지도 모른다

5Over the course (of its evolutionary history), / an organism's remote ancestors may have evolved / *a set of characteristics* — / evolutionary 'baggage' — / [that subsequently constrain future evolution].

S V O = 주격 관계대명사

과정 동안 (진화 역사의) / 생물체의 먼 조상들은 진화시켰을지도 모른다 / 일련의 특성들을 / 즉 진화의 '짐' / [나중에 미래의 진화를 제한하는]

(A) 조상들은 미래의 진화를 제한하는 특성들을 진화시켰을 수도 있음.

↳ **문제점 2:** 조상들이 미래의 진화를 제한하는 '짐'이 되는 특성을 진화시켰을 것임.

6For many millions of years, / the evolution (of vertebrates) / has been limited / to what can be achieved / by organisms (with a vertebral column).

S(단수) V(단수) to의 O(명사절)

수백만 년 동안 / 진화는 (척추동물의) / 제한되어 왔다 / 달성될 수 있는 것으로 / 생물체에 의해 (척추를 가진)

↳ **예:** 척추동물의 진화는 척추동물이 할 수 있는 것에 제한됨.

*<see A as B>: A를 B로 보다[여기다]

7Moreover, / much (of what we now see / as precise matches ([between] an organism [and] its environment)) / may equally be seen / as constraints: //

S_1 of의 O(what이 이끄는 명사절) V_1

(A) 현재 환경과 일치하는 생물의 특성이 제약이 될 수도 있음.

게다가 / 대부분은 (우리가 현재 보는 것의 / 정확한 일치로 (생물체와 그 환경 간의)) / 똑같이 보일 수도 있다 / 제약으로도 //

koala bears live successfully on *Eucalyptus foliage*, // [but], from another perspective, / koala bears cannot live / without *Eucalyptus foliage*.

S_2 V_2 S_3 V_3

(B) 코알라는 유칼립투스 잎 없이는(→ 환경이 바뀌면) 살 수 없음.

코알라는 유칼립투스 잎을 먹고 잘 산다 // 그러나 다른 관점에서 볼 때 / 코알라는 살 수 없다 / 유칼립투스 잎 없이는

↳ **문제점 3:** 생물체와 환경의 정확한 일치는 제약으로도 보일 수 있음.

↓

8*The survival characteristics* [that an organism currently carries] / may act as a(n) **(A) obstacle** / to its adaptability //

S 목적격 관계대명사 V

생존 특성은 [한 생물체가 현재 지니는] / (A) 장애물의 역할을 할 수도 있다 / 그것의 적응성에 //

when the organism finds itself coping with *changes* [that arise / in its **(B) surroundings**].

부사절 접속사 S′ V′ O′ C′ 주격 관계대명사 *<find+O+v-ing>: O가 v하고 있는 것을 깨닫다

그 생물체가 변화에 대처하는 상황에 있을 때 [발생하는 / 그것의 (B) 환경에서]

환경과 다른 과거 환경에서 유래한 것이기 때문에 현재 환경에 적합하지 않은 것이 일부 있다는 의미) 5진화 역사의 과정 동안 생물체의 먼 조상들은 나중에 미래의 진화를 제한하는 일련의 특성들, 즉 진화의 '짐'을 진화시켰을지도 모른다.(▶ 과거의 진화로 인해 미래에 적합한 진화를 제한하는 특성을 가지고 있을 수 있다는 의미) 6수백만 년 동안 척추동물의 진화는 척추를 가진 생물체에 의해 달성될 수 있는 것으로 제한되어 왔다. 7게다가, 우리가 현재 생물체와 그 환경 간의 정확한 일치로 보는 것의 대부분은 똑같이 제약으로도 보일 수도 있는데, 코알라는 유칼립투스 잎을 먹고 잘 살지만, 다른 관점으로 볼 때, 코알라는 유칼립투스 잎 없이는 살 수 없다.(▶ 유칼립투스 잎을 먹고 살도록(현재의 생존 특성) 진화했지만, 미래에 유칼립투스 잎이 사라지는 환경 변화가 일어나면 생존할 수 없게 된다는 의미)

↓

8한 생물체가 현재 지니는 생존 특성은 그 생물체가 (B) 환경에서 발생하는 변화에 대처하는 상황에 있을 때 적응성에 (A) 장애물의 역할을 할 수도 있다.

어휘

evolutionary 진화의
cf. evolution 진화; 발전
genetic 유전(학)의
variation 변이; 변화, 차이
available (즉각적 사용이 가능한 상태로) 존재하고 있는, 이용 가능한
It follows that ~ 따라서 ~이다
natural selection 자연 선택
fit 적합한, 알맞은; 적합(성)
arise 발생하다, 나타나다
property 특성; 재산; 부동산
originate 유래하다; 발명[고안]하다
respect (측)면; 존경(하다)
remote (시간·공간적으로) 먼; 외진
subsequently 나중에, 그 후에
constrain 제한[제약]하다; 강요하다
cf. constraint 제약, 제한
vertebral column 척추
precise 정확한; 명확한
live on ~을 먹고 살다
foliage (나뭇)잎
perspective 관점, 시각
[요약문] adaptability 적응[순응]성
cope with ~에 대처[대응]하다

정답 가이드

요약문으로 보아 생물체가 현재 가지고 있는 생존 특성이 그 생물체가 '어디'에서 발생하는 변화에 대처해야 할 때 적응성에 '어떤' 역할을 하는지를 찾아야 한다. 글을 읽어보면, 현재 생존 특성은 현재 환경에 적합하도록 진화한 것이며, 완전히 이상적인 최상의 상태는 아니라고 했다. 즉 생물체가 환경에 맞춰 진화시킨 생존 특성은 '환경'이 바뀌면 적응성에 '방해'가 될 수 있다는 내용이므로, 요약문의 빈칸 (A)와 (B)에 각각 들어갈 말로 가장 적절한 것은 ② 'obstacle(장애물) - surroundings(환경)'이다.

오답 클리닉

(A) (B)
① improvement - diet (12%) 개선 - 음식
③ advantage - genes (19%) 장점 - 유전자
④ regulator - mechanisms (8%) 조절 장치 - 메커니즘
⑤ guide - traits (8%) 안내서 - 형질
①, ③, ④, ⑤ 모두 (A)와 (B) 둘 다 틀림.

01 + 요약문 〈23학년도 대수능 40번 | 정답률 75%〉 ①

구문분석 & 직독직해 사회 사회적, 경제적 한계에 마주한 장인 정신

¹"Craftsmanship" may suggest *a way of life* [that declined with the arrival of industrial society] — // but this is misleading.
(S / V / O / 주격 관계대명사 / (= 앞 절))
'장인 정신'은 삶의 방식을 연상시킬지도 모른다 [산업 사회의 도래와 함께 쇠퇴한] // 하지만 이는 오해의 소지가 있다
↳ **통념과 사실:** 장인 정신은 쇠퇴한 삶의 방식이 아님.

²Craftsmanship names an enduring, basic human impulse, / the desire (to do a job well / for its own sake). 🔑 (A) 장인 정신은 지속되어 온 인간의 기본 욕구임.
장인 정신은 지속적이고 기본적인 인간의 욕구를 말한다 / 즉 욕망인 (일을 잘하고 싶은 / 일 자체를 위해)
↳ **상술:** 장인 정신은 일을 잘하고 싶어 하는 지속적인 인간의 욕망임.

³Craftsmanship cuts a far wider swath / than skilled manual labor; // it serves the computer programmer, the doctor, and the artist; // parenting improves / when it is practiced as a skilled craft, // as does citizenship.
(far: 비교급 수식 부사 / it (= craftsmanship) / it (= parenting) / as: 전치사(~로(서)) / as: 부사절 접속사(~처럼) / does (= improves))
*as 이하에 앞에서 언급된 내용이 반복될 때, be동사/대동사로 대체하고 도치가 일어남.
장인 정신은 훨씬 더 넓은 구획을 가른다 / 숙련된 육체노동보다 // 그것(장인 정신)은 컴퓨터 프로그래머, 의사, 예술가에게 도움이 된다 // 육아는 향상된다 / 그것(육아)이 숙련된 기술로서 실행될 때 // 시민 정신이 향상되는 것처럼

⁴In all these domains, / craftsmanship focuses on objective standards, / on the thing in itself.
이 모든 영역에서 / 장인 정신은 객관적 기준에 초점을 맞춘다 / 즉 그 자체의 것에
↳ 장인 정신은 광범위한 영역에서 도움이 되며, 일 그 자체, 즉 객관적인 기준에 집중함.

🔑 (B) 사회·경제적 조건이 장인 정신을 방해함.
⁵Social and economic conditions, / however, / often stand in the way of the craftsman's discipline and commitment: // schools may fail to provide *the tools* (to do good work), // and workplaces may not truly value the aspiration for quality.
(S_1 / V_1 / O_1 / S_2 / V_2 / O_2 / S_3 / V_3 / O_3)
사회적, 경제적 조건은 / 그러나 / 흔히 장인의 단련과 전념을 방해한다 // 즉 학교는 도구를 제공하지 못할 수 있다 (일을 잘하기 위한) // 그리고 일터는 품질에 대한 열망을 진정으로 가치 있게 여기지 않을 수 있다
↳ **문제점 1:** 사회적, 경제적 조건이 장인의 단련과 전념을 방해함.

⁶And though craftsmanship can reward an individual / with a sense of pride in work, // this reward is not simple. 🔑 (B) 장인 정신은 보상이 간단하지 않음.
(though: 부사절 접속사(양보) / S′ / V′ / O′ / S / V / C)
그리고 비록 장인 정신이 개인에게 보상할 수는 있지만 / 일에 대한 자부심으로 // 이 보상은 간단하지 않다
↳ **문제점 2:** 장인 정신의 보상은 자부심인데 이를 얻기는 간단하지 않음.

⁷The craftsman often faces conflicting objective standards (of excellence); // the desire (to do something well for its own sake) / can be weakened / by competitive pressure, by frustration, or by obsession. 🔑 (B) the desire ~ own sake는 craftsmanship을 의미. 장인 정신이 여러 요인으로 인해 약화됨.
(S_1 / V_1 / O / S_2 / V_2)
장인은 흔히 상충되는 객관적 기준에 직면한다 (탁월함에 대한) // 욕망은 (어떤 일 그 자체를 위해 잘하려는) / 약화될 수 있다 / 경쟁적 압력에 의해, 좌절에 의해, 또는 집착에 의해
↳ **문제점 3:** 탁월함에 대한 상충되는 객관적 기준에 직면함.

↓

⁸Craftsmanship, / *a human desire* [that has **(A) persisted** over time / in diverse contexts], / often encounters / *factors* [that **(B) limit** its full development].
(S / 주격 관계대명사 / V / O / 주격 관계대명사 / its (= craftsmanship's))
장인 정신은 / 인간의 욕망인 [오랜 시간에 걸쳐 (A) 존속되어 온 / 다양한 상황에서] / 흔히 마주친다 / 요인들과 [그것(장인 정신)의 완전한 발전을 (B) 제한하는]

해석

¹'장인 정신'은 산업 사회의 도래와 함께 쇠퇴한 삶의 방식을 연상시킬지도 모르지만, 이는 오해의 소지가 있다. ²장인 정신은 지속적이고 기본적인 인간의 욕구, 즉 일 자체를 위해 일을 잘하고 싶은 욕망을 말한다. ³장인 정신은 숙련된 육체노동보다 훨씬 더 넓은 구획을 가르는데, 그것(장인 정신)은 컴퓨터 프로그래머, 의사, 예술가에게 도움이 되고, 시민 정신이 향상되는 것처럼 육아는 숙련된 기술로서 실행될 때 향상된다. ⁴이 모든 영역에서 장인 정신은 객관적 기준, 즉 그 자체의 것에 초점을 맞춘다. ⁵그러나 사회적, 경제적 조건은 흔히 장인의 단련과 전념을 방해하는데, 즉 학교는 일을 잘하기 위한 도구를 제공하지 못할 수 있고, 일터는 품질에 대한 열망을 진정으로 가치 있게 여기지 않을 수 있다. ⁶그리고 비록 장인 정신이 일에 대한 자부심으로 개인에게 보상할 수는 있지만 이 보상은 간단하지 않다. ⁷장인은 흔히 탁월함에 대한 상충되는 객관적 기준에 직면하며, 어떤 일 그 자체를 위해 잘하려는 욕망(▶ 장인 정신을 의미)은 경쟁적 압력에 의해, 좌절에 의해, 또는 집착에 의해 약화될 수 있다.

↓

⁸다양한 상황에서 오랜 시간에 걸쳐 (A) 존속되어 온 인간의 욕망인 장인 정신은 흔히 그것의 완전한 발전을 (B) 제한하는 요인들과 마주친다.

어휘

craftsmanship 장인 정신
cf. craft 기술; 공예; 공예품을 만들다
cf. craftsman 장인
misleading 오해의 소지가 있는
enduring 지속적인, 오래가는
impulse 욕구, 충동; 충격; 자극
for one's own sake ~ 자체를 위한
manual 육체노동의, 손으로 하는
serve 도움이 되다; ~의 역할을 하다
parenting 육아, 양육
citizenship 시민 정신; 시민권
domain 영역, 분야
objective 객관적인; 목적, 목표
stand in the way of ~을 방해하다
discipline 단련, 수양; 학과; 훈련; 규율
commitment 전념, 헌신; 공약
aspiration 열망, 갈망
conflicting 상충[상반]되는
obsession 집착, 강박 관념
[요약문] diverse 다양한
context 상황, 배경; 문맥
encounter 마주치다, 만나다; (위험에) 직면하다

정답 가이드

요약문을 통해 장인 정신의 정의와 장인 정신이 마주하는 어떤 요인에 관한 글임을 알 수 있다. 장인 정신은 일 자체를 잘 하고 싶어 하는 '지속적'이고 기본적인 인간의 욕구로, 여러 영역에서 도움이 된다고 했는데, however를 포함한 문장 5부터는 장인 정신을 '약화시키는' 여러 요인을 설명하고 있다. 따라서 요약문의 빈칸 (A)와 (B)에 각각 들어갈 말로 가장 적절한 것은 ① 'persisted(존속되었다) - limit(제한하다)'이다.

오답 클리닉

② persisted - cultivate (8%) 존속되었다 - 양성하다
(A)는 맞지만, (B)는 글의 내용과 반대됨.

③ evolved - accelerate (3%) 발달했다 - 가속화하다
(A)는 맞지만, (B)는 여러 요소가 발전을 막는다는 내용이 되어야 하므로 틀림.

④ diminished - shape (4%) 감소했다 - 형성하다
(A)와 (B) 모두 틀림.

⑤ diminished - restrict (10%) 감소했다 - 제한하다
(A)는 글의 내용과 반대되며, (B)는 맞음.

The 주의 글의 도입 부분은 'Myth(근거 없는 믿음)-Truth(사실)' 구조로 문장 1에서 장인 정신을 쇠퇴한 삶의 방식이라고 보는 것은 오해라고 한 후, 문장 2에서 이는 지속적인 인간의 기본 욕망이라고 하고 있다. Myth에 해당하는 내용만 보고 (A)를 옳은 것으로 판단하지 않도록 주의하자.

02 + 요약문 〈23학년도 9월 모평 40번 | 정답률 71%〉 ①

구문분석 & 직독직해 직업 업무 규모에 따라 다른 디자이너의 기능

[1]A striving (to demonstrate individual personality / through designs) / should not be surprising.
S V C
노력은 (개인의 개성을 보여주려는 / 디자인을 통해) / 놀라운 것이 아닐 것이다 *여기서 should는 추측(~일 것이다)의 의미.
↳ 도입: 디자인으로 개성을 보여주려는 노력은 놀랍지 않음.

[2]Most designers are educated to work as individuals, // and design literature contains / countless references (to 'the designer').
S_1 V_1 C S_2 V_2 O
대부분의 디자이너는 개인으로서 작업하도록 교육받는다 // 그리고 디자인 문헌은 담고 있다 / 무수히 많은 언급을 ('그 디자이너'에 대한)

(A) 작은 상품에서는 디자이너의 개인적 재능이 필수적임.
[3]Personal flair is (without doubt) an absolute necessity / in some product categories, / particularly relatively small objects, (with a low degree of technological complexity), (such as furniture, lighting, small appliances, and housewares).
S V 전치사구 삽입 C
개인적 재능은 (의심할 여지 없이) 절대적인 필수품이다 / 일부 상품 범주에서 / 특히 비교적 작은 물건들에서 (낮은 수준의 기술적 복잡성을 가진) (가구, 조명, 소형 가전과 가정용품들과 같은)
↳ 대조 A(작은 프로젝트): 디자이너의 개인적 재능이 절대적으로 필요함.

[4]In larger-scale projects, / however, / even where a strong personality exercises powerful influence, // the fact // that substantial numbers of designers are employed / in implementing a concept / can easily be overlooked.
부사절 접속사(~한 곳) S′ V′ O′
S = 동격 접속사 V
(A) 더 큰 규모의 프로젝트에는 수많은 디자이너가 참여함.
더 큰 규모의 프로젝트에서 / 그러나 / 심지어 강한 개성이 강력한 영향력을 발휘하는 곳에서조차도 // 사실이 // 상당한 수의 디자이너가 투입된다는 / 구상을 이행하는 데 / 쉽게 간과될 수 있다

[5]The emphasis (on individuality) / is therefore problematic — // rather than actually designing, / many successful designer 'personalities' function more / as creative managers.
S_1 V_1 C S_2 V_2 전치사(~로(서))
(B) 유명 디자이너들이 관리자로서 기능함.
강조는 (개성에 대한) / 그러므로 문제가 있다 // 즉 실제로 디자인하기보다는 / 많은 성공한 디자이너 '유명 인사들'은 더 많이 기능한다 / 창의적인 관리자로서
↳ 대조 B(큰 프로젝트): 여러 디자이너가 함께 일하므로 개성에 대한 강조가 문제가 됨.

주제문
[6]A distinction needs to be made / between designers (working truly alone) / and those (working in a group).
S V O 명사구 병렬 현재분사구 현재분사구
구별이 이뤄져야 한다 / 디자이너 사이에 (진정으로 혼자 작업하는) / 디자이너와 (집단으로 작업하는)

해석

[1]디자인을 통해 개인의 개성을 보여주려는 노력은 놀라운 것이 아닐 것이다. [2]대부분의 디자이너는 개인으로서 작업하도록 교육받고, 디자인 문헌은 '그 디자이너'에 대한 무수히 많은 언급을 담고 있다. [3]개인적 재능은 의심할 여지 없이 일부 상품 범주에서 절대적인 필수품인데, 가구, 조명, 소형 가전과 가정용품들과 같은, 낮은 수준의 기술적 복잡성을 가진 비교적 작은 물건들에서 특히 그렇다. [4]그러나, 더 큰 규모의 프로젝트에서, 심지어 강한 개성이 강력한 영향력을 발휘하는 곳에서조차도, 상당한 수의 디자이너가 구상을 이행하는 데 투입된다는 사실이 쉽게 간과될 수 있다. [5]그러므로 개성에 대한 강조는 문제가 있는데, 즉 실제로 디자인하기보다는 많은 성공한 디자이너 '유명 인사들'은 창의적인 관리자로서 더 많이 기능한다. [6]진정으로 혼자 작업하는 디자이너와 집단으로 작업하는 디자이너 사이에 구별이 이뤄져야 한다. [7]후자의 경우, 관리 조직과 절차가 디자이너들의 창의성만큼 똑같이 의미 있을 수 있다.

↓

[8]프로젝트의 (A) 크기에 따라 팀 기반의 작업 환경을 (B) 조정하는 디자이너의 능력이 그들의 개인적 특성만큼 중요할 수 있다.

어휘

demonstrate 보여주다, 입증하다
personality 개성; 유명 인사; 성격, 인격
literature 문헌; 문학
countless 무수히 많은
reference 언급; 참고, 참조
absolute 절대적인; 확실한, 확고한
relatively 비교적, 상대적으로
complexity 복잡성

🔑 (B) 집단으로 일하는 디자이너에게 관리 조직과 절차가 창의성만큼 중요함.

[7] In the latter case, / management organization and processes can be equally as relevant / as designers' creativity.
(= designers working in a group) S V C
★<A as 원급 as B>: A는 B만큼 ~한[하게]

후자의 경우 / 관리 조직과 절차가 똑같이 의미 있을 수 있다 / 디자이너들의 창의성만큼

↳ **결론:** 혼자 일하는 디자이너와 집단으로 일하는 디자이너 간의 구분이 필요하며, 후자의 경우 관리 조직과 절차는 창의성 못지않게 의미 있음.

↓

[8] Depending on the **(A) size** of a project, / *the capacity of designers* (to **(B) coordinate** team-based working environments) / can be just as important / as their personal qualities.
S V C

프로젝트의 (A) 크기에 따라 / 디자이너의 능력이 (팀 기반의 작업 환경을 (B) 조정하는) / 중요할 수 있다 / 그들의 개인적 특성만큼

appliance 가전(제품); 적용, 응용
housewares 가정용품
exercise (힘을) 발휘[행사]하다; 운동(하다)
substantial (양·가치·중요성이) 상당한
implement 이행[실행]하다
concept 구상, 발상; 개념
overlook 간과하다; 눈감아 주다
emphasis 강조; 중점
individuality 개성, 특성
function 기능(하다)
distinction 구별, 구분; 차이
latter 후자(의)
relevant 의미 있는; 관련 있는
[요약문] capacity 능력, 역량; 용량

정답 가이드

요약문을 통해 프로젝트에 따른 디자이너의 능력에 관한 글임을 알 수 있다. 기술적 복잡성이 낮은 작은 물건을 만드는 데에는 디자이너의 개인적 재능이 절대적으로 필요하지만, 여럿이 함께 일하는 큰 규모의 프로젝트에서는 성공한 디자이너가 실제로 디자인을 하기보다는 관리자로 더 기능한다고 했다. 마지막 문장에서 '집단'으로 작업하는 디자이너의 경우, '관리 조직과 절차'가 창의성만큼 의미 있다고 강조하고 있으므로 요약문의 빈칸 (A)와 (B)에 각각 들어갈 말로 가장 적절한 것은 ① 'size(크기) - coordinate(조정하다)'이다.

오답 클리닉

② cost - systematize (4%) 비용 - 체계화하다
(A)는 틀리며, (B)는 맞음.
③ size - identify (20%) 크기 - 확인하다
(A)는 맞지만, (B)는 틀림. 집단으로 일할 때 디자이너가 팀 기반의 작업 환경을 관리한다는 내용이 되어야 하며, identify는 신원 등을 확인하거나 알아보는 의미이므로 적절하지 않음.
④ cost - innovate (4%) 비용 - 혁신하다
(A)와 (B) 둘 다 틀림.
⑤ goal - investigate (1%) 목표 - 조사하다
(A)와 (B) 둘 다 틀림.

03 + 요약문 ⟨23학년도 6월 모평 40번 | 정답률 62%⟩ ①

구문분석 & 직독직해 사회 이동성과 관련된 사회적 불평등

[1] Mobilities in transit offer / *a broad field* (to be explored / by different disciplines (in all faculties)), / in addition to the humanities.
S V O
~뿐만 아니라

횡단의 이동성은 제공한다 / 광범위한 분야를 (탐구되는 / 여러 학과에 의해 (모든 학부의)) / 인문학뿐만 아니라

↳ **도입:** 횡단의 이동성은 탐구할 분야가 많음.

[2] In spite of increasing acceleration, / (for example / in travelling through geographical or virtual space), / our body becomes more and more *a passive non-moving container*, //
전치사(~에도 불구하고) S V C

증가하는 가속에도 불구하고 / (예를 들어 / 지리적인 공간이나 가상의 공간을 이동하는 데 있어) / 우리의 몸은 점점 수동적이고 움직이지 않는 컨테이너가 된다 //

which is transported by artefacts / or loaded up with inner feelings (of being mobile / in the so-called information society).
관계대명사(보충 설명)

그것은 인공물에 의해 수송된다 / 또는 내적 느낌이 가득 실린다 (이동한다는 / 소위 정보 사회에서)

★<turn A into B>: A를 B로 바꾸다

[3] Technical mobilities turn human beings / into *some kind of terminal creatures*, //
S V O

기술적 이동성은 인간을 바꾼다 / 일종의 불치병에 걸린 존재로 //

🔑 (A) 기술적 이동성으로 인간은 움직이지 않고 시간을 보냄.

who spend most of their time at rest / and who need to participate in sports / in order to balance their daily disproportion (of motion and rest).
관계사절(보충 설명) 병렬 목적(~하기 위해)

그 존재는 대부분의 시간을 움직이지 않으며 보낸다 / 그리고 그 존재(인간)는 스포츠에 참여할 필요가 있다 / 그들의 일상적인 불균형을 균형 맞추기 위해 (활동과 휴식의)

↳ 기술적 이동성으로 인간은 움직이지 않게 됨.

해석

[1] 횡단의 이동성은 인문학뿐만 아니라 모든 학부의 여러 학과에 의해 탐구되는 광범위한 분야를 제공한다. [2] 예를 들어, 지리적인 공간이나 가상의 공간을 이동하는 데 있어 증가하는 가속에도 불구하고 우리의 몸은 점점 수동적이고 움직이지 않는 컨테이너가 되는데, 그것은 인공물에 의해 수송되거나 소위 정보 사회에서 이동한다는 내적 느낌이 가득 실린다. [3] 기술적 이동성은 인간을 일종의 불치병에 걸린 존재로 바꾸는데, 그 존재는 대부분의 시간을 움직이지 않으며 보내고 그들의 일상적인 활동과 휴식의 불균형을 균형 맞추기 위해 스포츠에 참여할 필요가 있다. [4] 엘리트들이 자신들은 전혀 움직일 필요가 없으면서 돈, 사물, 사람을 움직이는 힘을 행사할 때, 우리는 Aristotle의 부동의 동자(움직이지 않은 채 움직이는 존재)로서의 신(神)의 이미지에 더 가까워졌는가? [5] 이 힘의 아래에 있는(▶ 이 힘이 없다는 것을 의미) 다른 사람들은 이동성으로 구조화된 사회적 배제의 희생자들이다. [6] 그들은 어떻게 그리고 어디로 이동해야 할지를 결정할 수 없지만, 이동할 권리나 머무를 권리 없이 그저 여기저기 옮겨지거나 들어가지 못하게 되거나 심지어 갇히기도 한다.

↓

[4]Have we come closer / to Aristotle's image of God (as the immobile mover), // when elites exercise *their power* (to move money, things and people), // while they themselves do not need to move at all? ⊶ (A) 엘리트들은 움직이지 않고서 돈, 사물, 사람을 움직이는 힘을 행사함.

우리는 더 가까워졌는가 / Aristotle의 신(神)의 이미지에 (부동의 동자(움직이지 않은 채 움직이는 존재)로서의) // 엘리트들이 자신들의 힘을 행사할 때 (돈, 사물, 사람을 움직이는) // 자신들은 전혀 움직일 필요가 없으면서

↳ **대조 A(엘리트):** 자신은 움직이지 않으면서 다른 것들을 움직이는 힘을 행사함.

[5]Others, / (at the bottom of this power), / are victims (of mobility-structured social exclusion).

다른 사람들은 / (이 힘의 아래에 있는) / 희생자들이다 (이동성으로 구조화된 사회적 배제의)

⊶ (B) 사회에서 배제된 사람들은 이동에 대한 결정이나 권리가 없음.

[6]They cannot decide / how and where to move, // but are just moved around or locked out or even locked in / without either *the right* (to move) or *the right* (to stay).

그들은 결정할 수 없다 / 어떻게 그리고 어디로 이동해야 할지를 // 하지만 그저 여기저기 옮겨지거나 들어가지 못하게 되거나 심지어 갇히기도 한다 / (이동할) 권리나 (머무를) 권리 없이

↳ **대조 B(이동성이 배제된 사람들):** 이동에 대한 결정권이나 권리가 없음.

↓

[7]In a technology and information society, / *human beings*, // whose bodily movement is less **(A) necessary**, / appear to have gained increased mobility and power, // and such a mobility-related human condition raises / the issue (of social **(B) inequality**).

기술과 정보 사회에서 / 인간은 // 신체의 움직임이 덜 (A) 필요한 / 증가된 이동성과 힘을 얻은 것처럼 보인다 // 그리고 이동성과 관련된 그러한 인간의 상태는 제기한다 / 문제를 (사회적 (B) 불평등이라는)

[8]기술과 정보 사회에서, 신체의 움직임이 덜 (A) 필요한 인간은 증가된 이동성과 힘을 얻은 것처럼 보이며, 이동성과 관련된 그러한 인간의 상태는 사회적 (B) 불평등이라는 문제를 제기한다.

어휘

mobility 이동성
cf. mobile 이동하는, 이동식의; 기동성 있는 (↔immobile 움직이지 않는)
transit 횡단, 통행; 운반, 수송
faculty 학부; 교수단; 능력
humanities 인문학
acceleration 가속(도)
artefact 인공물, 가공품
load A up with B A에 B를 가득 싣다
terminal 불치병에 걸린; 불치의, 말기의
at rest 움직이지 않고
disproportion 불균형
lock out (문을 잠가) 들어가지 못하게 하다
lock in (감방에) 가두다
⊕ **부동의 동자(immobile mover): 자신은 움직이지도 변화하지도 않으면서 다른 존재를 움직이고 변화시키는 존재로 아리스토텔레스가 신(神)으로 규정한 개념.**

정답 가이드

요약문을 통해 기술과 정보 사회의 이동성이 사회에 미친 영향에 관한 글임을 알 수 있다. 기술적 이동성으로 인간은 신체를 움직일 '필요성이 줄어들었고', 엘리트들은 몸을 움직이지 않고서도 다른 것들을 움직이는 힘을 행사할 수 있게 되었다. 한편, 힘이 없는 다른 이들은 이동성으로 구조화된 사회의 '희생자'라고 했다. 따라서 요약문의 빈칸 (A)와 (B)에 각각 들어갈 말로 가장 적절한 것은 ① 'necessary(필요한) - inequality(불평등)'이다.

오답 클리닉

② necessary - growth (16%) 필요한 - 성장
(A)는 맞지만, (B)는 틀림. 사회적 성장이 문제가 된다는 내용이 아님.
③ limited - consciousness (5%) 제한된 - 의식
(A)와 (B) 둘 다 틀림.
④ desirable - service (8%) 바람직한 - 봉사
(A)와 (B) 둘 다 틀림.
⑤ desirable - divide (9%) 바람직한 - 분열
(A)는 틀리며, (B)는 맞음.

01 + 글의 순서 〈23학년도 대수능 36번 | 정답률 60%〉 ②

구문분석 & 직독직해

생물 물벼룩의 적응적 가소성

주제문

<call+O+C(O를 C라고 부르다)>에서 O가 선행사임.

[1] A fascinating species (of water flea) / exhibits *a kind of flexibility* [that evolutionary biologists call *adaptive plasticity*].

S = V O 목적격 관계대명사

굉장히 흥미로운 종은 (물벼룩이라는) / 일종의 유연성을 보인다 [진화 생물학자들이 '적응적 가소성'이라고 부르는]

↳ 물벼룩은 '적응적 가소성'을 보임.

주어진 글의 적응적 가소성을 새끼 물벼룩을 예로 들어 설명함.

(B) [2] If the baby water flea is developing into an adult / in *water* [that includes the chemical signatures (of *creatures* [that prey on water fleas])], //

부사절 접속사(조건) S′ V′ 주격 관계대명사 주격 관계대명사

만약 새끼 물벼룩이 성체로 발달하고 있으면 / 물에서 [화학적 특징을 포함하는 (생물의 [물벼룩을 잡아먹는])] //

(= the baby water flea)

it develops a helmet and spines / to defend itself against predators.

S V O 목적(~하기 위해)

그것(새끼 물벼룩)은 투구와 가시 돌기를 발달시킨다 / 자신을 포식자로부터 방어하기 위해

(= the baby water flea)

[3] If the water around it doesn't include / the chemical signatures (of predators), //

부사절 접속사(조건) S′ V′ O′

만일 그것(새끼 물벼룩) 주위의 물이 포함하지 않으면 / 화학적 특징을 (포식자의) //

the water flea doesn't develop these protective devices.

S V O

그 물벼룩은 이러한 보호 장치를 발달시키지 않는다

↳ 예: 새끼 물벼룩은 포식자가 있는 물에서만 투구와 가시 돌기를 발달시킴.

That은 물에 포식자가 없는 경우 보호 장치를 발달시키지 않는다는 (B)의 내용을 가리킴.

(A) [4] That's a clever trick, // because producing spines and a helmet is costly, / (in terms of energy), // and conserving energy is essential / for an organism's ability (to survive and reproduce).

S V C 부사절 접속사(이유) S′₁(동명사구) V′₁ C′₁ 전치사구 삽입 S′₂(동명사구) V′₂ C′₂ =

그것은 영리한 책략인데 // 가시 돌기와 투구를 만드는 것은 손실이 크기 때문이다 / (에너지 면에서) //

그리고 에너지를 보존하는 것은 필수적이기 때문이다 / 유기체의 능력에 있어 (살아남고 번식하는)

[5] The water flea only expends *the energy* (needed to produce spines and a helmet) //

S V O 과거분사구

물벼룩은 에너지를 쏟는다 (가시 돌기와 투구를 만드는 데 필요한) //

(= the water flea)

when it needs to (expend the energy).

부사절 접속사(시간) 반복어구 생략

그것(물벼룩)이 그래야 할 때만

↳ 부연 설명: 에너지를 보존과 생존과 번식의 면에서 필요할 때만 보호 장치를 발달시키는 물벼룩의 책략은 영리함.

(A)를 바탕으로 가소성이 번식에 대한 적응이라고 결론을 내림.

(C) [6] So / it may well be // that this plasticity is an adaptation: / *a trait* [that came to exist in a species // because it contributed to reproductive fitness].

S V ★<may well+동사원형>: 아마 ~일 것이다 C(명사절) = 주격 관계대명사 ★<come to-v>: v하게 되다

부사절 접속사(이유) (= the trait)

그러므로 / 아마도 ~일 것이다 // 이 가소성은 적응이다 / 즉 특성 [종에 존재하게 된 //

그것(특성)이 번식의 적합성에 기여했기 때문에]

[7] There are many cases, / (across many species), / (of adaptive plasticity).

V S 전치사구 삽입

많은 사례가 있다 / (많은 종에 걸쳐) / (적응적 가소성의)

[8] Plasticity is conducive to fitness // if there is sufficient variation / in the environment.

S V C 부사절 접속사(조건)

가소성은 적합성에 도움이 된다 // 충분한 차이가 있는 경우 / 환경에

↳ 결론: 적응적 가소성은 환경에 충분한 차이가 있을 때 번식의 적합성에 도움이 되는 특성임.

해석

[1] 물벼룩이라는 굉장히 흥미로운 종은 진화 생물학자들이 '적응적 가소성'이라고 부르는 일종의 유연성을 보인다. (B) [2] 만약 새끼 물벼룩이 물벼룩을 잡아먹는 생물의 화학적 특징을 포함하는 물에서 성체로 발달하고 있으면, 그것은 자신을 포식자로부터 방어하기 위해 투구와 가시 돌기를 발달시킨다. [3] 만일 그것(새끼 물벼룩) 주위의 물이 포식자의 화학적 특징을 포함하지 않으면, 그 물벼룩은 이러한 보호 장치를 발달시키지 않는다. (A) [4] 그것은 영리한 책략인데, 가시 돌기와 투구를 만드는 것은 에너지 면에서 손실이 크고, 에너지를 보존하는 것은 살아남고 번식하는 유기체의 능력에 있어 필수적이기 때문이다. [5] 물벼룩은 그래야 할 때만 가시 돌기와 투구를 만드는 데 필요한 에너지를 쏟는다. (C) [6] 그러므로 아마도 이 가소성은 적응, 즉 번식의 적합성에 기여했기 때문에 종에 존재하게 된 특성이다. [7] 많은 종에 걸쳐 적응적 가소성의 많은 사례가 있다. [8] 가소성은 환경에 충분한 차이가 있는 경우 적합성에 도움이 된다.

어휘

- fascinating 굉장히 흥미로운; 매혹적인
- water flea 물벼룩
- flexibility 유연성
- adaptive 적응하는
- *cf.* adaptation 적응; 각색
- signature 특징; 서명
- prey on ~을 잡아먹다
- helmet 투구(모양의 것); 헬멧
- predator 포식자
- costly 손실[희생]이 큰; 많은 돈이 드는
- in terms of ~ 면에서
- conserve 보존[보호]하다; 절약하다
- reproduce 번식하다; 재생하다
- *cf.* reproductive 번식의
- expend (시간·노력 등을) 쏟다[들이다]
- contribute 기여하다; ~의 원인이 되다
- fitness 적합(성); 건강
- variation 차이, 변화

⊕ 가소성(plasticity): 환경 변화에 적응하고 대처할 수 있는 능력. 어떤 유전자형의 발현이 특정한 환경 요인을 따라 특정 방향으로 변화하는 성질을 의미함.

정답 가이드

물벼룩의 '적응적 가소성'에 대해 언급한 주어진 글 뒤에는 구체적으로 새끼 물벼룩이 포식자의 화학적 특징을 포함한 물에서만 보호 장치를 발달시킨다는 예를 설명하는 (B)가 오는 것이 적절하다. (B)의 마지막 문장을 That으로 받아 필요할 때만 보호 장치를 발달시키는 것은 생존과 번식을 위한 영리한 책략이라는 내용의 (A)가 (B) 뒤에 이어져야 한다. 그다음 (A) 내용에 대한 결과로, 적응적 가소성이 번식의 적합성에 기여한 적응이라고 결론짓는 (C)가 마지막에 오는 것이 자연스럽다.

오답 클리닉

① (A) - (C) - (B) (2%)
(A)의 That이 가리키는 것은 (B)의 마지막 문장이므로 (A)는 (B) 뒤에 와야 한다.
③ (B) - (C) - (A) (7%)
(A)는 물벼룩이 가소성을 보이는 이유이고, (C)는 (A)를 바탕으로 적응적 가소성에 대해 결론을 내리고 일반화된 설명을 하고 있으므로 (A) 뒤에 와야 한다.
④ (C) - (A) - (B) (8%) / ⑤ (C) - (B) - (A) (23%)
(C)의 this plasticity가 주어진 글의 adaptive plasticity와 연결된다고 생각할 수 있으나, (C)는 결과를 나타내는 So로 시작하므로 앞에 결과를 도출할 만한 내용이 선행되어야 한다.

02~03 + 복합 유형 (24학년도 대수능 41~42번 | 정답률 02 59%, 03 58%)

02 ② 03 ⑤

구문분석 & 직독직해

미디어 언론 접촉에 대한 과학자들의 개인적 경향

[1]One way (to avoid contributing to overhyping a story) / would be to say nothing.
S V C
한 가지 방법은 (이야기를 과대광고하는 것에 기여하는 것을 피하는) / 아무 말도 하지 않는 것일 것이다

(= to say nothing)
[2]However, / that is not a realistic option / for *scientists* [who feel a strong sense of responsibility (to inform the public and policymakers and/or to offer suggestions)].
S V C 주격 관계대명사 / to-v구 병렬
그러나 / 그것(아무 말도 하지 않는 것)은 현실적인 선택이 아니다 / 과학자들에게는 [강한 책임감을 느끼는 (대중과 정책 입안자에게 정보를 알리고/알리거나 제안을 내놓아야 한다는)]
↳ **도입:** 과학자가 대중과 정치권에 아무 말도 하지 않는 것은 현실적인 선택이 아님.

02-(a) 메시지를 알리고 호의적인 인정을 받는 것은 언론 접촉의 '장점'임.
[3]Speaking with members of the media has **(a) advantages** (in getting a message out / and perhaps receiving favorable recognition), //
S_1(동명사구) V_1(단수) O_1 in의 O(동명사구 병렬)
언론 구성원들과 대화하는 것은 장점이 있다 (메시지를 밖으로 내보내는 / 그리고 아마 호의적인 인정을 받을 수 있다는) //
(= speaking with members of the media)
but it runs the risk (of misinterpretations, the need for repeated clarifications, and entanglement in never-ending controversy).
S_2 V_2 O_2
그러나 그것(언론 구성원들과 대화하는 것)은 위험이 있다 (오해, 반복적인 해명의 필요, 그리고 끝없는 논란에 얽힘의)
↳ **세부 사항:** 과학자들이 언론과 접하는 것에는 장단점이 있음.

주제문
*<whether to-v>: v인지 어떤지
[4]Hence, / the decision (of whether to speak with the media) / tends to be highly individualized.
S V
따라서 / 결정은 (언론과 대화할지에 대한) / 아주 개별화되는 경향이 있다
↳ **결과:** 과학자들은 언론과의 접촉 여부를 개별적으로 결정함.

02-(b) 과학자가 언론의 흥미를 끄는 연구 결과를 얻는 일이 '드물어서' 언론 접촉은 거의 없었을 것임.
[5]Decades ago, / it was **(b) unusual** / for Earth scientists to have *results* [that were of interest to the media], // and consequently few media contacts were expected or encouraged.
가주어 V_1 C to-v의 의미상 주어 진주어(to-v구) 주격 관계대명사 / *few: (준부정어) 거의 ~없는 S_2 V_2
수십 년 전에 / (~은) 드물었다 / 지구과학자들이 연구 결과를 얻는 것은 [언론의 흥미를 끄는] // 그리고 따라서 언론과의 접촉은 거의 기대되거나 권장되지 않았다
↳ **대조 A(과거):** 언론의 흥미를 끄는 결과가 드물어 언론 접촉이 기대되거나 권장되지 않았음.

02-(c) 언론 접촉이 권장되지 않았던 시대에 언론과 자주 대화하는 과학자들은 '비난받았을' 것임.
[6]In the 1970s, / *the few scientists* [who spoke frequently with the media] / were often **(c) criticized** / by their fellow scientists / for having done so.
S 주격 관계대명사 V
1970년대에 / 소수의 과학자들은 [언론과 자주 대화하는] / 흔히 비난받았다 / 동료 과학자들로부터 / 그렇게 한 것에 대해
↳ **예:** 1970년대에는 언론과 대화하는 과학자들이 동료 과학자들로부터 비난받았음.

해석

[1]이야기를 과대광고하는 것에 기여하는 것을 피하는 한 가지 방법은 아무 말도 하지 않는 것일 것이다. [2]그러나 그것(아무 말도 하지 않는 것)은 대중과 정책 입안자에게 정보를 알리고/알리거나 제안을 내놓아야 한다는 강한 책임감을 느끼는 과학자들에게는 현실적인 선택이 아니다. [3]언론 구성원들과 대화하는 것은 메시지를 밖으로 내보내고 아마 호의적인 인정을 받을 수 있다는 (a) 장점이 있지만, 그것은 오해, 반복적인 해명의 필요, 그리고 끝없는 논란에 얽힘의 위험이 있다. [4]따라서 언론과 대화할지에 대한 결정은 아주 개별화되는 경향이 있다. [5]수십 년 전에 지구과학자들이 언론의 흥미를 끄는 연구 결과를 얻는 것은 (b) 드물었고, 따라서 언론과의 접촉은 거의 기대되거나 권장되지 않았다. [6]1970년대에, 언론과 자주 대화하는 소수의 과학자들은 흔히 그렇게 한 것에 대해 동료 과학자들로부터 (c) 비난받았다. [7]지금은 상황이 아주 다른데, 많은 과학자가 지구 온난화와 관련 문제의 중요성 때문에 공개적으로 말해야 한다는 책임감을 느끼며 많은 기자도 이런 감정들을 공유하기 때문이다. [8]게다가, 많은 과학자는 자신들이 언론의 주목과 그에 따른 대중의 인정을 (d) 즐긴다는 것을 알아 가고 있다. [9]동시에, 다른 과학자들은 기자들과 대화하는 것에 계속해서 반대하는데, 그렇게 함으로써 자신의 과학을 위한 더 많은 시간을 보존하고, 잘못 인용되는 위험과 언론 보도와 관련된 다른 불쾌한 상황을 (e) 무릅쓴다(→ 피한다).

어휘

contribute to A A에 기여하다
public 대중(의); 공공의
policymaker 정책 입안자[담당자]
get out ~을 밖으로 내보내다; 입 밖에 내다
favorable 호의적인; 유리한
recognition 인정; 알아봄, 인식

⁷The situation now is quite different, // as many scientists feel a responsibility (to speak out) / because of the importance (of global warming and related issues), // and many reporters share these feelings.

S V C 부사절 접속사(~ 때문에) S'₁ V'₁ O'₁ = S'₂ V'₂ O'₂

지금은 상황이 아주 다르다 // 많은 과학자가 책임감을 느끼기 때문이다 (공개적으로 말해야 한다는) / 중요성 때문에 (지구 온난화와 관련 문제의) // 그리고 많은 기자도 이런 감정들을 공유하기 (때문이다)

⁸In addition, / many scientists are finding // that they (d) enjoy / the media attention and *the public recognition* [that comes with it].

(→ are finding의 O) S V 명사절 접속사 S' V' O' 주격 관계대명사 (= the media attention)

🔑 02-(d) 언론과 접촉하는 과학자들은 또한 언론의 주목과 대중의 인정을 '즐길' 것임.

게다가 / 많은 과학자는 알아 가고 있다 // 자신들이 즐긴다는 것을 / 언론의 주목과 대중의 인정을 [그(언론의 주목)에 따른]

🔑 02-(e) 언론 접촉에 반대함으로써 과학자들은 잘못 인용되는 위험을 '피할' 것임.

⁹At the same time, / other scientists continue to resist speaking with reporters, /

S V O

동시에 / 다른 과학자들은 기자들과 대화하는 것에 계속해서 반대한다 /

thereby preserving more time (for their science) / and (e) **running(→ avoiding)** / the risk (of being misquoted) / and *the other unpleasantries* (associated with media coverage).

분사구문(= and thereby they preserve ~) 분사구문(= and they avoid ~) 현재분사 avoiding의 O 과거분사구

그렇게 함으로써 더 많은 시간을 보존한다 (자신의 과학을 위한) / 그리고 무릅쓴다(→ 피한다) / 위험을 (잘못 인용되는) / 그리고 다른 불쾌한 상황을 (언론 보도와 관련된)

↳ **대조 B(현재):** 공개적으로 말해야 한다는 책임감을 느끼고 언론의 관심과 대중의 인정을 즐기는 많은 과학자가 있지만, 여전히 기자와 대화하는 것을 반대하는 과학자들도 있음.

run the risk of ~의 위험이 있다[위험을 무릅쓰다]
misinterpretation 오해; 오역
clarification 해명, 설명; 정화, 깨끗하게 함
controversy 논란, 논쟁
individualized 개별화된
be of interest to A A에게는 흥미가 있다
consequently 따라서, 그 결과
encourage 권장[장려]하다; 격려하다
fellow 동료(의)
speak out 공개적으로 말하다[밝히다]
resist v-ing v에 반대[저항]하다
thereby 그렇게 함으로써
preserve 보존[관리]하다; 지키다
misquote (말·글을) 잘못 인용하다
unpleasantry 불쾌한 상황[사건]; 불쾌한 말
coverage (언론의) 보도[방송]; 범위
[선택지] expose 노출시키다; 드러내다
cautious 조심하는, 신중한
dilemma 딜레마 ((두 개의 판단 사이에 끼어 어느 쪽도 결정할 수 없는 상태에 빠져 있는 것))

정답 가이드

02 과학자들이 언론인들과 대화하는 것은 메시지를 알리고 인정을 받을 수 있다는 장점이 있지만, 여러 위험(오해, 반복적인 해명의 필요, 논란에 얽힘)도 존재하기 때문에 언론과 대화할지에 대한 결정은 과학자 개인에 따라 다른 경향이 있다고 했다. 이어지는 세부 사항은 과거와 현재 과학자들의 언론 접촉에 대한 입장을 비교하는데, 언론 접촉이 기대되거나 권장되지 않았던 과거와 달리 현재는 많은 과학자가 언론에 말해야 한다는 책임감을 느끼고 주목과 인정을 즐기기도 하지만 여전히 기자들과 대화하는 것을 반대하는 과학자들도 있다고 했다. 이처럼 현재 과학자의 언론 접촉 여부는 과학자 개인의 판단의 문제로 볼 수 있으므로, 글의 제목으로 가장 적절한 것은 ② 'A Scientist's Choice: To Be Exposed to the Media or Not?(과학자의 선택, 언론에 노출될 것인가, 말 것인가?)'이다.

03 과거와 달리 지금은 언론과 접촉하는 과학자들이 많지만 다른 과학자들은 여전히 기자들과 대화하는 것을 반대한다고 했다. 그렇게 함으로써 이들은 잘못 인용되는 위험과 언론 보도와 관련된 불쾌한 상황을 피하는 것이므로 ⑤의 'running(무릅쓰는)'을 'avoiding(피하는)'과 같은 단어로 바꾸어야 한다.

오답 클리닉

02 ① The Troubling Relationship Between Scientists and the Media (18%) 과학자와 언론 간의 골치 아픈 관계(×)
과학자와 언론 간의 관계가 나쁘다는 내용이 아님.

The 주의 오해, 반복적인 해명 필요, 논란에 얽힘 등의 위험은 언론 접촉의 단점으로 언급된 것이다.

③ Scientists! Be Cautious When Talking to the Media (10%)
과학자여! 언론에 말할 때 조심하라(×)
언론에 말할 때 조심해야 한다고 당부하는 내용이 아님.
④ The Dilemma over Scientific Truth and Media Attention (10%)
과학적 진실과 언론의 주목에 대한 딜레마(×)
과학자들이 과학적 진실을 알리는 것과 언론의 주목을 받는 것 사이에서 결정을 내리지 못하는 내용이 아님.
⑤ Who Are Responsible for Climate Issues, Scientists or the Media? (4%) 과학자와 언론 중 누가 기후 문제에 책임이 있나(×)?
지문에 언급된 global warming을 활용한 오답. 기후 문제에 대한 책임을 따지는 내용이 아님.

03 ① advantages (2%) 장점
메시지를 알리고 호의적인 인정을 받는 것은 과학자들이 언론 구성원들과 대화하는 것의 '장점'이라 할 수 있다.
② unusual (10%) 드문
과거에 언론 접촉이 기대되거나 권장되지 않은 것은 과학자들이 언론의 흥미를 끄는 연구 결과를 얻는 일이 '드물었기' 때문이었을 것이다.
③ criticized (9%) 비난받다
언론 접촉이 권장되지 않았던 당시 언론과 자주 대화하는 과학자들은 '비난받았을' 것이다.
④ enjoy (22%) 즐기다
첨가 연결어 In addition으로 이어지는 내용은 오늘날 언론과 접촉하는 과학자들에 관한 내용이므로 이들이 언론의 주목과 대중의 인정을 '즐긴다'는 것은 자연스럽다.

01 + 문장 넣기 (23학년도 대수능 39번 | 정답률 56%) ④

구문분석 & 직독직해

협상 문제를 작게 나누는 협상 방법

주제문

[1]Negotiators should try to find *ways* (to slice a large issue / into smaller pieces), / (known as using *salami tactics*).
S V O
협상가들은 방법을 찾으려고 노력해야 한다 (큰 문제를 나누는 / 더 작은 조각들로) / ('살라미 전술'을 사용하는 것으로 알려진)
↳ 협상가는 문제를 작게 나누려고 노력해야 함.

(①) [2]*Issues* [that can be expressed / in quantitative, measurable units] / are easy to slice.
S 주격 관계대명사 V C 형용사 easy 수식
문제들은 [표현될 수 있는 / 양적이고 측정 가능한 단위로] / 나누기 쉽다
↳ 쟁점 세분화 방법 1: 측정 가능한 단위로 나눔.

(②) [3]For example, / compensation demands can be divided / into cents-per-hour increments // or lease rates can be quoted / as dollars per square foot.
S1 V1 S2 V2
예를 들어 / 보상금 요구는 나눠질 수 있다 / 시간당 센트 증가로 // 또는 임대료는 매겨질 수 있다 / 제곱 피트당 달러로
↳ 방법 1의 예: 보상금 요구와 임대료는 단위당 금액으로 나눠질 수 있음.

(③) [4]When working / to fractionate issues (of principle or precedent), /
(= When they work ~) 접속사를 생략하지 않은 분사구문 목적(~하기 위해)
작업을 할 때 / 쟁점을 세분하기 위해 (원칙이나 전례의) /

parties may use the time horizon / (when the principle goes into effect // or how long it will last) / as *a way* (to fractionate the issue).
S V O 전치사(~로(서))
🔑 원칙이 발효하는 때는 합의 조건이 이행되는 시기를 뜻함.
당사자들은 시간 지평을 사용할 수 있다 / (언제 원칙이 발효하는지 // 또는 얼마나 오래 지속될지와 같은) / 방법으로 (그 쟁점을 세분하는)
↳ 쟁점 세분화 방법 2: 시간 지평을 사용함.

🔑 the time horizon을 사용하는 예에 해당함.

(④ [5]It may be easier / to reach an agreement // when settlement terms don't have to be implemented / until months in the future.)
가주어 진주어(to-v구) 부사절 접속사(시간) S′ V′
(~은) 더 쉬울지도 모른다 / 합의에 이르는 것은 // 합의 조건이 이행될 필요가 없을 때 / 이후의 몇 달까지
↳ 방법 2의 예: 합의 조건을 당장 이행할 필요가 없는 쟁점은 합의에 이르기 더 쉬울 수 있음.

[6]Another approach is to vary / the number of *ways* [that the principle may be applied].
S V C 관계부사 S′ V′
또 다른 접근법은 다양화하는 것이다 / 방법의 수를 [원칙이 적용될 수 있는]
↳ 쟁점 세분화 방법 3: 원칙이 적용될 수 있는 방법의 수를 다양화함.

(⑤) [7]For example, / a company may devise / *a family emergency leave plan* [that allows employees *the opportunity* (to be away from the company / for a period (of no longer than three hours, / and no more than once a month), / for illness in the employee's immediate family)].
S V O 주격 관계대명사 V′ IO′ DO′ =
예를 들어 / 기업은 고안할 수 있다 / 가족 긴급 휴가 계획을 [직원들에게 기회를 주는 (회사로부터 떠나 있을 / 기간 동안 (세 시간 이내의 / 그리고 한 달에 한 번 이내의) / 직원의 직계 가족의 질병에 대해)]
↳ 방법 3의 예: 기간, 빈도, 사유, 가족 범위 등으로 세분화한 가족 긴급 휴가 계획을 고안함.

해석

[1]협상가들은 '살라미 전술'을 사용하는 것으로 알려진, 큰 문제를 더 작은 조각들로 나누는 방법을 찾으려고 노력해야 한다. (①) [2]양적이고 측정 가능한 단위로 표현될 수 있는 문제들은 나누기 쉽다. (②) [3]예를 들어, 보상금 요구는 시간당 센트 증가로 나뉘거나 임대료는 제곱 피트당 달러로 매겨질 수 있다. (③) [4]원칙이나 전례의 쟁점을 세분하기 위해 작업을 할 때, 당사자들은 그 쟁점을 세분하는 방법으로 (언제 원칙이 발효하는지 또는 얼마나 오래 지속될지와 같은) 시간 지평을 사용할 수 있다. (④ [5]합의 조건이 이후의 몇 달까지 이행될 필요가 없을 때 합의에 이르는 것은 더 쉬울지도 모른다.) [6]또 다른 접근법은 원칙이 적용될 수 있는 방법의 수를 다양화하는 것이다. (⑤) [7]예를 들어, 기업은 직원들에게 직원의 직계 가족의 질병에 대해 세 시간 이내의 그리고 한 달에 한 번 이내의 기간 동안 회사로부터 떠나 있을 기회를 주는 가족 긴급 휴가 계획을 고안할 수 있다.

어휘

negotiator 협상가
slice 나누다, 자르다; 조각
quantitative 양적인
compensation 보상(금)
demand 요구(하다); 필요로 하다
lease 임대(하다)
quote 시세를 매기다; 인용하다
precedent 전례; 관례
go into effect 발효하다, 실시되다
settlement 합의; 해결
term 조건; 용어; 학기
implement (계약 등을) 이행[시행]하다
devise 고안하다
immediate 직계[직속]의; 즉각적인
⊕ 살라미 전술(salami tactics): 협상에서 한 번에 목표를 달성하는 것이 아니라 문제를 부분별로 세분하고 쟁점화하여 각각에 대한 대가를 받아 냄으로써 이익을 극대화하는 전술.

정답 가이드

주어진 문장은 합의 조건 이행까지 시간이 더 있다면 (시간이 없을 때보다) 합의에 이르기가 더 쉬울 수 있다는 내용이다. 이는 합의 도달을 쉽게 할 수 있는 '방법'으로 '시간'을 더 주어야 한다고 제시한 것이다. 첫 문장부터 보면, 협상가들이 살라미 전술, 즉 큰 문제를 더 작은 조각들로 나누는 방법을 찾아야 한다고 했고, ③ 뒤 문장에 시간 지평으로 쟁점을 세분하는 방법이 제시되었는데, 주어진 문장은 이 문장을 구체적으로 뒷받침하므로 ④에 들어가는 것이 가장 적절하다.

오답 클리닉

① (2%) 협상가는 문제를 작게 나눠야 한다는 문장 뒤에 나누기 쉬운 문제의 속성을 설명하는 내용이다.
② (6%) 문제가 양적으로 측정 가능한 단위로 나눠지는 예가 자연스럽게 연결된다.
③ (14%) 쟁점을 세분화하기 위해 시간 지평을 사용하는 또 다른 방법을 설명한다.
⑤ (23%) 앞 문장에서 언급된 원칙 적용 방법을 다양화하는 예로 직원의 가족 긴급 휴가를 기간, 빈도, 사유, 가족 범위로 세분화해 적용하는 내용이 이어진다.

The 주의 ⑤ 뒤의 three hours, once a month가 시간과 관련된 쟁점 세분화 방법이 아닌 휴가 원칙 적용 방법을 다양화하는 예에 해당됨을 이해해야 한다.

02~03 복합 유형 (24학년도 9월 모평 41~42번 | 정답률 02 51%, 03 49%)

02 ① 03 ⑤

구문분석 & 직독직해

인지 잊어버리기 쉬운 맥락 정보

[1] *One reason* [(why) we think // (that) we forget most of what we learned / in school] / is // that we underestimate what we actually remember.
(S / 관계부사 생략 S′ V′ 명사절 접속사 생략 S″ V″ O″ / V / 명사절 접속사 S′ V′ O′(명사절); think의 O(명사절); is의 C(명사절))
한 가지 이유는 [우리가 생각하는 // 우리가 배운 것의 대부분을 잊어버린다고 / 학교에서] / ~이다 // 우리는 우리가 실제로 기억하는 것을 과소평가한다는 것

[2] Other times, / we know // (that) we remember something, //
(S_1 V_1 O_1(명사절))
다른 때에 / 우리는 안다 // 우리가 어떤 것을 기억한다는 것을 //
but we don't recognize // that we learned it / in school.
(S_2 V_2 O_2(명사절))
그러나 우리는 인식하지 못한다 // 우리가 그것을 배웠다는 것을 / 학교에서
↳ **도입:** 우리는 배운 내용은 기억하지만 그것을 학교에서 배웠다는 사실은 인식하지 못함.

[3] Knowing / where and when you learned something / is usually called *context information*, //
(S_1(동명사구) 동명사 knowing의 O(명사절) V_1(단수) C)
아는 것은 / 여러분이 무언가를 어디에서 언제 배웠는지를 / 보통 '맥락 정보'라고 불린다 //
and context is handled / by **(a) different** memory processes / than memory for the content.
(S_2 V_2 전치사((different 뒤에서) ~와는))
그리고 맥락은 다루어진다 / 다른 기억 절차에 의해 / 그 내용에 대한 기억과는
🔑 02-(a) 맥락은 기억하지 않고 내용을 기억하는 것이 가능한 이유는 맥락이 내용과는 '다른' 기억 절차에 의해 다뤄지기 때문임.

[4] Thus, / it's quite possible to retain content / without remembering the context.
(가주어 진주어(to-v구) without의 O(동명사구))
따라서 / 내용을 기억해 두는 것은 충분히 가능하다 / 맥락을 기억하지 않고
↳ **세부 사항 1:** 맥락 정보는 내용에 대한 기억과는 다른 기억 절차에 의해 처리되므로 맥락은 잊더라도 내용을 기억하는 것이 가능함.

[5] For example, / if someone mentions a movie // and you think to yourself // that you heard (that) it was terrible / but can't remember **(b) where** you heard that, //
(부사절 접속사(조건) S'_1 V'_1 O′ S'_2 V'_2 명사절 접속사 S″ V''_1 O''_1(명사절) V''_2 O''_2(명사절); think의 O(명사절))
예를 들어 / 만약 누군가가 어떤 영화에 대해 언급한다면 // 그리고 여러분이 마음속으로 생각한다면 // 그 영화가 끔찍하다고 들었다고 / 그러나 그것을 어디에서 들었는지는 기억할 수 없다고 //
you're recalling the content, // but you've lost the context.
(S_1 V_1 O_1 S_2 V_2 O_2)
🔑 03-(b) 맥락을 잃었다는 것은 내용을 '어디에서' 언제 들었는지를 기억하지 못함을 의미함.
여러분은 그 내용을 상기하고 있는 것이다 // 그러나 여러분은 맥락은 잃어버린 것이다
↳ **예:** 어떤 영화가 끔찍하다고 들은 것은(내용) 기억하지만 그것을 어디에서 들었는지는(맥락) 기억하지 못함.

[6] Context information is frequently **(c) easier** to forget / than content, // and it's the source (of a variety of memory illusions).
(S_1 V_1 C_1 형용사 easier 수식 S_2 V_2 C_2; (= 앞 내용))
맥락 정보는 흔히 잊어버리기 더 쉽다 / 내용보다 // 그리고 그것(맥락 정보가 잊어버리기 더 쉬운 것)이 근원이다 (다양한 기억 착각의)
↳ **세부 사항 2:** 맥락 정보는 내용보다 잊기 쉽고 기억 착각을 일으킴.

해석

[1]우리가 학교에서 배운 것의 대부분을 잊어버린다고 생각하는 한 가지 이유는 우리가 실제로 기억하는 것을 과소평가한다는 것이다. [2]다른 때에, 우리는 우리가 어떤 것을 기억한다는 것은 알지만, 우리는 우리가 그것을 학교에서 배웠다는 것을 인식하지 못한다. [3]여러분이 무언가를 어디에서 언제 배웠는지를 아는 것은 보통 '맥락 정보'라고 불리며, 맥락은 그 내용에 대한 기억과는 (a) 다른 기억 절차에 의해 다루어진다. [4]따라서, 맥락을 기억하지 않고 내용을 기억해 두는 것은 충분히 가능하다. [5]예를 들어, 만약 누군가가 어떤 영화에 대해 언급하고 여러분이 그 영화가 끔찍하다고 들었지만, 그것을 (b) 어디에서 들었는지는 기억할 수 없다고 마음속으로 생각한다면, 여러분은 그 내용을 상기하고 있지만 맥락은 잃어버린 것이다. [6]맥락 정보는 흔히 내용보다 잊어버리기 (c) 더 쉬우며, 그것이 다양한 기억 착각의 근원이다. [7]예를 들어, 만약 설득력 있는 주장이 별로 신뢰할 수 없는 어떤 사람(예를 들면, 그 주제에 대한 확실한 금전상의 이익을 가진 사람)에 의해 쓰인다면 사람들은 그것에 대해 (d) 납득하지 못한다. [8]하지만 이윽고 독자의 태도는 대체로 그 설득력 있는 주장의 방향으로 변화한다. [9]왜일까? 독자는 그 주장의 내용은 기억하지만 그 출처, 즉 신뢰할 수 없는 사람은 잊어버릴 가능성이 있기 때문이다. [10]만약 지식의 출처를 기억하는 것이 어렵다면, 여러분은 여러분이 학교에서 배운 많은 것을 기억하지 못한다고 결론 내리는 것이 얼마나 (e) 어려울(→ 쉬울)지를 알 수 있다.

어휘

underestimate 과소평가(하다)
recognize 인식하다; 알아보다; 인정하다
context 맥락, 문맥
handle 다루다; 취급하다
content 내용; 목차; 만족한
retain 기억해 두다; 유지[보유]하다
recall 상기하다, 기억해 내다

[7]For instance, / people are (d) unconvinced / by a persuasive argument //
S V C
예를 들어 / 사람들은 납득하지 못한다 / 설득력 있는 주장에 대해 //

(= the persuasive argument)
if it's written / by *someone* [who is not very credible] (e.g., someone (with a clear financial interest in the topic)).
부사절 접속사(조건) 주격 관계대명사
03-(d) 설득력 있는 주장이라도 신뢰할 수 없는 사람이 쓴다면 사람들은 '납득하지 못할' 것임.
만약 그것(설득력 있는 주장)이 쓰인다면 / 어떤 사람에 의해 [별로 신뢰할 수 없는] (예를 들면, 사람 (그 주제에 대한 확실한 금전상의 이익을 가진))

[8]But in time, / readers' attitudes, (on average), change / in the direction (of the persuasive argument).
S 전치사구 삽입 V
하지만 이윽고 / 독자의 태도는 (대체로) 변화한다 / 방향으로 (그 설득력 있는 주장의)
↳ **예:** 우리는 신뢰할 수 없는 사람의 설득력 있는 주장을 처음에 믿지 않지만, 머지않아 믿게 됨.

03-(c) 독자는 내용의 출처(맥락 정보)를 잊기 '쉬움'
[9]Why? // Because readers are likely / to remember the content (of the argument) / but (to) forget the source — / *someone* [who is not credible].
= S V C to-v구 병렬
주격 관계대명사
왜일까? // 독자는 (~할) 가능성이 있기 때문이다 / 내용은 기억할 (그 주장의) / 그러나 그 출처는 잊어버릴 / 즉 사람 [신뢰할 수 없는]
↳ **예의 부연 설명:** 내용은 기억해도 그 내용의 출처가 신뢰할 수 없는 사람이라는 것은 잊어버리기 때문임.

주제문 03-(e) 지식의 출처가 학교라는 것을 기억하기 어렵다면 학교에서 배운 것의 대부분을 잊었다고 결론 내리기 '쉬울' 것임.
can see의 O(명사절)
[10]If remembering the source of knowledge is difficult, // you can see // how it would be (e) challenging(→ easy) / to conclude // (that) you don't remember much (from school).
부사절 접속사(조건) S'(동명사구) V'(단수) C' S V 의문사 가주어' V'
to conclude의 O(명사절)
C' 진주어' 명사절 접속사 생략 S'' V'' O''
만약 지식의 출처를 기억하는 것이 어렵다면 // 여러분은 알 수 있다 // (~이) 얼마나 어려울(→ 쉬울)지를 / 결론 내리는 것이 // 여러분이 많은 것을 기억하지 못한다고 (학교에서 배운)
↳ **결론:** 지식의 출처(맥락 정보)를 기억하는 것이 어렵다면 학교에서 배운 많은 것을 기억하지 못한다고 결론 내리기 쉬움.

source 근원; 출처
unconvinced 납득[확신]하지 못하는
persuasive 설득력 있는
argument 주장; 논쟁
credible 신뢰할[믿을] 수 있는
cf. credibility 신뢰성
financial 금전상의; 금융[재정]의
interest 이익; 관심(을 끌다); 이해관계
in time 이윽고, 조만간
on average 대체로
challenging 어려운, 힘든; 도전적인
[선택지] trick 속이다; 속임수
selectively 선택적으로
constant 끊임없는; 불변의
shift 바꾸다; 이동(하다); 변화

정답 가이드

02 도입 내용 중 우리가 기억하더라도 학교에서 배웠다는 것을 인식하지 못한다는 것에 대해, 그 이유를 상세히 설명하는 글이다. 즉, 학교는 맥락 정보인데, 맥락 정보는 잊어버리기 쉬워서 학교에서 배운 것이 없다고 결론 내린다는 것이다. 따라서 글의 제목으로 가장 적절한 것은 ① 'Learned Nothing in School?: How Memory Tricks You(학교에서 배운 것이 없는가? 기억이 어떻게 여러분을 속이는가)'이다.

03 지식의 출처를 기억하는 것이 어렵다면 배운 내용은 기억해도 그것을 학교에서 배웠다는 것은 잊어버릴 것이므로 학교에서 배운 많은 것을 기억하지 못한다고 결론 내리기가 쉬울 것이다. 따라서 ⑤의 'challenging(어려운)'을 'easy(쉬운)'로 바꾸어야 한다.

오답 클리닉

02 ② Why We Forget Selectively: Credibility of Content (27%)
우리가 선택적으로 잊어버리는 이유인 내용의 신뢰성(×)
내용의 신뢰성이 기억에 영향을 준다는 내용은 없음.

The 주의 설득력 있는 주장은 기억해도 그 출처가 신뢰할 수 없는 사람인 것은 잊어버린다는 예는 내용보다 맥락 정보를 잊기 쉽다는 특징을 설명하는 지엽적인 내용이다.

③ The Constant Battle Between Content and Context (11%)
내용과 맥락 사이의 끊임없는 싸움(×)
맥락과 내용이 충돌한다는 내용이 아님. 내용과 맥락은 서로 다른 기억 절차에 의해 다루어진다고 했음.

④ How Students Can Learn More and Better in School (4%)
학생들이 학교에서 더 많이 그리고 더 잘 배울 수 있는 방법(×)
학생들의 효율적인 학습법에 관한 글이 아님.

⑤ Shift Your Focus from Who to What for Memory Building (7%)
기억 형성(×)을 위해 여러분의 초점을 누구에서 무엇으로 바꾸어라
기억을 형성하는 방법에 대한 글이 아님.

03 ① different (3%) 다른
문장 4의 맥락은 기억하지 않고 내용을 기억하는 것이 가능하다는 결과를 통해 맥락이 내용과는 '다른' 기억 절차에 의해 다루어진다고 유추할 수 있다.
② where (7%) 어디에서
맥락은 무언가를 언제 어디에서 배웠는지에 관한 것이므로 맥락을 잃어버렸다는 것은 내용을 '어디에서' 들었는지 기억하지 못함을 의미한다.
③ easier (10%) 더 쉬운
문장 9에서 독자는 내용은 기억해도 출처를 잊기 쉽다고 했으므로 맥락 정보는 잊어버리기가 '더 쉬운' 것이다.
④ unconvinced (30%) 납득하지 못하는
신뢰할 수 없는 사람이 쓴 설득력 있는 주장을 사람들은 납득하지 못하지만 결국에 그 출처를 잊고 주장을 믿게 된다는 맥락이 되어야 하므로 '납득하지 못하는'은 적절하다.

The 주의 설득력 있는 주장에 납득이 된다는 상식에 기반해 선택하지 않도록 주의한다. 뒤에 이어지는 조건(별로 신뢰할 수 없는 사람에 의해 쓰인다면)에 근거해 선택해야 한다.

01 + 밑줄 어법 (24학년도 대수능 29번 | 정답률 57%) ②

구문분석 & 직독직해

심리 아기의 타인을 모방하려는 욕구

[1] A number of studies provide / substantial evidence (of *an innate human disposition* (to respond differentially / to social stimuli)).

S(복수) V(복수) O

많은 연구가 제시한다 / 상당한 증거를 (타고난 인간 성향에 대한 (달리 반응하는 / 사회적 자극에))

[2] From birth, / infants will orient preferentially / towards the human face and voice, /

S V

태어날 때부터 / 아기들은 우선적으로 향한다 / 사람의 얼굴과 목소리 쪽으로 /

(= the human face and voice)

① **seeming** to know // that such stimuli are particularly meaningful / for them.

분사구문(= and they will seem ~) to know의 O(명사절) (= infants)

그리고 그들은 알고 있는 것 같다 // 그러한 자극(사람의 얼굴과 목소리)이 특히 의미가 있다는 것을 / 자신들에게

(= infants)

[3] Moreover, / they register this connection actively, / imitating *a variety of facial gestures* [that are presented to them] — / tongue protrusions, lip tightenings, mouth openings.

S V O 분사구문(= while they imitate ~) 주격 관계대명사 (= infants)

게다가 / 그들(아기)은 이러한 (자극과 의미의) 연결을 적극적으로 기억한다 / 다양한 표정들을 모방하면서 [자신들에게 보여지는] / 혀 내밀기, 입술 꽉 다물기, 입 벌리기와 같이

[4] They will even try to match / *gestures* ② [**which(→ with which)** they have some difficulty], /

S V O 전치사+관계대명사 S′ V′ O′

심지어 그들은 일치시키려고 노력한다 / 표정과 [자신들이 다소 어려워하는] /

experimenting with their own faces // until they succeed.

분사구문(= and they will experiment ~) 부사절 접속사(시간)

그리고 자기 자신의 얼굴로 실험한다 // 성공할 때까지

[5] When they ③ **do** succeed, // they show pleasure / by a brightening of their eyes; //

부사절 접속사(시간) 일반동사 강조 S_1 V_1 O_1

when they fail, // they show distress.

부사절 접속사(시간) S_2 V_2 O_2

그들이 정말 성공할 때 // 그들은 기쁨을 드러낸다 / 눈을 반짝이면서 //

그리고 그들이 실패할 때 // 그들은 괴로움을 드러낸다

[6] In other words, / they not only have / an innate capacity (for matching their own kinaesthetically experienced bodily movements / with ④ ***those*** *of others* [that are visually perceived]); // they have an innate drive (to do so).

S_1 V_1 O_1 ★세미콜론(;)이 <not only A but (also) B>의 but을 대신함.

(= bodily movements) 주격 관계대명사 S_2 V_2 O_2

다시 말해 / 그들은 가지고 있을 뿐만 아니라 / 타고난 능력을 (그들 자신의 운동감각적으로 경험한 신체 움직임을 일치시키는 / 다른 사람의 그것들(신체 움직임)과 [시각적으로 지각되는]) // 그들은 타고난 욕구도 가지고 있다 (그렇게 하려는)

주제문

[7] That is, / they seem to have an innate drive (to imitate *others* [whom they judge ⑤ **to be** 'like me']).

S V C 목적격 관계대명사 S′ V′ C′

즉 / 그들은 타고난 욕구가 있는 것으로 보인다 (타인을 모방하려는 [자신들이 '나와 비슷하다'라고 판단하는])

해석

[1]많은 연구가 사회적 자극에 달리 반응하는 타고난 인간 성향에 대한 상당한 증거를 제시한다. [2]태어날 때부터, 아기들은 사람의 얼굴과 목소리 쪽으로 우선적으로 향하는데, 그러한 자극(사람의 얼굴과 목소리)이 특히 자신들에게 의미가 있다는 것을 알고 있는 것 같다. [3]게다가, 그들(아기)은 혀 내밀기, 입술 꽉 다물기, 입 벌리기와 같이 자신들에게 보여지는 다양한 얼굴 표정들을 모방하면서 이러한 (자극과 의미의) 연결을 적극적으로 기억한다. [4]심지어 그들은 자신들이 다소 어려워하는 표정과 일치시키려고 노력하고, 성공할 때까지 자기 자신의 얼굴로 실험한다. [5]그들은 정말 성공할 때 눈을 반짝이면서 기쁨을 드러내고, 실패할 때 괴로움을 드러낸다. [6]다시 말해, 그들은 운동감각적으로 경험한 그들 자신의 신체 움직임을 시각적으로 지각되는 다른 사람의 신체 움직임과 일치시키는 타고난 능력을 가지고 있을 뿐만 아니라, 그렇게 하려는 타고난 욕구도 가지고 있다. [7]즉, 그들은 자신들이 '나와 비슷하다'라고 판단하는 타인을 모방하려는 타고난 욕구가 있는 것으로 보인다.

어휘

substantial (양이) 상당한; 실질[실체]의
differentially 달리, 구별하여; 특이하게
stimulus (*pl.* stimuli) 자극
infant 아기, 유아; 초기의
orient (어떤 방향으로) 향하다
preferentially 우선적으로
register 기억하다; 등록(하다)
actively 적극적으로; 활발히, 활동적으로
imitate 모방하다, 흉내 내다
present 보여 주다; 제공하다; 현재(의); 참석[출석]한
protrusion 내밀기; 돌출
tighten 꽉 다물다; 팽팽하게 하다
distress 괴로움, 고통; 괴롭히다
capacity 능력; 용량, 수용력
visually 시각적으로
perceive 지각하다, 인지하다
drive 욕구; 동기; 몰아가다

정답 가이드

② **[전치사+관계대명사]** 밑줄 친 관계대명사 which 뒤에 주어(they), 동사(have), 목적어(some difficulty)로 이뤄진 완전한 구조의 절이 왔으므로 관계대명사는 쓸 수 없다. 문맥상 선행사인 gestures를 수식하는 것은 맞는데, 관계부사(when, where, why, how)는 gestures를 선행사로 할 수 없으며 <전치사+관계대명사>는 완전한 절을 이끌어 선행사를 수식할 수 있다. <have some difficulty in/with ~>는 '~을 약간 어려워하다'란 의미를 나타내는 것으로, 원래 문장이 They have some difficulty in/with them(= gestures).임을 고려하여 which를 in[with] which로 고쳐야 한다.

The 핵심 ★ <전치사+관계대명사>는 관계부사와 마찬가지로 뒤에 완전한 절이 온다.

오답 클리닉

① **[분사구문]** (10%)
부대상황을 나타내는 분사구문의 생략된 주어는 문장의 주어와 같은 infants이고 이들이 알고 '있는 것 같다'는 능동의 의미이므로 현재분사 seeming은 어법상 적절하다.

③ **[강조구문]** (8%)
일반동사 succeed를 강조하기 위해 조동사 do가 쓰였다. 주어(they)가 복수이고 주절의 시제가 현재이므로 수와 시제의 일치도 적절하다.

④ **[명사-대명사의 수일치]** (14%)
앞에서 언급된 복수명사 bodily movements를 가리키기 위한 지시대명사로 those를 쓴 것은 적절하다.

⑤ **[목적격보어를 이끄는 to부정사]** (11%)
<judge+O+to be C>는 'O를 C라고 판단하다'의 의미로 목적어는 관계대명사 whom이 대신하기에 빠져 있으며, to be 뒤에 판단하는 내용인 목적격보어가 따르는 것은 적절하다. 이때 to be는 생략 가능하다.

02 + 밑줄 어법 (24학년도 9월 모평 29번 | 정답률 62%) ③

구문분석 & 직독직해

심리 스트레스 반응을 자원으로 보는 전략

★<view A as B>: A를 B로 보다[여기다]

[1]Viewing the stress response as a resource (S(동명사구)) / can transform (V) / the physiology (of fear) (O) / into the biology (of courage).
★<transform[turn] A into B>: A를 B로 바꾸다
스트레스 반응을 자원으로 보는 것은 / 바꿀 수 있다 / 생리 기능을 (두려움이라는) / 생명 작용으로 (용기라는)

[2]It (S) (= Viewing the stress response as a resource) can turn (V_1) a threat (O_1) / into a challenge / and can help (V_2) you (O_2) ① do your best (C) / under pressure.
그것(스트레스 반응을 자원으로 보는 것)은 위협을 바꿀 수 있다 / 도전으로 / 그리고 여러분이 최선을 다하도록 도울 수 있다 / 압박감 속에서

[3]Even when (부사절 접속사(시간)) the stress (S′) doesn't feel (V′) helpful (C′) — / (as in the case of anxiety) (전치사구 삽입; as → 전치사(~처럼)) — //
스트레스가 도움이 되지 않는다고 느껴질 때조차도 / (불안감의 경우에서처럼) //
welcoming it (S(동명사구); it → (= the stress)) can transform (V) ② it (O; → (= the stress)) / into *something* [that (주격 관계대명사) is helpful] : / more energy, more confidence, and *a greater willingness* (to take action).
그것(스트레스)을 기꺼이 받아들이는 것은 그것(스트레스)을 바꿀 수 있다 / 어떤 것으로 [도움이 되는] / 즉 더 많은 에너지, 더 많은 자신감, 그리고 더 기꺼이 하는 마음 (조치를 취하려는)

[4]You (S) can apply (V) this strategy (O) / in your own life // anytime (부사절 접속사(= whenever)) you notice signs of stress.
여러분은 이 전략을 적용할 수 있다 / 여러분 자신의 삶에 // 스트레스의 징후를 알아차릴 때마다

★<지각동사 feel+O+v-ing>: O가 v하고 있는 것을 느끼다
[5]When (부사절 접속사(시간)) you feel (V′) your heart (O'_1) beating (C'_1) or your breath (O'_2) quickening (C'_2), //
여러분의 심장이 뛰거나 호흡이 빨라지는 것을 느낄 때 //
③ **realizing(→ realize)** (V(명령문)) // that (명사절 접속사; → realize의 O(명사절)) it (S′) is (V′) your body's way (C′) (of trying to give you more energy).
깨달아라 // 그것이 여러분의 몸의 방식이라는 것을 (여러분에게 더 많은 에너지를 주려고 하는)

[6]If (부사절 접속사(조건)) you notice tension / in your body, // remind (V(명령문)) yourself (IO) // ④ **that** (명사절 접속사; → remind의 DO(명사절)) the stress response (S′) gives (V′) you (IO′) access to your strength (DO′).
여러분이 긴장을 알아차린다면 / 여러분의 몸에서 // 자신에게 상기시켜라 // 스트레스 반응이 여러분에게 여러분의 힘을 이용할 권리를 준다는 것을

[7]Sweaty palms?
손바닥에 땀이 나는가

해석

[1]스트레스 반응을 자원으로 보는 것은 두려움이라는 생리 기능을 용기라는 생명 작용으로 바꿀 수 있다. [2]그것은 위협을 도전으로 바꿀 수 있고 여러분이 압박감 속에서 최선을 다하도록 도울 수 있다. [3]불안감의 경우에서처럼 스트레스가 도움이 되지 않는다고 느껴질 때조차도 그것(스트레스)을 기꺼이 받아들이는 것은 그것(스트레스)을 도움이 되는 어떤 것, 즉 더 많은 에너지, 더 많은 자신감, 그리고 더 기꺼이 조치를 취하려는 마음으로 바꿀 수 있다. [4]여러분은 스트레스의 징후를 알아차릴 때마다 여러분의 삶에 이 전략을 적용할 수 있다. [5]여러분의 심장이 뛰거나 호흡이 빨라지는 것을 느낄 때, 그것이 여러분에게 더 많은 에너지를 주려고 하는 여러분의 몸의 방식이라는 것을 깨달아라. [6]여러분이 몸에서 긴장을 알아차린다면 스트레스 반응이 여러분에게 여러분의 힘을 이용할 권리를 준다는 것을 자신에게 상기시켜라. [7]손바닥에 땀이 나는가? [8]첫 데이트하러 가는 것이 어떤 기분이었는지를 기억하라. 즉 여러분이 원하는 어떤 것에 가까이 있을 때 손바닥에 땀이 난다.

어휘

resource 자원; 재료
biology 생명 작용[활동]; 생물학
anxiety 불안(감); 갈망
welcome 기꺼이 받아들이다; 환영하다, 맞이하다
willingness 기꺼이 하는 마음
take action 조치를 취하다, 행동에 옮기다
strategy 전략
beat (심장이) 뛰다; 치다; 이기다
quicken 빨라지다
remind 상기시키다, 일깨우다; 생각나다

↱ remember의 O(명사절)
[8]Remember // what it felt like ⑤ **to go** on your first date — //
V₁(명령문) 의문사 가주어' V' 진주어'(to-v구)
기억하라 // 첫 데이트하러 가는 것이 어떤 기분이었는지를 //

palms sweat // when you're close / to *something* [(that) you want].
S₂ V₂ 부사절 접속사(시간) 목적격 관계대명사 생략
즉 손바닥에 땀이 난다 // 여러분이 가까이 있을 때 / 어떤 것에 [여러분이 원하는]

access 이용할 권리[기회]; 접근(하다)
strength 힘; 강점
sweaty 땀이 나는
cf. sweat 땀(이 나다)
palm 손바닥

정답 가이드

③ **[정동사 자리 vs. 준동사 자리]** When이 이끄는 부사절 다음에 주절이 이어져야 하는데 realizing 뒤에 다른 술어 동사가 없다. 문맥상 '~을 깨달아라'라는 명령문이 자연스러우므로 realizing을 동사원형 realize로 고쳐야 한다.

The 주의 콤마(,) 뒤에 위치한 realizing을 분사구문을 이끄는 현재분사로 착각하지 않도록 주의한다.

오답 클리닉

① **[목적격보어로 쓰이는 원형부정사]** (7%)
<help+O+(to-)v>는 'O가 v하도록 돕다'라는 뜻으로, 준사역동사 help의 목적격보어에는 원형부정사와 to-v가 모두 올 수 있으므로 원형부정사 do는 어법상 적절하다.

② **[명사-대명사의 수일치]** (9%)
문맥상 앞의 부사절에 나온 단수명사 the stress의 반복을 피하기 위한 대명사로 it은 어법상 적절하다.

④ **[명사절 접속사 that]** (9%)
<remind+O+that ...>의 구조로 remind의 직접목적어인 명사절을 이끄는 접속사 that은 어법상 적절하다.

⑤ **[가주어 it - 진주어(to-v)]** (12%)
앞의 it은 형식상의 주어인 가주어이고 to go on your first date가 내용상의 주어인 진주어에 해당하므로, 명사 역할을 하는 to-v인 to go는 어법상 적절하다.

03 밑줄 어법 (24학년도 6월 모평 29번 | 정답률 40%) ③

구문분석 & 직독직해

심리 <오즈의 마법사>로 본 동기 부여

★<consider A (as) B>: A를 B로 생각하다
[1]Consider *The Wizard of Oz* / as a psychological study (of motivation).
<오즈의 마법사>를 생각해 보라 / 심리학적 연구로 (동기 부여에 관한)

[2]Dorothy and her three friends work hard / to get to the Emerald City, /
S V 목적(~하기 위해)
Dorothy와 그녀의 세 친구들은 열심히 노력한다 / 에메랄드 시로 가기 위해 /

overcoming barriers, persisting against all adversaries.
분사구문(= and they overcome ~ and persist ~)
그리고 장벽을 극복하고, 모든 적에게 끈질기게 맞선다

★<expect+O+to-v>: O가 v할 거라고 기대하다
[3]They do so // because they expect the Wizard to give ① **them** what they are missing.
S V 부사절 접속사(이유) S' V' O' C' to give의 IO to give의 DO(명사절)
그들은 그렇게 한다 // 그들은 마법사가 그들에게 없는 것을 자신들에게 줄 거라고 기대하기 때문에

★<aware that ~>: ~을 깨닫고[알고] 있는
[4]Instead, / the wonderful (and wise) Wizard makes them aware // that they, (not he), / always had / *the power* ② (**to fulfill** their wishes).
S V O C 명사절 접속사 S' V' O'
대신에 / 그 멋진 (그리고 현명한) 마법사는 그들이 깨닫게 한다 // 그들이 (자신(마법사)이 아니라) / 항상 가지고 있었다는 것을 / 힘을 (자신들의 소원을 실현할)

★<not A but B>: A가 아니라 B
[5]For Dorothy, / *home* is not a place / but a feeling of security, of comfort with *people* [(whom[that]) she loves]; // it is wherever her heart is.
S₁ V₁ C₁₋₁ C₁₋₂ 목적격 관계대명사 생략 S₂ V₂ C₂
Dorothy에게 / '집'은 장소가 아니라 / 안전감, 사람들과 함께하는 편안감이다 [그녀가 사랑하는] //
그녀의 마음이 있는 곳이면 어디든지가 그것(집)이다

[6]*The courage* [(which[that]) the Lion wants], / *the intelligence* [(which[that]) the Scarecrow longs for], / and *the emotions* [(which[that]) the Tin Man dreams of] /
S₁ 목적격 관계대명사 생략 S₂ 목적격 관계대명사 생략 S₃ 목적격 관계대명사 생략
용기는 [사자가 원하는] / 지성은 [허수아비가 간절히 바라는] / 그리고 감정은 [양철 나무꾼이 꿈꾸는] /
③ **being(→ are)** *attributes* [(which[that]) they already possess].
V(복수) C 목적격 관계대명사 생략
속성이다 [그들이 이미 가지고 있는]

해석

[1]<오즈의 마법사>를 동기 부여에 관한 심리학적 연구로 생각해 보라. [2]Dorothy와 그녀의 세 친구는 에메랄드 시로 가기 위해 열심히 노력하면서, 장벽을 극복하고, 모든 적에게 끈질기게 맞선다. [3]그들은 마법사가 그들에게 없는 것을 자신들에게 줄 거라고 기대하기 때문에 그렇게 한다. [4]대신에, 그 멋진 (그리고 현명한) 마법사는 자신(마법사)이 아니라 그들이 자신들의 소원을 실현할 힘을 항상 가지고 있었다는 것을 그들이 깨닫게 한다. [5]Dorothy에게, '집'은 장소가 아니라 안전감, 그녀가 사랑하는 사람들과 함께하는 편안감이며, 그녀의 마음이 있는 곳이면 어디든지가 집이다. [6]사자가 원하는 용기, 허수아비가 간절히 바라는 지성, 양철 나무꾼이 꿈꾸는 감정은 그들이 이미 가지고 있는 속성이다. [7]그들은 이러한 속성에 대해 내적인 조건으로가 아니라 그들이 이미 다른 이들과 관계를 맺고 있는 긍정적인 방식으로 생각할 필요가 있다.(▶ 용기, 지성, 감정은 조건적으로 생기는 것이 아니라 다른 이들과 긍정적으로 관계를 맺는 여정에서 발현됨을 의미) [8]결국, 그들은 자신들이 원하는 뭔가를 얻을 수 있을 거라는 미래의 가능성에 관한 생각, 즉 어떤 '기대'에 지나지 않은 것에 의해 동기가 부여된 여행인, 오즈로 가는 여정에서 그러한 자질들을 보여주지 않았는가?

어휘

wizard 마법사
psychological 심리(학)적인

[7] They need to think about these attributes / not as internal conditions / but as *positive ways* ④ [**in which** they are already relating / to others].

(S: They, V: need, O: to think about these attributes; 전치사(~로(서)); 전치사구 병렬; in which: 전치사+관계대명사)

그들은 이러한 속성에 대해 생각할 필요가 있다 / 내적인 조건으로가 아니라 / 긍정적인 방식으로 [그들이 이미 관계를 맺고 있는 / 다른 이들과]

[8] After all, / didn't they demonstrate those qualities / on the journey to Oz, / *a journey* ⑤ (**motivated** / by little more than *an expectation*), / an idea (about the future likelihood (of getting *something* [(which[that]) they wanted]))?

(V: didn't ... demonstrate, S: they, O: those qualities; 과거분사구; 목적격 관계대명사 생략)

결국 / 그들은 그러한 자질들을 보여주지 않았는가 / 오즈로 가는 여정에서 / 즉 여행인 (동기가 부여된 / 어떤 '기대'에 지나지 않은 것에 의해) / 즉 생각 (미래의 가능성에 관한 (뭔가를 얻을 수 있을 거라는 [자신들이 원하는]))

motivation 동기 부여; 자극
cf. motivate 동기를 부여하다
barrier 장벽, 장애물
persist 끈질기게 계속하다; 지속되다
fulfill 실현[성취]하다; 이행하다; 달성하다
scarecrow 허수아비
long for ~을 간절히 바라다
attribute 속성, 자질; (~을 …의) 탓으로 하다
possess 가지다, 소유하다
internal 내적인; 내부의
relate to A A와 관계가 있다
demonstrate 보여주다; 입증하다
quality 자질; 특성, 특징
journey 여정, 여행
little more than ~에 지나지 않은
likelihood 가능성, 있음직함

정답 가이드

③ **[정동사 자리 vs. 준동사 자리]** 준동사(분사, 동명사, to부정사)는 문장에서 동사 역할을 할 수 없음에 주의한다. 문장의 주어는 The courage ~ dreams of로 복수이고, attributes 이하를 보어로 이끌 be동사가 빠져 있으므로 being을 복수 be동사 are로 고쳐야 한다. being을 전치사 of의 목적어인 동명사로 오해할 수 있으나, the Tin Man dreams of는 앞에 목적격 관계대명사 which[that]가 생략된 관계사절이다.

오답 클리닉

① **[인칭대명사 vs. 재귀대명사]** (6%)
밑줄이 them에 있으므로, 대신하는 명사와 수가 같은지 또는 재귀대명사 themselves의 자리가 아닌지를 문맥으로 판단해야 한다. to give를 행하는 의미상 주어는 the Wizard이고 to give의 간접목적어 them은 Dorothy and her three friends를 지칭한다. to give의 의미상 주어와 목적어가 서로 다르므로(S≠O) 재귀대명사는 적절하지 않으며, 복수명사를 대신하므로 복수 인칭대명사 them은 어법상 적절하다.

② **[to-v의 형용사적 용법]** (9%)
to fulfill은 명사 the power를 수식하는 형용사 역할의 to-v로 쓰였으므로 어법상 적절하다. have가 사역의 의미일 때 목적격보어 자리에 동사원형을 쓰지만 여기서 have는 '가지다'의 의미이고, 목적어 the power와 to fulfill이 주어-서술 관계인 것도 아니므로 to fulfill은 목적격보어가 아니다.

④ **[전치사+관계대명사]** (25%)
<전치사+관계대명사>는 관계부사와 마찬가지로 뒤에 완전한 구조(SV)의 절이 와야 한다. 밑줄 친 in which 뒤에 주어(they), 자동사(are relating), 전치사구(to others)로 이루어진 완전한 구조의 절이 왔고, 이 절이 '방법'을 뜻하는 positive ways를 수식하므로 in which는 어법상 적절하다.

> The 주의 목적어가 없는 SV나 SVC문형이 완전한 구조의 절로 자주 출제되므로 주의해야 한다.

⑤ **[능동(v-ing) vs. 수동(p.p.)]** (20%)
분사의 수식을 받는 명사 a journey가 기대에 의해 '동기가 부여되는' 수동의 의미이므로 과거분사 motivated는 어법상 적절하다.

01 밑줄 어법 (23학년도 대수능 29번 | 정답률 40%) ②

구문분석 & 직독직해

생활 변화의 기반으로서 패션의 중요성

[1] Trends constantly suggest / *new opportunities* (for individuals to restage themselves), / representing occasions for change.
(S: Trends / V: suggest / O: new opportunities / for individuals: to-v의 의미상 주어 / representing ~: 분사구문(= and they represent ~))
유행은 끊임없이 제안한다 / 새로운 기회를 (사람들이 자신을 재실현할) / 그리고 변화를 위한 때를 나타낸다

주제문
[2] To understand // how trends can ultimately give individuals power and freedom, / one must first discuss fashion's importance / as a basis for change.
(To understand: 목적(~하기 위해) / how ~ freedom: To understand의 O(명사절) / how: 의문사 / trends: S′ / can ~ give: V′ / individuals: IO′ / power and freedom: DO′ / one: S / must ~ discuss: V / fashion's importance: O / as: 전치사(~로(서)))
이해하기 위해서는 // 유행이 어떻게 궁극적으로 개인에게 힘과 자유를 줄 수 있는지를 / 우선 패션의 중요성에 대해 논의해야 한다 / 변화를 위한 기반으로서

[3] *The most common explanation* (offered by my informants) (as to why fashion is so appealing) is // ① **that** it constitutes a kind of theatrical costumery.
(The most common explanation: S / offered ~: 과거분사구 / as to: (= about) / is: V / that ~: is의 C(명사절) / that: 명사절 접속사)
가장 일반적인 설명은 (나의 정보원들에 의해 제공된) (왜 패션이 그렇게 매력적인지에 관해) ~이다 // 그것이 일종의 연극 의상을 구성한다는 것

[4] Clothes are part (of how people present ② **them(→ themselves)** to the world), // and fashion locates them in the present, / relative to what is happening in society [and] to fashion's own history.
(how: 의문사 / people: S′ / present: V′ / them: O′ (people = themselves) / them: (= people) / to what ~ and to fashion's own history: 전치사구 병렬)
옷은 일부이다 (사람들이 자신을 세상에 보여주는 방식의) // 그리고 패션은 그들(사람들)을 현재에 자리 잡게 한다 / 사회에서 일어나고 있는 일과 패션 자체의 역사와 관련하여

[5] As a form of expression, / fashion contains a host of ambiguities, / enabling individuals to recreate *the meanings* (③ **associated** with specific pieces of clothing).
(As: 전치사(~로(서)) / enabling ~: 분사구문(= so (that) it enables ~) / ★<enable+O+to-v>: O가 v하도록 하다 / associated ~: 과거분사구)
표현의 한 형태로서 / 패션은 다수의 모호함을 포함한다 / (그 결과) 개인이 의미를 재창조할 수 있게 한다 (특정한 옷과 연관된)

[6] Fashion is among the simplest and cheapest methods (of self-expression): // clothes can be ④ **inexpensively** purchased / while making it easy to convey notions (of wealth, intellectual stature, relaxation or environmental consciousness), // even if none of these is true.
(Fashion: S_1 / is: V_1 / among ~: C / clothes: S_2 / can be ~ purchased: V_2 / while making ~: 접속사를 생략하지 않은 분사구문(= while they make ~) / it: 가목적어′ / to convey ~: 진목적어′ / these: (= notions of ~ consciousness) / even if: 부사절 접속사(양보))
패션은 가장 단순하고 저렴한 방법 중 하나이다 (자기표현의) // 즉 옷은 값싸게 구매될 수 있다 / 개념을 전달하기 쉽게 하면서 (부, 지적 능력, 휴식, 또는 환경 의식에 대한) // 비록 이것들 중 어느 것도 사실이 아닐지라도

[7] Fashion can also strengthen agency / in various ways, / ⑤ **opening** up space for action.
(Fashion: S / can ~ strengthen: V / agency: O / opening ~: 분사구문(= as it opens up ~))
패션은 또한 활동성을 강화시킬 수 있다 / 다양한 방법으로 / 활동을 위한 공간을 열어주면서

해석

[1] 유행은 사람들이 자신을 재실현할 새로운 기회를 끊임없이 제안하고 변화를 위한 때를 나타낸다. [2] 유행이 어떻게 궁극적으로 개인에게 힘과 자유를 줄 수 있는지를 이해하기 위해서는 우선 변화를 위한 기반으로서 패션의 중요성에 대해 논의해야 한다. [3] 왜 패션이 그렇게 매력적인지에 관해 나의 정보원들에 의해 제공된 가장 일반적인 설명은 그것이 일종의 연극 의상을 구성한다는 것이다.(▶ 연극에서 배역에 따라 의상이 달라지듯이 사람들도 패션을 통해 자신을 표현한다는 의미) [4] 옷은 사람들이 자신을 세상에 보여주는 방식의 일부이며 패션은 사회에서 일어나고 있는 일과 패션 자체의 역사와 관련하여 그들(사람들)을 현재에 자리 잡게 한다.(▶ 사람들이 입는 옷은 그 사회상을 반영하기 때문에 패션은 사람과 현재를 연결하는 역할을 한다고 볼 수 있음) [5] 표현의 한 형태로서 패션은 다수의 모호함을 포함하여 (그 결과) 개인이 특정한 옷과 연관된 의미를 재창조할 수 있게 한다. [6] 패션은 자기표현의 가장 단순하고 저렴한 방법 중 하나로, 즉 옷은 부, 지적 능력, 휴식, 또는 환경 의식에 대한 개념을, 비록 이것들 중 어느 것도 사실이 아닐지라도 전달하기 쉽게 하면서 값싸게 구매될 수 있다. [7] 패션은 또한 활동을 위한 공간을 열어주면서 다양한 방법으로 활동성을 강화시킬 수 있다.

어휘

restage 재실현하다; 재조직하다; 재상연하다
informant 정보원
appealing 매력적인, 흥미로운; 호소하는
constitute 구성하다
theatrical 연극[공연]의
costumery 의상, 복장
relative to A A에 관련하여; A에 비례하여
a host of 다수의
ambiguity 모호함
associate 연관 짓다, 연상하다
convey 전달하다; 나르다
notion 개념, 관념
consciousness 의식, 자각
strengthen 강화하다[되다]
agency 활동성, 발동력, 힘; 대리[대행]점

정답 가이드

② **[인칭대명사 vs. 재귀대명사]** how가 이끄는 간접의문문 형태의 명사절에서 주어 people이 세상에 보여주는 것은 자기 자신을 의미한다. 주어와 목적어가 서로 같으므로(S=O) 목적어 자리에는 재귀대명사인 themselves가 와야 한다. present는 '(물건을) 주다'라는 의미로 많이 쓰이지만 여기서는 present oneself의 형태로 '자신을 나타내다, 보여주다'의 의미로 쓰인 것이다. 이어지는 and fashion locates them에 의거하여 밑줄 친 them을 어법상 옳은 것으로 판단하지 말고, 서로 다른 절이므로 각각의 주어와 목적어로 판단해야 한다.

오답 클리닉

① **[명사절 접속사 that]** (7%)
be동사 is의 보어인 명사절을 이끄는 것으로 접속사 that은 어법상 적절하다.

③ **[능동(v-ing) vs. 수동(p.p.)]** (19%)
문맥상 '연관된, 관련된'을 의미하므로 associated가 적절하다. associating with는 '~와 어울리는'의 의미로 쓰인다.

④ **[형용사 vs. 부사]** (11%)
동사 can be purchased를 수식하는 부사 자리이므로 inexpensively는 어법상 적절하다. be동사 뒤에 나오는 주격보어가 아님에 유의한다.

⑤ **[분사구문]** (24%)
문맥상 부사절 as it(= fashion) opens up space for action을 분사구문으로 전환한 것이므로 현재분사 opening은 어법상 적절하다.

The 주의 콤마 뒤 분사 형태는 분사구문의 의미가 적절한지를 우선 판단하고, 분사구문의 의미상의 주어와 동사의 의미 관계에 따라 능동이면 v-ing, 수동이면 p.p.인지를 판단하면 된다.

02 + 밑줄 어법 <23학년도 9월 모평 29번 | 정답률 57%> ②

구문분석 & 직독직해

윤리 윤리적 문제 인식과 의사 결정

주제문

[1] Recognizing ethical issues / is the most important step / in understanding business ethics.
S(동명사구) V(단수) C
윤리적 문제를 인식하는 것은 / 가장 중요한 단계이다 / 비즈니스 윤리를 이해하는 데

★<require+O+to-v>: O가 v하도록 요구하다

[2] An ethical issue is / *an identifiable problem, situation, or opportunity* [that requires a person to choose / from among *several actions* [that may ① **be evaluated** / as right or wrong, ethical or unethical]].
S V C 주격 관계대명사 V' O' C' 주격 관계대명사
윤리적 문제는 ~이다 / 식별 가능한 문제, 상황 또는 기회 [한 사람이 선택하도록 요구하는 / 여러 가지 행동들 사이에서 [평가될 수 있는 / 옳거나 그르다고, 윤리적이거나 비윤리적이라고]]

★동명사 Learning 또는 to부정사 To learn의 목적어로 <의문사+to-v> 형태의 명사구가 옴.

[3] ② **Learn(→ Learning[To learn])** / how to choose from alternatives and make a decision / requires / not only good personal values, / but also knowledge competence (in the business area of concern).
S <how to-v>: 어떻게 v할지를 V(단수) O₁(명사구 병렬) ★<not only A but also B>: A뿐만 아니라 B도 O₂(명사구 병렬)
배우는 것은 / 대안 중에서 어떻게 선택하고 결정을 내릴지를 / 필요로 한다 / 훌륭한 개인적 가치관뿐만 아니라 / 지식 역량도 (관계가 있는 비즈니스 분야에서의)

→ to know의 O(명사구)

[4] Employees also need to know / when to rely on their organizations' policies and codes of ethics / or (when to) ③ **have** discussions / with co-workers or managers / on appropriate conduct.
S V O <when to-v>: 언제 v(해야) 할지를
또한 직원들은 알 필요가 있다 / 언제 자신이 속한 조직의 정책과 윤리 강령에 의존해야 할지를 / 혹은 언제 논의해야 할지를 / 동료 또는 관리자와 / 적절한 행동에 대해

[5] Ethical decision making is not always easy // because there are always *gray areas* [④ **that** create dilemmas, // no matter how decisions are made].
S V C 부사절 접속사(이유) V' S' 주격 관계대명사 V'' O'' (= however) ★양보의 부사절을 이끄는 no matter how는 '어떻게 ~하더라도'의 의미.
윤리적 의사 결정이 항상 쉬운 것은 아니다 // 왜냐하면 애매한 영역이 항상 있기 때문이다 [딜레마를 만드는 // 어떻게 결정이 내려지더라도]

[6] For instance, / should an employee report / on *a co-worker* (engaging in time theft)?
V S 현재분사구
예를 들어 / 직원은 보고해야 하는가 / 동료에 대해 (시간 절도를 벌이는)

[7] Should a salesperson leave out / facts (about a product's poor safety record) / in his presentation to a customer?
V S O
판매원은 생략해야 하는가 / 사실을 (어떤 제품의 좋지 않은 안전 기록에 대한) / 고객에게 하는 프레젠테이션에서

해석

[1]윤리적 문제를 인식하는 것은 비즈니스 윤리를 이해하는 데 가장 중요한 단계이다. [2]윤리적 문제는 옳거나 그르다고, 윤리적이거나 비윤리적이라고 평가될 수 있는 여러 가지 행동들 사이에서 한 사람이 선택하도록 요구하는 식별 가능한 문제, 상황 또는 기회이다. [3]대안 중에서 어떻게 선택하고 결정을 내릴지를 배우는 것은 훌륭한 개인적 가치관뿐만 아니라 관계가 있는 비즈니스 분야에서의 지식 역량도 필요로 한다. [4]또한 직원들은 언제 자신이 속한 조직의 정책과 윤리 강령에 의존해야 할지를 혹은 언제 동료 또는 관리자와 적절한 행동에 대해 논의해야 할지를 알 필요가 있다. [5]윤리적 의사결정이 항상 쉬운 것은 아닌데, 왜냐하면 어떻게 결정이 내려지더라도 딜레마를 만드는 애매한 영역이 항상 있기 때문이다. [6]예를 들어, 직원은 시간 절도를 벌이는 동료에 대해 보고해야 하는가? [7]판매원은 고객에게 하는 프레젠테이션에서 어떤 제품의 좋지 않은 안전 기록에 대한 사실을 생략해야 하는가? [8]그러한 질문은 의사 결정자가 자신이 선택한 윤리를 평가하여 지도를 요청할지를 결정하도록 요구한다.

어휘

ethical 윤리적인, 도덕상의
cf. ethics 윤리, 도의; 윤리학
identifiable 식별 가능한
alternative 대안, 선택 가능한 것
competence 역량, 능력
rely on ~에 의존하다
code of ethics 윤리 강령 ((어떤 집단에서 내세우는 윤리적인 행동 규범))
conduct 행동(하다), 처신(하다)
gray area 애매한 영역, 중간 영역
engage in ~에 관여[참여]하다; ~에 종사하다

[8]Such questions require the decision maker / to evaluate the ethics (of his or her choice) /
S V O C1
and (to) decide / ⑤ **whether** to ask for guidance.
→ (to) decide의 O(명사절)
C2 (= whether he/she should ask for guidance)
그러한 질문은 의사 결정자가 (~하도록) 요구한다 / 윤리를 평가하도록 (자신이 선택한) /
그리고 결정하도록 / 지도를 요청할지를

time theft 시간 절도 ((일을 하지 않고 근무 시간을 부적절하게 보내는 행위))
leave out ~을 생략하다
guidance 지도, 안내

정답 가이드

② **[정동사 자리 vs. 준동사 자리]** and 뒤의 make와 병렬 연결되어 명령문을 이끄는 동사로 오해할 수 있으나, 문장의 동사는 requires이고 make는 to choose와 and로 병렬 연결된 것이다. 따라서 Learn을 주어 역할을 할 수 있는 동명사 Learning이나 to부정사 To learn으로 고쳐야 한다.

오답 클리닉

① **[관계대명사절의 능동태 vs. 수동태]** (3%)
주격 관계대명사절의 태는 선행사와 동사의 의미 관계로 판단해야 한다. 선행사는 several actions이고 그것이 '평가되는' 것이므로 evaluate와 수동관계이다. 따라서 be evaluated는 어법상 적절하다.

③ **[병렬구조]** (14%)
문맥상 <when to-v>의 to rely on과 or로 연결된 병렬구조로 이해하는 것이 자연스러우므로 have는 어법상 적절하다. 등위접속사 뒤에 연결되는 to-v구에서 to는 생략이 가능하다.

④ **[관계대명사의 격과 선행사 구분]** (11%)
주어가 빠진 불완전한 구조의 절을 이끌면서 그 절이 gray areas(선행사)를 수식하므로 주격 관계대명사 that은 적절하다.

⑤ **[의문사+to-v]** (15%)
(to) decide의 목적어 자리에 <whether to-v: v할지를>의 명사구가 쓰인 것은 어법상 적절하다.

03 + 밑줄 어법 〈23학년도 6월 모평 29번 | 정답률 54%〉 ③

구문분석 & 직독직해

생물 생태계의 다양성과 특징

주제문

[1]Ecosystems differ / in composition and extent.
S V
생태계들은 서로 다르다 / 구성과 범위에 있어

[2]They can be defined / as ranging /
S(= Ecosystems) V ★<define A as B(A를 B로 정의하다)>의 수동형
그것(생태계)들은 정의될 수 있다 / 범위가 이르는 것으로 /

from the communities and interactions (of organisms (in your mouth)) / or ① **those** (in the canopy (of a rain forest)) / to all those (in Earth's oceans).
★<from A to B>: A에서부터 B까지 (= the communities ~ of organisms)
(= the communities ~ of organisms)
군집과 상호 작용에서부터 (유기체들의 (여러분의 입 안에 있는)) / 혹은 그것들(유기체들의 군집과 상호 작용)에서부터 (덮개 안에 있는 (열대 우림의)) / 모든 그것들(유기체들의 군집과 상호 작용)까지 (지구의 바다에 있는)

[3]*The processes* (② **governing** them) / differ / in complexity and speed.
→ (= ecosystems)
S 현재분사구 V
과정들은 (그것들(생태계)을 지배하는) / 서로 다르다 / 복잡성과 속도에 있어

[4]There are *systems* [that turn over in minutes], // and there are *others* [③ **which(→ whose)** rhythmic time extends / to hundreds of years].
V1 S1 주격 관계대명사 V′ V2 S2(= other systems) 소유격 관계대명사
S′ V′
체계가 있다 [몇 분 안에 바뀌는] // 그리고 다른 것들(체계)도 있다 [규칙적으로 순환하는 시간이 늘어나는 / 수백 년까지]

[5]Some ecosystems are extensive ('biomes', such as the African savanna); // some cover regions (river basins); //
S1 V1 C1 S2 V2 O2
어떤 생태계는 광범위하다 (아프리카 사바나와 같은 '생물군계') // 어떤 생태계는 지역들에 걸쳐 있다 (강의 유역) //

many involve clusters of villages (micro-watersheds); // others are confined / to the level of a single village (the village pond).
S3 V3 O3 S4 V4
많은 생태계는 마을 군집을 포함한다 (작은 분수령들) // 다른 생태계들은 국한된다 / 단 하나의 마을 수준으로 (마을 연못)

해석

[1]생태계들은 구성과 범위에 있어 서로 다르다. [2]그것들(생태계)은 범위가 여러분의 입 안에 있는 유기체들의 군집과 상호 작용 혹은 열대 우림의 덮개 안에 있는 그것들(유기체들의 군집과 상호 작용)에서부터 지구의 바다에 있는 모든 그것들(유기체들의 군집과 상호 작용)까지 이르는 것으로 정의될 수 있다. [3]그것들(생태계)을 지배하는 과정들은 복잡성과 속도에 있어 서로 다르다. [4]몇 분 안에 바뀌는 체계가 있고, 규칙적으로 순환하는 시간이 수백 년까지 늘어나는 다른 것들(체계)도 있다. [5]어떤 생태계는 광범위하고 (아프리카 사바나와 같은 '생물군계'), 어떤 생태계는 지역들에 걸쳐 있으며(강의 유역), 많은 생태계가 마을 군집을 포함하고(작은 분수령들), 다른 생태계들은 단 하나의 마을 수준으로 국한된다(마을 연못). [6]각각의 사례에는 불가분성(나눌 수가 없음)이라는 요소가 있다. [7]장벽을 만듦으로써 어떤 생태계를 부분들로 나누어라, 그러면 그 부분들의 생산성의 총합이 일반적으로, 다른 것이 동일하다면, 전체의 생산성보다 더 낮다는 것이 알려질 것이다. [8]생물학적 개체군의 이동성이 한 가지 이유이다. (▶ 생태계를 나누고 장벽을 만들어 생물들의 이동을 불가능하게 하면 이동이 가능할 때보다 생산성이 낮아진다는 의미) [9]예를 들어, 안전한 통행은 이동하는 종들이 살아남을 수 있게 한다.

어휘

composition 구성; 작곡; 작품

[6]In each example / there is an element (of indivisibility).
V S
각각의 사례에는 / 요소가 있다 (불가분성이라는)

★<명령문+and S+V ...>: ~하라, 그러면 S는 V할 것이다
[7]Divide an ecosystem into parts / by creating barriers, //
V1 O <by v-ing>: v함으로써
어떤 생태계를 부분들로 나누어라 / 장벽을 만듦으로써 //

★<find+O+(to be) C(O가 C임을 알다)>의 수동형
and the sum (of the productivity (of the parts)) / will typically be found / to be lower / than the productivity (of the whole), / other things ④ **being** equal.
S2 V2 C 분사구문(= if other things are equal)
그러면 총합이 (생산성의 (그 부분들의)) / 일반적으로 알려질 것이다 / 더 낮다는 것이 / 생산성보다 (전체의) / 다른 것이 동일하다면

[8]The mobility (of biological populations) is a reason.
S V C
이동성이 (생물학적 개체군의) / 한 가지 이유이다

[9]Safe passages, / for example, / enable migratory species ⑤ **to survive**.
S V O C
안전한 통행은 / 예를 들어 / 이동하는 종들이 살아남을 수 있게 한다

range from A to B A에서부터 B까지 이르다
community 《생물》 군집; 공동체
turn over 바뀌다; 뒤집히다
rhythmic 규칙적으로 순환하는; 주기적인
extend 늘어나다; 연장하다; 확대[확장]하다
cf. extensive 광범위한; 대규모의
biome (숲·사막 같은 특정 환경 내의) 생물군계
cluster 군집, 무리
watershed (강물이 갈라지는 경계가 되는) 분수령
confine 국한[제한]하다
indivisibility 불가분성
barrier 장벽, 장애물
mobility 이동성, 기동성
population 《생태》 개체군, 집단; 인구
passage 통행; 통로, 길
migratory 이동[이주]하는

정답 가이드

③ **[관계대명사의 격]** 뒤에 완전한 구조(SVM)의 절이 왔는데, 문맥상 이 절이 앞의 others를 선행사로 수식하고 있다. others가 주어 rhythmic time을 소유하는 의미(다른 체계의 규칙적으로 순환하는 시간)이므로 which를 소유격 관계대명사 whose로 고쳐야 한다.

오답 클리닉

① **[명사-대명사의 수일치]** (3%)
앞에 있는 복수명사 the communities and interactions of organisms의 반복을 피하기 위해 대명사 those가 적절히 쓰였다.
② **[능동(v-ing) vs. 수동(p.p.)]** (16%)
분사의 수식을 받는 명사 The processes가 them(= ecosystems)을 '지배하는' 것이므로 능동을 뜻하는 현재분사 governing은 어법상 적절하다.
④ **[주의해야 할 분사구문]** (23%)
조건을 나타내는 부사절 if other things are equal을 분사구문으로 바꾼 형태이다. 접속사 if를 생략하고, 분사구문의 의미상의 주어 other things는 명령문인 문장의 생략된 주어(you)와 일치하지 않아 남겨졌으며, 능동태 be동사 are를 현재분사 being으로 바꾼 것은 어법상 적절하다.
⑤ **[목적격보어로 쓰이는 부정사]** (4%)
<enable+O+to-v(O가 v하는 것을 가능하게 하다)> 구문으로, enable 다음의 목적격보어 to survive는 어법상 적절하다.

01 + 낱말 쓰임 〈24학년도 대수능 30번 | 정답률 66%〉 ④

구문분석 & 직독직해 경제 시장 경제의 가격 설정 메커니즘

주제문 ⑤ 공유된 문화를 바탕으로 가격이 정해지는 것이므로 서로가 '비슷한' 문화적·경제적 세상에 속해있는 것임.

[1] Bazaar economies feature / *an apparently flexible price-setting mechanism* [that sits / atop more enduring ties (of shared culture)].
S V O 주격 관계대명사 =

시장 경제는 특징으로 한다 / 겉보기에 융통성 있는 가격 설정 메커니즘을 [놓여 있는 / 더 지속적인 유대의 꼭대기에 (공유된 문화라는)]

[2] Both the buyer and seller are aware / of each other's ① **restrictions**.
S V C

구매자와 판매자 둘 다 알고 있다 / 서로의 제약을

① 시장의 구매자와 판매자는 재정적인 '제약'을 가지고 있음.

[3] In Delhi's bazaars, / buyers and sellers can ② **assess** / (to a large extent) / *the financial constraints* [that other actors have / in their everyday life].
S V 전치사구 삽입 O 목적격 관계대명사 S' V'

델리의 시장에서 / 구매자와 판매자는 평가할 수 있다 / (대부분) / 재정적인 제약을 [다른 행위자들이 가지는 / 그들의 일상생활에서]

② 구매자와 판매자가 서로의 재정적 제약을 '평가'하여 서로가 필수품과 사치품으로 여기는 것을 아는 것임.

[4] *Each actor* (belonging to a specific economic class) / understands // what the other sees / as a necessity and a luxury.
S 현재분사구 V O(명사절) ★<see A as B>: A를 B로 여기다[보다]

각 행위자는 (특정 경제 계층에 속하는) / 이해한다 // 상대방이 여기는 것을 / 필수품과 사치품으로

[5] In the case of electronic products (like video games), / they are not a ③ **necessity** (at the same level / as other household purchases (such as food items)).
전치사(~같은) S(→ (= electronic products)) V C

③ 비디오 게임은 식품과 동일한 '필수품'이 아님.

전자 제품의 경우 (비디오 게임 같은) / 그것들(전자 제품)은 필수품이 아니다 (동일한 수준의 / 다른 가정 구매품과 (식품과 같은))

[6] So, / the seller (in Delhi's bazaars) / is careful / not to directly ask for very ④ **low(→ high)** prices / for video games //
S V C 형용사 careful 수식

따라서 / 판매자는 (델리 시장의) / 주의한다 / 직접적으로 매우 낮은(→ 높은) 가격을 요구하지 않으려고 / 비디오 게임에 대해 //

④ 비디오 게임은 절대적인 필수품이 아니므로 판매하려는 판매자는 매우 '높은' 가격을 요구하지 않을 것임.

because at no point will the buyer see possession of them / as an absolute necessity.
부사절 접속사(이유) 부정어 포함어구 조동사' S' V' O' (= video games) 전치사(~로(서))

★부정어 포함 어구 at no point(전혀 ~않다)가 문장 앞에 와서 <조동사+주어+동사> 어순으로 도치됨.

구매자가 그것들(비디오 게임)의 소유를 여길 이유가 전혀 없기 때문에 / 절대적인 필수품으로

[7] Access (to this type of knowledge) / establishes a price consensus / by relating to each other's preferences and limitations (of belonging to a ⑤ **similar** cultural and economic universe).
S V O <by v-ing>: v함으로써 of의 O(동명사구)

접근은 (이러한 유형의 지식에 대한) / 가격 합의를 이룬다 / 서로의 선호와 한계를 관련지음으로써 (비슷한 문화적 경제적 세상에 속하는 것에서 나온)

해석

[1]시장 경제는 공유된 문화라는 더 지속적인 유대의 꼭대기에 놓여 있는, 겉보기에 융통성 있는 가격 설정 메커니즘을 특징으로 한다. [2]구매자와 판매자 둘 다 서로의 ① 제약을 알고 있다. [3]델리의 시장에서, 구매자와 판매자는 대부분 다른 행위자들이 그들의 일상생활에서 가지는 재정적인 제약을 ② 평가할 수 있다. [4]특정 경제 계층에 속하는 각 행위자는 상대방이 필수품과 사치품으로 여기는 것을 이해한다. [5]비디오 게임 같은 전자 제품의 경우, 그것들(전자 제품)은 식품과 같은 다른 가정 구매품과 동일한 수준의 ③ 필수품이 아니다. [6]따라서 델리 시장의 판매자는 비디오 게임에 대해 직접적으로 매우 ④ 낮은(→ 높은) 가격을 요구하지 않으려고 주의하는데, 구매자가 비디오 게임의 소유를 절대적인 필수품으로 여길 이유가 전혀 없기 때문이다. [7]이러한 유형의 지식에 대한 접근은 ⑤ 비슷한 문화적 경제적 세상에 속하는 것에서 나온 서로의 선호와 한계를 관련지음으로써 가격 합의를 이룬다.

어휘

bazaar 시장, 상점가; 자선 시장
feature 특징(으로 삼다); 특집 기사
apparently 겉보기에; 명백히
flexible 융통성 있는; 유연한
mechanism 메커니즘, 방법; 기제
atop ~의 꼭대기에
enduring (오래) 지속되는
tie 유대; 묶다
to a large extent 대부분, 주로
specific 특정한; 구체적인
luxury 사치(품)
household 가정(의)
possession 소유(물), 소지(품)
establish 정하다, 수립하다
relate to A A를 관련짓다
preference 선호, 애호
limitation 한계; 제한

정답 가이드

시장 경제는 겉보기에 융통성 있는 가격 설정 메커니즘을 특징으로 하는데 이 융통성 있어 보이는 가격 설정 메커니즘은 공유된 문화의 영향을 받는다는 내용이다. 즉, 공유된 문화를 통해 서로의 재정적 제약과 경제 계층을 알고, 구매자가 여기는 필수품과 사치품을 구별하여 사치품에는 높은 가격을 요구하지 않으려고 주의한다는 것이다. 따라서 ④의 'low(낮은)'를 'high(높은)'와 같은 낱말로 바꿔야 한다.

오답 클리닉

① restrictions (2%) 제약
문장 3에서 시장의 구매자와 판매자는 서로가 갖는 재정적 제약을 평가할 수 있다고 했으므로 서로의 '제약'을 알고 있다고 볼 수 있다.

② assess (3%) 평가하다
구매자와 판매자가 서로 상대가 필수품과 사치품으로 여기는 것을 아는 것은 서로의 재정적인 제약을 '평가할' 수 있어서이다.

③ necessity (5%) 필수품
비디오 게임은 식품과 비교하여 같은 '필수품'이라 할 수 없으므로 문맥상 적절하다.

⑤ similar (25%) 비슷한
시장의 가격 설정 메커니즘이 공유된 문화라는 유대를 바탕으로 서로의 제약을 이해함으로써 가격 합의를 이루는 것이라고 했으므로 구매자와 판매자가 '비슷한' 문화적, 경제적 세상에 속해있다는 것은 적절하다.

02 + 낱말 쓰임 (24학년도 9월 모평 30번 | 정답률 57%) ④

구문분석 & 직독직해

산업 섬유 산업을 통해 본 장소 가치의 중요성

주제문
[1]Why is the value of *place* so important?
왜 '장소'의 가치는 그렇게 중요한가

[2]From a historical perspective, / until the 1700s / textile production was *a hand process*
S V C
역사적 관점에서 볼 때 / 1700년대까지 / 직물 생산은 수동식 공정이었다
(using *the fibers* (available within a ① **particular** geographic region), / for example, cotton, wool, silk, and flax).
현재분사구 형용사구
(섬유를 사용하는 (특정한 지리적 지역 내에서 구할 수 있는) / 예를 들면, 면, 양모, 견, 그리고 아마 섬유)

①, ② 지역 간 무역이 '특정한' 지역에서 구할 수 있는 섬유로 만든 직물의 이용 가능성을 '증가시켰음'.
[3]Trade (among regions) / ② **increased** the availability (of these fibers and *associated textiles* (made from the fibers)).
S V O 과거분사구
무역은 (지역 간의) / 이용 가능성을 증가시켰다 (이러한 섬유들과 관련 직물의 (그 섬유들로 만들어진))

③ 무역에 이어 산업과 기술 발달은 섬유와 직물이 장소에 얽매이지 않는다는 사실을 '더했을' 것임.
[4]The First Industrial Revolution [and] subsequent technological advancements (in manufactured fibers) / ③ **added** to the fact // that fibers and textiles were no longer "place-bound."
S₁ S₂ V O (=) 동격 접속사 S′ V′ C′
1차 산업 혁명과 뒤이은 기술 발달은 (제조 섬유에서의) / 사실을 더했다 // 섬유와 직물이 더 이상 '장소에 얽매이지' 않는다는

④ 장소에 관계 없이 직물 제품을 제작하고 구입하는 것은 제품에 대한 단절, 상실, 경시를 '초래했을' 것임.
[5]Fashion companies created / [and] consumers could acquire / textiles and *products* (made from textiles) / with little or no connection / to where, how, or by whom the products were made.
S₁ V₁ S₂ V₂ created와 could acquire의 공통 O 과거분사구 to의 O(명사절)
패션 회사들은 만들었다 / 그리고 소비자들은 얻을 수 있었다 / 직물들과 제품들을 (직물들로 만들어진) / 거의 또는 전혀 관계 없이 / 제품이 어디서, 어떻게, 또는 누구에 의해 만들어졌는지에

(= 앞 문장)
[6]This ④ **countered(→ resulted in)** / a disconnect ([between] consumers [and] *the products* [(which[that]) they use on a daily basis]), /
S V O₁ 목적격 관계대명사 생략 (= consumers)
이것이 반박했다(→ 초래했다) / 단절을 (소비자와 제품 간의 [그들이 매일 사용하는]) /
a loss (of understanding and appreciation (in *the skills and resources* (necessary to create these products))), /
O₂ 형용사구
상실을 (이해와 인정의 (기술과 자원에 대한 (이러한 제품을 만드는 데 필요한)))
[and] an associated disregard (for *the human and natural resources* (necessary for the products' creation)).
O₃ 형용사구
그리고 관련된 경시를 (인간과 천연자원에 대한 (제품의 제작에 필요한))

해석

[1]왜 '장소'의 가치는 그렇게 중요한가? [2]역사적 관점에서 볼 때, 1700년대까지 직물 생산은 ① 특정한 지리적 지역 내에서 구할 수 있는 섬유, 예를 들면, 면, 양모, 견, 아마 섬유를 사용하는 수동식 공정이었다. [3]지역 간의 무역은 이러한 섬유들과 그 섬유들로 만들어진 관련 직물의 이용 가능성을 ② 증가시켰다. [4]1차 산업 혁명과 뒤이은 제조 섬유에서의 기술 발달은 섬유와 직물이 더 이상 '장소에 얽매이지' 않는다는 사실을 ③ 더했다. [5]제품이 어디서, 어떻게, 또는 누구에 의해 만들어졌는지에 대해 거의 또는 전혀 관계 없이 패션 회사들은 직물들과 직물들로 만들어진 제품들을 만들었고 소비자들은 그것들을 얻을 수 있었다. [6]이것이 소비자와 그들이 매일 사용하는 제품 간의 단절, 이러한 제품을 만드는 데 필요한 기술과 자원에 대한 이해와 인정의 상실, 그리고 제품의 제작에 필요한 인간과 천연자원에 대한 관련된 경시를 ④ 반박했다(→ 초래했다). [7]따라서 '장소'의 가치를 새롭게 하는 것은 회사와 소비자를 특정 장소의 사람, 지리 그리고 문화와 ⑤ 다시 연결한다.

어휘

perspective 관점; 전망
fiber 섬유(질)
available 구할[이용할] 수 있는
cf. availability 이용 가능성
geographic 지리(학)적인, 지리학의
cf. geography 지리(학)
flax 아마 (섬유)
associated 관련[연합]된
Industrial Revolution 산업 혁명
subsequent 뒤이은, 그 다음[후]의
advancement 발달, 진보
manufacture 제조[제작](하다)
add to ~을 더하다[보태다]; ~을 늘리다
-bound ~에 얽매인[묶인]; ~로 향하는

⊶ ⑤ 장소의 가치를 새롭게 하는 것은 회사와 소비자를 특정 장소의 사람, 지리, 문화와 '다시 연결할' 것임.

7 Therefore, / renewing a value on *place* / ⑤ **reconnects** the company and the consumer / with the people, geography, and culture (of a particular location).
S(동명사구) V(단수) O

따라서 / '장소'의 가치를 새롭게 하는 것은 / 회사와 소비자를 다시 연결한다 / 사람, 지리 그리고 문화와 (특정 장소의)

acquire 얻다; 획득하다
counter 반박하다; 대응하다; 계산대
disconnect 단절; 연결[공급]을 끊다
on a daily basis 매일
appreciation (진가의) 인정; 감상; 감사
disregard 경시[무시](하다); 재개하다
renew 새롭게 하다; 갱신하다; 재개하다

정답 가이드

섬유와 직물이 특정 장소에 얽매이지 않고 생산과 구입이 가능해지면서 장소의 가치가 상실되었고, 이는 제품과 소비자를 단절시키는 부정적인 결과를 초래하므로 장소 가치의 회복이 필요하다는 내용의 글이다. 문장 6의 This는 앞 문장의 내용을 지칭하므로, 제품에 대한 단절, 상실, 경시는 패션 회사와 소비자가 어디서, 어떻게, 누구에 의해 만들어졌는지에 관계없이 제품을 만들고 구입할 수 있었던 것의 결과로 봐야 한다. 따라서 ④의 'countered(반박했다)'를 'resulted in(초래했다)'으로 바꿔 써야 한다.

오답 클리닉

① particular (2%) 특정한
장소 가치의 중요성을 설명하는 내용이므로 직물 생산에 사용한 섬유는 지리적으로 '특정한' 지역에서 구할 수 있는 것이었을 것이다.

② increased (7%) 증가시켰다
지역 간의 무역은 특정 지역에서만 생산되는 섬유와 직물의 이용 가능성을 '증가시켰을' 것이다.

③ added (13%) 더했다
무역으로 특정 섬유와 직물의 이용 가능성이 증가한 것에 이어, 1차 산업 혁명과 기술 발달은 섬유와 직물이 더 이상 장소에 얽매이지 않는다는 사실을 '더했을' 것이다.

⑤ reconnects (22%) 다시 연결하다
문장 6에서 언급된 장소 가치의 상실로 인한 소비자와 제품의 단절은 장소의 가치를 새롭게 함으로써 소비자를 특정 장소의 사람, 지리, 문화와 '다시 연결할' 것이다.

03 + 낱말 쓰임 〈24학년도 6월 모평 30번 | 정답률 46%〉 ④

구문분석 & 직독직해

기술 합리적 에이전트의 학습과 자율성

1 To *the extent* [that an agent relies / on the prior knowledge (of its designer) / rather than on its own percepts], / we say // that the agent lacks autonomy.
~일 경우에 관계부사(= where) S′ V′ 전치사구 병렬 S V O(명사절)
★<A rather than B>: B라기보다는 A

경우에 [에이전트가 의존하는 / 사전 지식에 (설계자의) / 그것이 지각한 것보다] / 우리는 말한다 // 그 에이전트가 자율성이 부족하다고

주제문

2 A rational agent should be autonomous — // it should learn what it can (learn) / to (A) **compensate** for partial or incorrect prior knowledge.
S₁ V₁ C (= the rational agent) S₂ V₂ O(명사절) 목적(~하기 위해)

⊶ (A) 합리적인 에이전트가 학습해야 하는 이유는 불완전한 지식을 '보완하기' 위함임.

합리적 에이전트는 자율적이어야 한다 // 그것(합리적 에이전트)은 학습할 수 있는 것을 학습해야 한다 / 불완전하거나 부정확한 사전 지식을 보완하기 위해

3 For example, / *a vacuum-cleaning agent* [that learns to foresee where and when additional dirt will appear] / will do better / than *one* [that does not].
S 주격 관계대명사 to foresee의 O(명사절) V 주격 관계대명사

예를 들어 / 진공 청소 에이전트는 [또 다른 먼지가 어디에서 그리고 언제 나타날지 예측하는 것을 학습하는] / 더 잘할 것이다 / (~한) 것보다 [그렇게 하지 않는]

4 As a practical matter, / one seldom requires complete autonomy / from the start: // when the agent has had little or no experience, // it would have to act (B) **randomly** // unless the designer gave some assistance.
전치사(~로(서)) (= an agent) S₁ V₁ O 부사절 접속사(시간) S₂(= the agent) V₂ 부사절 접속사(= if not)
★가정법 과거 <If+S′+동사의 과거형 ~, S+would+동사원형 ...>: 만약 ~라면, …할 텐데

현실적으로 / 에이전트는 완전한 자율성을 거의 필요로 하지 않는다 / 처음부터 //

⊶ (B) 경험이 없는 에이전트에 설계자의 지원이 없다면 그것은 '임의로' 작동할 것임.

에이전트가 거의 또는 전혀 경험이 없을 때 // 그것(에이전트)은 임의로 작동해야 할 것이다 // 설계자가 약간의 지원을 제공하지 않는다면

해석

1 에이전트가 그것이 지각한 것보다 설계자의 사전 지식에 의존하는 경우에, 우리는 그 에이전트가 자율성이 부족하다고 말한다. 2 합리적 에이전트는 자율적이어야 하는데, 그것(합리적 에이전트)은 불완전하거나 부정확한 사전 지식을 (A) 보완하기 위해 학습할 수 있는 것을 학습해야 한다. 3 예를 들어, 또 다른 먼지가 어디에서 그리고 언제 나타날지 예측하는 것을 학습하는 진공 청소 에이전트는 그렇게 하지 않는 것(진공 청소 에이전트)보다 더 잘할 것이다. 4 현실적으로 에이전트는 처음부터 완전한 자율성을 거의 필요로 하지 않는데, 에이전트가 거의 또는 전혀 경험이 없을 때, 설계자가 약간의 지원(▶ 사전 지식)을 제공하지 않는다면, 그것은 (B) 임의로 작동해야 할 것이다. 5 따라서 꼭 진화가 동물에게 스스로 학습할 수 있을 만큼 충분히 오래 생존하도록 충분한 내재된 반사 신경을 제공하는 것처럼, 인공지능 에이전트에게 학습하는 능력뿐만 아니라 약간의 초기 지식을 제공하는 것이 합리적일 것이다. 6 환경을 충분히 경험한 후, 합리적 에이전트의 행동은 그것의 사전 지식에서 사실상 (C) 독립적이게 될 수 있다. 7 따라서 학습의 결합은 아주 다양한 환경에서 성공할 단일한 합리적 에이전트를 설계할 수 있게 한다.(▶ 에이전트에 학습 능력을 결합시키면, 다양한 환경에서 효과적으로 수행할 에이전트를 만들 수 있다는 의미)

★<provide A with B>: A에게 B를 제공하다 ★<형용사/부사+enough to-v>: v할 만큼 충분히 ~한/하게

[5]So, / just as evolution provides animals / with enough built-in reflexes / to survive long enough / to learn for themselves, //

부사절 접속사((꼭) ~인 것처럼) 목적(~하기 위해)

따라서 / 꼭 진화가 동물에게 제공하는 것처럼 / 충분한 내재된 반사 신경을 / 충분히 오래 생존하도록 / 스스로 학습할 수 있을 만큼 //

it would be reasonable / to provide an artificial intelligent agent / with some initial knowledge / as well as an ability (to learn).

가주어 V C 진주어(to-v구) 명사구 병렬

(~이) 합리적일 것이다 / 인공 지능 에이전트에게 제공하는 것이 / 약간의 초기 지식을 / 능력뿐만 아니라 (학습하는)

(C) 환경을 충분히 경험한 뒤에 합리적 에이전트의 행동은 사전 지식에서 '독립할'수 있을 것임.

[6]After sufficient experience of its environment, / the behavior (of a rational agent) / can become effectively (C) **independent** / of its prior knowledge.

전치사(~ 후에) S V C

환경을 충분히 경험한 후 / 행동은 (합리적 에이전트의) / 사실상 독립적이게 될 수 있다 / 그것의 사전 지식에서

★<allow+O+to-v>: O가 v할 수 있게 하다

[7]Hence, / the incorporation (of learning) / allows one to design / *a single rational agent* [that will succeed / in a vast variety of environments].

S V O C 주격 관계대명사

따라서 / 결합은 (학습의) / 사람이 설계할 수 있게 한다 / 단일한 합리적 에이전트를 [성공할 / 아주 다양한 환경에서]

어휘

percept 지각[인지]된 것
autonomy 자율성; 자치권
cf. autonomous 자율[자주]적인
rational 합리적인; 이성적인
partial 불완전한, 부분적인
foresee 예측하다
practical 현실적인; 실용적인
seldom 거의 ~않는
assistance 지원, 도움
evolution 진화; 발전, 진전
built-in 내재된, 타고난
reflexes 반사 신경
reasonable 합리적인, 타당한
artificial 인공의; 인위적인; 거짓의
initial 초기의, 처음의
sufficient 충분한
effectively 사실상; 효과적으로
incorporation 결합, 통합, 합병; 회사

⊕ 에이전트(agent): 사용자 대신 주변 환경을 탐지해 자율적으로 작업을 수행하는 장치 또는 프로그램. 지능형 에이전트의 예로는 질병 진단 시스템, 인공지능 스피커, 자율 주행 자동차 등이 있음.

정답 가이드

(A) 합리적 에이전트가 학습할 수 있는 것을 학습해야 하는 이유를 불완전하거나 부정확한 사전 지식을 '보완하기(compensate)' 위한 것으로 보는 것이 적절하다. compensate for(~을 보완하다) 뒤에는 보완해야 할 대상(부족, 결점, 손실 등)에 해당하는 내용이 와야 한다.
(B) 에이전트에게 참고할 경험이 없을 때 설계자의 지원(사전지식)이 없다면 '임의로(randomly)' 작동할 수밖에 없을 것이다.
(C) 처음에는 자율성을 거의 필요로 하지 않지만, 환경을 충분히 경험한 후에 에이전트의 행동은 사전 지식에서 벗어나 '독립적(independent)'이게 될 것이다.

오답 클리닉

① (A) compensate - (B) randomly - (C) protective (23%)
(C)의 protective (of)는 '(~을) 보호하는'의 의미. 에이전트가 환경을 충분히 경험하고 학습한 후에는 사전 지식을 보호하기보다 그것에서 벗어나 독립적으로 행동하는 자율성을 갖게 될 것이다.

The 주의 문장 5의 인공 지능 에이전트에게 약간의 초기 지식을 제공하는 것이 합리적이라는 내용에서 사전 지식을 보호해야 할 것으로 생각할 수 있으나, 결국 에이전트 설계가 지향하는 것은 사전 지식에 의존하지 않는 자율성임을 파악해야 한다.

② (A) compensate - (B) purposefully - (C) protective (9%)
(B)의 purposefully는 '목적 의식을 가지고, 의도적으로'의 의미. 어떠한 경험과 사전 지식도 없는 상태에서 에이전트의 행동에는 목적이나 의도는 없을 것이다.
③ (A) prepare - (B) randomly - (C) protective (14%)
⑤ (A) prepare - (B) purposefully - (C) independent (8%)
(A)의 prepare (for)는 '(~을) 준비하다'의 의미. 불완전하거나 부정확한 사전 지식을 '준비하기' 위해 학습해야 하는 것으로 볼 수 없다. prepare for 뒤에는 준비하고 대비해야 할 대상이 온다.

01 + 낱말 쓰임 (23학년도 대수능 30번 | 정답률 58%) ⑤

구문분석 & 직독직해

기술 인간 중심적 기술의 융합과 발전

[1] Everywhere we turn // we hear about almighty "cyberspace"!
우리가 고개를 돌리는 곳 어디에서나 // 우리는 대단한 '사이버공간'에 대해 듣는다

[2] The hype promises // that we will leave our boring lives, / put on goggles and body suits, / and enter some metallic, three-dimensional, multimedia otherworld.
(S: The hype / V: promises / 명사절 접속사: that / S′: we / V′1: will leave / O′1: our boring lives / V′2: put on / O′2: goggles and body suits / V′3: enter / O′3: some metallic, three-dimensional, multimedia otherworld; that절: promises의 O(명사절))
과대광고는 약속한다 // 우리가 지루한 삶을 떠나 / 고글과 전신 수영복을 입고 / 어떤 금속성의 3차원인 멀티미디어로 이루어진 다른 세계로 들어갈 것을

[3] When the Industrial Revolution arrived with its great innovation, the motor, // we didn't leave our world / to go to some ① **remote** motorspace! ⊶ ① 우리가 살고 있는 세상과 '동떨어진' 모터 공간이 대비됨.
(부사절 접속사(시간): When / S′: the Industrial Revolution / V′: arrived / its great innovation = the motor / S: we / V: didn't leave / O: our world / 목적(~하기 위해): to go)
위대한 혁신인 모터와 함께 산업 혁명이 도래했을 때 // 우리는 우리의 세상을 떠나지 않았다 / 어떤 동떨어진 모터 공간으로 가기 위해

⊶ ② 모터를 삶에 들여와 활용한 것을 '흡수'로 표현.
[4] On the contrary, / we brought the motors into our lives, / as automobiles, refrigerators, drill presses, and pencil sharpeners.
(S: we / V: brought / O: the motors / 전치사(~와 같은): as)
오히려 / 우리는 모터를 우리 삶에 가져왔다 / 자동차, 냉장고, 드릴 프레스, 그리고 연필깎이와 같은 것으로

*<so ~ that ...>: 아주 ~해서 …하다
[5] This ② **absorption** has been so complete // that we refer to all these tools / with *names* [that declare their usage, / not their "motorness."]
(S: This absorption / V: has been / C: so complete / S′: we / V′: refer to / O′: all these tools / 주격 관계대명사: that)
이 흡수는 아주 완전해서 // 우리는 이 모든 도구를 지칭한다 / 이름들로 [그것들의 쓰임새를 나타내는 / 그것들의 '모터성'이 아닌]

⊶ ③ 혁신들이 주요 사회 경제적 운동을 야기한 것은 그것들이 우리 일상에 '영향을 미쳤기' 때문임.
[6] These innovations led to a major socioeconomic movement // precisely because they entered and ③ **affected** profoundly our everyday lives.
(S: These innovations / V: led to / O: a major socioeconomic movement / 부사절 접속사(이유): because / S′: they / V′1: entered / V′2: affected / entered와 affected의 공통 O: our everyday lives)
이 혁신들은 주요 사회 경제적 운동으로 이어졌다 // 바로 그것들이 우리 일상생활에 들어와 깊이 영향을 미쳤기 때문에

[7] People have not changed fundamentally / in thousands of years.
사람들은 근본적으로 변하지 않았다 / 수천 년 동안

[8] Technology changes constantly. ⊶ ④ 인간은 변하지 않기 때문에 기술이 인간에 '적응하고' 변화해야 함(인간 중심적 관점).
기술은 끊임없이 변화한다

[9] It's *the one* [that must ④ **adapt** to us].
(It (= Technology) / 주격 관계대명사: that)
그것(기술)은 바로 (~한) 것이다 [우리에게 적응해야 하는]

[10] That's exactly what will happen with information technology and its devices / under human-centric computing.
(S: That (= 앞 문장) / V: 's / what: 관계대명사, is의 C(명사절))
그것(기술이 인간에게 적응하는 것)이 바로 정보 기술과 그 장치들에 일어날 일이다 / 인간 중심적 컴퓨터 사용하에서

[11] The longer we continue to believe // that computers will take us to a magical new world, //
(S1: we / V1: continue / O1: to believe / 명사절 접속사: that; that절: to believe의 O(명사절))
우리가 계속 더 오래 믿을수록 // 컴퓨터가 우리를 마법의 신세계로 데려다줄 것을 //
*<The 비교급 ~, the 비교급 ...>: ~하면 할수록 더욱 …하다
the longer we will ⑤ **maintain(→ delay)** their natural fusion with our lives, // (which is) the hallmark of *every major movement* [that aspires to be called a socioeconomic revolution].
(S2: we / V2: will maintain / O2: their natural fusion / 주격 관계대명사+be동사 생략: (which is) / 주격 관계대명사: that)
우리는 우리 삶과 그것(컴퓨터)의 자연스러운 융합을 더 오래 유지시킬(→ 지연시킬) 것인데 // (자연스러운 융합은) 모든 주요 운동의 특징이다 [사회 경제적 혁명이라 불리길 열망하는] ⊶ ⑤ 기술이 인간을 신세계로 데려다줄 거라는 과대광고를 믿는 것은 기술을 인간 삶에 가져와 적응시키는 융합을 '지연시킬' 뿐임.

해석

[1]우리가 고개를 돌리는 곳 어디에서나 우리는 대단한 '사이버공간'에 대해 듣는다! [2]과대광고는 우리가 지루한 삶을 떠나 고글과 전신 수영복을 입고, 어떤 금속성의 3차원인 멀티미디어로 이루어진 다른 세계로 들어갈 것을 약속한다. [3]위대한 혁신인 모터와 함께 산업 혁명이 도래했을 때 우리는 어떤 ① 동떨어진 모터 공간으로 가기 위해 우리의 세상을 떠나지 않았다!(▶ 인간이 기술에 따라 변화하지 않았다는 의미) [4]오히려, 우리는 모터를 자동차, 냉장고, 드릴 프레스, 연필깎이와 같은 것으로 우리 삶에 가져왔다. [5]이 ② 흡수는 아주 완전해서 우리는 그것들의 '모터성'이 아닌 그것들의 쓰임새를 나타내는 이름들로 이 모든 도구를 지칭한다. [6]이 혁신들은 바로 우리의 일상생활에 들어와 깊이 ③ 영향을 미쳤기 때문에 주요 사회 경제적 운동으로 이어졌다. [7]사람들은 수천 년 동안 근본적으로 변하지 않았다. [8]기술은 끊임없이 변화한다. [9]우리에게 ④ 적응해야 하는 것은 바로 기술이다. [10]그것(기술이 인간에게 적응하는 것)이 바로 인간 중심의 컴퓨터 사용하에서 정보 기술과 그 장치들에 일어날 일이다. [11]컴퓨터가 우리를 마법의 신세계로 데려다줄 것을 계속 더 오래 믿을수록 우리는 우리 삶과 그것(컴퓨터)의 자연스러운 융합을 더 오래 ⑤ 유지시킬(→ 지연시킬) 것인데, (자연스러운 융합은) 사회 경제적 혁명이라 불리길 열망하는 모든 주요 운동의 특징이다.

어휘

almighty 대단한, 굉장한; 전능하신
metallic 금속성의; 금속으로 된
dimensional 차원의
remote 동떨어진; 멀리 떨어진
absorption 흡수; 통합
declare 나타내다; 선언하다
usage 쓰임새, 사용
socioeconomic 사회 경제적인
profoundly 깊이; 완전히
fundamentally 근본[본질]적으로
adapt 적응하다; 맞추다, 조정하다
-centric ~ 중심의
fusion 융합, 결합
aspire 열망하다; 동경하다

정답 가이드

기술은 인간을 새로운 곳으로 데려가는 것이 아니라 인간에게 맞춰 변화하고 융합될 때 사회 경제적 발전을 가져온다는 내용의 글이다. 문장 11의 기술(컴퓨터)이 우리를 신세계로 데려다줄 것이라고 믿는 것은 그것을 우리 삶에 들여와 적응시키는 것과 반대된다. 따라서 그러한 믿음은 삶과 기술의 자연스러운 융합을 ⑤ 'maintain(유지시키기)'보다는 'delay(지연시킴)' 것이라 보는 것이 적절하다.

오답 클리닉

① remote (4%) 동떨어진
모터라는 신기술이 나왔을 때, 우리는 사는 세상을 떠나지 않고(삶의 방식을 바꾸지 않고) 모터를 생활 속으로 가져왔다고 했다. 이때, 모터 공간을 우리가 현재 살고 있는 공간과 대조되는 '동떨어진' 곳으로 표현한 것은 문맥상 자연스럽다.

② absorption (8%) 흡수
모터를 우리 삶에 들여와 여러 쓰임에 맞게 활용한 것은 기술을 삶에 '흡수'시킨 것으로 볼 수 있다.

③ affected (9%) 영향을 미치다
삶에 들여온 기술이 일상에 크게 '영향을 미쳐서' 주요 사회 경제적 운동으로 이어졌다는 인과 관계가 자연스럽다.

④ adapt (20%) 적응하다
주어 It이 Technology를 지칭한다는 것을 정확히 파악해야 한다. 인간은 변하지 않지만 기술은 변한다는 앞 문장을 통해 기술이 인간에게 '적응해야' 함을 추론할 수 있으며 이러한 인간 중심적 관점은 뒤에 이어지는 문장 10의 흐름과도 잘 이어진다.

The 주의 기술이 계속 변화한다는 바로 앞 문장만 보고 그 변화하는 기술에 인간이 적응해야 한다고 정반대로 생각할 수 있다. 그러나 인간은 변하지 않는다는 내용이 앞에 있고, 인간의 삶에 맞게 기술을 들여온다는 것이 글의 요지임에 주의한다.

02 + 낱말 쓰임 〈23학년도 9월 모평 30번 | 정답률 61%〉 ⑤

구문분석 & 직독직해 기술 인터넷의 부정적인 이면

주제문

★<provide A with B>: A에게 B를 제공하다

[1] Although the wonders (of modern technology) have provided people / with opportunities (beyond the wildest dreams of our ancestors), //

부사절 접속사(양보) S'(복수) V'(복수) O'

(현대 기술의) 경이로움은 사람들에게 제공했지만 / 기회를 (우리 조상들은 꿈에도 생각지 못한) //

★<the+형용사 = 추상명사>

the good, as usual, is weakened / by a downside.

S V

늘 그렇듯이 좋은 것은 약화된다 / 부정적인 것에 의해

[2] One (of those downsides) / is // that anyone [who so chooses] / can pick up *the virtual megaphone* [that is the Internet] / and (can) put in their two cents / on any of an infinite number of topics, / regardless of their ① **qualifications**.

S(단수) V(단수) 명사절 접속사 S' 주격 관계대명사 V'₁ O'₁ / is의 C(명사절)

주격 관계대명사 V'₂ O'₂ / 전치사(~에 상관없이)

하나는 (그 부정적인 것들 중) / ~이다 // 누구든 [그렇게 선택한] / 가상의 확성기를 집어 들을 수 있다는 것 [인터넷이라는] / 그리고 자신의 의견을 말할 수 있다는 것 / 무한히 많은 주제 중 어떤 것에 대해서라도 / 자신의 자격과는 상관없이

★<prevent A from v-ing>: A가 v하는 것을 막다

[3] After all, / on the Internet, / there are no *regulations* (② **preventing** a kindergarten teacher from offering medical advice / or a physician from suggesting *ways* (to safely make structural changes to your home)).

현재분사구

①, ② 인터넷상에서 '자격'과 상관없이 의견을 제시하는 예로 사람들이 자신의 분야가 아닌 것에 의견을 제시해도 '막을' 규정이 없음을 보여줌.

결국 / 인터넷에는 / 규정이 없다 (유치원 교사가 의료 자문을 제공하는 것을 막는 / 또는 의사가 방법을 제안하는 것을 막는 (여러분의 집에 안전하게 구조상의 변화를 줄))

③ 잘못된 정보가 정보로 퍼지게 되면 그 둘을 '구별하기'가 어려울 것임.

[4] As a result, / misinformation gets disseminated as information, // and it is not always easy / to ③ **differentiate** the two.

S₁ V₁ C₁ 전치사(~로(서)) 가주어 V₂ C₂ / (= misinformation and information) / 진주어(to-v구)

결과적으로 / 잘못된 정보가 정보로 퍼지게 된다 // 그리고 (~이) 항상 쉽지는 않다 / 그 둘을 구별하는 것이

(= 앞 문장)

[5] This can be particularly frustrating for *scientists*, //

이것은 과학자들에게 특히 좌절감을 줄 수 있다 //

★<spend+시간+v-ing>: v하는 데 시간을 보내다

who spend their lives learning / how to understand the intricacies of the world around them, /

관계대명사(보충 설명) learning의 O(명사구)

그들은 배우는 데 일생을 보낸다 / 자기 주변 세상의 복잡성을 이해하는 방법을 /

해석

[1]현대 기술의 경이로움은 사람들에게 우리 조상들은 꿈에도 생각지 못한 기회를 제공했지만, 늘 그렇듯이 좋은 것은 부정적인 것에 의해 약화된다. [2]그 부정적인 것들 중 하나는 그렇게 선택한(현대 기술을 사용하기로 선택한) 누구든 자신의 ① 자격과는 상관없이 인터넷이라는 가상의 확성기를 집어 들어 무한히 많은 주제 중 어떤 것에 대해서라도 자신의 의견을 말할 수 있다는 것이다. [3]결국 인터넷에는 유치원 교사가 의료 자문을 제공하거나 의사가 여러분의 집에 안전하게 구조상의 변화를 줄 방법을 제안하는 것을 ② 막는 규정이 없다. [4]결과적으로, 잘못된 정보가 정보로 퍼지게 되고, 그 둘을 ③ 구별하는 것이 항상 쉽지는 않다. [5]이것은 과학자들에게 특히 좌절감을 줄 수 있는데, 그들은 자기 주변 세상의 복잡성을 이해하는 방법을 배우는 데 일생을 보내지만, 결국 그들의 연구는 그 주제에 대한 경험이 분 단위로 측정될 수 있는(▶ 경험이 아주 적음을 의미) 사람들에 의해 즉석에서 ④ 도전받게 된다. [6]그리고 (과학자들의) 이러한 좌절감은 일반 대중들에게, 과학자와 도전자 둘 다에게 동등한 신뢰성이 부여된다는 사실에 의해 ⑤ 줄어든다(→ 증폭된다).

어휘

beyond one's wildest dreams 꿈에도 생각지 못한
weaken 약화시키다; 약화되다
downside 부정적인[불리한] 면
megaphone 확성기
infinite 무한한
qualification 자격(증), 면허; 자질
regulation 규정; 규제
physician (내과) 의사

★<사역동사 have+O+p.p.>: O가 ~되도록 하다[시키다] / ↱ 소유격 관계대명사

only to have their work summarily ④ **challenged** / by *people* [whose experience with the topic / can be measured / in minutes].

결과((그러나 결국) v하다)

🔑 ④ 과학자들에게 좌절감을 주는 것은 일생의 연구가 경험이 적은 비전문가들에 의해 '도전받게' 되는 것임.

그러나 결국 그들의 연구는 즉석에서 도전받게 된다 / 사람들에 의해 [그 주제에 대한 경험이 / 측정될 수 있는 / 분 단위로]

[6] This frustration is then ⑤ **diminished(→ amplified)** / by the fact // that, to the general public, / both the scientist and the challenger are awarded equal credibility.

(S / V / 동격 접속사 / S′ / V′ / DO′)

🔑 ⑤ 과학자와 비전문가의 정보가 동등한 신뢰성을 가진다면 과학자의 좌절감은 '증폭될' 것임.

그리고 이러한 좌절감은 줄어든다(→ 증폭된다) / 사실에 의해 // 일반 대중들에게 / 과학자와 도전자 둘 다에게 동등한 신뢰성이 부여된다는

structural 구조상의
differentiate 구별하다
summarily 즉석에서; 간소하게
diminish 줄어들다; 줄이다, 약화시키다
general public 일반 대중
credibility 신뢰성

정답 가이드

현대 기술의 좋은 점이 부정적인 점에 의해 약화된다고 한 후, 누구든 의견을 제시할 수 있는 인터넷상에서 잘못된 정보가 퍼지지 않게 하는 규정이 없다는 점을 지적하고 있다. 이는 일생을 연구한 과학자들이 그 주제에 대해 경험이 적은 비전문가들에 의해 도전받는 좌절감을 주며, 일반 대중들이 과학자의 정보와 비전문가의 정보를 구별하지 못하고 동등하게 신뢰할 때 이 좌절감은 ⑤ 'diminished(줄어들기)'보다는 'amplified(증폭될)' 것이라 보는 것이 적절하다.

오답 클리닉

① qualifications (3%) 자격
'자격'에 상관없이 인터넷에서 어떤 주제에 대해서든 자신의 의견을 말하는 예가 다음 문장에서 나오고 있으므로 문맥상 자연스럽다.

② preventing (8%) 막는
인터넷에서는 자신의 의견을 말할 수 있다고 했고, 그 예로 의료 자문을 하는 유치원 교사, 인테리어 변화 방법을 제안하는 의사를 들고 있으므로 사람들이 자신의 분야가 아닌 것에 의견을 제시하는 것을 '막을' 규정이 없는 것으로 볼 수 있다.

③ differentiate (11%) 구별하다
인터넷을 통해 잘못된 정보가 정보로 퍼지게 되면 두 정보를 서로 '구별하는' 것이 쉽지 않을 것이다.

④ challenged (17%) 도전받는
과학자들에게 좌절감을 주는 경우는 그들의 일생에 걸친 연구가 단지 그 주제를 잠시 살펴본 비전문가에 의해 '도전받는' 경우일 것으로 문맥상 자연스럽다.

03 + 낱말 쓰임 (23학년도 6월 모평 30번 | 정답률 54%) ④

구문분석 & 직독직해

환경 자동차 수요 관리의 필요성

주제문

[1] In recent years / urban transport professionals globally have largely acquiesced to the view // that automobile demand (in cities) / needs to be managed / rather than accommodated.

(S / V / 동격 접속사 / S′(단수) / V′(단수) / ★<A rather than B>: B라기보다 A / p.p. 병렬)

최근 몇 년 동안 / 전 세계적으로 도시 교통 전문가들은 의견에 대체로 따랐다 // 자동차 수요가 (도시의) / 관리되어야 한다는 / 수용되기보다는

[2] Rising incomes inevitably lead to increases (in motorization).
소득 증가는 필연적으로 증가로 이어진다 (자동차화의)

[3] Even without the imperative (of climate change), /
불가피성 없이도 (기후 변화라는) /

🔑 ① 도시의 물리적 압박과 사람들의 요구사항은 도로망을 확장시키는 것을 '제한할' 것임.

the physical constraints (of densely inhabited cities) / and the corresponding demands (of accessibility, mobility, safety, air pollution, and urban livability all) /

(S_1 / S_2)

물리적 압박 (인구가 조밀한 도시의) / 그리고 그에 상응하는 요구가 (접근성, 이동성, 안전, 대기 오염, 그리고 도시의 거주 적합성 모두에 대한) /

① **limit** the option (of expanding road networks / purely to accommodate this rising demand).

(V / O / 목적(~하기 위해))

선택권을 제한한다 (도로망을 확장시키는 / 단지 이 증가하는 수요를 수용하기 위해)

↱ 부사절 접속사(~하면서) / ↱ (= cities)

[4] As a result, / as cities develop and their residents become more prosperous, //

(S'_1 / V'_1 / S'_2 / V'_2 / C′)

결과적으로 / 도시가 발전하고 그것(도시)의 주민들이 더 부유해지면서 //

🔑 ② 도시가 발전하고 주민들이 부유해지면 자동차 수요를 관리하기 위해 자동차를 사용하지 않도록 '설득할' 것임.

해석

[1]최근 몇 년 동안 전 세계적으로 도시 교통 전문가들은 도시의 자동차 수요가 수용되기보다는 관리되어야 한다는 의견에 대체로 따랐다. [2]소득 증가는 필연적으로 자동차화의 증가로 이어진다. [3]기후 변화라는 불가피성 없이도, 인구가 조밀한 도시의 물리적 압박과 그에 상응하는 접근성, 이동성, 안전, 대기 오염, 그리고 도시의 거주 적합성 모두에 대한 요구가 단지 이 증가하는 수요를 수용하기 위해 도로망을 확장시키는 선택권을 ① 제한한다. [4]결과적으로, 도시가 발전하고 도시의 주민들이 더 부유해지면서, 사람들이 자동차를 사용하지 '않을' 것을 선택하도록 ② 설득하는 것은 도시 관리인과 설계자들의 점점 더 핵심적인 중점 사항이 된다. [5]걷기, 자전거 타기, 그리고 대중교통과 같은 ③ 대안적인 선택 사항의 질을 향상시키는 것은 이 전략의 가장 중요한 요소이다. [6]그러나 자동차 수요를 ④ 수용하는 것(→ 관리하는 것)에 대한 가장 직접적인 접근법은 자동차 이동을 더 비싸게 만들거나 그것을 행정 규칙으로 제한하는 것이다. [7]자동차 이동의 기후 변화에 대한 원인 제공은 이러한 불가피성(자동차 수요를 관리하는 것)을 ⑤ 강화한다.

*<persuade+O+to-v>: O가 v하도록 설득하다

② **persuading** people to choose *not* to use cars / becomes an increasingly key focus (of city managers and planners).
S(동명사구) V(단수) C

사람들이 자동차를 사용하지 '않을' 것을 선택하도록 설득하는 것은 / 점점 더 핵심적인 중점 사항이 된다 (도시 관리인과 설계자들의)

🔑 ③ 걷기, 자전거 타기, 대중교통은 자동차에 대한 '대안'임.

5 Improving the quality (of ③ **alternative** options), / (such as walking, cycling, and public transport), / is a central element (of this strategy).
S(동명사구) V(단수) C

질을 향상시키는 것은 (대안적인 선택 사항의) / (걷기, 자전거 타기, 그리고 대중교통과 같은) / 가장 중요한 요소이다 (이 전략의)

🔑 ④ 자동차 이동을 더 비싸게 만들고 행정 규칙으로 제한하는 것은 자동차 수요를 '관리하는' 접근법임.

6 However, / the most direct approach (to ④ **accommodating(→ managing)** automobile demand) / is / making motorized travel more expensive / or restricting it with administrative rules.
S *<make+O+C(형용사)>: O를 C하게 만들다 ↱ (= motorized travel)
V C(동명사구 병렬)

그러나 / 가장 직접적인 접근법은 (자동차 수요를 수용하는 것(→ 관리하는 것)에 대한) / ~이다 / 자동차 이동을 더 비싸게 만드는 것 / 또는 그것(자동차 이동)을 행정 규칙으로 제한하는 것

🔑 ⑤ 자동차 이동이 기후 변화의 원인이므로 자동차 수요 관리의 불가피성을 '강화할' 것임.

7 The contribution (of motorized travel) / to climate change / ⑤ **reinforces** this imperative.

원인 제공은 (자동차 이동의) / 기후 변화에 대한 / 이러한 불가피성(자동차 수요를 관리하는 것)을 강화한다

어휘

manage 관리[경영]하다; 간신히 해내다
accommodate (의견 등을) 수용하다; 공간을 제공하다
inevitably 필연적으로, 불가피하게
motorization 자동차화 ((자동차가 사회생활 속에 밀접하게 관련되어 광범위하게 보급된 현상))
densely 조밀하게, 밀집하여
inhabited (사람·동물이) 사는
corresponding 그에 상응하는, ~에 해당하는
accessibility 접근 가능성
mobility 이동성, 기동성
livability 거주 적합성, 살기 좋음
prosperous 부유한; 번영하는
alternative 대안적인; 대체의
restrict 제한하다; 방해하다
administrative 행정[관리]상의
contribution 원인 제공; 기여
reinforce 강화하다

정답 가이드

증가하는 자동차 수요를 수용하기보다는 규제를 통해 관리해야 한다는 내용의 글이다. 문장 6의 자동차 이동을 더 비싸게 만들거나 행정 규칙으로 제한하는 것은 자동차 수요를 ④ 'accommodating(수용하는 것)'이 아닌 'managing(관리하는 것)'에 대한 접근법으로 보는 것이 적절하다.

The 주의 문장 6이 However로 시작하지만 앞 문장(자동차 사용을 대체할 대안의 질을 높여야 한다)과 반대되는 내용이 아닌 자동차 수요 관리의 보다 더 직접적인 방법을 말하는 것임에 주의한다.

오답 클리닉

① limit (9%) 제한하다
도시의 물리적인 제약과 그에 상응하는 사람들의 요구사항은 도로망을 확장시킬 선택권을 '제한할' 것이다.

② persuading (7%) 설득하는 것
문장 1에서 도시의 자동차 수요가 관리되어야 한다고 했고, 도시가 발전하고 주민들이 부유해질수록 자동차 수요가 더 많아질 것이라고 했다. 이를 관리하기 위해 자동차를 사용하지 않도록 '설득하는 것'이 도시 관리인과 설계자들의 중점 사안이 된다는 연결은 자연스럽다.

③ alternative (7%) 대안적인
걷기, 자전거 타기, 대중교통은 자동차 사용에 대한 '대안적인' 선택 사항들이므로 문맥상 자연스럽다.

⑤ reinforces (23%) 강화하다
this imperative가 자동차 수요 관리의 불가피성을 의미한다는 것을 정확히 파악해야 한다. 자동차 이동이 기후 변화를 야기하는 것은 자동차 수요를 관리해야 하는 불가피성을 '강화할' 것이다.

01 ✦ 글의 주제 〈22학년도 대수능 23번 | 정답률 77%〉 ⑤

구문분석 & 직독직해

과학 과학 연구에서 패러다임의 기능적 활용

주제문

[1]Scientists *use* paradigms / rather than believing them.
S V O (= instead of) (= paradigms)
과학자들은 패러다임을 '사용한다' / 그것(패러다임)을 믿는 것이 아니라
↳ 과학자들은 패러다임을 믿지 않고 사용함.

🔑 과학자들은 패러다임을 사용해서 문제를 다룸.

[2]The use (of a paradigm) / in research / typically addresses related problems / by employing / shared concepts, symbolic expressions, experimental and mathematical tools and procedures, / and even some of the same theoretical statements.
S V O <by v-ing>: v함으로써 / 동명사 employing의 O
사용은 (패러다임의) / 연구에서 / 관련 문제들을 처리하는 것이 일반적이다 / 사용함으로써 / 공유된 개념, 상징적 표현, 실험 및 수학적 도구와 절차를 / 그리고 심지어 동일한 이론적 진술의 일부를
↳ 연구 문제를 처리하는 데 사용되는 패러다임의 요소들.

★need가 조동사로 쓰여 뒤에 동사원형이 옴.
[3]Scientists need only understand / *how* to use these various elements / in *ways* [that others would accept].
S V ★<how to-v>: v하는 방법 O 목적격 관계대명사
과학자들은 이해하기만 하면 된다 / 이런 다양한 요소들을 사용하는 '방법'을 / 방식으로 [다른 사람들이 받아들일]
↳ 과학자들은 패러다임을 사용하는 방법만 이해하면 됨.

[4]These elements (of shared practice) / thus / need not presuppose any comparable unity / in scientists' beliefs (about what they are doing // when they use them).
S V (= scientists) O (= scientists) 부사절 접속사(시간) (= these elements ~ practice)
이러한 요소들은 (공유된 실행의) / 따라서 / 그 어떤 유사한 통일성을 전제로 할 필요는 없다 / 과학자들의 믿음에서 (그들이 하고 있는 것에 관한 // 그것들을 사용할 때)
↳ 과학자들이 패러다임에 대해 통일성 있는 믿음을 가질 필요는 없음.

🔑 패러다임은 상세한 설명 없이 성공적으로 연구할 수 있도록 해줌.

[5]Indeed, / one role of a paradigm is / to enable scientists to work successfully / without having to provide a detailed account (of what they are doing or what they believe about it).
S V C (to-v구) ★<enable + O + to-v>: O가 v할 수 있게 하다 / 명사절 병렬
실제로 / 패러다임의 한 가지 역할은 ~이다 / 과학자들이 성공적으로 일할 수 있게 하는 것 / 상세한 설명을 제공할 필요 없이 (자신들이 하고 있는 것이나 자신들이 그것(패러다임)에 대해 믿고 있는 것에 대해)
↳ **패러다임의 역할:** 과학자들이 상세한 설명을 할 필요 없이 연구할 수 있게 해줌.

🔑 완전한 해석이나 이론적 설명에 동의하지 않아도 인정하는 것에는 동의 → 기능적 용도로 활용.

[6]Thomas Kuhn noted // that scientists "can agree / in their *identification* of a paradigm / without agreeing on, or even attempting to produce, / a full *interpretation* or *rationalization* of it.
S V noted의 O(명사절) 명사절 접속사 S' V' / 동명사구 병렬 / agreeing on과 to produce의 공통 O
Thomas Kuhn이 언급하기를 // 과학자들은 "동의할 수 있다 / 패러다임의 '인정'에 / ~에 동의하지 않거나 ~을 만들어 내려고 시도조차 하지 않으면서 / 그것(패러다임)에 대한 완전한 '해석'이나 '이론적 설명'
↳ 과학자들은 패러다임의 해석이나 설명에 동의하지는 않아도 패러다임의 인정에 동의할 수는 있음.

[7]Lack (of a standard interpretation or of an agreed reduction to rules) / will not prevent a paradigm / from guiding research." ★<prevent+A+from v-ing>: A가 v하는 것을 방해하다
S 전치사구 병렬 V O
결여는 (표준화된 해석이나 규칙 축소에 대한 합의의) / 패러다임이 (~하는 것을) 방해하지 못할 것이다 / 연구를 이끄는 것을"
↳ 표준적인 해설이 없어도 인정하여 연구에 활용함.

해석

[1]과학자들은 패러다임을 믿는 것이 아니라 그것을 '사용한다'. [2]연구에서 패러다임의 사용은 공유된 개념, 상징적 표현, 실험 및 수학적 도구와 절차, 그리고 심지어 동일한 이론적 진술의 일부를 사용함으로써 관련 문제들을 처리하는 것이 일반적이다. [3]과학자들은 다른 사람들이 받아들일 방식으로 이런 다양한 요소들(공유된 개념, 상징적 표현, 실험 및 수학적 도구와 절차, 동일한 이론적 진술의 일부)을 사용하는 '방법'을 이해하기만 하면 된다. [4]따라서 이러한 공유된 실행의 요소들은 과학자들이 그것들을 사용할 때 그들이 하고 있는 것에 관한 그들의 믿음에서 그 어떤 유사한 통일성을 전제로 할 필요는 없다.(▶ 패러다임을 사용할 때 과학자들의 그것에 대한 믿음은 서로 달라도 된다는 의미) [5]실제로, 패러다임의 한 가지 역할은 과학자들이 자신들이 하고 있는 것이나 자신들이 그것(패러다임)에 대해 믿고 있는 것에 대해 상세한 설명을 제공할 필요 없이 성공적으로 일할 수 있게 하는 것이다.(▶ 패러다임에 대한 과학자들의 믿음이 서로 달라도 성공적으로 일할 수 있다는 의미) [6]Thomas Kuhn이 언급하기를, 과학자들은 "패러다임에 대한 완전한 '해석'이나 '이론적 설명'에 동의하지 않거나 만들어 내려고 시도조차 하지 않으면서 패러다임의 '인정'에 동의할 수 있다.(▶ 패러다임에 동의하지 않아도 그것을 받아들여 연구에 사용할 수 있다는 의미) [7]표준화된 해석이나 규칙 축소에 대한 합의의 결여는 패러다임이 연구를 이끄는 것을 방해하지 못할 것이다."

어휘

typically 일반적으로, 보통
address (문제 등을) 처리하다, 다루다
symbolic 상징적인
theoretical 이론적인
statement 진술, 서술
presuppose 전제로 하다
comparable 유사한; 비교할 만한
unity 통일성; 통합; 일치
account 설명; (예금) 계좌; 간주하다
note 언급하다; 주목하다
identification 인정, 검증, 확인; 식별
attempt to-v v하려고 시도하다
interpretation 해석
rationalization 이론적 설명
[선택지] draw A from B B에서 A를 끌어내다
innovative 혁신적인
functional 기능적인; 실용적인; 가동되는
aspect 측면, 양상

⊕ 패러다임(paradigm): 어떤 한 시대 사람들의 견해나 사고를 지배하는 이론적 틀이나 개념의 집합체.

정답 가이드

첫 문장에서 과학자들이 패러다임을 믿지 않고 '사용'한다고 했다. 이어지는 내용에서도, 패러다임의 어떤 구체적 요소들이 연구 문제를 '처리'하는지와 과학자들이 패러다임에 대해 통일된 믿음이 없어도 패러다임이 연구에 성공할 수 있게 하는 '역할'을 한다는 것을 서술하고 있다. Thomas Kuhn이 언급한 내용도 이를 뒷받침한다. 즉, 이 글은 과학 연구에서 패러다임에 대한 과학자들의 통일된 믿음보다는 패러다임의 사용과 역할을 강조하는 것이므로, 글의 주제로 가장 적절한 것은 ⑤ 'functional aspects of a paradigm in scientific research(과학 연구에서 패러다임의 기능적 측면)'이다.

오답 클리닉

① difficulty in drawing novel theories from existing paradigms (3%)
기존의 패러다임으로부터 새로운 이론을 도출(×)하는 데 있어서의 어려움
기존 패러다임에서 새로운 이론을 도출하는 내용이 아님.

② significant influence of personal beliefs in scientific fields (6%)
과학 분야에서 개인 신념의 상당한 영향력(×)
패러다임 사용에서 과학자 개인의 믿음은 중요하지 않다고 했음.

③ key factors that promote the rise of innovative paradigms (6%)
혁신적 패러다임의 출현(×)을 고취하는 핵심 요인
혁신적 패러다임이나 이를 고취하는 요인에 대해 언급된 바 없음.

④ roles of a paradigm in grouping like-minded researchers (8%)
생각이 비슷한 연구원들을 분류(×)하는 데 있어서 패러다임의 역할
패러다임이 연구원들을 분류한다는 내용이 아니며, 사용에 있어서 과학자들의 생각은 통일될 필요가 없다고 했음.

02 + 빈칸 추론 〈23학년도 6월 모평 34번 | 정답률 36%〉 ②

구문분석 & 직독직해

예술 단순한 음을 다양하게 전개하는 클래식 음악

주제문

[1] Development can get very complicated and fanciful.
S V C
전개부는 매우 복잡하고 기상천외할 수 있다
↳ 음악의 전개부는 매우 복잡하거나 기발함.

[2] A fugue (by Johann Sebastian Bach) / illustrates // how far this process could go, //
S V O(명사절)
푸가는 (Johann Sebastian Bach의) / 분명히 보여준다 // 이 과정이 어디까지 갈 수 있을지를 //

when a single melodic line, / (sometimes just a handful of notes), / was *all* [that the composer needed / to create *a brilliant work* (containing lots of intricate development / within a coherent structure)].
부사절 접속사(시간) S′ 명사구 삽입 V′ C′ 목적격 관계대명사 목적(~하기 위해) 현재분사구
하나의 선율이 ~할 때 / (때로는 단지 소수의 음이) / 전부였(을 때) [그 작곡가가 필요로 한 / 훌륭한 작품을 만들기 위해 (많은 복잡한 전개부를 포함하는 / 통일성 있는 구조 내에서)]
↳ 예 1: Bach의 푸가는 하나의 선율만으로 전개부가 복잡하게 만들어짐.

🔑 클래식 작곡가는 소수의 음과 단순한 리듬에서 많은 이익을 얻어냄.

[3] Ludwig van Beethoven's famous Fifth Symphony provides / an exceptional example (of how much mileage a classical composer can get / out of a few notes and a simple rhythmic tapping).
S V O of의 O(명사절)
Ludwig van Beethoven의 유명한 5번 교향곡은 제공한다 / 이례적일 정도로 우수한 예를 (얼마나 많은 이익을 클래식 작곡가가 얻어낼 수 있는지에 대한 / 몇 개의 음과 단순하며 리드미컬한 두드림에서)
↳ 예 2: Beethoven의 5번 교향곡은 소수의 음과 단순하며 리드미컬한 두드림으로 다양하게 전개됨.

[4] *The opening da-da-da-DUM* [that everyone has heard somewhere or another] / **appears in an incredible variety of ways** /
S 목적격 관계대명사 V
시작 부분의 다-다-다-덤은 [모든 사람들이 어디선가 들어본] / 엄청나게 다양한 방식으로 나타난다 /

throughout not only the opening movement, but the remaining three movements, / like a kind of motto or a connective thread.
<not only A but (also) B>: A뿐만 아니라 B도 전치사(~처럼)
🔑 다-다-다-덤의 음이 악장 전체에서 다양한 방식으로 나타남.
시작 악장뿐만 아니라 나머지 3악장 내내 / 일종의 주제구나 연결하는 실처럼
↳ 예 2의 부연 설명: 다-다-다-덤이 4악장 모두에 다양한 방식으로 등장함.

*<not always>: ((부분 부정)) 항상 ~인 것은 아닌

[5] Just as we don't always see / the intricate brushwork [that goes into the creation of a painting], //
부사절 접속사(~인 것처럼) S′ V′ O′ 주격 관계대명사
우리가 항상 볼 수 있는 것이 아닌 것처럼 / 복잡한 붓놀림을 [그림 하나의 창작에 들어가는] //

해석

[1]전개부는 매우 복잡하고 기상천외할 수 있다. [2]Johann Sebastian Bach의 푸가는 하나의 선율, 때로는 단지 소수의 음이 그 작곡가가 통일성 있는 구조 내에서 많은 복잡한 전개부를 포함하는 훌륭한 작품을 만들기 위해 필요로 한 전부였을 때, 이 과정이 어디까지 갈 수 있을지를 분명히 보여준다.(▶ 하나의 선율이 푸가의 전개부를 복잡하고 기발하게 전개시킴을 의미) [3]Ludwig van Beethoven의 유명한 5번 교향곡은 클래식 작곡가가 몇 개의 음과 단순하며 리드미컬한 두드림에서 얼마나 많은 이익을 얻어낼 수 있는지에 대한 이례적일 정도로 우수한 예를 제공한다. [4]모든 사람들이 어디선가 들어본 시작 부분의 다-다-다-덤은 일종의 주제구나 연결하는 실처럼, 시작 악장뿐만 아니라 나머지 3악장 내내 엄청나게 다양한 방식으로 나타난다. [5]우리가 그림 하나의 창작에 들어가는 복잡한 붓놀림을 항상 볼 수 있는 것이 아닌 것처럼, 우리는 Beethoven이 어떻게 계속 자신의 주제구를 새롭게 사용하는 것을 찾는지 또는 어떻게 그의 자재(음악 요소들)를 거대하고 결합력 있는 진술로 전개하는지를 항상 알아보지는 못할 수도 있다. [6]그러나 그 위대한 교향곡에서 우리가 얻는 많은 즐거움은 그 이면의 독창성, 즉 음악적 아이디어의 인상적인 전개에서 생겨난다.

어휘

development ((음악)) 전개(부); 발달; 개발
cf. develop ((음악)) (주제를) 전개하다; 발달하다; 개발하다
fanciful 기상천외한, 기발한
illustrate 분명히 보여주다
a handful of 소수의
note 음(표); 주목하다
exceptional 이례적일 정도로 우수한; 극히 예외적인

we may not always notice // how Beethoven keeps finding fresh uses (for his motto) / or how he develops his material / into a large, cohesive statement.

S V O₁(명사절) O₂(명사절)

🔑 베토벤은 주제구를 다양한 방식으로 새롭게 만들어 사용함.

우리는 항상 알아보지는 못할 수도 있다 // Beethoven이 어떻게 계속 새로운 사용(새롭게 사용하는 것)을 찾는지를 (자신의 주제구에 대한) / 또는 그의 자재를 어떻게 전개하는지를 / 거대하고 결합력 있는 진술로

↳ Beethoven의 주제구는 새롭게 사용되어 못 알아차릴 수도 있음.

[6]But / *a lot of the enjoyment* [(which[that]) we get / from that mighty symphony] / stems from the inventiveness (behind it), / the impressive development (of musical ideas).

S 목적격 관계대명사 생략 V O =

그러나 / 많은 즐거움은 [우리가 얻는 / 그 위대한 교향곡에서] / 독창성에서 생겨난다 (그 이면의) / 즉 인상적인 전개인 (음악적 아이디어의)

↳ 하나의 선율을 독창적으로 전개시킨 교향곡에서 즐거움을 얻음.

mileage 이익; (자동차의) 주행 거리
tap 가볍게 두드리다
movement ((음악)) (교향곡의) 악장; 움직임
motto ((음악)) 주제구; 좌우명
thread 실
brushwork (화가의) 붓놀림
cohesive 결합력 있는
mighty 위대한; 강력한; 거대한
stem from ~에서 생겨나다
inventiveness 독창성
[선택지] contradictory 모순되는
extensive 광범위한; 대규모의
associated with ~와 관련된

정답 가이드

시작 부분의 다-다-다-덤이 시작 악장과 나머지 3악장 내내 '어떠한지'를 추론해야 한다. 이는 마치 일종의 주제구나 연결하는 실 같다고 했고, 이어지는 설명에서 우리가 Beethoven이 어떻게 계속 자신의 주제구를 새롭게 사용하는 것을 찾는지를 항상 알아보지는 못할 수도 있다고 했으므로 빈칸에 들어갈 말로 가장 적절한 것은 ② 'appears in an incredible variety of ways(엄청나게 다양한 방식으로 나타난다)'이다.

오답 클리닉

① makes the composer's musical ideas contradictory (18%)
작곡가의 음악적 아이디어를 모순되게 만든다
다-다-다-덤이 모순된 음악적 아이디어를 만든다는 내용은 없음.

③ provides extensive musical knowledge creatively (13%)
광범위한 음악적 지식을 창의적으로 제공한다
다-다-다-덤이 음악적 지식을 제공하는 것이 아님.

④ remains fairly calm within the structure (15%)
구조 내에서 상당히 조용하게 남아 있다
다-다-다-덤은 거대하고 결합력 있게 전개된다고 했으므로 틀림.

⑤ becomes deeply associated with one's own enjoyment (18%)
자기 자신의 즐거움과 깊이 관련된다
다-다-다-덤이 즐거움을 주는 것이 아니라 그것의 인상적인 전개 방식에서 나오는 독창성에서 즐거움을 얻는 것임.

03 + 글의 순서 (23학년도 9월 모평 37번 | 정답률 57%) ③

구문분석 & 직독직해 문화 문화가 작동하는 두 가지 방식

주제문

[1]Culture operates / in *ways* [(which[that]) we can consciously consider and discuss] / but also in *ways* [of which we are far less cognizant].

S V 목적격 관계대명사 생략 전치사+관계대명사 S′ V′ C′

문화는 작동한다 / 방식으로 [우리가 의식적으로 고려하고 논의할 수 있는] / 뿐만 아니라 방식으로도 [우리가 훨씬 덜 인식하는]

↳ 문화는 의식하거나 덜 인식하는 방식으로 작동함.

🔑 문화가 작동하는 두 가지 방식 중 먼저 의식적 방식을 설명함.

(B) [2]When we have to offer an account (of our actions), // we consciously understand // which excuses might prove acceptable, / given *the particular circumstances* [(which[that]) we find ourselves in].

부사절 접속사(시간) S V S′ V′ C′ 전치사(~을 고려해 볼 때) 목적격 관계대명사 생략 → understand의 O(명사절)

우리가 설명을 해야 할 때 (우리의 행동에 대한) // 우리는 의식적으로 이해한다 // 어떤 변명이 받아들일 만하다고 판명될 수 있을지를 / 특정한 상황을 고려해 볼 때 [우리가 처해 있는]

[3]In such situations, / we use cultural ideas // as we would use a particular tool.

S V O 부사절 접속사(~처럼)

그런 상황에서 / 우리는 문화적 관념을 사용한다 // 우리가 특정 도구를 사용하는 것처럼

↳ 대조 A(의식적 방식): 문화적 관념을 사용해 우리의 행동을 설명함.

해석

[1]문화는 우리가 의식적으로 고려하고 논의할 수 있는 방식뿐만 아니라 우리가 훨씬 덜 인식하는 방식으로도 작동한다. (B) [2]우리의 행동에 대한 설명을 해야 할 때, 우리는 우리가 처해 있는 특정한 상황을 고려해 볼 때 어떤 변명이 받아들일 만하다고 판명될 수 있을지를 의식적으로 이해한다. [3]그런 상황에서 우리는 특정 도구를 사용하는 것처럼 문화적 관념을 사용한다. (C) [4]우리가 스크루드라이버를 선택하듯이 우리는 문화적 개념을 선택하는데, 어떤 일은 십자 홈이 난 나사못을 필요로 하는 반면에 다른 일은 육각 렌치를 필요로 한다. [5]우리의 행동을 정당화하기 위해 대화에 어떤 (문화적) 관념을 집어넣든, 요점은 우리의 동기가 우리에게 만연하게 이용 가능하다는 것이다. [6]그것들(우리의 동기)은 숨겨져 있지 않다.(▶ 우리 행동을 정당화하는 동기를 문화적 관념을 사용하여 설명할 수 있다는 의미)

(B)의 특정 도구의 사용을 스크루드라이버 사용에 비유함.

(C) [4]We select the cultural notion // as we would select a screwdriver: //
S1 V1 O1 부사절 접속사(~듯이)
우리는 문화적 개념을 선택한다 // 우리가 스크루드라이버를 선택하듯이 //
(= other jobs)
certain jobs call for a Phillips head // while others require an Allen wrench.
S2 V2 O2 부사절 접속사(반면에)
어떤 일은 십자 홈이 난 나사못을 필요로 한다 // 반면에 다른 일은 육각 렌치를 필요로 한다
↳ 예: 상황에 알맞은 도구를 선택하듯이 우리는 문화적 개념을 선택함.

[5]Whichever idea we insert into the conversation / to justify our actions, //
양보 부사절(= no matter which ~) 목적(~하기 위해)
대화에 어떤 (문화적) 관념을 집어넣든 / 우리의 행동을 정당화하기 위해 //
is의 C(명사절)
the point is // that our motives are discursively available / to us.
S V 명사절 접속사 S′ V′ C′
요점은 ~이다 // 우리의 동기가 만연하게 이용 가능하다는 것 / 우리에게

(= Our motives)
[6]They are not hidden.
S V
그것들(우리의 동기)은 숨겨져 있지 않다
↳ 부연 설명: 행동을 정당화하는 데 어떤 문화적 관념을 사용하든 우리에게는 타당한 동기가 있음.

문화가 작동하는 덜 인식하는 방식에 대한 설명이 역접으로 이어짐.

(A) [7]In some cases, / however, / we are far less aware / of why we believe a certain claim to be true,
*여기서 <be to-v>는 '의무'를 뜻함. S V C of의 O1(명사절)
/ or how we are to explain // why certain social realities exist.
of의 O2(명사절) to explain의 O(명사절)
어떤 경우 / 하지만 / 우리는 훨씬 덜 알고 있다 / 왜 우리가 어떤 주장을 사실이라고 믿는지에 대해
/ 또는 어떻게 우리가 설명해야 할지에 대해 // 왜 어떤 사회적 현실이 존재하는지를
↳ 대조 B(덜 인식하는 방식): 어떤 경우, 우리는 어떤 생각을 하는 이유를 잘 알지 못함.

[8]Ideas (about the social world) / become part (of our worldview) /
S(복수) V(복수) C
관념은 (사회적 세계에 대한) / 일부가 된다 (우리 세계관의) /
without our necessarily being aware / of the source of the particular idea / or that we even hold the idea at all.
동명사의 의미상 주어 without의 O(동명사구) of의 O1(명사구) of의 O2(명사절)
우리가 반드시 알고 있지 않은 채로 / 특정한 관념의 출처에 대해서 / 혹은 심지어 우리가 그 관념을 갖고 있다는 것조차
↳ 부연 설명: 사회적 세계에 대한 관념은 우리가 잘 알지 못하는 채로 작동함.

(A) [7]하지만 어떤 경우, 우리는 왜 우리가 어떤 주장을 사실이라고 믿는지에 대해 또는 왜 어떤 사회적 현실이 존재하는지를 어떻게 우리가 설명해야 할지에 대해 훨씬 덜 알고 있다. [8]사회적 세계에 대한 관념은 우리가 특정한 관념의 출처에 대해서 혹은 심지어 우리가 그 관념을 갖고 있다는 것조차 반드시 알고 있지 않은 채로 우리 세계관의 일부가 된다.

어휘

operate 작동하다; 수술하다
consciously 의식적으로
account 설명(하다); 계좌
excuse 변명(하다); 용서(하다)
prove (~임이) 판명되다[드러나다]; 입증하다
acceptable 받아들일 만한, 용인되는
notion 개념, 관념
call for ~을 필요로 하다; 요구하다
insert 집어넣다, 삽입하다
justify 정당화하다
motive 동기(를 주다)
aware of ~을 알고[의식하고] 있는
claim 주장(하다); 요구(하다)
worldview 세계관
necessarily 반드시

정답 가이드

문화는 우리가 의식하는 방식뿐만 아니라 덜 인식하는 방식으로도 작동한다는 주어진 글 뒤에는 둘 중 의식적으로 작동하는 방식을 설명하는 (B)가 먼저 오는 것이 적절하다. 우리가 상황에 따라 특정한 도구를 사용하듯이 의식적으로 문화적 개념을 사용한다는 (B)의 마지막 문장을 스크루드라이버를 예로 들어 설명하는 (C)가 이어진 후, 덜 인식하는 방식으로 문화적 관념이 작동하기도 한다고 설명하는 (A)가 역접 연결어 however로 연결되는 것이 자연스럽다.

오답 클리닉

① (A) - (C) - (B) (2%)
주어진 글의 문화가 작동하는 방식 중 덜 인식하는 방식이 (A)에서 역접 연결어 however로 이어지므로, 의식적으로 작동하는 방식을 설명하는 (B)가 먼저 와야 한다.
② (B) - (A) - (C) (23%) / ④ (C) - (A) - (B) (10%) / ⑤ (C) - (B) - (A) (8%)
(C)의 스크루드라이버를 선택하는 것은 (B)의 특정한 도구를 사용한다는 내용을 부연 설명하는 것이므로 (B) 바로 뒤에 (C)가 와야 한다.

01 + 글의 제목 (22학년도 대수능 24번 | 정답률 53%) ①

구문분석 & 직독직해 기술 사람이 해야 하는 물건 수리

주제문

[1]Mending and restoring objects often require even more creativity / than original production.
(S / V / O; even: 비교급 강조 부사)
물건을 고치고 복원하는 것은 흔히 훨씬 더 많은 창의력을 필요로 한다 / 최초의 제작보다
(창의력 비교: 물건 수리 > 물건 제작)
↳ 물건을 처음 만드는 것보다 고치는 것에 창의력이 더 필요함.

[2]The preindustrial blacksmith made things to order / for people in his immediate community; //
(S_1 / V_1 / O; ★<make A to order>: A를 주문에 따라 만들다)
산업화 이전의 대장장이는 물건들을 주문에 따라 만들었다 / 가까운 지역 사회에 사는 사람들을 위해 //
customizing the product, / modifying or transforming it according to the user, / was routine.
(S_2(단수) = 동격 삽입어구 / V_2(단수) / C)
물건을 주문 제작하는 것 / 즉 사용자에 맞춰 물건을 수정하거나 변형시키는 것은 / 일상적이었다

[3]Customers would bring things back // if something went wrong; // repair was thus an extension (of fabrication).
(S_1 / V_1 / O / 부사절 접속사(조건) / S_2 / V_2 / C; ★<would+동사원형>: ~하곤 했다 (과거의 습관))
고객들은 물건을 다시 가져오곤 했다 // 무언가 고장 나면 // 따라서 수리는 연장이었다 (제작의)
↳ **산업화 이전:** 주문 제작과 수리를 모두 사람이 했음.

[4]With industrialization / and eventually with mass production, / making things became the province (of machine tenders (with limited knowledge)).
(전치사구 병렬 / S / V / C)
산업화와 함께 / 그리고 결국 대량 생산과 함께 / 물건을 만드는 것은 영역이 되었다 (기계 감독의 (한정적 지식을 지닌))
↳ **산업화 이후:** 물건 제작을 기계가 하게 됨.

[5]But / repair continued to require / a larger grasp (of design and materials), / an understanding (of the whole) / and a comprehension (of the designer's intentions).
(S / V / O / to require의 O =; 수리는 이해가 수반되어야 함.)
그러나 / 수리는 계속해서 요구했다 / 더 큰 이해를 (설계와 재료에 대한) / 즉 이해 (전체에 대한) / 그리고 이해 (설계자의 의도에 대한)
↳ 물건 수리는 더 큰 이해를 필요로 함.

[6]"Manufacturers all work / by machinery or by vast subdivision of labour / and not, (so to speak,) by hand," // an 1896 *Manual of Mending and Repairing* explained.
(S_1 / V_1 / 전치사구 병렬 / 전치사구 병렬 / 전치사구 병렬 / S_2 / V_2)
"제조업자들은 모두 일한다 / 기계나 노동의 방대한 세분화로 / 그리고 (말하자면) 손으로는 (일하지) 않는다" // 1896년의 <Manual of Mending and Repairing>이 설명했다
↳ 물건 제작은 수작업이 아닌 기계나 분업으로 이루어짐.

[7]"But / all repairing *must* be done / by hand.
(S / V; 수리는 사람이 해야 함.)
"그러나 / 모든 수리는 '행해져야 한다' / 손으로
↳ 수리는 수작업으로 해야 함.

[8]We can make every detail (of a watch or of a gun) / by machinery, //
(S_1 / V_1 / O_1)
우리는 모든 세밀한 부분을 만들 수 있다 (손목시계나 총의) / 기계로 //
but the machine cannot mend it // when (it is) broken, / much less a clock or a pistol!"
(S_2 / V_2 / O_2(= machinery); ★<much[still] less>: ((부정문)) ~(이 아님)은 더 말할 것도 없다)
하지만 기계는 그것(기계)을 고칠 수 없다 // 고장 났을 때 / 시계나 권총은 더 말할 것도 없다!"
↳ **부연 설명:** 기계로 제작은 해도 수리는 못함.

해석

[1]물건을 고치고 복원하는 것은 흔히 최초의 제작보다 훨씬 더 많은 창의력을 필요로 한다. [2]산업화 이전의 대장장이는 가까운 지역 사회에 사는 사람들을 위해 물건들을 주문에 따라 만들었고, 물건을 주문 제작하는 것, 즉 사용자에 맞춰 물건을 수정하거나 변형시키는 것은 일상적이었다. [3]고객들은 무언가 고장 나면 물건을 다시 가져오곤 했고, 따라서 수리는 제작의 연장이었다. [4]산업화와 함께 그리고 결국 대량 생산과 함께, 물건을 만드는 것은 한정적 지식을 지닌 기계 감독의 영역이 되었다. [5]그러나 수리는 설계와 재료에 대한 더 큰 이해, 즉 전체에 대한 이해와 설계자의 의도에 대한 이해를 계속해서 요구했다. [6]"제조업자들은 모두 기계나 노동의 방대한 세분화로 일하고, 말하자면 손으로는 일하지 않는다."라고 1896년의 <Manual of Mending and Repairing>이 설명했다. [7]"그러나 모든 수리는 손으로 '행해져야 한다'. [8]우리는 기계로 손목시계나 총의 모든 세밀한 부분을 만들 수 있지만, 고장 났을 때 기계는 그것(기계)을 고칠 수 없으며, 시계나 권총은 더 말할 것도 없다!"

어휘

mend 고치다, 수리하다; 개선하다
restore 복원[복구]하다; 회복시키다
preindustrial 산업화 이전의
blacksmith 대장장이
immediate 가까운, 인접한; 즉각적인
customize 주문 제작하다
modify 수정[변경]하다, 바꾸다
transform 변형시키다
go wrong 고장 나다; (일이) 잘못되다
extension 연장, 확장
fabrication 제작, 제조; 꾸며낸 것; 위조(물)
industrialization 산업화
mass production 대량 생산
province 영역, 분야; 지역, 지방
tender 감독, 감시인; 부드러운, 연한
grasp 이해(= comprehension); 꽉 잡다
intention 의도, 목적
manufacturer 제조업자, 제작자
machinery 기계(류); 기계 장치
subdivision 세분화; (세분된) 일부분
[선택지] art 기술, 요령; 예술
survey 개괄; 조사
evolve 발전[진화]하다; 발전[진화]시키다
repairperson 수리공

정답 가이드

과거에 제조와 수리를 모두 제작자(대장장이)가 하던 것과 대조하여, 현재는 제조를 기계가 하더라도 수리는 여전히 사람이 맡아서 해야 한다는 내용의 글이다. 따라서 글의 제목으로 가장 적절한 것은 ① 'Still Left to the Modern Blacksmith: The Art of Repair(현대 대장장이에게 여전히 맡겨진 것, 즉 수리의 기술)'이다.

오답 클리닉

② A Historical Survey of How Repairing Skills Evolved (8%)
수리 기술이 어떻게 발전했는지에 관한(×) 역사적 개괄
산업화에 따른 제작의 변화는 언급되었으나, 수리 기술의 발전에 대한 내용은 없음.

③ How to Be a Creative Repairperson: Tips and Ideas (5%)
창의적인 수리공이 되는 방법(×), 즉 조언과 아이디어
창의적인 수리공이 되는 방법을 설명하는 내용이 아님.

④ A Process of Repair: Create, Modify, Transform! (23%)
수리의 과정(×), 즉 만들고, 수정하고, 변형시켜라!
수리를 하는 구체적인 과정에 대한 내용은 없음.

⑤ Can Industrialization Mend Our Broken Past? (11%)
산업화가 우리의 망가진 과거(×)를 고칠 수 있을까?
industrialization과 mending을 활용한 오답. 산업화는 물건 제작 방식의 변화를 설명하기 위해 언급한 것으로 망가진 과거를 고치는 것과는 관련 없음.

02 ✦ 빈칸 추론 ⟨23학년도 6월 모평 33번 | 정답률 34%⟩ ②

구문분석 & 직독직해

상업 리드유저가 개발한 혁신을 거부하는 제조업자

주제문

*[ ]는 the way를 수식하는 관계부사절임.

[1]Manufacturers design their innovation processes / around *the way* [(they think) the process works].
(S: Manufacturers / V: design / O: their innovation processes / 전치사(~에 맞춰): around / 삽입절: they think)

제조업자들은 자신들의 혁신 과정을 설계한다 / 방식에 맞춰 [(자신들이 생각하기에) 그 과정이 작동되는]

↳ 제조업자들은 혁신 과정을 설계하는 자신들만의 방식이 있음.

[2]The vast majority (of manufacturers) / still think // that product development and service development are always done / by manufacturers, / and that their job is always to find a need and (to) fill it / rather than to sometimes find and commercialize *an innovation* [that **lead users have already developed**].
(S: The vast majority / V: think / → think의 O_1(명사절): 명사절 접속사 that / S′: product development and service development / V′: are always done / → think의 O_2(명사절): 명사절 접속사 that / S′: their job / V′: is / *<A rather than B>: B라기보다는 A / C′(to-v구 병렬) / 목적격 관계대명사 that)

🔑 제품을 개발하는 것이 제조업자 자신의 일이라 생각함.

대다수는 (제조업자의) / 여전히 생각한다 // 제품 개발과 서비스 개발이 항상 이루어진다고 / 제조업자들에 의해 / 그리고 자신들의 일은 항상 필요를 발견하고 그것을 채우는 것이라고 / 가끔 혁신을 발견하고 상업화하기보다는 [리드유저들이 이미 개발한]

↳ **세부 사항:** 제조업자들은 리드유저들이 이미 개발한 혁신을 찾아 상업화하는 것은 자신들의 일이 아니라고 여김.

🔑 제조업자는 자체적으로 시장을 분석하고 제품을 개발하려 함.

[3]Accordingly, / manufacturers have set up / *market-research departments* (to explore the needs (of users in the target market)), / *product-development groups* (to think up suitable products / to address those needs), / and so forth.
(S: manufacturers / V: have set up / O_1: market-research departments / O_2: product-development groups / 목적(~하기 위해): to address those needs)

그래서 / 제조업자들은 설립해 왔다 / 시장 연구 부서를 (필요를 탐구하기 위한 (표적 시장 사용자들의)) / 제품 개발 집단을 (적절한 제품을 고안하기 위한 / 그러한 필요를 다루기 위해) / 그리고 기타 등등을

↳ **결과:** 제조업자들은 시장을 분석하고 제품을 개발하기 위한 부서를 만들었음.

🔑 제조업자는 리드유저의 요구와 시제품 해답을 거부함.

[4]The needs and prototype solutions (of lead users) — // if (they are) encountered at all — / are typically rejected / as outliers (of no interest).
(S: The needs and prototype solutions / 부사절 접속사: if / 주어+be동사 생략: they are (= 문장의 S) / V′: encountered / V: are typically rejected)

*<of+추상명사>는 형용사와 같으며, 앞의 명사를 수식함.

필요와 시제품 해답은 (리드유저들의) // 맞닥뜨려진다 하더라도 / 보통 거부된다 / 이상치로 (전혀 흥미롭지 않은)

↳ **결론:** 리드유저들의 필요와 시제품 해답은 무시됨.

해석

[1]제조업자들은 자신들이 생각하기에 그 과정이 작동되는 방식에 맞춰 자신들의 혁신 과정을 설계한다. [2]제조업자의 대다수는 제품 개발과 서비스 개발이 항상 제조업자들에 의해 이루어지며, 자신들의 일은 가끔 리드유저들이 이미 개발한 혁신을 발견하고 상업화하기보다는 항상 필요를 발견하고 그것을 채우는 것이라고 여전히 생각한다. [3]그래서, 제조업자들은 표적 시장 사용자들의 필요를 탐구하기 위한 시장 연구 부서를, 그러한 필요를 다루기 위해 적절한 제품을 고안하기 위한 제품 개발 집단 및 기타 등등을 설립해 왔다. [4]리드유저들의 필요와 시제품 해답은, 맞닥뜨려진다 하더라도, 보통 전혀 흥미롭지 않은 이상치로 거부된다. [5]실제로, 리드유저들의 혁신이 한 회사의 제품 라인에 정말로 들어가게 될 때, 그것은 많은 회사의 여러 주요 혁신의 실질적인 원천이 되는 것으로 보여져 왔는데, 그것은 보통 지연되어, 그리고 이례적이고 비체계적인 경로를 통해 도달한다.

어휘

manufacturer 제조업자
the vast majority of ~의 대다수
commercialize 상업화하다
set up ~을 설립하다
department 부서; 부문; 학과
think up ~을 고안하다, 생각해 내다
suitable 적절한, 알맞은
address (문제를) 다루다, 처리하다; 연설하다
and so forth 기타 등등
prototype 시제품 ((시험 삼아 만들어본 제품))
lead user 리드유저 ((시장 트렌드를 선도하는 사용자))
if ~ at all ~한다고 하더라도
encounter 마주치다, 접하다
reject 거부하다
outlier 이상치 ((평균치에서 크게 벗어나 다른 대상들과 구분되는 표본))

[5]Indeed, / when lead users' innovations do enter a firm's product line — // and they have been shown / to be the actual source (of many major innovations (for many firms)) — //

(→ (enter 강조), (= lead users' innovations) ←, 부사절 접속사(시간), S'1, V'1, O', S'2, V'2, C')

실제로 / 리드유저들의 혁신이 한 회사의 제품 라인에 정말로 들어가게 될 때 // 그리고 그것(리드유저들의 혁신)은 보여져 왔다 / 실질적인 원천이 되는 것으로 (여러 주요 혁신의 (많은 회사의)) //

(→ (= lead users' innovations))

they typically arrive / with a lag and by an unusual and unsystematic route.

(S, V, 전치사구 병렬)

그것(리드유저들의 혁신)은 보통 도달한다 / 지연되어 그리고 이례적이고 비체계적인 경로를 통해

↳ 리드유저들의 혁신이 회사의 제품 라인에 들어가더라도 어렵게 들어감.

unsystematic 비체계적인
route 경로, 길; 노선
[선택지] overlook 간과하다; 못 본 체하다
put into use 활용하다, 사용하다

정답 가이드

제조업자들이 '어떤' 혁신을 발견하기보다는 항상 필요를 발견하는지를 추론해야 한다. 이어지는 설명에서, 리드유저들의 필요와 시제품은 흥미 대상이 아니라고 했고, 리드유저들의 혁신은 제품 라인에 들어가기 힘들다고 했으므로, 제조업자들은 ② 'lead users have already developed(리드유저들이 이미 개발한)' 혁신을 찾아 상업화하는 것을 자신들의 일로 여기지 않음을 알 수 있다.

오답 클리닉

① lead users tended to overlook (19%)
리드유저들이 간과하는 경향이 있었다
리드유저들이 놓친 혁신이 아니라 그들이 개발한 혁신을 거부한다고 했음.

③ lead users encountered in the market (27%)
리드유저들이 시장에서 마주쳤다
if encountered at all을 활용한 오답. 리드유저들이 시장에서 본 혁신이 아니라 그들이 직접 개발한 혁신을 거부하는 것임.

④ other firms frequently put into use (11%)
다른 회사들이 자주 활용했다
다른 회사가 활용한 혁신이 아닌 리드유저의 혁신을 거부하는 것임.

⑤ both users and firms have valued (9%)
사용자와 회사 둘 다 가치 있게 여겼다
사용자와 회사가 모두 가치 있게 여긴 혁신은 언급되지 않음.

03 + 문장 넣기 (23학년도 대수능 38번 | 정답률 54%)

⑤

구문분석 & 직독직해

건축 도시와 분리감을 주는 공원 설계

[1]Parks take / *the shape* (demanded by the cultural concerns (of their time)).

(S, V, O, 과거분사구)

공원은 취한다 / 형태를 (문화적 관심사에 의해 요구되는 (그 당대의))

[2]Once parks are in place, // they are no inert stage — // their purposes and meanings are made and (are) remade / by planners and by park users.

(부사절 접속사(일단 ~하면), S1, V1, C, S2, V2-1, V2-2)

일단 공원이 마련되면 // 그것은 비활성화된 단계가 아니다 // 그것의 목적과 의미는 만들어지고 다시 만들어진다 / (공원) 계획자와 공원 이용자에 의해

↳ 공원은 그 시대의 문화적 관심사의 형태를 띠고 계획자와 이용자에 의해 목적과 의미가 만들어짐.

[3]Moments (of park creation) / are particularly telling, / however, // for they reveal and actualize / ideas (about nature and its relationship to urban society).

(→ (= moments of park creation), S(복수), V(복수), C, 부사절 접속사(이유), about의 O(명사구))

순간들은 (공원 조성의) / 특히 인상적이다 / 그러나 // 그것들(공원 조성의 순간들)이 드러내고 실현하기 때문에 / 생각을 (자연과 그것(자연)이 도시 사회와 갖는 관계에 대한)

↳ 공원을 조성할 때 자연, 그리고 자연과 도시 사회의 관계에 대한 생각이 드러남.

★<distinguish A from B>: A를 B와 구별하다

(①) [4]Indeed, / what distinguishes a park / from the broader category of public space / is the representation (of *nature* [that parks are meant to embody]).

(S(명사절), V(단수), C, 목적격 관계대명사)

실제로 / 공원을 구별하는 것은 / 더 넓은 범주인 공공 공간과 / 표현이다 (자연의 [공원이 구현하기로 되어 있는])

(②) [5]Public spaces include / parks, concrete plazas, sidewalks, even indoor atriums.

(S, V, O1, O2, O3, O4)

공공 공간은 포함한다 / 공원, 콘크리트 광장, 보도, 심지어 실내 아트리움도

해석

[1]공원은 그 당대의 문화적 관심사에 의해 요구되는 형태를 취한다. [2]일단 공원이 마련되면, 그것은 비활성화된 단계가 아닌데, 그것의 목적과 의미는 (공원) 계획자와 공원 이용자에 의해 만들어지고 다시 만들어진다. [3]그러나 공원 조성의 순간들은 특히 인상적인데, 자연과 그것(자연)이 도시 사회와 갖는 관계에 대한 생각을 드러내고 실현하기 때문이다. (①) [4]실제로 공원을 더 넓은 범주인 공공 공간과 구별하는 것은 공원이 구현하기로 되어 있는 자연의 표현이다. (②) [5]공공 공간은 공원, 콘크리트 광장, 보도, 심지어 실내 아트리움도 포함한다. (③) [6]일반적으로 공원에는 그것들의 중심적인 특색으로 나무, 풀, 그리고 다른 식물들이 있다. (④) [7]도시 공원에 들어갈 때 사람들은 흔히 거리, 자동차, 그리고 건물로부터의 뚜렷한 분리를 상상한다. (⑤ [8]그것에는 이유가 있는데, 전통적으로 공원 설계자들은 공원 경계에 키 큰 나무를 심고, 돌담을 쌓고, 다른 칸막이 수단을 세움으로써 그런 느낌을 만들어 내려고 했다.) [9]이 생각의 뒤에 있는 것은 미적으로 시사하는 바가 많은 공원 공간을 설계하려는 조경가의 욕망뿐만이 아니라 도시와 자연을 대조적인 공간과 대립적인 세력으로 상상하는 훨씬 더 오래된 서구 사상의 역사이다.

(③) [6]Parks typically have trees, grass, and other plants / as their central features.
S V O 전치사(~로(서))
일반적으로 공원에는 나무, 풀, 그리고 다른 식물들이 있다 / 그것들(공원)의 중심적인 특색으로
↳ 공원과 공공 공간을 구별하는 것은 나무, 풀, 식물들을 특징으로 하는 자연의 표현임.

(④) [7]When entering a city park, / people often imagine / a sharp separation (from streets, cars, and buildings).
접속사를 생략하지 않은 분사구문(= When they enter ~) S V O
🔑 주어진 문장의 that과 such a feeling이 지칭하는 내용.
도시 공원에 들어갈 때 / 사람들은 흔히 상상한다 / 뚜렷한 분리를 (거리, 자동차, 그리고 건물로부터의)
↳ 사람들은 공원에 들어갈 때 도시와의 분리를 상상함.

↱ (= 앞 문장) 🔑 that과 such a feeling이 지칭하는 내용이 앞에 제시되어야 함.
(⑤ [8]There's a reason for that: // traditionally, / park designers attempted to create such a feeling /
V_1 S_1 S_2 V_2 O_2
그것에는 이유가 있다 // 전통적으로 / 공원 설계자들은 그런 느낌을 만들어 내려고 했다 /
★<by v-ing>: v함으로써
by planting tall trees at park boundaries, / building stone walls, / and constructing other means of partition.)
by의 O_1(동명사구) by의 O_2(동명사구) by의 O_3(동명사구)
공원 경계에 키 큰 나무를 심음으로써 / 돌담을 쌓음으로써 / 그리고 다른 칸막이 수단을 세움으로써
↳ **이유:** 분리감을 위해 공원 설계자들은 공원 경계에 키 큰 나무를 심고, 돌담을 쌓고, 다른 칸막이를 세웠음.

🔑 주어진 문장의 도시와 공원을 분리하려는 설계자의 생각을 의미함.
[9]What's behind this idea is / not only landscape architects' desire (to design aesthetically suggestive park spaces), /
S(명사절) V(단수) C_1(명사구 병렬) =
이 생각의 뒤에 있는 것은 ~이다 / 조경가의 욕망뿐만이 아니라 (미적으로 시사하는 바가 많은 공원 공간을 설계하려는) /
but a much longer history (of *Western thought* [that envisions cities and nature / as antithetical spaces and oppositional forces]).
C_2(명사구 병렬) 주격 관계대명사 전치사(~로(서))
훨씬 더 오래된 역사 (서구 사상의 [도시와 자연을 상상하는 / 대조적인 공간과 대립적인 세력으로])
↳ **이유 부연 설명:** 도시와 공원을 분리하는 생각에는 미적 공간을 설계하려는 조경가의 욕망뿐만 아니라 도시와 자연을 대조적인 공간으로 상상하는 서구 사상의 역사가 깔려있음.

어휘

inert 비활성의; 기력이 없는
telling 인상적인; 효과적인
reveal 드러내다; 밝히다
representation 표현, 묘사; 대표
be meant to-v v하기로 되어 있다; v할 생각[의도]이다
embody 구현[상징]하다
atrium 아트리움 ((현대식 건물 중앙 높은 곳에 유리로 지붕을 한 넓은 공간))
separation 분리; 분류
attempt to-v v하려고 시도하다
boundary 경계(선)
construct 세우다, 건설하다; 구성하다
partition 칸막이; 분할
landscape architect 조경가
suggestive 시사[암시]하는 바가 많은; 연상시키는
envision 상상하다
oppositional 대립적인; 반대의
force 세력, 힘; 강요하다

정답 가이드

주어진 문장은 그것(that)의 이유가 공원 경계에 칸막이 수단을 세움으로써 그런 느낌(such a feeling)을 만들려고 했기 때문이라고 설명한다. that과 such a feeling이 지칭하는 내용을 찾아야 하는데, 문맥상 that은 ⑤의 앞 문장인 도시 공원에 들어갈 때 사람들이 거리, 자동차, 건물과의 뚜렷한 분리를 상상하는 것이며, such a feeling 역시 도시 공원에 들어갈 때 사람들이 느끼는 도시로부터의 분리감을 의미함을 알 수 있다. 즉 주어진 문장은 ⑤ 앞에 있는 문장의 이유에 해당하므로 ⑤에 들어가는 것이 가장 적절하다. 또한 ⑤ 뒤에 이어지는 문장은 주어진 문장에서 언급된 공원 설계자들의 시도를 this idea로 받아 그 이면에 깔려 있는 것들을 서술하는 것으로 글을 끝맺고 있다.

오답 클리닉

① (2%) 공원을 조성할 때 자연, 그리고 자연과 도시 사회의 관계에 대한 생각이 드러나고 실현된다는 앞 문장에 대해 공원이 자연을 구현한다는 부연 설명이 이어진다.
② (5%) / ③ (6%) 앞에서 언급된 공공 공간과 공원의 구별에 대한 설명이 차례로 이어진다.
④ (33%) 나무, 풀, 그리고 다른 식물들이 있는 공원의 중심적 특색을 제시한 다음 사람들이 이러한 공원에 들어갈 때 도시로부터 분리됨을 느낀다는 내용이 자연스럽게 이어진다.

The 주의 주어진 문장이 ④에 들어갈 경우, 주어진 문장의 that과 such a feeling이 가리키는 내용을 앞에서 찾을 수 없음에 주의한다.

01 ✦ 함의 추론 〈22학년도 9월 모평 21번 | 정답률 34%〉 ②

구문분석 & 직독직해 비즈니스 조직 리더의 개별적 근무 환경 조성의 필요성

[1] **Flicking the collaboration light switch** / is *something* [that leaders are uniquely positioned to do], //
S(동명사구) V(단수) C 목적격 관계대명사
협업의 전등 스위치를 탁 내리는 것은 / 무언가이다 [리더들이 유일하게 할 위치에 있는] //
because several obstacles stand in the way / of *people* (voluntarily working alone).
부사절 접속사(이유) S′ V′ 현재분사구
왜냐하면 여러 장애물이 방해하기 때문이다 / 사람들을 (자발적으로 혼자 일하는)
↳ 혼자 일하는 사람들을 방해하지 않도록 리더는 협업을 멈춰야 함.

[2] For one thing, / the fear (of being left out of the loop) / can keep them glued to their enterprise social media.
S = V O C (them = people ~ working alone)
우선 / 두려움은 (혼자만 모르게 남겨지는) / 그들(자발적으로 혼자 일하는 사람들)이 계속 자신들의 기업 소셜 미디어에 열중하게 할 수 있다

[3] Individuals don't want to be — or appear to be — isolated.
S V O
개인들은 고립되거나 고립된 듯 보이는 것을 원하지 않는다
↳ **협업의 방해 1:** 고립을 두려워해 소셜 미디어 활동에 매달리게 됨.

[4] For another, / knowing what their teammates are doing / provides a sense of comfort and security, //
S 동명사 knowing의 O(명사절) V O
또 다른 것으로는 / 자신들의 팀 동료들이 무엇을 하고 있는지 아는 것이 / 편안함과 안전감을 제공한다 //
because people can adjust their own behavior / to be in harmony with the group.
부사절 접속사 S′ V′ O′ 목적(~하기 위해)
왜냐하면 사람들은 그들 자신의 행동을 조절할 수 있기 때문이다 / 집단과 조화를 이루도록

[5] It's risky / to go off on their own / to try *something new* [that will probably not be successful / right from the start].
가주어 V C 진주어(to-v구) 목적(~하기 위해) 주격 관계대명사
(~은) 위험하다 / 홀로 벗어나는 것은 / 무언가 새로운 것을 시도하기 위해 [아마도 성공적이지 않을 / 바로 처음부터]
↳ **협업의 방해 2:** 집단에 맞춰 자신의 행동을 조절하고 홀로 새로운 시도를 안 함.

[6] But / even though it feels reassuring / for individuals to be hyper-connected, //
부사절 접속사(양보) 가주어′ V′ C′ to-v의 의미상 주어 진주어′(to-v구)
하지만 / (~이) 안심된다고 느낄지라도 / 개개인이 과잉 연결되는 것이 //
🔑 주기적으로 혼자 일하는 것이 조직에 이로움.
it's better for the organization // if they periodically go off [and] think for themselves [and] generate diverse — if not quite mature — ideas.
S V C 부사절 접속사(조건) (they = individuals) V'_1 V'_2 V'_3 ~하지는 않더라도
*it은 막연한 상황을 의미하며, if절이 그 상황을 설명함.
조직에 더 좋다 // 그들(개개인)이 주기적으로 (조직을) 벗어나 스스로 생각하여 그다지 성숙하지는 않더라도 다양한 아이디어를 만들어 내는 것이
↳ **해결책:** 집단에서 벗어나 개개인이 스스로 생각해 아이디어를 만드는 것이 기업에 더 좋음.

🔑 리더의 일 = 전체에게 유익한 환경 조성 = 간헐적 상호 작용 시행.
[7] Thus, / it becomes the leader's job / to create *conditions* [that are good for the whole] / by enforcing intermittent interaction //
가주어 V C 진주어(to-v구) 주격 관계대명사 <by v-ing>: v함으로써
따라서 / (~이) 리더의 임무가 된다 / 환경을 만드는 것이 [전체에게 유익한] / 간헐적인 상호 작용을 시행함으로써 //
even when people wouldn't choose it for themselves, / without making it seem like a punishment.
부사절 접속사 S′ V′ O′(= intermittent interaction) = without의 O(동명사구)
사람들이 그것(간헐적인 상호 작용)을 스스로 선택하지 않는 때에도 / 그것을 처벌처럼 보이게 하지 않으면서
↳ **결론:** 리더는 간헐적 상호 작용(집단과의 교류를 쉴 수 있는) 환경을 만들어야 함.

해석

[1]협업의 전등 스위치를 탁 내리는 것은 리더들이 유일하게 할 위치에 있는 무언가인데, 왜냐하면 여러 장애물이 자발적으로 혼자 일하는 사람들을 방해하기 때문이다. [2]우선, 혼자만 모르게 남겨지는 두려움은 그들이 계속 자신들의 기업 소셜 미디어에 열중하게 할 수 있다. [3]개인들은 고립되거나 고립된 듯 보이는 것을 원하지 않는다. [4]또 다른 것으로는, 자신들의 팀 동료들이 무엇을 하고 있는지 아는 것이 편안함과 안전감을 제공하는데, 왜냐하면 사람들은 그들 자신의 행동을 집단과 조화를 이루도록 조절할 수 있기 때문이다. [5]아마도 바로 처음부터 성공적이지 않을 무언가 새로운 것을 시도하기 위해 홀로 벗어나는 것은 위험하다. [6]하지만 개개인이 과잉 연결되는 것이 안심된다고 느낄지라도, 그들이 주기적으로 (조직을) 벗어나 스스로 생각하여 그다지 성숙하지는 않더라도 다양한 아이디어를 만들어 내는 것이 조직에 더 좋다. [7]따라서, 사람들이 그것(간헐적인 상호작용)을 스스로 선택하지 않는 때에도, 처벌처럼 보이게 하지 않으면서 간헐적인 상호 작용을 시행함으로써, 전체에게 유익한 환경을 만드는 것이 리더의 임무가 된다.

어휘

flick (스위치를) 탁 내리다
collaboration 협업
position (특정한 위치에) 두다; 위치; 입장
obstacle 장애(물)
stand in the way of ~을 방해하다
voluntarily 자발적으로
out of the loop 혼자만 모르는, 소외된
glue ~에 열중[집중]하다; (접착제로) 붙이다
enterprise 기업
isolated 고립된
adjust 조절하다
go off 자리를 벗어나다
reassuring 안심시키는
hyper-connected 과잉 연결된
periodically 주기적으로
diverse 다양한
mature 성숙한, 무르익은
enforce 시행하다
punishment 처벌
[선택지] barrier 장벽, 장애물
norms 규범, 규준
prohibit 방해하다; 금지하다
devote A to B A를 B에 쏟다
productivity 생산성

정답 가이드

협업이 방해가 되는 요인으로 사람들이 소외되는 것을 원하지 않고 집단에 맞춰 개인의 행동을 조절하며 새로운 것을 시도하지 않는 것을 언급했다. 문장 6의 역접 연결어 But 이후에는 개인이 집단에서 벗어나 스스로 생각하며 다양한 아이디어를 만들어 내는 것이 조직에 유익하므로 리더는 집단과 연결을 잠시 끊는 것을 허용하는 간헐적 상호 작용을 해야 한다고 결론짓는다. 따라서 밑줄 친 부분이 의미하는 바로 가장 적절한 것은 ② 'having people stop working together and start working individually(사람들이 함께 일하는 것을 멈추고 개인적으로 일하기 시작하도록 하는 것)'이다.

The 핵심 ★ 밑줄 친 부분만으로는 협업을 시작하게 하는 것인지 그만두게 하는 것인지를 알 수 없다. 협업이 안도감을 주다는 내용에서 필자가 협업을 긍정적으로 여긴다고 착각할 수 있지만 주기적으로 집단에서 벗어나 생각하는 것이 조직에 좋다는 입장이므로 밑줄 친 부분이 내포하는 바는 협업을 그만두게 하는 것임을 추론할 수 있다.

오답 클리닉

① breaking physical barriers and group norms that prohibit cooperation
협력을 방해하는(×) 물리적 장벽과 집단 규범을 타파하는 것 (21%)
협력을 방해하는 요소를 없애려는 것이 아니라 오히려 협력이 혼자 일하는 사람을 방해한다고 했으므로 글의 내용과 반대됨.

③ encouraging people to devote more time to online collaboration
사람들이 온라인 협업(×)에 더 많은 시간을 쏟도록 격려하는 것 (7%)
온라인 협업에 관해서는 전혀 언급된 바가 없음.

④ shaping environments where higher productivity is required
더 높은 생산성이 요구되는 환경(×)을 조성하는 것 (11%)
간헐적 상호 작용을 하는 것은 직원의 생산성을 높일 수 있는 환경을 조성하는 것이지 더 높은 생산성, 즉 성과를 요구하는 환경을 조성하는 것이 아님.

⑤ requiring workers to focus their attention on group projects
직원들이 집단 프로젝트(×)에 관심을 집중하도록 요구하는 것 (28%)
집단에서 벗어나 혼자 일하도록 환경을 조성하라는 글의 내용과 반대됨.

02 + 빈칸 추론 〈23학년도 6월 모평 32번 | 정답률 46%〉

④

구문분석 & 직독직해

문학 작품의 내부 요소를 탐구하는 형식주의

주제문

[1] *The critic* [who wants to write about literature / from a formalist perspective] /
(S: The critic / 주격 관계대명사: who)
비평가는 [문학에 관해 쓰길 원하는 / 형식주의자의 관점에서] /

must first be *a close and careful reader* [who examines all the elements of a text individually / and questions // how they come together / to create a work of art].
(V: must first be / C: a close and careful reader / 주격 관계대명사: who / V'₁: examines / O'₁: all the elements of a text / V'₂: questions / O'₂(명사절): how they come together)
*결과(~해서 (결국) v하다)를 나타내는 to-v.

먼저 면밀하고도 주의 깊은 독자가 되어야 한다 [글의 모든 요소를 개별적으로 검토하는 / 그리고 질문하는 // 어떻게 그것들이 모여 / 예술 작품을 만드는지를]

↳ 형식주의 관점의 비평가는 면밀하고 주의 깊은 독자가 되어야 함.

[2] *Such a reader*, // who respects the autonomy of a work, / achieves an understanding of it / by **looking inside it, / not outside it or beyond it**.
(S: Such a reader / 관계대명사(보충 설명): who / V: achieves / O: an understanding of it / it = the work)
<by v-ing>: v함으로써

그러한 독자는 // 작품의 자율성을 존중하는 / 그것(작품)에 대한 이해를 달성한다 / 그것의 안을 들여다봄으로써 / 그것의 밖이나 그것을 넘어서가 아니라

↳ **세부 사항:** 작품의 자율성을 존중하는 형식주의 관점의 독자는 작품의 내부를 보고 이해함.

🔑 작품의 외적 요소가 아닌 내적 요소를 통해 작품을 이해하려 함.

[3] Instead of examining historical periods, author biographies, or literary styles, /
(전치사(~ 대신에): Instead of / Instead of의 O(동명사구))
역사적 시대, 작가의 전기, 또는 문체를 검토하는 대신에 /

for example, / he or she will approach a text / with the assumption // that it is a self-contained entity / and that he or she is looking for / *the governing principles* [that allow the text to reveal itself].
(S: he or she / V: will approach / that: 동격 접속사 / it = the text / 동격 접속사: that / S': he or she / V': is looking for / O': the governing principles / 주격 관계대명사: that)
*<allow+O+to-v>: O가 v하도록 하다

예를 들어 / 그 사람은 글에 접근할 것이다 / 가정을 가지고 // 그것(글)이 자족적인 실체라는 / 그리고 그는 찾고 있다는 / 지배적인 원칙을 [그 글이 스스로를 드러내도록 해주는]

↳ **부연 설명:** 형식주의 관점의 독자는 작품을 그 자체로 충족적이라 여기며 지배 원칙을 찾아 이해하려 함.

해석

[1]형식주의자의 관점에서 문학에 관해 쓰길 원하는 비평가는 먼저 글의 모든 요소를 개별적으로 검토하고 어떻게 그것들이 모여 예술 작품을 만드는지를 질문하는 면밀하고도 주의 깊은 독자가 되어야 한다. [2]작품의 자율성을 존중하는 그러한 독자는 그것의 밖이나 그것을 넘어서가 아니라 그것의 안을 들여다봄으로써 작품에 대한 이해를 달성한다. [3]예를 들어, 역사적 시대, 작가의 전기, 또는 문체를 검토하는 대신에, 그 사람은 글이 자족적인 실체이며, 그는 그 글이 스스로를 드러내도록 해주는 지배적인 원칙을 찾고 있다는 가정을 가지고 글에 접근할 것이다. [4]예를 들어, James Joyce의 단편 소설인 <Araby> 속의 등장인물들과 그가 개인적으로 알았던 사람들 사이의 관련성은 흥미로울 수도 있지만, 그 형식주의자에게 그것들(그 관련성)은 그 이야기가 그 안에 담고 있는 다른 종류의 정보보다 어떻게 그 이야기가 의미를 만들어내는지를 이해하는 데 덜 관련되어 있다.

어휘

critic 비평가, 평론가
literature 문학
cf. literary 문학의
formalist 형식주의(자)
perspective 관점, 시각
element 요소; 원소
come together 모이다
autonomy 자율성, 자주성; 자치권
biography 전기, 일대기
assumption 추정, 가정

[4]For example, / the correspondences (between the characters in James Joyce's short story "Araby" and the people [(who(m)[that]) he knew personally]) / may be interesting, //

S1 / 목적격 관계대명사 생략 / V1 / C1

예를 들어 / 관련성은 (James Joyce의 단편 소설인 <Araby> 속의 등장인물들 그리고 사람들 사이의 [그가 개인적으로 알았던]) / 흥미로울 수도 있다 //

(= the correspondences) 형식주의자에게는 작품 속 정보가 작품을 이해하는 데 중요함.

but for the formalist / they are less relevant / to understanding // how the story creates meaning // than are other kinds of information [that the story contains within itself]. *than 뒤에 앞에서 언급된 내용이 반복될 때 주어와 동사가 도치됨.

S2 V2 C2 / to의 O(동명사구) / understanding의 O(명사절) / V' S' / 목적격 관계대명사

그러나 그 형식주의자에게 / 그것들(그 관련성)은 덜 관련되어 있다 / 이해하는 데 // 어떻게 그 이야기가 의미를 만들어내는지를 // 다른 종류의 정보보다 [그 이야기가 그 안에 담고 있는]

↳ **예:** 형식주의자가 작품을 이해하는 데 작품의 외적 요소보다 그 안에 담긴 정보가 더 중요함.

self-contained 자족적인, 자기 충족의
governing 지배적인; 통치하는, 관리하는
principle 원칙, 원리; 신조
correspondence 관련성, 유사함; 일치, 조화
[선택지] middle ground 중간 지점; 타협안, 절충안

정답 가이드

빈칸 문장의 Such a reader가 형식주의 관점을 가진 독자임을 파악하고 이들이 작품을 이해하는 방식을 추론해야 한다. 그들은 작품을 자족적 실체로 여기며 '그 속의' 지배 원칙을 찾아 이해하려 한다고 했고, 마지막 문장의 예에서도 작품을 이해하는 데 작품의 외적 요소보다 '이야기 안에 담긴' 정보를 더 중시한다고 했다. 따라서 빈칸에 들어갈 말로 가장 적절한 것은 ④ 'looking inside it, not outside it or beyond it(그것의 밖이나 그것을 넘어서가 아니라 그것의 안을 들여다봄)'이다.

오답 클리닉

① putting himself or herself both inside and outside it (20%)
자신을 그것의 안과 밖 모두에 놓음
작품의 외적 요소보다 내적 정보가 작품 이해에 더 관련있다고 했으므로 틀림.

② finding a middle ground between it and the world (15%)
그것과 세상 사이에서 중간 지점을 찾음
세상은 외적 요소로 볼 수 있으며 세상과 타협안을 찾는 내용도 없음.

③ searching for historical realities revealed within it (13%)
그 안에서 드러난 역사적인 사실을 찾아봄
역사적 시대와 같은 외적 요소는 검토하지 않고 작품 자체만 본다고 했음.

⑤ exploring its characters' cultural relevance (6%)
그것의 등장인물들의 문화적인 관련성을 탐구함
문화적 관련성과 같은 외적 요소는 검토하지 않는다고 했음.

03 + 무관 문장 (22학년도 대수능 35번 | 정답률 75%) ④

구문분석 & 직독직해

경영 정보 시스템이 가져온 사업 수행 방식의 변화

주제문

[1]Since their introduction, / information systems have substantially changed / the way [(that) business is conducted].

전치사(~이후) / S / V / O / 관계부사 생략

정보 시스템이 변화시킨 사업 수행 방식에 관한 내용임.

도입 이후 / 정보 시스템은 상당히 변화시켜 왔다 / 방식을 [사업이 수행되는]

↳ 정보 시스템이 사업 수행 방식을 크게 변화시켜 옴.

(= 앞 문장) 기업 간 협력하는 형태의 사업에 해당됨.

① [2]This is particularly true / for business (in the shape and form of cooperation (between *firms* [that involves an integration of value chains / across multiple units])).

S V C / 주격 관계대명사

이는 특히 해당된다 / 사업에 (협력 형태와 유형의 (기업들 간의 [가치 체인의 통합을 수반하는 / 여러 부문들에 걸쳐]))

↳ **세부 사항:** 특히 기업 간 협력하는 사업에 변화를 가져옴.

→ 동사 강조 *<not only A but (also) B>: A뿐만 아니라 B도

② [3]The resulting networks / do not only cover the business units (of a single firm) / but typically also include multiple units (from different firms).

S / V1 / O1 / V2 / O2

그 결과로 생긴 네트워크는 / 사업 부문을 포함할 뿐만 아니라 (단일 기업의) / 일반적으로 여러 부문도 포함한다 (서로 다른 기업들의)

↳ 그 결과로 생긴 네트워크 연결망은 기업 안팎의 많은 부문들을 포함함.

해석

[1]도입 이후, 정보 시스템은 사업이 수행되는 방식을 상당히 변화시켜 왔다. ① [2]이는 여러 부문들에 걸쳐 가치 체인의 통합을 수반하는 기업들 간의 협력 형태와 유형의 사업에 특히 해당된다. ② [3]그 결과로 생긴 네트워크는 단일 기업의 사업 부문을 포함할 뿐만 아니라 일반적으로 서로 다른 기업들의 여러 부문도 포함한다. ③ [4]결과적으로, 기업들은 지속 가능한 사업 성과를 보장하기 위해 자신들의 내부 조직에 주의를 기울일 필요가 있을 뿐만 아니라, 자신들을 둘러싸고 있는 부문들의 전체 생태계를 고려할 필요도 있다. ④ [5]많은 주요 기업들은 수익성이 있는 부문에 집중하고 수익성이 덜한 부문은 잘라 냄으로써 자신들의 사업 모델을 근본적으로 변화시키고 있다. ⑤ [6]이 서로 다른 부문들이 성공적으로 협력하도록 하기 위해서는 공동 플랫폼의 존재가 매우 중요하다.

③ [4]As a consequence, / firms do [not only] need / to consider their internal organization / in order to ensure sustainable business performance[;] // *<not only A but (also) B>의 but을 대신하는 세미콜론(;)

↱ 동사 강조 / S / V_1 / 목적(~하기 위해)

결과적으로 / 기업들은 필요가 있을 뿐만 아니라 / 자신들의 내부 조직에 주의를 기울일 /
지속 가능한 사업 성과를 보장하기 위해 //

they [also] need to take into account / *the entire ecosystem of units* (surrounding them).

(= firms) V_2 현재분사구 (= firms)

그것들(기업)은 고려할 필요도 있다 / 부문들의 전체 생태계를 (자신들을 둘러싸고 있는)

↳ **주장:** 지속 가능한 사업 성과를 내기 위해서는 내부 조직뿐만 아니라 외부 전체의 생태계를 고려해야 함.

전체 부문들의 생태계 전반을 고려하는 협력 사업 방식과 무관한 내용.

④ [5]Many major companies are fundamentally changing / their business models / by focusing on profitable units / [and] cutting off less profitable ones.

S / V / O / by의 O(동명사구 병렬) / (= units)

많은 주요 기업들은 근본적으로 변화시키고 있다 / 자신들의 사업 모델을 /
수익성이 있는 부문에 집중함으로써 / 그리고 수익성이 덜한 부문은 잘라 냄으로써

↳ 많은 주요 기업이 수익성을 고려해 사업 모델을 변화시킴.

*<allow+O+to-v>: O가 v하도록 (허락)하다

⑤ [6]In order to allow these different units to cooperate successfully, / the existence (of a common platform) / is crucial.

목적(~하기 위해) / S / V / C

이 서로 다른 부문들이 성공적으로 협력하도록 하기 위해서는 / 존재가 (공동 플랫폼의) / 매우 중요하다

↳ **맺음말:** 서로 다른 부문들의 성공적 협력을 위해서는 공동 플랫폼이 필요함.

어휘

introduction 도입; 소개
substantially 상당히, 많이
conduct 수행하다; 행위, 행실
integration 통합
business unit 사업 부문
typically 일반적으로, 보통
internal 내부의
ensure 보장하다, 확실하게 하다
sustainable 지속 가능한
take into account ~을 고려하다
ecosystem 생태계
fundamentally 근본[본질]적으로
profitable 수익성이 있는, 이득이 되는
cut off ~을 잘라 내다; 차단하다
common 공동의, 공통의; 흔한

⊕ 가치 체인(value chain): 생산, 판매, 원료 관리, 연구개발, 인적 자원, 정보 시스템 등 제품이나 서비스를 생산하기 위한 일련의 가치 창조 활동. 이는 고객이 지불하고자 하는 가치를 창출하고 사슬처럼 연결되므로 가치 체인 또는 가치 사슬이라고 함.

정답 가이드

첫 문장으로 보아, 정보 시스템이 사업 수행 방식을 어떻게 변화시켜왔는지에 대한 내용이 구체적으로 전개될 것임을 예측할 수 있다. 정보 시스템이 도입되면서 기업 간 협력 형태가 기업 안팎의 여러 부문을 아우르게 되었고, 그 결과 내부 조직뿐만 아니라 기업 외부 부문들의 전체 생태계도 고려하도록 사업 수행 방식이 변화하게 되었다는 내용의 글이다. 하지만 ④는 수익성을 고려해 사업 모델을 변화시킨다는 내용이므로 글의 흐름과 무관하다.

오답 클리닉

① (1%) This는 앞 문장의 내용을 의미하며, 정보 시스템이 특히 기업 간 협력 형태의 사업 방식을 변화시켰다고 구체적인 설명을 시작하는 문장이다.
② (4%) 정보 시스템 도입으로 기업 간 협력 형태의 사업이 변화했고 그 결과로 생긴 네트워크가 기업 안팎의 여러 부문을 포함한다는 연결은 자연스럽다.
③ (16%) 앞 문장의 결과로 지속 가능한 사업 성과를 내기 위해서는 그 네트워크에 있는 기업 내외의 모든 협력 부문들을 고려할 필요가 있다고 주장하는 내용이다.
⑤ (3%) 서로 다른 부문들이 성공적으로 협력하려면 공동 플랫폼이 중요하다고 덧붙이며 끝맺고 있다.

01 + 글의 요지 〈23학년도 대수능 22번 | 정답률 78%〉 ①

구문분석 & 직독직해

사회 도시의 효율적인 운송 수단인 자전거

[1] Urban delivery vehicles (S) can be adapted (V) / to better suit the density (of urban distribution) (목적(~하기 위해)), // which (관계대명사(보충 설명)) often involves (V′) smaller vehicles (such as vans) (O′), / including bicycles.
*which는 앞 절 전체를 보충 설명하는 관계대명사절을 이끎.

도시의 배달 운송 수단은 조정될 수 있다 / 밀도에 더 잘 맞도록 (도시 유통의) //
이것은 흔히 더 작은 운송 수단을 포함한다 (밴(소형 트럭)과 같은) / 자전거도 포함해

↳ **도입:** 도시에는 소형 운송 수단이 적합함.

주제문 자전거는 혼잡 지역에서 선호되는 운송 수단임.

[2] The latter (= Bicycles) have the potential (to become a preferred 'last-mile' vehicle), / particularly in high-density and congested areas.

후자(자전거)는 잠재력이 있다 (선호되는 '최종 단계' 운송 수단이 될) / 특히 밀도가 높고 혼잡한 지역에서

↳ 혼잡 지역에서는 자전거가 선호됨.

[3] In *locations* [where (관계부사) bicycle use is high], / (such as the Netherlands), / delivery bicycles (S) are also used (V) / to carry personal cargo (e.g. groceries) (목적(~하기 위해)).

지역에서 [자전거 사용이 많은] / (네덜란드와 같이) /
배달 자전거는 또한 사용된다 / 개인 짐(예를 들면 식료품)을 운반하기 위해

↳ **예 1:** 도시에서 자전거는 개인 짐 운반에도 사용됨.

집 자전거는 구매와 유지 비용이 낮아 잠재력이 많음.

[4] Due to (전치사(~ 덕분에)) their low acquisition and maintenance costs, / cargo bicycles (S) convey (V) much potential (O) / in developed and developing countries alike, / such as the *becak* (a three-wheeled bicycle) in Indonesia.

낮은 매입 및 유지 비용 덕분에 / 짐 자전거는 많은 잠재력을 나타낸다 /
선진국과 개발도상국에서 똑같이 / 인도네시아의 '베짝(바퀴가 세 개 달린 자전거)'과 같이

↳ **예 2:** 자전거는 매입과 유지 비용이 낮아 개발도상국에서도 유용함.

[5] *Services* (S) (using electrically assisted delivery tricycles) (현재분사구) / have been successfully implemented (V_1) in France / and are gradually being adopted (V_2) across Europe / for services as varied as parcel and catering deliveries.
*<A as 형용사/부사 as B>: A는 B만큼 ~한/하게

서비스는 (전기 보조 배달용 세발자전거를 이용하는) / 프랑스에서 성공적으로 시행되었다 /
그리고 유럽 전역에 점차 도입되고 있다 / 소포나 음식 배달과 같이 다양한 서비스를 위해

↳ **예 3:** 전기 자전거도 활용됨.

[6] Using bicycles (as cargo vehicles) (S(동명사구 주어)) / is particularly encouraged (V(단수)) /

자전거를 사용하는 것은 (짐 운송 수단으로) / 특히 장려된다 /

when combined (접속사를 생략하지 않은 분사구문 (= when it is combined ~)) / with *policies* [that (주격 관계대명사) restrict motor vehicle access / to specific areas of a city, (such as downtown or commercial districts)], / or with the extension of dedicated bike lanes.
*combined에 뒤에는 with로 시작하는 전치사구 두 개가 or로 연결됨.

결합될 때 / 정책과 [자동차 접근을 제한하는 / 도시의 특정 지역에
(도심이나 상업 지구와 같은)] / 또는 자전거 전용 도로의 확장과

↳ **예 4:** 여러 정책적 배려와 맞물려 자전거의 매력도 증가함.

해석

[1] 도시의 배달 운송 수단은 도시 유통의 밀도에 더 잘 맞도록 조정될 수 있는데, 이것은 흔히 밴(소형 트럭)과 같은 더 작은 운송 수단을 포함하며, 자전거도 포함한다. [2] 후자(자전거)는 특히 밀도가 높고 혼잡한 지역에서 선호되는 '최종 단계' 운송 수단이 될 잠재력이 있다.(▶ 혼잡 지역은 이동이 용이한 자전거로 배송이 마무리됨을 의미) [3] 네덜란드와 같이 자전거 사용이 많은 지역에서 배달 자전거는 또한 개인 짐(예를 들면 식료품)을 운반하기 위해 사용된다. [4] 낮은 매입 및 유지 비용 덕분에 인도네시아의 '베짝(바퀴가 세 개 달린 자전거)'과 같이 짐 자전거는 선진국과 개발도상국에서 똑같이 많은 잠재력을 나타낸다. [5] 전기 보조 배달용 세발자전거를 이용하는 서비스는 프랑스에서 성공적으로 시행되었고 소포나 음식 배달과 같이 다양한 서비스를 위해 유럽 전역에 점차 도입되고 있다. [6] 자전거를 짐 운송 수단으로 사용하는 것은 도심이나 상업 지구와 같은 도시의 특정 지역에 자동차 접근을 제한하는 정책이나 자전거 전용 도로의 확장과 결합될 때 특히 장려된다.

어휘

urban 도시의
vehicle 운송 수단
density 밀도, 밀집 상태
distribution 유통; 분배, 배급
congested 혼잡한, 붐비는
cargo 짐, 화물
acquisition 매입; 습득
maintenance 유지; 지속; 정비
convey 나타내다; 전달하다; 운반하다
implement 시행하다
adopt 도입하다, 채택하다; 입양하다
combine 결합하다
restrict 제한하다
commercial district 상업 지구
extension 확장, 확대; 연장
dedicated 전용의; 전념하는, 헌신적인

⊕ 라스트 마일(last mile): 제조사에서 소비자까지 물품이 배송되는 단계는 흔히 first mile, middle mile, last mile로 구분됨. last mile, 또는 final mile은 그 지역 보관 창고까지 운송된 물품이 소비자에게 배송되는 최종 배송 단계를 말함.

정답 가이드

주제문에서 자전거가 혼잡한 도시 환경에서 선호되는 배송 수단이 될 잠재력이 있다고 한 후, 이어지는 예들로 이 잠재력을 구체적으로 설명하고 있다. 따라서 글의 요지로 가장 적절한 것은 ① '도시에서 자전거는 효율적인 배송 수단으로 사용될 수 있다.'이다.

The 핵심 ★ 문장 2의 The latter가 가리키는 것은 바로 앞 문장에서 언급된 vans와 bicycles 중 후자인 자전거임을 파악할 수 있어야 한다.

오답 클리닉

② 자전거는 출퇴근 시간을 줄이기 위한 대안(×)으로 선호되고 있다. (1%)
자전거는 배송 수단으로 선호되는 것이지, 출퇴근 용도로 쓰인다는 내용은 없음.

③ 자전거는 배송 수단으로의 경제적 장단점(×)을 모두 가질 수 있다. (4%)
경제적 장점(낮은 매입 및 유지 비용)은 언급되었으나 단점은 언급되지 않음.

④ 수요자의 요구(×)에 부합하는 다양한 용도의 자전거가 개발(×)되고 있다. (9%)
배송 수단으로서의 자전거 외의 다른 용도의 자전거들은 언급되지 않음.

The 주의 네덜란드의 자전거, 인도네시아의 '베짝', 프랑스의 전기 보조 배달용 세발자전거는 모두 배송을 위해 자전거를 사용하는 예로 언급된 것이다.

⑤ 세계 각국에서는 전기 자전거 사용을 장려하는 정책(×)을 추진하고 있다. (8%)
electrically assisted delivery tricycles와 policies를 활용한 오답. 전기 자전거는 유럽 국가에서 배송 수단으로 활용된다는 예로 언급된 것으로, 전체 내용을 포괄하지 못함.

02 + 빈칸 추론 (22학년도 9월 모평 32번 | 정답률 63%) ②

구문분석 & 직독직해

인지 TV 시청을 통한 불편한 감정의 완화

주제문 ★<A as 형용사/부사 as B>: A는 B만큼 ~한/하게

[1]Even as mundane a behavior / as watching TV (S) / may be (V) *a way* (C) / (for some people [to-v의 의미상 주어] to **escape painful self-awareness / through distraction**).

평범한 행동조차도 / TV를 보는 것만큼 / 방법일 수 있다 (어떤 사람들이 고통스러운 자기 인식에서 벗어나는 / 주의 전환을 통해)

↳ TV 시청과 같은 평범한 행동도 주의 전환을 통해 고통스러운 자각에서 벗어나는 방법일 수 있음.

[2]To test this idea, (목적(~하기 위해)) / Sophia Moskalenko and Steven Heine (S) gave (V_1) participants (IO) false feedback (about their test performance) (DO), /

이 생각을 시험하기 위해 / Sophia Moskalenko와 Steven Heine은 참가자들에게 거짓 피드백을 주었다 (그들의 시험 성적에 관한) /

and then seated (V_2) each one (O) (= participant) in front of a TV set / to watch a video (목적(~하도록)) / as the next part of the study.

그런 다음에 각 참가자를 TV 앞에 앉혔다 / 영상를 시청하도록 / 연구의 다음 부분으로서

[3]When the video came on, (부사절 접속사(시간)) / showing nature scenes (분사구문(= and it showed ~)) / with a musical soundtrack, //
the experimenter (S) exclaimed (V_1) // that this was the wrong video (O(명사절)) / and went (V_2) supposedly to get the correct one (목적(~하기 위해)) (= video), / leaving the participant alone (분사구문(= and the experimenter left ~)) // as the video played (부사절 접속사(~하는 동안)). ★<leave+O+C>: O를 C한 상태로 남겨두다

영상이 나오자 / 자연 풍경을 보여 주는 / 음악 사운드트랙과 함께 //
실험자는 소리쳤다 // 이것은 잘못된 영상이라고 / 그리고 아마도 맞는 것(영상)을 가지러 가기 위해 나갔다 / 참가자를 홀로 남겨두고 // (잘못된) 영상이 재생되는 동안

↳ **실험 내용:** 참가자에게 시험 성적에 관해 거짓 피드백을 준 다음, 잘못 재생된 영상을 얼마나 오래 시청하는지 실험함.

⊶ 부정적인 피드백을 받은 참가자들이 더 오래 영상을 시청함.

[4]*The participants* (S) [who (주격 관계대명사) had received failure feedback] / watched (V) the video (O) much (비교급 강조 부사) longer / than *those* (= participants) [who (주격 관계대명사) thought (that) (명사절 접속사 생략) they had succeeded].

참가자들은 [(시험에) 실패했다는 피드백을 받았던] / 영상을 훨씬 더 오래 시청했다 / 참가자들보다 [자신이 성공했다고 생각하는]

↳ **실험 결과:** 부정적인 피드백을 받은 참가자들이 영상을 더 오래 시청함.

해석

[1]TV를 보는 것만큼 평범한 행동조차도 어떤 사람들이 주의 전환을 통해 고통스러운 자기 인식에서 벗어나는 방법일 수 있다. [2]이 생각을 시험하기 위해, Sophia Moskalenko와 Steven Heine은 참가자들에게 그들의 시험 성적에 관한 거짓 피드백을 준 다음에 연구의 다음 부분으로서 영상을 시청토록 각 참가자를 TV 앞에 앉혔다. [3]음악 사운드트랙과 함께 자연 풍경을 보여 주는 영상이 나오자, 실험자는 이것은 잘못된 영상이라고 소리쳤고, (잘못된) 영상이 재생되는 동안 참가자를 홀로 남겨두고 아마도 맞는 것을 가지러 가기 위해 나갔다. [4](시험에) 실패했다는 피드백을 받았던 참가자들은 자신이 성공했다고 생각하는 참가자들보다 영상을 훨씬 더 오래 시청했다. [5]연구자들은 텔레비전 시청을 통한 주의 전환이 고통스러운 실패나 자신과 자기 규준 사이의 부조화와 관련된 불편함을 효과적으로 완화할 수 있다고 결론지었다. [6]대조적으로, 성공한 참가자들은 자기 자신과 관련된 생각에서 주의가 딴 데로 돌려지기를 거의 바라지 않았다!

어휘

self-awareness 자기 인식, 자각
distraction 주의 전환, 주의가 흩어짐
cf. distract (주의를) 딴 데로 돌리다
performance 성적, 성과; 공연
exclaim 소리치다
supposedly 아마도, 추정상
relieve 완화하다; 안심시키다
discomfort 불편(함)
associated with ~와 관련된
mismatch 부조화

conclude의 O(명사절) 텔레비전 시청을 통한 주의 전환이 실패로 인한 고통을 완화시켜줌.

[5] The researchers concluded // that distraction (through television viewing) / can effectively relieve *the discomfort* (associated with painful failures or mismatches (between the self and self-guides)).

S V 명사절 접속사 S' V' O' 과거분사구

연구자들은 결론지었다 // 주의 전환이 (텔레비전 시청을 통한) / 불편함을 효과적으로 완화할 수 있다고 (고통스러운 실패나 부조화와 관련된 (자신과 자기 규준 사이의))

↳ **결론:** TV 시청을 통한 주의 전환이 불편한 감정을 완화시킴.

*little: (준부정어) 거의 없는

[6] In contrast, / successful participants had *little wish* (to be distracted / from their self-related thoughts)!

S V O =

대조적으로 / 성공한 참가자들은 거의 바라지 않았다 (주의가 딴 데로 돌려지기를 / 자기 자신과 관련된 생각에서)

↳ **부연 설명:** 긍정적인 피드백을 받은 참가자들은 TV 시청으로 주의가 환기되기를 바라지 않음.

[선택지] comment 지적, 비판; 논평
peer 동료
constructive 건설적인; 구조적인
refocus 다시 집중하다
divided 분열된; 분할된
attention 주의(력); 관심
task 과업, 일
engage in ~에 참여[관여]하다
intense 격렬한, 심한; 강렬한
self-reflection 자기 반성

정답 가이드

빈칸 문장의 핵심은 사람들에게 TV 시청이 '어떠한' 방법일 수 있다는 것이다. 이에 대한 실험 내용에서 나쁜 시험 성적 결과를 받은 사람들이 좋은 성적을 받은 사람들보다 TV 영상을 훨씬 더 오래 시청했다. 결론은 TV 시청이 자신과 관련된 불편한 생각에서 벗어나 주의를 다른 곳으로 옮긴다는 것이므로, 빈칸에 들어갈 말로 가장 적절한 것은 ② 'escape painful self-awareness through distraction(주의 전환을 통해 고통스러운 자기 인식에서 벗어나다)'이다.

오답 클리닉

① ignore uncomfortable comments from their close peers (10%)
가까운 동료의 불편한 지적을 무시한다
동료가 지적한다거나 그 지적을 무시한다는 내용은 없음.

③ receive constructive feedback from the media (10%)
미디어로부터 건설적인 피드백을 받는다
미디어로부터 피드백을 받는다는 내용은 없음.

④ refocus their divided attention to a given task (7%)
분열된 주의력을 주어진 과업에 다시 집중한다
문장 5에서 텔레비전 시청은 주의를 딴 데로 돌린다고 했으므로, 다시 집중하는 것과 반대됨.

⑤ engage themselves in intense self-reflection (10%)
격렬한 자기 반성에 참여한다
TV 시청을 통해 자기 반성을 한다는 내용은 없음.

03 + 글의 순서 〈23학년도 9월 모평 36번 | 정답률 69%〉 ⑤

구문분석 & 직독직해 공학 운하 건설 시 수위 차이를 해결하는 로크

[1] When two natural bodies of water stand at different levels, //

부사절 접속사(시간) S' V'

두 개의 자연 수역(水域)이 서로 다른 높이에 있을 때 //

(= two natural bodies of water)

building a canal (between them) / presents a complicated engineering problem.

S(동명사구) V(단수) O

운하를 건설하는 것은 (그것들(두 개의 자연 수역) 사이에) / 복잡한 공학 문제를 야기한다

↳ **문제점:** 서로 다른 높이의 수역 사이에 운하를 세우는 데 복잡한 공학 문제가 있음.

주제문 주어진 글의 문제를 해결하는 방법을 제시함.

(C) [2] To make up for the difference in level, / engineers build one or more *water* "*steps*," / (called locks), / [that carry ships or boats / up or down / between the two levels].

목적(~하기 위해) S V O 과거분사구 삽입 주격 관계대명사

높이의 차이를 벌충하기 위해 / 공학자들은 하나 이상의 물 '계단'을 만든다 / (로크라고 불리는) / [배나 보트를 운반하는 / 위 또는 아래로 / 두 높이 사이에서]

↳ **해결책:** 로크라는 물 계단을 만들어 수역의 높이 차이를 벌충함.

[3] A lock is an artificial water basin.

S V C

로크는 인공적인 물웅덩이이다

(= A lock)

[4] It has / a long rectangular shape (with concrete walls and a pair of gates at each end).

S V O with의 O(명사구 병렬)

그것(로크)은 되어 있다 / 긴 직사각형 모양으로 (콘크리트 벽과 양 끝에 한 쌍의 문이 있는)

↳ **부연 설명:** 로크는 콘크리트 벽과 양 끝에 문이 있는 긴 직사각형 모양의 인공 물웅덩이임.

해석

[1] 두 개의 자연 수역(水域)이 서로 다른 높이에 있을 때, 그것들(두 개의 자연 수역) 사이에 운하를 건설하는 것은 복잡한 공학 문제를 야기한다. (C) [2] 높이의 차이를 벌충하기 위해 공학자들은 두 높이 사이에서 배나 보트를 위 또는 아래로 운반하는, 로크라고 불리는 하나 이상의 물 '계단'을 만든다. [3] 로크는 인공적인 물웅덩이이다. [4] 그것(로크)은 콘크리트 벽과 양 끝에 한 쌍의 문이 있는 긴 직사각형 모양으로 되어 있다. (B) [5] 선박이 상류로 가는 경우, 배가 더 낮은 수위에 있는 로크에 들어오는 동안 위쪽 문은 닫혀 있다. [6] 그러고 나서 하류의 문이 닫히고 더 많은 물이 웅덩이 안으로 쏟아 부어진다. [7] 상승하는 물이 선박을 위쪽 수역의 높이까지 끌어올린다. (A) [8] 그다음에 위쪽 문이 열리고 배가 빠져나간다. [9] 하류 통행의 경우, 그 과정은 정반대로 작동한다. [10] 배가 위쪽 높이에서의 로크로 들어오고, 배가 더 낮은 높이와 비슷해질 때까지 물이 로크로부터 퍼내진다.

🔑 선박이 상류로 올라갈 때 로크의 작동 방식을 설명함.

(B) [5]When a vessel is going upstream, // the upper gates stay closed // as the ship enters the lock (at the lower water level).

부사절 접속사(조건) / S / V / C / 부사절 접속사(~ 동안에)

선박이 상류로 가는 경우 // 위쪽 문은 닫혀 있다 // 배가 로크에 들어오는 동안 (더 낮은 수위에 있는)

[6]The downstream gates are then closed // and more water is pumped into the basin.

S_1 / V_1 / S_2 / V_2

그러고 나서 하류의 문이 닫힌다 // 그리고 더 많은 물이 웅덩이 안으로 쏟아 부어진다

[7]The rising water lifts the vessel / to the level (of the upper body of water).

S / V / O

상승하는 물이 선박을 끌어올린다 / 높이까지 (위쪽 수역의)

🔑 선박이 상류 수위까지 올라온 (B) 다음의 과정을 설명함.

(A) [8]Then / the upper gates open // and the ship passes through.

S_1 / V_1 / S_2 / V_2

그다음에 / 위쪽 문이 열린다 // 그리고 배가 빠져나간다

↳ **예 1(선박이 상류로 올라가는 경우):** 선박이 하류에서 로크로 들어오면 물을 채워 상류 수역 높이까지 끌어올린 다음 내보냄.

🔑 선박이 하류로 가는 반대 경우를 설명함.

[9]For downstream passage, / the process works the opposite way.

S / V

하류 통행의 경우 / 그 과정은 정반대로 작동한다

[10]The ship enters the lock (from the upper level), // and water is pumped / from the lock // until the ship is in line / with the lower level.

S_1 / V_1 / O_1 / S_2 / V_2 / 부사절 접속사(시간)

배가 로크로 들어온다 (위쪽 높이에서의) // 그리고 물이 퍼내진다 / 로크로부터 //
배가 비슷해질 때까지 / 더 낮은 높이와

↳ **예 2(선박이 하류로 내려가는 경우):** 선박이 상류에서 로크로 들어오면 물을 퍼내서 하류의 수위와 맞춤.

어휘

canal 운하, 수로
present 야기하다; 제시하다; 출석[참석]하다; 현재의
complicated 복잡한
engineering 공학 (기술)
cf. engineer 공학자
make up for ~을 벌충[만회]하다
artificial 인공적인
basin (물)웅덩이; 대야; 분지
vessel (대형) 선박; 그릇
upstream 상류로; 상류의
(↔ downstream 하류의; 하류로)
upper 위쪽의
pump A into[from] B A를 B로[에서] 쏟아 붓다[퍼내다]
passage 통행, 통과; 통로
opposite 정반대의; 반대(되는 것)
in line with ~와 비슷한

정답 가이드

두 개의 수역이 서로 다른 높이에 있을 때 운하를 건설하는 것은 복잡한 공학 문제를 야기한다는 주어진 글 뒤에는 '로크'라는 물 계단을 만들어 수역의 높이 차이를 벌충한다는 해결책을 제시하는 (C)가 이어져야 한다. (C)에서 로크는 콘크리트 벽과 양 끝에 문(gate)이 있다고 했으므로, 선박이 상류로 올라가는 경우 로크의 문이 작동하는 방식을 설명하는 (B)가 오고, 그와 반대로 선박이 하류로 내려가는 경우를 설명하는 (A)가 마지막에 오는 것이 자연스럽다.

오답 클리닉

① (A) - (C) - (B) (1%) / ④ (C) - (A) - (B) (15%)
(A)의 Then은 로크에 물을 채워 선박이 상류 높이까지 올라온 다음의 과정을 보여주는 연결어이므로 (A)는 (B) 뒤에 와야 한다. 또한 (A)의 the opposite way를 통해서 (A)와 반대되는 경우가 먼저 제시되어야 함을 알 수 있다.
② (B) - (A) - (C) (9%) / ③ (B) - (C) - (A) (5%)
주어진 글의 문제점에 대한 해결책으로 로크를 제시하고 설명한 다음에 배가 상류와 하류로 가는 경우를 예로 들어 구체적인 작동 방식을 설명하는 흐름이 가장 적절하다.

01 + 필자 주장 〈23학년도 대수능 20번 | 정답률 80%〉 ③

구문분석 & 직독직해

생활 직관보다 확률 분석을 통한 선택이 더 나음

[1] At every step in our journey through life / we encounter junctions (with *many different pathways* (leading into the distance)).
현재분사구
평생 우리 여정의 모든 단계에서 / 우리는 분기점을 만난다 (많은 다른 길들이 있는 (먼 곳으로 이어지는))
↳ **도입:** 살면서 선택할 일이 많음.

[2] Each choice involves uncertainty (about which path will get you to your destination).
S V O S′ V′ O′
각각의 선택은 불확실성을 포함한다 (어떤 길이 여러분을 목적지로 데려다줄지에 대한)
↳ 어떤 선택이 원하는 결과를 가져올지는 알 수 없음.

[3] Trusting our intuition / to make the choice / often ends up / with us making a suboptimal choice.
S(동명사구) 목적(~하기 위해) V(단수) 동명사 making의 의미상 주어
우리의 직관을 믿는 것은 / 선택을 하기 위해 / 흔히 결국 끝난다 / 우리가 차선의 선택을 하는 것으로
↳ **문제점:** 직관적인 선택은 최선의 선택이 아님.

주제문
🔑 수치화하는 것에 대한 긍정적 입장이 드러남.
[4] Turning the uncertainty into numbers / has proved a potent way (of analyzing the paths and finding the shortcut to your destination).
S V O of의 O(동명사구 병렬)
불확실성을 숫자로 바꾸는 것은 / 강력한 방법으로 입증되었다 (길을 분석하고 여러분의 목적지로 가는 지름길을 찾는)
↳ **해결책:** 선택지를 분석해 수치화하는 것이 좋은 방법임.

[5] The mathematical theory of probability hasn't eliminated risk, // but it allows us to manage that risk more effectively. 🔑 확률 분석이 위험 관리에 이로움.
S_1 V_1 O_1 S_2 V_2 O_2 C
확률에 대한 수학적 이론은 위험을 제거하지는 않았다 // 하지만 그것은 우리가 그 위험을 더 효과적으로 관리할 수 있게 해준다
↳ **논거(장점):** 확률적으로 선택하는 게 위험 관리에 효과적임.

[6] The strategy is / to analyze *all the possible scenarios* [that the future holds] / and then to see // what proportion of them lead to success or failure.
S V C_1(to-v구 병렬) 목적격 관계대명사 S′ V′ C_2(to-v구 병렬)
to see의 O(명사절)
그 전략은 ~이다 / 모든 가능한 시나리오를 분석하는 것 [미래가 안고 있는] / 그러고 나서 살펴보는 것 // 그것들의 비율이 얼마만큼 성공이나 실패로 이어지는지를
↳ **부연 설명:** 즉 모든 경우의 수를 분석해 성공/실패율을 확인하는 것임.

★<base A on B>: A의 근거를 B에 두다
[7] This gives you / *a much better map of the future* [on which to base your decisions (about which path to choose)]. 🔑 확률적 분석이 더 나은 판단을 도움.
S V IO DO (← ~ a much better map of the future to base your decisions on)
이것은 여러분에게 제공한다 / 미래에 대한 훨씬 더 좋은 지도를 [여러분의 결정의 근거로 삼을 (어떤 길을 선택할 것인지에 관한)]
↳ **결론:** 확률적 분석이 최선의 선택을 이끎.

해석

[1] 평생 우리 여정의 모든 단계에서 우리는 먼 곳으로 이어지는 많은 다른 길들이 있는 분기점을 만난다. [2] 각각의 선택은 어떤 길이 여러분을 목적지로 데려다줄지에 대한 불확실성을 포함한다. [3] 선택을 하기 위해 우리의 직관을 믿는 것은 흔히 결국 우리가 차선의 선택을 하는 것으로 끝난다. [4] 불확실성을 숫자로 바꾸는 것은 길을 분석하고 여러분의 목적지로 가는 지름길을 찾는 강력한 방법으로 입증되었다. [5] 확률에 대한 수학적 이론은 위험을 제거하지는 않았지만, 그것은 우리가 그 위험을 더 효과적으로 관리할 수 있게 해준다.(▶ 문장 4의 '불확실성을 숫자로 바꾸는 것(Turning the uncertainty into numbers)'이 문장 5에서 '확률에 대한 수학적 이론(The mathematical theory of probability)'으로 말바꿈 됨.) [6] 그 전략은 미래가 안고 있는 모든 가능한 시나리오를 분석하고 나서 그것들의 비율이 얼마만큼 성공이나 실패로 이어지는지를 살펴보는 것이다. [7] 이것은 어떤 길을 선택할 것인지에 관한 여러분의 결정의 근거로 삼을 미래에 대한 훨씬 더 좋은 지도를 여러분에게 제공한다.

어휘

journey 여정, 여행; 여행하다
encounter 만나다, 마주치다; 접촉, 만남
uncertainty 불확실(성)
destination 목적지, 도착지
intuition 직관(력)
end up with 결국 ~하게 되다
potent 강한[강력한]
shortcut 지름길
probability 확률, 있음직함[가망]; 개연성(있는 것)
eliminate 제거하다, 없애다; 탈락시키다
proportion 비율, 부분; 균형

정답 가이드

인생의 많은 선택의 기로에서 우리가 하는 선택은 불확실성을 포함하는데, 이때 직관적으로 선택하는 것보다 불확실성을 수치로 바꿔 분석하는 방법이 위험 관리에 효과적이며 이는 더 나은 선택의 근거를 제공해준다는 내용의 글이므로 필자가 주장하는 바로 가장 적절한 것은 ③ '더 나은 선택을 위해 성공 가능성을 확률적으로 분석해야 한다.'이다.

The 핵심 ★ 주장을 나타내는 표현인 must, should 등의 조동사를 써서 직접적으로 주장을 드러내고 있지는 않지만, a potent way, more effectively, much better와 같은 표현에서 필자가 확률을 분석해 선택하는 것을 긍정적으로 여기고 있음을 유추할 수 있다.

오답 클리닉

① 성공적인 삶을 위해 미래에 대한 구체적인 계획(×)을 세워야 한다. (4%)
선택의 기로에서 성공적인 삶을 위해 어떻게 결정을 내려야 하는지 설명하는 글이며, 구체적인 계획을 세우라는 내용은 언급되지 않음.

② 중요한 결정을 내릴 때에는 자신의 직관(×)에 따라 판단해야 한다. (11%)
오히려 직관을 따르면 차선의 선택으로 끝난다고 했으므로 글의 내용과 반대됨.

④ 빠른 목표 달성(×)을 위해 지름길로 가고자 할 때 신중해야(×) 한다. (3%)
지문에 언급된 shortcut을 활용한 오답. 빠른 목표 달성에 대한 내용이 아니며 신중하라는 언급도 없음.

⑤ 인생의 여정에서 선택에 따른 결과를 스스로 책임져야(×) 한다. (3%)
인생의 여정에서 많은 선택을 하게 된다고 했지만, 그에 따른 결과를 스스로 책임져야 한다는 내용은 아님.

02 + 빈칸 추론 (22학년도 9월 모평 33번 | 정답률 41%)

①

구문분석 & 직독직해

철학 새로운 사상 발전의 기반

[1]It is important to recognise / the interdependence (between individual, culturally formed actions and the state of cultural integration).
(가주어 / 진주어(to-v구) / ★<between A and B>: A와 B 사이의)
인식하는 것은 중요하다 / 상호 의존성을 (개별적이고 문화적으로 형성된 행동과 문화적 통합의 상태 사이의)
↳ 개인의 행동과 문화적 통합 사이의 상호 의존성을 인식해야 함.

[2]People work / within *the forms* (provided by *the cultural patterns* [that they have internalised]), // however contradictory these may be.
(S / V / 과거분사구 / 목적격 관계대명사 / (= no matter how) C′ / these(= the forms) S′ / V′)
사람들은 일한다 / 형태 내에서 (문화적 패턴에 의해 제공되는 [자신들이 내면화한]) // 아무리 이것(형태)이 모순될지라도
↳ 사람들은 내면화된 문화적 패턴의 형태 안에서 행동함.

🔑 사상은 다른 수용된 사상으로부터 나오며, 이러한 방식으로 문화적 혁신과 발견이 이루어짐.

[3]Ideas are worked out / as logical implications or consequences (of other accepted ideas), // and it is in this way // that cultural innovations and discoveries are possible.
(S / V / 전치사(~로(서)) / <it is ~ that ...> 강조구문)
사상은 산출된다 / 논리적 영향이나 결과로 (다른 수용된 사상의) // 그리고 바로 이러한 방식으로이다 // 문화적 혁신과 발견이 가능한 것은
↳ 어떤 사상은 다른 수용된 사상으로부터 나와 문화적 혁신을 가능케 함.

[4]New ideas are discovered / through logical reasoning, //
(S_1 / V_1)
새로운 사상은 발견된다 / 논리적 추론을 통해 //

🔑 기존 개념 체계를 수용해야 새로운 사상을 발견할 수 있음.

but such discoveries are inherent in and integral to / the conceptual system / and are made possible / only because of the acceptance (of its premises).
(S_2 / V_2 / in과 to의 공통 O / V_2 / 전치사(~ 때문에))
그러나 그러한 발견은 ~에 내재되고 내장되어 있다 / 개념 체계(에) / 그리고 가능해진다 / 오직 수용 때문에 (그 전제의)
↳ 기존 개념 체계의 전제를 수용해야만 새로운 사상을 발견할 수 있음.

[5]For example, / the discoveries (of new prime numbers) / are 'real' consequences (of *the particular number system* (employed)).
(S / V / C / 과거분사)
예를 들어 / 발견은 (새로운 소수의) / '실제' 결과이다 (특정 숫자 체계의 (사용되는))
↳ **예:** 새로운 소수는 이미 사용되는 특정 숫자 체계로부터 나온 결과물임.

주제문

[6]Thus, / cultural ideas show 'advances' and 'developments' // because they **are outgrowths (of previous ideas)**.
(S / V / O / 부사절 접속사(이유) / they(= cultural ideas) S′ / V′ / C′)
따라서 / 문화적 사상은 '진보'와 '발전'을 보여 준다 // 그것(문화적 사상)이 결과물이기 때문에 (이전 사상의)
↳ **결론:** 문화적 사상은 이전 사상이 발전한 결과물임.

해석

[1]개별적이고 문화적으로 형성된 행동과 문화적 통합의 상태 사이의 상호 의존성을 인식하는 것은 중요하다. [2]사람들은 아무리 이것(형태)이 모순될지라도 자신들이 내면화한 문화적 패턴에 의해 제공되는 형태 내에서 일한다. [3]사상은 다른 수용된 사상의 논리적 영향이나 결과로 산출되고, 문화적 혁신과 발견이 가능한 것은 바로 이러한 방식으로이다. [4]새로운 사상은 논리적 추론을 통해 발견되지만, 그러한 발견은 개념 체계에 내재되고 내장되어 있으며, 오직 그 전제의 수용 때문에 가능해진다. [5]예를 들어, 새로운 소수의 발견은 사용되는 특정 숫자 체계의 '실제' 결과이다. [6]따라서, 문화적 사상은 그것이 이전 사상의 결과물이기 때문에 '진보'와 '발전'을 보여 준다. [7]많은 개인의 누적된 일은 특정 '발견'이 가능해지거나 가능성이 높아지는 지식의 집적을 생산한다. [8]그러한 발견은 (일어나도록) '무르익으며', 더 일찍 발생할 수 없었을 것이며, 또한 다수의 개인에 의해 동시에 이루어질 가능성이 있다.

어휘

interdependence 상호 의존(성)
integration 통합, 합병
internalise[internalize] 내면화하다
contradictory 모순되는
work out ~을 산출[계산]하다
implication 영향, 결과; 함축
accept 수용하다
cf. acceptance 수용
reasoning 추론, 추리
inherent 내재하는; 본래부터의, 선천적인
integral 내장된, 일부로 들어가 있는; 필수적인
conceptual 개념의
premise (주장의) 전제
prime number 《수학》 소수(素數) 《1과 자신만이 나눌 수 있는 수》
advance 진보, 전진; 다가가다
outgrowth 결과물

[7]The cumulative work (of many individuals) / produces *a corpus of knowledge* [within which certain 'discoveries' become possible or more likely].
S(단수) V(단수) O 전치사+관계대명사 S' V' C'
누적된 일은 (많은 개인의) / 지식의 집적을 생산한다 [특정 '발견'이 가능해지거나 가능성이 높아지는]
↳ 집적된 지식을 통해 새로운 발견이 가능해짐.

★<could have p.p.>: ~했을 수도 있다
[8]Such discoveries are 'ripe' / and could not have occurred earlier / and are also likely to be made simultaneously / by numbers of individuals.
S V_1 C_1 V_2 V_3 C_3
★의미상 주어인 such discoveries가 만들어지는 것이므로 to-v의 수동형 <to be p.p.>가 쓰임.
그러한 발견은 (일어나도록) '무르익는다' / 그리고 더 일찍 발생할 수 없었을 것이다 / 그리고 또한 동시에 이루어질 가능성이 있다 / 다수의 개인에 의해
↳ 새로운 사상의 발견은 일어날 시기가 되면 이루어짐.

previous 이전의
cumulative 누적되는
ripe 무르익다; 익은, 숙성한
[선택지] stem from ~에서 비롯되다
abstract 추상적인
basis 토대, 기초; 근거
universalism 보편성
emerge 나타나다
promote 촉진하다; 홍보하다; 승진시키다

정답 가이드

빈칸 문장을 통해 문화적 사상이 '무엇'이기 때문에 '진보'와 '발전'을 보여주는지를 추론해야 함을 알 수 있다. 빈칸 문장은 결론을 나타내는 연결어 Thus가 이끌고 있으므로 바로 앞 예시 문장과 함께 무엇에 대한 예시와 결론인지 앞에서 단서를 찾아야 한다. 문장 3에서 문화적 혁신과 발견은 사상과 마찬가지로, 다른 수용된 사상의 논리적 영향이나 결과로 산출된다고 했다. 따라서 빈칸에 들어갈 말로 가장 적절한 것은 ① 'are outgrowths of previous ideas(이전 사상의 결과물이다)'이다.

오답 클리닉

② stem from abstract reasoning ability (17%)
추상적 추론 능력에서 비롯되다
새로운 사상은 논리적 추론을 통해 발견된다고 했음.

③ form the basis of cultural universalism (15%)
문화적 보편성의 토대를 형성하다
문화적 보편성에 관한 언급은 없음.

④ emerge between people of the same age (10%)
같은 시대의 사람들 사이에서 나타나다
문화적 사상이 같은 시대의 사람들 사이에서 나온다는 내용은 없음.

⑤ promote individuals' innovative thinking (18%)
개인들의 혁신적 사고를 촉진하다
어떤 사상적 기반도 없이 개인의 혁신적 사고로 문화적 사상이 발전한다는 내용이 아님.

03 + 문장 넣기 〈23학년도 9월 모평 39번 | 정답률 40%〉 ⑤

구문분석 & 직독직해

기술 양립하기 어려운 보안과 사용자 편의

주제문
★<intend+O+to-v(O가 v하도록 의도하다)>의 수동형
[1]Each new wave of technology is intended / to enhance user convenience, / as well as (to) improve security, // but sometimes these do not necessarily go hand-in-hand.
S_1 V_1(단수) C S_2 V_2 ★<not necessarily>: ((부분 부정)) 반드시[꼭] ~은 아닌
각각의 새로운 기술의 물결은 의도된다 / 사용자 편의를 향상하도록 / 보안을 향상할 뿐만 아니라 //
그러나 때때로 이것들이 반드시 밀접히 연관되지는 않는다
↳ 새 기술로 사용자 편의와 보안의 향상을 모두 이루기는 어려움.

<from A to B>: A에서 B로
[2]For example, / the transition (from magnetic stripe to embedded chip) / slightly slowed down transactions, / sometimes frustrating customers (in a hurry).
S V O 분사구문(= and it sometimes frustrated ~)
예를 들어 / 전환은 (마그네틱 띠에서 내장형 칩으로의) / 거래(의 속도)를 조금 늦춰서 / 때로 고객을 좌절시켰다 (바쁜)
↳ 예: 내장형 칩으로의 전환은 거래 속도 면에서 사용자 편의를 향상시키지 못함.

★<명령문+and S+V>: ~하라, 그러면 S는 V할 것이다
(①) [3]Make a service too burdensome, / and the potential customer will go elsewhere.
V_1(명령문) O C S_2 V_2
서비스를 너무 부담스럽게 만들어라 / 그러면 잠재 고객은 다른 곳으로 갈 것이다
↳ 문제점: 서비스가 사용하기 부담스럽다면 고객은 다른 선택을 할 것임.

(②) [4]This obstacle applies / at several levels.
S V
이런 장애물은 적용된다 / 여러 수준에서

해석

[1]각각의 새로운 기술의 물결은 보안을 향상할 뿐만 아니라 사용자 편의를 향상하도록 의도되지만, 때때로 이것들이 반드시 밀접히 연관되지는 않는다. [2]예를 들어 마그네틱 띠에서 내장형 칩으로의 전환은 거래(의 속도)를 조금 늦춰 때로 바쁜 고객을 좌절시켰다. (①) [3]서비스를 너무 부담스럽게 만들면, 잠재 고객은 다른 곳으로 갈 것이다. (②) [4]이런 장애물은 여러 수준에서 적용된다. (③) [5]비밀번호, 이중 키 확인, 지문, 홍채 및 음성 인식과 같은 생체 인식은 모두 잠재적인 사기꾼으로부터 계좌 내역을 숨기는, 즉 여러분의 데이터를 비밀로 유지하는 방법이다. (④) [6]하지만 그것들은 모두 불가피하게 계좌 이용에 부담을 가중한다. (⑤ [7]자신의 돈에 접근하는 데 도입된 난관에 더해, 만약 의심이 가는 사기가 감지되면, 계좌 소유자는 본인이 그 수상쩍은 거래를 했는지 묻는 전화를 처리해야만 한다.) [8]이것(수상쩍은 거래를 했는지 묻는 전화)은 모두 어느 정도 도움이 되며, 실제로, 여러분의 은행이 여러분을 보호하기 위해 경계를 늦추지 않고 있다는 것을 아는 것은 안심이 될 수 있지만, 그러한 전화를

(③) [5]Passwords, double-key identification, and biometrics (such as fingerprint-, iris-, and voice recognition) / are all ways (of keeping the account details hidden / from potential fraudsters, / of keeping your data dark).

S1 S2 S3 V(복수) C *<keep+O+C(형용사)>: O를 ~하게 만들다[유지하다]

비밀번호, 이중 키 확인, 생체 인식은 (지문, 홍채 및 음성 인식과 같은) /
모두 방법이다 (계좌 내역을 숨기는 / 잠재적인 사기꾼으로부터 / 즉 여러분의 데이터를 비밀로 유지하는)

(④) [6]But / they all inevitably add a burden / to the use of the account.

(= passwords, ~ and biometrics) S V O

보안 기술들은 계좌 이용에 부담을 줌.

하지만 / 그것들(비밀번호, 이중 키 확인, 생체 인식)은 모두 불가피하게 부담을 가중한다 / 계좌 이용에

↳ 첫 번째 난관: 비밀번호, 이중 키 확인, 생체 인식은 계좌 보안에 도움이 되지만 이용에 부담을 가중함.

앞에 계좌 접근에 도입된 난관이 언급되어야 함.

(⑤ [7]On top of *the hurdles* (introduced in accessing his or her money), / if a suspected fraud is detected, // the account holder has to deal with / *the phone call* (asking // if he or she made the suspicious transactions).)

~에 더하여 과거분사구 부사절 접속사(조건) S' V' S V O 현재분사구 asking의 O(명사절)

*if가 명사절을 이끌면 '~인지 (아닌지)'를 의미함.

난관에 더해 (자신의 돈에 접근하는 데 도입된) / 만약 의심이 가는 사기가 감지되면 //
계좌 소유자는 처리해야만 한다 / 전화를 (묻는 // 본인이 그 수상쩍은 거래를 했는지를)

[8]This is all useful at some level — // indeed, / it can be reassuring / knowing // that your bank is keeping alert / to protect you — //

(= The phone call ~ transactions) S1 V1 C1 가주어 V2 C2 진주어(동명사구) 동명사 knowing의 O(명사절)

이것(수상쩍은 거래를 했는지 묻는 전화)은 모두 어느 정도 도움이 된다 // 실제로 / (~은) 안심이 될 수 있다 / 아는 것은 // 여러분의 은행이 경계를 늦추지 않고 있다는 것을 / 여러분을 보호하기 위해 //

but it becomes tiresome // if too many such calls are received.

S3 V3 C3 부사절 접속사(조건)

주어진 문장의 '수상쩍은 거래를 했는지 묻는 전화'를 지칭함.

그러나 그것은 귀찮은 일이 된다 // 그러한 전화를 너무 많이 받게 되면

↳ 두 번째 난관: 사기가 감지된 거래에 대해 묻는 전화는 안심이 되지만 너무 많으면 귀찮음.

너무 많이 받게 되면 그것은 귀찮은 일이 된다.

어휘

convenience 편의
go hand-in-hand 밀접히 연관되다; 함께 가다
transition 전환, 변화
embed 끼워 넣다, 파묻다
transaction 거래
in a hurry 바쁜; 서둘러
burdensome 부담스러운
cf. burden 부담, 짐
identification 확인, 식별
biometrics 생체 인식
iris (안구의) 홍채
fraudster 사기꾼
dark 비밀의; 어두운
inevitably 불가피하게
hurdle 난관, 장애; (경기용) 허들
suspected 의심이 가는
cf. suspicious 수상쩍은, 의심스러운
reassuring 안심시키는
alert 경계(하는); 민첩한
tiresome 귀찮은, 성가신

정답 가이드

주어진 문장은 On top of hurdles ~ money로 시작하여 계좌에 접근하는 데 도입된 여러 난관들에 더해 계좌 소유자는 수상쩍은 거래를 했는지 묻는 전화도 처리해야 한다는 내용이다. 이를 통해 주어진 문장 앞에는 계좌에 접근하는 데 거쳐야 할 여러 난관들이 언급되어야 하고, 뒤에는 전화 처리라는 추가된 난관에 대한 부연 설명이 이어질 것임을 예상할 수 있다. ⑤의 앞부분은 여러 계좌 보안 기술(비밀번호, 이중 키 확인, 생체 인식)의 예를 들어 이들이 계좌 이용에 부담을 가중한다고 했고, ⑤ 뒤의 내용은 주어진 문장에서 언급한 은행의 확인 전화를 This와 such calls로 받아 부연 설명하므로 주어진 문장이 들어가기에 가장 적절한 곳은 ⑤이다.

오답 클리닉

① (3%) 보안의 향상이 사용자 편의를 줄인 예로 마그네틱 띠에서 내장형 칩으로의 전환을 언급한 뒤, 서비스를 너무 부담스럽게 만들면 잠재 고객은 그 서비스를 이용하지 않을 것이라고 지적하는 내용이 이어지는 것은 적절하다.
② (10%) 서비스를 너무 부담스럽게 만드는 것을 This obstacle로 받아 이것이 여러 수준에서 부담이 된다고 진술하는 것은 자연스럽다.
③ (12%) 서비스 이용을 부담스럽게 만드는 예로 여러 계좌 보안 서비스를 소개하는 것은 자연스럽다.
④ (34%) 앞에서 언급한 방법이 계좌 보안에는 도움이 되지만 계좌 이용에는 부담을 가중시킨다는 상반되는 내용이 역접 연결어 But으로 이어지는 것은 자연스럽다.

The 주의 주어진 문장이 ④ 뒤의 문장과 역접 관계가 아님을 파악해야 한다.

01 + 요약문 〈22학년도 대수능 40번 | 정답률 69%〉 ①

구문분석 & 직독직해 과학 과학적 설명에 대한 두 가지 관점

주제문

[1]Philip Kitcher and Wesley Salmon(S) have suggested(V) // that there are two possible alternatives(O(명사절)) / among philosophical theories of explanation.

Philip Kitcher와 Wesley Salmon은 제안했다 // 두 가지 가능한 대안이 있다고 / (과학적) 설명에 대한 철학 이론 중에

↳ 과학적 설명에 대한 철학적 이론 중 두 가지 대안이 있음.

(A) 최소한으로 적은 수의 일반화로 광범위한 많은 현상을 통합함.

[2]One(S) is(V) the view(C) // that(동격 접속사) scientific explanation(S′) consists in(V′) / the *unification*(O′) (of broad bodies of phenomena) (under a minimal number of generalizations).

하나는 관점이다 // 과학적 설명이 ~에 있다는 / '통합' (광범위하게 많은 현상들의) (아주 적은 수의 일반화에 따른)

↳ **대안 1:** 일반화로 광범위한 현상을 통합함.

(A) 모든 현상을 포괄하는 법칙이나 일반화의 간결한 틀을 구성함.

[3]According to this view, / the (or perhaps, a) goal of science(S) / is(V) to construct / an economical framework(C) (of *laws or generalizations* [that(주격 관계대명사) are capable of subsuming / all observable phenomena]).

이 관점에 따르면 / 과학의 목표(혹은 어쩌면 한 가지 목표)는 / 구성하는 것이다 / 간결한 틀을 (법칙이나 일반화의 [포섭할 수 있는 / 모든 관찰할 수 있는 현상을])

[4]Scientific explanations(S) organize and systematize(V) / our knowledge(O) (of the empirical world); //

과학적 설명은 조직하고 체계화한다 / 우리의 지식을 (경험적 세계에 대한) //

the more economical the systematization(S_1) (is)(V_1), // the deeper our understanding(S_2) (of what is explained)(of의 O(명사절)) (is)(V_2). ★<the+비교급 ~, the+비교급...>: ~할수록 더욱 …하다 비교급 뒤의 be동사가 생략되기도 함.

체계화가 더 간결할수록 // 우리의 이해는 더욱 깊어진다 (설명되는 것에 대한)

↳ **부연 설명:** 모든 현상을 포섭하는 간결한 일반화의 틀을 구축하여 지식을 조직하고 체계화함.

[5]The other view(S) is(V) the *causal/mechanical* approach(C).

다른 관점은 '인과 관계적/기계론적' 접근이다

↳ **대안 2:** 인과 관계적/기계론적 접근.

[6]According to it, / a scientific explanation (of a phenomenon)(S) / consists of(V) uncovering *the mechanisms*(O(동명사구)) [that(주격 관계대명사) produced(V′) the phenomenon(O′) of interest]. ★<of+추상명사>는 형용사로 쓰이므로, 앞의 명사를 수식함.

그것에 따르면 / 과학적인 설명은 (어떤 현상에 대한) / 메커니즘을 밝혀내는 것으로 구성된다 [관심 있는 그 현상을 만들어 낸]

↳ **부연 설명:** 어떤 현상의 메커니즘(생성 원리)을 밝힘.

(B) 일반화는 개별 사건에 대한 설명에서 나옴.

[7]This view(S) sees(V) / the explanation(O) (of individual events) / as primary, / ★<see A as B>: A를 B로 여기다[보다]

이 관점은 여긴다 / 설명을 (개별적인 사건들에 대한) / 근본적인 것으로 /

with the explanation of generalizations flowing from them(= individual events). ★<with+O′+v-ing>: O′가 ~하여[~하면서] (능동관계)

일반화에 대한 설명이 그것들(개별적인 사건들)로부터 흘러나와서

(B) 일반화는 규칙성을 만들어 내는 인과적 메커니즘에서 비롯됨.

[8]That is, / the explanation (of scientific generalizations)(S) / comes from(V) / *the causal mechanisms*(O) [that(주격 관계대명사) produce(V′) the regularities(O′)].

즉 / 설명은 (과학적 일반화에 대한) / ~에서 비롯된다 / 인과적 메커니즘 [규칙성을 만들어 내는]

↳ **부연 설명:** 개별 사건의 설명에서 일반화의 설명이 나오는데, 이것은 인과적 메커니즘이 만들어 내는 규칙성임.

해석

[1]Philip Kitcher와 Wesley Salmon은 (과학적) 설명에 대한 철학 이론 중에 두 가지 가능한 대안이 있다고 제안했다. [2]하나는 과학적 설명이 아주 적은 수의 일반화에 따른 광범위하게 많은 현상들의 '통합'에 있다는 관점이다. [3]이 관점에 따르면, 과학의 목표(혹은 어쩌면 한 가지 목표)는 모든 관찰할 수 있는 현상을 포섭할 수 있는 법칙이나 일반화의 간결한 틀을 구성하는 것이다. [4]과학적 설명은 경험적 세계에 대한 우리의 지식을 조직하고 체계화하는데, 체계화가 더 간결할수록, 설명되는 것에 대한 우리의 이해는 더욱 깊어진다.(▶ 체계가 간결할수록[통합될수록] 그것이 포함할 수 있는 현상은 많아지므로 이해가 깊어진다는 의미. 예를 들어 상대성 이론 하나로 수많은 물리 현상을 설명하고 이해할 수 있음.) [5]다른 관점은 '인과 관계적/기계론적' 접근이다. [6]그것에 따르면, 어떤 현상에 대한 과학적 설명은 관심 있는 그 현상을 만들어 낸 메커니즘을 밝혀내는 것으로 구성된다. [7]이 관점은 일반화에 대한 설명이 개별적인 사건들로부터 흘러나와서 개별적인 사건들에 대한 설명을 근본적인 것으로 여긴다. [8]즉, 과학적 일반화에 대한 설명은 규칙성을 만들어 내는 인과적 메커니즘에서 비롯된다.

↓

[9]과학적 설명은 모든 관찰을 포함하는 (A) 아주 적은 수의 원리를 찾거나 개별적인 현상으로부터 도출된 일반적인 (B) 패턴을 발견함으로써 이루어질 수 있다.

어휘

alternative 대안(적인)
philosophical 철학의
consist in ~에 있다
unification 통합, 통일
body 많은 양[모음]; 신체
phenomenon (*pl.* phenomena) 현상
minimal 아주 적은, 최소한의
generalization 일반화
economical (말·문체 등이) 간결한; 경제적인
framework 틀, 뼈대, 체계
be capable of ~할 수 있다
observable 관찰할 수 있는
cf. observation 관찰; 준수
systematize 체계화하다
cf. systematization 체계화
causal 인과 관계의, 원인이 되는
mechanical 기계(론)적인, 기계로 작동되는
consist of ~로 구성되다[이루어지다]
uncover 밝히다, 폭로하다; 덮개를 벗기다

↓

[9] Scientific explanations can be made / either by seeking the **(A) least** number of *principles* (covering all observations) / or by finding *general* **(B)** ***patterns*** (drawn from individual phenomena).

S V 전치사구 병렬 현재분사구 전치사구 병렬 과거분사구

과학적 설명은 이루어질 수 있다 / (A) 아주 적은 수의 원리를 찾음으로써 (모든 관찰을 포함하는) / 혹은 일반적인 (B) 패턴을 발견함으로써 (개별적인 현상으로부터 도출된)

primary 근본적인; 주요한
regularity 규칙성, 규칙적임
[요약문] draw (결론 등을) 도출해 내다, 얻다; 끌어당기다

정답 가이드

요약문을 통해 과학적 설명의 두 가지 관점에 대한 글임을 알 수 있다. 그중 하나는 관찰할 수 있는 모든 현상을 '아주 적은' 수의 일반화로 통합하는 것이고, 다른 하나는 개별적인 사건들에 대한 설명의 '규칙성'에서 일반화의 설명이 도출된다는 것이다. 따라서 요약문의 빈칸 (A)와 (B)에 각각 들어갈 말로 가장 적절한 것은 ① 'least(아주 적은) - patterns(패턴)'이다.

오답 클리닉

(A) (B)
② fixed - features (12%) 고정된 - 특징
(A)는 일반화 법칙의 수를 최소화하는 것이지 일정한 수로 고정하는 것이 아니므로 틀리며, (B)는 맞음.
③ limited - functions (3%) 제한된 - 기능
(A)는 일반화 법칙의 수에 제한을 두는 것이 아니므로 틀리며, (B)도 틀림.
④ fixed - rules (10%) 고정된 - 규칙
(A)는 틀리며, (B)는 맞음.
⑤ least - assumptions (6%) 아주 적은 - 가정
(A)는 맞고, (B)는 틀림.

02~03 + 복합 유형 〈24학년도 6월 모평 41~42번 | 정답률 02 57%, 03 36%〉

02 ③ 03 ②

구문분석 & 직독직해

사회 협상을 고정된 파이로 보는 잘못된 통념

[1] Many negotiators assume // that all negotiations involve a fixed pie.

S V 명사절 접속사(→ assume의 O(명사절)) S′ V′ O′

많은 협상가들이 가정한다 // 모든 협상이 고정된 (양의) 파이를 수반한다고

[2] Negotiators often approach integrative negotiation opportunities / as zero-sum situations or win-lose exchanges.

S V O 전치사(~로(서)) 명사구 병렬

협상가들은 흔히 통합적인 협상 기회에 접근한다 / 제로섬 상황이나 승패 교환으로

↳ **도입(통념):** 많은 협상가들은 협상을 고정된 파이를 나눠 갖는 것으로 생각함.

⊶ 03-(a) 합의와 절충의 가능성이 없다고 여기면 그것들을 찾으려는 노력을 '억누를' 것임.

[3] *Those* [who believe in the mythical fixed pie] / assume // that parties' interests stand in opposition, / with no possibility (for integrative settlements and mutually beneficial trade-offs), //

S₁ 주격 관계대명사 V₁ 명사절 접속사(→ assume의 O(명사절)) S′ V′ 명사구 병렬

사람들은 [가공의 고정된 파이를 믿는] / 가정한다 // 당사자들의 이해관계가 반대에 있다고 / 가능성 없이 (통합적 합의와 상호 간에 이익이 되는 절충에 대한) //

so they (a) suppress / *efforts* (to search for them).

부사절 접속사 S′ V′ O′ (them = integrative ~ trade-offs)

그래서 그들은 억누른다 / 노력을 (그것들을 찾으려는)

↳ **세부 사항 1:** 고정된 파이를 믿는 사람들은 당사자들의 이해관계가 반대된다고 가정하기 때문에 합의나 절충안을 찾으려 하지 않음.

[4] In a hiring negotiation, / *a job applicant* [who assumes // that salary is the only issue] / may insist on $75,000 // when the employer is offering $70,000.

S 주격 관계대명사 V′ O′(명사절) V O 부사절 접속사(시간) S′ V′ O′

고용 협상에서 / 구직자는 [간주하는 // 급여가 유일한 문제라고] / 7만 5천 달러를 요구할 수 있다 // 고용주가 7만 달러를 제시할 때

해석

[1]많은 협상가들이 모든 협상이 고정된 (양의) 파이를 수반한다고 가정한다. [2]협상가들은 흔히 통합적인 협상 기회에 (한쪽이 이득을 보는 만큼 반드시 다른 한쪽은 손해를 보는) 제로섬 상황이나 승패 교환으로 접근한다. [3]가공의 고정된 파이를 믿는(▶ 파이의 양이 고정적이라고 근거 없이 믿음을 의미) 사람들은 당사자들의 이해관계가 통합적 합의와 상호 간에 이익이 되는 절충에 대한 가능성 없이 반대에 있다고 가정하므로 그들은 그것들을 찾으려는 노력을 (a) 억누른다.(▶ 파이 양이 고정되어 있다고 생각하는 사람들은 어느 한쪽이 이익을 보면 다른 한쪽은 반드시 손해를 보게 되며 둘 다 이익을 보는 절충은 가능하지 않다고 가정한다는 의미) [4]고용 협상에서 급여가 유일한 문제라고 간주하는 구직자는 고용주가 7만 달러를 제시할 때 7만 5천 달러를 요구할 수 있다. [5]두 당사자(구직자와 고용주)가 가능성에 관해 더 논의하고 나서야 그들은 이사 비용과 시작 날짜 또한 협상될 수 있다는 것을 발견하는데, 이는 급여 문제의 해결을 (b) 방해할(→ 촉진할) 수도 있다.
[6]협상을 고정된 파이 측면에서 보는 경향은 사람들이 주어진 갈등 상황의 본질을 어떻게 보느냐에 따라 (c) 달라진다. [7]이는 Harinck, de Dreu와 Van Vianen의, 징역형에 대한 검사와 피고 측 변

*only(준부정어)를 포함하는 부사절이 문장 앞에 오면서 <조동사+주어+동사> 어순으로 도치가 일어남. ↱ discover의 O(명사절)

[5]Only when the two parties discuss the possibilities further // do they discover // that moving expenses and starting date can also be negotiated, //

부사절 접속사(시간) S′ V′ O′ 조동사 S V 명사절 접속사 S′ V′

🔑 03-(b) 다른 부분들 또한 협상될 수 있음은 급여 문제의 해결을 '촉진할' 수 있음.

두 당사자(구직자와 고용주)가 가능성에 관해 더 논의하고 나서야 // 그들은 발견한다 // 이사 비용과 시작 날짜 또한 협상될 수 있다는 것을 //

which may **(b) block(→ facilitate)** / resolution (of the salary issue).

관계대명사(앞 절 보충 설명)

그리고 이는 방해할(→ 촉진할) 수도 있다 / 해결을 (급여 문제의)

↳ **예(고용 협상):** 구직자와 고용주의 급여 의견에 차이가 있을 때 다른 부분들(이사 비용, 시작 날짜)의 협상 가능성을 아는 것은 급여 문제의 해결을 촉진할 수 있음.

🔑 03-(c) 갈등 상황을 바라보는 관점에 따라 고정된 파이 측면에서 협상을 보는 경향은 '달라질' 것임.

[6]The tendency (to see negotiation / in fixed-pie terms) / **(c) varies** / depending on how people view the nature (of a given conflict situation).

S(단수) = V(단수) on의 O(명사절)

경향은 (협상을 보는 / 고정된 파이 측면에서) / 달라진다 / 사람들이 본질을 어떻게 보느냐에 따라 (주어진 갈등 상황의)

↳ **세부 사항 2:** 협상을 고정된 파이 측면에서 보는 경향은 주어진 갈등 상황의 본질을 보는 방식에 따라 달라짐.

↱ (= 앞 문장)

[7]This was shown / in *a clever experiment* (by Harinck, de Dreu, and Van Vianen) (involving a simulated negotiation / between prosecutors and defense lawyers / over jail sentences).

S V 현재분사구(a clever experiment 수식)

이는 보였다 / 기발한 실험에서 (Harinck, de Dreu와 Van Vianen의) (모의 협상을 포함하는 / 검사와 피고 측 변호인 간의 / 징역형에 대한)

[8]Some participants were told to view their goals / in terms of personal gain / (e.g., arranging a particular jail sentence will help your career), //

S_1 V_1 C_1

어떤 참가자들은 그들의 목표를 보라는 말을 들었다 / 개인적 이득의 측면에서 / (예를 들어, 특정 징역형을 결정짓는 것이 당신의 경력에 도움이 될 것이다) //

others were told to view their goals / in terms of effectiveness / (a particular sentence is most likely to prevent recidivism), //

S_2 V_2 C_2

다른 참가자들은 그들의 목표를 보라는 말을 들었다 / 효과성의 측면에서 / (특정 형은 상습적 범행을 방지할 가능성이 가장 크다) //

and still others were told to focus on values / (a particular jail sentence is fair and just).

S_3 V_3 C_3

그리고 또 다른 참가자들은 가치에 초점을 두라는 말을 들었다 / (특정 징역형은 공정하고 정당하다)

↳ **예(실험):** 징역형 모의 협상에서 참가자들은 집단별로 목표를 각각 개인적 이득, 효과성, 가치로 봄.

🔑 03-(c) 개인적 이득에 초점을 두느냐 가치에 초점을 두느냐에 따라 고정된 파이 통념의 영향은 '달라질' 수 있음.

[9]*Negotiators* (focusing on personal gain) / were most likely / to come under the influence (of fixed-pie beliefs) / and (to) approach the situation **(d) competitively**.

S 현재분사구 V C to-v구 병렬

협상가들은 (개인적 이득에 초점을 둔) / 가능성이 가장 많았다 / 영향을 받을 (고정된 파이에 대한 믿음의) / 그리고 상황에 경쟁적으로 접근할

🔑 03-(d) 가치에 초점을 둔 협상가와 대조되는 개인적 이득에 초점을 둔 협상가들은 상황에 '경쟁적으로' 접근했을 것임.

[10]*Negotiators* (focusing on values) / were least likely to see the problem / in fixed-pie terms / and (were) more inclined to approach the situation cooperatively.

S 현재분사구 V C_1 *<be inclined to-v>: v하는 경향이 있다 C_2

협상가들은 (가치에 초점을 둔) / 문제를 볼 가능성이 가장 적었다 / 고정된 파이 측면에서 / 그리고 상황에 협조적으로 접근하는 경향이 더 많았다

↳ **실험 결과:** 개인적 이득에 중점을 둔 협상가들은 협상을 고정된 파이로 보고 경쟁적으로 접근한 반면, 가치에 중점을 둔 협상가들은 협상에 협조적으로 접근함.

🔑 03-(e) 고정된 파이에 대한 통념은 부정적인 영향을 미치므로 '덜' 통합적인 합의를 초래할 것임.

[11]Stressful conditions (such as time constraints) / contribute to *this common misperception*, // which in turn may lead to **(e) less** integrative agreements.

S V (= fixed-pie beliefs)

관계대명사(보충 설명)

스트레스가 많은 조건은 (시간 제약과 같은) / 이러한 흔한 오해의 원인이 된다 // 그리고 이는 결국 덜 통합적인 합의로 이어질 수 있다

↳ **첨가:** 스트레스가 많은 조건은 고정된 파이 통념의 원인이 되며, 결국 덜 통합적인 합의로 이어짐.

호인 간의 모의 협상을 포함하는 기발한 실험에서 보였다. [8]어떤 참가자들은 개인적 이득의 측면에서 그들의 목표를 보라는 말을 들었고(예를 들어, 특정 징역형을 결정짓는 것이 당신의 경력에 도움이 될 것이다), 다른 참가자들은 그들의 목표를 효과성의 측면에서 보라는 말을 들었으며(특정 형은 상습적 범행을 방지할 가능성이 가장 크다), 그리고 또 다른 참가자들은 가치에 초점을 두라는 말을 들었다(특정 징역형은 공정하고 정당하다). [9]개인적 이득에 초점을 둔 협상가들은 고정된 파이에 대한 믿음의 영향을 받아 상황에 (d) 경쟁적으로 접근할 가능성이 가장 많았다. [10]가치에 초점을 둔 협상가들은 문제를 고정된 파이 측면에서 볼 가능성이 가장 적었으며 상황에 협조적으로 접근하는 경향이 더 많았다. [11]시간 제약과 같은 스트레스가 많은 조건은 이러한 흔한 오해의 원인이 되며, 이는 결국 (e) 덜 통합적인 합의로 이어질 수 있다.

어휘

negotiator 협상가
cf. negotiation 협상
cf. negotiate 협상[교섭]하다
integrative 통합적인, 통합하는
mythical 가공의, 사실이 아닌; 신화적인
cf. myth 근거 없는 믿음; 신화
party 당사자; 정당
interest 이해관계; 관심(을 끌다); 이익
opposition 반대; 대립
settlement 합의, 해결; 정착
mutually 상호 간에, 서로
trade-off 절충(안)
insist on ~을 요구[고집]하다
resolution 해결; 결의, 결심
in ~ terms ~ 측면에서(= in terms of)
simulated 모의[모조]의
defense 피고 측; 방어, 수비
jail sentence 징역형, 실형
arrange 결정짓다; 배열하다; 정리하다
come under (무엇의 통제·영향을) 받다
cooperatively 협조적으로
condition 조건; 상태
constraint 제약; 제한
contribute to A A의 원인이 되다; A에 기여하다
misperception 오해, 오인
in turn 결국
agreement 합의; 일치
[선택지] stick to A A를 고수하다; A를 계속하다
maximize 극대화하다
⊕ 제로섬(zero-sum): 한쪽이 이득을 보면 다른 한쪽은 반드시 손해를 보는 득과 실의 차가 0인 상태.

정답 가이드

02 도입에서 모든 협상을 고정된 (양의) 파이를 수반하는 것으로 가정하는 잘못된 생각이 통합적인 합의와 상호 간에 이익이 되는 절충에 이르지 못하게 한다고 했다. 또한 징역형 모의 협상의 실험을 예로 들어 개인적 이득에 초점을 둔 협상가들이 고정된 파이 믿음의 영향을 받아 상황에 경쟁적으로 접근할 가능성이 가장 많았다고 설명한다. 이는 모두 협상가들이 협상을 고정된 파이로 보는 통념의 부정적 영향에 해당하므로 글의 제목으로 가장 적절한 것은 ③ 'Negotiators, Wake Up from the Myth of the Fixed Pie!(협상가들이여, 고정된 파이라는 근거 없는 믿음에서 깨어나라!)'이다.

03 구직자와 고용주 간의 고용 협상에는 급여 문제만 있는 것이 아니라 이사 비용이나 시작 날짜와 같은 다른 협상 가능한 문제들도 있으므로 이것들의 논의는 급여 문제 해결에 도움이 될 것이다. 따라서 ②의 'block(방해하다)'을 'facilitate(촉진하다)' 등으로 바꾸어야 한다.

오답 클리닉

02 ① Fixed Pie: A Key to Success in a Zero-sum Game (16%)
고정된 파이는 제로섬 게임에서 성공의 비결(×)
고정된 파이 관점을 부정적으로 보는 글의 내용과 반대됨.
② Fixed Pie Tells You How to Get the Biggest Salary (10%)
고정된 파이는 여러분에게 가장 높은 급여를 받는 방법(×)을 알려 준다
급여 문제는 고용 협상에서 고정된 파이 관점이 문제 해결에 도움이 되지 않는 예로 언급된 것임.
④ Want a Fairer Jail Sentence? Stick to the Fixed Pie (7%)
더 공정한 징역형(×)을 원하는가? 고정된 파이를 고수하라(×)
지문에 언급된 jail sentence를 활용한 오답. 고정된 파이 관점을 고수하라는 내용이 아님.
⑤ What Alternatives Maximize Fixed-pie Effects? (10%)
어떤 대안이 고정된 파이 효과를 극대화하는가?(×)
고정된 파이 관점을 부정적으로 보고 있으므로 이를 극대화하는 것은 틀림.

03 ① suppress (5%) 억누르다
통합적 합의나 상호 간에 이익이 되는 절충 가능성이 전혀 없다고 여기면 그것을 찾으려는 노력을 하지 않고 '억누를' 것이다.
③ varies (12%) 달라지다
문장 9와 10에서 협상 가 개인적 이득에 초점을 두면 고정된 파이의 영향을 가장 많이 받고, 가치에 초점에 두면 가장 적게 받았다고 한 것에서 갈등 상황의 본질을 어떻게 보느냐에 따라 고정된 파이의 측면에서 보는 경향이 '달라짐'을 알 수 있다.
④ competitively (22%) 경쟁적으로
개인적 이득에 초점을 둔 협상가와 가치에 초점을 둔 협상가를 대조해 설명한 실험 결과에서 가치에 초점을 둔 협상가는 문제를 고정된 파이의 관점으로 볼 가능성이 낮으며 상황에 협조적으로 접근한다고 했으므로 개인적 이득에 초점을 둔 협상가는 고정된 파이의 영향을 많이 받아 상황에 '경쟁적으로' 접근할 것을 유추할 수 있다.
⑤ less (24%) 덜
this common misperception은 고정된 파이 통념을 의미하는데, 이는 부정적인 영향을 미칠 것이므로 '덜' 통합적인 합의로 이어질 것이다.

01 + 빈칸 추론 〈22학년도 9월 모평 31번 | 정답률 43%〉 ③

구문분석 & 직독직해

역사 고고학적 기록의 불완전성

주제문

[1]When examining the archaeological record (of human culture), / one has to consider // that it is vastly incomplete.

접속사를 생략하지 않은 분사구문(= When one examines ~) / one: S / has to consider: V / that it is ~: O(명사절)

고고학적 기록을 살펴볼 때 (인류 문화의) / 그 사람은 고려해야 한다 // 그것이 대단히 불완전하다는 것을

🔑 인류 문화의 여러 측면이 고고학적 기록으로 식별하기 어려움.

[2]Many aspects (of human culture) / have what archaeologists describe / as low archaeological visibility, / meaning // (that) they are difficult to identify archaeologically.

S(복수) / ↱명사절 접속사 생략 / V(복수) / O(명사절) / 전치사(~로(서)) / 분사구문(= and it means ~) / (= many aspects of human culture) / 형용사 difficult 수식

많은 측면은 (인류 문화의) / 고고학자들이 묘사하는 것을 지니고 있다 / 낮은 고고학적 가시성으로 / 이것은 의미한다 / 그것들(인류 문화의 많은 측면)이 (무엇인지를) 고고학적으로 식별하기 어렵다는 것을

↳ 인류 문화의 많은 측면이 고고학적 기록으로는 식별하기 어려움.

[3]Archaeologists tend to focus / on tangible (or material) aspects of culture: / things [that can be handled and photographed], / (such as tools, food, and structures).

S / V / = / 주격 관계대명사

고고학자들은 초점을 맞추는 경향이 있다 / 문화의 유형적인 (혹은 물질적인) 측면에 / 즉 (~한) 것들 [만져지고 사진이 찍힐 수 있는] / (도구, 음식, 구조물처럼)

↳ **세부 사항 1:** 고고학자들은 비교적 식별이 쉬운 문화의 유형적인 측면에 초점을 맞춤.

🔑 더 많은 추론이 요구되기 때문에 인류 문화의 무형적인 측면을 재구성하는 것은 더 어려움.

[4]Reconstructing intangible aspects of culture is more difficult, / requiring // that one (should) draw more inferences / from the tangible.

S(동명사구) / V(단수) / C / 분사구문(= because it requires ~) / 현재분사 requiring의 O(명사절)

*주장·요구·제안·명령 등의 동사가 '~해야 한다'라는 당위성의 의미를 가질 때, 목적어로 쓰인 that절의 동사는 <(should+)동사원형> 형태로 씀.

문화의 무형적인 측면을 재구성하는 것은 더 어렵다 / 이것이 요구하기 때문에 // 사람들이 더 많은 추론을 끌어낼 것을 / 유형적인 것에서

↳ **세부 사항 2:** 문화의 무형적 측면은 추론을 해야 해서 재구성하는 것이 어려움.

[5]It is relatively easy, / for example, / for archaeologists / to identify and (to) draw inferences about technology and diet) / from stone tools and food remains.

가주어 / to-v의 의미상 주어 / to-v구 병렬(진주어)

(~은) 비교적 쉽다 / 예를 들어 / 고고학자들이 / 확인하고 추론을 끌어내는 것은 (기술과 식습관을[에 관한]) / 석기와 음식 유물로부터

↱ (stone tools and food remains의 말바꿈 표현)

[6]Using the same kinds of physical remains / to draw inferences (about social systems and what people were thinking about) / is more difficult.

S(동명사구) / 목적(~하기 위해) / about의 O₁(명사구) / about의 O₂(명사절) / V(단수) / C

같은 종류의 물질적인 유물을 사용하는 것은 / 추론을 끌어내기 위해 (사회 체계와 사람들이 무엇에 대해 생각하고 있었는지에 관한) / 더 어렵다

↳ **예:** 물질적 유물(석기와 음식 유물)에서 유형적인 측면(기술과 식습관)을 추론하는 것보다 무형적인 측면(사회 체계 및 사람들의 사고 방식)을 추론하는 것이 더 어려움.

↱ (= using the same ~ thinking about) 🔑 물질적 유물에서 무형적인 측면을 연구하는 데 더 많은 추론이 필요함.

[7]Archaeologists do it, // but there are necessarily *more inferences* (involved in getting / from *physical remains* (recognized as trash) / to making interpretations (about belief systems)).

S₁ / V₁ / O / V₂ / S₂ / 과거분사구 / 과거분사구

고고학자들은 그것을 한다 // 그러나 더 많은 추론이 불가피하게 있다 (가는 데 수반되는 / 물질적 유물로부터 (쓸모없는 것으로 인식되는) / 해석을 하는 것까지 (신념 체계에 관한))

↳ **맺음말:** 쓸모없는 유물을 보고 문화의 무형적인 측면을 해석하는 데에는 더 많은 추론이 필요함.

해석

[1]인류 문화의 고고학적 기록(물질적 유물)을 살펴볼 때, 그 사람은 그것이 대단히 불완전하다는 것을 고려해야 한다. [2]인류 문화의 많은 측면은 고고학자들이 낮은 고고학적 가시성으로 묘사하는 것을 지니고 있는데, 이것은 그것들이 (무엇인지를) 고고학적으로 식별하기 어렵다는 것을 의미한다. [3]고고학자들은 문화의 유형적인 (혹은 물질적인) 측면, 즉 도구, 음식, 구조물처럼 만져지고 사진이 찍힐 수 있는 것들에 초점을 맞추는 경향이 있다. [4]문화의 무형적인 측면을 재구성하는 것은 더 어려운데, 이것은 (사람들이) 유형적인 것에서 더 많은 추론을 끌어낼 것을 요구하기 때문이다. [5]예를 들어, 고고학자들이 석기와 음식 유물로부터 기술과 식습관을 확인하고 그것에 관한 추론을 끌어내는 것은 비교적 쉽다. [6]사회 체계와 사람들이 무엇에 대해 생각하고 있었는지에 관한 추론을 끌어내기 위해 같은 종류의 물질적인 유물을 사용하는 것은 더 어렵다. [7]고고학자들은 그것을 하지만, 쓸모없는 것으로 인식되는 물질적 유물로부터 신념 체계에 관한 해석을 하는 것까지 가는 데 수반되는 더 많은 추론이 불가피하게 있다.(▶ 물질적 유물로 무형적인 측면을 연구하려면 추론을 더 많이 할 수밖에 없다는 의미)

어휘

examine 살펴보다, 조사하다
vastly 대단히; 광대하게
incomplete 불완전한
aspect 측면, 국면, 양상
visibility 가시성, 눈에 잘 보임
identify 식별하다; 확인하다; 동일시하다
tangible 유형의, 실체적인 (↔ intangible 무형의)
material 물질적인; 물질, 재료
structure 구조(물); 구성하다
reconstruct 재구성[재현]하다
draw 끌어내다, 끌다; 추첨하다
inference 추론, 추리
relatively 비교적, 상대적으로
stone tool 석기
remains 유물, 유적
physical 물질[물리]적인; 육체의
necessarily 불가피하게, 필연적으로
recognize 인식하다, 알아보다; 인정하다
interpretation 해석

정답 가이드

인류 문화의 고고학적 기록(물질적 유물)을 살펴볼 때 '어떤' 점을 고려해야 하는지를 추론해야 한다. 이어지는 설명과 예에서는 인류 문화의 많은 측면이 무엇인지를 고고학적으로 식별하기가 어려운데, 그중에서 문화의 무형적인 측면은 물질적인 유물에서 추론해야 하기 때문에 재구성하는 것이 더 어렵다고 했다. 이는 곧 고고학적 기록들이 옛 인류 문화를 온전히 알 수 있게 해주지 못한다는 것이므로, 빈칸에 들어갈 말로 가장 적절한 것은 ③ 'incomplete(불완전한)'이다.

오답 클리닉

① outdated (12%) 구식인
인류 문화의 고고학 기록이 구식이라는 내용은 없음.
② factual (19%) 사실에 기반을 둔
고고학 기록이 사실인지 아닌지를 가리는 내용이 아님.
④ organized (13%) 체계적인
인류 문화의 고고학 기록이 체계적이라는 언급은 없음.
⑤ detailed (13%) 상세한
고고학 기록이 얼마나 상세한지에 관한 내용이 아님.

02 + 글의 순서 〈23학년도 6월 모평 37번 | 정답률 46%〉 ②

구문분석 & 직독직해

심리 매몰 비용 오류

[1]In economics, / there is *a principle* (known as the *sunk cost fallacy*).
(is: V / a principle: S / known as ~: 과거분사구)
경제학에 / 원리가 있다 ('매몰 비용 오류'라고 알려진)

[2]The idea is // that when you are invested and have ownership in something, // you overvalue that thing.
(↱ is의 C(명사절) / The idea: S / is: V / that: 명사절 접속사 / when ~ something: 부사절(시간) / you: S′ / overvalue: V′ / that thing: O′)
그 개념은 ~이다 // 여러분이 어떤 것에 몰입되고 소유권을 가질 때 // 여러분은 그것에 지나치게 가치를 둔다는 것
↳ **매몰 비용 오류의 정의:** 우리가 관심을 쏟고 소유권을 얻은 대상을 과대평가하는 것.

(🔑 문장 2의 that절을 가리킴.)
(B) [3]This leads people to continue / on *paths or pursuits* [that should clearly be abandoned].
(This: S / leads: V / people: O / to continue: C / that: 주격 관계대명사)
이것은 사람들이 계속하게 한다 / 계획이나 일을 [분명히 그만두어야 하는]
↳ **문제점:** 매몰 비용 오류는 우리가 그만둬야 하는 계획이나 일을 계속하게 함.

[4]For example, / people often remain / in terrible relationships //
(people: S / remain: V)
예를 들어 / 사람들은 종종 남아 있다 / 끔찍한 관계에 //
simply because they've invested a great deal of themselves / into them.
(because: 부사절 접속사(이유) / they: S′ / 've invested: V′ / a great deal of themselves: O′ / them: (= terrible relationships))
그저 그들이 그들이 자신의 많은 것을 투자했기 때문에 / 그것들(끔찍한 관계)에

[5]Or / someone may continue pouring money / into *a business* [that is clearly a bad idea / in the market].
(someone: S / may continue: V / pouring money: O(동명사구) / that: 주격 관계대명사)
또는 / 누군가는 계속 돈을 쏟아 부을지도 모른다 / 사업에 [분명히 나쁜 아이디어인 / 시장에서]
↳ **예:** 사람들은 많은 것을 투자했다는 이유로 끔찍한 관계나 수익성이 없는 사업을 버리지 못함.

(🔑 (B)의 문제점에 대한 해결책을 제시함.)
(A) [6]Sometimes, / *the smartest thing* [(which[that]) a person can do] / is (to) quit.
(the smartest thing: S / (which[that]): 목적격 관계대명사 생략 / is: V / (to) quit: C)
때때로 / 가장 현명한 일은 [한 사람이 할 수 있는] / 그만두는 것이다
★주어를 수식하는 관계사절이 do로 끝나고 be동사가 이어지면 보어로 to를 생략한 원형부정사를 사용하는 경우가 많음.
↳ **해결책:** 그만둬야 하는 일을 그만두어야 함.

[7]Although this is true, // it has also become a tired and played-out argument.
(this: (= 앞 문장) / Although: 부사절 접속사(양보) / it: S / has also become: V / a tired and played-out argument: C)
이것이 진실이기는 하지만 // 그것은 또한 진부하고 낡은 주장이 되었다

(★<not always>: ((부분 부정)) 항상 ~인 것은 아닌)
[8]Sunk cost doesn't always have to be a bad thing.
(Sunk cost: S / doesn't always have to be: V / a bad thing: C)
매몰 비용이 항상 나쁜 것이어야 할 필요는 없다
↳ **장점:** 매몰 비용이 항상 나쁜 것은 아님.

해석

[1]경제학에 '매몰 비용 오류'라고 알려진 원리가 있다. [2]그 개념은 여러분이 어떤 것에 몰입되고 소유권을 가질 때, 그것에 지나치게 가치를 둔다는 것이다. (B) [3]이것은 사람들이 분명히 그만두어야 하는 계획이나 일을 계속하게 한다. [4]예를 들어, 사람들은 그저 자신의 많은 것을 끔찍한 관계에 투자했기 때문에 그것들 속에 종종 남아 있다. [5]또는 누군가는 시장에서 분명히 나쁜 아이디어인 사업에 계속 돈을 쏟아 부을지도 모른다. (A) [6]때때로 한 사람이 할 수 있는 가장 현명한 일은 그만두는 것이다. [7]이것이 진실이기는 하지만, 그것은 또한 진부하고 낡은 주장이 되었다. [8]매몰 비용이 항상 나쁜 것이어야 할 필요는 없다. (C) [9]실제로, 여러분은 이런 인간의 성향을 여러분에게 이득이 되도록 이용할 수 있다. [10]누군가가 자신의 약속을 완수하는 것을 확실히 하기 위해 개인 트레이너에게 많은 돈을 투자하는 것처럼, 여러분 또한 여러분이 있고 싶은 길에 머무르는 것을 확실히 하기 위해 선불로 많은 것을 투자할 수 있다.

어휘

invest (시간·노력 등을) 쏟다; 투자하다
ownership 소유(권)
overvalue 지나치게 가치를 두다, 과대평가하다
path (행동) 계획; 길, 방향
pursuit 일, 활동; 추구
abandon 그만두다; 버리다
played-out 낡은, 효력이 떨어진; 지쳐버린
argument 주장; 논쟁
ensure 확실히 하다, 보장하다
follow through on ~을 완수하다
commitment 약속; 전념
up front 선불로

(A)의 매몰 비용이 항상 나쁜 것은 아니라는 내용을 부연 설명함.

(C) [9]Actually, / you can leverage this human tendency / to your benefit.
S V O

실제로 / 여러분은 이런 인간의 성향을 이용할 수 있다 / 여러분에게 이득이 되도록

↳ **부연 설명:** 매몰 비용을 우리에게 이득이 되도록 이용할 수 있음.

[10]Like someone invests a great deal of money / in a personal trainer / to ensure // (that) they follow through on their commitment, //

부사절 접속사(~처럼) / 목적(~하기 위해) / to ensure의 O(명사절) / 명사절 접속사 생략 S′ V′ O′

누군가가 많은 돈을 투자하는 것처럼 / 개인 트레이너에게 / 확실히 하기 위해 // 자신이 자신의 약속을 완수하는 것을 //

you, too, can invest a great deal / up front / to ensure // (that) you stay / on the path [(which[that]) you want to be on].

S V O / 목적(~하기 위해) / to ensure의 O(명사절) / 명사절 접속사 생략 S′ V′ / 목적격 관계대명사 생략

여러분 또한 많은 것을 투자할 수 있다 / 선불로 / 확실히 하기 위해 // 여러분이 머무르는 것을 / 길에 [여러분이 있고 싶은]

↳ 목표로 하는 것에 미리 투자함으로써 계속 목표를 추구하게 함.

⊕ 매몰 비용 오류(sunk cost fallacy): 돈이나 시간, 노력 등을 투입한 일에 대해 성공 여부와 관계없이 그 일을 지속하려는 현상. 매몰 비용은 이미 지출되어 회수할 수 없는 비용을 의미함.

정답 가이드

매몰 비용 오류에 대해 정의하는 주어진 글 뒤에는 정의 내용을 This로 받아 그로 인한 문제점과 예를 제시하는 (B)가 이어지는 것이 적절하다. 그다음에는 (B)의 문제를 해결하는 방법으로 '그만두는 것'을 언급하는 (A)가 와야 한다. (A) 마지막에 매몰 비용이 항상 나쁜 것은 아니라고 내용이 전환되는데, 그 뒤에는 이를 구체적으로 설명하는 (C)가 오는 것이 흐름상 가장 자연스럽다.

오답 클리닉

① (A) - (C) - (B) (3%)

주어진 글에는 매몰 비용 오류로 인한 어떤 문제점도 언급되지 않았으므로 해결책을 제시하는 (A)가 주어진 글 바로 뒤에 오는 것은 어색하다.

③ (B) - (C) - (A) (24%) / ④ (C) - (A) - (B) (11%) / ⑤ (C) - (B) - (A) (16%)

매몰 비용을 이득이 되도록 이용할 수 있다고 설명하는 (C)는 매몰 비용이 항상 나쁜 것은 아니라고 내용이 전환되는 (A) 뒤에 오는 것이 적절하다.

03 + 문장 넣기 〈23학년도 9월 모평 38번 | 정답률 39%〉 ②

구문분석 & 직독직해

사회 '집단'의 정확한 정의

★<see A as B>: A를 B로 간주하다[여기다]

[1]In everyday life, / we tend to see any collection of people / as a group.
S V

일상생활에서 / 우리는 어떤 사람들의 무리라도 간주하는 경향이 있다 / 하나의 집단으로

↳ 우리는 일상에서 무리를 하나의 집단으로 간주함.

주어진 문장의 they가 지칭하는 것.

(①) [2]However, / social psychologists use this term / more precisely.
S V O(= a group)

그러나 / 사회 심리학자들은 이 용어를 사용한다 / 더 정확하게

주제문 they가 지칭할 대상이 앞에 있어야 함. ★<define A as B>: A를 B로 정의하다

(② [3]In particular, / they define a group / as two or more people [who interact with, and exert mutual influences on, / each other].)
S V O 전치사(~로(서)) 주격 관계대명사 동사구 병렬 with와 on의 공통O

특히 / 그들(사회 심리학자들)은 집단을 정의한다 / 둘 이상의 사람들로 [상호 작용하고 상호 영향력을 발휘하는 / 서로]

↳ 사회 심리학자들은 집단을 서로 상호 작용하고, 상호 영향력을 행사하는 둘 이상의 사람들로 정의함.

주어진 문장에서 집단을 정의한 내용을 부연 설명함.

[4]It is this sense of mutual interaction or inter-dependence / for a common purpose // which distinguishes the members of a group / from a mere aggregation of individuals.

<It is ~ which[that] ...> 강조구문: …하는 것은 바로 ~이다 / V′ O′ / ★<distinguish A from B>: A를 B와 구별하다

바로 이 서로의 상호 작용감 또는 상호 의존감이다 / 공동의 목적을 위한 //

집단의 구성원들을 구별하는 것은 / 단순한 개인들의 집합과

↳ 집단을 개인들의 집합과 구별하는 것은 공동의 목적을 위한 상호 작용감 또는 상호 의존감임.

부사절 접속사(~처럼) ★<happen to-v>: 우연히 v하다

(③) [5]For example, / (as Kenneth Hodge observed), // a collection (of people [who happen to go for a swim after work / on the same day each week]) /

부사절 삽입 S 주격 관계대명사

예를 들어 / (Kenneth Hodge가 말한 것처럼) // 무리는 (사람들의 [우연히 일을 마치고 수영을 하러 가는 / 매주 같은 날에]) /

해석

[1]일상생활에서 우리는 어떤 사람들의 무리라도 하나의 집단으로 간주하는 경향이 있다. (①) [2]그러나 사회 심리학자들은 이 용어를 더 정확하게 사용한다. (② [3]특히, 그들(사회 심리학자들)은 집단을 서로 상호 작용하고, 상호 영향력을 발휘하는 둘 이상의 사람들로 정의한다.) [4]집단의 구성원들을 단순한 개인들의 집합과 구별하는 것은 바로 이 공동의 목적을 위한 서로의 상호 작용감 또는 상호 의존감이다. (③) [5]예를 들어, Kenneth Hodge가 말한 것처럼, 우연히 매주 같은 날에 일을 마치고 수영을 하러 가는 사람들의 무리는 엄밀히 말하면 집단을 구성하지 않는데, 이 수영하는 사람들은 구조화된 방식으로 서로 상호 작용하지 않기 때문이다. (④) [6]대조적으로, 매일 아침 학교에 가기 전에 훈련하는 경쟁을 하는 어린 수영 선수들의 팀은 공동의 목표(경기를 위한 훈련)를 공유할 뿐만 아니라 공식적인 방식으로 (예를 들면, 미리 함께 준비 운동을 함으로써) 서로 상호 작용도 하기 때문에 집단'이다'. (⑤) [7]'팀'을 정의하는 것은 바로 공동의 목표를 달성하기 위해 사람들이 함께 모이는 이러한 관념이다.

어휘

collection (물건·사람의) 무리, 더미; 수집(품)

term 용어; 기간; 조건

does not, (strictly speaking), constitute a group // because these swimmers do not interact with each other / in a structured manner. *strictly speaking은 분사구문의 관용적 표현으로 '엄밀히 말하면'을 뜻함.

V / O / 부사절 접속사(이유) / S′ / V′ / O′

(엄밀히 말하면) 집단을 구성하지 않는다 // 이 수영하는 사람들은 서로 상호 작용하지 않기 때문이다 / 구조화된 방식으로

↳ **예 1:** 일을 마치고 수영하러 가는 사람들은 구조화된 방식으로 서로 상호 작용하지 않으므로 집단이 아님.

(④) [6]By contrast, / a squad (of *young competitive swimmers* [who train / every morning before going to school]) / *is* a group //

S / 주격 관계대명사 / V / C

대조적으로 / 팀은 (경쟁을 하는 어린 수영 선수들의 [훈련하는 / 학교에 가기 전에 매일 아침]) / 집단'이다' //

because they not only share a common objective (training for competition) / but also interact with each other / in formal ways (e.g., by warming up together beforehand).

부사절 접속사(이유) / V′₁ / O′₁ / *<not only A but also B>: A뿐만 아니라 B도 / V′₂ / O′₂ / <by v-ing>: v함으로써

그들이 공동의 목표(경기를 위한 훈련)를 공유할 뿐만 아니라 (~하기) 때문에 / 서로 상호 작용도 하기 (때문에) / 공식적인 방식으로 (예를 들면, 미리 함께 준비 운동을 함으로써)

↳ **예 2:** 어린 수영 선수들의 팀은 공동의 목표를 공유하고 서로 공식적인 방식으로 상호 작용하기 때문에 집단임.

(⑤) [7]It is this sense (of people coming together / to achieve a common objective) // that defines a "team".

→ 동명사의 의미상 주어 / = / of의 O(동명사구) / 목적(~하기 위해) / V′ / O′

바로 이러한 관념이다 (사람들이 함께 모이는 / 공동의 목표를 달성하기 위해) // '팀'을 정의하는 것은

↳ **결론:** '팀'은 공동의 목표를 위해 사람들이 함께 모이는 것을 뜻함.

precisely 정확하게
mutual 상호 간의, 서로의
mere 단순한; ~에 불과한
observe 말하다; 목격하다; (규칙을) 준수하다
constitute 구성하다; 설립하다
structure 구조(화하다)
manner 방식; 태도; 예의
squad (스포츠) 팀, 선수단; (군대의) 분대
objective 목표, 목적; 객관적인
formal 공식적인; 형식적인
warm up 준비 운동을 하다
beforehand 미리

정답 가이드

주어진 문장은 그들(they)이 집단을 서로 상호 작용하고, 상호 영향력을 발휘하는 둘 이상의 사람들로 정의한다는 내용이다. ② 앞 문장의 사회 심리학자들이 집단이라는 용어를 더 정확하게 사용한다는 내용에서 주어진 문장의 집단을 정의하는 주체가 사회 심리학자들임을 알 수 있다. ② 뒤의 문장은 주어진 문장의 서로 상호 작용하고 상호 영향력을 발휘한다는 내용을 this sense of mutual interaction or interdependence로 받아 부연 설명하고 뒤이어 이에 대한 구체적인 예가 서술되고 있으므로, 주어진 문장이 들어가기에 가장 적절한 곳은 ②이다.

오답 클리닉

① (4%) '우리'가 생각하는 것과 다른 '사회 심리학자들'이 생각하는 집단에 관한 내용이 역접 연결어 However로 연결되는 것은 자연스럽다.
③ (24%) 집단을 개인의 집합과 구별하는 공동의 목적을 위한 상호 작용감 또는 상호 의존감을 예를 들어 보여주는 내용이다.
④ (16%) 역접 연결어 By contrast로 앞의 예와 상반되는 예가 자연스럽게 이어진다.
⑤ (17%) 예를 통해 '팀'에 대한 정의를 내리며 글을 마무리하고 있다.

01 + 글의 주제 (22학년도 9월 모평 23번 | 정답률 69%) ⑤

구문분석 & 직독직해

철학 제약되지 않는 것에서 얻는 심미적 즐거움

★<too ~ to-v>: 너무 ~해서 v할 수 없는

[1]In Kant's view, / geometrical shapes(S) are(V) too perfect(C) / to induce an aesthetic experience.

칸트의 관점에서 / 기하학적 모양은 너무 완벽해서 / 심미적 경험을 유발할 수 없다

↳ 대조 A: 완벽한 것은 심미적 경험을 유발할 수 없음.

★대시(—) 사이에 삽입된 내용은 Insofar as에 연결되어 조건을 나타냄.

[2]Insofar as(부사절 접속사(~하는 한)) they(= geometrical shapes) agree with the underlying concept or idea — / thus possessing *the precision*(분사구문(= and thus they possess ~)) [that(목적격 관계대명사) the ancient Greeks sought and celebrated] — // geometrical shapes(S1) can be grasped(V1), //

그것들(기하학적 모양)이 근본적인 개념이나 생각과 일치하는 한 / 그래서 '정확성'을 가지는 한 [고대 그리스인들이 추구하고 찬양했던] // 기하학적 모양은 이해될 수 있다 //

but they(S2, = geometrical shapes) do not give rise to(V2) emotion(O2), // and, most importantly, / they(S3) do not move(V3) the imagination(O3) / to free and new (mental) lengths.

하지만 그것들(기하학적 모양)은 감정을 불러일으키지 않는다 // 그리고 가장 중요하게는 / 그것들은 상상력을 움직이게 하지 않는다 / 자유롭고 새로운 (정신적인) 범위로

↳ 기하학적 모양은 이해는 가능하지만 감정과 상상력을 자극하지는 않음.

주제문 — 인간의 심미적 경험과 상상력을 유발하는 것은 완벽함, 정확함과 정반대되는 것임.

[3]*Forms or phenomena*(S), / on the contrary, / [that possess a degree of immeasurability], or [that do not appear constrained], /(주격 관계대명사절 병렬)

형태나 현상은 / 그와는 반대로 / [어느 정도의 측정이 불가능한 특징을 지닌] 또는 [제약이 없어 보이는] /

stimulate(V) the human imagination(O) — / hence their(= forms' or phenomena's) ability (to induce a sublime aesthetic experience).

인간의 상상력을 자극한다 / 이 때문에 그것들(형태와 현상)의 능력이 나타난다 (숭고한 심미적인 경험을 유발하는)

↳ 대조 B: 측정할 수 없고 제약이 없는 형태나 현상들이 인간의 상상력을 자극함.

즐거움 = 명확하게 규정할 수 없는 대상을 이해하려는 정신적 활동을 즐기는 것.

[4]*The pleasure*(S) (associated with experiencing immeasurable objects — indefinable or formless objects —)(과거분사구) / can be defined(V) / as(전치사(~으로)) enjoying one's own emotional and mental activity.

즐거움은 (측정이 불가능한 대상, 즉 규정할 수 없거나 형태가 없는 대상을 경험하는 것과 연관된) / 정의될 수 있다 / 자신의 감정적이고 정신적인 활동을 즐기는 것으로

↳ 측정할 수 없는 대상을 경험하면서 얻는 즐거움은 정신적 활동을 즐기는 것임.

[5]Namely, / the pleasure(S) consists of(V) / being challenged / and struggling(of의 O(동명사구 병렬)) / to understand and (to)(to 생략) decode *the phenomenon* (present to view).

다시 말해 / 그 즐거움은 ~로 구성된다 / 도전 받는 것(으로) / 그리고 애쓰는 것(으로) / 현상을 이해하고 해독하려고 (보도록 존재하는)

↳ 현상을 이해하고 해독하려는 노력에서 즐거움이 생김.

★<사역동사 have+O+p.p.(O가 ~된 상태이다)>가 동명사구로 쓰임.

[6]Furthermore, / part of the pleasure(S) comes from(V) / having one's comfort zone(O) (momentarily) violated.

게다가 / 그 즐거움의 일부는 ~로부터 온다 / 익숙한 곳이 (일시적으로) 침해된 상태(로부터) /

↳ 익숙하지 않은 것을 경험하는 것에서 즐거움을 느낌.

해석

[1]칸트의 관점에서, 기하학적 모양(예: 원, 직사각형, 정육면체, 원뿔 등)은 너무 완벽해서 심미적 경험을 유발할 수 없다. [2]그것들(기하학적 모양)이 근본적인 개념이나 생각과 일치해서 고대 그리스인들이 추구하고 찬양했던 '정확성'을 가지는 한 기하학적 모양은 이해될 수 있지만, 그것들은 감정을 불러일으키지 않으며, 가장 중요하게는 상상력을 자유롭고 새로운 (정신적인) 범위로 움직이게 하지 않는다. [3]그와는 반대로, 어느 정도의 측정이 불가능한 특징을 지니거나 제약이 없어 보이는(자유로운) 형태나 현상(예: 광활한 자연 경치, 천문 현상, 자연 현상 등)은 인간의 상상력을 자극하며, 이 때문에 숭고한 심미적인 경험을 유발하는 그것들(형태와 현상)의 능력이 나타난다. [4]측정이 불가능한 대상, 즉 규정할 수 없거나 형태가 없는 대상을 경험하는 것과 연관된 즐거움은 자신의 감정적이고 정신적인 활동을 즐기는 것으로 정의될 수 있다. [5]다시 말해, 그 즐거움은 도전 받는 것과 보도록 존재하는 현상을 이해하고 해독하려고 애쓰는 것으로 구성된다. [6]게다가, 그 즐거움의 일부는 익숙한 곳이 (일시적으로) 침해된 상태로부터 온다. (▶ 익숙하지 않은 것을 경험하는 것도 즐거움에 일조한다는 의미)

어휘

induce 유발하다, 유도하다
underlying 근본적인
possess 가지다, 소유하다
precision 정확성
celebrate 찬양하다; 축하하다
grasp 이해하다
give rise to A A를 일으키다, A를 초래하다
length (의견 등의) 범위, 정도; 길이
phenomenon (*pl.* phenomena) 현상
immeasurability 측정할 수 없음
constrained 제약된; 강요된
stimulate 자극하다
indefinable 규정[정의]할 수 없는
formless 형태가 없는
namely 다시 말해, 즉
decode 해독하다
comfort zone 익숙한 곳
momentarily 일시적으로
violate 침해하다; 위반하다
[선택지] inherent 내재적인
inclination 경향, 성향

정답 가이드

기하학적 모양은 인간의 감정과 상상력을 자극하지 않는 반면에, 측정할 수 없고 자유로운 형태나 현상은 인간의 상상력을 자극하며 그것들을 이해하려고 애쓰는 것에서 즐거움이 온다는 내용의 글이다. 두 개의 대상인 A와 B를 대조하여 서술하는 구조지만 대조 자체보다는 B를 더 강조하기 위해 대조되는 A를 도입에 서술한 경우에 해당한다. 따라서 글의 주제로 가장 적절한 것은 ⑤ 'aesthetic pleasure from things unconstrained(제약되지 않은 것으로부터 얻는 심미적 즐거움)'이다.

오답 클리닉

① diversity of aesthetic experiences in different eras (6%)
시로 다른 시대에(×) 심미적인 경험의 다양성
고대 그리스인들이 정확성을 추구하고 찬양했다는 언급 외에 다른 시대의 심미적 경험에 대한 언급은 없음.

② inherent beauty in geometrically perfect shapes (11%)
기하학적으로 완벽한 모양의 내재적 아름다움(×)
기하학적 모양은 너무 완벽해서 감정을 불러일으키지 않는다고 했으므로 오답임.

③ concepts of imperfection in modern aesthetics (7%)
현대 미학(×)에서 불완전함의 개념(×)
현대 미학에 국한된 내용이 아니며 불완전함의 개념을 정의한 내용도 없음.

④ natural inclination towards aesthetic precision (7%)
심미적 정확성(×)을 향한 자연스러운 경향
정확성을 갖는 기하학적 모양이 아닌, 측정할 수 없고 제약이 없는 것들이 심미적 경험을 유발한다는 내용임.

02 + 빈칸 추론 〈22학년도 6월 모평 32번 | 정답률 52%〉 ②

구문분석 & 직독직해 인지 전략적 자기 무지

주제문 ★<some of+N(~ 중 일부)>은 of 뒤에 오는 명사에 수 일치하여 단수동사 emphasizes가 옴.

[1]Some (of the most insightful work (on information seeking)) / emphasizes "*strategic self-ignorance*," /
S / V(단수) / O
일부는 (가장 통찰력 있는 연구 중 (정보 탐색에 관한)) / '전략적 자기 무지'를 강조한다 /

(which is) understood / as "the use of ignorance / as *an excuse* (to engage excessively in *pleasurable activities* [that may be harmful / to one's future self])."
주격 관계대명사+be동사 생략 / 전치사(~로(서)) / 전치사(~로(서)) / 주격 관계대명사
🔑 미래에 해로울 수도 있는 즐거운 활동을 하려는 핑계로 무지를 이용함.
이는 이해된다 / '무지의 이용으로 / 핑계로서 (즐거운 활동에 과도하게 참여하려는 [해로울 수도 있는 / 자신의 미래 자아에])'

↳ **'전략적 자기 무지'의 정의:** 미래에 해로울 수 있는 즐거운 활동을 하기 위한 핑계로 무지를 이용하는 것.

[2]The idea here is // that if people are present-biased, // they might avoid / *information* [that would make current activities less attractive] — // ★<make+O+C(형용사)>: O를 C하게 만들다
S / V / is의 C(명사절) / 명사절 접속사 / 부사절(조건) / S′ / V′ / O′ / 주격 관계대명사
여기서의 생각은 ~이다 // 만약 사람들이 현재에 편향되어 있다면 // 그들은 피할지도 모른다는 것 / 정보를 [현재의 활동을 덜 매력적으로 만들] //
🔑 정보가 죄책감과 수치심을 유발하고 활동을 하지 못하도록 충고하기 때문에 피함.

perhaps because it would produce guilt or shame, / perhaps because it would suggest / *an aggregate trade-off* [that would counsel / against engaging in such activities].
(= information) / S'_1 / V'_1 / O'_1 / S'_2 / V'_2 / O'_2 / 주격 관계대명사 / (= pleasurable activities)
아마도 그것(정보)이 죄책감이나 수치심을 유발할 것이기 때문에 / 아마도 그것이 제안할 것이기 때문에 / 집합적 절충을 [충고할 / 그러한 활동을 하지 말라고]

↳ **상술:** 현재에 편향된 사람들은 현재의 활동을 즐기지 못하게 하는 정보를 피함.

[3]St. Augustine famously said, // "God give me chastity — / tomorrow."
V / IO / DO
성 아우구스티누스는 ~라는 유명한 말을 했다 // "하나님 제게 정결을 주시옵소서 / 내일"

★<사역동사 let+O+원형부정사(v)>: O가 v하게 하다
[4]Present-biased agents think: // "Please let me know the risks — / tomorrow."
현재에 편향되어 있는 행위자들은 ~라고 생각한다 // "제가 위험을 알게 해주세요 / 내일"

↳ **예(인용):** 사람들은 정보를 아는 것을 내일로 미룸.

해석

[1]정보 탐색에 관한 가장 통찰력 있는 연구 중 일부는 '전략적 자기 무지'를 강조하는데, 이는 '자신의 미래 자아에 해로울 수도 있는 즐거운 활동에 과도하게 참여하려는 핑계로서 무지의 이용'으로 이해된다. [2]여기서의 생각은 만약 사람들이 현재에 편향되어 있다면, 그들이 현재의 활동을 덜 매력적으로 만들 정보를 피할지도 모른다는 것인데, 아마도 그것(정보)이 죄책감이나 수치심을 유발할 것이고, 아마도 그것이 그러한 활동을 하지 말라고 충고할 집합적 절충을 제안할 것이기 때문이다. [3]성 아우구스티누스는 "하나님 제게 정결을 내일 주시옵소서."라는 유명한 말을 했다. [4]현재에 편향되어 있는 행위자들은 "제가 위험을 내일 알게 해주세요."라고 생각한다. [5]사람들이 단기적인 혜택은 있지만 장기적인 대가가 있는 활동에 참여하는 것에 대해 생각하고 있을 때마다, 그들은 중요한 정보의 수령을 미루는 것을 선호할 수도 있다. [6]사람들을 슬프게 하거나 화나게 할 수 있는 정보에 관해서도 똑같은 점이 적용될 수 있다. 즉 "제가 알아야 할 것을 제게 내일 말해 주세요."

어휘

insightful 통찰력 있는
emphasize 강조하다(= highlight)
strategic 전략적인
ignorance 무지, 무식
excuse 핑계, 구실; 용서하다
engage in ~에 참여[관여]하다
excessively 과도하게
biased 편향된, 선입견이 있는

[5]Whenever people are thinking / about engaging in an activity (with short-term benefits but long-term costs), // they might prefer to delay / receipt (of important information).
부사절 접속사(~할 때마다) about의 O(동명사구) S V O(to-v구)
사람들이 생각하고 있을 때마다 / 활동에 참여하는 것에 대해 (단기적인 혜택은 있지만 장기적인 대가가 있는) //
그들은 미루는 것을 선호할 수도 있다 / 수령을 (중요한 정보의)
↳ **결론:** 사람들은 즐거운 활동을 할 때, 중요한 정보는 피함.

[6]The same point might hold / about *information* [that could make people sad or mad]: //
S V 주격 관계대명사 V′ O′ C′
"Please tell me // what I need to know — / tomorrow."
V IO DO(명사절)
똑같은 점이 적용될 수 있다 / 정보에 관해서도 [사람들을 슬프게 하거나 화나게 할 수 있는] //
즉 "제게 말해 주세요 // 제가 알아야 할 것을 / 내일"
↳ **추가 결론:** 슬프거나 화나게 하는 정보 또한 피함.

current 현재의; 통용되는
guilt 죄책감
shame 수치심; 유감스러운 일
trade-off (상호) 절충
counsel 충고(하다); 상담(하다)
agent 행위자; 대리인
short-term 단기적인(↔long-term 장기적인)
delay 미루다, 연기하다; 연기
receipt 수령, 받기; 영수증
hold 적용되다, 효력이 있다; 잡다, 쥐다
[선택지] attachment 애착; 부착(물); 첨부 파일
potentially 잠재적으로

정답 가이드

현재에 편향된 사람들이 '어떤' 정보를 피하려고 할지를 추론해야 한다. 빈칸 뒤에서 이 정보가 죄책감이나 수치심을 갖게 하여 그런 활동을 하지 말라고 하기 때문에 그 정보를 피하려 한다고 했으므로, 자신이 즐기고 있는 활동을 덜 매력적으로 만드는 활동을 피하는 것임을 추론할 수 있다. 따라서 빈칸에 들어갈 말로 가장 적절한 것은 ② 'make current activities less attractive(현재의 활동을 덜 매력적으로 만든다)'이다.

오답 클리닉

① highlight the value of preferred activities (17%)
선호되는 활동의 가치를 강조하다
즐거운 활동을 하지 말라고 충고하는 정보이므로 활동의 가치를 떨어뜨릴 것임.

③ cut their attachment to past activities (13%)
과거 활동에 대한 자신들의 애착을 끊다
현재의 즐거운 활동을 위해 전략적 자기 무지를 사용한다는 내용임.

④ enable them to enjoy more activities (9%)
그들이 더 많은 활동을 즐기게 해주다
죄책감을 유발하고 활동을 하지 말라고 충고하는 정보는 활동을 즐기지 못하게 한다고 볼 수 있음.

⑤ potentially become known to others (8%)
다른 사람들에게 잠재적으로 알려지게 되다
다른 사람들에게 알려지게 될 정보를 피한다는 내용이 아님.

03 + 글의 순서 (23학년도 6월 모평 36번 | 정답률 55%) ⑤

구문분석 & 직독직해

과학 진화론을 뒷받침하는 화석 기록

[1]The fossil record provides / evidence (of evolution).
S V O
화석 기록은 제공한다 / 증거를 (진화의)
↳ **화석 기록의 기능 1:** 진화의 증거를 제공함.

[2]*The story* [(which[that]) the fossils tell] / is one (of change).
S(단수) 목적격관계대명사 생략 V(단수) C (one → (= the story))
이야기는 [화석이 알려주는] / 것이다 (변화에 관한)

[3]*Creatures* existed in the past [that are no longer with us].
S V 주격 관계대명사
생물들이 과거에는 존재했다 [더는 우리와 함께하지 않는]

[4]Sequential changes are found / in *many fossils* (showing the change (of certain features) / over time / from a common ancestor), / as in the case of the horse.
S V 현재분사구 전치사(~처럼)
잇따른 변화가 발견된다 / 많은 화석에서 (변화를 보여주는 (특정한 특징의) / 시간이 흐름에 따라 / 공통의 조상으로부터) / 말의 경우에서처럼
↳ **부연 설명:** 화석은 생물들의 변화를 알려줌.

⊶ 주어진 글의 화석이 진화의 증거를 제공한다는 내용. (did → 일반동사 강조)
(C) [5]Apart from demonstrating // that evolution did occur, /
전치사(~외에도) 동명사 demonstrating의 O(명사절)
증명하는 것 외에도 // 진화가 정말 일어났다는 것을 /

해석

[1]화석 기록은 진화의 증거를 제공한다. [2]화석이 알려주는 이야기는 변화에 관한 것이다. [3]더는 우리와 함께하지 않는 생물들이 과거에는 존재했다. [4]말의 경우에서처럼, 시간이 흐름에 따라 공통의 조상으로부터 특정한 특징의 변화를 보여주는 많은 화석에서 잇따른 변화가 발견된다. (C) [5]진화가 정말 일어났다는 것을 증명하는 것 외에도, 화석 기록은 또한 진화론에서 만들어진 예측에 대한 검증을 제공한다. [6]예를 들어, 그 이론(진화론)은 단세포 생물이 다세포 생물 이전에 진화했다고 예측한다. (B) [7]화석 기록은 이 예측을 뒷받침하는데, 다세포 생물은 단세포 생물의 최초 출현 수백만 년 후에 지구 지층에서 발견된다. [8]그 반대가 발견될 수도 있다는 가능성이 항상 남아 있음에 주목하라. (A) [9]다세포 생물이 단세포 생물 이전에 진화했다고 실제로 밝혀진다면, 진화론은 거부될 것이다. [10]좋은 과학 이론은 항상 거부의 가능성을 고려한다. [11]화석 기록에 대한 무수한 조사에서 우리가 그러한 경우를 발견하지 못했다는 사실은 진화론을 위한 논거를 강화한다.

🔑 주어진 글에 이어 화석 기록의 다른 기능을 추가로 제시함.
the fossil record also provides / tests (of *the predictions* (made from evolutionary theory)).
S V O 과거분사구
화석 기록은 또한 제공한다 / 검증을 (예측에 대한 (진화론에서 만들어진))
↳ **화석 기록의 기능 2:** 진화론의 예측에 대한 검증을 제공함.

(= the evolutionary theory) predicts의 O(명사절)
[6]For example, / the theory predicts // that single-celled organisms evolved / before multicelled organisms.
S V 명사절 접속사 S′ V′ 전치사(~전에)
예를 들어 / 그 이론(진화론)은 예측한다 // 단세포 생물이 진화했다고 / 다세포 생물 이전에

🔑 (C)의 단세포 생물이 다세포 생물보다 먼저 진화했다는 진화론의 예측을 지칭함.
(B) [7]The fossil record supports this prediction — // multicelled organisms are found / in layers of earth / millions of years after the first appearance (of single-celled organisms).
S_1 V_1 O S_2 V_2
화석 기록은 이 예측을 뒷받침한다 // 다세포 생물은 발견된다 / 지구 지층에서 / 최초 출현 수백만 년 후에 (단세포 생물이)
↳ **예:** 단세포 생물이 다세포 생물보다 먼저 진화했다는 진화론의 예측을 화석 기록이 뒷받침함.

[8]Note // that the possibility always remains // that the opposite could be found.
V(명령문) O(명사절) 동격 접속사
주목하라 // 가능성이 항상 남아 있음에 // 그 반대가 발견될 수도 있다는
★첫 번째 that은 Note의 목적어인 명사절을, 두 번째 that은 the possibility와 동격인 명사절을 이끄는 접속사임.
↳ 화석 기록에서 예측과 반대되는 것이 발견될 수도 있음.

🔑 (B)의 반대가 발견될 가능성을 구체적으로 설명함.
(A) [9]If multicelled organisms were indeed found to have evolved / before single-celled organisms, // then the theory of evolution would be rejected.
부사절 접속사(가정) S′ V′ C′ S V
★<If+S′+과거동사 ~, S+조동사 과거형+동사원형 ...>은 '만약 ~한다면, …할 것이다(현재 사실의 반대)'를 뜻하는 가정법 과거.
다세포 생물이 진화했다고 실제로 밝혀진다면 / 단세포 생물 이전에 // 진화론은 거부될 것이다
↳ **예:** 다세포 생물이 단세포 생물보다 먼저 진화했다고 화석에서 밝혀지면 진화론은 받아들여지지 않을 것임.

[10]A good scientific theory always allows for / the possibility (of rejection).
S V O
좋은 과학 이론은 항상 ~을 고려한다 / 가능성 (거부의)
↳ 좋은 과학 이론은 거부될 가능성이 있음을 받아들임.

(= 다세포 생물이 먼저 진화했다는 것)
[11]The fact // that we have not found such a case / in countless examinations (of the fossil record) / strengthens the case (for evolutionary theory).
S 동격 접속사 S′ V′ O′ V O
사실은 // 우리가 그러한 경우를 발견하지 못했다는 / 무수한 조사에서 (화석 기록에 대한) /
논거를 강화한다 (진화론을 위한)
↳ 수많은 화석 기록 조사에서 진화론의 예측과 반대되는 경우가 발견되지 않았다는 사실이 진화론의 논거를 강화함.

어휘

fossil 화석
evolution 진화; 발전
cf. evolutionary 진화의
cf. evolve 진화하다
creature 생물; 창조물
sequential 잇따른, 순차적인
demonstrate 증명[논증]하다; 설명하다
single-celled 단세포의(↔ multicelled 다세포의)
organism 생물(체), 유기체
layer 지층; 층, 겹, 막
appearance 출현; (겉)모습
note 주목[주의]하다; 언급하다
opposite 반대(의)
indeed 실제로, 정말로
allow for ~을 고려[감안]하다
countless 무수한, 셀 수 없이 많은
examination 조사; 검토; 시험
strengthen 강화하다
case 논거, 주장; 사례, 경우

정답 가이드

화석 기록이 진화의 증거를 제공한다는 주어진 글 뒤에는 그 외에도 진화론에서 만들어진 예측에 대한 검증을 제공한다는 화석 기능의 다른 기능을 also로 덧붙이는 (C)가 이어져야 한다. 이어서 (C)의 마지막 문장에서 예로 든 단세포 생물이 다세포 생물 이전에 진화했다는 진화론의 예측을 (B)에서 this prediction으로 받아 화석 기록이 이를 뒷받침한다고 설명하며, (B)의 끝에서 언급한 그 반대 경우를 구체적으로 설명하는 (A)가 마지막에 오는 것이 자연스럽다.

오답 클리닉

① (A) - (C) - (B) (2%)
(A)는 다세포 생물이 단세포 생물보다 먼저 진화했다는 진화론의 반대 경우를 설명하는데, 주어진 글에는 진화론이나 단세포, 다세포 생물에 대한 언급이 없으므로 (A)는 주어진 글 바로 뒤에 올 수 없다.
② (B) - (A) - (C) (9%) / ③ (B) - (C) - (A) (16%)
주어진 글에는 (B)의 this prediction을 지칭할 내용이 없으므로 (B)는 주어진 글 바로 뒤에 올 수 없다.
④ (C) - (A) - (B) (19%)
(A)는 (B)의 the opposite의 발견 가능성에 대한 설명이므로 (B) 뒤에 와야 한다.

01 ✦ 글의 제목 〈22학년도 9월 모평 24번 | 정답률 68%〉 ③

구문분석 & 직독직해

사회 정부의 서비스 제공에 따른 시민 참여 감소

[1]The world has become / *a nation of laws and governance* [that has introduced a system (of public administration and management) / to keep order].
(S: The world / V: has become / C: a nation ... / that: 주격 관계대명사 / to keep: 목적(~하기 위해))

세계는 되었다 / 법과 통치의 나라가 [체계를 도입한 (공공 행정과 관리의) / 질서를 유지하기 위해]

↳ **도입:** 세계는 질서를 유지하기 위해 법과 통치의 나라가 됨.

[2]With this administrative management system, / urban institutions of government have evolved / to offer *increasing levels of services* / to their citizenry, / (which are) provided / through a taxation process and/or fee for services (e.g., police and fire, street maintenance, utilities, waste management, etc.).
(S(복수): urban institutions of government / V(복수): have evolved / to offer: 결과((~해서) v하다) / (which are): (= increasing levels of services) 주격 관계대명사+be동사 생략)

이 행정적인 관리 체계와 함께 / 도시의 정부 기관들은 진화해서 / 점점 더 수준 높은 서비스를 제공했다 / 자신들의 시민에게 / 이는 제공된다 / 과세 과정 그리고/또는 서비스(예를 들어, 치안과 소방, 도로 정비, 공익사업, 쓰레기 관리 등)에 대한 수수료를 통해 /

↳ **원인:** 정부는 행정 관리 체계를 도입하여 시민들로부터 세금과 수수료를 받아서 다양한 서비스를 제공함.

주제문 ⊶ 정부의 서비스 제공이 시민 참여를 대신함.

[3]Frequently this has displaced citizen involvement.
(S: this (= 앞 문장) / V: has displaced / O: citizen involvement)

빈번히 이것은 시민 참여를 대체했다

↳ **결과:** 시민의 공적 참여가 없어짐.

[4]Money (for services) / is not a replacement (for citizen responsibility and public participation).
(S: Money / V(단수): is / C: a replacement)

돈은 (서비스를 위한) / 대체물이 아니다 (시민의 책임과 공적 참여의)

[5]Responsibility (of the citizen) / is slowly being supplanted / by *government* (being the substitute provider).
(S: Responsibility / V: is being supplanted / being: 현재분사구)

책임은 (시민의) / 천천히 대체되고 있다 / 정부에 의해 (대리 제공자인)

↳ **결과 상술:** 시민은 돈을 내는 대신 사회에 참여하지 않고 정부가 시민의 책임을 대신함.

[6]Consequentially, / there is a philosophical and social change / in *attitude and sense of responsibility* (of our urban-based society) (to become involved).
(V: is / S: a philosophical and social change)

결과적으로 / 철학적이고 사회적인 변화가 있다 / 태도와 책임 의식에 (도시를 기반으로 하는 우리 사회의) (참여해야 한다는)

[7]The sense of community and *associated responsibility* (of all citizens) (to be active participants) / is therefore diminishing. ⊶ 시민의 공동체 의식 및 책임감이 줄어듦.
(S: The sense of community and associated responsibility / V: is diminishing)

공동체 의식과 관련된 책임감은 (모든 시민의) (적극적인 참여자가 되어야 한다는) / 그 결과 약해지고 있다

↳ 도시 기반 사회 행정 시스템이 시민의 공동체 의식과 책임 의식을 약화시킴.

[8]Governmental substitution (for citizen duty and involvement) / can have serious implications.
(S: Governmental substitution / V: can have / O: serious implications)

정부의 대리는 (시민의 의무와 참여에 대한) / 심각한 영향을 미칠 수 있다

↳ **맺음말:** 시민의 의무와 참여를 정부가 대신하는 것은 문제임.

[9]This impedes / *the nations of the world* (to be responsive / to natural and man-made disasters / as part of global preparedness).
(S: This (= Governmental substitution ~ involvement) / V: impedes / O: the nations of the world)

이것은 방해한다 / 세계의 국가들을 (반응하는 / 자연재해와 인간이 만든 재해에 / 전면적인 준비의 일부로)

↳ **예:** 시민의 책임과 참여가 없으면 재난 대비를 할 수 없음.

해석

[1]세계는 질서를 유지하기 위해 공공 행정과 관리 체계를 도입한 법과 통치의 나라가 되었다. [2]이 행정적인 관리 체계와 함께 도시의 정부 기관들은 진화해서 자신들의 시민에게 점점 더 수준 높은 서비스를 제공했는데, 이는 과세 과정 그리고/또는 서비스(예를 들어, 치안과 소방, 도로 정비, 공익사업, 쓰레기 관리 등)에 대한 수수료를 통해 제공된다. [3]빈번히 이것은 시민 참여를 대체했다. [4]서비스를 위한 돈은 시민의 책임과 공적 참여의 대체물이 아니다.(▶ 서비스를 위한 돈을 내는 것으로 시민의 책임과 공적 참여를 대신할 수 없다는 의미) [5]시민의 책임은 대리 제공자인 정부에 의해 천천히 대체되고 있다. [6]결과적으로, 도시를 기반으로 하는 우리 사회의 참여해야 한다는 태도와 책임 의식에 철학적이고 사회적인 변화가 있다. [7]공동체 의식과 적극적인 참여자가 되어야 한다는 모든 시민의 관련된 책임감은 그 결과 약해지고 있다. [8]시민의 의무와 참여에 대한 정부의 대리는 심각한 영향을 미칠 수 있다. [9]이것은 전면적인 준비의 일부로 자연재해와 인간이 만든 재해에 반응하는 세계의 국가들을 방해한다. (▶ 시민 참여의 부재는 각기 다른 나라들과 방대한 지역에 영향을 미치는 재해를 대비하는 데 방해가 된다는 의미)

어휘

governance 통치, 지배
administration 행정[관리] 업무
cf. administrative 행정적인
order 질서; 순서; 명령; 주문
institution 기관, 단체; (사회) 제도
citizenry 시민
taxation 과세, 징세
fee 수수료, 요금
maintenance 정비, 유지 (관리)
utility (전기·가스 등의) 공익사업; 유용(성)
displace 대체[대신]하다; 추방하다
involvement 참여, 관여
replacement 대체(물)
substitute 대리[대체]의; 대용물
cf. substitution 대리(인); 대용품
diminish 약해지다, 줄어들다
implication 영향, 결과; 함축, 암시
responsive to A A에 반응하는
global 전면적인; 세계적인
[선택지] sound (신체·정신이) 건전한, 건강한
contemporary 현대의; 동시대의
maximize 최대[극대]화하다

정답 가이드

시민이 정부에 세금이나 수수료를 주고 정부로부터 여러 공공 서비스를 제공받음에 따라, 시민의 책임이 줄어드는 문제점을 낳았다는 내용의 글이다. 따라서 글의 제목으로 가장 적절한 것은 ③ 'Decreased Citizen Involvement: A Cost of Governmental Services(줄어든 시민 참여, 즉 정부 서비스의 대가)'이다.

오답 클리닉

① A Sound Citizen Responsibility in a Sound Government (12%)
건전한 정부(×)에 건전한 시민의 책임감
정부가 건전해야 시민의 책임감이 건전해진다는 내용이 아님.

② Always Better than Nothing: The Roles of Modern Government (6%) 없는 것보다 항상 더 낫다(×), 즉 현대 정부의 역할
정부의 역할을 긍정적으로 보는 것이 아니라 정부의 역할이 커질수록 시민의 참여가 줄어든다는 문제점을 지적하는 내용이므로 틀림.

④ Why Does Global Citizenship Matter in Contemporary Society? (10%) 세계 시민권(×)은 현대 사회에서 왜 중요한가?
세계 시민권에 관한 언급은 없음.

⑤ How to Maximize Public Benefits of Urban-Based Society (4%)
도시를 기반으로 하는 사회의 공적인 혜택을 최대화하는 방법(×)
공적인 혜택, 즉 정부의 서비스가 문제가 된다는 내용임.

02 ✦ 빈칸 추론 〈21학년도 대수능 34번 | 정답률 42%〉 ②

구문분석 & 직독직해 — 교육 | 교육 기술의 성공적 통합

주제문

[1]Successful integration (of an educational technology) / is marked / by that technology being regarded by users / as an unobtrusive facilitator (of learning, instruction, or performance).
(S: Successful integration … / V: is marked / 동명사의 의미상 주어: that technology / by의 O(동명사구): being regarded / 전치사(~로(서)): as)
🔑 교육 기술은 눈에 띄지 않는 촉진제여야 함.
성공적인 통합은 (교육 기술의) / 특징지어진다 / 그 기술이 사용자에 의해 여겨지는 것으로 / 눈에 띄지 않는 촉진제로 (학습이나 교육, 또는 수행의)
↳ 교육 기술의 통합은 눈에 띄지 않으면서 목적 달성을 촉진하는 경우에 이루어짐.

🔑 기술보다 목적에 초점을 둬야 함.

[2]When the focus shifts / from the technology (being used) / to the educational purpose [that technology serves], //
(부사절 접속사(시간): When / <from A to B>: A에서 B로 / 현재분사구: being used / 목적격 관계대명사: that)
초점이 옮겨가면 / 기술에서 (사용되고 있는) / 교육적 목적으로 [기술이 도움이 되는] //
then that technology is becoming a comfortable and trusted element, / and can be regarded / as being successfully integrated.
(S: that technology / V_1: is becoming / C: a comfortable and trusted element / V_2: can be regarded / 전치사(~로(서)): as / as의 O(동명사구): being successfully integrated)
그러면 그 기술은 편하고 신뢰받는 요소가 되어 간다 / 그리고 여겨질 수 있다 / 성공적으로 통합되는 것으로
↳ **상술:** 사용자의 초점이 기술보다 교육 목적에 있어야 함.

*few: 거의 없는 (준부정어)

[3]Few people give a second thought / to the use of a ball-point pen // although the mechanisms (involved) vary — //
(S: Few people / V: give / O: a second thought / 부사절 접속사(양보): although / S′: the mechanisms / 과거분사: involved / V′: vary)
더 생각하는 사람은 거의 없다 / 볼펜 사용에 대해 // (관련된) 방법이 가지각색이지만 //
some use a twist mechanism // and some use a push button on top, // and there are other variations as well.
(S'_1: some / V'_1: use / O'_1: a twist mechanism / S'_2: some / V'_2: use / O'_2: a push button / V'_3: are / S'_3: other variations)
어떤 것들은 돌리는 방법을 사용한다 // 그리고 어떤 것들은 위에 달린 누르는 버튼을 사용한다 // 또한 다른 변형(된 방법)들도 있다
↳ **예 1:** 볼펜의 사용 방법(기술)보다 용도(목적)를 신경 씀 → 완전한 교육 기술의 통합에 이름.

[4]Personal computers have reached a similar level of familiarity / for a great many users, / but certainly not for all.
(S: Personal computers / V: have reached / O: a similar level of familiarity)
개인 컴퓨터는 비슷한 수준의 친숙함에 도달했다 / 아주 많은 사용자들에게 / 하지만 분명 모두에게는 아니다
↳ **예 2:** 컴퓨터 기술은 모두에게 친숙하지는 않음 → 완전한 교육 기술의 통합에 이르지는 못함.

[5]New and emerging technologies often introduce / both fascination and frustration / with users.
(S: New and emerging technologies / V: introduce / O: both fascination and frustration)
새롭고 최근에 만들어진 기술은 흔히 접하게 한다 / 매력과 좌절감 둘 다를 / 사용자들에게
↳ **예 2의 부연 설명:** 새로운 기술은 매력적이지만 친숙해지기 전에는 좌절감을 주기도 함.

해석

[1]교육 기술의 성공적인 통합은 그 기술이 사용자에 의해 학습이나 교육, 또는 수행의 눈에 띄지 않는 촉진제로 여겨지는 것으로 특징지어진다. [2]사용되고 있는 기술에서 기술이 도움이 되는 교육적 목적으로 초점이 옮겨가면, 그러면 그 기술은 편하고 신뢰받는 요소가 되어 가며, 성공적으로 통합되는 것으로 여겨질 수 있다. [3]어떤 것들은 돌리는 방법을 사용하고, 어떤 것들은 위에 달린 누르는 버튼을 사용하며, 또한 다른 변형(된 방법)들도 있듯이 관련된 방법이 가지각색이지만, 볼펜 사용에 대해 더 생각하는 사람은 거의 없다.(▶ 더 생각할 것 없이 볼펜을 친숙하게 사용한다는 의미) [4]개인 컴퓨터는 아주 많은 사용자들에게 (볼펜과) 비슷한 수준의 친숙함에 도달했지만, 분명 모두에게는 아니다. [5]새롭고 최근에 만들어진 기술은 흔히 사용자들에게 매력과 좌절감 둘 다를 접하게 한다. [6]학습, 교육 또는 수행을 촉진하는 데 있어서 사용자의 초점이 기술의 사용이 아니라 기술 그 자체에 맞춰져 있는 한, 그러면 적어도 그 사용자에게는 그 기술이 성공적으로 통합되었다고 결론을 내려서는 안 된다.

어휘

integration 통합
cf. integrate 통합하다[되다]; 전체로 합치다
mark 특징짓다; 표시(하다)
facilitator 촉진제
instruction 교육; 설명; 지시
serve 도움이 되다; 봉사하다, 섬기다
element 요소, 성분; 원소
second thought 다시 생각함, 재고(再考)
mechanism 방법, 메커니즘; 기계 장치; 구조
vary 가지각색이다; 다르다; 바꾸다
cf. variation 변형; 변화
twist 돌리다, 비틀다; 구부리다
familiarity 친숙함; 친밀감
emerging 최근에 만들어진, 신흥의, 신생의

[6] As long as **the user's focus is on the technology itself / rather than its use** / in promoting learning, instruction, or performance, //
부사절 접속사(~하는 한) (= the technology's) in의 O(동명사구)
사용자의 초점이 기술 그 자체에 맞춰져 있는 한 / 그것(기술)의 사용이 아니라 / 학습, 교육 또는 수행을 촉진하는 데 있어서 //

then one ought not to conclude // that the technology has been successfully integrated — / at least for that user.
S V 명사절 접속사 S' V' (ought not to conclude의 O(명사절))
그러면 결론을 내려서는 안 된다 // 그 기술이 성공적으로 통합되었다고 / 적어도 그 사용자에게는
↳ **결론:** 사용자의 초점이 목적보다 기술에 있는 경우 교육 기술이 성공적으로 통합되었다고 볼 수 없음.

introduce (모르던 것을) 접하게 하다, 소개하다
fascination 매력(있는 것)
A rather than B B라기보다는 A
promote 촉진하다; 홍보하다; 승진시키다
[선택지] employ 사용하다; 고용하다
outdated 시대에 뒤진, 구식인
involuntarily 무의식중에, 모르는 사이에
get used to A A에 익숙해지다
misuse 오용(하다); 악용[남용]하다

정답 가이드

빈칸 문장으로 보아, 학습 등을 촉진하는 데 있어서, '어떤 조건 하에서는' 그 기술이 성공적으로 통합된 것이 아니라는 것인지를 추론해야 한다. 교육 기술의 성공적인 통합은 그 기술이 눈에 띄지 않는 촉진제가 되는 것이라고 했다. 즉 초점이 기술의 교육적 목적으로 옮겨가야 한다는 것이다. 이는 볼펜의 사용법(기술)을 특별히 염두에 두지 않고 볼펜을 사용하는(기술의 교육적 목적) 예와 같다. 따라서 기술이 성공적으로 통합되었다고 볼 수 없는 조건으로 적절한 것은 이와 반대되는 내용인 ② 'the user's focus is on the technology itself rather than its use(사용자의 초점이 기술의 사용이 아니라 기술 그 자체에 맞춰져 있다)'이다.

오답 클리닉

① the user successfully achieves familiarity with the technology (31%)
사용자가 성공적으로 그 기술에 대한 친숙함을 얻는다
사용자가 기술에 친숙해진 것은 오히려 교육 기술이 성공적으로 통합된 경우로 볼 수 있으므로 글의 내용과 반대됨.

The 주의 빈칸이 있는 문장을 해석한 후, 글의 주제와 반대되는 내용이 빈칸에 들어가야 함을 파악해야 한다.

③ the user continues to employ outdated educational techniques (13%) 사용자가 계속해서 시대에 뒤진 교육 기술을 사용한다
교육 기술이 구식인지 신식인지에 따라 통합 여부가 달라지는 것이 아님.
④ the user involuntarily gets used to the misuse of the technology (10%) 사용자가 무의식중에 그 기술의 오용에 익숙해진다
기술을 잘못 사용하는 것에 대해서는 언급되지 않음.
⑤ the user's preference for interaction with other users persists (4%)
다른 사용자와의 상호 작용에 대한 사용자의 선호가 지속된다
사용자 간 상호 작용이 기술 통합에 영향을 준다는 내용은 없음.

03 + 문장 넣기 〈23학년도 6월 모평 39번 | 정답률 40%〉 ③

구문분석 & 직독직해 생물 집단 탐지 역학의 특징

주제문
[1] The dynamics (of collective detection) / have an interesting feature.
S V O
역학은 (집단 탐지의) / 흥미로운 특징이 있다
↳ 집단 탐지의 역학은 흥미로움.

[2] Which cue(s) do individuals use / as evidence (of predator attack)?
O S 전치사(~로(서)) as의 O(명사구) (V: do ... use)
개체들은 어느 단서를 사용하는가 / 증거로 (포식자 공격의)

[3] In some cases, / when an individual detects a predator, // its best response is to seek shelter.
부사절 접속사(시간) S' V' O' S V C (its = an individual's)
어떤 경우에는 / 개체가 포식자를 탐지할 때 // 그것(개체)의 최선의 반응은 피난처를 찾는 것이다

(①) [4] Departure (from the group) / may signal danger / to nonvigilant animals /
S V_1 O_1
이탈은 (무리로부터의) / 위험 신호를 보낼 수도 있다 / 경계하지 않는 동물들에게 /
and (may) cause // what appears to be a coordinated flushing of prey / from the area.
V_2 관계대명사 V' C' ((may) cause의 O(명사절))
그리고 야기할 수도 있다 // 먹잇감(동물)의 조직화된 날아오름으로 보이는 것을 / 그 구역에서
↳ **세부 사항:** 개체는 포식자를 발견하면 무리를 이탈해 경계하지 않는 동물에게 위험 신호를 보낼 수 있음.

(②) [5] Studies (on dark-eyed juncos (a type of bird)) / support the view // that nonvigilant animals attend / to departures (of individual group mates) //
S(복수) V(복수) O 동격 접속사 S' V' (= 동격절)
연구는 (검은 눈을 가진 검은방울새(새의 한 종류)에 관한) / 견해를 뒷받침한다 // 경계하지 않는 동물들이 주목한다는 / 이탈에 (개별적인 무리 친구들의) //

해석

[1]집단 탐지의 역학은 흥미로운 특징이 있다. [2]개체들은 어느 단서를 포식자 공격의 증거로 사용하는가? [3]어떤 경우에는 개체가 포식자를 탐지할 때 그것(개체)의 최선의 반응은 피난처를 찾는 것이다. (①) [4]무리로부터의 이탈은 경계하지 않는 동물들에게 위험 신호를 보내서 먹잇감(동물)의 조직화된 날아오름으로 보이는 것을 그 구역에서 야기할 수도 있다. (②) [5]검은 눈을 가진 검은방울새(새의 한 종류)에 관한 연구는 경계하지 않는 동물들이 개별적인 무리 친구들의 이탈에 주목하지만 여러 개체의 이탈은 경계하지 않는 개체에 더 큰 도망 반응을 일으킨다는 견해를 뒷받침한다. (③ [6]이것은 정보 신뢰성의 관점에서 타당하다.) [7]무리 구성원 하나가 이탈한다면, 그것은 포식 위협과 거의 관련이 없는 여러 이유로 그렇게 했을지도 모른다. (④) [8]경계하지 않는 동물들이 단 하나의 구성원이 무리를 떠날 때마다 도망한다면, 그것들(경계하지 않는 동물들)은 포식자가 전혀 없는 (거짓 경보인) 때에도 자주 반응할 것이다.(▶ 한 개체가 이탈할 때마다 달아난다면 거짓 경보에 너무 자주 반응하는 것이 되어 정보 신뢰성은 떨어짐을 의미) (⑤) [9]반면에 여러 개체가 동시에 무리를 이탈할 때, 진짜 위협이 존재할 가능성이 훨씬 더 크다.

↱ 동격절₂ ⊶ 주어진 문장의 This가 가리키는 내용.

but that the departure (of multiple individuals) / causes a greater escape response / in the nonvigilant individuals.

동격 접속사 S′(단수) V′(단수) O′

그러나 이탈은 (여러 개체의) / 더 큰 도망 반응을 일으킨다는 / 경계하지 않는 개체에

↳ **예:** 검은방울새의 무리 내 경계하지 않는 동물들은 여러 개체가 이탈할수록 더 큰 도망 반응을 보임.

⊶ This가 가리키는 내용이 앞에 제시되어야 함.

(③ [6]This makes sense / from the perspective (of information reliability).)

S V

이것은 타당하다 / 관점에서 (정보 신뢰성의)

↳ 여러 개체의 이탈이 더 큰 도망 반응을 일으키는 것은 정보 신뢰성 관점에서 타당함.

★<might have p.p.>: ~했을지도 모른다 ★<have little to do with>: ~와 거의 관련이 없다

[7]If one group member departs, // it might have done so / for *a number of reasons* [that have little to do with predation threat].

부사절 접속사(조건) S V 주격 관계대명사

무리 구성원 하나가 이탈한다면 // 그것은 그렇게 했을지도 모른다 / 여러 이유로 [포식 위협과 거의 관련이 없는]

★가정법 과거 <If+S′+동사의 과거형, S+would+동사원형>으로 현재 사실의 반대를 가정함.

(④) [8]If nonvigilant animals escaped // each time a single member left the group, //

부사절 접속사(~할 때마다) S″ V″ O″

경계하지 않는 동물들이 도망한다면 // 단 하나의 구성원이 무리를 떠날 때마다 //

↱ (= nonvigilant animals)

they would frequently respond // when there was no predator (a false alarm).

S V 부사절 접속사(시간) V′ S′

그것들(경계하지 않는 동물들)은 자주 반응할 것이다 // 포식자가 전혀 없는 (거짓 경보인) 때에도

↳ **대조 A(한 개체의 개별 이탈):** 포식 위협 때문이 아닐 수도 있음.

(⑤) [9]On the other hand, / when several individuals depart the group at the same time, // a true threat is much more likely to be present.

부사절 접속사(시간) S′ V′ O′

S V C

반면에 / 여러 개체가 동시에 무리를 이탈할 때 // 진짜 위협이 존재할 가능성이 훨씬 더 크다

↳ **대조 B(여러 개체의 동시 이탈):** 진짜 위협이 존재할 가능성이 더 큼.

어휘

dynamics 역학; 원동력
collective 집단의; 공동의
detection 탐지, 간파
cf. detect 탐지하다
feature 특징(으로 삼다); 특집 (기사)
cue 단서, 신호
shelter 피난(처)
departure 이탈; 출발
cf. depart 이탈하다; 출발하다
signal 신호(를 보내다)
coordinate 조직화하다; 조화를 이루게 하다
attend 주목[주의]하다; 참석하다
make sense 타당하다; 이해가 되다
perspective 관점
reliability 신뢰성, 신빙성
alarm 경보(음)
present 존재하는; 현재의; 참석한

정답 가이드

주어진 문장은 이것(This)이 정보 신뢰성의 관점에서 타당하다는 내용으로, 주어진 문장 앞에는 This가 가리키는 내용이 제시되어야 하고, 뒤로는 그것이 타당하다고 말할 수 있는 이유가 설명되어야 한다. 글의 첫 부분부터 읽어보면, 개체가 포식자를 탐지할 때 피난처를 찾거나 무리로부터 이탈해서 경계하지 않은 동물들이 조직화된 날아오름을 하게 한다고 했다. 이에 대한 예로 검은방울새의 연구가 제시되었고 이 연구는 여러 개체의 이탈이 더 큰 도망 반응을 일으킨다고 했으므로, 주어진 문장을 ③에 넣고 앞 내용을 This로 받아 정보 신뢰성의 관점에서 타당함을 언급하는 흐름이 자연스럽다. ③ 뒤부터는 그것이 왜 타당한지를 설명하므로 주어진 문장이 들어가기에 가장 적절한 곳은 ③이다.

오답 클리닉

① (3%) 포식자를 발견하면 피난처를 찾는다는 내용이 무리 이탈로 연결되며, 이는 위험 신호로 작용할 수 있다고 설명한다.

② (14%) 검은방울새를 예로 들어 여러 개체가 이탈하면 더 큰 도망 반응을 보인다는 앞 문장의 견해를 설명한다.

④ (27%) 한 개체의 개별 이탈은 포식 위협과 관계가 거의 없을 수 있어서 경계하지 않는 동물들이 매번 도망하지 않는 것이라고 부연 설명하는 내용이다.

⑤ (17%) On the other hand가 문장을 이끌며 앞 문장과 대조되는, 여러 개체가 동시에 이탈하는 경우의 정보 신뢰성을 설명하는 내용이다.

01 ✦ 함의 추론 (22학년도 6월 모평 21번 | 정답률 56%) ②

구문분석 & 직독직해

비즈니스 대응적인 일은 보류하고 창조적인 일에 집중하기

주제문

[1] *The single most important change* [(which[that]) you can make / in your working habits] / is to switch to creative work first, reactive work second. 🔑 일을 할 때, 창조적인 일 먼저, 대응적인 일을 그 이후에 해야 함.
(S / 목적격 관계대명사 생략 / V / C)

단 한 가지 가장 중요한 변화는 [여러분이 만들어 낼 수 있는 / 일하는 습관에서] / 창조적인 일 먼저, 대응적인 일은 그다음으로 전환하는 것이다

↳ 일할 때 창조적인 일 먼저, 대응적인 일은 나중에 해야 함.

(= to switch ~ second)
[2] This means / blocking off a large chunk of time every day / for creative work / on your own priorities, / with the phone and e-mail off.
(S / V / O)

이것은 의미한다 / 매일 상당히 많은 시간을 차단하는 것을 / 창조적인 일을 위해 / 여러분 자신의 우선순위에 따라 / 전화기와 이메일을 끈 채

↳ **부연 설명:** 창조적인 일을 위해 외부 접촉을 차단함을 의미함.

★<used to+동사원형>: 예전에는 ~였다((과거의 상태)); ~하곤 했다((과거의 습관))
[3] I used to be a frustrated writer.
나는 예전에는 좌절감을 느끼는 작가였다

[4] Making this switch / turned me into a productive writer.
(S(동명사구) / V / O)
이런 전환을 하는 것이 / 나를 생산적인 작가가 되게 했다

↳ **필자의 예:** 이 전환이 자신을 생산적인 작가로 변화시킴.

[5] Yet / there wasn't *a single day* [when I sat down / to write an article, blog post, or book chapter / without a string of people waiting for me to get back to them].
(관계부사 / 목적(~하기 위해) / 동명사 waiting의 의미상 주어 / to get back의 의미상 주어 / (= a string of people))

하지만 / 단 하루도 없었다 [내가 앉아 있던 날은 / 기사나 블로그 게시글 혹은 책의 한 챕터를 쓰기 위해 / 일련의 사람들이 내가 그들에게 나중에 다시 연락하기를 기다리는 것 없이]

↳ 창조적인 일을 할 때 계속해서 대응적인 일이 생김.

[6] It wasn't easy, / and it still isn't (easy), // particularly when I get *phone messages* (beginning "I sent you an e-mail *two hours ago*...!")
(반복어 생략 / 현재분사구)

그것은 쉽지 않았다 / 그리고 아직도 쉽지 않다 // 특히 내가 전화 메시지를 받을 때는 ("'2시간 전에' 이메일을 보냈어요…!"라고 시작하는)

↳ 연락에 답하지 않는 것은 쉬운 일이 아님.

[7] By definition, / this approach goes against the grain / of others' expectations and *the pressures* [(which[that]) they put on you].
(목적격 관계대명사 생략 (= others))

당연히 / 이러한 접근 방식은 맞지 않는다 / 다른 사람들의 기대와 압박에 [그들이 여러분에게 가하는]

↳ 답을 기다리는 사람들의 기대에 어긋나기 때문임.

[8] It takes willpower / to switch off the world, / even for an hour.
(가주어 V / O / 진주어)
(~은) 의지가 필요하다 / 세상에 대해 신경을 끄는 것에는 / 단 한 시간 동안이라도

[9] It feels uncomfortable, // and sometimes people get upset.
(= to switch ~ world)
그것은 불편한 느낌이 든다 // 그리고 때로 사람들이 화가 나기도 한다

↳ 답을 하지 않는 데에는 의지가 필요하고 편하지 않음.

해석

[1]여러분이 일하는 습관에서 만들어 낼 수 있는 단 한 가지 가장 중요한 변화는 창조적인 일 먼저, 대응적인 일은 그다음으로 전환하는 것이다. [2]이것은 전화기와 이메일을 끈 채, 여러분 자신의 우선순위에 따라 창조적인 일을 위해 매일 상당히 많은 시간을 차단하는 것을 의미한다. [3]나는 예전에는 좌절감을 느끼는 작가였다. [4]이런 전환을 하는 것이 나를 생산적인 작가가 되게 했다. [5]하지만 일련의 사람들이 내가 그들에게 나중에 다시 연락하기를 기다리는 것 없이 기사나 블로그 게시글 혹은 책의 한 챕터를 쓰기 위해 내가 앉아 있던 날은 단 하루도 없었다. [6]그것은 쉽지 않았고, 특히 "'2시간 전에' 이메일을 보냈어요…!"라고 시작하는 전화 메시지를 받을 때는 아직도 쉽지 않다. [7]당연히, 이러한 접근 방식은 다른 사람들의 기대와 그들이 여러분에게 가하는 압박에 맞지 않는다. [8]단 한 시간 동안이라도 세상에 대해 신경을 끄는 것에는 의지가 필요하다. [9]그것은 불편한 느낌이 들고, 때로 사람들이 화가 나기도 한다. [10]그러나 빈 수신함을 위해(▶ 모든 외부 연락에 대응해 수신함을 비운다는 의미) 여러분의 꿈을 포기하는 것보다, 사소한 것에 대해 소수의 사람들을 실망시키는 것이 낫다. [11]그렇게 하지 않으면, 여러분은 전문성이라는 환상을 위해 자신의 잠재력을 희생하고 있는 것이다.

어휘

switch to ~로 전환하다
cf. switch off 신경을 끄다; 스위치를 끄다
reactive 대응적인; 반응을 나타내는
block off ~을 차단하다[막다]
chunk 상당히 많은 양; 덩어리
priority 우선순위
productive 생산적인
article 기사, 글
a string of 일련의
get back to ~에게 나중에 다시 연락하다; ~로 돌아가다
by definition 당연히, 분명히; 정의상, 의미상
go against the grain 맞지 않다, 거스르다
willpower 의지(력)
abandon 포기하다, 버리다
sacrifice 희생하다; 희생(물)
illusion 환상, 환각
professionalism 전문성
[선택지] innovative 혁신적인, 획기적인
attempt to-v v하려고 시도하다

🔑 문장 1의 주제가 반복됨.

[10]But / it's better / to disappoint a few people over small things, / than to abandon your dreams / for an empty inbox.

가주어 V C　진주어(to-v구)　★진주어에서 to disappoint와 to abandon이 비교됨.

그러나 / (~이) 낫다 / 사소한 것에 대해 소수의 사람들을 실망시키는 것이 / 여러분의 꿈을 포기하는 것보다 / 빈 수신함을 위해

↳ **결론:** 꿈을 포기하느니 사람들을 실망시키는 것이 나음.

[11]Otherwise, / you're sacrificing your potential / for the illusion of professionalism.

(= If not)

그렇게 하지 않으면 / 여러분은 자신의 잠재력을 희생하고 있는 것이다 / 전문성이라는 환상을 위해

↳ 대응적인 일을 우선시하는 것은 어리석음.

정답 가이드

창조적인 일을 할 때는 방해받지 않도록 전화기나 이메일을 꺼 두라는 내용의 글이다. 같은 맥락에서 빈 수신함을 위해, 즉 모든 외부 연락에 대응해서 수신함을 비워내면서 자신의 꿈을 포기하는 것보다 답을 기다리는 소수의 사람을 실망시키는 것이 낫다고 했다. 따라서 밑줄 친 부분이 의미하는 바로 가장 적절한 것은 ② 'attempting to satisfy other people's demands(다른 사람들의 요구를 충족하려고 시도하는 것)'이다.

오답 클리닉

① following an innovative course of action (9%)
혁신적인 행동 방침(×)을 따르는 것 (9%)
혁신적인 행동에 대해서는 언급되지 않음.

③ completing challenging work without mistakes (7%)
실수 없이(×) 도전적인 일(×)을 완수하는 것 (7%)
실수 없이 완벽하게 도전적인 일을 완수하는 것은 언급되지 않음.

④ removing social ties to maintain a mental balance (17%)
정신적 균형을 유지하기 위해(×) 사회적 유대를 제거(×)하는 것 (17%)
빈 수신함은 바로바로 답하는 것을 뜻하며 이는 사회적 유대를 제거하기보다는 유지하는 쪽에 가까움. 또한 정신적 균형은 언급되지 않은 내용임.

The 주의 창의적인 일을 우선하기 위해 답을 미뤄두라는 내용을 사회적 유대를 없애라는 것으로 오해하지 않도록 주의가 필요하다.

⑤ securing enough opportunities for social networking (11%)
소셜 네트워킹을 위한 충분한 기회를 확보하는 것(×)
사람들에게 답을 보내는 것을 소셜 네트워킹으로 본다고 해도 그것을 위해 기회를 확보하라는 내용은 유추할 수 없음.

02 + 빈칸 추론 〈21학년도 대수능 33번 | 정답률 54%〉　①

구문분석 & 직독직해　과학 환경과 경험에 따라 다르게 발달하는 뇌

[1]Thanks to newly developed neuroimaging technology, /
새로 개발된 신경 촬영법 기술 덕분에 /

we now have access (to *the specific brain changes* [that occur during learning]).

S V O　주격 관계대명사

우리는 이제 접근 방법이 있다 (특정한 뇌 변화에의 [학습 중에 일어나는])

↳ **도입:** 학습 중 일어나는 뇌 변화를 알 수 있음.

주제문

[2]Even though all of our brains contain the same basic structures, // our neural networks are as unique / as our fingerprints.

부사절 접속사(양보) S′ V′ O′　S V C

우리의 뇌는 모두 같은 기본 구조를 가지고 있긴 하지만 // 우리의 신경망은 독특하다 / 우리의 지문처럼

↳ 뇌의 기본 구조는 같아도 신경망은 사람마다 다름.

[3]The latest developmental neuroscience research has shown // that the brain is much more malleable throughout life / than previously assumed; //

S V　→ has shown의 O(명사절)　명사절 접속사 S′ V′ C′

★much는 비교급을 수식하는 부사이며, 이 외에도 far, a lot, even 등이 있음.

최근의 발달 신경과학 연구는 보여 줬다 // 뇌가 평생 동안 훨씬 더 순응성이 있다는 것을 / 이전에 생각되었던 것보다 //

it develops / in response to its own processes, / to its immediate and distant "environments," / and to its past and current situations.

→ (= the brain)　S V　전치사구 병렬　전치사구 병렬　전치사구 병렬

🔑 뇌는 개인의 환경에 따라 다르게 발달함.

그것(뇌)은 발달한다 / 그것 자신의 처리 과정에 응하여 / 그것에 아주 가까이에 있는 '환경'과 먼 '환경'에 (응하여) / 그리고 그것의 과거와 현재의 상황에 (응하여)

↳ **논거 1(연구 내용):** 순응성이 높은 뇌는 개인이 처한 환경에 따라 변화함.

해석

[1]새로 개발된 신경 촬영법 기술 덕분에, 우리는 이제 학습 중에 일어나는 특정한 뇌 변화에의 접근 방법이 있다. [2]우리의 뇌는 모두 같은 기본 구조를 가지고 있긴 하지만, 우리의 신경망은 우리의 지문처럼 독특하다. [3]최근의 발달 신경과학 연구는 뇌가 이전에 생각되었던 것보다 평생 동안 훨씬 더 순응성이 있다는 것을 보여 줬으며, 그것(뇌)은 그것 자신의 처리 과정, 그것에 아주 가까이에 있는 '환경'과 먼 '환경', 그리고 그것의 과거와 현재의 상황에 응하여 발달한다. [4]뇌는 기존의 신경망을 확립하거나 개선하는 것을 통해 의미를 만들어 내려고 한다. [5]우리가 새로운 사실이나 기술을 배울 때, 우리의 뉴런들은 연결된 정보망을 형성하기 위해 소통한다. [6]이러한 지식이나 기술을 사용하는 것은 유사한 미래 자극이 다른 것들보다 더 빠르고 효율적으로 이동하게 하기 위해 구조적 변화를 야기한다. [7]고활동 시냅스 연결이 안정되고 강화되는 반면에, 사용이 상대적으로 적은 연결은 약해지고 결국에는 잘린다. [8]이런 방식으로, 우리의 뇌는 우리 자신의 경험의 이력에 의해 형태가 만들어진다.

🔑 뇌는 기존 신경망을 확립하거나 개선함.

[4]The brain seeks to create meaning / through establishing or refining existing neural networks.
S V O
뇌는 의미를 만들어 내려고 한다 / 기존의 신경망을 확립하거나 개선하는 것을 통해
↳ **논거 2:** 뇌는 기존 신경망을 확립하거나 개선해 의미를 만들어 냄.

[5]When we learn a new fact or skill, // our neurons communicate / to form networks of connected information. 🔑 새로운 것을 배울 때 정보망을 형성함.
부사절 접속사(시간) S V 목적(~하기 위해)
우리가 새로운 사실이나 기술을 배울 때 // 우리의 뉴런들은 소통한다 / 연결된 정보망을 형성하기 위해

🔑 새로 배운 지식과 기술 사용으로 구조적 변화가 일어남. ★<allow+O+to-v>: O가 v하게 하다
[6]Using this knowledge or skill / results in structural changes / to allow similar future impulses / to travel more quickly and efficiently / than others.
S(동명사구) V(단수) O 목적(~하기 위해)
이러한 지식이나 기술을 사용하는 것은 / 구조적 변화를 야기한다 / 유사한 미래 자극이 (~하게) 하기 위해 / 더 빠르고 효율적으로 이동하게 / 다른 것들보다

[7]High-activity synaptic connections are stabilized and strengthened, // while connections (with relatively low use) / are weakened and eventually pruned.
S V 부사절 접속사(대조) S′(복수) V′(복수)
고활동 시냅스 연결이 안정되고 강화된다 // 반면에 연결은 (사용이 상대적으로 적은) / 약해지고 결국에는 잘린다
↳ **논거 2의 부연 설명(뇌의 변화 과정):** 새로운 지식 학습 → 정보망 형성 → 고활동 시냅스 강화/저활동 시냅스 약화 → 뇌의 구조적 변화

[8]In this way, / our brains are **sculpted / by our own history of experiences.**
S V
이런 방식으로 / 우리의 뇌는 형태가 만들어진다 / 우리 자신의 경험의 이력에 의해
↳ **결론(주제문 재진술):** 뇌는 개인의 경험에 따라 다르게 발달함.

어휘

neuroimaging 신경 촬영법
specific 특정한; 구체적인, 명확한
neural 신경의
cf. neuron 뉴런, 신경세포
fingerprint 지문
in response to ~에 응하여[답하여]
immediate 아주 가까이에 있는; 즉각적인; 당면한
distant 먼, (멀리) 떨어져 있는
establish 확립하다; 설립[수립]하다
refine 개선하다; 정제하다
existing 기존의
impulse 자극, 충격; 충동
stabilize 안정시키다
strengthen 강화하다
relatively 상대적으로, 비교적
sculpt 형태[형상]을 만들다; 조각하다
[선택지] gear (맞게) 조정[조절]하다; 준비하다; 《기계》 기어, 톱니바퀴
twin 밀접하게 연결시키다; 쌍둥이
organ 기관, 장기
portray 그리다, 묘사하다; (역할을) 연기하다
seat 근원; 기저(부); 자리

정답 가이드

빈칸 문장이 In this way로 시작하므로 직전 문장을 통해 this way가 '활동이 활발하면 시냅스 연결이 강화되고, 그렇지 않으면 약해지는 방식'을 의미한다는 것을 먼저 파악한다. 이후 이런 방식으로 우리의 뇌가 '어떠하다'는 것인지를 추론해야 한다. 앞부분에서 뇌는 지문처럼 독특하며 환경에 반응하여 변화하는 존재로서, 의미 형성을 위해 기존 신경망을 확립하거나 개선시켜 나간다고 했다. 더 자세히 말하면, 우리는 새로운 것을 배울 때 연결된 정보망을 구축하는데, 미래에 유사한 정보가 더 효율적으로 전달될 수 있도록 뇌에 구조적 변화가 일어난다. 시냅스 연결이 자주 사용된 곳은 강해지고 그렇지 않은 곳은 약해지거나 없어지는데, 이는 '뇌가 우리 경험에 따라 변화한다'는 것이므로 빈칸에 들어갈 말로 가장 적절한 것은 ① 'sculpted by our own history of experiences(우리 자신의 경험의 이력에 의해 형태가 만들어진다)'이다.

오답 클리닉

② designed to maintain their initial structures (18%)
그것의 최초의 구조를 유지하도록 설계된다
뇌는 구조적으로 변화한다고 했으므로 글의 내용과 반대됨.
③ geared toward strengthening recent memories (16%)
최근의 기억을 강화하도록 조정된다
뇌의 기억력 강화는 구조 변화와 관계 없음.
④ twinned with the development of other organs (5%)
다른 기관의 발달과 밀접하게 연결된다
다른 신체 기관은 언급되지 않음.
⑤ portrayed as the seat of logical and creative thinking (7%)
논리적이고 창의적인 사고의 근원으로 그려진다
뇌의 논리성이나 창의성에 관한 내용이 아님.

03 ✦ 무관 문장 (22학년도 9월 모평 35번 | 정답률 79%) ③

구문분석 & 직독직해 경제 경제학의 관점에서 본 이민 결정

[1]A variety of theoretical perspectives provide insight (into immigration).
S V O
다양한 이론적 관점은 통찰을 제공한다 (이민에 대한)

주제문 🔑 경제학의 관점에서 이민을 설명함.
[2]*Economics*, // (which assumes // that actors engage in utility maximization), / represents one framework.
S 관계대명사(보충 설명) V′ O′(명사절) V O
경제학은 // (추정하는 // 행위자들이 효용 극대화에 참여한다고) / 하나의 틀을 설명한다
↳ 경제학이 이민에 관한 하나의 틀을 제시함.

해석

[1]다양한 이론적 관점은 이민에 대한 통찰을 제공한다. [2]행위자들이 효용 극대화에 참여한다고 추정하는 경제학은 하나의 틀을 설명한다. ① [3]이 관점에서 개인은 합리적인 행위자라고, 즉 그들이 떠나는 것의 비용 및 편익과 비교하여 주어진 지역(본국)에 남는 것의 편익뿐만 아니라 비용에 대한 자신의 평가에 근거하여 이주 결정을 내린다고 추정된다. ② [4]편익은 단기적이고 장기적인 금전적 이득, 안전, 그리고 문화적 표현의 더 큰 자유를 포함할 수

① [3]From this perspective, / it is assumed // that individuals are rational actors, //
가주어 V 진주어(명사절)
이 관점에서 / (~라고) 추정된다 // 개인은 합리적인 행위자라고 //
*<A as well as B>: B뿐만 아니라 A도
i.e., that they make migration decisions / based on their assessment (of the costs as well as benefits of remaining in a given area / versus the costs and benefits of leaving).
즉, 그들이 이주 결정을 내린다고 / 자신의 평가에 근거하여 (주어진 지역(본국)에 남는 것의 편익뿐만 아니라 비용에 대한 / 떠나는 것의 비용 및 편익과 비교하여))
↳ **세부 사항:** 경제학의 관점에서 개인은 떠나는 것과 남는 것의 비용 및 편익을 비교 평가해서 이주를 결정하는 합리적 행위자임.

② [4]Benefits may include / but are not limited to / short-term and long-term monetary gains, safety, and greater freedom of cultural expression.
S V1 V2 may include와 are not limited to의 공통 O
편익은 포함할 수도 있다 / 그러나 ~에 국한되지는 않는다 / 단기적이고 장기적인 금전적 이득, 안전, 그리고 문화적 표현의 더 큰 자유
↳ **부연 설명(편익):** 장단기적 금전적 이득, 안전, 문화적 표현의 자유 등을 포함.

🔑 이주의 비용-편익과 무관한 돈이 많은 사람의 소비 경향에 관한 내용.

③ [5]People (with greater financial benefits) / tend to use their money / to show off their social status / by purchasing luxurious items.
S V 목적(~하기 위해)
<by v-ing>: v함으로써
사람들은 (더 큰 재정상의 이득을 가진) / 돈을 쓰는 경향이 있다 / 자신의 사회적 지위를 과시하기 위해 / 사치품을 구입함으로써
↳ 돈이 많은 사람들은 사치품을 구입해 사회적 지위를 과시하는 경향이 있음.

④ [6]Individual costs include / but are not limited to / the expense (of travel), / uncertainty (of living in a foreign land), / difficulty (of adapting to a different language), / uncertainty (about a different culture), / and the great concern (about living in a new land).
S V1 V2 include와 are not limited to의 공통 O
개인적 비용은 포함한다 / 그러나 ~에 국한되지는 않는다 / 비용 (이동의) / 불확실성 (외국에서 사는 것의) / 어려움 (다른 언어에 적응하는 것의) / 불확실성 (다른 문화에 대한) / 그리고 큰 염려 (새로운 나라에서 사는 것에 대한)
↳ **부연 설명(개인적 비용):** 이동 비용, 각종 불확실성과 어려움, 염려 등을 포함.

⑤ [7]*Psychic costs* (associated with separation (from family, friends), / and the fear of the unknown) / also should be taken into account / in cost-benefit assessments.
S 과거분사구 V
심적 비용은 (헤어짐과 관련된 (가족, 친구와의) / 그리고 미지의 것에 대한 두려움(과 관련된)) / 또한 고려되어야 한다 / 비용-편익 평가에서
↳ **부연 설명(심적 비용):** 부정적인 심적 비용도 고려해야 함.

도 있으나 이에 국한되지는 않는다. ③ [5]더 큰 재정상의 이득을 가진 사람들은 사치품을 구입함으로써 자신의 사회적 지위를 과시하기 위해 돈을 쓰는 경향이 있다. ④ [6]개인적 비용은 이동 비용, 외국에서 사는 것의 불확실성, 다른 언어에 적응하는 것의 어려움, 다른 문화에 대한 불확실성, 그리고 새로운 나라에서 사는 것에 대한 큰 염려를 포함하지만 이에 국한되지는 않는다. ⑤ [7]가족, 친구와의 헤어짐과 미지의 것에 대한 두려움과 관련된 심적 비용 또한 비용-편익 평가에서 고려되어야 한다.

어휘

theoretical 이론적인; 이론상으로 (가능한)
perspective 관점, 시각
insight 통찰(력); 이해
immigration 이민, 이주
engage in ~에 참여하다; ~에 종사하다
utility 효용, 유용성
maximization 극대화, 최대 활용
represent 설명하다; 대표하다
framework 틀, 뼈대, 구조
rational 합리적인, 이성적인
migration 이주, 이동
assessment 평가
versus ~와 비교하여
monetary 금전적인
financial 재정(상)의; 금융(상)의
show off ~을 과시하다
status 지위, 신분
expense 비용, 경비
associated with ~와 관련된
separation 헤어짐; 분리, 구분
take A into account A를 고려하다

정답 가이드

도입 부분에서 행위자들이 효용을 극대화하려 한다고 상정하는 경제학의 관점에서 이민에 대한 하나의 틀을 설명한다고 했으므로 이에 대한 설명이 이어져야 한다. 개인은 합리적인 행위자로서 이민을 떠나는 것과 본국에 남는 것의 비용과 편익을 고려해 이민을 결정한다고 한 후, 편익과 비용에 포함되는 구체적인 요소들의 예를 나열하여 설명하고 있다. 그런데, ③은 큰 재정상의 이익을 가진 사람들이 사회적 지위를 과시하기 위해 사치품을 구입한다는 내용으로 글의 흐름과 무관하다.

The 주의 ③ 앞의 두 문장에서 반복된 benefits를 무관 문장에서 financial benefits로 넣어 마치 내용이 연결되는 것처럼 보이도록 한 것에 주의한다.

오답 클리닉

① (1%) this perspective는 앞에서 언급된 경제학의 관점을 의미하며, 그 관점에서 개인의 이민 결정을 설명하는 내용이 자연스럽게 연결된다.
② (5%) 앞에서 이민 결정 시 평가한다고 언급한 편익과 비용 중, 편익에 포함되는 요소를 설명한다.
④ (11%) 이어서 비용에 포함되는 요소를 설명한다.
⑤ (3%) 추가로 고려해야 할 심적 비용을 설명한다.

01 ✦ 글의 요지 〈23학년도 9월 모평 22번 | 정답률 92%〉 ⑤

구문분석 & 직독직해

법 조세 입법에 도덕적 목표 설정의 중요성

[1]Historically, / drafters of tax legislation(S) are(V) attentive(C1) to questions (of economics and history), / and less attentive(C2) to moral questions.

역사상, / 조세 입법 입안자들은 문제에 주의를 기울인다 (경제학과 역사의) / 그리고 도덕적 문제에는 주의를 덜 기울인(다)

[2]Questions of morality(S) are often pushed(V) to the side / in legislative debate, / labeled too controversial, too difficult to answer, or, worst of all, irrelevant to the project.

분사구문(= as they are labeled ~)

도덕성에 관한 문제는 종종 옆으로 밀려난다 / 입법 토론에서 /

너무 논란이 많거나, 답변하기 너무 어렵거나, 아니면 최악의 경우, 계획과 무관한 것으로 분류되면서

↳ **잘못된 경향:** 조세 입법 시 도덕적 문제는 경시됨.

주제문 ⊶ 조세의 도덕적 문제는 세법을 만드는 데 매우 핵심적임.

[3]But, in fact, / the moral questions of taxation(S) are(V) at the very heart (of the creation of tax laws).

하지만, 사실 / 조세의 도덕적 문제는 가장 핵심에 있다 (세법 제정의)

⊶ 세금 부과에 도덕적 문제가 근본적임.

[4]Rather than (= Instead of) irrelevant, / moral questions(S) are(V) fundamental(C) to the imposition of tax.

무관하다기보다 / 도덕적 문제는 세금 부과에 근본적이다

★rather than은 부사구를 이끄는전치사로 쓰였으며, irrelevant 앞에는 being이 생략됨.

↳ **바람직한 경향:** 조세에서 도덕적 문제는 매우 중요함.

[5]Tax(S) is(V) the application(C) (of a society's theories of distributive justice).

세금은 적용이다 (사회의 분배 정의 이론의)

↳ **논거:** 세금은 사회의 분배 정의에 따라 부과됨.

★전치사 towards의 목적어로 온 동명사구 helping ~ goal이 <help+O+(to-)v(O가 v하는 것을 돕다)> 구조로 쓰임.

[6]Economics(S1) can go(V1) a long way / towards(전치사) helping(V′) a legislature(O′) determine(C′) // whether or not a particular tax law will help achieve a particular goal(determine의 O(명사절)), //

경제학이 크게 도움이 될 수 있다 / 입법부가 결정하는 것을 돕는 것에 // 특정 세법이 특정 목표를 달성하는 데 도움이 될지 안 될지를 //

but economics(S2) cannot, (in a vacuum), identify(V2) the goal(O).

하지만 경제학은 (외부와 단절된 상태로는) 그 목표를 밝혀낼 수 없다

↳ 경제학만으로는 세법의 목표를 규명할 수 없음.

⊶ 조세 정책을 만들 때 도덕적 목표를 규명하는 것이 필요함.

[7]Creating tax policy(S) requires(V) *identifying a moral goal*(O), // which(↱ 관계대명사(보충 설명)) is(V′) *a task*(C′) [that(주격 관계대명사) must involve ethics and moral analysis].

조세 정책을 만드는 것은 도덕적 목표를 밝히는 것을 요구한다 // 그런데 그것(도덕적 목표를 밝히는 것)은 과업이다 [윤리학과 도덕적 분석을 수반해야 하는]

↳ **주제문 재진술:** 조세 입법에는 도덕적 목표의 규명을 위한 연구가 필요함.

해석

[1]역사상, 조세 입법 입안자들은 경제학과 역사의 문제에 주의를 기울이고, 도덕적 문제에는 주의를 덜 기울인다. [2]도덕성에 관한 문제는 너무 논란이 많거나, 답변하기 너무 어렵거나, 아니면 최악의 경우, 계획과 무관한 것으로 분류되면서 종종 입법 토론에서 옆으로 밀려난다. [3]하지만, 사실, 조세의 도덕적 문제는 세법 제정의 가장 핵심에 있다. [4]무관하다기보다, 도덕적 문제는 세금 부과에 근본적이다. [5]세금은 사회의 분배 정의 이론의 적용이다. [6]경제학이 입법부가 특정 세법이 특정 목표를 달성하는 데 도움이 될지 안 될지를 결정하는 것을 돕는 것에 크게 도움이 될 수 있지만, 경제학은 외부와 단절된 상태로는 그 목표를 밝혀낼 수 없다. [7]조세 정책을 만드는 것은 도덕적 목표를 밝히는 것을 요구하는데, 그것은 윤리학과 도덕적 분석을 수반해야 하는 과업이다.

어휘

drafter 입안자, 초안 작성자
attentive to A A에 주의를 기울이는
moral 도덕적인; 교훈
cf. morality 도덕성
legislative 입법의, 법률을 제정하는
cf. legislature 입법부
label 분류하다; 라벨을 붙이다; 표[라벨]
controversial 논란이 많은; 논쟁(의 여지가 있는)
irrelevant to ~와 무관한
taxation 조세; 과세제도
rather than ~보다, ~대신에
fundamental 근본적인; 핵심적인
application 적용, 응용; 지원(서)
go a long way toward(s) ~에 크게 도움이 되다
in a vacuum 외부와 단절된 상태에서
identify 찾다, 발견하다; 확인하다
ethics 윤리(학)
analysis 분석

⊕ 분배 정의(distributive justice): 각자가 정당한 몫을 누릴 수 있게 하고, 아무도 불만을 제기하지 않는 방식으로 분배하는 것. 분배의 기준은 사회 제도에 따라 업적, 능력, 필요에 따른 분배 등으로 나뉨.

정답 가이드

조세 입법 입안자들이 도덕적 문제에 주의를 덜 기울여 왔지만, 도덕적 문제는 세법 제정의 가장 핵심에 있음을 주장한 뒤 이에 대한 부연 설명이 뒤따르고 있다. 따라서 글의 요지로 가장 적절한 것은 ⑤ '세법을 만들 때 도덕적 목표를 설정하는 것이 중요하다.'이다.

오답 클리닉

① 분배 정의를 실현하려면 시민 단체의 역할(×)이 필요하다. (1%)
distributive justice를 활용한 오답. 시민 단체의 역할에 대해서는 전혀 언급되지 않음.
② 사회적 합의(×)는 민주적인 정책 수립(×)의 선행 조건이다. (1%)
조세 입법에 관한 내용이며 사회적 합의가 필요하다는 내용도 언급되지 않음.
③ 성실한 납세(×)는 안정적인 정부 예산 확보의 기반이 된다. (2%)
조세 입법에 관한 내용이며 성실한 납세의 필요성은 언급되지 않음.
④ 경제학(×)은 세법을 개정할 때 이론적 근거를 제공한다. (3%)
경제학이 입법부의 결정에 도움을 준다고는 했으나, 도덕적 문제를 고려해야 한다는 글의 중심 내용에서 벗어남.

02 + 빈칸 추론 (21학년도 대수능 32번 | 정답률 56%) ③

구문분석 & 직독직해

사회 비슷한 사람과 어울리는 생존 전략의 한계점

[1]Choosing similar friends / can have a rationale.
S(동명사구) V O
비슷한 친구를 선택하는 것은 / 논리적 근거가 있을 수 있다
↳ 비슷한 친구를 선택하는 것은 논리적 근거가 있음.

[2]Assessing the survivability (of an environment) / can be risky / (if an environment turns out to be deadly, / for instance, // it might be too late // by the time you found out), // so humans have evolved the desire (to associate with similar individuals) / as *a way* (to perform this function efficiently).
S₁(동명사구) V₁ C / 부사절 접속사(조건) S′ V′ C′ / S V C / 부사절 접속사(~할 때쯤) / S₂ V₂ O = / 전치사(~로(서))
생존 가능성을 평가하는 것은 (어떤 환경의) / 위험할 수 있다 / (어떤 환경이 치명적인 것으로 드러나면 / 예를 들어 // 너무 늦을 수도 있다 // 당신이 알 때쯤에는) //
그래서 인간은 욕구를 발달시켜 왔다 (비슷한 개인들과 어울리려는) / 한 가지 방법으로 (이 기능을 효율적으로 수행하기 위한)
↳ 인간은 생존 가능성을 높이기 위해 비슷한 사람들과 어울리고자 함.

[3]This is especially useful / to *a species* [that lives / in so many different sorts of environments].
(= The desire ~ similar individuals) S V C 주격 관계대명사
이것(비슷한 개인들과 어울리려는 욕구)은 특히 유용하다 / 종에게 [사는 / 매우 다양한 유형의 환경에]
↳ 이 욕구는 매우 다양한 환경에 사는 종에게 유용함.

주제문
[4]However, / the carrying capacity (of a given environment) / **places a limit / on this strategy**.
S V O
그러나 / 수용력은 (주어진 환경에 대한) / 제한을 둔다 / 이 전략(비슷한 사람과 어울리려는 생존 전략)에
↳ 주어진 환경에 대한 수용력이 이 전략을 제한함.

🔑 자원이 한정된 환경에서 사람은 똑같은 방식으로 살아갈 수 없음.
[5]If resources are very limited, // *the individuals* [who live in a particular place] / cannot all do the exact same thing /
부사절 접속사(조건) S 주격 관계대명사 V O
자원이 매우 한정되어 있다면 // 개인은 [특정 장소에 사는] / 모두 똑같은 것을 할 수는 없다 /
(for example, / if there are few trees, // people cannot all live in tree houses, //
부사절 접속사(조건) S₁ V₁
(예를 들어 / 나무가 거의 없다면 // 사람들이 모두 나무집에서 살 수는 없다 //
or if mangoes are in short supply, // people cannot all live / solely on a diet of mangoes).
부사절 접속사(조건) S₂ V₂
또는 망고의 공급이 부족하면 // 사람들이 모두 살 수는 없다 / 오직 망고만 먹고)
↳ **세부 사항:** 자원이 한정된 환경에서 모두가 똑같은 방식으로 생존할 수는 없음.

🔑 때로 생존을 위한 합리적인 전략은 자신과 비슷한 사람들을 '피하는' 것임.
[6]A rational strategy would therefore sometimes be to *avoid* / similar members (of one's species).
S V C
그러므로 합리적인 전략은 때로는 '피하는' 것일 것이다 / 비슷한 구성원들을 (자기 종의)
↳ **결론:** 때로는 자신과 비슷한 사람들을 '피하는' 것이 합리적인 생존 전략임.

해석

[1]비슷한 친구를 선택하는 것은 논리적 근거가 있을 수 있다. [2]어떤 환경의 생존 가능성을 평가하는 것은 위험할 수 있는데 (예를 들어, 어떤 환경이 치명적인 것으로 드러나면, 당신이 알 때쯤에는 너무 늦을 수도 있다), 그래서 인간은 이 기능을 효율적으로 수행하기 위한 한 가지 방법으로 비슷한 개인들과 어울리려는 욕구를 발달시켜 왔다. [3]이것(비슷한 개인들과 어울리려는 욕구)은 매우 다양한 유형의 환경에 사는 종에게 특히 유용하다. [4]그러나 주어진 환경에 대한 수용력은 이 전략(비슷한 사람과 어울리려는 생존 전략)에 제한을 둔다. [5]자원이 매우 한정되어 있다면, 특정 장소에 사는 개인은 모두 똑같은 것을 할 수는 없다 (예를 들어, 나무가 거의 없다면, 사람들이 모두 나무집에서 살 수는 없으며, 또는 망고의 공급이 부족하면, 사람들이 모두 오직 망고만 먹고 살 수는 없다). [6]그러므로 합리적인 전략은 때로는 자기 종의 비슷한 구성원들을 '피하는' 것일 것이다.

어휘

rationale 논리적 근거[이유]
cf. rational 합리적인, 이성적인
assess 평가하다; 재다[가늠하다]
survivability 생존 가능성
risky 위험한
turn out (~인 것으로) 드러나다[밝혀지다]
deadly 치명적인
evolve 발달[진전]시키다
associate 어울리다; 연상하다, 연관짓다
species ((생물)) 종(種)
solely 오직, 단지
[선택지] exceed 초과하다, 넘다
means 수단, 방법
suitable 적합한, 알맞은
tie 유대[관계]; 묶다; 동점을 이루다
⊕ 환경 수용력(carrying capacity): 어떤 환경 내에서 생존·존속할 수 있는 특정 개체군의 개체 수.

정답 가이드

빈칸 문장을 However가 이끌고 있으므로 앞선 내용과는 역접 관계인 내용이 와야 한다. 앞 내용에서는 인간이 생존 가능성을 높이기 위해 비슷한 개인들과 어울리려는 욕구가 있다고 했고, 빈칸 문장 뒤에서는 '자원이 한정된 환경'이라면 비슷한 구성원들을 피하는 것이 합리적이라고 했다. 이를 달리 표현하면 '주어진 환경에 대한 수용력'에 따라 비슷한 개인들과 어울리는 전략은 적절하지 않을 수도 있다는 것이다. 따라서 빈칸에 들어갈 말로 가장 적절한 것은 ③ 'places a limit on this strategy(이 전략에 제한을 둔다)'이다.

오답 클리닉

① exceeds the expected demands of a community (17%)
공동체의 예상 수요를 초과한다
환경 수용력이 공동체의 동일한 수요를 충족하기에 부족한 경우를 설명함.

② is decreased by diverse means of survival (17%)
다양한 생존 수단에 의해 감소된다
환경 수용력이 사람들의 생존 전략에 영향을 미치는 것이지 영향을 받아 감소하는 것이 아님.

④ makes the world suitable for individuals (5%)
세상을 개인들에게 적합하게 만든다
생존하기 위해 개인이 환경 수용력에 맞춰 세상에 적응해야 함.

⑤ prevents social ties to dissimilar members (5%)
비슷하지 않은 구성원들과의 사회적 유대를 방해한다
환경 수용력이 비슷한 사람들과 어울리는 생존 전략을 방해하는 것이므로 글의 주제와 반대됨.

03 + 글의 순서 〈22학년도 대수능 37번 | 정답률 67%〉 ⑤

구문분석 & 직독직해

예술 허구 세계와 현실 세계 간의 차이

주제문

[1]In spite of the likeness (between the fictional and real world), / the fictional world deviates / from the real one / in one important respect.
전치사(~에도 불구하고) / A와 B 사이의 / S / V / (= world)
유사성에도 불구하고 (허구와 현실 세계 사이의) / 허구의 세계는 벗어난다 / 현실 세계로부터 / 한 가지 중요한 측면에서
↳ 허구 세계는 한 가지 측면에서 현실 세계와 다름.

🔑 주어진 글의 real world를 설명함.
(C) [2]*The existing world* (faced by the individual) / is in principle an infinite chaos (of events and details) // before it is organized / by a human mind.
S / (= the existing world) / 과거분사구 / V / C / 부사절 접속사(시간) S′ V′
현재의 세계는 (개인이 직면한) / 이론상으로는 끝없는 혼돈 상태이다 (사건들과 세부 사항들의) // 그것(현재의 세계)이 체계화되기 전에는 / 인간의 정신에 의해

[3]This chaos only gets processed and modified / when perceived / by a human mind.
S / V / C / 접속사를 생략하지 않은 분사구문(= when it is perceived ~)
이 혼돈 상태는 오직 처리되고 수정된다 / 인식될 때 / 인간의 정신에 의해
↳ **대조 A(현실 세계):** 인간의 정신에 의해 인식되고 체계화되기 전에 현실 세계는 혼돈 상태에 불과함.

(B) [4]Because of *the inner qualities* [with which the individual is endowed / through heritage and environment], / the mind functions as a filter; // 🔑 (C)에서 언급한 a human mind의 기능을 설명함.
전치사+관계대명사 / S′ / V′ / S_1 / V_1
내적 특성으로 인해 [개인이 부여받은 / 유산과 환경을 통해] / 정신은 여과기의 역할을 한다 //
every outside impression [that passes through it] / is filtered and interpreted.
S_2 / 주격 관계대명사 / (= the mind) / V_2
모든 외부의 인상이 [그것(정신)을 거쳐 가는] / 걸러지고 해석된다
↳ **대조 A의 부연 설명:** 인간의 정신은 외부의 인상을 거르고 해석하는 여과기 역할을 함.

[5]However, / *the world* [(which[that]) the reader encounters / in literature] / is already processed and filtered / by another consciousness. 🔑 현실 세계와 다른 허구 세계에 대한 설명이 역접으로 이어짐.
S / 목적격 관계대명사 생략 / V
그러나 / 세계는 [독자가 접하는 / 문학에서] / 이미 처리되고 걸러져 있다 / 또 다른 의식에 의해
↳ **대조 B(허구 세계):** 문학을 통해 접하는 허구 세계는 또 다른 의식에 의해 처리되고 걸러져 있음.

해석

[1]허구와 현실 세계 사이의 유사성에도 불구하고 허구의 세계는 한 가지 중요한 측면에서 현실 세계로부터 벗어난다. (C) [2]개인이 직면한 현재의 세계는 인간의 정신에 의해 그것이 체계화되기 전에는 이론상으로는 사건들과 세부 사항들의 끝없는 혼돈 상태이다. [3]이 혼돈 상태는 오직 인간의 정신에 의해 인식될 때 처리되고 수정된다. (B) [4]개인이 유산과 환경을 통해 부여받은 내적 특성으로 인해 정신은 여과기의 역할을 하는데, 그것(정신)을 거쳐 가는 모든 외부의 인상이 걸러지고 해석된다. [5]그러나 문학에서 독자가 접하는 세계는 또 다른 의식에 의해 이미 처리되고 걸러져 있다. (A) [6]작가는 중립적이고 객관적이고자 하는, 또는 세계에 대한 주관적인 견해를 전달하려는 시도에서 자신의 세계관과 적절성에 대한 자신의 개념에 따라 내용을 선정해 왔다. [7]동기가 무엇이든, 세계에 대한 작가의 주관적인 개념은 독자와 이야기의 기반이 되는 원래의 본래 그대로의 세계 사이에 있다.

어휘

likeness 유사성, 닮음
fictional 허구의; 소설적인
respect (측)면; 존경(하다); 존중(하다)
existing 현재의, 현존하는; 기존의
in principle 이론상으로는
infinite 끝없는, 무한한
chaos 혼돈(된 상태); 혼란
modify 수정하다, 변경하다
perceive 인식[인지]하다; 여기다

🔑 (B)의 another consciousness를 가리킴.

(A) [6]The author has selected the content / according to his own worldview [and] his own conception (of relevance), / in an attempt (to be neutral and objective / [or] (to) convey a subjective view (on the world)).

S / V / O / 전치사(~에 따라) / 명사구 병렬 / = / to-v구 병렬

작가는 내용을 선정해 왔다 / 자신의 세계관과 자신의 개념에 따라 (적절성에 대한) / 시도에서 (중립적이고 객관적이고자 하는 / 또는 주관적인 견해를 전달하려는 (세계에 대한))

★부사절에서 whatever가 be동사의 보어일 때 be동사는 생략 가능함.

[7]Whatever the motives (are), // the author's subjective conception (of the world) / stands / [between] the reader [and] *the original, untouched world* [on which the story is based].

양보 부사절(= No matter what ~) / S / V / 명사구 병렬 / 전치사+관계대명사 / S' / V'

동기가 무엇이든 // 작가의 주관적인 개념은 (세계에 대한) / 있다 / 독자와 원래의 본래 그대로의 세계 사이에 [이야기의 기반이 되는]

↳ **대조 B의 부연 설명:** 허구 세계는 작가의 세계관이 반영된 세계임.

function as ~의 역할을 하다
filter 여과기, 필터; 거르다, 여과하다
interpret 해석하다; 통역하다
encounter 접하다, 마주치다; 만남
literature 문학
consciousness 의식
conception 개념, 생각; 구상
relevance 적절[타당]성; 관련성
neutral 중립(적인)
objective 객관적인(↔ subjective 주관적인)
untouched 본래 그대로의; 손대지 않은

정답 가이드

허구 세계와 현실 세계가 한 가지 중요한 측면에서 서로 다르다고 언급한 주어진 글 다음에는 그 측면이 무엇인지에 대한 설명이 나올 것임을 예측할 수 있다. 먼저 현실 세계에 대해 설명하는 (C)가 이어지고, 이후에는 (C)의 a human mind를 the mind로 받아 현실 세계를 처리하는 인간 정신의 역할을 부연 설명하고 뒤이어 역접 연결어 However와 함께 현실 세계와 대조되는 문학의 허구 세계를 설명하는 (B)가 와야 한다. 허구 세계는 또 다른 의식(작가)에 의해 이미 처리되고 걸러진 것이라고 현실 세계와의 차이를 설명한 (B) 뒤에는 작가가 어떻게 허구 세계를 처리하는지를 구체적으로 설명하는 (A)가 이어지는 것이 자연스럽다.

오답 클리닉

① (A) - (C) - (B) (2%) / ④ (C) - (A) - (B) (12%)
(A)의 The author는 (B)의 문학에서 독자가 접하는 허구 세계를 처리하고 여과하는 another consciousness에 연결되는 것이므로 (B) 뒤에 와야 한다.
② (B) - (A) - (C) (10%) / ③ (B) - (C) - (A) (8%)
(B)에서 설명하는 정신에 관한 내용이 주어진 글에 없으므로 (B)는 주어진 글 뒤에 올 수 없다.

01 ✦ 필자 주장 〈23학년도 9월 모평 20번 | 정답률 94%〉 ①

구문분석 & 직독직해

문화 문화의 기반 이해의 중요성

★접속사 if가 이끄는 명사절이 to see의 목적어로 옴. if가 명사절을 이끌면 '~인지 (아닌지)'의 의미.

[1]Becoming competent in another culture (S) / means (V) looking beyond behavior (O) / to see (목적(~하기 위해)) // if (명사절 접속사) we (S′) can understand (V′) / *the attitudes, beliefs, and values* [that (주격 관계대명사) motivate (V″) what we observe (O″(명사절))].

다른 문화에 유능해진다는 것은 / 행동을 넘어 살펴보는 것을 의미한다 / 알아보기 위해 // 우리가 이해할 수 있는지 / 태도, 신념, 가치를 [우리가 목격하는 것의 이유가 되는]

↳ **도입:** 다른 문화를 잘 알려면 눈에 보이는 것 이상을 봐야 함.

★대시(—)로 삽입된 내용은 the visible aspects of culture에 대한 추가 정보를 제공함.

[2]By looking (<by v-ing>: v함으로써) only at the visible aspects (of culture) — / customs, clothing, food, and language — / we (S) develop (V) a short-sighted view (of intercultural understanding) (O) — / just the tip of the iceberg, really.

눈에 보이는 면만 봄으로써 (문화의) / 즉 관습, 의복, 음식, 언어 / 우리는 근시안적 시각을 키운다 (다른 문화 간의 이해에 대해) / 정말로 그저 빙산의 일각에 불과한

↳ **문제점:** 우리는 문화의 일부에 불과한 눈에 보이는 면만 봄.

주제문

[3]If we are to be successful (be to-v(의도)) / in our business interactions (with *people* [who (주격 관계대명사) have different values and beliefs (about how the world is ordered (about의 O(명사절)))]), //

★의문사가 이끄는 명사절이 목적어로 쓰일 경우 <의문사+S+V>의 간접의문문 어순을 사용함.

우리가 성공하고자 한다면 / 사업상의 교류에서 (사람들과의 [다른 가치관과 신념을 가진 (세상이 어떻게 질서 잡혀 있는지에 대해)]) //

then we must go (V_1) below the surface (of what it means to understand culture (of의 O(명사절))) / and attempt (V_2) to see (O) what Edward Hall calls the "hidden dimensions." (to see의 O(명사절))

🔑 타 문화권 사람과의 교류에서 성공하려면 문화의 숨겨진 차원을 알려고 해야 함.

그러면 우리는 그 표면 아래로 들어가야 한다 (문화를 이해한다는 게 무엇을 의미하는지의) / 그리고 Edward Hall이 '숨겨진 차원'이라고 일컫는 것을 보려고 시도해야 한다

↳ **해결책:** 타 문화권 사람과 잘 교류하려면 문화의 숨겨진 이면을 봐야 함.

🔑 숨겨진 측면인 문화의 기반을 아는 것이 중요함.

[4]Those hidden aspects (S) are (V_1) the very foundation of culture (C_1) / and are (V_2) *the reason* (C_2) [why (관계부사) culture is actually more than meets the eye].

그 숨겨진 측면이 바로 문화의 기반이다 / 그리고 이유이다 [문화가 실제로는 눈에 보이는 것 이상인]

↳ **부연 설명:** '숨겨진 차원'은 문화의 기반임.

[5]We tend not to notice those cultural norms // until they (S′) (= those cultural norms) violate (V′) what we consider to be common sense, good judgment, or the nature of things (O′).

★<not A until B>: B할 때까지 A하지 않다, B하고 나서야 비로소 A하다

★<consider+O+(to be) C(O를 C라고 여기다)>에서 what이 목적어를 대신해 뒤에 보어만 남음.

우리는 그런 문화적 규범들을 알아차리지 못하는 경향이 있다 // 그것들(문화적 규범들)이 우리가 상식, 올바른 판단 또는 사물의 본질이라고 여기는 것을 위반할 때까지

↳ **부연 설명:** 문화적 규범은 미리 알기 어려움.

해석

[1]다른 문화에 유능해진다는 것은 우리가 목격하는 것의 이유가 되는 태도, 신념, 가치를 이해할 수 있는지 알아보기 위해 행동을 넘어 살펴보는 것을 의미한다. [2]문화의 눈에 보이는 면, 즉 관습, 의복, 음식, 언어만 봄으로써, 우리는 다른 문화 간의 이해에 대해 정말로 그저 빙산의 일각에 불과한 근시안적 시각을 키운다. [3]세상이 어떻게 질서 잡혀 있는지에 대해 다른 가치관과 신념을 가진 사람들과의 사업상의 교류에서 우리가 성공하고자 한다면, 우리는 문화를 이해한다는 게 무엇을 의미하는지의 그 표면 아래로 들어가야 하고, Edward Hall이 '숨겨진 차원'이라고 일컫는 것을 보려고 시도해야 한다. [4]그 숨겨진 측면이 바로 문화의 기반이며 문화가 실제로는 눈에 보이는 것 이상인 이유이다. [5]우리는 그런 문화적 규범들이 우리가 상식, 올바른 판단 또는 사물의 본질이라고 여기는 것을 위반할 때까지 그것들을 알아차리지 못하는 경향이 있다.

어휘

competent 유능한; 능숙한; 자격을 갖춘
motivate 이유[원인]가 되다; 동기를 부여하다
observe 목격하다, 보다; 관찰하다
visible (눈에) 보이는; 가시적인, 뚜렷한
aspect (측)면; 양상, 외관
custom 관습, 풍습
short-sighted 근시안적인, 근시안의
intercultural 다른 문화 간의
the tip of the iceberg 빙산의 일각
interaction 교류, 상호 작용
order 질서를 세우다; 명령하다; 주문하다; 순서
surface 표면
attempt 시도(하다)
dimension 차원; 관점; 규모; 크기
foundation 기반, 토대; 재단; 설립
meet the eye 눈에 보이다[띄다]
norm 규범; 표준
violate 위반하다; 침해하다; 훼손하다
common sense 상식
judg(e)ment 판단(력); 판결
nature 본질; 자연; 본성

정답 가이드

다른 문화권 사람들과 성공적으로 교류하기 위해서는 눈에 보이는 면만이 아니라 그 아래에 숨겨진 측면, 즉 신념과 가치관과 같은 문화의 기반까지도 알아야 한다는 내용이다. 따라서 필자가 주장하는 바로 가장 적절한 것은 ① '타 문화 사람들과 교류를 잘 하려면 그 문화의 이면을 알아야 한다.'이다.

The 핵심 the "hidden dimensions(숨겨진 차원)"는 이어지는 문장에서 각각 Those hidden aspects, the very foundation of culture, those cultural norms로 말바꿈해 설명되었다.

오답 클리닉

② 문화 배경이 다른 직원과 협업할 때 공정하게 업무를 나눠야(×) 한다. (1%)
공정한 업무 배분은 언급되지 않음.

③ 여러 문화에 대한 이해를 통해 공동체 의식(×)을 길러야 한다. (4%)
문화 이해를 통한 공동체 의식 함양은 언급되지 않음.

④ 원만한 대인 관계(×)를 위해서는 서로의 공통점(×)을 우선 파악해야 한다. (1%)
타 문화권 사람들과의 사업상의 교류를 잘하고자 하는 것을 원만한 대인 관계로 바꿔 말하는 것은 너무 포괄적이며, 서로의 공통점이 아니라 오히려 문화적 차이를 파악하고 이해하라는 내용임.

⑤ 문화적 갈등(×)을 줄이려면 구성원 간의 소통을 활성화(×)해야 한다. (1%)
문화적 갈등을 줄이는 것이 아닌 문화적 이해를 더 깊이 해야 한다는 내용임. 또 이를 위해 구성원 간 소통을 하라는 내용도 없음.

02 + 빈칸 추론 〈21학년도 대수능 31번 | 정답률 53%〉

②

구문분석 & 직독직해

역사 수메르의 문자 발달

[1]In the classic model (of the Sumerian economy), / the temple functioned / as *an administrative authority* (governing commodity production, collection, and redistribution).

(S: the temple, V: functioned, 전치사(~로(서)): as, 현재분사구: governing ~)

전형적 모델에서 (수메르 경제의) / 사원은 기능했다 / 행정 당국으로서 (상품의 생산, 수집, 그리고 재분배를 관리하는)

↳ 수메르 경제에서 사원은 행정 당국의 기능을 했음.

[2]The discovery (of administrative tablets (from the temple complexes at Uruk)) / suggests // that token use and consequently writing evolved / as a tool (of centralized economic governance).

(S: The discovery, V: suggests, → suggests의 O(명사절), 명사절 접속사: that, S′: token use and consequently writing, V′: evolved, 전치사(~로(서)): as)

발견은 (행정 (점토)판의 (우루크에 있는 사원 단지에서 나온)) / 시사한다 //
상징 사용과 결과적으로 문자가 발달했다는 것을 / 도구로 (중앙집권화된 경제 지배의)

↳ 경제의 중앙 집권을 위한 도구로 문자가 발달됨.

[3]Given the lack (of archaeological evidence (from Uruk-period domestic sites)), /

(전치사(~을 고려하면): Given)

없음을 고려하면 (고고학적 증거가 (우루크 시대 가정집 터에서 나온)) /

*whether가 명사절을 이끌면 '~인지 (아닌지)'를 의미함.

it is not clear // whether individuals also used the system / for **personal agreements**.

(가주어: it, 진주어(명사절): whether ~)

(~은) 명확하지 않다 // 개인들도 그 체계를 사용했는지는 / 사적인 합의를 위해

↳ 개인도 사적인 합의를 목적으로 문자를 사용했는지는 명확하지 않음.

🔑 초기에 이 목적을 위해 읽고 쓸 수 있는 능력이 얼마나 퍼져 있었는지는 명확하지 않음.

[4]For that matter, / it is not clear // how widespread literacy was / at its beginnings.

(가주어: it, 진주어(명사절): how ~)

그 문제와 관련하여 / (~은) 명확하지 않다 // 읽고 쓰는 능력이 얼마나 널리 퍼져 있었는지는 / 그것(그 체계)의 초기에

↳ 초기에 얼마나 많은 사람들이 읽고 쓸 수 있었는지 명확하지 않음.

🔑 그림 문자의 사용은 상호 간에 이해 가능한 어휘 목록이 필요했음을 보여줌.

[5]The use (of identifiable symbols and pictograms / on the early tablets) / is consistent / with administrators needing *a lexicon* [that was mutually intelligible / by literate and nonliterate parties].

(S(단수): The use, V(단수): is, C: consistent, 동명사 needing의 의미상 주어: administrators, with의 O(동명사구): needing ~)

사용은 (인식 가능한 기호와 그림 문자의 / 초기의 (점토)판에서의) / 일치한다 /
행정가들이 어휘 목록을 필요로 했던 것과 [서로 이해할 수 있는 / 읽고 쓸 줄 아는 측과 읽고 쓸 수 없는 측이]

↳ 초기 기호와 그림 문자의 사용은 읽고 쓸 수 있는 능력에 상관없이 서로 이해할 수 있는 어휘가 필요했음을 의미함.

해석

[1]수메르 경제의 전형적 모델에서, 사원은 상품의 생산, 수집, 그리고 재분배를 관리하는 행정 당국으로서 기능했다. [2]우루크에 있는 사원 단지에서 나온 행정 (점토)판의 발견은 상징 사용과 결과적으로 문자가 중앙집권화된 경제 지배의 도구로 발달했다는 것을 시사한다. [3]우루크 시대 가정집 터에서 나온 고고학적 증거가 없음을 고려하면, 개인들도 사적인 합의를 위해 그 체계를 사용했는지는 명확하지 않다. [4]그 문제와 관련하여, 읽고 쓰는 능력이 그것(그 체계)의 초기에 얼마나 널리 퍼져 있었는지는 명확하지 않다. [5]초기의 (점토)판에서의 인식 가능한 기호와 그림 문자의 사용은 행정가들이 읽고 쓸 줄 아는 측과 읽고 쓸 수 없는 측이 서로 이해할 수 있는 어휘 목록을 필요로 했던 것과 일치한다. [6]쐐기 문자가 더욱 추상적이게 되면서, 읽고 쓰는 능력이 한 사람이 자신이 합의했던 것을 이해했다는 것을 확실히 하기 위해 점점 더 중요해졌음이 틀림없다.

어휘

classic 전형적인; 고전적인; 일류의
administrative 행정[관리]의
cf. administrator 행정가
authority 당국; 권한; 권위
commodity 상품, 물품; 원자재
redistribution 재분배
tablet (점토)판
complex (건물) 단지; 복잡한
token 상징, 표시; (화폐 대용으로 쓰는) 토큰
centralize 중앙집권화하다
domestic 가정의; 국내의
literacy (글을) 읽고 쓰는 능력
cf. literate (글을) 읽고 쓸 줄 아는

🔑 서로 합의한 내용을 확실히 이해하고자 읽고 쓰는 능력이 중요해졌음.

[6] As cuneiform script became more abstract, // literacy must have become increasingly important / to ensure // (that) one understood // what he or she had agreed to. *<must have p.p.>: ~했음이 틀림없다

부사절 접속사(~하면서) S V C / 목적(~하기 위해) 명사절 접속사 생략 S′ V′ O′(명사절)

쐐기 문자가 더욱 추상적이게 되면서 // 읽고 쓰는 능력이 점점 더 중요해졌음이 틀림없다 / 확실히 하기 위해 // 한 사람이 이해했다는 것을 // 자신이 합의했던 것을

↳ 서로의 합의를 이해하기 위해 읽고 쓰는 능력이 점점 더 중요해졌음.

identifiable 인식 가능한, 알아 볼 수 있는
pictogram 그림 문자
consistent with ~와 일치하는
mutually 서로, 상호간에
intelligible (쉽게) 이해할 수 있는, 알기 쉬운
abstract 추상적인
[선택지] communal 공동의, 공용의
shift 이동, 변화

정답 가이드

빈칸 문장의 the system은 앞서 나온 상징과 그로 발달한 문자 체계를 의미하는데, 개인들도 '어떤 목적'을 위해 이 체계를 사용했는지 명확히 알 수 없다고 한 것으로 보아 그 체계의 다른 사용 주체로 언급된 행정가들은 '어떤 목적'으로 이 체계를 사용했는지를 확인해야 한다. 이어지는 설명에서 초기 기호와 그림 문자의 사용은 행정가들이 상호 간에 이해할 수 있는 어휘 목록을 필요로 했던 것과 일치하는데, 서로 합의한 내용을 이해했다는 것을 확실히 하기 위해 이 체계를 읽고 쓰는 능력이 중요해졌다고 했다. 그런데 초기에 이 체계를 읽고 쓰는 능력이 얼마나 퍼져 있었는지는 명확하지 않다고 했으므로, 개인들도 ② 'personal agreements(사적인 합의)'를 위해 문자 체계를 사용했는지는 명확하지 않다고 볼 수 있다.

오답 클리닉

① religious events (13%) 종교 행사
temple을 활용한 오답. 종교적인 목적은 언급되지 않음.
③ communal responsibilities (10%) 공동 책임
공동 책임을 진다는 내용은 언급되지 않음.
④ historical records (22%) 역사적 기록
archaeological evidence를 활용한 오답. 역사적 기록을 남기기 위해 문자 체계를 사용한 것이 아님.
⑤ power shifts (2%) 권력 이동
권력과 관련된 내용은 없음.

03 ✦ 문장 넣기 〈23학년도 6월 모평 38번 | 정답률 52%〉 ④

구문분석 & 직독직해 — 농업 살충제의 대안을 고려하는 이유

[1] Simply maintaining yields / at current levels / often requires new cultivars and management methods, //

S(동명사구) V(단수) O

그저 수확량을 유지하는 것만도 / 현재 수준으로 / 흔히 새로운 품종과 관리 기법을 필요로 한다 //

since pests and diseases continue to evolve, // and aspects (of the chemical, physical, and social environment) / can change / over several decades.

부사절 접속사(~ 때문에) S′₁ V′₁ O′ S′₂ V′₂

해충과 질병이 계속 진화하기 때문에 // 그리고 양상이 (화학적, 물리적, 사회적 환경의) / 변할 수 있기 (때문에) / 수십 년에 걸쳐

↳ 도입: 수확량을 현재 수준으로 유지하기 위해서는 새로운 품종 및 관리 기법이 필요함.

*<consider+O+(to be) C>: O가 C하다고 여기다

(①) [2] In the 1960s, / many people considered / pesticides to be mainly beneficial / to mankind.

S V O C

1960년대에 / 많은 사람들은 여겼다 / 살충제가 대체로 유익하다고 / 인간에게

(②) [3] Developing new, broadly effective, and persistent pesticides / often was considered / to be *the best way* (to control pests (on crop plants)).

S(동명사구) V(단수) C

새롭고 널리 효과가 있고 지속성 있는 살충제를 개발하는 것은 / 흔히 여겨졌다 / 최고의 방법으로 (해충을 통제하는 (농작물에 있는))

↳ 대조 A(1960년대): 살충제를 유익하다고 여기고 해충을 통제하는 데 효과가 더 좋은 것을 개발함.

(③) [4] Since that time, / it has become apparent // that broadly effective pesticides can have harmful effects / on beneficial insects, // which can negate their effects / in controlling pests, //

전치사(~이후로) 가주어 V C 명사절 접속사(진주어₁(명사절)) S′₁ V′₁ O′₁ 관계사절(진주어₁ 보충 설명)

그때 이후로 / (~이) 분명해졌다 // 널리 효과가 있는 살충제가 해로운 영향을 미칠 수 있다는 것이 / 유익한 곤충에 // 그리고 이는 그것(살충제)의 효과를 무효화할 수 있다 / 해충을 통제함에 있어 //

🔑 살충제가 익충과 비표적 생물에 해를 끼침.

and that persistent pesticides can damage / non-target organisms (in the ecosystem), / (such as birds and people).

명사절 접속사(진주어₂(명사절)) S′₂ V′₂ O′₂

그리고 지속성 있는 살충제는 해칠 수 있다는 것이 / 비표적 생물을 (생태계의) / (새와 사람 같은)

↳ 대조 B(1960년대 이후): 살충제가 익충과 생태계의 비표적 생물에 해를 끼칠 수 있음.

해석

[1] 그저 현재 수준으로 수확량을 유지하는 것만도 해충과 질병이 계속 진화하고 화학적, 물리적, 사회적 환경의 양상이 수십 년에 걸쳐 변할 수 있기 때문에, 흔히 새로운 품종과 관리 기법을 필요로 한다. (①) [2] 1960년대에 많은 사람들은 살충제가 인간에게 대체로 유익하다고 여겼다. (②) [3] 새롭고 널리 효과가 있고 지속성 있는 살충제를 개발하는 것은 흔히 농작물에 있는 해충을 통제하는 최고의 방법으로 여겨졌다. (③) [4] 그때 이후로, 널리 효과가 있는 살충제가 유익한 곤충에 해로운 영향을 미칠 수 있어서 해충을 통제함에 있어 살충제의 효과를 무효화할 수 있고, 지속성 있는 살충제는 새와 사람 같은 생태계의 비표적 생물을 해칠 수 있다는 것이 분명해졌다. (④ [5] 또한, 기업들이 새로운 살충제를 개발하는 것이 어려워졌는데, 주요한 이로운 효과가 있지만 부정적인 효과는 거의 없을 수 있는 것들조차 그러하다.) [6] 매우 높은 비용이 새로운 살충제에 대한 정부의 승인을 얻는 데 필요한 모든 절차를 따르는 것에 수반된다. (⑤) [7] 결과적으로, 다른 생물학적 통제 기법을 개량하여 사용함으로써 더 강한 해충 저항력을 품종에 집어넣는 것 같은, 해충을 관리하는 다른 방법들에 더 많은 고려가 주어지고 있다.

어휘

yield 수확량; 생산하다; 항복하다; 양보하다
current 현재의; 흐름, 해류
pest 해충
decade 10년
beneficial 유익한, 이로운

🔑 살충제 개발의 어려움이 Also로 추가됨.

(④) [5]Also, / it has become difficult / for companies to develop new pesticides, / even *those* [that can have major beneficial effects / and few negative effects].)

(가주어 / V / C / to-v의 의미상 주어 / 진주어(to-v구) / (= pesticides) / 주격 관계대명사)

★few: ((준부정어)) 거의 없는

또한 / (~이) 어려워졌다 / 기업들이 새로운 살충제를 개발하는 것이 / 것들(살충제)조차 [주요한 이로운 효과가 있을 수 있는 / 그리고 부정적인 효과는 거의 없을 수 있는]

[6]Very high costs are involved / in following *all of the procedures* (needed to gain government approval (for new pesticides)).

(S / V / in의 O(동명사구) / 과거분사구)

매우 높은 비용이 수반된다 / 모든 절차를 따르는 것에 (정부의 승인을 얻는 데 필요한 (새로운 살충제에 대한))

↳ 새로운 살충제에 대한 정부의 승인을 얻는 데 높은 비용이 수반되어 기업들이 새로운 살충제를 개발하기 어려워짐.

(⑤) [7]Consequently, / more consideration is being given / to *other ways* (to manage pests), / such as incorporating greater resistance to pests into cultivars / by breeding and using other biological control methods).

(S / V / ★<incorporate A into B>: A를 B에 집어넣다 / <by v-ing>: v함으로써)

결과적으로 / 더 많은 고려가 주어지고 있다 / 다른 방법들에 (해충을 관리하는) / (더 강한 해충 저항력을 품종에 집어넣는 것 같은 / 다른 생물학적 통제 기법을 개량하여 사용함으로써)

↳ **결과:** 살충제 대신 해충을 관리하는 다른 방법들이 고려되고 있음.

mankind 인간, 사람들; 인류
persistent 지속성 있는; 끈질긴
crop 농작물
apparent 분명한
negate 무효화하다; 부정하다
procedure 절차
approval 승인; 찬성, 동의
resistance 저항(력)
biological 생물학적인

⊕ 비표적 생물(non-target organism): 농약으로 방제하는 생물 이외의 생물. 즉 해충 이외의 곤충, 천적, 토양 서식 소동물 등을 말함.

정답 가이드

주어진 문장은 '첨가'를 뜻하는 Also가 이끌고 있는데, 기업들이 새로운 살충제를 개발하기 어려워졌다고 했으므로 살충제와 관련한 어려운 상황을 먼저 언급한 뒤에 나와야 함을 알 수 있다. 첫 문장부터 보면, 현재 수준으로 수확량을 유지하려면 새 품종과 관리 기법이 필요한데, 살충제에 대한 과거 1960년대의 긍정적 인식이 ③ 이후 문장에서는 부정적으로 바뀌었다고 했다. 이는 살충제와 관련된 어려운 상황에 해당한다. 따라서 ④에 주어진 문장을 넣어 기업들의 새로운 살충제 개발에 어려움이 있다는 일반적인 서술 뒤에 문장 6에서 새로운 살충제에 대한 정부 승인을 얻는 데 (기업이) 높은 비용을 들여야 한다는 구체적 어려움을 덧붙이는 순서가 자연스럽다. 따라서 주어진 문장이 들어가기에 가장 적절한 곳은 ④이다.

오답 클리닉

① (2%) / ② (5%) 해충과 질병에 대한 새로운 관리 기법이 필요하다는 문장 뒤에 살충제 사용을 긍정적으로 여겼던 1960년대를 설명하는 내용이다.

③ (14%) that time은 앞서 설명한 1960년대를 가리키며, 그 이후 살충제를 부정적으로 여기게 된 문제점을 제시해 앞의 내용과 대조를 이루는 것은 자연스럽다.

⑤ (27%) 살충제의 해로운 영향과 개발의 어려움 때문에 다른 관리 방법들이 고려되고 있다는 결과가 마지막에 이어진다.

The 주의 ⑤ 앞의 문장은 주어진 문장(새로운 살충제 개발의 어려움)의 이유(높은 비용)를 부연 설명하는 내용이므로, 주어진 문장이 그 뒤에 오는 것은 어색하다.

01 + 요약문 〈22학년도 9월 모평 40번 | 정답률 50%〉 ①

구문분석 & 직독직해

기술 컴퓨터 정보 처리의 장단점

[1]The computer has, (to a considerable extent), solved / the problem (of acquiring, preserving, and retrieving information). 🔑 (A) 컴퓨터가 정보 처리의 문제를 많이 해결함.

S / V / 전치사구 삽입 / O / of의 O(동명사구)

컴퓨터는 (상당한 정도로) 해결했다 / 문제를 (정보를 얻고, 보존하고, 추출하는)

↳ **도입:** 컴퓨터가 정보 처리에서의 문제를 상당히 해결함.

[2]Data can be stored / in effectively unlimited quantities / and in manageable form.

S / V / 전치사구 병렬

데이터는 저장될 수 있다 / 사실상 무한한 양으로 / 그리고 관리할 수 있는 형태로

*SVOC 문형에서 O의 길이에 비해 C의 길이가 짧으면 CO의 구조가 되기도 함.

[3]The computer makes available / *a range of data* (unattainable in the age of books).

S / V / C / O / 형용사구

컴퓨터는 이용 가능하게 만든다 / 다양한 데이터를 (책의 시대에서는 얻을 수 없는)

[4]It packages it effectively; // style is no longer needed / to make it accessible, // nor is memorization. *<nor+V+S>: ((부정문 뒤)) S도 역시 ~ 않다

(= The computer) / ↱(= a range of data) / S₁ / V₁ / 목적(~하기 위해) / ↱(= a range of data) / V₂ / S₂

그것(컴퓨터)은 그것(다양한 데이터)을 효과적으로 꾸린다 // 더 이상 (특수한) 방식이 필요하지 않다 / 그것(다양한 데이터)을 이용할 수 있게 만들기 위해 // 암기도 역시 필요하지 않다

↳ **장점:** 컴퓨터는 다양한 데이터를 효과적으로 저장해 쉽게 이용할 수 있게 함.

[5]In dealing with *a single decision* (separated from its context), /

과거분사구

단일한 결정을 처리할 때 (그것의 맥락과 분리된) /

the computer supplies / *tools* (unimaginable / even a decade ago). 🔑 (A) 컴퓨터는 맥락과 분리된 결정을 처리하는 데 유용함.

S / V / O / 형용사구

컴퓨터는 제공한다 / 도구들을 (상상할 수 없었던 / 10년 전만 해도)

↳ **장점 부연 설명:** 컴퓨터는 맥락과 분리된 하나의 결정 처리에 놀라운 도구들을 제공함.

[6]But it also diminishes perspective. 🔑 (B) 컴퓨터가 관점을 약화시킴.

↱(= the computer) S / V / O

하지만 그것(컴퓨터)은 또한 관점을 약화시킨다

↳ **단점:** 컴퓨터는 관점을 약화시킴.

[7]Because information is so accessible / and communication (is so) instantaneous, // there is a diminution of focus (on its significance, / or even on the definition (of what is significant)).

부사절 접속사(이유) S′₁ V′₁ C′₁ / S′₂ 반복어구 생략 C′₂ / V / S / 전치사구 병렬 / of의 O(명사절)

정보가 매우 접근하기 쉽기 때문에 / 그리고 의사소통은 매우 즉각적이기 때문에 // 초점이 감소된다 (그것(정보)의 중요성에 관한 / 혹은 심지어 정의에 관한 (중요한 것의))

↳ **단점 부연 설명:** 정보 접근이 쉽고 의사소통이 즉각적이어서 정보의 중요성이나 중요한 것의 정의에 대한 관심이 줄어듦.

*<encourage+O+to-v>: O가 v하도록 부추기다[고무하다]

[8]This dynamic may encourage policymakers / to wait for an issue to arise / rather than anticipate it, / and to regard moments of decision / as a series of isolated events / rather than part of a historical continuum.

S / V / O / C₁(to-v구 병렬) / (= an issue) / C₂(to-v구 병렬) / *<regard A as B>: A를 B로 여기다[간주하다]

🔑 (B) 결정의 순간을 연속으로 연결되는 일이라기보다 고립된 일로 여기게 함.

이런 역학은 정책 입안자들이 (~하도록) 부추길 수 있다 / 쟁점이 발생하기를 기다리도록 / 그것(쟁점)을 예상하기보다는 / 그리고 결정의 순간을 여기도록 / 일련의 고립된 일들로 / 역사적인 연속체의 일부라기보다는

[9]When this happens, // manipulation of information replaces / reflection (as the principal policy tool).

↱부사절 접속사(시간) / (= 앞 문장) / S / V / O / 전치사(~로서)

이런 일이 일어나면 // 정보 조작이 대체한다 / 숙고를 (주요한 정책 도구로서의)

↳ **문제점:** 정책 입안자들은 결정의 순간을 역사적인 연속체의 일부가 아닌 고립된 것으로 여김 → 숙고하기보다 정보를 조작함.

해석

[1]컴퓨터는 정보를 얻고, 보존하고, 추출하는 문제를 상당한 정도로 해결했다. [2]데이터는 사실상 무한한 양으로, 그리고 관리할 수 있는 형태로 저장될 수 있다. [3]컴퓨터는 책의 시대에서는 얻을 수 없는 다양한 데이터를 이용 가능하게 만든다. [4]그것(컴퓨터)은 그것(다양한 데이터)을 효과적으로 꾸리는데, 그것(다양한 데이터)을 이용할 수 있게 만들기 위해 더 이상 (특수한) 방식이 필요하지 않으며, 암기도 역시 필요하지 않다. [5]그것의 맥락과 분리된 단일한 결정을 처리할 때, 컴퓨터는 10년 전만 해도 상상할 수 없었던 도구들을 제공한다. [6]하지만 그것은 또한 관점을 약화시킨다. [7]정보가 매우 접근하기 쉽고 의사소통은 매우 즉각적이기 때문에, 그것(정보)의 중요성이나 심지어 중요한 것의 정의에 관한 초점이 감소된다. [8]이런 역학은 정책 입안자들이 쟁점을 예상하기보다는 발생하기를 기다리도록, 그리고 결정의 순간을 역사적인 연속체의 일부라기보다는 일련의 고립된 일들로 여기도록 부추길 수 있다. [9]이런 일이 일어나면, 정보 조작이 주요한 정책 도구로서의 숙고를 대체한다.(▶ 숙고하여 정책을 마련하지 않고 정책에 맞게 정보를 조작한다는 의미)

↓

컴퓨터는 분명히 탈맥락화된 방식으로 정보를 처리하는 데 있어서 (A) 유능하지만, 정책 결정 과정에서 보여질 수 있는 것처럼 우리가 더 광범위한 맥락과 관련된 (B) 종합적 판단을 하는 것을 방해한다.

어휘

considerable 상당한, 많은
extent 정도, 규모, 크기
effectively 사실상; 효과적으로
manageable 관리[처리]할 수 있는
a range of 다양한
unattainable 얻을 수 없는
package 꾸리다, 포장하다; 상자; 꾸러미
accessible 이용[접근] 가능한; 접근이 쉬운
deal with ~을 처리하다[다루다]
diminish 약화시키다, 줄이다; 감소하다
perspective 관점, 시각
instantaneous 즉각적인, 순간적인
dynamic 역학; 역동적인
policymaker 정책 입안자
A rather than B B라기보다는 A
anticipate 예상하다; 기대하다
a series of 일련의
isolated 고립된, 분리된
continuum 연속(체)

↓

[10]Although the computer is clearly **(A) competent** / at handling information / in a decontextualized way, // it interferes with / our making **(B)** ***comprehensive*** *judgments* (related to the broader context), // as can be seen / in policymaking processes.

부사절 접속사(양보) / at의 O(동명사구) / (= the computer) V 동명사 making의 의미상 주어 / with의 O(동명사구) / 과거분사구

컴퓨터는 분명히 (A) 유능하지만 / 정보를 처리하는 데 있어서 / 탈맥락화된 방식으로 //
그것(컴퓨터)은 방해한다 / 우리가 (B) 종합적 판단을 하는 것을 (더 광범위한 맥락과 관련된) //
보여질 수 있는 것처럼 / 정책 결정 과정에서

manipulation 조작; 조종
reflection 숙고; 반사; 반영
principal 주요한
[요약문] decontextualize 탈맥락화하다
interfere with ~을 방해하다

정답 가이드

요약문을 통해 컴퓨터의 탈맥락화된 정보 처리 방식이 정책 결정 과정에서의 판단에 미치는 영향에 관한 글임을 알 수 있다. 정보를 효과적으로 관리하고 저장하는 컴퓨터는 맥락과 분리된 결정을 처리할 때 '유용한 도구들을 제공한다고' 했다. 역접 연결어 But 이후로는 컴퓨터가 전체적인 상황을 바라보는 관점을 약화시킨다는 단점을 제시하며, 정책 입안자들이 결정의 순간을 연속체의 일부라기보다 '고립된' 일로 여기게 하는 것과 같은 문제를 야기한다고 했다. 따라서 요약문의 (A)와 (B)에 각각 들어갈 말로 가장 적절한 것은 ① 'competent(유능한) - comprehensive(종합적인)'이다.

오답 클리닉

(A) (B)
② dominant - biased (24%) 우세한 - 편향된
(A)는 맞지만, (B)는 글의 내용과 반대됨. 컴퓨터의 탈맥락화된 정보 처리 방식이 방해하는 것은 편향된 판단이 아닌 균형 잡힌 판단이어야 함.
③ imperfect - informed (10%) 불완전한 - 잘 아는
(A)와 (B) 모두 틀림.
④ impressive - legal (11%) 인상적인 - 합법적인
(A)는 맞지만, (B)는 틀림. 정책 결정의 합법성을 논하는 내용이 아님.
⑤ inefficient - timely (5%) 비효율적인 - 시기적절한
(A)는 글의 내용과 반대되고, (B)도 틀림.

02~03 + 복합 유형 〈23학년도 대수능 41~42번 | 정답률 02 57%, 03 62%〉

02 ① 03 ④

구문분석 & 직독직해

기술 인간의 능력을 능가하는 간단한 공식

[1]There is evidence // that even very simple algorithms can outperform / expert judgement (on simple prediction problems). ⊶ 03-(a) 알고리즘이 전문가의 판단을 능가할 수 있음은 인간보다 더 '정확한' 것임.

V S = 동격 접속사 S′ V′ O′

증거가 있다 // 매우 간단한 알고리즘조차도 능가할 수 있다는 / 전문가의 판단을 (간단한 예측 문제에 대한)

↳ **도입:** 간단한 알고리즘이 전문가보다 예측을 더 잘할 수 있음.

⊶ 03-(b) 알고리즘과 마찬가지로 간단한 공식은 인간보다 '더 잘' 예측할 것임.

[2]For example, / algorithms have proved more **(a) accurate** / than humans / in predicting // whether *a prisoner* (released on parole) / will go on to commit another crime, /

S V C 전치사구 병렬 / 동명사 predicting의 O(명사절)

예를 들어 / 알고리즘이 더 정확하다는 것이 입증되었다 / 인간보다 / 예측하는 데 //
죄수가 (가석방으로 풀려난) / 계속해서 다른 범죄를 저지를 것인지 /

*whether는 명사절을 이끌 때 '~인지 (어떤지)'를 의미함.

or in predicting // whether a potential candidate will perform well / in a job / in future.

전치사구 병렬 / 동명사 predicting의 O(명사절)

또는 예측하는 데 // 잠재적인 후보자가 일을 잘할 것인지 / 직장에서 / 앞으로

↳ **도입의 예:** 범죄자의 재범률과 후보자의 역량 판단은 알고리즘이 더 정확하게 예측함.

주제문

*<half of+N>과 같은 부분 표현에서는 of 뒤의 명사에 수일치를 함.

[3]In over 100 studies (across many different domains), / half of all cases show //

S_1 V_1

100개가 넘는 연구에서 (많은 다른 영역에 걸친) / 전체 사례의 절반은 보여준다 //

↱ show의 O(명사절)

(that) simple formulas make **(b) better** significant predictions / than human experts, //

명사절 접속사 생략 S′ V′ O′

간단한 공식이 중요한 예측을 더 잘한다는 것을 / 인간 전문가보다 //

and the remainder / (except a very small handful), / show a tie (between the two).

S_2 V_2 O_2 (= simple formulas and human experts)

그리고 그 나머지(사례)는 / (아주 적은 소수를 제외하고) / 무승부를 보여준다 (둘 사이의)

↳ 간단한 공식이 인간 전문가보다 예측을 더 잘함.

해석

[1]매우 간단한 알고리즘조차도 간단한 예측 문제에 대한 전문가의 판단을 능가할 수 있다는 증거가 있다. [2]예를 들어, 가석방으로 풀려난 죄수가 계속해서 다른 범죄를 저지를 것인지 예측하거나 잠재적인 후보자가 앞으로 직장에서 일을 잘할 것인지 예측하는 데 알고리즘이 인간보다 더 (a) 정확하다는 것이 입증되었다. [3]많은 다른 영역에 걸친 100개가 넘는 연구에서, 전체 사례의 절반은 간단한 공식이 인간 전문가보다 중요한 예측을 (b) 더 잘한다는 것을 보여주고, (아주 적은 소수를 제외하고) 그 나머지(사례)는 둘 사이의 무승부를 보여준다. [4]관련된 많은 다른 요인이 있고 상황이 매우 불확실할 때, 가장 중요한 요소에 초점을 맞추고 일관성을 유지함으로써 간단한 공식이 승리할 수 있는 반면, 인간의 판단은 특히 두드러지고 아마도 (c) 관련 없는 고려 사항에 의해 너무 쉽게 영향을 받는다. [5]사람들이 (d) 편안하다고(→ 일이 너무 많다고) 느낄 때 중요한 조치나 고려 사항이 누락되지 않도록 확실히 함으로써 '체크리스트'가 다양한 영역에서 전문가 결정의 질을 향상할 수 있다는 추가적인 증거로 유사한 생각(▶ 간단한 공식이 인간의 판단을 능가함을 의미)이 뒷받침된다. [6]예를 들어, 집중 치료 중인 환자를 치료하는 것은 하루에 수백 가지의 작은 조치를 필요로 할 수 있으며, 작은 실수 하나가 목숨

4 When there are *a lot of different factors* (involved) / and a situation is very uncertain, //
부사절 접속사(시간) V'1 S'1 과거분사 S'2 V'2 C'
많은 다른 요인이 있을 때 (관련된) / 그리고 상황이 매우 불확실할 때 //

03-(c) 간단한 공식이 중요한 것에 집중하는 것과 인간의 판단이 '관련 없는' 것에 영향받는 것이 대조됨.

simple formulas can win out / by focusing on the most important factors / and being consistent, //
S V by의 O(동명사구 병렬)
간단한 공식이 승리할 수 있다 / 가장 중요한 요소에 초점을 맞춤으로써 / 그리고 일관성을 유지함으로써 //

while human judgement is too easily influenced / by particularly salient and perhaps **(c) irrelevant** considerations.
부사절 접속사(~인 반면에) S' V'
반면에 인간의 판단은 너무 쉽게 영향을 받는다 / 특히 두드러지고 아마도 관련 없는 고려 사항에 의해

↳ 세부 사항: 관련 요인이 많고 상황이 불확실할 때 인간보다 간단한 공식이 더 나음.

03-(e) 체크리스트는 다양한 영역에서 결정의 질을 향상시키므로 의학적 상황에서도 '효과적'일 것임.

5 A similar idea is supported / by further evidence // that 'checklists' can improve the quality (of expert decisions / in a range of domains) / by ensuring // that important steps or considerations aren't missed // when people are feeling **(d) relaxed(→ overloaded)**.
S V = 동격 접속사 <by v-ing>: v함으로써 동명사 ensuring의 O(명사절)
유사한 생각이 뒷받침된다 / 추가적인 증거로 // '체크리스트'가 질을 향상할 수 있다는 (전문가 결정의 / 다양한 영역에서) / 확실히 함으로써 // 중요한 조치나 고려 사항이 누락되지 않도록 // 사람들이 편안하다고(→ 일이 너무 많다고) 느낄 때

↳ 추가 세부 사항: 체크리스트는 일이 많을 때 중요한 조치나 고려 사항을 누락하지 않게 해줌.

03-(d) 수백 가지의 조치가 필요한 환자를 치료하는 예는 사람이 편안한 때가 아닌 '일에 압도된' 때임.

6 For example, / treating patients (in intensive care) / can require hundreds of small actions / per day, // and one small error could cost a life.
S1(동명사구) V1 O1 S2 V2 O2
예를 들어 / 환자를 치료하는 것은 (집중 치료 중인) / 수백 가지의 작은 조치를 필요로 할 수 있다 / 하루에 // 그리고 작은 실수 하나가 목숨을 잃게 할 수 있다

7 Using checklists / to ensure // that no crucial steps are missed / has proved to be remarkably **(e) effective** / in a range of medical contexts, / from preventing live infections to reducing pneumonia.
S(동명사구) 목적(~하기 위해) to ensure의 O(명사절) V(단수) C 동명사구 병렬
체크리스트를 사용하는 것은 / 확실히 하기 위해 // 어떠한 중대한 조치도 누락되지 않도록 / 현저하게 효과적이라는 것이 입증되었다 / 다양한 의학적 상황에서 / 당면한 감염을 예방하는 것에서부터 폐렴을 줄이는 것에 이르기까지

↳ 예: 수많은 조치가 취해져야 하는 의학적 상황에서 체크리스트 사용은 유용함.

을 잃게 할 수 있다. 7 어떠한 중대한 조치라도 누락되지 않도록 확실히 하기 위해 체크리스트를 사용하는 것은 당면한 감염을 예방하는 것에서부터 폐렴을 줄이는 것에 이르기까지 다양한 의학적 상황에서 현저하게 (e) 효과적이라는 것이 입증되었다.

어휘

outperform 능가하다
accurate 정확한
release 풀어주다, 석방하다; 발표하다
go on to-v 계속해서 v를 하다
commit (범죄를) 저지르다
potential 잠재적인; 잠재력, 가능성
candidate 후보(자); 지원자
domain 영역, 분야
formula 공식, 법칙
remainder 나머지; 재고품
handful 소수; 한 움큼
consistent 일관성이 있는, 한결같은; ~와 일치하는
irrelevant 관련이 없는
step 조치; 단계
intensive care 집중 치료
cost 잃게 하다; (비용이) ~이다
remarkably 현저하게
live 당면한; 살아 있는
infection 감염
[선택지] prioritise 우선순위를 매기다
simplicity 단순함, 간단함

정답 가이드

02 도입에서 알고리즘의 예측 능력이 전문가를 능가할 수 있다고 한 후, 간단한 공식이 인간 전문가보다 중요한 예측을 더 잘한다고 설명했다. 이어지는 세부 사항에서 인간의 판단은 다른 영향에 취약하며, 그에 반해 간단한 공식은 가장 중요한 요소에 초점을 두고 일관성을 유지하기 때문에 의사 결정에 강점이 있다고 설명하므로 글의 제목으로 가장 적절한 것은 ① 'The Power of Simple Formulas in Decision Making(의사 결정을 할 때의 간단한 공식의 힘)'이다.

03 (d) 뒤에 이어지는 예는 집중 치료 중인 환자에게 하루에 수백 가지의 작은 조치들이 필요하고 작은 실수에도 환자가 목숨을 잃을 수 있는 상황이므로 ④의 'relaxed(편안한)'를 'overloaded(과부하된)' 또는 'overwhelmed((너무 많은 일로) 어쩔 줄 모르는)'와 같은 단어로 바꾸어야 한다.

오답 클리닉

02 ② Always Prioritise: Tips for Managing Big Data (7%)
항상 우선 사항(×)을 결정하라는 빅 데이터(×) 관리 요령
우선 사항이나 빅 데이터에 관한 내용이 아님.

③ Algorithms' Mistakes: The Myth of Simplicity (7%)
알고리즘의 실수(×)인 단순함의 신화
알고리즘이 인간보다 낫다고 긍정적으로 보는 글의 내용과 반대됨.

④ Be Prepared! Make a Checklist Just in Case (20%)
준비하라! 만일의 경우를 대비해(×) 체크리스트를 만들어라
지문에 언급된 checklist를 활용한 오답. 만일의 경우를 대비하기 위함이 아닌 중요한 것을 놓치지 않기 위해 체크리스트를 만들라고 했음.

The 주의 ⓒ 체크리스트는 간단한 공식의 강점과 대비되는 인간 판단의 약점을 보완해 주는 도구로 언급된 것이므로 전체 내용을 포괄하지 못한다.

⑤ How Human Judgement Beats Algorithms (9%)
인간의 판단이 알고리즘을 이기는 방법(×)
인간이 알고리즘을 이겨야 한다는 내용이 아님.

03 ① accurate (2%) 정확한
문장 1에서 간단한 알고리즘조차도 예측에 있어 인간을 능가한다고 했으므로 알고리즘이 인간보다 '정확하다'는 것은 문맥상 자연스럽다.

② better (4%) 더 잘 하는
문장 2에서 알고리즘과 인간의 예측 능력을 비교한 것과 같이 간단한 공식과 인간 전문가를 비교하고 있으므로 간단한 공식이 예측을 '더 잘한다'고 유추할 수 있다. 문장 4에서 간단한 공식들이 승리할 수 있다는 내용 또한 이를 뒷받침한다.

③ irrelevant (28%) 관련 없는
가장 중요한 것에 집중하는 간단한 공식과 대조되는 내용이므로, 인간의 판단은 '관련 없는' 것들에 쉽게 영향을 받는다고 할 수 있다.

⑤ effective (4%) 효과적인
문장 5에서 체크리스트가 결정의 질을 높여준다고 하였고 문장 6, 7에서 의학적 상황의 예를 들어 이를 뒷받침한다. 따라서 체크리스트를 사용하는 것이 '효과적'이라는 내용은 문맥상 자연스럽다.

01 + 빈칸 추론 (21학년도 9월 모평 34번 | 정답률 38%) ④

구문분석 & 직독직해

철학 작은 진보의 과정을 나타내는 프로토피아

주제문

*<A rather than B>: B라기보다는 A

1 Protopia is a state of becoming, / rather than a destination.
S V C1 C2
프로토피아는 되어감의 상태이다 / 목적지라기보다는

2 It is a process.
(= Protopia)
그것(프로토피아)은 과정이다
↳ 정의: 프로토피아는 결과가 아닌 되어가는 과정임.

*부사절의 주어가 주절의 주어와 같고 동사가 be동사일 경우 생략 가능함.

3 In the protopian mode, / things are better today // than they were yesterday, // although (they are) only a little better.
S V C / 부사절 접속사(양보) / <주어+be동사> 생략 / C'
프로토피아적 방식에서는 / 상황이 오늘 더 낫다 // 그것들이 어제 그랬던 것보다 // 비록 그저 약간 더 나을 뿐이라도
↳ 프로토피아 방식에서 미미하긴 하나 상황은 어제보다 오늘 더 나음.

(= Protopia)
4 It is incremental improvement or mild progress.
S V C
그것(프로토피아)은 점진적 개선이나 가벼운 진보이다

5 The "pro" in protopian / stems from the notions (of process and progress).
프로토피아적이라는 말에서 '프로'는 / 개념에서 유래한다 (과정과 진보라는)

6 This subtle progress is not dramatic, not exciting.
이 미묘한 진보는 극적이지도 자극적이지도 않다
↳ 프로토피아의 진보는 미미함.

(= Protopia)

🔑 새로운 이익만큼 문제도 발생하여 진보를 놓치기 쉬움.

7 It is easy to miss // because a protopia generates almost as many new problems / as new benefits.
S 형용사 easy 수식 부사절 접속사(이유) S' V' O'
그것(프로토피아)은 놓치기 쉽다 // 프로토피아는 거의 (~만큼) 많은 새로운 문제를 만들어 내기 때문에 / 새로운 이익만큼
↳ 프로토피아는 새로운 이익만큼이나 새로운 문제를 발생시키므로 놓치기 쉬움.

8 The problems of today were caused / by yesterday's technological successes, //
S1(복수) V1(복수)
and the technological solutions to today's problems will cause / the problems of tomorrow.
S2 V2 O2
오늘의 문제는 유발되었다 / 어제의 기술적 성공에 의해 //
그리고 오늘의 문제에 대한 기술적 해결책은 유발할 것이다 / 내일의 문제를
↳ 부연 설명: 문제 발생과 해결이 꼬리에 꼬리를 물고 이어짐.

9 This circular expansion (of both problems and solutions) / **hides a steady accumulation (of small net benefits) / over time.**
S(단수) V(단수) O
이러한 순환적 팽창은 (문제와 해결책의) / 꾸준한 축적을 감춘다 (작은 순이익의) / 시간이 지남에 따라
↳ 결과: 문제와 해결의 반복은 작은 이점이 꾸준히 축적되는 것을 못 보게 함.

🔑 인간은 점진적으로 발전해 왔음.

10 Ever since the Enlightenment and the invention of science, / we've managed to create / a tiny bit more // than we've destroyed each year.
전치사(~이래 죽) S V O
*<manage to-v>: 어떻게든 v하다
계몽주의와 과학의 발명 이래로 죽 / 우리는 어떻게든 만들어왔다 / 아주 조금 더 많이 // 매년 우리가 파괴해 온 것보다
↳ 인간은 아주 조금씩 점진적으로 발전해 왔음.

해석

1 프로토피아는 목적지라기보다는 되어감의 상태이다. 2 그것은 과정이다. 3 프로토피아적 방식에서는 비록 그저 약간 더 나을 뿐이라도 상황이 어제 그랬던 것보다 오늘 더 낫다. 4 그것은 점진적 개선이나 가벼운 진보이다. 5 프로토피아적이라는 말에서 '프로'는 과정과 진보라는 개념에서 유래한다. 6 이 미묘한 진보는 극적이지도, 자극적이지도 않다. 7 프로토피아는 거의 새로운 이익만큼 많은 새로운 문제를 만들어 내기 때문에 놓치기 쉽다. 8 오늘의 문제는 어제의 기술적 성공에 의해 유발되었고, 오늘의 문제에 대한 기술적 해결책은 내일의 문제를 유발할 것이다. 9 문제와 해결책의 이런 순환적 팽창은 시간이 지남에 따라 작은 순이익의 꾸준한 축적을 감춘다. 10 계몽주의와 과학의 발명 이래로 죽, 우리는 어떻게든 매년 우리가 파괴해 온 것보다 아주 조금 더 많이 만들어왔다. 11 그러나 그 작은 몇 퍼센트의 긍정적인 차이는 수십 년에 걸쳐 우리가 문명이라고 부를 수 있는 것으로 조합된다. 12 그것의 이익은 영화에서 결코 주연을 맡지 않는다.(▶ 프로토피아의 이익은 부각되지 않는다는 의미)

어휘

state 상태; 국가; 말하다, 진술하다
destination 목적지
mode 방식, 방법
mild 가벼운, 순한; 온화한
progress 진보, 발전; 나아가다
stem from ~에서 유래하다
notion 개념, 관념
subtle 미묘한, 포착하기 어려운; 교묘한
dramatic 극적인
circular 순환적인; 원형의
expansion 팽창, 확대
steady 꾸준한; 안정된
accumulation 축적, 누적
net (돈의 액수에 대해) 순(純)-; 그물(망)
the Enlightenment 계몽주의
civilization 문명 (사회)
star 주연을 맡다
[선택지] conceal 감추다, 숨기다
innovation 혁신, 획기적인 것
motivate 동기를 부여하다
considerable 상당한, 많은

[11]But that few percent positive difference is compounded / over decades / into what we might call civilization. 점진적 발전이 오랜 기간 쌓여 문명을 이룸 → 이익이 바로 드러나지 않음을 의미함.

(S: that few percent positive difference, V: is compounded, into의 O(명사절): what we might call civilization, S': we, V': might call, C': civilization) ★<call+O+C>: O를 C라고 부르다

그러나 그 작은 몇 퍼센트의 긍정적인 차이는 조합된다 / 수십 년에 걸쳐 / 우리가 문명이라고 부를 수 있는 것으로

↳ 오랜 기간 작은 발전이 모여 문명을 형성함.

[12]Its benefits never star / in movies. 프로토피아의 이익은 두드러지지 않음.

(Its = Protopia's)

그것(프로토피아)의 이익은 결코 주연을 맡지 않는다 / 영화에서

↳ 프로토피아의 이익은 눈에 띄지 않음.

정답 가이드

빈칸 문장의 문제와 해결책의 순환적 팽창이란 바로 앞 문장에서 설명한, 해결책이 또 다른 문제를 유발한다는 것을 의미하는데, 이것이 '무엇을 하는지'를 추론해야 한다. 이어지는 설명에서 우리가 어떻게든 만들어내는 아주 작은 개선들(해결책)이 오랜 시간에 걸쳐 조합되어 문명이 되며, 영화에서 결코 주연을 맡지 않는다고 했다. 즉, 해결책이 또 다른 문제를 유발하므로 개선이 '드러나지 않게' 된다는 것을 의미하므로, 빈칸에 들어갈 말로 가장 적절한 것은 ④ 'hides a steady accumulation of small net benefits over time(시간이 지남에 따라 작은 순이익의 꾸준한 축적을 감춘다)'이다.

오답 클리닉

① conceals the limits of innovations at the present time (16%)
현재의 혁신의 한계를 감춘다
어제의 기술적 성공이 오늘의 문제를 유발한다고 했으므로 한계를 감춘다고 볼 수 없음.

② makes it difficult to predict the future with confidence (16%)
자신감 있게 미래를 예측하는 것을 어렵게 만든다
미래 예측에 관한 내용이 아님.

③ motivates us to quickly achieve a protopian civilization (12%)
프로토피아적인 문명을 빨리 이루도록 우리에게 동기를 부여한다
점진적 발전이 오랜 기간 쌓여 문명을 이룬다고 했으므로 빨리 이루도록 한다는 내용은 틀림.

⑤ produces a considerable change in technological successes (19%)
기술적 성공에서 상당한 변화를 만든다
technological successes를 활용한 오답. 프로토피아는 작은 진보를 의미함.

02 + 글의 순서 〈22학년도 대수능 36번 | 정답률 71%〉 ②

구문분석 & 직독직해

경제 과세를 통한 가격 인상의 영향

주제문

[1]According to the market response model, / [it is] increasing prices // [that] drive providers to search for new sources, / innovators to substitute, / consumers to conserve, / [and] alternatives to emerge.

(According to: 전치사(~에 따르면), <it is A that ...>: …한 것은 바로 A이다, V': drive, O'₁: providers, C'₁: to search for new sources, O'₂: innovators, C'₂: to substitute, O'₃: consumers, C'₃: to conserve, O'₄: alternatives, C'₄: to emerge) ★<drive+O+to-v>: O가 (할 수 없이) v하게 하다

시장 반응 모형에 따르면 / 바로 증가하는 가격이다 // 공급자가 새로운 공급원을 찾게 하는 것은 / 혁신가가 대체하게 (하는 것은) / 소비자가 아껴 쓰게 (하는 것은) / 그리고 대안이 생기게 (하는 것은)

↳ 가격 인상은 시장에 많은 영향을 미침.

(B) [2]Taxing certain goods or services, / [and] so increasing prices, / should result in / [either] decreased use (of these resources) / [or] creative innovation (of new sources or options). 주어진 글의 가격 인상이 세금 부과로 인한 것임을 설명함.

(S(동명사구 병렬): Taxing certain goods or services, and so increasing prices, V: should result in, O: either decreased use ... or creative innovation ...) ★<either A or B>: A와 B 둘 중 하나

특정 재화나 서비스에 세금을 부과하는 것은 / 그래서 가격을 인상시키는 것은 / 야기할 것이다 / 감소된 사용이나 (이러한 자원의) / 창조적 혁신 중 하나를 (새로운 공급원 또는 선택 사항의)

↳ **세부 사항:** 세금 부과로 인한 가격 인상은 소비 감소 및 새로운 원천 개발을 야기함.

[3]*The money* (raised through the tax) / can be used directly by the government / [either] to supply services [or] to search for alternatives.

(S: The money, 과거분사구: raised through the tax, V: can be used, to-v구 병렬: to supply services or to search for alternatives)

돈은 (세금으로 모아진) / 정부에 의해 직접 사용될 수 있다 / 서비스를 공급하거나 대안을 모색하는 데

↳ 세금으로 모은 돈은 정부가 서비스를 공급하거나 대안을 모색하는 데 사용함.

해석

[1]시장 반응 모형에 따르면, 공급자가 새로운 공급원을 찾게 하고, 혁신가가 대체하게 하고, 소비자가 아껴 쓰게 하고, 대안이 생기게 하는 것은 바로 증가할 가격이다. (B) [2]특정 재화나 서비스에 세금을 부과해서 가격을 인상시키는 것은 이러한 자원의 사용 감소나 새로운 공급원 또는 선택 사항의 창조적 혁신 중 하나를 야기할 것이다. [3]세금으로 모아진 돈은 정부에 의해 직접 서비스를 공급하거나 대안을 모색하는 데 사용될 수 있다. (A) [4]그러한 '환경세'의 많은 예가 존재한다. [5]예를 들어, 쓰레기 매립 비용, 노동비, 쓰레기 처리 준비에 관련된 비용에 직면하면서 일부 도시는 가정이 모든 폐기물을 소비자에 의해 직접 구입된, 흔히 각각 1달러 또는 그 이상이 드는 특별 쓰레기봉투에 담아 처리하도록 요구해 왔다. (C) [6]그 결과는 크게 증가된 재활용과 포장과 폐기물에 대한 소비자의 더 세심한 주의였다. [7]소비자에게 쓰레기 비용을 자신의 것으로 하도록 함으로써, 가정에서 나오는 쓰레기의 양에서 관찰된 감소가 있었다.

(A) [4]Many examples (of such "green taxes") / exist. (B)에서 언급한 과세를 '환경세'로 지칭함.
S V
많은 예가 (그러한 '환경세'의) / 존재한다
↳ 부연 설명: 정부가 특정 재화나 서비스에 부과하는 환경세가 있음.

[5]Facing / landfill costs, labor expenses, and related costs (in the provision of garbage disposal), /
분사구문(= As they have faced)
for example, / some cities have required / households to dispose of all waste /
S V O C
직면하면서 / 쓰레기 매립 비용, 노동비, 관련된 비용에 (쓰레기 처리 준비에) /
예를 들어 / 일부 도시는 (~하도록) 요구해 왔다 / 가정이 모든 폐기물을 처리하도록
in *special trash bags*, / (purchased by consumers themselves), / and (often costing a dollar or more each).
과거분사구 현재분사구
특별 쓰레기봉투에 담아 / (소비자에 의해 직접 구입된) / 그리고 (흔히 각각 1달러 또는 그 이상이 드는)
↳ 예: 가정의 쓰레기 처리 비용을 소비자가 직접 부담하게 함.

(A)의 쓰레기봉투를 구입해 폐기물을 처리하게 한 예시에 대한 결과가 이어짐.
(C) [6]The results have been greatly increased recycling and more careful attention (by consumers) / to packaging and waste.
S V C
그 결과는 크게 증가된 재활용과 더 세심한 주의였다 (소비자의) / 포장과 폐기물에 대한

[7]By internalizing the costs of trash to consumers, / there has been an observed decrease / in the flow of garbage (from households).
<by v-ing>: v함으로써 V S
소비자에게 쓰레기 비용을 자기 것으로 하도록 함으로써 / 관찰된 감소가 있었다 / 쓰레기의 양에서 (가정에서 나오는)
↳ 예의 결과: 재활용이 늘고 소비자가 포장과 폐기물에 세심한 주의를 기울여, 가정의 쓰레기 배출량이 감소함.

어휘

substitute 대체[대용]하다; 대체[대용]물
conserve 아껴 쓰다; 보존하다
alternative 대안(적인)
tax 세금(을 부과하다)
raise (돈을) 모으다; 올리다; 기르다
face 직면하다; 마주보다
landfill 쓰레기 매립(지)
provision 준비; 공급
disposal 처리
cf. dispose of ~을 처리하다[없애다]
household 가정(의), 가족(의)
waste 폐기물, 쓰레기; 낭비(하다)
packaging 포장(재)
internalize 자기 것으로 하다, 내면화하다
observe 관찰하다; 말하다; 준수하다
⊕ 환경세(green tax): 환경을 오염시키거나 파괴하는 행위에 부과하는 세금

정답 가이드

가격 인상이 시장에 여러 영향을 미친다는 주어진 글 다음에는 세금 부과로 인한 가격 인상의 결과를 설명하는 (B)가 이어지는 것이 적절하다. (B)에서 언급된 특정 재화나 서비스에 부과된 '세금'을 (A)에서 such "green taxes"로 지칭하며 소비자에게 직접 가정 폐기물 처리비를 부과하는 예를 든 다음 그로 인한 결과를 The results 이하로 설명하는 (C)가 마지막에 오는 것이 자연스럽다.

오답 클리닉

① (A) - (C) - (B) (3%)
주어진 글에는 세금 부과에 관한 내용이 없으므로 (A)의 such "green taxes"가 연결될 수 없다.
③ (B) - (C) - (A) (12%) / ④ (C) - (A) - (B) (8%) / ⑤ (C) - (B) - (A) (6%)
(C)는 쓰레기 처리 비용을 소비자가 부담하도록 한 (A)의 결과에 해당하므로 (A) 뒤에 와야 한다.

03 + 문장 넣기 (22학년도 대수능 39번 | 정답률 47%) ④

구문분석 & 직독직해

예술 영화적 환상을 파괴하는 기술 혁신

주제문
★<not A but B>: A가 아니라 B
[1]Cinema is valuable / not for its ability (to make visible the hidden outlines of our reality), /
S V C V' C' O'
영화는 가치가 있다 / 능력 때문이 아니라 (우리 현실의 숨겨진 윤곽을 보이게 만드는) /
but for its ability (to reveal // what reality itself veils — / the dimension of fantasy).
to reveal의 O(명사절)
능력 때문에 (드러내는 // 현실 자체가 가리고 있는 것을 / 즉 환상의 차원을)
↳ 영화는 현실이 아닌 환상의 차원(현실이 가리고 있는 것)을 보여주기 때문에 가치가 있음.

(= 앞 문장) is의 C(명사절)
(①) [2]This is // why, to a person, the first great theorists of film decried / the introduction (of *sound* and *other technical innovations* (*such as color*) [that pushed film / in the direction of realism]).
S V 관계부사 S' V' O'
주격 관계대명사
이것이 ~이다 // 최초의 위대한 영화 이론가들이 하나같이 비난한 이유 / 도입을
(소리와 다른 기술 혁신의 (색채와 같은) [영화를 밀어붙였던 / 사실주의 쪽으로])

해석

[1]영화는 우리 현실의 숨겨진 윤곽을 보이게 만드는 능력 때문이 아니라 현실 자체가 가리고 있는 것, 즉 환상의 차원을 드러내는 능력 때문에 가치가 있다. (①) [2]이것이 최초의 위대한 영화 이론가들이 영화를 사실주의 쪽으로 밀어붙였던 소리와 (색채와 같은) 다른 기술 혁신의 도입을 하나같이 비난한 이유이다. (②) [3]영화는 전적으로 환상적인 예술이었기 때문에 이러한 혁신들(소리와 색채)은 완전히 불필요했다. (③) [4]그리고 설상가상으로 그것들(이러한 혁신)은 잠재적으로 영화를 현실의 표현을 위한 단순한 전달 장치로 변형시키면서, 영화 제작자와 관객을 영화의 환상적인 차원으로부터 멀어지게 할 수 있을 뿐이었다. (④ [5]무성 흑백 영화의 비현실주의가 지배하는 한 누구든 영화적 환상을 현실

(②) [3]Since cinema was an entirely fantasmatic art, // these innovations were completely unnecessary.

부사절 접속사(~ 때문에) S′ V′ C′ S V C

영화는 전적으로 환상적인 예술이었기 때문에 // 이러한 혁신들(소리와 색채)은 완전히 불필요했다

↳ 영화를 사실주의로 만드는 기술 혁신들은 불필요했음.

(③) [4]And what's worse, / they could do nothing but turn filmmakers and audiences away / from the fantasmatic dimension of cinema, /

(they = these innovations) S V ★<do nothing but+동사원형>: 단지 ~할 뿐이다

그리고 설상가상으로 / 그것들(이러한 혁신)은 영화 제작자와 관객을 멀어지게 할 수 있을 뿐이었다 /

영화의 환상적인 차원으로부터 / ★<transform A into B>: A를 B로 변형시키다

potentially transforming film / into a mere delivery device (for representations of reality).

분사구문(= as they potentially transformed ~)

잠재적으로 영화를 변형시키면서 / 단순한 전달 장치로 (현실의 표현을 위한)

↳ 기술적인 혁신은 영화를 환상적인 것에서 현실 표현을 위한 수단으로 변형시킴 → 기술 혁신에 대한 부정적 시각.

★<take A for B>: A를 B로 착각하다

(④ [5]As long as the irrealism of the silent black and white film predominated, // one could not take filmic fantasies / for representations of reality.)

부사절 접속사(~하는 한) S′ V′ S V O

🔑 문장 6의 such an illusion이 가리키는 내용.

무성 흑백 영화의 비현실주의가 지배하는 한 // 누구든 영화적 환상을 착각할 수 없었다 / 현실의 표현으로

↳ 무성 흑백 영화에서는 영화적 환상을 현실의 표현으로 착각할 수 없었음.

🔑 기술 혁신(소리와 색채)을 부정적으로 보는 내용이 But으로 이어짐.

[6]But / sound and color threatened / to create just such an illusion, / thereby destroying the very essence of film art.

S V O 분사구문(= and thereby they destroyed ~)

★<threaten to-v>: v하겠다고 위협하다

그러나 / 소리와 색채는 위협했다 / 바로 그러한 착각을 만들겠다고 / 그 때문에 영화 예술의 바로 그 본질을 파괴했다

↳ 소리 및 색채(기술 혁신들)가 영화를 현실의 표현으로 착각하게 만들어 영화 예술의 본질(환상의 차원)을 파괴함.

(⑤) [7]As Rudolf Arnheim puts it, // "The creative power of the artist can only come into play // where reality and the medium of representation do not coincide."

부사절 접속사(~처럼) S′ V′ O′ S V

부사절 접속사 S′₁ S′₂ V′

Rudolf Arnheim이 표현한 것처럼 // "예술가의 창의적 힘은 오직 작동할 수 있다 //

현실과 표현의 매체가 일치하지 않는 곳에서만"

↳ **맺음말(인용):** 현실과 표현의 매체가 일치하지 않는 곳에서 예술가의 창의적 힘이 발현될 수 있음.

의 표현으로 착각할 수 없었다.(▶ 무성 흑백 영화에는 사실적 요소인 소리와 색채가 빠져 있기 때문에 사람들은 영화적 환상을 현실의 표현으로 착각할 수 없었다는 의미)) [6]그러나 소리와 색채는 바로 그러한 착각을 만들겠다고 위협했고, 그 때문에 영화 예술의 바로 그 본질을 파괴했다. (⑤) [7]Rudolf Arnheim이 표현한 것처럼, "예술가의 창의적 힘은 오직 현실과 표현의 매체가 일치하지 않는 곳에서만 작동할 수 있다."

어휘

visible (눈에) 보이는
outline 윤곽; 개요(를 서술하다)
reveal 드러내다, 밝히다
veil 가리다; 장막
dimension 차원; 크기; 규모
to a parson[man] 하나같이, 만장일치로
turn A away from B B에 들어오지 못하게 A를 돌려보내다[쫓아내다]
mere 단순한; (한낱) ~에 불과한
representation 표현, 묘사; 대표(자)
silent 무성 (영화)의; 조용한
predominate 지배하다; 우세하다
illusion 착각; 환상
put (특정한 방식으로) 표현[말]하다
come into play 작동[활동]하다
medium 매체, 매개(물); 수단
coincide 일치하다; 동시에 일어나다

정답 가이드

주어진 문장은 무성 흑백 영화의 비현실주의로 인해 영화적 환상을 현실의 표현으로 착각할 수 없었다는 내용이다. 첫 문장은 주어진 문장을 일반적으로 서술한 것으로, 영화는 현실보다는 환상의 차원을 드러내야 한다는 주장이다. 이어지는 문장들은 이를 부연 설명하는데, 기술 혁신을 부정적으로 보는 ④ 앞 문장과 ④ 뒤 문장이 역접 연결어 But으로 이어지는 연결이 부자연스러우며, ④ 앞 문장에서는 ④ 뒤 문장의 소리와 색채가 만들겠다고 위협한 such an illusion이 지칭하는 내용도 찾을 수 없다. 주어진 문장을 ④에 넣으면, 무성 흑백 영화로 사람들은 영화적 환상을 현실의 표현으로 착각할 수 없었지만, 소리와 색채가 그러한 착각(such an illusion)을 만들겠다고 위협했다는 내용이 되므로 글의 흐름이 자연스럽다. 마지막 문장은 맺음말로서 주제문을 재진술한 것이다. 따라서 주어진 문장이 들어가기에 가장 적절한 곳은 ④이다.

오답 클리닉

① (5%) 영화는 환상의 차원을 드러낸다는 점에서 가치 있다는 앞의 내용을 This로 받아 영화 이론가들이 왜 기술 혁신을 비난했는지를 설명하는 내용이다.

② (8%) 앞 문장의 sound and other technical innovations를 these innovations로 받아 기술 혁신에 대한 부정적인 논조를 이어가는 내용이다.

③ (24%) And what's worse를 통해 기술 혁신이 현실을 잘 표현해 영화 제작자와 관객을 영화의 환상적인 차원에서 멀어지게 했다는 부정적인 점을 추가로 제시하는 것은 자연스럽다.

⑤ (15%) 소리와 색채가 예술의 본질을 파괴한다는 내용에 이어 전문가의 말을 인용해 현실과 표현 매체가 일치하지 않을 때 창의성이 발현된다고 하며 글을 맺고 있다.

01 + 글의 주제 〈22학년도 6월 모평 23번 | 정답률 66%〉 ④

구문분석 & 직독직해

아동 발달 아동기 이후에도 지속되는 역할 놀이

[1]Children can move effortlessly / between play and absorption in a story, // as if both are forms (of the same activity).
(S: Children / V: can move / as if: 부사절 접속사 (마치 ~인 것처럼))

아이들은 쉽게 이동할 수 있다 / (역할) 놀이와 이야기에의 몰입 사이를 // 마치 그 둘이 형태인 것처럼 (같은 활동의)

↳ **도입:** 아이들에게 (역할) 놀이와 이야기 몰입은 비슷함.

[2]The taking of roles / in a narratively structured game of pirates / is not very different / than the taking of roles / in identifying with characters // as one watches a movie.
(S: The taking of roles ... pirates / V: is not / C: different / as: 부사절 접속사(~하면서))

역할을 맡는 것은 / 이야기식으로 구조화된 해적 게임에서 / 그다지 다르지 않다 /
역할을 맡는 것과 / 등장인물과 동일시하며 // (어떤 사람이) 영화를 보면서

↳ **상술:** 게임에서 역할을 맡는 것(= 역할 놀이)과 영화의 등장인물과 자신을 동일시하는 것(= 몰입)은 비슷함.

주제문

[3]It might be thought // that, as they grow towards adolescence, // people give up childhood play, // but this is not so. 🔑 청소년기에도 아동기 놀이는 계속됨.
(It: 가주어 / V: might be thought / that: 진주어(명사절), 명사절 접속사 / as: 부사절 접속사(~하면서) / they (= people) / so (= 앞의 that절))

(~라고) 여겨질 수도 있다 // 사람들이 청소년기로 성장하면서 // 사람들이 아동기의 놀이를 그만둔다고 //
하지만 이는 그렇지 않다

↳ 아동기 이후에도 놀이는 계속됨.

[4]Instead, / the bases and interests (of this activity) / change and develop / to playing and watching sports, / to the fiction (of plays, novels, and movies), / and nowadays to video games.
(S: the bases and interests / V: change and develop / 전치사구 병렬)

🔑 놀이의 기반과 흥미가 다른 것으로 바뀌어 발전함.

대신에 / 기반과 흥미가 (이런 활동의) / 바뀌어 발전한다 / 스포츠 활동과 관람으로 /
허구로 (연극, 소설, 영화의) / 그리고 오늘날에는 비디오 게임으로

↳ **부연 설명:** 아동기 이후에는 놀이의 기반과 흥미가 새로운 방식들로 바뀌어 발전함.

[5]In fiction, / one can enter possible worlds.
(S: one / V: can enter / O: possible worlds)

허구에서 / 사람들은 있을법한 세계로 들어갈 수 있다

[6]When we experience emotions / in such worlds, // this is not a sign // that we are being incoherent or regressed.
(When: 부사절 접속사(시간) / S: this / V: is not / C: a sign = that: 동격 접속사)

우리가 감정들을 경험할 때 / 그런 세계에서 // 이는 신호가 아니다 //우리가 일관되지 않다거나 퇴행하고 있다는

↳ 허구 속에서 감정을 느끼는 것은 퇴행의 신호가 아님.

[7]It derives / from trying out metaphorical transformations (of our selves) / in new ways, / in new worlds, / in *ways* [that can be moving and important to us].
(It (= To experience emotions in such worlds): S / V: derives / from의 O(동명사구) / that: 주격 관계대명사 / V′: can be / C′: moving and important)

그것은 기인한다 / 은유적 변신을 시도하는 것에서 (우리 자신의) / 새로운 방식으로 / 새로운 세계에서 /
방식으로 [우리에게 감동적이고 중요할 수 있는]

↳ 자신을 허구 속 인물과 동일시(= 은유적 변신)하여 감정을 느끼는 것임.

해석

[1]아이들은 마치 (역할) 놀이와 이야기에의 몰입이 같은 활동의 형태인 것처럼 그 둘 사이를 쉽게 이동할 수 있다. [2]이야기식으로 구조화된 해적 게임에서 역할을 맡는 것은 영화를 보면서 등장인물과 동일시하며 역할을 맡는 것과 그다지 다르지 않다. [3]사람들이 청소년기로 성장하면서 아동기의 놀이를 그만둔다고 여겨질 수도 있겠지만, 이는 그렇지 않다. [4]대신에, 이런 활동의 기반과 흥미가 스포츠 활동과 관람으로, 연극, 소설, 영화의 허구로, 그리고 오늘날에는 비디오 게임으로 바뀌어 발전한다. [5]허구에서 사람들은 있을법한 세계로 들어갈 수 있다. [6]우리가 그런 세계에서 감정들을 경험할 때(▶ 예를 들어, 허구 속 죽음이 진짜가 아님에도 슬픔을 느끼는 경우), 이는 우리가 일관되지 않다거나 퇴행하고 있다는 신호가 아니다. [7]그것은 새로운 방식으로, 새로운 세계에서, 우리에게 감동적이고 중요할 수 있는 방식으로 우리 자신의 은유적 변신을 시도하는 것에서 기인한다.

어휘

effortlessly 쉽게, 노력하지 않고
absorption 몰입, 몰두; 흡수
narratively 이야기식으로
cf. narrative 이야기(의); 서술
identify with ~와 동일시하다
adolescence 청소년기
cf. adolescent 청소년
childhood 아동[유년]기; 어린 시절
base 기반, 기초
fiction 허구, 상상; 꾸며낸 이야기
regress 퇴행[퇴보]시키다
derive from ~에서 기인[유래]하다
try out ~을 시도하다, ~을 시험 삼아 해보다
metaphorical 은유적인
transformation 변신, 변화, 탈바꿈
[선택지] stability 안정(감), 안정성
imaginary 가상[상상]의
engagement 참여; 약속; 약혼
alter 변하다; 바꾸다

정답 가이드

아이들이 청소년기로 성장하면서 아동기의 (역할) 놀이를 그만두는 것이 아니라 그 놀이의 기반과 흥미를 스포츠 활동과 관람, 비디오 게임 등으로 바꾸어 발전시켜 계속해서 놀이에 참여한다고 했다. 따라서 글의 주제로 가장 적절한 것은 ④ 'continued engagement in altered forms of play after childhood(아동기 이후 변화된 형태의 놀이에의 지속적 참여)'이다.

오답 클리닉

① relationship between play types and emotional stability (8%)
놀이 유형과 정서적 안정(×) 간의 관계
정서적 안정에 대한 언급은 없음.

② reasons for identifying with imaginary characters in childhood (15%) 아동기에 가상의 등장인물과 동일시하는 이유(×)
아동기에 가상의 등장인물과 동일시한다는 내용은 있으나 그 이유는 언급되지 않음.

The 주의 ⓑ 글 후반부의 허구 세계에서 감정을 느끼는 것이 은유적 변신의 시도에서 기인한다는 내용에서 감정 경험은 허구 속 등장인물과 동일시한 '결과'로 볼 수 있다.

③ ways of helping adolescents develop good reading habits (4%)
청소년이 좋은 독서 습관(×)을 개발하도록 돕는 방법
좋은 독서 습관 개발에 대한 내용은 언급되지 않음.

⑤ effects of narrative structures on readers' imaginations (7%)
독자의 상상력에 이야기 구조가 미치는 영향(×)
독자의 상상력에 이야기 구조가 영향을 미친다는 내용은 없음.

02 + 빈칸 추론 〈21학년도 9월 모평 33번 | 정답률 55%〉 ①

구문분석 & 직독직해 사회 유사성과 차이점을 모두 고려한 평등

주제문
[1] Since human beings are at once both similar and different, // they should be treated equally / because of both.
(Since: 부사절 접속사(~ 때문에), human beings: S′, are: V′, both similar and different: C′, they: S, should be treated: V)
인간은 동시에 비슷하기도 하고 다르기도 하기 때문에 // 그들은 동등하게 대우받아야 한다 / 둘 모두로 인해
↳ 인간은 비슷하지만 다르기도 해서 동등하게 대우받아야 함.

[2] *Such a view*, // which grounds equality / not in human uniformity / but in the interplay (of uniformity and difference), /
(Such a view: S, which: 관계대명사(보충 설명), grounds: V′, equality: O′, not ~ but ~: 전치사구 병렬)
★<not A but B>: A가 아니라 B
그러한 견해는 // 평등의 근거를 두는 / 인간의 획일성이 아니라 / 상호 작용에 (획일성과 차이의) /
★<build A into B>: A를 B의 일부로 만들다
builds difference / into the very concept of equality, / breaks the traditional equation of equality (with similarity), / and is immune / to monist distortion.
(builds: V_1, difference: O_1, breaks: V_2, the traditional equation of equality: O_2, is: V_3, immune: C_3)
차이를 만들어낸다 / 평등이라는 바로 그 개념의 일부로 / 평등의 전통적인 동일시를 깨뜨린다 (유사성과) / 그리고 영향을 받지 않는다 / 일원론적 왜곡의
↳ 부연 설명: 평등의 근거를 획일성(절대적 평등)에 두지 않고, 획일성과 차이의 상호 작용(상대적 평등)에 두는 견해임.

★<so+V+S>: S도 역시 그렇다
[3] Once the basis of equality changes // so does its content.
(Once: 부사절 접속사(일단 ~하면), does: V(= changes), its content: S)
일단 평등의 기준이 바뀌면 // 그것의 내용도 바뀐다

[4] Equality involves / equal freedom or *opportunity* (to be different), // and treating human beings equally / requires us to take into account / both their similarities and differences.
(Equality: S_1, involves: V_1, equal freedom or opportunity: O_1, treating human beings equally: S_2(동명사구), requires: V_2(단수), us: O_2, to take into account ~: C_2)
평등은 포함한다 / 동등한 자유나 기회를 (서로 다를 수 있는) // 그리고 인간을 동등하게 대하는 것은 / 우리가 고려하도록 요구한다 / 그들의 유사성과 차이점을 둘 다
↳ 세부 사항: 평등은 유사성과 차이점을 모두 고려해야 함.

[5] When the latter are not relevant, // equality entails uniform or identical treatment; // when they are (relevant), // it requires differential treatment. ⊶ 차이가 있을 때는 다른 대우가 필요함.
(the latter: (= differences), equality: S_1, entails: V_1, uniform or identical treatment: O_1, they: (= differences), are: 대동사, it: S_2 (= equality), requires: V_2, differential treatment: O_2)
후자(차이점)가 관련이 없을 때 // 평등은 균등하거나 똑같은 대우를 수반한다 //
차이점이 관련이 있을 때 // 그것(평등)은 차등을 두는 대우를 필요로 한다
↳ 예: 차이가 없을 때는 똑같이 대우하면 되지만, 차이점이 있을 때는 차등을 두는 대우가 필요함.

해석

[1]인간은 동시에 비슷하기도 하고 다르기도 하기 때문에 그들은 둘 모두로 인해 동등하게 대우받아야 한다. [2]그러한 견해는 평등의 근거를 인간의 획일성이 아니라 획일성과 차이의 상호 작용에 두는데, 평등이라는 바로 그 개념의 일부로 차이를 만들어내고, 유사성과 평등의 전통적인 동일시를 깨뜨리며, 일원론적 왜곡(▶ 절대 차별을 해서는 안 된다)의 영향을 받지 않는다. [3]일단 평등의 기준이 바뀌면 그것의 내용도 바뀐다. [4]평등은 동등한 자유나 서로 다를 수 있는 기회를 포함하고, 인간을 동등하게 대하는 것은 우리가 그들의 유사성과 차이점을 둘 다 고려하도록 요구한다. [5]후자(차이점)가 관련이 없을 때 평등은 균일하거나 똑같은 대우를 수반하고, 차이점이 관련이 있을 때 그것(평등)은 차등을 두는 대우를 필요로 한다. [6]평등한 권리는 똑같은 권리를 의미하지 않는데, 서로 다른 문화적 배경과 요구를 가진 개인들이 그들 권리의 내용이 되는 모든 것에 관해 평등을 누리기 위해 다른 권리를 요구할지도 모르기 때문이다. [7]평등은 흔히 주장되듯이 무관한 차이들에 대한 거부뿐만 아니라 합법적이고 관련 있는 차이들에 대한 완전한 인정도 포함한다.

어휘

at once 동시에
ground A in B A의 근거를 B에 두다
uniformity 획일(성); 일관(성)
cf. uniform 균등한; 획일적인
interplay 상호 작용
equation 동일시; 방정식
immune ~의 영향을 받지 않는; 면역성이 있는
distortion 왜곡
content 내용; 목차
take into account ~을 고려하다

앞 문장의 identical treatment가 말바꿈됨.

[6]Equal rights do not mean identical rights, //
S V O

평등한 권리는 똑같은 권리를 의미하지 않는다 //

부사절 접속사(이유) / 앞 문장의 identical treatment가 말바꿈됨.

for individuals (with different cultural backgrounds and needs) / might **require different rights** /
S′ V′ O′

to enjoy equality / in respect of whatever happens to be the content of their rights.

목적(~하기 위해) ~에 관해 in respect of의 O(명사절)

개인들이 (~하기) 때문에 (서로 다른 문화적 배경과 요구를 가진) / 다른 권리를 요구할지도 모르기 (때문에) / 평등을 누리기 위해 / 그들 권리의 내용이 되는 모든 것에 관해

↳ 차이가 있는 경우, 개인은 평등을 누리기 위해 서로 다른 권리를 요구할 것임.

🔑 서로 다른 문화 배경과 요구를 가진 이들은 똑같은 권리가 아닌 차이를 고려한 권리를 요구할 것임.

★<not just A but also B>: A뿐만 아니라 B도

[7]Equality involves / not just rejection (of irrelevant differences) // (as is commonly argued), /
S V O₁ 부사절 삽입

but also full recognition (of legitimate and relevant ones).
O₂ (= differences)

평등은 포함한다 / 거부뿐만 아니라 (무관한 차이들에 대한) // (흔히 주장되듯이) / 완전한 인정도 (합법적이고 관련 있는 것들(차이들)에 대한)

↳ **맺음말:** 평등은 차이를 두지 않는 것뿐만 아니라 차이를 인정하는 것도 포함함.

latter 후자(의); 마지막(의)
relevant 관련이 있는(↔ irrelevant 무관한)
identical 똑같은, 동일한
differential 차등을 두는, 차별하는
rejection 거부, 거절
cf. reject 거부[거절]하다
recognition 인정, 승인; 알아봄, 인식
legitimate 합법적인, 합당한
[선택지] abandon 포기하다; 버리다
perception 인식; 지각

정답 가이드

빈칸 문장의 주절에서 평등이 똑같은 권리를 의미하지 않는다고 했고, 빈칸이 있는 부사절은 그 이유를 설명하는데, 주어가 서로 다른 문화적 배경과 요구를 가진 개인들이므로 빈칸에는 '평등을 위해 서로 다른 권리가 필요'할지도 모른다는 맥락의 내용이 들어가야 한다. 또한 이어지는 문장에서 평등은 차이를 인정하는 것도 포함한다고 했으므로, 빈칸에 들어갈 말로 가장 적절한 것은 ① 'require different rights to enjoy equality(평등을 누리기 위해 다른 권리를 요구한다)'이다.

오답 클리닉

② abandon their own freedom for equality (13%)
평등을 위해 자신의 자유를 포기한다
평등은 동등한 자유를 포함한다고 했으므로 틀림.

③ welcome the identical perception of inequality (9%)
불평등에 관한 동일한 인식을 기꺼이 받아들인다
차이에 따라 다르게 대우하는 평등에 관한 내용이며, 불평등을 받아들인다는 내용은 없음.

④ accept their place in the social structure more easily (15%)
사회 구조에서 자신의 위치를 더 쉽게 받아들인다
사회적 위치를 받아들인다는 내용은 없음.

⑤ reject relevant differences to gain full understanding (9%)
온전한 이해를 얻기 위해 관련이 있는 차이점을 거부한다
문장 7에서 평등은 차이에 대한 인정도 포함한다고 했으므로 틀림.

03 + 글의 순서 (22학년도 9월 모평 37번 | 정답률 45%) ②

구문분석 & 직독직해

기술 개인용 가정 보조로서 소셜 로봇의 특징

★<a number of+복수명사>: 많은 ~

[1]Recently, / *a number of commercial ventures* have been launched [that offer social robots / as personal home assistants], / perhaps eventually to rival existing smart-home assistants.
S V 주격 관계대명사 전치사(~로(서)) 결과((결국) ~하다)

최근에 / 많은 상업적인 벤처 사업들이 시작되었다 [소셜 로봇을 제공하는 / 개인용 가정 보조로] / 아마도 결국 기존의 스마트 홈 보조와 경쟁하게 될 것이다

↳ **도입:** 소셜 로봇을 개인용 가정 보조로 제공하는 다양한 사업들이 시작됨.

🔑 주어진 글에 언급한 로봇을 설명함.

(B) [2]Personal robotic assistants are *devices* [that have no physical manipulation or locomotion capabilities.
S V C 주격 관계대명사

개인용 로봇 보조는 장치이다 [물리적 조작이나 이동 능력이 없는]

↳ **특징 1:** 물리적 조작 및 이동 능력이 없음.

(= personal robotic assistants)

[3]Instead, / they have a distinct social presence / and have *visual features* (suggestive of their ability (to interact socially)), / such as eyes, ears, or a mouth.
S V₁ O₁ V₂ O₂ 형용사구

대신에 / 그것들(개인용 로봇 보조)에는 뚜렷한 사회적 실재감이 있다 / 그리고 시각적 특징을 가지고 있다 (그것들의 능력을 암시하는 (사회적으로 상호 작용하는)) / 눈, 귀 또는 입과 같은

↳ **특징 2:** 사회적 실재감이 뚜렷하고 사회적 상호 작용을 보여주는 시각적 특징이 있음.

해석

[1]최근에, 소셜 로봇을 개인용 가정 보조로 제공하는 많은 상업적인 벤처 사업들이 시작되어서, 아마도 결국 기존의 스마트 홈 보조와 경쟁하게 될 것이다. (B) [2]개인용 로봇 보조는 물리적 조작이나 이동 능력이 없는 장치이다. [3]대신에, 그것들(개인용 로봇 보조)에는 뚜렷한 사회적 실재감이 있고 눈, 귀 또는 입과 같은 사회적으로 상호 작용하는 그것들의 능력을 암시하는 시각적 특징을 가지고 있다. (A) [4]그것들(개인용 로봇 보조)은 동력화될 수 있으며 방 안의 사용자를 추적할 수 있어서, 주위에 있는 사람들을 감지한다는 인상을 준다. [5]개인용 로봇 보조가 스마트 홈 보조의 서비스와 유사한 서비스를 제공할지라도, 그들의 사회적 실재감은 소셜 로봇 특유의 기회를 제공한다. (C) [6]예를 들어, 음악을 틀어주는 것뿐 아니라, 소셜 개인용 보조 로봇은 마치 사용자가 로봇과 함께 그 음악을 듣고 있는 것처럼 느끼도록 음악과의 교감을 표현할 것이다. [7]이러한 로봇들은 보안 감시 장치로 사용될 수 있거나, 통신 매개체의

↱ (= personal robotic assistants) ⊶ (B)의 로봇 특징을 부연 설명함.

(A) [4]They might be motorized / and can track the user (around the room), /
S V₁ V₂ O₂

그것들(개인용 로봇 보조)은 동력화될 수 있다 / 그리고 사용자를 추적할 수 있다 (방 안의) /

giving the impression (of being aware of the people (in the environment)).

분사구문(= so they give ~) =

그래서 인상을 준다 (사람들을 감지한다는 (주위에 있는))

↳ **특징 3:** 동력화될 수 있고 공간에 있는 사용자를 탐지함.

[5]Although personal robotic assistants provide / *services* (similar to those of smart-home assistants), //

부사절 접속사(양보) S′ V′ O′ (= services)

개인용 로봇 보조가 제공할지라도 / 서비스를 (스마트 홈 보조의 그것(서비스)과 유사한) //

their social presence offers / *an opportunity* [that is unique to social robots].

S V O 주격 관계대명사

그들의 사회적 실재감은 제공한다 / 기회를 [소셜 로봇 특유의]

↳ **특징 4:** 사회적 실재감이 소셜 로봇 특유의 기회를 제공함.

⊶ (A)의 소셜 로봇의 사회적 실재감이 제공하는 기회의 예를 제시함.

(C)[6]For instance, / in addition to playing music, / a social personal assistant robot would express /

~뿐 아니라 S V

its engagement (with the music) //

O

예를 들어 / 음악을 틀어주는 것뿐 아니라 / 소셜 개인용 보조 로봇은 표현할 것이다 / 교감을 (음악과의) //

so that users would feel // like they are listening to the music / together with the robot.

부사절 접속사(~하도록) 부사절 접속사(마치 ~인 것처럼)

사용자가 느끼도록 // 마치 자신들이 그 음악을 듣고 있는 것처럼 / 로봇과 함께

↳ **특징 4의 예 1:** 음악을 틀어줄 뿐만 아니라 사용자와 함께 음악을 듣고 있는 것처럼 음악과의 교감을 표현함.

[7]These robots can be used / as surveillance devices, / (can) act as communicative intermediates, /

S V₁ 전치사(~로(서)) V₂

(can) engage in richer games, / (can) tell stories, / or (can) be used / to provide encouragement or incentives.

V₃ V₄ V₅ 목적(~하는 데)

이러한 로봇들은 사용될 수 있다 / 보안 감시 장치로 / 통신 매개체의 역할을 할 수 있다 /
더 풍부한 게임에 참여할 수 있다 / 이야기를 들려줄 수 있다 / 또는 사용될 수 있다 / 격려나 동기를 제공하는 데

↳ **특징 4의 예 2:** 보안 감시 장치, 통신 매개체, 게임 참여, 이야기 전달, 격려 및 동기 제공 등에 사용될 수 있음.

역할을 하거나, 더 풍부한 게임에 참여하거나, 이야기를 들려주거나, 격려나 동기를 제공하는 데 사용될 수 있다.

어휘

commercial 상업적인; 광고 (방송)
venture 벤처 사업; 모험; 위험을 무릅쓰고 ~하다
launch 시작하다; 출시하다; 발사하다
rival 경쟁하다; 경쟁자
device 장치, 기구
manipulation (기계·기구의) 조작, 조종; 속임(수)
distinct 뚜렷한, 분명한; 별개의
feature 특징(을 이루다); 특집 (기사)
suggestive of ~을 암시[시사]하는
motorize 동력화하다
track 추적하다; 탐지하다
unique to A A 특유의, 고유의
engagement 교감, 참여; 약속; 약혼
cf. engage in ~에 참여하다, ~에 종사하다
intermediate 매개체; 중간의; 중급의
incentive 동기, 유인; 장려책

⊕ 소셜 로봇(social robot): 사람을 대신하여 물리적인 일을 하는 산업용 로봇이나 서비스 로봇과 달리, 사람과 상호 작용하고 소통하기 위해 설계된 로봇으로 인간의 행동, 감정 등을 인지하고 반응할 수 있음.

⊕ 사회적 실재감(social presence): 누군가와 함께 교류하고 있다고 느끼는 것.

정답 가이드

소셜 로봇을 개인용 가정 보조로 제공하는 사업의 시작을 언급한 주어진 글 뒤에는 그 로봇에 대한 구체적인 설명에 해당하는 (A), 또는 (B)가 이어질 수 있다. 한편, (C)는 스마트 홈 보조와 대조되는, 소셜 로봇이 제공하는 사회적 실재감의 예인데, (A)의 마지막에 언급된 소셜 로봇 특유의 기회에 대한 구체적 설명으로 볼 수 있다. 따라서 (B) - (A) - (C)의 순서가 적절하다.

오답 클리닉

① (A) - (C) - (B) (3%)
(B)에서 이동 능력이 없지만 (A)에서 동력화될 수 있다고 했고, (B)에서 언급한 사회적으로 상호 작용하는 시각적 특징과 뚜렷한 사회적 실재감을 (A)에서 사용자를 추적할 수 있고 소셜 로봇에만 특유한 기회를 제공한다고 부연 설명하고 있으므로 (A)는 (B) 뒤에 와야 한다.

③ (B) - (C) - (A) (34%)
음악을 틀어줄 뿐만 아니라 음악과의 교감을 표현한다는 (C)는 (A)의 소셜 로봇의 사회적 실재감이 제공하는 특유한 기회의 예에 해당하므로 (C)는 (A) 뒤에 와야 한다.

The 주의 (C)를 (B)의 사회적으로 상호 작용하는 능력을 보여주는 예로 생각할 수도 있으나, 스마트 홈 보조가 제공하는 서비스(음악을 틀어주는 것)와 대조되는 소셜 로봇만의 특유한 서비스(음악과의 교감을 표현)에 대해 설명하고 있으므로 (A)의 마지막 문장의 예로 보는 것이 적절하다.

④ (C) - (A) - (B) (10%) / ⑤ (C) - (B) - (A) (8%)
(C)는 소셜 로봇의 기능의 구체적인 예에 해당하므로 기능에 대한 전반적인 설명이 먼저 제시된 다음에 오는 것이 흐름상 적절하다.

01 + 글의 제목 〈22학년도 6월 모평 24번 | 정답률 65%〉 ①

구문분석 & 직독직해

인지 노년기 사회 지각의 이점

주제문

[1]Although cognitive and neuropsychological approaches emphasize / *the losses with age* [that might impair social perception], //
부사절 접속사(양보) S′ V′ O′ 주격 관계대명사 V″ O″
비록 인지적 접근법과 신경심리학적 접근법이 강조할지라도 / 노화에 따른 손실을 [사회적 지각을 해칠지도 모르는] //

motivational theories indicate // that there may be some gains or qualitative changes.
S V 명사절 접속사 V′ S′ (indicate의 O(명사절)) 노화에 이점이나 질적 변화가 있을 수 있음.
동기 이론은 보여 준다 // 어떤 이점이나 질적인 변화가 있을 수 있다는 것을
↳ **노화에 관한 대조적인 이론:** 인지적/신경심리학적 접근법(손실이 있음) ↔ 동기 이론(이점이 있음).

[2]Charles and Carstensen review / *a considerable body of evidence* (indicating // that, /
S V O 현재분사구 명사절 접속사 (indicating의 O(명사절))
Charles와 Carstensen은 재검토한다 / 상당한 양의 증거를 (보여 주는 // (~라는) 것을 /
*( )는 명사절 접속사와 주어 사이에 삽입된 부사절임.
(as people get older), // they tend / to prioritize close social relationships, / (to) focus more on achieving emotional well-being, / [and] (to) attend more to positive emotional information /
부사절 접속사(~할수록) S′ V′ to-v구 병렬 to-v구 병렬 to-v구 병렬
while ignoring negative information).
접속사를 생략하지 않은 분사구문(= while they ignore ~)
(사람들이 나이가 들수록) // 그들은 (~하는) 경향이 있다는 / 친밀한 사회적 관계를 우선시하는 / 정서적 행복을 달성하는 데 더 집중하는 / 그리고 긍정적인 정서적 정보에 더 주의를 기울이는 / 부정적인 정보는 무시하는 반면에
↳ **동기 이론 논거 1(노화에 따른 변화):** 친목 관계, 정서적 행복, 긍정적 정보를 중시함.

[3]These changing motivational goals (in old age) / have implications /
S V O
for attention to [and] processing of / social cues (from the environment).
전치사 for의 O(명사구 병렬) 전치사 to와 of의 공통 O
이 변화하는 동기 부여의 목표는 (노년의) / 영향을 미친다 / ~에의 주목과 처리에 / 사회적 신호 (주변 환경에서 오는)
↳ **동기 변화의 결과:** 사회 지각에 영향을 미침.

*<of+추상명사=형용사>이므로 of particular importance는 particularly important와 같음.
[4]Of particular importance / in considering emotional changes (in old age) / is the presence of a positivity bias: // 노년기의 긍정 편향은 사회 지각에 있어 이점임.
C V S
*형용사 역할의 보어가 문두에 와서 주어와 동사가 도치됨.
특히 중요한 / 정서적 변화를 고려할 때 (노년에서의) / 긍정 편향의 존재가 ~이다 //
that is, a tendency (to notice, attend to, and remember / more positive (information) / compared to negative information).
즉, 경향 (인지하고, 주의를 기울이고, 기억하는 / 더 많은 긍정적 정보를 / 부정적 정보에 비해)
↳ **결과 부연 설명:** 노년기에 부정적 정보보다 긍정적 정보에 집중하는 경향이 특히 중요함.

[5]The role (of life experience in social skills) / also indicates // that older adults might show gains /
S(단수) V(단수) 명사절 접속사 S′ V′ O′ (indicates의 O(명사절))
in some aspects (of social perception). 사회적 경험은 노인의 사회 지각에 긍정적으로 작용함.
역할은 (사회적 기술에 관한 인생 경험의) / 또한 보여준다 // 노인이 이점을 보일지도 모른다는 것을 / 일부 측면들에서 (사회적 지각의)
↳ **동기 이론 논거 2:** 사회적 경험이 노년기 사회 지각에 이점이 됨.

해석

[1]비록 인지적 접근법과 신경심리학적 접근법이 사회적 지각을 해칠지도 모르는 노화에 따른 손실을 강조할지라도, 동기 이론은 어떤 이점이나 질적 변화가 있을 수 있다는 것을 보여 준다.(▶ 나이가 들어감에 따라 인지적/신경심리학적으로는 손실이 있지만, 동기 이론에 의하면 이점이나 질적 변화가 있다는 의미) [2]Charles와 Carstensen은 사람들이 나이가 들수록 가까운 사회적 관계를 우선시하고, 정서적 행복을 달성하는 데 더 집중하고, 부정적인 정보는 무시하는 반면에 긍정적인 정서적 정보에 더 주의를 기울이는 경향이 있다는 것을 보여 주는 상당한 양의 증거를 재검토한다. [3]노년의 이 변화하는 동기 부여의 목표는 주변 환경에서 오는 사회적 신호에의 주목과 처리에 영향을 미친다. [4]노년에서의 정서적 변화를 고려할 때 긍정 편향, 즉, 부정적 정보에 비해 더 많은 긍정적 정보를 인지하고, 주의를 기울이고, 기억하는 경향의 존재가 특히 중요하다. [5]사회적 기술에 관한 인생 경험의 역할은 또한 노인이 사회적 지각의 일부 측면들에서 이점을 보일지도 모른다는 것을 보여 준다.

어휘

neuropsychological 신경심리학의
emphasize 강조하다
perception 지각; 인식(력)
indicate 보여 주다, 나타내다; 가리키다
qualitative 질적인
considerable 상당한, 많은
tend to-v v하는 경향이 있다
prioritize 우선시하다; 우선순위를 매기다
well-being 행복, 안녕, 복지
attend to A A에 주의를 기울이다
implication 영향, 결과; 함축, 암시
cue 신호, 단서; 신호를 주다
presence 존재, 현존; 참석
bias 편향, 편견
tendency 경향; 성향
aspect 측면; 관점, 견해
[선택지] block out ~을 차단하다[막다]
sharpen 단련시키다, 연마하다; 날카롭게 하다
maturity 성숙(기)
objectivity 객관성
reverse 역으로 돌리다; 뒤집다; 반대(의); 뒷면(의)

정답 가이드

첫 문장에서 노화가 사회적 지각을 해친다는 인지적/신경심리학적 접근법과 반대로, 동기 이론은 노화가 사회적 지각에 이점이 있을 수 있다는 것을 보여준다고 했다. 이어지는 내용은 긍정적인 정보에 주목하는 긍정 편향과 풍부한 사회적 경험을 근거로 동기 이론을 뒷받침한다. 따라서 글의 제목으로 가장 적절한 것은 ① 'Social Perception in Old Age: It's Not All Bad News!(노년의 사회적 지각, 이는 전부 나쁜 소식은 아니다!)'이다.

오답 클리닉

② Blocking Out the Negative Sharpens Social Skills (9%)
부정적인 것을 차단하는 것이 사회적 기술을 단련시킨다(×)
부정적인 것을 차단하는 것과 사회적 기술은 각각 노년기의 사회적 지각에 작용하는 이점으로 언급된 것이며, 서로 인과관계에 있지 않음.

③ Lessons on Life-long Goals from Senior Achievers (6%)
크게 성공한 노인들로부터의 평생 목표(×)에 대한 교훈
성공한 노인들로부터 평생 목표에 대한 교훈을 얻는 내용이 아님.

④ Getting Old: A Road to Maturity and Objectivity (8%)
나이가 드는 것, 즉 성숙과 객관성(×)에 이르는 길
나이가 들수록 긍정적인 것에 주목한다고 했지만, 성숙해진다거나 객관성을 얻게 된다는 내용은 없음.

⑤ Positive Mind and Behavior: Tips for Reversing Aging (12%)
긍정적인 마음과 행동, 즉 노화를 역으로 돌리기 위한 조언(×)
나이가 들면서 긍정적인 것에 주목한다고 했지만, 이는 노화를 되돌리기 위한 방법이 아님.

02 + 빈칸 추론 (21학년도 9월 모평 32번 | 정답률 38%)

②

구문분석 & 직독직해

생물 생물 다양성의 위협이 아닌 유전 공학

[1] *Genetic engineering* (followed by *cloning* (to distribute many identical animals or plants)) / is sometimes seen / as a threat (to the diversity of nature).

S: Genetic engineering / 과거분사구: followed by ... / V: is sometimes seen / 전치사(~로(서)) as / *<see A as B(A를 B로 여기다[간주하다])>의 수동형

유전 공학은 (생물 복제로 이어지는 (많은 똑같은 동물이나 식물을 퍼뜨리기 위한)) / 때때로 여겨진다 / 위협으로 (자연의 다양성에 대한)

↳ **통념(Myth):** 유전 공학이 자연의 다양성을 위협한다고 생각함.

[2] However, / humans have been replacing diverse natural habitats / with artificial monoculture / for millennia.

S: humans / V: have been replacing / O: diverse natural habitats / *<replace A with B>: A를 B로 대체하다

그러나 / 인간은 다양한 자연 서식지를 대체해 오고 있다 / 인위적인 단일 경작으로 / 수천 년간

↳ **사실(Truth):** 인간의 인위적인 단일 경작이 자연의 다양성을 대체함.

[3] Most natural habitats (in the advanced nations) / have already been replaced / with some form of *artificial environment* (based on mass production or repetition).

S: Most natural habitats / V: have already been replaced / 과거분사구: based on ...

대부분의 자연 서식지는 (선진국의) / 이미 대체되었다 / 인위적인 환경의 어떤 형태로 (대량 생산이나 반복에 기반을 둔)

↳ **부연 설명:** 식량의 대량 생산을 위해 자연 서식지가 인위적인 환경으로 바뀜.

[4] The real threat (to biodiversity) / is surely *the need* (to convert ever more of our planet / into production zones / to feed the ever-increasing human population).

S: The real threat / V: is / C: the need / *<convert A into B>: A를 B로 전환하다 / 목적(~하기 위해): to feed

진짜 위협은 (생물 다양성에 대한) / 분명히 필요성이다 (지구의 더욱더 많은 부분을 전환해야 할 / 생산 구역으로 / 계속 증가하는 인구를 먹여 살리기 위해)

↳ 식량 공급을 위해 지구의 많은 부분을 생산 구역으로 바꾸는 것이 생물 다양성을 위협함.

[5] The cloning and transgenic alteration (of domestic animals) / makes little difference / to the overall situation.

S(단수): The cloning and transgenic alteration / V(단수): makes / O: little difference

생물 복제와 이식 유전자에 의한 변화는 (가축의) / 변화를 거의 가져오지 않는다 / 전반적인 상황에

↳ **통념 반박:** 유전 공학은 생물 다양성에 거의 위협을 주지 않음.

해석

[1] 많은 똑같은 동물이나 식물을 퍼뜨리기 위한 생물 복제로 이어지는 유전 공학은 때때로 자연의 다양성에 대한 위협으로 여겨진다. [2] 그러나 인간은 수천 년간 인위적인 단일 경작으로 다양한 자연 서식지를 대체해 오고 있다. [3] 선진국의 대부분의 자연 서식지는 대량 생산이나 반복에 기반을 둔 인위적인 환경의 어떤 형태로 이미 대체되었다. [4] 생물 다양성에 대한 진짜 위협은 분명히 계속 증가하는 인구를 먹여 살리기 위해 지구의 더욱더 많은 부분을 생산 구역으로 전환해야 할 필요성이다. [5] 가축의 생물 복제와 이식 유전자에 의한 변화는 전반적인 상황에 변화를 거의 가져오지 않는다. [6] 반대로, 유전학에 대한 새로워진 관심은 다양한 아직 알려지지 않은 목적을 위해서 이용될 수 있는 흥미롭거나 유용한 유전적 특성을 가진 많은 야생 동식물이 있다는 증가하는 인식으로 이어졌다. [7] 이는 결국 자연 생태계가 암, 말라리아 또는 비만에 맞서는 미래의 약의 거처가 될 수도 있기 때문에 우리가 자연 생태계를 파괴하는 것을 피해야 한다는 깨달음으로 이어졌다.

어휘

genetic engineering 유전 공학
cloning 생물 복제
distribute 퍼뜨리다; 분배하다, 나누어 주다
identical 똑같은, 동일한
diversity 다양성
cf. diverse 다양한
cf. biodiversity 생물 다양성
habitat 서식지; 거주지

🔑 아직 알려지지 않은 목적으로 이용될 수 있는 유용한 유전적 특성을 가진 야생 동식물이 많다는 인식을 늘림.

[6]Conversely, / the renewed interest (in genetics) / has led to a growing awareness // that there are many wild plants and animals (with *interesting or useful genetic properties* [that could be used / for a variety of as-yet-unknown purposes]).

S(단수) V(단수) O = 동격 접속사 주격 관계대명사

반대로 / 새로워진 관심은 (유전학에 대한) / 증가하는 인식으로 이어졌다 // 많은 야생 동식물이 있다는 (흥미롭거나 유용한 유전적 특성을 가진 [이용될 수 있는 / 다양한 아직 알려지지 않은 목적을 위해서])

↳ 유전 공학이 유용한 유전적 특성을 가진 동식물에 대한 인식을 높임.

(= The growing awareness)

[7]This has led in turn to a realization // that **we should avoid destroying natural ecosystems** //

S V O = 동격 접속사

이(증가하는 인식)는 결국 깨달음으로 이어졌다 // 우리가 자연 생태계를 파괴하는 것을 피해야 한다는 //

(= natural ecosystems)

because they may harbor tomorrow's drugs (against cancer, malaria, or obesity).

부사절 접속사(이유)

그것(자연 생태계)이 미래의 약의 거처가 될 수도 있기 때문에 (암, 말라리아 또는 비만에 맞서는)

🔑 질병 치료의 거처가 될 수도 있으므로 생물 다양성을 유지해야 할 것임.

↳ **결론:** 유전 공학은 생물 다양성의 필요를 깨닫게 함.

artificial 인위적인; 인공의
millennium (*pl.* millennia) 천년(간)
mass 대량의, 대규모의; 대중의
feed 먹여 살리다; 먹이를 주다
transgenic 이식 유전자에 의한
alteration 변화; 개조, 수정
domestic animal 가축
conversely 반대로, 역으로
renewed 새로워진, 재개된
awareness 인식, 자각; 의식
property 특성, 속성; 재산; 부동산
harbor (동물 등의) 거처가 되다; 항구
obesity 비만
[선택지] modify 변경[수정]하다; 수식하다
adapt 적응하다; 맞추다, 조정하다

정답 가이드

빈칸 문장과 직전 문장으로 보아 This(다양한 목적으로 이용될 수 있는 야생 동식물이 있다는 인식)는 '어떤' 깨달음을 이끌었고, 그 이유는 they(자연 생태계)에 질병을 치료할 약이 있을 수 있기 때문이다. 글 앞부분부터 살펴보면 유전 공학이 똑같은 생물을 복제하기 때문에 자연의 다양성을 위협한다고 여겨지지만, 사실 진짜 위협은 인간이 식량 공급을 위해 자연 서식지를 인위적인 생산지로 바꾸는 것이며 유전 공학은 오히려 유용한 유전적 특성을 가진 야생 동식물에 대한 인식을 높였다는 것이다. 즉 이런 인식이 '야생 동식물을 보존해야 할' 깨달음을 주었다는 문맥이 되는 것이 가장 적절하다. 따라서 빈칸에 들어갈 말로 가장 적절한 것은 ② 'we should avoid destroying natural ecosystems(우리가 자연 생태계를 파괴하는 것을 피해야 한다)'이다. 이는 because 이하의 they(자연 생태계)가 질병을 치료할 약의 거처가 될 수 있기 때문이라는 내용과도 잘 연결된다.

오답 클리닉

① ecological systems are genetically programmed (16%)
생태계는 유전적으로 프로그램되어 있다
생태계가 유전적으로 프로그램되어 있다는 언급은 없음.

③ we need to stop creating genetically modified organisms (20%)
우리가 유전자 변형 생물을 만드는 것을 중단할 필요가 있다
유전자 변형 생물을 만드는 것을 비판하는 내용이 아님. 복제와 유전자 변형은 생물 다양성에 위협이 아니라고 했음.

④ artificial organisms can survive in natural environments (17%)
인위적인 유기체는 자연환경에서 생존할 수 있다
인위적 유기체의 생존 가능성은 언급되지 않음.

⑤ living things adapt themselves to their physical environments (8%)
생물은 자신의 물리적 환경에 적응한다
생물의 물리적 환경에 대한 적응성은 언급되지 않음.

03 + 문장 넣기 (22학년도 9월 모평 38번 | 정답률 51%) ④

구문분석 & 직독직해

과학 물질에 관한 이해의 발달

[1]The earliest humans had access / to only a very limited number of materials, / *those* [that occur naturally]: / stone, wood, clay, skins, and so on.

S V O = 주격 관계대명사

초기 인류는 접근했었다 / 매우 제한된 수의 물질들에만 / 즉 것들 [자연적으로 존재하는] / 돌, 나무, 찰흙, 가죽 등의

(= the earliest humans)

(①) [2]With time, / they discovered / techniques (for producing *materials* [that had *properties* (superior to those of the natural ones)); // these new materials included pottery and various metals.

S_1 V_1 O_1 주격 관계대명사 (= properties) (= materials) S_2 V_2 O_2

시간이 흐르면서 / 그들(초기 인류)은 발견했다 / 기술을 (물질을 만들어 내는 [특성을 가진 (자연적인 물질의 특성보다 더 우수한)]) // 이 새로운 물질은 도자기와 다양한 금속을 포함했다

↳ **세부 사항 1(초기 인류):** 제한된 자연적인 물질만 이용 → 더 우수한 물질(도자기, 금속)을 만들어 냄.

진주어(명사절)

(②) [3]Furthermore, / it was discovered // that the properties of a material could be altered / by heat treatments and by the addition of other substances.

가주어 V 명사절 접속사 S' V' 전치사구 병렬

게다가 / (~이) 발견되었다 // 물질의 특성이 바뀔 수 있다는 것이 / 열처리와 다른 물질의 첨가로

해석

[1]초기 인류는 매우 제한된 수의 물질들, 즉 돌, 나무, 찰흙, 가죽 등의 자연적으로 존재하는 것들에만 접근했었다. (①) [2]시간이 흐르면서 그들(초기 인류)은 자연적인 물질의 특성보다 더 우수한 특성을 가진 물질을 만들어 내는 기술을 발견했는데, 이 새로운 물질은 도자기와 다양한 금속을 포함했다. (②) [3]게다가, 물질의 특성이 열처리와 다른 물질의 첨가로 바뀔 수 있다는 것이 발견되었다. (③) [4]이 시점에, 물질 이용은 전적으로 주어진 상당히 제한된 물질의 집합 중에서 물질의 특성에 근거하여 용도에 가장 적합한 물질을 결정하는 것을 수반하는 선택의 과정이었다. (④ [5]비교적 최근에서야 비로소 과학자들이 물질의 구조적 요소와 특성 사이의 관계를 이해하게 되었다.) [6]이 지식은 대략 지난 100년 동안 획득되었는데, 그들(과학자들)이 상당한 정도로 물질의 특성을 형성할 수 있게 했다. (⑤)

주어진 문장의 recent times와 대비되는 과거 발견의 시기를 지칭함.

(③) [4]At this point, / materials utilization was totally *a selection process* [that involved deciding / from a given, rather limited set of materials, / the one (best suited for an application / based on its characteristics)].

S V C 주격 관계대명사 (= the material) deciding의 O(명사구)

이 시점에 / 물질 이용은 전적으로 선택의 과정이었다 [결정하는 것을 수반하는 / 주어진 상당히 제한된 물질의 집합 중에서 / 물질을 (용도에 가장 적합한 / 물질의 특성에 근거하여)]

↳ **추가 설명:** 물질의 특성을 바꿀 수 있게 되면서 특성에 근거해 용도에 맞는 적합한 물질을 결정해야 했음.

(④) [5]It was not until relatively recent times // that scientists came to understand / the relationships (between the structural elements of materials and their properties).)

*<it is[was] not until A that B>: A하고 나서야 비로소 B하다[했다] S′ V′ 현대 과학자들의 이해가 이어짐.

비교적 최근에서야 // 비로소 과학자들이 이해하게 되었다 / 관계를 (물질의 구조적 요소와 특성 사이의)

↳ **세부 사항 2(현대 과학자):** 최근에서야 과학자들이 물질의 구조적 요소와 특성 간의 관계를 이해하게 됨.

This knowledge는 주어진 문장의 현대 과학자들의 이해를 가리킴. *<empower+O+to-v>: O가 v할 수 있게 하다

[6]This knowledge, / (being) acquired over approximately the past 100 years, / has empowered them to fashion, / (to a large degree), / the characteristics of materials.

S(단수) 분사구문(= and it has been acquired ~) V(단수) O (= scientists) C 삽입어구

이 지식은 / 대략 지난 100년 동안 획득되었는데 / 그들(과학자들)이 형성할 수 있게 했다 / (상당한 정도로) / 물질의 특성을

(⑤) [7]Thus, / tens of thousands of different materials have evolved / (with *rather specialized characteristics* [that meet the needs (of our modern and complex society)]), / including metals, plastics, glasses, and fibers.

S V 전치사구(주어 수식) 주격 관계대명사 전치사(~을 포함하여)

따라서 / 수만 가지의 다양한 물질이 생성되었다 / (상당히 특수화된 특성을 가진 [요구를 충족하는 (현대적이고 복잡한 우리 사회의)]) / 금속, 플라스틱, 유리, 섬유를 포함하여

↳ **결과:** 물질의 특성을 형성하게 되어 현대 사회의 요구를 충족하는 수만 가지의 다양한 물질이 생성됨.

[7]따라서 금속, 플라스틱, 유리, 섬유를 포함하여 현대적이고 복잡한 우리 사회의 요구를 충족하는 상당히 특수화된 특성을 가진 수만 가지의 다양한 물질이 생성되었다.

어휘

access 접근(권); 접근하다; 이용하다
material 물질(적인); 재료
property 특성; 재산; 부동산
superior to A A보다 더 우수한
pottery 도자기
alter 바꾸다, 변경하다
treatment (약품에 의한) 처리; 치료; 대우
addition 첨가; 추가
substance 물질
utilization 이용, 활용
suited 적합한; 어울리는
application (특정의) 용도; 지원(서); 적용
fashion 형성하다, 만들다; 유행
degree 정도
evolve 생성되다; 발전[진화]하다
specialized 특수화[분화]된; 전문적인
meet (필요 등을) 충족시키다; 만나다
fiber 섬유

정답 가이드

주어진 문장은 최근에서야 비로소 과학자들이 물질의 구조적 요소와 특성 간의 관계를 이해하게 되었다는 내용으로, 앞에는 이 관계를 이해하지 못한 '과거 시절'이 서술되어야 한다. ④ 앞은 과거 인류가 제한된 물질의 집합 중에서 물질을 이용했다는 설명이고, ④의 뒤 문장의 This knowledge는 주어진 문장의 과학자가 이해하게 된 물질의 구조적 요소와 특성 간의 관계를, them은 과학자를 가리키므로 주어진 문장이 들어가기에 가장 적절한 곳은 ④이다.

오답 클리닉

① (4%) 초기 인류가 자연적으로 존재하는 물질만 이용하는 것에서 자연 물질보다 더 우수한 물질을 만들어 내게 되었다는 발전을 서술하는 내용이다.
② (12%) 앞 문장의 발전에 더해 물질의 특성이 바뀔 수 있음을 발견했다는 내용이 첨가의 연결어 Furthermore로 이어지는 것은 적절하다.
③ (21%) 앞 문장의 발견을 한 시기를 At this point로 가리키며 물질 이용은 전적으로 제한된 물질 중에서 선택하는 과정이었다고 부연 설명하는 내용이다.
⑤ (12%) 과학자들이 물질의 특성을 형성할 수 있게 되었다는 앞 문장의 결과가 Thus로 이어지는 것은 적절하다.

01 + 함의 추론 (21학년도 대수능 21번 | 정답률 62%) ②

구문분석 & 직독직해

미디어 환경을 대변해야 하는 환경 저널리스트의 역할

[1] There is *an African proverb* [that says, // 'Till the lions have their historians, // tales of hunting will always glorify the hunter'].
주격 관계대명사 / 부사절 접속사(시간)
아프리카 속담이 있다 [~라고 하는 // "사자들이 자신들의 역사가를 갖게 될 때까지 // 사냥 이야기는 언제나 사냥한 자를 미화할 것이다"]

[2] The proverb is about power, control and law making.
S V C
이 속담은 권력, 통제, 법 제정에 관한 것이다
↳ **도입:** 사자(= 약자)의 입장을 대변하는 역사가는 없다는 뜻의 아프리카 속담은 권력, 통제, 법 제정과 관련됨.

주제문
[3] Environmental journalists have to play **the role (of the 'lion's historians')**.
S V O
환경 저널리스트는 그 역할을 수행해야 한다 ('사자의 역사가'의)
↳ **주장:** 환경 저널리스트는 환경을 대변하는 역할을 해야 함.

(= Environmental journalists) / 환경 저널리스트들의 구체적인 역할을 언급함.
[4] They have to put across the point of view (of the environment) / to *people* [who make the laws].
S V O / 주격 관계대명사
그들은 관점을 이해시켜야 한다 (환경에 대한) / 사람들에게 [법을 만드는]
↳ **역할 1:** 입법자들이 환경을 생각할 수 있도록 해야 함.

(= Environmental journalists)
[5] They have to be the voice of wild India.
S V C
그들은 인도 야생의 대변인이 되어야 한다
↳ **역할 2:** 야생의 자연 보호를 위해 목소리를 내야 함.

[6] The present rate (of human consumption) / is completely unsustainable.
S V C
현재 속도는 (인간 소비의) / 전적으로 지속 불가능하다

*<see A as B(A를 B로 여기다)>의 수동형
[7] Forest, wetlands, wastelands, coastal zones, eco-sensitive zones, they are all seen / as disposable / for the accelerating demands (of human population).
S = V
숲, 습지, 황무지, 해안 지역, 환경 민감 지역 모두 여겨진다 / 마음대로 쓸 수 있는 것으로 / 가속화되고 있는 수요를 위해 (인구의)
↳ **비판 1:** 인간 마음대로 자연을 빠르게 소비하고 있음.

*whether it be는 가정법 현재로 현재나 미래의 단순 가정을 나타냄. whether를 생략하고 주어와 동사가 도치된 be it으로도 쓸 수 있음.
[8] But / to ask for any change in human behaviour — // whether it be to cut down on consumption, (to) alter lifestyles or (to) decrease population growth — / is seen as a violation (of human rights).
S(to-v구) / 부사절 접속사(양보) S' V' C'1 / C'2 / C'3 / V(단수)
그러나 / 인간의 행동에 어떤 변화든 요구하는 것은 // 소비를 줄이는 것이든, 생활 방식을 바꾸는 것이든, 인구 증가를 줄이는 것이든 / 침해로 여겨진다 (인권의)

[9] But / at some point / human rights become 'wrongs'.
S V C
하지만 / 어느 시점에 / 인권은 '옳지 않은 것'이 된다
↳ **비판 2:** 자연을 파괴하면서 인권만 우선시하는 것은 옳지 않음.

명사절 접속사 생략 / 인권만 우선시하는 우리 생각을 바꿔야 함.
[10] It's time // (that) we changed our thinking // so that there is no difference / between the rights of humans and the rights of the rest of the environment.
S V C / S' V' O' / 부사절 접속사(목적) / 명사구 병렬
*<It is time (that)+S'+과거동사(~해야 할 때다)>의 that절에 가정법이 쓰여 '바꿔야 했지만 아직 바뀌지 않음'을 의미하며 should change로도 쓸 수 있음.
(~할) 때이다 // 우리가 생각을 바꿔야 할 // 차이가 없도록 / 인간의 권리와 나머지 환경의 권리 사이에
↳ **결론:** 환경권을 인권과 동등하게 존중해야 함.

해석

[1]"사자들이 자신들의 역사가를 갖게 될 때까지, 사냥 이야기는 언제나 사냥한 자를 미화할 것이다."라고 하는 아프리카 속담이 있다. [2]이 속담은 권력, 통제, 법 제정에 관한 것이다. [3]환경 저널리스트는 그 '사자의 역사가'의 역할을 수행해야 한다. [4]그들은 법을 만드는 사람들에게 환경에 대한 관점을 이해시켜야 한다. [5]그들은 인도 야생의 대변인이 되어야 한다. [6]현재 인간 소비의 속도는 전적으로 지속 불가능하다. [7]숲, 습지, 황무지, 해안 지역, 환경 민감 지역 모두 가속화되고 있는 인구의 수요를 위해 마음대로 쓸 수 있는 것으로 여겨진다. [8]그러나 소비를 줄이는 것이든, 생활 방식을 바꾸는 것이든, 인구 증가를 줄이는 것이든, 인간의 행동에 어떤 변화든 요구하는 것은 인권의 침해로 여겨진다. [9]하지만 어느 시점에 인권은 '옳지 않은 것'이 된다. [10]인간의 권리와 나머지 환경의 권리 사이에 차이가 없도록 우리가 생각을 바꿔야 할 때이다.

어휘

proverb 속담
tale 이야기, 소설
glorify 미화하다, 찬양하다
put across A to B A를 B에게 이해시키다
voice 대변인; 목소리
consumption 소비[소모](량); 소진
unsustainable 지속 불가능한
(↔ sustainable 지속 가능한)
wetland 습지(대)
wasteland 황무지, 불모지
disposable 마음대로 쓸 수 있는; 일회용의
accelerate 가속화되다[하다]
cut down on ~을 줄이다
alter 바꾸다, 고치다
violation 침해, 위반
[선택지] uncover 밝히다, 알아내다; 뚜껑[덮개]을 벗기다
species ((생물)) 종(種)
evolution 진화; 발전[진전]
shift 변화; 교체, 교대; 이동(하다)
underrepresented 소외된, 불충분하게 대표된
restrict 제한[통제]하다

정답 가이드

환경에 대한 인간의 행동과 생각 변화를 이끄는 데 있어 환경 저널리스트의 역할에 관한 내용이다. 인간이 무분별하게 환경을 착취하며 이를 당연한 권리로 여기는 것을 비판하며, 인권만큼 환경을 존중하고 보호해야 한다고 했다. 이러한 맥락에서 환경 저널리스트의 역할을 뜻하는 밑줄 친 부분이 의미하는 바로 가장 적절한 것은 ② 'urging a shift to sustainable human behaviour for nature(자연을 위한 인간의 지속 가능한 행동으로의 변화를 촉구하는 것)'이다.

The 핵심 도입에 나온 아프리카 속담의 the hunter는 '강자'인 human을, the lions는 '약자'인 environment를 의미함을 파악하고, 인간에게 이용당하기만 하는 환경을 대변하는 환경 저널리스트의 역할로 적절한 것을 선택한다.

오답 클리닉

① uncovering the history of a species' biological evolution (3%)
어떤 종의 생물학적 진화의 역사(×)를 밝혀내는 것
종의 생물학적 진화에 대해서는 전혀 언급되지 않음.

③ fighting against widespread violations of human rights (15%)
만연한 인권 침해(×)에 맞서 싸우는 것
환경보다 인권이 중시되는 실태를 비판하는 내용이므로 글의 내용과 반대됨.

④ rewriting history for more underrepresented people (4%)
더 소외된 사람들을(×) 위해서 역사를 다시 쓰는 것(×)
소외된 사람들에 대한 언급은 없으며, 역사를 다시 쓰는 것이 아니라 환경의 입장을 대변하는 것에 대한 글임.

⑤ restricting the power of environmental lawmakers (16%)
환경법 입법자들의 권한을 제한하는 것(×)
입법자들이 환경을 이해할 수 있도록 해야 한다고 했지만 권한을 제한해야 한다는 내용은 없음.

02 + 빈칸 추론 〈21학년도 9월 모평 31번 | 정답률 44%〉 ⑤

구문분석 & 직독직해 예술 미술품의 해석에 영향을 미치는 제목

★<call+O+C>: O를 C라고 부르다
[1]"What's in a name? *That* [which we call a rose], / by any other name / would smell as sweet."
(S: That / 목적격 관계대명사: which / V: would smell)
"이름이 뭐가 중요한가? 그것은 [우리가 장미라고 부르는] / 다른 어떤 이름으로든 / 똑같이 향기로울 것이다"

[2]This thought (of Shakespeare's) / points up a difference (between roses and, say, paintings).
(S / V / O) ★<between A and B>: A와 B 사이의
이 생각은 (Shakespeare의) / 차이를 강조한다 (장미와 이를테면 그림 사이의)
↳ **도입(인용):** 장미(자연물)와 그림(미술품) 간의 차이를 대조함.

주제문
[3]Natural objects, / (such as roses), / are not **interpreted**.
(S / V)
자연물은 / (장미와 같은) / 해석되지 않는다
↳ **대조 A(자연물):** 자연물은 해석되지 않음.

(They = Natural objects)
[4]They are not taken / as vehicles (of meanings and messages). — 자연물은 의미와 메시지를 전달하는 매개체 역할을 하지 않음.
(S / V / 전치사(~로(서)))
그것들(자연물)은 받아들여지지 않는다 / 매개체로 (의미와 메시지의)
↳ **세부 사항 1:** 자연물은 의미와 메시지를 전달하지 않음.

(They = Natural objects)
[5]They belong to no tradition, / strictly speaking have no style / and are not understood / within a framework (of culture and convention). — 자연물은 문화와 관습의 틀 안에서 이해되지 않음.
(S / V_1 / O_1 / V_2 / O_2 / V_3)
그것들(자연물)은 어떤 전통에도 속하지 않는다 / 엄밀히 말하면 양식이 없다 / 그리고 이해되지 않는다 / 틀 안에서 (문화와 관습의)
↳ **세부 사항 2:** 자연물은 문화와 관습의 틀 안에서 이해되지 않음.

— 자연물은 지적 매개 없이 직접적으로 감상됨.
(they = natural objects)
[6]Rather, / they are sensed and (are) savored relatively directly, / without intellectual mediation, // and so what they are called, / either individually or collectively, / has little bearing / on our experience of them.
(S_1: they / V_1: are sensed and (are) savored / S_2(명사절): what they are called / A이든 B든: either ~ or / V_2 준부정어(거의 없는): has little bearing / them = natural objects)
좀 더 정확하게 말하면 / 그것들(자연물)은 비교적 직접적으로 감지되고 음미된다 / 지성을 필요로 하는 매개 없이 // 그리고 따라서 그것들이 불리는 것은 / 개별적으로든 집합적으로든 / 관련이 거의 없다 / 그것들(자연물)에 대한 우리의 경험과는
↳ **세부 사항 3:** 자연물은 지적 매개와 상관없이 그 자체로 감상되므로 무엇으로 불리든 상관없음.

해석

[1]"이름이 뭐가 중요한가? 우리가 장미라고 부르는 그것은 다른 어떤 이름으로든 똑같이 향기로울 것이다." [2]이 Shakespeare의 생각은 장미와, 이를테면 그림 사이의 차이를 강조한다. [3]장미와 같은 자연물은 해석되지 않는다. [4]그것들은 의미와 메시지의 매개체로 받아들여지지 않는다. [5]그것들은 어떤 전통에도 속하지 않고, 엄밀히 말하면 양식이 없으며, 문화와 관습의 틀 안에서 이해되지 않는다. [6]좀 더 정확하게 말하면, 그것들은 지성을 필요로 하는 매개 없이 비교적 직접적으로 감지되고 음미되며, 따라서 개별적으로든 집합적으로든, 그것들이 불리는 것은 그것들에 대한 우리의 경험과는 관련이 거의 없다. [7]반면에 미술 작품이 무엇이라고 제목이 붙는지는 그것이 나타내는 미학적 면과 그것에서 우리가 올바르게 인지하는 특징에 상당한 영향을 미친다. [8]가지고 있는 것과는 다른 이름으로 불리는 장미 한 송이의 그림은, 미학적으로 말해, 아마 매우 향기가 다를 것이다. [9]'Rose of Summer'라고 제목 붙여진 그림과 'Vermillion Womanhood'라고 제목 붙여진 식별하기 어려운 그림은 물리적으로, 또한 의미적으로나 미학적으로도 별개의 미술품이다.

어휘

point up ~을 강조하다[두드러지게 하다]
interpret 해석하다, 이해하다
vehicle 매개체[수단]; 차량, 탈것
belong to A A에 속하다
strictly speaking 엄밀히 말하면
framework 틀, 뼈대
convention 관습, 관례

[7]What a work of art is titled, / on the other hand, / has a significant effect / on *the aesthetic face* [(which[that]) it presents] / and on *the qualities* [(which[that]) we correctly perceive in it].

S(명사절) V(단수) O 전치사구 병렬
목적격 관계대명사 생략 (= a work of art) 전치사구 병렬 목적격 관계대명사 생략

미술 작품이 무엇이라고 제목이 붙는지는 / 반면에 / 상당한 영향을 미친다 / 미학적 면에 [그것(미술 작품)이 나타내는] / 그리고 특징에 [그것에서 우리가 올바르게 인지하는]

↳ **대조 B(미술품):** 미술 작품의 제목은 우리가 작품을 이해하는 데 영향을 미침.

[8]A painting of a rose, / (by a name other than *the one* [(which[that]) it has]), / might very well smell different, / aesthetically speaking.

(= the painting of a rose)
S 전치사구 삽입 (= name) 목적격 관계대명사 생략 V C

장미 한 송이의 그림은 / (것(이름)과는 다른 이름으로 불리는 [그것(장미 한 송이의 그림)이 가지고 있는]) / 아마 매우 향기가 다를 것이다 / 미학적으로 말해

[9]*The painting* (titled *Rose of Summer*) / and *an indiscernible painting* (titled *Vermillion Womanhood*) / are physically, but also semantically and aesthetically, / distinct objects of art.

S_1 과거분사구 S_2 과거분사구 V C

그림 ('Rose of Summer'라고 제목 붙여진) / 그리고 식별하기 어려운 그림은 ('Vermillion Womanhood'라고 제목 붙여진) / 물리적으로, 또한 의미적으로나 미학적으로도 ~이다 / 별개의 미술품

↳ **예:** 같은 장미 그림이라도 서로 제목이 다르면 물리적, 의미적, 미학적으로 별개의 작품으로 여겨짐.

relatively 비교적, 상대적으로
intellectual 지성을 필요로 하는, 지적인
mediation 매개, 중개
collectively 집합적으로; 일괄하여
have a bearing on ~와 관련이 있다
cf. bearing 관련, 영향
aesthetic 미학적인; 미적 감각이 있는
cf. aesthetically 미학적으로
face 면; 직면하다
quality 특징, 특성; 질
perceive 인지[감지]하다
other than ~와 다른, ~이 아닌
might (very) well 아마 ~일 것이다; (~하는 것도) 당연하다
physically 물리적으로
distinct 별개의, 다른; 뚜렷한
[선택지] classify 분류[구분]하다

정답 가이드

장미와 같은 자연물이 '어떻지 않다'는 것인지를 찾아야 한다. 이어지는 설명을 요약하면 자연물은 그것을 이해하는 데 지적 매개 없이 직접적으로 감지, 음미되는 것이기에 그것이 무엇이라고 불리든 그것에 대한 감상(경험)은 변하지 않는다는 것이다. 이와 대조적으로 미술 작품에 붙여진 제목은 그것을 이해하는 것에 영향을 미친다고 했다. 즉 자연물은 직접적으로 이해되는 것이므로 '해석되지' 않는 것이고 미술 작품은 제목에 영향받아 '해석되는' 것이다. 따라서 빈칸에 들어갈 말로 가장 적절한 것은 ⑤ 'interpreted(해석되는)'이다.

오답 클리닉

① changed (21%) 변하는
자연물이 변하지 않는 반면, 미술품은 변한다는 내용이 아님.
② classified (22%) 분류되는
자연물을 분류한다는 내용은 없음.
③ preserved (6%) 보존되는
자연물이나 미술품이 보존된다는 내용은 없음.
④ controlled (6%) 통제되는
자연물에 대한 통제 여부는 언급되지 않음.

03 + 무관 문장 (22학년도 6월 모평 35번 | 정답률 84%) ④

구문분석 & 직독직해 사회 수정 확대 가족의 특징

[1]Kinship ties continue to be important / today.

S V O

친족 유대 관계는 계속해서 중요하다 / 오늘날에

[2]In modern societies (such as *the United States* [(where) people frequently have family get-togethers]), / they telephone their relatives regularly, // and they provide their kin with a wide variety of services.

관계부사 생략 S′ V′ O′
S_1 V_1 O_1 S_2 V_2 O_2
★<provide A with B>: A에게 B를 제공하다

현대 사회에서 (미국과 같은 [사람들이 가족 모임을 자주 갖는]) / 그들은 자신의 친척들에게 정기적으로 전화한다 // 그리고 그들은 자신의 친족에게 매우 다양한 도움을 제공한다

↳ **도입:** 친척에게 정기적으로 연락하고 도움을 제공하는 등 친족 유대 관계는 현대에서도 중요함.

주제문
★<refer to A as B>: A를 B라고 부르다

① [3]Eugene Litwak has referred to this pattern of behaviour / as the 'modified extended family'.

S V
🔑 수정 확대 가족의 특징에 관한 글임.

Eugene Litwak은 이 행동 패턴을 불렀다 / '수정 확대 가족'이라고

↳ 현대의 친족 유대 관계의 행동 패턴을 '수정 확대 가족'이라고 함.

해석

[1]친족 유대 관계는 오늘날에 계속해서 중요하다. [2]사람들이 가족 모임을 자주 갖는 미국과 같은 현대 사회에서, 그들은 자신의 친척들에게 정기적으로 전화하며, 그들은 친족에게 매우 다양한 도움을 제공한다. ① [3]Eugene Litwak은 이 행동 패턴을 '수정 확대 가족'이라고 불렀다. ② [4]그것은 다세대의 유대 관계가 유지되기 때문에 확대 가족 구조이지만, 그것이 일반적으로 세대 간의 공동 거주에 기초하지 않고 대부분의 확대 가족이 공동 집단으로서 기능하지 않기 때문에 수정된다. ③ [5]비록 수정 확대 가족의 구성원들이 흔히 가까이 살긴 하지만, 수정 확대 가족은 지리적 근접을 필요로 하지 않으며, 유대 관계는 친족이 상당한 거리로 떨어져 있을 때에도 유지된다. ④ [6]가족 구성원들이 서로 아

(=The modified extended family)

② [4]It is an extended family structure // because multigenerational ties are maintained, //

S₁ V₁ C 부사절 접속사(이유) S′ V′

그것은 확대 가족 구조이다 // 다세대의 유대 관계가 유지되기 때문에 //

but it is modified // because it does not usually rest on co-residence (between the generations) //

S₂ V₂ 부사절 접속사(이유)

and most extended families do not act / as corporate groups.

전치사(~로(서))

그러나 그것은 수정된다 // 그것이 일반적으로 공동 거주에 기초하지 않기 때문에 (세대 간의) //

그리고 대부분의 확대 가족이 기능하지 않기 때문에 / 공동 집단으로서

↳ **세부 사항 1:** 다세대 유대 관계가 유지되지만, 같이 거주하거나 공동 집단으로 기능하지 않음.

③ [5]Although modified extended family members often live close by, //

부사절 접속사(양보) S′ V′

비록 수정 확대 가족의 구성원들이 흔히 가까이 살긴 하지만 //

the modified extended family does not require geographical proximity // and ties are maintained

S₁ V₁ O S₂ V₂

// even when kin are separated / by considerable distances.

부사절 접속사(시간) S′(복수) V′(복수)

수정 확대 가족은 지리적 근접을 필요로 하지 않는다 // 그리고 유대 관계는 유지된다

// 친족이 떨어져 있을 때에도 / 상당한 거리로

↳ **세부 사항 2:** 가까이 살지 않아도 유대 관계가 유지됨.

수정 확대 가족의 특징과 무관한 최고령자의 결정 권한에 관한 내용임.

④ [6]The oldest member (of the family) / makes the decisions / on important issues, //

S V O

no matter how far away family members live from each other.

아무리 ~하더라도 S′ V′

최고령자가 (가족의) / 결정을 내린다 / 중요한 문제에 관해 //

가족 구성원들이 서로 아무리 멀리 떨어져 살지라도

↳ 구성원들이 멀리 떨어져 살더라도 중요 문제는 가족의 최고 연장자가 결정함.

⑤ [7]In contrast to *the traditional extended family* [where kin always live in close proximity], //

관계부사 S′ V′

전통적인 확대 가족과는 대조적으로 [친족이 항상 아주 가까이에 사는] //

the members (of modified extended families) / may freely move away from kin / to seek

S V 목적(~하기 위해)

opportunities (for occupational advancement).

구성원들은 (수정 확대 가족의) / 친족으로부터 떠나 자유롭게 이주할 수도 있다 / 기회를 추구하기 위해 (직업상의 발전을 위한)

↳ **부연 설명:** 수정 확대 가족의 구성원들은 직업을 위해 친족들과 떨어져 멀리 이주할 수 있음.

무리 멀리 떨어져 살지라도, 가족의 최고령자가 중요한 문제에 관해 결정을 내린다. ⑤ [7]친족이 항상 아주 가까이에 사는 전통적인 확대 가족과는 대조적으로, 수정 확대 가족의 구성원들은 직업상의 발전을 위한 기회를 추구하기 위해 친족으로부터 떠나 자유롭게 이주할 수도 있다.

어휘

kinship 친족, 친척 관계
tie 유대 (관계), 연줄; 묶다
get-together 모임
relative 친척; 비교상의, 상대적인
modify 수정[변경]하다; 수식하다
extended family 확대 가족, 대가족
structure 구조, 구성; 구조물
multigenerational 다세대의
rest on ~에 기초하다; ~에 의지하다
co-residence 공동 거주; 남녀 공동 기숙사
act 기능[역할]을 하다; 행동하다
corporate 공동의, 단체의; 법인 조직의
geographical 지리적인, 지리학(상)의
considerable 상당한, 많은
occupational 직업(상)의
advancement 발전, 진보; 승진

정답 가이드

도입 부분에서 오늘날에도 계속해서 중요한 친족 유대 관계에 대해 설명한 뒤, 그런 유대관계를 가진 행동 패턴이 '수정 확대 가족'이며 이는 공동 거주에 기초하지 않는다는 설명이 끝까지 이어지고 있다. 그런데 ④는 가족의 최고령자가 중요한 문제를 결정한다는 '의사 결정의 권한'에 초점을 둔 내용이므로 글의 전체 흐름과 무관하다.

오답 클리닉

① (2%) 앞 문장에 언급된 정기적으로 친척들에게 전화하고 도움을 제공하는 것이 this pattern of behaviour로 연결되며, 이러한 현대 가족의 행동 패턴을 수정 확대 가족이라 부른다고 정의하고 있다.
② (4%) 수정 확대 가족의 특징을 설명하는 세부 사항이다.
③ (8%) 수정 확대 가족이 공동으로 거주하지 않는다는 앞 문장의 특징을 이어서 설명하는 내용이다.
⑤ (3%) 수정 확대 가족은 가까이 살지 않아도 되기 때문에 직업을 위해 멀리 이주할 수 있다는 부연 설명이다.

01 + 글의 요지 〈23학년도 6월 모평 22번 | 정답률 61%〉 ①

구문분석 & 직독직해

생활 소비자의 개인 정보 제공의 속성 이해

[1]Often overlooked, but just as important a stakeholder, / is / *the consumer* [who plays a large role / in the notion (of the privacy paradox)].

C / V / S / 주격 관계대명사

*강조를 위해 보어가 문장 맨 앞에 와서 <V+S> 어순으로 도치가 일어남. <as+형용사+a(n)+명사>는 부사 as가 형용사를 수식해서 형용사가 관사 a(n) 앞에 온 구조임.

흔히 간과되지만 못지않게 중요한 이해관계자 / ~이다 / 소비자는 [큰 역할을 하는 / 개념에서 (프라이버시 역설이라는)]

↳ 소비자는 프라이버시 역설에 큰 역할을 함.

[2]Consumer engagement levels / in all manner (of digital experiences and communities) / have simply exploded — // [and] they show little or no signs of slowing.

S1 / V1 / (= consumer engagement levels) S2 / V2 / O

소비자의 참여 수준은 / 모든 방식에서 (디지털 경험과 커뮤니티의) / 그야말로 폭발적으로 증가해 왔다 // 그리고 그것(소비자의 참여 수준)은 (증가하는) 속도를 늦출 기미를 거의 또는 전혀 보이지 않는다

↳ 소비자의 디지털 참여가 엄청나게 늘고 있음.

[3]There is an awareness among consumers, //

V / S

소비자들 사이에는 인식이 있다 // *an awareness와 동격을 이루는 두 개의 that절이 <not only A but also B>로 연결됨.

[not only] that their personal data helps / to drive *the rich experiences* [that these companies provide], //

동격 접속사 / 목적격 관계대명사

자신들의 개인 정보가 도움이 된다는 것뿐만 아니라 / 풍부한 경험을 추진하는 데 [이러한 회사들이 제공하는] //

[but also] that sharing this data is *the price* [(which[that]) you pay for these experiences], / in whole or in part.

동격 접속사 / (= their personal data) / 목적격 관계대명사 생략 / (= the rich experiences)

이 정보를 공유하는 것이 대가이기도 하다는 [이러한 경험에 대해 지불하는] / 전체로든 부분으로든

↳ 소비자는 개인 정보 제공이 좋은 서비스 이용에 대한 대가라고 인식함.

[4]Without a better understanding (of the what, when, and why (of data collection and use)), / the consumer is often left feeling vulnerable and conflicted. ⊶ 소비자는 개인 정보 수집, 활용에 대해 잘 알아야 함.

전치사(~이 없으면) / S / V / C

더 나은 이해가 없으면 (내용, 시기, 그리고 이유에 대한 (정보 수집 및 이용의)) / 소비자는 종종 상처를 입기 쉽고 갈등을 겪는다고 느끼게 된다

↳ 소비자는 개인 정보가 어떻게 수집되고 활용되는지를 모르면 취약함을 느낌.

*첫 번째 if는 조건의 부사절을 이끄는 접속사이고, 두 번째 if는 when 부사절의 동사 am asked의 목적어 역할을 하는 명사절을 이끄는 접속사임.

[5]"I love this restaurant-finder app on my phone, // [but] what happens to my data // if I press 'ok' // when (I am) asked // if that app can use my current location?"

부사절 접속사 / 부사절 접속사(시간) / S′ / V′ / 명사절 접속사 / O′

'내 전화기에 있는 이 식당 검색 앱이 마음에 들어 // 그런데 내 정보에는 무슨 일이 일어날까 // 내가 'ok'를 누르면 // 질문받을 때 // 그 앱이 내 현재 위치를 이용해도 되는지'

↳ 예: 소비자는 개인 정보가 어떻게 활용될지 잘 몰라서 걱정함.

[6]Armed with *tools* [that can provide them options], / the consumer moves / [from] passive bystander [to] active participant. ⊶ 소비자에게 선택권이 생기면 능동적 참여자가 됨.

분사구문(= As the customer is armed ~) / 주격 관계대명사 / (= consumers) / S / V

도구로 무장하여 [그들(소비자들)에게 선택권을 제공할 수 있는] / 소비자는 이동한다 / 수동적 방관자에서 능동적 참여자로

↳ (정보 제공의) 선택권이 있으면 소비자는 능동적 참여자가 됨.

해석

[1]프라이버시 역설이라는 개념에서 큰 역할을 하는 소비자는 흔히 간과되지만 (다른 이해관계자) 못지않게 중요한 이해관계자이다. [2]디지털 경험과 커뮤니티의 모든 방식에서 소비자의 참여 수준은 그야말로 폭발적으로 증가해 왔으며, 그것(소비자의 참여 수준)은 (증가하는) 속도를 늦출 기미를 거의 또는 전혀 보이지 않는다. [3]소비자들 사이에는 이러한 회사들이 제공하는 풍부한 경험을 추진하는 데 자신들의 개인 정보가 도움이 된다는 것뿐만 아니라, 이 정보를 공유하는 것이 전체로든 부분으로든, 이러한 경험에 대해 지불하는 대가이기도 하다는 인식이 있다. [4]정보 수집 및 이용의 내용, 시기, 그리고 이유에 대한 더 나은 이해가 없으면, 소비자는 종종 상처를 입기 쉽고 갈등을 겪는다고 느끼게 된다. [5]'내 전화기에 있는 이 식당 검색 앱이 마음에 드는데, 그 앱이 내 현재 위치를 이용해도 되는지 질문 받을 때 내가 'ok'를 누르면 내 정보에는 무슨 일이 일어날까?' [6]그들(소비자들)에게 선택권을 제공할 수 있는 도구로 무장하여 소비자는 수동적 방관자에서 능동적 참여자로 이동한다.

어휘

overlook 간과하다; 못 본 체하다
notion 개념, 관념, 생각
engagement 참여, 관여
simply ((강조)) 그야말로, 정말로; 그저(단순히)
explode 폭발적으로 증가하다; 폭발하다
awareness 인식
drive 추진시키다; 추진(력); (차를) 운전하다
in whole or in part 전체로든 부분으로든
conflicted 갈등을 겪는
current 현재의
arm 무장하다[시키다]
passive 수동적인(↔ active 능동적인)
bystander 방관자, 구경꾼
⊕ 프라이버시 역설(privacy paradox): 어떤 서비스를 이용하기 위해 개인 정보 활용을 스스로 허락해야 하는 상황을 빗대는 말

정답 가이드

첫 문장에서 프라이버시 역설에 소비자가 큰 역할을 한다고 했는데, 이어지는 설명으로 이는 디지털 서비스를 이용하기 위해 개인 정보를 기업에 공유하는 상황을 말하는 것임을 알 수 있다. 이런 상황에서, 기업의 정보 수집, 활용 등에 대해 소비자가 더 잘 이해하고, 정보 제공에 대해 선택권을 가지면 능동적 소비자가 된다는 글의 핵심 내용이 이어지고 있다. 따라서 글의 요지로 가장 적절한 것은 ① '개인 정보 제공의 속성을 심층적으로 이해하면 주체적 소비자가 된다.'이다.

오답 클리닉

② 소비자는 디지털 시대에 유용한 앱(×)을 적극 활용하는 자세가 필요하다. (6%)
유용한 앱의 활용을 권장하는 내용은 없음.

③ 현명한 소비자가 되려면 다양한 디지털 데이터(×)를 활용해야 한다. (9%)
다양한 디지털 데이터를 활용하라는 내용은 없음.

④ 기업의 디지털 서비스를 이용하면 상응하는 대가(×)가 뒤따른다. (20%)
지문에서 해당 내용이 언급되기는 했지만, 이는 프라이버시 역설을 설명하는 부분이며 글의 요지로 볼 수는 없음.

The 주의 글의 세부 사항을 요지로 착각하지 않도록 주의한다.

⑤ 타인과의 정보 공유로 인해 개인 정보가 유출(×)되기도 한다. (4%)
회사에 개인 정보를 제공하는 것을 타인과의 정보 공유로 볼 수도 있으나 개인 정보 유출에 대해서는 언급되지 않음.

02 + 빈칸 추론 〈21학년도 6월 모평 34번 | 정답률 50%〉 ②

구문분석 & 직독직해

인지 보길 기대한 것을 보여주는 뇌의 시각적 전략

주제문

[1]A large part (of what we see) / is what we expect to see.
(S / of의 O(명사절) / V / C(명사절))
🔑 우리는 우리가 보길 기대한 것을 봄.
많은 부분은 (우리가 보는 것의) / 우리가 보기를 기대하는 것이다
↳ 우리는 마음속 기대를 바탕으로 무언가를 봄.

[2]This explains // why we "see" faces and figures / in a flickering campfire, [or] in moving clouds.
(S / V / O(명사절) / 전치사구 병렬)
이것은 설명한다 // 우리가 얼굴과 형상을 '보는' 이유를 / 흔들리는 모닥불 속이나 움직이는 구름 속에서

[3]This is // why Leonardo da Vinci advised artists to discover their motifs / by staring at patches (on a blank wall).
(S / V / C(명사절) / ★<advise+O+to-v>: O가 v하도록 조언하다 / <by v-ing>: v함으로써)
이것이 ~이다 // Leonardo da Vinci가 화가들에게 그들의 주제를 발견하라고 조언한 이유 / 부분들을 응시함으로써 (빈 벽의)
↳ **세부 사항:** 우리는 변화화는 대상(모닥불, 구름)과 변화하지 않는 대상(빈 벽)에서 얼굴과 형상을 봄.

[4]A fire provides a constant flickering change / in *visual information* [that never integrates into anything solid] / [and] thereby allows the brain to engage in a play of hypotheses.
(S / V_1 / O_1 / 주격 관계대명사 / V_2 / O_2 / C_2)
불은 끊임없이 흔들리는 변화를 제공한다 / 시각 정보에 [일정한 어떤 것에도 절대 통합되지 않는] / 그리고 그렇게 함으로써 뇌가 가설 놀이에 참여하게 한다
↳ **대조 A(불):** 불의 변화하는 시각 정보는 뇌가 가설 놀이를 하게 함.

[5]On the other hand, / the wall does not present us / with very much / in the way of visual clues, // [and] so the brain begins to make more and more hypotheses / [and] desperately searches for confirmation.
(S_1 / V_1 / S_2 / V_{2-1} / O_{2-1} / V_{2-2})
🔑 뇌가 가설을 만들고 확인하는 이미지는 우리가 마음속으로 보길 기대한 이미지임.
반면에 / 벽은 우리에게 주지 않는다 / 그리 많은 것을 / 시각적인 단서의 형태로 //
그래서 뇌는 점점 더 많은 가설을 세우기 시작한다 / 그리고 필사적으로 확인을 구한다
↳ **대조 B(벽):** 시각 정보를 많이 주지 않는 벽은 뇌가 더 많은 가설을 만들게 함.

[6]A crack in the wall looks / a little like the profile (of a nose) // [and] suddenly a whole face appears, / [or] a leaping horse (appears), [or] a dancing figure (appears).
(S_1 / V_1 / 전치사(~처럼) / C / S_2 / V_2 / S_3 / V_3(생략) / S_4 / V_4(생략))
벽의 갈라진 틈은 보인다 / 약간 옆모습처럼 (코의) // 그리고 갑자기 얼굴 전체가 나타난다
/ 또는 뛰는 말이나 춤추는 형상이 (나타난다)
↳ **가설 놀이의 예:** 벽의 갈라진 틈에서 다양한 형상을 보게 됨.

해석

[1]우리가 보는 것의 많은 부분은 우리가 보기를 기대하는 것이다. [2]이것은 우리가 흔들리는 모닥불 속이나 움직이는 구름 속에서 얼굴과 형상을 '보는' 이유를 설명한다. [3]이것이 Leonardo da Vinci가 화가들에게 빈 벽의 부분들을 응시함으로써 그들의 주제를 발견하라고 조언한 이유다. [4]불은 일정한 어떤 것에도 절대 통합되지 않는 시각 정보에 끊임없이 흔들리는 변화를 제공하고, 그렇게 함으로써 뇌가 가설 놀이에 참여하게 한다. [5]반면에, 벽은 우리에게 시각적인 단서의 형태로 그리 많은 것을 주지 않고, 그래서 뇌는 점점 더 많은 가설을 세우기 시작하고 필사적으로 확인을 구한다. [6]벽의 갈라진 틈은 약간 코의 옆모습처럼 보이고 갑자기 얼굴 전체가 나타나거나 뛰는 말이나 춤추는 형상이 나타난다. [7]이와 같은 경우에 뇌의 시각적 전략은 마음속에서 바깥 세상으로 이미지를 투영하는 것이다.

어휘

figure 형상, 형체; 인물; 수치
motif (문학·예술 작품의) 주제[모티프]
stare at ~을 응시하다
patch (다른 것과 달라 보이는) 부분; (헝겊) 조각
visual 시각의
integrate into ~에 통합되다
solid 한결같은, 고른; 단단한; 고체(의)
thereby 그렇게 함으로써
engage in ~에 참여하다
hypothesis (*pl.* hypotheses) 가설
present 주다; 제출하다; 현재의; 참석한
desperately 필사적으로, 절박하게
confirmation 확인
crack 갈라진 틈; 갈라지다
profile 옆모습, 옆얼굴

[7]In cases like these / the brain's visual strategies are **projecting images / from within the mind out onto the world**.

S(= the play of hypotheses) V C(동명사구)

이와 같은 경우에 / 뇌의 시각적 전략은 이미지를 투영하는 것이다 / 마음속에서 바깥 세상으로

↳ **결론:** 우리가 보는 것은 뇌가 마음속 이미지를 밖으로 투영한 것임.

leap 뛰다, 뛰어오르다
strategy 전략, 전술
project 투영하다, 비추다; 계획(하다)
[선택지] distract (정신이) 산만하게 하다, (주의를) 딴 데로 돌리다
categorize 분류하다
strengthen 강화하다
remove 제거하다, 없애다

정답 가이드

빈칸 문장과 직전 문장으로 보아 벽의 틈이 코의 옆모습으로 보이는 등의 경우, 뇌의 시각적 전략이 '어떠하다'는 것인지를 추론해야 한다. 첫 문장에서 우리는 우리가 보기를 기대하는 것을 본다고 하고, 이어서 뇌는 모닥불, 구름, 벽 등에서 가설(마음속으로 보길 기대한 이미지)을 세우고 확인하며 형상을 본다고 했다. 따라서 벽의 갈라진 틈에서 본 코의 옆모습, 뛰는 말과 같은 형상은 우리가 '보길 기대한' 마음속 이미지가 투영된 것이므로, 이와 같은 경우에 뇌의 시각적 전략은 ② 'projecting images from within the mind out onto the world(마음속에서 바깥 세상으로 이미지를 투영하는 것)'이 가장 적절하다.

오답 클리닉

① ignoring distracting information unrelated to visual clues (17%)
시각적 단서와 관련 없는 정신을 산만하게 하는 정보를 무시하는 것
visual clues를 활용한 오답. 시각적 단서와 관련 없는 정보를 무시한다는 내용은 없음.

③ categorizing objects into groups either real or imagined (10%)
사물을 실제이거나 상상한 그룹 중 하나로 분류하는 것
사물을 두 부류로 분류한다는 내용은 없음.

④ strengthening connections between objects in the real world (15%)
현실 세계에서 사물들 사이의 관련성을 강화하는 것
뇌가 이미지의 가설을 세우는 것을 실제 사물 간의 관련성을 강화하는 것으로 볼 수 없음.

⑤ removing the broken or missing parts of an original image (8%)
원래의 이미지에서 부서지거나 없어진 부분을 제거하는 것
a crack in the wall(벽의 갈라진 틈)을 활용한 오답. 이미지의 일부를 제거하는 것은 유추할 수 없음.

03 + 글의 순서 (22학년도 9월 모평 36번 | 정답률 39%)

⑤

구문분석 & 직독직해

비즈니스 친환경 제품 투자를 꺼리는 이유

[1]Green products involve, / (in many cases), / higher ingredient costs / than those (of mainstream products).

S V 전치사구 삽입 O (= ingredient costs)

친환경 제품은 수반한다 / (많은 경우) / 더 높은 원료비를 / 것(원료비)보다 (주류 제품의)

↳ **친환경 제품의 문제점 1:** 주류 제품보다 원료비가 더 높음.

🗝 주어진 글에 이어 친환경 제품의 다른 문제점을 추가함.

(C) [2]Furthermore, / *the restrictive ingredient lists and design criteria* [that are typical of such products] / may make green products inferior / to mainstream products / on core performance dimensions (e.g., less effective cleansers).

S 주격 관계대명사 (= green products) V O C

게다가 / 제한 성분 목록과 디자인 기준이 [그런 제품(친환경 제품)의 전형적인] / 친환경 제품을 열등하게 만들 수 있다 / 주류 제품보다 / 핵심 성능 면에서 (예를 들어, 덜 효과적인 세척제)

↳ **친환경 제품의 문제점 2:** 주류 제품보다 성능 면에서 열등함.

[3]In turn, / the higher costs and lower performance (of some products) / attract only a small portion (of the customer base), / leading to lower economies of scale / in procurement, manufacturing, and distribution.

S V O 분사구문(= so that it leads ~)

결과적으로 / 더 높은 비용과 더 낮은 성능은 (일부 제품의) / 오직 적은 부분만 유인한다 (고객층의) / 그래서 더 낮은 규모의 경제로 이어진다 / 조달, 제조, 유통에서의

↳ **결과:** 끌어들이는 고객이 적어서 수익이 낮음.

해석

[1]많은 경우 친환경 제품은 주류 제품의 원료비보다 더 높은 원료비를 수반한다. (C) [2]게다가 그런 제품(친환경 제품)의 전형적인 제한 성분 목록과 디자인 기준이 친환경 제품을 주류 제품보다 핵심 성능 면에서 열등하게 만들 수 있다(예를 들어, 덜 효과적인 세척제). [3]결과적으로, 일부 제품의 더 높은 비용과 더 낮은 성능은 고객층의 오직 적은 부분만 유인해서, 조달, 제조, 유통에서의 더 낮은 규모의 경제로 이어진다. (B) [4]친환경 제품이 성공한다 할지라도 그것(친환경 제품)은 기업의 수익이 더 높은 주류 제품을 잡아먹을 수 있다. [5]이런 부정적인 면을 고려해 볼 때, 성공적인 주류 제품을 주류 소비자에게 공급하는 기업들은 너무 뻔한 투자 결정처럼 보이는 것에 직면한다. (A) [6]그들은 현재 고객이 아닌 사람들을 만족시킬 수도 있는 위험하고 수익성이 더 낮은 소량의 제품보다는, 다수의 고객층을 만족시키는 이미 알려져 있고 수익성이 있는 다량의 제품에 차라리 돈과 시간을 투자하고 싶어 한다. [7]그런 선택을 고려해 볼 때, 이 기업들은 작은 틈새 경쟁사들에게 시장의 친환경 부문을 맡기기를 선택할 수 있다.

(B) [4]Even if the green product succeeds, // it may cannibalize the company's higher-profit mainstream offerings.

(= the green product) 부사절 접속사(양보) S' V' S V O

🔑 (C)의 고객이 적은 경우와 반대되는 고객이 많은 성공한 경우의 문제점을 제시함.

친환경 제품이 성공한다 할지라도 // 그것(친환경 제품)은 기업의 수익이 더 높은 주류 제품을 잡아먹을 수 있다

↳ **친환경 제품의 문제점 3:** 성공하면 자사 주류 제품의 매출 감소를 가져올 수 있음.

🔑 앞서 언급된 높은 원료비, 낮은 성능, 주류 제품 잠식을 가리킴. ★<serve A with B>: A에게 B를 공급하다

[5]Given such downsides, / *companies* (serving mainstream consumers / with successful mainstream products) / face // what seems like an obvious investment decision.

전치사(~을 고려해 볼 때) S 현재분사구 V O(명사절)

이런 부정적인 면을 고려해 볼 때 / 기업들은 (주류 소비자에게 공급하는 / 성공적인 주류 제품을) / 직면한다 // 너무 뻔한 투자 결정처럼 보이는 것에

↳ **결론:** 여러 부정적인 면을 고려하면 기업들은 친환경 제품보다 고수익 주류 제품에 투자할 수밖에 없음.

🔑 (B)의 companies ~ mainstream products를 They로 받아 (B)의 마지막에 언급된 뻔한 투자 결정을 설명함.

(A) [6]They'd rather put money and time / into *known, profitable, high-volume products* [that serve populous customer segments] / than into *risky, less-profitable, low-volume products* [that may serve current noncustomers].

S V O 전치사구 병렬 주격 관계대명사

★<would rather A than B>: B 하기보다는 차라리 A 하고 싶다[하겠다] 전치사구 병렬 주격 관계대명사

그들은 차라리 돈과 시간을 투자하고 싶어 한다 / 이미 알려져 있고 수익성이 있는 다량의 제품에 [다수의 고객층을 만족시키는] / 위험하고 수익성이 더 낮은 소량의 제품보다는 [현재 고객이 아닌 사람들을 만족시킬 수도 있는]

[7]Given that choice, / these companies may choose / to leave the green segment of the market / to small niche competitors.

전치사(~을 고려해 볼 때) S V O

그런 선택을 고려해 볼 때 / 이 기업들은 선택할 수 있다 / 시장의 친환경 부문을 맡기기를 / 작은 틈새 경쟁사들에게

↳ **부연 설명:** 기업은 친환경 제품보다 주류 제품에 투자하고 싶어하며 친환경 부분은 작은 경쟁사들에게 맡겨버림.

어휘

ingredient cost 원료비
mainstream 주류(의)
restrictive 제한[한정]하는
criterion (*pl.* criteria) 기준
typical 전형적인; 일반적인
inferior to A A보다 열등한
dimension 면; 차원
portion 부분; (음식의) 1인분; 몫
customer base 고객층
distribution 유통; 분배
offering 팔 물건; 제공된 것
downside 부정적인[불리한] 면
profitable 수익성이 있는; 유익한
serve 만족시키다; (서비스를) 제공하다
populous 다수의; 인구가 많은
niche (시장의) 틈새

⊕ 규모의 경제(economies of scale): 산출량을 늘릴수록 한 단위당 생산 비용이 줄어들어 수익이 증가하는 현상.

정답 가이드

친환경 제품의 원료비가 주류 제품보다 높다는 문제점을 제시한 주어진 글 뒤에는 첨가를 나타내는 연결어 Furthermore로 친환경 제품의 또 다른 문제점인 핵심 성능 면에서의 열등함을 제시하는 (C)가 이어져야 한다. (B)는 친환경 제품이 성공하더라도 고수익 주류 제품을 잠식할 수 있다는 또 다른 문제점에 해당하고 주어진 문장과 (C)에서 언급된 문제점 전체를 묶어 such downsides로 통칭했으므로 (C) 뒤에 나와야 한다. (A)에서 설명되는 그들(they)은 수익성 있는 다량의 제품에 투자하고 싶어 한다고 했으므로 (B)의 마지막 부분에 언급된 기업들(companies serving mainstream consumers)을 지칭하는 것이다. 따라서 (B)-(A)의 순서가 되어야 한다.

오답 클리닉

① (A) - (C) - (B) (3%) / ④ (C) - (A) - (B) (16%)

(A)의 They는 (B)의 companies를 지칭하므로 주어진 글이나 (C) 뒤에 올 수 없다.

② (B) - (A) - (C) (26%) / ③ (B) - (C) - (A) (15%)

(B)의 such downsides는 앞서 언급한 친환경 제품의 여러 부정적인 면들을 통틀어 지칭하는 것이므로 (B)는 높은 원료비와 낮은 성능을 문제로 언급한 주어진 글과 (C) 뒤에 와야 한다.

01 + 필자 주장 〈23학년도 6월 모평 20번 | 정답률 70%〉 ②

구문분석 & 직독직해

스포츠 추진력이 운동선수에게 미치는 영향

[1]Consider *two athletes* [who both want to play in college].
주격 관계대명사
두 명의 운동선수를 생각해 보라 [둘 다 대학에서 뛰고 싶어 하는]

★<one ~, the other ~>: (둘 중) 한쪽은 ~ 다른 한쪽은 …
[2]One says // (that) she has to work very hard // and the other uses goal setting / to create *a plan* (to stay on track and (to) work on *specific skills* [where she is lacking]).
S1 V1 명사절 접속사 생략 O1(명사절) S2 V2 O2 목적(~ 하기 위해) 관계부사 S′ V′ C′
한 선수는 말한다 // 아주 열심히 노력해야 한다고 // 그리고 다른 선수는 목표 설정을 이용한다 / 계획을 세우기 위해 (계속 순조롭게 나아가고 특정 기술을 연습할 [자신이 부족한])
↳ 예: 한 선수는 그저 열심히 하고 다른 한 선수는 목표를 설정함.

[3]Both are working hard // but only the latter is working smart.
(= an athlete who uses goal setting)
둘 다 열심히 하고 있다 // 하지만 후자만이 영리하게 하고 있다
↳ 예의 결론: 목표 설정을 이용하는 선수(후자)가 영리함.

★진주어에서 to work와 make가 but으로 연결되었고 make 앞의 반복되는 to는 생략됨.
[4]It can be frustrating / for athletes to work extremely hard / but not (to) make *the progress* [(which[that]) they wanted].
가주어 to-v의 의미상 주어 진주어(to-v구) 목적격 관계대명사 생략
(~은) 좌절감을 줄 수 있다 / 운동선수가 아주 열심히 하는 것은 / 하지만 진전을 이루지 못하는 것은 [자신이 원했던]
↳ 문제점: 열심히 하는데 성과가 없으면 좌절할 수 있음.

주제문 ⊶ 추진력에서 차이가 드러남.
[5]What can make the difference / is drive — / utilizing the mental gear / to maximize *gains* (made in the technical and physical areas).
S V C 목적(~하기 위해) 과거분사구
차이를 만들어낼 수 있는 것은 / 추진력이다 / 즉 정신적 장치를 활용하는 것 / 증진을 극대화하기 위해 (기술과 신체 영역에서 얻은)
↳ 해결책: 운동선수에게 추진력이 있는지가 차이를 만듦.

[6]Drive provides direction (goals), / sustains effort (motivation), / and creates *a training mindset* [that goes beyond simply working hard]. ★공통주어 Drive에 동사 세 개가 콤마(,)와 and로 연결됨.
S V1 O1 V2 O2 V3 O3 주격 관계대명사
추진력은 방향(목표)을 제공한다 / 노력(동기부여)을 유지시킨다 / 그리고 훈련의 마음가짐을 만든다 [단순히 열심히 하는 것을 넘어서는]
↳ 논거 1: 추진력은 목표, 동기, 마음가짐을 형성함.

[7]Drive applies direct force / on your physical and technical gears, / strengthening and polishing them // so they can spin with vigor and purpose.
S V O 분사구문(= and it[drive] strengthens and polishes ~) (= your ~ gears) S′ V′
추진력은 직접적인 힘을 가한다 / 여러분의 신체적 그리고 기술적 장치에 / 그리고 그것들을 강화하고 다듬는다 // 그것들이 활력과 목적을 가지고 회전할 수 있도록
↳ 논거 2: 추진력은 신체와 기술을 발전시킴.

[8]While desire might make you spin those gears faster and harder // as you work out or practice, // drive is what built them / in the first place. ★what이 이끄는 명사절이 동사 is의 보어 역할을 함.
부사절 접속사(~하지만) S′ V′ O′ (= your physical and technical gears) C′ 부사절 접속사(~할 때) S V C (= those gears)
욕망이 그러한 장치를 더 빨리, 그리고 더 열심히 회전시키게 만들지도 모르지만 // 여러분이 운동하거나 연습할 때 // 추진력은 그것들을 만든 것이다 / 애초에
↳ 논거 2의 부연 설명: 욕망보다 추진력이 더 근본적인 동력임.

해석

[1]둘 다 대학에서 뛰고 싶어 하는 두 명의 운동선수를 생각해 보라. [2]한 선수는 아주 열심히 노력해야 한다고 말하고, 다른 한 선수는 계속 순조롭게 나아가고 자신이 부족한 특정 기술을 연습할 계획을 세우기 위해 목표 설정을 이용한다. [3]둘 다 열심히 하고 있지만 후자만이 영리하게 하고 있다. [4]운동선수가 아주 열심히 하지만 자신이 원했던 진전을 이루지 못하는 것은 좌절감을 줄 수 있다. [5]차이를 만들어낼 수 있는 것은 추진력, 즉 기술과 신체 영역에서 얻은 증진을 극대화하기 위해 정신적 장치를 활용하는 것이다. [6]추진력은 방향(목표)을 제공하고, 노력(동기부여)을 유지시키며, 단순히 열심히 하는 것을 넘어서는 훈련의 마음가짐을 만든다. [7]추진력은 여러분의 신체적 그리고 기술적 장치에 직접적인 힘을 가해 그것들이 활력과 목적을 가지고 회전할 수 있도록 그것들을 강화하고 다듬는다. [8]욕망이 여러분이 운동을 하거나 연습할 때 그러한 장치를 더 빨리, 그리고 더 열심히 회전시키게 만들지도 모르지만, 추진력은 애초에 그것들을 만든 것이다.

어휘

athlete 운동선수
on track 순조롭게 나아가는
specific 특정한; 구체적인, 명확한
lack 부족하다, ~이 없다; 결핍[부족]
extremely 아주, 극도로
progress 진전, 진보; 진행하다; 나아가다
utilize 활용[이용]하다
gear 장치, 장비
maximize 극대화하다
gain 증진, 증가; 이득, 이점; 얻다
sustain 유지시키다; 견디다, 지탱하다
mindset 마음가짐, 사고방식, 태도
apply 힘을 가하다; 적용하다; 지원하다
strengthen 강화하다
polish 다듬다; (윤이 나도록) 닦다
work out 운동하다
in the first place 애초에, 맨 처음에

정답 가이드

그냥 열심히 하는 선수와 목표 설정을 이용하는 운동선수의 예를 들고 정신적 추진력이 뒷받침될 때 선수가 신체와 기술 영역에서 얻은 증진을 극대화할 수 있다는 주제문이 나왔다. 그 이후에는 정신적 추진력이 어떻게 도움이 되는지 설명하는 논거가 이어지므로 필자가 주장하는 바로 가장 적절한 것은 ② '선수들은 최고의 성과를 얻기 위해 정신적 추진력을 잘 활용해야 한다.'이다.

오답 클리닉

① 선수들의 훈련 방식(×)은 장점을 극대화하는 방향으로 이루어져야 한다. (4%)
선수들의 훈련 방식에 대한 언급은 없으며, 추진력으로 극대화하는 것은 장점이 아니라 신체와 기술 영역에서 이룬 증진임.

③ 선수들은 단기적 훈련 성과보다 장기적(×) 목표 달성에 힘써야 한다. (6%)
선수들이 목표 설정을 이용해야 한다는 내용은 있으나 단기적 성과와 장기적 성과를 비교하는 내용은 없음.

④ 선수들은 육체적 훈련과 정신적 훈련(×)을 균형 있게 병행(×)해야 한다. (13%)
정신적 훈련에 대한 언급은 없으며 육체적 훈련과 균형 있게 병행해야 한다는 내용도 없음.

The 주의 추진력이 목표를 제공하고 동기를 부여하는 '정신적 장치'로 설명된 것을 '정신적 훈련'으로 혼동하지 않도록 주의한다.

⑤ 선수들은 수립한 계획을 실행하면서 꾸준히 수정(×)하여야 한다. (7%)
계획을 세우기 위해 목표를 설정하는 선수가 영리하다고 했지만 계획을 꾸준히 수정해야 한다는 내용은 없음.

02 + 빈칸 추론 〈21학년도 6월 모평 33번 | 정답률 46%〉 ⑤

구문분석 & 직독직해

인지 도구로의 자아 확장

주제문 ↱ 부사절 접속사(시간) *수식을 받는 명사가 -thing, -body, -one으로 끝나는 경우 수식어(구)가 뒤에서 수식함.

[1]Even when we(S′) do(V′) something(O′) (as apparently simple / as picking up a screwdriver), // our brain(S) automatically **adjusts**(V) / **what it**(↱ = our brain) **considers body**(O(명사절)) / **to include the tool.**(목적(~하도록))

우리가 무언가를 할 때조차도 (겉보기에는 간단한 / 나사돌리개를 집는 것만큼) //
우리의 뇌는 무의식적으로 조정한다 / 그것(뇌)이 신체로 여기는 것을 / 도구를 포함하도록
↳ 뇌는 우리가 사용하는 도구까지 신체로 여기려고 함.

[2]We(S) can literally feel(V) things(O) / with the end of the screwdriver.
우리는 말 그대로 사물을 느낄 수 있다 / 나사돌리개의 끝부분으로

[3]When(부사절 접속사(시간)) we extend a hand, / holding the screwdriver,(분사구문(= as we hold ~)) // we(S) automatically take(V) the length(O) of the latter into account. 🔑 나사돌리개를 들고 손을 뻗을 때 그 길이도 계산에 넣음 → 나사돌리개까지 손에 포함함.
우리가 손을 뻗을 때 / 나사돌리개를 들고 // 우리는 무의식적으로 후자(나사돌리개)의 길이를 계산에 넣는다

[4]We(S) can probe(V_1) difficult-to-reach places(O_1) / with its(= screwdriver's) extended end, / and (can) comprehend(V_2) what we are exploring(O_2(명사절)).
우리는 닿기 어려운 곳을 탐색할 수 있다 / 그것(나사돌리개)의 확장된 끝으로 / 그리고 우리가 더듬어 살피고 있는 것을 이해할 수 있다

*<regard A as B>: A를 B로 간주하다[여기다]

[5]Furthermore, / we(S) instantly regard(V_1) *the screwdriver*(O) [(which[that])(목적격 관계대명사 생략) we are holding] / as(전치사(~로(서))) "our" screwdriver, / and get(V_2) possessive(C) about it(= the screwdriver we are holding).
게다가 / 우리는 나사돌리개를 즉시 간주한다 [우리가 들고 있는] / '우리의' 나사돌리개로 /
그리고 그것(우리가 들고 있는 나사돌리개)에 대해 소유욕이 강해진다
↳ **예 1(나사돌리개):** 나사돌리개 끝으로 탐색할 때, 그 길이만큼 계산에 넣고 나사돌리개를 '자신의' 일부로 여김.

[6]We(S) do(V) the same / with *the much*(비교급 강조 부사) *more complex tools* [(which[that])(목적격 관계대명사 생략) we use], / in much more complex situations.
우리는 똑같이 한다 / 훨씬 더 복잡한 도구에도 [우리가 사용하는] / 훨씬 더 복잡한 상황에서

🔑 운전하는 자동차가 자기 자신이 됨.

[7]*The cars*(S(복수)) [(which[that])(목적격 관계대명사 생략) we pilot] / instantaneously and automatically become(V(복수)) ourselves(C).
자동차는 [우리가 조종하는] / 순간적이면서도 무의식적으로 우리 자신이 된다

해석

[1]우리가 나사돌리개를 집는 것만큼 겉보기에는 간단한 무언가를 할 때조차도, 우리의 뇌는 무의식적으로 그것(뇌)이 신체로 여기는 것을 도구를 포함하도록 조정한다.(▶ 도구를 우리 신체의 일부로 인식한다는 것을 의미) [2]우리는 말 그대로 나사돌리개의 끝부분으로 사물을 느낄 수 있다. [3]나사돌리개를 들고 손을 뻗을 때 우리는 무의식적으로 후자(나사돌리개)의 길이를 계산에 넣는다. [4]우리는 그것의 확장된 끝으로 닿기 어려운 곳을 탐색할 수 있고, 우리가 더듬어 살피고 있는 것을 이해할 수 있다. [5]게다가, 우리는 우리가 들고 있는 나사돌리개를 '우리의' 나사돌리개로 즉시 간주하고, 그것에 대해 소유욕이 강해진다. [6]우리는 훨씬 더 복잡한 상황에서 우리가 사용하는 훨씬 더 복잡한 도구에도 똑같이 한다. [7]우리가 조종하는 자동차는 순간적이면서도 무의식적으로 우리 자신이 된다. [8]이것 때문에, 우리가 횡단보도에서 어떤 사람을 짜증나게 한 이후에 그가 우리 자동차의 덮개를 주먹으로 쾅 하고 칠 때, 우리는 그것을 개인적으로 받아들인다. [9]이것은 항상 합리적인 것은 아니다. [10]그럼에도 불구하고 기계로까지 자신을 확장하지 않는다면 운전하는 것은 불가능할 것이다.(▶ 기계를 우리 자신으로 여기지 않으면 사용할 수 없다는 의미)

어휘

apparently 겉보기에는; 명백히, 분명하게
screwdriver 나사돌리개
automatically 무의식적으로; 자동으로
adjust 조정[조절]하다
literally 말 그대로, 문자 그대로
extend (손·발 등을) 뻗다; 확장하다
cf. extension 확장
take A into account A를 계산에 넣다[고려하다]
latter 후자(의)

[8]Because of this, / when someone bangs his fist / on our car's hood // after we have irritated him / at a crosswalk, // we take it personally.

부사절 접속사(시간) / 부사절 접속사(시간) / S V O

이것 때문에 / 어떤 사람이 주먹으로 쾅 하고 칠 때 / 우리 자동차의 덮개를 // 우리가 그를 짜증 나게 한 이후에 / 횡단보도에서 // 우리는 그것을 개인적으로 받아들인다

↳ **예 2(자동차):** 운전하는 자동차를 '자기 자신'으로 여김.

(= 앞 문장) ★<not always>: ((부분 부정)) 항상 ~한 것은 아니다

[9]This is not always reasonable.

이것이 항상 합리적인 것은 아니다

자신을 기계로까지 확장시킴.

[10]Nonetheless, / without the extension of self into machine, / it would be impossible to drive.

(= if it were not for) 가주어 V C 진주어

그럼에도 불구하고 / 기계로까지 자신을 확장하지 않는다면 / 운전하는 것은 불가능할 것이다

↳ **결론:** 자동차에까지 자신을 확장시키는 것이 운전하는 데 필요함.

explore (손 등으로) 더듬어 살피다; 탐구하다
possessive 소유욕이 강한; 소유의
pilot 조종하다; 조종사, 파일럿
instantaneously 순간적으로; 즉각적으로
bang 쾅 하고 치다[때리다]
fist 주먹; 주먹으로 때리다
hood (자동차 등의) 덮개
irritate 짜증나게 하다, 거슬리다
take A personally A를 개인적으로[기분 나쁘게] 받아들이다
reasonable 합리적인; 이성적인
[선택지] recall 상기하다, 생각해내다
utilize 활용하다
cf. utility 효용, 유용성

정답 가이드

우리가 나사돌리개를 집을 때 뇌가 무의식적으로 '어떻게' 하는지를 추론해야 한다. 우리가 나사돌리개를 들고 손을 뻗을 때 손이 닿을 수 있는 거리에 나사돌리개의 길이도 계산에 넣고, 자동차를 운전할 때 그 자동차가 우리 자신이 된다고 했다. 이러한 예는 우리가 사용하는 도구를 우리 자신으로 여긴다는 것을 보여주므로, 빈칸에 들어갈 말로 가장 적절한 것은 ⑤ 'adjusts what it considers body to include the tool(그것이 신체로 여기는 것을 도구를 포함하도록 조정한다)'이다.

오답 클리닉

① recalls past experiences of utilizing the tool (18%)
그 도구를 활용했던 지난 경험을 상기한다
어떤 도구를 활용했던 경험을 떠올린다는 내용은 없음.

② recognizes what it can do best without the tool (11%)
그 도구 없이 그것이 가장 잘할 수 있는 것을 인지한다
나사돌리개와 자동차의 예는 도구를 사용하는 것과 관련됨.

③ judges which part of our body can best be used (13%)
우리 신체의 어느 부분이 가장 잘 활용될 수 있는지를 판단한다
신체가 아니라 도구를 활용하는 내용임.

④ perceives what limits the tool's functional utility (11%)
무엇이 그 도구의 기능적 효용을 제한하는지를 인식한다
도구의 기능성을 제한하는 내용은 없음.

03 + 문장 넣기 (22학년도 6월 모평 39번 | 정답률 37%) ⑤

구문분석 & 직독직해 생물 진화에서 잠이 하는 역할

주제문

[1]*The role* [that sleep plays / in evolution] / is still under study.

S 목적격 관계대명사 V C

역할은 [잠이 하는 / 진화에서] / 여전히 연구 중이다

↳ 잠이 진화에 미치는 영향에 관한 연구는 진행 중임.

(①) [2]One possibility is // that it is an advantageous adaptive state (of decreased metabolism) / for an animal // when there are no more pressing activities.

S V (is의 C(명사절)) 명사절 접속사 S′ V′ C′ 부사절 접속사(시간) V″ S″

한 가지 가능성은 ~이다 // 그것(잠)이 유리한 적응적 상태라는 것 (신진대사가 줄어든) / 동물에게 // 더 이상 긴급한 활동이 없을 때

↳ **세부 사항 1:** 잠은 긴급한 활동이 없을 때 신진대사가 줄어든 동물의 유리한 적응 상태임.

(②) [3]This seems true / for deeper states of inactivity (such as hibernation / during *the winter* [when there are few food supplies, / and a high metabolic cost / to maintaining adequate temperature]).

S V C ★few: 거의 ~없는(준부정어) 관계부사 V′ S′1 S′2 to의 O(동명사구)

이것은 해당하는 것처럼 보인다 / 더 깊은 무활동 상태에도 (겨울잠과 같은 / 겨울 동안의 [식량 공급이 거의 없는 / 그리고 높은 신진대사 비용이 드는 / 적절한 체온을 유지하는 것에])

해석

[1]진화에서 잠이 하는 역할은 여전히 연구 중이다. (①) [2]한 가지 가능성은 그것(잠)이 더 이상 긴급한 활동이 없을 때 신진대사가 줄어든, 동물에게 유리한 적응적 상태라는 것이다. (②) [3]이것은 식량 공급이 거의 없고 적절한 체온을 유지하는 것에 높은 신진대사 비용이 드는 겨울 동안의 겨울잠과 같은, 더 깊은 무활동 상태에도 해당하는 것처럼 보인다. (③) [4]그것은, 예를 들어 먹이 생물종이 어두워진 이후에 포식자를 피하려는 것처럼, 일상 상황에도 해당될지도 모른다. (④) [5]다른 한편으로는, 잠의 분명한 보편성, 그리고 고래목의 동물들과 같은 포유동물들이 한 번에 적어도 뇌의 한쪽에서는 잠을 유지하는 매우 고도로 복잡한 기제를 발전시켰다는 관찰 결과는 잠이 생명체에게 생명 유지에 필수적인 어떤 도움(들)을 부가적으로 제공한다는 것을 시사한다. (⑤ [6]잠의 한 가지 측면은 환경에 대한 감소된 반응성이기 때문에 이것은 특히 사실이다.) [7]이러한 잠재적인 대가가 치러져야 할 때조차도 잠이 보편적이라면, 그 함의는 조용한, 깨어있는 휴식

(③) [4]It may be true / in daily situations as well, / for instance for a prey species to avoid predators / after dark.

S V C to-v의 의미상 주어 목적(~하려고)

그것은 해당될지도 모른다 / 일상 상황에도 / 예를 들어 먹이 생물종이 포식자를 피하려는 것처럼 / 어두워진 이후에

↳ **부연 설명:** 겨울잠 같은 무활동 상태뿐만 아니라 어두워진 후에 잠을 자는 것은 동물의 유리한 적응 상태임.

(④) [5]On the other hand, / the apparent universality (of sleep), / (and the observation // that mammals (such as cetaceans) / have developed / *such highly complex mechanisms* (to preserve sleep) / on at least one side of the brain / at a time), /

S =

다른 한편으로는 / 분명한 보편성 (잠의) / (그리고 관찰 결과는 //

동격 접속사 S′ V′ O′

포유동물들이 (고래목의 동물들과 같은) / 발전시켰다는 / 매우 고도로 복잡한 기제를 (잠을 유지하는) / 적어도 뇌의 한쪽에서는 / 한 번에) /

suggests의 O(명사절) 🔑 주어진 문장의 This가 가리키는 내용.

suggests // that sleep additionally provides / some vital service(s) / for the organism.

V 명사절 접속사 S′ V′ O′

시사한다 // 잠이 부가적으로 제공한다는 것을 / 생명 유지에 필수적인 어떤 도움(들)을 / 생명체에게

↳ **세부 사항 2:** 잠은 생명 유지에 필수적인 도움을 줌.

(= sleep additionally ~ the organism) 🔑 This는 앞 문장의 잠이 생명 유지에 필수적인 도움을 제공한다는 시사점을 지칭함.

(⑤ [6]This is particularly true // since one aspect of sleep is / decreased responsiveness (to the environment).)

S V C 부사절 접속사(이유) S′ V′ C′

이것은 특히 사실이다 // 잠의 한 가지 측면은 ~이기 때문에 / 감소된 반응성 (환경에 대한)

🔑 주어진 문장의 환경에 대한 감소된 반응성을 가리킴.

[7]If sleep is universal // even when this potential price must be paid, //

부사절 접속사(조건) 부사절 접속사(시간) S″ V″

잠이 보편적이라면 // 이러한 잠재적인 대가가 치러져야 할 때조차도 //

may be의 C(명사절)

the implication may be // that it has *important functions* [that cannot be obtained / just by quiet, wakeful resting].

S V 명사절 접속사 S′ (= sleep) V′ O′ 주격 관계대명사

그 함의는 ~일 수도 있다 // 그것(잠)이 중요한 기능을 갖고 있다는 것 [얻어질 수 없는 / 조용한, 깨어있는 휴식만으로는]

↳ **부연 설명:** 환경에 대한 반응성을 감소시킴에도 잠이 보편적인 이유는 휴식만으로는 얻을 수 없는 중요 기능이 있을 수 있기 때문임.

만으로는 얻어질 수 없는 중요한 기능을 그것(잠)이 갖고 있다는 것일 수도 있다.

어휘

play a role 역할을 하다
advantageous 유리한, 이로운
adaptive 적응성의; 조정의
pressing 긴급한
inactivity 무활동
hibernation 겨울잠
metabolic 신진대사의
adequate 적절한, 알맞은
apparent 분명한, 명백한
universality 보편성
cf. universal 보편적인
observation (관찰의) 결과; 관찰; 감시
cetacean 고래목의 동물
mechanism 기제[구조]; 기계 장치
preserve 유지하다; 보호하다; 보존하다
vital 생명 유지에 필수적인
service 도움; 제공하다
responsiveness 반응성
implication 함의; 함축
function 기능(하다)
wakeful 깨어 있는

정답 가이드

주어진 문장은 바로 앞에 말한 내용이 특히 사실인 것은 잠의 환경에 대한 감소된 반응성, 즉 잠이 들면 환경 변화에 잘 반응하기 힘들기 때문이라는 것이므로 이 이유가 어떤 내용을 사실로 설명하는 것인지를 찾아야 한다. ④ 앞은 신진대사 비용을 줄이거나 포식자를 피할 수 있다는 점에서 잠의 긍정적 역할을 서술하고 있고, on the other hand 뒤에 이어지는 내용은 잠의 보편성이 생명 유지에 잠이 필수적인 도움을 제공한다는 것을 시사한다는 것이다. 이 내용은 주어진 문장에서 말한, 환경 변화에 반응하지 못한다는 잠의 부정적 측면 때문에 특히 사실인 것에 해당한다. ⑤ 뒤에 이어지는 내용은 이 환경에 대한 감소된 반응성을 this potential price로 받아 주어진 문장을 부연 설명한다. 따라서 주어진 문장이 들어가기에 가장 적절한 곳은 ⑤이다.

오답 클리닉

① (2%) 진화에서 잠이 하는 역할에 대한 첫 번째 세부 사항으로 신진대사를 줄이는 유리한 적응적 상태라고 설명하는 내용이다.

② (10%) 잠은 신진대사를 줄이는, 동물에게 유리한 적응적 상태라는 내용을 This로 받으면서, 이는 겨울잠과 같은 무활동 상태에 해당된다고 부연 설명하는 것은 자연스럽다.

③ (21%) 내용을 첨가하는 부사 as well을 사용해 잠은 일상 상황에도 유리하게 작용한다는 내용이 이어진다.

④ (30%) 앞에서 설명한 잠의 긍정적인 역할과는 다른 내용을 연결어 on the other hand를 사용해 제시하고 있다.

The 주의 주어진 문장의 This는 ④의 뒤 문장에서 suggests의 목적어로 쓰인 명사절을 지칭함을 파악해야 한다.

01 + 요약문 (22학년도 6월 모평 40번 | 정답률 58%) ③

구문분석 & 직독직해

역사 영국의 귀족들에게 있어 나무 심기의 의미

주제문

[1]The idea // that *planting* trees could have a social or political significance / appears to have been invented / by the English, // though it has since spread widely.

(S = that절: 동격 접속사 / V: appears / C(to-v의 완료 수동형) / ★ <appear to-v>: v인 것처럼 보인다 / though: 부사절 접속사(양보) / it (= the idea) / has spread: V')

생각은 // 나무를 '심는 것'이 사회적이거나 정치적인 의미를 가질 수 있다는 / 고안된 것처럼 보인다 / 영국인들에 의해 // 비록 그 생각이 이후에 널리 퍼지긴 했지만

↳ 나무 심기가 사회적, 정치적 의미를 가질 수 있다는 것은 영국인이 만든 생각임.

[2]According to Keith Thomas's history *Man and the Natural World*, / seventeenth- and eighteenth-century aristocrats began planting hardwood trees, / (usually in lines), /

(S: seventeenth- and eighteenth-century aristocrats / V: began / O: planting hardwood trees / 전치사구 삽입: usually in lines)

Keith Thomas의 역사서 <Man and the Natural World>에 의하면 / 17세기와 18세기의 귀족들은 활엽수를 심기 시작했다 / (보통 일렬로) /

🔑 (A) 귀족들은 토지에 대한 권리의 영속성을 나타내려고 나무를 심음.

to declare / the extent of their property [and] the permanence of their claim to it.

(목적(~하기 위해) / to declare의 O(명사구 병렬) / it (= their property))

나타내기 위해 / 자신들의 소유지 범위와 그것(자신들의 소유)에 대한 자신들의 권리의 영속성을

↳ **세부 사항 1:** 영국 귀족들은 소유지 범위와 그 권리의 영속성을 보여주려고 활엽수를 심음 → 사회적 의미.

[3]"What can be more pleasant," / (the editor of a magazine for gentlemen asked his readers), /

(삽입절)

"더 기쁠 수 있는 일이 무엇이 있겠습니까" / (신사들을 위한 어떤 잡지의 편집자는 자신의 독자들에게 물었다) /

"than to have the bounds and limits of your own property preserved and continued / from age to age / by the testimony (of such living and growing witnesses)?"

(★<사역동사 have+O+p.p.>: O가 ~되도록 하다[시키다] / witnesses (= trees))

"귀하 소유의 토지의 경계와 한계가 보존되고 지속되도록 하는 것보다 / 대대로 / 증언으로 (그런 살아 있고 자라나는 증인들의)"

↳ **부연 설명:** 나무로 토지의 경계와 한계를 보존하고 지속하는 것이 가장 즐거움.

🔑 (B) 나무를 심는 것은 애국적인 행동으로 여겨짐.

[4]Planting trees had the additional advantage (of being regarded as a patriotic act), // for the Crown had declared / a severe shortage (of *the hardwood* [on which the Royal Navy depended]).

(S: Planting trees / V: had / O: the additional advantage / as: 전치사(~로(서)) / for: 부사절 접속사(이유) / S': the Crown / V': had declared / O': a severe shortage / on which: 전치사+관계대명사)

나무를 심는 것은 추가적인 이점을 가졌다 (애국적인 행동으로 여겨지는) // 군주가 선언했기 때문에 / 심각한 부족을 (견목의 [영국 해군이 의존하는])

↳ **세부 사항 2:** 나무 심기는 애국적 행동으로 여겨짐 → 정치적 의미.

↓

[5]For English aristocrats, / planting trees served as *statements* (to mark the **(A) lasting** ownership (of their land)), // [and] it was also considered / to be an **(B) exhibition** of their loyalty (to the nation).

(S_1: planting trees / V_1: served / it (= planting trees): S_2 / V: was considered / C_2: to be an exhibition / ★<consider A (to be) B(A를 B로 여기다)>의 수동형)

영국의 귀족들에게 / 나무를 심는 것은 표현의 역할을 했다 ((A) 지속적인 소유권을 표시하는 (자신의 땅에 대한)) // 그리고 그것(나무를 심는 것)은 또한 여겨졌다 / 그들의 충성심의 (B) 표현으로 (국가에 대한)

해석

[1]나무를 '심는 것'이 사회적이거나 정치적인 의미를 가질 수 있다는 생각은, 비록 그 생각이 이후에 널리 퍼지긴 했지만, 영국인들에 의해 고안된 것처럼 보인다. [2]Keith Thomas의 역사서 <Man and the Natural World>에 의하면, 17세기와 18세기의 귀족들은 자신들의 소유지 범위와 그것(자신들의 소유)에 대한 자신들의 권리의 영속성을 나타내기 위해 보통 일렬로 활엽수를 심기 시작했다. [3]신사들을 위한 어떤 잡지의 편집자는 자신의 독자들에게 "그런 살아 있고 자라나는 증인들(나무들)의 증언으로 귀하 소유의 토지의 경계와 한계가 대대로 보존되고 지속되도록 하는 것보다 더 기쁠 수 있는 일이 무엇이 있겠습니까?"라고 물었다. [4]나무를 심는 것은 애국적인 행동으로 여겨지는 추가적인 이점을 가졌는데, 군주가 영국 해군이 의존하는 견목(활엽수에서 얻은 단단한 목재)의 심각한 부족을 선언했기 때문이었다.

↓

[5]영국의 귀족들에게, 나무를 심는 것은 자신의 땅에 대한 (A) 지속적인 소유권을 표시하는 표현의 역할을 했고, 그것(나무를 심는 것)은 또한 국가에 대한 그들의 충성심의 (B) 표현으로 여겨졌다.

어휘

significance 의미; 중요성
hardwood 활엽수; 견목, 경재; 견목의
in line 일렬로 늘어선; 직렬의
declare 나타내다, 밝히다; 선언[선포]하다
extent 범위, 정도, 규모
property (소유의) 토지; 재산, 소유물
permanence 영속성, 영구성
claim 권리; 주장(하다); 요구하다
bound 경계(선); 한도, 범위
testimony 증언, 증거
witness 증인, 참고인; 목격자
advantage 장점, 이점; (~에게) 유리하게 하다
shortage 부족
the Royal Navy 영국 해군
[요약문] statement 표현; 성명(서), 진술(서)
ownership 소유(권)

정답 가이드

요약문을 통해 영국 귀족들이 나무를 심는 의미에 대한 글임을 알 수 있다. 첫 번째 문장에서 나무 심기는 사회적이거나 정치적인 의미를 가질 수 있다고 한 후, 귀족들이 활엽수를 심어 토지 소유권의 '영속성'을 나타냈으며, 영국 해군이 의존하는 견목이 부족했던 상황에서 이는 또한 '애국적인 행동'으로도 여겨졌다고 설명한다. 따라서 요약문의 빈칸 (A)와 (B)에 각각 들어갈 말로 가장 적절한 것은 ③ 'lasting(지속적인) - exhibition(표현)'이다.

오답 클리닉

(A) (B)

① unstable - confirmation (15%) 불안정한 - 확인

(A)는 틀리며, (B)는 맞음. 귀족들은 나무를 심어 대대로 땅에 대한 소유권의 표시를 견고히 한 것이므로 '불안정한'은 적절하지 않음.

② unstable - exaggeration (7%) 불안정한 - 과장

(A)와 (B) 모두 틀림.

④ lasting - manipulation (14%) 지속적인 - 조작

(A)는 맞지만, (B)는 틀림.

⑤ official - justification (6%) 공식적인 - 정당화

(A)와 (B) 모두 틀림. 나무를 심어 소유지의 경계를 표시하는 것이 공식적으로 인정되는 것인지는 알 수 없음.

02~03 + 복합 유형 (23학년도 9월 모평 41~42번 | 정답률 02 62%, 03 60%)

02 ③ 03 ③

구문분석 & 직독직해

환경 기후 변화를 표현하지 못하는 상상력

[1] Climate change experts and environmental humanists / alike agree //

기후 변화 전문가들과 환경 인문주의자들은 / 똑같이 동의한다 //

that the climate crisis is, / (at its core), / a crisis (of the imagination) // and much of the popular imagination is shaped / by fiction.

(↱ agree의 O(명사절); 명사절 접속사, S′1, V′1, 삽입어구, C′1, S′2, V′2)

기후 위기가 ~라는 것에 / (근원적으로) / 위기 (상상력의) // 그리고 대중적 상상력의 많은 부분이 형성된다는 것에 / 소설에 의해

03-(a) 기후 위기 인식에 영향을 미치는 소설이 기후 변화를 그럴듯하게 표현하지 '못해' 대응에 실패함.

↳ **도입:** 기후 위기는 상상력의 위기이며, 대중적 상상력의 많은 부분은 소설로 형성됨.

[2] In his 2016 book *The Great Derangement*, / anthropologist and novelist Amitav Ghosh takes on / this relationship (between imagination and environmental management), /

(S, V, O)

자신의 2016년도 책 <The Great Derangement>에서 / 인류학자이자 소설가인 Amitav Ghosh는 논한다 / 이러한 관계를 (상상과 환경 관리 사이의) /

arguing // that humans have failed to respond to climate change / at least in part // because fiction **(a) fails** to believably represent it.

(분사구문(= as he argues ~); 현재분사 arguing의 O(명사절); 부사절 접속사(이유); it = climate change)

주장하면서 // 인간이 기후 변화에 대응하지 못했다고 / 적어도 부분적으로는 // 소설이 그것(기후 변화)을 그럴듯하게 표현하지 못하기 때문에

[3] Ghosh explains // that climate change is largely absent / from contemporary fiction //

(S, V, ↱ explains의 O(명사절); 명사절 접속사, S′, V′, C′)

Ghosh는 설명한다 // 기후 변화가 대체로 부재하다고 / 현대 소설에서 //

03-(b) 사이클론, 홍수, 큰 재해가 다음 문장에서 '엄청난' 사건들로 말바꿈됨.

because *the cyclones, floods, and other catastrophes* [(which[that]) it brings to mind] / simply seem too "improbable" / to belong in stories (about everyday life).

(부사절 접속사(이유), S″, 목적격 관계대명사 생략, V″, C″; ★<too ~ to-v>: v하기에는 너무 ~한)

사이클론, 홍수, 그리고 다른 큰 재해들이 ~이기 때문에 [그것(기후 변화)이 상기시키는] / 그야말로 너무 '있을 것 같지 않은' 것처럼 보이(기 때문에) / 이야기에 속하기에는 (일상생활에 관한)

↳ **부연 설명:** 소설은 실제 기후 변화를 그럴듯하게 표현하지 못하고 큰 재해들은 일상 이야기에 있을 것 같지 않아 보여서 현대 소설에서 없어짐.

[4] But climate change does not only reveal itself / as a series of **(b) extraordinary** events.

(S, V, O(itself = climate change), 전치사(~로(서)))

그러나 기후 변화는 자신을 오로지 드러내지 않는다 / 일련의 엄청난 사건들로만

↳ 기후 변화가 엄청난 사건들로만 드러나는 것은 아님.

해석

[1] 기후 변화 전문가들과 환경 인문주의자들은 기후 위기가 근원적으로 상상력의 위기이며 대중적 상상력의 많은 부분이 소설에 의해 형성된다는 것에 똑같이 동의한다.(▶ 소설이 기후 위기에 대한 대중의 인식에 영향을 미친다는 의미) [2] 인류학자이자 소설가인 Amitav Ghosh는 자신의 2016년도 책 <The Great Derangement>에서 적어도 부분적으로는 소설이 그것(기후 변화)을 그럴듯하게 표현하지 (a) 못하기 때문에 인간이 기후 변화에 대응하지 못했다고 주장하며, 이러한 상상과 환경 관리 사이의 관계를 논한다. [3] Ghosh는 그것(기후 변화)이 상기시키는 사이클론, 홍수, 그리고 다른 큰 재해들이 그야말로 일상생활에 관한 이야기에 속하기에는 너무 '있을 것 같지 않은' 것처럼 보이기 때문에 기후 변화가 현대 소설에 대체로 부재하다고 설명한다. [4] 그러나 기후 변화는 오로지 일련의 (b) 엄청난 사건들로만 자신을 드러내지 않는다. [5] 사실, Rachel Carson에서 Rob Nixon에 이르는 환경론자들과 생태 비평가들이 지적했듯이, 환경 변화는 '감지할 수 없을' 수 있는데, 즉 그것은 (c) 빠르게(→ 점진적으로) 진행되며, 단지 이따금 '폭발적이고 극적인' 사건들을 만들어 낼 뿐이다. [6] 대부분의 기후 변화의 영향은 매일 관찰될 수는 없지만, 우리가 그것들의 축적된 영향에 직면할 때 그것들은 (d) 가시화된다.

[7] 기후 변화는 그것이 상당한 표현상의 문제를 제기하기 때문에 우리의 상상에서 벗어난다.(▶ 기후 변화를 정확히 나타내기 어렵기 때문에 우리가 상상할 수 없다는 의미) [8] 그것은 '인간의 시간' 동안에는 관찰될 수 없는데, 그것이 빙하와 산호초에 미치는 기후 변화의 영향을 추적하는 다큐멘터리 영화 제작자 Jeff Orlowski가 서서히 일어난 변화를 (e) 강조하기 위해 같은 장소에서 수개월 간격으로 찍힌 '전과 후' 사진을 이용하는 이유이다.

[5]In fact, / as environmentalists and ecocritics (from Rachel Carson to Rob Nixon) / have pointed out, // environmental change can be "imperceptible"; //
부사절 접속사(~하듯이) S′ V′ S_1 V_1 C_1
사실 / 환경론자들과 생태 비평가들이 ~하듯이 (Rachel Carson에서 Rob Nixon에 이르는) / 지적했(듯이) // 환경 변화는 '감지할 수 없을' 수 있다 //

🔑 03-(c) 환경 변화를 감지할 수 없는 것은 '점진적으로' 진행되기 때문임.

(= environmental change)
it proceeds (c) rapidly(→ gradually), / only occasionally producing "explosive and spectacular" events.
S_2 V_2 분사구문 (= as it only occasionally produces ~)
그것은 빠르게(→ 점진적으로) 진행된다 / 단지 이따금 '폭발적이고 극적인' 사건들을 만들어 내며

[6]Most climate change impacts cannot be observed day-to-day, // but they become (d) visible // when we are confronted with their accumulated impacts.
S_1 V_1 S_2 V_2 C_2 부사절 접속사(시간)
대부분의 기후 변화의 영향은 매일 관찰될 수는 없다 // 하지만 그것들은 가시화된다 // 우리가 그것들의 축적된 영향에 직면할 때

🔑 03-(d) 매일 '관찰될 수 없다'와 but으로 연결되어 기후 변화의 영향이 축적되면 '보인다'는 흐름이 적절함

↳ **세부 사항:** 기후 변화는 점진적으로 일어나 매일 감지할 수 없으며, 변화가 축적되어야만 보임.

주제문
[7]Climate change evades our imagination // because it poses significant representational challenges.
S V O 부사절 접속사(이유) S′ V′ O′
기후 변화는 우리의 상상에서 벗어난다 // 그것이 상당한 표현상의 문제를 제기하기 때문에

↳ **결론:** 기후 변화는 표현의 문제 때문에 우리의 상상으로 표현할 수 없음.

(= Climate change)
[8]It cannot be observed in "human time," // which is (the reason) why documentary filmmaker *Jeff Orlowski*, // (who tracks climate change effects / on glaciers and coral reefs), /
S V 관계대명사(앞 절 보충 설명) 선행사 생략 관계부사 S′ 관계사절 삽입(보충 설명)
그것(기후 변화)은 '인간의 시간' 동안에는 관찰될 수 없다 // 그리고 그것이 다큐멘터리 영화 제작자 Jeff Orlowski가 ~하는 이유이다 // (기후 변화의 영향을 추적하는 / 빙하와 산호초에 미치는) /

uses *"before and after" photographs* (taken several months apart / in the same place) / to (e) **highlight** *changes* [that occurred gradually].
V′ O′ 과거분사구 주격 관계대명사 목적(~하기 위해)
'전과 후' 사진을 이용하는 (수개월 간격으로 찍힌 / 같은 장소에서) / 변화를 강조하기 위해 [서서히 일어난]

🔑 03-(e) 같은 장소에서 수개월 간격으로 찍은 전과 후 사진은 서서히 일어난 변화를 '강조해' 보여줌.

↳ **대안:** 다큐멘터리 영화의 '전과 후' 사진이 점진적인 기후 변화의 영향을 잘 보여줌.

어휘

climate 기후; 분위기, 풍조
humanist 인문주의자
core 근원, 핵심; 핵심적인
take on ~을 논하다, 다루다[떠맡다]
believably 그럴듯 하게, 믿을만 하게
represent 표현하다, 나타내다; 대표하다
largely 대체로, 주로
absent 부재한, 존재하지 않는; 결석한
contemporary 현대의, 당대의; 동시대의
cyclone 사이클론 ((열대지방에서 발생하는 저기압))
bring to mind ~을 상기시키다
improbable 있을 것[사실] 같지 않은, 희한한
reveal 드러내다, 보여주다
a series of 일련의, 연속적인
imperceptible 감지할 수 없는
proceed 진행되다; 나아가다
explosive 폭발적인; 폭발(성)의; 폭발물
spectacular 극적인; 장관을 이루는
impact 영향, 충격
be confronted with ~에 직면하다
accumulated 축적된
pose (위협·문제 등을) 제기하다
track 추적하다; 길
glacier 빙하
coral reef 산호초
apart (거리·시간·공간상으로) 떨어져; 따로
[선택지] movement (정치·사회적) 운동; 움직임, 동작
vivid 뚜렷한, 선명한; 생생한

정답 가이드

02 첫 문장에서 기후 위기가 근원적으로 상상력의 위기이며 상상력은 소설에 의해 생긴다고 했다. 그러나 소설은 기후 변화를 그럴듯하게 표현하지 못하고 큰 재해 같은 것은 일상 이야기에 있을 것 같지 않으므로 현대 소설에 나오지 않는다고 설명했다. 또한 기후 변화는 점진적으로 진행되므로 표현상 문제가 있기 때문에 상상할 수 없다고 설명한다. 따라서 글의 제목으로 가장 적절한 것은 ③ 'The Silence of Imagination in Representing Climate Change(기후 변화를 표현하는 데 있어서의 상상력의 침묵)'이다.

03 환경 변화는 감지할 수 없을 수 있다는 앞 내용을 부연 설명하고 있으므로 ③의 'rapidly(빠르게)'를 'gradually(점진적으로)' 또는 'slowly(느리게)'와 같은 단어로 바꾸어야 한다.

오답 클리닉

02 ① Differing Attitudes Towards Current Climate Issues (14%)
현재의 기후 문제에 대한 상이한 태도(×)
기후 문제에 대한 다른 태도들을 설명하는 글이 아님.
② Slow but Significant: The History of Ecological Movements (15%)
느리지만 중요한 생태 운동의 역사(×)
생태 운동의 역사에 관한 글이 아님.
④ Vivid Threats: Climate Disasters Spreading in Local Areas (7%)
뚜렷한 위협으로 지역에서 확산되는(×) 기후 재앙들
큰 기후 재해들이 지역에서 퍼져나간다는 내용이 아님.
⑤ The Rise and Fall of Environmentalism and Ecocriticism (2%)
환경주의와 생태 비평의 흥망성쇠(×)
environmentalists and ecocritics를 활용한 오답. 환경주의와 생태 비평에 관한 내용이 아님.

03 ① fails (6%) ~하지 못하다
문장 1에서 소설이 기후 위기에 대한 사람들의 인식에 영향을 미친다고 했다. 따라서 인간이 기후 변화에 대응하지 못한 것은 소설이 기후 변화를 그럴듯하게 표현하지 '못했기' 때문이다.
② extraordinary (12%) 엄청난
문장 3에서 언급한 the cyclones, floods, and other catastrophes를 받아 기후 변화가 이런 '엄청난' 사건들로만 나타나는 것이 아니라고 내용을 전환하는 것은 적절하다.
④ visible (14%) 가시적인
앞 절과 but으로 연결되어 기후 변화의 영향은 매일 관찰될 수 없지만, 영향이 축적되면 '가시화'된다고 대조되는 흐름이 자연스럽다.
⑤ highlight (7%) 강조하다
같은 장소에서 수개월 간격으로 찍은 사진을 이용하는 것은 감지하기 어려운 변화를 한 눈에 볼 수 있도록 '강조하기' 위해서이다.

01 ✦ 빈칸 추론 〈21학년도 6월 모평 32번 | 정답률 40%〉 ③

구문분석 & 직독직해

언어 독자가 편견을 갖게 하는 글쓰기 위험 요소

주제문

[1]One (of the great risks of writing) / is // that even the simplest of choices (regarding wording or punctuation) / can sometimes **prejudice** **your audience** / **against you** / in *ways* [that may seem unfair].

S(단수) V(단수) 명사절 접속사 S′ V′ O′ 주격 관계대명사 (→ is의 C(명사절))

하나는 (글쓰기의 큰 위험 중) / ~이다 // 가장 단순한 선택조차 (단어 선택이나 구두점과 관련한) / 때때로 독자가 편견을 갖게 할 수 있다는 것 / 여러분에 대해 / 방식으로 [부당해 보일 수도 있는]

↳ 글쓰기에 있어 어떤 단순한 선택조차 독자가 편견을 갖게 할 수 있음.

[2]For example, / look again at / *the old grammar rule* (forbidding the splitting of infinitives).

V(명령문) O 현재분사구

예를 들어 / 다시 보라 / 옛날 문법 규칙을 (부정사를 분리하는 것을 금지하는)

[3]After decades (of telling students / to never split an infinitive (something just done in this sentence)), / most composition experts now acknowledge // that a split infinitive is *not* a grammar crime.

of의 O(동명사구) S V 명사절 접속사 S′ V′ C′ (→ acknowledge의 O(명사절))

수십 년간 ~한 후에 (학생들에게 말한 / 부정사를 절대 분리하지 말라고 (바로 이 문장에서 행해진 것인)) / 대부분의 작문 전문가들은 이제 인정한다 // 분리된 부정사가 문법적 죄가 '아니'라는 것을

↳ 예: 현재와 달리 과거에는 분리부정사를 사용하는 것이 금지되었음.

*<convince A of B>: A에게 B를 납득[확신]시키다

[4]Suppose // (that) you have written *a position paper* (trying to convince your city council / of *the need* (to hire security personnel for the library)), /

V(명령문) 명사절 접속사 생략 S'_1 V'_1 O'_1 현재분사구 (→ suppose의 O(명사절))

가정해 보라 // 여러분이 의견서를 작성했다고 (시의회에 납득시키려고 하는 / 필요를 (도서관을 위한 보안 요원을 고용할)) /

and half (of the council members) — / *the people* [(who(m)|that) you wish to convince] — / remember their eighth-grade grammar teacher's warning (about splitting infinitives).

S'_2 = 목적격 관계대명사 생략 V'_2 O'_2

그리고 절반이 (시의회 의원 중) / 사람들인 [여러분이 납득시키고 싶어 하는] / 자신들의 8학년 문법 교사의 경고를 기억한다고 (부정사를 분리하는 것에 대한)

[5]How will they respond // when you tell them, / (in your introduction), // that librarians are compelled "to always accompany" visitors / to the rare book room / because of the threat of damage?

의문사 V S → 부사절 접속사(시간) S′ V′ IO′ 전치사구 삽입 DO′(명사절)

*<compel+O+to-v(O에게 v하도록 강요하다)>의 수동형.

그들은 어떻게 반응할까 // 여러분이 그들에게 말할 때 / (여러분의 도입부에서) // 도서관 사서는 방문객과 '항상 동행해야' 한다고 / 희귀 서적이 있는 방에 / 손상의 위험 때문에

[6]How much of their attention have you suddenly lost / because of their automatic recollection (of what is now a nonrule)?

O V S of의 O(명사절)

🗝 분리부정사가 과거에 금지된 문법 규칙이었던 것을 기억한 독자는 글에 대한 관심을 잃음.

여러분은 그들의 관심을 얼마나 많이 갑작스럽게 잃었는가 / 그들의 자동적인 기억 때문에 (지금은 규칙이 아닌 것에 대한)

↳ 가상의 상황: 과거에 금지되었던 분리부정사("to always accompany")를 사용한 것이 읽는 이의 관심을 잃게 함.

*진주어의 to write와 (to) offend가 and로 연결됨.

[7]It is possible, / in other words, / to write correctly and still (to) offend your readers' notions (of your language competence).

가주어 V C 진주어(to-v구)

🗝 글을 올바르게 쓰더라도 글쓴이의 사소한 선택이 독자에게 불쾌감을 줄 수 있음.

(~이) 가능하다 / 다른 말로 하면 / 올바르게 글을 쓰면서도 독자의 생각에 불쾌감을 주는 것 (여러분의 언어 능력에 대한)

↳ 요약: 분리부정사의 사용은 현재 문법적으로 올바르나, 그것이 한때 금지되었던 것을 기억하는 독자는 불쾌감을 느낄 수 있음.

해석

[1]글쓰기의 큰 위험 중 하나는 단어 선택이나 구두점과 관련한 가장 단순한 선택조차 부당해 보일 수도 있는 방식으로 때때로 독자가 여러분에 대해 편견을 갖게 할 수 있다는 것이다. [2]예를 들어, 부정사를 분리하는 것을(▶ to-v를 to+부사+v의 형태로 쓰는 것을 의미) 금지하는 옛날 문법 규칙을 다시 보라. [3]학생들에게 (바로 이 문장에서 행해진 것인(to never split)) 부정사를 절대 분리하지 말라고 수십 년간 말한 후에, 대부분의 작문 전문가들은 이제 분리된 부정사가 문법적 죄가 '아니'라는 것을 인정한다. [4]여러분이 시의회에 도서관을 위한 보안 요원을 고용할 필요를 납득시키려고 하는 의견서를 작성했고 여러분이 납득시키고 싶어 하는 사람들인 시의회 의원 중 절반이 부정사를 분리하는 것에 대한 자신들의 8학년 문법 교사의 경고를 기억한다고 가정해 보라. [5]여러분이 여러분의 도입부에서 손상의 위험 때문에 희귀 서적이 있는 방에 도서관 사서는 방문객과 '항상 동행해야(to always accompany)' 한다고 그들에게 말할 때 그들은 어떻게 반응할까? [6]지금은 규칙이 아닌 것에 대한 그들의 자동적인 기억 때문에 여러분은 그들의 관심을 얼마나 많이 갑작스럽게 잃었는가? [7]다른 말로 하면, 올바르게 글을 쓰면서도 여러분의 언어 능력에 대한 독자의 생각에 불쾌감을 주는 것이 가능하다.

어휘

regarding ~에 관련하여
wording 단어 선택, 표현(법)
forbid 금지하다
split 분리하다; 분리된
composition 작문; 작곡; 구성(물)
acknowledge 인정하다, 승인하다
position paper 의견서, 성명서
city council 시의회
security personnel 보안 요원
introduction 도입(부)
accompany 동행하다, 동반하다
rare 희귀한, 드문
recollection 기억(력); 회상
offend 불쾌감을 주다; 위반하다
notion 생각, 관념, 개념
competence 능력; 적성, 자격
[선택지] intention 의도, 의사
distort 왜곡하다; 일그러지게 하다, 비틀다
prejudice 편견(을 갖게 하다)
comprehension 이해(력)
fierce 격렬한; 사나운
debate 논쟁; 토론

정답 가이드

글쓰기에서 가장 단순한 선택조차 부당한 방식으로 '어떠할' 수 있다는 것인지를 찾아야 한다. 이어지는 예에서, 과거에 금지되었던 분리부정사를 지금 사용하면 독자들이 글쓴이의 언어 능력을 불쾌하게 여길 수 있다고 했다. 이는 분리부정사를 사용하는 것과 같은 '단순한 선택'이 올바른 것임에도 불구하고 독자들의 기억 때문에 글쓴이의 능력이 잘못 판단될 수 있다는 것을 의미하므로, 빈칸에 들어갈 말로 가장 적절한 것은 ③ 'prejudice your audience against you(독자가 여러분에 대해 편견을 갖게 하다)'이다.

오답 클리닉

① reveal your hidden intention (13%)
여러분의 숨겨진 의도를 드러내다
숨겨진 의도에 대한 언급은 없음.

② distort the meaning of the sentence (29%)
문장의 의미를 왜곡하다
분리부정사의 사용이 문장의 의미 자체를 왜곡한 것이 아님.

The 주의 독자에게 글쓴이의 언어 능력에 문제가 있다는 인상을 줄 수 있는 예로 분리부정사의 사용이 언급된 것이다.

④ test your audience's reading comprehension (11%)
독자의 독해력을 시험하다
독자의 독해력에 관한 언급은 없음.

⑤ create fierce debates about your writing topic (7%)
여러분의 작문 주제에 관한 격렬한 논쟁을 만들어 내다
작문 주제에 대해 서로 논쟁한다는 내용은 없음.

02 + 글의 순서 (22학년도 6월 모평 37번 | 정답률 38%) ⑤

구문분석 & 직독직해

경제 투자와 관련된 복수균형

*<whether to-v>: v할지

[1]A firm is deciding / whether to invest in shipbuilding.
(S: A firm / V: is deciding / O(명사구): whether to invest in shipbuilding)
한 회사가 결정 중이다 / 조선업에 투자할지를

[2]If it can produce at sufficiently large scale, // it knows // (that) the venture will be profitable.
(If: 부사절 접속사(조건) / it (= a firm) / S: it (= a firm) / V: knows / (that): 명사절 접속사 생략 / knows의 O(명사절) / S′: the venture / V′: will be / C′: profitable)
만약 그것(회사)이 충분히 대규모로 생산할 수 있다면 // 그것(회사)은 알고 있다 // 그 모험이 수익성이 있을 거라는 것을
↳ **도입:** 조선업에의 투자 여부를 결정하는 회사는 대규모 생산이 가능하다면 투자는 수익성이 있을 것임을 앎.

(C) [3]But / one key input is low-cost steel, // and it must be produced nearby.
(S₁: one key input / V₁: is / C: low-cost steel / S₂: it (= low-cost steel) / V₂: must be produced)
그러나 / 한 가지 핵심 투입 요소는 저가의 강철이다 // 그리고 그것(저가의 강철)은 근처에서 생산되어야 한다

주어진 글에 언급된 회사의 조선업 투자 결정의 요건을 제시함.

[4]The company's decision boils down to this: // if there is a steel factory close by, // invest in shipbuilding; // otherwise, don't invest (in shipbuilding).
(S₁: The company's decision / V₁: boils down / if: 부사절 접속사(조건) / V₂(명령문): invest in / V₃(명령문): don't invest / (in shipbuilding): 반복어구 생략)
그 회사의 결정은 결국 다음과 같이 된다 // 즉 만약 강철 공장이 가까이에 있다면 // 조선업에 투자하라 // 그렇지 않으면(강철 공장이 가까이에 없다면) 투자하지 마라
↳ **조선소 투자 요건:** 근처에 저가의 강철을 조달할 수 있는 공장이 있어야 함.

[5]Now consider / the thinking (of potential steel investors / in the region).
(V(명령문): consider / O: the thinking)
이제 고려해 보라 / 생각을 (잠재적 강철 투자자들의 / 그 지역에 있는)

(B) [6]Assume // that shipyards are the only potential customers (of steel).
(V(명령문): Assume / that: 명사절 접속사, assume의 O(명사절) / S′: shipyards / V′: are / C′: the only potential customers)
가정하라 // 조선소가 유일한 잠재적 고객이라고 (강철의)
↳ **가정:** 조선소가 유일한 강철의 잠재 고객인 상황.

(C)의 마지막에 언급된 잠재적 강철 투자자들의 생각을 설명함.

[7]Steel producers figure // (that) they'll make money // if there's a shipyard (to buy their steel), // but (they will) not (make money) otherwise.
(S: Steel producers / V: figure / (that): 명사절 접속사 생략, figure의 O(명사절) / S′: they / V′: 'll make / O′: money / if: 부사절 접속사(조건) / V″: 's / S″: a shipyard)
강철 생산자들은 생각한다 // 자신들이 돈을 벌 것이라고 // 조선소가 있으면 (자신들의 강철을 구매할) // 하지만 그렇지 않으면 (돈을 벌지) 못할 것이라고
↳ **강철 투자의 요건:** 강철을 구매해 줄 조선소가 근처에 있어야 함.

*<call+O+C>: O를 C라고 부르다

[8]Now we have two possible outcomes — // what economists call "multiple equilibria."
(S: we / V: have / O: two possible outcomes / = 동격절(명사절): what economists call "multiple equilibria.")
이제 우리는 두 가지 가능한 결과를 갖게 된다 // 경제학자들이 '복수균형'이라고 부르는 것
↳ 두 가지 가능한 결과(복수균형)를 갖게 됨.

해석

[1]한 회사가 조선업에 투자할지를 결정 중이다. [2]만약 충분히 대규모로 생산할 수 있다면, 회사는 그 (사업) 모험이 수익성이 있을 거라는 것을 알고 있다. (C) [3]그러나 한 가지 핵심 투입 요소는 저가의 강철이며, 그것은 근처에서 생산되어야 한다. [4]그 회사의 결정은 결국 다음과 같이 되는데, 즉 만약 강철 공장이 가까이에 있다면, 조선업에 투자하고, 그렇지 않으면(강철 공장이 가까이에 없다면) 투자하지 말라는 것이다. [5]이제 그 지역에 있는 잠재적 강철 투자자들의 생각을 고려해 보라. (B) [6]조선소가 강철의 유일한 잠재적 고객이라고 가정하라. [7]강철 생산자들은 자신들의 강철을 구매할 조선소가 있으면 돈을 벌겠지만 그렇지 않으면(강철을 구매할 조선소가 없으면) 돈을 벌지 못할 것이라고 생각한다. [8]이제 우리는 두 가지 가능한 결과, 즉 경제학자들이 '복수균형'이라고 부르는 것을 갖게 된다. (A) [9]'좋은' 결과가 있는데, 그 결과 내에서는 투자의 두 가지 형태가 모두 이루어지며, 조선소와 제강업자 모두 결국 이득을 얻고 만족하게 된다. [10]균형이 이루어진다. [11]그다음에 '나쁜' 결과가 있는데, 그 결과 내에서는 둘 중 어떤 투자 형태도 이루어지지 않는다. [12]이 두 번째 결과 또한 균형 상태인데, 왜냐하면 투자하지 않겠다는 결정이 서로를 강화하기 때문이다.

어휘

firm 회사; 딱딱한; 확고한
shipbuilding 조선(업)
sufficiently 충분히
scale 규모; 등급; 저울
venture (사업상의) 모험; 위험을 무릅쓰고 ~하다
profitable 수익성이 있는; 이득이 되는
input 투입; 입력(하다)
steel 강철; 철강업

🗝 (B)의 두 가지 가능한 결과를 좋은 결과와 나쁜 결과로 상술함.

(A) [9]There is *a "good" outcome*, // in which both types of investments are made, // and both the shipyard and the steelmakers end up profitable and happy.

V S 전치사+관계대명사(보충 설명) S′₁ V′₁ S′₂ V′₂ C′

'좋은' 결과가 있다 // 그 결과 내에서는 투자의 두 가지 형태가 모두 이루어진다 // 그리고 조선소와 제강업자 모두 결국 이득을 얻고 만족하게 된다

[10]Equilibrium is reached.

S V

균형이 이루어진다

↳ **좋은 결과:** 투자가 모두 이루어지고 조선소와 제강업자 둘 다 이득을 얻음.

★<neither+단수명사>: (둘 중) 어느 것도 ~아닌

[11]Then there is *a "bad" outcome*, // in which neither type of investment is made.

V S 전치사+관계대명사(보충 설명) S′ V′

그다음에 '나쁜' 결과가 있다 // 그 결과 내에서는 둘 중 어떤 투자 형태도 이루어지지 않는다

↳ **나쁜 결과:** 어떤 투자도 이루어지지 않음.

[12]This second outcome also is an equilibrium // because *the decisions* (not to invest) / reinforce each other.

S(= A "bad" outcome) V C 부사절 접속사(이유) S′(복수) V′(복수) O′

이 두 번째 결과('나쁜' 결과) 또한 균형 상태이다 // 왜냐하면 결정이 (투자하지 않겠다는) / 서로를 강화하기 때문이다

↳ **부연 설명:** 투자하지 않겠다는 결정이 서로를 강화시켜 균형을 이룸.

boil down to A 결국 A가 되다; A로 요약하다
assume 가정[추정]하다; (역할·임무 등을) 맡다
shipyard 조선소
figure 생각하다; 계산하다; 수치; 인물
outcome 결과
steelmaker 제강업자
end up 결국 ~하게 되다
reach (목적 등을) 이루다; 도달하다
reinforce 강화하다

정답 가이드

한 회사가 조선업에 투자할지를 결정 중인데 충분히 생산하면 수익성이 있을 것이라는 주어진 글 이후, 역접 연결어 But으로 이어져서 저가의 강철이 근처에서 생산되어야 한다는 투자 요건과 그렇지 않으면 투자하지 않는다는 회사의 최종 결정이 설명된 (C)가 이어져야 한다. (C)의 마지막 문장은 그다음에 잠재적 강철 투자자들의 생각을 고려해 보라는 것인데, (B)는 강철을 구매할 조선소가 있으면 강철 생산자가 돈을 벌고 그렇지 않으면 돈을 벌지 못할 것이라는 내용으로, 강철 투자자들의 생각을 구체적으로 설명하므로 (C) 뒤에 이어져야 한다. (A)는 균형이 이루어지는 두 가지 결과에 대한 것으로 (B)의 마지막에 언급된 multiple equilibria에 대한 설명에 해당하므로 마지막에 와야 한다.

오답 클리닉

① (A) - (C) - (B) (2%)
(A)의 both types of investments는 (C)와 (B)에서 언급된 조선업과 강철에 대한 투자를 지칭하는 것이므로 (A)는 (C)와 (B) 뒤에 와야 한다.

② (B) - (A) - (C) (33%) / ③ (B) - (C) - (A) (18%)
주어진 글에는 조선업에 투자할지를 결정 중인 한 회사만 언급되어 있으므로 강철 생산자들의 생각을 설명하는 (B)가 바로 이어지는 것은 어색하다.

The 주의 글의 흐름을 알려주는 연결어나 대명사의 단서가 없는 경우, 한 단락의 뒷부분에 언급된 내용이 다음 단락의 앞부분으로 이어지는지 등 글의 전개상 내용의 흐름이 자연스러운지 파악해야 한다.

④ (C) - (A) - (B) (9%)
(C)의 마지막에서 언급한 강철 투자자들의 생각을 구체적으로 설명하는 (B)가 그 뒤에 온 후, 결과인 (A)가 이어지는 것이 적절하다.

03 + 문장 넣기 〈22학년도 6월 모평 38번 | 정답률 53%〉 ②

구문분석 & 직독직해

경영 다면 평가 시행의 배경

[1]In most organizations, / the employee's immediate supervisor evaluates the employee's performance.

S V O

대부분의 조직에서 / 직원의 직속 관리자는 그 직원의 성과를 평가한다

↱ is의 C(명사절) ★접속사 because는 명사절을 이끌기도 하며 '이유'를 의미함.

(①) [2]This is // because the supervisor is responsible for the employee's performance, /

S(= 앞 문장) V S′ V′ C′

이것은 ~이다 // 그 관리자가 그 직원의 성과를 책임지기 때문 /

★세 개의 현재분사구가 콤마(,)와 and로 연결됨.

providing supervision, handing out assignments, and developing the employee.

분사구문(= as he/she provides ~, hands out ~, and develops ~)

감독을 제공하고, 업무를 나눠주고, 그 직원을 계발하면서

↳ **도입:** 직속 관리자는 직원의 성과를 책임지기 때문에 직원을 평가함.

해석

[1]대부분의 조직에서, 직원의 직속 관리자는 그 직원의 성과를 평가한다. (①) [2]이것은 그 관리자가 감독을 제공하고, 업무를 나눠주고, 그 직원을 계발하면서, 그 직원의 성과를 책임지기 때문이다. (② [3]하지만, 문제는 관리자가 흔히 자신의 직원과 떨어진 위치에서 일해서 자신의 부하 직원들의 성과를 관찰할 수 없다는 것이다.) [4]관리자는 자신이 관찰할 수 없는 성과 범위에 대해 직원들을 평가해야 하는가? (③) [5]이 딜레마를 없애기 위해, 점점 더 많은 조직이 '다면 평가'라고 불리는 평가를 시행하고 있다. (④) [6]직원들은 자신의 관리자에 의해

🗝 관리자가 직원을 평가한다는 앞 내용의 문제점이 however와 함께 제시됨.

(②) [3]A problem, however, is // that supervisors often work / in locations (apart from their employees) / and therefore are not able to observe their subordinates' performance.)

S V 명사절 접속사 S' V'₁ V'₂ C'₂ (→ is의 C(명사절))

하지만 문제는 ~이다 // 관리자가 흔히 일한다는 것 / 위치에서 (자신의 직원과 떨어진) / 그래서 자신의 부하 직원들의 성과를 관찰할 수 없다(는 것)

🗝 주어진 문장에 제시된 문제로 인해 관리자가 겪는 딜레마.

[4]Should supervisors rate employees / on *performance dimensions* [(which[that]) they cannot observe]?

V(의문문) S O 목적격 관계대명사 생략

관리자는 직원들을 평가해야 하는가 / 성과 범위에 대해 [자신이 관찰할 수 없는]

↳ **문제점:** 관리자는 직원들과 떨어져 있어 그들의 성과를 관찰할 수 없음에도 평가해야 하는 딜레마가 있음.

주제문

(③) [5]To eliminate this dilemma, / more and more organizations are implementing / *assessments* (referred to as *360-degree evaluations*).

목적(~하기 위해) S V O 과거분사구

★<비교급 and 비교급>: 점점 더 ~한 ★<refer to A as B>: A를 B라고 부르다

이 딜레마를 없애기 위해 / 점점 더 많은 조직이 시행하고 있다 / 평가를 ('다면 평가'라고 불리는)

(④) [6]Employees are rated / not only by their supervisors / but by coworkers, clients or citizens, / *professionals in other agencies* [with whom they work], / and subordinates.

S V 전치사구 병렬 전치사+관계대명사

★<not only A but (also) B>: A뿐만 아니라 B도

직원들은 평가받는다 / 자신의 관리자에 의해서뿐만 아니라 / 동료, 고객이나 시민에 의해서도 / 다른 대행사의 전문가들 [그들(직원들)이 함께 일하는] / 그리고 부하 직원들(에 의해서도)

↳ **해결책:** 관리자뿐만 아니라 동료, 고객 등의 평가를 받는 '다면 평가'를 시행함.

(⑤) [7]The reason (for this approach) is // that often coworkers and clients or citizens have *a greater opportunity* (to observe an employee's performance) / and are in *a better position* (to evaluate many performance dimensions).

S V 명사절 접속사 S' V'₁ O' V'₂ (→ is의 C(명사절))

이유는 (이 접근법에 대한) ~이다 // 동료와 고객 또는 시민들이 흔히 더 많은 기회를 가지기 (때문) (어떤 직원의 성과를 관찰할) / 그리고 더 나은 위치에 있기 (때문) (많은 성과 범위를 평가할 수 있는)

↳ **이유:** 관리자보다 동료와 고객 또는 시민들이 직원의 성과를 관찰할 기회가 더 많음.

서뿐만 아니라, 동료, 고객이나 시민, 그들(직원들)이 함께 일하는 다른 대행사의 전문가들, 그리고 부하 직원들에 의해서도 평가받는다. (⑤) [7]이 접근법에 대한 이유는 동료와 고객 또는 시민들이 흔히 어떤 직원의 성과를 관찰할 더 많은 기회를 가지며, 많은 성과 범위를 평가할 수 있는 더 나은 위치에 있기 때문이다.

어휘

immediate 직속의; 즉각적인
supervisor 관리자
cf. supervision 감독, 관리
evaluate 평가하다
cf. evaluation 평가(= assessment)
performance 성과, 실적; 수행; 공연
hand out 나눠주다, 배포하다
assignment 업무; 과제; 배정
observe 관찰하다; 보다; 말하다
rate 평가하다; 속도
dimension 범위, 규모; 차원
eliminate 없애다, 제거하다
implement 시행하다; 도구
agency 대행사; 기관
approach 접근법; 다가가다

정답 가이드

주어진 문장은 역접 연결어 however를 포함하여, 부하 직원들과 떨어진 곳에서 일하는 관리자는 그들의 성과를 관찰할 수 없다는 문제점을 지적하는 내용이다. ②의 앞은 관리자가 직원을 평가한다는 내용이고, 그 뒤는 관리자가 관찰할 수 없는 성과에 대해 평가해야 하는지에 대한 의문을 제기하고 있으므로 그 사이에는 관리자가 성과를 관찰할 수 없다는 문제점이 제시되어야 한다. 따라서 주어진 문장이 들어가기에 가장 적절한 곳은 ②이다.

오답 클리닉

① (2%) 직속 관리자가 직원의 성과를 평가하는 이유가 연결되는 내용이다.
③ (19%) 앞 문장의 의문을 this dilemma로 받으면서, 다면 평가를 해결책으로 제시하는 것은 적절하다.
④ (17%) 다면 평가의 평가 방법을 부연 설명하는 내용이다.
⑤ (8%) 다면 평가를 시행하는 이유를 설명하는 내용이다.

01 ✦ 글의 주제 〈21학년도 대수능 23번 | 정답률 61%〉 ③

구문분석 & 직독직해

기술 자동화 시스템 내 인간 업무의 부적합성

주제문

★<think of A as B>: A를 B로 생각하다[여기다]

[1] Difficulties arise // when we do not think of people and machines / as collaborative systems, / but assign whatever tasks can be automated / to the machines / and leave the rest / to people.

(S, V, 부사절 접속사, S′, V′₁, O′₁, V′₂, O′₂ (= any tasks that can be automated), V′₃, O′₃)

어려움이 발생한다 // 우리가 사람과 기계를 생각하지 않을 때 / 협업 시스템으로 / 하지만 자동화될 수 있는 작업은 무엇이든 할당할 (때) / 기계에 / 그리고 나머지를 맡길 (때) / 사람들에게

↳ 자동화 업무를 모두 기계에 맡기고 나머지를 모두 인간이 맡을 경우 문제가 생김.

★<require+O+to-v>: O가 v하도록 요구하다

[2] This ends up requiring people to behave / in machine-like fashion, / in ways [that differ from human capabilities]. 🔑 문제점: 인간의 능력에 맞지 않는 기계적 업무를 맡게 됨.

(S(= 앞 문장), =, 주격 관계대명사)

이것은 결국 사람들이 행동하도록 요구하게 된다 / 기계와 같은 방식으로 / 즉 방식으로 [인간의 능력과 다른]

↳ **문제점:** 인간에게도 기계적 업무를 요구하게 됨.

🔑 인간이 잘하지 못하는 일 1: 기계 감시하기. ↱ 관계대명사(보충 설명)

[3] We expect people *to monitor machines*, // which means keeping alert / for long periods, / *something* [(that) we are bad at].

(S, V, O, C, V′, O′, =, 목적격 관계대명사 생략)

우리는 사람들이 기계를 감시하기를 기대한다 // 그리고 이것은 경계 상태를 유지하는 것을 의미한다 / 오랫동안 / 어떤 것 [우리가 못하는]

↳ **기계적 업무의 예 1:** 오랫동안 기계 감시하기.

[4] We require people to do repeated operations / with *the extreme precision and accuracy* (required by machines), / again *something* [(that) we are not good at]. 🔑 인간이 잘하지 못하는 일 2: 반복 작업하기.

(S, V, O, C, 과거분사구, =, 목적격 관계대명사 생략)

우리는 사람들에게 반복적인 작업을 할 것을 요구한다 / 극도의 정밀함과 정확성을 가지고 (기계에 의해 요구되는) / 이 또한 어떤 것 [우리가 잘하지 못하는]

↳ **기계적 업무의 예 2:** 정밀하고 정확하게 반복 작업하기.

[5] When we divide up / the machine and human components (of a task) / in this way, //

(부사절 접속사, S′, V′, O′)

우리가 나눌 때 / 기계적 요소와 인간적 요소를 (어떤 일의) / 이런 식으로 //

we fail to take advantage of / human strengths and capabilities / but instead rely upon / *areas* [where we are genetically, biologically unsuited]. 🔑 인간에게 분배된 업무가 인간의 강점과 능력에 맞지 않게 됨.

(S, V₁, O₁, V₂, O₂, 관계부사)

우리는 ~을 이용하지 못한다 / 인간의 강점과 능력(을) / 그러나 그 대신 ~에 의존한다 / 영역(에) [우리가 유전적으로, 생물학적으로 부적합한]

↳ **결론:** 자동화를 기준으로 기계와 인간의 업무를 나누면 인간의 능력은 제대로 발휘될 수 없음.

[6] Yet, / when people fail, // they are blamed.

(부사절 접속사(시간), S, V)

그런데도 / 사람들이 기대에 못 미치면 // 그들은 비난을 받는다

↳ **비판:** 부적합한 업무를 맡아 제대로 하지 못하는 것인데도 비난을 받게 됨.

해석

[1]우리가 사람과 기계를 협업 시스템으로 생각하지 않지만 자동화될 수 있는 작업은 무엇이든 기계에 할당하고 나머지를 사람들에게 맡길 때 어려움이 발생한다. [2]이것은 결국 사람들이 기계와 같은 방식으로, 즉 인간의 능력과 다른 방식으로 행동하도록 요구하게 된다. [3]우리는 사람들이 기계를 감시하기를 기대하는데, 이는 오랫동안 경계 상태를 유지하는 것을 의미하며, 이것은 우리가 못하는 것이다. [4]우리는 사람들에게 기계에 의해 요구되는 극도의 정밀함과 정확성을 가지고 반복적인 작업을 할 것을 요구하며, 이 또한 우리가 잘하지 못하는 것이다. [5]우리가 이런 식으로 어떤 일의 기계적 요소와 인간적 요소를 나눌 때, 우리는 인간의 강점과 능력을 이용하지 못하고, 그 대신 우리가 유전적으로, 생물학적으로 부적합한 영역에 의존한다. [6]그런데도, 사람들이 기대에 못 미치면, 그들은 비난을 받는다.

어휘

arise 발생하다, 생기다; 일어나다
collaborative system 협업 시스템
assign 할당하다, 부여하다
automate 자동화하다
leave (관리 등을) 맡기다; 떠나다; 남기다
end up v-ing 결국 v하게 되다
fashion (유행하는) 방식, 방법; 유행
monitor 감시[관리]하다
alert (위험 등을) 경계하는; 기민한; (위험을) 알리다, 경보를 발하다
be bad[good] at ~을 못[잘]하다
precision 정밀함; 정확(성); 신중함
accuracy 정확성
component (구성)요소, 부품
take advantage of ~을 이용하다
rely (up)on ~에 의지하다
genetically 유전적으로
unsuited 부적합한, 어울리지 않는
fail (기대에) 못 미치다; 실패하다
blame 비난하다, 탓하다
[선택지] overcome 극복하다
allocate 할당하다, 배분하다
unfit 부적합한

정답 가이드

첫 문장인 주제문에서 자동화될 수 있는 작업은 무엇이든 기계에 할당하고 그 나머지를 인간에게 맡길 때 어려움이 발생한다고 한 후, 그 어려움은 인간이 잘할 수 없는 기계적 업무를 인간이 하게 만드는 것이라고 했다. 따라서 글의 주제로 가장 적절한 것은 ③ 'issues of allocating unfit tasks to humans in automated systems(자동화된 시스템에서 인간에게 부적합한 과제를 할당하는 것의 문제)'이다.

오답 클리닉

① difficulties of overcoming human weaknesses to avoid failure (4%)
실패를 피하기 위해 인간의 약점을 극복하는 것의 어려움(×)
인간이 잘하지 못하는 일들이 언급되었으나, 이를 극복하는 것이 어렵다는 언급은 없음.

② benefits of allowing machines and humans to work together (13%)
기계와 인간이 함께 일하게 하는 것의 이점(×)
기계와 인간이 함께 일할 때 생기는 문제점에 관한 글임.

④ reasons why humans continue to pursue machine automation (11%) 인간이 기계 자동화를 계속 추구(×)하는 이유
인간이 기계 자동화를 추구한다는 내용은 없음.

⑤ influences of human actions on a machine's performance (10%)
인간의 행동이 기계의 성능(×)에 미치는 영향
인간의 행동이 기계의 성능에 영향을 미친다는 내용이 아님.

02 + 빈칸 추론 〈21학년도 6월 모평 31번 | 정답률 40%〉 ①

구문분석 & 직독직해 과학 인간의 다리 강직도 조정 능력

주제문

1 Research (with human runners) / challenged conventional wisdom /
S V₁ O
연구는 (달리는 사람에 관한) / 사회적 통념에 이의를 제기했다 /

(→ found의 O(명사절))
and found // that the ground-reaction forces at the foot / and *the shock* (transmitted up the leg and through the body / after impact with the ground) / **varied little** //
V₂ 명사절 접속사 S′₁ S′₂ 과거분사구 V′
그리고 알아냈다 // 발에서 일어나는 지면 반발력 / 그리고 충격은 (다리 위로 몸을 관통하여 전달되는 / 지면과의 충돌 후에) / 거의 달라지지 않았다는 것을 //

(<from A to B>: A에서 B로)
as runners moved / from extremely compliant to extremely hard running surfaces.
부사절 접속사(~할 때)
달리는 사람이 이동했을 때 / 매우 말랑말랑한 활주면에서 / 매우 단단한 활주면으로
↳ **연구 결과:** 말랑말랑한 활주면과 단단한 활주면에서 달리는 사람이 받는 충격은 비슷함.

(→ to believe의 O(명사절))
2 As a result, / researchers gradually began to believe // that runners are subconsciously able to adjust leg stiffness / prior to foot strike / based on their perceptions (of the hardness or stiffness of *the surface* [on which they are running]).
S V O 명사절 접속사 S′ V′ C′ (→ (= where)) 전치사+관계대명사
그 결과 / 연구자들은 점차 믿기 시작했다 // 달리는 사람은 다리의 강직도를 잠재의식적으로 조정할 수 있다고 / 발의 (지면을) 치기 전에 / 자신의 인식에 근거하여 (지표면의 견고함이나 단단함에 대한 [자신이 달리고 있는])

(→ suggests의 O(명사절))
3 This view suggests // that runners create / *soft legs* [that soak up impact forces] // when they are running on very hard surfaces / and (runners create) stiff legs // when they are moving along on yielding terrain.
S V 명사절 접속사 S′ V′ O′₁ 주격 관계대명사 부사절₁ O′₂ 부사절₂
이 견해는 시사한다 // 달리는 사람이 만든다는 것을 / 푹신한 다리를 [충격력을 흡수하는] // 그들이 매우 단단한 지표면에서 달리고 있을 때 / 그리고 단단한 다리를 // 그들이 물렁한 지형에서 움직이고 있을 때
↳ **시사점:** 달리는 사람은 지표면의 단단함에 따라 다리의 강직도를 조정할 수 있음.

(🔑 활주면의 유형에 따른 충격력은 strikingly simiar 함 → 별 차이 없음.)
4 As a result, / *impact forces* (passing through the legs) / are strikingly similar / over a wide range of running surface types.
S 현재분사구 V C
그 결과 / 충격력은 (다리를 통해 전해지는) / 눈에 띄게 비슷하다 / 다양한 활주면 유형에 걸쳐서
↳ **결론:** 활주면의 유형이 달라져도 다리에 전해지는 충격력은 비슷함.

해석

1 달리는 사람에 관한 연구는 사회적 통념(▶ 푹신한 모래 위보다 콘크리트 위를 달리는 것이 다리에 더 해롭다는 생각)에 이의를 제기하고, 발에서 일어나는 지면 반발력과 지면과의 충돌 후에 다리 위로 몸을 관통하여 전달되는 충격은 달리는 사람이 매우 말랑말랑한 활주면에서 매우 단단한 활주면으로 이동했을 때 거의 달라지지 않았다는 것을 알아냈다. 2 그 결과, 연구자들은 달리는 사람은 자신이 달리고 있는 지표면의 견고함이나 단단함에 대한 자신의 인식에 근거하여 발의 (지면을) 치기 전에 다리의 강직도를 잠재의식적으로 조정할 수 있다고 점차 믿기 시작했다. 3 이 견해는 달리는 사람이 매우 단단한 지표면에서 달리고 있을 때 충격력을 흡수하는 푹신한 다리를 만들고 물렁한 지형에서 움직이고 있을 때 단단한 다리를 만든다는 것을 시사한다. 4 그 결과, 다리를 통해 전해지는 충격력은 다양한 활주면 유형에 걸쳐서 눈에 띄게 비슷하다. 5 일반적인 생각과는 반대로, 콘크리트 위를 달리는 것은 푹신한 모래 위를 달리는 것보다 다리에 더 해롭지 않다.

어휘

challenge 이의를 제기하다; 도전(하다)
conventional wisdom 사회적 통념
ground-reaction force 지면 반발력
transmit 전달하다; 나르다, 운송하다
impact 충돌, 충격; 충돌하다
vary 달라지다; 바꾸다, 변경하다
gradually 점차
subconsciously 잠재 의식적으로
adjust 조정[조절]하다
stiffness 단단함; 완고함
cf. stiff 딱딱한, 경직된
prior to A A 전에, A에 앞서
strike 치기, 때리기; 부딪치다, 치다
perception 인식; 지각, 자각
soak up 흡수하다, 빨아들이다
yielding 물렁한, 유연한
strikingly 눈에 띄게, 두드러지게

[5]Contrary to popular belief, / running on concrete is not more damaging to the legs / than running on soft sand.
S(동명사구) V(단수) C
일반적인 생각과는 반대로 / 콘크리트 위를 달리는 것은 다리에 더 해롭지 않다 / 푹신한 모래 위를 달리는 것보다
↳ **주제문 재진술:** 콘크리트에서 달리는 것이 푹신한 모래에서 달리는 것보다 다리에 더 해롭지 않음.

a wide range of 다양한, 광범위한
contrary to A A와 반대로
[선택지] peak 최고조[절정](에 달하다)
hardly 거의 ~않다

정답 가이드

빈칸 문장은 간단히 말해, 지면의 단단함에 따라 다리에 전달되는 충격이 '어떠한지'를 연구 결과로 알아냈다는 것이다. 이어지는 설명에서 그 충격이 어떠한지에 대한 연구 결과를 찾아야 한다. 달리는 사람은 지면의 단단함에 따라 다리 강직도를 조정하기 때문에 충격도 눈에 띄게 '비슷하다'고 했고, 마지막 문장에서도 단단한 지면이 푹신한 지면보다 더 해로운 것은 아니라고 했다. 따라서 빈칸에 들어갈 말로 가장 적절한 것은 ① 'varied little(거의 달라지지 않았다)'이다.

The 주의 ⓑ little(거의 ~없는)이 쓰여 '거의 달라지지 않았다'를 의미함에 유의한다.

오답 클리닉

② decreased a lot (17%) 많이 감소했다
③ suddenly peaked (12%) 갑자기 최고조에 달했다
여러 활주면 유형에서 전해지는 충격력은 비슷하다고 했으므로, 충격이 감소하거나 증가했다는 내용은 틀림.
④ gradually appeared (14%) 점차 나타났다
⑤ were hardly generated (17%) 거의 발생되지 않았다
활주면의 유형에 따라 발생하는 충격력의 정도를 비교하는 내용이므로, 충격이 없다가 나타나거나 발생하지 않는 것이 아님.

03 + 글의 순서 〈21학년도 대수능 37번 | 정답률 48%〉 ⑤

구문분석 & 직독직해

경제 에너지 효율의 비용 효율성 산정의 어려움

[1]Experts have identified *a large number of measures* [that promote energy efficiency].
S V O 주격 관계대명사
전문가들은 다수의 대책을 발견해 왔다 [에너지 효율을 증진하는]

[2]Unfortunately / many of them are not cost effective.
S V C
유감스럽게도 / 그중 많은 것들이 비용 효율이 높지 않다

(= Being cost effective)
[3]This is a fundamental requirement (for energy efficiency investment) / from an economic perspective.
S V C
이것(비용 효율이 높은 것)은 기본 요건이다 (에너지 효율성 투자의) / 경제적 관점에서
↳ **도입:** 에너지 효율을 증진하는 대책의 비용 효율이 높지 않은데, 높은 비용 효율은 에너지 효율성 투자의 기본 요건임.

주제문 — 주어진 글에서 언급한 비용 효율성의 계산에 있어서의 어려움이 However로 이어짐.

(C) [4]However, / the calculation (of such cost effectiveness) / is not easy: // it is not simply a case (of looking at private costs / and comparing them / to *the reductions* (achieved)).
S_1 V_1 C_1 S_2 V_2 C_2
*<compare A to B>: A를 B와 비교하다 (= private costs)
of의 O(동명사구 병렬) 과거분사
그러나 / 계산은 (그러한 비용 효율성의) / 쉽지 않다 // 그것은 단순히 경우가 아니기 때문에 (사적 비용을 살펴보는 / 그리고 그것(사적 비용)을 비교하는 / 절감액과 (달성된))
↳ 비용 효율성은 계산하기 쉽지 않음.

— 비용 효율성 계산이 쉽지 않다는 (C)의 이유를 제시함.

(B) [5]There are *significant externalities* (to take into account) // and there are also macroeconomic effects.
V_1 S_1 V_2 S_2
상당한 외부 효과가 있다 (고려해야 할) // 그리고 거시 경제적 효과도 있다
↳ **세부 사항:** 외부 효과 및 거시 경제적 효과를 고려해야 함.

[6]For instance, / at the aggregate level, / improving the level (of national energy efficiency) / has positive effects / on macroeconomic issues (such as energy dependence, climate change, health, national competitiveness and reducing fuel poverty).
S(동명사구) V(단수) O
예를 들어 / 집합적 차원에서 / 수준을 높이는 것은 (국가 에너지 효율의) / 긍정적인 영향을 미친다 / 거시 경제적 문제에 (에너지 의존성, 기후 변화, 보건, 국가 경쟁력, 연료 빈곤을 감소시키는 것과 같은)
↳ **예 1(집합적 차원):** 국가 에너지 효율 수준을 높이는 것은 거시 경제적 문제에 긍정적 영향을 미침.

해석

[1]전문가들은 에너지 효율을 증진하는 다수의 대책을 발견해 왔다. [2]유감스럽게도 그중 많은 것들이 비용 효율이 높지 않다. [3]이것(비용 효율이 높은 것)은 경제적 관점에서 에너지 효율성 투자의 기본 요건이다. (C) [4]그러나 그러한 비용 효율성의 계산은 쉽지 않은데, 그것은 단순히 사적 비용을 살펴보고 그것을 달성된 절감액과 비교하는 경우가 아니기 때문이다. (B) [5]고려해야 할 상당한 외부 효과가 있으며 거시 경제적 효과도 있다. [6]예를 들어 집합적 차원에서, 국가 에너지 효율의 수준을 높이는 것은 에너지 의존성, 기후 변화, 보건, 국가 경쟁력, 연료 빈곤을 감소시키는 것과 같은 거시 경제적 문제에 긍정적인 영향을 미친다. (A) [7]그리고 이것은 개별적 차원에서 직접적인 영향을 미치는데, 가정은 전기와 가스 요금 고지서의 비용을 줄이고 그들의 건강과 안락을 증진할 수 있는 반면에, 회사는 자체 경쟁력과 생산성을 증대시킬 수 있다. [8]결국, 에너지 효율을 위한 시장은 일자리와 기업 창출을 통해 경제에 기여할 수 있다.

어휘

identify 발견하다, 찾다; 확인하다; 동일시하다
measure 대책, 조치; 측정(하다)
efficiency 효율(성)
cost effective 비용 효율이 높은
fundamental 기본의, 근본적인; 필수적인
requirement 요건, 필요(조건)
perspective 관점; 원근법
reduction 절감(액), 감소(량)
externality 외부 효과; 외부성
take into account ~을 고려하다

(= 앞 문장) (B)의 집합적 차원에서의 긍정적 영향이 개별적 차원에도 영향을 미침을 설명함.

(A) [7]And this has direct repercussions / at the individual level: //
S1 V1 O1

그리고 이것은 직접적인 영향을 미친다 / 개별적 차원에서 //

households can reduce / the cost (of electricity and gas bills), / and improve their health and comfort, // while companies can increase their competitiveness and their productivity.
S2 V2-1 O2-1 V2-2 O2-2 부사절 접속사(~인 반면에) S′ V′ O′

가정은 줄일 수 있다 / 비용을 (전기와 가스 요금 고지서의) / 그리고 그들의 건강과 안락을 증진할 수 있다 // 반면에 회사는 자체 경쟁력과 생산성을 증대시킬 수 있다

↳ **예 2(개별적 차원):** 가정은 비용 및 건강 측면에서, 회사는 경쟁력 및 생산성 측면에서 긍정적인 영향을 받음.

[8]Finally, / the market (for energy efficiency) / could contribute to the economy / through job and firms creation.
S V

결국 / 시장은 (에너지 효율을 위한) / 경제에 기여할 수 있다 / 일자리와 기업 창출을 통해

↳ 에너지 효율 시장은 일자리와 기업을 창출함으로써 경제에 기여함.

macroeconomic 거시 경제(학)의
competitiveness 경쟁력
poverty 빈곤, 가난; 부족
household 가정
comfort 안락; 위안(하다)
productivity 생산성
contribute to A A에 기여하다; A의 원인이 되다

정답 가이드

주어진 글은 높은 비용 효율은 에너지 효율성 투자의 기본 요건이라는 내용이다. 그 뒤에는 역접 연결어 However로 그러한 비용 효율성(such cost effectiveness)을 계산하는 것이 쉽지 않다는 어려움을 제시하는 (C)가 와야 한다. (C)에서 계산이 쉽지 않은 이유는 단순히 사적 비용과 절감액을 비교하는 차원이 아니기 때문이라고 하였고, (B)는 그 이유를 설명하며 상당한 외부 효과와 거시 경제적 효과가 있다고 하고 '집합적 차원'의 예를 들었으므로 (C) 뒤에 이어져야 한다. 마지막으로, (B)에서 말한 내용을 this로 받아 '개별적 차원'에 영향을 미친다는 내용을 설명하는 (A)가 마지막에 오는 것이 자연스럽다.

오답 클리닉

① (A) - (C) - (B) (2%)
(A)의 this가 가리키는 내용이 주어진 글에 없으므로 (A)는 주어진 글 뒤에 이어질 수 없다.
② (B) - (A) - (C) (18%) / ③ (B) - (C) - (A) (21%)
(B)는 비용 효율성을 계산하기 쉽지 않다는 (C)의 이유에 해당하므로 (C) 뒤에 오는 것이 자연스럽다.
④ (C) - (A) - (B) (10%)
(B)의 집합적 차원에서의 영향을 예로 언급한 뒤에 And로 (A)의 개별적인 차원에서의 영향이 이어지는 것이 자연스럽다.

01 ✦ 글의 제목 〈21학년도 대수능 24번 | 정답률 52%〉 ②

구문분석 & 직독직해

인지 시간에 기반을 둔 촉각

주제문 ⊶ 촉각은 시간에 기반을 둠.

[1] People don't usually think of touch / as a temporal phenomenon, // but it is every bit as time-based / as it is spatial. ★<A as 형용사/부사 as B>: A는 B만큼 ~한[하게]

S₁ V₁ O 전치사(~로(서)) S₂(= touch) V₂ C (= touch)

사람들은 보통 촉각을 생각하지 않는다 / 시간적 현상으로 // 그러나 그것은 전적으로 시간을 기반으로 한다 / 그것이 공간적인 만큼

↳ **통념과 반박:** 촉각은 공간적인 만큼 시간적임.

[2] You can carry out an experiment / to see for yourself.

S V O 목적(~하기 위해)

당신은 실험을 수행할 수 있다 / 직접 확인하기 위해

★<ask+O+to-v>: O가 v하도록 요청[요구]하다

[3] Ask a friend / to cup his hand, / palm face up, / and (to) close his eyes.

V(명령문) O C₁(to-v구 병렬) 부사구(= with the palm face up) to 생략 C₂(to-v구 병렬)

친구에게 요청하라 / 손을 컵 모양으로 오므리라고 / 손바닥이 위로 향하게 / 그리고 눈을 감으라고

[4] Place a small ordinary object in his palm — / a ring, an eraser, anything will do — // and ask him to identify it / without moving any part of his hand.

V₁(명령문) O₁ V₂(명령문) O₂ C (= the small ordinary object)

그의 손바닥에 작은 평범한 물건을 놓아라 / 반지, 지우개, 어느 것이든 괜찮다 // 그리고 그에게 그것을 식별하도록 요청하라 / 손의 어느 부분도 움직이지 않은 채로

[5] He won't have a clue / other than weight and maybe overall size.

S V O (= except for)

그는 전혀 알지 못할 것이다 / 무게와 어쩌면 전반적인 크기 외에

↳ **논거(실험 내용 1):** 손가락을 움직이지 않고 손바닥 위의 물건을 식별할 수 없음.

[6] Then / tell him / to keep his eyes closed / and (to) move his fingers / over the object.

V(명령문) O C(to-v구) 병렬

그러고 나서 / 그에게 말하라 / 계속 눈을 감고 있으라고 / 그리고 손가락을 움직이라고 / 그 물건 위로

[7] He'll most likely identify it / at once.

S V O(= the object)

그는 아마도 틀림없이 그것을 식별할 것이다 / 즉시

↳ **논거(실험 내용 2):** 손가락이 움직이면 손바닥 위의 물건을 식별할 수 있음.

★<allow+O+to-v>: O가 v하도록 (허락)하다 ⊶ 촉각에 시간이 더해져 물건을 식별하게 됨.

[8] By allowing the fingers to move, / you've added time / to the sensory perception (of touch).

<by v-ing>: v함으로써 S V O =

손가락이 움직이게 함으로써 / 당신은 시간을 더했다 / 감각적 지각에 (촉각이라는)

↳ **실험 시사점:** 손가락이 움직이면서 시간도 흐름.

[9] There's a direct analogy (between *the fovea at the center of your retina* and *your fingertips*), // both of which have high acuity. ★부분 표현인 both of와 주격 관계대명사 which가 선행사 the fovea ~ fingertips를 보충 설명함.

V S (= and both of them) V′ O′

직접적인 유사점이 있다 (망막의 중심에 있는 중심와(窩)와 손가락 끝 사이에) // 그것 둘 다 예민함이 높다

↳ **추가 내용:** 촉각은 시각과 같이 예민함.

[10] Your ability (to make complex use of touch), / such as buttoning your shirt or unlocking your front door / in the dark, / depends on continuous time-varying patterns (of touch sensation).

S = 동명사구 병렬 V

⊶ 시간에 따라 변하는 촉각에 의존해 일을 수행함.

당신의 능력은 (촉각을 복잡하게 활용하는) / 셔츠 단추를 잠그는 것 또는 현관문을 여는 것과 같이 / 어둠 속에서 / 지속적인, 시간에 따라 변하는 패턴에 의존한다 (촉각이라는 감각의)

↳ **촉각의 활용:** 시간에 따라 달라지는 촉각으로 복잡한 일을 할 수 있음.

해석

[1]사람들은 보통 촉각을 시간적 현상으로 생각하지 않지만, 그것은 그것이 공간적인 만큼 전적으로 시간을 기반으로 한다. [2]당신은 직접 확인하기 위해 실험을 수행할 수 있다. [3]친구에게 손바닥이 위로 향하게, 손을 컵 모양으로 오므리고, 눈을 감으라고 요청하라. [4]그의 손바닥에 반지, 지우개, 어느 것이든 괜찮은데, 작은 평범한 물건을 놓고 손의 어느 부분도 움직이지 않은 채로 그에게 그것을 식별하도록 요청하라. [5]그는 무게와 어쩌면 전반적인 크기 외에 전혀 알지 못할 것이다. [6]그러고 나서 그에게 계속 눈을 감고 있고 그 물건 위로 손가락을 움직이라고 말하라. [7]그는 아마도 틀림없이 그것을 즉시 식별할 것이다. [8]손가락이 움직이게 함으로써 당신은 촉각이라는 감각적 지각에 시간을 더했다. [9]망막의 중심에 있는 중심와(窩)와 손가락 끝 사이에 직접적인 유사점이 있는데, 그것 둘 다 예민함이 높다는 것이다. [10]어둠 속에서 셔츠 단추를 잠그는 것 또는 현관문을 여는 것과 같이 촉각을 복잡하게 활용하는 당신의 능력은 촉각이라는 감각의 지속적인, 시간에 따라 변하는 패턴에 의존한다.

어휘

temporal 시간적, 시간의; 일시적인, 잠시의
phenomenon 현상; 경이(로운 사람[것])
every bit 전적으로; 모두, 전부
spatial 공간적인, 공간의
carry out 수행하다; (과업을) 완수하다
cup 손을 컵 모양으로 오므리다; 컵; 한 잔 (분량)
palm 손바닥
ordinary 평범한, 보통의
identify 식별하다; 확인하다
not have a clue 전혀 알지 못하다
other than ~외에, ~을 제외하고
overall 전반[종합]적인
sensory 감각적인, 감각의
perception 지각; 인지, 이해, 통찰력
acuity (지각의) 예민함, 날카로움
make use of ~을 활용하다
continuous 지속적인, 계속되는
vary 변화하다, 달라지다; 서로 다르다
[선택지] matter 중요하다; 문제되다; 문제, 사안
timely 시기적절한, 때맞춘; 이른
manner 방식, 태도
booster 촉진제; (자신감 등을) 높이는 것

정답 가이드

촉각은 시간에 기반을 둔다는 것을 실험을 통해 보여주며 손가락을 움직이게 함으로써 촉각에 시간을 더해 물건을 식별할 수 있다고 했다. 또한 촉각 능력은 시간에 따라 변하는 패턴에 의존한다고 했으므로 글의 제목으로 가장 적절한 것은 ② 'Time Does Matter: A Hidden Essence of Touch(시간은 정말로 중요하다, 즉 촉각의 숨겨진 본질)'이다.

오답 클리닉

① Touch and Movement: Two Major Elements of Humanity (11%)
촉각과 움직임, 즉 인간의 두 가지 주요한 요소(×)
손가락을 움직여 사물을 식별할 수 있다는 내용은 있지만 핵심어인 시간을 포괄하지 않음.

③ How to Use the Five Senses in a Timely Manner (4%)
시기적절한 방법으로 오감(×)을 사용하는 방법
오감 중 하나인 촉각에 대한 글임.

④ The Role of Touch in Forming the Concept of Time (21%)
시간 개념 형성(×)에 있어 촉각의 역할
촉각이 시간 개념을 형성하는 것이 아니라 시간을 기반으로 하는 것임.

The 주의 핵심어인 touch와 time이 모두 포함되어 있지만 글의 중심 내용과 전혀 다름에 유의한다.

⑤ The Surprising Function of Touch as a Booster of Knowledge (12%)
지식의 촉진제(×)로서 촉각의 놀라운 기능
촉각이 지식을 촉진한다는 내용은 없음.

02 + 빈칸 추론 〈20학년도 대수능 34번 | 정답률 44%〉 ②

구문분석 & 직독직해

예술 음악을 정의하려는 시도

[1]There have been many attempts (to define what music is / in terms of the specific attributes (of musical sounds)).
(V: have been / S: many attempts / to define의 O(명사절): what music is)

많은 시도가 있었다 (음악이 무엇인가를 정의하려는 / 특정한 속성이라는 관점에서 (악음(樂音)의))

↳ **도입:** 악음의 특정한 속성으로 음악을 정의하려는 시도들이 있었음.

[2]The famous nineteenth-century critic Eduard Hanslick regarded 'the measurable tone' / as 'the primary and essential condition of all music.'
(S: The famous nineteenth-century critic Eduard Hanslick / V: regarded / O: 'the measurable tone' / as: 전치사(~로(서)))
*<regard A as B>: A를 B로 간주하다[여기다]

19세기의 유명 평론가인 Eduard Hanslick은 '측정할 수 있는 음조'를 간주했다 / '모든 음악의 주요하고 본질적인 조건'으로

↳ **세부 사항 1:** 유명 평론가가 '측정할 수 있는 음조'를 음악의 주된 조건으로 간주했음.

[3]Musical sounds, / (he was saying), / can be distinguished from those of nature / by the fact // that they involve the use (of fixed pitches), // whereas virtually all natural sounds consist of / constantly fluctuating frequencies. 음악은 정해진 음높이를 사용함.
(S: Musical sounds / 삽입절: he was saying / V: can be distinguished / those (= sounds) / 동격 접속사: that / they (= musical sounds) / 부사절 접속사(대조): whereas)
*<distinguish A from B(A와 B를 구별하다)>의 수동형

악음은 / (그가 말하기를) / 자연의 소리와 구별될 수 있다 / 사실에 의해 // 그것들(악음)이 사용을 수반한다는 (정해진 음높이의) // 사실상 모든 자연의 소리가 ~로 구성되어 있는 것에 반해 / 끊임없이 변동하는 주파수

↳ **논거:** 정해진 음높이를 사용하는 음악은 변동하는 주파수로 이루어진 자연의 소리와 구별됨.

[4]And a number of twentieth-century writers have assumed, / (like Hanslick), // that fixed pitches are / among the defining features of music. 작곡가들도 고정된 음높이를 음악을 규정하는 특징으로 추정함.
(S: a number of twentieth-century writers / V(복수): have assumed / 전치사구 삽입: like Hanslick / 명사절 접속사: that / S′: fixed pitches / V′: are / C′: among the defining features of music / have assumed의 O(명사절))
*<a number of+복수명사>: 많은[다수의] ~

그리고 20세기의 많은 작곡가들은 (~라고) 추정했다 / (Hanslick과 마찬가지로) // 정해진 음높이가 ~라고 / 음악을 규정하는 특징 중의 하나

↳ **세부 사항 2:** 20세기의 작곡가도 정해진 음높이를 음악을 규정하는 특징으로 추정함.

[5]Now it is true // that in most of the world's musical cultures, / pitches are not only fixed, / but (are) organized / into a series of discrete steps.
(가주어: it / V: is / C: true / 진주어(명사절): that ... / 전치사구: in most of the world's musical cultures / S′: pitches / V′1: are ... fixed / V′2: (are) organized)
*<not only A but (also) B>: A뿐만 아니라 B도

이제 (~은) 사실이다 // 대부분의 세계 음악 문화에서 / 음높이는 정해져 있을 뿐만 아니라 / 조직되어 있다는 것은 / 일련의 별개 음정으로

↳ **결론:** 음높이는 정해져 있으며 일련의 별개 음정들로 조직되어 있음.

해석

[1]악음(樂音)의 특정한 속성이라는 관점에서 음악이 무엇인가를 정의하려는 많은 시도가 있었다. [2]19세기의 유명 평론가인 Eduard Hanslick은 '측정할 수 있는 음조'를 '모든 음악의 주요하고 본질적인 조건'으로 간주했다. [3]악음은, 그가 말하기를, 사실상 모든 자연의 소리가 끊임없이 변동하는 주파수로 구성되어 있는 것에 반해, 그것들(악음)이 정해진 음높이의 사용을 수반한다는 사실에 의해 자연의 소리와 구별될 수 있다. [4]그리고 20세기의 많은 작곡가들은 Hanslick과 마찬가지로 정해진 음높이가 음악을 규정하는 특징 중의 하나라고 추정했다. [5]이제 대부분의 세계 음악 문화에서 음높이는 정해져 있을 뿐만 아니라 일련의 별개 음정으로 조직되어 있다는 것은 사실이다. [6]하지만 이것은 음악에 관한 일반화이지 그것에 관한 정의는 아닌데, 왜냐하면 반례(反例)를 제기하는 것이 쉽기 때문이다. [7]예를 들어, 일본의 '샤쿠하치' 음악과 한국의 '산조' 음악은 그 음악이 구성된 관점인 이론상의 음높이 주위에서 끊임없이 변동한다.

어휘

in terms of ~의 관점에서
attribute 속성, 특성; (원인을) ~에 돌리다
critic 평론가, 비평가
measurable 측정할 수 있는(↔immeasurable 측정할 수 없는)
primary 주요한, 주된; 기본적인; 초기의
condition (전제) 조건; 상태
pitch 음높이, 음조; 던지다, 팽개치다
virtually 사실상; 가상으로
consist of ~로 구성되다
fluctuate 변동하다
frequency 주파수, 진동수; 빈도
defining (본질적인 의미를) 규정하는
a series of 일련의
discrete 별개의
step 음정; (발)걸음; 단계

주제문

[6]However, / this is a generalization about music / and not a definition of it, //
(this: = 앞 문장의 that절 / S: this / V: is / C1: a generalization about music / C2: a definition of it / it: = music)
하지만 / 이것은 음악에 관한 일반화이다 / 그리고 그것(음악)에 관한 정의는 아니다 //
for it is easy / to put forward counter-examples.
(for: 부사절 접속사(이유) / it: 가주어 / to put forward counter-examples: 진주어(to-v구))
왜냐하면 (~이) 쉽기 때문이다 / 반례(反例)를 제기하는 것이
↳ 반례가 있어 정해진 음높이는 음악의 정의가 못 됨.

[7]Japanese *shakuhachi* music and the *sanjo* music of Korea, / for instance, / fluctuate constantly / around *the notional pitches* [in terms of which the music is organized].
(S: Japanese shakuhachi music and the sanjo music of Korea / V: fluctuate / in terms of which: 전치사+관계대명사 / S′: the music / V: is organized)
일본의 '샤쿠하치' 음악과 한국의 '산조' 음악은 / 예를 들어 / 끊임없이 변동한다 /
이론상의 음높이 주위에서 [그 음악이 구성된 관점인]
↳ **반례:** 일본과 한국의 음악은 음높이가 끊임없이 변동함.

generalization 일반화
put forward ~을 제기하다[내다]
counter- 반-, 역-
notional 관념[이론, 개념]상의
[선택지] not so much A as B A라기보다는 B
artificially 인위적으로, 인공적으로
compositional 구성의
vehicle 수단, 매체; 차량, 탈것

정답 가이드

세계의 음악 문화에서 음높이가 어떻게 여겨지는지를 추론해야 하는데, 이어지는 '반례'에서는 이론상의 음높이 주위에서 '끊임없이 변동하는' 음악이 제시되었다. 이와 반대로, 빈칸에는 정해진 음높이를 하나하나 정확히 지키는 음악에 대한 내용이 나와야 한다. 따라서 빈칸에 들어갈 말로 가장 적절한 것은 ② 'not only fixed, but organized into a series of discrete steps(정해져 있을 뿐만 아니라 일련의 별개 음정으로 조직된)'이다.

오답 클리닉

① not so much artificially fixed as naturally fluctuating (29%)
인위적으로 정해져 있기보다는 자연적으로 변동하는
음악은 정해진 음높이를 사용하고 자연의 소리가 끊임없이 변동한다고 했음.

③ hardly considered a primary compositional element of music (11%)
음악의 주된 구성 요소로 거의 여겨지지 않는
문장 4에서 정해진 음높이가 음악을 규정하는 특징 중 하나라고 했으므로 글의 내용과 반대됨.

④ highly diverse and complicated, and thus are immeasurable (8%)
매우 다양하고 복잡하고, 그래서 측정할 수 없는
음높이는 측정할 수 있다고 했으므로 틀림.

⑤ a vehicle for carrying unique and various cultural features (9%)
독특하고 다양한 문화적 특징을 전달하는 수단
음높이가 문화적 특징을 전달한다는 내용은 언급되지 않음.

03 + 문장 넣기 〈21학년도 대수능 39번 | 정답률 70%〉 ④

구문분석 & 직독직해 법 저작권이 보호하는 대상

[1]Designers draw on their experience of design // when approaching a new project.
(S: Designers / V: draw on / O: their experience of design / when approaching: 접속사를 생략하지 않은 분사구문(= when they approach ~))
디자이너는 자신의 디자인 경험을 이용한다 // 새로운 프로젝트에 접근할 때

[2]This includes / the use (of *previous designs* [that (they know) work] — / both *designs* [that they have created themselves] / and *those* [that others have created]).
(S: This (= 앞 문장) / V: includes / O: the use / that: 주격 관계대명사 / they know: 삽입절 / that they: 목적격 관계대명사 / those: (= designs) / that others: 목적격 관계대명사)
이것은 포함한다 / 활용을 (이전의 디자인의 [(그들이 알기에) 효과가 있는] / 디자인 둘 다 [그들이 직접 만들었던] /
그리고 그것들(디자인) [다른 사람들이 만들었던])
↳ **도입:** 디자이너는 본인 및 다른 사람의 디자인을 활용하여 새로운 프로젝트에 접근함.

(①) [3]Others' creations often spark / *inspiration* [that also leads to new ideas and innovation].
(S: Others' creations / V: spark / O: inspiration / that: 주격 관계대명사)
다른 사람들의 창작물은 흔히 일으킨다 / 영감을 [새로운 아이디어와 혁신으로도 이어지는]

(②) [4]This is well known and understood.
(This: = 앞 문장)
이는 잘 알려져 있고 이해된다
↳ **도입의 부연 설명:** 다른 사람의 창작물은 흔히 새로운 아이디어와 혁신으로 이어지는 영감을 일으킴.

주제문

(③) [5]However, / the expression (of an idea) / is protected by copyright, //
(S1: the expression / V1: is protected)
그러나 / 표현은 (한 아이디어의) / 저작권에 의해 보호된다 //

해석

[1]디자이너는 새로운 프로젝트에 접근할 때 자신의 디자인 경험을 이용한다. [2]이것은 그들이 알기에 효과가 있는 이전의 디자인, 즉 그들이 직접 만들었던 디자인과 다른 사람들이 만들었던 디자인 둘 다의 활용을 포함한다. (①) [3]다른 사람들의 창작물은 흔히 새로운 아이디어와 혁신으로도 이어지는 영감을 일으킨다. (②) [4]이는 잘 알려져 있고 이해된다. (③) [5]그러나 한 아이디어의 표현은 저작권에 의해 보호되며, 그 저작권을 침해하는 사람들은 법정에 소환되어 기소될 수 있다. (④ [6]저작권은 아이디어의 표현을 보호하며, 아이디어 그 자체를 보호하지는 않는다는 것에 유의하라.) [7]이것은 예를 들어, 전부 유사한 기능을 가진 많은 스마트폰이 있지만, 그 아이디어가 서로 다른 방식으로 표현되었고 저작권 보호를 받은 것은 바로 그 표현이기 때문에 이것이 저작권 침해를 나타내지 않는다는 것을 의미한다. (⑤) [8]저작권은 무료이며 저작자, 예를 들어 어떤 책의 저자나 프로그램을 개발하는 프로그래머에게 자동으로 부여되는데, 그들이 서명하여 저작권을 다른 누군가에게 양도하지 않는 한 그러하다.

and people [who infringe on that copyright] / can be taken to court and prosecuted.

S_2 주격 관계대명사 V_2

그리고 사람들은 [그 저작권을 침해하는] / 법정에 소환되어 기소될 수 있다

↳ 아이디어의 표현은 저작권에 의해 법적으로 보호되며 저작권을 침해하면 기소될 수 있음.

↱ note의 O(명사절) 🔑 뒤 문장의 This가 가리키는 내용.

(④) [6]Note // that copyright covers the expression of an idea / and not the idea itself.)

V(명령문) 명사절 접속사 S′ V′ O'_1 O'_2

~에 유의하라 // 저작권은 아이디어의 표현을 보호한다는 것 / 그리고 아이디어 그 자체를 보호하지는 않는다는 것

↳ 저작권은 아이디어 자체가 아닌 아이디어의 표현을 보호함.

↱ (= 앞 문장) ↱ means의 O(명사절) 🔑 주어진 문장을 예를 들어 설명함.

[7]This means, / for example, // that / while there are numerous smartphones (all with similar functionality), // this does not represent an infringement of copyright //

S V 명사절 접속사 부사절 접속사(~하지만) V″ S″ S′ V′ O′

이것은 의미한다 / 예를 들어 // ~라는 것을 / 많은 스마트폰이 있지만 (전부 유사한 기능을 가진) // 이것이 저작권 침해를 나타내지 않는다(는 것을) //

★<it is ~ that ...> 강조구문: …한 것은 바로 ~이다

as the idea has been expressed in different ways // and it is the expression that has been copyrighted.

부사절 접속사(~ 때문에) 강조구문

그 아이디어가 서로 다른 방식으로 표현되었기 때문에 // 그리고 저작권 보호를 받은 것은 바로 그 표현이기 (때문에)

↳ 예: 많은 스마트폰은 유사한 기능을 가졌지만, 아이디어의 표현 방식이 다르므로 저작권 침해에 해당되지 않음.

(⑤) [8]Copyright is free / and is automatically invested in the author, / for instance, / the writer of a book or *a programmer* [who develops a program], // unless they sign the copyright over to someone else.

S V_1 C V_2 ★<sign A over (to B)>: (서명 절차를 거쳐) A를 (B에게) 양도하다

주격 관계대명사 부사절 접속사(조건) S′ V′ O′

저작권은 무료이다 / 그리고 저작자에게 자동으로 부여된다 / 예를 들어 / 어떤 책의 저자나 프로그래머 [프로그램을 개발하는] // 그들이 서명하여 저작권을 다른 누군가에게 양도하지 않는 한

↳ 저작권은 무료이며, 타인에게 양도하지 않는 한 자동으로 저작자에게 부여됨.

어휘

draw on ~을 이용하다; ~에 의지하다
approach 접근하다; 접근법
spark 일으키다, 유발하다; 불꽃
inspiration 영감, 기발한 생각; 고무, 고취
copyright 저작권; ~의 저작권을 보호하다
court 법정, 법원
note ~에 유의하다
cover 보호하다; 덮다; 포함하다
functionality 기능
represent 나타내다; 대표[대신]하다
invest 부여하다; 투자하다

정답 가이드

주어진 문장은 저작권이 아이디어 자체가 아닌 아이디어의 표현을 보호한다는 것에 유의하라는 내용이다. ③ 뒤는 아이디어 표현이 저작권에 의해 보호되고 침해 시 기소될 수 있다는 내용이고, ④ 뒤의 for example로 이어지는 내용은 기능이 전부 유사한 스마트폰들이 많지만 그 표현 방식이 다르기 때문에 저작권 침해가 아니라는 것이므로, 주어진 문장을 This로 받아 그 의미를 부연 설명하는 예에 해당한다. 따라서 이는 저작권 침해로 기소될 수 있다는 ④ 앞의 내용에 대한 예로 볼 수 없으므로, 주어진 문장이 들어가기에 가장 적절한 곳은 ④이다.

오답 클리닉

① (1%) 디자이너가 다른 사람들이 만들었던 디자인도 활용한다는 앞 문장에 이어 다른 사람들의 창작물이 영감을 일으킨다는 설명은 자연스럽다.

② (7%) This는 다른 사람들의 창작물이 새로운 아이디어와 혁신으로 이어지는 영감을 일으킨다는 앞 문장의 내용을 받아 이어지는 내용이다.

③ (11%) 다른 사람의 창작물을 활용한다는 앞의 언급에 대해 역접 연결어 However를 사용하여 아이디어의 표현이 저작권에 의해 보호된다는 상반된 내용이 이어지는 것은 자연스럽다.

⑤ (10%) 저작권이 아이디어의 표현을 보호한다는 내용에 덧붙여 저작권의 다른 속성들을 설명하며 글을 끝맺고 있다.

01 + 함의 추론 〈21학년도 9월 모평 21번 | 정답률 50%〉 ①

구문분석 & 직독직해

생활 예측 가능한 방식의 이로움

[1]By expecting / what's likely to happen next, / you prepare for the few most likely scenarios //
by v-ing: v함으로써 / expecting의 O(명사절) / S V
예상함으로써 / 다음에 일어날 것 같은 일을 / 여러분은 가장 가능성이 높은 몇 가지 시나리오에 대비한다 //
→ 부사절 접속사(목적) / V′ / → 부사절 접속사(~ 동안에)
so that you don't have to figure things out // while they're happening.
S′ O′ S″(= things) V″
여러분이 상황 파악을 할 필요가 없도록 하기 위해 // 그것들이 일어나는 동안에
↳ **도입:** 우리는 일어날 가능성이 높은 시나리오를 예상해 둠으로써 대비함.

[2]It's therefore not a surprise // when a restaurant server offers you a menu.
가주어 V C 진주어(명사절) S′ V′ IO′ DO′
그러므로 (~는) 놀랄 일이 아니다 // 음식점 종업원이 여러분에게 메뉴를 제공하는 경우는

→ 부사절 접속사(시간) / *if가 명사절 목적어를 이끌면 '~인지 (아닌지)'의 뜻 / → (= a clear fluid)
[3]When she brings you a glass (with a clear fluid in it), // you don't have to ask // if it's water.
S′ V′ IO′ DO′ (= a glass) S V O(명사절)
그녀가 여러분에게 유리잔을 가져다줄 때 (안에 투명한 액체가 담긴) // 여러분은 물을 필요가 없다 // 그것이 물인지

[4]After you eat, // you don't have to figure out // why you aren't hungry anymore.
S V O(명사절)
식사를 한 후에 // 여러분은 알아낼 필요가 없다 // 왜 더 이상 배가 고프지 않은지

[5]All these things are expected / and are therefore not *problems* (to solve).
S V_1 V_2 C
이 모든 것들은 예상된다 / 따라서 문제가 아니다 (해결해야 할)
⊶ 예상 가능한 일은 문제되지 않음 → 긍정적 입장.
↳ **예 1:** 예상 가능한 일은 문제가 되지 않음.

→ imagine의 O(명사절)
[6]Furthermore, / imagine // how demanding it would be / to always consider all the possible uses (for *all the familiar objects* [with which you interact]).
V 의문사 가주어 진주어(to-v구)
*with which는 <전치사+관계대명사> 형태로 all the familiar objects를 수식함.
더욱이 / 상상해 보라 // (~이) 얼마나 힘들 것인지 / 모든 가능한 용도들을 항상 고려하는 것이 (모든 친숙한 물건들에 대한 [여러분이 상호 작용하는])

[7]*Should I use my hammer or my telephone / to pound in that nail?*
목적(~하기 위해)
"나의 망치나 전화기 중 어떤 것을 사용해야 할까? / 저 못을 박기 위해서"

[8]On a daily basis, / functional fixedness is a relief, / not a curse.
매일 / 기능의 고정성은 안도이다 / 저주가 아니라
⊶ 용도가 고정되어 있는 물건은 안도감을 줌 → 긍정적 입장.
↳ **예 2:** 정해져 있는 용도가 우리에게 안도감을 줌.

주제문 → is의 C(명사절 / ⊶ 당연한 일에 모든 선택지와 가능성을 따지지 말아야 함.
[9]That's // why you shouldn't even attempt / to consider all your options and possibilities.
S V 관계부사
그것이 ~이다 // 여러분이 시도조차 해서는 안 되는 이유 / 여러분의 모든 선택지와 가능성을 고려하기를
↳ **결론:** 모든 선택지와 가능성을 고려하지 말아야 함.

[10]You can't (consider all your options and possibilities).
여러분은 그럴(여러분의 모든 선택지와 가능성을 고려할) 수도 없다

→ 부사절 접속사(조건)
[11]If you tried to (consider all your options and possibilities), // then you'd never get anything done.
S′ V′ O′ S V O C
여러분이 그렇게 하려고(여러분의 모든 선택지와 가능성을 고려하려고) 한다면 // 여러분은 절대 아무것도 완수할 수 없을 것이다
↳ **이유:** 모든 선택지와 가능성을 고려하면 아무것도 제대로 할 수 없음.

[12]So / **don't knock the box.**
그러므로 / 상자를 두드리지 말아라
↳ **주제문 재진술:** 모든 선택지와 가능성을 고려하지 말아야 함.

해석

[1]다음에 일어날 것 같은 일을 예상함으로써, 여러분은 그것들이 일어나는 동안에 상황 파악을 할 필요가 없도록 하기 위해 가장 가능성이 높은 몇 가지 시나리오에 대비한다. [2]그러므로 음식점 종업원이 여러분에게 메뉴를 제공하는 경우는 놀랄 일이 아니다. [3]그녀가 여러분에게 안에 투명한 액체가 담긴 유리잔을 가져다줄 때, 여러분은 그것이 물인지 물을 필요가 없다. [4]식사를 한 후에, 여러분은 왜 더 이상 배가 고프지 않은지 알아낼 필요가 없다. [5]이 모든 것들은 예상되며 따라서 해결해야 할 문제가 아니다. [6]더욱이, 여러분이 상호 작용하는 모든 친숙한 물건들에 대한 모든 가능한 용도들을 항상 고려하는 것이 얼마나 힘들 것인지 상상해 보라. [7]"저 못을 박기 위해서 나의 망치나 전화기 중 어떤 것을 사용해야 할까?" [8]매일, 기능의 고정성은 저주가 아니라 안도이다. [9]그것이 여러분의 모든 선택지와 가능성을 고려하기를 시도조차 해서는 안 되는 이유이다. [10]여러분은 그럴 수도 없다. [11]여러분이 그렇게 하려고 한다면, 여러분은 절대 아무것도 완수할 수 없을 것이다. [12]그러므로 상자를 두드리지 말아라. [13]역설적으로, 그것이 여러분의 사고를 제한하기는 하지만, 그것은 여러분을 똑똑하게도 만들어 준다. [14]그것은 현실보다 한발 앞서 있도록 여러분을 도와준다.(▶ 뻔하고 당연한 일은 신경 쓰지 않고 처리함으로써 정말 생각이 많이 필요한 일을 잘 처리할 수 있게 된다는 의미)

어휘

figure out ~을 알아내다
fluid 액체, 유동체
demanding 힘든, 부담이 큰; 요구가 많은
familiar 친숙한, 익숙한
interact with ~와 상호 작용하다
pound (물건을) 치다, 두들기다
functional 기능의, 기능적인
relief 안도(감)
curse 저주(하다)
attempt 시도(하다)
ironically 역설적으로, 반어적으로
[선택지] deal with ~을 처리하다, ~을 다루다
habitual 늘 하는, 습관적인; 상습적인
predetermined 미리 정해진
routine (판에 박힌) 일상
outcome 결과
given 주어진, 정해진; ~을 고려해 볼 때
boundary 경계, 한계(선)

(= not knocking the box)
[13]Ironically, / although it limits your thinking, // it also makes you smart.
부사절 접속사(양보) S' V' O' S V O C
역설적으로 / 그것(상자를 두드리지 않는 것)이 여러분의 사고를 제한하기는 하지만 // 그것은 여러분을 똑똑하게도 만들어 준다

(= Not knocking the box)
[14]It helps you / to stay one step ahead of reality.
S V O C
그것(상자를 두드리지 않는 것)은 여러분을 도와준다 / 현실보다 한발 앞서 있도록
↳ **이점:** 예상 가능하고 정해진 기능에 기대는 것이 효율적임.

정답 가이드

예상 가능한 일과 사물의 고정적인 기능은 우리가 때마다 상황을 파악할 필요 없이 일상생활을 할 수 있게 해준다고 했다. 만약 우리가 어떤 상황마다 모든 선택지와 가능성을 고민해야 한다면 아무것도 제대로 해낼 수 없을 것이므로 당연한 일에 대해서는 이미 아는 정해진 방식에 따라 처리하는 것이 낫다고 이야기한다. 이러한 맥락에서 밑줄 친 부분이 의미하는 바로 가장 적절한 것은 ① 'Deal with a matter based on your habitual expectations.(늘 하는 예상을 바탕으로 문제를 처리하라.)'이다.

오답 클리닉

② Question what you expect from a familiar object. (12%)
여러분이 익숙한 물건으로부터 기대하는 것에 대해 이의를 제기하라(×)
물건의 다른 용도에 대해 고민할 필요 없이 정해진 용도대로 사용하면 된다는 글의 내용과 반대됨.

③ Replace predetermined routines with fresh ones. (5%)
미리 정해진 일상을 새로운 일상으로 교체하라(×)
정해진 일상을 새로운 것으로 교체하라는 언급은 없음.

④ Think over all possible outcomes of a given situation. (25%)
주어진 상황의 모든 가능한 결과에 대해 숙고하라(×)
모든 가능한 선택지와 가능성을 고려하지 말라는 글의 내용과 반대됨.

The 주의 밑줄 친 부분이 부정문이라고 해서 문장 9의 주장(모든 선택지와 가능성을 고려하지 말라)을 반대하는 것으로 판단하지 않도록 주의한다.

⑤ Extend all the boundaries that guide your thinking to insight. (8%)
사고를 통찰력(×)으로 이끄는 모든 경계를 확대하라(×)
정해진 방식 안에서 문제를 파악하라고 했으므로 경계를 확대하는 것으로 보기 어려우며 통찰력은 언급되지 않은 내용임.

02 + 빈칸 추론 (20학년도 대수능 33번 | 정답률 47%) ①

구문분석 & 직독직해

기술 첨단 기술 개발을 위한 재료 확보의 필요성

주제문
★<not A but B>: A가 아니라 B
[1]The future (of our high-tech goods) / may lie / not in the limitations (of our minds), / but in our ability (to secure *the ingredients* (to produce them)).
S V 전치사구 병렬 / 전치사구 병렬 = (= our high-tech goods)
미래는 (우리 첨단 기술 제품의) / 있을지도 모른다 / 한계가 아니라 (우리 생각의) / 우리의 능력에 (재료를 확보하는 (그것(우리 첨단 기술 제품)을 생산하기 위한))
↳ 첨단 기술 제품을 생산하는 재료를 확보하는 능력이 중요함.

[2]In previous eras, / (such as the Iron Age and the Bronze Age), / the discovery (of new elements) / brought forth seemingly unending numbers of new inventions.
전치사구 삽입 S V O
이전 시대에 / (철기 시대와 청동기 시대와 같은) / 발견은 (새로운 원소의) / 끝이 없어 보이는 수의 새로운 발명품을 낳았다
↳ **과거:** 새로운 원소(재료)의 발견이 새로운 발명품을 만듦.

[3]Now / the combinations may truly be unending.
S V C
현재 / 그 조합은 정말로 끝이 없을지도 모른다

[4]We are now witnessing a fundamental shift / in our resource demands.
S V O
우리는 이제 근본적인 변화를 목격하고 있다 / 우리의 자원 수요에 있어서

★부정어를 포함한 부사구가 강조를 위해 문두에 오면서 <조동사+S+V> 어순으로 도치가 일어남.
[5]At no point in human history have we used *more* elements, / in *more* combinations, / and in increasingly refined amounts.
부정어 포함 어구 조동사 S V O 전치사구 병렬 전치사구 병렬
인류 역사의 어느 시점에서도 우리가 '더 많은' 원소를 사용한 적은 없었다 / '더 많은' 조합으로 / 그리고 점차 정밀한 양으로
↳ **현재:** 어느 때보다 많은 양의 자원을 다양한 조합으로 사용하고 있음.

해석

[1]우리 첨단 기술 제품의 미래는 우리 생각의 한계가 아니라, 그것을 생산하기 위한 재료를 확보하는 우리의 능력에 있을지도 모른다. [2]철기 시대와 청동기 시대와 같은 이전 시대에, 새로운 원소의 발견은 끝이 없어 보이는 수의 새로운 발명품을 낳았다. [3]현재 그 조합은 정말로 끝이 없을지도 모른다. [4]우리는 이제 우리의 자원 수요에 있어서 근본적인 변화를 목격하고 있다. [5]인류 역사의 어느 시점에서도 우리가 '더 많은' 원소를 '더 많은' 조합으로, 그리고 점차 정밀한 양으로 사용한 적은 없었다. [6]우리의 창의력은 곧 우리의 물질적인 공급을 앞지를 것이다. [7]이 상황은 세계가 화석 연료에 대한 의존을 줄이려고 분투하고 있는 결정적인 시점에 온다. [8]다행히, 희귀 금속들이 전기 자동차, 풍력 발전용 터빈, 태양 전지판과 같은 친환경 기술의 핵심 재료이다. [9]친환경 기술들은 태양과 바람과 같은 무료 천연 자원을 우리의 생활에 연료를 공급하는 동력으로 전환하는 데 도움을 준다. [10]하지만 오늘날의 제한된 공급을 늘리지 않고는, 우리는 기후 변화를 늦추기 위해 우리가 필요로 하는 친환경 대체 기술을 개발할 가망이 없다.

어휘

high-tech 첨단 기술의
limitation 한계; 제한

[6]Our ingenuity will soon outpace / our material supplies. (S / V / O) 🔑 문장 1의 our minds가 our ingenuity로, our ability ~ them이 our material supplies로 말바꿈됨.
우리의 창의력은 곧 앞지를 것이다 / 우리의 물질적인 공급을
↳ **문제점:** 인간의 창의력에 비해 재료 공급이 부족해짐.

[7]This situation comes / at *a defining moment* [when the world is struggling to reduce / its reliance on fossil fuels]. (S(= 앞 문장) / V / 관계부사 / S′ / V′ / 목적(~하기 위해))
이 상황은 온다 / 결정적인 시점에 [세계가 줄이려고 분투하고 있는 / 화석 연료에 대한 의존을]
↳ **부연 설명:** 세계는 화석 연료 사용을 줄이려고 함.

[8]Fortunately, / rare metals are key ingredients / in green technologies (such as electric cars, wind turbines, and solar panels). (S / V / C)
다행히 / 희귀 금속들이 핵심 재료이다 / 친환경 기술의 (전기 자동차, 풍력 발전용 터빈, 태양 전지판과 같은)

(= Green technologies) ★<convert A into B>: A를 B로 전환하다
[9]They help to convert / free natural resources (like the sun and wind) / into *the power* [that fuels our lives]. (S / V / O / 주격 관계대명사)
그것들(친환경 기술)은 전환하는 데 도움을 준다 / 무료 천연 자원을 (태양과 바람과 같은) / 동력으로 [우리의 생활에 연료를 공급하는]
↳ **대안점:** 희귀 금속들(재료)을 이용해 친환경 기술을 개발해 천연 자원으로 동력을 만들 수 있음.

🔑 친환경 대체 기술을 대체하려면 제한된 자원 공급을 늘려야 함.
[10]But without increasing today's limited supplies, / we have no chance (of developing *the alternative green technologies* [(which[that]) we need] / to slow climate change). (without의 O(동명사구) / S / V / O / = / 목적격 관계대명사 생략 / 목적(~하기 위해))
하지만 오늘날의 제한된 공급을 늘리지 않고는 / 우리는 가망이 없다 (친환경 대체 기술을 개발할 [우리가 필요로 하는] / 기후 변화를 늦추기 위해)
↳ **주제문 재진술:** 재료 공급을 늘려야 친환경 대체 기술을 개발할 수 있음.

secure 확보하다; 안전하게 지키다
ingredient 재료[성분]; 구성 요소
the Iron Age 철기 시대
the Bronze Age 청동기 시대
element 원소; 요소, 성분
bring forth ~을 낳다[생산하다]
seemingly 겉보기에는
combination 조합[결합]
witness 목격하다; 목격자
fundamental 근본적인; 필수적인
shift 변화; 옮기다, 이동하다; 바뀌다
increasingly 점차, 더욱 더
refined 정밀한; 세련된
outpace 앞지르다
defining moment 결정적인 시점
struggle to-v v하려고 분투하다
reliance 의존, 의지
fossil fuel 화석 연료
wind turbine 풍력 발전용 터빈
solar panel 태양 전지판
alternative 대체의
[선택지] eco-friendly 친환경적인
distribution 배급, 분배
innovative 혁신적인, 획기적인

정답 가이드

첨단 기술의 미래가 '무엇'에 있을지를 추론해야 한다. 우리는 어느 때보다도 많은 자원을 다양하게 사용하고 있는데, 우리의 창의력이 곧 물질적인 공급을 앞지를 것이라고 했고, 마지막 문장에서 '제한된 공급을 늘리지 않고는' 친환경 대체 기술을 개발할 수 없다고 했다. '자원', '물질 공급', '제한된 공급'은 모두 첨단 기술 실현을 위한 '원료, 즉 재료'를 의미하며 이를 확보하는 것이 필요하다는 것이므로 빈칸에 들어갈 말로 가장 적절한 것은 ① 'our ability to secure the ingredients to produce them(그것을 생산하기 위한 재료를 확보하는 우리의 능력)'이다.

오답 클리닉

② our effort to make them as eco-friendly as possible (33%)
그것을 가능한 한 친환경적이게 만들려고 하는 우리의 노력
친환경적인 미래 기술을 만들어야 한다는 내용이 아님.

The 주의 친환경 대체 기술은 미래 첨단 기술의 예로 언급된 것임에 유의해야 한다.

③ the wider distribution of innovative technologies (6%)
혁신 기술의 더 광범위한 배급
혁신 기술을 더욱 널리 전파해야 한다는 내용은 없음.
④ governmental policies not to limit resource supplies (6%)
자원 공급을 제한하지 않는 정부 정책
자원 공급을 늘려야 한다는 내용이지만 정부 정책에 관한 언급은 없음.
⑤ the constant update and improvement of their functions (7%)
그것의 기능의 지속적인 업데이트와 개선
첨단 기술의 지속적인 개선이 필요하다는 내용이 아님.

03 + 무관 문장 (21학년도 대수능 35번 | 정답률 83%) ③

구문분석 & 직독직해 생활 조직을 단결하는 유머와 웃음의 공유

주제문 🔑 공유된 사건에 같이 웃으면서 직원들이 단결된다는 내용임.
[1]Workers are united / by laughing at shared events, / even *ones* [that may initially spark anger or conflict]. (S / V / <by v-ing>: v함으로써 / (= events) 주격 관계대명사)
직원들은 단결된다 / 공유된 사건에 웃음으로써 / 심지어 (~한) 것들(사건)에도 [처음에는 분노나 갈등을 유발할 수 있는]
↳ 직원들은 공유된 사건에 같이 웃음으로써 단결됨.

해석

[1]직원들은 공유된 사건, 심지어 처음에는 분노나 갈등을 유발할 수 있는 사건에도 웃음으로써 단결된다. [2]유머는 분열을 일으킬 가능성이 있는 사건들을 조직 구성원들에 의해 보유되는 통합 가치에 도움이 되는 것으로 (제대로) 보여지는 그저 '우스운' 사

★<reframe A into B>: A를 B로 재구성하다

[2]Humor reframes potentially divisive events / into merely "laughable" *ones* [which are put in perspective / as subservient / to *unifying values* (held by organization members)].

S / V / O / (= events) 주격 관계대명사 / 전치사(~로(서)) / 과거분사구

유머는 분열을 일으킬 가능성이 있는 사건들을 재구성한다 / 그저 '우스운' (~한) 것들(사건)로 [(제대로) 보여지는 / 도움이 되는 것으로 / 통합 가치에 (조직 구성원들에 의해 보유되는)]

↳ **세부 사항 1:** 유머는 문제가 될 수 있는 사건을 구성원들의 통합 가치에 도움이 되도록 재구성함.

[3]Repeatedly recounting humorous incidents reinforces / *unity* (based on key organizational values).

S(동명사구) / V(단수) / O / 과거분사구

유머러스한 사건들을 되풀이하여 자세히 말하는 것은 강화한다 / 단결을 (핵심적인 조직의 가치에 근거를 둔)

↳ **세부 사항 2:** 유머러스한 사건들을 반복해서 공유하는 것이 조직을 단결시킴.

① [4]One team told repeated stories (about a dumpster fire), / *something* [that does not seem funny on its face], // but the reactions of *workers* (motivated to preserve safety) / sparked laughter //

S_1 / V_1 / O_1 / = / 주격 관계대명사 / V′ / C′ / S_2 / 과거분사구 / V_2 / O_2

어떤 팀이 되풀이되는 이야기를 했다 (엄청난 재앙에 관한) / 어떤 것 [표면적으로는 재미있어 보이지 않는] // 하지만 직원들의 반응이 (안전을 지키도록 동기를 부여받은) / 웃음을 유발했다 //

as the stories were shared / multiple times / by multiple parties in the workplace.

부사절 접속사(~하면서)

그 이야기가 공유되면서 / 여러 번 / 직장의 여러 당사자들에 의해

↳ **예:** 나쁜 사건이 여러 번 공유되면서 조직의 단결이라는 안전성을 지키려는 직원들에게 웃음을 유발함.

② [5]*Shared events* [that cause laughter] / can indicate a sense of belonging // since "you had to be there" / to see the humor in them, // and non-members were not (there) and do not (see the humor in them).

S / 주격 관계대명사 / V / O / 부사절 접속사(~ 때문에) / S′₁ / V′₁ / 목적(~하려면) / (= shared events) / S′₂ / V′₂ / 반복어 생략 / V′₃ / 반복어구 생략

공유된 사건은 [웃음을 유발하는] / 소속감을 나타낼 수 있다 // '여러분은 그곳에 있어야 했기' 때문에 / 그 사건 속의 유머를 이해하려면 // 그리고 조직 구성원이 아닌 사람들은 그러지 않아서(그곳에 없어서) 그러지(사건 속의 유머를 이해하지) 못하기 때문에

↳ **세부 사항 3:** 웃음을 유발하는 사건을 공유하는 것은 소속감을 나타냄.

'유머'라는 소재만 같고 직원들을 단결시키는 유머의 공유와는 무관한 내용임.

③ [6]Since humor can easily capture people's attention, // commercials tend to contain humorous elements, / such as funny faces and gestures.

부사절 접속사(~ 때문에) / S / V

유머는 사람들의 관심을 쉽게 사로잡을 수 있기 때문에 // 광고 방송은 유머러스한 요소들을 포함하는 경향이 있다 / 웃긴 표정과 몸짓 같은

↳ 광고에서 사람들의 관심을 사로잡기 위해 유머러스한 요소를 사용함.

④ [7]Instances of humor serve to enact bonds (among organization members).

S / V

유머의 사례는 유대감을 일으키는 데 도움이 된다 (조직 구성원들 간의)

⑤ [8]Understanding the humor may even be required / as an informal badge of membership (in the organization).

S(동명사구) / V / 전치사(~로(서))

유머를 이해하는 것은 심지어 요구될 수도 있다 / 회원 신분의 비공식 증표로 (그 조직의)

↳ **부연 설명:** 공유된 유머는 조직 구성원들 간의 유대감을 조성하고, 조직에 소속되려면 그 유머를 이해할 수 있어야 함.

건들로 재구성한다. [3]유머러스한 사건들을 되풀이하여 자세히 말하는 것은 핵심적인 조직의 가치에 근거를 둔 단결을 강화한다. ① [4]어떤 팀이 엄청난 재앙에 관한 되풀이되는 이야기를 했는데, 표면적으로는 재미있어 보이지 않는 어떤 것이지만, 그 이야기가 직장의 여러 당사자들에 의해 여러 번 공유되면서 안전을 지키도록 동기를 부여받은 직원들의 반응이 웃음을 유발했다.(▶ 여러 번 공유된 나쁜 사건 이야기에 직원들은 웃음으로써 조직의 안전(단결)을 지키려 했다는 의미) ② [5]웃음을 유발하는 공유된 사건은 소속감을 나타낼 수 있는데, 그 사건 속의 유머를 이해하려면 '여러분은 그곳에 있어야 했고' 조직 구성원이 아닌 사람들은 그러지 않아서(그곳에 없어서) 그러지(사건 속의 유머를 이해하지) 못하기 때문이다. ③ [6]유머는 사람들의 관심을 쉽게 사로잡을 수 있기 때문에, 광고 방송은 웃긴 표정과 몸짓 같은 유머러스한 요소들을 포함하는 경향이 있다. ④ [7]유머의 사례는 조직 구성원들 간의 유대감을 일으키는 데 도움이 된다. ⑤ [8]유머를 이해하는 것은 심지어 그 조직의 회원 신분의 비공식 증표로 요구될 수도 있다.

어휘

unite 단결[결속]시키다
cf. unity 단결, 조화; 통합, 통일
spark 유발하다, 촉발시키다; 불꽃
divisive 분열을 일으키는; 구별하는
merely 그저, 단지
put A in perspective A를 (제대로) 보다, A를 이해하다
unify 통합[통일]하다
recount 자세히 말하다; 다시 세다
incident 사건, 일
reinforce 강화하다; 보강하다
dumpster fire 엄청난 재앙, 극도로 혼란스러운 상황
motivate 동기를 부여하다; 이유가 되다
party 당사자; 정당; 파티
sense of belonging 소속감
capture (관심을) 사로잡다; 포획하다
commercial 광고 방송; 상업의
tend to-v v하는 경향이 있다
serve 도움이 되다; 봉사하다
enact (사건을) 일으키다; (법을) 제정하다
bond 유대, 결속; 접착시키다[되다]
badge 증표, 상징; 배지, 훈장

정답 가이드

공유된 사건에 같이 웃음으로써 직원들이 단결된다는 내용의 첫 문장 이후로 공유된 유머를 이해하고 같이 웃는 것이 조직 구성원들의 소속감과 유대감을 형성한다는 설명이 끝까지 이어진다. 그런데 ③은 광고에서 유머를 사용하는 이유에 해당하므로 전체 글의 흐름과 무관하다.

오답 클리닉

① (2%) 유머러스한 사건을 반복해서 공유하는 것이 단결을 강화한다는 앞 문장의 예로, 공유된 이야기가 조직의 안전을 지키려는 직원들에게 웃음을 유발했다는 내용이다.
② (5%) 공유된 유머가 소속감을 나타내는 이유를 설명한다.
④ (9%) 공유된 유머를 이해하는 것이 소속감을 나타낸다는 앞의 내용에 이어서 유머가 유대감을 조성한다고 재차 설명한다.
⑤ (2%) 유머의 이해는 조직의 일원임을 나타내는 비공식 증표의 역할까지도 할 수 있다고 덧붙이는 내용이다.

01 ✦ 글의 요지 〈22학년도 대수능 22번 | 정답률 90%〉 ①

구문분석 & 직독직해

환경 사회적 대응이 요구되는 환경 위험 요인

[1]Environmental hazards (S) include (V) biological, physical, and chemical ones (O) (= hazards), / along with *the human behaviors* [that (주격 관계대명사) promote or allow exposure].

환경 위험 요소는 생물학적, 물리적, 화학적 위험 요소를 포함한다 / 인간 행동과 함께 [(유해 환경에) 노출되는 것을 조장하거나 허용하는]

↳ **도입:** 환경 위험 요소는 다양함.

[2]Some environmental contaminants (S_1) are (V_1) difficult (C_1) to avoid (형용사 difficult 수식) / (the breathing (of polluted air), / the drinking (of chemically contaminated public drinking water), / noise (in open public spaces)); //

일부 환경 오염 물질은 피하기 어렵다 / (호흡 (오염된 공기의) / 음용 (화학적으로 오염된 공공 식수의) / 소음 (개방된 공공장소에서의)) //

in these circumstances, / exposure (S_2) is (V_2) largely involuntary (C_2).

이러한 상황에서 / 노출은 대개 자기도 모르게 하는 것이다

↳ **문제점:** 환경 오염 물질에의 노출은 피하기 어려우며 자기도 모르게 이루어짐.

주제문

🔑 피하기 어려운 환경 오염 물질들을 줄이려면 사회적 행동이 요구됨.

[3]Reduction or elimination (of these factors (= unavoidable environmental contaminants)) (S) / may require (V) societal action (O), / such as public awareness and public health measures.

감소 또는 제거는 (이러한 요인의) / 사회적 행동을 필요로 할지도 모른다 / 대중의 인식 및 공중 보건 조치와 같은

↳ **해결책:** 피하기 어려운 환경 오염 물질을 줄이거나 없애려면 사회적 행동이 필요함.

[4]In many countries, / the fact (S) // that (동격 접속사) some environmental hazards are difficult to avoid at the individual level // is felt (V) to be more morally egregious (C) / than *those hazards* [that (주격 관계대명사) can be avoided].

많은 국가에서, / 사실은 // 일부 환경적 위험 요소가 개인 수준에서 피하기 어렵다는 // 도덕적으로 더 매우 나쁜 것으로 느껴진다 / 위험 요소보다 [피해질 수 있는]

↳ 개인이 피하기 어려운 환경 위험 요소는 도덕적으로 더 나쁘게 여겨짐.

[5]Having no choice but to drink *water* (contaminated with very high levels of arsenic) (S_1 / 과거분사구), / or being forced to passively breathe in tobacco smoke in restaurants (S_2), / outrages (V) people (O) more / than the personal choice (of whether an individual smokes tobacco (of의 O(명사절))).

어쩔 수 없이 물을 마실 수밖에 없는 것 (매우 높은 수준의 비소로 오염된) / 또는 식당에서 담배 연기를 간접적으로 들이마시도록 강요당하는 것은 / 사람들을 더 격분하게 만든다 / 개인적 선택보다 (개인이 담배를 피울지에 대한)

↳ **예:** 선택권 없이 오염된 물을 마시는 것, 피하기 어려운 간접흡연은 사람들을 더 격분하게 함.

[6]These factors (= unavoidable environmental contaminants) are important // when (부사절 접속사(시간)) one (S′) considers (V′) how change (risk reduction) happens (O′(명사절)).

이러한 요인들은 중요하다 // 변화(위험 감소)가 일어날 방법을 고려할 때

↳ 피하기 어려운 환경 위험 요인들은 위험 감소가 일어날 방법을 고려하는 상황에서 중요함.

해석

[1]환경 위험 요소는 (유해 환경에) 노출되는 것을 조장하거나 허용하는 인간 행동과 함께 생물학적, 물리적, 화학적 위험 요소를 포함한다. [2](오염된 공기의 호흡, 화학적으로 오염된 공공 식수의 음용, 개방된 공공장소에서의 소음처럼) 일부 환경 오염 물질은 피하기 어렵고, 이러한 상황에서 노출은 대개 자기도 모르게 하는 것이다. [3]이러한 요인의 감소 또는 제거는 대중의 인식 및 공중 보건 조치와 같은 사회적 행동을 필요로 할지도 모른다. [4]많은 국가에서, 일부 환경적 위험 요소가 개인 수준에서 피하기 어렵다는 사실은 피해질 수 있는 위험 요소보다 도덕적으로 더 매우 나쁜 것으로 느껴진다. [5]어쩔 수 없이 매우 높은 수준의 비소로 오염된 물을 마실 수밖에 없는 것이나, 식당에서 담배 연기를 간접적으로 들이마시도록 강요당하는 것은 개인이 담배를 피울지에 대한 개인적 선택보다 사람들을 더 격분하게 만든다. [6]이러한 요인들은 변화(위험 감소)가 일어날 방법을 고려할 때 중요하다.(▶ 개인 수준에서 피하기 어려운 환경 위험 요소는 개인적 선택에 의한 위험 요소와 구별해서 해결해야 한다는 의미)

어휘

hazard 위험 (요소)
along with ~와 함께
promote 조장하다, 촉진하다; 홍보하다; 승진시키다
exposure 노출; 폭로
contaminant 오염 물질
avoid 피하다
involuntary 자기도 모르게 하는, 무의식의
reduction 감소; 축소, 삭감; 할인
elimination 제거
societal 사회적인, 사회의
awareness 인식; 의식[관심]
measure 조치, 방책; 양; 측정하다[재다]
morally 도덕적으로
have no choice but to-v (어쩔 수 없이) v하는 수밖에 없다
arsenic 《화학》 비소
outrage 격분하게 만들다; 격노, 격분

정답 가이드

사회적 행동을 필요로 하는 환경 위험 요소들을 설명하고, 이는 개인이 피하기 어려울 수 있다는 점을 이어서 보충 설명하고 있다. 따라서 글의 요지로 가장 적절한 것은 ① '개인이 피하기 어려운 유해 환경 요인에 대해서는 사회적 대응이 필요하다.'이다.

오답 클리닉

② 환경 오염으로 인한 피해자들에게 적절한 보상(×)을 하는 것이 바람직하다. (1%)
환경 오염 피해자들에게 보상해야 한다는 내용은 없음.

③ 다수의 건강을 해치는 행위에 대해 도덕적 비난 이상의 조치(×)가 요구된다. (4%) 개인이 피하기 어려운 환경 위험 요인은 도덕적으로 더 나쁘게 여겨진다고 했으나 비난 이상의 조치에 대한 언급은 없음.

④ 환경 오염 문제를 해결하기 위해서는 사후 대응보다 예방(×)이 중요하다. (4%)
환경 오염 예방에 관한 내용이 아님.

⑤ 대기 오염(×) 문제는 인접 국가들과의 긴밀한 협력(×)을 통해 해결할 수 있다. (1%) 대기 오염에 한정된 내용이 아니며 국가들 간의 협력에 대한 언급도 없음.

02 + 빈칸 추론 〈20학년도 대수능 32번 | 정답률 64%〉 ①

구문분석 & 직독직해

인지 아동의 시간 및 공간 차원 혼동

[1]The Swiss psychologist Jean Piaget frequently analyzed / children's conception of time / via their ability (to compare or (to) estimate *the time* (taken by pairs of events)).

(S: The Swiss psychologist Jean Piaget / V: analyzed / O: children's conception of time / 전치사(~을 통해): via / to compare = (to) estimate / 과거분사구: taken by pairs of events)

스위스의 심리학자 Jean Piaget는 자주 분석했다 / 아이들의 시간 개념을 / 아이들의 능력을 통해 (시간을 비교하거나 추정하는 (짝 지은 사건들에 걸리는))

↳ **도입:** 아이들의 시간 개념을 분석함.

[2]In a typical experiment, / two toy cars were shown running synchronously / on parallel tracks, / **one running faster and stopping further down the track.**

(S: two toy cars / V: were shown / C: running synchronously / ★<show+O+v-ing(O가 v하고 있는 것을 보여 주다)>의 수동형 / one (= a car) / 분사구문(= and one ran faster and stopped ~) / ★분사구문의 의미상 주어(one)와 문장의 주어(two toy cars)가 서로 달라 의미상의 주어를 생략하지 않음.)

한 대표적인 실험에서 / 두 대의 장난감 자동차가 같은 시간에 달리고 있는 것이 보여졌는데 / 평행 경주로에서 / 한 대가 더 빠르게 달려 경주로 더 멀리 아래쪽에 멈춰 섰다

↳ **실험 내용:** 두 대의 장난감 자동차가 같은 시간에 달리는데, 한 대가 더 빨리 달려 더 멀리에 멈춰 섰음.

[3]The children were then asked / to judge // whether the cars had run for the same time / and to justify their judgment.

(S: The children / V: were ... asked / C_1(to-v구 병렬): to judge ... / C_2(to-v구 병렬): to justify their judgment / to judge의 O(명사절): whether ... time)

그리고 나서 아이들은 요청받았다 / 판단하도록 // 그 자동차들이 같은 시간 동안 달렸는지를 / 그리고 자신들의 판단이 옳음을 보여주도록

↳ 아이들에게 장난감 자동차들이 같은 시간 동안 달렸는지를 판단하고 증명하도록 요청함.

주제문

[4]Preschoolers and young school-age children confuse temporal and spatial dimensions: //

(🔑 아이들은 시간 차원과 공간 차원을 혼동함. / S_1: Preschoolers and young school-age children / V_1: confuse / O: temporal and spatial dimensions)

미취학 아동과 어린 학령기 아동은 시간 차원과 공간 차원을 혼동한다 //

Starting times are judged by starting points, / stopping times (are judged) by stopping points / and durations (are judged) by distance, // though each (of these errors) does not necessitate the others.

(S_2: Starting times / V_2: are judged / S_3: stopping times / V_3 생략 / S_4: durations / V_4 생략 / 부사절 접속사(양보): though / S'(단수): each / V'(단수): does not necessitate / O': the others)

시작 시각은 시작 지점에 의해 판단된다 / 정지 시각은 정지 지점에 의해 (판단된다) / 그리고 지속 시간은 거리에 의해 (판단된다) // 각각이 (이 오류들의) 나머지 오류들을 필연적으로 동반하지는 않지만

↳ **실험 결과:** 아이들이 시간과 공간 개념을 혼동함.

[5]Hence, / a child may claim // that the cars started and stopped running together (correct) / and that *the car* [which stopped further ahead], / ran for more time (incorrect).

(S: a child / V: may claim / 명사절 접속사: that / S'_1: the cars / V'_1: started and stopped / O': running together / may claim의 O_1(명사절) / may claim의 O_2(명사절) / 명사절 접속사: that / S'_2: the car / 주격 관계대명사: which / V'_2: ran / 🔑 자동차 두 대 중 한 대가 더 멀리서 멈춤.)

따라서 / 아이는 (~라고) 주장할 수도 있다 // 그 자동차들이 같이 달리기 시작해서 멈췄다고 (옳음) / 그리고 자동차가 [더 멀리 앞에 멈춘] / 더 오랜 시간 동안 달렸다고 (틀림)

↳ **실험 결과의 부연 설명:** 장난감 자동차 두 대를 동시에 출발시키고 멈추게 한 것은 옳게 인식하면서, 더 빨리 달려 더 멀리에 멈춘 자동차가 더 오래 달렸다고 틀리게 판단할 수 있음.

해석

[1]스위스의 심리학자 Jean Piaget는 짝 지은 사건들에 걸리는 시간을 비교하거나 추정하는 아이들의 능력을 통해 그들의 시간 개념을 자주 분석했다. [2]한 대표적인 실험에서, 두 대의 장난감 자동차가 같은 시간에 평행 경주로에서 달리고 있는 것이 보여졌는데, 한 대가 더 빠르게 달려 경주로 더 멀리 아래쪽에 멈춰 섰다. [3]그러고 나서 아이들은 그 자동차들이 같은 시간 동안 달렸는지를 판단하고 자신들의 판단이 옳음을 보여주도록 요청받았다. [4]미취학 아동과 어린 학령기 아동은 시간 차원과 공간 차원을 혼동하는데, 이 오류들의 각각이 나머지 오류들을 필연적으로 동반하지는 않지만 시작 시각은 시작 지점에 의해, 정지 시각은 정지 지점에 의해, 그리고 지속 시간은 거리에 의해 판단된다. [5]따라서 아이는 그 자동차들이 같이 달리기 시작해서 멈췄고 (옳음) 더 멀리 앞에 멈춘 자동차가 더 오랜 시간 동안 달렸다고 (틀림) 주장할 수도 있다.

어휘

psychologist 심리학자
conception 개념, 관념; 구상
estimate 추정하다; 추정, 추산
typical 대표적인, 전형적인; 일반적인
parallel 평행의
justify 옳음을 보여 주다; 정당화하다
preschooler 미취학 아동
school-age 학령기의
confuse 혼동하다; 혼란스럽게 만들다
temporal 시간의; 속세의; 일시적인
spatial 공간의
dimension 차원; 규모
duration 지속 시간
necessitate 필연적으로 동반하다; 필요로 하다
[선택지] alternate 번갈아 하다; 번갈아 하는
identical 동일한

정답 가이드

빈칸 문장은 구체적인 실험 내용에 해당하므로 이어지는 실험 결과를 통해 빈칸을 추론해야 한다. 아동은 시간 차원과 공간 차원을 혼동하여, 실험에서 두 대의 자동차가 같은 시간을 달리고 멈췄어도 그 중 더 멀리 앞에 멈춘 자동차가 더 오래 달렸다고 주장할 수도 있다고 했다. 따라서 구체적인 실험 내용에 자동차 한 대가 더 멀리 가서 멈춘 내용이 있어야 하므로 빈칸에 들어갈 말로 가장 적절한 것은 ① 'one running faster and stopping further down the track(한 대가 더 빠르게 달려 경주로 더 멀리 아래쪽에 멈춰 섰다)'이다.

오답 클리닉

② both stopping at the same point further than expected (13%)
두 대 모두 예상보다 더 먼 곳의 같은 지점에서 멈춰 섰다
두 대 중 더 멀리 앞에 멈춘 자동차가 더 오래 달렸다고 틀리게 판단했으므로 두 대가 모두 같은 지점에서 멈췄다는 것은 틀림.

③ one keeping the same speed as the other to the end (6%)
한 대는 다른 한 대와 끝까지 같은 속도를 유지했다
두 대가 같이 출발하고 멈췄는데, 한 대가 더 멀리 간 것은 속도가 더 빨랐기 때문임을 알 수 있음.

④ both alternating their speed but arriving at the same end (12%)
두 대 모두 번갈아 속도를 바꿨지만 같은 목표점에 도착했다
한 대가 더 먼 지점에 멈췄다고 했으므로 틀림.

⑤ both slowing their speed and reaching the identical spot (4%)
두 대 모두 속도를 늦춰 동일한 지점에 도착했다
한 대가 더 먼 지점에 멈췄다고 했으므로 틀림.

03 + 글의 순서 〈 21학년도 대수능 36번 | 정답률 76% 〉 ②

구문분석 & 직독직해

정치 전쟁의 정치적 목표

[1]The objective of battle, / to "throw" the enemy and to make him defenseless, /
S =
전투의 목표는 / 즉 적군을 '맹렬히 쓰러뜨려' 무방비하게 만드는 것 /

may temporarily blind commanders and even strategists / to the larger purpose of war.
V O
일시적으로 지휘관과 심지어 전략가까지도 보지 못하게 만들 수도 있다 / 전쟁의 더 큰 목적을

*<nor+V+S>는 '~도 (또한) 아니다'의 의미로 부정어 nor 뒤에 도치가 일어남.

[2]War is never an isolated act, // nor is it ever only one decision.
S V C 부정어 V S(= war) C
전쟁은 결코 단일 행위가 아니다 // 또한 단 하나의 결정도 결코 아니다

↳ **도입:** 전쟁에는 적군을 쓰러뜨리는 것보다 더 큰 목표가 있으며, 전쟁은 단일한 이유로 일어나지 않음.

주제문 ⊶ 주어진 글에서 언급한 전쟁의 더 큰 목적을 설명함.

(B) [3]In the real world, / war's larger purpose is always a political purpose.
S V C
현실 세계에서 / 전쟁의 더 큰 목적은 언제나 정치적 목적이다

[4]It transcends the use of force.
S V O
그것은 물리력의 사용을 초월한다

[5]This insight was famously captured / by Clausewitz's most famous phrase, // "War is a mere continuation of politics / by other means."
S V S' V' C'
이 통찰은 훌륭하게 표현되었다 / Clausewitz의 가장 유명한 한마디에 의해 // "전쟁은 단지 정치를 계속하는 것에 불과하다 / 다른 수단으로"라는

↳ 전쟁의 더 큰 목적은 정치적 목적이며, 전쟁은 정치의 다른 수단일 뿐임.

⊶ (B)에서 언급된 전쟁의 정치적 목적을 부연 설명하며 정치적 목적의 조건을 제시함.

(A) [6]To be political, / a political entity or a representative of a political entity, // whatever its constitutional form (is), / has to have an intention, a will.
목적(~하려면) S(단수) 양보 부사절 (= no matter what ~) V(단수) O =
정치적이려면 / 정치적 실체나 정치적 실체의 대표자는 // 그 조직상의 형태가 무엇이든지 / 의도, 즉 의지가 있어야 한다

↳ **정치적 목적의 조건 1:** 의지(의도)가 있어야 함.

[7]That intention has to be clearly expressed.
S V
그 의도는 분명히 표현되어야 한다

↳ **정치적 목적의 조건 2:** 의도가 분명히 표현되어야 함.

해석

[1]전투의 목표, 즉 적군을 '맹렬히 쓰러뜨려' 무방비하게 만드는 것은 일시적으로 지휘관과 심지어 전략가까지도 전쟁의 더 큰 목적을 보지 못하게 만들 수도 있다. [2]전쟁은 결코 단일 행위가 아니며, 또한 단 하나의 결정도 결코 아니다. (B) [3]현실 세계에서 전쟁의 더 큰 목적은 언제나 정치적 목적이다. [4]그것은 물리력의 사용을 초월한다. [5]이 통찰은 "전쟁은 다른 수단으로 단지 정치를 계속하는 것에 불과하다."라는 Clausewitz의 가장 유명한 한마디에 의해 훌륭하게 표현되었다. (A) [6]정치적이려면, 정치적 실체나 정치적 실체의 대표자는, 그 조직상의 형태가 무엇이든지, 의도, 즉 의지가 있어야 한다. [7]그 의도는 분명히 표현되어야 한다. (C) [8]그리고 한쪽의 의지는 대치하는 동안 어느 시점에 적에게 전달되어야 한다(그것이 공개적으로 전달될 필요는 없다). [9]폭력적인 행위와 그것의 더 큰 정치적 의도는 또한 대치하는 동안 어느 시점에 한쪽의 탓으로 돌려져야 한다. [10]역사는 궁극적 귀인이 없는 전쟁 행위에 대해 알지 못한다.(▶ 역사상 궁극적 귀인(정치적 목적)이 없는 전쟁은 존재하지 않는다는 의미)

어휘

objective 목표; 객관적인
throw 맹렬히 쓰러뜨리다; 던지다
defenseless 무방비의, 방어할 수 없는
temporarily 일시적으로
blind A to B A에게 B를 보지 못하게 만들다
commander 지휘관, 사령관
strategist 전략가
isolated 단 하나[한 번]의; 외딴; 고립된

(A)의 마지막 문장을 부연 설명함.

(C) [8]And / one side's will has to be transmitted to the enemy / at some point / during the confrontation // (it does not have to be publicly communicated).

S (= one side's will) V S' V'

그리고 / 한쪽의 의지는 적에게 전달되어야 한다 / 어느 시점에 / 대치하는 동안 //
(그것(한쪽의 의지)이 공개적으로 전달될 필요는 없다)

↳ **부연 설명:** 한쪽의 의지가 반드시 적에게 전달되어야 함.

★<attribute A to B(A를 B의 탓으로 돌리다)>의 수동형

[9]A violent act and its larger political intention / must also be attributed to one side / at some point / during the confrontation.

S V

폭력적인 행위와 그것의 더 큰 정치적 의도는 / 또한 한쪽의 탓으로 돌려져야 한다 / 어느 시점에 / 대치하는 동안

↳ **정치적 목적의 조건 3:** 폭력적 행위와 정치적 의도가 한쪽의 탓으로 돌려져야 함.

[10]History does not know / of acts of war (without eventual attribution).

S V

역사는 알지 못한다 / 전쟁 행위에 대해 (궁극적인 귀인이 없는)

↳ 모든 전쟁에는 궁극적 귀인(정치적 목적)이 있음.

famously 훌륭하게, 멋지게
capture 표현[포착]하다; 붙잡다
phrase (간결한) 한마디; 어구
mere 단지 ~에 불과한; 단순한
continuation 계속; 존속
representative 대표(자); 대표하는
constitutional 조직상의; 헌법(상)의; 합법적인
transmit 전달하다; 전송하다
confrontation 대치, 대립
publicly 공개적으로
eventual 궁극[최종]적인
attribution 귀인, (원인에) 돌리기; 속성

정답 가이드

전투의 목표가 전쟁의 더 큰 목적을 보지 못하게 할 수 있다는 주어진 글 뒤에는 그 전쟁의 더 큰 목적이 정치적 목적이라고 설명하는 (B)가 이어져야 한다. 그런 다음, 목적이 정치적이려면 정치적 실체 및 대표자는 의도(의지)를 가져야 하고 그 의도는 분명히 표현되어야 한다고 설명하는 (A)가 오고, 이를 And로 연결하여 한쪽의 의지가 적에게 전달되어야 한다는 것을 첨언하는 (C)가 마지막에 오는 것이 가장 적절하다.

오답 클리닉

① (A) - (C) - (B) (2%)
주어진 글에는 전쟁이 정치적 목적을 갖는다는 내용이 없으므로, 정치적 목적을 구체적으로 설명하는 (A)가 바로 이어질 수 없다.
③ (B) - (C) - (A) (9%)
And로 연결되는 (C)의 첫 문장은 (A)의 마지막 문장을 부연 설명하므로, (C)는 (A) 뒤에 와야 한다.
④ (C) - (A) - (B) (5%) / ⑤ (C) - (B) - (A) (7%)
(C)는 전쟁의 정치적 목적의 조건을 구체적으로 설명하므로, 주어진 글 바로 뒤에 올 수 없다.

01 ✦ 필자 주장 〈22학년도 대수능 20번 | 정답률 83%〉 ③

구문분석 & 직독직해

비즈니스 목표에 중점을 둔 기업 소셜 미디어 활용의 필요성

★<consider v-ing>: v할 것을 고려하다

[1] One of *the most common mistakes* (made by organizations // when they first consider experimenting with social media) is // that they focus too much on social media tools and platforms / and not (focus) enough on their business objectives.

(S: One of ~ social media) / V: is / 부사절 접속사 (= organizations) / is의 C(명사절))

가장 일반적인 실수 중 하나는 ~이다 (조직에 의해 행해지는 // 그들이 소셜 미디어로 실험하는 것을 처음 고려할 때) // 그들이 소셜 미디어 도구와 플랫폼에 너무 지나치게 중점을 두는 것 / 그리고 조직의 사업 목표에는 충분히 중점을 두지 않는 것

🔑 기업의 소셜 미디어가 사업 목표에 중점을 두지 않는 것이 문제임.

↳ **문제점:** 조직이 사업 목표보다 소셜 미디어 자체에 더 중점을 둠.

주제문

[2] The reality of success (in the social web for businesses) / is // that creating a social media program begins / not with insight into the latest social media tools and channels / but with a thorough understanding (of the organization's own goals and objectives).

(S / V / is의 C(명사절) / 명사절 접속사 / S′ / V′ / ★<not A but B>: A가 아니라 B / 전치사구 병렬)

성공의 실제는 (기업을 위한 소셜 웹에서) / 이다 // 소셜 미디어 프로그램을 만드는 것이 시작된다는 것 / 최신 소셜 미디어 도구와 채널에 대한 통찰력으로가 아니라 / 철저한 이해로 (조직 자체의 목적과 목표에 대한)

🔑 조직의 목표를 이해하고 소셜 미디어를 만들어야 함.

↳ **해결책:** 조직의 목표 이해를 바탕으로 소셜 미디어를 사용해야 성공할 수 있음.

[3] A social media program / is not merely the fulfillment (of a vague need (to manage a "presence" on popular social networks // because "everyone else is doing it."))

(S / V / C / =)

소셜 미디어 프로그램은 / 그저 충족이 아니다 (막연한 필요의 (인기 소셜 네트워크상에서 '존재'를 관리해야 하는 // '다른 모두가 하고 있기' 때문에)

[4] "Being in social media" / serves no purpose / in and of itself.

'소셜 미디어에 있는 것'은 / 아무 도움이 되지 않는다 / 그 자체로는

↳ **해결책 상술:** 목적이 없는 기업 소셜 계정 운영은 의미가 없음.

★<either A or B>: A와 B 둘 중 하나

[5] In order to serve any purpose at all, / a social media presence must either solve a problem for the organization and its customers / or result in an improvement of some sort (preferably a measurable one).

(목적(~하기 위해) / S / V_1 / O_1 / V_2 / O_2 / (= improvement))

🔑 기업이 소셜 미디어로 달성해야 할 목적이 드러남.

조금이라도 어떤 도움이 되기 위해 / 소셜 미디어상의 존재는 조직과 조직의 고객을 위해 문제를 해결해야 한다 / 또는 어떤 종류의 개선(되도록 측정 가능한 개선)이라는 결과를 내야 한다

↳ 조직의 소셜 미디어는 문제 해결 또는 개선과 같은 목적을 달성해야 함.

[6] In all things, / purpose drives success.

(S / V / O)

어떤 일이든 / 목적이 성공을 이끌어낸다

[7] The world of social media is no different.

소셜 미디어의 세계도 다르지 않다

↳ **맺음말(결론):** 목적을 가지고 소셜 미디어를 활용해야 함.

해석

[1] 소셜 미디어로 실험하는 것을 처음 고려할 때 조직에 의해 행해지는 가장 일반적인 실수 중 하나는 그들이 소셜 미디어 도구와 플랫폼에 너무 지나치게 중점을 두고 조직의 사업 목표에는 충분히 중점을 두지 않는 것이다. [2] 기업을 위한 소셜 웹에서 성공의 실제는 소셜 미디어 프로그램을 만드는 것이 최신 소셜 미디어 도구와 채널에 대한 통찰력으로가 아니라 조직 자체의 목적과 목표에 대한 철저한 이해로 시작된다는 것이다. [3] 소셜 미디어 프로그램은 그저 '다른 모두가 하고 있기' 때문에 인기 소셜 네트워크상에서 '존재'를 관리해야 하는 막연한 필요의 충족이 아니다. [4] '소셜 미디어에 있는 것'은 그 자체로는 아무 도움이 되지 않는다. [5] 조금이라도 어떤 도움이 되기 위해, 소셜 미디어상의 존재는 조직과 조직의 고객을 위해 문제를 해결하거나 어떤 종류의 개선(되도록 측정 가능한 개선)이라는 결과를 내야 한다. [6] 어떤 일이든, 목적이 성공을 이끌어낸다. [7] 소셜 미디어의 세계도 다르지 않다.

어휘

organization 조직(체), 기구; 구조; 구성
platform 플랫폼 ((누구나 사용할 수 있는 정보 시스템을 제공하는 기반 서비스))
objective 목표; 객관적인
insight 통찰력; 이해, 간파
thorough 철저한, 빈틈없는
merely 그저, 단지
fulfillment 충족, 실현; 이행
vague 막연한, 모호한; 희미한
manage 관리[운영]하다; 간신히 해내다
serve a purpose 도움이 되다, 유용하다
in and of itself 그것 자체로는
result in (결과적으로) ~을 낳다[야기하다]
improvement 개선, 향상
preferably 되도록, 가급적이면; 차라리
measurable 측정할 수 있는; 예측 가능한
drive 이끌어내다, 추진시키다; (어떤 방향으로) 몰다

정답 가이드

조직이 소셜 미디어 프로그램을 만들 때 사업 목표가 아닌 소셜 미디어 도구나 플랫폼 자체에 중점을 두는 문제점을 지적하며, 성공하기 위해서는 조직의 목표에 대한 철저한 이해를 바탕으로 문제를 해결하거나 개선을 가져올 수 있도록 소셜 미디어를 운영해야 한다고 했다. 따라서 필자가 주장하는 바로 가장 적절한 것은 ③ '기업은 소셜 미디어를 활용할 때 사업 목표를 토대로 해야 한다.'이다.

오답 클리닉

① 기업 이미지에 부합(×)하는 소셜 미디어를 직접 개발(×)하여 운영해야 한다. (6%)
기업이 소셜 미디어를 활용하는 것에 대한 내용이지만 기업 이미지에 맞는 미디어를 직접 개발해야 한다는 내용은 언급되지 않음.

The 주의 문장 2에 소셜 미디어 프로그램을 만든다는 내용이 있으나 뒤에 이어지는 내용을 통해 프로그램의 '개발'이 아닌 소셜 미디어 프로그램 사용을 시작하는 것으로 이해하는 것이 적절하다.

② 기업은 사회적 가치와 요구를 반영(×)하여 사업 목표를 수립해야 한다. (5%)
기업이 소셜 미디어를 활용할 때 조직 목표에 중점을 둬야 한다는 내용은 있으나, 이 목표에 사회적 가치와 요구를 반영해야 한다는 내용은 없음.

④ 소셜 미디어로 제품을 홍보(×)할 때는 구체적인 정보를 제공해야 한다. (2%)
소셜 미디어로 제품을 홍보하는 내용이 아님.

⑤ 소비자의 의견을 수렴(×)하기 위해 소셜 미디어를 적극 활용해야 한다. (4%)
소비자의 의견 수렴이 아닌 문제 해결과 개선을 위해 활용해야 한다고 했음.

02 + 빈칸 추론 〈20학년도 대수능 31번 | 정답률 41%〉 ②

구문분석 & 직독직해

철학 과학만능주의와 과학 철학

[1]The role of science can sometimes be overstated, / with its advocates slipping / into scientism.
(S: The role of science / V: can sometimes be overstated / <with+O+v-ing.>: O가 ~하면서)
과학의 역할은 때때로 과장될 수 있다 / 그것의 옹호자들이 빠지면서 / 과학만능주의에

[2]Scientism is the view // that the scientific description (of reality) / is *the only truth* [(that) there is]. 🔑 과학적 서술만 진실로 여김.
(S: Scientism / V: is / C: the view = 동격 접속사 that / S′: the scientific description / V′: is / C′: the only truth / 주격 관계대명사 생략)
과학만능주의는 견해이다 // 과학적 서술이 (현실에 대한) / 유일한 진실이라는 [존재하는]
↳ 과학만능주의는 과학적 설명만을 진실로 여김.

[3]With the advance of science, / there has been a tendency (to slip into scientism, / and (to) assume // that any factual claim can be authenticated // if and only if the term 'scientific' can correctly be ascribed / to it). ★<ascribe A to B(A가 B에 속한다고 생각하다)>의 수동형
(V: has been / S: a tendency / (to) assume의 O(명사절) / 명사절 접속사 that / S′: any factual claim / V′: can be authenticated / 부사절 접속사(조건) if and only if / S″: the term 'scientific' / V″: can correctly be ascribed / it = factual claim)
과학의 발전과 함께 / 경향이 있어 왔다 (과학만능주의에 빠지는 / 그리고 간주하는 // 사실에 입각한 어떠한 주장도 입증될 수 있다고 // '과학적'이라는 용어가 정확하게 속하는 것으로 생각될 수 있는 경우에 그리고 오직 그런 경우에만 / 그것(사실에 입각한 주장)에)
↳ **문제점:** '과학적'이란 용어가 들어가야 사실에 입각한 주장이 입증될 수 있다고 생각함.

[4]The consequence is // that non-scientific approaches (to reality) — //
(S: The consequence / V: is / is의 C(명사절) / 명사절 접속사 that / S′: non-scientific approaches)
결과는 ~이다 // 비과학적 접근 방식은 ~라는 것 (현실에 대한) //

and that can include / all the arts, religion, / and personal, emotional and value-laden ways (of encountering the world) — /
(S″: that (= 의미상 non-scientific approaches를 지칭) / V″: can include / O″: all the arts, ... ways / of의 O(동명사구))
그리고 그것은 포함할 수 있다 / 모든 예술, 종교를 / 그리고 개인적, 감정적, 가치 판단적인 방식을 (세상을 접하는) /

may become labelled / as merely subjective, / and therefore of little account / in terms of describing *the way* [(that) the world is]. 🔑 비과학적 접근 방식을 경시함.
(V′: may become labelled / 전치사(~로(서)) as / C′: merely subjective / ★<of+추상명사>는 형용사로 쓰임. / in terms of: ~라는 면에서 / 관계부사 생략)
꼬리표가 붙여질지도 모른다(는 것) / 그저 주관적일 뿐이라고 / 그리고 따라서 거의 중요하지 않다고 / 방식을 서술하는 면에서 [세상이 존재하는]
↳ **결과:** 현실에 대한 비과학적 접근은 주관적이어서 중요하지 않은 것으로 여겨질 수 있음.

[5]The philosophy of science seeks / to avoid crude scientism / and (to) get a balanced view (on what the scientific method can and cannot achieve).
(S: The philosophy of science / V: seeks / O(to-v구 병렬) / on의 O(명사절))
과학 철학은 노력한다 / 투박한 과학만능주의를 피하려고 / 그리고 균형 잡힌 생각을 가지려고 (과학적 방법이 성취할 수 있는 것과 성취할 수 없는 것에 관해)
↳ **대안책:** 과학 철학은 과학만능주의를 지양하고 균형 잡힌 시각을 가지려 노력함.

해석

[1]과학의 역할은 그것의 옹호자들이 과학만능주의에 빠지면서 때때로 과장될 수 있다. [2]과학만능주의는 현실에 대한 과학적 서술이 존재하는 유일한 진실이라는 견해이다. [3]과학의 발전과 함께, 과학만능주의에 빠져 '과학적'이라는 용어가 정확하게 사실에 입각한 주장에 속하는 것으로 생각될 수 있는 경우에 그리고 오직 그런 경우에만 사실에 입각한 어떠한 주장도 입증될 수 있다고 간주하는 경향이 있어 왔다. [4]그 결과, 현실에 대한 비과학적 접근 방식은 모든 예술, 종교, 그리고 세상을 접하는 개인적, 감정적, 가치 판단적인 방식을 포함할 수 있는데, 그저 주관적일 뿐이고, 따라서 세상이 존재하는 방식을 서술하는 면에서 거의 중요하지 않다고 꼬리표가 붙여질지도 모른다. [5]과학 철학은 투박한 과학만능주의를 피하고 과학적 방법이 성취할 수 있는 것과 성취할 수 없는 것에 관한 균형 잡힌 생각을 가지려고 노력한다.

어휘

overstate 과장하다
advocate 옹호자; 지지[옹호]하다
slip (좋지 못한 상황에) 빠지다; 미끄러지다
scientism 과학만능주의
description 서술, 기술, 묘사
cf. describe 서술하다, 말하다
advance 발전, 진전; 나아가게 하다
assume 간주하다, 가정하다
factual 사실에 입각한; 실제의
authenticate 입증하다; 인증하다
term 용어; 기간; 학기
value-laden 가치 판단적인
encounter 접하다[마주치다]; 만남
label 꼬리표를 붙이다; 분류하다
subjective 주관적인
account 중요성, 가치; 설명; 계좌

정답 가이드

빈칸 문장은 The consequence is that ~으로 시작하여 '결과'를 이끌며, 요약하면 비과학적 접근 방식은 주관적인 것에 불과하여 세상이 존재하는 방식을 서술하는 면에서 거의 '~하지' 않다는 것이다. 문맥상 과학 철학이 균형 잡힌 생각을 가지려고 노력한다는 이어지는 설명과는 대조되는 부정적 내용의 문장이어야 한다. 빈칸 문장의 결과가 무엇을 근거로 하는지 앞부분 내용을 보면, 과학만능주의에 의해 과학의 역할이 과장될 수 있는데, 이는 현실에 대한 과학적 서술만이 유일한 진실이라는 견해이며, 과학의 발전에 따라 사람들이 그 견해에 빠져 들었다고 했다. 그 결과, 비과학적 접근 방식은 주관적일 뿐이고, 세상이 존재하는 방식을 기술할 때 '중요하지 않다'는 문맥이 되어야 하므로, 빈칸에 들어갈 말로 가장 적절한 것은 ② 'account(중요성)'이다.

The 주의 앞에 준부정어 little(거의 ~않는)이 있어 빈칸을 부정하는 의미가 됨에 주의한다.

오답 클리닉

① question (18%) 의문
의문이 거의 없다는 것은 과학만능주의에 입각한 견해이므로 글의 내용과 반대됨.
③ controversy (9%) 논쟁
비과학적 접근 방식이 주관적이라고 했으므로 논쟁의 여지가 없다고 볼 수 없음.
④ variation (15%) 변화
비과학적인 접근 방식의 변화 유무는 언급되지 않음.
⑤ bias (17%) 편견
비과학적 접근 방식이 주관적이라고 했으므로 편견이 없다고 볼 수 없음.

03 + 문장 넣기 〈21학년도 대수능 38번 | 정답률 53%〉 ④

구문분석 & 직독직해

언어 'bad'와 'wicked'의 차이

[1]Imagine // (that) I tell you // that Maddy is bad.
(Imagine: V(명령문) / (that) ~: imagine의 O(명사절) / I: S′ / tell: V′ / you: IO′ / that Maddy is bad: DO′(명사절))
생각해 보라 // 내가 여러분에게 말한다고 // Maddy가 나쁘다고

[2]Perhaps you infer / from my intonation, or the context [in which we are talking], // that I mean (she is) morally bad.
(you: S / infer: V / my intonation, or the context: from의 O(명사구 병렬) / in which: 전치사+관계대명사(= where) / that: 명사절 접속사, infer의 O(명사절) / I: S′ / mean: V′ / (she is) morally bad: O′)
여러분은 추론할지도 모른다 / 나의 억양이나 맥락으로부터 [우리가 말하고 있는] // 내가 (그녀가) 도덕적으로 나쁘다는 것을 뜻한다고

[3]Additionally, / you will probably infer // that I am disapproving of Maddy, / or (I am) saying // that (I think) you should disapprove of her, or similar, /
(you: S / will infer: V / that: 명사절 접속사, will infer의 O(명사절) / I: S′ / am disapproving: V′1 / (I am) saying: V′2 / (I think): 삽입절 / that ~: saying의 O(명사절))
게다가 / 여러분은 아마 추론할 것이다 // 내가 Maddy를 못마땅해하고 있다고 / 또는 말하고 있다고 // (내가 생각하기에) 여러분이 그녀를 못마땅해하거나 그와 비슷해야 한다고 /

given typical linguistic conventions / and assuming // (that) I am sincere.
(given: 전치사(~을 고려해 볼 때) / assuming: 접속사(~라고 가정하면) / (that) I am sincere: assuming의 O(명사절))
일반적인 언어 관행을 고려해 볼 때 / 그리고 가정한다면 // 내가 진심이라고

↳ **대조 A:** Maddy가 '나쁘다'고 말하면, 보통 그녀가 도덕적으로 나쁘거나 화자가 그녀를 못마땅해한다고 추론함.

(①) [4]However, / you might not get a more detailed sense (of *the particular sorts of way* [in which Maddy is bad], / her typical character traits, / and the like), //
(you: S / might not get: V / a more detailed sense: O / the particular sorts of way: of의 O1(명사구) / in which: 전치사+관계대명사 / her typical character traits: of의 O2(명사구) / the like: of의 O3(명사구))
하지만 / 여러분은 더 자세한 인식을 얻지 못할 수도 있다 (특정 유형의 방식에 대해 [Maddy가 나쁜] / 그녀의 일반적인 성격 특성 / 등(에 대해)) //

since people can be bad / in many ways.
(since: 부사절 접속사(~ 때문에))
사람들이 나쁠 수 있기 때문이다 / 여러 방면에서

↳ **A의 부연 설명:** 사람들은 여러 방면으로 나쁠 수 있기 때문에 Maddy가 정확히 어떤 유형의 나쁜 사람인지는 알 수 없음.

(②) [5]In contrast, / if I say // that Maddy is wicked, // then you get more of a sense (of her typical actions and attitudes / to others).
(if: 부사절 접속사(조건) / say: V′ / that Maddy is wicked: O′(명사절) / you: S / get: V / more of a sense: O)
그에 반해서 / 만일 내가 말한다면 // Maddy는 사악하다고 // 그러면 여러분은 더 많은 인식을 얻게 된다 (그녀의 일반적인 행동과 태도에 대해 / 다른 사람들에 대한)

↳ **대조 B:** Maddy가 '사악하다'고 말하면, 타인에 대한 그녀의 행동과 태도를 더 인식하게 됨.

해석

[1]내가 여러분에게 Maddy가 나쁘다고 말한다고 생각해 보라. [2]아마 여러분은 나의 억양이나 우리가 말하고 있는 맥락으로부터 내가 (그녀가) 도덕적으로 나쁘다는 것을 뜻한다고 추론할지도 모른다. [3]게다가 여러분은 아마, 일반적인 언어 관행을 고려하고 내가 진심이라고 가정한다면, 내가 Maddy를 못마땅해하고 있거나 내가 생각하기에 여러분이 그녀를 못마땅해하거나 그와 비슷해야 한다고 말하고 있다고 추론할 것이다. (①) [4]하지만 여러분은 Maddy가 나쁜 특정 유형의 방식, 그녀의 일반적인 성격 특성 등에 대해 더 자세한 인식을 얻지 못할 수도 있는데, 사람들이 여러 방면에서 나쁠 수 있기 때문이다. (②) [5]그에 반해서, 만일 내가 Maddy는 사악하다고 말한다면, 여러분은 다른 사람들에 대한 그녀의 일반적인 행동과 태도에 대해 더 많은 인식을 얻게 된다. (③) [6]'사악한'이라는 낱말은 '나쁜'보다 더 구체적이다. (④ [7]사악함은 여러 형태를 띠기 때문에 나는 여전히 Maddy의 성격을 정확히 묘사하지 않았다.) [8]그러나 그럼에도 불구하고 더 많은 세부 사항, 아마도 Maddy라는 사람의 유형에 대한 더 두드러진 함축이 있다. (⑤) [9]게다가, 그리고 다시 일반적인 언어 관행을 가정하면, 여러분은 또한, 우리가 여전히 그녀의 도덕적 성격을 논의하고 있다고 가정하면서, 내가 Maddy를 못마땅해하고 있다고, 또는 여러분이 그녀를 못마땅해하거나 그와 비슷해야 한다고 말하고 있다는 인식을 얻을 것이다.

어휘

infer 추론[추측]하다
intonation 억양
context 맥락; 문맥
morally 도덕적으로
cf. moral 도덕적인

🔑 '사악한'이 '나쁜'보다 더 구체적임.

(③) [6]The word 'wicked' is more specific / than 'bad'.

'사악한'이라는 낱말은 더 구체적이다 / '나쁜'보다

🔑 '사악한'이 더 구체적인 표현이어도 Maddy의 성격을 정확히 나타낸 것은 아님.

(④) [7]I have still not exactly pinpointed Maddy's character // since wickedness takes many forms.)

나는 여전히 Maddy의 성격을 정확히 묘사하지 않았다 // 사악함은 여러 형태를 띠기 때문에

↳ B의 부연 설명: '나쁜'보다 '사악한'이라는 낱말이 더 구체적이긴 하지만, Maddy의 성격을 정확히 나타내지는 못함.

🔑 정확하게 묘사한 것은 아니더라도 그 사람의 유형에 대한 세부 사항을 파악할 수 있음.

[8]But / there is more detail nevertheless, / perhaps a stronger connotation (of *the sort of person* [(that) Maddy is]).

관계대명사 생략

그러나 / 그럼에도 불구하고 더 많은 세부 사항이 있다 / 아마도 더 두드러진 함축 (사람의 유형에 대한 [Maddy라는])

(⑤) [9]In addition, / and again assuming typical linguistic conventions, / you should also get a sense // that I am disapproving of Maddy, /

분사구문(if you assume ~) / 동격 접속사

게다가 / 그리고 다시 일반적인 언어 관행을 가정하면 / 여러분은 또한 인식을 얻을 것이다 // 내가 Maddy를 못마땅해하고 있다는 /

or saying // that you should disapprove of her, or similar, / assuming // that we are still discussing her moral character.

saying의 O(명사절) / 분사구문(= as you assume ~) / 현재분사 assuming의 O(명사절)

또는 말하고 있다는 // 여러분이 그녀를 못마땅해하거나 그와 비슷해야 한다고 / 가정하면서 // 우리가 여전히 그녀의 도덕적 성격을 논의하고 있다고

↳ 부연 설명(재반박): 그럼에도 불구하고 '사악하다'는 표현에는 더 많은 세부 사항과 함축이 있음.

disapprove 못마땅해하다; 승인하지 않다
typical 일반적인; 전형적인
linguistic 언어(학)의
convention 관행, 관습
assume 가정[추정]하다; 맡다
sincere 진심 어린, 진실된
detailed 자세한
cf. detail 세부 사항
sense 인식, 인지
sort 유형, 종류, 부류
character 성격
trait 특성, 특징
and the like 등 ((etc.보다 형식적인 표현))
wicked 사악한, 못된
cf. wickedness 사악함
specific 구체적인; 특정한
pinpoint 정확히 묘사[기술]하다; 정확히 찾아내다

정답 가이드

주어진 문장은 '사악함(wickedness)'이 여러 형태가 있으므로 Maddy의 성격이 사악하다고 하는 것은 여전히 그녀의 성격을 정확히 설명하는 것이 아니라는 내용이다. 즉 주어진 문장은 '사악한'이라는 낱말 사용에 관한 내용이므로 관련 설명이 시작하는 ② 이후에 들어가야 한다. ④ 앞에서는 '사악한'이라는 낱말이 '나쁜'보다 더 구체적이라고 했는데, 그 뒤에 더 많은 세부 사항이 있다는 같은 맥락의 내용이 역접 연결어 But과 nevertheless로 이어지는 것은 부자연스럽다. 흐름상 ④의 앞 문장을 여전히 Maddy의 성격을 정확하게 묘사한 것은 아니라고 주어진 문장이 부정한 다음, 주어진 문장을 ④ 뒤의 문장이 다시 반박하는 흐름이 적절하다. 따라서 주어진 문장이 들어가기에 가장 적절한 곳은 ④이다.

오답 클리닉

① (2%) '나쁜'이라는 낱말 사용에 관한 내용이다.

② (9%) '나쁜'과 대조되는 '사악한'이라는 낱말 사용에 대해 In contrast로 설명을 시작하는 내용이다.

③ (16%) Maddy가 사악하다는 말을 들었을 때, 다른 사람들에 대한 그녀의 행동과 태도를 더 많이 인식할 수 있게 된다는 앞 문장의 내용을 '사악한'이라는 낱말이 더 구체적인 의미를 전달해서라고 부연 설명하는 것은 자연스럽다.

⑤ (19%) 첨가를 나타내는 In addition(게다가)을 사용하여 일반적인 언어 관행이나 도덕적 성격을 논하는 상황을 가정할 때 우리가 인식하게 되는 것을 덧붙이는 내용은 자연스럽다.

01 + 요약문 〈21학년도 대수능 40번 | 정답률 57%〉 ③

구문분석 & 직독직해 문화 문화 간 정치권력의 개념 차이

[1]From a cross-cultural perspective / the equation (between public leadership and dominance) / is questionable.
S V C
비교 문화적 관점에서 / 동일시는 (공적 리더십과 지배의) / 의문의 여지가 있다
↳ **도입:** 비교 문화적 관점에서 대중적인 지도력과 지배력은 같지 않음.

[2]What does one mean / by 'dominance'?
의미하려는 바는 무엇인가 / '지배'로

[3]Does it indicate coercion? // Or control (over 'the most valued')?
(it = dominance) ★<the+형용사>: ~한 것[사람들]
그것(지배)은 강제를 나타내는가? // 아니면 통제(를 나타내는가) ('가장 가치 있는 것'에 대한)
↳ **질문:** 지배력은 강제인가 혹은 가치 있는 것에 대한 통제인가?

주제문
[4]'Political' systems may be / about both, either, or conceivably neither.
'정치' 체제는 ~일 수도 있다 / 둘 다에 관한 것, 둘 중 하나에 관한 것, 아니면 아마도 어느 쪽에 관한 것도 아닐
↳ **대답:** 정치적 체제가 강제나 통제에 관한 것인지 정해진 것은 없음.

[5]The idea (of 'control') / would be a bothersome one / for many peoples, //
S = V C (one = idea)
생각은 ('통제'라는) / 괴로운 생각일 것이다 / 많은 민족들에게 //
as (for instance) among many native peoples of *Amazonia* [where all members (of a community) / are fond of their personal autonomy / and notably allergic / to any obvious expression (of control or coercion)].
(as 전치사(~처럼)) 삽입어구 ★<as among ~>: ~사이에서처럼 관계부사 S' V' C'1 C'2
(예를 들어) 아마존의 많은 원주민 부족들 사이에서처럼 [모든 구성원이 (공동체의) / 개인의 자율을 좋아하는 / 그리고 특히 몹시 싫어하는 / 어떤 명백한 표현도 (통제나 강제의)]
↳ **세부 사항 1('통제'라는 생각):** 아마존 원주민 부족과 같은 많은 민족들이 통제를 싫어함.

[6]The conception (of political power / as a *coercive* force), / (while it may be a Western fixation), / is not a universal. 🔑 (B) '강제적인' 힘으로서의 정치권력은 보편적인 것이 아님.
S = 양보 부사절 삽입 V C
개념은 (정치권력이라는 / '강제적' 힘으로서의) / (서양의 고정관념일지도 모르겠지만) / 보편적인 것이 아니다
↳ **세부 사항 2('강제적인' 힘으로서의 정치권력):** 서양의 고정관념으로 보편적인 것이 아님.

[7]It is very unusual / for an Amazonian leader to give an order.
가주어 to-v의 의미상 주어 진주어(to-v구)
(~은) 아주 드물다 / 아마존의 지도자가 명령을 내리는 것은

★<view A as B>: A를 B로 여기다[생각하다] ★<nor>: ((부정문 뒤)) ~도 또한 아니다
[8]If many peoples do not view political power / as a coercive force, / nor *as the most valued domain*, //
부사절 접속사(조건) 전치사구 병렬
많은 부족원이 정치권력을 여기지 않는다면 / 강제적인 힘으로 / 또한 '가장 가치 있는 영역'으로도 //
then the leap (from 'the political' to 'domination' (as coercion), / *and from there* to 'domination of women'), / is a shaky one. 🔑 (A) 서양과 달리 아마존에서 '정치적인 것'에서 '지배'로의 비약은 불안정한 것임.
S (there = 'domination') 전치사구 병렬 V C (one = leap)
그렇다면 비약은 ('정치적인 것'에서 (강제로서의) '지배'로 / '그리고 거기(지배)에서' '여성에 대한 지배'로의) / 불안정한 것(비약)이다
↳ **부연 설명:** 정치 권력을 강제적인 힘으로 여기지 않으면, '정치적인 것'에서 '(여성에 대한) 지배'로의 비약은 불안정함.

해석

[1]비교 문화적 관점에서 공적 리더십과 지배를 동일시하는 것은 의문의 여지가 있다. [2]'지배'로 의미하려는 바는 무엇인가? [3]그것은 강제를 나타내는가? 아니면 '가장 가치 있는 것'에 대한 통제(를 나타내는가)? [4]'정치' 체제는 둘 다에 관한 것일 수도, 둘 중 하나에 관한 것일 수도, 아니면 아마도 어느 쪽에 관한 것도 아닐 수 있다. [5]'통제'라는 생각은 많은 민족들에게 괴로운 생각일 것인데, 예를 들어 공동체의 모든 구성원이 개인의 자율을 좋아하고 통제나 강제의 어떤 명백한 표현도 몹시 싫어하는 아마존의 많은 원주민 부족들 사이에서처럼 말이다. [6]서양의 고정관념일지도 모르겠지만, 정치권력이 '강제적' 힘이라는 개념은 보편적인 것이 아니다. [7]아마존의 지도자가 명령을 내리는 것은 아주 드물다. [8]많은 부족원이 정치권력을 강제적인 힘으로도, '가장 가치 있는 영역'으로도 여기지 않는다면, '정치적인 것'에서 (강제로서의) '지배'로, '그리고 거기(지배)에서' '여성에 대한 지배'로의 비약은 불안정한 것(비약)이다. [9]Marilyn Strathern이 말한 것처럼, '정치적인 것'과 '정치적 인격'이라는 개념은 우리 자신의 문화적 강박 관념, 즉 인류학상의 구성 개념에 오랫동안 반영된 편견(▶ 인류학자들이 다른 문화를 이해하는 이론을 만드는 데 영향을 미쳤다는 의미)이다.

↓

[10]정치권력에 대한 우리 자신의 개념을 통해 다른 문화의 정치권력을 이해하는 것은 (A) 잘못 이해된 것인데, 왜냐하면 정치권력에 관한 생각은 여러 문화에 걸쳐 (B) 동일하지 않기 때문이다.

어휘

cross-cultural 비교 문화의; 이(異)문화 간의
perspective 관점, 시각
equation 동일시; 등식, 방정식
dominance 지배(력); 우월
cf. domination 지배, 통치
questionable 의심스러운, 미심쩍은
conceivably 아마도, 생각건대
bothersome 괴로운, 성가신
be fond of ~을 좋아하다
allergic to A A를 몹시 싫어하는; A에 알레르기가 있는

🔑 (A) 우리가 이해하는 정치 개념들은 편견에 불과함.

[9]As Marilyn Strathern has remarked, // the notions (of 'the political' and 'political personhood') / are cultural obsessions of our own, / *a bias* (long reflected / in anthropological constructs).

(부사절 접속사(~처럼) / S / V / C / 과거분사구)

Marilyn Strathern이 말한 것처럼 // 개념은 ('정치적인 것'과 '정치적 인격'이라는) / 우리 자신의 문화적 강박 관념이다 / 즉 편견 (오랫동안 반영된 / 인류학상의 구성 개념에)

↳ **결론:** '정치적인 것'이나 '정치적 인격'이라는 개념은 문화적 강박 관념이자 오랜 편견임.

↓

[10]It is **(A) misguided** / to understand political power in other cultures / through our own notion of it // because ideas of political power are not **(B) uniform** / across cultures.

(가주어 / 진주어(to-v구) / (= political power) / 부사절 접속사(이유))

(~은) (A) 잘못 이해된 것이다 / 다른 문화의 정치권력을 이해하는 것은 / 정치권력에 대한 우리 자신의 개념을 통해 // 왜냐하면 정치권력에 관한 생각은 (B) 동일하지 않기 때문이다 / 여러 문화에 걸쳐

conception 개념; 구상
fixation 고정관념, 집착; 고정
universal 보편적인 (것); 우주의
domain 영역, 범위
leap 비약, 도약; (껑충) 뛰다
shaky 불안정한; 흔들리는
remark 말하다, 언급하다
personhood 인격; 개성
obsession 강박 (관념); 집착
bias 편견, 선입견
anthropological 인류학(상)의
construct 구성 개념; 구성하다

정답 가이드

요약문을 통해 문화에 따른 정치권력에 대한 생각과 이해에 관한 글임을 알 수 있다. 서양에서는 정치권력을 강제적인 힘으로 여기지만, 아마존 부족은 그렇지 않다고 하며 서양의 정치 개념이 '보편적인 것'은 아니라고 했다. 이는 서양의 개념으로 아마존의 정치권력을 이해하는 것이 '적절하지 않음'을 의미한다. 따라서 요약문의 빈칸 (A)와 (B)에 각각 들어갈 말로 적절한 것은 ③ 'misguided(잘못 이해된) - uniform(동일한)'이다.

오답 클리닉

(A) (B)

① rational - flexible (16%) 합리적인 - 유연한
(A)는 틀리며, (B)는 글의 내용과 반대됨.

The 주의 요약문에 부정어 not이 있는 것에 주의한다.

② appropriate - commonplace (14%) 적절한 - 흔한
(A)와 (B) 모두 틀림.

④ unreasonable - varied (8%) 불합리한 - 다양한
(A)는 맞지만, (B)는 글의 내용과 반대됨.

⑤ effective - objective (5%) 효과적인 - 객관적인
(A)는 틀리며, (B)는 맞음. 정치권력에 관한 생각은 문화마다 다르다고 했으므로 객관적이지 않다고도 볼 수 있음.

02~03 + 복합 유형 〈23학년도 6월 모평 41~42번 | 정답률 02 66%, 03 55%〉

02 ① 03 ③

구문분석 & 직독직해

심리 상황 판단에 미치는 군중의 영향

[1]Once an event is noticed, // an onlooker must decide // if it is truly an emergency.

(부사절 접속사(일단 ~하면) / S / V / O(명사절) / 명사절 접속사(~인지))

일단 어떤 사건이 목격되면 // 구경하는 사람은 결정해야 한다 // 그것(그 사건)이 정말로 비상 상황인지를

↳ **도입:** 어떤 사건을 보면 그것이 정말 비상 상황인지를 결정해야 함.

🔑 03-(a) 예로 든 '연기'는 비상 상황이 항상 명확하게 '꼬리표가 붙어 있는' 것이 아님을 보여줌.

[2]Emergencies are not always clearly **(a) labeled** / as such; // "*smoke*" (pouring into a waiting room) / may be caused by fire, // or it may merely indicate / a leak (in a steam pipe).

(S / V / 전치사(~로) / S₁ / 현재분사구 / V₁ / S₂ / V₂ / O₂)

비상 상황은 항상 명확하게 꼬리표가 붙어 있는 것은 아니다 / 그와 같은 것으로 // '연기'는 (대기실로 쏟아져 들어오는) / 화재에 의해 야기될 수도 있다 // 또는 그것(연기)은 단순히 나타낼 수도 있다 / 누출을 (증기 파이프의)

[3]Screams (in the street) / may signal an attack or a family quarrel.

(S / V / O)

비명은 (거리에서의) / 폭행이나 가족 간의 다툼을 나타낼 수도 있다

[4]*A man* (lying in a doorway) / may be having a coronary — // or he may simply be sleeping off a drunk.

(S₁ / 현재분사구 / V₁ / O₁ / S₂ / V₂ / O₂)

한 남자는 (출입구에 누워 있는) / 관상 동맥증을 앓고 있을 수도 있다 // 또는 그는 그저 술을 깨려고 잠을 자는 중일 수도 있다

↳ 비상 상황은 항상 명확하게 구분될 수 있는 것이 아님. (예: 연기, 거리에서의 비명, 출입구에 누워 있는 남자)

해석

[1]일단 어떤 사건이 목격되면, 구경하는 사람은 그것이 정말로 비상 상황인지를 결정해야 한다. [2]비상 상황은 항상 명확하게 그와 같은 것으로 (a) 꼬리표가 붙어 있는 것은 아닌데, 대기실로 쏟아져 들어오는 '연기'는 화재에 의해 야기될 수도 또는 단순히 증기 파이프의 누출을 나타낼 수도 있다. [3]거리에서의 비명은 폭행이나 가족 간의 다툼을 나타낼 수도 있다. [4]출입구에 누워 있는 한 남자는 관상 동맥증을 앓고 있을 수도 있고 또는 그저 술을 깨려고 잠을 자는 중일 수도 있다.

[5]어떤 상황을 판단하려고 하는 사람은 자신이 어떻게 반응해야 하는지 알기 위해 흔히 자기 주변에 있는 사람들을 본다. [6]만약 다른 모든 사람이 침착하고 무관심하다면, 그는 그런 상태를 유지하려는 경향이 있을 것이고, 만약 다른 모든 사람이 강하게 반응하고 있다면, 그는 경계하게 될 가능성이 있다. [7]이러한 경향은 단순히 맹목적인 순응이 아닌데, 보통 우리는 우리 주변의 다른 사람들이 어떻게 행동하는지로부터 새로운 상황에 관한 많은 귀중한 정

주제문

[5]*A person* (trying to interpret a situation) / often looks at those around him / to see how he should react.

S 현재분사구 V (= people) 목적(~하기 위해)

사람은 (어떤 상황을 판단하려고 하는) / 흔히 자기 주변에 있는 사람들을 본다 / 자신이 어떻게 반응해야 하는지 알기 위해

↳ 주변 사람을 보고 상황에 맞는 반응을 함.

[6]If everyone else is calm and indifferent, // he will tend to remain so; //

부사절 접속사(조건) S V (= calm and indifferent)

만약 다른 모든 사람이 침착하고 무관심하다면 // 그는 그런 상태를 유지하려는 경향이 있을 것이다 //

if everyone else is reacting strongly, // he is likely to become alert.

부사절 접속사(조건) S V C

만약 다른 모든 사람이 강하게 반응하고 있다면 // 그는 경계하게 될 가능성이 있다

★<derive A from B>: B로부터 A를 얻다

[7]This tendency is not merely blind conformity; // ordinarily we derive much valuable information (about new situations) / from how others around us behave.

S_1 V_1 C_1 S_2 V_2 O_2 from의 O(명사절)

🔑 03-(b) 우리는 타인의 행동에서 정보를 얻으므로 손님이 없는 식당을 이용하는 여행객은 '드문' 것임.

이러한 경향은 단순히 맹목적인 순응이 아니다 // 보통 우리는 많은 귀중한 정보를 얻는다

(새로운 상황에 관한) / 우리 주변의 다른 사람들이 어떻게 행동하는지로부터

↳ **세부 사항 1:** 주변 사람을 보고 비슷하게 반응하는 것은 타인의 행동에서 귀중한 정보를 얻는 것임.

★<It is A who[that] ~>: ~하는 사람[것]은 바로 A이다

[8]It's a **(b) rare** traveler // who, (in picking a roadside restaurant), / chooses to stop / at *one* [where no other cars appear / in the parking lot].

강조구문 <in v-ing>: v할 때 V′ O′

→ (= a roadside restaurant) 관계부사 S″ V″

바로 보기 드문 여행객이다 // (길가의 식당을 고를 때) / 멈추기로 결정하는 사람은 /

곳에 [다른 차가 보이지 않는 / 주차장에]

↳ **예:** 식당을 고를 때 주차장에 차가 없는 곳(다른 사람들이 안 가는 곳)에 가는 여행객은 드묾.

[9]But occasionally the reactions of others provide / **(c) accurate (→ false)** information.

S V O

그러나 때때로 다른 사람들의 반응은 제공한다 / 정확한(→ 거짓된) 정보를

↳ **세부 사항 2:** 타인의 반응이 거짓 정보를 제공하기도 함.

🔑 03-(c) 내면의 불안을 무관심으로 표현하는 것은 '거짓' 정보를 제공하는 것임.

[10]The studied nonchalance (of patients in a dentist's waiting room) / is a poor indication (of their inner anxiety).

S V C

관찰된 무관심은 (치과 병원 대기실 환자의) / 잘못된 지표이다 (그들의 내적 불안의)

↳ **예:** 치과 병원 대기실 환자는 속으로 불안해하면서 무관심한 척함.

[11]It is considered embarrassing / to "lose your cool" in public.

가주어 V C 진주어(to-v구)

🔑 03-(d) 사람들은 냉정을 잃는 것을 창피해하므로 심각한 상황에서 실제보다 '태연한' 척할 것임.

(~은) 창피한 일로 여겨진다 / 사람들이 있는 데서 '냉정을 잃는' 것은

[12]In a potentially acute situation, / then, / *everyone* (present) / will appear more **(d) unconcerned** // than he is (unconcerned) in fact.

S V C 반복어 생략

잠재적으로 심각한 상황에서 / 그렇다면 / 모든 사람은 (그곳에 있는) / 더 태연한 것처럼 보일 것이다 //

그가 실제로 그러한 것보다

↳ **부연 설명:** 냉정을 잃는 것을 창피하게 여겨 사람들은 심각한 상황에서 실제보다 더 태연해 보일 것임.

[13]A crowd can thus force **(e) inaction** / on its members / by implying, / (through its passivity), // that an event is not an emergency.

S V O <by v-ing>: v함으로써 전치사구 삽입

동명사 implying의 O(명사절)

🔑 03-(e) 군중이 '아무것도 하지 않음'으로써 비상 상황이 아니라고 암시하면 구성원도 따를 것임.

따라서 군중은 가만히 있는 것을 강제할 수 있다 / 구성원들에게 / 넌지시 비춤으로써 / (수동성을 통해) //

사건이 비상 상황이 아님을

→ fears의 O(명사절)

[14]Any individual (in such a crowd) / fears // that he may appear a fool // if he behaves // as though it were (an emergency).

S V 명사절 접속사 부사절 접속사(조건) 반복어구 생략

★<as though[if]+가정법 과거>: 앞 절 behaves의 현재시제에 맞춰 '마치 ~인 것처럼 …한다'로 해석함.

어떤 개인이든 (그러한 군중 속에 있는) / 두려워한다 // 자신이 바보처럼 보일 수도 있을까 봐 // 그가 행동하면 //

그 사건이 마치 비상 상황인 것처럼

↳ **결과:** 비상 상황에서 군중은 수동성(가만히 있는 것)을 통해 개인들이 가만히 있도록 할 수 있음.

보를 얻는다. [8]길가의 식당을 고를 때 주차장에 다른 차가 보이지 않는 곳에 멈추기로 결정하는 사람은 바로 (b) 보기 드문 여행객이다. [9]그러나 때때로 다른 사람들의 반응은 (c) 정확한(→ 거짓된) 정보를 제공한다. [10]치과 병원 대기실 환자의 관찰된 무관심은 그들의 내적 불안의 잘못된 지표이다.(▶ 불안감을 정확히 전달하지 않는다는 의미) [11]사람들이 있는 데서 '냉정을 잃는' 것은 창피한 일로 여겨진다. [12]그렇다면, 잠재적으로 심각한 상황에서, 그곳에 있는 모든 사람은 실제로 그러한 것보다 더 (d) 태연한 것처럼 보일 것이다. [13]따라서 군중은 수동성을 통해 사건이 비상 상황이 아님을 넌지시 비춤으로써 구성원들에게 (e) 가만히 있는 것을 강제할 수 있다. [14]그러한 군중 속에 있는 어떤 개인이든 그 사건이 마치 비상 상황인 것처럼 행동하면 자신이 바보처럼 보일 수도 있을까 봐 두려워한다.

어휘

onlooker 구경하는 사람
indicate 나타내다, 보여 주다
cf. indication 지표, 표시; 암시
leak 누출(시키다); 누설(하다)
signal 나타내다, 신호(를 보내다)
quarrel (말)다툼[싸움]; 다투다
sleep A off 잠을 자서 A가 낫게 하다[A를 떨쳐 버리다]
interpret 판단[이해]하다; 해석하다
indifferent 무관심한
alert 경계하는, 기민한; 경보를 발하다
tendency 경향, 성향; 동향
blind 맹목적인; 눈이 먼
conformity 순응, 따름
occasionally 때때로, 이따금
lose one's cool 냉정을 잃다
acute 심각한, 중대한; 급성의
imply 넌지시 비추다, 암시하다
passivity 수동성
fool 바보; 속이다, 기만하다
[선택지] independently 독립적으로, 자주적으로
emergent 긴급한; 신생의, 신흥의

정답 가이드

02 목격한 상황이 비상 상황인지를 판단할 때, 개인은 주위에 있는 사람들을 살펴 어떻게 반응해야 할지를 결정한다고 했다. 이때 주변 사람들의 반응으로부터 얻은 정보는 정확할 수도 그렇지 않을 수도 있으며, 군중은 실제와 다르게 행동해서 개인의 판단을 방해할 수도 있다고 했다. 따라서 글의 제목으로 가장 적절한 것은 ① 'Do We Judge Independently? The Effect of Crowds(우리는 독립적으로 판단을 하는가? 군중의 영향)'이다.

03 (c)가 있는 문장 9는 역접 연결어 But으로 시작하므로 흐름상 앞 내용과 반대되는 내용이 와야 함을 알 수 있다. 문장 9 앞은 주변 사람들의 행동에서 상황에 대한 귀중한 정보를 얻는 예로 손님이 없는 식당에는 가지 않는 것을 들었다. 문장 9 뒤는 치과 대기실 환자들이 내적 불안이 아닌 무관심함을 보이는 예를 들었으므로 타인의 반응이 때때로 잘못된, 거짓 정보를 전달한다는 내용이다. 따라서 ③ 'accurate(정확한)'를 'false(거짓된)'로 바꿔야 한다.

오답 클리닉

02 ② Winning Strategy: How Not to Be Fooled by Others (6%)
승리 전략인 다른 사람에 의해 속지 않는(×) 방법
타인에게 속지 않는 방법에 관한 내용이 아님.
③ Do Emergencies Affect the Way of Our Thinking? (17%)
비상 상황(×)이 우리의 사고방식에 영향을 끼치는가?
비상 상황이 아니라 타인의 반응이 우리의 상황 판단에 영향을 끼친다는 내용임.
④ Stepping Towards Harmony with Your Neighbors (4%)
이웃과의 조화(×)를 향해 발걸음을 내딛기
주변에 있는 사람들을 살펴 상황을 판단한다고 했지만, 그들과 조화를 이룬다는 내용은 없음.
⑤ Ways of Helping Others in Emergent Situations (7%)
긴급한 상황에서 다른 사람을 돕는 방법(×)
긴급한 상황에서 다른 사람들을 돕는 내용이 아님.

03 ① labeled (2%) 꼬리표가 붙어 있는
연기, 거리에서의 비명, 출입구에 누워 있는 남자의 예는 모두 그것이 비상 상황일 수도 있고 아닐 수도 있다는 설명이므로, 언제나 명확하게 그런 것들에 비상 상황이라는 '꼬리표가 붙어 있는' 것은 아니라는 문맥은 적절하다.
② rare (12%) 보기 드문
문장 8은 주변 사람의 행동을 보고 새로운 상황에 대한 귀중한 정보를 얻는 예에 해당하므로, 주차장에 차가 없는 식당에 가는 사람은 '보기 드문' 여행객일 것이다.
④ unconcerned (23%) 태연한
앞에서 사람들은 냉정을 잃는 것을 창피해한다고 했으므로 심각한 상황이라도 사람들은 실제보다 더 '태연한' 듯이 보일 것이다.
⑤ inaction (8%) 가만히 있는 것
개인은 타인의 행동에 따라 반응하기 때문에 군중이 비상 상황에 수동적으로 있으면 개인도 따라서 '가만히 있는 것'이 강제될 것이다.

01 ✦ 빈칸 추론 〈20학년도 9월 모평 34번 | 정답률 38%〉 ②

구문분석 & 직독직해

사회 사회 인류학과 문화 인류학의 논쟁

주제문

★<not A but B>: A가 아니라 B

[1]The debates (between social and cultural anthropologists) / concern / not the differences between the concepts but the analytical priority: //

S V O_1 O_2

논쟁은 (사회 인류학자와 문화 인류학자 사이의) / ~에 관한 것이다 / 개념들 간의 차이가 아니라 분석적 우선 사항 //

which should come first, / the social chicken or the cultural egg?

의문대명사

즉 어느 것이 먼저인가 / 사회적 닭 혹은 문화적 달걀

↳ 사회 인류학과 문화 인류학의 분석적 우선 사항은 각기 다름.

★<the+형용사>: ~한 것[사람들]

[2]British anthropology emphasizes the social.

영국의 인류학은 사회적인 것을 강조한다

↱ assumes의 O_1(명사절)

[3]It assumes // that social institutions determine culture //

S V 명사절 접속사 S'₁ V'₁ O'₁

그것(영국의 인류학)은 추정한다 // 사회 제도가 문화를 결정한다고 //

↱ assumes의 O_2(명사절)

and that universal domains of society (such as kinship, economy, politics, and religion) / are represented /

명사절 접속사 S'₂ V'₂

그리고 사회의 보편적인 영역이 (친척 관계, 경제, 정치, 그리고 종교와 같은) / 나타난다고 /

by *specific institutions* (such as the family, subsistence farming, the British Parliament, and the Church of England) [which can be compared cross-culturally].

주격 관계대명사

구체적인 제도에 의해 (가족, 자급 농업, 영국 의회, 그리고 영국 국교회와 같은) [비교 문화적으로 비교될 수 있는]

↳ **대조 A(영국 인류학):** 사회 제도가 문화를 결정함. (사회 우선)

[4]American anthropology emphasizes the cultural.

미국의 인류학은 문화적인 것을 강조한다

[5]It assumes // that culture shapes social institutions / ⊶ 미국 인류학은 문화가 사회 제도를 형성한다고 봄.

S V O(명사절)

그것(미국의 인류학)은 추정한다 // 문화가 사회 제도를 형성한다고 /

★<사역동사 make+O+C(형용사)>: O가 C하게 만들다

by providing *the shared beliefs, the core values, the communicative tools, and so on* [that make social life possible].

<by v-ing: v함으로써> 주격 관계대명사 V' O' C'

공유된 믿음, 핵심적 가치관, 의사소통 도구 등을 제공함으로써 [사회생활을 가능하게 만드는]

↳ **대조 B(미국 인류학):** 문화가 사회 제도를 형성함. (문화 우선)

↱ does not assume의 O(명사절)

[6]It does not assume // that there are universal social domains, /

S V 명사절 접속사 V' S'

그것(미국의 인류학)은 추정하지 않는다 // 보편적인 사회적 영역이 있다고 /

preferring instead to discover domains empirically / as aspects (of each society's own classificatory schemes — / in other words, its culture). ⊶ 미국 인류학은 문화 측면에서 사회 영역을 경험적으로 발견하는 것을 선호함.

분사구문(= and it prefers ~) 전치사(~로(서))

그리고 대신에 영역들을 경험적으로 발견하는 것을 선호한다 / 측면으로서 (각 사회 자체의 분류 체계의 / 다른 말로, 그것의 문화의)

↳ **미국 인류학의 부연 설명 1:** 사회 영역을 문화의 측면에서 발견하는 것을 선호함.

[7]And / it rejects *the notion* // that any social institution can be understood / **in isolation from its own context.**

S V O = 동격 접속사 S' V'

그리고 / 그것은 개념을 거부한다 // 어떤 사회 제도든 이해될 수 있다는 / 그것 자체의 맥락에서 분리되어

↳ **미국 인류학의 부연 설명 2:** 문화적 맥락을 고려하지 않고 사회 제도를 이해할 수 없음.

해석

[1]사회 인류학자와 문화 인류학자 사이의 논쟁은 개념들 간의 차이가 아니라 분석적 우선 사항에 관한 것인데, 즉 사회적 닭 혹은 문화적 달걀, 어느 것이 먼저냐는 것이다. [2]영국의 인류학은 사회적인 것을 강조한다. [3]그것은 사회 제도가 문화를 결정하고 (친척 관계, 경제, 정치, 그리고 종교와 같은) 사회의 보편적인 영역이 (가족, 자급 농업, 영국 의회, 그리고 영국 국교회와 같은) 비교 문화적으로 비교될 수 있는 구체적인 제도에 의해 나타난다고 추정한다. [4]미국의 인류학은 문화적인 것을 강조한다. [5]그것은 문화가 사회생활을 가능하게 만드는 공유된 믿음, 핵심적 가치관, 의사소통 도구 등을 제공함으로써 사회 제도를 형성한다고 추정한다. [6]그것은 보편적인 사회적 영역이 있다고 추정하지 않고 대신에 각 사회 자체의 분류 체계, 다른 말로, 그것의 문화의 측면으로서 영역들을 경험적으로 발견하는 것을 선호한다. [7]그리고 그것은 어떤 사회 제도든 그것 자체의 맥락에서 분리되어 이해될 수 있다는 개념을 거부한다.

어휘

debate 논쟁[토론](하다)
anthropologist 인류학자
concern ~에 관한 것이다; 우려[걱정](하다)
analytical 분석적인
priority 우선 사항, 우선(권)
emphasize 강조하다, 중시하다
assume 추정[가정]하다; (책임을) 떠맡다
institution 제도; 기관, 단체
universal 보편적인; 전 세계의
domain 영역, 분야; 영토
kinship 친척 관계; 유사, 근사
represent 나타내다, 표현하다; 대표[대신]하다
specific 구체적인; 특정한
parliament 의회, 국회
cross-culturally 비교 문화적으로
core 핵심적인, 가장 중요한; 중심부
classificatory 분류(상)의
scheme 체계; 계획, 설계; 개요
reject 거부[거절]하다
isolation 분리, 격리, 고립(된 상태)
context 맥락, 상황
[선택지] in relation to A A에 관련하여
regardless of ~에 상관없이
on the basis of ~을 기반으로, ~에 근거하여

정답 가이드

빈칸 문장으로 보아, it은 사회 제도가 '어떻게' 이해될 수 없다고 보는 것인지를 추론해야 한다. 첫 문장에서 사회 인류학자와 문화 인류학자의 차이를 설명하고 영국의 사회 인류학과 미국의 문화 인류학을 대조하는 설명이 이어진다. 내용상 빈칸 문장의 it은 미국의 문화 인류학을 뜻하므로 이를 중심으로 읽으면, 미국의 인류학은 문화가 사회 제도를 형성한다고 여기며 문화의 측면에서 사회 영역을 경험적으로 발견하는 것을 선호한다고 했다. 이는 미국 인류학이 사회 제도를 문화적 맥락 속에서 이해한다는 것을 의미하므로, 그것은 ② 'in isolation from its own context(그것 자체의 맥락에서 분리되어)' 사회 제도를 이해할 수 있다고 보는 개념을 거부할 것이다.

오답 클리닉

① in relation to its cultural origin (33%)
그것의 문화적 기원과 관련하여
문화적 기원과 관련해 사회 제도를 이해하는 것이 미국의 인류학이므로 이 개념을 거부하게 되면 글의 내용과 정반대가 됨.

The 주의 빈칸 문장의 주어 it이 American anthropology(미국의 인류학)를 지칭함을 파악하고 그것이 거부하는 개념, 즉 그 이론과 반대되는 것을 찾아야 한다.

③ regardless of personal preferences (11%)
개인적인 선호에 상관없이
개인적인 선호가 사회 제도를 형성한다는 내용은 없음.

④ without considering its economic roots (7%)
그것의 경제적인 뿌리를 고려하지 않은 채로
경제에 관한 언급은 없음.

⑤ on the basis of British-American relations (10%)
영국과 미국 사이의 관계를 기반으로
영국과 미국의 인류학을 대조해 설명하는 내용이며, 두 나라의 관계에 대한 내용이 아님.

02 ✦ 글의 순서 (21학년도 9월 모평 37번 | 정답률 55%) ⑤

구문분석 & 직독직해 — 예술 미술의 기록 보관적 가치

주제문

[1] It can be difficult / to decide the place of fine art, / (such as oil paintings, watercolours, sketches or sculptures), / in an archival institution.
(가주어 It, V can be, C difficult, 진주어(to-v구))
(~은) 어려울 수 있다 / 순수 미술의 위치를 정하는 것은 / (유화, 수채화, 스케치, 또는 조각과 같은) / 기록 보관 기관에서
↳ **도입:** 기록 보관 기관에서 미술품의 위치를 결정하기란 어려움.

주어진 글의 미술의 위치를 결정짓는 것과 관련해 미술의 역할을 설명함.

(C) [2] Art can serve as documentary evidence, // especially when the items were produced // before photography became common.
(S Art, V can serve, when: 부사절 접속사(~할 때), before: 부사절 접속사(~전에))
미술은 증거 서류의 역할을 할 수 있다 // 특히 그 품목들이 만들어졌을 때 // 사진술이 흔해지기 전에
↳ **미술의 역할 1:** 증거 서류의 역할을 할 수 있음.

[3] Sketches (of soldiers on a battlefield), / paintings (of English country villages) / or portraits (of Dutch townspeople) / can provide the only visual evidence (of a long-ago place, person or time).
(S_1, S_2, S_3, V can provide, O the only visual evidence)
스케치 (전쟁터에 있는 군인들의) / 그림 (영국 시골 마을의) / 또는 초상화는 (네덜란드 시민들의) / 유일한 시각적 증거를 제공할 수 있다 (옛날의 장소, 사람 또는 시절의)
↳ **예:** 스케치, 그림, 초상화 등이 과거에 대한 시각적 증거를 제공함.

also로 (A)에 이어 미술의 다른 역할을 추가함.

(B) [4] But / art can also carry *aesthetic value*, // which elevates the job of evaluation / into another realm.
(S art, V can carry, O aesthetic value, which: 관계대명사(보충 설명))
그러나 / 미술은 또한 미적 가치를 지닐 수 있다 // 그런데 그것은 (가치) 평가라는 일을 승격시킨다 / 다른 영역으로
↳ **미술의 역할 2:** 미적 가치를 지님.

[5] Aesthetic value and the notion (of artistic beauty) / are important considerations, //
(S_{1-1}, S_{1-2}, V_1, C_1)
미적 가치와 개념은 (예술적 아름다움의) / 중요한 고려 사항이다 //
but they are not // what motivates archival preservation / in the first instance.
(S_2 they, V_2 are not, C_2(명사절))
그러나 그것들(미적 가치와 예술적 아름다움의 개념)이 (~은) 아니다 // 기록 보존의 이유가 되는 것은 / 우선적으로
↳ **부연 설명:** 미적 가치는 중요하지만 미술을 보존하는 우선적인 이유는 아님.

해석

[1]기록 보관 기관에서 유화, 수채화, 스케치, 또는 조각과 같은 순수 미술의 위치를 정하는 것은 어려울 수 있다. (C) [2]미술은, 특히 사진술이 흔해지기 전에 그 품목들이 만들어졌을 때, 증거 서류의 역할을 할 수 있다. [3]전쟁터에 있는 군인들의 스케치, 영국 시골 마을의 그림 또는 네덜란드 시민들의 초상화는 옛날의 장소, 사람 또는 시절의 유일한 시각적 증거를 제공할 수 있다. (B) [4]그러나 미술은 또한 미적 가치를 지닐 수 있는데, 그것은 (가치) 평가라는 일을 다른 영역으로 승격시킨다. (▶ 미적 가치를 미술의 위치 결정에 고려하는 것은 보다 높은 차원에서 평가가 이뤄져야 한다는 의미. 즉, 평가가 매우 어려움을 나타냄.) [5]미적 가치와 예술적 아름다움의 개념은 중요한 고려 사항이지만, 그것들이 우선적으로 기록 보존의 이유가 되는 것은 아니다. (A) [6]미술에 관한 최선의 기록 보관 결정은 영역권(이 물건은 내가 그것을 돌볼 자원이 없더라도 내 기관에 속해 있다)이나 금전적 가치나 위신의 문제(이 물건은 내 기관의 문화적 지위를 높인다)에 초점을 두지 않는다. [7]최선의 결정은 어떤 증거 가치가 존재하는지 그리고 그 품목에 무엇이 최선인지에 초점을 둔다.

어휘

fine art (순수) 미술(품)
sculpture 조각(품)
institution 기관[단체]; 제도
serve as ~의 역할을 하다
documentary 서류[증서]의; 기록물
portrait 초상화; 묘사

(A) ⁶The best archival decisions (about art) / do not focus / on territoriality /
　　　　　　　　　　　　　　S　　　　　　　　　　　　V　　　　　전치사구 병렬
최선의 기록 보관 결정은 (미술에 관한) / 초점을 두지 않는다 / 영역권에 /

(this object belongs in my institution // even though I do not have *the resources* (to care for it)) /
　　　　　　　　　　　　　　　　부사절 접속사(양보)　　　　　　　　　　　　　　(= the object)
(이 물건은 내 기관에 속해 있다 // 내가 자원이 없더라도 (그것을 돌볼)) /

or on questions (of monetary value or prestige) (this object raises / the cultural standing of my
　　전치사구 병렬
institution).
또는 문제에 (금전적 가치나 위신의) / (이 물건은 높인다 / 내 기관의 문화적 지위를)
↳ 단순 소유권이나 금전적 가치 또는 위신 때문에 미술품을 보관하는 것도 아님.

　　　　　　　　　　　☞ (B)의 미적 가치 외에 기록 보존을 결정하는 요소를 설명함.
⁷The best decisions focus / on what evidential value exists and what is best for the item.
　　　S　　　　　　　V　　　　　　　　　　　　　　　on의 O(명사절 병렬)
최선의 결정은 초점을 둔다 / 어떤 증거 가치가 존재하는지 그리고 그 품목에 무엇이 최선인지에
↳ 결론: 최고의 기록 보관 결정은 미술의 증거 가치가 있는지와 그 품목에 무엇이 최선인지에 초점을 둠.

townspeople 시민
aesthetic 미적인; 미학의
elevate 승격시키다, 높이다; 올리다
evaluation 평가, 감정
notion 개념, 관념
consideration 고려 사항; 숙고
motivate ~의 이유[원인]가 되다; 동기를 부여하다
in the first instance 우선[먼저]
territoriality 영역권
monetary 금전(상)의; 화폐[통화]의
standing 지위, 평판

정답 가이드

기록 보관 기관에서 미술의 위치를 정하는 것이 어려울 수 있다는 주어진 글 뒤에는 그 위치를 결정짓는 미술의 가치로서 미술이 증거 서류의 역할을 할 수 있다고 설명하는 (C)가 와야 한다. 다음으로는 also를 사용해 미술의 미적 가치 역할을 추가로 제시하는 (B)가 이어지는데, 미적 가치가 기록 보존의 우선적인 이유는 아니라고 했다. 이어서 (A)에서 영역권, 금전적 가치 등과 같은 다른 고려 사항들도 초점이 아니라고 언급한 후, 이 모든 내용에 대해 최선의 기록 보관 결정은 미술에 어떤 증거 가치가 있고 무엇이 그 미술품에 최선인지에 초점을 둔다고 결론짓는 순서가 되는 것이 가장 자연스럽다.

오답 클리닉

① (A) - (C) - (B) (11%)
(A)는 최선의 기록 보관 결정이 무엇인지 설명하는 결론에 해당하므로 주어진 글 뒤에 바로 이어지는 것은 어색하다.
② (B) - (A) - (C) (8%) / ③ (B) - (C) - (A) (7%)
(B)는 내용을 첨가하는 also와 함께 쓰였으므로 앞에 미적 가치와 다른 미술의 다른 역할이 제시되어야 한다.
④ (C) - (A) - (B) (20%)
미적 가치가 기록 보관의 우선적인 이유가 아니라는 (B)의 마지막 문장 내용을 받아서 (A)에서 최선의 기록 보관 결정이 무엇에 중점을 두는지 설명하고 있으므로 (A)는 (B) 뒤에 와야 한다.

---

03 + 문장 넣기 〈21학년도 9월 모평 39번 | 정답률 64%〉　　　　　　　④

구문분석 & 직독직해　　　　　　　문화 자연스럽게 발전한 영화 문법　　　**해석**

¹Film has no grammar.
영화에는 문법이 없다

(①) ²There are, however, some vaguely defined rules (of usage in cinematic language), //
　　　　　　　　　　V₁　　　　　　　　　　　S₁
그러나 막연하게 정의된 몇 가지 규칙이 있다 (영화 언어 사용에 관한) //

and the syntax of film — / its systematic arrangement — / orders these rules /
　　　　　　S₂　　　　　　(= these rules)　　　　　　V₂₋₁　O₂₋₁
and indicates relationships among them.
　　V₂₋₂　　　　O₂₋₂
그리고 영화의 문장 구조 / 그것(문장 구조)의 체계적인 (처리) 방식은 / 이러한 규칙을 정리한다 /
그리고 그것들(이러한 규칙) 사이의 관계를 보여준다
↳ 영화에 문법은 없으나 영화 언어 사용에 관한 막연한 몇 가지 규칙이 있음.

　　　　　　　　　　　　　　　　　　　　　　　　　　→ to remember의 O(명사절)
(②) ³As with written and spoken languages, / it is important to remember // that the syntax of
　　　~와 마찬가지로　　　　　　　　　　가주어 V　　C　　진주어(to-v구)　명사절 접속사　S′
film is a result of its usage, / not a determinant of it.
　　V′　　C′　　　　　　　(= the syntax of film)
문어와 구어에서와 마찬가지로 / 기억하는 것이 중요하다 // 영화의 문장 구조는 그것(그 문장 구조)을 사용한 결과라는 것을 /
그것(그 문장 구조)의 결정 요인이 아니라
↳ 영화 문법은 미리 정해진 것이 아님.

(③) ⁴There is *nothing* (preordained about film syntax).
　　　　　　　V　　S　　　　　과거분사구
(~것은) 아무것도 없다 (영화의 문장 구조에 관해 미리 정해진)
↳ 영화의 문장 구조는 미리 결정된 것이 아닌 사용을 통해 얻어진 결과임.

¹영화에는 문법이 없다. (①) ²그러나 영화 언어 (▶ 영화에서 의미, 감정, 이야기 등을 시청자에게 전달하기 위해 독특하게 사용되는 특별한 기술이나 요소들을 의미) 사용에 관한 막연하게 정의된 몇 가지 규칙이 있고, 영화의 문장 구조, 문장 구조의 체계적인 (처리) 방식은 이러한 규칙을 정리하고 그것들(이러한 규칙) 사이의 관계를 보여준다. (②) ³문어와 구어에서와 마찬가지로, 영화의 문장 구조는 그 문장 구조의 결정 요인이 아니라 그것을 사용한 결과라는 것을 기억하는 것이 중요하다. (③) ⁴영화의 문장 구조에 관해 미리 정해진 것은 아무것도 없다. (④ ⁵오히려, 그것(영화의 문장 구조)은 특정 방법(▶ 영화를 찍는 기술, 도구, 장치 등을 의미)이 실제로 운용할 수 있고 유용하다는 것이 밝혀지면서 자연스럽게 발전했다.) ⁶문어와 구어의 문장 구조처럼 영화의 문장 구조는 자연스러운 발전의 결과이고, 규범적(미리 설정된 규칙에 따르는 것)이기보다는 기술적(이미 사용된 것을 있는 그대로 설명하는 것)이며, 여러 해에 걸쳐 상당히 변화해 왔다. (⑤) ⁷할리우드식 문법은 이제 우습게 들릴지도 모르지만, 30년대, 40년대, 그리고 50년대 초반

주제문

(④ 5Rather, / it evolved naturally // as certain devices were found / in practice to be both workable and useful.)

(it = film syntax) S V / 부사절 접속사(~하면서) S′ V′ C′

Rather(오히려)로 앞 문장과 상반되는 내용이 이어짐.

*<find+O+(to be) C(O가 C임을 알게 되다)>의 수동형

오히려 / 그것(영화의 문장 구조)은 자연스럽게 발전했다 // 특정 방법이 밝혀지면서 / 실제로 운용할 수 있고 유용하다는 것이

↳ 영화의 문장 구조는 자연스럽게 발전한 것임.

주어진 문장에 대한 부연 설명이 이어짐.

6Like the syntax of written and spoken language, / the syntax of film is an organic development, / (descriptive rather than prescriptive), // and it has changed considerably / over the years.

전치사(~처럼) *<A rather than B>: B라기보다는 A / S1 V1 C / 삽입어구 / S2 V2

문어와 구어의 문장 구조처럼 / 영화의 문장 구조는 자연스러운 발전의 결과이다 / (규범적이기보다는 기술적이며) // 그리고 그것(영화의 문장 구조)은 상당히 변화해 왔다 / 여러 해에 걸쳐

↳ **부연 설명:** 영화의 문장 구조는 자연스럽게 생긴 발전물로 기술적이며, 여러 해에 걸쳐 변화함.

(⑤) 7"Hollywood Grammar" may sound laughable now, // but during the thirties, forties, and early fifties / it was an accurate model (of *the way* [(that) Hollywood films were constructed]).

S1 V1 C1 / S2 V2 C2 / 관계부사 생략

'할리우드식 문법'은 이제 우습게 들릴지도 모른다 // 그러나 30년대, 40년대, 그리고 50년대 초반에 / 그것('할리우드식 문법')은 정확한 모델이었다 (방식의 [할리우드 영화가 구성되는])

↳ **예:** '할리우드식 문법'이 과거에는 영화를 구성하는 방식이었음.

에 그것은 할리우드 영화가 구성되는 방식의 정확한 모델이었다.

어휘

vaguely 막연하게; 희미하게
cinematic 영화의
syntax 문장 구조, 구문 규칙
systematic 체계적인
arrangement (처리) 방식; 준비; 배치; 정리
order 정리(하다); 순서; 명령(하다)
determinant 결정 요인
device 방법; 장치
in practice 실제로
workable 운용[실행]할 수 있는
organic 자연스러운, 서서히 생기는; 유기농의
laughable 우스운, 터무니없는
accurate 정확한
construct 구성하다; 건설하다

정답 가이드

주어진 문장이 앞서 말한 내용과 다르거나 반대되는 말을 도입할 때 사용하는 Rather(오히려)로 시작하는 것으로 보아, 그 앞에는 영화의 문장 구조가 자연스럽게 발전했다는 주어진 문장과 반대되는 내용이 나와야 한다. 그러므로 ④ 앞의 영화의 문장 구조에 관해 미리 정해진 것은 아무것도 없다는 내용 다음에 오히려 영화 문장 구조는 자연스럽게 발전했다는 주어진 문장이 이어지는 것이 적절하며, 이는 ④ 뒤의 영화 문장 구조는 자연스러운 발전의 결과라는 부연 설명과도 자연스럽게 연결된다. 따라서 주어진 문장이 들어가기에 가장 적절한 곳은 ④이다.

오답 클리닉

① (2%) 영화는 문법이 없으나 영화 언어 사용에 관한 몇 가지 규칙이 있다는 상반되는 내용이 역접 연결어 however로 이어지는 것은 자연스럽다.
② (7%) 영화에서의 규칙의 특징을 설명하는 내용이 이어진다.
③ (16%) 영화의 문장 구조가 실제 사용을 통해 얻어진 결과라는 내용 뒤에 영화의 문장 구조에 관해 미리 정해진 것은 없다고 부연 설명하는 내용이 이어지는 것은 자연스럽다.
⑤ (11%) 영화의 문장 구조가 여러 해에 걸쳐 상당히 변화했다는 앞 문장에 대한 예로 '할리우드식 문법'을 제시하는 내용이다.

01 + 글의 주제 〈21학년도 9월 모평 23번 | 정답률 69%〉 ①

구문분석 & 직독직해 철학 사회문화적 산물인 개인

[1] *Conventional wisdom in the West,* / (influenced by philosophers from Plato to Descartes), / credits individuals and especially geniuses / with creativity and originality.
(S / 과거분사구 삽입 / V / ★<credit A with B>: A에게 B가 있다고 믿다)
서양의 통념은 / (Plato에서 Descartes에 이르는 철학자들의 영향을 받은) / 개인, 특히 천재들에게 (~이) 있다고 믿는다 / 창의력과 독창성이
↳ **서양의 통념(Myth):** 창의력과 독창성은 개인, 특히 천재들에게 있음.

[2] Social and cultural influences and causes / are minimized, / (are) ignored, / or (are) eliminated from consideration at all.
(S / V1 / V2 / V3)
사회적, 문화적 영향과 원인은 / 최소화되거나 / 무시되거나 / 또는 고려에서 완전히 배제된다
↳ **부연 설명 1:** 사회적, 문화적 영향은 고려되지 않음.

[3] Thoughts, / (original and conventional), / are identified with individuals, //
(S1 / 삽입어구 / V1)
생각은 / (독창적인 그리고 관습적인) / 개인과 동일시된다 //
and *the special things* [that individuals are and do] / are traced / to their genes and their brains.
(S2 / 관계대명사 / V2)
그리고 특별한 것은 [개인이라는 존재와 (개인이) 하는] / 기원이 밝혀진다 / 그 개인의 유전자와 두뇌에서
↳ **부연 설명 2:** 생각은 곧 개인과 동일시되며, 특별한 업적은 유전자와 두뇌에서 비롯되었다고 여김.

주제문
[4] The "trick" here is to recognize // that individual humans are social constructions themselves, /
(S / V / C / → to recognize의 O(명사절) / 명사절 접속사 / S' / V' / C' / 주어 강조(생략 가능))
여기서 '비결'은 인식하는 것이다 // 개개의 인간이 사회적 구성 그 자체라는 것을 /
embodying and reflecting / *the variety* (of social and cultural influences) [(which[that]) they have been exposed to / during their lives].
(분사구문(= as they embody and reflect ~) / 목적격 관계대명사 생략 / (= individual humans))
⊶ 인간은 사회적 구성체이며 사회 문화적 영향을 구현하고 반영하는 존재임.
구현하고 반영하며 / 다양성을 (사회적, 문화적 영향의) [그들이 접해온 / 생애 동안]
↳ **사실(Truth):** 개인은 사회적으로 구성되며 사회 문화적 영향을 받음.

[5] Our individuality is not denied, // but it is viewed / as a product (of specific social and cultural experiences).
(★<not A but B>: A가 아니라 B / → (= our individuality) / S1 / V1 / S2 / V2 / 전치사(~로(서)))
⊶ 개인은 사회적, 문화적 경험의 산물임.
우리의 개인성은 부인되는 것이 아니라 // 그것은 여겨진다 / 산물로 (특정한 사회적, 문화적 경험의)
↳ **논거 1:** 개인성은 특정한 사회 문화적 경험의 결과임.

⊶ 뇌도 사회 환경의 영향을 받음.
[6] The brain itself is a social thing, / influenced structurally and at the level (of its connectivities / by social environments).
(S / V / C / 분사구문(= and it is influenced ~))
뇌는 그 자체로 사회적인 것이다 / 그리고 그것은 구조적으로 그리고 수준에서 영향을 받는다 (그것의 연결성의 / 사회 환경에 의한)
↳ **논거 2:** 뇌는 사회 환경의 영향을 받는 사회적인 것임.

[7] The "individual" is a legal, religious, and political fiction // just as the "I" is a grammatical illusion.
(S / V / C / 부사절 접속사 (꼭 ~인 것처럼) / S' / V' / C')
'개인'은 법적, 종교적, 그리고 정치적 허구이다 // 꼭 '나'가 문법적 환상인 것처럼
↳ **논거 3:** 개별적 존재로 여겨지는 '개인'은 허상에 불과하며, 사회 문화적 영향을 받지 않는 개인은 없음.

해석

[1]Plato에서 Descartes에 이르는 철학자들의 영향을 받은 서양의 통념은 개인, 특히 천재들에게 창의력과 독창성이 있다고 믿는다. [2]사회적, 문화적 영향과 원인은 최소화되거나 무시되거나 고려에서 완전히 배제된다. [3]독창적인 그리고 관습적인 생각은 개인과 동일시되며, 개인이라는 특별한 존재와 개인이 하는 특별한 것은 그 개인의 유전자와 두뇌에서 기원이 밝혀진다. [4]여기서 '비결'은 개개의 인간이 사회적 구성 그 자체이며 그들이 생애 동안 접해온 사회적, 문화적 영향의 다양성을 구현하고 반영한다는 것을 인식하는 것이다. [5]우리의 개인성은 부인되는 것이 아니라 특정한 사회적, 문화적 경험의 산물로 여겨진다. [6]뇌는 그 자체로 사회적인 것이며, 구조적으로, 그리고 그것의 사회 환경에 의한 연결성 수준에서 영향을 받는다. [7]'개인'은 꼭 '나'가 문법적 환상인 것처럼 법적, 종교적, 그리고 정치적 허구이다.

어휘

conventional wisdom (일반) 통념
cf. conventional 관습적인; 전통적인, 종래의
originality 독창성, 창의력; 진짜[진품]임
minimize 최소화하다
eliminate 배제하다, 제거하다
consideration 고려, 숙고; 고려 사항
be identified with ~와 동일시되다
trace (기원을) 밝혀내다, 추적하다; 흔적
recognize 인식[인정]하다; 알아보다
construction 구성; 구조물; 건설, 공사
embody 구현하다, 구체화하다; 포함하다
expose 접하게[경험하게] 하다; 드러내다, 폭로하다
individuality 개인성; 개성, 특성
deny 부인[부정]하다
connectivity 연결(성)
legal 법률상의; 합법의
fiction 허구; 소설
illusion 환상; 착각[오해]; 환각
[선택지] inherent 내재하는, 고유의
collectivity 집단성
separate 구분 짓다; 분리하다; 분리된
acknowledgement 인정, 승인; 감사
interdependence 상호 의존

정답 가이드

서양의 통념은 창의력과 독창성을 개인 고유의 특질로 여기며 특별한 것(업적)은 개인의 유전자와 두뇌에서 나온 것으로 보지만, 사실 모든 인간은 사회적으로 구성되는 사회적, 문화적 경험의 산물이라는 내용의 글이다. 따라서 글의 주제로 가장 적절한 것은 ① 'recognition of the social nature inherent in individuality(개인성에 내재한 사회적 속성의 인식)'이다.

The 핵심 ★ Myth-Truth 구조의 글로, 글의 주제가 드러나는 Truth(사실)에 주목한다.

오답 클리닉

② ways of filling the gap between individuality and collectivity (3%)
개인성과 집단성(×)의 간격을 채우는 방법
개인성에 대한 글이며 집단성에 대한 언급은 없음.

③ issues with separating original thoughts from conventional ones (7%) 독창적인 생각과 관습적인 생각을 구분 짓는 것(×)에 관한 문제
독창적인 그리고 관습적인 생각이 개인과 동일시된다는 내용은 있으나 그 둘을 구분하는 내용은 아님.

④ acknowledgment of the true individuality embodied in human genes (16%)
인간 유전자에 구현된(×) 진정한 개인성의 인정
개인성이 사회 문화적으로 구성된 것이라는 글의 내용과 반대됨.

The 주의 서양의 통념에서는 개인성을 유전자와 두뇌에서 비롯된 것으로 봤다고 했지만, 이후에 사회 문화적 영향이 있음을 인정하는 내용이 나오므로 지문의 전체 내용을 포괄하는 선택지를 골라야 한다.

⑤ necessity of shifting from individualism to interdependence (5%)
개인주의에서 상호 의존으로 전환(×)할 필요성
개인주의와 상호 의존에 대한 언급은 전혀 없음.

02 ✦ 빈칸 추론 (20학년도 9월 모평 33번 | 정답률 50%) ⑤

구문분석 & 직독직해

사회 탈진실이 일어나는 이유

★<not so much A as B>: A라기보다는 B인

[1] If one looks at the Oxford definition, // one gets the sense // that post-truth is [not so much] a claim // that truth *does not exist* / [as] (a claim) // that *facts are subordinate to our political point of view.*
(부사절 접속사(조건) / one: S / gets: V / the sense: O = that: 동격 접속사 / post-truth: S′ / is: V′ / a claim: C′ = that: 동격 접속사 / (a claim) = that: 동격 접속사)

Oxford 사전의 정의를 보면 // 누구나 이해를 하게 된다 // 탈진실은 주장이라기보다는 // 진실이 '존재하지 않는다'라는 / 주장이라는 것을 // '사실이 우리의 정치적 관점에 종속되어 있다'라는

[2] The Oxford definition focuses / on "*what*" post-truth is: // the idea // that feelings sometimes matter / more than facts.
(The Oxford definition: S / focuses: V / "what" post-truth is: on의 O(명사절) / the idea = that: 동격 접속사)

Oxford 사전의 정의는 초점을 둔다 / 탈진실이란 '무엇'인가에 // 생각 // 때로는 감정이 더 중요하다는 / 사실보다

↳ **탈진실의 사전적 정의:** 객관적인 사실보다 개인의 관점과 감정이 중요하다는 생각임.

★보어가 문장 앞에 오면서 <V+S> 어순으로 도치됨.

[3] But / just as important *is the next question*, // which is *why* this ever occurs.
(just as important: C / is: V / the next question: S / which: 관계대명사 (보충 설명) / is: V′ / why this ever occurs: C′(명사절))

하지만 / 그다음 질문이 그만큼 중요한데 // 이는 도대체 '왜' 이것(때로는 감정이 사실보다 더 중요한 것)이 발생하는가이다

↳ 사실보다 개인의 관점과 감정을 더 중요시하게 되는 이유도 중요함.

[4] Someone does not argue / against an obvious or easily confirmable fact / for no reason; // he or she does so // when it is to his or her advantage. ⊶ 사람들은 자신의 이익을 위해 사실에 반박함.
(Someone: S_1 / does not argue: V_1 / against: 전치사(~에 반대하여) / he or she: S_2 / does so: V_2 / when: 부사절 접속사(시간))

어떤 사람은 의견을 주장하지 않는다 / 명백하거나 쉽게 확인할 수 있는 사실에 반대하여 / 아무런 이유 없이 // 그 사람은 그렇게 한다 // 그것이 자신에게 이익이 될 때

↳ **탈진실이 일어나는 이유 1:** 이익을 얻기 위함.

⊶ 사람들은 불편한 사실에 의해 자신의 믿음이 위협받으면 사실에 반박함.

[5] When a person's beliefs are threatened / by an "inconvenient fact," // sometimes it is preferable / to challenge the fact.
(When: 부사절 접속사(시간) / it: 가주어 / is: V / preferable: C / to challenge the fact: 진주어(to-v구))

어떤 사람의 믿음이 위협받을 때 / '불편한 사실'에 의해 // 때로는 (~이) 선호된다 / 그 사실에 이의를 제기하는 것이

↳ **탈진실이 일어나는 이유 2:** 자신의 신념을 지키기 위함.

해석

[1]Oxford 사전의 정의를 보면, 누구나 탈진실은 진실이 '존재하지 않는다'라는 주장이라기보다는, '사실이 우리의 정치적 관점에 종속되어 있다'라는 주장이라는 것을 이해하게 된다. [2]Oxford 사전의 정의는 탈진실이란 '무엇'인가에 초점을 두는데, 때로는 감정이 사실보다 더 중요하다는 생각이다. [3]하지만 그다음 질문이 그만큼 중요한데, 이는 도대체 '왜' 이것이 발생하는가이다. [4]어떤 사람은 아무런 이유 없이 명백하거나 쉽게 확인할 수 있는 사실에 반론을 펴지 않고, 그 사람은 그것이 자신에게 이익이 될 때 그렇게 한다. [5]어떤 사람의 믿음이 '불편한 사실'에 의해 위협받을 때, 때때로 그 사실에 이의를 제기하는 것이 선호된다. [6]이것은 의식적인 수준이나 무의식적인 수준에서 일어날 수 있지만 (왜냐하면 때때로 우리가 납득시키려고 시도하고 있는 사람이 우리 자신이기 때문에), 핵심은 사실에 대한 이러한 종류의 탈진실 관계가 우리가 진실 그 자체보다 우리에게 더 중요한 어떤 것을 주장하려고 시도하고 있을 때만 발생한다는 것이다.

어휘

post-truth 탈진실 ((객관적 사실보다 개인의 감정이 여론 형성에 더 큰 영향을 미치는 현상))
claim 주장(하다); 청구[신청](하다)
point of view 관점
matter 중요하다, 문제가 되다; 문제
occur 일어나다, 발생하다
obvious 명백한, 분명한
confirmable 확인할 수 있는

↱ (= Arguing against or challenging the fact)
[6]This can happen / at either a conscious or unconscious level // (since sometimes the person [(who(m)[that]) we are seeking to convince] / is ourselves), //
S1 V1 A와 B 둘 중 하나 부사절 접속사(~ 때문에) S′ 목적격 관계대명사 생략 V′ C′

이것은 발생할 수 있다 / 의식적인 수준이나 무의식적인 수준에서 // (왜냐하면 때때로 사람이 [우리가 납득시키려고 시도하고 있는] / 우리 자신이기 때문에) //

주제문

↱ is의 C(명사절)
but the point is // that this sort of post-truth relationship to facts occurs // only when we are seeking to assert / *something* [**that is more important to us / than the truth itself**].
S2 V2 명사절 접속사 S′ V′ 부사절 접속사(시간) S″ V″ O″ 주격 관계대명사

하지만 핵심은 ~이다 // 사실에 대한 이러한 종류의 탈진실 관계가 발생한다는 것 // 우리가 주장하려고 시도하고 있을 때만 / 어떤 것을 [우리에게 더 중요한 / 진실 그 자체보다]

↳ **결론:** 탈진실은 우리에게 사실보다 더 중요한 것이 있을 때 일어남.

threaten 위협[협박]하다
inconvenient 불편한, 곤란한
preferable 선호되는; 더 좋은
challenge 이의를 제기하다; 도전(하다)
conscious 의식적인; 의식[자각]이 있는
(↔unconscious 무의식적인; 의식을 잃은)
seek to-v v하려고 (시도)하다
convince 납득시키다; 설득하다
assert 주장하다, 단언하다
[선택지] hold back 억제[저지]하다
give way to A A에게 양보하다[항복하다]
constant 변함없는; 끊임없는

정답 가이드

빈칸 문장으로 보아, 사실에 대한 탈진실 관계는 우리가 '어떤' 것을 주장하려고 시도할 때 발생하는 것인지를 추론해야 한다. 탈진실이란 사실보다 개인의 관점과 감정을 중시하는 생각인데, 이것은 사실에 반박하는 것이 자신에게 이익이 될 때와 불편한 사실로부터 자신의 신념을 지키려 할 때 일어난다고 설명한다. 이를 종합하면 탈진실은 우리가 주장하는 것이 ⑤ 'that is more important to us than the truth itself(진실 그 자체보다 우리에게 더 중요한)' 것일 때 발생함을 추론할 수 있다.

오답 클리닉

① to hold back our mixed feelings (14%)
우리의 뒤섞인 감정들을 억제하는
감정을 억제하기보다 중시할 때 탈진실이 일어남.

② that balances our views on politics (13%)
정치에 관한 우리 견해들의 균형을 잡는
our political point of view(우리의 정치적 관점)를 활용한 오답.

③ that leads us to give way to others in need (10%)
어려움에 처한 다른 사람들에게 우리가 양보하도록 하는
어려운 사람들에게 양보하는 것에 대한 내용은 없음.

④ to carry the constant value of absolute truth (13%)
절대적 진실의 변함없는 가치를 지니기 위한
탈진실은 절대적인 진실보다 감정과 신념을 중시하므로 글의 내용과 반대됨.

03 ✦ 글의 순서 〈21학년도 9월 모평 36번 | 정답률 55%〉 ②

구문분석 & 직독직해

철학 인간을 만물의 척도로 보는 관념

[1]In the fifth century *B.C.E.*, / the Greek philosopher Protagoras pronounced, // "Man is the measure of all things."
S V S′ V′ C′

기원전 5세기에 / 그리스의 철학자 Protagoras는 선언했다 // "인간은 만물의 척도이다"라고

[2]In other words, / we feel entitled / to ask the world, // "What good are you?"
S V C

다시 말해서 / 우리는 자격이 있다고 느낀다 / 세상에 물어볼 // "당신은 무슨 쓸모가 있는가?"라고

↳ 우리는 인간을 만물을 평가하는 기준으로 봄.

🔑 인간이 만물의 척도라는 주어진 글의 내용과 연결됨.
↱ 동격 접속사
(B) [3]We assume // that we are the world's standard, // that all things should be compared to us.
S V O(명사절) =

우리는 추정한다 // 우리가 세상의 기준이라고 // 즉 모든 것이 우리와 비교되어야 한다고

↳ 우리는 인간을 세상의 기준으로 여기고 모든 것을 인간과 비교함.

주제문

[4]Such an assumption makes us overlook a lot.
S V O C

그런 추정은 우리가 많은 것을 간과하게 만든다

↳ **문제점:** 인간을 모든 것의 척도로 삼으면 많은 것을 간과하게 됨.

해석

[1]기원전 5세기에, 그리스의 철학자 Protagoras는 "인간이 만물의 척도이다."라고 선언했다. [2]다시 말해서, 우리는 세상에 "당신은 무슨 쓸모가 있는가?"라고 물어볼 자격이 있다고 느낀다. (B) [3]우리는 우리가 세상의 기준이라고, 즉 모든 것이 우리와 비교되어야 한다고 추정한다. [4]그런 추정은 우리가 많은 것을 간과하게 만든다. (A) [5]'우리를 인간답게 만든다고' 일컬어지는 능력들, 즉 공감, 의사소통, 슬픔, 도구 제작 등은 우리와 세상을 공유하는 다른 존재들 사이에도 다양한 정도로 모두 존재한다. [6]척추를 가진 동물들(어류, 양서류, 파충류, 조류, 포유류)은 모두 동일한 기본 골격, 장기, 신경계, 호르몬, 행동을 공유한다. (C) [7]꼭 다양한 자동차 모델들이 각각 엔진, 동력 전달 장치, 네 바퀴, 문, 좌석을 가지고 있는 것처럼, 우리는 주로 우리의 외부 윤곽과 몇 가지 내부적인 조정 면에서 다르다. [8]하지만 고지식한 자동차 구매자들처럼, 대부분의 사람들은 오직 동물들의 다양한 겉모습만을 본다.(▶ 인간을 만물

(B)의 마지막에 언급한 간과하는 것을 설명함.

(A) [5] *Abilities* (said to "make us human") — / empathy, communication, grief, toolmaking, and so on — / all exist / to varying degrees / among *other minds* (sharing the world with us).

S 과거분사구 = V 현재분사구

능력들은 ('우리를 인간답게 만든다고' 일컬어지는) / 공감, 의사소통, 슬픔, 도구 제작 등 / 모두 존재한다 / 다양한 정도로 / 다른 존재들 사이에도 (우리와 세상을 공유하는)

↳ **세부 사항:** 인간을 인간답게 만드는 능력을 다른 존재들도 가지고 있음.

[6] Animals with backbones (fishes, amphibians, reptiles, birds, and mammals) / all share / the same basic skeleton, organs, nervous systems, hormones, and behaviors.

S V O

척추를 가진 동물들은 (어류, 양서류, 파충류, 조류, 포유류) / 모두 공유한다 / 동일한 기본 골격, 장기, 신경계, 호르몬, 행동을

↳ 척추동물들은 달라 보여도 공유하는 부분들이 있음.

(A)의 내용을 자동차에 비유해 설명함.

(C) [7] Just as different models of automobiles each have / an engine, drive train, four wheels, doors, and seats, //

부사절 접속사(꼭 ~인 것처럼) S′ V′ O′

꼭 다양한 자동차 모델들이 각각 가지고 있는 것처럼 / 엔진, 동력 전달 장치, 네 바퀴, 문, 그리고 좌석을 //

we differ / mainly in terms of our outside contours and a few internal tweaks.

S V

우리(인간을 포함해 척추를 가진 동물)는 다르다 / 주로 우리의 외부 윤곽과 몇 가지 내부적인 조정 면에서

↳ **부연 설명(비유):** 서로 달라 보이는 자동차들이 공통점을 가지고 있는 것처럼 우리도 다른 동물들과 일부만 다르고 공통점을 가짐.

[8] But / like naive car buyers, / most people see only animals' varied exteriors.

전치사(~처럼) S V O

하지만 / 고지식한 자동차 구매자들처럼 / 대부분의 사람들은 오직 동물들의 다양한 겉모습만을 본다

↳ **주제문 재언급:** 사람들은 인간과 동물의 외적인 차이만 보고 공유하는 특성을 간과함.

의 척도로 여기는 관념은 인간과 동물이 공유하는 많은 부분을 간과하고 겉모습의 차이에만 중점을 두게 한다는 의미)

어휘

pronounce 선언하다; 발음하다
measure 척도; 조치; 측정하다
entitled to-v v할 자격[권리]이 있는
standard 기준[표준](의)
overlook 간과하다; 내려다보다
empathy 공감, 감정 이입
varying 다양한, 가지각색의(= varied)
degree 정도; (각도·온도계 등의) 도; 학위
backbone 척추, 등뼈; 중추
amphibian 양서류
reptile 파충류
mammal 포유류
nervous system 신경계
drive train 동력 전달 장치
in terms of ~라는 면에서
internal 내부적인; 내적인
naive 고지식한, 지식[경험]이 없는; 순진한
exterior 겉모습; 외부(의)

정답 가이드

인간이 만물의 척도라는 주어진 글 다음에는 이를 재서술하여 우리가 인간을 세상의 기준으로 여긴다는 내용의 (B)가 연결되는 것이 적절하다. (B)의 끝부분에서는 이 관점이 많은 것을 간과하게 만든다는 문제점을 제기하는데, (A)에서 이 문제점을 더 자세히 설명하므로 (B) 뒤에 이어져야 한다. (A)는 인간을 인간답게 만든다고 여겨지는 능력이 척추동물들 모두가 공유하는 부분이라고 설명하므로 그 뒤에는 이것을 사람들이 자동차를 구매할 때 겉모습만을 보는 것에 비유하며 인간과 동물은 많은 부분을 공유하지만 사람들이 겉모습의 차이만 본다고 지적하는 내용의 (C)가 오는 것이 자연스럽다.

오답 클리닉

① (A) - (C) - (B) (4%)
인간이 만물의 척도라는 주어진 글 다음에 인간이 간과하는 부분을 설명하는 (A)가 이어지는 것은 어색하다. (A) 앞에는 인간을 만물의 척도로 보는 관념의 문제를 제기하는 (B)가 먼저 와야 한다.

③ (B) - (C) - (A) (30%)
(C)는 Just as(꼭 ~인 것처럼)로 이어지며 자동차에 비유해 인간과 동물이 많은 부분을 공유한다는 (A)의 내용을 부연 설명하며, (C)의 we는 인간을 포함해 척추를 가진 동물을 함께 지칭하므로 앞에 (A)가 먼저 와야 한다.

④ (C) - (A) - (B) (8%) / ⑤ (C) - (B) - (A) (3%)
인간이 만물의 척도라는 주어진 글은 인간을 다른 존재들과 구별되는 세상의 기준으로 본다는 것을 뜻하므로, 바로 뒤에 인간과 척추동물이 공유하는 부분이 많으며 이를 인간이 간과한다고 지적하는 (C)가 이어지는 것은 어색하다.

01 ✦ 글의 제목 (21학년도 9월 모평 24번 | 정답률 54%) ①

구문분석 & 직독직해 인지 인간의 불완전한 지식

[1]The discovery // that man's knowledge is not, and never has been, perfectly accurate / has had a humbling and perhaps a calming effect / upon the soul (of modern man).
S 동격 접속사 S′ V′1 V′2 C′ V O
발견은 // 인간의 지식이 완벽하게 정확하지 않고 '결코 그런 적도 없다'는 / 겸손하게 하고 아마도 진정시키는 효과를 미쳐왔다 / 영혼에 (현대 인간의)
↳ 인간의 지식은 결코 완벽하게 정확할 수 없음.

[2]The nineteenth century, // (as we have observed), / was the last (to believe // that the world, as a whole as well as in its parts, / could ever be perfectly known).
S 삽입절 V C 명사절 접속사 S′ V′ (→ to believe의 O(명사절))
<A as well as B>: B뿐만 아니라 A도
19세기는 // (우리가 목격했듯이) / 마지막이었다 (믿은 // 세상이 그것의 부분들에서뿐만 아니라 전체로서도 / 언제나 완벽하게 이해될 수 있다고)
↳ **과거(~ 19세기):** 세상을 완벽하게 알 수 있다고 믿음.

[3]We realize now // that this is, and always was, impossible.
S V 명사절 접속사 S′ V′1 V′2 C′ (→ realize의 O(명사절))
우리는 이제 이해한다 // 이것이 불가능하며, 언제나 불가능했다는 것을
↳ **현재:** 세상을 완벽하게 아는 것은 불가능하다는 것을 이해함.

[4]We know within limits, / not absolutely, // even if the limits can usually be adjusted / to satisfy our needs.
S V 부사절 접속사(~일지라도) S′ V′ 목적(~하기 위해)
우리는 한도 내에서 알고 있다 / 완전히가 아니라 // 비록 그 한도가 대개 조정될 수 있을지라도 / 우리의 필요를 충족시키기 위해
↳ **부연 설명:** 우리는 한도 내에서만 세상을 알 수 있음.

주제문
[5]Curiously, / from this new level of uncertainty / even greater goals emerge / and appear to be attainable.
S V1 V2 C (→ 비교급 수식 부사)
🔑 불확실성(한정된 지식)으로 더 원대한 목표를 열망하게 됨.
이상하게도 / 이 새로운 수준의 불확실성에서 / 훨씬 더 큰 목표가 나온다 / 그리고 달성할 수 있어 보인다
↳ 불확실성에서 더 큰 목표가 나타남.

[6]Even if we cannot know the world / with absolute precision, // we can still control it.
(→ 부사절 접속사(비록 ~일지라도)) S′ V′ O′ S V O(= the world)
비록 우리가 세상을 알 수는 없을지라도 / 절대적인 정확성을 가지고 // 우리는 여전히 그것(세상)을 제어할 수 있다
↳ **예:** 불완전한 지식(불확실성)으로도 세상을 제어할 수 있음.

[7]Even our inherently incomplete knowledge / seems to work / as powerfully as ever.
S V C
★<as ~ as ever>: 여전히[변함 없이] ~로
심지어 우리의 본질적으로 불완전한 지식도 / 작동하는 것처럼 보인다 / 여전히 강력하게
↳ 불완전한 지식이라도 많이 활용됨.

[8]In short, / we may never know precisely // how high is the highest mountain, // but we continue to be certain // that we can get to the top nevertheless.
S1 V1 O1(명사절) S2 V2 O2(to-v구) 명사절 접속사 S′ V′
★간접의문문 형태인 명사절의 주어와 동사가 도치됨.
🔑 지식에 한계가 있지만 목표를 이룰 수 있다고 생각함.
간략하게 말하자면 / 우리는 아마 절대 정확하게 알 수 없을 것이다 // 가장 높은 산이 얼마나 높은지를 // 하지만 우리는 계속 확신한다 // 그럼에도 불구하고 우리가 정상에 닿을 수 있다는 것을
↳ **요약:** 지식의 한계(산 높이를 알지 못함)가 있어도 목표(정상)에 도달할 수 있다고 확신함.

해석

[1]인간의 지식이 완벽하게 정확하지 않고 '결코 그런 적도 없다'는 발견은 현대 인간의 영혼에 겸손하게 하고 아마도 진정시키는 효과를 미쳐왔다. [2]우리가 목격했듯이, 19세기는 세상이 그것의 부분들에서뿐만 아니라 전체로서도, 언제나 완벽하게 이해될 수 있다고 믿은 마지막이었다. [3]우리는 이것이 불가능하며, 언제나 불가능했다는 것을 이제 이해한다. [4]우리는 완전히가 아니라, 비록 그 한도가 대개 우리의 필요를 충족시키기 위해 조정될 수 있을지라도, 한도 내에서 알고 있다. [5]이상하게도, 이 새로운 수준의 불확실성에서 훨씬 더 큰 목표가 나오고 달성할 수 있어 보인다. [6]비록 우리가 절대적인 정확성을 가지고 세상을 알 수는 없을지라도, 우리는 여전히 그것(세상)을 제어할 수 있다. [7]심지어 우리의 본질적으로 불완전한 지식도 여전히 강력하게 작동하는 것처럼 보인다. [8]간략하게 말하자면, 우리는 가장 높은 산이 얼마나 높은지를 아마 절대 정확하게 알 수 없을 것이지만, 우리는 그럼에도 불구하고 우리가 정상에 닿을 수 있다는 것을 계속 확신한다.

어휘

- accurate 정확한; 정밀한
- humble 겸손하게 하다; 겸손한
- observe 목격하다, 보다; 관찰[관측]하다
- limit 한도, 한계; 제한하다
- adjust 조정[조절]하다; 적응하다
- uncertainty 불확실(성); 불확실한 것[상황]
- emerge 나오다, 나타나다
- appear ~인 것 같이 보이다; 나타내다
- attainable 달성할 수 있는
- precision 정확(성); 정밀(성); 신중함
- inherently 본질적으로; 선천적으로
- incomplete 불완전한
- nevertheless 그럼에도 불구하고
- [선택지] summit (산의) 정상, 꼭대기; 정점
- onward 앞으로 나아가는; 전방으로(의)
- integrate 통합하다

정답 가이드

인간의 지식에는 한계가 있는데, 그 지식의 불확실성에서 달성할 수 있어 보이는 더 큰 목표가 나온다고 했다. 그렇기 때문에 우리는 세상을 정확하게 알 수는 없더라도 제어할 수 있으며, 마지막 문장에서 이를 산의 높이를 알지 못해도 정복할 수 있다고 믿는 것에 비유한다. 즉, 계속해서 세상에 대한 정확한 지식을 갖기 위해 나아가고 있는 것이므로 글의 제목으로 가장 적절한 것은 ① 'Summits Yet to Be Reached: An Onward Journey to Knowledge(아직 도달되지 못한 정상, 즉 지식을 향해 나아가는 여정)'이다.

오답 클리닉

② Over the Mountain: A Single But Giant Step to Success (15%)
산을 넘어, 즉 성공을 향한 단 하나이지만 거대한 발걸음(×)
산은 비유적 표현으로 등장한 것이며, 그것이 성공에 이르는 방법이라는 내용도 아님.

③ Integrating Parts into a Whole: The Road to Perfection (9%)
부분들을 하나의 전체로 통합하기(×), 즉 완벽으로 가는 길
as a whole, in its parts를 활용한 오답. 통합에 대한 언급은 없음.

④ How to Live Together in an Age of Uncertainty (16%)
불확실의 시대에서 함께 사는 방법(×)
세상을 완전히 알 수 없다는 점에서 불확실성이 있지만, 공존에 대한 내용은 없음.

⑤ The Two Faces of a Knowledge-Based Society (6%)
지식 기반 사회의 두 얼굴(×)
지식 기반 사회가 가진 양면성에 대한 내용이 아님.

02 + 빈칸 추론 〈20학년도 9월 모평 32번 | 정답률 52%〉 ①

구문분석 & 직독직해

경제 소득 증가에 따른 동물성 식품 소비 증대

[1]With population growth slowing, / *the strongest force* (increasing demand for more agricultural production) / will be *rising incomes*, //
<with+O'+v-ing>: O'가 ~하면서, ~한 채로 / S / 현재분사구 / V / C
인구 증가가 둔화되면서 / 가장 강력한 힘은 (더 많은 농업 생산에 대한 수요를 늘리는) / '증가하는 소득'일 것이다 //

which are desired / by practically all governments and individuals.
관계대명사(보충 설명)
이를 원한다 / 사실상 모든 정부와 개인이

↳ **도입:** 농업 생산에 대한 수요를 늘리는 것은 '소득 증가'임.

★<spend A on B>: A를 B에 소비하다
[2]Although richer people spend / smaller proportions (of their income) / on food, //
부사절 접속사(양보) S' V' O'
비록 더 부유한 사람들이 소비하지만 / 더 작은 비율을 (자신들의 소득의) / 음식에 //

in total they consume more food — / and *richer food*, // which contributes to various kinds of disease and debilitation.
S V O₁ O₂ 관계대명사(보충 설명)
🔑 사람들은 부유할수록 더 기름진 음식을 섭취함.
통틀어서 그들은 더 많은 음식을 먹는다 / 그리고 더 기름진 음식을 // 그리고 이것은 다양한 종류의 질병과 건강 악화의 원인이 된다

↳ 부유한 사람들은 더 많고 기름진 음식을 먹음.

[3]*The changes in diet* [that usually accompany higher incomes] / will require relatively greater increases / in the production (of feed grains, / rather than food grains), //
S 주격 관계대명사 ★<A rather than B>: B보다는 A V O
명사구 병렬
식단의 변화는 [보통 더 높은 소득에 수반하는] / 상대적으로 더 큰 증가를 요구할 것이다 / 생산에서 (사료용 곡물의 / 식용 곡물보다는) //

→ 부사절 접속사(~ 때문에)
as foods of animal origin partly **displace** / **plant-based foods** / **in people's diets**.
S'(복수) V'(복수) O'
왜냐하면 동물성 식품이 어느 정도 대체하기 때문이다 / 식물에 기반한 식품을 / 사람들의 식단에서

↳ 소득이 높아지면 식물성 식품보다 동물성 식품을 더 섭취해 사료용 곡물 생산을 늘려야 함.

🔑 동물성 식품 생산에 더 많은 곡물이 필요함.
[4]It takes two to six times more grain / to produce food value through animals / than to get the equivalent value directly from plants.
<It takes A to-v: v하는 데 A가 필요하다> / to-v구 병렬
두 배에서 여섯 배 더 많은 곡물이 필요하다 / 동물을 통해 영양가를 생산하는 데 / 식물에서 직접 동등한 영양가를 얻는 것보다

↳ **부연 설명:** 식물성 식품보다 동물성 식품 생산에 곡물이 더 많이 필요함.

해석

[1]인구 증가가 둔화되면서, 더 많은 농업 생산에 대한 수요를 늘리는 가장 강력한 힘은 '증가하는 소득'일 것인데, 사실상 모든 정부와 개인이 이를 원한다. [2]비록 더 부유한 사람들이 자신들의 소득의 더 작은 비율을 음식에 소비하지만, 통틀어서 그들은 더 많은 음식을 그리고 더 기름진 음식을 먹는데, 이것은 다양한 종류의 질병과 건강 악화의 원인이 된다. [3]보통 더 높은 소득에 수반하는 식단의 변화는 식용 곡물보다는 사료용 곡물의 생산에서 상대적으로 더 큰 증가를 요구할 것인데, 왜냐하면 동물성 식품이 어느 정도 사람들의 식단에서 식물에 기반한 식품을 대체하기 때문이다.(▶ 사람들이 식물성 식품보다 동물성 식품을 더 많이 먹는다는 의미) [4]동물을 통해 영양가를 생산하는 데 식물에서 직접 동등한 영양가를 얻는 것보다 두 배에서 여섯 배 더 많은 곡물이 필요하다. [5]따라서 향후 30년에서 50년 안에 경제적 그리고 사회적 요구를 충족시키기 위해서는 세계가 현재의 두 배 넘는 만큼 많은 곡물과 농작물을 생산하되, 이것들이 식량이 부족한 사람들에게 이용 가능한 방식으로 해야 한다고 추정하는 것은 꽤 설득력이 있다.

어휘

agricultural 농업의, 농경의
income 소득, 수입
practically 사실상, 거의
proportion 비율, 부분
in total 통틀어, 전체로서
consume 먹다; 소비하다
contribute to A A의 원인이 되다
accompany 수반[동반]하다; 동행하다
relatively 상대적으로, 비교적

주제문

[5]It is thus quite credible to estimate //
가주어 V C 진주어
따라서 (~라고) 추정하는 것은 꽤 설득력이 있다 //

→ to estimate의 O(명사절)
that in order to meet economic and social needs / within the next three to five decades, /
명사절 접속사 목적(~하기 위해)
경제적 그리고 사회적 요구를 충족시키기 위해 / 향후 30년에서 50년 안에 /

★<A 배수사 as ~ as B>: A는 B의 …배만큼 ~한
the world should be producing / more than twice as much grain and agricultural products / as at present, / but in *ways* [that these are accessible to the food-insecure].
S′ V′ O′ 관계부사 <the+형용사>: ~한 사람들
세계가 생산해야 한다고 / 두 배 넘는 만큼 많은 곡물과 농작물을 / 현재의 /
그러나 방식으로 [이것들이 식량이 부족한 사람들에게 이용 가능한]

↳ **결론(시사점):** 경제적, 사회적 요구를 충족하되, 식량이 부족한 사람들이 이용할 수 있도록 농작물을 두 배 넘게 많이 생산해야 함.

feed grain 사료용 곡물
food grain 식용 곡물
food of animal origin 동물성 식품
partly 어느 정도; 부분적으로
displace 대체[대신]하다
food value (식품의) 영양가
equivalent 동등한; 상당하는 (것)
credible 설득력 있는; 신뢰할 수 있는
accessible 이용[접근] 가능한
food-insecure 식량이 부족한
[선택지] eco-friendly 친환경적인
nutritional 영양(상)의
imbalance 불균형
status 지위; 신분

정답 가이드

빈칸이 포함된 절의 주어인 동물성 식품이 '무엇을 하는' 것인지를 추론해야 한다. 주절의 내용은 식단 변화로 사료용 곡물의 생산 증가가 요구된다는 것이다. 빈칸 문장 뒤 이어지는 설명에서 동등한 영양가를 만드는 데 식물 기반 식품보다 동물성 식품 생산에 더 많은 곡물이 필요하다고 했다. 이를 통해, 동물성 식품 수요가 증가하기 때문에 사료용 곡물의 생산 증가가 요구된다는 의미임을 알 수 있으므로 빈칸에 들어갈 말로 가장 적절한 것은 ① 'displace plant-based foods in people's diets(사람들의 식단에서 식물에 기반한 식품을 대체하다)'이다.

오답 클리닉

② demand eco-friendly processing systems (9%)
친환경적인 처리 시스템을 요구하다
환경에 대한 내용이 아님.

③ cause several nutritional imbalances (14%)
여러 가지 영양 불균형을 유발하다
동물성 식품 위주로 식단이 바뀌는 것이 영양 불균형을 일으킨다는 내용은 없음.

The 주의 문장 2의 더 기름진 음식을 먹는 것이 다양한 질병과 건강 악화로 이어진다는 내용을 보고 영양 불균형이 발생할 것이라고 넘겨짚지 않도록 주의한다.

④ indicate the consumers' higher social status (14%)
소비자의 더 높은 사회적 지위를 나타내다
소득 증가와 동물성 식품 소비 증가를 연관 지어 설명하고 있지만, 소득 증가가 높은 사회적 지위를 나타낸다고 볼 수 없음.

⑤ play an important role in population growth (10%)
인구 증가에 있어 중요한 역할을 하다
동물성 식품이 인구 증가에 기여한다는 내용은 없으며, 첫 번째 문장에서 인구 증가가 둔화된다고 했음.

03 + 문장 넣기 〈21학년도 9월 모평 38번 | 정답률 49%〉 ③

구문분석 & 직독직해

수학 상대적 크기 비교에 효과적인 숫자 사용

★<without v-ing>: v하지 않고; v함이 없이
[1]We sometimes solve number problems / almost without realizing it.
S V O (= solving number problems)
우리는 가끔 숫자 문제를 푼다 / 거의 그것(숫자 문제를 풀고 있다는 것)을 인식하지 못한 채

↳ **도입:** 우리는 거의 무의식적으로 숫자 문제를 풀 때가 있음.

→ V(명령문) → suppose의 O₁(명사절) → suppose의 O₂(명사절)
(①) [2]For example, / suppose // (that) you are conducting a meeting // and (that) you want to ensure // that everyone there has a copy of the agenda.
명사절 접속사 생략 S′₁ V′₁ O′₁ S′₂ V′₂ O′₂ to ensure의 O(명사절)
예를 들어 / 가정해 보라 // 당신이 회의를 주관하고 있다고 // 그리고 당신이 확실히 하고 싶어 한다고 //
그곳에 있는 모든 사람이 의제에 관한 사본을 갖는 것을

🔑 주어진 문장의 this process가 지칭하는 내용임.
(②) [3]You can deal with this / by labelling each copy of the handout / in turn / with the initials (of each of *those* (present)).
S V O <by v-ing>: v함으로써 형용사
여러분은 이것을 처리할 수 있다 / 그 유인물의 각 사본에 적음으로써 / 차례로 / 이름의 첫 글자들을 (사람들 각각의 (참석한))

해석

[1]우리는 가끔 (숫자 문제를 풀고 있다는 것을) 거의 인식하지 못한 채 숫자 문제를 푼다. (①) [2]예를 들어, 당신이 회의를 주관하고 있고 그곳에 있는 모든 사람이 의제에 관한 사본을 갖는 것을 당신이 확실히 하고 싶어 한다고 가정해 보라. (②) [3]여러분은 그 유인물의 각 사본에 참석한 사람들 각각의 이름의 첫 글자들을 차례로 적음으로써 이것을 처리할 수 있다. (③ [4]이 과정을 완료하기 전에 사본이 다 떨어지지 않는 한, 여러분은 사람들에게 돌아갈 충분한 수의 사본이 있다는 것을 알 것이다.) [5]그렇다면 여러분은 산수에 의존하지 않고, 명시적인 계산 없이 이 문제를 해결한 것이다. (④) [6]그래도 여기에는 우리에게 영향을 미치는 숫자가 있고 그것(숫자)이 하나의 집합과 다른 집합의 정확한 비교를 가능하게 하는데, 그 집합을 구성하는 요소들이 한 세

앞 문장의 회의 참석자 각각의 이름 첫 글자를 유인물에 적는 것을 지칭함.

(③) [4]As long as you do not run out of copies / before completing this process, //
부사절 접속사(~하는 한)
여러분에게 사본이 다 떨어지지 않는 한 / 이 과정을 완료하기 전에 //

will know의 O(명사절)
you will know // that you have *a sufficient number* (to go around).)
S V 명사절 접속사 S′ V′ O′
여러분은 알 것이다 // 충분한 수의 사본이 있다는 것을 (사람들에게 돌아갈)
↳ 예: 유인물에 회의 참석자들 각각의 이름 첫 글자들을 적고도 모자라지 않는다면 유인물은 충분히 있는 것임.

[5]You have then solved this problem / without resorting to arithmetic / and without explicit counting.
S V O 전치사구 병렬
그렇다면 여러분은 이 문제를 해결한 것이다 / 산수에 의존하지 않고 / 그리고 명시적인 계산 없이
↳ 예의 부연 설명: 명시적인 계산 없이 문제를 해결함

주제문
(④) [6]There are numbers (at work for us) / here all the same // and they allow precise comparison (of one collection with another), //
V₁ S₁ (= numbers) S₂ V₂ O
숫자가 있다 (우리에게 영향을 미치는) / 그래도 여기에는 // 그리고 그것(숫자)이 정확한 비교를 가능하게 한다 (하나의 집합과 다른 집합의) //

부사절 접속사(양보)
even though *the members* [that make up the collections] / could have entirely different characters,
S′ 주격 관계대명사 V′ O′
부사절 접속사(~처럼)
// as is the case *here*, // where one set is a collection of people, // while the other consists of pieces of paper.
V″ S″ 관계부사절(보충 설명) 부사절 접속사(~인 한편)
*접속사 as가 비교(~처럼)를 뜻할 때, 주어와 동사가 도치될 수 있음.
요소들이 ~임에도 [그 집합을 구성하는] / 완전히 다른 특징을 가질 수 있음(에도) // 여기의 경우처럼 // 한 세트는 사람들의 집합인 // 다른 세트는 종이로 구성된 한편

(⑤) [7]What numbers allow us to do / is to compare the relative size of one set / with another.
S(명사절) V(단수) C(to-v구)
숫자가 우리로 하여금 할 수 있게 하는 것은 / 한 세트의 상대적인 크기를 비교하는 것이다 / 다른 세트와
↳ 숫자는 여전히 다른 특징을 지닌 두 집합의 상대적 크기를 정확하게 비교할 수 있게 함.

트는 사람들의 집합인 한편 다른 세트는 종이로 구성된 여기의 경우처럼 완전히 다른 특징을 가질 수 있음에도 그러하다. (⑤) [7]숫자가 우리로 하여금 할 수 있게 하는 것은 한 세트의 상대적인 크기를 다른 세트와 비교하는 것이다.

어휘

conduct 이끌다; 행동(하다)
agenda 의제, 안건
deal with ~을 처리하다; ~을 다루다
label (이름·라벨을) 적다, 붙이다; 분류하다
in turn 차례로; 결국
initial 이름의 첫 글자; 처음의
run out of ~이 다 떨어지다
go around (사람들에게 몫이) 돌아가다
resort to A A에 의존하다
explicit 명시적인, 명백한
counting 계산, 셈
at work (영향이) 작용하여
all the same 그래도, 여전히
precise 정확한
collection 집합; 수집(품)
make up ~을 구성하다; 지어내다
consist of ~로 구성되다
relative 상대적인; 친척

정답 가이드

주어진 문장은 이 과정(this process)을 완료하기 전에 사본이 다 떨어지지 않는다면 사람들에게 돌아갈 사본이 충분히 있다는 것을 알 수 있다는 내용으로, 주어진 문장 앞에는 this process가 지칭하는 내용이 제시되어야 할 것이다. 회의 참석자 모두에게 유인물을 나눠주고자 하는 상황을 예로 들며, ③ 앞에서 참석자의 이름 첫 글자들을 각각 유인물에 적는 과정을 설명하고 있고, 이를 주어진 문장에서 this process로 받아 그 과정을 마저 설명하고 있다. 또한 ③ 뒤에서 그런 과정으로 문제를 해결한 것이라고 했으므로 주어진 문장은 ③에 들어가는 것이 가장 적절하다.

오답 클리닉

① (2%) 우리는 가끔 인식하지 못한 채 숫자 문제를 푼다는 앞 문장에 대한 예를 제시하는 내용이다.
② (6%) 회의에 참석한 모든 사람들에게 의제의 사본을 나눠주고자 하는 상황을 뒤에서 this로 받으면서, 해결 과정에 대한 설명이 이어진다.
④ (31%) 계산 없이도 문제를 해결할 수 있다는 예 뒤에 all the same(그래도)을 사용하여 서로 다른 집합을 정확하게 비교할 수 있게 숫자가 여전히 영향을 미친다는 상반되는 내용이 이어진다.

The 주의 주어진 문장은 명시적인 계산 없이도 문제를 해결할 수 있다는 예에 해당하는 내용임에 주의한다.

⑤ (12%) 앞 문장을 재진술한 내용으로 연결이 자연스럽다.

01 ✦ 함의 추론 (21학년도 6월 모평 21번 | 정답률 65%) ⑤

구문분석 & 직독직해

비즈니스 고객의 일을 대신 해주는 보조 사업

주제문

[1] *Many ancillary businesses* [that today seem almost core] / at one time started out / as **journey edges**.
(S: Many ancillary businesses / 주격 관계대명사: that / V′: seem / C′: core / V: started out)

많은 보조 사업들이 [오늘날 거의 핵심인 것처럼 보이는] / 한때는 시작했다 / 여정의 가장자리로

↳ 현재 주요해 보이는 보조 사업들(추가 서비스)은 처음에 주요하지 않았음.

🔑 조립과 설치는 상품 구매에 따라오는 추가 서비스임.

[2] For example, / retailers often boost sales / with accompanying support (such as assembly or installation services).
(S: retailers / V: boost / O: sales)

예를 들어 / 소매상들은 흔히 매출을 끌어올린다 / 수반하는 지원으로 (조립이나 설치 서비스와 같은)

↳ **예 1:** 소매상들은 추가 지원을 제공함으로써 판매를 촉진함.

[3] Think of *a home goods retailer* (selling an unassembled outdoor grill as a box of parts / and leaving its customer's mission incomplete).
(V: Think / 현재분사구 병렬: selling ~ and leaving ~ / ★<leave+O+C>: O를 ~한 상태로 두다)

가정용품 소매상을 생각해 보라 (조립되지 않은 야외 그릴을 부품 상자로 판매하는 / 그리고 고객의 임무를 미완성 상태로 두는)

↳ **미조립 제품을 판매하는 경우:** 고객은 바로 제품을 사용할 수 없음.

[4] When that retailer also sells assembly and delivery, // it takes another step in the journey / to the customer's true mission (of cooking in his backyard).
(부사절 접속사: When / S′: that retailer / V₁: sells / O′: assembly and delivery / S: it (= that retailer) / V: takes / O: another step / the customer's true mission = cooking in his backyard)

그 소매상이 조립과 배달도 판매할 때 // 그것(그 소매상)은 여정에서 또 다른 한 걸음을 나아간다 / 고객의 진정한 임무를 향해 (자신의 뒤뜰에서 요리하기라는)

↳ **조립과 배달을 제공하는 경우:** 고객은 바로 제품을 사용할 수 있음.

[5] Another example is *the business-to-business service contracts* [that are layered / on top of software sales].
(S: Another example / V: is / C: the business-to-business service contracts / 주격 관계대명사: that)

또 다른 예는 기업 대 기업 간 서비스 계약이다 [층층이 쌓이는 / 소프트웨어 판매에 더해]

↳ **예 2:** 기업 간 거래에서도 부가 서비스를 끼워 계약함.

🔑 고객이 직접 할 일을 대신 해주는 서비스임.

[6] *Maintenance, installation, training, delivery, anything at all* [that turns do-it-yourself into a do-it-for-me solution] / originally resulted / from exploring the edge (of where core products intersect with customer journeys).
(S: Maintenance, ~ anything at all / 주격 관계대명사: that / V: resulted / of의 O(명사절): where ~ journeys)

유지, 설치, 교육, 배달, 무엇이든 [손수 하는 것을 나를 위해 해주는 해결책으로 바꿔주는] / 원래 비롯되었다 / 가장자리를 탐구하는 것에서 (핵심 제품이 고객의 여정과 교차하는 곳의)

↳ **주제문 재진술:** 보조 사업은 고객의 일을 덜어주기 위해 생겨남.

해석

[1] 오늘날 거의 핵심인 것처럼 보이는 많은 보조 사업들이 한때는 여정의 가장자리로 시작했다. [2] 예를 들어, 소매상들은 흔히 조립이나 설치 서비스와 같은 수반하는 지원으로 매출을 끌어올린다. [3] 조립되지 않은 야외 그릴을 부품 상자로 판매해서 고객의 임무를 미완성 상태로 두는 가정용품 소매상을 생각해 보라.(▶ 바로 사용이 불가능해서 고객이 제품으로 하려던 일을 하지 못함을 의미) [4] 그 소매상이 또한 조립과 배달도 판매할 때, 그것은 자신의 뒤뜰에서 요리하기라는 그 고객의 진정한 임무를 향해 여정에서 또 다른 한 걸음을 나아간다. [5] 또 다른 예는 소프트웨어 판매에 더해 층층이 쌓이는 기업 대 기업 간 서비스 계약이다. [6] 손수 하는 것을 나를 위해 해주는 해결책으로 바꿔주는 유지, 설치, 교육, 배달, 무엇이든 핵심 제품이 고객의 여정과 교차하는 곳의 가장자리를 탐구하는 것에서 원래 비롯되었다.

어휘

edge 가장자리, 모서리; (칼 등의) 날
retailer 소매상, 소매업자
boost 끌어 올리다; 신장시키다, 북돋우다
accompanying 수반하는
assembly (기계 부품의) 조립; 집회
cf. assemble 조립하다; 모이다
installation 설치[설비]
home goods 가정용품
mission 임무, 사명
incomplete 미완성의
contract 계약(서); 계약하다
layer 층층이 쌓다; 층[막, 겹]
on top of ~에 더하여, ~외에; ~ 위에
maintenance 유지, 지속
turn A into B A를 B로 바꾸다
result from ~에서 비롯되다, ~이 원인이다
[선택지] dependence 의존(성), 의지
end product 완제품, 최종 결과물[제품]
component 부품, (구성) 요소
breakthrough 획기적 발전; (문제 해결의) 돌파구
primary 기본적인; 최초의

정답 가이드

첫 문장에서 핵심 사업으로 보이는 보조 사업들이 여정의 가장자리로 시작했다고 설명한 뒤 예가 이어지므로, 주제문임을 알 수 있다. 예를 통해 이것이 고객이 편리하게 제품을 사용하도록 소매상이 조립과 배달과 같은 서비스를 제공하는 것임을 알 수 있다. 마지막 문장에서도 이것이 고객이 직접 할 일을 대신 해주는 해결책으로 나왔다고 했으므로 밑줄 친 부분이 의미하는 바로 가장 적절한 것은 ⑤ 'providing extra services beyond customers' primary purchase(고객의 기본적인 구매를 넘어 추가 서비스를 제공하는 것)'이다.

The 핵심 ★ journey edges가 보조 사업이었다는 것에서 주된 판매에 덧붙여 고객의 임무 완수를 위한 가장자리 업무 대행, 즉 추가 서비스 제공임을 추론할 수 있다.

오답 클리닉

① requiring customers to purchase unnecessary goods (7%)
고객이 불필요한 상품을 구매하도록(×) 요구하는 것
고객이 불필요한 상품을 사게 한다는 내용은 언급되지 않음.

② decreasing customers' dependence on business services (10%)
비즈니스 서비스에 대한 고객의 의존을 줄이는 것(×)
보조 사업은 고객이 직접 할 일을 대신 해주므로 오히려 고객의 의존도를 높인다고 볼 수 있음.

③ focusing more on selling end products than components (11%)
부품보다 완제품 판매(×)에 더 중점을 두는 것
parts, assembly를 활용한 오답. 완제품 판매에 대한 언급은 없음.

④ adding a technological breakthrough to their core products (7%)
핵심 제품에 기술의 획기적 발전을 추가하는 것(×)
고객 편의를 위해 추가 서비스를 제공한 것이지 기술의 획기적 발전을 추가한 것이 아님.

02 + 빈칸 추론 (20학년도 9월 모평 31번 | 정답률 37%)

①

구문분석 & 직독직해

생활 반복하는 이야기가 기억이 되는 과정

[1] When you begin to tell *a story* again [that you have retold many times], // what you retrieve from memory is the index to the story itself.
(When: 부사절 접속사(시간) / that: 목적격 관계대명사 / what you retrieve from memory: S(명사절) / is: V / the index to the story itself: C)
🔑 이야기는 우리 기억에서 나옴.
여러분이 이야기를 다시 말하기 시작할 때 [여러분이 여러 번 다시 말했던] // 여러분이 기억으로부터 회수하는 것은 그 이야기 자체에 대한 지표이다
↳ **도입:** 같은 이야기를 다시 할 때 우리가 기억해 내는 것은 이야기 그 자체의 지표임.

[2] That index can be embellished / in a variety of ways.
(That index: S / can be embellished: V)
그 지표는 윤색(과장이나 미화)될 수 있다 / 다양한 방식으로

[3] Over time, / even the embellishments become standardized.
(the embellishments: S / become: V / standardized: C)
시간이 흐르면서 / 그 윤색된 것들까지도 표준화된다

[4] *An old man's story* [that he has told hundreds of times] / shows little variation, // and *any variation* [that does exist] / becomes part (of the story itself), / regardless of its origin.
(An old man's story: S_1 / that: 목적격 관계대명사 / shows: V_1 / variation: O_1 / *little: 거의 없는 / any variation: S_2 / that: 주격 관계대명사 / does → exist 강조 / becomes: V_2 / part: C_2 / regardless of: 전치사(~와 상관없이))
한 노인의 이야기는 [그가 수백 번 말한] / 변형을 거의 보이지 않는다 // 그리고 어떤 변형이든 [정말로 존재하는] / 일부가 된다 (이야기 자체의) / 그것의 기원과 상관없이
🔑 반복해서 말한 이야기의 변형이 이야기의 일부가 됨.
↳ **이야기의 윤색과 변형:** 여러 번 반복하다 보면 이야기의 일부가 됨.

[5] People add *details* / to their stories / [that may or may not have occurred].
(People: S / add: V / details: O / that: 주격 관계대명사 / may or may not have occurred: V′)
사람들은 세부 사항을 더한다 / 자신들의 이야기에 / [일어났을 수도, 또는 일어나지 않았을 수도 있는]

[6] They are recalling indexes / and (are) reconstructing details.
(They: S(= People) / are recalling: V_1 / indexes: O_1 / (are) reconstructing: V_2 / details: O_2)
그들은 지표들을 기억해 내고 있다 / 그리고 세부 사항들을 재구성하고 있다

[7] If at some point they add a nice detail, / not (being) really certain of its validity, // telling the story (with that same detail) / a few more times / will ensure its permanent place / in the story index.
(If: 부사절 접속사(조건) / they: S′ / add: V′ / a nice detail: O′ / not (being) really certain: 분사구문(= while they are not really certain ~) / *형용사 앞의 현재분사 being이 생략됨. / telling the story: S(동명사구) / will ensure: V / its permanent place: O)
🔑 더해진 세부 사항은 반복적으로 말하다 보면 이야기의 일부가 됨.
만약 어느 시점에 그들이 훌륭한 세부 사항을 더한다면 / 그것의 타당성에 대해 정말로 확신하지 못한 채로 // 그 이야기를 말하는 것은 (동일한 그 세부 사항과 함께) / 몇 번 더 / 그것의 영구적인 위치를 보장할 것이다 / 그 이야기 지표에서
↳ **이야기에 더해진 세부 사항:** 여러 번 반복하다 보면 이야기에 영구적으로 편입됨.

해석

[1]여러분이 여러 번 다시 말했던 이야기를 다시 말하기 시작할 때, 기억으로부터 회수하는 것은 그 이야기 자체에 대한 지표이다. [2]그 지표는 다양한 방식으로 윤색될 수 있다. [3]시간이 흐르면서, 그 윤색된 것들까지도 표준화된다. [4]수백 번 말한 한 노인의 이야기는 변형을 거의 보이지 않으며, 정말로 존재하는 어떤 변형이든 그것의 기원과 상관없이 이야기 자체의 일부가 된다. [5]사람들은 일어났을 수도, 또는 일어나지 않았을 수도 있는 세부 사항을 자신들의 이야기에 더한다. [6]그들은 지표들을 기억해 내고 세부 사항들을 재구성하고 있다. [7]만약, 그것의 타당성에 대해 정말로 확신하지 못한 채로 어느 시점에 그들이 훌륭한 세부 사항을 더한다면, 동일한 그 세부 사항과 함께 그 이야기를 몇 번 더 말하는 것은 그 이야기 지표에서 그것의 영구적인 위치를 보장할 것이다. [8]다시 말해, 우리가 되풀이하여 말하는 이야기는 그 이야기와 관련이 있는 사건들에 대해 우리가 가지고 있는 기억과 일치한다.

어휘

index 지표; 색인
standardize 표준화하다
variation 변형; 변화, 변동
detail 세부 사항; 상세히 알리다
recall 기억해 내다, 상기하다[시키다]; 회수[리콜]하다
reconstruct 재구성하다; 재건[복원]하다
validity 타당성, 정당성; 유효함
ensure 보장하다; 확보하다
permanent 영구[영속]적인
time and again 되풀이하여, 몇 번이고

주제문

[8]In other words, / the stories [we tell time and again] / are **identical** / to the memory [(which[that]) we have] (of the events [that the story relates]).

S V C / 목적격 관계대명사 생략 / 목적격 관계대명사

다시 말해 / 이야기는 [우리가 되풀이하여 말하는] / 일치한다 / 기억과 [우리가 가지고 있는] (사건들에 대해 [그 이야기와 관련이 있는])

↳ **결론:** 우리가 말하는 이야기는 우리가 가지고 있는 기억과 같음.

정답 가이드

빈칸 문장은 우리가 되풀이하는 이야기는 우리 기억과 '어떠하다'는 것인지를 묻고 있는데, 마지막 문장이 In other words로 시작하므로 앞서 길게 말한 내용을 다른 말로 바꿔 간단히 표현한 것임을 알 수 있다. 반드시 직전 문장을 말바꿈할 때에만 In other words를 사용하는 것은 아니라는 것에 주의해야 한다. 첫 문장에서 이야기를 되풀이 할 때 '기억'으로부터 회수한다고 했으므로 이야기와 기억은 서로 '일치하는' 것임을 알 수 있다. 뒤이어 시간이 흐르면서 윤색된 것들도 이야기의 일부가 된다고 더 자세히 설명한다. 타당성(윤색된 세부 사항이 실제 사실인지)에 대한 확신 없이 세부 사항을 더해 되풀이하다 보면 그 세부 사항이 이야기 속에 영원히 자리 잡는다는 것이다. 따라서 빈칸에 들어갈 말로 가장 적절한 것은 ① 'identical(일치하는)'이다.

오답 클리닉

② beneficial (20%) 유익한
되풀이하여 말하는 이야기가 기억에 유익하다는 내용이 아님.

③ alien (25%) 이질적인
되풀이해서 말하는 이야기의 변형은 결국 이야기의 일부가 되어 기억되는 것이므로 글의 내용과 반대됨.

④ prior (12%) 앞선
이야기와 기억의 선후 관계를 따지는 내용이 아니므로 알 수 없는 내용임.

⑤ neutral (6%) 중립적인
되풀이하여 말하는 이야기는 반복되면서 윤색되거나 변형될 수 있으므로 중립적이라는 말은 적절하지 않음.

03 + 무관 문장 〈21학년도 9월 모평 35번 | 정답률 84%〉 ③

구문분석 & 직독직해

경제 상품으로 여겨지는 경관의 정체성

주제문

[1]In a highly commercialized setting (such as the United States), / it is not surprising // that many landscapes are seen / as commodities. ⊶ 경관을 상품으로 여기는 것에 관한 내용임.

★<see A as B(A를 B로 여기다)>의 수동형 / 가주어 V C / 진주어(명사절)

고도로 상업화된 환경에서는 (미국과 같이) / (~은) 놀라운 일이 아니다 // 많은 경관이 여겨지는 것은 / 상품으로

[2]In other words, / they are valued / because of their market potential.

→ (= landscapes) S V

다시 말해 / 그것들(경관)은 가치 있게 여겨진다 / 그것들의 시장 잠재력 때문에

↳ 경관은 시장 잠재력 때문에 상품으로 가치 있게 여겨짐.

[3]Residents develop an identity / in part based on // how the landscape can generate income / for the community.

S V O / → based on의 O(명사절) 의문사 S' V' O'

주민들은 정체성을 발전시킨다 / 부분적으로 ~에 기초하여 // 경관이 어떻게 소득을 만들어 낼 수 있는지 / 지역 사회를 위해

↳ **세부 사항 1:** 주민들은 소득 창출에 기반해 경관 정체성을 발전시킴.

① [4]This process involves / more than the conversion of the natural elements / into commodities.

S V O

이 과정은 포함한다 / 자연적인 요소의 전환 그 이상을 / 상품으로의

② [5]The landscape itself, / (including the people and their sense of self), / takes on the form of a commodity.

S 전치사구 삽입 V O

경관 자체가 / (사람들과 그들의 자아감을 포함하여) / 상품의 형태를 띤다

↳ **부연 설명:** 지역 주민의 자아감을 포함해 자연 경관이 상품화됨.

⊶ 경관의 상품화와 무관한 경관 보호에 관한 내용임.

③ [6]Landscape protection in the US traditionally focuses / on protecting areas of wilderness, (typically in mountainous regions).

S V on의 O(동명사구)

미국에서 경관 보호는 전통적으로 초점을 둔다 / 황무지 지역을 보호하는 것에 (일반적으로 산악 지역에 있는)

↳ 미국의 경관 보호는 황무지 지역 보호에 초점을 둠.

해석

[1]미국과 같이 고도로 상업화된 환경에서는 많은 경관이 상품으로 여겨지는 것이 놀라운 일이 아니다. [2]다시 말해, 그것들(경관)은 그것들의 시장 잠재력 때문에 가치 있게 여겨진다. [3]주민들은 경관이 지역 사회를 위해 어떻게 소득을 만들어 낼 수 있는지에 부분적으로 기초하여 정체성을 발전시킨다. ① [4]이 과정은 자연적인 요소의 상품으로의 전환 그 이상을 포함한다. ② [5]사람들과 그들의 자아감을 포함하여 경관 자체가 상품의 형태를 띤다. ③ [6]미국에서 경관 보호는 일반적으로 산악 지역에 있는 황무지 지역을 보호하는 것에 전통적으로 초점을 둔다. ④ [7]시간이 지나면서, 경관 정체성은 경관에 대한 이야기를 선전하기 위해 사용될 수 있는 일종의 '로고'로 발전할 수 있다. ⑤ [8]따라서 캘리포니아의 'Wine Country', 플로리다의 'Sun Coast', 혹은 사우스다코타의 'Badlands'는 외부인과 주민 둘 다 장소를 인식하는 방식을 형성하고, 이 호칭들은 그곳에 사는 사람들의 문화와 관련된 일련의 기대감을 형성한다.

어휘

commercialize 상업화하다
landscape 경관, 풍경
commodity 상품, 물품; (유용한) 것
resident 주민; 거주하는
in part 부분적으로, 어느 정도
based on ~에 기초하여
conversion 전환, 변환

④ [7]Over time, / the landscape identity can evolve / into *a sort of "logo"* [that can be used / to sell the stories (of the landscape)].

(S: the landscape identity / V: can evolve / 주격 관계대명사: that / V′: can be used / 목적(~하기 위해): to sell)

시간이 지나면서 / 경관 정체성은 발전할 수 있다 / 일종의 '로고'로 [사용될 수 있는 / 이야기를 선전하기 위해 (경관에 대한)]

↳ **세부 사항 2:** 경관 정체성은 일종의 로고로 발전 가능함.

⑤ [8]Thus, California's "Wine Country," Florida's "Sun Coast," or South Dakota's "Badlands" shape // how both outsiders and residents perceive a place, //

(S_1 / V_1: shape / O_1(명사절): how both outsiders and residents perceive a place)

따라서 캘리포니아의 'Wine Country', 플로리다의 'Sun Coast', 또는 사우스다코타의 'Badlands'는 형성한다 // 외부인과 주민 둘 다 장소를 인식하는 방식을 //

and these labels build / *a set of expectations* (associated with the culture (of *those* [who live there])).

(S_2: these labels / V_2: build / O_2(명사구): a set of expectations / 과거분사구: associated with ... / 주격 관계대명사: who)

그리고 이 호칭들은 형성한다 / 일련의 기대감을 (문화와 관련된 (사람들의 [그곳에 사는]))

↳ **부연 설명(예):** 경관 정체성이 발전하여 사람들이 그 장소를 인식하는 방식과 그곳의 문화에 대한 기대감을 형성함.

sense of self 자아감, 자의식
take on (양상을) 띠다, 나타내다; (일을) 떠맡다
wilderness 황무지, 황야
mountainous region 산악 지역
evolve 발전하다; 진화하다
perceive 인식하다, 감지하다
associated with ~와 관련된

⊕ 캘리포니아의 Wine Country는 유명 와인 생산지, 플로리다의 Sun Coast는 플로리다 반도의 남서쪽 해변 지역, 사우스다코타의 badlands는 바위투성이의 침식 지역으로 협곡, 언덕, 뾰족한 산봉우리 등으로 이루어진 불모지임.

정답 가이드

도입 부분에서 미국처럼 고도로 상업화된 환경에서는 경관도 상품으로 여겨지며, 주민들이 경관으로 소득을 올리는 방법에 기반하여 정체성을 발전시킨다고 했다. 즉 경관을 상품화하고 경관 정체성을 발전시키는 것에 대한 내용이 주 흐름인데, ③은 경관 보호에 대한 내용이므로 흐름이 어색하다. 반면, ④, ⑤는 경관 정체성이 경관을 선전하는 로고로 발전할 수 있음을 예를 들어 설명하는 것이므로 경관을 상품화한다는 글의 흐름에 알맞다.

오답 클리닉

① (2%) This process는 앞 문장에 언급된 경관 정체성의 발전 과정을 의미하며, 그 과정이 단순한 상품으로의 전환 이상을 포함한다는 내용이다.
② (4%) 앞 문장의 내용을 지역 주민들의 자아감을 포함해 경관 자체가 상품이 되는 것이라고 구체적으로 설명한다.
④ (8%) 경관 정체성이 경관에 대한 이야기를 선전하는 '로고'로 발전할 수 있다는 내용이다.
⑤ (2%) 경관 정체성이 로고로 발전한 예를 보여주며, 그것이 지역을 인식하는 방식과 그곳의 문화에 대한 기대감을 형성한다고 설명한다.

01 ✦ 글의 요지 〈22학년도 9월 모평 22번 | 정답률 54%〉 ①

구문분석 & 직독직해

사회 전문직의 자율성에 따르는 사회적 책임

[1]Historically, / the professions and society have engaged / in *a negotiating process* (intended to define / the terms of their relationship).
(S: the professions and society / V: have engaged / 과거분사구: intended to define)

역사적으로 / 전문직과 사회는 참여해 왔다 / 협상 과정에 (규정하고자 의도된 / 그들 관계의 조건을)

*장소 부사구가 문장 맨 앞에 오면서 주어와 동사가 도치됨.

[2]At the heart of this process / is the tension (between the professions' pursuit of autonomy and the public's demand for accountability).
(장소 부사구 / V / S / 명사구 병렬)

이 (협상) 과정의 핵심에는 / 긴장이 있다 (전문직의 자율성 추구와 책임에 대한 공공의 요구 사이의)

↳ **도입:** 전문직은 자율성을, 사회는 (전문직의) 책임을 원함.

주제문

[3]Society's granting of power and privilege / to the professions / is premised / on *their willingness and ability* (to contribute to social well-being / and to conduct their affairs / in *a manner* (consistent with broader social values)).
(동명사 granting의 의미상 주어 / S / V / = / to-v구 병렬 / 형용사구)

🔑 사회 기여와 책무 수행을 전제로 전문직은 권한을 부여받음.

사회가 권한과 특권을 부여한 것은 / 전문직에 / 전제로 한다 / 그들(전문직)의 자발성과 능력을 (사회 복지에 기여하는 / 그리고 자신의 일을 수행하는 / 방식으로 (더 광범위한 사회적 가치와 일치하는))

↳ 전문직이 부여받은 특권은 사회 기여의 책임을 수반함.

[4]It has long been recognized // that the expertise and privileged position of professionals / confer *authority and power* [that could readily be used / to advance their own interests / at the expense of *those* [(who(m)[that]) they serve]].
(가주어 / V / 진주어(명사절) / 명사절 접속사 / S′ / V′ / O′ / 주격 관계대명사 / 목적(~하기 위해) / (= people) 목적격 관계대명사 생략)

(~라고) 오랫동안 인식되어 왔다 // 전문직의 전문 지식과 특권적 지위가 / 권위와 권한을 준다고 [쉽게 이용될 수 있는 / 그들 자신의 이익을 향상시키기 위해 / 사람들을 희생시켜 [그들이 돕는]]

↳ **지금까지의 인식:** 전문직의 권한이 사적 이익 추구에 이용될 수 있음.

[5]As Edmund Burke observed two centuries ago, //
(부사절 접속사(~듯이) / S′ / V′)

Edmund Burke가 2세기 전에 말했듯이 //

"Men are qualified for civil liberty / in exact proportion to *their disposition* (to put moral chains upon their own appetites)."

🔑 도덕적 제약(= 책임)을 따르는 만큼 자유(= 자율성)를 얻을 수 있음.

"인간은 시민의 자유를 위한 자격을 얻는다 / 그들의 성향에 정확히 비례해서 (자신의 욕구에 도덕적 사슬을 매는)"

↳ 자유를 누리고 싶은 만큼 개인의 욕구를 제어해야 함.

🔑 자율성은 그냥 주어지는 것이 아님.

[6]Autonomy has never been a one-way street / and is never granted absolutely and irreversibly.
(S / V_1 / V_2)

자율성은 일방통행로였던 적이 없었다 / 그리고 결코 절대적이고 뒤집을 수 없게 주어지는 것이 아니다

↳ **결론:** 자율성은 일방적으로 주어지지 않으므로 책임을 다해야 함.

해석

[1]역사적으로 전문직과 사회는 그들 관계의 조건을 규정하고자 의도된 협상 과정에 참여해 왔다. [2]이 (협상) 과정의 핵심에는 전문직의 자율성 추구와 책임에 대한 공공의 요구 사이의 긴장이 있다. [3]사회가 전문직에 권한과 특권을 부여한 것은 사회 복지에 기여하고 더 광범위한 사회적 가치와 일치하는 방식으로 자신의 일을 수행하는 그들(전문직)의 자발성과 능력을 전제로 한다. [4]전문직의 전문 지식과 특권적 지위가 그들이 돕는 사람들을 희생시켜 그들 자신의 이익을 향상시키기 위해 쉽게 이용될 수 있는 권위와 권한을 준다고 오랫동안 인식되어 왔다. [5]Edmund Burke가 2세기 전에 말했듯이, "인간은 자신의 욕구에 도덕적 사슬을 매는 그들의 성향에 정확히 비례해서 시민의 자유를 위한 자격을 얻는다." [6]자율성은 일방통행로였던 적이 없었으며 결코 절대적이고 뒤집을 수 없게 주어지는 것이 아니다.

어휘

profession (*pl.*) 전문직; 직업, 직종
engage in ~에 참여하다
negotiate 협상하다
define 규정하다, 정의하다
term (*pl.*) 조건, 조항; 용어; 학기
tension 긴장 (상태); 갈등
accountability 책임, 책무
grant 부여하다, 주다; 승인하다
willingness 자발성, 기꺼이 하기
contribute to A A에 기여하다
conduct 수행하다
affair (*pl.*) 일, 업무; 사건
consistent with ~와 일치하는
expertise 전문 지식
confer 주다, 수여[부여]하다
authority 권위, 권한
readily 쉽게, 순조롭게; 선뜻, 기꺼이
advance 향상시키다
at the expense of ~을 희생시키면서
serve 돕다; 봉사하다
observe 말하다; 보다; 관찰하다
qualify 자격을 주다
in proportion to A A에 비례하여
disposition 성향, 기질[성격]
appetite 욕구; 식욕
irreversibly 뒤집을 수 없게

정답 가이드

사회가 전문직에 부여한 권한은 그들이 사회 복지에 기여하고 더 폭넓은 사회적 가치와 일치하는 방식으로 임무를 수행하는 것, 즉 사회적 책임을 전제로 하는 것이라고 했다. 이어지는 문장들은 모두 이를 뒷받침하는 것으로, 자율성을 개인적인 이익이나 욕구 충족에 이용하는 것을 비판하고 있다. 따라서 글의 요지로 가장 적절한 것은 ① '전문직에 부여되는 자율성은 그에 상응하는 사회적 책임을 수반한다.'이다.

오답 클리닉

② 전문직의 권위는 해당 집단의 이익을 추구(×)하는 데 이용되어 왔다. (24%)
문장 4를 이용한 오답. 전문직의 지식과 특권적 지위가 그들 자신의 이익을 추구하는 권한을 준다고 인식되어 왔다는 내용은 있으나 글의 요지에서 벗어남.

The 주의 글의 일부 내용을 담은 오답을 요지로 착각하지 않도록 주의한다.

③ 전문직의 사회적 책임을 규정할 수 있는 제도 정비(×)가 필요하다. (2%)
전문직의 사회적 책임이 필요한 것은 맞으나 그에 관한 제도 정비에 대한 언급은 없음.

④ 전문직이 되기 위한 자격 요건(×)은 사회 경제적 요구에 따라 변화해 왔다. (4%)
전문직이 되기 위한 자격 요건에 대한 언급은 없음.

⑤ 전문직의 업무 성과(×)는 일정 수준의 자율성과 특권이 부여될 때 높아진다. (16%) 전문직의 업무 성과와 자율성과 특권의 관계는 언급되지 않음.

02 + 빈칸 추론 (20학년도 6월 모평 33번 | 정답률 46%) ①

구문분석 & 직독직해

기술 비물질화 현상

주제문

[1]Digital technology accelerates dematerialization / by hastening the migration (from products to services).
S / V / O / <by v-ing>: v함으로써

디지털 기술은 비물질화를 가속화한다 / 이동을 촉진함으로써 (제품에서 서비스로의)

[2]The liquid nature (of services) / means // (that) they don't have to be bound to materials.
S(단수) / V(단수) / 명사절 접속사 생략 / (that) → (= services) / O(명사절)

유동적인 특성은 (서비스의) / 의미한다 // 그것들(서비스)이 물질에 얽매일 필요가 없다는 것을

↳ **비물질화 현상:** 디지털 기술 발전으로 제품이 서비스화 됨.

[3]But dematerialization is not just about digital goods.
S / V / C

그러나 비물질화는 단지 디지털 상품에 관한 것만은 아니다

[4]*The reason* [(why) even solid physical goods (— like a soda can —) / can deliver more benefits / while inhabiting less material] / is //
S / 관계부사 생략 / S′ / V′ / O′ / 접속사를 생략하지 않은 분사구문 (= while they inhabit ~) / V

이유는 [고체의 물리적 상품조차도 (탄산음료 캔과 같은) / 더 많은 이익을 내놓을 수 있는 / 더 적은 양의 물질을 가지고 있으면서] / ~이다 //

because their heavy atoms are substituted / by weightless bits.
부사절 접속사(이유) / their → (= solid physical goods') / S′ / V′

그것들(고체의 물리적 상품)의 무거운 원자가 대체되기 때문에 / 무게가 없는 비트로

↳ **세부 사항 1:** 비물질화는 고체의 물리적 상품(탄산음료 캔)에도 일어남.

유형의 것이 무형의 것들로 대체됨.

[5]The tangible is replaced / by *intangibles* (— intangibles (like better design, innovative processes, smart chips, and eventually online connectivity) —) /
S / V / 주격 관계대명사 that의 선행사 / 전치사(~ 같은)

유형의 것들은 대체된다 / 무형의 것들에 의해 (즉 무형의 것들 (더 나은 설계, 혁신적인 과정, 스마트 칩, 그리고 궁극적으로 온라인 연결성과 같은)) /

[that do *the work* [that more aluminum atoms used to do]].
→ 주격 관계대명사 / V′ / O′ / 목적격 관계대명사 / S″ / V″ / *<used to v>: v하곤 했다((과거의 상태))

[일을 하는 [더 많은 알루미늄 원자들이 하곤 했던]]

↳ **세부 사항 2:** 기술로 무형의 것들이 유형의 것들을 대체함.

해석

[1]디지털 기술은 제품에서 서비스로의 이동을 촉진함으로써 비물질화를 가속화한다. [2]서비스의 유동적인 특성은 그것들이 물질에 얽매일 필요가 없다는 것을 의미한다. [3]그러나 비물질화는 단지 디지털 상품에 관한 것만은 아니다. [4]탄산음료 캔과 같은 고체의 물리적 상품조차도 더 적은 양의 물질을 가지고 있으면서 더 많은 이익을 내놓을 수 있는 이유는 그것들의 무거운 원자가 무게가 없는 비트로 대체되기 때문이다.(▶ 예를 들어 1950년대 73g이었던 캔의 무게는 오늘날 13g으로 가벼워지면서 물질 사용이 현저히 줄어듦.) [5]유형의 것들은 더 많은 알루미늄 원자들이 하곤 했던 일을 하는 무형의 것들, 즉 더 나은 설계, 혁신적인 과정, 스마트 칩, 그리고 궁극적으로 온라인 연결성과 같은 무형의 것들에 의해 대체된다. [6]따라서 딱딱한 물건들이 더 소프트웨어같이 작용하게 만드는, 지능과 같이 부드러운 것들이 알루미늄과 같은 딱딱한 물건에 내장된다. [7]비트가 주입된 물질적 상품들은 점점 마치 그것들이 무형의 서비스인 것처럼 행동한다. [8]명사가 동사로 변한다.(▶ 유형의 것인 명사가 무형의 동사(서비스)가 된다는 의미) 하드웨어가 소프트웨어처럼 작동한다. [9]실리콘 밸리에서 사람들은 그것을 이렇게 말한다. "소프트웨어가 모든 것을 먹는다."

어휘

accelerate 가속화하다
dematerialization 비물질화
hasten 촉진하다, 재촉하다
migration 이동, 이주
liquid 유동적인; 액체(의)(↔ solid 고체(의); 견고한)
bound 얽매인; ~할 가능성이 큰; ~행(行)의

유형의 것(알루미늄)에 무형의 것(지능)이 내장되면 무형의 것과 같은 역할(소프트웨어)을 함.

[6]*Soft things*, / (like intelligence), / are thus embedded / into hard things, / (like aluminum), / [that make hard things behave more like software].

S / 삽입어구 / V / 삽입어구 / 주격 관계대명사 / V′ / O′ / C′

부드러운 것들이 / (지능과 같이) / 따라서 내장된다 / 딱딱한 물건에 / (알루미늄과 같은) / [딱딱한 물건들이 더 소프트웨어같이 작용하게 만드는]

↳ **예:** 딱딱한 물건(알루미늄)에 부드러운 것(지능)이 심어져 소프트웨어로 작동함 → 유형의 것이 무형의 것의 기능을 함.

→ Material goods는 hard things를, bits는 soft things를 의미함. / → 부사절 접속사(마치 ~처럼)

[7]*Material goods* (infused with bits) / increasingly act // as if **they were intangible services**.

S / 과거분사구 / V / S′ / V′ / C′

물질적 상품들은 (비트가 주입된) / 점점 행동한다 // 마치 그것들이 무형의 서비스인 것처럼

↳ **결과:** 물질적 상품이 무형의 서비스 기능을 함.

[8]Nouns morph to verbs. // Hardware behaves / like software.

명사가 동사로 변한다 // 하드웨어가 작동한다 / 소프트웨어처럼

[9]In Silicon Valley / they say it like this: // "Software eats everything."

S_1 V_1 O_1 / S_2 V_2 O_2

실리콘 밸리에서 / 사람들은 그것을 이렇게 말한다 // "소프트웨어가 모든 것을 먹는다"

↳ **맺음말(인용):** 유형의 것이 무형의 것으로 바뀌어 감 → 비물질화 현상.

deliver 내놓다, 산출하다; 배달하다; 출산하다
inhabit 차지하다; 살다
atom 원자
substitute 대체[교체]하다; 대신하는 사람[것]
tangible 유형의(↔ intangible 무형의)
innovative 혁신적인
connectivity 연결성, 접속 가능성
embed 내장하다, 끼워 넣다[박다]
infuse (사상 등을) 주입하다, 불어넣다
⊕ 비트(bit): 디지털 세상을 구성하는 비물질적 전기 신호 뭉치.

정답 가이드

빈칸 문장으로 보아 비트가 주입된 물질적 상품이 마치 '~처럼' 행동하는지를 추론해야 한다. 빈칸을 as if가 이끌고 선택지 동사가 모두 과거형이므로 '실제로는 그렇지 않은' 행동임을 의미한다. 이어지는 설명이 매우 구체적이므로 빈칸 문장의 예임을 이해할 수 있는데, 명사, 하드웨어는 물질적 상품들을 의미하고 동사와 소프트웨어가 빈칸을 의미한다. 앞에서부터 읽어보면, 디지털 기술로 인해 제품에서 서비스로 이동이 촉진되어 비물질화를 가속화하는데, 단지 디지털 상품이 아니라 고체인 물리적 상품도 무거운 원자가 무게 없는 비트로 대체되어 비물질화가 이루어진다고 했다. 즉, 비물질적인 것처럼 행동한다는 내용이 되어야 하므로, 빈칸에 들어갈 말로 가장 적절한 것은 ① 'they are intangible services(그것들이 무형의 서비스이다)'이다.

오답 클리닉

② they replaced all digital goods (20%)
그것들이 모든 디지털 상품들을 대체한다
물질적 상품이 디지털 상품을 대체하는 것이 아니라, 물질적 상품이 무형의 서비스화 된다는 내용임.

③ hardware could survive software (16%)
하드웨어가 소프트웨어보다 더 오래 존속할 수 있다
하드웨어와 소프트웨어의 유지 기간을 비교하는 내용이 아님.

④ digital services were not available (8%)
디지털 서비스가 사용될 수 없다
물질이 디지털 서비스처럼 작용하는 비물질화에 관한 내용임.

⑤ software conflicted with hardware (10%)
소프트웨어가 하드웨어와 충돌한다
소프트웨어가 하드웨어를 대체한다고는 했지만, 둘의 충돌은 언급되지 않음.

03 + 글의 순서 〈21학년도 6월 모평 37번 | 정답률 45%〉 ⑤

구문분석 & 직독직해

과학 과일 숙성의 문제와 해결책

[1]The fruit ripening process brings about / the softening of cell walls, / sweetening / and the production (of *chemicals* [that give colour and flavour]).

S / V / O_1 / O_2 / O_3 / 주격 관계대명사

과일 숙성 과정은 야기한다 / 세포벽의 연화(軟化)를 / 단맛을 / 그리고 생산을 (화학 물질의 [색과 맛을 주는])

[2]The process is induced / by the production (of *a plant hormone* (called ethylene)).

S / V / 과거분사구

그 과정은 유발된다 / 생산에 의해 (식물 호르몬의 (에틸렌이라고 불리는))

↳ **도입:** 과일 숙성 과정은 에틸렌이라는 식물 호르몬에 의해 유발됨.

주어진 문장에서 언급한 과일 숙성에 따르는 문제점과 해결책을 설명함.

(C) [3]The problem (for growers and retailers) / is // that ripening is followed sometimes quite rapidly / by deterioration and decay / and (that) the product becomes worthless.

S(단수) / V(단수) / C_1(명사절) / 명사절 접속사 생략 / C_2(명사절)

문제는 (재배자와 소매업자에게) / ~이다 // 숙성 뒤에 때로 아주 빠르게 뒤따른다는 것 / 품질 저하와 부패가 / 그리고 제품이 가치 없게 된다는 것

↳ **문제점 1:** 빠른 숙성은 품질을 저하시켜 상품 가치를 떨어뜨림.

해석

[1]과일 숙성 과정은 세포벽의 연화(軟化), 단맛, 그리고 색과 맛을 주는 화학 물질의 생산을 야기한다. [2]그 과정은 에틸렌이라고 불리는 식물 호르몬의 생산에 의해 유발된다. (C) [3]재배자와 소매업자에게 문제는 숙성 뒤에 때로 아주 빠르게 품질 저하와 부패가 뒤따라서 제품이 가치 없게 된다는 것이다. [4]그러므로 토마토와 다른 과일은 대개 익지 않았을 때 수확되어 운송된다. (B) [5]일부 국가에서는 그다음에 숙성을 유도하기 위해 소비자에게 판매하기 전에 그것들에 에틸렌이 뿌려진다. [6]그러나 익기 전에 수확된 과일은 식물에서 익은 상태로 수확된 과일보다 맛이 덜하다. [7]따라서 생명공학자들은 과일의 숙성 및 연화 과정을 지연시키는 데 있어서 기회를 보았다. (A) [8]에틸렌 생산을 방해하거나 에틸렌에 반응하는 과정을 방해함으로써 숙성이 늦춰질 수 있다면, 과일은 익어서 풍미가 가득할 때까지 식

[4]Tomatoes and other fruits are, therefore, usually picked and (are) transported // when they are unripe.

S / V1 / V2 / 부사절 접속사(시간)

그러므로 토마토와 다른 과일은 대개 수확되어 운송된다 // 그것들이 익지 않았을 때

they는 (C)의 Tomatoes and other fruits를 가리킴.

(B) [5]In some countries / they are then sprayed with ethylene / before sale to the consumer / to induce ripening.

S / V / 전치사(~ 전에) / 목적(~하기 위해)

일부 국가에서는 / 그다음에 그것들(토마토와 다른 과일)에 에틸렌이 뿌려진다 / 소비자에게 판매하기 전에 / 숙성을 유도하기 위해

↳ **해결책 1:** 토마토와 다른 과일은 익기 전에 수확해서 운송한 다음 판매 전에 숙성을 위해 에틸렌을 뿌림.

[6]However, / *fruit* (picked before it is ripe) / has less flavour / than *fruit* (picked ripe from the plant).

S / 과거분사구 / V / O / 과거분사구

그러나 / 과일은 (익기 전에 수확된) / 맛이 덜하다 / 과일보다 (식물에서 익은 상태로 수확된)

↳ **문제점 2:** 익기 전에 딴 과일은 익었을 때 딴 과일보다 맛이 없음.

[7]Biotechnologists / therefore / saw an opportunity / in delaying the ripening and softening process in fruit.

S / V / O / in의 O(동명사구)

생명공학자들은 / 따라서 / 기회를 보았다 / 과일의 숙성 및 연화 과정을 지연시키는 데 있어서

↳ **해결책 2:** 생명공학자들이 과일의 숙성 및 연화 과정을 지연시킴.

(B)의 마지막에 언급한 과일의 숙성을 지연시키는 생각을 부연 설명함.

(A) [8]If ripening could be slowed down / by interfering / with ethylene production / or with *the processes* [that respond to ethylene], //

부사절 접속사(조건) / <by v-ing>: v함으로써 / 전치사구 병렬 / 주격 관계대명사

숙성이 늦춰질 수 있다면 / 방해함으로써 / 에틸렌 생산을 / 또는 과정을 [에틸렌에 반응하는] //

fruit could be left on the plant // until it was ripe and full of flavour / but would still be in good condition // when it arrived at the supermarket shelf.

S / V1 / 부사절 접속사(~할 때까지) / V2 / 부사절 접속사(시간)

과일은 식물에 남아 있을 수 있다 // 그것이 익어서 풍미가 가득할 때까지 / 하지만 여전히 좋은 상태일 것이다 // 슈퍼마켓 진열대에 도착할 때

↳ **부연 설명:** 에틸렌 생산과 반응을 막아 숙성을 늦춘다면 과일이 익었을 때 따더라도 판매될 때까지 신선할 것임.

물에 남아 있을 수 있지만, 슈퍼마켓 진열대에 도착할 때 여전히 좋은 상태일 것이다.

어휘

ripen 숙성하다, 익다; 숙성시키다
cf. ripe 익은(↔ unripe 익지 않은)
bring about ~을 야기[초래]하다
soften 연하게[부드럽게] 하다
flavo(u)r 맛, 풍미
induce 유발[초래]하다; 유도하다
retailer 소매업자
be followed by ~이 뒤따르다
decay 부패(하다)
worthless 가치 없는
transport 운송(하다)
spray 뿌리다[살포하다]; 분무(기)
biotechnologist 생명공학자
delay 지연(시키다); 미루다, 연기하다
interfere with ~을 방해하다
condition 상태; 조건

정답 가이드

에틸렌이라는 식물 호르몬에 의해 과일의 숙성 과정이 유발된다는 주어진 글 이후에, 숙성 때문에 재배자와 소매업자가 겪는 문제점과 해결책을 소개하는 (C)가 이어져야 한다. (B)의 they는 (C)의 Tomatoes and other fruits를 받아 해결책을 이어서 설명하고, 그것이 근본적인 해결책이 될 수 없는 다른 문제점과 생명공학자들이 생각한 해결책을 제시한다. 이어서 과일의 숙성을 늦춰 풍미를 높이고 판매될 때까지 신선도를 유지하는 해결 방안을 구체적으로 설명하는 (A)가 마지막에 오는 것이 가장 적절하다.

오답 클리닉

① (A) - (C) - (B) (4%) / ④ (C) - (A) - (B) (11%)
(A)는 (B)의 마지막에 언급한 해결책을 부연 설명하므로, (B) 뒤에 와야 한다.
② (B) - (A) - (C) (22%) / ③ (B) - (C) - (A) (18%)
주어진 글에는 (B)의 they가 지칭할 대상이 없으므로, (B)는 주어진 글 뒤에 올 수 없다.

01 ✦ 필자 주장 (22학년도 9월 모평 20번 | 정답률 89%) ①

구문분석 & 직독직해

교육 상호 작용을 통한 교육의 중요성

[1] We live in *a time* [when everyone seems to be looking for quick and sure solutions].
관계부사 S′ V′ C′
우리는 시대에 살고 있다 [모두가 빠르고 확실한 해결책을 찾고 있는 것 같은]
↳ **도입:** 오늘날 모두가 빠르고 확실한 해결책을 원함.

★선행사 ways는 관계부사 how와 함께 쓰일 수 없으며 that이나 in which와는 쓰일 수 있음.

[2] Computer companies have even begun to advertise / *ways* [in which computers can replace parents].
S V O 전치사+관계대명사
컴퓨터 회사들은 심지어 광고하기 시작했다 / 방법들을 [컴퓨터가 부모를 대신할 수 있는]
↳ **예:** 컴퓨터가 부모를 대신할 수 있다는 광고가 나옴.

[3] They are too late — // television has already done that.
(= Computer companies) (= replacing parents)
그들(컴퓨터 회사)은 너무 늦었다 // 텔레비전이 이미 그것(부모를 대신하는 것)을 하고 있다
↳ **예:** 텔레비전이 이미 부모를 대신하고 있음.

[4] Seriously, however, / in *every branch of education*, / including moral education, / we make a mistake //
S V O
하지만 진지하게 / 교육의 모든 분야에서 / 도덕 교육을 포함한 / 우리는 실수를 범한다 //
↱ 부사절 접속사(시간) ↱ suppose의 O(명사절)
when we suppose // that a particular batch of content [or] a particular teaching method [or] a particular configuration (of students and space) / will accomplish our ends.
S′ V′ 명사절 접속사 S″ V″ O″
(~라고) 가정할 때 // 특정한 내용 묶음이나 특정 교육 방법 또는 특정 배치가 (학생과 공간의) / 우리의 목적을 달성할 것이라고
↳ **문제점:** 특정하게 설계된 교육이 모든 학습에 효과적일 것이라는 생각은 잘못됨.

[5] The answer is both harder and simpler.
S V C
정답은 더 어렵고 더 단순하다
↳ **해결책:** 교육 목적을 달성할 수 있는 방법은 더 어려운 동시에 더 단순함.

주제문
★조동사 have to 뒤의 동사원형 다섯 개가 콤마(,)와 and로 연결됨.
[6] We, parents and teachers, / have to live with our children, talk to them, listen to them, enjoy their company, / [and] show them /
S = V1 V2 V3 V4 V5 IO
우리, 부모와 교사는 / 우리의 아이들과 생활하고, 그들에게 말을 건네고, 그들의 말에 귀를 기울이고, 그들과 함께하는 것을 즐기고, 그들에게 보여주어야 한다 /
↱ show의 DO(명사절)
by what we do [and] how we talk // that it is possible / to live appreciatively or, at least, nonviolently with most other people.
by의 O(명사절 병렬) 명사절 접속사 가주어 진주어(to-v구)
🔑 교육에서 부모와 교사의 중요한 역할이 드러남.
우리가 하는 것과 말하는 방식으로 // (~이) 가능하다는 것을 / 감사하며 살거나 적어도 대부분의 다른 사람들과 비폭력적으로 사는 것이
↳ **해결책 상술:** 부모와 교사가 아이들과 상호 작용하는 것이 교육에 있어 가장 중요함.

해석

[1] 우리는 모두가 빠르고 확실한 해결책을 찾고 있는 것 같은 시대에 살고 있다. [2] 컴퓨터 회사들은 심지어 컴퓨터가 부모를 대신할 수 있는 방법들을 광고하기 시작했다. [3] 그들은 너무 늦었는데, 텔레비전이 이미 그것(부모를 대신하는 것)을 하고 있다.(▶ 빠르고 확실한 해결책의 예로 컴퓨터와 텔레비전을 언급함.) [4] 하지만 진지하게, 도덕 교육을 포함한 교육의 모든 분야에서, 우리는 우리가 특정한 내용 묶음이나 특정 교육 방법 또는 학생과 공간의 특정 배치가 우리의 목적을 달성할 것이라고 가정할 때 실수를 범한다. [5] 정답은 더 어렵고 더 단순하다. [6] 우리, 부모와 교사는, 우리의 아이들과 생활하고, 그들에게 말을 건네고, 그들의 말에 귀를 기울이고, 그들과 함께하는 것을 즐기고, 우리가 하는 것과 말하는 방식으로 감사하며 살거나 적어도 대부분의 다른 사람들과 비폭력적으로 사는 것이 가능하다는 것을 그들에게 보여주어야 한다.

어휘

advertise 광고하다
replace 대신[대체]하다; 바꾸다
branch 분야, 부문; (나뭇)가지
moral 도덕의; 도의적인; 교훈
particular 특정한, 특별한
batch 한 묶음, 한 회분
content 내용(물); 목차; 만족(한)
method 방법; 체계성
configuration 배치, 배열
end 목적, 목표; 끝; 종료(하다)
company 함께함, 동반; 회사; 단체
appreciatively 감사하며, 고마워하면서
nonviolently 비폭력적으로

정답 가이드

텔레비전이나 컴퓨터가 가르침을 주는 부모의 역할을 대신할 수 있다고 생각하지만 특정한 내용이나 방법을 통해 교육의 모든 분야를 가르칠 수 있다고 생각하는 것은 잘못되었으며, 삶에 대한 가르침은 부모나 교사가 아이들과 함께 생활하고 소통함으로써 일깨워 줄 수 있다는 내용의 글이다. 따라서 필자가 주장하는 바로 가장 적절한 것은 ① '교육은 일상에서 아이들과의 상호 작용을 통해 이루어져야 한다.'이다.

The 핵심 부모와 교사가 범하는 교육 실수를 언급한 후, 올바른 방법을 제시하는 '문제점-해결책' 구조에서는 주제문에 해당하는 '해결책' 부분에 주목하여 필자의 주장을 파악한다.

오답 클리닉

② 도덕 교육을 강화(×)하여 타인을 배려하는 공동체 의식(×)을 높여야 한다. (3%)
도덕 교육에 한정된 내용이 아니며, 공동체 의식에 대해서는 언급되지 않음.
③ 텔레비전의 부정적 영향(×)을 줄이려는 사회적 노력이 있어야 한다. (1%)
텔레비전이 부정적 영향을 준다는 내용은 언급되지 않음.
④ 다양한 매체(×)를 활용하여 학교와 가정 교육의 한계(×)를 보완해야 한다. (4%)
컴퓨터나 텔레비전 같은 특정한 매체로 교육 목적을 달성할 수 있다는 생각는 잘못된 것이라고 했으므로 글의 내용과 반대됨.
⑤ 아이들의 온라인 예절 교육(×)을 위해 적절한 콘텐츠를 개발(×)해야 한다. (2%)
온라인 교육보다는 부모, 교사와 직접적으로 소통하며 배우는 것이 중요하다는 내용이며, 콘텐츠 개발의 필요성에 대한 내용은 언급되지 않음.

02 + 빈칸 추론 〈20학년도 6월 모평 32번 | 정답률 55%〉 ①

구문분석 & 직독직해

고고학 가설 검증 절차를 지키지 않는 고고학자들

[1]Through recent decades / academic archaeologists have been urged / to conduct their research and excavations / according to hypothesis-testing procedures.
S V C
*<urge+O+to-v(O가 v하도록 촉구[권고]하다)>의 수동형
최근 몇십 년 동안 내내 / 학계의 고고학자들은 촉구되어 왔다 / 연구와 발굴을 수행하도록 / 가설 검증 절차에 따라

→ 진주어(명사절) *조동사 should 뒤의 동사원형이 콤마(,)와 and로 연결됨.
[2]It has been argued // that we should construct our general theories, / deduce testable propositions / and prove or disprove them / against the sampled data.
가주어 V 명사절 접속사 S' V'₁ O'₁ V'₂ O'₂ V'₃ O'₃(= testable propositions)
(~라고) 주장되어 왔다 // 우리가 일반적인 이론을 구축해야 한다고 / 검증할 수 있는 명제를 추론해야 한다고 / 그리고 그것들을 증명하거나 틀렸음을 증명해야 한다고 / 샘플로 추출된 자료와 비교하여
↳ **도입:** 고고학 연구는 '이론 구축 → 명제 추론 → 자료 증명'의 가설 검증 절차가 필요함.

[3]In fact, / the application (of this 'scientific method') / often ran into difficulties.
S V O
사실 / 적용은 (이런 '과학적 방법'의) / 자주 어려움을 겪었다

[4]The data have a tendency (to lead to unexpected questions, problems and issues).
S V O =
자료는 경향이 있다 (예기치 않은 질문, 문제 그리고 쟁점으로 이어지는)
↳ **문제점:** 예기치 않은 문제가 많이 생겨서 가설 검증 방법을 적용하기가 어려움.

주제문
*<find+oneself+v-ing>: 자신도 모르게 v하고 있다
[5]Thus, / *archaeologists* (claiming / to follow hypothesis-testing procedures) / found themselves having to create a fiction.
S 현재분사구 V O C
따라서 / 고고학자들은 (주장하는 / 가설 검증 절차를 따른 것이 사실임을) / 자신도 모르게 꾸며낸 이야기를 써야 했다
↳ **결과:** 고고학자들이 가설 검증 절차를 따른 것처럼 꾸며냄.

[6]In practice, / their work and theoretical conclusions partly developed / **from *the data* [which they had discovered]**.
S V 목적격 관계대명사
(= archaeologists)
실제로 / 그들의 연구물과 이론적 결론이 부분적으로 발전했다 / 자료에서 [그들이 발견했던]

자료를 이미 알고 이론을 구축함.
[7]In other words, / they already knew the data // when they decided upon an interpretation.
S(= archaeologists) V O 부사절 접속사 S' V' O'
다시 말해서 / 그들은 이미 그 자료를 알고 있었다 // 그들이 어떤 해석으로 결정지을 때

해석

[1]최근 몇십 년 동안 내내 학계의 고고학자들은 가설 검증 절차에 따라 연구와 발굴을 수행하도록 촉구되어 왔다. [2]우리가 일반적인 이론을 구축하고, 검증할 수 있는 명제를 추론해서, 그것들을 샘플로 추출된 자료와 비교하여 증명하거나 틀렸음을 증명해야 한다고 주장되어 왔다. [3]사실 이런 '과학적 방법'의 적용은 자주 어려움을 겪었다. [4]자료는 예기치 않은 질문, 문제 그리고 쟁점으로 이어지는 경향이 있다. [5]따라서 가설 검증 절차를 따른 것이 사실임을 주장하는 고고학자들은 자신도 모르게 꾸며낸 이야기를 써야 했다. [6]실제로, 그들의 연구물과 이론적 결론이 부분적으로 그들이 발견했던 자료에서 발전했다. [7]다시 말해서, 그들이 어떤 해석으로 결정지을 때 그들은 이미 그 자료를 알고 있었다. [8]그러나 연구물을 발표할 때, 그들은 실험실 조건하의 실험에서와 같이 이론을 앞세우고 그것(이론)을 자신들이 발견한 자료와 비교하여 검증했다고 주장하면서 대본을 다시 썼다.

어휘

academic 학계의, 학문의
archaeologist 고고학자
conduct 수행하다; 행동
hypothesis 가설; 추정
construct 구축[구성]하다; 건설하다
theory 이론, 학설
cf. theoretical 이론적인
proposition 명제, 진술; 제안
prove 증명하다(↔ disprove 틀렸음을 증명하다)
application 적용; 지원[신청](서)
run into (곤경 등을) 겪다, 만나다
tendency 경향, 성향

🔑 연구 발표에서 이론을 정립하고 나서 검증한 것처럼 지어냄. 문장 5의 create a fiction이 말바꿈 됨.

[8] But / in presenting their work / they rewrote the script, / placing the theory first / and claiming to have tested it / against *data* [which they discovered], / (= as they placed ~) (= as they claimed ~)

<in v-ing>: v할 때 / S / V / O / 분사구문1 / 분사구문2 / (= theory) / 목적격 관계대명사

그러나 / 연구물을 발표할 때 / 그들은 대본을 다시 썼다 / 이론을 앞세우면서 / 그리고 그것(이론)을 검증했다고 주장하면서 / 자료와 비교하여 [자신들이 발견한] /

as in an experiment (under laboratory conditions).

~의 경우(에서)와 같이

실험에서와 같이 (실험실 조건하의)

↳ **부연 설명:** 이미 알고 있는 자료로 이론을 구축하지만, 마치 이론을 구축한 다음에 검증한 것처럼 연구를 발표함.

unexpected 예기치 않은, 의외의
fiction 꾸며낸 이야기, 허구; 소설
interpretation 해석, 이해, 설명
[선택지] framework 틀, 뼈대; 체계
observe (규칙을) 준수하다; 관찰하다

정답 가이드

빈칸 문장과 빈칸 앞 문장으로 보아 their는 고고학자들의 소유격이며, 그들의 연구물과 이론적 결론의 발전과 관련된 정보를 추론해야 한다. 빈칸 뒤에서 고고학자들은 어떤 해석을 내릴 때 '그 자료'를 이미 알았지만(그 자료를 해석하여 이론을 만듦), 연구물을 발표할 때는 이론을 먼저 세우고 나서 발견한 자료로 비교 검증했다고 주장한다고 했다. 따라서 그들의 연구물과 이론적 결론의 발전은 '그 자료의 발견'에 의한 것임을 알 수 있다. 또한, 앞에서 고고학자들은 가설 검증 절차를 따라야 하는데, 이는 먼저 일반적 이론을 만들어 검증할 명제를 추론한 뒤 샘플로 추출된 자료와 비교하여 증명하는 것이라고 했다. 그런데 그 샘플 자료는 예기치 않은 문제로 이어지는 경향이 있어서 고고학자들이 자료에서부터 이야기를 지어냈으므로, 연구물과 이론적 결론은 부분적으로 '그 샘플 자료'에서 발전한 것이라 할 수 있다. 따라서 빈칸에 들어갈 말로 가장 적절한 것은 ① 'from the data which they had discovered(그들이 발견했던 자료에서)'이다.

오답 클리닉

② from comparisons of data in other fields (10%)
다른 분야의 자료와의 비교로부터
고고학 이외의 다른 분야에 관한 언급은 없음.

③ to explore more sites for their future studies (6%)
향후 연구를 위한 더 많은 장소를 탐색하기 위해서
미래 연구나 장소 탐색에 관한 언급은 없음.

④ by supposing possible theoretical frameworks (16%)
가능한 이론적 틀을 가정함으로써
이론적 틀을 구축해서 검증하지 않고 이미 아는 자료로 이론을 구축한다고 했으므로 글의 내용과 반대됨.

⑤ by observing the hypothesis-testing procedures (13%)
가설 검증 절차를 준수함으로써
과학적 방법 적용의 어려움 때문에 검증 절차를 반대 순서로 연구한다고 했으므로 준수한다고 볼 수 없음.

03 + 문장 넣기 〈21학년도 6월 모평 39번 | 정답률 50%〉 ⑤

구문분석 & 직독직해 생물 반딧불이가 빛을 내는 이유

주제문 ★<not just A (but) also B>: A뿐만 아니라 B도

[1] Fireflies don't just light up their behinds / to attract mates, // they also glow / to tell bats not to eat them. ★<tell+O+to-v>: O에게 v하라고 말하다

S1 / V1 / O1 / 목적(~하기 위해) / S2 / V2 / 목적(~하기 위해) / (= fireflies)

반딧불이는 꽁무니를 빛나게 만들 뿐만 아니라 / 짝을 유혹하기 위해서 // 그것들은 빛을 내기도 한다 / 박쥐에게 자기들을 먹지 말라고 말하기 위해

↳ 반딧불이는 짝짓기를 위해서뿐만 아니라, 박쥐에게 잡아먹히지 않기 위해 꽁무니에 빛을 냄.

[2] This twist (in the tale (of *the trait* [that gives fireflies their name])) / was discovered / by Jesse Barber and his colleagues.

S / 주격 관계대명사 V′ / IO′ / DO′ / V

이 반전은 (이야기의 (특성에 대한 [반딧불에게 그것들의 이름을 지어주는])) / 발견되었다 / Jesse Barber와 그의 동료들에 의해

↳ **세부 사항:** 반딧불이가 빛을 내는 다른 목적을 알아낸 발견에 대해 설명함.

[3] The glow's warning role benefits both fireflies and bats, // because these insects taste disgusting / to the mammals.

S / V / O / 부사절 접속사(이유) / S′ / V′ / C′ / (= bats)

그 빛의 경고 역할은 반딧불이와 박쥐 모두에게 유익하다 // 왜냐하면 이 곤충(반딧불이)은 역겨운 맛이 나기 때문이다 / 그 포유동물(박쥐)에게는

(①) [4] When (they are) swallowed, // *chemicals* (released by fireflies) / cause bats to throw them back up.

<주어+동사> 생략 / S / 과거분사구 / V / O / C / (= fireflies)

삼켜지면 // 화학 물질은 (반딧불이에 의해 발산된) / 박쥐가 그것(반딧불이)을 다시 토해내게 한다

↳ **발견점:** 반딧불이는 박쥐에게 역겨운 맛이 나기 때문에 반딧불이의 빛이 하는 경고는 반딧불이와 박쥐 모두에게 유익함.

해석

[1]반딧불이는 짝을 유혹하기 위해서 꽁무니를 빛나게 만들 뿐만 아니라, 박쥐에게 자기들을 먹지 말라고 말하기 위해 빛을 내기도 한다. [2]반딧불이에게 그것들의 이름을 지어주는 특성에 대한 이야기의 이 반전은 Jesse Barber와 그의 동료들에 의해 발견되었다. [3]그 빛의 경고 역할은 반딧불이와 박쥐 모두에게 유익한데, 왜냐하면 이 곤충(반딧불이)은 그 포유동물(박쥐)에게는 역겨운 맛이 나기 때문이다. (①) [4]삼켜지면, 반딧불이에 의해 발산된 화학물질은 박쥐가 그것(반딧불이)을 다시 토해내게 한다. (②) [5]그 팀(Jesse Barber와 그의 동료들)은 여덟 마리의 박쥐를 서너 마리의 반딧불이와, (그것의) 세 배가 많은 딱정벌레와 나방을 포함하여 맛이 좋은 곤충들과 함께 어두운 방에 나흘 동안 두었다. (③) [6]첫날 밤 동안에, 모든 박쥐는 적어도 한 마리의 반딧불이를 잡았다. (④) [7]그러나 네 번째 밤쯤에, 대부분의 박쥐는 반딧불이를 피하고 대신에 다른 모든 먹이를 잡는 법을 배웠다. (⑤ [8]그 팀이 반딧불이의 빛이 나는 기관을 어둡게 칠했을 때, 새로운 한 무리의 박쥐는 그것들을 피하는 법을 배우는 데 두 배의 시간이 걸렸다.) [9]반딧불이의 생물 발광(發光)은 주로 짝짓기 신호의 역할을 한다고 오랫동안 생각되었지만, 그 새로운 연구 결과는 짝짓기를 하기에 미숙함에도 불구하고 왜 반딧불이 애벌레도 빛을 내는지를 설명해 준다.

(②) [5]The team placed eight bats in a dark room / with three or four fireflies / plus three times as many tasty insects (as fireflies), / (including beetles and moths), / for four days.

S V O

★<배수사 as ~ as ...>: …의 몇 배가 ~한 / 전치사구 삽입

그 팀은 여덟 마리의 박쥐를 어두운 방에 두었다 / 서너 마리의 반딧불이와 /
(그것의) 세 배가 많은 맛이 좋은 곤충들과 함께 / (딱정벌레와 나방을 포함하여) / 나흘 동안

↳ **실험 내용:** 어두운 방에 박쥐들을 서너 마리의 반딧불이와 그보다 세 배 많은 맛이 좋은 곤충들과 함께 둠.

(③) [6]During the first night, / all the bats captured at least one firefly.

S V O

첫날 밤 동안에 / 모든 박쥐는 적어도 한 마리의 반딧불이를 잡았다

🔑 박쥐가 반딧불이를 피하게 되는 데 나흘 정도 걸림.

(④) [7]But / by the fourth night, / most bats had learned / to avoid fireflies / and (to) catch all the other prey / instead.

S V O(to-v 병렬)

그러나 / 네 번째 밤쯤에 / 대부분의 박쥐는 배웠다 / 반딧불이를 피하는 법을 / 그리고 다른 모든 먹이를 잡는 법을 / 대신에

★<take+시간+to-v>: v하는 데 시간이 걸리다

(⑤ [8]When the team painted fireflies' light organs dark, // a new set of bats took twice as long / to learn to avoid them.)

부사절 접속사(시간) S' V' O' C' S V

🔑 시간이 두 배 더 걸렸다는 것과 비교할 내용이 앞에 있어야 함.

(= fireflies painted dark)

그 팀이 반딧불이의 빛이 나는 기관을 어둡게 칠했을 때 // 새로운 한 무리의 박쥐는 두 배의 시간이 걸렸다 /
그것들(빛이 나는 기관을 어둡게 칠한 반딧불이)을 피하는 법을 배우는 데

↳ **실험 결과:** 박쥐는 초반에는 반딧불이를 잡았으나 곧 반딧불이를 피했는데, 빛이 나는 기관을 어둡게 칠한 반딧불이를 피하는 데는 더 오래 걸림.

↱ 진주어(명사절)

[9]It had long been thought // that firefly bioluminescence mainly acted as a mating signal, //

가주어 V_1 명사절 접속사 S' V'

(~라고) 오랫동안 생각되었다 // 반딧불이의 생물 발광(發光)은 주로 짝짓기 신호의 역할을 한다고 //

🔑 주어진 문장의 실험 결과를 지칭함. ↱ explains의 O(명사절)

but the new finding explains // why firefly larvae also glow / despite being immature for mating.

S_2 V_2 관계부사 S' V' ~에도 불구하고 despite의 O(동명사구)

그러나 그 새로운 연구 결과는 설명해 준다 // 왜 반딧불이 애벌레도 빛을 내는지를 / 짝짓기를 하기에 미숙함에도 불구하고

↳ **결론:** 반딧불이 발광(發光)은 짝짓기 신호 외에 잡아먹지 말라는 경고이기도 함.

어휘

firefly 반딧불이
light up 빛나게 만들다; 빛이 나다
mate (쌍을 이루는 것의) 짝
cf. mating 짝짓기
glow 빛(을 내다); 불타다
twist 반전, (예상 밖의) 전개; 비틀다
trait 특성, 특징
colleague 동료
disgusting 역겨운; 혐오스러운
mammal 포유동물
swallow 삼키다
release 발산[방출]하다; 풀어 주다
throw up 토하다
beetle 딱정벌레
moth 나방
capture (붙)잡다
prey 먹이; 희생자
organ (생물의) 기관, 장기
act as ~의 역할을 하다
immature 미숙한, 미성숙의

정답 가이드

주어진 문장은 연구팀이 반딧불이의 빛이 나는 기관을 어둡게 칠하자 새로운 한 무리의 박쥐가 반딧불이를 피하는 데 두 배의 시간이 걸렸다는 내용으로, 그 앞에는 걸린 시간을 비교할 수 있는 다른 실험 결과가 제시되어야 함을 알 수 있다. <twice+as ~ (as ...)> 등의 비교구문에서 비교 대상인 <as ...>가 생략되는 것은 주로 앞에 언급되어 명확하기 때문이다. ⑤의 앞은 반딧불이의 빛이 나는 기관을 어둡게 칠하지 않은 조건하에 얻은 시간 결과이고, ⑤ 뒤는 주어진 문장의 내용을 the new finding으로 받아 설명하므로, 주어진 문장이 들어가기에 가장 적절한 곳은 ⑤이다.

오답 클리닉

① (3%) 반딧불이가 역겨운 맛이 나서 박쥐가 토한다는 내용이 자연스럽게 연결된다. 아직 실험에 관한 내용이 제시되지 않았으므로 주어진 문장은 들어갈 수 없다.
② (10%) 실험 설명을 시작하기 전에 실험 결과에 해당하는 주어진 문장이 오는 것은 적절하지 않다.
③ (16%) 앞에서 설명한 실험에 따른 결과가 시간의 경과 순서로 초반 것부터 제시되었다.
④ (22%) 실험 초반의 결과와 상반되는 나중의 결과가 역접 연결어 But으로 이어지는 것은 자연스럽다.

01 + 요약문 (21학년도 9월 모평 40번 | 정답률 51%) ②

구문분석 & 직독직해

사회 물질주의에 대한 공통적인 우려

[1] Research (from the Harwood Institute for Public Innovation in the USA) shows // that people feel // that 'materialism' somehow comes / between them and the satisfaction of their social needs.

연구는 (미국 Harwood Institute for Public Innovation에서의) 보여준다 // 사람들이 느낀다는 것을 // '물질주의'가 어떻게든 끼어든다고 / 자신과 자신의 사회적 욕구 충족 사이에

↳ 사람들은 '물질주의'가 자신과 자신의 사회적 욕구의 충족 사이에 끼어든다고 느낌.

🔑 (A) 사람들은 물질주의가 사회적 욕구 충족을 방해한다고 느낌.

[2] *A report* (entitled *Yearning for Balance*), / based on a nationwide survey of Americans, / concluded // that they were 'deeply ambivalent / about wealth and material gain'.

보고서는 (<Yearning for Balance>라는 제목의) / 미국인에 대한 전국적인 설문 조사를 토대로 한 / 결론지었다 // 그들이 '매우 양면 가치적이라고 / 부와 물질적 이익에 관해'

↳ **세부 사항:** 미국인들은 부와 물질적 이익에 관해 양면 가치적임.

[3] A large majority of people wanted / society to 'move / away from greed and excess / toward *a way of life* (more centred / on values, community, and family)'.

*<want+O+to-v>: O가 v하기를 원하다

대다수의 사람은 원했다 / 사회가 '움직이기를 / 탐욕과 과잉에서 벗어나 / 삶의 방식을 향해 (더 중심을 둔 / 가치, 공동체, 가족에)'

[4] But they also felt // that these priorities were not shared / by *most of their fellow Americans*, // who, / (they believed), / had become 'increasingly atomized, selfish, and irresponsible'.

그러나 그들(조사를 받은 대다수의 사람)은 또한 느꼈다 // 이러한 우선순위가 공유되지 않는다고 / 대부분의 동료 미국인에 의해 // 그런데 이들(대부분의 동료 미국인)은 / (그들이 생각하기에) / '점점 더 개별화되고, 이기적이며, 무책임하게' 되었다

↳ **원인:** 개인은 사회가 물질주의에서 벗어나 사회적 가치를 추구하길 바람 ↔ 다른 사람들은 자신들과 같은 생각을 공유하지 않는다고 느낌.

[5] As a result / they often felt isolated.

그 결과 / 그들은 종종 소외감이 들었다

↳ **결과:** 소외감을 느낌.

🔑 (B) 다른 사람들도 같은 생각을 공유함.

[6] However, / the report says, // that when (they were) brought together in focus groups / to discuss these issues, // people were 'surprised and excited to find // that others share[d] their views'.

하지만 / 보고서는 (~라고) 한다 // 포커스 그룹으로 모였을 때 / 이러한 문제를 논의하기 위해 // 사람들은 '알게 되어서 놀라고 흥분했다고 // 다른 사람들이 그들의 생각을 공유한[했]다는 것을'

↳ **사실:** 다른 사람들도 자신과 같은 생각을 하고 있었음 → 물질주의적 사회에 대한 우려는 공통적임.

[7] Rather than uniting us with others / in a common cause, / *the unease* [(which[that]) we feel / about the loss of social values / and *the way* [(that) we are drawn into the pursuit of material gain]] / is often experienced // as if it were *a purely private ambivalence* [which cuts us off from others].

(= Instead of)

우리를 다른 사람들과 결속시키기보다는 / 공동의 대의로 / 불안감은 [우리가 느끼는 / 사회적 가치의 상실에 대해 / 그리고 방식에 대해 [우리가 물질적 이익의 추구로 빠지는]] / 흔히 느껴진다 // 마치 그것이 순전히 개인적인 양면 가치인 것처럼 [우리를 다른 사람들로부터 단절시키는]

*<as if+가정법 과거>는 주절과 때(현재)를 일치시켜, '마치 ~인 것처럼 …한다'로 해석함.

↳ 불안감은 우리를 다른 사람들로부터 단절시키는 사적인 양면 가치인 것처럼 느껴짐.

해석

[1] 미국 Harwood Institute for Public Innovation에서의 연구는 사람들이 '물질주의'가 어떻게든 자신과 자신의 사회적 욕구 충족 사이에 끼어든다고 느낀다는 것을 보여준다. [2] 미국인에 대한 전국적인 설문 조사를 토대로 한 <Yearning for Balance>라는 제목의 보고서는 그들이 '부와 물질적 이익에 관해 매우 양면 가치적'이라고 결론지었다. [3] 대다수의 사람은 사회가 '탐욕과 과잉에서 벗어나 가치, 공동체, 가족에 더 중심을 둔 삶의 방식을 향해 움직이기'를 원했다. [4] 그러나 그들은 또한 이러한 우선순위가 대부분의 동료 미국인에 의해 공유되지 않는다고 느꼈는데, 그들(조사를 받은 대다수의 사람)이 생각하기에 이들(대부분의 동료 미국인)은 '점점 더 개별화되고, 이기적이며, 무책임하게' 되었다. [5] 그 결과 그들(조사를 받은 대다수의 사람)은 종종 소외감이 들었다. [6] 하지만, 보고서는 이러한 문제를 논의하기 위해 사람들이 포커스 그룹으로 모였을 때, 그들은 '다른 사람들이 그들의 생각을 공유한[했]다는 것을 알게 되어서 놀라고 흥분했다'고 한다. [7] 우리가 사회적 가치의 상실과 물질적 이익의 추구로 빠지는 방식에 대해 느끼는 불안감은 공동의 대의로 우리를 다른 사람들과 결속시키기보다는, 마치 그것이 우리를 다른 사람들로부터 단절시키는 순전히 개인적인 양면 가치인 것처럼 흔히 느껴진다.(▶ 다른 사람들 역시 물질주의적 사회에 대해 우려하지만, 개인은 그 감정이 개인만의 감정인 것처럼 느끼며 소외감을 느낀다는 의미)

↓

[8] 물질주의가 자신이 사회적 가치를 (A) 추구하는 것을 막는다고 믿으며 많은 미국인은 대다수의 다른 사람들로부터 분리된 것처럼 느끼지만, 이것은 실제로 상당히 (B) 공통적인 우려이다.

어휘

materialism 물질(만능)주의
somehow 어떻게든; 어쩐지, 웬일인지
come between ~ 사이에[를] 끼어들다[갈라놓다]
entitled (~라는) 제목의
nationwide 전국적인
greed 탐욕, 욕심
excess 과잉, 과다; 초과량
centre 중심(을 두다) (= center)
priority 우선순위[사항]
atomize 개별화하다, 세분화하다; 원자화하다
irresponsible 무책임한
rather than ~보다는, ~ 대신에
unite 결속[통합]시키다; 결합하다
cause 대의, 목적; 원인(이 되다)

↓

[8]Many Americans, / believing that materialism keeps them from **(A) pursuing** social values, //
S1 분사구문(= as they believe ~) ↱(= believing ~ values) ★<keep A from v-ing>: A가 v하는 것을 막다
feel detached from most others, // but this is actually a fairly **(B) common** concern.
V1 C1 S2 V2 C2
많은 미국인은 / 물질주의가 자신이 사회적 가치를 (A) 추구하는 것을 막는다고 믿으며 //
대다수의 다른 사람들로부터 분리된 것처럼 느낀다 // 하지만 이것(물질주의가 사회적 가치를 추구하는 것을 막는다고 믿는 것)은 실제로 상당히 (B) 공통적인 우려이다

unease 불안(감), 우려
purely 순전히, 전적으로
cut A off from B A를 B로부터 단절시키다
[요약문] detached 분리된, 고립된; 공정한, 초연한
⊕ 포커스 그룹(focus group): 시장 조사나 여론 조사를 위해 각 계층을 대표하도록 뽑은 소수의 사람들로 이뤄진 그룹
⊕ 양면 가치(ambivalence): 어떤 것에 대해 동시에 상충하여 일어나는 감정과 태도

정답 가이드

요약문을 통해 물질주의와 사회적 가치, 미국인들이 느끼는 단절감에 대한 글임을 알 수 있다. 사람들은 사회가 물질주의에서 벗어나 사회적 가치에 중점을 둔 삶을 '지향하길' 원하지만, 다른 사람들은 이러한 생각을 공유하지 않는다고 생각해서 소외감을 느낀다고 했다. 하지만 알고 보면 다른 사람들도 마찬가지로 사회에 대해 그들과 '같은 생각'을 공유했다고 했다. 따라서 요약문의 빈칸 (A)와 (B)에 각각 들어갈 말로 가장 적절한 것은 ② 'pursuing(추구하는 것) - common(공통적인)'이다.

오답 클리닉

(A) (B)
① pursuing - unnecessary (26%) 추구하는 것 - 불필요한
(A)는 맞지만, (B)는 틀림. 물질주의에 대한 우려의 필요성을 판단하는 내용이 아님.
③ holding - personal (7%) 지니는 것 - 개인적인
(A)는 맞지만, (B)는 글의 내용과 반대됨. 다른 사람들도 우려를 공유한다고 했으므로 개인적이지 않음.
④ denying - ethical (6%) 부정하는 것 - 윤리적인
(A)는 글의 내용과 반대되며, (B)는 틀림. 물질주의에 대한 사람들의 우려를 윤리적 측면에서 가치 판단하고 있지 않음.
⑤ denying - primary (10%) 부정하는 것 - 주된
(A)는 글의 내용과 반대되며, (B)는 맞음.

02~03 + 복합 유형 (22학년도 대수능 41~42번 | 정답률 02 64%, 03 61%)

02 ② 03 ③

구문분석 & 직독직해

언어 언어에 내재된 분류 체계

★<classify A into B>: A를 B로 분류하다
[1]Classifying things together into groups is / *something* [(that) we do all the time], //
S(동명사구) V O 목적격 관계대명사 생략
물건들을 묶어서 그룹으로 분류하는 것은 ~이다 / 일 [우리가 항상 하는] //
↱ to see의 O(명사절)
and it isn't hard to see // why (we classify things together into groups).
가주어 V C 진주어 반복어구 생략
그리고 이해하는 것은 어렵지 않다 // 이유를
↳ **도입:** 사물을 묶어 그룹으로 분류하는 데에는 이유가 있음.

[2]Imagine / trying to shop in *a supermarket* [where the food was arranged / in random order / on the shelves]: // 🔑 03-(a) 식품이 마구잡이로 진열된 곳에서 원하는 물건을 찾는 데 '시간이 걸릴' 것임.
V(명령문) Imagine의 O(동명사구) 관계부사 S′ V′
상상해 보라 / 슈퍼마켓에서 쇼핑하려고 하는 것을 [식품이 배열된 / 마구잡이로 / 진열대에] //
tomato soup (next to the white bread / in one aisle), / chicken soup (in the back / next to the 60-watt light bulbs), / one brand of cream cheese (in front) / and another (in aisle 8 near the cookies).
토마토수프 (흰 빵 옆에 / 한 통로에서는) / 치킨 수프 (뒤쪽에 있는 / 60와트 백열전구 옆에)
/ 한 크림치즈 브랜드 (앞쪽에 있는) / 또 다른 하나 / (쿠키 근처의 8번 통로에 있는)

[3]The task (of finding // what you want) / would be **(a) time-consuming** and extremely difficult, // if not impossible.
S = 동명사 finding의 O(명사절) V C
일은 (찾는 // 여러분이 원하는 것을) / 시간이 걸리고 매우 어려울 것이다 // 불가능하지는 않더라도
↳ **예:** 슈퍼마켓에 분류 체계가 없으면 원하는 물건을 찾기 힘듦.

[4]In the case of a supermarket, / someone had to **(b) design** the system of classification.
S V O
슈퍼마켓의 경우 / 누군가는 분류 체계를 고안해야 했다
↳ **대조 A:** 슈퍼마켓의 경우 분류 체계를 만드는 것이 필요함.

주제문 🔑 03-(b) 언어에는 분류 체계가 포함되어 있으나 슈퍼마켓은 그렇지 않으므로 누군가가 '고안해야' 함.
[5]But there is also *a ready-made system of classification* (embodied in our language).
V S 과거분사구
하지만 또한 이미 만들어져 있는 분류 체계도 있다 (우리 언어에 포함된)
↳ **대조 B:** 언어에는 이미 만들어진 분류 체계가 있음.

해석

[1]물건들을 묶어서 그룹으로 분류하는 것은 우리가 항상 하는 일이며, 이유를 이해하는 것은 어렵지 않다. [2]식품이 진열대에 마구잡이로 배열된 슈퍼마켓에서 쇼핑하려고 하는 것을 상상해 보라. 한 통로에서는 흰 빵 옆에 토마토수프가 있고, 치킨 수프는 뒤쪽에 있는 60와트 백열전구 옆에 있고, 한 크림치즈 브랜드는 앞쪽에, 또 다른 하나는 쿠키 근처의 8번 통로에 있다. [3]여러분이 원하는 것을 찾는 일은 불가능하지는 않더라도 (a) 시간이 걸리고 매우 어려울 것이다.
[4]슈퍼마켓의 경우, 누군가는 분류 체계를 (b) 고안해야 했다. [5]하지만 또한 우리 언어에 포함된 이미 만들어져 있는 분류 체계도 있다. [6]예를 들어, '개'라는 단어는 특정 부류의 동물들을 함께 묶어 그것들을 다른 동물들과 구별한다. [7]분류라고 불리기에는 그러한 묶음이 너무 (c) 추상적으로(→ 명백하게) 보일 수 있지만, 이것은 단지 여러분이 이미 그 단어를 숙달했기 때문이다. [8]말하기를 배우는 아이로서, 여러분은 여러분의 부모님이 여러분에게 가르치려 애썼던 분류 체계를 (d) 익히기 위해 열심히 노력해야 했다. [9]여러분이 그것을 이해하기 전에는, 아마 고양이를 개라고 부르는 것과 같은 실수를 했을 것이다. [10]만약 여러분이 말하기를 배우지 않았다면, 온 세상이 (e) 정돈되지 않은 슈퍼마켓처럼 보일 것이며, 여러분은 모든 물건이 새롭고 익숙지 않은 유아의 상태에 있을 것이다. [11]그러므로 분류의 원리를 배울 때, 우리는 우리 언어의 핵심에 있는 구조에 대해 배우고 있는 것이다.

[6]The word "dog," / for example, / groups together a certain class of animals / and distinguishes them from other animals.
S V1 O1 V2 O2

'개'라는 단어는 / 예를 들어 / 특정 부류의 동물들을 함께 묶는다 / 그리고 그것들을 다른 동물들과 구별한다

[7]Such a grouping may seem too (c) **abstract(→ obvious)** / to be called a classification, //
S1 V1 C1 ★<too ~ to-v>: v하기에는 너무 ~한

그러한 묶음이 너무 추상적으로(→ 명백하게) 보일 수 있다 / 분류라고 불리기에는 //

↱ is의 C(명사절) ★because절이 명사절로 사용되기도 하며, '~때문'이라는 의미

but this is only // because you have already mastered the word. ⊶ 03-(c) 단어를 이미 숙달한 상태이므로 분류가 '명확해' 보일 것임.
S2 V2 S' V' O'

하지만 이것은 단지 // 여러분이 이미 그 단어를 숙달했기 때문이다

↳ **부연 설명:** 언어에서의 분류(예: 단어 '개'가 특정 동물과 다른 동물을 구별하는 것)는 너무 명확해 보임.

⊶ 03-(d) 말하기를 배우는 아이는 부모가 가르치려는 분류 체계를 '익히기' 위해 노력했을 것임.

[8]As *a child* (learning to speak), / you had to work hard / to (d) **learn** *the system of classification* [(which[that]) your parents were trying to teach you].
전치사(~로(서)) 현재분사구 S V 목적(~하기 위해) 목적격 관계대명사 생략 S' V' O'

아이로서 (말하기를 배우는) / 여러분은 열심히 노력해야 했다 / 분류 체계를 익히기 위해 [여러분의 부모님이 여러분에게 가르치려 애썼던]

↱ (= the system of classification) ★<call+O+C>: O를 C라고 부르다

[9]Before you got the hang of it, // you probably made mistakes, / like calling the cat a dog.
부사절 접속사(시간) S V O like의 O(동명사구)

여러분이 그것을 이해하기 전에는 // 여러분은 아마 실수를 했을 것이다 / 고양이를 개라고 부르는 것과 같은

⊶ 03-(e) 말하기 즉, 언어의 분류 체계를 배우지 않은 상태는 분류 체계가 없는 '정돈되지 않은' 슈퍼마켓과 같을 것임.

[10]If you hadn't learned to speak, // the whole world would seem / like the (e) **unorganized** supermarket; //
부사절 접속사(조건) S1 V1 ★혼합가정법 <If+S'+had p.p. ~, S+조동사 과거형+동사원형 ...>: (과거에) 만약 ~했더라면, (지금) …할 텐데

만약 여러분이 말하기를 배우지 않았다면 // 온 세상이 보일 것이다 / 정돈되지 않은 슈퍼마켓처럼 //

you would be in the position of *an infant*, // for whom every object is new and unfamiliar.
S2 V2 전치사+목적격 관계대명사 S' V' C'

여러분은 유아의 상태에 있을 것이다 // 모든 물건이 새롭고 익숙지 않은

↳ 말하기를 배우는 것은 언어의 분류 체계를 배우는 것이며, 말하기를 배우지 않은 것은 분류 체계도 배우지 않음을 의미함.

[11]In learning the principles of classification, / therefore, / we'll be learning / about *the structure* [that lies at the core of our language].
<in v-ing>: v할 때, v함에 있어 주격 관계대명사

분류의 원리를 배울 때 / 그러므로 / 우리는 배우고 있는 것이다 / 구조에 대해 [우리 언어의 핵심에 있는]

↳ **결론:** 분류 원리를 배우는 것이 언어의 핵심 구조를 배우는 것임.

어휘

classify 분류하다, 범주화하다
cf. classification 분류; 유형, 범주
arrange 배열하다, 정리하다
random 마구잡이로 하는, 무작위의, 임의의
aisle 통로; 복도
light bulb 백열전구
task 일, 과제, 과업
ready-made 이미 만들어진, 기성(품)의
embody 포함하다, 담다; 구현하다
class 부류, 종류; 반; 수업; 계층
distinguish A from B A를 B와 구별하다
abstract 추상적인
master 숙달하다, 완전히 익히다
get the hang of ~을 이해하다
infant 유아
unfamiliar 익숙지 않은, 낯선
principle 법칙, 원리; 원칙
structure 구조(물)
lie (위치해) 있다; 눕다, 누워 있다
core 핵심(적인); 중심부
[선택지] similarity 유사성, 닮음
linguistic 언어(학)의
inherent 내재된, 고유한
categorization 범주화
dilemma 딜레마, 진퇴양난

정답 가이드

02 슈퍼마켓에서는 누군가가 물건을 분류하는 체계를 만들어야 하지만, 언어에는 이미 만들어진 분류 체계가 포함되어 있다고 했다. 말하기를 배우는 아이는 이 분류 체계를 배우는 것이라고 하며, 마지막 문장에서 분류 원리를 배울 때 언어의 핵심에 있는 구조를 배우는 것이라고 정리하고 있으므로, 글의 제목으로 가장 적절한 것은 ② 'Classification: An Inherent Characteristic of Language(분류는 언어의 내재된 특성)'이다.

03 '개'라는 단어를 이미 숙달한 상태에서 개를 다른 동물과 구별하는 것은 분류라고 하기에 너무 명백할 것이다. 따라서 ③ 'abstract(추상적인)'를 'obvious(명백한)'로 고쳐야 한다.

오답 클리닉

02 ① Similarities of Strategies in Sales and Language Learning (17%)
판매와(×) 언어 학습의 전략(×)의 유사성
판매와 언어 학습의 전략을 비교하여 서로 유사성이 있음을 설명하는 글이 아님.
③ Exploring Linguistic Issues Through Categorization (5%)
범주화를 통한 언어학 문제 탐색(×)
범주화로 언어학적 문제를 탐색하는 내용이 아님.
④ Is a Ready-Made Classification System Truly Better? (6%)
이미 만들어진 분류 체계가 정말 더 나은가(×)?
언어에 이미 만들어진 분류 체계가 있다고 언급되긴 했지만 다른 것과 비교해 더 나은지를 판단하는 내용이 아님.
⑤ Dilemmas of Using Classification in Language Education (7%)
언어 교육에서 분류 활용의 딜레마(×)
언어 학습으로 분류 체계를 익히는 내용은 있지만, 분류 활용의 딜레마는 언급되지 않음.

03 ① time-consuming (3%) 시간이 걸리는
물건이 마구잡이로 진열되어 있는 슈퍼마켓에서 원하는 물건을 찾는 데에는 '시간이 걸릴' 것이다.
② design (5%) 고안하다
(b)가 포함된 문장 4는 문장 5와 But으로 연결되어 분류 체계가 포함되어 있는 언어와 그렇지 않은 슈퍼마켓을 대조하고 있다. 따라서 슈퍼마켓에서는 누군가가 분류 체계를 '고안해야' 할 것이다.
④ learn (15%) 익히다
말하기를 배우는 아이가 부모님이 가르치려는 체계를 '익히기' 위해 노력하는 것은 자연스럽다.
⑤ unorganized (15%) 정돈되지 않은
말하기를 배우지 않은 상태는 언어의 분류 체계를 배우지 않은 것과 같으므로 세상이 '정돈되지 않은' 슈퍼마켓처럼 보일 것이다.

01 ✦ 빈칸 추론 (20학년도 6월 모평 31번 | 정답률 63%) ②

구문분석 & 직독직해

동물 야생 동물 피해 관리

*<define A as B>: A를 B로 정의하다

[1]Some people have defined wildlife damage management / as the science and management (of overabundant species), // but this definition is too narrow.

S₁ V₁ O 전치사(~로(서)) S₂ V₂ C

어떤 사람들은 야생 동물 피해 관리를 정의했다 / 과학과 관리로 (과다한 종들에 대한) // 하지만 이 정의는 너무 한정적이다

↳ **통념과 반박:** 야생 동물 피해 관리를 과다한 종의 관리로 보는 것은 한정적인 정의임.

[2]All wildlife species act / in *ways* [that harm human interests].

S V 주격 관계대명사

모든 야생 동물 종들은 행동한다 / 방식으로 [인간의 이익에 해를 끼치는]

주제문

[3]Thus, / all species cause wildlife damage, / not just overabundant ones.

S V O (= species)

따라서 / 모든 종이 야생 동물 피해를 일으킨다 / 단지 과다한 것(종)뿐만 아니라

↳ 모든 종의 야생 동물이 피해를 일으킴.

🔑 멸종 위기 종이 다른 멸종 위기 종에 피해를 일으킴.

[4]One interesting example of this involves / *endangered peregrine falcons in California,* // which prey on another endangered species, / the California least tern.

S V O 관계대명사(보충 설명) V′ O′ =

이것의 흥미로운 한 사례는 포함한다 / 캘리포니아의 멸종 위기에 처한 송골매를 // 그리고 이것들은 또 다른 멸종 위기에 처한 종을 먹이로 삼는다 / 캘리포니아 작은 제비갈매기라는

*<consider A as B>: A를 B로 여기다 🔑 송골매는 멸종 위기 종이므로 개체 수를 줄여 관리할 수 없음.

[5]Certainly, / we would not consider peregrine falcons / as being overabundant, // but we wish // that they would not feed on an endangered species.

S₁ V₁ O₁ 전치사(~로(서)) as의 O(동명사구)

틀림없이 / 우리는 송골매를 여기지는 않을 것이다 / 과다한 상태라고 //

↱ wish의 O(명사절) S₂ V₂ 명사절 접속사 S′ V′ O′

그러나 우리는 바란다 // 그것들이 멸종 위기에 처한 종을 먹지 않기를

[6]In this case, / one (of *the negative values* (associated with a peregrine falcon population)) / is // that its predation reduces / the population (of another endangered species).

↱ is의 C(명사절) S(단수) 과거분사구 V(단수) 명사절 접속사 S′ V′ O′

이런 경우에 / 하나는 (부정적인 평가들 중 (송골매 개체 수와 관련된)) / ~이다 // 그것의 포식이 감소시킨다는 것 / 개체 수를 (또 다른 멸종 위기에 처한 종의)

↳ **예:** 멸종 위기 종(송골매)이 다른 멸종 위기 종(작은 제비갈매기)을 잡아먹음 → 멸종 위기 종도 피해를 일으키면 관리가 필요함.

*<stop+O+from v-ing>: O가 v하지 못하게 하다

[7]The goal (of wildlife damage management) / in this case / would be to stop the falcons from eating the terns / without **harming** the falcons.

S V C

목표는 (야생 동물 피해 관리의) / 이런 경우에 / 송골매가 작은 제비갈매기를 먹지 못하게 하는 것일 것이다 / 송골매에 해를 끼치지 않으면서

↳ **멸종 위기 종 관리 목표:** 피해를 주는 종(송골매)에 해를 주지 않으면서 다른 멸종 위기 종(작은 제비갈매기)을 보호해야 함.

해석

[1]어떤 사람들은 야생 동물 피해 관리를 (개체 수가) 과다한 종들에 대한 과학과 관리로 정의했지만, 이 정의는 너무 한정적이다. [2]모든 야생 동물 종들은 인간의 이익에 해를 끼치는 방식으로 행동한다. [3]따라서 단지 과다한 종뿐만 아니라 모든 종이 야생 동물 피해를 일으킨다. [4]이것의 흥미로운 한 사례는 캘리포니아의 멸종 위기에 처한 송골매를 포함하는데, 이것들은 캘리포니아 작은 제비갈매기라는 또 다른 멸종 위기에 처한 종을 먹이로 삼는다. [5]틀림없이 우리는 송골매를 과다한 상태라고 여기지는 않겠지만, 우리는 그것들이 멸종 위기에 처한 종을 먹지 않기를 바란다. [6]이런 경우에, 송골매 개체 수와 관련된 부정적인 평가들 중 하나는 그것의 포식이 또 다른 멸종 위기에 처한 종의 개체 수를 감소시킨다는 것이다. [7]이런 경우에 야생 동물 피해 관리의 목표는 송골매에 해를 끼치지 않으면서 송골매가 작은 제비갈매기를 먹지 못하게 하는 것일 것이다.

어휘

define 정의하다; 규정하다
cf. definition 정의; 의미
wildlife 야생 동물
management 관리; 경영(진)
overabundant 과다한, 과잉의
species ((생물)) 종(種)
narrow 한정된[제한된]; 좁은
involve 포함하다, 수반하다
endangered 멸종 위기에 처한
prey on ~을 먹이로 삼다
value 평가; 가치; 값; 소중하게 여기다
associated with ~와 관련된
population 개체수; 인구; 집단
predation 포식 (관계)
[선택지] clone 복제하다; 복제 (생물)
domesticate (동물을) 길들이다, 사육하다

정답 가이드

빈칸 문장으로 보아 송골매의 사례에 적용될 야생 동물 피해 관리의 목표가 송골매에 '무엇을 하지' 않으면서 송골매가 작은 제비갈매기를 먹지 못하게 하는 것인지를 찾아야 한다. 앞에서 야생 동물 관리는 개체 수가 과다한 종뿐만 아니라 야생 동물 피해를 일으키는 모든 종이 관리의 대상이라고 하며, 멸종 위기 종인 송골매가 또 다른 멸종 위기 종인 작은 제비갈매기를 먹이로 삼는 것을 예로 들었다. 송골매의 개체 수가 과다한 상태가 아니므로, 송골매와 작은 제비갈매기 모두가 보호해야 할 대상이 된다. 따라서 빈칸에 들어갈 말로 가장 적절한 것은 ② 'harming(해를 끼치는 것)'이다.

오답 클리닉

① cloning (6%) 복제하는 것
종 복제에 관한 내용이 아님.
③ training (8%) 훈련시키는 것
송골매를 훈련시키는 관리 방법을 지양해야 한다는 글이 아님.
④ overfeeding (18%) 먹이를 너무 많이 주는 것
송골매에게 얼마나 많은 양의 먹이를 줘야 하는지에 대한 내용이 아님.
⑤ domesticating (5%) 길들이는 것
야생 동물인 송골매를 길들이는 것에 관한 내용이 아님.

02 ✦ 글의 순서 〈21학년도 6월 모평 36번 | 정답률 56%〉 ④

구문분석 & 직독직해

심리 적당한 양의 스트레스가 갖는 이점

[1]Studies (of *people* (struggling with major health problems)) / show // that the majority of respondents report // (that) they derived benefits / from their adversity.

(S: Studies / 현재분사구: struggling with major health problems / V: show / 명사절 접속사: that / → show의 O(명사절) / S′: the majority of respondents / V′: report / O′(명사절): (that) they derived benefits from their adversity / *<derive A from B>: B에서 A를 얻다)

연구는 (사람들에 대한 (중대한 건강 문제와 씨름하는)) / 보여준다 // 대다수의 응답자가 보고한다는 것을 // 그들이 이익을 얻었다고 / 자신들의 역경으로부터

↳ **도입(예):** 건강 문제와 싸우는 대다수의 사람들이 역경으로부터 이익을 얻었다고 응답함.

*<force+O+to-v>: (어쩔 수 없이) O가 v하게 만들다[강요하다]

[2]Stressful events sometimes force people / to develop new skills, / (to) reevaluate priorities, / (to) learn new insights, / and (to) acquire new strengths.

(S: Stressful events / V: force / O: people / C₁: to develop new skills / C₂: (to) reevaluate priorities / C₃: (to) learn new insights / C₄: (to) acquire new strengths)

스트레스를 주는 사건들은 때때로 사람들이 ~하게 만든다 / 새로운 기술을 개발하게 / 우선 사항을 재평가하게 / 새로운 통찰을 배우게 / 그리고 새로운 강점을 얻게

주제문 🔑 주어진 글과 비슷한 스트레스의 좋은 점이 이어짐.

(C) [3]In other words, / *the adaptation process* (initiated by stress) / can lead to personal changes (for the better).

(S: the adaptation process / 과거분사구: initiated by stress / V: can lead to / O: personal changes)

다시 말해 / 적응 과정은 (스트레스에 의해 시작된) / 개인적 변화로 이어질 수 있다 (더 나은 쪽으로의)

↳ 스트레스에 의한 적응 과정이 개인에게 좋은 변화를 가져옴.

[4]*One study* [that measured participants' exposure / to thirty-seven major negative events] / found a curvilinear relationship (between lifetime adversity and mental health).

(S: One study / 주격 관계대명사: that / V: found / O: a curvilinear relationship)

한 연구는 [참가자들의 경험을 측정한 / 서른일곱 가지 주요 부정적인 사건에 대한] / 곡선 관계를 발견했다 (일생의 역경과 정신 건강 사이의)

↳ **논거 1:** 한 연구에서 일생의 역경과 정신 건강 사이의 곡선 관계를 발견함.

🔑 (C)의 역경과 정신 건강의 곡선 관계를 부연 설명함.

(A) [5]High levels of adversity predicted poor mental health, / as (it is) expected, // but *people* [who had faced intermediate levels of adversity] / were healthier / than *those* [who experienced little adversity], / suggesting // that moderate amounts of stress can foster resilience.

(S₁: High levels of adversity / V₁: predicted / O₁: poor mental health / 부사절 접속사(~대로): as / S₂: people / 주격 관계대명사: who / V₂: were / C₂: healthier / 주격 관계대명사: who / 준부정어(거의 ~않는): little / 분사구문(= and it suggests ~): suggesting / 현재분사 suggesting의 O(명사절): that moderate amounts of stress can foster resilience)

높은 수준의 역경은 나쁜 정신 건강을 예측했다 / 예상대로 // 그러나 사람들은 [중간 수준의 역경에 직면했던] / 더 건강했다 / 사람들보다 [역경을 거의 경험하지 않았던] / 이는 시사한다 // 적당한 양의 스트레스가 회복력을 촉진할 수 있다는 것을

↳ **결과:** 중간 수준의 역경을 경험한 사람이 너무 높거나 낮은 역경을 경험한 사람들보다 더 건강함.

해석

[1]중대한 건강 문제와 씨름하는 사람들에 대한 연구는 대다수의 응답자가 자신들의 역경으로부터 이익을 얻었다고 보고한다는 것을 보여준다. [2]스트레스를 주는 사건들은 때때로 사람들이 새로운 기술을 개발하고, 우선 사항을 재평가하고, 새로운 통찰을 배우고, 새로운 강점을 얻게 만든다. (C) [3]다시 말해, 스트레스에 의해 시작된 적응 과정은 더 나은 쪽으로의 개인적 변화로 이어질 수 있다. [4]서른일곱 가지 주요 부정적인 사건에 대한 참가자들의 경험을 측정한 한 연구는 일생의 역경과 정신 건강 사이의 곡선 관계를 발견했다. (A) [5]높은 수준의 역경은 예상대로 나쁜 정신 건강을 예측했지만, 중간 수준의 역경에 직면했던 사람들은 역경을 거의 경험하지 않았던 사람들보다 더 건강했는데, 이는 적당한 양의 스트레스가 회복력을 촉진할 수 있다는 것을 시사한다. [6]후속 연구는 일생의 역경의 양과 실험용 스트레스 요인에 대한 피실험자들의 반응 사이에서 비슷한 관계를 발견했다. (B) [7]중간 수준의 역경이 가장 큰 회복력을 예측했다. [8]따라서 적당한 양의 스트레스를 다뤄야 하는 것은 장래의 스트레스에 직면할 때의 회복력을 기를 수 있다.

어휘

struggle with ~와 씨름하다, ~와 싸우다
adversity 역경, 불운
reevaluate 재평가하다
priority 우선 (사항)
acquire 얻다, 습득하다
adaptation 적응; 각색
initiate 시작하다; 착수시키다
measure 측정하다; 치수; 조치
exposure 경험[체험]하기; 노출; 폭로
curvilinear 곡선의
intermediate 중간의; 중급의

[6]A follow-up study found / a similar link (between the amount of lifetime adversity / and subjects' responses to laboratory stressors).
S V O

후속 연구는 발견했다 / 비슷한 관계를 (일생의 역경의 양과 / 실험용 스트레스 요인에 대한 피실험자들의 반응 사이에서)

↳ **논거 2:** 후속 연구에서 역경의 양과 스트레스 요인에 대한 반응 사이에서도 비슷한 관계를 발견함.

(A)의 후속 연구가 발견한 비슷한 결과가 이어짐.

(B) [7]Intermediate levels of adversity were predictive / of the greatest resilience.
S V C

중간 수준의 역경이 예측했다 / 가장 큰 회복력을

↳ **결과:** 후속 연구에서도 중간 수준의 역경을 겪었을 때 회복력이 가장 좋음.

[8]Thus, / having to deal with a moderate amount of stress / may build resilience / in the face of future stress.
S(동명사구) V O ~에 직면하여

따라서 / 적당한 양의 스트레스를 다뤄야 하는 것은 / 회복력을 기를 수 있다 / 장래의 스트레스에 직면할 때의

↳ **결론(주제문 재진술):** 적당한 양의 스트레스가 회복력을 높여줌.

moderate 적당한; 보통의; (기후가) 온화한
foster 촉진하다, 육성하다; 기르다
follow-up 후속의
subject 피실험자; 주제; 과목
stressor 스트레스 요인
predictive 예측[예언]하는; 전조가 되는
deal with ~을 다루다; 처리하다

정답 가이드

주어진 글은 사람들이 스트레스를 주는 사건들을 겪으며 새로운 강점을 얻는다는 내용으로 스트레스의 긍정적 영향을 서술한 것이다. 그 뒤에는 연결어 In other words를 사용해 스트레스에 의한 적응 과정이 더 나은 개인적 변화로 이어질 수 있다고 바꿔 말하는 (C)가 이어지는 것이 적절하다. 일생의 역경과 정신 건강 간의 곡선 관계를 논거로 언급한 (C) 다음에는 그 관계를 부연 설명하고 비슷한 관계를 발견한 후속 연구를 추가로 제시하는 (A)가 와야 한다. 끝으로 후속 연구의 결과와 결론을 설명하는 (B)가 마지막에 오는 것이 가장 자연스럽다.

오답 클리닉

① (A) - (C) - (B) (4%)
(A)는 (C)에서 언급된 역경과 정신 건강 사이의 곡선 관계를 설명하는 내용이므로 (C) 뒤에 와야 한다.

② (B) - (A) - (C) (8%) / ③ (B) - (C) - (A) (10%)
(B)는 후속 연구의 결과를 설명하고, 연결어 Thus로 두 연구 결과를 종합해 결론을 내리는 내용이므로 주어진 글 뒤에 올 수 없다.

⑤ (C) - (B) - (A) (9%)
일생의 역경과 정신 건강 사이의 곡선 관계를 발견한 연구의 결과 → 후속 연구 → 후속 연구의 결과로 이어지는 것이 자연스러우므로 (B)는 (A) 뒤에 와야 한다.

03 + 문장 넣기 〈21학년도 6월 모평 38번 | 정답률 38%〉 ②

구문분석 & 직독직해

인문 지도자의 결정이 명료하기 어려운 이유

주제문

[1]Clarity is often *a difficult thing* (for a leader to obtain).
S V C to-v의 의미상 주어

명료성은 흔히 어려운 것이다 (지도자가 얻기)

↳ 지도자가 명료성을 얻기는 어려움.

[2]Concerns (of the present) / tend to seem larger / than *potentially greater concerns* [that lie farther away].
S(복수) V(복수) 주격 관계대명사

우려들은 (현재의) / 더 커 보이는 경향이 있다 / 잠재적으로 더 큰 우려들보다 [더 멀리 떨어져 있는]

↳ **논거 1:** 현재의 우려가 미래의 잠재적인 우려보다 더 커 보임.

(①) [3]*Some decisions* / by their nature / present great complexity, // whose many variables must come together a certain way / for the leader to succeed.
S V O 관계대명사(보충 설명)
to-v의 의미상 주어 목적(~하기 위해)

몇몇 결정은 / 그 본질상 / 엄청난 복잡성을 보여준다 // 그리고 그것(몇몇 결정)의 많은 변수들이 특정한 방식으로 합쳐져야 한다 / 지도자가 성공하기 위해서는

↳ **논거 2:** 일부 결정은 본질적으로 복잡함.

해석

[1]명료성은 흔히 지도자가 얻기 어려운 것이다. [2]현재의 우려들은 더 멀리 떨어져 있는, 잠재적으로 더 큰 우려들보다 더 커 보이는 경향이 있다. (①) [3]몇몇 결정은 그 본질상 엄청난 복잡성을 보여주는데, 지도자가 성공하기 위해서는 그것(몇몇 결정)의 많은 변수들이 특정한 방식으로 합쳐져야 한다. (② [4]그 어느 때보다도 지금 그 어려움의 정도를 더하는 것은 인간 공학자들이 정보 과부하라고 부르는 것으로, 그 경우 지도자는 자신의 생각을 흐트러뜨리고 혼란스럽게 할 뿐인 이메일, 회의, 통화를 통한 조언에 압도당한다.) [5]그렇지 않다면, 지도자의 정보는 그저 단편적일 수도 있으며, 이는 지도자가 때로는 엄밀한 의미의 그런 추정으로 인식하지 못하면서 (정보의) 공백을 추정으로 채우게 할지도 모른다. (③) [6]그리고 지도자의 가장 중요한 결정의 가치는 그 본질상 보통 명확하지 않다. (④) [7]대신에 그러

🔑 '어려움을 더하는 것'으로 문장이 시작하려면, 앞에 다른 어려움이 제시되어야 함.

↱ is의 C(명사절)

(②) [4]Compounding the difficulty, / now more than ever, / is // what ergonomists call *information overload*, // where a leader is overrun / with *inputs* — / (via e-mails, meetings, and phone calls) — / [that only distract and confuse her thinking].)

S(동명사구) V(단수) 관계대명사 S′ V′ C′ 관계부사(보충 설명) 전치사(~을 통해) 주격 관계대명사

그 어려움의 정도를 더하는 것은 / 그 어느 때보다도 지금 / ~이다 // 인간 공학자들이 정보 과부하라고 부르는 것 // 그리고 그 경우 지도자는 압도된다 / 조언에 / (이메일, 회의, 통화를 통한) / [자신의 생각을 흐트러뜨리고 혼란스럽게 할 뿐인]

↳ **논거 3:** 지도자는 정보 과부하에 압도됨.

🔑 주어진 문장의 정부 과부하와 연관된 정보가 단편적인 경우가 대조됨.

[5]Alternatively, / the leader's information might be only fragmentary, //

S V C

그렇지 않다면 / 지도자의 정보는 그저 단편적일 수도 있다 //

★<cause+O+to-v>: O가 v하게 하다

which might cause her to fill in the gaps / with assumptions — / sometimes without recognizing them as such.

관계대명사(앞 절 보충 설명) (= assumptions)

그리고 이는 지도자가 공백을 채우게 할지도 모른다 / 추정으로 / 때로는 엄밀한 의미의 그런 그것(추정)으로 인식하지 못하면서

↳ **논거 3의 대조:** 정보가 단편적인 경우 정보의 공백을 추정으로 채워야 할 수도 있음.

(③) [6]And / the merits (of a leader's most important decisions), / by their nature, / typically are not clear-cut.

S V C

그리고 / 가치는 (지도자의 가장 중요한 결정의) / 그 본질상 / 보통 명확하지 않다

↳ **논거 4:** 지도자의 결정에 대한 가치가 명확하지 않음.

★<assign A to B>: A에 B를 부여하다

(④) [7]Instead / those decisions involve a process (of assigning weights to competing interests, / and then determining, / based upon some criterion, // (that) which one predominates.

S V O ↱ determining의 O(명사절) of의 O(동명사구 병렬) 명사절 접속사 생략 ★which는 대명사 one을 수식하는 의문형용사임.

대신에 / 그러한 결정들은 과정을 포함한다 (상충하는 이익에 가중치를 부여하는 / 그런 다음 결정하는 / 어떤 기준을 근거로 // 어떤 것이 우위를 차지하는지

↳ **논거 4의 부연 설명:** 결정은 상충하는 이익을 비교해서 어느 것이 우세한가를 기준으로 내려짐.

(⑤) [8]The result is one of judgment, / (one) of shades of gray; /

S V C

↱ 동명사 saying의 O(명사절)

like saying // that Beethoven is a better composer / than Brahms.

명사절 접속사 S′ V′ C′

그 결과는 판단에 따른 것이다 / 즉 회색의 미묘한 차이를 띤 (것) /

그것은 말하는 것과 같다 // Beethoven이 더 훌륭한 작곡가라고 / Brahms보다

↳ **논거 4의 결과:** 지도자의 결정은 미묘한 판단에 의한 것임.

한 결정들은 상충하는 이익에 가중치를 부여한 다음, 어떤 기준을 근거로 어떤 것이 우위를 차지하는지 결정하는 과정을 포함한다. (⑤) [8]그 결과는 판단에 따른 것, 즉 회색의 미묘한 차이를 띤 것으로, 그것은 Beethoven이 Brahms보다 더 훌륭한 작곡가라고 말하는 것과 같다.

어휘

clarity 명료성; 명확성
by nature 본질상, 본래
variable 변수; 가변적인
come together (하나로) 합치다
compound ~의 정도를 더하다, 악화시키다; 혼합물
overload 과부하; 과적하다
overrun 압도하다; 초과하다; 침략하다
input 조언; 투입
alternatively 그렇지 않다면, (~아니면) 그 대신에
assumption 추정, 가정
as such 엄밀한 의미의[보통 말하는] 그런
merit 가치, 우수성; 장점; 공로
clear-cut 명확한
weight 가중치(를 주다); 중요성; 무게
competing (이해 등이) 상충하는, 모순된
criterion (*pl.* criteria) 기준, 규범
predominate 우위를 차지하다
shade 미묘한 차이; 그늘
composer 작곡가

정답 가이드

주어진 문장은 '그 어려움'에 더해서 지도자가 그 어느 때보다 지금 정보 과부하로 인해 혼란스럽다는 내용이다. 따라서 주어진 문장 앞에는 지도자의 다른 어떤 '어려움'이 제시되어야 한다. ② 앞에 지도자의 몇몇 결정은 본질적으로 복잡성이 있다는 '어려움'이 제시되었고, ② 뒤는 지도자의 정보가 단편적일 수 있음을 설명하는데, 이는 주어진 문장의 정보 과부하와 의미상 대조를 이루는 것이며 부사 Alternatively(그렇지 않다면)가 이끌고 있으므로 주어진 문장이 들어가기에 가장 적절한 곳은 ②이다.

오답 클리닉

① (5%) 지도자가 명료성을 얻기 어려운 이유로 결정이 본질적으로 복잡함을 들고 있다.
③ (22%) 정보가 단편적인 경우 지도자가 명료성을 얻지 못한다고 설명한 후, 또 다른 이유를 And로 추가하는 것은 자연스럽다.
④ (25%) 지도자의 가장 중요한 결정을 those decisions로 받으면서 부연 설명하는 내용이다.
⑤ (10%) 지도자가 결정을 내리는 과정에 이어 그에 따른 결과를 설명하는 것은 자연스럽다.

01 + 글의 주제 (21학년도 6월 모평 23번 | 정답률 75%) ⑤

구문분석 & 직독직해

사회 문제 이해와 해결에 영향을 미치는 문제의 표현

[1] *Problem framing* amounts / to defining // *what* problem you are proposing to solve.

S V 전치사 to의 O(동명사구) 동명사 defining의 O(명사절)

'문제 표현하기'는 해당한다 / 규정하는 것에 // 여러분이 '어떤' 문제를 해결하려고 하는지를

↳ **도입:** 문제 표현은 해결하려는 문제를 규정하는 것임.

주제문

[2] This is a critical activity // because *the frame* [(which[that]) you choose] / strongly influences your understanding (of the problem), //

(= Problem framing) 부사절 접속사(이유) S′ 목적격 관계대명사 생략 V′ O′

🔑 문제의 표현은 문제 이해와 접근 방식에 영향을 미침.

이것(문제의 표현)은 중대한 행위이다 // 왜냐하면 표현이 [여러분이 선택하는] / 여러분의 이해에 강하게 영향을 미치기 때문에 (그 문제에 대한) //

thereby conditioning your approach (to solving it).

분사구문(= and thereby it conditions ~) (= the problem)

그로 인해 여러분의 접근 방식을 좌우한다 (그것을 해결하는)

↳ 문제의 표현은 문제 이해와 해결 방식에 영향을 미치므로 중요함.

[3] For an illustration, / consider / *Thibodeau and Broditsky's series of experiments* [in which they asked people / for *ways* (to reduce crime / in a community)].

V O 전치사+관계대명사 (= where) S′ V′ O′

하나의 예로 / 생각해 보라 / Thibodeau와 Broditsky의 일련의 실험을 [사람들에게 물어본 / 방법을 (범죄를 줄이는 / 지역사회 내의)]

↳ **예(실험):** 지역사회 범죄를 줄이는 방법을 사람들에게 물었음.

(= Thibodeau and Broditsky)

[4] They found // that the respondents' suggestions changed significantly / depending on // whether *the metaphor* (used to describe crime) / was as a virus or as a beast.

S V O(명사절) 전치사 on의 O(명사절) *<whether A or B>: A인지 B인지 명사절 접속사 S″ 과거분사구 V″

🔑 문제의 표현에 따라 응답자들이 제시한 해결 방법도 달라짐.

그들은 발견했다 // 응답자들의 제안이 크게 달라졌다는 것을 / ~에 따라 // 은유가 (범죄를 묘사하는 데 사용된) / 바이러스였는지 짐승이었는지

↳ **실험 결과:** 범죄 묘사 방식에 따라 응답이 달라짐.

*presented ~ city는 People을, comparing ~ city는 a metaphor를, invading their city는 a virus를 수식하는 분사구임.

[5] *People* (presented with *a metaphor* (comparing crime / to *a virus* (invading their city))) / emphasized / prevention and addressing the root causes (of the problem), / such as eliminating poverty and improving education.

S V O 동명사구 병렬

사람들은 (은유를 제공받은 (범죄를 비유하는 / 바이러스에 (자신들의 도시에 침입한))) / 강조했다 / 예방과 근본 원인을 다루는 것을 (문제의) / 빈곤을 없애는 것과 교육을 향상시키는 것 같은

↳ **응답 A(범죄를 바이러스에 은유한 경우):** 예방과 근본 원인 해결에 초점을 둠.

[6] On the other hand, / *people* (presented with the beast metaphor) / focused on remediations: / increasing the size (of the police force and prisons).

S 과거분사구 V =

*콜론(:)이 앞서 언급된 어구에 대한 구체적인 내용을 부연 설명함.

반면에 / 사람들은 (짐승의 은유를 제공받은) / 교정 조치에 초점을 맞추었다 / 즉 규모를 늘리는 것 (경찰력과 교도소의)

↳ **응답 B(범죄를 짐승에 은유한 경우):** 교정 조치에 초점을 둠.

해석

[1]'문제 표현하기'는 여러분이 '어떤' 문제를 해결하려고 하는지를 규정하는 것에 해당한다. [2]여러분이 선택하는 표현이 그 문제에 대한 여러분의 이해에 강하게 영향을 미치며, 그로 인해 그것을 해결하는 여러분의 접근 방식을 좌우하기 때문에 이것(문제의 표현)은 중대한 행위이다. [3]하나의 예로, 사람들에게 지역사회 내의 범죄를 줄이는 방법을 물어본 Thibodeau와 Broditsky의 일련의 실험을 생각해 보라. [4]그들은 범죄를 묘사하는 데 사용된 은유가 바이러스였는지 짐승이었는지에 따라 응답자들의 제안이 크게 달라졌다는 것을 발견했다. [5]범죄를 자신들의 도시에 침입한 바이러스에 비유하는 은유를 제공받은 사람들은 빈곤을 없애는 것과 교육을 향상시키는 것 같은, 예방과 문제의 근본 원인을 다루는 것을 강조했다. [6]반면에, 짐승의 은유를 제공받은 사람들은 교정 조치, 즉 경찰력과 교도소의 규모를 늘리는 것에 초점을 맞추었다.

어휘

frame (특정한 방식으로) 표현하다; 구조, 틀
amount to A A에 해당하다, A와 마찬가지이다; (합계가) A에 이르다
propose (~을 하려고) 작정[의도]하다; 제안하다
thereby 그것에 의해, 그렇게 함으로써
condition 좌우하다, 영향을 미치다; 상태; 조건
illustration 예, 실례; 삽화
metaphor 은유, 비유
invade 침입하다; 침해하다
emphasize 강조하다
address (문제 등을) 다루다, 처리하다
eliminate 없애다, 제거하다
remediation 교정(조치), 개선; 치료 교육
[선택지] preventive 예방의, 예방[방지]을 위한
measure 조치, 정책; 측정하다

정답 가이드

주제문에서 문제를 어떻게 표현하느냐가 문제 이해와 접근 방식에 영향을 미치기 때문에 중요하다고 한 후, 범죄를 바이러스 또는 짐승으로 표현한 것에 따라 해결 방식에 대한 응답이 달라진 것을 예로 들어 설명하는 글이다. 따라서 글의 주제로 가장 적절한 것은 ⑤ 'effect of problem framing on approaching and solving problems(문제 접근 및 해결에 문제 표현이 미치는 영향)'이다.

오답 클리닉

① importance of asking the right questions for better solutions (3%)
더 나은 해결책(×)을 위해 올바른 질문을 하는 것(×)의 중요성
질문에 따라 해결책이 더 나빠지거나 나아진다는 내용이 아님.

② difficulty of using a metaphor to find solutions to a problem (9%)
문제에 대한 해결책을 찾기 위해 은유를 사용하는 것의 어려움(×)
metaphor를 이용한 오답. 은유는 문제를 표현하는 범죄 묘사 방식의 하나로 언급된 것으로 중심 내용이 아님.

③ reasons why problem framing prevents solutions from appearing (7%) 문제 표현이 해결책이 출현하는 것을 막는 이유(×)
문제 표현이 문제 해결 방식에 영향을 미치는 것이지 해결책 출현 자체를 막는다는 내용은 없음.

④ usefulness of preventive measures in reducing community crime (5%) 지역 사회 범죄를 줄이는 데 있어서 예방 조치의 유용성(×)
지역 사회 범죄 예방 조치는 문제 표현에 따라 달라지는 응답의 예로 언급된 내용일 뿐임.

02 + 빈칸 추론 〈19학년도 대수능 33번 | 정답률 30%〉 ②

구문분석 & 직독직해 문화 현재에 따라 가치가 결정되는 유산

[1]Heritage(S) is concerned(V) / with *the ways* [in which(전치사+관계대명사) very selective material artefacts, mythologies, memories and traditions(S′) become(V′) resources(C′) (for the present)].
유산은 관련이 있다 / 방식과 [매우 선별적인 물질적 인공물, 신화, 기억, 그리고 전통이 자원이 되는 (현재를 위한)]
↳ 유산은 현재와 관련이 있음.

🔑 유산은 현재의 요구에 따라 선택된 과거의 자원임.

[2]The contents, interpretations and representations (of the resource)(S_1) / are selected(V_1) / according to the demands of the present; //
내용, 해석, 표현은 (그 자원의) / 선택된다 / 현재의 요구에 따라 //
an imagined past(S_2) provides(V_2) / resources(O) (for *a heritage* [that(주격 관계대명사) is to be passed / onto an imagined future]).
상상된 과거는 제공한다 / 자원을 (유산을 위한 [전달될 / 상상된 미래로])

🔑 유산의 의미와 기능도 현재를 기준으로 함.

[3]It follows too // that the meanings and functions of memory and tradition are defined / in the present.
★<It follows that ~>은 논리적인 결과를 말하는 표현.
또한 (~라는) 결론이 된다 // 기억과 전통의 의미와 기능들이 정의된다는 / 현재에서
↳ **세부 사항 1:** 현재의 요구와 기준으로 유산이 선택되고 그 의미와 기능들이 정의됨.

[4]Further, / heritage(S) is more concerned(V) with meanings / than material artefacts.
게다가 / 유산은 의미와 더 관련 있다 / 물질적 인공물보다

강조구문 ★강조된 주어 the former는 단수이지만, the former가 meanings를 지칭하므로 복수형 동사가 쓰임.
[5]It is the former(= meanings) // that give(V'_1) value(O'_1), / either cultural or financial, / to the latter(= material artefacts) / and explain(V'_2) why they(= material artefacts) have been selected / from the near infinity (of the past)(O'_2).
바로 전자(의미)이다 // 가치를 부여하는 것은 / 문화적 또는 재정상의 / 후자(물질적 인공물)에 / 그리고 왜 그것들이 선택되었는지를 설명하는 것은 / 거의 무한에 가까운 것들로부터 (과거의)
↳ **세부 사항 2:** 유산은 그 자체보다는 가치를 부여하는 의미가 중요함.

🔑 유산은 현재의 요구 변화에 따라 버려지기도[잊혀지기도] 함.

[6]In turn, / they(S)(= material artefacts) may later be discarded(V) // as(부사절 접속사(~함에 따라)) the demands of present societies(S′) change(V′), //
결국 / 그것들은 나중에 버려지지도 모른다 // 현재 사회의 요구가 변화함에 따라 //
★<as is>: ~이듯이, 있는 그대로
or even, / as is presently occurring(V′) / in the former Eastern Europe, // when(부사절 접속사(시간)) pasts have to be reinvented / to reflect new presents(목적(~하기 위해)).
혹은 심지어 / 현재 일어나고 있듯이 / 구 동유럽에서 // 과거가 다시 만들어져야 할 때 / 새로운 현재를 반영하기 위해서
↳ 현재 사회의 요구에 맞지 않으면 유산은 버려질 수도 있음.

해석

[1]유산은 매우 선별적인 물질적 인공물, 신화, 기억, 그리고 전통이 현재를 위한 자원이 되는 방식과 관련이 있다. [2]그 자원의 내용, 해석, 표현은 현재의 요구에 따라 선택되며, 상상된 과거는 상상된 미래로 전달될 유산을 위한 자원을 제공한다. [3]또한 기억과 전통의 의미와 기능들이 현재에서 정의된다는 결론이 된다. [4]게다가, 유산은 물질적 인공물보다 의미와 더 관련 있다. [5]후자(물질적 인공물)에 문화적 또는 재정상의 가치를 부여하고 거의 무한에 가까운 과거의 것들로부터 왜 그것들이 선택되었는지를 설명하는 것은 바로 전자(의미)이다. [6]결국, 현재 사회의 요구가 변화함에 따라, 혹은 심지어, 구 동유럽에서 현재 일어나고 있듯이, 새로운 현재를 반영하기 위해서 과거가 다시 만들어져야 할 때, 그것들은 나중에 버려지지도 모른다. [7]따라서 유산은 과거를 기억하는 것만큼 과거를 잊는 것에 관한 것이다.

어휘

heritage (국가, 사회의) 유산, 전통; 세습 재산
be concerned with ~와 관계가 있다
artefact (특히 역사적·문화적 의미가 있는) 인공물, 가공품
mythology 신화
representation 표현, 묘사; 대표(자)
pass onto A A에게 전달하다[넘겨주다]
the former 전자
cf. former 과거[이전]의
financial 재정(상)의
the latter 후자
infinity 무한히 많음; 무한(성)
discard 버리다, 폐기하다
[선택지] neither A nor B A도 B도 아닌
universal 보편적인; 일반적인
⊕ 구 동유럽(former Eastern Europe): Eastern bloc(동구권)이라고도 하며, 1945년에서 1990년에 이르기까지 소련 통치하에 있었던 체코슬로바키아, 동독, 헝

주제문

[7]Thus / heritage is **as much about forgetting / as remembering the past.**
따라서 / 유산은 (과거를) 잊는 것에 관한 것이다 / 과거를 기억하는 것만큼
↳ **결론:** 유산은 과거의 것이지만 현재의 가치와 의미를 반영하여 선택되는 것임.

가리, 폴란드, 루마니아, 유고슬라비아 등을 의미함. 이들 국가들은 소련 붕괴 후 20세기 말에 극심한 정치적, 사회적, 경제적 변화를 겪었는데, 이 글의 내용으로 보아, 이들 국가에서는 많은 유산이 버려지고 새로운 유산이 가치를 부여받았을 것으로 이해할 수 있음.

정답 가이드

빈칸 문장이 Thus로 시작하므로 '유산'에 대한 필자의 결론이 무엇인지를 추론해야 한다. 앞 내용에서 유산은 현재의 요구에 따라 선택된 과거의 자원이며, 그것의 의미와 기능은 현재를 기준으로 정의된다고 했다. 결국 현재 사회의 요구가 변하면 새로운 현재를 반영하기 위한 과거가 다시 만들어지고 이전 것들은 버려질 수도 있다는 것이다. 따라서 빈칸에 들어갈 말로 가장 적절한 것은 ② 'as much about forgetting as remembering the past(과거를 기억하는 것만큼 과거를 잊는 것에 관한 것)'이다.

오답 클리닉

① a collection of memories and traditions of a society (39%)
한 사회의 기억과 전통을 모아놓은 것
유산은 축적되기만 하는 것이 아니라 버려지기도 한다고 했으므로 틀림.

The 주의 유산의 일반적인 개념에 따라 빈칸을 추론하려 해서는 안 된다.

③ neither concerned with the present nor the future (11%)
현재에도 미래에도 관련되지 않은 것
미래로 전달될 의미와 가치를 가진 유산이 현재를 기준으로 선택되는 것이므로 글의 내용과 반대됨.

④ a mirror reflecting the artefacts of the past (13%)
과거의 인공물들을 반영하는 거울
유산은 과거만이 아니라 현재의 의미와 가치도 반영한다고 볼 수 있음.

⑤ about preserving universal cultural values (6%)
보편적인 문화적 가치를 보존하는 것에 관한 것
가치와 의미는 시대에 따라 변화한다고 했고 그에 따라 보존되지 않고 버려지기도 한다고 했으므로 틀림.

03 + 글의 순서 (20학년도 대수능 37번 | 정답률 51%) ②

구문분석 & 직독직해

역사 과학 사학자의 전통적 목표의 결함

[1]Traditionally, / (Kuhn claims), // the primary goal (of historians of science) / was /
(삽입절) (S) (V)
전통적으로 / (Kuhn이 주장하기를) // 주된 목표는 (과학 사학자의) / ~이었다 /
'to clarify and (to) deepen / an understanding (of *contemporary* scientific methods or concepts) / by displaying their evolution'.
(C)
<by v-ing>: v함으로써
'명확하게 하고 깊게 하는 것 / 이해를 ('당대의' 과학적 방법이나 개념에 대한) / 그것들의 점진적 발전을 보여줌으로써'
↳ 과학 사학자의 목표는 과학의 점진적 발전을 밝혀서 과학에 대한 이해를 높이는 것임.

This는 주어진 글의 kuhn이 주장한 목표를 가리킴.
(B) [2]This entailed / relating the progressive accumulation (of breakthroughs and discoveries).
(S) (V) (O(동명사구))
이것은 수반했다 / 점진적인 축적에 대하여 이야기하는 것을 (획기적인 발전과 발견의)

[3]Only *that* [which survived in some form / in the present] / was considered relevant.
(S) (주격 관계대명사) (V) (C)
(~한) 것만이 [어떤 형태로 살아남은 / 현재에] / 유의미하다고 여겨졌다
↳ **부연 설명:** 과학의 획기적 발전 및 발견의 점진적인 축적을 이야기하고 현재까지 남아있는 정보들만 유의미하다고 여김.

주제문
★<a number of+N>: 많은 ~
[4]In the mid-1950s, / however, / a number of faults / in this view of history / became apparent.
(S) (V) (C)
1950년대 중반에 / 하지만 / 많은 결함이 / 역사에 대한 이러한 관점에서 / 분명해졌다
↳ **문제점:** 과학 사학자들의 전통적 관점에는 결함이 있음.

→ to ask의 O(명사절)
[5]Closer analysis (of scientific discoveries), / for instance, / led historians to ask // whether the dates of discoveries [and] their discoverers can be identified precisely.
(S) (V) (O) (C) (명사절 접속사 (~인지)) (S'1) (S'2) (V')
더 면밀한 분석은 (과학적 발견에 대한) / 예를 들어 / 사학자들로 하여금 묻도록 했다 // 발견 날짜와 그것들의 발견자가 정확하게 확인될 수 있는지
↳ **결함 1:** 과학적 발견의 발견일과 발견자를 정확히 확인하려 함.

해석

[1]Kuhn이 주장하기를, 전통적으로 과학 사학자의 주된 목표는 '당대의' 과학적 방법이나 개념의 점진적 발전을 보여줌으로써 그것에 대한 이해를 명확하게 하고 깊게 하는 것이었다. (B) [2]이것은 획기적인 발전과 발견의 점진적인 축적에 대하여 이야기하는 것을 수반했다. [3]현재에 어떤 형태로 살아남은 것만이 유의미하다고 여겨졌다. [4]하지만 1950년대 중반에, 역사에 대한 이러한 관점에서 많은 결함이 분명해졌다. [5]예를 들어, 과학적 발견에 대한 더 면밀한 분석은 사학자들로 하여금 발견 날짜와 그것들의 발견자가 정확하게 확인될 수 있는지를 묻도록 했다. (A) [6]몇몇 발견은 무수한 단계와 발견자들을 수반하는 것처럼 보이는데, 그중에서 어느 것도 확정적인 것으로 확인될 수 없다. [7]게다가, 오늘날의 기준에 따라 과거의 발견과 발견자들을 평가하는 것은 우리가 그것들이 당시에 얼마나 중요했을지를 알 수 없게 한다. (C) [8]전통적인 관점은 또한 비지성적인 요인들, 특히 제도적 요인과 사회 경제적 요인들이 과학 발전에서 하는 역할을 인식하지 못한다. [9]하지만 가장 중요한 것은, 전통적인 과학 사학자가 과거를 구상하기 위해 사용하는 개념, 질문, 기준 그 자체가 역사적 변화의 영향을 받는다는 사실을 알지 못하는 것처럼 보인다는 것이다.

어휘

primary 주된; 최초의

(B)의 마지막에 언급한 결함에 대해 구체적으로 설명함.

(A) [6]Some discoveries seem to entail / *numerous phases and discoverers*, // none of which can be identified / as (being) definitive.
S V C 관계사절(보충 설명)

몇몇 발견은 수반하는 것처럼 보인다 / 무수한 단계와 발견자들을 // 그중에서 어느 것도 확인될 수 없다 / 확정적인 것으로

↳ **부연 설명:** 몇몇 발견들은 많은 단계 및 발견자들을 수반해서 확인될 수 없음.

[7]Furthermore, / the evaluation (of past discoveries and discoverers) / according to present-day standards /
S(단수)

게다가 / 평가하는 것은 (과거의 발견과 발견자들을) / 오늘날의 기준에 따라 /

does not allow us to see // how significant they may have been / in their own day.
V(단수) O C to see의 O(명사절)

우리가 알 수 없게 한다 // 그것들(과거 발견과 발견자들)이 얼마나 중요했을지를 / 당시에

↳ **결함 2:** 과거의 발견을 현대의 기준으로 평가해 발견 당시의 중요도를 알 수 없음.

(A)의 마지막 문장인 부정문과 Nor로 연결되며 다른 결함을 추가함.

(C) [8]Nor does the traditional view recognise / *the role* [that non-intellectual factors, / especially institutional and socio-economic ones, / play in scientific developments].
부정어 조동사(도치) S V O 목적격 관계대명사 (= factors)

전통적인 관점은 또한 인식하지 못한다 / 역할을 [비지성적인 요인들이 / 특히 제도적인 것 그리고 사회 경제적인 것들(요인들) / 과학 발전에서 하는]

↳ **결함 3:** 과학 발전에 비지성적 요인들이 미치는 영향을 인식하지 못함.

[9]Most importantly, / however, / the traditional historian of science seems blind /
S V C

가장 중요한 것은 / 하지만 / 전통적인 과학 사학자가 알지 못하는 것처럼 보인다는 것이다 /

to the fact // that *the concepts, questions and standards* [that they use / to frame the past] / are themselves subject to historical change.
= 동격 접속사 S′ 목적격 관계대명사 목적(~하기 위해) V′ C′

사실을 // 개념, 질문, 기준이 [그들이 사용하는 / 과거를 구상하기 위해] / 그 자체가 역사적 변화의 영향을 받는다는

↳ **결함 4:** 전통 과학 사학자는 그들이 사용하는 개념, 질문, 기준이 역사적 변화의 영향을 받음을 인식하지 못함.

contemporary 당대의, 현대의; 동시대의
evolution (점진적인) 발전; 진화
entail 수반하다
relate ~에 대하여 이야기하다; 관련시키다
progressive 점진적인; 진보[혁신]적인
accumulation 축적, 누적
breakthrough 획기적 발전; 돌파(구)
relevant 유의미한; 관련 있는, 적절한
identify 확인하다; 식별하다; 동일시하다
precisely 정확하게; 바로
phase 단계[국면]; 양상
definitive 확정적인, 최종적인
significant 중요한; 상당한
institutional 제도적인; 기관의
socio-economic 사회경제적
blind to A A를 알지 못하는
frame 구상하다; 표현하다; 틀; 구조
be subject to A A의 영향을 받다[받기 쉽다]; A의 대상이다

정답 가이드

주어진 글은 전통 과학 사학자가 가졌던 주된 목표에 대한 Kuhn의 주장을 설명하는 내용이므로 이를 This로 받아 부연 설명하는 (B)가 뒤에 이어져야 한다. (B)의 뒷부분부터 전통 과학 사학자의 관점에 대한 결함이 설명되고 그 예로 과학적 발견(discoveries)에 대한 면밀한 분석으로 발견 날짜와 발견자를 정확히 확인하는 분석이 언급된다. 그 뒤에 몇몇 발견(Some discoveries)은 확인될 수 없다고 서술하는 (A)가 이어져야 하며, 마지막으로 부정어 nor(~도 또한 아니다)를 통해 전통적 관점이 가지는 추가적인 결함을 설명하는 (C)가 오는 것이 흐름상 자연스럽다.

오답 클리닉

① (A) - (C) - (B) (2%)
(A)는 (B)에서 지적한 결함을 부연 설명하는 내용이므로 (B) 뒤에 와야 한다.

③ (B) - (C) - (A) (20%)
(C)가 부정의 연속을 나타내는 nor로 시작하므로 앞 문장이 부정문이어야 하는데 (B)의 마지막 문장은 부정문이 아니므로 (B) 뒤에 (C)가 올 수 없다.

④ (C) - (A) - (B) (13%) / ⑤ (C) - (B) - (A) (14%)
(C)는 전통적 관점의 결함을 추가로 제시하는 내용이므로 앞에 다른 결함에 대한 내용이 있어야 한다. 따라서 주어진 글 바로 뒤에 올 수 없다.

01 ✦ 글의 제목 〈21학년도 6월 모평 24번 | 정답률 69%〉 ①

구문분석 & 직독직해

생물 유전적 적응에 선행하는 행동적 적응

[1]A common error (in current Darwinian thinking) / is the assumption // that "selfish genes" are the prime mover in evolution.
(S / V / C = 동격 접속사 S′ V′ C′)
흔한 오류는 (현재의 다윈적 사고에서) / 가정이다 // '이기적 유전자'가 진화의 원동력이라는
↳ **다윈적 사고의 오류:** 이기적 유전자를 진화의 원동력으로 여김.

[2]In strict Darwinism / the prime mover is environmental threat.
(S V C)
엄밀한 (의미의) 다윈설에서 / (진화의) 원동력은 환경적 위협이다
↳ **사실:** 진화의 원동력은 환경적 위협임.

[3]In the absence of threat, / natural selection tends to *resist* change.
(S V)
위협이 없을 때에 / 자연 선택은 변화에 '저항하는' 경향이 있다
↳ **부연 설명:** 환경적 위협이 없으면 자연 선택에 의한 변화도 없음.

*<explain A as B>: A를 B로 설명하다
[4]It is un-biological / to "explain" behavioural change / as *resulting from* genetic change / or the *ex vacuo* emergence (of domain-specific brain modules).
(가주어 V C / 진주어 / 전치사(~로(서)) / 명사구 병렬)
(~은) 생물학적이지 않다 / 행동 변화를 '설명하는' 것은 / 유전적 변화에서 '비롯되는' 것으로 / 또는 '무(無)에서의' 출현에서 '비롯되는' 것으로 (영역 특수적 뇌 모듈의)
↳ **행동 변화 설명:** 유전적이지도 무(無)에서 생겨나지도 않음.

[5]Evolutionary psychologists surely know why brains evolved: //
(S_1 V_1 O(명사절))
진화 심리학자들은 뇌가 왜 진화했는지 분명히 안다 //
as Cosmides and Tooby point out, // brains are found / only in *animals* [that move].
(부사절 접속사(~듯이) / S_2 V_2 / 주격 관계대명사)
Cosmides와 Tooby가 언급하듯이 // 뇌는 발견된다 / 동물들에게서만 [움직이는]
↳ **논거(연구 내용):** 움직이는 동물만이 뇌를 가지고 있음.

*being ~ non-random은 behavioural adaptation을 부연 설명하는 분사구문
[6]Brains are behavioural organs, // and behavioural adaptation, / being immediate and non-random / is vastly more efficient / than genetic adaptation. ⊶ 행동적 적응과 유전적 적응을 비교함.
(S_1 V_1 O / S_2 / 분사구문(= and it is ~) / V_2 C)
뇌는 행동 기관이다 // 그리고 행동적 적응[변화]은 / 즉각적이며 임의적이지 않은 / 매우 더 효율적이다 / 유전적 적응[변화]보다
↳ 행동적 적응이 즉각적이고 체계적이기 때문에 유전적 적응보다 효율적임.

주제문
[7]So, / in animals (with brains), / behavioural change is the usual first response (to environmental threat).
(S V C)
그래서 / 동물들에게서 (뇌를 가진) / 행동 변화는 흔히 있는 첫 번째 대응이다 (환경적 위협에 대한)
⊶ 유전적 적응은 행동적 적응 뒤에 일어남.

[8]If the change is successful, // genetic adaptation (to the new behaviour) / will follow more gradually.
(부사절 접속사(조건) / S / V)
만약 그 변화가 성공적이라면 // 유전적 적응이 (그 새로운 행동에 대한) / 더 서서히 뒤이어 일어날 것이다
↳ **결론(적응 순서):** 환경적 위협에 대한 즉각적인 행동 변화(행동적 적응) → 유전적 적응.

[9]Animals do not evolve carnivore teeth and then (do not) decide // (that) it might be a good idea / to eat meat.
(S V_1 O / V_2 / ↱ decide의 O(명사절) / 명사절 접속사 생략 / 가주어 V′ C′ / 진주어′(to-v구))
동물들은 육식 동물의 이빨을 진화시킨 다음에 결정하지 않는다 // 좋은 생각일지도 모른다고 / 고기를 먹는 것이
↳ **예:** 행동 변화(고기를 먹음)가 유전적 적응(이빨 진화)으로 이어짐.

해석

[1]현재의 다윈적 사고(자연 선택에 의한 진화론적 사고)에서 흔한 오류는 '이기적 유전자'가 진화의 원동력이라는 가정이다. [2]엄밀한 (의미의) 다윈설에서 (진화의) 원동력은 환경적 위협이다. [3]위협이 없을 때에 자연 선택은 변화에 '저항하는' 경향이 있다. [4]행동 변화를 유전적 변화 또는 영역 특수적 뇌 모듈의 '무(無)에서의' 출현에서 '비롯되는' 것으로 '설명하는' 것은 생물학적이지 않다.(▶ 생물학적으로 행동 변화는 유전적 변화나 무에서 출현하지 않는다는 의미) [5]진화 심리학자들은 뇌가 왜 진화했는지 분명히 아는데, Cosmides와 Tooby가 언급하듯이, 뇌는 움직이는 동물들에게서만 발견된다. [6]뇌는 행동 기관이고, 즉각적이며 임의적이지 않은 행동적 적응[변화]이 유전적 적응[변화]보다 매우 더 효율적이다. [7]그래서 뇌를 가진 동물들에게서 행동적 변화는 환경적 위협에 대한 흔히 있는 첫 번째 대응이다. [8]만약 그 변화가 성공적이라면, 그 새로운 행동에 대한 유전적 적응이 더 서서히 뒤이어 일어날 것이다. [9]동물들은 육식 동물의 이빨을 진화시킨 다음에 고기를 먹는 것이 좋은 생각일지도 모른다고 결정하지 않는다.

어휘

assumption 가정, 추정
prime mover 원동력
evolution 진화; 발달, 발전
cf. evolutionary 진화의
strict 엄밀한, 정확한; 엄격한
in the absence of ~이 없을 때에
tend to-v v하는 경향이 있다
resist 저항[반항]하다; 참다[견디다]
result from ~에서 비롯되다[기인하다]
genetic 유전의, 유전학의
emergence 출현, 발생
point out (주의를 기울이도록) 언급[지적]하다
behavioural 행동적인, 행동의
adaptation 적응; 각색 (작품)
vastly 매우, 대단히; 광대하게
[선택지] superior 우수한, 뛰어난; 상위의

⊕ 이기적 유전자(selfish gene): 생물학자 Richard Dawkins가 사용한 비유적 표현. 생물이 유기체에 유리하도록 자연 선택에 의해 진화한 것이 아니라, 유전자의 생존이나 증식에 유리하도록 진화한 것이라는 견해.
⊕ 다윈설(Darwinism): 자연 선택에 의한 생물의 진화를 주장한 이론.
⊕ 영역 특수적 뇌 모듈(domain-specific brain modules): 두뇌가 경험으로 발달하는 것이 아니라 특정 기능을 실행하도록 진화한 선천적 신경 조직을 가지고 태어난다는 주장. 예를 들어 언어적 추론 기제는 오직 언어적 영역의 정보를 처리할 때만 이용 가능하다는 것.

정답 가이드

행동적 적응이 즉각적이고 임의적이지 않아서 유전적 적응보다 더 효율적이므로, 환경적 위협에 대해 행동적 적응이 우선되고 그다음에 그에 대한 유전적 적응이 일어난다는 글이다. 따라서 글의 제목으로 가장 적절한 것은 ① 'Which Adapts First, Behaviour or Genes?(행동 또는 유전자 중 어느 것이 먼저 적응하는가?)'이다.

오답 클리닉

② The Brain Under Control of Selfish Genes (15%)
이기적 유전자의 통제 하에 있는(×) 뇌
뇌는 행동 기관이라고 했으므로 이기적 유전자의 통제를 받는다고 볼 수 없음.

③ Why Animals Eat Meat: A Story of Survival (3%)
동물들이 고기를 먹는 이유, 즉 생존의 이야기(×)
마지막 문장에 언급된 육식 동물들은 행동적 적응이 유전적 적응보다 먼저 일어남을 보여주기 위한 예로, 육식과 생존에 대한 글이 아님.

④ Genes Always Win the Battle Against Nature! (3%)
유전자가(×) 항상 자연과의 전투에서 승리한다(×)!
유전자가 항상 자연을 이기는지는 유추할 수 없음.

⑤ The Superior Efficiency of Genetic Adaptation (11%)
유전적 적응(×)의 우수한 효율성
유전적 적응보다 행동적 적응이 더 효율적이라고 했으므로 틀림.

02 ✦ 빈칸 추론 (19학년도 대수능 32번 | 정답률 62%) ①

구문분석 & 직독직해

사회 소수 집단이 영향력을 행사하는 방법

[1]Minorities tend not to have / much power or status / and may even be dismissed / as troublemakers, extremists or simply 'weirdos'.
(S: Minorities, V₁: tend, V₂: may even be dismissed, as: 전치사(~로(서)))
소수 집단은 가지고 있지 않은 경향이 있다 / 많은 힘이나 지위를 / 그리고 심지어 일축될 수도 있다 / 말썽꾼, 극단주의자, 또는 단순히 '별난 사람'으로

[2]How, then, do they ever have any influence / over the majority?
(they = minorities)
그렇다면 그들(소수 집단)은 도대체 어떻게 영향을 미치는가 / 다수 집단에
↳ **도입(질문):** 힘이나 지위를 가지고 있지 않은 소수 집단은 어떻게 다수 집단에게 영향력을 행사하는가?

주제문
[3]The social psychologist Serge Moscovici claims // that the answer lies in their *behavioural style*, / i.e. *the way* [**the minority gets its point across**].
(S: The social psychologist Serge Moscovici, V: claims, that: 명사절 접속사 → claims의 O(명사절), S′: the answer, V′: lies)
★관계부사 how와 the way는 함께 쓰일 수 없으므로 the way만 쓰임.
사회 심리학자 Serge Moscovici는 주장한다 // 그 답이 그들의 '행동 양식'에 있다고 / 즉 '방식' [소수 집단이 자신의 의견을 이해시키는]
↳ **답변:** 소수 집단은 자신의 의견을 이해시키는 '행동 양식'이 있음.

[4]The crucial factor (in the success of the suffragette movement) / was that its supporters were *consistent* / in their views, // and this created a considerable degree of social influence.
(S₁: The crucial factor, V₁: was, that: 명사절 접속사 → was의 C(명사절), S′: its supporters, V′: were, C′: consistent; S₂: this (= 앞 절의 that절), V₂: created, O₂: a considerable degree of social influence)
🔑 소수 집단은 일관된 관점을 지지했음.
결정적인 요인은 (여성 참정권 운동의 성공에서) / 그 지지자들이 '일관적'이었다는 것이었다 / 자신들의 관점에서 //
그리고 이것이 상당한 정도의 사회적 영향력을 만들어 냈다
↳ **세부 사항(예):** 여성 참정권 운동에서 소수 집단의 '일관된' 관점이 영향력을 만들어 냄.

🔑 소수 집단은 일관된 입장을 지지하며 다수 집단의 생각을 변화시킬 틈을 만들어냄.
[5]*Minorities* [that are active and organised], // who support and defend their position *consistently*, / can create social conflict, doubt and uncertainty / among members of the majority, // and ultimately this may lead to social change.
(S₁: Minorities, that: 주격 관계대명사, who: 관계대명사(보충 설명), V′: support and defend, O′: their position, V₁: can create, O₁: social conflict, doubt and uncertainty; S₂: this (= 앞 절), V₂: may lead, O₂: social change)
소수 집단은 [활동적이고 조직적인] // 그들(소수 집단)은 자신들의 입장을 '일관되게' 옹호하고 방어하는데 / 사회적 갈등, 의심, 그리고 불확신을 만들어 낼 수 있다 / 다수 집단의 구성원 사이에 //
그리고 궁극적으로 이것이 사회 변화로 이어질 수도 있다
↳ **부연 설명:** 소수 집단의 '일관된' 입장이 다수 집단에 갈등과 의심을 만들어 변화를 이끎.

해석

[1]소수 집단은 많은 힘이나 지위를 가지고 있지 않은 경향이 있고 심지어 말썽꾼, 극단주의자, 또는 단순히 '별난 사람'으로 일축될 수도 있다. [2]그렇다면 그들은 도대체 어떻게 다수 집단에 영향을 미치는가? [3]사회 심리학자 Serge Moscovici는 그 답이 그들의 '행동 양식', 즉 소수 집단이 자신의 의견을 이해시키는 '방식'에 있다고 주장한다. [4]여성 참정권 운동의 성공에서 결정적인 요인은 그 지지자들이 자신들의 관점에서 '일관적'이었다는 것이었고, 이것이 상당한 정도의 사회적 영향력을 만들어 냈다. [5]활동적이고 조직적인 소수 집단은 자신들의 입장을 '일관되게' 옹호하고 방어하는데, 다수 집단의 구성원 사이에 사회적 갈등, 의심, 그리고 불확신을 만들어 낼 수 있고, 궁극적으로 이것이 사회 변화로 이어질 수도 있다. [6]소수 집단이 다른 사람들을 자신의 관점으로 변하게 했기 때문에 그러한 변화는 흔히 일어났다. [7]소수 집단의 영향력이 없다면 우리에게는 어떤 혁신, 어떤 사회 변화도 없을 것이다. [8]우리가 현재 '주요' 사회 운동(예를 들어, 기독교 신앙, 노동조합 운동, 또는 남녀평등주의)으로 여기는 것의 다수는 본래 거침없이 밀하는 소수 집단의 영향력으로 인한 것이었다.

어휘

minority 소수 (집단)(↔ majority 다수 (집단))
status 지위, 신분; 상태
troublemaker 말썽꾼
extremist 극단주의자
i.e. 즉 ((라틴어 id est의 축약어))
get a point across 의견[논지, 요점]을 이해시키다
movement (정치적·사회적) 운동
consistent 일관된
cf. consistently 일관되게
considerable 상당한, 많은
ultimately 궁극적으로, 결국

🗝 사회 변화는 다수의 생각을 소수의 생각으로 변화시키면서 일어남. ★<convert A (in)to B>: A를 B로 변하게 하다, 전환하다

[6]Such change has often occurred // because a minority has converted others / to its point of view.
S(= Social change) V 부사절 접속사(이유) S′ V′ O′
그러한 변화(사회 변화)는 흔히 일어났다 // 소수 집단이 다른 사람들을 변하게 했기 때문에 / 자신의 관점으로

[7]Without the influence of minorities, / we would have no innovation, no social change.
(= If it were not for) ★If절을 대신하는 가정법 과거 표현으로 '~가 없다면, …할 것이다'의 의미
소수 집단의 영향력이 없다면 / 우리에게는 어떤 혁신, 어떤 사회 변화도 없을 것이다

★<regard A as B>: A를 B로 여기다[생각하다]
[8]Many (of what we now regard / as 'major' social movements / (e.g. Christianity, trade unionism or feminism)) / were originally due to the influence (of an outspoken minority).
S(복수) of의 O(명사절) V(복수) C
다수는 (우리가 현재 여기는 것의 / '주요' 사회 운동으로 / (예를 들어, 기독교 신앙, 노동조합 운동, 또는 남녀평등주의)) / 본래 영향력으로 인한 것이었다 (거침없이 말하는 소수 집단의)

↳ **맺음말:** 소수 집단의 영향력 덕분에 사회가 변화할 수 있었음.

Christianity 기독교 신앙
trade unionism 노동조합 운동
outspoken 거침없이 말하는; 솔직한
[선택지] tone down (음성을) 낮추다
cultivate 양성하다; 경작하다
bring about 야기하다, 초래하다
cooperate 협동[협력]하다

정답 가이드

소수 집단이 어떤 방식으로 다수 집단에 영향력을 행사하는지를 추론해야 한다. 빈칸 문장 뒤에서 여성 참정권 운동의 성공을 예로 들어, 소수 집단은 '일관된' 입장을 옹호하고 방어함으로써 다수 집단의 생각을 변화시켜 사회 변화를 이룬 것이라고 설명한다. 이는 소수 집단이 지지하는 의견을 다수 집단이 수용하도록 한 것이므로, 빈칸에 들어갈 말로 가장 적절한 것은 ① 'the minority gets its point across(소수 집단이 자신의 의견을 이해시키다)'이다.

The 핵심 ★ 빈칸에 들어갈 적절한 말을 추론했다고 해도 막상 선택지 어휘가 낯선 경우 정답을 고르기 난감할 수 있으므로 어휘 학습을 게을리 하지 말아야 한다. get something across와 같이 <get+명사+부사>의 구조일 때는 '부사'가 의미 파악에 큰 역할을 한다. '명사(its point)가 건너편으로 건너가게 하다'라는 의미는 곧 '자신의 의견을 상대방에게 전달하다[이해시키다]'로 추론할 수 있어야 한다.

오답 클리닉

② the minority tones down its voice (8%)
소수 집단이 자신의 목소리를 낮추다
소수 집단은 자신의 의견을 일관되게 지지했다고 했으므로 글의 내용과 반대됨.

③ the majority cultivates the minority (6%)
다수 집단이 소수 집단을 양성하다
다수 집단이 소수 집단에 영향을 미치는 내용이 아님.

④ the majority brings about social change (16%)
다수 집단이 사회적 변화를 야기하다
소수 집단의 일관된 입장이 사회 변화를 가져왔다고 했으므로 글의 내용과 반대됨.

⑤ the minority cooperates with the majority (8%)
소수 집단이 다수 집단과 협동하다
두 집단 간의 협동에 관한 언급은 없음.

03 + 문장 넣기 (20학년도 대수능 39번 | 정답률 38%) ③

구문분석 & 직독직해

광고 광고주가 텔레비전 광고에서 얻는 이점

[1]*The fragmentation* (of television audiences / during recent decades), // which has happened throughout the globe // as new channels have been launched everywhere, / has caused advertisers much concern.
S(단수) 관계대명사(보충 설명) 부사절 접속사(~하면서) S′ V′ V(단수) IO DO
★<cause+IO+DO>: IO에게 DO를 (안겨)주다
분산은 (텔레비전 시청자의 / 최근 몇십 년 동안) // 이는 전 세계적으로 일어났는데 // 도처에서 새로운 채널들이 생겨나면서 / 광고주들에게 많은 우려를 안겨주었다

↳ **도입:** 새로운 채널이 많아지면서 시청자들이 분산되자 광고주들이 우려함.

(①) [2]Advertisers look back nostalgically / to *the years* [when a single spot transmission would be seen / by the majority of the population / at one fell swoop].
S V 관계부사 S′ V′
광고주들은 향수에 젖어 회상한다 / 시절을 [한 곳에서의 방송이 시청되었던 / 대부분의 사람들에 의해 / 한 번에]

★<make+O+C(형용사)>: O를 ~하게 만들다
(②) [3]This made / the television advertising (of mass consumer products) / relatively straightforward — / not to say easy — //
S(= 앞 문장) V O C
이것은 만들었다 / 텔레비전 광고를 (대량 소비재의) / 비교적 간단하게 / 쉬웠다고 말하는 것은 아니지만 //

해석

[1]최근 몇십 년 동안 텔레비전 시청자의 분산은 도처에서 새로운 채널들이 생겨나면서 전 세계적으로 일어났는데, 이는 광고주들에게 많은 우려를 안겨주었다. (①) [2]광고주들은 한 곳에서의 방송이 대부분의 사람들에 의해 한 번에 시청되었던 시절을 향수에 젖어 회상한다. (②) [3]이것은 대량 소비재의 텔레비전 광고를, 쉬웠다고 말하는 것은 아니지만 비교적 간단하게 만들었는데, 반면에 오늘날에는 광고주들이 개별 시청자가 있는 다수의 채널에 광고를 함으로써, 시간을 두고 자신들의 목표 시장의 (광고) 도달 범위를 늘리는 것이 필요하다. (③ [4]그럼에도 불구하고, 다른 매체에서의 광고들은 늘 단편적이었기 때문에, 이 문제에 대해 광고주들이 오히려 너무 많이 걱정한다고 주장할 수 있다.) [5]게다가, 광고주들은 수많은 방송국들 간의 가격 경쟁으로부터 상당한 이익을 얻는다. (④) [6]그리고 텔레비전은 새로운 브랜드나 새로운 캠페인에

주어진 문장의 this problem이 지칭하는 내용.
whereas today / it is necessary / for advertisers / to build up coverage (of their target markets) /
부사절 접속사(대조) 가주어 V' C' to-v의 의미상 주어 진주어(to-v구)
over time, / by advertising on a host of channels (with separate audiences).
<by v-ing>: v함으로써
반면에 오늘날에는 / (~이) 필요하다 / 광고주들이 / (광고) 도달 범위를 늘리는 것이 (자신들의 목표 시장의) / 시간을 두고 / 다수의 채널에 광고를 함으로써 (개별 시청자가 있는)

↳ **우려점:** 채널이 하나였던 과거와 달리 오늘날은 다수의 채널에 광고해야 함.

주제문 광고주들이 걱정한다는 앞 내용과 역접으로 이어짐.
(③ [4]Still, / it is arguable // that advertisers worry rather too much / about this problem, //
가주어V C 진주어(명사절)
부사절 접속사(~ 때문에)
as advertising (in other media) / has always been fragmented.)
S' V'
그럼에도 불구하고 / (~라고) 주장할 수 있다 // 광고주들이 오히려 너무 많이 걱정한다고 / 이 문제에 대해 // 광고들은 (~하기) 때문에 (다른 매체에서의) / 늘 단편적이었기 (때문에)

↳ 광고주들은 여러 텔레비전 채널에 광고해야 하는 문제에 대해 지나치게 걱정할 필요는 없음.

광고할 방송국이 많으면 광고주들이 이익을 얻는다는 내용이 연결됨.
[5]Moreover, / advertisers gain considerable benefits / from the price competition (between the numerous broadcasting stations).
S V O
게다가 / 광고주들은 상당한 이익을 얻는다 / 가격 경쟁으로부터 (수많은 방송국들 간의)

↳ **논거 1:** 여러 방송국들 간의 가격 경쟁에서 이익을 얻음.

*much는 최상급 강조 부사로 쓰임.
(④) [6]And television remains / *much the fastest way* (to build up public awareness (of a new brand or a new campaign)).
S V C
그리고 텔레비전은 남아 있다 / 단연코 가장 빠른 방법으로 (대중의 인식을 형성하는 (새로운 브랜드나 새로운 캠페인에 대한))

*준부정어(seldom)가 문두에 위치해 <조동사+주어+동사> 어순으로 도치가 일어남.
(⑤) [7]Seldom does / *a new brand or new campaign* [that solely uses other media, / without using television], / reach high levels of public awareness / very quickly.
준부정어 조동사 S 주격 관계대명사 V O
거의 없다 / 새로운 브랜드나 새로운 캠페인이 [오로지 다른 매체를 이용하는 / 텔레비전을 이용하지 않고] / 높은 수준의 대중 인지도에 도달하는 경우는 / 아주 빠르게

↳ **논거 2:** 텔레비전은 대중 인지도를 쌓는 데 있어 가장 효과적인 광고 방법임.

대한 대중의 인식을 형성하는 단연코 가장 빠른 방법으로 남아 있다. (⑤) [7]텔레비전을 이용하지 않고, 오로지 다른 매체를 이용하는 새로운 브랜드나 새로운 캠페인이 아주 빠르게 높은 수준의 대중 인지도에 도달하는 경우는 거의 없다.

어휘

fragmentation 분산; 분열; 파편화
channel (텔레비전의) 채널; 경로; 수단, 방법
launch 시작[착수]하다; 진출시키다; 발사하다
concern 우려, 걱정; 관심
look back 회상하다
nostalgically 향수에 젖어
transmission 방송; 전송; 전염
mass 대량의; 덩어리
consumer product 소비재
relatively 비교적, 상대적으로
straightforward 간단한; 솔직한
coverage (광고의) 도달 범위; 보도[방송]
target market 목표 시장
a host of 다수의
arguable 주장할 수 있는; 논쟁의 소지가 있는
considerable 상당한
broadcasting station 방송국
awareness 인식; 인지도
seldom 좀처럼 ~않는
solely 오로지

정답 가이드

주어진 문장은 Still이라는 역접 연결어가 이끌며 광고주들이 '이 문제(this problem)'에 대해 너무 많이 걱정한다고 주장하므로 앞에는 광고주들이 걱정하는 어떤 '문제'가 나와야 하고 주어진 문장과 역접으로 연결되어야 한다. ③의 앞부분은 텔레비전 채널이 많아지고 시청자들도 분산됨에 따라 광고주들이 여러 채널에 광고를 해야 하는 어려움, 즉 문제가 있다는 내용이고, 뒷부분은 텔레비전으로 광고하는 것에는 이점이 있다는 내용이다. 즉 ③을 기점으로 글의 내용이 대조적으로 전환되어, 앞부분은 텔레비전의 채널 다양화로 인한 광고주들의 걱정, 뒤에는 광고주들의 이익을 다루므로, 주어진 문장이 들어가기에 가장 적절한 곳은 ③이다.

오답 클리닉

① (4%) 최근 새로운 채널이 생겨나고 시청자가 분산되어 광고주들이 걱정한다는 내용에 과거 텔레비전 채널이 하나였던 때를 그리워한다는 내용이 이어지는 것은 자연스럽다.
② (18%) 앞 문장의 내용을 This로 받아 과거의 텔레비전 광고와 오늘날의 광고 방법을 비교하는 내용이 이어진다.
④ (18%) 앞 문장에 이어 텔레비전 광고의 이점을 And로 추가 제시하고 있다.
⑤ (21%) 텔레비전이 대중의 인식을 형성하는 데 가장 빠른 방법이라는 내용을 부연 설명하는 내용이 이어진다.

01 + 함의 추론 (20학년도 대수능 21번 | 정답률 71%) ⑤

구문분석 & 직독직해 학습 지식 또는 창의력에 치우친 학습의 실패

주제문

[1]*Any learning environment* [that deals with only the database instincts or only the improvisatory instincts] / ignores one half (of our ability).
S 주격 관계대명사 V O
어떤 학습 환경이든 [데이터베이스 직감만을 혹은 즉흥적인 직감만을 다루는] / 절반을 무시한다 (우리 능력의)

[2]It is bound to fail.
(= Any ~ instincts) ★<be bound to-v>: 반드시 v하다
그것은 반드시 실패한다
↳ 데이터베이스 또는 즉흥적인 직감만 쓰는 학습은 실패함.

[3]It makes me think of jazz guitarists: //
S₁ V₁ O C
그것은 내게 재즈 기타리스트를 생각나게 한다 //

(= jazz guitarists) 부사절 접속사(조건)
They're not going to make it // if they know a lot about music theory / but don't know / how to jam in a live concert.
S₂ V₂ S' V'₁ V'₂ O'
그들은 성공하지 못할 것이다 // 그들이 음악 이론에 대해 많이 알고 있다면 / 그러나 모른다(면) / 라이브 콘서트에서 즉흥 연주하는 법을
↳ **세부 사항(예):** 이론만 알고 즉흥 연주는 못하는 재즈 기타리스트 → 데이터베이스 직감만 있는 음악가.

[4]Some schools and workplaces emphasize / a stable, rote-learned database.
S V O
어떤 학교와 직장은 강조한다 / 안정적이고 기계적으로 암기한 데이터베이스를

(= Some schools and workplaces)
[5]They ignore *the improvisatory instincts* (drilled into us / for millions of years).
S V O 과거분사구
그들은 즉흥적인 직감을 무시한다 (우리에게 주입된 / 수백만 년 동안)

[6]Creativity suffers.
S V
창의력이 악화된다
↳ **대조 A:** 데이터베이스 암기만 중시하면 창의력이 악화됨.

(= Other schools and workplaces)
[7]Others emphasize creative usage (of a database), / without installing a fund of knowledge / in the first place.
S V O <without v-ing>: v하지 않고
다른 곳(다른 학교와 직장)은 창의적인 사용을 강조한다 (데이터베이스의) / 지식의 축적을 자리 잡게 하지 않고 / 애초에

[8]They ignore our need (to obtain a deep understanding of a subject), // which includes / memorizing and storing a richly structured database.
S V O = 관계대명사(보충 설명) V' O'(동명사구)
그들은 우리의 욕구를 무시한다 (어떤 주제에 대한 깊은 이해를 얻고자 하는) // 그리고 그것은 포함한다 / 풍부하게 구조화된 데이터베이스를 암기하고 저장하는 것을

[9]You get *people* [who are great improvisers / but don't have depth of knowledge].
S V O 주격 관계대명사
여러분은 사람들을 얻게 된다 [훌륭한 즉흥 연주자인 / 그러나 지식의 깊이는 없는]
🔑 즉흥적 직감은 있고 깊은 지식은 없음.
↳ **대조 B:** 창의력만 중시하면 지식의 깊이는 없어짐.

(= people who ~ knowledge)
[10]You may know someone like this // where you work.
부사절 접속사
여러분은 이런 누군가를 알지도 모른다 // 여러분이 일하는 곳에서

해석

[1]데이터베이스(에 기반한) 직감만을 혹은 즉흥적인 직감만을 다루는 어떤 학습 환경이든 우리 능력의 절반을 무시한다. [2]그것은 반드시 실패한다. [3]그것은 내게 재즈 기타리스트를 생각나게 하는데, 그들이 음악 이론에 대해 많이 알고 있지만 라이브 콘서트에서 즉흥 연주하는 법을 모른다면, 그들은 성공하지 못할 것이다. [4]어떤 학교와 직장은 안정적이고, 기계적으로 암기한 데이터베이스를 강조한다. [5]그들은 수백만 년 동안 우리에게 주입된 즉흥적인 직감을 무시한다. [6](그 결과) 창의력이 악화된다. [7]다른 곳(다른 학교와 직장)은 애초에 지식의 축적을 자리 잡게 하지 않고 데이터베이스의 창의적인 사용을 강조한다. [8]그들은 풍부하게 구조화된 데이터베이스를 암기하고 저장하는 것을 포함하는, 어떤 주제에 대한 깊은 이해를 얻고자 하는 우리의 욕구를 무시한다. [9](그 결과) 여러분은 훌륭한 즉흥 연주자이지만 지식의 깊이는 없는 사람들을 얻게 된다. [10]여러분은 여러분이 일하는 곳에서 이런 누군가를 알지도 모른다. [11]그들은 재즈 음악가처럼 보이고 즉흥 연주를 하는 모습을 지니고 있을지 모르지만, 결국 그들은 아무것도 모른다. [12]그들은 지적인 기타 연주 흉내를 내고 있다.

어휘

deal with ~을 다루다
instinct 직감, 본능
improvisatory 즉흥의, 즉석의
cf. improviser 즉흥 연주자
make it 성공하다
jam (다른 연주자들과 미리 연습해 보지 않고) 즉흥 연주를 하다
emphasize 강조하다
stable 안정적인
drill A into B B에게 A를 주입시키다
install 자리를 잡게 하다; 설치[설비]하다
fund (지식 등의) 축적; 자금(을 대다)
appearance (겉)모습, 외양
intellectual 지적인, 총명한
air guitar 기타 연주 흉내 ((록 음악 등을 들으며 기타를 치는 것처럼 흉내 내는 것))
[선택지] acquire 습득하다, 얻다
enhance (능력·질 등을) 향상시키다, 높이다
exhibit 보이다; 전시하다
couple A with B A와 B를 결합시키다[연결짓다]

[11]They may look like jazz musicians / and have the appearance of jamming, //
S V₁ C V₂ O
그들은 재즈 음악가처럼 보일지 모른다 / 그리고 즉흥 연주를 하는 모습을 지니고 있을지 모른다 //

but in the end / they know nothing. 🔑 즉흥 연주를 하는 것처럼 보여도 지식은 없음.
그러나 결국 / 그들은 아무것도 모른다

[12]They're **playing intellectual air guitar.**
그들은 지적인 기타 연주 흉내를 내고 있다
↳ **대조 B의 결론:** 겉보기에는 즉흥 연주를 하는 것 같아도 지식은 없음.

solid 탄탄한, 견고한; 고체(의)
pose as ~인 체하다
demonstrate 보여주다; 입증하다
seemingly 겉보기에는

정답 가이드

밑줄 친 부분이 있는 문장의 주어 They는 바로 앞 문장에서 재즈 음악가처럼 보이고 즉흥 연주를 하는 것처럼 보이지만, 결국 아무것도 모르는 사람들이라고 했다. 즉 그들은 아는 것은 없으면서 즉흥적인 직감만 있는 사람들이므로, 밑줄 친 부분이 의미하는 바로 가장 적절한 것은 ⑤ 'displaying seemingly creative ability not rooted in firm knowledge(확실한 지식에 뿌리를 두지 않은 겉보기에만 창의적인 능력을 보여주고 있는)'이다.

The 핵심 ★ the database instincts와 the improvisatory instincts의 의미는 글에서 같은 맥락으로 쓰인 표현을 통해 유추할 수 있다.

the database instincts	the improvisatory instincts
- music theory	- to jam in a live concert
- a stable, rote-learned database	- creativity
- a fund of knowledge	- creative usage of a database
- memorizing and storing a richly structured database	- improvisers
- intellectual	- jazz musicians

오답 클리닉

① acquiring necessary experience to enhance their creativity (5%)
자신들의 창의력을 향상시키기 위해(×) 필요한 경험을 습득하고 있는
즉흥적 직감이 있는 사람들은 창의력을 이미 가지고 있다고 볼 수 있으므로 창의력을 향상시키는 것이 아님.
② exhibiting artistic talent coupled with solid knowledge of music (8%) 탄탄한 음악 지식(×)과 결합된 예술적 재능을 보이고 있는
즉흥 연주를 해도 아는 것은 없다고 했으므로 글의 내용과 반대됨.
③ posing as experts by demonstrating their in-depth knowledge (11%) 자신들의 깊이 있는 지식을 보여줌으로써(×) 전문가인 체하고 있는
즉흥 연주자이지만 깊은 지식은 없다고 했으므로 글의 내용과 반대됨.
④ performing musical pieces to attract a highly educated audience (4%) 고학력 청중을 끌어들이기 위해(×) 음악 작품을 공연하고 있는
고학력 청중에 대한 내용은 전혀 언급되지 않음.

02 + 빈칸 추론 〈19학년도 대수능 31번 | 정답률 55%〉 ③

구문분석 & 직독직해 인지 사회적 공유를 통한 나쁜 소식의 수용

[1]Finkenauer and Rimé investigated / the memory (of the unexpected death (of Belgium's King Baudouin in 1993)) / in a large sample of Belgian citizens.
S V O
Finkenauer와 Rimé는 조사했다 / 기억을 (예기치 않은 죽음에 대한 (1993년 벨기에 왕 Baudouin의)) / 벨기에 시민들의 대규모 표본을 대상으로
↳ **도입:** 벨기에 왕의 갑작스러운 죽음에 대한 시민들의 기억을 조사함.

↱ revealed의 O(명사절) ★<of는 동격을 이끄는 전치사로, the news와 the king's death가 동격 관계임.
[2]The data revealed // that the news of the king's death had been widely socially shared.
S V 명사절 접속사 S' V
그 자료는 밝혔다 // 왕의 죽음이라는 소식이 널리 사회적으로 공유되었다는 것을

[3]By talking about the event, / people gradually constructed / a social narrative and a collective memory (of the emotional event).
<by v-ing>: v함으로써 S V O (= the king's death)
그 사건에 관해 이야기함으로써 / 사람들은 서서히 구성했다 / 사회적 이야기와 집단 기억을 (그 감정적인 사건에 대한)
↳ **조사 결과 1:** 사회적 공유를 통해 사람들은 사건을 다 같이 기억하게 됨.

[4]At the same time, / they consolidated their own memory (of *the personal circumstances* [in which the event took place]), / *an effect* (known as "flashbulb memory)."
S(= people) V O 전치사+관계대명사 과거분사구
동시에 / 그들은 자신들의 기억을 공고히 했다 (개인적 상황에 대한 [그 사건이 일어났던]) / 효과 ('섬광 기억'으로 알려진)
↳ **조사 결과 2:** 사건 당시의 개인적 상황도 함께 기억됨.

해석

[1]Finkenauer와 Rimé는 벨기에 시민들의 대규모 표본을 대상으로 1993년 벨기에 왕 Baudouin의 예기치 않은 죽음에 대한 기억을 조사했다. [2]그 자료는 왕의 죽음이라는 소식이 널리 사회적으로 공유되었다는 것을 밝혔다. [3]그 사건에 관해 이야기함으로써 사람들은 그 감정적인 사건에 대한 사회적 이야기와 집단 기억을 서서히 구성했다. [4]동시에 그들은 그 사건이 일어났던 개인적 상황에 대한 자신들의 기억을 공고히 했는데, 이는 '섬광 기억'으로 알려진 효과이다. [5]한 사건이 사회적으로 더 많이 공유될수록, 그것은 사람들의 마음에 더 많이 새겨질 것이다. [6]사회적 공유는 이런 식으로 사람들이 갖고 있을지도 모르는 어떤 자연적인 성향을 중화시키는 것을 도울지도 모른다. [7]자연적으로 사람들은 달갑지 않은 사건을 '잊도록' 이끌릴 것이다. [8]그래서 방금 나쁜 소식 한 가지를 들은 누군가는 처음에는 흔히 일어난 일을 부정하는 경향이 있다. [9]나쁜 소식의 반복적인 사회적 공유는 현실성에 기여한다.

주제문 ★<the + 비교급 ~, the + 비교급 ...>: ~하면 할수록 더욱 …하다 🔑 많이(자주) 공유될수록 기억에 더 남음.

[5]The more an event is socially shared, // the more it will be fixed in people's minds.
S₁ V₁ S₂ V₂
한 사건이 사회적으로 더 많이 공유될수록 // 그것(그 사건)은 사람들의 마음에 더 많이 새겨질 것이다
↳ **결론:** 사회적 공유가 더 많을수록 사람들의 기억은 더 공고화됨.

🔑 사회적 공유가 사람들의 믿지 않으려는 성향을 중화시킴.

[6]Social sharing may in this way help / to counteract *some natural tendency* [(which[that]) people may have].
S V O 목적격 관계대명사 생략
사회적 공유는 이런 식으로 도울지도 모른다 / 어떤 자연적인 성향을 중화시키는 것을 [사람들이 갖고 있을지도 모르는]

★여기서 조동사 should는 추측(아마 ~일 것이다)의 의미로 쓰임.
[7]Naturally, / people should be driven / to "forget" undesirable events.
S V C
자연적으로 / 사람들은 이끌릴 것이다 / 달갑지 않은 사건을 '잊도록'

🔑 사람은 나쁜 소식을 처음 들으면 일어난 일(현실)을 부정하려 함.

[8]Thus, / *someone* [who just heard a piece of bad news] / often tends initially to deny / what happened.
S 주격 관계대명사 V to deny의 O(명사절)
그래서 / 누군가는 [방금 나쁜 소식 한 가지를 들은] / 처음에는 흔히 부정하는 경향이 있다 / 일어난 일을
↳ **사회적 공유의 이점:** 달갑지 않은 사건을 부정하고 잊으려 하는 사람들의 자연적 성향을 중화시킴[줄임].

[9]The **repetitive** social sharing (of the bad news) / contributes to realism.
S V
반복적인 사회적 공유는 (나쁜 소식의) / 현실성에 기여한다
↳ **주제문 재진술:** 나쁜 소식이 많이 공유될수록 현실로 받아들이게 됨.

어휘

construct 구성[구축]하다; 건설하다
narrative 이야기, 묘사
collective 집단의; 공동의
flashbulb 섬광[플래시] 전구
fix (기억에) 새겨 두다; 고정시키다, 박다; 수리하다
counteract (효력 등을) 중화하다; ~에 반대로 행동하다, 대응하다
undesirable 달갑지 않은; 바람직하지 않은
initially 처음에
contribute to A A에 기여하다
realism 현실성; 사실주의
[선택지] biased 선입견이 있는, 편향된
temporary 일시적인, 순간의
⊕ 섬광 기억(flashbulb memory): ((심리학)) 아주 중요하거나 놀라운 사건을 경험했을 때 이와 관련된 내용, 그 당시의 상황 등에 대해 매우 자세하고 선명하게 기억하는 것.

정답 가이드

나쁜 소식의 '어떤' 사회적 공유가 현실성에 기여하는지를 찾아야 한다. 앞에서부터 살펴보면, 나쁜 소식의 예인 벨기에 왕의 죽음이라는 소식이 '널리 사회적으로 공유되고 이야기되어' 집단 기억을 구성했다고 했고, 사회적 공유는 나쁜 소식을 잊으려는 사람들의 자연적 성향을 '중화'시킨다고(나쁜 소식이 기억된다는 의미) 했다. '사회적으로 더 많이 공유되고 이야기되는' 것은 곧 '반복적'으로 이야기된다는 의미이고, 사람들의 나쁜 소식을 잊고 부정하려는 성향을 중화시켜 그것을 기억하게 만드는 것은 곧 '현실성에 기여하는' 것으로 볼 수 있다. 따라서 빈칸에 들어갈 말로 가장 적절한 것은 ③ 'repetitive(반복적인)'이다.

오답 클리닉

① biased (22%) 선입견을 가진
사람들이 선입견을 가지고 소식을 공유한다는 내용이 아님.

The 주의 달갑지 않은 사건을 부정하고 잊으려 하는 사람들의 성향을 나쁜 소식에 대한 선입견으로 볼 수도 있지만, 빈칸은 사람들의 성향이 아닌 널리 알려지는 사회적 공유의 속성을 설명하는 것임에 주의해야 한다.

② illegal (7%) 불법적인
불법적인 사회적 공유가 이루어졌다는 내용은 없음.
④ temporary (11%) 일시적인
문장 8에서 오히려 나쁜 소식을 방금 전해 들은 사람은 부정하려는 경향을 보인다고 했으므로 일시적인 사회적 공유가 현실성에 기여한다고 볼 수 없음.
⑤ rational (6%) 이성적인
감정적인 사건을 공유했다는 내용이 있을 뿐, 이성적 사회적 공유에 대한 언급은 전혀 없음.

03 + 무관 문장 〈21학년도 6월 모평 35번 | 정답률 64%〉 ④

구문분석 & 직독직해 환경 친환경적 생활 양식에 대한 통념

[1]One (of the most widespread, / (and sadly mistaken), / environmental myths) / is // that living "close to nature" (out in the country or in a leafy suburb) / is the best "green" lifestyle.
S(단수) 삽입어구 V(단수) ↱ is의 C(명사절)
명사절 접속사 S'(동명사구) V'(단수) C'
하나는 (가장 널리 퍼져 있는 / (그리고 유감스럽게도 잘못된) / 환경에 대한 근거 없는 통념들 중의) / ~이다 // '자연과 가까이' 사는 것이 (시골에서 혹은 녹음이 우거진 교외에서) / 최고의 '친환경적인' 생활 방식이라는 것

[2]Cities, / on the other hand, / are often blamed / as a major cause (of ecological destruction) — / *artificial, crowded places* [that suck up precious resources].
S V 전치사(~로(서)) 주격 관계대명사 V' O'
도시들은 / 반면에 / 자주 비난받는다 / 주요한 원인으로 (생태계 파괴의) / 인공적이고 혼잡한 장소 [귀중한 자원을 빨아들이는]
↳ **통념(Myth):** 시골이나 교외에서 사는 것이 가장 친환경적이며 도시는 생태계 파괴의 주범이라고 비난함.

해석

[1]가장 널리 퍼져 있는, 그리고 유감스럽게도 잘못된, 환경에 대한 근거 없는 통념들 중의 하나는 시골에서 혹은 녹음이 우거진 교외에서 '자연과 가까이' 사는 것이 최고의 '친환경적인' 생활 방식이라는 것이다. [2]반면에 도시들은 귀중한 자원을 빨아들이는 인공적이고 혼잡한 장소, 즉 생태계 파괴의 주요한 원인으로 자주 비난받는다. [3]그러나 사실들을 살펴보면, 아무것도 진실로부터 더 멀 수 없다(전혀 사실이 아니다). ① [4]시골과 대부분의 교외에서의 생활 양식은 출근하고, 식료품을 사고, 아이들을 학교와 활동들에 데리고 가기 위해 연료를 소모하고 배기가스를 쏟아 내면서 매주 자동차 안에서 오랜 시

주제문

[3]Yet, / when you look at the facts, // nothing could be farther / from the truth.

부사절 접속사(~하면)

그러나 / 사실들을 살펴보면 // 아무것도 더 멀 수 없다 / 진실로부터

↳ **사실(Truth):** 실제로 위의 통념은 사실이 아님.

🔑 시골이나 교외 생활이 도시 생활보다 더 친환경적이라는 통념에 대한 반박이 이어질 것임.

① [4]The pattern of life (in the country and most suburbs) / involves / long hours in the automobile / each week, / burning fuel [and] pumping out exhaust / to get to work, (to) buy groceries, and (to) take kids to school and activities.

S(단수) V(단수) O 분사구문(= as it burns ~ and pumps out ~) 목적(~하기 위해)

생활 양식은 (시골과 대부분의 교외에서의) / 포함한다 / 자동차 안에서 오랜 시간 있는 것을 / 매주 / 연료를 소모하고 배기가스를 쏟아 내면서 / 출근하고, 식료품을 사고, 아이들을 학교와 활동들에 데리고 가기 위해

② [5]City dwellers, / on the other hand, / have the option (of walking [or] taking transit / to work, shops, and school).

S V O └of의 O(동명사구 병렬)┘

도시 거주자들은 / 반면에 / 선택권이 있다 (걸어가기나 대중교통 이용과 같은 / 직장, 상점, 학교로)

↳ **논거 1:** 시골과 교외에서는 자동차를 많이 이용하지만, 도시에서는 걷거나 대중교통을 이용할 수 있음.

③ [6]*The larger yards and houses* (found outside cities) / also create / an environmental cost / in terms of energy use, water use, and land use.

S 과거분사구 V O

더 큰 마당과 집들은 (도시 밖에서 발견되는) / 또한 만들어 낸다 / 환경적인 대가를 / 에너지 사용, 물 사용, 토지 사용의 측면에서

↳ **논거 2:** 교외의 큰 마당과 집들은 많은 자원을 사용함.

🔑 도시 생활이 더 친환경적일 수 있다는 글의 흐름과 무관함.

④ [7]This illustrates / the tendency // that most city dwellers get tired of urban lives [and] decide to settle in the countryside.

↱ 동격 접속사

S V O └ = ┘ S′ V′₁ V′₂

이는 보여준다 / 경향을 // 대부분의 도시 거주자들이 도시 생활에 지쳐서 시골에 정착하기로 결심하는

↳ 도시 사람들이 시골에 정착하려는 경향을 보여줌.

⑤ [8]It's clear // that the future of the Earth depends on / more people gathering together / in compact communities.

가주어 V C 진주어(명사절) 동명사 gathering의 의미상 주어

(~은) 분명하다 // 지구의 미래가 ~에 달려 있다는 것은 / 더 많은 사람들이 모이는 것 / 밀집한 공동체들 속에

↳ **결론:** 지구 환경은 더 많은 사람들이 밀집 공동체(도시)에 사는 것에 달려 있음.

간 있는 것을 포함한다. ② [5]반면에 도시 거주자들은 직장, 상점, 학교로 걸어가기나 대중교통 이용과 같은 선택권이 있다. ③ [6]도시 밖에서 발견되는 더 큰 마당과 집들은 에너지 사용, 물 사용, 토지 사용의 측면에서 환경적인 대가를 또한 만들어 낸다. ④ [7]이는 대부분의 도시 거주자들이 도시 생활에 지쳐서 시골에 정착하기로 결심하는 경향을 보여준다. ⑤ [8]지구의 미래가 더 많은 사람들이 밀집한 공동체들 속에 모이는 것에 달려 있다는 것은 분명하다.(▶ 도시에 사는 것이 환경을 지키는 것이라는 의미)

어휘

widespread 널리 퍼진, 일반적인
myth 근거 없는 통념; 신화
leafy 녹음이 우거진, 잎이 무성한
suburb 교외 ((도심을 벗어난 주택 지역))
ecological 생태계[학]의, 생태상의
suck up ~을 빨아들이다[삼키다]
pump out (대량의) ~을 쏟아 내다
exhaust 배기가스; 기진맥진하게 하다; 고갈시키다
dweller 거주자, 주민
transit 대중교통; 운반, 운송
in terms of ~의 측면에서
illustrate 보여주다, 설명하다; 삽화를 넣다
get tired of ~에 지치다, 싫증이 나다
settle 정착하다; 해결하다

정답 가이드

도입 부분에서 시골이나 교외에 사는 것이 친환경적이고 도시 생활은 환경 파괴적이라는 통념은 사실이 아니라고 주장했으므로 이를 뒷받침하는 내용이 전개되어야 한다. ①, ②, ③은 시골이나 교외 생활이 환경에 해를 끼치는 점과 도시 생활은 그렇지 않은 점을 설명하므로 글의 흐름이 자연스럽다. 그러나 ④는 앞의 내용으로 인해 도시 거주자들이 시골에 정착하기를 결심하는 경향이 드러난다는 내용이므로 글의 흐름과 무관하다. 마지막으로 ⑤는 사람들이 도시에 모이는 것이 미래를 위해 바람직하다는 것이므로 글의 전체 흐름상 알맞다.

오답 클리닉

① (2%), ② (7%) 통념을 반박하는 논거로 시골과 교외의 오랜 자동차 사용과 도시의 걷기나 대중교통 사용을 대조해 보여주는 내용이다.
③ (19%) 교외 생활의 부정적인 환경 영향(더 많은 자원 소비)을 추가 논거로 제시하는 내용이다.
⑤ (7%) 앞의 두 논거를 바탕으로 도시 생활이 환경에 더 좋다는 결론을 내리고 있다.

01 ✦ 밑줄 어법 〈22학년도 대수능 29번 | 정답률 54%〉 ④

구문분석 & 직독직해 생물 세포의 성장과 변화

[1] Like whole individuals, / cells(S) have(V) a life span(O).
모든 개체와 마찬가지로 / 세포는 수명을 가지고 있다

[2] During their life cycle (cell cycle), / cell size, shape, and metabolic activities(S) can change(V) dramatically.
그것의 생명 주기(세포 주기) 동안에 / 세포 크기, 모양, 물질대사 활동이 극적으로 변할 수 있다

[3] A cell(S) is "born"(V) as a twin // when(부사절 접속사(시간)) its mother cell(S′) divides(V′), / ① **producing** two daughter cells(분사구문(= and it produces ~)).
세포는 쌍둥이로 '탄생'한다 // 모세포가 분열될 때 / (그리고) 두 개의 딸세포를 생성한다

[4] Each daughter cell(S_1) is(V_1) smaller(C_1) / than the mother cell, //
각각의 딸세포는 더 작다 / 모세포보다 //

and except for unusual cases, / each(S_2) grows(V_2) // until(부사절 접속사(시간)) it(S′) becomes(V′) as large(C′) // as the mother cell(S″) ② **was**(V″(대동사)).
★<A as 형용사/부사 as B>: A는 B만큼 ~한[하게]
그리고 특이한 경우를 제외하고는 / 각각 자란다 // 커질 때까지 // 모세포(가 컸던 것)만큼

[5] During this time, / the cell(S) absorbs(V_1) water, sugars, amino acids, and other nutrients(O_1) / and assembles(V_2) them(O_2(= water ~ nutrients)) / into new, living protoplasm.
이 기간 동안 / 세포는 물, 당, 아미노산, 그리고 다른 영양소들을 흡수한다 /
그리고 그것들을 조합해 (~로) 만든다 / 새로운 살아있는 원형질로

[6] After(부사절 접속사(시간)) the cell has grown to the proper size, // its metabolism(S) shifts(V) // as(부사절 접속사(~하면서)) it(S′(= the cell)) either prepares(V'_1) to divide / or matures(V'_2) and ③ **differentiates** into a specialized cell.
★<either A or B>: A와 B 둘 중 하나
세포가 적절한 크기로 성장한 후 // 그것의 물질대사는 변화한다 // 그것(그 세포)이 분열할 준비를 하면서 /
혹은 성숙하여 특화된 세포로 분화하면서

[7] Both growth and development(S) require(V) / *a complex and dynamic set of interactions*(O) (involving all cell parts(현재분사구)).
성장과 발달 둘 다 필요로 한다 / 복잡하고 역동적인 일련의 상호 작용을 (모든 세포 부분을 포함하는)

[8] ④ **What(→ That)** cell metabolism and structure should be complex(S_1(명사절)) / would not be(V_1) surprising(C_1), //
★여기서 should는 '~일 것이다'라는 '추측'의 의미
but actually, they(S_2(= cell metabolism and structure)) are(V_2) rather simple and logical(C_2).
세포의 물질대사와 구조가 복잡할 것임은 / 놀랍지 않을 것이다 //
그러나 실제로 그것들은 꽤 간단하고 논리적이다

[9] Even the most complex cell(S) has(V) / only a small number of parts(O), /
each (being) ⑤ **responsible** / for a distinct, well-defined aspect (of cell life)(분사구문(= and each is responsible ~)).
가장 복잡한 세포조차도 가지고 있다 / 그저 소수의 부분만을 /
(그리고) 각각은 책임지고 있다 / 뚜렷하고, 명확한 측면을 (세포 생명의)

해석

[1]모든 개체와 마찬가지로, 세포는 수명을 가지고 있다. [2]그것의 생명 주기(세포 주기) 동안에, 세포 크기, 모양, 물질대사 활동이 극적으로 변할 수 있다. [3]세포는 모세포가 분열될 때 쌍둥이로 '탄생'하여, 두 개의 딸세포를 생성한다. [4]각각의 딸세포는 모세포보다 더 작으며, 특이한 경우를 제외하고는 모세포(가 컸던 것)만큼 커질 때까지 각각 자란다. [5]이 기간 동안, 세포는 물, 당, 아미노산, 그리고 다른 영양소들을 흡수하고 그것들을 조합해 새로운 살아있는 원형질로 만든다. [6]세포가 적절한 크기로 성장한 후, 그것이 분열할 준비를 하거나 혹은 성숙하여 특화된 세포로 분화하면서 그것의 물질대사는 변화한다. [7]성장과 발달 둘 다 모든 세포 부분을 포함하는 복잡하고 역동적인 일련의 상호 작용을 필요로 한다. [8]세포의 물질대사와 구조가 복잡할 것임은 놀랍지 않겠지만, 실제로 그것들은 꽤 간단하고 논리적이다. [9]가장 복잡한 세포조차도 그저 소수의 부분만을 가지고 있으며, 각각은 세포 생명의 뚜렷하고, 명확한 측면을 책임지고 있다.

어휘

life span 수명
cycle 주기, 순환
dramatically 극적으로
divide 분열되다, 갈라지다; 나누다
absorb 흡수하다, 빨아들이다
amino acid 아미노산
nutrient 영양소, 영양분
assemble A into B A를 조합해 B로 만들다
metabolism 물질[신진]대사
mature 성숙해지다, 다 자라다; 성숙한
differentiate 분화하다; 구별[식별]하다
specialized 《생물》 특화[분화]된
rather 꽤, 약간; 오히려, 차라리
logical 논리적인; 타당한
distinct 뚜렷한, 분명한; 구별되는
well-defined 명확한, 알기[이해하기] 쉬운
aspect 측면, 양상

정답 가이드

④ **[what vs. 접속사 that]** 문장의 주어 역할을 하는 완전한 구조(SVC)의 절을 이끌고 있으므로 What을 명사절을 이끄는 접속사인 That으로 고쳐야 한다. what도 주어절을 이끌 수 있지만, 뒤에 주어나 목적어가 빠진 불완전한 구조의 절을 이끈다.

오답 클리닉

① **[분사구문]** (4%)
when절의 주어(its mother cell)를 의미상의 주어로 하는 분사구문이며, '모세포'가 딸세포를 '생성하는' 능동의 의미이므로 현재분사 producing은 어법상 적절하다.

② **[대동사]** (22%)
앞에 나온 일반동사(구)를 대신할 때는 대동사 do, does, did를 쓰고, be동사(구)를 대신할 때는 be동사를 쓴다. 문맥상 앞에 쓰인 becomes large를 대신하는 것인데, large라는 주격보어를 취할 수 있는 be동사 was를 대동사로 사용한 것은 어법상 적절하다.

The 주의 대동사는 대동사가 쓰인 절의 주어의 수와 인칭, 시제에 맞게 사용하므로, 대신하는 동사와 일치하지 않을 수 있다.

③ **[병렬구조]** (8%)
<either A or B> 구조에서 B가 <동사 and 동사> 구조인 문장이다. A 자리의 prepares와 문법상 대등해야 하므로 matures and differentiates는 어법상 적절하다.

⑤ **[주의해야 할 분사구문]** (12%)
부대상황을 의미하는 절 and each is responsible을 분사구문으로 바꾼 형태이다. 접속사 and를 생략하고 분사구문의 의미상의 주어는 문장의 주어와 일치하면 생략하고 일치하지 않으면 남겨야 한다. 문장의 주어가 the most complex cell이므로 each는 남았다. 그 뒤 능동형 be동사 are이 현재분사 being으로 바뀌는데, 분사구문의 being은 종종 생략되므로 responsible은 어법상 적절하다.

02 + 빈칸 추론 (19학년도 9월 모평 34번 | 정답률 51%)

②

구문분석 & 직독직해

심리 개인의 지식으로 구성되는 주관적 세계 이해

[1]Modern psychological theory states // that the process of understanding is a matter of construction, / not reproduction, //
(S: Modern psychological theory / V: states / 명사절 접속사: that — states의 O(명사절) / S′: the process of understanding / V′: is / C′: a matter of construction)

현대의 심리학 이론은 말한다 // 이해의 과정은 구성의 문제라고 / 재현이 아니라 //

🔑 이해는 외부에서 오는 정보와 정신에서 생성되는 정보를 해석하는 것임.

which means // that the process of understanding takes / the form of the interpretation of *data* (coming from the outside and generated by our mind).
(관계대명사(보충 설명): which / means의 O(명사절): that ~ / 현재분사구: coming from the outside / 과거분사구: generated by our mind)

그것은 의미한다 // 이해의 과정이 취한다는 것을 / 정보 해석의 형태를 (외부로부터 들어오고 우리 정신에 의해 생성되는)

↳ **도입:** 이해는 외부 및 내부 정보를 해석하는 것임.

[2]For example, / the perception of a moving object / as a car / is based on an interpretation (of incoming data) / within the framework of our knowledge (of the world).
(S: the perception of a moving object as a car / V: is based)

예를 들어 / 움직이는 물체를 인식하는 것은 / 차로 / 해석에 근거한다 (들어오는 정보의) / 우리 지식의 틀 안에서 (세상에 대한)

↳ **예:** 움직이는 물체를 차로 인식하는 것은 들어온 정보를 지식의 틀 안에서 해석하는 것임.

[3]While the interpretation (of simple objects) / is usually an uncontrolled process, //
(부사절 접속사(~인 반면에): While / S′(단수): the interpretation / V′(단수): is / C′: an uncontrolled process)

해석이 (단순한 물체의) / 보통 통제되지 않는 과정인 반면에 //

the interpretation (of more complex phenomena), / such as interpersonal situations, / usually requires active attention and thought.
(S(단수): the interpretation / V(단수): requires / O: active attention and thought)

해석은 (더 복잡한 현상에 대한) / 대인 관계 상황과 같은 / 보통 적극적인 주의와 사고를 필요로 한다

↳ 복잡한 현상에 대한 해석은 더 많은 주의와 사고를 필요로 함.

🔑 개인의 지식을 바탕으로 자극을 해석하므로 주관적임.

[4]Psychological studies indicate // that it is *knowledge* (possessed by the individual) // that determines //
(S: Psychological studies / V: indicate / 명사절 접속사: that — indicate의 O(명사절) / 과거분사구: possessed by the individual / V′₁: determines)

★<It ~ that ...: …인 것은 바로 ~이다> 강조구문이 주어인 knowledge ~ individual을 강조함.

심리학 연구는 보여준다 // 바로 지식이라는 것을 (개인에 의해 보유된) // 결정하는 것은 //

해석

[1]현대의 심리학 이론은 이해의 과정은 재현이 아니라 구성의 문제라고 말하는데, 그것은 이해의 과정이 외부로부터 들어오고, 우리 정신에 의해 생성되는 정보의 해석이라는 형태를 취한다는 것을 의미한다. [2]예를 들어, 움직이는 물체를 차로 인식하는 것은 세상에 대한 우리 지식의 틀 안에서 들어오는 정보의 해석에 근거한다. [3]간단한 물체의 해석이 보통 통제되지 않는 과정인 반면에, 대인 관계 상황과 같은 더 복잡한 현상에 대한 해석은 보통 적극적인 주의와 사고를 필요로 한다. [4]심리학 연구는 어떤 자극이 그 개인의 주의의 초점이 되는지, 그 사람이 이 자극에 어떤 의미를 부여하는지, 그리고 그 자극들이 어떻게 더 커다란 전체로 결합되는지를 결정하는 것은 바로 개인에 의해 보유된 지식이라는 점을 보여준다. [5]특정한 방식으로 해석되는 이러한 주관적 세계는 우리에게 '객관적' 세계인데, 우리는 우리 자신의 해석의 결과로 우리가 알고 있는 세계 외에는 그 어떤 세계도 알 수 없다.

어휘

state 말하다, 진술하다; 상태; 국가(의)
construction 구성; 건설; 건축[구조]물
reproduction 재현, 재생; 복제(물)
interpretation 해석, 이해, 설명
cf. interpret 해석하다, 이해하다
perception 인식, 지각
cf. perceptual 인식[지각]의

which stimuli become the focus (of that individual's attention), / what significance he or she assigns to these stimuli, / and how they are combined into a larger whole.

O'₁(명사절 병렬) (= these stimuli) O'₂(명사절 병렬) O'₃(명사절 병렬)

어떤 자극이 초점이 되는지 (그 개인의 주의력의) / 그 사람이 이 자극에 어떤 의미를 부여하는지 / 그리고 그 자극들이 어떻게 더 커다란 전체로 결합되는지를

↳ 외부 자극의 해석은 개인이 보유한 지식에 달려 있음.

주제문 ⊶ 개인의 지식에 의해 특정한 방식으로 해석된 주관적 세상이 우리에게는 객관적 세계가 됨.

[5] *This subjective world,* / interpreted in a particular way, / is for us the "objective" world; //

S 분사구문(= and it is interpreted ~) V C

이러한 주관적 세계는 / 특정한 방식으로 해석되는 / 우리에게 '객관적' 세계이다 //

we cannot know any world / other than ***the one*** [(which[that]) **we know / as a result of our own interpretations**].

S V O (= except for) (= the world) 목적격 관계대명사 생략

우리는 그 어떤 세계도 알 수 없다 / 세계 외에는 [우리가 알고 있는 / 우리 자신의 해석의 결과로]

↳ **결론:** 우리는 개인의 지식으로 해석한 주관적 세계만 알 수 있음.

framework 틀; 체제
uncontrolled 통제[제어]되지 않는
phenomenon (*pl.* phenomena) 현상
indicate 보여 주다, 나타내다
stimulus (*pl.* stimuli) 자극(제)
significance 의미; 중대성
assign 부여하다; 맡기다, 배정하다
combine A into B A를 B로 결합하다
subjective 주관적인(↔ objective 객관적인)
[선택지] convention 관습, 관례
filter 거르다, 여과하다
external 외부의

정답 가이드

빈칸 문장을 정리하면, 어떤 주관적 세계는 우리에게 객관적 세계이며, 우리가 오로지 '어떤' 세계만을 알 수 있다는 것이다. 즉 우리가 알 수 있는(이해하는) 그것이 무엇인지를 추론해야 한다. 첫 문장에서 이해는 재현이 아니라 구성의 문제, 즉 외부에서 들어온 것을 '우리 정신이 해석'하는 것이라고 했다. 이에 대한 구체적인 예가 나온 뒤, 심리학 연구는 자극에 대한 해석이 개인이 보유한 지식으로 결정된다고 했다. 따라서 우리가 알 수 있는 세계는 결국 ② 'the one we know as a result of our own interpretations(우리 자신의 해석의 결과로 우리가 알고 있는 세계)'라고 할 수 있다.

오답 클리닉

① the reality placed upon us through social conventions (11%)
사회 관습을 통해 우리에게 놓여진 현실
사회 관습에 관한 내용이 아님.

③ the world of images not filtered by our perceptual frame (14%)
우리의 인식 틀에 의해 걸러지지 않은 모습의 세계
우리의 인식 틀, 즉 지식에 속하지 않는 모습의 세계는 우리가 알 수 없으므로 틀림.

④ the external world independent of our own interpretations (20%)
우리 자신의 해석과는 관계없는 외부 세계
우리는 우리 자신이 해석한 세계밖에 알 수 없으므로 틀림.

The 주의 빈칸 앞의 조동사 부정형(cannot)만 보고 주관적 세계와 반대되는 선택지를 고르지 않도록 주의한다. 이중 부정 표현이 들어가는 경우에는 주제와 빈칸 어구의 관계를 신중히 파악해야 한다.

⑤ the physical universe our own interpretations fail to explain (5%)
우리 자신의 해석이 설명하지 못하는 물리적 세계
우리가 해석하지 못하는 세계는 우리가 알 수 없으므로 틀림.

03 + 글의 순서 〈20학년도 대수능 36번 | 정답률 61%〉 ⑤

구문분석 & 직독직해 예술 우리가 영화를 즐기는 이유

[1]Movies may be said / to support the dominant culture / and to serve as a means (for its reproduction) / over time.

S V C(to-v구 병렬)

영화는 ~라고 할 수 있다 / 지배적인 문화를 지지한다고 / 그리고 수단의 역할을 한다고 (그것(문화)의 재생산을 위한) / 시간이 지남에 따라

↳ 영화는 지배적인 문화를 지지하고 재생산함.

⊶ 역접 연결어 But으로 주어진 글과 상반되는 영화의 즐거움에 대해 질문함. such movies는 주어진 글에서 언급된 영화를 의미함.

(C) [2]But / one may ask // why audiences would find such movies enjoyable //

S V 의문사 S' V' O' C' (may ask의 O(명사절))

그러나 / 누군가는 물을 수도 있다 // 왜 관객들이 그러한 영화가 즐겁다고 느끼는지 //

if *all* [(that) they do] / is (to) give cultural directives and prescriptions (for proper living).

S" 목적격 관계대명사 생략 V" C" (= movies)

모든 것이 ~이라면 [그것(영화)이 하는] / 문화적 지시와 처방을 전달하는 것뿐(이라면) (제대로 된 삶에 대한)

↳ **질문:** 영화가 문화적 지시와 처방을 전달하기만 한다면 관객들은 왜 영화를 재미있어하는가?

[3]Most of us would likely grow tired of such didactic movies /

S V₁ C

우리 중 대부분은 그러한 교훈적인 영화에 싫증나게 될 것이다 /

해석

[1]영화는 지배적인 문화를 지지하고 시간이 지남에 따라 그것의 재생산을 위한 수단의 역할을 한다고 할 수 있다. (C) [2]그러나 영화가 하는 모든 것이 제대로 된 삶에 대한 문화적 지시와 처방을 전달하는 것뿐이라면 왜 관객들이 그러한 영화가 즐겁다고 느끼는지 누군가는 물을 수도 있다. [3]우리 중 대부분은 그러한 교훈적인 영화에 싫증나게 될 것이고, 아마도 그것들을 소련 그리고 다른 독재 사회에서 흔했던, 문화적 예술 작품과 유사한 선전으로 보게 될 것이다. (B) [4]이 질문에 대한 간단한 답은 영화가 책임 있는 행동에 관한 두 시간짜리 국민 윤리 교육이나 사설을 제시하는 것보다 더 많은 것을 한다는 것이다. [5]그것들은 또한 우리가 결국 만족스럽다고 느끼는 이야기를 한다. (A) [6]나쁜 사람들은 보통 벌을 받고, 낭만적인 커플은 진정한 사랑에 이르는 길에서 맞닥뜨리는 장애물과 어려움에도 불구하

*<come to-v>: v하게 되다

and would probably come to see them / as *propaganda*, (similar to *the cultural artwork* [that was common / in the Soviet Union and other autocratic societies]).

V₂ (= such didactic movies) 형용사구 주격 관계대명사

그리고 아마도 그것들(그러한 교훈적인 영화)을 보게 될 것이다 / 선전으로 (문화적 예술 작품과 유사한 [흔했던 / 소련 그리고 다른 독재 사회에서])

↳ **부연 설명:** 교훈적인 영화들은 싫증나고 선전으로 인식될 뿐임.

(C)의 질문에 대한 답을 제시함.

(B) [4]The simple answer to this question is // that movies do more / than present two-hour civics lessons or editorials (on responsible behavior).

S V C(명사절)

이 질문에 대한 간단한 답은 ~이다 // 영화가 더 많은 것을 한다는 것 / 두 시간짜리 국민 윤리 교육이나 사설을 제시하는 것보다 (책임 있는 행동에 관한)

(= Movies) *관계사절 내의 <find+O+C>에서 빠져있는 목적어가 선행사 stories임.

[5]They also tell *stories* [that, in the end, we find satisfying].

S V O 목적격 관계대명사 S′ V′ C′

그것들(영화)은 또한 이야기를 한다 [우리가 결국 만족스럽다고 느끼는]

↳ **답변:** 영화는 교훈을 주는 것보다 더 많은 것을 하며, 관객이 만족스러워할 만한 이야기를 함.

(B)의 마지막에 언급한 우리가 만족스러워하는 이야기의 예를 제시함.

(A) [6]The bad guys are usually punished; // the romantic couple almost always find each other / despite *the obstacles and difficulties* [(which[that]) they encounter / on the path to true love]; //

S₁ V₁ S₂ V₂ O₂ 전치사(~에도 불구하고) 목적격 관계대명사 생략

나쁜 사람들은 보통 벌을 받는다 // 낭만적인 커플은 거의 항상 서로를 만나게 된다 / 장애물과 어려움에도 불구하고 [그들이 맞닥뜨리는 / 진정한 사랑에 이르는 길에서] //

→ is의 C(명사절)

and *the way* [(that) we wish the world to be] / is // how, (in the movies), it more often than not winds up being.

S₃ 관계부사 생략 S′ V′ O′ C′ V₃ 의문사 S′(= the world) V′

그리고 방식은 [우리가 세상이 되길 바라는] / ~이다 // (영화 속에서) 대개 결국 그것(세상)이 되게 되는 방식

↳ **예:** 관객들은 권선징악, 해피엔딩, 유토피아를 보여주는 영화에 만족함.

주제문

[7]No doubt / it is this utopian aspect of movies // that accounts for why we enjoy them so much.

<it is ~ that ...> 강조구문: …한 것은 바로 ~이다 V′ O′(명사절)

의심할 여지 없이 / 바로 영화의 이 이상적인 측면이다 // 우리가 왜 그렇게 많이 그것들(영화)을 즐기는지를 설명해 주는 것은

↳ 우리가 영화를 즐기는 이유는 영화의 이상적인 측면 때문임.

고 거의 항상 서로를 만나게 되며, 우리가 세상이 되길 바라는 방식은 영화 속에서 대개 결국 그것(세상)이 되게 되는 방식이다. [7]우리가 왜 그렇게 많이 그것들(영화)을 즐기는지를 설명해 주는 것은 의심할 여지 없이 바로 영화의 이 이상적인 측면이다.

어휘

dominant 지배적인, 우세한
serve as ~의 역할을 하다
means 수단, 방법
reproduction 재생산; 번식; 복제
directive 지시[명령](하는)
prescription 처방(전)
propaganda 선전 (활동)
civics 국민 윤리(과)
editorial 사설, 논설; 편집의
obstacle 장애(물)
more often than not 대개, 자주
wind up 결국 ~하게 되다, (어떤 상황에) 처하게 되다
utopian 이상적인, 유토피아적인
account for ~을 설명하다; (부분·비율을) 차지하다

정답 가이드

영화가 지배적인 문화를 지지하고 재생산하는 역할을 한다는 주어진 글 다음에는 그런데도 관객들이 그러한 영화를 즐기는 이유에 대해 질문을 제기하는 (C)가 역접 연결어 But으로 이어지는 것이 적절하다. 이어서 질문에 대한 답변인 (B)가 오고, 영화가 우리가 만족스러워하는 이야기를 한다는 (B)의 마지막 내용 뒤에는 그 예를 구체적으로 설명하는 (A)가 연결되는 것이 자연스럽다.

오답 클리닉

① (A) - (C) - (B) (7%) / ④ (C) - (A) - (B) (16%)
(A)는 (B)의 마지막에서 언급한 우리가 만족스럽게 느끼는 이야기의 예에 해당하므로 (B) 뒤에 와야 한다.
② (B) - (A) - (C) (9%) / ③ (B) - (C) - (A) (7%)
주어진 글에는 (B)의 this question이 가리킬 대상이 없으므로 (B)는 주어진 글 뒤에 바로 올 수 없다.

01 ✦ 낱말 쓰임 〈22학년도 대수능 30번 | 정답률 55%〉 ③

구문분석 & 직독직해

환경 '유기농' 농법의 단점과 장점

[1]It has been suggested // that "organic" methods, / defined as *those* [in which only natural products can be used as inputs], / would be less damaging to the biosphere.
(가주어 V / 진주어(명사절) / 명사절 접속사 S′ / 분사구문(= and they are defined ~) / (= methods) 전치사+관계대명사 / V′ C′)

(~라고) 시사되어 왔다 // '유기농' 방식은 / 방식으로 정의되는 [천연 제품들만 투입물로 사용될 수 있는] / 생물권에 덜 해로울 것이라고

🔑 ① 역접 연결어 however로 이어지므로 유기농 농경 방식의 단점인 수확량의 '감소'가 나와야 함.

[2]Large-scale adoption (of "organic" farming methods), / however, / would ① **reduce** yields and increase production costs / for many major crops.
(S / V_1 / V_2)

대규모 채택은 ('유기농' 농경 방식의) / 그러나 / 수확량을 줄이고 생산비를 늘릴 것이다 / 많은 주요 작물에 대한

[3]Inorganic nitrogen supplies are ② **essential** / for maintaining moderate to high levels of productivity (for many of the non-leguminous crop species), //
(S V C / for의 O(동명사구))

무기 질소 (비료) 공급은 필수적이다 / 중상 수준의 생산성을 유지하는 데 (많은 비(非) 콩과 작물 종의) //

★<either A or B>: A와 B 둘 중 하나

because organic supplies (of nitrogenous materials) / often are either limited or more expensive / than inorganic nitrogen fertilizers. 🔑 ② 무기 질소 비료가 유기 비료보다 효율적이기 때문에 생산성 유지에 '필수적'으로 봄.
(부사절 접속사(이유) S′ / V′ / C'_1 / C'_2)

왜냐하면 유기 (비료) 공급이 (질소 물질의) / 흔히 한정되거나 더 비싸기 때문이다 / 무기 질소 비료보다

[4]In addition, / there are ③ **benefits(→ constraints)** / to the extensive use (of either manure / or legumes as "green manure" crops). 🔑 ③ 앞과 유사한 내용을 덧붙이는 In addition(게다가)으로 이어지므로 유기농 농법의 '제약'이 나와야 함.
(전치사(~로(서)))

게다가 / 이점(→ 제약)이 있다 / 광범위한 사용에는 (거름 / 또는 '친환경 거름' 작물로 콩과 식물의)

🔑 ④ 잡초 방제가 매우 힘들다고 했으므로 부유한 사회에서 그 일을 하려는 사람은 '더 적어질' 것임.

[5]In many cases, / weed control can be very difficult or (can) require much hand labor // if chemicals cannot be used, //
(S_1 / V_{1-1} / C / V_{1-2} / O / 부사절 접속사(조건))

많은 경우 / 잡초 방제가 매우 힘들거나 많은 손일을 필요로 할 수 있다 // 화학 물질이 사용될 수 없다면 //

and ④ **fewer** people are willing to do this work // as societies become wealthier.
(S_2 / V_2 / O_2 (= weed control) / 부사절 접속사(~함에 따라))

그리고 더 적은 사람들이 이 일(잡초 방제)을 기꺼이 하려 할 것이다 // 사회가 더 부유해짐에 따라

🔑 ⑤ 역접 연결어 however로 이어지므로 유기농 농경 방식의 이점인 농업 생태계에의 '기여'가 언급될 것임.

[6]*Some methods* (used in "organic" farming), / however, / (such as the sensible use (of crop rotations) / and specific combinations (of cropping and livestock enterprises)), /
(S / 과거분사구 / 명사구 병렬 / 명사구 병렬)

몇몇 방법들은 ('유기농' 농경에서 사용되는) / 그러나 / (합리적인 사용 (돌려짓기의) / 그리고 특정한 조합과 같은 (경작과 가축 사업의)) /

can make important ⑤ **contributions** / to the sustainability (of rural ecosystems).
(V / O)

중요한 기여를 할 수 있다 / 지속 가능성에 (농업 생태계의)

해석

[1]천연 제품들만 투입물로 사용될 수 있는 방식으로 정의되는 '유기농' 방식은 생물권에 덜 해로울 것이라고 시사되어 왔다. [2]그러나 '유기농' 농경 방식의 대규모 채택은 많은 주요 작물에 대한 수확량을 ① 줄이고 생산비를 늘릴 것이다. [3]무기 질소 공급은 많은 비(非) 콩과 작물 종의 중상 수준의 생산성을 유지하는 데 ② 필수적인데, 왜냐하면 질소 물질의 유기 공급이 무기 질소 비료보다 흔히 한정되거나 더 비싸기 때문이다. [4]게다가, 거름이나 '친환경 비료' 작물로 콩과 식물을 광범위하게 사용하는 것은 ③ 이점(→ 제약)이 있다. [5]많은 경우, 화학 물질이 사용될 수 없다면 잡초 방제가 매우 힘들거나 많은 손일을 필요로 할 수 있는데, 사회가 더 부유해짐에 따라 ④ 더 적은 사람들이 이 일을 기꺼이 하려 할 것이다. [6]그러나 돌려짓기의 합리적인 사용과 경작과 가축 사업의 특정한 조합과 같은 '유기농' 농경에서 사용되는 몇몇 방법들은 농업 생태계의 지속 가능성에 중요한 ⑤ 기여를 할 수 있다.

어휘

organic 유기농의; 유기의(↔ inorganic 무기의)
input 투입(물); 입력
biosphere 생물권
large-scale 대규모의
adoption 채택; 입양
yield 수확[산출]량
production cost 생산비
moderate 중간의, 보통의
productivity 생산성
extensive 광범위한; 아주 넓은, 대규모의
weed control 잡초 방제
be willing to-v 기꺼이 v하다
sensible 합리적인, 분별 있는
crop rotation 돌려짓기, 윤작 ((같은 땅에 여러 가지 농작물을 해마다 바꾸어 심는 일))
combination 조합, 결합
livestock 가축
enterprise 사업; 회사
contribution 기여, 이바지
sustainability 지속[유지] 가능성
rural 농업의; 시골의

정답 가이드

'유기농' 농경 방식은 수확량이 줄고 생산비가 증가하는 등의 단점이 있지만 합리적 방법으로 사용하면 농업 생태계의 지속 가능성에 기여하는 장점도 있다는 내용의 글이다. 문장 4가 In addition(게다가)으로 시작하므로 앞 문장과 비슷한 맥락의 내용이 전개될 것임을 알 수 있는데, 앞에서 유기 질소 비료가 무기 질소 비료보다 한정적이거나 비싸다는 단점을 언급했으므로 문장 4도 유기 비료의 단점을 말하는 내용이 나와야 한다. manure나 legumes as "green manure" crops는 모두 유기 비료의 예이므로, 이것들을 광범위하게 사용하는 것에는 문제, 즉 제약이 있을 것이다. 따라서 ③ 'benefits(이점)'를 'constraints(제약)'로 바꿔 써야 한다. 문장 5에서 무기(화학) 비료를 사용하지 못하는 것에 따른 어려움을 설명하는 것과도 잘 이어진다.

오답 클리닉

① reduce (5%) 줄이다
첫 문장과 역접 연결어 however로 이어졌으므로 '유기농' 농경 방식의 단점이 나와야 한다. 따라서 생산비를 늘리고 수확량은 '줄일' 것으로 추론할 수 있다.

② essential (5%) 필수적인
유기 질소 비료가 무기 질소 비료보다 한정적이거나 비싸기 때문에 생산성 유지를 위해 무기 질소 비료 공급이 '필수적'이라는 인과 관계가 자연스럽다.

④ fewer (27%) 더 적은
this work가 weed control을 지칭하고 유기 비료 사용의 단점을 계속해서 설명하는 맥락임을 파악해야 한다. 앞 절에서 잡초 방제는 매우 힘들고 많은 손일을 필요로 한다고 했으므로 사회가 더 부유해짐에 따라 '더 적은' 사람이 그 일을 하려고 할 것이라는 문제점으로 이어져야 자연스럽다.

⑤ contributions (9%) 기여
역접 연결어 however가 있으므로 앞서 언급된 단점들과 반대되는 내용으로 유기농 농법의 장점이 나와야 한다. 따라서 농업 생태계의 지속 가능성에 '기여'한다는 내용이 이어지는 것은 문맥상 자연스럽다.

02 ✦ 빈칸 추론 〈19학년도 9월 모평 33번 | 정답률 58%〉 ④

구문분석 & 직독직해

문화 집단을 통합하고 지속시키는 음식

주제문

★<A as well as B>: B뿐만 아니라 A도 / → 부사절 접속사(이유) / 🗝 음식은 먹는 사람들을 하나로 만듦.

[1] Food(S) unites(V₁) / [as well as] distinguishes(V₂) eaters(O) // because what and how one eats(S′(명사절)) forms(V′(단수)) / much(O′) (of one's emotional tie (to a group identity)), // be it (= a group identity) a nation or an ethnicity. ★부사절 접속사 whether가 생략되어 <V+S>로 도치됨.

음식은 통합하기도 한다 / 먹는 사람들을 구별할 뿐만 아니라 // 사람이 먹는 것과 먹는 방식이 형성하기 때문에 / 대부분을 (사람의 정서적 유대의 (집단 정체성에 대한)) // 그것(집단 정체성)이 국가든 민족성이든

↳ 음식은 집단을 통합함.

[2] The famous twentieth-century Chinese poet and scholar Lin Yutang(S) remarks(V), //

저명한 20세기 중국의 시인이자 학자인 Lin Yutang은 말한다 //

"Our love for fatherland(S′₁) is(V′₁) largely / a matter of recollection (of the keen sensual pleasure (of our childhood))(C′₁).

"조국에 대한 우리의 사랑은 대개 ~입니다 / 기억의 문제 (강렬한 감각적 즐거움에 대한 (우리 유년기의))

The loyalty(S′₂) (to Uncle Sam) / is(V′₂) the loyalty(C′₂) (to American doughnuts), //

충성은 (미국 정부에 대한) / 충성입니다 (미국 도넛에 대한) //

[and] the loyalty(S′₃) (to the *Vaterland*) / is(V′₃) the loyalty(C′₃) (to *Pfannkuchen* and *Stollen*)."

그리고 충성은 ('Vaterland(독일어로 '조국'을 의미)'에 대한) / 충성입니다 ('Pfannkuchen(독일의 새해맞이에 먹는 도넛)'과 'Stollen(크리스마스 시즌에 먹는 독일식 빵)'에 대한)"

↳ **예(인용):** 애국심은 유년기의 감각적 즐거움(음식 문화)과 관련 있음.

[3] Such keen connection(S) ([between] food [and] national or ethnic identification) (A와 B 사이의) / clearly indicates(V) /

그러한 강렬한 연관성은 (음식과 국가 혹은 민족 동일시 사이의) / 분명히 보여 준다 /

the truth(O) // that(= 동격 접속사) cuisine and table narrative(S′₁) occupy(V′₁) a significant place(O′) / in the training grounds (of a community and its civilization), // 🗝 요리와 식탁 이야기는 공동체와 그 문화를 가르쳐줌 → 집단 통합과 유지의 역할.

진리를 // 요리와 식탁 이야기가 중요한 위치를 차지한다는 / 훈련장에서 (한 공동체와 그것의 문화의) //

[and] thus, eating, cooking, and talking about one's cuisine(S′₂) / are(V′₂) vital(C′) / to **a community's wholeness and continuation**.

그래서 먹고, 요리하고, 누군가의 요리에 대해서 이야기하는 것이 / 매우 중요하다는 / 한 공동체의 완전함과 지속에

↳ **세부 사항:** 음식은 공동체와 문화를 가르치는 데 중요하므로, 공동체를 결속하고 유지하는 데 필수적임.

해석

[1]사람이 먹는 것과 먹는 방식이 집단 정체성에 대한, 그것이 국가든 민족성이든, 사람의 정서적 유대의 대부분을 형성하기 때문에 음식은 먹는 사람들을 구별할 뿐만 아니라 통합하기도 한다. [2]저명한 20세기 중국의 시인이자 학자인 Lin Yutang은 "조국에 대한 우리의 사랑은 대개 우리 유년기의 강렬한 감각적 즐거움에 대한 기억의 문제입니다. (▶ 국가 정체성이 이른 시기에 음식 문화를 통해 형성됨을 의미) 미국 정부에 대한 충성은 미국 도넛에 대한 충성이고, 'Vaterland(독일어로 '조국'을 의미)'에 대한 충성은 'Pfannkuchen(독일의 새해맞이에 먹는 도넛)'과 'Stollen(크리스마스 시즌에 먹는 독일식 빵)'에 대한 충성입니다."라고 말한다. [3]음식과 국가 혹은 민족 동일시 사이의 그러한 강렬한 연관성은 요리와 식탁 이야기가 한 공동체와 그것의 문화의 훈련장에서 중요한 위치를 차지하고, 그래서 먹고, 요리하고, 누군가의 요리에 대해서 이야기하는 것이 한 공동체의 완전함과 지속에 매우 중요하다는 진리를 분명히 보여 준다. [4]다시 말해서, 한 공동체의 운명은 그것이 얼마나 잘 그 구성원들을 기르는지에 달려 있다.

어휘

unite 통합[결속]시키다
tie 유대, 관계; 묶다
identity 정체(성), 신원; 동일감
ethnicity 민족성
cf. ethnic 민족[종족]의
fatherland 조국
recollection 기억(력)
keen 강렬한; 날카로운, 예민한
sensual 감각적인
identification 동일시; 신분 증명[확인]

음식은 공동체의 존망에 중요한 역할을 함.

[4]In other words, / the destiny (of a community) / depends on // how well it nourishes its members.
S / V / O(명사절)
다시 말해서 / 운명은 (한 공동체의) / ~에 달려 있다 // 그것(공동체)이 얼마나 잘 그 구성원들을 기르는지
↳ **주제문 재진술:** 공동체는 음식으로 결속되고 지속됨.

cuisine 요리(법)
occupy 차지하다; 사용하다
civilization 문화, 문명
wholeness 완전(함); 전체[총체]
continuation 지속, 존속; 계속
[선택지] dominance 우월성; 지배
⊕ 미국 (정부)/전형적인 미국인(Uncle Sam): 1812년 미영전쟁 때 군부대에 고기를 납품한 실존 인물 Samuel Wilson(1766~1854)에서 유래함. 납품한 고기에는 미국을 표시하는 U.S.가 찍혀 있었는데, 이것이 Wilson의 별명인 'Uncle Sam'으로 알려지면서 연방 정부에 납품하는 모든 군수물자엔 Uncle Sam이라는 이름이 붙게 됨.

정답 가이드

빈칸 문장 앞에서 음식이 국가나 민족 동일시와 강한 연관성이 있고, 요리와 식탁 이야기가 공동체와 그것의 문화를 훈련시키는 데 중요한 위치를 차지한다고 했다. 따라서 먹고 요리하는 등의 행위가 '무엇'에 매우 중요하다는 것인지를 추론해야 한다. 이어지는 In other words로 시작하는 문장은 한 '공동체의 운명'이 얼마나 구성원들을 잘 기르는지에 달려 있다고 했다. 구성원들을 잘 기르는 것은 먹고 요리하는 등의 행위라 볼 수 있고, 그 행위가 '공동체의 운명'에 매우 중요하다는 것으로 추론할 수 있다. 따라서 빈칸에 들어갈 말로 가장 적절한 것은 ④ 'a community's wholeness and continuation(한 공동체의 완전함과 지속)'이다. 글의 앞부분에 제시되는 음식이 사람들을 통합하는 예를 통해서도 정답을 확신할 수 있다.

오답 클리닉

① an individual's dietary choices (9%)
한 개인의 식단 선택
개인이 아닌 음식과 공동체를 연결짓는 내용이므로 틀림.
② one's diverse cultural experiences (14%)
사람의 다양한 문화적 경험
음식으로 다양한 문화적 경험을 한다는 내용은 유추할 수 없음.
③ one's unique personality and taste (10%)
사람의 특유한 성격과 미각
음식을 개인의 특성과 관련짓는 내용이 아님.
⑤ a community's dominance over other cultures (9%)
한 공동체의 다른 문화에 대한 우월성
문화의 우월성을 비교하는 내용이 아님.

03 + 문장 넣기 (20학년도 대수능 38번 | 정답률 69%) ④

구문분석 & 직독직해

생물 서식지 선택에 있어 텃새와 철새의 차이

[1]Resident-bird habitat selection is seemingly *a straightforward process*
S / V / C
텃새들의 서식지 선택은 겉보기에는 간단한 과정이다
[in which a young dispersing individual moves // until it finds / *a place* [where it can compete successfully / to satisfy its needs]].
전치사+관계대명사 / S′ / V′ / 부사절 접속사(시간) / 관계부사 / 목적(~하기 위해)
[흩어지는 어린 개체가 옮겨 다니는 // 그것(흩어지는 어린 개체)이 찾을 때까지 / 장소를 [성공적으로 경쟁할 수 있는 / 필요를 충족시키기 위해]]
↳ **대조 A(텃새):** 텃새들의 생존을 위한 서식지 선택은 겉보기에 간단해 보임.

(①) [2]Initially, / these needs include only food and shelter.
S / V / O
처음에는 / 이러한 필요는 음식과 은신처만 포함한다
↳ **서식지 조건 1:** 처음에는 생존의 필요만 포함함.

(②) [3]However, / eventually, / the young must locate, identify, and settle in /
S / V_1 / V_2 / V_3
그러나 최종적으로 / 그 어린 새는 찾아내고, 확인하고, 정착해야 한다 /
a habitat [that satisfies not only survivorship but reproductive needs as well].
O / 주격 관계대명사 / *<not only A but B as well>: A뿐만 아니라 B도
서식지를 [생존뿐만 아니라 번식의 필요도 충족시키는]
↳ **서식지 조건 2:** 생존뿐만 아니라 번식의 필요도 충족해야 함.

해석

[1]텃새들의 서식지 선택은 흩어지는 어린 개체가 필요를 충족시키기 위해 성공적으로 경쟁할 수 있는 장소를 찾을 때까지 옮겨 다니는 겉보기에는 간단한 과정이다. (①) [2]처음에는, 이러한 필요는 음식과 은신처만 포함한다. (②) [3]그러나 최종적으로, 그 어린 새는 생존뿐만 아니라 번식의 필요도 충족시키는 서식지를 찾아내고, 확인하고, 그곳에 정착해야 한다. (③) [4]일부의 경우, 번식기의 특수한 요건들 때문에, 생존을 위한 최고의 기회를 제공하는 서식지가 최고의 번식 능력을 준비하는 서식지와 같은 서식지가 아닐 수도 있다. (④ [5]따라서 많은 텃새 종의 개체들은 다산(多産)의 번식지를 장악하는 것이 갖는 합목적성에서 오는 이득에 직면할 때, 가장 높은 번식 성공이 일어나는 특정 서식지에 머물러 있음으로써 더 낮은 비번식기 생존율의 형태로 대가의 균형을 맞추도록 강요될 수도 있다.) [6]그러나 철새들은 비번식기 동안에는 생존을 위한 최적의 서식지를, 번식기 동안에는 번식을 위한 최적의 서식지를 자유롭게 선택한다. (⑤) [7]이와 같이

🔑 주어진 문장의 원인에 해당함.

(③) [4]In some cases, / *the habitat* [that provides the best opportunity for survival] / may not be the same habitat / as *the one* [that provides for highest reproductive capacity] / because of *requirements* (specific to the reproductive period).

★<the same A as B>: B와 같은 A / S / 주격 관계대명사 / V / C / (= the habitat) / 주격 관계대명사 / 전치사(~ 때문에) / 형용사구

일부의 경우 / 서식지가 [생존을 위한 최고의 기회를 제공하는] / 같은 서식지가 아닐 수도 있다 /
그 서식지와 [최고의 번식 능력을 준비하는] / 요건들 때문에 (번식기의 특수한)

↳ **부연 설명(원인):** 생존에 유리한 서식지와 번식에 유리한 서식지가 같지 않을 수 있음.

🔑 번식에 유리한 서식지에는 낮은 생존율이라는 대가가 있다는 결과가 Thus로 이어짐.

(④) [5]Thus, / individuals (of many resident species), / confronted / with the fitness benefits (of control over a productive breeding site), / may be forced to balance costs /

S / 분사구문(= when they are confronted ~) / V / C / ★<force+O+to-v(O가 v하도록 강요하다)>의 수동형

따라서 / 개체들은 (많은 텃새 종의) / 직면할 때 / 합목적성에서 오는 이득에
(다산(多産)의 번식지를 장악하는 것이 갖는) / 대가의 균형을 맞추도록 강요될 수도 있다 /

in the form of lower nonbreeding survivorship / by remaining / in *the specific habitat* [where highest breeding success occurs].)

<by v-ing>: v함으로써 / 관계부사 / S' / V'

더 낮은 비번식기 생존율의 형태로 / 머물러 있음으로써 / 특정 서식지에 [가장 높은 번식 성공이 일어나는]

↳ **부연 설명(결과):** 번식 성공률이 높은 서식지에 남음으로써 이득을 취하는 대신 낮은 비번식기 생존율이라는 대가를 치러야 함.

[6]Migrants, / however, / are free to choose / the optimal habitat for survival / during the nonbreeding season / and (the optimal habitat) for reproduction / during the breeding season.

S / V / C / to choose의 O_1 / 반복어구 생략 / to choose의 O_2

철새들은 / 그러나 / 자유롭게 선택한다 / 생존을 위한 최적의 서식지를 / 비번식기 동안에는 /
그리고 번식을 위한 (최적의 서식지를) / 번식기 동안에는

↳ **대조 B(철새):** 철새들은 서식지 선택이 자유로움.

(⑤) [7]Thus, / habitat selection (during these different periods) / can be quite different / for migrants / as opposed to residents, / even among closely related species.

S / V / C / ~와는 대조적으로

이와 같이 / 서식지 선택은 (이 서로 다른 시기 동안의) / 상당히 다를 수 있다 /
철새들에게 있어서 / 텃새들과는 대조적으로 / 심지어 밀접하게 관련이 있는 종들 사이에서조차도

↳ 철새들의 서식지 선택은 텃새와 상당히 다름.

서로 다른 시기 동안의 서식지 선택은, 철새들에게 있어서 텃새들과는 대조적으로 심지어 밀접하게 관련이 있는 종들 사이에서조차도, 상당히 다를 수 있다.

어휘

resident bird 텃새
habitat 서식지
seemingly 겉보기에는
straightforward 간단한; 솔직한
shelter 은신처, 대피소; 주거지
locate (위치를) 찾아내다, 알아내다; (위치에) 두다
settle in ~에 정착하다
survivorship 생존
reproductive 번식[생식]의
cf. reproduction 번식, 생식; 복제
provide for ~을 준비[대비]하다
capacity 능력; 용량; 수용력
requirement 요건, 필요조건; 요구
specific 특수한, 특유한; 특정한; 구체적인
confront ~에 직면하다[마주치다]; 맞서다
fitness 합목적성 ((어떤 사물이 목적에 적합한 방식으로 존재하는 성질))
productive 다산(多産)의; 생산적인
breeding 번식(↔ nonbreeding 비번식)
migrant 철새; 이주자

정답 가이드

주어진 문장이 결과를 나타내는 Thus로 이어지는 것으로 보아 그 앞에는 주어진 문장의 내용이 귀결된 이유, 원인이 제시되어야 한다. 주어진 문장을 요약하면 텃새들은 번식 성공률이 높은 곳에 서식하면 비번식기에는 생존율이 낮을 수 있다는 것이다. ④의 앞 문장에서 생존에 유리한 서식지와 번식에 유리한 서식지가 같지 않을 수 있다고 했으므로, 그 결과로 주어진 문장이 이어지는 것이 자연스럽다. ④의 뒤부터는 텃새의 경우와 다르게, 번식과 생존에 각각 유리한 서식지를 자유롭게 선택하는 철새에 관한 내용이 이어진다. 따라서 주어진 문장이 들어가기에 가장 적절한 곳은 ④이다.

오답 클리닉

① (1%) 앞 문장의 its needs가 these needs로 이어지며 새들이 서식지를 선택할 때 충족시키고자 하는 필요를 구체적으로 설명하는 내용이 이어진다.
② (5%) 처음에는 생존을 위한 서식지를 찾지만 결국에는 번식을 위한 서식지도 찾아야 한다는 내용이 이어지는 것은 자연스럽다.
③ (18%) 생존을 위한 서식지와 번식을 위한 서식지가 각각 다를 수 있다고 부연 설명한다.
⑤ (6%) 텃새들과 대조되는 철새들의 비번식기와 번식기의 다른 서식지 선택을 설명하는 내용이다.

01 + 요약문 (21학년도 6월 모평 40번 | 정답률 64%) ③

구문분석 & 직독직해

생물 화석 기록의 한계성

주제문

*<be likely to-v>: v할 가능성이 있다
🔑 (A) 화석화 이후에 발견 가능성은 환경에 따름.

1 Some environments (S) are (V) more likely / to lead to fossilization and subsequent discovery (C) / than others. (= other environments)

어떤 환경은 (~할) 가능성이 더 높다 / 화석화와 차후의 발견으로 이어질 / 다른 환경보다

↳ 화석이 되고 추후 발견될 가능성은 환경의 영향을 받음.

2 Thus, we (S) cannot assume (V) // that (명사절 접속사) more fossil evidence (from a particular period or place) (S′) / means (V′) // that more individuals were present / at that time, or in that place. (→ cannot assume의 O(명사절); O′(명사절))

🔑 (B) 화석 증거가 많다고 그 개체가 많았을 것이라 추정할 수 없음.

따라서, 우리는 추정할 수 없다 // 더 많은 화석 증거가 (특정한 시기나 장소에서의) / 의미한다고 // 더 많은 개체가 있었음을 / 그 시기나 그 장소에

3 It (S) may just be (V) // that (명사절 접속사) the circumstances (at one period of time, or at one location), (S′1(복수)) / were (V′1(복수)) more favourable for fossilization (C′1) // than they (S′2, = the circumstances) were (V′2) at other times, [or] in other places. (→ may be의 C(명사절))

그저 ~일 수도 있다 // 상황이 (어느 시기나 어느 장소의) / 화석화에 더 유리했던 것 // 그것들(상황)이 다른 시기나 다른 장소에서 그랬던 것보다

↳ **세부 사항 1:** 어떤 환경이 화석화에 유리했던 것뿐일 수 있기 때문에 화석의 개수로 개체의 많고 적음을 추정할 수 없음.

4 Likewise, / the absence (of hominin fossil evidence (at a particular time or place)) (S) / does not have (V) the same implication (O) / as (→ 전치사(~와 같이)) its presence. (= hominin fossil evidence)

이와 마찬가지로 / 부재는 (인류 화석 증거의 (특정 시기나 장소에서의)) / 똑같은 암시를 갖지 않는다 / 그것(인류 화석 증거)의 존재와 같이

5 As (부사절 접속사(~듯이)) the saying goes, // 'absence of evidence is not evidence of absence.'

속담에서 말하듯이 // '증거의 부재가 부재의 증거는 아니다.'

↳ **세부 사항 2:** (어떤 환경이 화석화에 유리하지 않아서) 화석이 없는 것이 그 개체가 없었음을 암시하지 않음.

6 Similar logic (S) suggests (V) // that (명사절 접속사) taxa are likely to have arisen // before (→ 부사절 접속사(시간)) they (S″) first appear (V″) in the fossil record, // [and] they are likely to have survived / beyond the time of their most recent appearance / in the fossil record. (→ suggests의 O(명사절))

비슷한 논리는 시사한다 // 분류군이 생겼을 가능성이 있다는 것을 // 그것들(분류군)이 화석 기록에 처음 출현하기 전에 // 그리고 그것들(분류군)은 살아남았을 가능성이 있다는 것을 / 그것들의 가장 최근 출현 시기를 지나서도 / 화석 기록에서

↳ **시사점:** 분류군[생물]은 화석 기록에 나오기 전에 존재했을 수 있고, 마지막 화석 기록 이후에도 존재했을 수 있음.

7 Thus, / the first appearance datum, [and] the last appearance datum (of taxa) (in the hominin fossil record) (S(명사구 병렬)) / are (V) likely to be conservative statements (C) (about the times of origin and extinction of a taxon).

🔑 (B) 화석 기록 진술은 어떤 분류군의 발생과 멸종 시기를 적게 잡은 진술일 수 있음 → 부정확함.

따라서 / 첫 출현 자료와 마지막 출현 자료는 (분류군의) (인류 화석 기록에서) / 적게 잡은 진술일 가능성이 있다 (한 분류군의 발생과 멸종 시기에 대해)

↳ **결론:** 화석 기록 자료로 어떤 분류군[생물]의 발생과 멸종 시기를 정확히 알기 어려움.

↓

8 Since (부사절 접속사(~ 때문에)) fossilization and fossil discovery (S′) are affected (V′) / by **(A) environmental** conditions, // the fossil evidence (of a taxon) (S) / cannot definitely **(B) clarify** (V) / its population size [or] the times (of its appearance and extinction) (O(명사구 병렬)).

화석화와 화석의 발견은 영향을 받기 때문에 / (A) 환경적인 조건에 의해 // 화석 증거는 (한 분류군의) / 확실히 (B) 규명할 수 없다 / 그 개체군의 크기나 시기를 (그것의 출현과 멸종의)

해석

1어떤 환경은 다른 환경보다 화석화와 차후의 발견으로 이어질 가능성이 더 높다. 2따라서, 우리는 특정한 시기나 장소에 화석 증거가 더 많다는 것이 그 시기나 그 장소에 개체가 더 많이 있었음을 의미한다고 추정할 수 없다. 3그저 어느 시기나 어느 장소의 상황이 다른 시기나 다른 장소에서 그랬던 것보다 화석화에 더 유리했던 것일 수도 있다. 4이와 마찬가지로, 특정 시기나 장소에서의 인류 화석 증거의 부재는 그것의 존재와 똑같은 암시를 갖지 않는다.(▶ 인류 화석의 존재가 인류가 있었음을 암시한다고 해서 인류 화석의 부재가 인류가 없었음을 암시한다고 볼 수 없다는 의미) 5속담에서 말하듯이, '증거의 부재가 부재의 증거는 아니다.' 6비슷한 논리는 분류군이 화석 기록에 처음 출현하기 전에 생겼을 가능성이 있고, 그것들(분류군)은 화석 기록에서 그것의 가장 최근 출현 시기를 지나서도 살아남았을 가능성이 있다는 것을 시사한다. 7따라서 인류 화석 기록에서 분류군의 첫 출현 자료와 마지막 출현 자료는 한 분류군의 발생과 멸종 시기에 대해 적게 잡은 진술일 가능성이 있다.

↓

8화석화와 화석의 발견은 (A) 환경적인 조건에 의해 영향을 받기 때문에, 한 분류군의 화석 증거는 그 개체군의 크기나 그것의 출현과 멸종의 시기를 확실히 (B) 규명할 수 없다.

어휘

lead to A A로 이어지다
fossilization 화석화
cf. fossil 화석(의)
assume 추정[추측]하다; (책임을) 맡다
period 시기, 기간; 시대
circumstance 상황, 환경; 사정, 형편
favourable 유리한; 호의적인
absence 부재, 없음; 결석
implication 암시, 함축
saying 속담, 격언
logic 논리, 논법
arise 생기다, 발생하다; 유발되다
appear 출현하다, 나타나다
cf. appearance 출현; 겉모습, 외모
datum (*pl.* data) 자료
conservative (실제 수나 양보다) 적게 잡은; 보수적인
statement 진술, 성명
origin 발생, 기원
extinction 멸종; 소멸
[요약문] clarify 규명하다, 분명히 하다
population 개체군, 집단; 인구

정답 가이드

요약문을 통해 화석화와 화석의 발견에 영향을 미치는 조건과 그에 따른 결론에 대한 글임을 알 수 있다. 화석화된 후에 화석의 발견 가능성은 '환경'이 그것에 유리한지에 달려 있기 때문에 화석 증거가 많다고 해서 그 시기나 장소에 더 많은 개체가 있었다고 추정할 수 없으며 화석의 기록만으로 어떤 분류군의 생존 시기를 '정확히 진술할 수도 없다'고 했다. 따라서 요약문의 빈칸 (A)와 (B)에 각각 들어갈 말로 가장 적절한 것은 ③ 'environmental(환경적인) - clarify(규명하다)'이다.

오답 클리닉

(A) (B)

① experimental - confirm (11%) 실험적인 - 확인하다

화석화는 인위적인 실험이 아니라 그것에 유리한 환경, 상황의 영향을 받은 것이므로 (A)는 틀리며, (B)는 맞음.

② experimental - reveal (9%) 실험적인 - 밝히다

(A)는 틀리며, (B)는 맞음.

④ environmental - conceal (14%) 환경적인 - 감추다

(A)는 맞고, (B)는 틀림. 화석 증거가 개체군에 대한 정보를 감출 수 없는 것이 아니라 확실히 알려주지 못한다는 내용임.

⑤ accidental - mask (2%) 우연한 - 가리다

(A)는 맞고, (B)는 틀림.

02~03 + 복합 유형 (22학년도 9월 모평 41~42번 | 정답률 02 60%, 03 49%)

02 ② 03 ⑤

구문분석 & 직독직해

통계 실험 집단과 통제 집단 실험 설정의 주의점

[1]In *studies* (examining the effectiveness of vitamin C), / researchers typically divide the subjects / into two groups.

(현재분사구 / S / V / O) ★<divide A into B>: A를 B로 나누다

연구에서 (비타민 C의 효과를 조사하는) / 연구자들은 일반적으로 실험 대상자들을 나눈다 / 두 집단으로

[2]One group (the experimental group) receives a vitamin C supplement, // [and] the other (the control group) does not (receive a vitamin C supplement).

(S_1 / V_1 / O_1 / S_2 / V_2 / 반복어구 생략)

한 집단(실험 집단)은 비타민 C 보충제를 받는다 // 그리고 다른 집단(통제 집단)은 받지 않는다

[3]Researchers observe both groups / to determine // whether one group has fewer or shorter colds / than the other.

(S / V / O / 목적(~하기 위해) / 명사절 접속사 / S′ / V′ / O′) → to determine의 O(명사절)

연구자들은 두 집단 모두를 관찰한다 / 알아내기 위해 // 한 집단이 감기에 더 적게 또는 더 짧게 걸리는지를 / 다른 집단보다

↳ **도입:** 감기에 대한 비타민 C의 효과를 조사하는 연구를 실험 집단과 통제 집단으로 나눠 실시함.

주제문

03-(a) them은 some of the pitfalls를 가리키므로 이를 '피하는' 방법을 설명하는 흐름이 적절함.

[4]The following discussion describes / some (of *the pitfalls* (inherent in an experiment of this kind)) / [and] *ways* (to **(a) avoid** them).

(S / V / O_1 / 형용사구 / O_2)

이어지는 논의는 설명한다 / 일부를 (함정 중 (이러한 종류의 실험에 내재하는)) / 그리고 방법을 (그것들을 피하는)

↳ 실험 집단과 통제 집단을 이용한 실험에서의 일부 함정과 이를 피하는 방법을 설명함.

[5]In sorting subjects into two groups, / researchers must ensure // that each person has an **(b) equal** chance (of being assigned / to [either] the experimental group [or] the control group).

(<in v-ing>: ~할 때 / S / V / 명사절 접속사 / S′ / V′ / O′ / =) → must ensure의 O(명사절), <either A or B>: A나 B 둘 중 하나

실험 대상자를 두 집단으로 분류할 때 / 연구자들은 반드시 ~하게 해야 한다 // 각 개인이 동일한 확률을 갖게 (배정될 / 실험 집단 또는 통제 집단 둘 중 하나에)

03-(b) 실험 대상자는 실험 집단과 통제 집단에 임의로 선정되므로 배정 확률은 반반으로 '동일함'.

[6]This is accomplished by randomization; // that is, the subjects are chosen randomly / from the same population / by flipping a coin [or] *some other method* (involving chance).

(S(= 앞 문장) / V / S / V / by의 O(명사구 병렬) / 현재분사구)

이는 임의 추출에 의해 달성된다 // 즉 실험 대상자는 임의로 선정된다 / 동일 모집단에서 / 동전 던지기나 어떤 다른 방법에 의해 (우연을 포함하는)

↳ **세부 사항 1:** 실험 대상자를 실험 집단과 통제 집단으로 분류하는 것은 임의적이어야 함.

[7]Randomization helps to ensure // that results reflect the treatment / [and] not (reflect) *factors* [that might influence the grouping of subjects].

(S / V / O / 명사절 접속사 / 주격 관계대명사) → to ensure의 O(명사절)

임의 추출은 반드시 ~하게 하는 데 도움이 된다 // 결과가 처치를 반영하게 / 그리고 요인은 그러지(반영되지) 않게 [실험 대상자들을 집단으로 분류하는 데 영향을 줄지도 모르는]

↳ **부연 설명:** 임의 추출은 연구 결과가 실험 처치를 반영하고 다른 요인은 반영되지 않도록 함.

해석

[1]비타민 C의 효과를 조사하는 연구에서 연구자들은 일반적으로 실험 대상자들을 두 집단으로 나눈다. [2]한 집단(실험 집단)은 비타민 C 보충제를 받고 다른 집단(통제 집단)은 받지 않는다. [3]연구자들은 한 집단이 다른 집단보다 감기에 더 적게 또는 더 짧게 걸리는지를 알아내기 위해 두 집단 모두를 관찰한다. [4]이어지는 논의는 이러한 종류의 실험에 내재하는 함정 중 일부와 그것들을 (a) 피하는 방법을 설명한다. [5]실험 대상자를 두 집단으로 분류할 때, 연구자들은 반드시 각 개인이 실험 집단 또는 통제 집단 둘 중 하나에 배정될 (b) 동일한 확률을 갖게 해야 한다. [6]이는 임의 추출에 의해 달성되는데, 즉 실험 대상자는 동전 던지기나 우연을 포함하는 어떤 다른 방법에 의해 동일 모집단에서 임의로 선정된다. [7]임의 추출은 반드시 결과가 처치(실험 집단에 비타민 C 보충제를 섭취하게 하는 것)를 반영하되 실험 대상자들을 집단으로 분류하는 데 영향을 줄지도 모르는 요인(예: 나이, 성별, 건강 등)은 그러지(반영되지) 않게 하는 데 도움이 된다. [8]중요한 것은, 감기의 비율, 심각성, 또는 지속 기간에서 관찰된 차이가 어떤 식으로든 일어났을지도 모른다는 가능성을 (c) 배제하기 위해 두 집단의 사람들이 비슷해야 하고 감기에 관해 동일한 기록을 가지고 있어야 한다는 것이다. [9]예를 들어, 통제 집단이 실험 집단보다 보통 두 배만큼 많은 감기에 걸리곤 했다면, 그 연구 결과는 (d) 아무것도 입증하지 못한다.(▶ 원래 감기에 잘 걸리는 사람들로 통제 집단을 구성하면 안 된다는 의미) [10]영양분을 포함하는 실험에서, 두 집단의 식단은 특히 연구 중인 영양분에 관련해서 또한 (e) 달라야(→ 비슷해야) 한다. [11]실험 집단에 속한 사람들이 평소 식단에서 더 적은 비타민 C를 섭취하고 있었다면, 보충제의 어떤 효과도 분명하지 않을 수 있다.

어휘

subject 실험 대상자, 피실험자; 주제; 과목

supplement 보충제; 보충(하다)

determine 알아내다; 결정하다

8 Importantly, / the two groups of people must be similar / and must have the same track record / with respect to colds /

☞ 03-(c) 두 집단이 비슷해야 하는 것은 다른 변인이 감기에 미칠 영향을 '배제하기' 위함임.

S / V₁ C₁ / V₂ O₂ / ~에 관하여

중요한 것은 / 두 집단의 사람들이 비슷해야 한다 / 그리고 동일한 기록을 가지고 있어야 한다 / 감기에 관해 /

to **(c) rule out** the possibility // that observed differences (in the rate, severity, or duration of colds)
목적(~하기 위해) = 동격 접속사 S'

/ might have occurred anyway.
V'

가능성을 배제하기 위해 // 관찰된 차이가 (감기의 비율, 심각성, 또는 지속 기간에서) / 어떤 식으로든 일어났을지도 모른다는

↳ **세부 사항 2:** 실험 변인을 제외한 다른 변인이 두 집단 간에 비슷해야 함.

☞ 03-(d) 통제 집단이 감기에 걸리기 쉬운 사람들로 구성되면 비타민 C의 효과를 '아무것도' 입증 못 할 것임.

9 If, for example, the control group would normally catch / twice as many colds / as the
부사절 접속사 S' V' O'

experimental group, // then the findings prove **(d) nothing**.
★ <A 배수 as ~ as B>: A는 B의 …배만큼 ~한

예를 들어, 통제 집단이 보통 걸리곤 했다면 / 두 배만큼 많은 감기에 / 실험 집단보다 // 그렇다면 그 연구 결과는 아무것도 입증하지 못한다

↳ **예 1:** 평소 두 집단이 감기에 걸리는 확률이 비슷해야 함.

10 In *experiments* (involving a nutrient), / the diets (of both groups) / must also be **(e) different**(→
현재분사구 S V C

similar), / especially with respect to *the nutrient* (being studied).
~에 관하여 현재분사구

실험에서 (영양분을 포함하는) / 식단은 (두 집단의) / 또한 달라야(→ 비슷해야) 한다 / 특히 영양분에 관련해서 (연구 중인)

11 If those in the experimental group were receiving / less vitamin C / from their usual diet, //
부사절 접속사(조건) S' V' O'

then any effects of the supplement may not be apparent.
S V C

☞ 03-(e) 평소 비타민 C 섭취가 집단 간 다르면 보충제의 효과가 불분명해지므로 식단은 '비슷해야' 함.

실험 집단에 있는 사람들이 섭취하고 있었다면 / 더 적은 비타민 C를 / 평소 식단에서 // 그렇다면 보충제의 어떤 효과도 분명하지 않을 수 있다

↳ **예 2:** 평소 두 집단의 식단(비타민 C 섭취량)이 비슷해야 함.

---

inherent 내재하는, 고유한
sort A into B A를 B로 분류[구분]하다
ensure 반드시 ~하게 하다, 보장하다
assign 배정하다, 할당하다
randomization 임의[무작위] 추출
flip (동전 등을) 던지다; 홱 뒤집다
reflect 반영하다; 비추다; 반사하다
treatment 처치; 처리; 대우
track record (개인·기관의 모든) 기록[실적]
severity 심각성
duration 지속 (기간)
finding(s) 연구 결과
nutrient 영양분, 영양소
apparent 분명한, 명백한
[선택지] faulty 불완전한, 흠이 있는; 잘못된
irrelevant 상관없는, 무관한
in-depth 심층의, 면밀한
analysis 분석, 분해

⊕ 실험 집단(experimental group): 연구에서 관심을 두고 있는 처치를 받는 집단
⊕ 통제 집단(control group): 실험 집단과의 결과를 비교하기 위해 실험 처치를 하지 않은 집단
⊕ 모집단(population): 통계 조사의 대상이 되는 집단 전체. 결과가 가장 정확하려면 집단 전체인 모집단을 조사해야 하는데, 대부분의 경우 그것이 어렵기 때문에 모집단에서 일부(표본)를 추출하여 조사함.

정답 가이드

02 실험 집단과 통제 집단을 이용해 감기에 대한 비타민 C의 효과를 알아보는 실험에서 주의할 사항에 대해 설명하는 글이다. 각 집단의 실험 대상자들은 임의로 선정하여 결과가 처치만을 반영하게 해야 하며, 평소 감기에 대한 기록이나 식단이 두 집단 간 유사해야 유의미한 결과를 얻을 수 있다고 했다. 따라서 글의 제목으로 가장 적절한 것은 ② 'Don't Let Irrelevant Factors Influence the Results!(상관없는 요인이 결과에 영향을 미치지 않도록 하라!)'이다.

03 감기에 대한 비타민 C의 효과를 알아보는 실험에서 실험 집단과 통제 집단은 비타민 C 보충제 섭취를 제외한 다른 조건들이 비슷해야 그 효과를 분명히 알 수 있을 것이다. 따라서 ⑤의 'different(다른)'를 'similar(비슷한)'로 바꾸어야 한다.

> **The 핵심 ★** 두 집단이 비슷해야 한다는 문장 8의 예에 해당하므로 같은 문맥으로 이어져야 함을 알 수 있다.

오답 클리닉

02 ① Perfect Planning and Faulty Results: A Sad Reality in Research (13%)
완벽한 계획과 불완전한 결과(x)는 연구의 슬픈 현실
완벽한 계획을 세웠음에도 불완전한 결과가 나오는 내용이 아님.

> **The 주의 ◑** 불분명한 결과를 초래할 수 있는 요소들을 배제함으로써 온전한 연구 결과를 얻는 방법을 설명하는 글이다.

③ Protect Human Subjects Involved in Experimental Research! (9%)
실험 연구에 참여하는 인간 실험 대상자들을 보호하라(x)!
실험 대상자들을 보호하는 내용이 아님.

④ What Nutrients Could Better Defend Against Colds? (10%)
어떤 영양소가 감기를 더 잘 막을 수(x) 있을까?
감기에 대한 비타민 C의 효과를 알아보는 실험은 집단을 나눠 실험하는 연구의 주의 사항을 설명하는 예로 쓰인 것으로 글 전체를 포괄하는 제목이 될 수 없음.

⑤ In-depth Analysis of Nutrition: A Key Player for Human Health (8%)
인간의 건강을 위한 핵심 요소인 영양에 대한 심층 분석(x)
영양을 심층 분석하는 내용이 아님.

03 ① avoid (3%) 피하다
실험에 있을 수 있는 함정을 '피하는' 방법들에 대한 설명이 이어지므로 적절함.

② equal (10%) 동일한
문장 6에서 실험 대상자는 임의 추출에 의해 실험 집단과 통제 집단에 배정된다고 했으므로 배정 확률은 반반으로 '동일'하다고 볼 수 있음.

③ rule out (15%) 배제하다
두 집단의 사람들이 비슷한 조건이어야 하는 것은 실험 결과에 다른 조건들이 영향을 미칠 가능성을 '배제하기' 위함으로 보는 것이 적절함.

④ nothing (23%) 아무것도 (없음)
통제 집단과 실험 집단의 사람들은 비슷해야 하는데 그렇지 않으면 실험 결과는 '아무것도' 입증하지 못함.

> **The 주의 ◑** 통제 집단이 평소 감기에 잘 걸리는 사람들로 구성되면 실험 결과가 차이가 있다고 해도 원인이 비타민 C 보충제의 섭취 여부인지를 입증할 수 없다.

01 + 빈칸 추론 (19학년도 9월 모평 32번 | 정답률 50%) ①

구문분석 & 직독직해

사회 정치적 문제가 일으키는 서로 다른 정체성

[1] Although most people, / (including Europe's Muslims), / have numerous identities, //
부사절 접속사(양보) S′ 전치사구 삽입 V′ O′
비록 대부분의 사람들이 ~이긴 하지만 / (유럽의 이슬람교도들을 포함한) / 다수의 정체성을 가지(기는 하지만) //

(= these numerous identities) *few: (준부정어) 거의 없는
few of these are politically salient / at any moment.
S(복수) V(복수) C
이들 중에서 정치적으로 두드러지는 정체성은 거의 없다 / 언제 어느 때나
↳ **일반적 경향:** 정치적으로 항상 두드러지는 정체성은 거의 없음.

주제문
[2] It is only when a political issue affects the welfare (of those in a particular group) // that identity assumes importance.
<It is ~ that ...> 강조구문: …인 것은 바로 ~이다
S′ V′ O′
바로 어떤 정치적 문제가 안녕에 영향을 주는 경우뿐이다 (특정 집단의 사람들의) // 정체성이 중요성을 띠는 것은
↳ **예외적 사실:** 정체성은 어떤 정치적 문제가 특정 집단의 안녕에 영향을 미칠 때 중요해짐.

여성의 권리 문제가 생기면 여성이라는 정체성이 주요해짐. *<think of A as B>: A를 B로 생각하다
[3] For instance, / when *issues* arise [that touch on women's rights], // women start to think of gender / as their principal identity.
부사절 접속사 S′ V′ 주격 관계대명사 S V
예를 들어 / 문제가 생기는 경우 [여성의 권리에 관련해] // 여성들은 성(性)을 생각하기 시작한다 / 자신들의 주된 정체성으로

*<whether A or B>: A인지 B인지
[4] Whether such women are American or Iranian / or whether they are Catholic or Protestant / matters less / than the fact // that they are women.
S(명사절 병렬) V(단수) = 동격 접속사
그런 여성들이 미국인인지 이란인인지 / 혹은 그들이 가톨릭교도인지 개신교도인지는 / 덜 중요하다 / 사실보다 // 그들이 여성이라는
↳ **예 1:** 여성의 권리 문제가 생기면 여성은 성(性)을 주된 정체성으로 여김.

아프리카계 미국인들은 아프리카에 문제가 생기면 그곳과 연결되어 있는 혈족 관계를 상기함.
[5] Similarly, / when famine and civil war threaten people / in sub-Saharan Africa, //
부사절 접속사(시간) S′ V′ O′
마찬가지로 / 기아와 내전이 사람들을 위태롭게 하는 경우 / 사하라 사막 이남의 아프리카에서 //

*<remind A of B(A에게 B를 상기시키다)>의 수동형 (= where)
many African-Americans are reminded / of their kinship (with *the continent* [in which their ancestors originated / centuries earlier]), // and they lobby their leaders / to provide humanitarian relief.
S_1 V_1 전치사+관계대명사 S′ V′ S_2 V_2 O C
많은 아프리카계 미국인들은 상기하게 된다 / 혈족 관계를 (대륙과의 [자신들의 조상이 유래한 / 수세기 이전에]) // 그리고 그들은 자신들의 지도자들에게 압력을 가한다 / 인도주의적 구호를 제공하도록
↳ **예 2:** 아프리카에 문제가 생기면 아프리카계 미국인들은 그들이 뿌리를 둔 아프리카와의 혈족 관계를 주된 정체성으로 여김.

정체성은 문제에 관한 정치적 선호에 따라 다르게 나타남.
[6] In other words, / each issue calls forth / *somewhat different identities* [that help explain *the political preferences* [(which[that]) people have / regarding those issues]].
S V O 주격 관계대명사 목적격 관계대명사 생략
다시 말해서 / 각각의 문제는 불러일으킨다 / 다소 서로 다른 정체성을 [정치적인 선호를 설명하는 데 도움을 주는 [사람들이 갖는 / 그 문제들에 관하여]]
↳ **결론:** 각각의 문제는 사람들이 정치적 선호에 따라 서로 다른 정체성을 드러내게 함.

해석

[1]비록 유럽의 이슬람교도들을 포함한 대부분의 사람들이 다수의 정체성을 가지기는 하지만, 이들 중에서 언제 어느 때나 정치적으로 두드러지는 정체성은 거의 없다.(▶ 사람들은 종교, 민족, 인종, 언어, 문화, 직업 등등의 요소에 기초하여 많은 정체성을 가지는데, 그 많은 정체성들 중에서 항상 정치적으로 두드러지는 정체성은 거의 없다는 의미) [2]정체성이 중요성을 띠는 것은 바로 어떤 정치적 문제가 특정 집단의 사람들의 안녕에 영향을 주는 경우뿐이다. [3]예를 들어, 여성의 권리에 관련해 문제가 생기는 경우, 여성들은 성(性)을 자신들의 주된 정체성으로 생각하기 시작한다. [4]그런 여성들이 미국인인지 이란인인지, 혹은 그들이 가톨릭교도인지 개신교도인지는 그들이 여성이라는 사실보다 덜 중요하다. [5]마찬가지로 사하라 사막 이남의 아프리카에서 기아와 내전이 사람들을 위태롭게 하는 경우, 많은 아프리카계 미국인들은 자신들의 조상이 수세기 이전에 유래한 대륙과의 혈족 관계를 상기하게 되고, 자신들의 지도자들에게 인도주의적 구호를 제공하도록 압력을 가한다. [6]다시 말해서, 각각의 문제는 그 문제들에 관하여 사람들이 갖는 정치적인 선호를 설명하는 데 도움을 주는 다소 서로 다른 정체성을 불러일으킨다.(▶ 문제에 대해 사람들이 드러내는 정체성은 그 사람의 정치적 성향을 보여준다는 의미)

어휘

numerous 다수의, 수많은
welfare 안녕, 행복; 복지
assume (특질·양상을) 띠다; 추정하다
touch (up)on ~에 관련하다
principal 주된, 주요한
Catholic 가톨릭교도
Protestant (개)신교도
famine 기아, 굶주림
civil war 내전
kinship 혈족 관계
continent 대륙
originate 유래하다
lobby 압력을 가하다, (정치적인) 로비를 하다
humanitarian 인도주의적인
relief 구호(품); 안도, 안심
call forth ~을 불러일으키다
somewhat 다소, 약간
regarding ~에 관하여
[선택지] precede 우선하다; 앞서다
stability 안정성
nationality 국적
bear 가지다, 지니다; 견디다

정답 가이드

빈칸 문장은 '~은 바로 정치적 문제가 특정 집단 사람들의 안녕에 영향을 줄 때 뿐이다'라는 의미이므로, 정치적 문제가 있을 때 '어떤 일'이 일어나는지를 찾아야 한다. 이어지는 예에서, 여성의 권리와 아프리카 문제(좁은 의미로는 사회적, 인도적 문제이지만 정책 변화가 요구되는 것들이므로 넓은 의미에서 정치적 문제)가 생기면, 각각 성(性), 혈족 관계가 주요 정체성이 된다고 했으므로, 빈칸에 들어갈 말로 가장 적절한 것은 ① 'identity assumes importance(정체성이 중요성을 띠다)'이다.

오답 클리닉

② religion precedes identity (16%)
종교가 정체성에 우선하다
정체성보다 종교가 우선된다는 내용은 없음.

③ society loses stability (12%)
사회가 안정성을 잃다
여성의 권리, 아프리카의 기아와 내전이 언급되긴 했지만 안정성을 잃었다는 내용은 없음.

④ society supports diversity (17%)
사회가 다양성을 지지하다
사회가 다양성을 지지한다는 언급은 없음.

⑤ nationality bears significance (5%)
국적이 중요성을 갖다
국적은 하나의 정체성일 뿐이며, 각 문제에 따라 드러나는 정체성은 달라진다고 했음.

02 + 글의 순서 〈20학년도 9월 모평 37번 | 정답률 64%〉 ②

구문분석 & 직독직해 과학 인과 관계를 가정하는 결정론

[1]Because a main goal of science is / to discover lawful relationships, //
부사절 접속사(이유) S′ V′ C′
과학의 주요 목적이 ~이기 때문에 / 법칙적인 관계를 발견하는 것 //

↱ assumes의 O(명사절)
science assumes // that what is being investigated is lawful.
S V 명사절 접속사 S′(명사절) V′ C′
과학은 가정한다 // 연구되고 있는 것이 법칙적이라고

[2]For example, / the chemist assumes // that chemical reactions are lawful, // and the physicist assumes // that the physical world is lawful.
S_1 V_1 O_1(명사절) S_2 V_2 O_2(명사절)
예를 들어 / 화학자는 가정한다 // 화학 반응이 법칙적이라고 // 그리고 물리학자는 가정한다 // 물리적 세계가 법칙적이라고
↳ **도입:** 과학은 연구 대상의 법칙적 관계를 가정함.

주제문 🔑 주어진 글의 가정을 (B)에서 결정론으로 설명함.
(B) [3]The assumption // that what is being studied can be understood / in terms of causal laws / is called determinism.
S(단수) = 동격 접속사 S′(명사절) V′ ~의 관점에서 V(단수) C
가정은 // 연구되고 있는 것이 이해될 수 있다는 / 인과 법칙의 관점에서 / 결정론이라고 불린다
↳ 결정론은 연구 대상이 인과 법칙으로 이해될 수 있다고 가정함.

★<define A as B>: A를 B로 정의하다
[4]Richard Taylor defined determinism / as *the philosophical doctrine*
S V O
Richard Taylor는 결정론을 정의했다 / 철학적 교리로

↱ states의 O(명사절)
[that "states // that for *everything* [that ever happens] / there are conditions // such that, / given them, / nothing else could happen."]
주격 관계대명사 명사절 접속사 주격 관계대명사 V′ S′ 부사절 접속사(결과) (= conditions) S″ V″
[(~라고) '말하는 // 모든 일에 대해서 [항상 일어나는] / 조건들이 있다고 //
그래서 / 그것들(조건들)이 주어지면 / 그 밖의 것은 아무것도 일어날 수 없다고']
↳ **정의:** 항상 일어나는 일에는 그 일이 일어나는 조건이 있음 → 인과 관계의 법칙

🔑 (B)에 언급된 결정론의 정의에 따른 가정을 제시함. ↱ assumes의 O_1(명사절)
(A) [5]The determinist, / then, / assumes // that *everything* [that occurs] / is a function (of a finite number of causes) //
S V 명사절 접속사 S′ 주격 관계대명사 V′(단수) C′
결정론자는 / 그래서 / ~라고 가정한다 // 모든 일은 [일어나는] / 작용이라고 (유한한 수의 원인들의) //

↱ assumes의 O_2(명사절)
and that, (if these causes were known), an event could be predicted / with complete accuracy.
명사절 접속사 부사절 접속사(조건) S′ V′
그리고 (이 원인들이 알려지면) 사건은 예측될 수 있다고 / 완전히 정확하게
↳ 결정론자는 사건을 일으키는 원인(조건)을 밝히면 그 사건을 예측할 수 있다고 가정함.

해석

[1]과학의 주요 목적이 법칙적인 관계를 발견하는 것이기 때문에, 과학은 연구되고 있는 것이 법칙적이라고 가정한다. [2]예를 들어, 화학자는 화학 반응이 법칙적이라고 가정하고, 물리학자는 물리적 세계가 법칙적이라고 가정한다. (B) [3]연구되고 있는 것이 인과 법칙의 관점에서 이해될 수 있다는 가정은 결정론이라고 불린다. [4]Richard Taylor는 결정론을 '항상 일어나는 모든 일에 대해서 조건들이 있는데, 그래서 그 조건들이 주어지면 그 밖의 것은 아무것도 일어날 수 없다고 말하는' 철학적 교리로 정의했다. (A) [5]그래서 결정론자는 일어나는 모든 일은 유한한 수의 원인들의 작용이고 이 원인들이 알려지면 사건은 완전히 정확하게 예측될 수 있다고 가정한다. [6]그러나, 어떤 사건의 '모든' 원인을 아는 것이 필수적인 것은 아니어서, 결정론자는 그저 원인들이 존재하고 더 많은 원인들이 알려질수록 예측은 더 정확해진다고 가정한다. (C) [7]예를 들어, 거의 모든 사람이 날씨는 태양의 흑점, 높은 고도의 제트 기류, 그리고 기압과 같은 유한한 수의 변수들의 작용이라는 것에 동의할 것이지만, 일기 예보는 늘 확률적인데, 이러한 변수들 중 다수가 끊임없이 변하고 다른 변수들은 전혀 알려져 있지 않기 때문이다.

어휘

lawful 법칙적인
investigate 연구하다; 조사하다
chemist 화학자
cf. chemical 화학의; 화학 물질
physicist 물리학자
cf. physical 물리[물질]적인; 육체의
causal 인과적인, 인과 관계의
determinism 결정론
cf. determinist 결정론자(의)
philosophical 철학의

[6]However, / knowing *all* causes of an event is not necessary; //
S₁(동명사구) V₁(단수) C
그러나 / 어떤 사건의 '모든' 원인을 아는 것이 필수적인 것은 아니다 //

the determinist simply assumes // that they exist // and that as more causes are known, //
S₂ V₂ (they = causes) O(명사절 병렬) (as: 부사절 접속사(~할수록))
predictions become more accurate.

결정론자는 그저 가정한다 // 그것들(원인들)이 존재한다고 // 그리고 더 많은 원인들이 알려질수록 ~라고 //
예측은 더 정확해진다고

↳ 모든 원인을 알 필요는 없지만, 많이 알수록 예측이 정확해진다고 가정함.

(A)의 결정론자의 견지에서 날씨를 예측하는 예를 제시함. (→ would agree의 O(명사절))

(C) [7]For example / almost everyone would agree // that the weather is a function
S₁ V₁ 명사절 접속사 S' V' C'
(of a finite number of variables (such as sunspots, high-altitude jet streams, and barometric pressure)); //

예를 들어 / 거의 모든 사람이 동의할 것이다 // 날씨는 작용이라는 것에
(유한한 수의 변수들의 (태양의 흑점, 높은 고도의 제트 기류, 그리고 기압과 같은)) //

yet weather forecasts are always probabilistic // because many of these variables change constantly,
S₂ V₂ C 부사절 접속사(이유) S'₁ V'₁
// and others are simply unknown.
S'₂ V'₂ C'

하지만 일기 예보는 늘 확률적이다 // 이러한 변수들 중 다수가 끊임없이 변하기 때문에
// 그리고 다른 변수들은 전혀 알려져 있지 않기 (때문에)

↳ **예:** 많은 변수(원인)가 작용하는 일기 예보는 예측이 어려움

doctrine 교리, 신조
state 말하다; 상태; 국가
condition (전제) 조건; 상태
finite 유한한, 한정된
accuracy 정확(도)
cf. accurate 정확한
variable 변수; 가변적인
sunspot 태양의 흑점
probabilistic 확률(론)적인
constantly 끊임없이; 자주
simply 전혀, 절대로; 간단히

정답 가이드

주어진 글은 과학이 연구되고 있는 것을 법칙적이라고 가정한다는 내용과 그 예이므로 그 뒤에는 주어진 글의 가정, 즉 연구되고 있는 것이 인과 법칙의 관점에서 이해될 수 있다는 것을 결정론으로 설명하는 (B)가 이어지는 것이 자연스럽다. (B)에서 설명한 결정론에 따른 결정론자의 가정을 (A)에서 제시하고, 그 가정에 대한 구체적인 예를 드는 (C)가 마지막에 오는 것이 적절하다.

오답 클리닉

① (A) - (C) - (B) (3%)
주어진 글에는 결정론에 대한 언급이 없으므로 (A)의 The determinist가 바로 이어질 수 없다. 또한 (A)가 논리적인 결과를 나타내는 연결어 then과 함께 쓰인 것으로 보아 그 앞에는 결정론자가 가정을 내리는 근거, 즉 결정론의 정의를 설명하는 (B)가 먼저 와야 한다.
③ (B) - (C) - (A) (21%)
(C)는 (A)와 같은 견지에서 날씨는 유한한 수의 변수(원인)들의 작용이라고 설명하고 있으므로 (A) 뒤에 오는 것이 자연스럽다. (A)는 모든 원인을 알 필요는 없지만 많이 알수록 정확한 예측을 할 수 있다는 내용이고, (C)는 변수가 많아서 예측이 어려운 날씨를 예로 들고 있다.
④ (C) - (A) - (B) (6%) / ⑤ (C) - (B) - (A) (6%)
(C)는 결정론자의 견지에서 일기 예보가 확률적인 이유를 설명하고 있으므로 주어진 글 바로 뒤에 올 수 없다.

03 + 문장 넣기 〈20학년도 9월 모평 39번 | 정답률 31%〉 ③

구문분석 & 직독직해

예술 과학과 예술 각자의 소명

*<treat A as B>: A를 B로 취급하다[다루다]

[1]Representational theories of art treat the work of the artist / as similar to that of the scientist.
S V O (that = the work)
재현 예술 이론은 예술가가 하는 일을 취급한다 / 과학자가 하는 일과 유사한 것으로

(Both = The work of the artist and the scientist)
[2]Both, / so to speak, / are involved / in describing the external world.
S V in의 O(동명사구)
둘 다 / 말하자면 / 관련이 있다 / 외부 세계를 묘사하는 것과

↳ **19세기 이전:** 외부 세계를 묘사한다는 점에서 과학과 예술을 유사하게 취급함.

(①) [3]But / by the nineteenth century, / any comparison (between the scientist and the artist) /
S
*<be bound to-v>: v할 수밖에 없다, 반드시 v하다
was bound to make the artist look like a poor relation /
V
그러나 / 19세기 무렵에 / 어떤 비교든 (과학자와 예술가 사이의) /
예술가를 열등한 것처럼 보이게 만들 수밖에 없었다 /

in terms of making discoveries about the world or holding a mirror up to nature.
~ 면에 있어서 of의 O(동명사구 병렬)
세상에 관한 발견을 하거나 자연에 거울을 비추는 면에 있어서

해석

[1]재현 예술 이론은 예술가가 하는 일을 과학자가 하는 일과 유사한 것으로 취급한다. [2]말하자면, 둘 다 외부 세계를 묘사하는 것과 관련이 있다. (①) [3]그러나 19세기 무렵에, 과학자와 예술가 사이의 어떤 비교든 세상에 관한 발견을 하거나 자연에 거울을 비추는(자연을 있는 그대로 묘사하는) 면에 있어서 예술가를 열등한 것처럼 보이게 만들 수밖에 없었다. (②) [4]여기서, 과학은 분명히 우위를 가졌다. (③ [5]그래서 예술이 그것(예술)을 과학과 구별하는 동시에, 수준에 있어 그것(예술)을 과학과 동일하게 만드는 어떤 소명을 제시해야 한다는 사회적 압력이 있었다.) [6]예술이 감정의 표현을 전문으로 한다는 개념은 이런 관점에서 특히 매력적이었다. (④) [7]그것(그 개념)은 과학에 그 자체의 것, 즉 객관

(②) [4]Here, / science clearly had the edge. 예술이 사회적 압력을 받은 원인에 해당함.
여기서 / 과학은 분명히 우위를 가졌다
↳ **19세기:** 세상을 발견하고 자연을 있는 그대로 바라본다는 점에서 과학이 예술보다 우위를 가짐.

앞 문장에 대한 결과가 So로 이어짐. → to-v의 의미상 주어
(③ [5]So, / there was *a social pressure* (for art / to come up with *some vocation* [that both distinguished it from science / and, at the same time, / made it equal in stature / to science]).)
V S (= art) 주격 관계대명사 V'₁ (= art) V'₂ O'₂ C'₂
그래서 / 사회적 압력이 있었다 (예술이 / 어떤 소명을 제시해야 한다는 [그것(예술)을 과학과 구별하는 / 그리고 동시에 / 수준에 있어 그것(예술)을 동일하게 만드는 / 과학과])
↳ **결과:** 예술은 과학과 수준이 같다고 소명해야 하는 사회적 압력을 받음.

→ 동격 접속사
[6]The notion // that art specialized in the expression of the emotions / was particularly attractive / in this light. 앞 문장의 예술을 소명하는 관점임.
S(단수) = V(단수) C
개념은 // 예술이 감정의 표현을 전문으로 한다는 / 특히 매력적이었다 / 이런 관점에서
↳ **예술의 소명:** 감정 표현을 전문으로 한다는 점에서 예술은 매력적임.

주제문 → (= The notion)
(④) [7]It rendered unto science / its own — / the exploration of the objective world — /
S V O =
그것(그 개념)은 과학에 주었다 / 그 자체의 것을 / 즉 객관적 세계에 대한 탐구를 /
→ 접속사를 생략하지 않은 분사구문(= while it saved ~) → to-v의 의미상 주어
while saving *something comparably important* (for art to do) — / to explore the inner world of feeling.
동시에 (과학과) 동등하게 중요한 것을 남겨두었다 (예술이 해야 하는) / 즉 감정이라는 내적 세계를 탐구하는 것

(⑤) [8]If science held the mirror up to nature, // art turned a mirror / at the self and its experiences.
부사절 접속사(조건) S V O
만약 과학이 자연을 거울에 비추었다면 // 예술은 거울의 방향을 돌렸다 / 자아와 그것의 경험으로
↳ **결론:** 과학은 객관적 세계를 탐구하고 예술은 내적 세계를 탐구하는 것으로 구분됨.

적 세계에 대한 탐구를 주었고, 동시에 예술이 해야 하는 (과학과) 동등하게 중요한 것, 즉 감정이라는 내적 세계를 탐구하는 것을 남겨두었다. (⑤) [8]만약 과학이 자연을 거울에 비추었다면(보이는 그대로 묘사했다면), 예술은 거울의 방향을 자아와 그것의 경험으로 돌렸다.

어휘

representational 《미술》 재현적[묘사적]인
so to speak 말하자면
involve 관련시키다; 수반[포함]하다
external 외부의
poor relation 열등한 것[사람]
mirror 거울(을 비추다); (충실하게) 묘사하다
edge 우위, 유리함; 끝; (칼 등의) 날
come up with ~을 제시하다, 생각해 내다
distinguish A from B A를 B와 구별하다
notion 개념, 생각, 관념
specialize in ~을 전문으로 하다
light 관점, 견해; 빛
exploration 탐구; 답사[탐사]
cf. explore 탐구하다; 답사[탐사]하다
comparably 동등하게, 비교할 수 있을 정도로
⊕ 재현 예술 이론(representational theory of art): 주로 자연의 경치, 자연물 등의 눈에 보이는 세계를 그대로 재현하여 묘사하는 예술에 대한 이론임. 재현 예술은 자연주의 및 사실주의로 분류됨.

정답 가이드

주어진 문장은 결과를 나타내는 So가 이끌어, 예술이 과학과 동일하게 되는 어떤 소명을 제시해야 한다는 사회적 압력이 있었다는 내용이다. 따라서, 앞에는 그러한 결과를 이끈 원인이 나와야 할 것이다. ③의 앞은 자연을 있는 그대로 묘사하는 데 있어 과학이 예술보다 우위를 가졌다는 내용이므로, 주어진 문장에 대한 원인이라 할 수 있다. ③의 뒤 문장은 주어진 문장의 '예술이 어떤 소명을 제시해야 한다는 것'을 '이런 관점(this light)'으로 받아, 감정 표현이 예술의 소명으로 매력적이었음을 설명하고 있다. 따라서 주어진 문장이 들어가기에 가장 적절한 곳은 ③이다.

오답 클리닉

① (4%) 예술과 과학의 일을 유사한 것으로 여겼다는 내용과 19세기 무렵에는 예술이 과학보다 열등한 것처럼 보였다는 상반되는 내용이 역접 연결어 But으로 이어지는 것은 적절하다.
② (20%) Here는 앞에서 언급된 과학에 비해 예술이 열등하게 여겨진 상황을 가리킨다.
④ (27%) 앞 문장의 The notion을 It으로 받아 과학과 예술의 구별되는 소명을 밝히고 있다.
⑤ (18%) 앞 문장의 내용을 재진술하며 글을 마무리하는 문장이다.

01 ✦ 글의 주제 〈20학년도 대수능 23번 | 정답률 64%〉 ⑤

구문분석 & 직독직해

생물 도덕적 발달 과정에서 유전과 환경의 상호 작용

¹Human beings do not enter the world / as competent moral agents.
S V O 전치사(~로서)
인간은 세상에 나오지 않는다 / 유능한 도덕적 행위자로서

*부정어 nor(~도 (또한) 아니다)가 문두에 와서 <조동사+주어+동사> 어순으로 도치됨.
²Nor does everyone leave the world / in that state.
조동사 S V O
또한 모든 이가 세상을 떠나지도 않는다 / 그 (유능한 도덕적 행위자인) 상태로

³But / somewhere in between, / most people acquire / *a bit of decency* [that qualifies them for membership (in the community of moral agents)].
S V O 주격 관계대명사 (= most people)
하지만 / (태어나서 죽는) 그 사이의 어딘가에서 / 대부분의 사람들은 습득한다 / 약간의 예의를 [그들에게 구성원 자격을 주는 (도덕적 행위자 공동체의)]
↳ **도입:** 인간은 도덕적 존재는 아니지만 살면서 예의를 습득함.

주제문 🔑 도덕성 발달에 유전자와 학습이 모두 기여함.
⁴Genes, development, and learning all contribute / to the process (of becoming a decent human being).
S V
유전자, 발달, 그리고 학습은 모두 기여한다 / 과정에 (예의 바른 인간이 되는)
↳ 예의 습득에 유전자, 발달, 학습이 모두 영향을 미침.

🔑 genes가 nature로, learning이 nurture로 말바꿈됨.
⁵The interaction (between nature and nurture) / is, however, highly complex, //
S₁ V₁ C
상호 작용은 (천성과 양육 사이의) / 하지만 매우 복잡하다 //
↱ to grasp의 O(명사절)
and developmental biologists are only just beginning / to grasp // just how complex it is.
S₂ V₂ O(to-v구)
그리고 발생 생물학자들은 간신히 시작하고 있을 뿐이다 / 이해하는 것을 // 그저 그것(천성과 양육 사이의 상호 작용)이 얼마나 복잡한지
↳ 천성과 양육의 상호 작용은 매우 복잡해 이해하기 어려움.

⁶Without *the context* (provided by cells, organisms, social groups, and culture), / DNA is inert.
과거분사구 S V C
맥락이 없으면 (세포, 유기체, 사회 집단, 그리고 문화에 의해 제공되는) / DNA는 비활성이다
↳ **상호 작용 관계 설명:** DNA(유전자)를 활성화하려면 맥락(환경)이 있어야 함.

↱ says의 O(명사절)
⁷*Anyone* [who says // that people are "genetically programmed" / to be moral] / has an oversimplified view (of how genes work).
S 주격 관계대명사 명사절 접속사 S′ V′ C′ V O
of의 O(명사절)
누구든 [말하는 // 사람들은 '유전적으로 프로그램되어' 있다고 / 도덕적이도록] / 지나치게 단순화된 견해를 가지고 있다 (유전자가 작동하는 방식에 대한)
↳ (맥락 없이) 사람이 유전적으로 도덕적이라는 생각은 너무 단순함.

🔑 유전자와 환경이 상호 작용함. ↱ to think의 O(명사절)
⁸Genes and environment interact / in *ways* [that make it nonsensical / to think // that the process of moral development in children, or any other developmental process, can be discussed / in terms of nature *versus* nurture].
S V 주격 관계대명사 V′ 가목적어′ C′ 진목적어′ 명사절 접속사 S″₁ S″₂ V″
유전자와 환경은 상호 작용한다 / 방식으로 [(~을) 무의미하게 만드는 / 생각하는 것을 // 아이들의 도덕적 발달 과정, 또는 다른 어떤 발달 과정이든 논의될 수 있다고 / 천성 '대' 양육의 측면에서]
↳ 유전자(천성)와 환경(양육) 둘 중 한 가지 측면에서만 도덕적 발달을 논할 수 없음.

↱ (= the process ~ developmental process)
⁹Developmental biologists now know // that it is really both, / or nature *through* nurture.
S V know의 O(명사절) =
발생 생물학자들은 이제 알고 있다 // 그것이 진정 둘 다라는 것을 / 즉 양육을 '통한' 천성
↳ 도덕성은 양육과 천성의 상호 작용으로 발달함.

해석

¹인간은 유능한 도덕적 행위자로서 세상에 나오지 않는다. ²또한 모든 이가 그 상태로 세상을 떠나지도 않는다. ³하지만 (태어나서 죽는) 그 사이의 어딘가에서, 대부분의 사람들은 그들에게 도덕적 행위자 공동체의 구성원 자격을 주는 약간의 예의를 습득한다. ⁴유전자, 발달, 그리고 학습은 모두 예의 바른 인간이 되는 과정에 기여한다. ⁵하지만 천성과 양육 사이의 상호 작용은 매우 복잡하며, 발생 생물학자들은 그저 그것(천성과 양육 사이의 상호 작용)이 얼마나 복잡한지 이해하는 것을 간신히 시작하고 있을 뿐이다. ⁶세포, 유기체, 사회 집단, 그리고 문화에 의해 제공되는 맥락이 없으면, DNA는 비활성이다. ⁷사람들은 도덕적이도록 '유전적으로 프로그램되어' 있다고 말하는 누구든 유전자가 작동하는 방식에 대한 지나치게 단순화된 견해를 가지고 있다. ⁸유전자와 환경은 아이들의 도덕적 발달 과정, 또는 다른 어떤 발달 과정이든, 천성 '대' 양육의 측면에서 논의될 수 있다고 생각하는 것을 무의미하게 만드는 방식으로 상호 작용한다. ⁹발생 생물학자들은 이제 그것이 진정 둘 다라는 것, 즉 양육을 '통한' 천성이라는 것을 알고 있다. ¹⁰인간 종의 도덕적 진화와 발달에 대한 완전한 과학적 설명은 아주 멀리 떨어져 있다.(▶ 인간의 도덕적 발달에 대한 과학적 설명은 현재 불가능하다는 의미)

어휘

competent 유능한, 능력 있는
moral 도덕적인; 도덕의
cf. morality 도덕성
agent 행위자; 대리인
state 상태; 국가; 말하다, 진술하다
acquire 습득하다, 얻다
qualify 자격을 주다
contribute to A A에 기여하다
decent 예의 바른; (수준이) 괜찮은, 제대로 된
nature 천성, 본성; 자연
nurture 양육(하다)
grasp 이해하다, 파악하다; 꽉 잡다
oversimplify 지나치게 단순화하다
nonsensical 무의미한, 터무니없는
in terms of ~의 측면에서
complete 완전한; 완료하다, 끝마치다
evolution 진화
cf. evolutionary 진화의
a long way off 멀리 떨어진
[선택지] perspective 관점, 시각
controversy 논란, 논쟁
interplay 상호 작용

[10] A complete scientific explanation (of moral evolution and development (in the human species)) / is a very long way off.
(S: A complete scientific explanation ~ / V: is / C: a very long way off)

완전한 과학적 설명은 (도덕적 진화와 발달에 대한 (인간 종의)) / 아주 멀리 떨어져 있다
↳ 인간의 도덕적 발달 과정은 현재 과학적으로 완벽하게 설명할 수 없음.

⊕ 발생 생물학(developmental biology): 동식물이 자라고 발달하는 개체 발생의 과정을 연구하는 생물학의 한 분야. 발생 생리학, 비교 발생학, 발생 유전학 등이 있음.

정답 가이드

인간은 선천적으로 도덕적이지 않지만, 살아가는 어느 시점에 천성과 양육의 상호 작용을 통해 도덕적으로 발달하는데, 그 과정은 매우 복잡해서 과학적으로 완전히는 설명되지 않고 있다는 내용의 글이다. 따라서 이 글의 주제로 가장 적절한 것은 ⑤'complicated gene-environment interplay in moral development(도덕적 발달에 있어서 유전자-환경의 복잡한 상호 작용)'이다.

오답 클리닉

① evolution of human morality from a cultural perspective (6%)
문화적 관점으로부터의(×) 인간 도덕성의 진화
문화적 관점에 한정해 도덕성 진화를 설명하는 것이 아님.

② difficulties in studying the evolutionary process of genes (5%)
유전자의 진화 과정(×) 연구에서의 어려움
유전자 진화 과정이 아니라, 도덕성을 발달시키는 유전자와 환경의 상호 작용이 복잡해 연구가 어렵다고 했음.

③ increasing necessity of educating children as moral agents (3%)
도덕적 행위자로 아이들을 교육하는 것의(×) 필요성 증가
아이들이 도덕적이도록 교육해야 할 필요성은 언급되지 않음.

④ nature versus nurture controversies in developmental biology (21%) 발생 생물학에서의 천성 대 양육 논란(×)
천성 대 양육이라는 어구가 언급되기는 했지만, 그 관점에서 도덕적 발달을 논하는 것은 무의미하다고 했음.

The 주의 발생 생물학에서의 천성 대 양육 논란이 주제라면 각각의 입장을 주장하는 내용이 세부 사항으로 서술되어야 한다.

02 + 빈칸 추론 〈19학년도 9월 모평 31번 | 정답률 69%〉 ①

구문분석 & 직독직해

과학 체온 조절 행동의 개념 및 의의

주제문

*부사구(Among ~ behaviors)가 문장 앞에 위치하면서 주어(those ~ ants)와 동사(are)가 도치됨.

[1] Among the most fascinating natural temperature-regulating behaviors / are those (of social insects (such as bees and ants)).
(부사구: Among ~ behaviors / V: are / S: those (= behaviors))

가장 흥미진진한 자연의 체온 조절 행동 중에는 / 행동이 있다 (사회적 곤충들의 (벌과 개미와 같은))
↳ 사회적 곤충은 체온 조절 행동을 함.

[2] These insects are able to maintain / a nearly constant temperature / in their hives or mounds / throughout the year.
(S: These insects / V: are able to maintain / O: a nearly constant temperature)

이 곤충들은 유지할 수 있다 / 거의 일정한 온도를 / 자신들의 벌집이나 개밋둑에서 / 일 년 내내
↳ 군집 내 일정한 온도를 유지할 수 있음.

*<not just A but (also) B>: A뿐만 아니라 B도

[3] The constancy (of these microclimates) / depends [not just] on the location and insulation (of the habitat), / [but] **on the activity (of the insects in the colony).**
(S(단수): The constancy / V(단수): depends / 전치사구 병렬: on the location ~, on the activity ~)

항상성은 (이러한 미기후의) / 위치와 단열뿐에만 달려 있는 것이 아니라 (서식지의) / 활동에도 (달려 있다) (군집 내 곤충들의)
↳ **군집 내 온도 항상성에 영향을 미치는 요소들:** 1) 서식지의 위치 및 단열 2) 군집 내 활동.

주변 온도가 올라가면 활동을 줄여 신진대사로 발생하는 열의 양을 줄임.

[4] When the surrounding temperature increases, // the activity in the hive decreases, // which decreases the amount of *heat* (generated by insect metabolism).
(부사절 접속사(~하면): When / S': the surrounding temperature / V': increases / S: the activity in the hive / V: decreases / 관계대명사(앞 절 보충 설명): which / V': decreases / O': the amount of heat / 과거분사구: generated by insect metabolism)

주변 온도가 올라가면 // 벌집 내 활동은 줄어든다 // 그리고 이는 열의 양을 감소시킨다 (곤충의 신진대사에 의해 발생하는)
↳ **활동을 통한 온도 조절 원리:** 주변 온도 상승 → 활동 감소 → 신진대사에 의한 열의 양 감소.

해석

[1]가장 흥미진진한 자연의 체온 조절 행동 중에는 벌과 개미와 같은 사회적 곤충들의 행동이 있다. [2]이 곤충들은 일 년 내내 자신들의 벌집이나 개밋둑에서 거의 일정한 온도를 유지할 수 있다. [3]이러한 미기후의 항상성은 서식지의 위치와 단열뿐만 아니라, 군집 내 곤충들의 활동에도 달려 있다. [4]주변 온도가 올라가면, 벌집 내 활동은 줄어드는데, 이는 곤충의 신진대사에 의해 발생하는 열의 양을 감소시킨다. [5]사실, 많은 동물은 더위 속에서는 활동을 줄이고 추위 속에서는 활동을 늘리는데, 덥거나 추운 환경에서 신체 활동의 수준을 선택할 수 있는 인간은 체온에 맞춰 자신들의 작업량을 정확하게 조절한다. [6]이러한 행동은 저체온증과 고체온증 둘 다를 피하는 데 도움이 된다.

어휘

regulate 조절하다; 규정하다; 규제[통제]하다
constant 일정한, 변함없는; 끊임없는
cf. constancy 항상성, 불변(성)
hive 벌집
mound 개밋둑; 흙더미
microclimate 미기후 ((특정 좁은 지역의 기후))

🔑 동물은 더울 때는 활동을 감소시키고, 추울 때는 활동을 증가시킴.

[5]In fact, / many animals decrease their activity in the heat / and increase it in the cold, //
S1 V1-1 O1-1 V1-2 O1-2(= their activity)
사실 / 많은 동물은 더위 속에서는 활동을 줄인다 / 그리고 추위 속에서는 활동을 늘린다 //

and people [who are allowed to choose levels of physical activity / in hot or cold environments] / adjust their workload precisely / to body temperature.
S2 주격 관계대명사 V2 O2
그리고 인간은 [신체 활동의 수준을 선택할 수 있는 / 덥거나 추운 환경에서] / 자신들의 작업량을 정확하게 조절한다 / 체온에 맞춰

↳ 인간을 포함한 많은 동물이 온도에 따라 활동을 조절함.

[6]This behavior serves to avoid / both hypothermia and hyperthermia.
S(= 앞 문장) V
이러한 행동은 피하는 데 도움이 된다 / 저체온증과 고체온증 둘 다를

↳ **결론(의의):** 체온 조절 행동이 저체온증과 고체온증을 피하게 해줌.

habitat 서식지
colony 군집[집단]; 식민지
surrounding 주변의, 인근의
metabolism 신진[물질]대사
adjust 조절하다; 적응하다
workload 작업[업무]량
precisely 정확하게
serve to-v v하는 데 도움이 되다
[선택지] interaction 상호 작용
inhabitant 서식 동물; 주민, 거주자

정답 가이드

'미기후'의 항상성, 즉 벌집이나 개밋둑 같은 좁은 곳의 기후가 일정한 것이 서식지 위치와 단열 외에 '무엇'에도 달려 있는지를 추론해야 한다. 빈칸 문장의 다음 문장에서 벌을 예로 들어 주변 온도가 올라가면 벌집 내 활동을 줄여 신진대사로 발생하는 열의 양을 감소시킨다고 했다. 이 밖에도 인간을 포함한 많은 동물이 온도에 따라 활동을 조절한다고 했으므로 빈칸에 들어갈 말로 가장 적절한 것은 ① 'the activity of the insects in the colony(군집 내 곤충들의 활동)'이다.

오답 클리닉

② the interaction with other species (6%)
다른 종들과의 상호 작용
다른 종들과 상호 작용한다는 내용은 없음.

③ the change in colony population (4%)
군집 개체 수의 변화
군집 개체 수의 변화에 따른 온도 조절에 대한 내용은 없음.

④ the building materials of the habitat (7%)
서식지의 건축 재료
서식지 온도에 영향을 주는 요소로 언급된 것은 서식지의 위치와 단열임.

⑤ the physical development of the inhabitants (14%)
서식 동물의 신체 발달
levels of physical activity를 활용한 오답. 동물의 신체 발달 정도가 온도에 영향을 미친다는 내용은 없음.

The 주의 문장 5의 인간이 주위 온도에 따라 신체 활동의 수준을 선택할 수 있다는 내용을 신체 발달의 개념과 연결 짓지 않도록 주의한다.

03 + 글의 순서 (20학년도 9월 모평 36번 | 정답률 33%) ⑤

구문분석 & 직독직해 사회 주권과 시민권에 중요한 시간적 자유

★<define A as B(A를 B로 정의하다)>의 수동형 → (= a state)

[1]A sovereign state is usually defined / as one [whose citizens are free to determine their own affairs / without interference (from any agency / beyond its territorial borders)].
S V 소유격 관계대명사
주권 국가는 보통 정의된다 / 국가라고 [그것의 시민들이 자신들의 일을 자유롭게 결정하는 / 간섭 없이 (어떤 기관으로부터의 / 영토의 국경 너머)]

↳ **도입(정의):** 주권 국가란 타국의 간섭을 받지 않고 시민들이 자유롭게 결정할 수 있는 국가임.

(C) [2]But / freedom in space (and limits on its territorial extent) / is merely one characteristic (of sovereignty).
S V C
🔑 주어진 글의 '국경 너머의 간섭 없음'이 (B)의 공간의 자유로 이어짐. 역접 연결어 But으로 주권 국가의 다른 중요한 특징인 시간적 자유를 제시함.
하지만 / 공간적 자유는 (그리고 영토 범위에 대한 경계는) / 단지 한 가지 특징일 뿐이다 (주권의)

주제문
[3]Freedom in time (and limits on its temporal extent) / is equally important and probably more fundamental.
S V C
시간적 자유가 (그리고 시간의 범위에 대한 경계가) / 동등하게 중요하며 아마 더 근본적일 것이다

↳ 시간적 자유가 주권의 더 근본적인 특징임.

🔑 (C)의 시간의 자유를 구체적으로 설명함. ★<A as 원급 as B>: A는 B만큼 ~한/하게

(B) [4]Sovereignty and citizenship require / freedom from the past / at least as much as freedom from contemporary powers.
S V O
주권과 시민권은 필요로 한다 / 과거로부터의 자유를 / 최소한 동시대 권력으로부터의 자유만큼이나

↳ **세부 사항:** 주권과 시민권을 얻기 위해선 과거에서 벗어나는 것이 필요함.

해석

[1]주권 국가는 보통 그것의 시민들이 영토의 국경 너머 어떤 기관으로부터의 간섭 없이 자신들의 일을 자유롭게 결정하는 국가라고 정의된다. (C) [2]하지만 공간적 자유는 (그리고 영토 범위에 대한 경계는) 단지 주권의 한 가지 특징일 뿐이다. [3]시간적 자유가 (그리고 시간의 범위에 대한 경계가) 동등하게 중요하며 아마 더 근본적일 것이다. (B) [4]주권과 시민권은 최소한 동시대 권력으로부터의 자유만큼이나 과거로부터의 자유를 필요로 한다. [5]국민들이 과거에 그들의 조상들에 의해 채택된 행동 방침을, 또는 한때 그들이 전념했던 행동 방침조차도 바꿀 능력이 없다면 그 어떤 국가도 자주적일 수 없을 것이다. (A) [6]공동체가 깨뜨리기를 원할 수도 있는 선조의 전통에 매여 있는 한 어떤 시민도 그 공동체의 완전한 구성원이 될 수 없을 것인데, 이는 Sophocles의 비극에서 Antigone의 문제이다.(▶ Antigone가 왕과 대립하며 사회의 관습을 지키고 죽게 되는 비극으로 '전통'과 '국가[공동체]의 질서'가 대비됨.) [7]따라서 주권과 시민권은 공간의 경계뿐만 아니라 시간의 경계 또한 필요로 한다.

★<If+S'+동사의 과거형 ~, S+조동사 과거형+동사원형 ...>: 만약 ~라면, …할 텐데 (가정법 과거)

[5]No state could be sovereign // if its inhabitants lacked the ability (to change *a course of action* (adopted by their forefathers / in the past), / or even *one* [to which they once committed themselves]).

S V C 부사절 접속사 S' V' O' = 전치사+관계대명사 과거분사구 (= a course of action) S''(= its inhabitants) V''

그 어떤 국가도 자주적일 수 없을 것이다 // 국민들이 능력이 없다면 (행동 방침을 바꿀 (그들의 조상들에 의해 채택된 / 과거에) / 또는 행동 방침조차도 [한때 그들(국민들)이 전념했던])

↳ 국민들이 과거의 행동 방침을 바꾸지 못하는 국가는 자주적이라 할 수 없음.

(A) [6]No citizen could be a full member of the community // so long as she was tied / to *ancestral traditions* [with which the community might wish to break] — / the problem of Antigone / in Sophocles' tragedy.

S V C 부사절 접속사(~하는 한) 전치사+관계대명사 S' V' O'

어떤 시민도 그 공동체의 완전한 구성원이 될 수 없을 것이다 // 매여 있는 한 / 선조의 전통에 [공동체가 깨뜨리기를 원할 수도 있는] / Antigone의 문제 / Sophocles의 비극에서

🔑 (B)의 조상이 과거에 채택한 행동 방침이 ancestral traditions로 연결됨.

↳ **부연 설명:** 공동체가 원하지 않는 선조(과거)의 전통에 매여 있으면 그 공동체의 구성원이 될 수 없음.

<not only A but also B>: A뿐만 아니라 B도

[7]Sovereignty and citizenship / thus / require not only borders in space, but also borders in time.

S V O_1 O_2

주권과 시민권은 / 따라서 / 공간의 경계뿐만 아니라 시간의 경계도 필요로 한다

↳ **결론:** 주권과 시민권은 영토의 경계뿐만 아니라 과거와의 경계 또한 중요함.

어휘

affair 일[문제]; 사건
interference 간섭, 방해
agency (정부) 기관; 단체
border 국경; 경계
extent 범위, 정도; 크기, 규모
merely 단지, 그저
temporal 시간의; 세속적인; 일시적인
fundamental 근본적인
citizenship 시민권
contemporary 동시대의; 현대의
inhabitant 주민, 거주자
course of action 행동 방침
adopt 채택하다; 입양하다
forefather 조상[선조]
commit 전념[헌신]하다; (범죄를) 저지르다
ancestral 선조[조상]의
tragedy 비극 (작품)

⊕ 안티고네(Antigone): 고대 그리스의 비극작가 소포클레스가 쓴 희곡. 오이디푸스의 두 왕자가 왕위를 놓고 싸우다가 모두 죽자, 오이디푸스의 딸인 안티고네는 새로운 왕이자 삼촌인 크레온의 명령을 어기고 반역을 일으켜 죽은 왕자의 장례를 치르고 죽게 되는 비극.

정답 가이드

주어진 글은 주권 국가는 국경 너머의 기관으로부터 간섭을 받지 않고 시민들이 자신들의 일을 자유롭게 결정하는 국가라는 내용이다. 이러한 국경 안에서의 자유는 (C)의 freedom in space로 연결되는데, 역접 연결어 But이 함께 쓰여 공간적 자유는 주권의 한 가지 특징일 뿐이며 시간적 자유도 중요하다고 했다. (B)는 (C)의 시간적 자유를 구체적으로 설명하고 있으므로 (C) 뒤에 이어져야 한다. (A)는 (B)에서 말한 조상의 행동 방침, 즉 선조의 전통에 매여 비극을 초래한 구체적인 예를 들고 결론짓고 있으므로 마지막에 오는 것이 적절하다.

오답 클리닉

① (A) - (C) - (B) (3%)
(A)는 (B)에서 언급한 과거로부터의 자유에 대한 부연 설명에 해당하므로, 공간적 자유의 관점에서 주권을 설명한 주어진 글 뒤에 올 수 없다.

② (B) - (A) - (C) (25%) / ③ (B) - (C) - (A) (25%)
(B)의 과거로부터의 자유는 (C)의 시간적 자유를 구체적으로 설명하는 내용이므로 (C) 뒤에 와야 한다. 또한 (B)는 과거로부터의 자유에 대해 말하고 있으므로, 공간적 자유와 관련된 주어진 글 뒤에 바로 연결되는 것은 흐름상 어색하다.

④ (C) - (A) - (B) (14%)
(A)는 공동체가 깨길 원하는 전통에 매여 있으면 공동체의 일원이 될 수 없다며 (B)의 과거로부터의 자유를 부연 설명하므로 (B) 뒤에 와야 한다.

01 + 글의 제목 (20학년도 대수능 24번 | 정답률 68%) ②

구문분석 & 직독직해

환경 외래종의 침입을 막는 생물 다양성

[1]Invasions (of natural communities) (by non-indigenous species) / are currently rated / as one (of the most important global-scale environmental problems).
S / V / 전치사(~로(서))
★<rate A as B(A를 B로 여기다[평가하다])>의 수동형
침입은 (자연 군집의) (외래종에 의한) / 현재 여겨진다 / 하나로 (가장 중요한 세계적인 규모의 환경 문제 중의)

[2]The loss (of biodiversity) / has generated / concern (over the consequences for ecosystem functioning) //
S₁ / V₁ / O
손실은 (생물 다양성의) / 일으켰다 / 염려를 (생태계 기능에 대한 영향에 관해) //
↳ **문제점:** 외래종이 침입하면 생물 다양성이 줄어들어 생태계 기능에 영향을 주므로 큰 환경 문제임.

(both = the loss of biodiversity and ecosystem functioning)
and thus understanding the relationship (between both) / has become a major focus / in ecological research / during the last two decades.
S₂(동명사구) / V₂(단수) / C
그리하여 관계를 이해하는 것은 (둘 사이의) / 주된 초점이 되어왔다 / 생태계 연구에서 / 지난 20년 동안
↳ 생물 다양성 손실과 생태계 기능의 관계를 이해하는 것이 중요함.

주제문 🔑 군집의 생물 다양성이 높을수록 침입하기 어려움.
[3]The "biodiversity-invasibility hypothesis" (by Elton) / suggests // that high diversity increases the competitive environment (of communities) / and makes them more difficult to invade.
S / V / 명사절 접속사 / S′ / V′₁ / O′₁ / V′₂ / O′₂(= communities) / C′₂ (that절: suggests의 O(명사절))
'생물 다양성-침입 가능성 가설'은 (Elton에 의한) / 시사한다 // 높은 (생물) 다양성이 경쟁력 있는 환경을 증가시킨다는 것을 (군집의) / 그래서 (외래종이) 군집을 침입하기 더 어렵게 만든다(는 것을)
↳ **해결책:** 생물 다양성을 높이면 외래종이 침입하기 어려움. (생물 다양성-침입 가능성 가설)

[4]Numerous biodiversity experiments have been conducted / since Elton's time //
S₁ / V₁ / 전치사(~ 이후로)
수많은 생물 다양성 실험이 실행되어 왔다 / Elton의 시대 이후로 //

and several mechanisms have been proposed / to explain the often observed negative relationship (between diversity and invasibility).
S₂ / V₂ / 목적(~하기 위해)
그리고 여러 방법이 제안되어 왔다 / 종종 관찰되는 부적 관계성을 설명하기 위해 (다양성과 침입성 사이의)
↳ 생물 다양성과 침입 가능성 사이의 부적 관계성을 설명하기 위해 실험이 실시됨.

[5]Beside the decreased chance (of empty ecological niches) / but the increased probability (of *competitors* [that prevent invasion success]), /
전치사(~ 외에) / Beside의 O(명사구 병렬) / 주격 관계대명사
줄어든 가능성 외에도 (비어 있는 생태적 지위의) / 하지만 늘어난 가망성 (외에도) (경쟁자들의 [침입 성공을 막는]) /

diverse communities are assumed / to use resources more completely / and, therefore, (to) limit the ability of invaders (to establish).
S / V / C(to-v구 병렬)
🔑 종이 다양한 군집이 외래종의 침입 능력을 제한함.
다양한 군집은 간주된다 / 자원을 더 완전히 쓰는 것으로 / 그리고 따라서 침입자의 능력을 제한하는 것으로 (정착하는)
↳ **부연 설명 1:** 부적 관계성(생물 다양성이 크면 외래종의 정착이 어려움)의 이유(1. 외래종이 차지할 빈 생태적 지위가 적고 토착종들이 외래종의 침입을 막음. 2. 토착종들이 자원을 모두 써버려서 없음.)

[6]Further, / more diverse communities are believed / to be more stable //
S / V / C
뿐만 아니라 / 더 다양한 군집은 여겨진다 / 더 안정적인 것으로 //

(they = more diverse communities)
because they use a broader range of niches / than species-poor communities.
부사절 접속사 / S′ / V′ / O′
그것들이 더 폭넓은 범위의 생태적 지위를 이용하기 때문에 / 종이 빈약한 군집들보다
↳ **부연 설명 2:** 부적 관계성(생물 다양성이 크면 외래종의 정착이 어려움)의 이유(3. 사용하는 생태적 지위들이 더 광범위해서 생태적 기능이 더 안정적임.)

해석

[1]외래종에 의한 자연 군집의 침입은 현재 가장 중요한 세계적인 규모의 환경 문제 중의 하나로 여겨진다. [2]생물 다양성의 손실은 생태계 기능에 대한 영향에 관해 염려를 일으켰고 그리하여 둘 사이의 관계를 이해하는 것은 지난 20년 동안 생태계 연구에서 주된 초점이 되어왔다. [3]Elton에 의한 '생물 다양성-침입 가능성' 가설은 높은 (생물) 다양성이 군집의 경쟁력 있는 환경을 증가시키므로 (외래종이) 군집을 침입하기 더 어렵게 만든다는 것을 시사한다. [4]수많은 생물 다양성 실험이 Elton의 시대 이후로 실시되어 왔고, 종종 관찰되는 다양성과 침입성 사이의 부적 관계성을 설명하기 위해 여러 방법이 제안되어 왔다. [5]비어 있는 생태적 지위의 가능성은 줄어들지만 침입 성공을 막는 경쟁자들의 가망성은 늘어나는 것 외에도(▶ 기존의 종들이 이미 다양하게 있어서 외래종이 차지할 빈 생태적 지위가 있을 가능성이 없는데다가, 외래종의 침입을 막을 가능성도 큰 상황이라는 의미), 다양한 군집은 자원을 더 완전히 써서 침입자의 정착하는 능력을 제한하는 것으로 간주된다. [6]뿐만 아니라, 더 다양한 군집은 종이 빈약한 군집보다 더 폭넓은 범위의 생태적 지위를 이용하기 때문에 더 안정적인 것으로 여겨진다.

어휘

invasion 침입, 침략; (권리 등의) 침해
cf. invade 침입하다; 침해하다
community (생물의) 군집; 공동체
global-scale 세계적인 규모의
consequence 영향, 결과
ecological 생태계[학]의
numerous 수많은, 무수한
conduct (업무를) 실시하다, 수행하다; 행동하다
mechanism 방법, 기법; (기계) 장치
probability 가망성; 있을 법함
establish 정착하다; 설립[설치]하다
stable 안정적인; 변동이 없는
broad 폭넓은, 광범위한
[선택지] carve out (땅을) 개척하다; 잘라내다
resist (적을) 막아내다, 격퇴하다; 저항[반항]하다
secure 안정적인, 튼튼한
⊕ 생물 다양성-침입 가능성 가설(biodiversity-invasibility hypothesis): 생물 다양성이 풍부할수록, 외래종의 침입이 어렵다는 1950년대 Charles Elton의 가설.
⊕ 부적 관계성(negative relationship): 변인 X의 값이 커지면 변인 Y의 값이 작아지는 경우, 혹은 변인 X의 값이 작아지면 변인 Y의 값이 커지는 경우, X와 Y 간에 존재하는 관계. 이 지문에서 X와 Y는 각각 생물 다양성과 침입 가능성임.

정답 가이드

외래종의 자연 군집 침입은 현재 중요한 환경 문제 중 하나인데, Elton의 '생물 다양성-침입 가능성 가설'을 통해 생물 다양성이 높은 군집은 외래종이 침입하기 어렵다고 했다. 그 뒤에 생물 다양성이 어떻게 외래종의 침입을 막아내는지 설명하고 있으므로 글의 제목으로 가장 적절한 것은 ② 'Guardian of Ecology: Diversity Resists Invasion(생태계의 수호자, 즉 다양성이 침입을 막아낸다)'이다.

오답 클리닉

① Carve Out More Empty Ecological Spaces! (3%)
비어 있는 더 많은 생태 공간(×)을 개척하라!
비어 있는 생태 공간은 생물 다양성의 특징(비어 있는 생태적 지위가 적음)과 반대됨.

③ Grasp All, Lose All: Necessity of Species-poor Ecology (6%)
모든 것을 쥐면, 모든 것을 잃는다, 즉 종이 빈약한 생태계의 필요성(×)
생태계의 종이 다양할수록 외래종의 침입을 막는다고 했으므로 글의 내용과 반대됨.

④ Challenges in Testing Biodiversity-Invasibility Hypothesis (8%)
생물 다양성-침입 가능성 가설을 시험하는 것에서의 난제(×)
가설 시험에 있었던 어려움에 대한 내용이 아님.

⑤ Diversity Dilemma: The More Competitive, the Less Secure (15%)
다양성의 딜레마, 즉 더 경쟁력이 있을수록 덜 안정적이다(×)
종이 다양할수록 더 경쟁력 있고 더 안정적이라고 했으므로 글의 내용과 반대됨.

The 주의 핵심어들이 정적 관계인지 부적 관계인지 헷갈리지 않도록 유의한다.

02 + 빈칸 추론 〈19학년도 6월 모평 33번 | 정답률 39%〉 ①

구문분석 & 직독직해

예술 소설의 주관적 특징

주제문 소설을 전기(개인의 이야기)로 규정함.
*<define A as B>: A를 B로 규정하다 / 주격 관계대명사

[1]Theorists of the novel commonly define the genre / as *a biographical form* [that came to prominence / in the late eighteenth and nineteenth centuries] / (**to establish the individual character** / as a replacement for traditional sources (of cultural authority)).

S(복수) V(복수) O 전치사(~로(서)) 전치사(~로(서))

소설의 이론가들은 공통적으로 그 장르를 규정한다 / 전기(傳記) 형식으로 [두드러졌던 / 18세기 말과 19세기에] / (독자적인 등장인물을 설정하는 / 전통적인 원천에 대한 대체물로 (문화적 권위의))

↳ 소설을 다른 사람과 구별되는 독특한 등장인물에 대한 전기적 형식의 이야기로 규정함.

[2]The novel, / (Georg Lukács argues), / "seeks, / (by giving form), / to uncover [and] (to) construct the concealed totality of life" / in the interiorized life story (of its heroes).

S 삽입절 V 전치사구 삽입 O(to-v 병렬) to uncover와 (to) construct의 공통 O

소설은 / (Georg Lukács가 주장하기를) / "~하고자 한다 / (형식을 제공함으로써) / 삶의 숨겨진 전체를 드러내고 구성하(고자)" / 내면화된 삶의 이야기에서 (주인공들의)

↳ **특징 1:** 주인공의 내면화된 삶의 이야기로 삶의 전체를 보여줌.

주인공이 마음속 권위를 탐구하는 내용임. → 개인적 특징 *within은 전치사로 주인공 내면에 있는 권위를 의미함.

[3]The typical plot (of the novel) / is the protagonist's quest (for authority within), / therefore, // when that authority can no longer be discovered outside.

S V C 부사절 접속사(시간) S′ V′

전형적인 줄거리는 (소설의) / 주인공의 탐구이다 (마음속 권위에 대한) / 따라서 // 그 권위가 더 이상 외부에서 발견될 수 없을 때

↳ **특징 2:** 주인공이 외부가 아닌 내면의 권위를 탐구함.

[4]By this accounting, / there are no objective goals in novels, // (there is) only the subjective goal (of seeking *the law* [that is necessarily created / by the individual]).

V_1 S_1 S_2 = 주격 관계대명사

개인이 만든 법칙을 찾는 주관적 목표만 있음. → 주관적 특징

이 설명에 의하면 / 소설에 객관적인 목표는 없다 / 주관적 목표만 있을 뿐이다 (법칙을 찾는 [반드시 만들어지는 / 개인에 의해])

↳ **특징 3:** 객관적 목표가 아닌 주관적 목표만 있음.

개인의 의식에 의해 소설 속 행위가 주관적으로 판단됨.

[5]The distinctions (between crime and heroism), / therefore, / [or] (between madness and wisdom), / become purely subjective ones / in a novel, / (being) judged / by the quality or complexity (of the individual's consciousness).

S 전치사구 병렬 V C

구별은 (범죄와 영웅주의의) / 따라서 / 또는 (광기와 지혜의) / 전적으로 주관적인 것이 된다 / 소설에서 / 그리고 판단된다 / 특성이나 복잡성에 의해 (개인의 의식의)

분사구문(= and they are judged ~) *부대상황을 나타내는 분사구문으로 앞에는 being이 생략됨.

↳ **특징 3의 예:** 소설 속 행위의 구별은 개인의 의식에 의해 판단되는 주관적인 것임.

해석

[1]소설의 이론가들은 공통적으로 그 장르를 문화적 권위의 전통적인 원천에 대한 대체물로 독자적인 등장인물을 설정하는, 18세기 말과 19세기에 두드러졌던 전기(傳記) 형식으로 규정한다.(▶ 소설이 나온 이후부터 문화적 권위 원천이 개인으로 바뀌었다는 의미) [2]소설은, Georg Lukács가 주장하기를, 주인공들의 내면화된 삶의 이야기에서 "형식을 제공함으로써, 삶의 숨겨진 전체를 드러내고 구성하고자 한다." [3]따라서 소설의 전형적인 줄거리는 그 권위가 더 이상 외부에서 발견될 수 없을 때 마음속 권위에 대한 주인공의 탐구이다. [4]이 설명에 의하면 소설에 객관적인 목표는 없으며, 반드시 개인에 의해 만들어지는 법칙을 찾는 주관적 목표만 있을 뿐이다. [5]따라서 범죄와 영웅주의, 또는 광기와 지혜의 구별은 소설에서 전적으로 주관적인 것이 되고, 개인의 의식의 특성이나 복잡성에 의해 판단된다.

어휘

theorist 이론가
biographical 전기의, 일대기의
prominence 두드러짐, 현저함
replacement 대체[교체](물)
authority 권위, 권력; 영향력
construct 구성하다; 건설하다
totality 전체; 총액
interiorize 내면화하다
protagonist 주인공
quest 탐구, 탐색
account 설명하다, 밝히다; 생각하다
objective 객관적인(↔ subjective 주관적인)
distinction 구별; 차이
heroism 영웅주의
consciousness 의식, 생각
[선택지] cast doubt on ~을 의심하다
identity 신원, 신분; 동질감
collective 집단적인

정답 가이드

빈칸 문장과 선택지로 보면, 소설 장르는 전기 형식으로 규정되며, '무엇을' 문화적 권위의 전통적 원천의 대체물로 하는 전기 형식인지를 찾아야 한다. 즉, 18세기 말 이전까지의 문학 장르들이 가지고 있었던 전통적 원천을 소설이 다른 무엇인가로 대체한 것이다. 빈칸 문장에서 소설은 한 개인의 일생을 기록한 '전기'라 했고, 이어지는 설명에서 소설은 주인공의 내면, 마음속 권위에 대한 주인공의 탐구라고 했다. 또한, 소설은 주관적이며 범죄와 영웅주의 등을 구별하는 것도 개인 특성이나 복잡성에 의해 주관적으로 판단된다고 했다. 이를 종합하면 소설 장르는 다른 이들과 구별되는 독특하고 주관적인 등장인물을 설정하는 것이므로, 빈칸에 들어갈 말로 가장 적절한 것은 ① 'to establish the individual character(독자적인 등장인물을 설정하는)'이다.

오답 클리닉

② to cast doubt on the identity of a criminal (12%)
범죄자의 신원을 의심하는
범죄자의 신원에 관한 언급은 없음.

③ to highlight the complex structure of social consciousness (19%)
사회적 의식의 복잡한 구조를 강조하는
사회적 의식이 아닌 개인적이고 주관적인 의식을 강조하는 것이므로 틀림.

④ to make the objective distinction between crime and heroism (19%) 범죄와 영웅주의를 객관적으로 구별하는
문장 5에서 범죄와 영웅주의의 구별은 개인의 의식에 의해 주관적으로 판단된다고 했으므로, 글의 내용과 반대됨.

⑤ to develop the inner self of a hero into a collective wisdom (11%)
주인공의 내적 자아를 집단적 지혜로 발전시켜나가는
주인공의 내면을 이야기한다는 내용은 있으나 집단적 지혜로 확장된다는 내용은 없음.

03 ✦ 문장 넣기 〈20학년도 9월 모평 38번 | 정답률 56%〉 ④

구문분석 & 직독직해 사회 인권의 이상과 현실 간의 격차 이해

1 There is obviously a wide gap (between the promises of the Universal Declaration of Human Rights in 1948 and the real world of human-rights violations).
V(단수) S / 명사구 병렬
분명히 큰 격차가 있다 (1948년 세계 인권 선언의 약속과 인권 침해의 현실 세계 사이에는)

2 In so far as we sympathize with the victims, // we may criticize the UN and its member governments / for failing to keep their promises.
부사절 접속사(~하는 한) / S V O / for의 O(동명사구)
우리가 피해자들에게 공감하는 한 // 우리는 UN과 그 회원국 정부들을 비난할 수도 있을 것이다 / 약속을 지키지 못한 것에 대해
↳ **도입:** 우리는 세계 인권 선언과 인권 침해의 현실 사이의 큰 격차를 비난할 수도 있음.

(①) 3 However, / we cannot understand / the gap (between human-rights ideals and the real world of human-rights violations) / by sympathy or by legal analysis.
S V O / 명사구 병렬
그러나 / 우리는 이해할 수 없다 / 격차를 (인권의 이상과 인권 침해의 현실 세계 사이의) / 공감이나 법률 분석으로

주제문
(②) 4 Rather, / it requires investigation by the various social sciences (of the causes (of social conflict and political oppression), / and of the interaction (between national and international politics)).
(= understanding the gap) / S V O / 전치사구 병렬(investigation 수식)
오히려 / 그것(격차를 이해하는 것)은 다양한 사회 과학의 연구를 필요로 한다 (원인에 대한 (사회 갈등과 정치 억압의) / 그리고 상호 작용에 대한 (국내 정치와 국제 정치 사이의))
↳ 인권의 이상과 인권 침해의 현실 사이의 격차는 공감이나 법률 분석이 아닌 사회 과학 연구로 이해할 수 있음.

🔑 UN이 인권을 국제법과 국제 정치에 도입함.
(③) 5 The UN introduced the concept of human rights / into international law and politics.
S V O
UN은 인권이라는 개념을 도입했다 / 국제법과 국제 정치에

🔑 인권을 우선시하지 않는 내용이 역접 연결어 however로 이어짐.
(④ 6 The field (of international politics) / is, however, dominated / by *states and other powerful actors* (such as multinational corporations) [that have priorities (other than human rights)].
S(단수) V(단수) / 주격 관계대명사 / ~이외의
분야는 (국제 정치의) / 그러나 지배된다 / 국가 및 다른 영향력 있는 행위자들에 의해 (다국적 기업과 같은) [우선 사항들이 있는 (인권 이외의)]
↳ **원인:** 인권을 도입해도 국제 정치는 인권을 우선시하지 않는 국가와 기업에 의해 지배됨.

해석

1 1948년 세계 인권 선언의 약속과 인권 침해의 현실 세계 사이에는 분명히 큰 격차가 있다. 2 우리가 피해자들에게 공감하는 한, 우리는 UN과 그 회원국 정부들을 약속을 지키지 못한 것에 대해 비난할 수도 있을 것이다. (①) 3 그러나 우리는 인권의 이상과 인권 침해의 현실 세계 사이의 격차를 공감이나 법률 분석으로 이해할 수 없다. (②) 4 오히려 그것(격차를 이해하는 것)은 사회 갈등과 정치 억압의 원인과 국내 정치와 국제 정치 사이의 상호 작용에 대한 다양한 사회 과학의 연구를 필요로 한다. (③) 5 UN은 국제법과 국제 정치에 인권이라는 개념을 도입했다. (④ 6 그러나 국제 정치 분야는 인권 이외의 우선 사항들이 있는 국가 및 (다국적 기업과 같은) 다른 영향력 있는 행위자들에 의해 지배된다.) 7 세계 각국 정부가 인권을 선언하지만, 그것을 시행하는 데 매우 변동이 심한 기록을 갖고 있다는 것은 인권 분야의 주된 특징이다. (⑤) 8 우리는 이것이 왜 그런지를 이해해야 한다.

어휘

violation 침해; 위반
sympathize 공감하다; 동정하다
cf. sympathy 공감; 동정
ideal 이상(적인)
legal 법률의; 합법적인
investigation 연구; 수사
national 국내의, 국가의
introduce 도입하다; 소개하다
field 분야; 현장; 들판
dominate 지배하다; 우위를 차지하다
multinational 다국적의
corporation 기업, 회사
priority 우선 (사항)

[7]It is a leading feature (of the human-rights field) // that the governments of the world proclaim human rights / but have a highly variable record (of implementing them).

(진주어(명사절) / 가주어 V / C / 명사절 접속사 / S′ / V′₁ / O′₁ / V′₂ / O′₂ / (= human rights))

다른 우선순위들 때문에 인권이 변동적으로 시행됨.

(~은) 주된 특징이다 (인권 분야의) // 세계 각국 정부가 인권을 선언하는 것은 / 그러나 매우 변동이 심한 기록을 갖고 있는 것 (그것(인권)을 시행하는 데)

(⑤) [8]We must understand // why this is so.

(S / V / O(명사절))

우리는 이해해야 한다 // 이것이 왜 그런지를

↳ **결과:** 각국에서 인권을 선언해도 그 시행이 일정하지 않음.

leading 주된; 선두적인
feature 특징(을 이루다); 특집(으로 다루다)
proclaim 선언[선포]하다
variable 변동이 심한, 가변적인
implement 시행하다; 도구

⊕ 세계 인권 선언(Universal Declaration of Human Rights): 1948년 12월 10일 파리에서 개최된 제3회 UN 총회에서 채택된 인권에 대한 선언으로 제2차 세계 대전에서의 인권 침해에 대한 반성과 인간의 기본 권리 존중을 위해 채택됨.

정답 가이드

주어진 문장은 국제 정치 분야를 지배하는 국가 및 영향력 있는 행위자들에게 인권은 우선 사항이 아니라는 현실에 관한 내용이다. 역접 연결어 however로 이어진 것으로 보아 그 앞에는 반대로 국제 정치 분야에서 인권을 중요하게 여기는 내용이 제시되어야 한다. ④의 앞 문장은 UN이 국제 정치에 인권을 도입했다는 내용으로, 주어진 문장과 역접 연결어로 이어지는 것이 자연스럽다. 또한, ④의 뒤 문장은 주어진 문장의 내용으로 인해 세계 각국에서 인권이 변동적으로 시행된다는 결과에 해당하므로 주어진 문장이 들어가기에 가장 적절한 곳은 ④이다.

오답 클리닉

① (3%) 약속이 지켜지지 않은 것에 대해 UN과 회원국을 비난할 수도 있지만, 우리는 인권의 이상과 현실 사이의 격차를 이해할 수 없다는 내용 연결이 자연스럽다. 주어진 문장의 international politics가 언급되기 전이므로 정답이 될 수 없다.

② (7%) 격차를 이해하기 위해서는 공감이나 법률 분석보다 다양한 사회 과학 연구가 필요하다는 내용이다.

③ (22%) 사회 과학적 견지에서 국제 사회 인권의 이상과 현실을 설명하는 흐름은 자연스럽다. UN이 국제법과 국제 정치에 인권을 도입했다는 내용은 '이상'에 해당한다.

The 주의 인권의 '현실'에 해당하는 주어진 문장이 역접으로 이어지기 위해서는 앞에 '이상'이 먼저 제시되어야 한다.

⑤ (13%) 앞 내용을 this로 지칭하면서 이것이 왜 그런지 이해해야 한다고 마무리하는 내용이다.

01 ✦ 함의 추론 〈20학년도 9월 모평 21번 | 정답률 53%〉 ①

구문분석 & 직독직해

문화 관광업으로 인한 전통 문화 보존의 어려움

★<see A as B(A를 B로 여기다)>의 수동형

[1]For a long time, / tourism was seen / as *a huge monster* (invading the areas of indigenous peoples, / introducing them to the evils (of the modern world)).

(S / V / C; (= indigenous peoples); ★invading 이하는 a huge monster를 수식하는 현재분사구; ★<introduce A to B>: A에게 B를 접하게 하다[소개하다]; 분사구문(= and it introduced ~))

오랫동안 / 관광업은 여겨졌다 / 거대한 괴물로 (토착민의 영역을 침범한 / 그리고 그들(토착민)에게 악을 접하게 한 (현대 세계의))

[2]However, / research has shown // that this is not *the correct way* (to perceive it).

(S / V / 명사절 접속사 S' V' C'; has shown의 O(명사절); (= tourism))

그러나 / 연구는 보여주었다 // 이것이 올바른 방법이 아니라는 것을 (그것(관광업)을 인식하는)

[3]In most places, / tourists are welcome // and indigenous people see tourism / as a path (to modernity and economic development).

(S_1 V_1 C / S_2 V_2 O C)

대부분의 지역에서 / 관광객은 환영받는다 // 그리고 토착민은 관광을 여긴다 / 길로 (현대적인 것과 경제 발전에 이르는)

↳ **도입:** 관광업을 부정적으로 보는 시각과 긍정적으로 보는 시각이 있음.

주제문

[4]But / such development is always a two-edged sword.

(S / V / C)

그러나 / 그러한 발전은 언제나 양날의 칼이다

↳ 관광업을 통한 발전에는 양면성이 있음.

🔑 관광업으로 전통과 문화적 독특함을 상실함.

[5]Tourism can mean progress, // but most often also means the loss (of traditions and cultural uniqueness).

(S_1 V_1 O_1 / S_2 V_2 O_2)

관광업은 발전을 의미할 수 있다 // 하지만 대부분은 흔히 상실을 의미하기도 한다 (전통과 문화적 독특성의)

↳ **세부 사항:** 관광업으로 발전하지만, 전통과 문화적 독특성은 사라짐.

[6]And, of course, / there are examples (of 'cultural pollution', 'vulgarization' and 'phony-folk-cultures').

(V S)

그리고 물론 / 예들이 있다 ('문화 오염', '상스럽게 함(저속화)', 그리고 '가짜 민속 문화'와 같은)

[7]The background (for such characteristics) / is often more or less romantic / and the normative ideas (of a former or prevailing authenticity).

(S / V / C_1 / C_2; (= cultural pollution, ~ phony-folk-cultures))

배경은 (그러한 특징들의) / 흔히 다소 낭만적이다 / 그리고 규정하는 생각이다 (이전의 혹은 (현재) 지배적인 진짜(문화)에 대해)

↳ **부연 설명:** 문화 오염, 상스럽게 함, 가짜 민속 문화는 관광객들이 현대적인 것과 다른 전통 문화를 막연히 이상적인 것으로 여기고, 진짜 문화는 어떠해야 한다고 규정하는 생각으로 야기됨 → 있는 그대로의 전통 문화를 보존하기 어려움.

🔑 관광객이 방문해서 볼 수 있는 보존된 고대 문화가 있어야 함.

[8]Ideally (to some) / there should exist *ancient cultures* (for modern consumers / to gaze at, / or even (to) step into for a while, / while (they are) travelling or on holiday).

(V / S / to-v의 의미상 주어 / to-v구 병렬 / to-v구 병렬 / 부사절 접속사(~ 동안에))

이상적으로 (일부 사람들에게는) / 고대 문화가 존재해야 한다 (현대 소비자들이 / 바라볼 / 혹은 심지어 잠시라도 들어가 볼 수 있는 / 여행이나 휴가 동안에)

↳ 이상적으로 관광객들이 방문해서 볼 수 있는 문화적 독특성을 간직한 고대 문화가 있어야 한다고 생각함.

[9]This is *a cage model* [that is difficult to defend / in *a global world* [where we all, / (indigenous or not), / are part (of the same social fabric)]].

((= 앞 문장) / 주격 관계대명사 V' C' 형용사 difficult 수식 / 관계부사 S'' / 삽입어구 / V'' C'')

이것은 우리 모델이다 [지키기 어려운 / 지구촌 세계에서 [우리 모두가 / (토착민이든 아니든) / 일부인 (같은 사회 구조의)]]

↳ 우리 모델은 모두가 영향을 주고 받으며 같은 현대 사회를 살아가는 세상에서 지키기 힘듦 → 옛 문화를 있는 그대로 보존하기 어려움.

해석

[1]오랫동안 관광업은 토착민의 영역을 침범하고 그들(토착민)에게 현대 세계의 악을 접하게 한 거대한 괴물로 여겨졌다. [2]그러나 연구는 이것이 그것(관광업)을 인식하는 올바른 방법이 아니라는 것을 보여주었다. [3]대부분의 지역에서 관광객은 환영받고 토착민은 관광을 현대적인 것과 경제 발전에 이르는 길로 여긴다. [4]그러나 그러한 발전은 언제나 양날의 칼이다. [5]관광업은 발전을 의미할 수 있지만, 대부분은 흔히 전통과 문화적 독특성의 상실을 의미하기도 한다. [6]그리고 물론 '문화 오염', '상스럽게 함(저속화)', '가짜 민속 문화'와 같은 예들이 있다. [7]그러한 특징들의 배경은 흔히 다소 낭만적이고, 이전의 혹은 (현재) 지배적인 진짜(문화)에 대해 규정하는 생각이다.(▶ 관광객들이 갖고 있는 전통 문화에 대한 막연한 낭만적[이상적] 생각과 진짜 문화란 어떠해야 한다는 규범적 생각에 맞추기 위해 전통 문화가 오염되고 저속화, 가짜 문화 등이 생겨났다는 것. 즉 관광객의 구미에 맞추기 위해 가짜 문화가 등장했다는 의미) [8]이상적으로 (일부 사람들에게는) 현대 소비자들이 여행이나 휴가 동안에 바라보거나 혹은 심지어 잠시라도 들어가 볼 수 있는 고대 문화가 존재해야 한다. [9]이것은 토착민이든 아니든 우리 모두가 같은 사회 구조의 일부인 지구촌 세계에서 지키기 어려운 우리 모델이다.

어휘

invade 침범하다
perceive 인식하다
modernity 현대적인 것, 현대적임
two-edged sword 양날의 칼
uniqueness 독특성
phony-folk-culture 가짜 민속 문화
more or less 다소 어느 정도
normative 규정하는; 규범적인
former 이전[과거]의
prevailing 지배적인, 우세한
authenticity 진짜임; 진정성, 진실성
gaze at ~을 바라보다[응시하다]
cage 우리, 새장
fabric 구조; 직물, 천
[선택지] preserve 보존하다
restore 복원하다; 회복시키다
cultural heritage 문화 유산
neglect 방치하다; 도외시하다
conservation 보존, 보호
confine 제한[국한]하다
policy 정책
regulation 규정; 규제

정답 가이드

관광업에 의한 발전을 양날의 칼에 비유하며 관광업이 현대화와 경제 발전을 이뤄주지만, 전통과 문화적 독특성의 상실을 초래한다고도 했다. 일부는 이상적으로 관광객들이 방문해서 볼 수 있는 옛 문화적 독특성을 간직한 고대 문화가 있어야 한다고 여기지만, 이는 지구촌 세계에서 지키기 어려운 '우리 모델(a cage model)'이라 했으므로 밑줄 친 부분이 의미하는 바로 가장 적절한 것은 ① 'preserving a past culture in its original form for consumption(소비를 위해 과거 문화를 그것의 원래 형태로 보존하는 것)'이다.

오답 클리닉

② restoring local cultural heritages that have long been neglected (8%) 오랫동안 방치되어 있던(×) 지역 문화 유산을 복원하는 것(×)
문화 유산이 방치되었다는 내용은 없으며 이를 복원하는 내용도 아님.

③ limiting public access to prehistoric sites for conservation (15%)
보존을 위해(×) 선사시대 유적지에 대한 일반인의 접근을 제한하는 것(×)
관광객이 방문할 수 있는 보존된 고대 문화가 필요하다고 했으므로 글의 내용과 반대됨.

④ confining tourism research to authentic cultural traditions (20%)
관광 연구(×)를 진짜 문화적 전통에 제한하는 것(×)
a former ~ authenticity를 활용한 오답. 관광 연구 대상을 제한하는 내용이 아님.

⑤ maintaining a budget for cultural policies and regulations (4%)
문화 정책 및 규정에 대한 예산을 유지하는 것(×)
예산에 대한 내용은 없음.

02 + 빈칸 추론 〈19학년도 6월 모평 32번 | 정답률 40%〉 ②

구문분석 & 직독직해

심리 자기 효능감이 높은 사람들의 특징

[1]*An individual characteristic* [that moderates the relationship with behavior] / is self-efficacy, / or a judgment of one's capability (to accomplish a certain level of performance).
(S: An individual characteristic / that: 주격 관계대명사 / V: is / C: self-efficacy = a judgment of one's capability)

개인적인 특징은 [행동과의 관계를 조정하는] / 자기 효능감이다 /
즉 자신의 능력에 대한 판단 (특정한 수준의 성과를 달성하는)

↳ 자기 효능감은 행동을 조정하는 역할을 함.

[2]*People* [who have a high sense of self-efficacy] / tend to pursue / *challenging goals* [that may be outside the reach (of the average person)].
(S(복수): People / who: 주격 관계대명사 / V(복수): tend / that: 주격 관계대명사)

사람들은 [높은 자기 효능감을 가진] / 추구하는 경향이 있다 / 도전적인 목표를 [범위 밖에 있을 수도 있는 (보통 사람들의)]

↳ 자기 효능감이 높은 사람의 특징 1: 도전적인 목표를 추구함.

🔑 자기 효능감이 높은 사람들은 목표를 위해 문화적으로 규정된 행동 밖으로 나아가려 함.

[3]People (with a strong sense of self-efficacy), / therefore, / may be more willing to step / outside the culturally prescribed behaviors /
(S: People / V: may be / ★<be willing to-v>: 기꺼이 v하다)

사람들은 (강한 자기 효능감을 가진) / 그러므로 / 더 기꺼이 나아가려 할 수도 있다 / 문화적으로 규정된 행동 밖으로 /

to attempt *tasks or goals* [for which success is viewed / as improbable / by the majority of social actors (in a setting)].
(목적(~하기 위해): to attempt / 전치사+관계대명사: for which / S′: success / V′: is viewed / ★<view A as B(A를 B로 여기다)>의 수동형)

일이나 목표를 시도하기 위해 [성공이 여겨지는 / 있을 법 하지 않다고 / 사회 행위자들 대다수에 의해 (어떤 환경의)]

↳ 자기 효능감이 높은 사람의 특징 2: 목표를 위해서 문화적으로 규정된 행동을 벗어나려 함.

주제문

(these individuals = people with a strong sense of self-efficacy)

[4]**For these individuals, / culture will have little or no impact / on behavior.**
(S: culture / V: will have / O: little or no impact)

이런 사람들(강한 자기 효능감을 가진 사람들)에게 / 문화는 거의 혹은 전혀 영향을 주지 않을 것이다 / 행동에

↳ 문화는 자기 효능감이 높은 사람의 행동에 거의 영향을 미치지 않음.

[5]For example, / Australians tend to endorse / the "Tall Poppy Syndrome."
예를 들어 / 호주 사람들은 지지하는 경향이 있다 / '키 큰 양귀비 증후군'을

(that ~: suggests의 O(명사절))

[6]This saying suggests // that *any "poppy"* [that outgrows the others in a field] / will get "cut down;" //
(S: This saying / V: suggests / 명사절 접속사: that / S′₁: any "poppy" / 주격 관계대명사: that / V′₁: will get / C′₁: "cut down")

이 말은 시사한다 // 어떤 '양귀비'라도 [들판에서 다른 것들보다 더 크게 자라는] / '베이게' 될 것임을 //

in other words, / any overachiever will eventually fail.
(S′₂: any overachiever / V′₂: will eventually fail)

다시 말해 / 표준 이상의 성공을 거두는 사람은 누구든지 결국 실패할 것임을

↳ 예: 호주 사람들의 '키 큰 양귀비 증후군'(표준 이상의 성공을 이루는 사람은 결국 실패할 것이라고 생각함)

해석

[1]행동과의 관계를 조정하는 개인적인 특징은 자기 효능감, 즉 특정한 수준의 성과를 달성하는 자신의 능력에 대한 판단이다. [2]높은 자기 효능감을 가진 사람들은 보통 사람들의 범위 밖에 있을 수도 있는 도전적인 목표를 추구하는 경향이 있다. [3]그러므로 강한 자기 효능감을 가진 사람들은 어떤 환경의 사회적인 행위자들 대다수에 의해 성공이 있을 법 하지 않다고 여겨지는 일이나 목표를 시도하기 위해 더 기꺼이 문화적으로 규정된 행동 밖으로 나아가려 할 수도 있다. [4]이런 사람들에게 문화는 행동에 거의 혹은 전혀 영향을 주지 않을 것이다. [5]예를 들어, 호주 사람들은 '키 큰 양귀비 증후군'을 지지하는 경향이 있다. [6]이 말은 들판에서 다른 것들보다 더 크게 자라는 어떤 '양귀비'라도 '베이게' 될 것임을, 다시 말해 표준 이상의 성공을 거두는 사람은 누구든지 결국 실패할 것임을 시사한다. [7]면접과 관찰은 실제로 평균 이상을 성취하기 위해 이 문화적으로 규정된 행동 밖으로 나아가는 사람은 바로 높은 자기 효능감을 가진 호주 사람들이라는 것을 나타낸다.

어휘

moderate 조정하다; 완화하다; 보통의, 중간의
capability 능력, 역량
performance 성과, 실적; 수행
tend to-v v하는 경향이 있다
pursue 추구하다, 해나가다
challenging 도전적인
average 보통의; 평균의
prescribe 규정하다; 처방하다
improbable 있을 법 하지 않은
setting 환경, 배경
impact 영향(을 주다)

🔑 높은 자기 효능감을 가진 호주인들은 문화적으로 규정된 행동 밖으로 나아감.

[7]Interviews and observations suggest // that it is the high self-efficacy Australians // who step outside this culturally prescribed behavior / to actually achieve beyond average.

S V suggest의 O(명사절) 목적(~하기 위해)

★<It is A who[that] ~> 강조구문: ~하는 사람[것]은 바로 A이다

면접과 관찰은 나타낸다 // 바로 높은 자기 효능감을 가진 호주 사람들이라는 것을 //
이 문화적으로 규정된 행동(표준 이상의 성공을 지양하는 것) 밖으로 나아가는 사람은 / 실제로 평균 이상을 성취하기 위해

↳ 자기 효능감이 높은 호주인들은 더 성취하기 위해 문화적으로 규정된 행동을 벗어나고자 함.

syndrome 증후군
saying 말; 속담, 격언
outgrow ~보다 더 커지다
overachiever 표준 이상의 성공을 거두는 사람
[선택지] define 정의하다; 분명히 밝히다
typical 전형적인, 일반적인
quality 특성, 자질; (상품의) 품질

정답 가이드

빈칸 문장의 these individuals가 강한 자기 효능감을 가진 사람들을 지칭함을 파악한 후, 그들에게는 '무엇이 어떠하다'는 것인지를 추론해야 한다. 이어지는 예에서, 호주인들이 표준 이상의 성공을 거두는 사람은 결국 실패한다는 '키 큰 양귀비 증후군'을 지지하지만, 자기 효능감이 높은 호주인들은 평균 이상을 성취하고자 '문화적으로 규정된 행동 밖으로' 나아간다고 했다. 따라서 빈칸에 들어갈 말로 가장 적절한 것은 ② 'culture will have little or no impact on behavior(문화는 행동에 거의 혹은 전혀 영향을 주지 않을 것이다)'이다.

오답 클리닉

① self-efficacy is not easy to define (15%)
자기 효능감은 정의를 내리기 쉽지 않다
자기 효능감을 정의하려는 내용이 아님.

③ setting a goal is important before starting a task (17%)
일을 시작하기 전에 목표를 설정하는 것이 중요하다
문장 3에 나온 goals를 활용한 오답. 목표 설정에 관한 내용이 아님.

④ high self-efficacy is a typical quality of Australians (15%)
높은 자기 효능감은 호주 사람들의 전형적인 특성이다
호주인들이 모두 자기 효능감이 높은지는 알 수 없음.

⑤ judging the reaction from the community will be hard (14%)
공동체로부터의 반응을 판단하는 것은 어려울 것이다
자기 효능감이 높은 사람들이 공동체의 반응을 판단하는 내용은 없음.

03 + 무관 문장 〈20학년도 대수능 35번 | 정답률 67%〉 ③

구문분석 & 직독직해

인문 격언으로 보는 상식적 지식의 모순

주제문

[1]Although commonsense knowledge may have merit, // it also has *weaknesses*, //
부사절 접속사(양보) S'₁ V'₁ O'₁ S V O
비록 상식적인 지식에 장점이 있을 수도 있지만 // 그것에는 약점도 있다 //
★<not the least>: 중요한; 적지 않은, 막대한 (= commonsense knowledge)
not the least of which is // that it often contradicts itself. 🔑 상식적인 지식이 모순되는 점에 관한 내용임.
관계대명사(보충 설명) V'₂ C'₂
그중에서 중요한 것(약점)은 ~이다 // 그것(상식적인 지식)이 종종 모순된다는 것
↳ 상식적 지식은 모순되는 경우가 자주 있음.

[2]For example, / we hear // that *people* [who are similar] / will like one another / ("Birds of a feather flock together") //
S V 명사절 접속사 S'₁ 주격 관계대명사 V'₁ O'₁ (hear의 O₁(명사절))
예를 들어 / 우리는 듣는다 // 사람들이 [비슷한] / 서로를 좋아할 것이라고 / ('깃털이 같은 새들이 모인다(유유상종)') //
but also / that *persons* [who are dissimilar] / will like each other / ("Opposites attract").
명사절 접속사 S'₂ 주격 관계대명사 V'₂ O'₂ (hear의 O₂(명사절))
하지만 또한 / 사람들이 [비슷하지 않은] / 서로를 좋아할 것이라고 / ('정반대의 사람들은 서로에게 끌린다')
↳ 예 1: 끌리는 사람 유형에 대한 모순된 표현들.

① [3]We are told // that groups are wiser and smarter / than individuals / ("Two heads are better than one") //
S V 명사절 접속사 S'₁ V'₁ C'₁ (are told의 O₁(명사절))
우리는 듣는다 // 집단이 더 현명하고 더 똑똑하다고 / 개인보다 / ('백지장도 맞들면 낫다') //
but also / that group work inevitably produces poor results / ("Too many cooks spoil the broth").
명사절 접속사 S'₂ V'₂ O'₂ (are told의 O₂(명사절))
하지만 또한 // 집단 작업이 불가피하게 좋지 못한 결과를 만든다고 / ('요리사가 너무 많으면 수프를 망친다(사공이 많으면 배가 산으로 간다)')
↳ 예 2: 집단 작업의 효율에 대한 모순된 표현들.

해석

[1]비록 상식적인 지식에 장점이 있을 수도 있지만, 그것에는 약점도 있는데, 그중에서 중요한 것은 그것(상식적인 지식)이 종종 모순된다는 것이다. [2]예를 들어, 우리는 비슷한 사람들이 서로를 좋아할 것이라고('깃털이 같은 새들이 모인다(유유상종)') 듣지만, 또한 비슷하지 않은 사람들이 서로를 좋아할 것이라고('정반대끼리 서로 끌린다') 듣는다. ① [3]우리는 집단이 개인보다 더 현명하고 더 똑똑하다고('백지장도 맞들면 낫다') 듣지만, 또한 집단 작업이 불가피하게 좋지 못한 결과를 만든다고('요리사가 너무 많으면 수프를 망친다(사공이 많으면 배가 산으로 간다)') 듣는다. ② [4]이런 모순되는 말들의 각각은 특정한 상황에서는 사실일 수 있으나, 그것이 언제 적용되고 언제 적용되지 않는지에 관한 명확한 진술 없이는 격언은 사람들 사이의 관계에 대한 통찰력을 거의 제공하지 못한다. ③ [5]그것이 우리 삶의 긴 여정에서 어려움과 도전에 직면할 때마다 우리가 격언에 심하게 의존하는 이유이다. ④ [6]그것들은 우리가 결정을 내려야 하는 상황에서 훨씬 더 적은 지침을 제공한다. ⑤ [7]예를 들어, 위험을 수반하는 선택에 직면할 때, '위험을 무릅쓰지 않으면 아무것도 얻을 수 없다' 또는 '나중에 후회하는 것보다 조심하는 것이 낫다' 중에 우리는 어느 지침을 이용해야 하는가?

② [4]Each (of these contradictory statements) / may hold true / under particular conditions, //
S1 V1
각각은 (이런 모순되는 말들의) / 사실일 수 있다 / 특정한 상황에서는 //

but without a clear statement (of when they apply and when they do not (apply)), /
of의 O(명사절 병렬) 반복어 생략

aphorisms provide little insight (into relations among people).
S2 V2 O2
그러나 명확한 진술 없이는 (그것이 언제 적용되고 언제 적용되지 않는지에 관한) /
격언은 통찰력을 거의 제공하지 못한다 (사람들 사이의 관계에 대한)

↳ **세부 사항:** 격언들은 적용되는 상황이 명확히 제시되지 않으면 통찰력을 주지 못함.

격언이 통찰력을 제공해주지 못한다는 앞 내용과 상반됨.

③ [5]That is // (the reason) why we heavily depend on aphorisms //
↱ is의 C(명사절)
S V 선행사 생략 관계부사 S′ V′

whenever we face difficulties and challenges / in the long journey (of our lives).
복합관계부사(~할 때마다)
그것이 ~이다 // 우리가 격언에 심하게 의존하는 이유 //
어려움과 도전에 직면할 때마다 / 긴 여정에서 (우리 삶의)

↳ 삶에서 역경에 직면할 때마다 우리는 격언에 의존함.

↱ (= Aphorisms) ↱ 비교급 강조 부사 *관계부사 where의 선행사는 case(경우), circumstance(사정) 등의 추상적 공간도 될 수 있음.

④ [6]They provide even less guidance / in *situations* [where we must make decisions].
S V O 관계부사 S′ V′ O′
그것들(격언)은 훨씬 더 적은 지침을 제공한다 / 상황에서 [우리가 결정을 내려야 하는]

↳ **부연 설명:** 결정의 기로에서 격언은 더 도움이 안 됨.

⑤ [7]For example, / when facing *a choice* [that entails risk], // which guideline should we use — /
접속사를 생략하지 않은 분사구문(= when we face ~) 주격 관계대명사
예를 들어 / 선택에 직면할 때 [위험을 수반하는] // 우리는 어느 지침을 이용해야 하는가 /

"Nothing ventured, nothing gained" / or "Better safe than sorry"?
'위험을 무릅쓰지 않으면 아무것도 얻을 수 없다' / 또는 '나중에 후회하는 것보다 조심하는 것이 낫다' 중에

↳ **예:** 위험을 수반하는 선택에서 서로 모순되는 격언들 중 어느 것을 따라야 할지 알 수 없음.

어휘

commonsense 상식적인
merit 장점; 가치
contradict 모순되다; 반박하다
cf. contradictory 모순되는
flock 모이다, 떼를 짓다; 무리, 떼
inevitably 불가피하게, 필연적으로
spoil 망치다, 상하게 하다
broth 수프, 죽
hold true 사실이다; 딱 들어맞다
condition 상황; 상태; 조건
insight 통찰(력)
relation 관계
depend on ~에 의존하다
face 직면하다; 얼굴
guidance 지침, 지도
venture 위험을 무릅쓰고 하다; 모험

정답 가이드

도입 부분은 상식이 서로 모순된다는 주장에 이어서 서로 모순되는 격언을 예로 들어 설명했으므로, 이어서 선택지 문장에서 나열된 예들이 같은 주장을 뒷받침하는 예인지를 판단하면서 읽어나가야 한다. 그런데 ③은 앞선 내용이 우리가 어려움에 직면할 때마다 격언에 의존하는 이유라는 것이므로 글의 전체 흐름과 무관하다. 반면, 이어지는 ④, ⑤는 격언이 지침을 제공하지 못하는 경우를 설명하는 것이므로 ②에 이어지는 글의 전체 흐름에 맞다.

오답 클리닉

① (2%) 앞 문장의 예에 이어 격언이 모순되는 또 다른 예를 추가하고 있다.
② (6%) 앞에서 예로 든 모순되는 격언을 Each of these contradictory statements로 받아 이것들이 적용되는 상황이 명확하지 않아 통찰력을 제공하지 못한다고 지적하는 내용이다.
④ (21%) They는 ②의 명확한 진술이 없는 격언(aphorisms)을 받아, 그것이 결정을 내려야 하는 상황에서 도움이 되지 않는다고 부연 설명한다.
⑤ (3%) 위험을 수반하는 선택의 상황에서 어느 것을 적용해야 할지 알 수 없는 모순되는 격언을 예로 들었다.

01 + 밑줄 어법 〈22학년도 9월 모평 29번 | 정답률 61%〉 ③

구문분석 & 직독직해 생활 인간의 의사소통과 조건

[1] Accepting // whatever others are communicating / only pays off //
S₁(동명사구) (= anything that others are communicating) V₁(단수)
if their interests correspond to ours — // think cells in a body, bees in a beehive.
부사절 접속사 S′ V′ (= our interests) V₂(명령문) O
받아들이는 것은 // 다른 사람들이 전달하고 있는 것은 무엇이라도 / 성공할 뿐이다 //
그들의 관심사가 우리의 관심사와 일치할 경우에만 // 우리 몸의 세포, 벌집 속의 벌을 생각해보라

★<as[so] far as ~ be concerned>: ~에 관한 한
[2] As far as communication between humans is concerned, // such commonality (of interests) /
부사절 접속사(조건) S′ V′ S₁(단수)
① **is** rarely achieved; //
V₁(단수)
인간 사이의 의사소통에 관한 한 // 그러한 공통성은 (관심사의) / 좀처럼 이루어지지 않는다 //
even a pregnant mother has *reasons* (to mistrust *the chemical signals* (sent by her fetus)).
S₂ V₂ O 과거분사구
심지어 임산부도 이유가 있다 (화학적 신호를 불신하는 (태아에 의해 보내지는))

주제문
★전치사 of의 목적어로 쓰인 동명사구는 <make+O+원형부정사(v)(O가 v하게 하다)>의 구조.
[3] Fortunately, / there are ways (of making communication work) / even in the most adversarial of relationships.
V S of의 O(동명사구)
다행히도 / 방법이 있다 (의사소통이 이루어지도록 하는) / 가장 적대적인 관계에서도

★<convince+O+to-v>: O에게 v하도록 설득하다
[4] A prey can convince a predator / not to chase ② **it**.
S V O C (= the prey)
먹잇감은 포식자에게 설득할 수 있다 / 그것(자신)을 쫓지 말도록

[5] But / for such communication to occur, / there must be strong guarantees // ③ **which(→ that)**
to-v의 의미상 주어 목적(~하기 위해) V S = 동격 접속사
those [who receive the signal] / will be better off believing it.
주격 관계대명사 (= the signal)
그러나 / 그러한 의사소통이 일어나기 위해서는 / 강력한 보장이 있어야 한다 //
이들이 [신호를 받는] / 그것(그 신호)을 믿는 것이 더 좋을 것이라는
★<keep+O+C(형용사)(O를 C인 상태로 유지하다)>의 수동형
[6] The messages have to be kept, on the whole, ④ **honest**.
S V C
메시지는 전체적으로 정직한 상태로 유지되어야 한다

[7] In the case of humans, / honesty is maintained / by *a set of cognitive mechanisms* [that evaluate ⑤ **communicated** information].
S V 주격 관계대명사 V′ O′
인간의 경우 / 정직성은 유지된다 / 일련의 인지 기제에 의해 [전달된 정보를 평가하는]
★<allow+O+to-v>: O가 v하도록 하다
[8] These mechanisms allow us / to accept most beneficial messages — / to be open — /
S V O C
while rejecting most harmful messages — / to be vigilant.
접속사를 생략하지 않은 분사구문(= while they reject ~)
이러한 기제는 우리가 (~하도록) 한다 / 가장 유익한 메시지를 받아들이도록 / 즉 개방적이도록 /
한편 가장 해로운 메시지를 거부한다 / 즉 경계하도록

해석

[1]다른 사람들이 전달하고 있는 것은 무엇이라도 받아들이는 것은 그들의 관심사가 우리의 관심사와 일치할 경우에만 성공할 뿐인데, 우리 몸의 세포, 벌집 속의 벌을 생각해보라. [2]인간 사이의 의사소통에 관한 한, 관심사의 그러한 공통성은 좀처럼 이루어지지 않는데, 심지어 임산부도 태아에 의해 보내지는 화학적 신호를 불신하는 이유가 있다.(▶ 가장 가까운 관계인 임산부와 태아의 예로, 인간 사이의 의사소통은 관심사가 달라 이뤄지기 힘들다는 것을 설명) [3]다행히도, 가장 적대적인 관계에서도 의사소통이 이루어지도록 하는 방법이 있다. [4]먹잇감은 포식자에게 자신을 쫓지 말도록 설득할 수 있다. [5]그러나 그러한 의사소통이 일어나기 위해서는, 신호를 받는 이들이 그것을 믿는 것이 더 좋을 것이라는 강력한 보장이 있어야 한다. [6]메시지는 전체적으로 정직한 상태로 유지되어야 한다. [7]인간의 경우, 정직성은 전달된 정보를 평가하는 일련의 인지 기제에 의해 유지된다. [8]이러한 기제는 가장 해로운 메시지를 거부하는, 즉 경계하는 한편, 우리가 가장 유익한 메시지를 받아들이도록, 즉 개방적이도록 한다.

어휘

communicate (정보 등을) 전달하다; 의사소통을 하다
pay off 성공하다
correspond to A A와 일치하다, A에 상응하다
commonality 공통성
rarely 좀처럼 ~하지 않는
pregnant 임신한
mistrust 불신하다, 신뢰하지 않다
prey 먹잇감(↔ predator 포식자)
occur 일어나다, 발생하다
guarantee 보장(하다)
better off 더 좋은[나은]; 형편이 더 나은, 부유한
cognitive 인지의
mechanism 기제, 구조
evaluate 평가하다
beneficial 유익한, 이로운
reject 거부하다

정답 가이드

③ **[관계대명사 which vs. 동격 that]** 밑줄 친 which 뒤에 주어(those ~ signal), 동사(will be), 보어(better off ~ it)로 이루어진 완전한 구조의 절이 왔고, 그 절이 문맥상 strong guarantees와 동격 관계를 이루고 있다. 따라서 which를 동격절을 이끄는 접속사 that으로 고쳐야 한다.

> The 주의 guarantees와 같은 명사의 바로 뒤에 오는 which는 이를 선행사로 하는 관계대명사로 착각하기 쉬우므로 주의해야 한다.

오답 클리닉

① **[주어와 동사의 수일치]** (3%)
밑줄 친 동사 is의 주어는 단수명사인 such commonality이고 문맥상 현재 사실을 설명하는 것이므로 적절하다. 수식어구에 속하는 interests를 주어로 착각하지 않도록 해야 한다.

② **[인칭대명사 vs. 재귀대명사]** (9%)
it이 대신하는 명사와 수가 같은지 또는 재귀대명사 itself의 자리가 아닌지를 문맥으로 판단해야 한다. not to chase를 행하는 의미상의 주어는 a predator이고 대상이 되는 목적어는 a prey이다. 주어와 목적어가 서로 다르므로 재귀대명사는 적절하지 않으며, 단수명사인 a prey를 대신하므로 it은 적절하다.

④ **[형용사 vs. 부사]** (17%)
콤마 사이의 삽입구는 제외하고 판단하면 문장 구조를 더 잘 이해할 수 있다. 조동사 have to의 수동태는 <have to + be p.p.>의 형태이다. 문맥상 <keep+O+C> 구문이 수동태로 전환된 것인데, 수동태 문장에서 목적격보어는 동사 뒤에 그대로 두므로 honest는 적절하다. 보어 자리에 부사는 쓸 수 없다.

> The 주의 형용사 보어는 우리말에서 부사처럼 해석되기도 하지만 부사는 보어로 쓸 수 없음에 주의한다.

⑤ **[능동(v-ing) vs. 수동(p.p.)]** (9%)
'전달된 정보를 평가하다'라는 의미로, 분사의 수식을 받는 information이 '전달된' 수동의 의미이므로 과거분사 communicated는 적절하다.

02 + 빈칸 추론 〈 19학년도 6월 모평 31번 | 정답률 34% 〉 ④

구문분석 & 직독직해

경제 시장에 의한 소매가 변동

주제문

[1]Although prices in most retail outlets are set / by the retailer, // this does not mean // that these prices **do not adjust to market forces / over time.**
(부사절 접속사(양보) S′ V′ S V O(명사절))

비록 대부분의 소매점에서 가격은 정해지긴 하지만 / 소매상에 의해 // 이는 의미하는 것은 아니다 // 이 가격이 시장의 힘에 조정되지 않는다는 것을 / 시간이 지나면서

↳ 소매점의 가격은 소매상이 정하지만 시장에 의해 조정되기 함.

[2]On any particular day / we find // that all products have a specific price ticket / on them.
(S V find의 O(명사절) 명사절 접속사 S′ V′ O′ (= all products))

그 어느 특정한 날에도 / 우리는 안다 // 모든 상품은 명확한 가격표가 있다는 것을 / 그것에

[3]However, / this price may be different / from day to day or week to week. 소매 가격은 달라지기도 함.

그러나 / 이 가격은 다를 수도 있다 / 날마다 또는 주마다

↳ 상품의 가격표가 항상 같지는 않음.

[4]*The price* [that the farmer gets / from the wholesaler] / is much more flexible / from day to day / than *the price* [that the retailer charges consumers].
(S 목적격 관계대명사 V 비교급 강조 부사 C 목적격 관계대명사)

가격은 [농부가 받는 / 도매상에게서] / 훨씬 더 유연하다 / 그날그날 / 가격보다 [소매상이 소비자에게 청구하는]

↳ **세부 사항:** 도매상이 농부에게 지불하는 가격은 소매상의 가격보다 변동적임.

[5]If, for example, bad weather leads to a poor potato crop, // then *the price* [that supermarkets have to pay / to their wholesalers / for potatoes] / will go up //
(부사절 접속사(조건) S′ V′ O′ S_1 목적격 관계대명사 V_1)

예를 들어, 만약에 악천후가 부족한 감자 수확량을 초래한다면 // 가격은 [슈퍼마켓이 지불해야 하는 / 그들의 도매상에게 / 감자에 대해] / 상승할 것이다 //

감자 수확량 감소가 소매 가격에 영향을 미침.

and this will be reflected / in *the prices* [(which[that]) they mark on potatoes / in their stores].
((= 앞 절의 주절) S_2 V_2 목적격 관계대명사 생략 (= supermarkets))

그리고 이는 반영될 것이다 / 가격에 [그들(슈퍼마켓)이 감자에 붙이는 / 자신의 가게에 있는]

↳ **예:** 감자의 수확량이 줄면 도매 가격이 오르고, 이는 소매 가격에도 반영됨.

가격은 시장의 수요와 공급을 반영함.

[6]Thus, / these prices do reflect the interaction (of demand and supply (in the wider marketplace for potatoes)).
(S 동사 강조 V O)

따라서 / 이 가격들은 상호 작용을 정말로 반영한다 (수요와 공급의 (더 넓은 감자 시장에서의))

해석

[1]비록 대부분의 소매점에서 가격은 소매상에 의해 정해지긴 하지만, 이는 이 가격이 시간이 지나면서 시장의 힘에 조정되지 않는다는 것을 의미하는 것은 아니다. [2]그 어느 특정한 날에도 우리는 모든 상품은 그것에 명확한 가격표가 있다는 것을 안다. [3]그러나 이 가격은 날마다 또는 주마다 다를 수도 있다. [4]도매상에게서 농부가 받는 가격은 소매상이 소비자에게 청구하는 가격보다 그날그날 훨씬 더 유연하다. [5]예를 들어, 만약에 악천후가 부족한 감자 수확량을 초래한다면, 슈퍼마켓이 감자에 대해 그들의 도매상에게 지불해야 하는 가격은 상승할 것이고, 이는 그들(슈퍼마켓)이 자신의 가게에 있는 감자에 붙이는 가격에 반영될 것이다. [6]따라서 이 가격들은 더 넓은 감자 시장에서의 수요와 공급의 상호 작용을 정말로 반영한다. [7]비록 가격들이 수요와 공급에서의 지역적 변동을 반영하기 위해 슈퍼마켓에서 시간마다 바뀌지는 않지만, 그것들은 문제의 상품에 대한 전반적인 생산과 수요의 기저에 놓인 상황을 반영하기 위해 시간이 지나면서 정말로 바뀐다.

어휘

retail outlet 소매점
retailer 소매상
adjust to A A에 조정[조절]되다; A에 적응하다
specific 명확한, 구체적인; 특정한
wholesaler 도매상
flexible 유연한, 구부리기 쉬운; 융통성 있는
charge (요금을) 청구하다; 고소[고발]하다; 충전하다
lead to A A를 초래하다; A로 이어지다
crop (한 철에 거둔) 수확량; (농)작물
reflect 반영하다; 비추다
demand 수요; 요구 (사항); 요구하다
supply 공급(량); 공급(제공)하다

⁷Although they do not change in the supermarket from hour to hour / to reflect local variations (in demand and supply), //
(they = these prices) 부사절 접속사(양보) S′ V′ 목적(~하기 위해)

비록 그것들(가격들)이 슈퍼마켓에서 시간마다 바뀌지는 않지만 / 지역적 변동을 반영하기 위해 (수요와 공급에서의) //

they do change over time / to reflect the underlying conditions (of the overall production of [and] demand for / the goods in question). 🔑 상품의 생산와 수요를 반영해 가격이 변동됨.
(they = these prices) S V 목적(~하기 위해) of와 for의 공통 O(명사구)

그것들(가격들)은 시간이 지나면서 정말로 바뀐다 / 기저에 놓인 상황을 반영하기 위해 (~에 대한 전반적인 생산과 수요의 / 문제의 상품(에 대한))

↳ **결과:** 상품의 수요와 공급을 반영하기 위해 소매 가격이 변동됨.

marketplace 시장
local 지역적인, 현지의
variation 변동, 변화; 차이
underlying 기저의; 근원적인, 기초를 이루는
condition 《복수형》 상황, 환경
overall 전반적인, 전체의
in question 문제의, 논의가 되고 있는
[선택지] principle 원리, 원칙

정답 가이드

소매상이 정한 가격이 '무엇을' 의미하지 않는지를 파악해야 한다. 이어지는 설명에서 가격은 변동될 수 있으며 이는 수요와 공급의 상호 작용(즉 '시장'을 의미)을 반영하는 것이라고 했다. 따라서, 소매상의 가격이 '시장을 반영하지 않는 것'은 아니므로, 빈칸에 들어갈 말로 가장 적절한 것은 ④ 'do not adjust to market forces over time(시간이 지나면서 시장의 힘에 조정되지 않는다)'이다.

The 핵심 ★ 빈칸 문장이 부정어(not, no, never, seldom, neither, little, rarely 등)를 포함한 경우, 빈칸에서 그것을 다시 부정하면 이중 부정이 되어 긍정의 의미가 된다.

오답 클리닉

① reflect the principle of demand and supply (26%)
수요와 공급의 원리를 반영한다
문장 6에서 가격은 수요와 공급의 상호 작용을 반영한다고 했지만, 빈칸 문장이 부정어를 포함하고 있어 정반대의 의미가 되므로 틀림.

② may not change from hour to hour (24%)
시간마다 바뀌지 않을 수도 있다
문장 7의 가격이 시간마다 바뀌는 것은 아니라는 내용이 부정문을 포함한 빈칸 문장에 들어가면 시간마다 바뀔 수 있다는 의미가 되므로 틀림.

③ go up due to bad weather (7%)
악천후로 인해 오른다
감자 수확량 감소 사례를 활용한 오답.

⑤ can be changed by the farmer's active role (8%)
농부의 적극적인 역할에 의해 바뀔 수 있다
농부의 적극적인 역할이 소매 가격에 영향을 미친다는 내용은 없음.

03 + 글의 순서 (20학년도 6월 모평 37번 | 정답률 55%) ③

구문분석 & 직독직해

기술 인간 정신의 확장으로서의 기술

¹Marshall McLuhan, / among others, / noted // that clothes are people's extended skin, / wheels (are people's) extended feet, / camera and telescopes (are people's) extended eyes.
S V 명사절 접속사 S′₁ V′₁ C′₁ (noted의 O(명사절)) S′₂ 반복어구 생략 C′₂ S′₃ 반복어구 생략 C′₃

Marshall McLuhan은 / 특히 / 언급했다 // 옷은 사람들의 확장된 피부이고 / 바퀴는 확장된 발이고 / 카메라와 망원경은 확장된 눈이라고

²Our technological creations are / great extrapolations (of *the bodies* [that our genes build]).
S V C 목적격 관계대명사

우리의 기술적인 창조물들은 ~이다 / 위대한 연장 (신체의 [우리의 유전자가 만들어 낸])

🔑 기술적 창조물이 신체의 연장이라는 주어진 글의 내용을 지칭함.

(B) ³In this way, / we can think of technology / as our extended body.
S V O 전치사(~로(서)) ★<think of A as B>: A를 B로 생각하다[여기다]

이런 방식으로 / 우리는 기술을 생각할 수 있다 / 우리의 확장된 신체로

↳ 옷, 바퀴, 카메라와 같은 기술적 창조물을 인간의 유전자가 만든 신체의 연장으로 여김.

⁴During the industrial age / it was easy / to see the world this way.
가주어 V C 진주어(to-v구)

산업화 시대에 / (~이) 쉬웠다 / 세상을 이런 식으로 보는 것이

⁵Steam-powered shovels, locomotives, television, and the levers and gears of engineers / were *a fabulous exoskeleton* [that turned man into superman]. ★<turn A into B>: A를 B로 바꾸다
S V C 주격 관계대명사

증기를 동력으로 이용하는 굴착기, 기관차, 텔레비전, 그리고 엔지니어의 지렛대와 톱니바퀴는 / 엄청난 외골격이었다 [인간을 슈퍼맨으로 바꾼]

↳ **예:** 산업 시대에 기술적 창조물(증기 동력 굴착기, 기관차 등)은 인간의 유전자에서 비롯된 확장된 신체였음.

해석

¹특히 Marshall McLuhan은 옷은 사람들의 확장된 피부, 바퀴는 확장된 발, 카메라와 망원경은 확장된 눈이라고 언급했다. ²우리의 기술적인 창조물들은 우리의 유전자가 만들어 낸 신체의 위대한 연장이다. (B) ³이런 방식으로, 우리는 기술을 우리의 확장된 신체로 생각할 수 있다. ⁴산업화 시대에 세상을 이런 식으로 보는 것이 쉬웠다. ⁵증기를 동력으로 이용하는 굴착기, 기관차, 텔레비전, 그리고 엔지니어의 지렛대와 톱니바퀴는 인간을 슈퍼맨으로 바꾼 엄청난 외골격이었다.(▶ 기술적 창조물을 인간의 확장된 신체에 비유함.) (C) ⁶더 면밀한 검토는 이 비유의 결함을 드러낸다. 동물들의 확장된 의상은 그들의 유전자의 결과물이다. ⁷그것들은 자신들이 만드는 것의 기본 청사진을 물려받는다. ⁸인간은 그렇지 않다. (A) ⁹우리의 껍질에 대한 청사진은 우리의 정신에서 비롯되는데, 그것(우리의 정신)은 우리 조상들 중 어느 누구도 만들어 내거나 심지어 상상하지도 못했던 무언가를 자연스럽게 만들어 낼 수도 있다. ¹⁰기술이 인간의 확장이라면, 그것은 우리의 유전자의 확장이 아니라 우리의 정신의 확장이다. ¹¹그러므로 기술은 아이디어를 위한 확장된 신체이다.

🔑 this analogy는 (B)의 기술적 창조물을 외골격에 비유한 것을 가리킴.

(C) [6]A closer look reveals / the flaw (in this analogy): // The extended costume (of animals) / is the result of their genes.

S1 V1 O1 S2(단수) V2(단수) C2

더 면밀한 검토는 드러낸다 / 결함을 (이 비유의) // 확장된 의상은 (동물들의) / 그들의 유전자의 결과물이다

↳ **문제 제기:** 기술을 신체의 확장으로 보는 비유에는 결함이 있음.

(= Animals)

[7]They inherit / the basic blueprints (of what they make).

S V O of의 O(명사절)

그것들(동물들)은 물려받는다 / 기본 청사진을 (자신들이 만드는 것의)

[8]Humans don't (inherit the basic blueprints of what they make).

반복어구 생략

인간은 그렇지 않다

↳ 동물은 만드는 것의 청사진을 유전으로 물려받지만 인간은 그렇지 않음.

🔑 (C)에서 언급한 인간의 차이점을 부연 설명함.

(A) [9]The blueprints (for our shells) / spring from *our minds*, //

S V O

청사진은 (우리의 껍질에 대한) / 우리의 정신에서 비롯된다 //

which may spontaneously create / *something* [(that) none of our ancestors ever made or even imagined].

관계대명사(보충 설명) 목적격 관계대명사 생략

그리고 그것(인간의 정신)은 자연스럽게 만들어 낼 수도 있다 / 무언가를 [우리 조상들 중 어느 누구도 만들어 내거나 심지어 상상하지도 못했던]

↳ 인간이 만들어 내는 것은 정신으로부터 비롯됨.

주제문

*<not A but B>: A가 아니라 B

[10]If technology is an extension of humans, // it is not an extension of our genes / but (an extension) of our minds.

부사절 접속사(조건) S V C1 C2

기술이 인간의 확장이라면 // 그것은 우리의 유전자의 확장이 아니라 / 우리의 정신의 확장이다

[11]Technology is therefore the extended body (for ideas).

S V C

그러므로 기술은 확장된 신체이다 (아이디어를 위한)

↳ **결론:** 기술은 유전자의 확장이 아니라 정신의 확장임.

어휘

note 언급하다; ~에 주목하다
extended 확장된; 연장된
cf. extension 확장
telescope 망원경
creation 창조(물)
gene 유전자
steam 증기
powered ~을 (동력으로) 이용하는
shovel 굴착기; 삽
locomotive 기관차; 운동의
lever 지렛대, 지레
gear 톱니바퀴; 장치; 장비
fabulous 엄청난; 멋진
analogy 비유; 유추
costume 의상, 복장
inherit 물려받다; 상속하다
blueprint 청사진, 설계도; 계획
shell 껍질[껍데기]; 겉모습
spring from ~에서부터 비롯되다[야기되다]
spontaneously 자연스럽게, 자발적으로

정답 가이드

기술적 창조물이 우리 유전자가 만들어 낸 신체의 연장이라는 주어진 글 다음에는 이를 In this way로 받아 산업화 시대의 기술적 창조물을 예로 들어 구체적으로 설명하는 내용의 (B)가 와야 한다. 이어서 (B)에서 기술적 창조물을 외골격에 비유한 것을 (C)에서 this analogy로 받아 이러한 비유에 결함이 있다고 지적하며, 동물이 만들어 내는 것은 유전의 결과이지만 인간은 그렇지 않다고 설명하고, 마지막으로 (A)에서 이를 구체적으로 부연 설명하여 기술은 인간의 정신의 확장이라고 결론짓는 것이 가장 적절하다.

오답 클리닉

① (A) - (C) - (B) (3%)
기술적 창조물이 유전자가 만들어 낸 인간 신체의 연장이라는 주어진 글의 내용과 인간의 정신의 확장이라는 (A)의 내용이 상반되므로 (A)는 주어진 글 바로 뒤에 올 수 없다.

② (B) - (A) - (C) (16%)
(C)의 '인간은 그렇지 않다'라는 내용을 (A)에서 구체적으로 설명하므로 (A)는 (C) 뒤에 와야 한다.

④ (C) - (A) - (B) (21%) / ⑤ (C) - (B) - (A) (6%)
(C)는 기술을 인간의 신체의 확장에 비유한 (B)의 결함을 지적하는 내용이므로 (B) 뒤에 와야 한다. (B)에서 기술적 창조물을 a fabulous exoskeleton에 비유한 것을 (C)에서 this analogy로 가리키고 있다.

The 주의 (C)를 중심으로 기술을 보는 관점이 인간의 신체의 확장에서 정신의 확장으로 바뀌는 것에 주의한다.

01 + 낱말 쓰임 〈22학년도 9월 모평 30번 | 정답률 48%〉 ④

구문분석 & 직독직해 *what이 이끄는 명사절이 문장의 주어 역할을 함. 경제 운송 부문의 수요와 공급

[1]In economic systems / what takes place in one sector has impacts on another; // demand (for a good or service / in one sector) / is derived / from another.
관계대명사 S1(명사절) V1(단수) O S2 V2
① 한 부문의 재화나 서비스에 대한 수요는 다른 부문의 '수요'를 유발함.
경제 시스템에서는 / 한 부문에서 일어나는 일이 다른 부문에 영향을 미친다 // 그리고 수요가 (재화나 서비스에 대한 / 한 부문의) / 파생된다 / 다른 부문에서

[2]For instance, / *a consumer* (buying a good in a store) / will likely trigger / *the replacement* (of this product), //
S 현재분사구 V O
예를 들어 / 소비자는 (가게에서 제품을 구매하는) / 아마 촉발시킬 것이다 / 대체를 (이 제품의) //
which will generate / ① **demands** (for activities (such as manufacturing, resource extraction and, of course, transport)).
관계대명사(보충 설명) V′ O′
이는 만들어낼 것이다 / 수요를 (활동에 대한 (제조, 자원 추출, 그리고 물론 운송과 같은))

[3]What is different about transport is // that it cannot exist alone // and a movement cannot be ② **stored**.
S(명사절) V(단수) 명사절 접속사 → is의 C(명사절)
③ 이동은 저장될 수 없으므로 비행기 좌석이나 화물 용량은 팔리지 않으면 '나중에' 되돌려질 수 없음.
운송에 관해 다른 것은 ~이다 // 그것(운송)이 단독으로는 존재할 수 없다는 것 // 그리고 이동은 저장될 수 없다(는 것)

[4]An unsold product can remain on the shelf of a store / until bought (often with discount incentives), //
S1 V1 접속사를 생략하지 않은 분사구문(= until it is bought ~)
팔리지 않은 제품은 가게 선반에 남아 있을 수 있다 / 구매될 때까지 (흔히 할인 장려책으로) //
but an unsold seat on a flight or unused cargo capacity in the same flight / remains unsold and cannot be brought back / as additional capacity / ③ **later**.
S2 V2-1(단수) C V2-2(조동사+수동태) 전치사(~로(서))
② 비행기의 좌석 및 화물 용량은 팔리지 않은 채로 남겨지므로 '저장될' 수 없음.
그러나 비행기의 팔리지 않은 좌석이나 같은 비행기의 사용되지 않은 화물 적재량은 / 팔리지 않은 채로 남아 있고 되돌려질 수 없다 / 추가 용량으로 / 나중에

[5]In this case / an opportunity has been ④ **seized(→ missed)**, //
S V
④ 공급이 수요보다 많으면 남은 용량을 사용할 기회는 '상실됨'.
이 경우 / 기회는 포착되었다(→ 상실되었다) //
since *the amount of transport* (being offered) / has exceeded the demand for it.
부사절 접속사(~ 때문에) 현재분사구 (= the amount of transport being offered)
운송량이 (~하기) 때문에 (제공되는) / 그것에 대한 수요를 넘었기 (때문에)

[6]The derived demand (of transportation) / is often very difficult / to reconcile with an equivalent supply, //
S1 V1 C 형용사 difficult 수식
파생된 수요는 (운송에 대한) / 흔히 매우 어렵다 / 같은 양의 공급과 조화를 이루기 //
and actually transport companies would prefer / to have *some additional capacity* (to accommodate ⑤ **unforeseen** demand) / (often at much higher prices).
S2 V2 비교급 수식 부사
⑤ 운송 회사가 추가 용량을 갖길 원하는 것은 '예측하지 못한' 수요를 수용하기 위함임.
그래서 실제로 운송 회사들은 선호할 것이다 / 약간의 추가 용량을 갖는 것을 (예측하지 못한 수요를 수용할) / (흔히 훨씬 더 높은 가격으로)

해석

[1]경제 시스템에서는 한 부문에서는 일어나는 일이 다른 부문에 영향을 미치고, 한 부문의 재화나 서비스에 대한 수요가 다른 부문에서 파생된다. [2]예를 들어, 가게에서 제품을 구매하는 소비자는 아마 이 제품의 대체를 촉발시킬 것이고, 이는 제조, 자원 추출, 그리고 물론 운송과 같은 활동에 대한 ① 수요를 만들어낼 것이다. [3]운송에 관해 다른 것은 그것이 단독으로는 존재할 수 없고 이동은 ② 저장될 수 없다는 것이다. [4]팔리지 않은 제품은 (흔히 할인 장려책으로) 구매될 때까지 가게 선반에 남아 있을 수 있지만, 비행기의 팔리지 않은 좌석이나 같은 비행기의 사용되지 않은 화물 적재량은 팔리지 않은 채로 남아 있고 ③ 나중에 추가 용량으로 되돌려질 수 없다. [5]이 경우 제공되는 운송량(공급)이 그것에 대한 수요를 넘었기 때문에 (운송 공간이 이용될) 기회는 ④ 포착되었다(→ 상실되었다). [6]운송에 대한 파생된 수요(다른 부문의 수요로 인해 파생된 운송 수요)는 흔히 같은 양의 공급과 조화를 이루기 매우 어려워서, 실제로 운송 회사들은 (흔히 훨씬 더 높은 가격으로) ⑤ 예측하지 못한 수요를 수용할 약간의 추가 용량을 갖는 것을 선호할 것이다.(▶ 운송은 다른 부문에서 일어나는 판매에 의존하며 운송 공간은 저장해둘 수 없으므로, 공급이 수요를 초과하면 빈 공간은 그대로 둘 수밖에 없어 수익을 얻지 못함. 따라서, 수요가 공급보다 갑자기 커질 때는 수익을 높이기 위해 더 높은 가격에 공급하는 추가 운송 용량을 갖는 것을 선호한다는 의미)

어휘

take place 일어나다; 개최되다
sector 부문, 분야
demand 수요; 요구
derive from ~에서 파생하다, 유래하다
trigger 촉발시키다, 일으키다; (총의) 방아쇠
replacement 대체, 교체
generate 만들어 내다
extraction 추출
transport 운송(= transportation); 운송하다
incentive 장려[우대]책
cargo capacity 화물 적재량
additional 추가의
seize (기회 등을) 포착하다; (붙)잡다
exceed 넘다, 초과하다
equivalent 같은 양의, 동등한
supply 공급(하다)
accommodate 수용하다, 공간을 제공하다
unforeseen 예측하지 못한

정답 가이드

제품과 비교해 운송의 수요와 공급의 특징을 설명하는 글이다. 제품과 달리 비행기 좌석이나 화물 적재량과 같은 운송은 그때 팔리지 않으면 나중에 추가 용량으로 되돌려질 수 없다고 했다. 따라서 소비자에게 제공되는 운송량, 즉 공급이 수요를 넘어설 경우 남은 운송량이 이용될 기회는 '포착되는' 것이 아니라 '상실되는' 것이다. 따라서 ④ 'seized(포착되는)'를 'missed(상실되는)'로 고쳐야 한다.

오답 클리닉

① demands (3%) 수요
한 부문에서의 재화에 대한 수요는 다른 부문에서 유래된다고 했으므로 소비자가 제품을 구매하면 이는 제조, 자원 추출, 운송과 같은 활동에 대한 '수요'를 만들어낼 것으로 볼 수 있다.

② stored (9%) 저장된
비행기의 팔리지 않은 좌석이나 사용되지 않은 화물 적재량은 나중에 팔리지 않은 채 남아 있기 때문에 이동은 '저장될' 수 없다는 것이 적절하다.

③ later (11%) 나중에
이동은 저장될 수 없다고 했으므로 비행기 좌석이나 화물 적재량이 팔리지 않으면 '나중에' 추가 용량으로 되돌려질 수 없다는 것은 자연스럽다.

⑤ unforeseen (28%) 예측하지 못한
운송은 흔히 수요를 예측해서 공급을 맞추기 어렵다고 했으므로, 운송 회사가 더 높은 가격으로 추가 용량을 갖고자 하는 것은 '예측하지 못한' 갑작스러운 수요를 수용하기 위함으로 보는 것이 적절하다.

02 + 빈칸 추론 〈18학년도 대수능 34번 | 정답률 51%〉 ①

구문분석 & 직독직해

인문 AI의 도래로 인한 인간성의 재정의

주제문

[1]Over the past 60 years, / as mechanical processes have replicated / *behaviors and talents* [(which[that])(we thought) were unique to humans], // we've had to change our minds (about what sets us apart).

(as: 부사절 접속사(~ 때문에) / mechanical processes: S′ / have replicated: V′ / behaviors and talents: O′ / we thought: 삽입절 / were: V″ / unique: C″ / we: S / had to change: V / our minds: O / what sets us apart: about의 O(명사절))

*삽입절을 포함한 주격 관계대명사절의 관계대명사는 생략 가능함.

지난 60년 동안 / 기계식 공정이 복제해왔기 때문에 / 행동과 재능을 [(우리가 생각하기에) 인간에게 고유했던] // 우리는 우리의 생각을 바꿔야만 했다 (우리를 구별하는 것에 관한)

🔑 우리를 다르게 만드는 것, 즉 고유한 인간성에 대한 생각을 바꿔야 함.

↳ 기계가 인간의 고유한 특성을 복제하면서 인간을 다르게 구별하는 것에 대한 생각을 바꿔야 할 필요가 대두됨.

[2]As we invent more species of AI, // we will be forced to surrender / more (of what is supposedly unique about humans).

(As: 부사절 접속사(~함에 따라) / we: S / will be forced to surrender: V / more: C / what is supposedly unique about humans: of의 O(명사절))

*<be forced to-v>: 하는 수 없이 v하다

우리가 더 많은 종의 AI(인공지능)를 발명함에 따라 // 우리는 하는 수 없이 넘겨줘야 할 것이다 / 더 많은 것을 (아마도 인간에게 고유한 것 중)

[3]Each step (of surrender) — // we are not *the only mind* [that can play chess, fly a plane, make music, or invent a mathematical law] — / will be painful and sad.

(Each step: S / we: S′ / are: V′ / the only mind: C′ / that: 주격 관계대명사 / will be: V / painful and sad: C)

각 단계는 (양도(넘겨주는 것)의) // 우리가 유일한 존재가 아니라는 것은 [체스를 두거나, 비행기를 조종하거나, 음악을 만들거나, 수학 법칙을 발명할 수 있는] / 고통스럽고 슬플 것이다

↳ **원인:** 인공지능이 인간의 고유한 특징들을 갖게 됨.

[4]We'll spend the next three decades — / indeed, perhaps the next century — / in a permanent identity crisis, / continually asking ourselves // what humans are good for.

(We: S / 'll spend: V / the next three decades: O / continually asking: 분사구문(= and we'll continually ask ~) / ourselves: asking의 IO / what humans are good for: asking의 DO(명사절))

🔑 인간의 쓸모를 질문함.

우리는 다음 30년을 보낼 것이다 / 사실, 아마도 다음 한 세기를 / 영구적인 정체성 위기 속에서 / 우리 자신에게 계속해서 질문하면서 // 인간이 무엇에 쓸모가 있는지를

🔑 인간의 특별함을 고민함.

[5]If we aren't unique toolmakers, or artists, or moral ethicists, // then what, if anything, makes us special?

(If: 부사절 접속사(조건) / makes: V / us: O / special: C)

우리가 유일한 도구 제작자나 예술가, 혹은 도덕 윤리학자가 아니라면 // 그렇다면 대체 무엇이 우리를 특별하게 만드는가

↳ **결과:** 인간은 인간만의 고유한 특징에 관해 고민하게 됨.

해석

[1]지난 60년 동안, 기계식 공정이 우리가 생각하기에 인간에게 고유했던 행동과 재능을 복제해왔기 때문에, 우리는 우리를 (기계와) 구별하는 것에 관한 우리의 생각을 바꿔야만 했다. [2]우리가 더 많은 종의 AI(인공지능)를 발명함에 따라, 우리는 하는 수 없이 아마도 인간에게 고유한 것 중 더 많은 것을 넘겨줘야 할 것이다. [3]우리가 체스를 두거나, 비행기를 조종하거나, 음악을 만들거나, 수학 법칙을 발명할 수 있는 유일한 존재가 아니라는 양도(넘겨주는 것)의 각 단계는 고통스럽고 슬플 것이다. [4]우리는 다음 30년, 사실, 아마도 다음 한 세기를 인간이 무엇에 쓸모가 있는지를 우리 자신에게 계속해서 질문하면서 영구적인 정체성 위기 속에서 보낼 것이다. [5]우리가 유일한 도구 제작자나 예술가, 혹은 도덕 윤리학자가 아니라면, 그렇다면 대체 무엇이 우리를 특별하게 만드는가? [6]가장 아이러니하게도, 일상적이고 실용적인 AI의 가장 큰 이점은, 비록 그 모든 것이 일어날 것이지만, 증가된 생산성이나 풍요의 경제학, 혹은 과학을 행하는 새로운 방식이 아닐 것이다. [7]인공지능 도래의 가장 큰 이점은 AI가 인간성을 정의하는 데 도움을 줄 것이라는 것이다.

어휘

mechanical 기계에 의한; 기계(상)의
unique 고유의, 특유의; 독특한
set A apart (from B) A를 (B와) 구별하다[다르게 만들다]
surrender 넘겨주다[포기하다]; 양도; 항복(하다)
supposedly 아마, 추측건대
permanent 영구[영속]적인

[6]In the grandest irony of all, / the greatest benefit (of an everyday, utilitarian AI) / will not be increased productivity or an economics of abundance or a new way of doing science — // although all those will happen.

S V C 부사절 접속사(양보) S′ V′

가장 아이러니하게도 / 가장 큰 이점은 (일상적이고 실용적인 AI의) / 증가된 생산성이나 풍요의 경제학, 혹은 과학을 행하는 새로운 방식이 아닐 것이다 // 비록 그 모든 것이 일어날 것이지만

주제문

[7]The greatest benefit (of the arrival of artificial intelligence) / is // that **AIs will help define humanity**.

S V is의 C(명사절)

가장 큰 이점은 (인공지능 도래의) / ~이다 // AI가 인간성을 정의하는 데 도움을 줄 것이라는 것

↳ **AI의 역설적인 이점:** 인간성을 재정의하도록 함.

identity 정체성; 신원, 신분; 유사성
crisis 위기
moral 도덕(상)의; 교훈
ethicist 윤리학자
utilitarian 실용적인; 실용주의의
productivity 생산성
abundance 풍요; 과다
[선택지] liberate 해방시키다, 자유롭게 하다
compensate for ~을 보충[보상]하다
decline 쇠퇴(하다); 감소(하다)

정답 가이드

AI가 도래하여 생겨난 '이점'을 추론해야 한다. 첫 문장에서 기계식 공정이 인간 고유의 행동과 재능을 복제해서 우리는 '기계와 우리를 구별하는 것에 관한 생각을 바꿔야' 했다고 했다. 이어지는 구체적 설명과 예에서 우리 인간이 무엇에 쓸모가 있는지, 무엇이 인간을 특별하게 만드는지에 대한 물음이 제시되었다. 따라서, AI의 이점은 생산성 증가 등이 아니라, ① 'AIs will help define humanity(AI가 인간성을 정의하는 데 도움을 줄 것이다)'라는 문맥이 되어야 가장 적절하다.

오답 클리닉

② humans could also be like AIs (12%)
인간도 AI처럼 될 수 있다
AI가 인간의 능력을 가지게 된다고 했음.

③ humans will be liberated from hard labor (14%)
인간이 고된 노동으로부터 해방될 것이다
AI가 인간의 노동을 대신한다는 내용은 추론할 수 없음.

④ AIs could lead us in resolving moral dilemmas (10%)
AI가 우리를 도덕적 딜레마의 해결로 인도할 수 있다
moral ethicists를 활용한 오답. AI가 도덕적 딜레마를 해결한다는 내용은 언급되지 않음.

⑤ AIs could compensate for a decline in human intelligence (12%)
AI가 인간 지능의 쇠퇴를 보충할 수 있다
인간 지능이 쇠퇴했다는 내용은 없으며 AI가 이를 보충한다는 내용도 유추할 수 없음.

03 + 문장 넣기 (20학년도 6월 모평 39번 | 정답률 51%) ④

구문분석 & 직독직해 과학 위스퍼링 갤러리의 효과와 원리

주제문

[1]Whispering galleries are *remarkable acoustic spaces* (found / beneath certain domes or curved ceilings).

S V C 과거분사구

위스퍼링 갤러리는 놀라운 음향 공간이다 (발견되는 / 어떤 돔이나 곡선 모양의 천장 아래에서)

↳ 위스퍼링 갤러리는 놀라운 음향 공간임.

[2]A famous one is located / outside a well-known restaurant (in New York City's Grand Central Station).

S V

유명한 한 곳이 있다 / 잘 알려진 식당 밖에 (뉴욕시의 Grand Central 역에 있는)

↳ **예:** 뉴욕시 Grand Central 역에 있는 식당 밖에 유명한 위스퍼링 갤러리가 있음.

(①) [3]It's *a fun place* (to take a date): // the two of you can exchange romantic words //

S1 V1 C S2 V2 O

그곳은 재미있는 곳이다 (데이트하기에) // 여러분 두 사람은 낭만적인 말을 주고받을 수 있다 //

while you're forty feet apart / and separated by a busy passageway.

부사절 접속사(~동안에)

여러분이 40피트 떨어져 있는 동안에 / 그리고 혼잡한 통로로 분리되어 (있는 동안에)

(②) [4]You'll hear each other clearly, // but the passersby won't hear / *a word* [(which[that]) you're saying].

S1 V1 O1 S2 V2 O2 목적격 관계대명사 생략

여러분은 서로의 말이 분명하게 들릴 것이다 // 그러나 지나가는 사람들은 들리지 않을 것이다 / 한마디도 [여러분이 말하고 있는]

↳ **부연 설명:** 혼잡한 통로에 서로 떨어져 말을 주고받을 수 있으나, 지나가는 사람들은 그 말을 듣지 못함.

해석

[1]위스퍼링 갤러리는 어떤 돔이나 곡선 모양의 천장 아래에서 발견되는 놀라운 음향 공간이다. [2]유명한 한 곳이 뉴욕시의 Grand Central 역에 있는 잘 알려진 식당 밖에 있다. (①) [3]그곳은 데이트하기에 재미있는 곳으로, 혼잡한 통로로 분리되어 40피트 떨어져 있는 동안에 여러분 두 사람은 낭만적인 말을 주고받을 수 있다. (②) [4]여러분은 서로의 말이 분명하게 들릴 것이지만 지나가는 사람들은 여러분이 말하고 있는 한마디도 들리지 않을 것이다. (③) [5]이런 효과를 내려면 여러분 두 사람은 그 공간의 대각선으로 맞은편의 구석에서 벽을 마주 보고 서 있어야 한다. (④ [6]그것은 여러분 각자를 여러분의 목소리가 통로의 곡선 모양의 벽과 천장에서 반사될 때 집중되는 특별한 지점인 초점 가까이에 둔다.) [7]보통 여러분이 만드는 음파는 모든 방향으로 이동하고 각기 다른 시간과 장소에서 벽에 반사되어서, (그 결과) 이는 그것들(음파)을 너무 많이 뒤섞어서 그것들이 40피트 떨어져 있는 듣는 사람의 귀에 도달할 때는 들리지 않는다. (⑤) [8]그러나 여러분이 한쪽 '초점'에서 속삭일 때, 반사되는 음파는 전부 다른 한쪽 초점에 '동시에' 도달하며, 따라서 서로(반사되는 음파)를 강화하여 여러분의 말이 들리게 한다.

(③) 5To produce this effect, / the two of you should stand / at diagonally opposite corners (of the space), / facing the wall. 🔑 두 사람이 대각선 맞은편 구석에 벽을 보고 서 있어야 함.

목적(~하려면) S V 분사구문(= as the two of you face ~)

이런 효과를 내려면 / 여러분 두 사람은 서 있어야 한다 / 대각선으로 맞은편의 구석에서 (그 공간의) / 벽을 마주 보고

🔑 앞 문장의 조건을 가리킴.

(④) 6That puts you each near a focus, / *a special point* [at which the sound of your voice gets focused // as it reflects off the passageway's curved walls and ceiling]).

S V O = 전치사+관계대명사 S′ V′ C′ 부사절 접속사(~할 때)

그것은 여러분 각자를 초점 가까이에 둔다 / 특별한 지점인 [여러분의 목소리가 집중되는 // 그것이 통로의 곡선 모양의 벽과 천장에서 반사될 때]

↳ **조건:** 두 사람이 대각선으로 맞은편 구석에서 벽을 보고 서면 목소리가 집중되는 특별한 지점 가까이에 있게 됨.

7Ordinarily, / *the sound waves* [(which[that]) you produce] / travel in all directions / and bounce off the walls / at different times and places, /

S 목적격 관계대명사 생략 V_1 V_2

보통 / 음파는 [여러분이 만드는] / 모든 방향으로 이동한다 / 그리고 벽에 반사된다 / 각기 다른 시간과 장소에서 /

scrambling them so much that they are inaudible // when they arrive / at the ear of a listener forty feet away.

(= the sound waves) (= the sound waves)

분사구문(= so it scrambles ~) S′ V′ C′ 부사절 접속사(시간)

★<so+형용사[부사]+that+S′+V′ ...>: 너무 ~해서 …하다

이는 그것들(음파)을 너무 많이 뒤섞어서 들리지 않는다 // 그것들(음파)이 도달할 때는 / 40피트 떨어져 있는 듣는 사람의 귀에

↳ **일반적인 경우:** 음파는 모든 방향으로 이동하고 반사되어 뒤섞이므로 멀리 떨어진 사람에게 들리지 않음.

(⑤) 8But / when you whisper at a *focus*, // the reflected waves all arrive at the *same* time / at the other focus, /

부사절 접속사(시간) S V

그러나 / 여러분이 한쪽 '초점'에서 속삭일 때 // 반사되는 음파는 전부 '동시에' 도달한다 / 다른 한쪽 초점에 /

thus reinforcing one another and allowing your words to be heard.

분사구문(= and thus they reinforce ~ and allow ~) ★<allow+O+to-v>: O가 v하도록 하다

따라서 서로를 강화하여 여러분의 말이 들리게 한다

↳ **위스퍼링 갤러리의 경우:** '초점'에서 속삭여 반사되는 음파가 다른 초점에 동시에 도달하므로 소리를 들을 수 있음.

어휘

remarkable 놀라운, 주목할 만한
dome 돔, 반구형 지붕
curved 곡선의
ceiling 천장
locate (위치하고) 있다; 찾아내다
apart (시간·공간적으로) 떨어져
passageway 통로
passerby 지나가는 사람
focus 초점; 집중하다[시키다]
reflect 반사하다; (거울에 상을) 비추다; 반영하다
ordinarily 보통
sound wave 음파
travel 이동하다; 여행(하다)
bounce (소리가) 반사하다; (공이) 튀다
scramble 뒤섞다; 기어오르다
inaudible 들리지 않는
reinforce 강화하다

정답 가이드

주어진 문장의 That이 지칭하는 내용이 무엇인지를 찾아야 한다. 그것(That)이 목소리가 집중되는 초점 가까이에 여러분을 둔다고 했으므로 That은 목소리를 초점 가까이에 두도록 사람을 위치시키는 조건임을 알 수 있다. 따라서 주어진 문장은 이 조건을 제시하는 문장 5 뒤인 ④에 들어가는 것이 가장 적절하다.

오답 클리닉

① (3%) 앞에서 위스퍼링 갤러리의 예로 든 공간을 It으로 받아 부연 설명하는 내용이다.
② (11%) 앞 문장의 40피트 떨어져 혼잡한 통로에 분리된 동안 말을 주고받는 경험에 대해 설명을 덧붙이는 내용이다.
③ (20%) 앞 문장을 this effect로 받아 그 효과를 내기 위한 조건을 제시하는 내용이다.
⑤ (16%) 보통의 경우와 대조되는 '초점'에서 속삭일 때 소리가 들리는 원리가 역접 연결어 But으로 연결된다.

01 ✦ 요약문 〈20학년도 대수능 40번 | 정답률 69%〉 ⑤

구문분석 & 직독직해

생물 코끼리의 진화된 인사 행동

[1]Because elephant groups break up and reunite very frequently — / for instance, / in response to variation in food availability — // reunions are more important / in elephant society / than among primates.

부사절 접속사(이유) S′ V′ ~에 응하여 S V C

코끼리 집단은 매우 자주 헤어지고 재결합하기 때문에 / 예를 들어 / 먹이 이용 가능성의 변화에 응하여 // 재결합은 더 중요하다 / 코끼리 사회에서 / 영장류들 사이에서보다

↳ **도입:** 코끼리 집단에서 재결합은 중요함.

[2]And the species has evolved *elaborate greeting behaviors*, // the form (of which) reflects / the strength (of the social bond (between the individuals)) / 🔑 (A) 인사 형태는 유대감의 강도를 반영함.

→ (= elephant) S V O → 전치사+관계대명사(보충 설명) S′ V′ O′

그래서 그 종(種)(코끼리)은 정교한 인사 행동을 진화시켜 왔다 // 그리고 그 형태는 나타낸다 / 강도를 (사회적 유대감의 (개체들 사이의)) /

(much like // how you might merely shake hands / with a long-standing acquaintance // but hug *a close friend* [(who(m)[that]) you have not seen / in a while], / and maybe even tear up).

→ like의 O(명사절) 전치사 의문사 S″ V″₁ V″₂ 목적격 관계대명사 생략 V″₃

(마치 ~처럼 // 여러분이 단지 악수를 하는 것 / 오래된 지인들과 // 하지만 친한 친구는 껴안는 것 [여러분이 보지 못했던 / 한동안] / 그리고 어쩌면 눈물까지 흘릴 수도 있는 것)

↳ **세부 사항 1:** 코끼리 집단의 인사 행동은 개체들 사이의 사회적 유대감의 정도를 반영함.

[3]Elephants may greet each other / simply by reaching their trunks into each other's mouths, // (which is) possibly equivalent / to a human peck on the cheek.

S V O <by v-ing>: v함으로써 주격 관계대명사+be동사 생략(앞 절 보충 설명)

코끼리는 서로 인사할 수도 있다 / 단순히 코를 서로의 입 안에 갖다 댐으로써 // 그리고 이것은 아마도 같을 것이다 / 사람들이 뺨에 가볍게 입 맞추는 것과

↳ **예:** 코를 입 안에 대는 것은 가벼운 인사임.

🔑 (B) 오래 못 본 후에는 아주 극적인 표현으로 인사함.

[4]However, / after long absences, / members (of family and bond groups) / greet one another / with incredibly theatrical displays.

S V O

그러나 / 오랜 부재 후에 / 구성원들은 (가족과 유대 집단의) / 서로에게 인사한다 / 믿을 수 없을 만큼 극적인 표현으로

↳ **세부 사항 2:** 오랜 부재 후에는 아주 극적인 표현으로 인사함.

🔑 (A), (B) 인사의 격렬함은 친밀도뿐 아니라 헤어짐의 기간도 반영함.

[5]The fact // that the intensity reflects / the duration of the separation as well as the level of intimacy / suggests // that elephants have a sense of time as well.

S = 동격 접속사 명사구 병렬 V suggests의 O(명사절) *<A as well as B>: B뿐만 아니라 A도

사실은 // 격렬함이 반영한다는 / 친밀도뿐만 아니라 헤어짐의 기간도 / 암시한다 // 코끼리들도 시간 감각이 있다는 것을

↳ **시사점:** 헤어져 있던 기간에 따라 다른 인사의 격렬함은 코끼리에게 시간 감각이 있음을 의미함.

[6]To human eyes, / these greetings strike a familiar chord.

S V O

사람의 눈에 / 이 인사 행위(오랜 부재 후의 인사)는 친숙한 감정을 불러일으킨다

[7]I'm reminded / of *the joyous reunions* (so visible / in the arrivals area (of an international airport terminal).

형용사구

나는 연상된다 / 아주 기뻐하는 재회가 (잘 보이는 / 도착 구역에서 (국제공항 터미널의))

↳ **부연 설명(비유):** 긴 헤어짐 후 코끼리의 극적인 인사는 사람들이 공항에서 재회하는 장면을 연상시킴.

↓

[8]The evolved greeting behaviors (of elephants) / can serve as an indicator (of how much they are socially **(A) tied** and how long they have been **(B) parted**).

S V 전치사(~로(서)) of의 O₁(명사절 병렬) of의 O₂(명사절 병렬)

진화된 인사 행동은 (코끼리의) / 지표로 쓰일 수 있다 (그것들이 얼마나 많이 사회적으로 (A) 연결되어 있는지와 얼마나 오랫동안 (B) 헤어져 있었는지에 대한)

해석

[1]코끼리 집단은 예를 들어, 먹이 이용 가능성의 변화에 응하여, 매우 자주 헤어지고 재결합하기 때문에 재결합은 영장류들 사이에서보다 코끼리 사회에서 더 중요하다. [2]그래서 그 종(種)(코끼리)은 정교한 인사 행동을 진화시켜 왔는데, 그 형태는 (마치 여러분이 오래된 지인들과 단지 악수를 하지만 한동안 여러분이 보지 못했던 친한 친구는 껴안고, 어쩌면 눈물까지 흘릴 수도 있는 것처럼) 개체들 사이의 사회적 유대감의 강도를 나타낸다. [3]코끼리는 단순히 코를 서로의 입 안에 갖다 댐으로써 서로 인사할 수도 있는데, 이것은 아마도 사람들이 뺨에 가볍게 입 맞추는 것과 같을 것이다. [4]그러나 오랜 부재 후에 가족과 유대 집단의 구성원들은 믿을 수 없을 만큼 극적인 표현으로 서로에게 인사한다. [5]격렬함이 친밀도뿐만 아니라 헤어짐의 기간도 반영한다는 사실은 코끼리들도 시간 감각이 있다는 것을 암시한다. [6]사람의 눈에 이 인사 행위는 친숙한 감정을 불러일으킨다. [7]나는 국제공항 터미널의 도착 구역에서 잘 보이는 아주 기뻐하는 재회가 연상된다.

↓

[8]코끼리의 진화된 인사 행동은 그것들이 얼마나 많이 사회적으로 (A) 연결되어 있는지와 얼마나 오랫동안 (B) 헤어져 있었는지에 대한 지표로 쓰일 수 있다.

어휘

break up 헤어지다; 부서지다
reunite 재결합[재회]하다
cf. reunion 재회; 모임, 동창회
variation 변화, 변동; 변형
primate 영장류
evolve 진화[발달]시키다[하다]
elaborate 정교한; 자세히 설명하다
greeting 인사; 안부의 말
reflect 나타내다, 반영하다; (모습을) 비추다
bond 유대(감을 형성하다); 접착하다
long-standing 오래된
tear up 눈물을 흘리다
trunk (코끼리의) 코; 나무의 몸통; 여행용 큰 가방
equivalent to A A와 같은, A와 동등한
absence 부재 (기간); 없음, 결여
theatrical 극적인, 연극의; 과장된
display 표현, 드러냄; 전시[진열](하다)
intensity 격렬함, 강렬함; (빛 등의) 강도
intimacy 친밀함
strike a chord ~을 불러일으키다
[요약문] serve 쓰일 수 있다, 적합하다
indicator 지표, 척도; 표시기

정답 가이드

요약문을 통해 코끼리들의 진화된 인사 행동이 무엇을 보여주는 지표인지를 설명하는 글임을 알 수 있다. 코끼리들의 인사 행동의 격렬함이 '친밀도'뿐만 아니라 '헤어짐의 기간'도 반영한다고 했으므로, 요약문의 빈칸 (A)와 (B)에 각각 들어갈 말로 가장 적절한 것은 ⑤ 'tied(연결된) - parted(헤어진)'이다.

오답 클리닉

(A) (B)

① competitive - disconnected (15%) 경쟁력 있는 - 따로 떨어진
(A)는 틀리며, (B)는 맞음.

② tied - endangered (8%) 연결된 - 멸종 위기에 처한
(A)는 맞지만, (B)는 틀림.

③ responsible - isolated (3%) 책임감 있는 - 고립된
(A)는 틀리며, (B)는 맞음.

④ competitive - united (6%) 경쟁력 있는 - 통합된
(A)는 틀리며, (B)는 글의 내용과 반대됨.

02~03 + 복합 유형

22학년도 6월 모평 41~42번 | 정답률 02 70%, 03 49%

02 ③ 03 ②

구문분석 & 직독직해

사회 사생활 권리 개념의 변화

03-(a) 사생활권은 타인의 권리에 의해 제한되듯이 공공의 이익에 의해서도 '비슷하게' 제한됨.

[1]The right to privacy may extend / only to *the point* [where it does not restrict / someone else's right to freedom of expression or right to information].

S V 관계부사 S′ V′ O′

사생활권은 확장될 수 있다 / 정도까지만 [그것이 제한하지 않는 / 다른 사람의 표현의 자유에 대한 권리나 정보에 대한 권리를]

[2]The scope (of the right to privacy) / is **(a) similarly** restricted / by the general interest / in preventing crime or in promoting public health.

S V 전치사구 병렬

범위는 (사생활권의) / 비슷하게 제한된다 / 공공이익에 의해 / 범죄 예방이나 공중 보건 증진에서의

주제문

03-(b) 소유 기반에서 생활 범주로 사생활 개념이 확장 이동하면 그 한계를 설정하기가 '더 어려울' 것임.

[3]However, / when we move away / from *the property-based notion of a right* [(where the right to privacy would protect, / for example, / images and personality)], / to modern notions of private and family life, //

부사절 접속사(시간) ★<from A to B>: A에서 B로 관계부사 S″ V″ O″

하지만 / 우리가 옮겨갈 때 / 소유에 기반을 둔 권리 개념에서 [(사생활권이 보호할 것이라는 / 예를 들어 / 이미지와 인격을)] / 사생활과 가정생활이라는 현대적 개념으로 //

we find it **(b) easier(→ harder)** / to establish the limits (of the right).

S V 가목적어 C 진목적어(to-v구)

우리는 (~이) 더 쉽다는(→ 더 어렵다는) 것을 알게 된다 / 한계를 설정하기가 (그 권리의)

↳ 권리의 개념이 소유 기반에서 개인과 가정생활이라는 현대적 개념으로 옮겨가면서 권리의 한계 설정이 더 어려워짐.

(= 앞 문장의 주절)

[4]This is, (of course), / the strength (of the notion of privacy), // in that it can adapt / to meet changing expectations and technological advances.

S V C ~라는 점에서 (= the notion of privacy) 목적(~하기 위해) to meet의 O(명사구 병렬)

이것(사생활권의 한계를 설정하기 어려운 것)은 (물론) / 강점이다 (사생활 개념의) // 그것(사생활 개념)이 적응할 수 있다는 점에서 / 변화하는 기대와 기술 발전에 대응하기 위해

↳ **장점:** 변화하는 기대와 기술 진보에 따라 사생활 개념이 적응할[바뀔] 수 있음.

[5]In sum, / *what* is privacy today?

요컨대 / 오늘날 사생활이란 '무엇'인가

[6]The concept includes a claim // that we should be unobserved, // and that certain information and images (about us) / should not be **(c) circulated** / without our permission.

S V O = 동격절₁ 동격절₂

그 개념은 주장을 포함한다 // 우리가 다른 사람의 주목을 받지 않아야 한다는 // 그리고 특정 정보와 이미지가 (우리에 관한) / 유포되어서는 안 된다는 / 우리의 허락 없이

03-(c) 사생활 개념은 우리 허락 없이 정보가 '유포되지' 않아야 함을 의미함.

↳ **오늘날 사생활의 개념:** 우리가 타인에 의해 주시되지 않고 우리에 대한 특정 정보와 이미지가 허락 없이 유포되지 않는 것임.

해석

[1]사생활권은 다른 사람의 표현의 자유에 대한 권리나 정보에 대한 권리를 제한하지 않는 정도까지만 확장될 수 있다. [2]사생활권의 범위는 범죄 예방이나 공중 보건 증진에서의 공공이익에 의해 (a) 비슷하게 제한된다. [3]하지만 우리가 소유에 기반을 둔 권리 개념(예를 들어 사생활권이 이미지와 인격을 보호할 것이라는)에서 사생활과 가정생활이라는 현대적 개념으로 옮겨갈 때, 우리는 그 권리의 한계를 설정하기가 (b) 더 쉽다는(→ 더 어렵다는) 것을 알게 된다.(▶ 사생활 권리가 사적 소유 기반(예: 개인의 사진)에서 생활 범주로 확장되면 그 권리의 한계를 정하기 어려워진다는 의미) [4]이것은 물론 변화하는 기대와 기술 발전에 대응하기 위해 적응할 수 있다는 점에서, 사생활 개념의 강점이다.(▶ 권리의 한계를 설정하기 어려운 것은 사생활 개념이 세상의 변화에 맞춰 같이 변화할 수 있음을 의미) [5]요컨대, 오늘날 사생활이란 '무엇'인가? [6]그 개념은 우리가 다른 사람들의 주목을 받지 않아야 한다는 주장과, 우리의 허락 없이 우리에 관한 특정 정보와 이미지가 (c) 유포되어서는 안 된다는 주장을 포함한다. [7]'왜' 이러한 사생활 주장들이 생겼는가? [8]그것은 영향력 있는 사람들이 그런 주목에 불쾌감을 느꼈기 때문에 생겼다. [9]게다가 사생활은 가족, 가정, 그리고 서신을 임의의 (d) 간섭으로부터 보호할 필요성을 포함했고, 또한 명예와 평판을 보호하려는 결의가 있었다. [10]사생활은 '어떻게' 보호되는가? [11]역사적으로 사생활은 피해를 주는 자료의 유포를 제한함으로써 보호되었다. [12]그러나 사생활 개념이 사진과 신문을 통한 이미지 재생산에 대한 대응으로 처음 법적으로 관심을 끌게 되었다면, 자료 저장, 디지털 이미지, 그리고 인터넷과 같은 더 최근의 기술 발전은 사생활에 새로운 위협을 (e) 제기한다. [13]사생활권은 이제 그러한 문제들에 대처하기 위해 재해석되고 있다.

어휘

extend 확장[확대]하다
restrict 제한하다

[7] *Why* did these privacy claims arise?
'왜' 이러한(주목받지 않고 허락 없이 정보가 유포되면 안 된다는) 사생활 주장들이 생겼는가

(= these privacy claims)
[8] They arose // because powerful people took offence / at such observation.
S V 부사절 접속사(이유) S' V' O'
그것들은 생겼다 // 영향력 있는 사람들이 불쾌감을 느꼈기 때문에 / 그런 주목에

03-(d) 사생활 주장이 임의의 간섭으로부터 가족, 가정, 서신을 보호할 필요성에서 나왔다고 보는 것이 적절함.
[9] Furthermore, / privacy incorporated *the need* (to protect the family, home, and correspondence / from arbitrary **(d) interference**) // and, (in addition), / there has been *a determination* (to protect honour and reputation).
S₁ V₁ O V₂ S₂
게다가 / 사생활은 필요성을 포함했다 (가족, 가정, 그리고 서신을 보호할 / 임의의 간섭으로부터) // 그리고 (또한) / 결의가 있었다 (명예와 평판을 보호하려는)
↳ **사생활 주장의 배경:** 영향력 있는 사람들이 느끼는 주시에 대한 불쾌감, 간섭으로부터 생활을 보호할 필요성, 명예와 평판을 보호하려는 결의 때문임.

[10] *How* is privacy protected?
사생활은 '어떻게' 보호되는가

03-(c) 자료 '유포'를 제한해 사생활을 보호한다고 했음.
[11] Historically, / privacy was protected / by restricting circulation (of the damaging material).
S V <by v-ing>: v함으로써
역사적으로 / 사생활은 보호되었다 / 유포를 제한함으로써 (피해를 주는 자료의)

[12] But if the concept of privacy first became interesting legally / as a response to reproductions of images / through photography and newspapers, //
부사절 접속사(조건) S' V' C' 전치사(~으로)
그러나 사생활 개념이 처음 법적으로 관심을 끌게 되었다면 / 이미지 재생산에 대한 대응으로 / 사진과 신문을 통한 //
more recent technological advances, / (such as data storage, digital images, and the Internet), / **(e) pose** new threats / to privacy.
S V O
03-(e) 최근 기술 발전이 사생활 보호를 어렵게 하면서 새로운 위협을 '제기함'.
더 최근의 기술 발전은 / (자료 저장, 디지털 이미지, 그리고 인터넷과 같은) / 새로운 위협을 제기한다 / 사생활에
↳ **기존의 사생활 보호 방법과 새로운 위협:** 자료 유포를 제한했었지만, 최근 기술 발전으로 사생활에 대한 새로운 위협이 생김.

[13] The right to privacy / is now being reinterpreted / to meet those challenges.
V(현재진행 수동태) 목적(~하기 위해) (= new threats)
사생활권은 / 이제 재해석되고 있다 / 그러한 문제들에 대처하기 위해
↳ **결과:** 새로운 문제에 대처하기 위해 사생활권이 재해석되고 있음.

scope 범위
general interest 공공이익
promote 증진[촉진]하다; 진급시키다
property-based 소유[자산]에 기반을 둔
establish 설정하다; 수립하다
adapt 적응하다; 조정하다
meet 대응하다; 충족시키다; 만나다
advance 발전, 진전
unobserved 주목되지 않는
permission 허락, 허가
take offence 불쾌감을 느끼다
observation 주시, 관찰(력), 감시
incorporate 포함하다; 설립하다
correspondence 서신, 편지; 관련성
determination 결의, 결심
reputation 평판, 명성
damaging 피해를 주는, 해로운
legally 법적으로
reproduction 재생산
reinterpret 재해석하다
challenge (어려운) 문제, 도전; 이의를 제기하다
[선택지] side effect 부작용
domain 영역, 범위
evolve 발달하다; 진화하다
practice 실제; 실천, 실행; 연습
regulation 규정(된), 규제
intervention 개입, 간섭, 중재

정답 가이드

02 사생활권은 타인의 권리와 공공이익에 의해 제한되는데, 역접 연결어 However 이후부터 권리의 개념이 개인과 가족의 생활이라는 현대적 개념으로 옮겨가면서 한계를 설정하기가 어려워진다고 내용이 전환된다. 이는 변화하는 기대와 기술 진보에 맞춰 사생활 개념이 적응할 수 있다는 강점으로 볼 수 있으며, 마지막 문장에서 최근의 기술 발전이 제기한 사생활 보호 문제에 대처하기 위해 사생활권이 재해석되고 있다고 했다. 이를 통해 사생활 개념이 변화하고 발전함을 알 수 있으므로 글의 제목으로 가장 적절한 것은 ③ 'The Right to Privacy: Evolving Concepts and Practices(사생활권의 진화하는 개념과 실제)'이다.

03 사생활권이 타인의 권리와 공공이익에 의해 제한된다는 앞 내용과 역접 연결어 However로 이어지고 있고 소유에 기반을 둔 권리에서 현대적 권리 개념으로 이동하는 경우를 설명하는 것이므로, 권리의 한계를 설정하는 것이 '더 어려워졌다'는 의미가 되어야 자연스럽다. 따라서 ② 'easier(더 쉬운)'를 'harder(더 어려운)' 등으로 바꿔야 한다.

The 핵심 ★ 글의 요지는 사생활권의 개념이 변화하는 기대와 기술 발전에 따라 같이 바뀌고 재해석된다는 것이므로 그 변화에 맞춰 한계를 설정하는 것은 어려울 것이다.

오답 클리닉

02 ① Side Effects of Privacy Protection Technologies (11%)
사생활 보호 기술(×)의 부작용(×)
사생활 보호 기술이나 그 부작용에 대한 내용이 아님.
② The Legal Domain of Privacy Claims and Conflicts (10%)
사생활 주장과 갈등(×)의 법률적 영역
legally를 활용한 오답. 사생활 주장과 관련한 갈등에 대한 글이 아님.
④ Who Really Benefits from Looser Privacy Regulations? (5%)
더 느슨한(×) 사생활 규정으로부터 누가 정말 득을 보는가(×)?
느슨한 사생활 규정으로 이득을 보는 사람이나 집단에 대한 설명은 없음.
⑤ Less Is More: Reduce State Intervention in Privacy! (4%)
적을수록 좋으므로 사생활에 대한 국가의 개입(×)을 줄여라!
사생활에 대한 국가의 개입을 줄여야 한다고 주장하는 글이 아님.

03 ① similarly (5%) 비슷하게
사생활권이 타인의 권리를 제한하지 않는 정도에서 한정된다는 앞 문장과 '비슷하게' 공공이익에 의해서도 제한된다는 내용이 이어지는 것은 문맥상 적절하다.
③ circulated (9%) 유포되는
사생활 주장은 우리의 허락 없이 우리에 대한 정보가 '유포되어서는' 안 된다는 의미가 되는 것이 자연스럽다. 또한 문장 11의 피해를 주는 자료의 유포를 제한함으로써 사생활이 보호되었다는 내용과도 상응됨을 알 수 있다.
④ interference (26%) 간섭
사생활 주장이 가족, 가정, 서신을 임의의 '간섭'으로부터 보호하려는 필요성에서 나왔다는 흐름은 자연스럽다.
⑤ pose (11%) 제기하다
자료 저장, 디지털 이미지, 인터넷과 같은 최근 기술 발전이 사생활 보호를 어렵게 만들어 새로운 위협을 '제기한다'는 흐름은 자연스럽다.

01 + 빈칸 추론 〈18학년도 대수능 33번 | 정답률 51%〉 ①

구문분석 & 직독직해

농업 자본주의적 생산 방식의 문제점

[1]In the less developed world, / the percentage (of *the population* (involved in agriculture)) / is declining, //
S1 과거분사구 V1
저개발 세계에서 / 비율은 (인구의 (농업에 종사하는) / 감소하고 있다 //

but at the same time, / *those* (remaining in agriculture) / are not benefiting / from technological advances.
S2 현재분사구 V2
그러나 동시에 / 사람들은 (농업에 남아 있는) / 득을 보지 못하고 있다 / 기술의 발전으로부터

↳ **도입:** 저개발 국가의 농민들은 기술 발전의 혜택을 받지 못함.

[2]The typical scenario (in the less developed world) / is *one* [in which a very few commercial agriculturalists are technologically advanced // while the vast majority are incapable of competing].
S V C(→ (= the scenario)) 전치사+관계대명사 S′ V′ C′ 부사절 접속사(~인 반면에) S″ V″ C″
전형적인 시나리오는 (저개발 세계에서의) / 것(시나리오)이다 [아주 소수의 상업 농장주들이 기술적으로 앞서 있다는 // 대다수는 경쟁할 수 없는 반면에]

↳ 소수의 농장주들만 선진 기술을 사용함.

주제문

[3]Indeed, / this vast majority **have lost control** (**over their own production**) / because of larger global causes.
S V O 전치사(~ 때문에)
사실 / 이 대다수는 통제력을 잃었다 (자신들의 생산에 대한) / 더 큰 세계적인 원인 때문에

↳ **문제점:** 세계적인 문제로 소작농이 생산 통제력을 잃음.

[4]As an example, / in Kenya, / farmers are actively encouraged / to grow export crops (such as tea and coffee) / at the expense of basic food production.
전치사(~로(서)) S V C
★<encourage+O+to-v(O가 v할 것을 장려하다)>의 수동형
🔑 케냐 농부들이 수출 작물을 재배하도록 장려됨.
한 예로 / 케냐에서 / 농부들은 적극적으로 장려된다 / 수출 작물을 재배하도록 (차와 커피와 같은) / 기초식품 생산을 희생하면서

↳ **예:** 케냐 농부들은 기초식품이 아닌 수출 작물을 재배하도록 권장됨.

[5]The result is // that a staple crop, / such as maize, / is not being produced / in a sufficient amount.
S V 명사절 접속사(→ is의 C(명사절)) S′ V′(현재진행 수동태)
🔑 주요 식량 작물 생산이 부족해짐.
그 결과는 ~이다 // 주요 작물이 / 옥수수와 같은 / 생산되고 있지 않다는 것 / 충분한 양으로

↳ **예의 결과:** 케냐의 주요 작물이 충분히 생산되지 못함.

[6]The essential argument here is //
S V
여기에서 본질적인 논점은 ~이다 //

that the capitalist mode of production is affecting / peasant production (in the less developed world) / in such a way as to limit the production (of staple foods), / thus causing a food problem.
→ is의 C(명사절) 명사절 접속사 S′ V′ O′
🔑 자본주의적 생산 방식은 저개발 국가의 주요 식품 생산을 제한함.
<in such a way as to-v>: v하는 방식으로 분사구문(= and thus it is casuing ~)
자본주의적 생산 방식이 영향을 미치고 있다는 것 / 소농의 생산에 (저개발 세계의) / 생산을 제한하는 방식으로 (주요 식품의) / 그리고 따라서 식량 문제를 일으키고 있다(는 것)

↳ **결론:** 자본주의적 생산 방식이 식량 문제를 야기함.

해석

[1]저개발 세계에서, 농업에 종사하는 인구의 비율은 감소하고 있지만, 동시에 농업에 남아 있는 사람들은 기술의 발전으로부터 득을 보지 못하고 있다. [2]저개발 세계에서의 전형적인 시나리오는 아주 소수의 상업 농장주들이 기술적으로 앞서 있는 반면에 대다수는 경쟁할 수 없다는 것이다. [3]사실, 이 대다수는 더 큰 세계적인 원인 때문에 자신들의 생산에 대한 통제력을 잃었다. [4]한 예로, 케냐에서 농부들은 기초식품 생산을 희생하면서 차와 커피와 같은 수출 작물을 재배하도록 적극적으로 장려된다. [5]그 결과는 옥수수와 같은 주요 작물이 충분한 양으로 생산되고 있지 않다는 것이다. [6]여기에서 본질적인 논점은 자본주의적 생산 방식이 주요 식품의 생산을 제한하는 방식으로 저개발 세계의 소농의 생산에 영향을 미쳐 식량 문제를 일으키고 있다는 것이다.

어휘

involve 종사시키다; 포함하다
cf. involvement 개입, 관련
agriculture 농업
cf. agriculturalist 농장주, 농업 전문가
advance 발전, 진전
cf. advanced 앞선, 선진의; 고급의
typical 전형적인
commercial 상업의
incapable of ~할 수 없는
actively 적극적으로
crop (농)작물
at the expense of ~을 희생하면서
sufficient 충분한
essential 본질적인; 필수적인
argument 논점; 주장; 언쟁, 논쟁
capitalist 자본주의적인; 자본주의자
[선택지] turn to A A에 의지하다
cash crop 환금 작물 ((팔기 위해 재배하는 농작물))
regain 되찾다

정답 가이드

빈칸 문장의 this vast majority는 기술적으로 뒤처진 대다수의 농업 종사 인구를 말하며 이들이 세계적인 원인 때문에 '어떠했는지' 그 '결과'에 해당하는 내용을 추론해야 한다. 이어지는 설명에서 기초식품 생산 대신 수출 작물을 재배하게 되어, 그 결과 주요 작물이 충분히 생산되고 있지 않아 식량 문제가 일어난다고 했다. 자본주의적 생산 방식이 주요 식품의 생산을 제한한다는 것이므로, 빈칸에 들어갈 말로 가장 적절한 것은 ① 'have lost control over their own production(자신들의 생산에 대한 통제력을 잃었다)'이다.

오답 클리닉

② have turned to technology for food production (11%)
식품 생산을 위해 기술에 의지했다
대다수 농민들은 기술 혜택을 받지 못한다고 했으므로 틀림.

③ have challenged the capitalist mode of production (21%)
자본주의적 생산 방식에 이의를 제기했다
자본주의적 생산 방식을 따른 결과 식량 부족 문제가 생긴 것이므로 이의를 제기했다고 볼 수 없음.

④ have reduced their involvement in growing cash crops (12%)
환금 작물을 재배하는 것에 대한 개입을 줄였다
수출 작물 재배가 장려된다고 했으므로 개입을 줄였다고 볼 수 없음.

⑤ have regained their competitiveness in the world market (5%)
세계 시장에서 자신들의 경쟁력을 되찾았다
대부분의 저개발 국가 농부들은 경쟁력이 없다고 했으므로 틀림.

02 ✦ 글의 순서 〈20학년도 6월 모평 36번 | 정답률 56%〉 ②

구문분석 & 직독직해 예술 악보 표기법의 장단점

[1] Notation was more than a practical method (for preserving an expanding repertoire of music).
S V C
악보 표기법은 실용적인 방법 이상이었다 (음악의 확장되는 연주곡목을 보존하기 위한)
↳ **악보 표기법의 장점 1:** 연주곡목을 보존함.

(= Notation) 주어진 문장의 Notation을 (B)에서 It으로 받음.
(B) [2] It changed the nature (of the art itself).
S V O
그것(악보 표기법)은 본성을 바꾸었다 (예술 그 자체의)
↳ 악보 표기법은 예술의 본성을 바꿈.

[3] To write something down means // that people (far away in space and time) / can re-create it.
S(to-v구) V(단수) means의 O(명사절)
무언가를 적는다는 것은 의미한다 // 사람들이 (공간과 시간 면에서 멀리 떨어져 있는) / 그것을 재현할 수 있다는 것을
↳ **악보 표기법의 장점 2:** 악보를 통해 누구나 시공간에 상관없이 곡을 재현할 수 있음.

[4] At the same time, / there are downsides.
V S
동시에 / 불리한 면이 있다
↳ **대조:** 악보 표기법은 단점 또한 있음.

(B)의 마지막에 언급된 악보 표기법의 불리한 면을 구체적으로 설명함.
(A) [5] Written notes freeze the music / rather than allowing it to develop / in the hands (of individuals), // and it discourages improvisation.
S_1 V_1 O_1 (= the music) *<allow+O+to-v>: O가 v하도록 허용하다 전치사 rather than의 O(동명사구) S_2(= 앞 절) V_2 O_2
표기된 음은 그 음악을 고정시킨다 / 그것(그 음악)이 발전하도록 허용하기보다는 / 손에서 (개인들의) //
그리고 그것(표기된 음이 음악을 고정하는 것)은 즉흥 연주를 막는다
↳ **악보 표기법의 단점 1:** 음악을 고정시킴.

[6] Partly because of notation, / modern classical performance lacks / the depth (of *nuance* [that is part of aural tradition]).
전치사(~ 때문에) S V O 주격 관계대명사
부분적으로 악보 표기법 때문에 / 현대의 고전 음악 공연은 없다 / 깊이가 (음의 미묘한 차이의 [청각 전승의 일부인])
↳ **악보 표기법의 단점 2:** 청각으로 전승되는 음의 미묘한 차이의 깊이가 없음.

[7] Before notation arrived, // in all history / music was largely carried on / as an aural tradition.
부사절 접속사(시간) S V 전치사(~로(서))
악보 표기법이 등장하기 전에 // 역사를 통틀어 / 음악은 대체로 계속되었다 / 청각 전승으로
↳ 악보 표기법 이전의 상황을 대조시킴.

해석

[1]악보 표기법은 음악의 확장되는 연주곡목을 보존하기 위한 실용적인 방법 이상이었다. (B) [2]그것(악보 표기법)은 예술 그 자체의 본성을 바꾸었다. [3]무언가를 적는다는 것은 공간과 시간 면에서 멀리 떨어져 있는 사람들이 그것을 재현할 수 있다는 것을 의미한다. [4]동시에, 불리한 면이 있다. (A) [5]표기된 음은 그것(그 음악)이 개인들의 손에서 발전하도록 허용하기보다는 그 음악을 고정시키며, 그것(표기된 음이 음악을 고정하는 것)은 즉흥 연주를 막는다. [6]부분적으로 악보 표기법 때문에 현대의 고전 음악 공연은 청각 전승의 일부인 음의 미묘한 차이의 깊이가 없다. [7]악보 표기법이 등장하기 전에, 역사를 통틀어 음악은 대체로 청각 전승으로 계속되었다. (C) [8]인도 음악과 발리 음악과 같은 정교한 음악적인 전통을 포함하여 대부분의 세계 음악은 여전히 기본적으로 청각적이다. [9]재즈 음악가 대부분은 악보를 읽을 수 있지만 흔히 신경 쓰지 않으며, 그들의 예술은 즉흥 연주와 많이 연관된다. [10]많은 현대 대중음악가들은, Paul McCartney가 한 사례인데, 악보를 전혀 읽지 못한다.

어휘

notation 악보 표기(법), 기보법; 기록
practical 실용적인; 현실적인
preserve 보존하다; 지키다
expand 확장되다[하다]
repertoire 연주[노래]곡목, 레퍼토리
nature 본성, 천성; 자연
downside 불리한[부정적인] 면
note 음(표); 주목하다
freeze 고정시키다; 얼다[얼리다]
discourage 막다, 방해하다; 의욕을 꺾다

🔑 (A)의 마지막에 언급된 청각 전승 음악이 여전히 대부분임을 보충 설명함.

(C) [8]Most world music is still basically aural, / including sophisticated musical traditions (such as Indian and Balinese).
S V C 전치사(~을 포함하여)
대부분의 세계 음악은 여전히 기본적으로 청각적이다 / 정교한 음악적인 전통을 포함하여 (인도 음악과 발리 음악과 같은)
↳ 전 세계 대부분의 음악은 여전히 청각을 기반으로 함.

[9]Most jazz musicians can read music / but often don't bother, // and their art is much involved / with improvisation.
S₁ V₁₋₁ O V₁₋₂ S₂ V₂
재즈 음악가 대부분은 악보를 읽을 수 있다 / 하지만 흔히 신경 쓰지 않는다 // 그리고 그들의 예술은 많이 연관된다 / 즉흥 연주와

*문장의 주어(many modern pop music)와 분사구문의 의미상 주어가 달라 의미상 주어(one example)가 분사 앞에 위치함.
[10]Many modern pop musicians, / one example being Paul McCartney, / can't read music at all.
S 분사구문(= and one example is ~) V O
많은 현대 대중음악가들은 / Paul McCartney가 한 사례인데 / 악보를 전혀 읽지 못한다
↳ 대부분의 재즈 음악가는 악보를 신경 쓰지 않고 주로 즉흥 연주를 하며, 많은 현대 대중음악가들은 악보를 읽지 못하기도 함.

lack ~이 없다[부족하다]
nuance (음·빛깔·의미 등의) 미묘한 차이, 뉘앙스
tradition 전승; 전통
largely 대체로, 주로
carry on ~을 계속하다
sophisticated 정교한; 세련된
bother 신경 쓰다; 귀찮게 하다

정답 가이드

악보 표기법이 음악의 연주곡목을 보존하는 실용적인 방법이었다는 주어진 글 뒤에는 Notation을 대명사 It으로 받아 다른 장점을 추가로 설명하는 (B)가 오는 것이 적절하다. (B)의 마지막 문장에서 악보 표기법은 불리한 면도 있다고 내용이 전환되는데, 그다음에는 악보 표기법의 구체적인 단점을 설명하는 (A)가 이어져야 한다. (C)는 (A)에서 언급한 청각 전승에 대한 구체적인 예를 제시하므로 마지막에 오는 것이 가장 자연스럽다.

오답 클리닉

① (A) - (C) - (B) (5%)
주어진 글은 악보 표기법의 장점에 해당하고 (A)는 단점에 해당하므로, (A)가 주어진 글 뒤에 바로 오는 것은 흐름상 부적절하다.
③ (B) - (C) - (A) (9%)
(A)에서 언급한 청각 전승을 (C)에서 자세히 설명하고 있으므로 (C)는 (A) 뒤에 와야 한다.
④ (C) - (A) - (B) (18%) / ⑤ (C) - (B) - (A) (11%)
악보 표기법의 장점에 대한 주어진 글 뒤에 대부분의 음악이 청각적이어서 악보를 신경 쓰지 않는다는 (C)가 바로 오는 것은 흐름상 부적절하다.

03 + 문장 넣기 〈20학년도 6월 모평 38번 | 정답률 51%〉 ⑤

구문분석 & 직독직해 심리 부정적인 경험에서 얻는 강렬한 행복

[1]We seek out feel-good experiences, / (being) always on the lookout / for the next holiday, purchase or culinary experience.
S V O 분사구문(= as we are ~)
우리는 기분을 좋게 해주는 경험을 찾아낸다 / 항상 세심히 살피면서 / 다음 휴일, 물건 사기, 또는 요리 체험을

(= this approach to happiness)
[2]This approach (to happiness) / is relatively recent; // it depends on our capacity (both to pad our lives with material pleasures / and to feel // that we can control our suffering).
S₁ V₁ C S₂ V₂ O =
*to-v구 두 개가 <both A and B(A와 B 둘 다)>로 연결됨. to feel의 O(명사절)
이런 접근법은 (행복에 대한) / 비교적 최근의 것이다 // 그것(행복에 대한 이런 접근법)은 우리의 능력에 달려 있다 (우리의 삶을 물질적 즐거움으로 채워 넣고 / 그리고 느끼는 // 우리가 우리의 고통을 제어할 수 있다고)
↳ **대조 A:** 우리는 기분을 좋게 해주는 경험(물질적 즐거움과 고통의 제어)을 통해 행복을 추구함.

(①) [3]Painkillers, / (as we know them today), / are a relatively recent invention // and access (to material comfort) / is now within reach (of a much larger proportion (of the world's population)).
S₁ 부사절 삽입 V₁ C₁ S₂ V₂ 비교급 강조 부사
진통제는 / (오늘날 우리가 그것들을 알고 있는 것처럼) / 비교적 최근의 발명품이다 //
그리고 접근은 (물질적 안락에 대한) / 이제 손이 닿는 곳에 있다 (훨씬 더 큰 비율의 (전 세계 인구의))

(②) [4]These technological and economic advances have had significant cultural implications, / leading us to see our negative experiences / as a problem / and maximizing our positive experiences / as the answer.
S V O
*<lead+O+to-v>: O가 v하도록 이끌다
분사구문 병렬(= and they have led ~ and have maximized ~)
이런 과학 기술과 경제의 발전은 상당한 문화적 영향을 미쳤다 /
우리가 우리의 부정적인 경험을 보게 했다 / 문제로 / 그리고 우리의 긍정적인 경험을 극대화했다 / 그 해결책으로
↳ 과학 기술과 경제의 발전으로 우리는 부정적 경험을 고쳐야 할 문제로 보고, 긍정적 경험은 해결책으로 보고 극대화함.

해석

[1]우리는 항상 다음 휴일, 물건 사기, 또는 요리 체험을 세심히 살피면서 기분을 좋게 해주는 경험을 찾아낸다. [2]행복에 대한 이런 접근법은 비교적 최근의 것인데, 그것(행복에 대한 이런 접근법)은 우리의 삶을 물질적 즐거움으로 채워 넣고 우리가 우리의 고통을 제어할 수 있다고 느끼는 우리의 능력에 달려 있다. (①) [3]오늘날 우리가 알고 있는 것처럼 진통제는 비교적 최근의 발명품이며, 물질적 안락에 대한 접근은 이제 전 세계 인구의 훨씬 더 큰 비율의 손이 닿는 곳에 있다.(▶오늘날 많은 사람이 물질적 안락을 누릴 수 있다는 의미) (②) [4]이런 과학 기술과 경제의 발전은 상당한 문화적 영향을 미쳐서, 우리가 우리의 부정적인 경험을 문제로 보게 하고 그 해결책으로 우리의 긍정적인 경험을 극대화했다. (③) [5]하지만 이를 통해 우리는 인생에서 행복한 것이 단지 즐거움에 관한 것만은 아니라는 것을 잊게 되었다. (④) [6]편안함, 만족감 그리고 충족감이 행복의 특효약이었던 적은 절대 없었다. (⑤ [7]오히려, 행복은 우리가 가장 상처받기 쉽거나 혼자이거나 고통을 겪는 그런 순간에 자주 발견된다.) [8]행복은 거기에, 즉 이런 경험의 가장자리에 있고, 우리가 '그런' 종류의 행복을 언뜻 보게 될 때, 그것은 강력하고 뛰어나며 강렬하다.

(③) [5]Yet, / through this / we have forgotten // that being happy in life is not just about pleasure.
(= 앞 문장) S V 명사절 접속사 S'(동명사구) V' C'
(have forgotten의 O(명사절))
하지만 / 이를 통해 / 우리는 잊게 되었다 // 인생에서 행복한 것이 단지 즐거움에 관한 것만은 아니라는 것을

주어진 문장과 대조되는 행복을 얻는 긍정적 경험임.
(④) [6]Comfort, contentment and satisfaction have never been the elixir of happiness.
S(복수) V(복수) C
편안함, 만족감 그리고 충족감이 행복의 특효약이었던 적은 절대 없었다
↳ **대조 B:** 행복은 즐거움, 편안함, 만족감 등에만 관련된 것이 아님.

주제문
Rather로 이어지므로 행복을 얻는 긍정적 경험을 언급한 뒤에 와야 함.
(⑤) [7]Rather, / happiness is often found / in *those moments* [(when) we are most vulnerable, alone or in pain].)
S V 관계부사 생략
오히려 / 행복은 자주 발견된다 / 그런 순간에 [우리가 가장 상처받기 쉽거나 혼자이거나 고통을 겪는]

주어진 문장의 those moments ~ in pain을 가리킴.
[8]Happiness is there, / on the edges of these experiences, // and when we get a glimpse (of *that* kind of happiness) // it is powerful, transcendent and compelling.
S_1 V_1 = 부사절 접속사(시간) S' V' O' S_2 V_2 C
행복은 거기에 있다 / 즉 이런 경험의 가장자리에 // 그리고 우리가 언뜻 보게 될 때 ('그런' 종류의 행복을) //
그것은 강력하고 뛰어나며 강렬하다
↳ 행복은 오히려 힘든 순간에 자주 강력하게 나타남.

어휘

seek out ~을 찾아내다
be on the lookout for ~을 세심히 살피다
approach 접근(법); 다가가다[오다]
relatively 비교적
pad A with B A를 B로 채워 넣다
suffering 고통
painkiller 진통제
comfort 안락, 편안(함); 위안[위로](하다)
within reach 손이 닿는 곳에, 힘이 미치는 곳에
proportion 비율; 균형
advance 발전; 증진되다
significant 상당한; 중요한
implication 영향; 함축
contentment 만족(감)
vulnerable 상처를 받기 쉬운; 취약한
edge 가장자리; 우위[유리함]
get a glimpse of ~을 언뜻[힐끗] 보다
compelling 강렬한; 설득력 있는

정답 가이드

주어진 문장이 앞에서 말한 것과 반대되는 내용을 연결하는 Rather(오히려)로 이어진 것으로 보아, 그 앞에는 주어진 문장의 부정적 경험과 대조되는, 행복을 얻는 긍정적 경험이 언급되어야 함을 알 수 있다. 글은 ③ 뒤부터 행복이 즐거움에 관한 것만은 아니라는 내용으로 전환되는데, ⑤ 앞 문장의 긍정적 경험(편안함, 만족감, 충족감)을 주어진 문장이 반박하며 행복은 오히려 부정적 경험(가장 상처받기 쉽거나 혼자이거나 고통을 겪는 순간)에 자주 발견된다는 흐름이 되는 것이 자연스럽다. 아울러 주어진 문장의 '상처 받고 혼자이거나 고통을 겪는 것'은 ⑤ 뒤 문장의 these experiences로 연결되므로 주어진 문장은 ⑤에 들어가는 것이 가장 적절하다.

오답 클리닉

① (4%) 앞 문장의 고통을 제어할 수 있다고 느끼는 능력을 진통제의 발명으로 부연 설명한다.
② (5%) 앞 문장에서 제시된 진통제의 발명과 물질적 안락을 다음 문장에서 These technological and economic advances로 받으며 내용이 연결된다.
③ (12%) 앞 문장의 내용을 this로 받으며, 역접 연결어 Yet으로 행복이 즐거움에 관한 것만은 아니라는 내용으로 전환된다.
④ (28%) 행복이 단지 즐거움에 관련된 것만은 아니라는 앞 문장을 부연 설명하는 내용이다. 앞뒤 문장 모두 행복을 유발한다고 오인되는 것들을 제시하고 있으므로 연결이 자연스럽다.

The 주의 주어진 문장이 ④에 들어갈 경우 ⑤ 뒤 문장의 these experiences가 가리키는 것이 긍정적인 경험(편안함, 만족감, 충족감)이 됨에 주의해야 한다.

01 ✦ 글의 주제 (20학년도 9월 모평 23번 | 정답률 72%) ①

구문분석 & 직독직해

생활 도서관 소장 도서의 중요성

[1]Libraries are becoming increasingly interested / in *the services* [(which[that]) they are providing / for their users].
(S: Libraries, V: are becoming, C: interested / 목적격 관계대명사 생략, S′: they (= libraries), V′: are providing)
도서관들은 점점 더 많은 관심을 갖고 있다 / 서비스에 [그것들이 제공하고 있는 / 그것들의 이용자들에게]

[2]This is an important focus — // especially as more and more information becomes available electronically.
(This (= 앞 문장): S, is: V, an important focus: C / as: 부사절 접속사(~함에 따라), more and more information: S′, becomes: V′, available: C′)
이것은 중요한 주안점이다 // 특히 점점 더 많은 정보가 전자적으로 이용 가능하게 됨에 따라
↳ **도입:** 전자 정보가 이용 가능해지면서 도서관들은 제공 서비스에 많은 관심을 가짐.

주제문 ⊶ 도입부와 역접으로 이어지는 주제문에서 도서관은 소장 도서가 중요하다는 것을 드러냄.

[3]However, / the traditional strengths (of libraries) / have always been their collections.
(S: the traditional strengths, V: have always been, C: their collections)
하지만 / 전통적인 힘은 (도서관들의) / 항상 그것들의 소장 도서에 있어 왔다

⊶ 지금도 소장 도서가 중요함.

[4]This is true still today — / especially in research libraries.
(This (= 앞 문장): S, is: V, true: C)
이것은 오늘날에도 여전히 사실이다 / 특히 연구 도서관에서
↳ 도서관의 힘은 서비스가 아니라 소장 도서에 있음.

[5]Also, / collection makeup is / *the hardest thing* (to change quickly).
(S: collection makeup, V: is, C: the hardest thing)
또한 / 소장 도서의 구성은 ~이다 / 가장 어려운 것 (신속하게 바꾸기)
↳ **소장 도서의 특성 1:** 구성을 빠르게 바꾸기가 어려움.

[6]For example, / if a library has a long tradition (of heavily collecting *materials* (published in Mexico)), // then even if that library stops / purchasing all Mexican imprints, //
(if: 부사절 접속사(조건), a library: S′, has: V′, a long tradition: O′ = of heavily collecting materials / published in Mexico: 과거분사구 / even if: 부사절 접속사(~할지라도), that library: S′, stops: V′, purchasing all Mexican imprints: O′)
예를 들어 / 한 도서관이 오랜 전통을 갖고 있다면 (자료를 다량으로 수집하는 (멕시코에서 출판된)), // 그 도서관이 그만둘지라도 / 모든 멕시코 인쇄물을 구매하는 것을 //

its Mexican collection will still be large and impressive / for several years to come // unless they start withdrawing books.
(S: its Mexican collection, V: will still be, C: large and impressive / unless: 부사절 접속사(~하지 않는 한), they: S′, start: V′, withdrawing books: O′)
그것의 멕시코 소장 도서는 여전히 대규모이고 인상적일 것이다 / 향후 여러 해 동안 // 그들(도서관 직원)이 책들을 빼내기 시작하지 않는 한
↳ **예:** 도서관에서 다량으로 수집한 멕시코 자료들은 쉽게 바뀌지 않음.

[7]Likewise, / if a library has not collected much / in a subject, / and then decides to start collecting heavily / in that area //
(if: 부사절 접속사(조건), a library: S′, has not collected: V′1, much: O′1, decides: V′2, to start collecting: O′2)
마찬가지로 / 한 도서관이 많은 것을 수집하지 않았다면 / 한 주제에서 / 그런 다음 다량으로 수집하는 것을 시작하기로 결정한다면 / 그 분야에서 //

it will take several years / for the collection to be large enough and rich enough / to be considered an important research tool.
★ <It takes+시간+(for A)+to-v>: (A가) v하는 데 시간이 걸리다
<~ enough to-v>: v할 만큼 충분히 ~한
여러 해가 걸릴 것이다 / 그 소장 도서가 충분히 많고 충분히 풍부해지는 데에는 / 중요한 연구 도구로 여겨질 만큼
↳ **소장 도서의 특성 2:** 구성하는 데 시간이 오래 걸림.

해석

[1]도서관들은 이용자들에게 제공하고 있는 서비스에 점점 더 많은 관심을 갖고 있다. [2]이것은 중요한 주안점인데, 특히 점점 더 많은 정보가 전자적으로 이용이 가능하게 됨에 따라 그러하다. [3]하지만 도서관들의 전통적인 힘은 항상 소장 도서에 있어 왔다. [4]이것은 오늘날에도 여전히 사실이며, 특히 연구 도서관에서 그러하다. [5]또한 소장 도서의 구성은 신속하게 바꾸기 가장 어려운 것이다. [6]예를 들어, 한 도서관이 멕시코에서 출판된 자료를 다량으로 수집하는 오랜 전통을 갖고 있다면, 그 도서관이 모든 멕시코 인쇄물을 구매하는 것을 그만둘지라도, 그것의 멕시코 소장 도서는 도서관 직원들이 책들을 빼내기 시작하지 않는 한, 향후 여러 해 동안 여전히 대규모이고 인상적일 것이다. [7]마찬가지로 한 도서관이 한 주제에서 많은 것을 수집하지 않았고, 그런 다음 그 분야에서 다량으로 수집하는 것을 시작하기로 결정한다면, 그 소장 도서가 중요한 연구 도구로 여겨질 만큼 충분히 많고 충분히 풍부해지는 데에는 여러 해가 걸릴 것이다.

어휘

electronically 전자적으로, 컴퓨터로
strength 힘, 영향력; 강점
collection 소장 도서, 소장품; 수집
makeup 구성, 짜임새
heavily 다량으로, 많이
imprint 인쇄물; 찍다, 누르다; 각인시키다
withdraw 빼내다, 철수시키다; (약속을) 철회[취소]하다; (돈을) 인출하다
subject 주제; 학과, 과목
[선택지] lasting 지속적인, 영속적인
significance 중요성; 의미
analyze 분석하다
rare 드문, 희귀한
contribution 기여; 기부금
reputation 명성, 평판

정답 가이드

점점 더 많은 정보가 전자적으로 이용이 가능해지고 있는 오늘날까지도 도서관들의 전통적인 힘은 소장 도서에 있고, 그 소장 도서는 바꾸거나 새로 구성하기가 어려운 도서관의 중추적인 요소라고 했다. 따라서 글의 주제로 가장 적절한 것은 ① 'lasting significance of library collections even in the digital age(디지털 시대에도 지속되는 도서관 소장 도서의 중요성)'이다.

오답 클리닉

② changing roles of local libraries and their effects on society (10%)
지역 도서관들의 변화하는 역할(×)과 그것들이 사회에 미치는 영향(×)
도입에서 도서관이 제공하는 서비스에 관심이 많아지고 있다고 했지만, 핵심은 소장 도서가 여전히 중요하다는 것이며 사회에 미치는 영향도 언급되지 않음.

③ growing needs for analyzing a large volume of library data (9%)
도서관 자료의 방대한 양을 분석해야 할(×) 증가하는 필요성
소장 자료를 분석하는 것에 관한 내용이 아님.

④ online services as a key to the success of research libraries (4%)
연구 도서관의 성공 열쇠로서의 온라인 서비스(×)
특히 연구 도서관에서는 소장 도서가 중요하다고 했으므로 오답임.

⑤ rare book collectors' contributions to a library's reputation (5%)
도서관의 명성에 대한 희귀 서적 수집가들의 기여(×)
도서관의 소장 도서가 중요하다는 내용이며, 희귀 서적 수집가들의 기여에 대한 언급은 없음.

02 + 빈칸 추론 〈18학년도 대수능 32번 | 정답률 59%〉 ②

구문분석 & 직독직해

인지 지난주 점심을 떠올리기 어려운 이유

[1]How many of *the lunches* [that you ate / over the last week] / can you recall?
목적격 관계대명사
점심 중 얼마나 많이 [여러분이 먹은 / 지난주 동안] / 여러분은 기억해 낼 수 있는가

[2]Do you remember what you ate today? // I hope so.
V O(명사절)
여러분은 오늘 먹은 것을 기억하는가 // 나는 그러길 바란다

[3]Yesterday? // I bet // (that) it takes a moment's effort.
S V 명사절 접속사 생략 O(명사절)
어제는? // 틀림없이 // (기억해 내는 데) 잠깐의 노력이 필요할 것이다

[4]And what about the day before yesterday? // What about a week ago?
그리고 그저께는 어떤가? // 일주일 전은 어떤가?
↳ **질문:** 지난 점심에 먹은 것을 기억할 수 있는가?

주제문

[5]It's not so much // that your memory (of last week's lunch) / has disappeared; //
명사절 접속사 S′ V′
(~인) 것은 아니다 // 여러분의 기억이 (지난주 점심에 대한) / 사라진 // 적절한 단서가 주어지면 기억해 냄.
if provided with the right cue, / (like where you ate it, or whom you ate it with), //
접속사를 생략하지 않은 분사구문(= if you were provided ~) 전치사구 삽입
만약 적절한 단서가 제공된다면 / (어디에서 그것을 먹었는지, 혹은 그것을 누구와 함께 먹었는지와 같은) //
you would likely recall // what had been on your plate.
S V O(명사절)
여러분은 아마 기억해 낼 것이다 // 접시에 무엇이 담겨 있었는지를
↳ **답변:** 적절한 단서가 주어지면 기억해 낼 수 있음.

[6]Rather, / it's difficult to remember last week's lunch //
가주어 진주어(to-v구)
오히려 / 지난주의 점심을 기억하는 것이 어렵다 //
because your brain has filed it away / with *all the other lunches* [(which[that]) you've ever eaten] /
부사절 접속사(이유) S′ V′ O′(= last week's lunch) 목적격 관계대명사 생략
as *just another lunch.*
전치사(~로(서))
여러분의 뇌가 그것(지난주의 점심)을 정리해 두었기 때문에 / 모든 다른 점심들과 함께 [여러분이 먹어 본 적이 있는] /
'흔해 빠진 점심'으로
↳ 기억이 어려운 것은 지난주의 점심을 흔한 것 중 하나로 정리해 두었기 때문임.

*<try to-v>: v하려고 노력하다[애쓰다]
[7]When we try to recall something / from *a category* [that includes as many instances / as "lunch" or "wine,"] // many memories compete / for our attention.
부사절 접속사(시간) 주격 관계대명사 전치사(~와 같은) S V
우리가 어떤 것을 기억해 내려고 할 때 / 범주로부터 [많은 사례를 포함하는 / '점심'이나 '와인'과 같은] //
많은 기억이 경쟁한다 / 우리의 주목을 위해
↳ **부연 설명:** 많은 기억이 있는 범주 중에서 구체적인 하나를 떠올리는 것은 쉽지 않음.

해석

[1]여러분은 지난주 동안 여러분이 먹은 점심 중 얼마나 많이 기억해 낼 수 있는가? [2]여러분은 오늘 먹은 것을 기억하는가? 나는 그러길 바란다. [3]어제는? 틀림없이 (기억해 내는 데) 잠깐의 노력이 필요할 것이다. [4]그리고 그저께는 어떤가? 일주일 전은 어떤가? [5]지난주 점심에 대한 여러분의 기억이 사라진 것은 아닌데, 만약 어디에서 그것을 먹었는지, 혹은 그것을 누구와 함께 먹었는지와 같은 적절한 단서가 제공된다면, 여러분은 아마 접시에 무엇이 담겨 있었는지를 기억해 낼 것이다. [6]오히려, 여러분의 뇌가 그것(지난주의 점심)을 여러분이 먹어 본 적이 있는 모든 다른 점심들과 함께 '흔해 빠진 점심'으로 정리해 두었기 때문에 지난주의 점심을 기억하는 것이 어렵다. [7]우리가 '점심'이나 '와인'과 같은 많은 사례를 포함하는 범주로부터 어떤 것을 기억해 내려고 할 때, 많은 기억이 우리의 주목을 위해 경쟁한다. [8]지난 수요일 점심에 대한 기억이 반드시 사라진 것은 아닌데, 여러분은 점심시간의 기억이라는 바다 밖으로 그것(지난 수요일 점심에 대한 기억)을 끄집어 낼 적절한 낚싯바늘이 없는 것이다. [9]하지만 말하는 와인, 그것은 유일무이하다. 그것은 경쟁자가 없는 기억이다.

어휘

recall 기억해 내다, 상기하다
bet ~이 틀림없다[분명하다]; 돈을 걸다; 내기
cue 단서, 신호; 신호를 주다
file away (생각을 머릿속에) 정리해 두다
just another 흔해 빠진, 그렇고 그런
instance 사례, 경우
compete 경쟁하다; (경기 등에) 참가하다
cf. competitor 경쟁자; 참가자
unique 유일무이한, 독특한; 고유의
[선택지] channel 수로(水路); 경로
ordinary 평범한; 보통의
hook 낚싯바늘; 고리
glue 접착제

★<not necessarily>: ((부분 부정)) 반드시 ~인 것은 아닌

[8]The memory (of last Wednesday's lunch) / isn't necessarily gone; //
S1 V1
기억이 (지난 수요일 점심에 대한) / 반드시 사라진 것은 아니다 //
is의 C(명사절) (= the memory of last Wednesday's lunch)
it's // that you lack ***the right hook*** **(to pull it / out of a sea of lunchtime memories)**.
S2 V2 명사절 접속사 V' O'
~이다 // 여러분은 적절한 낚싯바늘이 없는 것 (그것(지난 수요일 점심에 대한 기억)을 끄집어 낼 / 점심시간의 기억이라는 바다 밖으로)
↳ 주제문 재진술: 기억이 아예 사라진 것은 아니며, 단지 떠올리는 데 단서가 되어줄 만한 것이 없는 것임.

[9]But / *a wine* [that talks]: // That's unique. // It's a memory (without rivals).
주격 관계대명사
하지만 / 와인 [말하는] // 그것은 유일무이하다 // 그것은 기억이다 (경쟁자가 없는)
↳ 반례: 유일무이한 기억은 떠올리기 쉬움.

attach 붙이다, 첨부하다
capacity 용량, 수용력; 능력
sufficient 충분한

정답 가이드

빈칸 문장으로 보아 지난 수요일 점심에 대한 기억이 반드시 사라진 것은 아닌데, '무엇'이 없다는 것인지를 추론해야 한다. 맺음말로, 말하는 와인은 독특하며 경쟁자가 없는 기억이라고 했는데, 비유적 표현일 것이므로 단서를 나머지 부분에서 찾도록 한다. 앞에서부터 읽어보면 점심에 대한 기억을 묻고는 지난주 점심에 대한 기억이 사라진 것은 아니며, '적절한 단서가 제공된다면' 기억해 낼 것이라고 했다. 우리가 먹은 점심이나 와인은 너무나 사례가 많은 것이기 때문에 기억해 낼 만한 '적절한 단서'가 없어서 기억하지 못한다는 의미이다. 하지만 '말하는 와인'과 같은 것은 경쟁할 다른 와인이 없는 아주 독특한 것으로, 기억해 내기 쉬운 예로 언급되었다. 따라서 빈칸에 들어갈 말로 가장 적절한 것은 ② 'the right hook to pull it out of a sea of lunchtime memories(점심시간의 기억이라는 바다 밖으로 그것을 끄집어 낼 적절한 낚싯바늘)'이다.

오답 클리닉

① the channel to let it flow into the pool of ordinary memories (18%)
그것이 평범한 기억의 못으로 흘러 들어가게 하는 경로
평범한 기억으로 분류하는 것은 기억을 저장하는 방법으로 언급된 것임.
③ the glue to attach it to just another lunch memory (10%)
그것을 흔해 빠진 점심 기억에 덧붙이는 접착제
지난 수요일 점심을 다른 점심과 연결 짓지 못해 기억하지 못하는 것이 아니고, 오히려 흔해 빠진 점심으로 분류해서 기억하기 어려운 것이라고 했음.
④ the memory capacity to keep a box of sleeping memories (5%)
한 상자의 잠자고 있는 기억을 보관할 수 있는 기억 용량
잠자고 있는 기억은 언급되지 않음.
⑤ the sufficient number of competitors in a battle for attention (8%)
주목을 받기 위한 싸움에서 충분한 수의 경쟁자들
경쟁 사례가 많기 때문에 지난 점심을 특정해 기억하기 어려운 것이라고 했으므로, 반대로 경쟁자들이 없으면 기억하기 쉬울 것임.

03 + 글의 순서 (19학년도 대수능 37번 | 정답률 34%) ⑤

구문분석 & 직독직해 인지 도식적 지식의 오류

[1]Clearly, / schematic knowledge helps you — / guiding your understanding / and enabling you to reconstruct / *things* [(that) you cannot remember].
S V O 분사구문 병렬(= as it guides ~ and enables ~)
★<enable+O+to-v>: O가 v할 수 있게 하다
목적격 관계대명사 생략
분명히 / 도식적 지식은 여러분을 돕는다 / 여러분의 이해를 이끌면서 / 그리고 여러분이 재구성할 수 있게 하면서 / (~한) 것들을 [여러분이 기억할 수 없는]
↳ 도입: 도식적 지식은 이해와 기억의 재구성을 도와줌.

주제문 ⊶ 주어진 글과 반대되는 내용이 But으로 이어짐.
(C) [2]But / schematic knowledge can also hurt you, / promoting errors / in perception and memory.
S V O 분사구문(= because it promotes ~)
하지만 / 도식적 지식은 또한 여러분에게 해를 끼칠 수 있다 / 오류를 조장하기 때문에 / 인식과 기억에
↳ 도식적 지식은 인식과 기억에 오류를 초래함.

[3]Moreover, / the *types* (of *errors* (produced by schemata)) / are quite predictable: //
S(복수) 과거분사구 V(복수) C
게다가 / '유형'은 (오류의 (도식에 의해서 생기는)) / 상당히 예측 가능하다 //
bear in mind의 O(명사절)
Bear in mind // that schemata summarize / the broad pattern (of your experience), //
V(명령문) 명사절 접속사 S'1 V'1 O'
(= schemata)
and so they tell you, / in essence, // what's typical or ordinary / in a given situation.
S'2 V'2 IO' DO'(명사절)
명심하라 // 도식이 요약한다는 것을 / 광범위한 패턴을 (여러분의 경험의) //
그래서 그것(도식)이 여러분에게 말해 준다는 것을 / 본질적으로 // 무엇이 전형적이거나 평범한 것인지 / 주어진 상황에서
↳ 부연 설명: 도식적 지식은 경험을 요약해 주어진 상황에서 전형적이거나 평범한 것을 말해줌.

해석

[1]분명히, 도식적 지식은 여러분의 이해를 이끌면서, 그리고 여러분이 기억할 수 없는 것들을 재구성할 수 있게 하면서 여러분을 돕는다. (C) [2]하지만 도식적 지식은 또한 인식과 기억에 오류를 조장하기 때문에 여러분에게 해를 끼칠 수 있다. [3]게다가, 도식에 의해서 생기는 오류의 '유형'은 상당히 예측 가능하다. 도식이 여러분의 경험의 광범위한 패턴을 요약하며 그래서 그것(도식)이 본질적으로 주어진 상황에서 무엇이 전형적이거나 평범한 것인지 여러분에게 말해 준다는 것을 명심하라. (B) [4]따라서, 도식적 지식에 대한 어떠한 의존이든 어떤 것이 '정상적인' 것인지에 대한 이러한 정보에 의해 형성될 것이다. [5]따라서 어떤 상황이나 사건을 보면서 여러분이 알아채지 못하는 것들이 있으면, 여러분의 도식이 그 상황에서 일반적으로 무엇이 적절한지에 관한 지식으로 이러한 '공백'을 채우도록 여러분을 이끌 것이다. (A) [6]마찬가지로, 여러분이 기억해 낼 수 없는 것들이 있으면, 여러분의 도식이 그 상황에서 어떤 것이 전형적인지에 대한 지식으로 그 공백을 채워 줄 것이다. [7]결과적으로, 도식에 대한 의존은 불

(B) [4]Any reliance (on schematic knowledge), / therefore, / will be shaped / by this information (about what's "normal.") (C)에서 설명한 도식의 작용으로 인해 도식적 지식에 대한 의존이 생긴다는 인과 관계가 성립함.
S / V
어떠한 의존이든 (도식적 지식에 대한) / 따라서 / 형성될 것이다 / 이러한 정보에 의해
(어떤 것이 '정상적인' 것인지에 대한)
↳ 도식이 알려주는 정보에 의존하게 됨.

[5]Thus, / if there are *things* [(that) you don't notice / while viewing a situation or event], //
부사절 접속사(조건) / 목적격 관계대명사 생략 / 접속사를 생략하지 않은 분사구문(= while you view ~)
따라서 / (~한) 것들이 있으면 [여러분이 알아채지 못하는 / 어떤 상황이나 사건을 보면서] //

your schemata will lead you to fill in these "gaps" / with knowledge (about what's normally in place / in that setting). *<lead+O+to-v>: O가 v하도록 이끌다
S / V / O / C / about의 O(명사절)
여러분의 도식이 이러한 '공백'을 채우도록 여러분을 이끌 것이다 / 지식으로 (일반적으로 무엇이 적절한지에 관한 / 그 상황에서)
↳ 예 1: 우리가 알아채지 못한 것을 도식이 채워줌.

(B)와 비슷한 예가 이어짐.
(A) [6]Likewise, / if there are *things* [(that) you can't recall], // your schemata will fill in the gaps / with knowledge (about what's typical / in that situation).
부사절 접속사(조건) / 목적격 관계대명사 생략 / S / V / O / about의 O(명사절)
마찬가지로 / (~한) 것들이 있으면 [여러분이 기억해 낼 수 없는] // 여러분의 도식이 그 공백을 채워 줄 것이다 / 지식으로 (어떤 것이 전형적인지에 대한 / 그 상황에서)
↳ 예 2: 우리가 기억하지 못하는 것을 도식이 채워줌.

[7]As a result, / a reliance on schemata will inevitably make the world seem more "normal" // than it really is //
S / V_1 / O_1 / C_1 / (= the world)
결과적으로 / 도식에 대한 의존은 불가피하게 세상을 더 '정상적인' 것으로 보이게 할 것이다 //
실제로 그것(세상)이 그런 것보다 //
and will make the past seem more "regular" // than it actually was.
V_2 / O_2 / C_2 / (= the past)
그리고 과거를 더 '통상적인' 것으로 보이게 할 것이다 // 실제로 그것(과거)이 그랬던 것보다
↳ 결과: 도식에 대한 의존은 불가피한 인식과 기억의 오류를 야기함.

가피하게 실제로 세상이 그런 것보다 그것을 더 '정상적인' 것으로 보이게 할 것이고, 실제로 과거가 그랬던 것보다 그것을 더 '통상적인' 것으로 보이게 할 것이다.

어휘

schematic 도식적인; 도식으로 나타낸
reconstruct 재구성하다; 재건[복원]하다
promote 조장하다; 촉진하다; 승진시키다
perception 인식; 지각, 자각
bear in mind ~을 명심[유념]하다
summarize 요약하다
in essence 본질적으로
typical 전형적인, 대표적인; 일반적인
reliance 의존, 의지
notice 알아채다, 인지하다; 통지, 통보
fill in ~을 채우다
in place 적절[적당]한
recall 기억해 내다, 상기하다
inevitably 불가피하게, 필연적으로
regular 통상적인; 정기적인
⊕ 도식[틀, 프레임](schema(*pl.* schemata)): 사람은 과거의 경험을 통해 어떤 것이 '전형적'이고 '정상적'인지에 대한 도식을 갖고 있으며, 이를 토대로 새롭게 접하는 현상을 효율적으로 이해함. 그러나 도식적 지식에만 의존해서 세상을 보고 과거를 기억하게 되면 이에 맞는 것, 즉 '정상적'인 것과 '통상적'인 것만 인지하게 되므로 결과적으로 오류를 낳는 역기능도 있음.

정답 가이드

주어진 글은 도식적 지식이 이해와 기억을 재구성하는 데 도움이 된다는 내용이다. 그 다음에는 인식과 기억에 오류를 일으키기 때문에 해가 될 수 있다는 반대 내용이 역접 연결어 But으로 이어지는 (C)가 와야 한다. (C)의 끝에서 도식이 주어진 상황에서 무엇이 '전형적'이거나 '평범한' 것인지를 알려준다고 했는데, 이를 (B)에서 this information about what's "normal"로 받으면서 상황을 이해할 수 있게 해주는 도식의 역할을 설명한다. (A)는 Likewise로 시작하여, 도식이 기억을 채워준다는 또 다른 역할을 제시하므로 마지막에 오는 것이 흐름상 적절하다.

오답 클리닉

① (A) - (C) - (B) (3%) / ④ (C) - (A) - (B) (27%)
(A)는 유사한 내용을 덧붙이는 Likewise로 이어지므로 그 앞에는 도식이 공백을 채운다는 비슷한 내용이 있어야 한다. 또한 (A)의 As a result 이하는 (B)에서 언급한 도식에 대한 의존으로 인한 결과에 해당하므로 (B) 뒤에 와야 한다.
② (B) - (A) - (C) (25%) / ③ (B) - (C) - (A) (11%)
주어진 글에 (B)의 this information about what's "normal"이 가리킬 대상이 없으므로 (B)는 주어진 글 뒤에 올 수 없다.

01 ✦ 글의 제목 〈20학년도 9월 모평 24번 | 정답률 59%〉 ④

구문분석 & 직독직해

사회 노인의 노화를 유발하는 사회적 배제

<from ~ on>: ~부터 계속[죽] ★<the+형용사>: ~한 사람들

[1]From the late nineteenth century on, / the dullness (found in the senile), / their isolation and withdrawal, / their clinging to the past / and lack of interest in worldly affairs /

(S1, 과거분사구, S2, 동명사 clinging의 의미상 주어, S3, S4)

19세기 후반부터 계속 / 둔함 (노쇠한 사람들에게서 발견되는) / 그들의 고립과 움츠림 / 과거에 대한 그들의 집착 / 그리고 세상일에 대한 관심 결여는 /

★<represent A as B(A를 B로 기술하다[표현하다])>의 수동형

were characteristically represented / as the *symptoms* (of senility) — / the social shame (of the inevitable deterioration of the brain).

(V, 전치사(~로서), =)

특징적으로 기술되었다 / '증상'으로서 (노쇠의) / 즉 사회적으로 애석한 일 (피할 수 없는 뇌의 노화라는)

↳ **도입(통념):** 노인들의 둔함 등은 뇌의 노화 증상으로 기술되었음.

[2]Following World War II, / academic discourse (on aging) / typically represented these / as the *causes* of senility.

(S, V, O(= 뒤 문장), 전치사(~로(서)))

제2차 세계 대전 후에 / 학술적 담론은 (노화에 대한) / 일반적으로 이것들을 기술했다 / 노쇠의 '원인'으로서

↳ 노화의 다른 원인이 지목됨.

주제문 ⊶ 노인의 정신 노화는 사회적 역할을 빼앗는 '사회' 때문임. ★<no longer A but B>: 더 이상 A가 아니라 B

[3]The location (of senile mental deterioration) was / no longer the aging brain / but *a society* [that, through involuntary retirement, social isolation, and the loosening of traditional family ties, / stripped the elderly / of *the roles* [that had sustained meaning in their lives]].

(S, V, C, 주격 관계대명사, ★<strip A of B>: A에게서 B를 빼앗다, V′, O′, 주격 관계대명사, V′, O′)

장소는 (노년의 정신 노화의) ~이었다 / 더 이상 노화하는 뇌가 아니라 / 사회 [원치 않는 퇴직, 사회적 고립, 그리고 전통적인 가족 유대의 약화를 통해 / 노인들에게서 빼앗은 / 역할을 [그들의 삶에서 의미를 유지했던]]

↳ **새로운 원인(사실):** 뇌의 노화가 아니라 사회적 원인(역할의 박탈)으로 노년의 정신 노화가 옴.

★<deprive A of B(A에게서 B를 빼앗다)>의 수동형

[4]When elderly people were deprived of these meaningful social roles, //

(부사절 접속사(시간), S′, V′) ⊶ 노화는 사회적 역할을 빼앗기고 고립될 때 일어남.

노인들이 이 의미 있는 사회적 역할을 빼앗겼을 때 //

when they became increasingly isolated and were cut off / from *the interests and activities* [that had earlier occupied them], //

(부사절 접속사(시간), S′, V′1, C′, V′2, 주격 관계대명사, (= elderly people))

그들이 점점 더 고립되고 단절되었을 때 / 관심사와 활동들로부터 [이전에 그들의 마음을 끌었던] //

not surprisingly their mental functioning deteriorated.

(S, V)

놀랄 것도 없이 그들의 정신 기능은 노화했다

↳ **상술:** 사회적 역할을 잃고 고립되면 노인의 정신 기능이 쇠퇴함.

★<not so much A as B>: A라기보다는 B

[5]The elderly did not so much lose their minds / as lose their place.

(S, V)

노인들은 그들의 정신을 잃었다기보다는 / 그들의 자리를 잃었다

↳ **결론:** 노인들은 뇌의 기능이 아니라 사회적 위치를 잃은 것임.

해석

[1]19세기 후반부터 계속, 노쇠한 사람들에게서 발견되는 둔함, 그들의 고립과 움츠림, 과거에 대한 그들의 집착, 그리고 세상일에 대한 관심 결여는 노쇠의 '증상', 즉 피할 수 없는 뇌의 노화라는 사회적으로 애석한 일로서 특징적으로 기술되었다. [2]제2차 세계 대전 후에, 노화에 대한 학술적 담론은 일반적으로 이것들을 노쇠의 '원인'으로서 기술했다. [3]노년의 정신 노화의 장소는 더 이상 노화하는 뇌가 아니라 원치 않는 퇴직, 사회적 고립, 그리고 전통적인 가족 유대의 약화를 통해 노인들에게서 그들의 삶에서 의미를 유지했던 역할을 빼앗은 사회였다. [4]노인들이 이 의미 있는 사회적 역할을 빼앗겼을 때, 그들이 이전에 그들의 마음을 끌었던 관심사와 활동들로부터 점점 더 고립되고 단절되었을 때, 놀랄 것도 없이 그들의 정신적 기능은 노화했다. [5]노인들은 그들의 정신을 잃었다기보다는 그들의 자리를 잃었다.

어휘

dullness 둔함; 활발치 못함
isolation 고립, 고독
cf. isolated 고립된
withdrawal 움츠림, 물러남; 취소, 철회
cling to A A에 집착하다[매달리다], A를 고수하다
worldly 세상의; 세속적인
affair 일, 사건
symptom 증상, 징후
senility 노쇠, 노년
shame 애석한[유감스러운] 일; 수치, 망신
inevitable 피할 수 없는; 필연적인, 당연한
discourse 담론, 이야기
involuntary 원치 않는, 본의 아닌
retirement 퇴직, 은퇴
sustain 유지하다; 계속하다
cut off 차단하다, 가로막다
occupy (주의를) 끌다; 차지하다, 점유하다
[선택지] in concert with ~와 연합[제휴]하여
unfailing 틀림없는, 확실한; 변하지 않는
discrimination 차별
intensify (정도·강도가) 심해지다; 심화시키다, 강화하다
leave A out A를 배제시키다[빼다]
disabled 무능력하게 된; 장애가 있는

정답 가이드

노인들의 정신 노화의 원인은 뇌가 아니라 노인들에게서 의미 있는 사회적 역할을 빼앗아 세상으로부터 단절시키는 사회라는 내용의 글이다. 따라서 글의 제목으로 가장 적절한 것은 ④ 'What Makes the Elderly Decline: Being Left Out Socially(무엇이 노인들을 쇠하게 만드는가, 바로 사회적으로 배제되는 것)'이다.

오답 클리닉

① Aged Mind in Concert with Aged Body: An Unfailing Truth (7%)
나이 든 신체와(×) 연합한 나이 든 정신, 틀림없는 진리
정신 노화를 신체 노화와 연관지어 설명하는 글이 아님.

② No Change from Past to Present: Social Images of Old Age (11%)
과거에서 현재까지 변함없음, 즉 노령에 대한 사회적 이미지(×)
노령에 대한 사회적 이미지에 관한 언급은 없음.

③ No Country for Old Men: Age Discrimination Intensified (15%)
노인들을 위한 나라는 없다, 즉 연령 차별이 심해졌다(×)
연령 차별이 아닌 노인들의 정신 노화를 일으키는 원인에 관한 내용임.

⑤ Not Disabled But Differently Abled: New Faces of Old Age (7%)
무능력해진 것이 아니라 다르게 능력이 있음(×), 즉 노년의 새로운 얼굴
노인들에게 생기는 다른 능력에 대한 언급은 없음.

02 + 빈칸 추론 (18학년도 대수능 31번 | 정답률 64%) ①

구문분석 & 직독직해

예술 영화 <Apocalypse Now>의 흥행 이유

주제문

[1] *Apocalypse Now*, / *a film* (produced and directed / by Francis Ford Coppola), / gained widespread popularity, / and for good reason.
(S = *a film*; 과거분사구; V: gained; O: widespread popularity)
<Apocalypse Now>는 / 영화인 (제작되고 연출된 / Francis Ford Coppola에 의해) / 광범위한 인기를 얻었다 / 그리고 충분한 이유가 있었다
↳ **도입:** 영화 <Apocalypse Now>의 인기에는 이유가 있었음.

[2] The film is an adaptation (of *Joseph Conrad's novel Heart of Darkness*), // which is set in the African Congo / at the end of the 19th century.
(S: The film; V: is; C: an adaptation ~; which: 관계대명사(보충 설명))
그 영화는 각색물이다 (Joseph Conrad의 소설인 <Heart of Darkness>의) // 그 작품은 아프리카의 콩고를 배경으로 한다 / 19세기 말

[3] Unlike the original novel, / *Apocalypse Now* is set in Vietnam and Cambodia / during the Vietnam War. ⊶ 원작 소설과 다른 배경을 씀.
(S: *Apocalypse Now*; V: is set)
원작 소설과 달리 / <Apocalypse Now>는 베트남과 캄보디아를 배경으로 한다 / 베트남 전쟁 중의
↳ **세부 사항1:** <Apocalypse Now>는 원작 소설의 배경을 그대로 쓰지 않음.

[4] The setting, time period, dialogue and other incidental details are changed //
(S_1; V_1: are changed)
배경, 시대, 대화, 그리고 다른 부수적인 세부 사항은 바뀌었다 //
but the fundamental narrative and themes (of *Apocalypse Now*) / are the same / as those (of *Heart of Darkness*).
(S_2: the fundamental narrative and themes; V_2: are; C: the same; those = the fundamental narrative and themes)
하지만 기본적인 이야기와 주제는 (<Apocalypse Now>의) / 같다 / 그것들(기본적인 이야기와 주제)과 (<Heart of Darkness>의)

[5] Both describe a physical journey, / reflecting the central character's mental and spiritual journey, / down a river / to confront *the deranged Kurtz character*, // who represents the worst aspects (of civilisation).
(Both = *Apocalypse Now* and *Heart of Darkness*; S: Both; V: describe; O: a physical journey; 분사구문(= and both reflect ~); 목적(~하기 위해); who: 관계대명사(보충 설명))
둘 다 물리적인 여정을 묘사한다 / 주인공의 정신적 그리고 영적인 여정을 나타내며 / 강을 따라 내려가는 / 제정신이 아닌 Kurtz라는 인물에 맞서기 위해 // 그리고 그는 최악의 측면을 나타낸다 (문명의)
↳ **세부 사항2:** 배경은 달라도 주인공의 여정을 묘사하는 줄거리와 주제는 원작 소설과 같음.

⊶ 영화 개봉 시기의 배경으로 각색한 것이 관객의 영화 몰입을 높임.
[6] By giving *Apocalypse Now a setting* [that was contemporary at the time of its release], /
(<by v-ing>: v함으로써; that: 주격 관계대명사; its = *Apocalypse Now*'s)
<Apocalypse Now>에 배경을 제공함으로써 [그것의 개봉 당시와 동시대의] /
audiences were able to experience and (to) identify with its themes / more easily //
(S: audiences; V: were; C: able; to-v 병렬; its themes: to experience와 (to) identify with의 공통 O)
관객들은 그것의 주제를 경험하고 그것과 동질감을 느낄 수 있었다 / 더 쉽게 //

해석

[1]Francis Ford Coppola에 의해 제작되고 연출된 영화인 <Apocalypse Now>는 광범위한 인기를 얻었는데, 충분한 이유가 있었다. [2]그 영화는 Joseph Conrad의 소설 <Heart of Darkness>의 각색물인데, 그 작품은 19세기 말 아프리카의 콩고를 배경으로 한다. [3]원작 소설과 달리 <Apocalypse Now>는 베트남 전쟁 중의 베트남과 캄보디아를 배경으로 한다. [4]배경, 시기, 대화, 그리고 다른 부수적인 세부 사항은 바뀌었지만 <Apocalypse Now>의 기본적인 이야기와 주제는 <Heart of Darkness>의 그것들과 같다. [5]둘 다 문명의 최악의 측면을 나타내는, 제정신이 아닌 Kurtz라는 인물에 맞서기 위해 강을 따라 내려가는 물리적인 여정을 묘사하고, 그것은 주인공의 정신적 그리고 영적인 여정을 나타낸다. [6]<Apocalypse Now>에 그것의 개봉 당시와 동시대의 배경을 제공함으로써, 관객들은 영화가 그 소설의 충실한 각색물이었다면 그들이 그랬을 것보다 더 쉽게 그것의 주제를 경험하고 그것과 동질감을 느낄 수 있었다.

어휘

widespread 광범위한, 널리 퍼진
for good reason 충분한 이유로, 정당한 사유로
adaptation 각색(물); 적응
incidental 부수적인; 우연의, 우발적인
fundamental 기본적인, 근본적인
narrative 이야기(체의); 서술 (기법)
theme 주제, 테마
spiritual 영적인; 정신적인; 종교적인
confront 맞서다; 직면하다
represent 나타내다, 상징하다; 대표하다
civilisation[civilization] 문명(화)
contemporary 동시대의; 현대의
release 개봉; 풀어 주다; 발표[공개]하다
identify with ~와 동질감을 느끼다, ~와 동일시하다
literal (원문에) 충실한(= faithful); 문자 그대로의

★<S+과거 조동사(would)+have p.p. ... if+S'+had p.p. ~(만약 ~했더라면 …했을 텐데)>의 가정법 과거완료가 쓰임.

than they would have (experienced and identified with its themes) // if the film had been **a literal adaptation of the novel**.

(= audiences) 반복어구 생략 부사절 접속사(조건)

그들이 그랬을 것보다(그것의 주제를 경험하고 그것과 동질감을 느꼈을 것보다) // 영화가 그 소설의 충실한 각색물이었다면

↳ **결론:** 동시대의 배경이 관객들로 하여금 더 쉽게 주제를 경험하게 하고 동질감을 유발함.

[선택지] inspiration 영감(을 주는 것)
depiction 묘사, 서술
vivid 생생한; 선명한, 강렬한
dramatisation[dramatization] 각색, 극화
interpretation 해석, 이해

정답 가이드

빈칸 문장에 과거 사실을 반대로 가정, 상상하는 표현인 가정법 과거완료가 쓰였으므로 '과거에 사실이 아닌 것'이 무엇인지를 추론해야 한다. 앞에서 원작 소설과 영화 <Apocalypse Now>의 '배경 등이 서로 다르다'고 했다. 영화 개봉 당시와 동시대의 배경을 제공하여 '원작 소설과 같은 배경이었을' 때보다 더 쉽게 주제를 경험하고 동질감을 느낄 수 있었다는 문맥이 되어야 하므로, 빈칸에 들어갈 말로 가장 적절한 것은 ① 'a literal adaptation of the novel(그 소설의 충실한 각색물)'이다.

오답 클리닉

② a source of inspiration for the novel (12%)
그 소설을 위한 영감의 원천
영화가 소설에 영감을 주었는지에 대한 내용은 없음.

③ a faithful depiction of the Vietnam War (8%)
베트남 전쟁에 관한 충실한 묘사
영화가 동시대인 베트남 전쟁 당시를 배경으로 각색된 것은 과거 사실과 반대되는 내용이 아니며, 배경 묘사의 정도에 관한 언급도 없음.

④ a vivid dramatisation of a psychological journey (7%)
심리적 여정의 생생한 각색
소설과 영화 모두 a physical journey(물리적인 여정)를 묘사하며 그것이 주인공의 mental and spiritual journey(정신적이고 영적인 여정)를 나타낸다고 했음.

⑤ a critical interpretation of contemporary civilisation (8%)
동시대 문명에 대한 비판적인 해석
contemporary와 civilisation을 이용한 오답. 문장 5에서 문명의 최악의 측면을 나타내는 인물에 맞서는 내용이라고 했으나, 이것이 영화 원작과 달리 관객에게 더 쉽게 다가간 이유는 아님.

03 + 문장 넣기 (19학년도 대수능 39번 | 정답률 35%) ③

구문분석 & 직독직해 지리 지도 제작자들의 지형 묘사 방법

[1] A major challenge (for map-makers) / is the depiction (of *hills and valleys, slopes and flatlands* (collectively called the *topography*)).

S(단수) V(단수) C 과거분사구

주된 문제는 (지도 제작자들의) / 묘사이다 (언덕과 계곡, 경사지와 평지의 (집합적으로 '지형'이라고 불리는))

주제문

[2] This can be done / in various ways.

(= The depiction of topography)

이것(지형 묘사)은 행해질 수 있다 / 여러 방법으로

↳ 지도 제작자들은 지형을 묘사하는 것을 어려워하는데, 지형 묘사에는 여러 방법이 있음.

[3] One is to create / an image (of sunlight and shadow) // so that wrinkles (of the topography) / are alternately lit and shaded, / creating a visual representation (of the shape of the land).

S V C 부사절 접속사(목적) S'(복수) V'(복수)

★<creating ~ the land>는 분사구문으로 to create ~ shaded를 부연 설명함.

하나는 만드는 것이다 / 이미지를 (햇빛과 그림자의) // 주름이 ~하도록 (지형의) / 번갈아 빛이 비치고 그늘지(도록) / 그리고 이는 시각적 표현을 만들어 내는 것이다 (땅 모양의)

↳ **방법 1:** 지형의 주름이 번갈아 빛나도록 햇빛과 그림자의 이미지를 만듦.

(①) [4] Another, technically more accurate way is to draw contour lines.

S V C(to-v구)

또 다른 기술적으로 더 정확한 방법은 등고선을 그리는 것이다

🔑 산의 등고선이 일련의 동심원으로 나타나는 이유.

(②) [5] A contour line connects / *all points* [that lie at the same elevation].

S V O 주격 관계대명사

등고선은 연결한다 / 모든 점을 [동일한 고도에 있는]

↳ **방법 2:** 동일한 고도에 있는 모든 점을 연결하는 등고선을 그림.

🔑 앞에 언급한 이유로 인해 산은 일련의 동심원으로 표현됨.

(③ [6] *A round hill* (rising above a plain), / therefore, / would appear on the map / as a set of concentric circles, / the largest at the base and the smallest near the top.)

S 현재분사구 V 전치사(~로(서)) =

둥그런 산은 (평야 위로 솟은) / 따라서 / 지도에 나타날 것이다 / 일련의 동심원으로 / 가장 큰 동심원이 맨 아랫부분에 그리고 가장 작은 동심원은 꼭대기 근처에 있는

↳ **예:** 둥그런 산의 경우, 가장 큰 동심원은 가장 아래에, 가장 작은 동심원은 꼭대기 근처에 위치함.

해석

[1] 지도 제작자들의 주된 문제는 집합적으로 '지형'이라고 불리는 언덕과 계곡, 경사지와 평지의 묘사이다. [2] 이것(지형 묘사)은 여러 방법으로 행해질 수 있다. [3] 하나는 지형의 주름이 번갈아 빛이 비치고 그늘지도록 햇빛과 그림자의 이미지를 만들어서, 땅 모양의 시각적 표현을 만들어 내는 것이다. (①) [4] 또 다른 기술적으로 더 정확한 방법은 등고선을 그리는 것이다. (②) [5] 등고선은 동일한 고도에 있는 모든 점을 연결한다. (③ [6] 따라서 평야 위로 솟은 둥그런 산은 가장 큰 동심원이 맨 아랫부분에 그리고 가장 작은 동심원은 꼭대기 근처에 있는 일련의 동심원으로 지도에 나타날 것이다.) [7] 등고선이 서로 가깝게 배치되면 산의 경사가 가파르고, 그것들이 더 멀리 떨어져 있으면 경사가 더 완만하다. (④) [8] 등고선은 지역 지형의 가파른 비탈, 분지, 그리고 계곡을 나타낼 수 있다. (⑤) [9] 한눈에, 그것들(등고선)은 지도로 그려진 지역의 고저가 큰지 작은지를 드러내는데, 즉 '복잡한' 등고선 지도는 많은 큰 고저를 의미한다.

어휘

challenge 문제, 과제; 도전(하다)
depiction 묘사
valley 계곡, 골짜기
slope 경사지; 경사면
collectively 집합적으로
topography 지형(학)
wrinkle 주름(을 잡다)
alternately 번갈아, 교대로

🔑 주어진 문장의 a round hill을 지칭함.

[7] When the contour lines are positioned closely together, // the hill's slope is steep; //
부사절 접속사(조건) S′ V′ S1 V1 C1
등고선이 서로 가깝게 배치되면 // 산의 경사가 가파르다 //
→ (= the contour lines)
if they lie farther apart, // the slope is gentler.
부사절 접속사(조건) S2 V2 C2
그것들(등고선)이 더 멀리 떨어져 있으면 // 경사가 더 완만하다

(④) [8] Contour lines can represent / scarps, hollows, and valleys (of the local topography).
S V O
등고선은 나타낼 수 있다 / 가파른 비탈, 분지, 그리고 계곡을 (지역 지형의)

→ (= contour lines) → reveal의 O(명사절)
(⑤) [9] At a glance, / they reveal // whether the relief (in the mapped area) / is great or small: //
S1 V1 명사절 접속사 S′ V′ C′
a "busy" contour map means lots of high relief.
S2 V2 O
한눈에 / 그것들(등고선)은 드러낸다 // 고저가 (지도로 그려진 지역의) / 큰지 작은지를 //
즉 '복잡한' 등고선 지도는 많은 큰 고저를 의미한다

↳ **부연 설명:** 등고선의 간격은 경사를 나타내며, 등고선은 여러 지형과 높낮이를 나타낼 수 있음.

shade 그늘(지게 하다)
representation 표현, 묘사; 대표, 대리
cf. represent 나타내다; 대표[대신]하다
accurate 정확한
contour line 《지리》 등고선
lie (위치해) 있다; 눕다; 거짓말(하다)
elevation 고도, 높이; 증가
plain 평야; 분명한; 보통의
a set of 일련의, 일습의
base 맨 아랫부분; 기초; 기반
position 배치하다; 위치; 자리(를 잡다)
steep 가파른; 급격한
gentle 완만한; 온화한
hollow 분지, (땅이) 움푹 꺼진 곳; 빈
at a glance 한눈에, 즉시
busy 복잡한; 바쁜

정답 가이드

주어진 문장은 산이 지도에 일련의 동심원으로 나타날 것이라는 내용인데, 결과를 나타내는 연결어 therefore가 쓰인 것으로 보아 그 앞에는 산의 등고선이 그렇게 나타나게 되는 이유가 제시되어야 한다. 따라서 주어진 문장은 등고선이 동일한 고도에 있는 모든 점을 연결한다는 내용 뒤인 ③에 들어가는 것이 적절하며, 그렇게 되면 주어진 문장의 A round hill이 다음 문장의 the hill로 이어지는 연결도 자연스럽다.

오답 클리닉

① (4%) 지형을 묘사하는 두 번째 방법으로 등고선을 그리는 것을 제시하는 내용이다.
② (5%) 앞에서 등고선을 소개한 뒤에 그것을 그리는 방법을 설명하는 것은 자연스럽다.
④ (32%) 등고선의 간격이 경사를 나타낸다는 내용 뒤에, 등고선은 여러 지형을 나타낼 수 있다고 부연 설명한다.

The 주의 ④ 앞 문장의 the hill은 주어진 문장의 a round hill을 지칭하므로 주어진 문장은 그 뒤에 올 수 없다.

⑤ (23%) 등고선으로 나타낼 수 있는 다른 정보(지역의 고저)를 부연 설명하는 내용이다.

01 ✦ 함의 추론 (20학년도 6월 모평 21번 | 정답률 49%) ⑤

구문분석 & 직독직해

경영 성과가 아닌 활동 중심 과정 설계의 문제

주제문

[1] Many companies confuse activities and results.
(S) (V) (O)
많은 회사들이 활동과 성과를 혼동한다

[2] As a consequence, / they (= many companies) make the mistake (of designing *a process* [that sets out milestones] / in the form of *activities* [that must be carried out / during the sales cycle]).
(S) (V) (O) (주격 관계대명사) (주격 관계대명사)
그 결과 / 그들은 실수를 범한다 (과정을 기획하는 [획기적인 일을 제시하는] / 활동의 형태로 [행해져야 하는 / 판매 주기 동안])
↳ **문제점:** 성과를 내기 위한 과정을 활동의 형태로 기획하는 것은 실수임.

[3] Salespeople have a genius (for doing what's compensated / rather than what's effective).
(S) (V) (O) (for의 O(동명사구))
판매원들은 특별한 재능이 있다 (보상받는 일을 하는 데 / 효과적인 일보다는)
↳ 판매원들은 활동이 효과적인지는 관심 없음.

[4] If your process has an activity (such as "submit proposal" or "make cold call,") // then that's (= an activity ~ call) just what your people will do.
(S) (V) (C(명사절))
만약 당신의 과정에 활동이 있다면 ('제안서 제출하기'나 '권유 전화 걸기'와 같은) // 그것이 바로 당신의 사람들(판매원들)이 할 일이다
↳ **예:** 과정을 활동으로 계획하는 경우.

*<No matter that ~>은 <It doesn't matter that ~>을 줄인 표현임.

[5] No matter // that the calls were to the wrong customer [or] went nowhere.
(명사절 접속사) (S') (V'₁) (V'₂)
~했어도 문제가 되지 않는다 // 전화가 잘못된 고객에게 갔거나 아무 성과를 보지 못했다

[6] No matter // that the proposal wasn't submitted at the right point in the buying decision / [or] contained inappropriate information.
(명사절 접속사) (S') (V'₁) (V'₂) (O'₂)
~했어도 문제가 되지 않는다 // 제안서가 구매 결정의 적절한 시점에 제출되지 않았다 / 또는 부적절한 정보를 포함했다
↳ 판매원들이 활동을 잘못 했어도 문제가 안 됨.

[7] The process asked for activity, // [and] activity was what it (= the process) got.
(S_1) (V_1) (S_2) (V_2) (C(명사절))
그 과정은 활동을 요구했다 // 그리고 그것(과정)이 얻은 것이 활동이었다
🔑 과정을 활동의 형태로 설계한 것은 잘못된 것임.

[8] Salespeople have done what was asked for.
(S) (V) (O)
판매원들은 요구받은 일을 했다
↳ 판매원들은 요구받은 대로 활동을 수행했을 뿐임.

*동명사 telling의 간접목적어는 you이고, 직접목적어인 "Garbage ~ out"은 강조를 위해 문두에 위치함.

[9] **"Garbage in, garbage out"** // they (= Salespeople) will delight in telling you.
(S) (V)
"쓰레기(같은 활동 형태의 과정)가 들어가면 쓰레기(같은 결과)가 나오지요" // 그들은 당신에게 ~라고 말하기를 즐길 것이다

[10] "It's not our problem, // it's this dumb process."
🔑 성과를 보지 못한 것은 잘못된 과정 설계의 결과임.
"그것은 우리의 문제가 아니라 // 이 바보 같은 (활동 형태의) 과정이에요"
↳ 활동의 형태로 과정을 요구해 놓고 성과를 바라면 안 됨.

해석

[1]많은 회사들이 활동과 성과를 혼동한다. [2]그 결과, 그들은 획기적인 일을 제시하는 과정을 판매 주기 동안 행해져야 하는 활동의 형태로 기획하는 실수를 범한다. [3]판매원들은 효과적인 일보다는 보상받는 일을 하는 데 특별한 재능이 있다. [4]만약 당신의 과정에 '제안서 제출하기'나 '권유 전화 걸기'와 같은 활동이 있다면, 그것이 바로 당신의 사람들(판매원들)이 할 일이다. [5]전화가 잘못된 고객에게 갔거나 아무 성과를 보지 못했어도 문제가 되지 않는다. [6]제안서가 구매 결정의 적절한 시점에 제출되지 않았거나 부적절한 정보를 포함했어도 문제가 되지 않는다. [7]과정이 활동을 요구했고, 그것(과정)이 얻은 것이 활동이었다. [8]판매원들은 요구받은 일을 했다. [9]그들은 당신에게 "쓰레기(같은 활동 형태의 과정)가 들어가면 쓰레기(같은 결과)가 나오지요."라고 당신에게 말하기를 즐길 것이다. [10]"그것은 우리의 문제가 아니라 이 바보 같은 (활동 형태의) 과정 때문이에요."

어휘

confuse 혼동하다; 혼란시키다
as a consequence 그 결과(로서)
set out ~을 제시하다; 출발하다; 착수하다
milestone 획기적인 일[사건]
carry out 수행하다
a genius for ~의 특별한 재능[소질]
compensate 보상하다
cf. compensation 보상
A rather than B B라기보다는 A
proposal 제안(서); 제의
cold call (상품을 팔기 위한) 권유 전화
go nowhere 아무 성과도 못보다
inappropriate 부적절한, 부적합한
delight in (다른 사람들이 불편해하는 일을) 즐기다
dumb 바보 같은
[선택지] seek 추구하다, 찾다
draw from (생각 등을) 도출해 내다
end up v-ing 결국 v하게 되다

정답 가이드

많은 회사에서 활동과 성과를 혼동하여 획기적인 일을 제시하는 과정을 활동 중심으로 만드는 실수를 범한다고 했다. 그러면 판매원들은 보상을 받기 위해 주어진 활동을 수행하긴 하지만, 그것이 매출에 효과적인 일인지는 신경 쓰지 않는다. 즉 그들은 과정이 요구한 비효과적인 활동을 할 뿐이다. 따라서 밑줄 친 부분이 의미하는 바로 가장 적절한 것은 ⑤ 'Processes focused on activities end up being ineffective.(활동에 초점을 맞춘 과정은 결국 효과적이지 않다.)'이다.

오답 클리닉

① In seeking results, compensation is the key to quality. (11%)
성과를 추구하는 데 있어서 보상(×)이 품질의 핵심이다.
직원이 보상받는 일을 하는 데 재능이 있다고 했지만 보상을 해서 성과를 높여야 한다는 내용이 아님.

② Salespeople should join in a decision-making process. (14%)
판매원들이 의사 결정 과정에 참여해야(×) 한다.
의사 결정 과정에 판매원들의 참여가 필요하다는 내용이 아님.

③ Shared understanding does not always result in success. (8%)
공유된 이해가(×) 항상 성공으로 이어지는 것은 아니다.
공유된 이해는 언급되지 않음.

④ Activities drawn from false information produce failure. (18%)
잘못된 정보에서(×) 도출된 활동은 실패를 낳는다.
inappropriate information을 활용한 오답. 잘못된 정보가 아니라 과정을 활동의 형태로 기획하는 것에서 실패가 발생한다는 내용임.

02 + 빈칸 추론 〈18학년도 9월 모평 34번 | 정답률 47%〉 ①

구문분석 & 직독직해

관광 산업 관광지 지역 주민들의 장소 정체성

[1] *The narratives* [that people create / to understand their landscapes] / come to be viewed / as marketable entities and a source of income (for residents).
S 목적격 관계대명사 목적(~하기 위해) V
★<view A as B(A를 B로 여기다)>의 수동형
이야기는 [사람들이 만들어 내는 / 자신들의 지역을 이해하기 위해] / 여겨지게 된다 / 시장성이 높은 실재이자 소득원으로 (주민들의)
↳ **대조 A:** 자신이 사는 지역을 이해하고자 만들어 내는 이야기는 이윤을 남김.

[2] Landscapes (with a strong place identity) / have an advantage in marketing to tourists, //
S(복수) V(복수) O
지역은 (강한 장소 정체성을 지닌) / 관광객들에게 마케팅하는 데 있어 이점이 있다 //
↱ 부사절 접속사(~ 때문에)
as it is relatively easy / to compartmentalize [and] (to) market their narratives.
가주어 진주어(to-v구)
왜냐하면 (~가) 비교적 쉽기 때문에 / (지역을) 구획하고 그것의 이야기를 시장에 내놓기가
↳ 특히 장소 정체성이 강한 지역 이야기는 마케팅 이점이 있음.

주제문
[3] Such places may have disadvantages as well, / however.
그런 장소들은 또한 불리한 점이 있을지도 모른다 / 그러나
↳ **대조 B:** 강한 장소 정체성을 지닌 곳은 약점도 있음.

[4] If place identity is tied / to a particular industry, // 🔑 특정 산업 지역의 주민들은 그 장소 정체성에 강한 애착을 느낌.
부사절 접속사(조건)
만약 장소 정체성이 결부되어 있다면 / 어떤 특정 산업과 //
local residents may feel strongly attached / to *the definitions of place* [that stem from involvement in that industry], //
S_1 V_1 C 주격 관계대명사
지역 주민들은 강한 애착을 느낄 수 있다 / 장소의 정의에 [그 산업에 대한 관여로 생겨나는] //
[and] they may **resist losing that identity** / in favor of *one* (based on a tourism industry).
S_2 V_2 O (= identity) 과거분사구
그리고 그들(지역 주민들)은 그 정체성을 잃는 것에 저항할 수도 있다 / 정체성을 지지하여 (관광 산업을 기반으로 하는)
↳ **세부 사항:** 특정 산업과 연관된 지역 주민들은 애착이 강해 관광 산업으로 기존 정체성을 잃는 것에 반대할 수도 있음.

[5] *People* (rooted in landscape) / may feel strong connections / to other community members /
S 과거분사구 V_1 O_1
사람들은 (지역에 뿌리를 둔) / 강한 연관성을 느낄 수 있다 / 다른 공동체 일원들에게 /
[and] may resent / the invasion (of *outsiders* [who (they believe) are different / [and] challenge their common identity]). 🔑 강한 장소 정체성을 지닌 사람들은 외부인에 적대적일 수 있음.
V_2 O_2 주격 관계대명사 삽입절 V'_1 C′ V'_2 O′
그리고 분개할 수도 있다 / 침입에 (외부인의 [(그들이 생각하기에) 다른 / 그리고 자신들의 공통된 정체성에 도전하는])
↳ **세부 사항:** 연대가 강한 지역 사람들은 외부인(관광객)이 들어오는 것에 적대적일 수 있음.

해석

[1]사람들이 자신들의 지역을 이해하기 위해 만들어내는 이야기는 시장성이 높은 실재이자 주민들의 소득원으로 여겨지게 된다. [2]강한 장소 정체성을 지닌 지역은 관광객들에게 마케팅하는 데 있어 이점이 있는데, 왜냐하면 (지역을) 구획하고 그것의 이야기를 시장에 내놓기가 비교적 쉽기 때문이다. [3]그러나 그런 장소들은 또한 불리한 점이 있을지도 모른다. [4]만약 장소 정체성이 어떤 특정 산업과 결부되어 있다면, 지역 주민들은 그 산업에 대한 관여로 생겨나는 장소의 정의에 강한 애착을 느낄 수 있고, 그들은 관광 산업을 기반으로 하는 정체성을 지지하여 그 정체성을 잃는 것에 저항할 수도 있다. [5]지역에 뿌리를 둔 사람들은 다른 공동체 일원들에게 강한 연관성을 느낄 수 있으며, 그들이 생각하기에 다르고 자신들의 공통된 정체성에 도전하는 외부인의 침입에 분개할 수도 있다. [6]결국, 지역 주민들은 이 과정이 자신들의 정체성을 단순한 상거래로 격하시킨다고 느낄 수도 있으며, 그들은 자신들의 장소에 관한 독특하고 특별한 것을 자신들이 희생한다고 여길 수도 있다.

어휘

narrative 이야기(체의); 서술 (기법)
landscape 지역, 장소; 풍경
marketable 시장성이 높은
income 소득, 수입
resident 주민, 거주자
relatively 비교적; 상대적으로
attached 애착을 가진; 부착된, 첨부된
definition 정의, 의미
stem from ~에서 생겨나다[유래하다]
resist 저항[반대]하다
in favor of ~에 지지하여
rooted ~에 뿌리[근원]를 둔

[6]Finally, / local residents may feel // that this process reduces their identities / to mere commercial transactions, //

(that: may feel의 O(명사절) / S1 V1 명사절 접속사 S′ V′ O′)

🗝 지역 주민들은 정체성이 격하되고 지역 특색이 사라진다고 생각할 수 있음.

결국 / 지역 주민들은 (~라고) 느낄 수도 있다 // 이 과정이 자신들의 정체성을 격하시킨다고 / 단순한 상거래로 //

and they may believe // (that) they sacrifice // what is unique and special about their place.

(S2 V2 명사절 접속사 생략 S′ V′ O′(명사절) / (that): may believe의 O(명사절))

그리고 그들은 (~라고) 여길 수도 있다 // 자신들이 희생한다고 // 자신들의 장소에 관한 독특하고 특별한 것을

↳ **결과:** 관광지의 지역 주민들이 느끼는 장소 정체성이 격하될 수 있음.

resent 분개하다
invasion 침입; 침략; 침해
mere 단순한
commercial 상업의
sacrifice 희생하다; 희생(물)
[선택지] persist 지속하다; 고집하다
tolerate 용인하다; 참다, 견디다
shift 변화; 바꾸다; 교대 근무
alienate 멀리하다, 따돌리다

정답 가이드

빈칸 문장의 의미로 보아, 지역 주민들이 장소 정체성이 결부된 어떤 특정 산업에 강한 애착을 느끼면 '무엇을 할' 수도 있는지를 추론해야 한다. 이어지는 설명은 특정 산업을 기반으로 하는 강한 정체성을 가진 공동체가 관광 산업으로 인해 자신들의 정체성이 도전받고 격하되며 희생된다고 느낄 수 있다는 것이므로 지역 주민들은 자신들의 정체성을 지키려고 할 것이다. 따라서 빈칸에 들어갈 말로 가장 적절한 것은 ① 'resist losing that identity(그 정체성을 잃는 것에 저항하다)'이다.

오답 클리닉

② stop persisting with the old tie (11%)
오래된 유대를 지속하기를 멈추다
지역 공동체 일원들과 강한 연관성을 느낀다고 했으므로 틀림.

③ tolerate the shift of that industry (12%)
그 산업의 변화를 용인하다
산업의 변화에 관한 언급은 없음.

④ alienate themselves from that place (17%)
그 장소로부터 자신들을 멀리하다
특정 산업과 연관된 장소 정체성에 강한 애착을 느낀다고 했으므로 글의 내용과 반대됨.

⑤ refuse the advantage of that industry (11%)
그 산업의 이익을 거부하다
주민들이 산업의 이익을 거부한다는 내용은 없음.

03 + 무관 문장 (20학년도 9월 모평 35번 | 정답률 89%) ④

구문분석 & 직독직해

생활 정신 에너지를 아껴주는 습관

[1]Much (of what we do each day) // is automatic and guided by habit, / requiring little conscious awareness, // and that's not a bad thing.

(what ~ day: of의 O(명사절) / S1 V1 C1 / 분사구문(= and it requires ~) / that: (= much ~ by habit) / S2 V2 C2)

대부분은 (우리가 매일 하는 일의) // 자동적이고 습관에 의해 이끌어진다 / 의식적인 인식을 거의 필요로 하지 않으면서 // 그리고 그것은 나쁜 것이 아니다

↳ **도입:** 매일 하는 습관적인 일은 생각을 요하지 않는데, 그렇다고 나쁜 것은 아님.

주제문 🗝 습관이 정신 에너지를 절약해 준다는 내용임.

[2]As Duhigg explains, // our habits are necessary mental energy savers.

(부사절 접속사(~듯이) / S V C)

Duhigg가 설명하듯이 // 우리의 습관은 필수적인 정신 에너지 절약 장치이다

↳ 습관은 필수적인 정신 에너지 절약 장치임.

① [3]We need to relieve our conscious minds // so (that) we can solve new problems // as they come up.

(S V O / 부사절 접속사 S′ V′ O′ / 부사절 접속사(~할 때) / *<so (that)>: ~하도록(= in order that))

우리는 의식적인 생각을 덜어야 한다 // 우리가 새로운 문제들을 해결할 수 있도록 // 그것들이 발생할 때

↳ **세부 사항:** 새로운 문제 해결을 위해 생각을 덜어야 함.

② [4]Once we've solved / the puzzle (of how to ballroom dance), / for example, // we can do it by habit, // and so (we can) be mentally freed / to focus on a conversation / while dancing instead.

(부사절 접속사(일단 ~하면) / <how to-v>: v하는 방법 / S1 V1 O / S2 V2 C / 접속사를 생략하지 않은 분사구문 (= while we are dancing))

일단 우리가 해결하고 나면 / 문제를 (사교댄스를 추는 방법에 대한) / 예를 들어 // 우리는 그것을 습관적으로 할 수 있다 // 그래서 정신적으로 자유로워질 수 있다 / 대화에 집중하도록 / 춤을 추면서도

↳ **예 1:** 사교댄스에 익숙해지면, 춤을 추며 대화에 집중할 수 있음.

해석

[1]우리가 매일 하는 일의 대부분은 자동적이고 습관에 의해 이끌어지며, 의식적인 인식을 거의 필요로 하지 않는데, 그것은 나쁜 것이 아니다. [2]Duhigg가 설명하듯이, 우리의 습관은 필수적인 정신 에너지 절약 장치이다. ① [3]우리는 새로운 문제들이 발생할 때 우리가 그것들을 해결할 수 있도록 의식적인 생각을 덜어야 한다. ② [4]예를 들어, 사교댄스를 추는 방법에 대한 문제를 일단 해결하고 나면, 우리는 그것을 습관적으로 할 수 있고, 그래서 춤을 추면서도 대화에 집중하도록 정신적으로 자유로워질 수 있다. ③ [5]하지만 탱고를 추는 법을 처음 배울 때 말하려고 해보면 그것은 엉망진창이 될 것인데, 스텝에 집중하기 위해 우리는 의식적인 주의를 필요로 하기 때문이다. ④ [6]탱고 음악가는 가지각색의 배경에서 더 다양한 청중을 끌어 모으기 위해 서로 다른 장르의 음악을 한데 모은다. ⑤ [7]만약 우리가 모든 행동, 예를 들어, 우리가 딛는 모든 (탱고) 스텝에서 발을 어디에 둘지에 의식적으로 집중해야 한다면 우리가 얼마나 적게 성취할지를 상상해 보라.

★<명령문, and S+V ...>: ~해라, 그러면 S는 V할 것이다

③ [5]But try to talk / when first learning to dance the tango, // and it's a disaster — //

V₁(명령문) 접속사를 생략하지 않은 분사구문(= when you first learn ~)

하지만 말하려고 해 보아라 / 탱고를 추는 법을 처음 배울 때 // 그러면 그것은 엉망진창이 될 것이다 //

we need our conscious attention / to focus on the steps.

목적(~하기 위해)

우리는 의식적인 주의를 필요로 하기 때문이다 / 스텝에 집중하기 위해

↳ **예 2:** 처음 춤을 배울 때는 스텝에 집중해야 해서 말하기 어려움.

앞 문장의 예로 사용된 tango를 활용한 무관한 문장.

④ [6]Tango musicians bring different genres of music together / to attract a more diverse audience (from varying backgrounds).

S V O 목적(~하기 위해)

탱고 음악가는 서로 다른 장르의 음악을 한데 모은다 / 더 다양한 청중을 끌어 모으기 위해 (가지각색의 배경에서)

↳ 탱고 음악가는 여러 청중을 끌어 모으기 위해 여러 장르의 음악을 모음.

★가정법 과거 <If+S'+동사의 과거형 ~, S+조동사의 과거형+동사원형 ...>: 만약 ~라면, …할 텐데

⑤ [7]Imagine // how little we'd accomplish // if we had to focus consciously / on every behavior — /

V(명령문) O

상상해 보라 // 우리가 얼마나 적게 성취할지를 // 만약 우리가 의식적으로 집중해야 한다면 / 모든 행동에 /

e.g., / on where to place our feet / for *each step* [(which[that]) we take].

<where to-v>: 어디에 v할지 목적격 관계대명사 생략

예를 들어 / 발을 어디에 둘지에 / 모든 (탱고) 스텝에서 [우리가 딛는]

↳ **결론:** 모든 행동에 의식적으로 집중해야 한다면 적게 성취할 것임 → 습관은 정신 에너지를 절약해 더 많이 성취할 수 있게 해줌.

어휘

automatic 자동의; 무의식적인
conscious 의식적인
awareness 인식, 자각
saver 절약 장치; 절약가
relieve (고통·부담을) 덜다, 완화하다
come up 발생하다, 생기다
ballroom dance 사교댄스(를 추다)
disaster 엉망진창인 것; 참사, 재난
bring A together A를 한데 모으다[합치다]
attract 끌어 모으다; 마음을 끌다
diverse 다양한
varying 가지각색의; 변화하는
background 배경

정답 가이드

도입 부분에서 우리의 일상은 습관에 의한 것이고 의식적으로 인식할 필요가 없다고 했다. 이는 나쁜 것이 아니라고 했으므로 습관에 의한 무의식적 행위를 긍정적으로 여기는 내용이 이어질 것을 예측할 수 있다. 이어지는 내용에서 습관이 우리의 정신 에너지를 절약해 다른 과업에 쓸 수 있게 해준다는 것을 사교댄스, 즉 탱고 배우기를 예로 들어 설명하고 있다. 하지만 ④는 탱고 음악가가 서로 다른 장르의 음악을 한데 모으는 이유를 설명하는 내용이므로 글의 흐름과 무관하다. 그 다음 문장은 우리가 모든 행동을 의식적으로 집중하면 성취가 적을 것이라는 내용이므로 글 전체 흐름과 일치한다.

오답 클리닉

① (2%) 앞에서 정신 에너지 절약 장치로 언급된 습관이 의식적인 생각을 덜어주는 것이라고 설명하는 연결은 자연스럽다.

② (2%) 의식적인 생각을 덜어낸 예로 사교댄스를 추면서 대화에 집중하는 것을 들고 있다.

③ (5%) 역접 연결어 But으로 이어져 앞과 반대되는 예로 탱고를 추면서 스텝에 집중하느라 대화하지 못하는 것을 들고 있다.

⑤ (2%) 모든 행동에 의식적으로 집중해야 한다면 많이 성취할 수 없을 것이라고 습관의 순기능을 강조하며 글을 끝맺고 있다.

01 + 밑줄 어법 〈22학년도 6월 모평 29번 | 정답률 58%〉 ⑤

구문분석 & 직독직해 천문학 스톤헨지의 천문학적 의미

[1]Most historians of science (S(복수)) / point to (V(복수)) the need for a reliable calendar (O) / to regulate agricultural activity (목적(~하기 위해)) / as (전치사(~로(서))) the motivation for learning (about what we now call astronomy, / the study of stars and planets) (about의 O(명사절)).

대부분의 과학 역사가들은 / 신뢰할 만한 달력의 필요성을 지적한다 / 농업 활동을 규정하기 위해 / 학습을 위한 동기로 (우리가 현재 천문학이라 부르는 것에 관한 / 별과 행성에 대한 연구)

주제문 *<when to-v>: 언제 v(해야) 할지*

[2]Early astronomy (S) provided (V₁) / information (O) (about when to plant crops (about의 O(명사구))) / [and] gave (V₂) humans (IO) / ① **their** (= humans') first formal method (DO) (of recording the passage of time).

초기 천문학은 제공했다 / 정보를 (언제 작물을 심어야 하는지에 대한) / 그리고 인간에게 제공했다 / 그들 최초의 공식적인 방법을 (시간의 흐름을 기록하는)

[3]Stonehenge (S(단수)), / the 4,000-year-old ring of stones in southern Britain, / ② **is** (V(단수)) perhaps the best-known monument (C) / to the discovery (of regularity and predictability) / in *the world* [(which[that]) (목적격 관계대명사 생략) we (S') inhabit (V')].

스톤헨지는 / 영국 남부에 있는 4,000년 된 원형의 돌들인 / 아마도 가장 잘 알려진 유적일 것이다 / 발견에 대한 (규칙성과 예측 가능성의) / 세계에서 [우리가 사는]

[4]The great markers (of Stonehenge) (S(복수)) / point to (V(복수)) *the spots on the horizon* (O) [③ **where** (관계부사) the sun (S') rises (V') / at the solstices and equinoxes — / *the dates* [(which[that]) (목적격 관계대명사 생략) we still use / to mark the beginnings of the seasons (목적(~하기 위해))]].

커다란 표식은 (스톤헨지의) / 지평선의 장소를 가리킨다 [태양이 뜨는 / 지점(至點)과 분점(分點)에서 / 날짜인 [우리가 여전히 사용하는 / 계절의 시작을 표시하기 위해]]

<may have p.p>: ~했을지도 모른다(약한 추측)

[5]The stones (S) may even have ④ **been used** (V) / to predict eclipses (목적(~하기 위해)).

그 돌들은 심지어 사용되었을지도 모른다 / (해·달의) 식(蝕)을 예측하기 위해

bear testimony to A: A에 대하여 증명[입증]하다

[6]The existence of Stonehenge (S), / (built by people without writing), / bears (V) silent testimony (O) / [both] to the regularity of nature / [and] to the ability of the human mind (to see behind immediate appearances / [and] ⑤ **discovers(→ (to) discover)** deeper meanings in events) (전치사구 병렬; to-v구 병렬).

스톤헨지의 존재는 / (글자가 없던 사람들에 의해 지어진) / 말없이 증명한다 / 자연의 규칙성에 대해 / 그리고 인간 정신 능력 (둘 다)에 대해 (눈앞에 보이는 모습의 이면을 보는 / 그리고 사건에서 더 깊은 의미를 발견하는)

해석

[1]대부분의 과학 역사가들은 별과 행성에 대한 연구, 즉 우리가 현재 천문학이라 부르는 것을 학습하는 동기로, 농업 활동을 규정하기 위해 신뢰할 만한 달력의 필요성을 지적한다. (▶ 천문학을 학습하게 된 동기는 농업 활동을 위한 달력을 만들기 위한 것이었다는 의미) [2]초기 천문학은 언제 작물을 심어야 하는지에 대한 정보를 제공했고 인간에게 시간의 흐름을 기록하는 그들 최초의 공식적인 방법을 제공했다. [3]영국 남부에 있는 4,000년 된 원형의 돌들인 스톤헨지는 아마도 우리가 사는 세계에서 규칙성과 예측 가능성의 발견에 대한 가장 잘 알려진 유적일 것이다. [4]스톤헨지의 커다란 표식은 우리가 계절의 시작을 표시하기 위해 여전히 사용하는 날짜인 지점(至點)과 분점(分點)에서 태양이 뜨는 지평선의 장소를 가리킨다. [5]그 돌들은 심지어 (해·달의) 식(蝕)을 예측하기 위해 사용되었을지도 모른다. [6]글자가 없던 사람들에 의해 지어진 스톤헨지의 존재는 자연의 규칙성과 눈앞에 보이는 모습의 이면을 보고 사건에서 더 깊은 의미를 발견하는 인간 정신 능력 둘 다에 대해 말없이 증명한다.

어휘

point to A A를 지적하다; A를 가리키다
reliable 신뢰할[믿을] 만한
regulate 규정[규제]하다; 조절하다
agricultural 농업의
astronomy 천문학
passage (시간의) 흐름, 경과
monument 유적, (역사적) 기념물
regularity 규칙성
predictability 예측 가능성
inhabit 살다, 거주하다
spot 장소; 점; 발견하다
horizon 지평선, 수평선
solstice 《천문》 지점(至點) 《하지점과 동지점을 통틀어 이르는 말》
equinox 《천문》 분점(分點) 《태양이 적도를 통과하는 점으로 춘분점과 추분점이 있음》
existence 존재, 실재, 현존

정답 가이드

⑤ **[병렬구조]** discovers는 3인칭 현재동사 형태이므로 문장의 동사가 있는지부터 살펴야 한다. 길고 복잡하지만 문장의 동사 bears가 이미 있다. both A and B 구문의 B를 이루는 the ability of the human mind와 동격인 to부정사구가 and로 연결된 구조로 보는 것이 문맥상 자연스럽다. to see와 문법상 대등한 형태여야 하므로 discovers를 (to) discover로 고쳐야 한다.

오답 클리닉

① **[대명사]** (12%)
문맥상 first formal method는 앞에 나온 복수명사 humans가 소유하는 것이므로 이를 대신하는 their는 어법상 적절하다.

② **[주어와 동사의 수일치]** (5%)
단수인 Stonehenge가 주어인 문장의 동사 자리이므로, 3인칭 단수 현재시제인 is는 어법상 적절하다. 주어를 부연 설명하는 동격어구가 콤마(,) 사이에 삽입되어 주어와 동사와의 거리가 멀어진 형태이다.

③ **[관계부사]** (12%)
뒤에 주어(the sun), 자동사(rises), 부사구(at the solstices and equinoxes)로 이루어진 완전한 구조의 절이 왔고, 이 절이 '장소'를 뜻하는 the spots on the horizon을 수식하므로 관계부사 where는 어법상 적절하다.

The 주의 목적어가 없는 SV나 SVC문형이 완전한 구조의 절로 자주 출제된다.

④ **[능동태 vs. 수동태]** (12%)
주어(The stones)가 사용을 당하는 대상이므로, 주어와 동사는 수동관계이다. 따라서 완료형(have p.p.)과 결합한 수동태 been used는 어법상 적절하다.

02 ✦ 빈칸 추론 〈18학년도 9월 모평 33번 | 정답률 35%〉 ①

구문분석 & 직독직해

심리 외재화하는 대화 상담 기법

주제문

[1]Externalization is *the foundation* [from which many narrative conversations are built].
S V C 전치사+관계대명사
외재화는 토대이다 [많은 이야기식 대화가 만들어지는]

(= Externalization)
[2]This requires a particular shift / in the use (of language).
S V O
이것은 특별한 변화를 필요로 한다 / 사용에 있어 (언어의)

↳ **도입:** 외재화는 이야기식 대화의 바탕이 되며, 언어 사용에 있어 변화를 요구함.

[3]Often externalizing conversations involve tracing / the influence (of the problem) / in a child's life / over time /
S V O 동명사 tracing의 O_1(명사구)
외재화하는 대화는 추적하는 것을 흔히 포함한다 / 영향을 (문제의) / 아동의 삶에 미친 / 시간이 지나는 동안 /
and how the problem has disempowered the child / by limiting his ability (to see things / in a different light).
동명사 tracing의 O_2(명사절) <by v-ing>: v함으로써 =
그리고 어떻게 그 문제가 아동으로부터 힘을 빼앗아 왔는지를 / 아동의 능력을 제한함으로써 (상황을 보는 / 다른 관점에서)

↳ **외재화하는 대화:** 문제가 아동의 삶에 미치는 영향을 추적함.

★<help+O+(to-)v>: O가 v하도록 돕다
[4]The counsellor helps the child to change / by deconstructing old stories / and reconstructing preferred stories (about himself and his life).
S V O C by의 O(동명사구 병렬)
상담사는 아동이 변화하도록 돕는다 / 옛 이야기를 해체함으로써 / 그리고 (아동이) 선호하는 이야기를 재구성함으로써 (아동 자신과 아동 자신의 삶에 관한)

↳ **상담 방법:** 문제가 있는 이야기는 해체하고, 아동 자신에 관해 선호하는 이야기는 재구성하도록 함.

🔑 문제가 없던 때를 생각하고 그때의 사고와 행동 방식이 어떻게 달랐는지에 주목함.
[5]To help the child to develop a new story, / the counsellor and child search / for *times* [when the problem has not influenced / the child or the child's life] /
목적(~하기 위해) S V_1 관계부사
아동이 새로운 이야기를 전개하도록 돕기 위해 / 상담사와 아동은 찾는다 / 때를 [그 문제가 영향을 미치지 않았던 / 아동이나 아동의 삶에] /
and focus / on *the different ways* [(that) the child thought, felt and behaved].
V_2 관계부사 생략
그리고 초점을 둔다 / 다른 방식에 [아동이 생각하고, 느끼고, 행동했던]

[6]These **exceptions** (**to the problem story**) / help the child create a new and preferred story.
S(복수) V(복수) O C
이러한 예외들은 (그 문제 이야기에 대한) / 아동이 새롭고 선호하는 이야기를 만들어 내도록 돕는다

↳ **부연 설명:** 문제가 없던 때를 떠올려 그때의 사고와 행동 방식에 초점을 두고 선호하는 이야기를 만들도록 함.

해석

[1]외재화는 많은 이야기식 대화가 만들어지는 토대이다. [2]이것은 언어의 사용에 있어 특별한 변화를 필요로 한다. [3]외재화하는 대화는 시간이 지나는 동안 아동의 삶에 미친 문제의 영향과 어떻게 그 문제가 다른 관점에서 상황을 보는 아동의 능력을 제한함으로써 아동으로부터 힘을 빼앗아 왔는지를 추적하는 것을 흔히 포함한다. [4]상담사는 아동 자신과 아동 자신의 삶에 관한 옛 이야기를 해체하고 (아동이) 선호하는 이야기를 재구성함으로써 아동이 변화하도록 돕는다. [5]아동이 새로운 이야기를 전개하도록 돕기 위해, 상담사와 아동은 그 문제가 아동이나 아동의 삶에 영향을 미치지 않았던 때를 찾아 아동이 생각하고, 느끼고, 행동했던 다른 방식에 초점을 둔다. [6]이러한 그 문제 이야기에 대한 예외들(그 문제 이야기에 해당되지 않는 것들)은 아동이 새롭고 선호하는 이야기를 만들어 내도록 돕는다. [7]새롭고 선호하는 이야기가 나오기 시작할 때, 아동이 그 새로운 이야기에 매달리도록, 즉 그 새로운 이야기와 연결된 상태를 유지하도록 돕는 것이 중요하다.

어휘

externalize 외재[표면]화하다
foundation 토대, 기초
narrative 이야기(식의); 묘사; 서술 (기법)
shift 변화(하다); 옮기다; 교대 근무
trace 추적하다; 자국, 흔적
disempower 힘[영향력]을 빼앗다
counsellor 상담사, 상담 전문가
deconstruct 해체[분해]하다
reconstruct 재구성하다; 재건하다
emerge 나오다; 생겨나다
hold on to A A에 매달리다, A를 고수하다[지키다]

[7]As a new and preferred story begins to emerge, //
부사절 접속사(~할 때) S' V' O'
새롭고 선호하는 이야기가 나오기 시작할 때 //

→ 진주어(to-v구) ★<assist+O+to-v>: O가 v하도록 돕다
it is important / to assist the child to hold on to, / or (to) stay connected to, / the new story.
가주어 V' O' C' =
(~이) 중요하다 / 아동이 ~에 매달리도록 돕는 것이 / 즉 ~와 연결된 상태를 유지하도록 / 그 새로운 이야기에([~와])
↳ **상담사의 역할:** 아동이 선호되는 이야기에 집중할 수 있도록 도와주어야 함.

⊕ 외재화(externalization): 상담 심리학에서 외재화란 문제를 밖으로 꺼내 이야기하거나 쓰는 행위를 말함.
⊕ 외재화하는 대화(externalizing conversation): 내담자의 문제를 밖으로 끌어내어 객관화시킴으로써, 새로운 시각으로 문제를 바라보고 가능성을 찾고자 하는 기법. 문제가 되는 이야기의 부정적 영향을 줄이고 내담자가 선호하는 방향으로 대안적 이야기를 쓰도록 함.
⊕ 선호하는 이야기(preferred story): 내담자의 다양한 삶의 이야기 중에서 내담자가 보다 만족해하고, 미래의 희망찬 삶을 위한 의미를 부여하려고 하는 이야기.

정답 가이드

빈칸 문장으로 보아 이러한 '무엇'이 아동이 새롭고 선호하는 이야기를 만들어 내도록 도와주는지를 추론해야 하는데, These로 시작하므로 앞에 단서가 있을 것으로 추측할 수 있다. 외재화하는 대화란 아동의 삶에 미친 문제의 영향을 해결하기 위해 아동의 삶에 관한 옛 이야기를 해체하고 선호하는 이야기를 만들어 내는 것인데, 이를 돕기 위해 '그 문제가 영향을 미치지 않았던 때'의 아동의 생각과 행동에 초점을 둔다고 했다. 따라서 빈칸에 들어갈 말로 가장 적절한 것은 ① 'exceptions to the problem story(그 문제 이야기에 대한 예외들)'이다.

오답 클리닉

② distances from the alternative story (13%)
대안적 이야기로부터의 거리
문제에서 벗어난 대안적 이야기는 새로운 선호되는 이야기를 의미하므로 그것과 거리를 두는 것은 글의 내용과 반대됨.

③ problems that originate from the counsellor (8%)
상담사로부터 나오는 문제들
상담사가 아이들을 돕는 과정을 설명하고 있으므로 틀림.

④ efforts to combine old and new experiences (20%)
옛 경험과 새 경험을 합치려는 노력
옛 경험인 문제 경험을 새로운 이야기로 대체한다고 했으므로 틀림.

⑤ methods of linking the child's stories to another's (22%)
아동의 이야기를 다른 사람의 이야기와 연결하는 방법
connect를 활용한 오답. 다른 사람들의 이야기가 아닌 아동이 만든 새 선호하는 이야기에 집중하게 해야 한다고 했음.

03 + 글의 순서 ⟨19학년도 대수능 36번 | 정답률 57%⟩ ③

구문분석 & 직독직해 심리학 과학적 연구의 어려움과 이점

[1]Researchers in psychology follow the scientific method / to perform *studies* [that help explain and may predict human behavior].
S(복수) V(복수) O 목적(~하기 위해) 주격 관계대명사
심리학 연구자들은 과학적인 방법을 따른다 / 연구를 수행하기 위해 [인간의 행동을 설명하는 데 도움을 주고 예측할 수 있는]

주제문
→ (= Following the scientific method in psychology)
[2]This is a much more challenging task / than studying snails or sound waves.
S V C
이는 훨씬 더 힘든 일이다 / 달팽이나 음파를 연구하는 것보다
↳ **도입:** 자연 현상과 달리 인간의 행동을 연구하는 심리학에서 과학적 방법을 사용하는 것은 매우 어려움.

→ (= Following the scientific method in psychology) ★<A rather than B>: B라기보다는 A
(B) [3]It often requires compromises, / such as testing behavior within laboratories / rather than natural settings, / ⊶ 심리학 연구에서 과학적 방법을 따르는 것이 힘든 작업임을 절충안을 제시함으로써 부연 설명함.
S V O 동명사구 병렬
그것은 종종 절충이 필요하다 / 실험실 내에서의 행동을 검사하는 것과 같은 / 자연적인 환경보다 /
★<ask+O+to-v>: O가 v하도록 요청하다
and asking *those* (readily available) / (such as introduction to psychology students) / to participate / rather than collecting data / from a true cross-section of the population.
동명사구 병렬 형용사구
그리고 (~한) 사람들에게 요청하는 것(과 같은) (손쉽게 구할 수 있는) / (심리학 입문 수업 학생들처럼) / 참여하도록 / 데이터를 모으는 것보다 / 모집단의 대표적인 실제 예에서
↳ **세부 사항 1:** 과학적 방법을 따르기 위해 심리학 연구는 절충(실험실 내에서의 검사, 주변인 참여 요청 등)이 필요함.

해석

[1]심리학 연구자들은 인간의 행동을 설명하는 데 도움을 주고 예측할 수 있는 연구를 수행하기 위해 과학적인 방법을 따른다. [2]이는 달팽이나 음파를 연구하는 것보다 훨씬 더 힘든 일이다. (B) [3]그것은 종종 자연적인 환경보다 실험실 내에서의 행동을 검사하는 것, 그리고 모집단의 대표적인 실제 예에서 데이터를 모으는 것보다 (심리학 입문 수업 학생들처럼) 손쉽게 구할 수 있는 사람들에게 참여하도록 요청하는 것과 같은 절충이 필요하다. [4]반응성(▶ 자신들이 관찰되고 있음을 인식하여 자신의 생각과는 다른 반응을 보이는 것을 의미)이라 불리는, 그들의 생각을 바꾸는 것 없이 사람들이 생각하고 있는 것에 접근할 방법을 생각해 내는 것은 대단한 교묘함[솜씨]을 필요로 한다. (C) [5]단순히 자신들이 관찰되고 있다는 것을 아는 것은 사람들이 (더욱 공손하게 하는 것처럼!) (평소와) 다르게 행동하도록 야기할 수 있다. [6]사람들은 자신들의 실제 생각보다 그들이 생각하기에 더 사회적으로 바람직한 답변을 줄지도 모른다. (A) [7]그러나 심리학에 대한 모든 이러한 어려움에도 불구하고, 과학적인 방법의 이득

⁴It often requires great cleverness / to conceive of *measures* [that tap into what people are thinking / without *altering their thinking*, // (which is) called reactivity].

가주어 V O 진주어(to-v구) 주격 관계대명사 into의 O(명사절) without의 O(동명사구)

(~은) 대단한 교묘함[솜씨]을 종종 필요로 한다 / 방법을 생각해 내는 것은 [사람들이 생각하고 있는 것에 접근할 / 그들의 생각을 바꾸는 것 없이 // 반응성이라 불리는]

↳ 세부 사항 2: 피험자의 생각에 영향을 미치지 않고 그들의 본래 생각을 파악하기는 어려움.

명사절 접속사 생략 / ★<cause+O+to-v>: O가 v하도록 야기하다

(C) ⁵Simply knowing // (that) they are being observed / may cause people to behave differently / (such as more politely!).

S(동명사구) 동명사 knowing의 O(명사절) V O C

🗝 피험자의 생각을 바꾸지 않고 연구하기가 어렵다는 (B)를 구체적으로 설명함.

단순히 아는 것은 // 자신들이 관찰되고 있다는 것을 / 사람들이 (평소와) 다르게 행동하도록 야기할 수 있다 / (더욱 공손하게 하는 것처럼!)

↳ 이유 1: 사람들은 본인이 관찰되고 있음을 알게 되면 본래 모습과 다르게 행동함.

⁶People may give / *answers* [that (they feel) are more socially desirable / than their true feelings].

S V O 주격 관계대명사 삽입절

사람들은 줄지도 모른다 / 답변을 [(그들이 생각하기에) 더 사회적으로 바람직한 / 자신들의 실제 생각보다]

↳ 이유 2: 실제 자신의 생각이 아닌 사회적으로 바람직한 답변을 함.

🗝 But으로 심리학에서 과학적 방법을 사용하는 어려움과 대조되는 장점이 이어짐.

(A) ⁷But / for all of these difficulties for psychology, / the payoff (of the scientific method) / is // that the findings are replicable; //

전치사(~에도 불구하고) S_1 V_1 C(명사절)

그러나 / 심리학에 대한 모든 이러한 어려움에도 불구하고 / 이득은 (과학적인 방법의) / ~이다 // 연구 결과가 반복 가능하다는 것 //

★<be likely to-v>: v할 가능성이 있다

that is, / if you run the same study again / following the same procedures, // you will be very likely to get the same results.

부사절 접속사(조건) 분사구문(= while you follow ~) S_2 V_2

즉 / 여러분이 같은 연구를 다시 진행한다면 / 같은 절차를 따르면서 // 여러분은 같은 결과를 얻을 가능성이 매우 클 것이다

↳ 과학적 연구의 이점: 같은 연구 결과를 반복해 얻을 수 있음.

은 연구 결과가 반복 가능하다는 것이다. 즉 여러분이 같은 절차를 따르면서 같은 연구를 다시 진행한다면, 같은 결과를 얻을 가능성이 매우 클 것이다.

어휘

challenging 힘든, 어려운; 도전적인
compromise 절충[타협](하다)
laboratory 실험실
readily 손쉽게
available 구할[이용할] 수 있는
introduction 입문(서); 도입; 소개
participate 참여하다, 참가하다
cross-section 대표적인 예; (횡)단면
population 모집단; 인구; 주민
cleverness 교묘함, 솜씨 좋음; 영리함
conceive of ~을 생각해 내다; ~을 상상하다
measure 방법, 조치; 측정하다
tap into ~에게 접근하다; ~을 활용하다
alter 바꾸다; 변하다
reactivity 반응성
observe 관찰하다; 준수하다; 말하다
desirable 바람직한
payoff 이득, 이익, 보상; 지불
finding 연구 결과
procedure 절차; 순서

정답 가이드

과학적인 방법을 사용하여 심리학 연구를 하기가 어렵다는 주어진 글 다음, 필요한 절충안을 제시하는 (B)가 오는 것이 적절하다. 이어서 (B)에서 서술한 '반응성'을 좀 더 구체적으로 설명한 (C)가 이어져야 한다. 마지막으로 역접 연결어 But과 함께 (C)에서 서술된 것들을 받는 '이러한 어려움들(these difficulties)'에도 불구하고 과학적 방법에 이점이 있음을 서술하는 (A)가 이어지는 것이 자연스럽다.

오답 클리닉

① (A) - (C) - (B) (3%)
주어진 글에는 (A)의 all of these difficulties for psychology에 해당하는 구체적인 내용이 없으므로 (A)는 주어진 글 바로 뒤에 올 수 없다.
② (B) - (A) - (C) (19%)
(A)의 for all of these difficulties를 통해 과학적 연구의 어려움이 모두 앞서 언급되어 있어야 함을 알 수 있다. 따라서 (C)는 (A) 앞에 와야 한다.
④ (C) - (A) - (B) (9%) / ⑤ (C) - (B) - (A) (13%)
(C)는 (B)의 피험자의 생각을 바꾸지 않고 연구하기가 어려운 이유를 구체적으로 설명하므로 (B) 뒤에 와야 한다.

01 ✦ 낱말 쓰임 〈22학년도 6월 모평 30번 | 정답률 64%〉 ④

구문분석 & 직독직해

스포츠 스포츠가 야기하는 열렬한 정서적 반응

[1]Sport can trigger an emotional response / in its consumers / of *the kind* (rarely brought forth / by other products).
S V O 과거분사구

스포츠는 정서적 반응을 일으킬 수 있다 / 그것의 소비자에게서 / 종류의 (좀처럼 야기되지 않는 / 다른 제품에 의해)

★<imagine+O+v-ing>: O가 v하는 것을 상상하다

[2]Imagine bank customers / buying memorabilia / to show loyalty to their bank, /
V(명령문) O_1 C_1 목적(~하기 위해)

은행 고객이 (~하는 것을) 상상해 보라 / 기념품을 구입하는 것을 / 그들 은행에 대한 충성심을 보여 주기 위해 /

or consumers / ① **identifying** so strongly with their car insurance company // that they get a tattoo / with its logo.
O_2 C_2 └identify with: ~와 동일시하다┘ ★<so+형용사/부사+that ...>: 매우 ~해서 …하다

🔑 ① 고객이 회사 로고로 문신을 새기는 것은 고객이 회사와 '동일시'하기 때문임.

또는 고객이 (~하는 것을) / 자신들의 자동차 보험 회사와 매우 강하게 동일시해서 // 문신을 새기는 것을 / 그 회사 로고로

↱ know의 O(명사절)

[3]We know // that some sport followers are so ② **passionate** / about players, teams and the sport itself // that their interest borders on obsession.
S V 명사절 접속사 S′ V′ C′ 재귀대명사(강조) S″ V″ O″

🔑 ② 일부 스포츠팬들이 매우 '열정적'이어서 그들의 관심이 집착에 가까운 것임.

우리는 알고 있다 // 일부 스포츠팬들이 매우 열정적이어서 / 선수, 팀, 그리고 스포츠 그 자체에 // 그들의 관심이 집착에 아주 가깝다는 것을

[4]This addiction provides / *the emotional glue* [that binds fans to teams], / and maintains loyalty / even in the face of on-field ③ **failure**.
S V_1 O_1 주격 관계대명사 V_2 O_2 ~에도 불구하고

🔑 ③ 팬을 팀에 결속시키는 정서적 접착제를 제공하여 경기에서 '실패'하더라도 충성심을 유지하게 할 것임.

이러한 중독은 제공한다 / 정서적 접착제를 [팬을 팀에 결속시키는] / 그리고 충성심을 유지하게 한다 / 구장 위의 실패에도 불구하고

주제문

★<A as 형용사/부사 as B>: A는 B만큼 ~한/하게

[5]While most managers can only dream of / having *customers* [that are as passionate about their products / as sport fans], //
부사절 접속사(~ 반면에) S′ V′ O′ 주격 관계대명사

대부분의 관리자들은 오직 ~만 꿈꿀 수 있는 반면에 / 고객을 가지기를 [그들의 제품에 열정적인 / 스포츠팬만큼] //

the emotion (triggered by sport) / can also have a negative impact.
S 과거분사구 V O

정서는 (스포츠에 의해 유발된) / 또한 부정적인 영향을 미칠 수 있다

↱ can mean의 O(명사절)

[6]Sport's emotional intensity can mean // that organisations have strong attachments to the past / through nostalgia and club tradition.
S V 명사절 접속사 S′ V′ O′

🔑 ④ 조직은 과거에 대한 애착이 강해 변화에 신속히 대응할 필요성을 '무시할' 것임.

스포츠의 정서적 강렬함은 의미할 수 있다 // 조직이 과거에 대한 강한 애착을 가지고 있다는 것을 / 향수와 구단 전통을 통해

↱ (= the organisations)

[7]As a result, / they may ④ **increase(→ ignore)** / efficiency, productivity and *the need* (to respond quickly / to changing market conditions).
S V O_1 O_2 O_3

그 결과 / 그것(조직)은 늘릴(→ 무시할) 수도 있다 / 효율성, 생산성, 그리고 필요성을 (신속하게 대응할 / 변화하는 시장 상황에)

[8]For example, / a proposal (to change club colours / in order to project a more attractive image) / may be ⑤ **defeated** // because it breaks a link with tradition.
S = 목적(~하기 위해) V 부사절 접속사(이유) (= the proposal)

🔑 ⑤ 구단 전통을 통해 과거에 강한 애착을 가진다고 했으므로 전통과의 관계를 끊는 제안은 '무산'될 것임.

예를 들어 / 제안은 (구단 색깔을 바꾸자는 / 더 매력적인 이미지를 투영하기 위해) / 무산될 수도 있다 // 그것(제안)이 전통과의 관계를 끊기 때문에

해석

[1]스포츠는 그것의 소비자에게서 다른 제품에 의해 좀처럼 야기되지 않는 종류의 정서적 반응을 일으킬 수 있다. [2]은행 고객이 그들 은행에 대한 충성심을 보여 주기 위해 기념품을 구입하는 것, 또는 고객이 자신들의 자동차 보험 회사와 매우 강하게 ① 동일시해서 그 회사 로고로 문신을 새기는 것을 상상해 보라.(▶ 다른 제품을 구매하는 소비자들은 스포츠팬들이 그러는 것처럼 기념품 구입을 하거나 로고 문신을 새기지는 않는다는 것을 의미) [3]우리는 일부 스포츠팬들이 선수, 팀, 그리고 스포츠 그 자체에 매우 ② 열정적이어서 그들의 관심이 집착에 아주 가깝다는 것을 알고 있다. [4]이러한 중독은 팬을 팀에 결속시키는 정서적 접착제를 제공하고 구장 위의 ③ 실패에도 불구하고 충성심을 유지하게 한다. [5]대부분의 관리자들(스포츠가 아닌 다른 산업에 종사하는 사람들)은 스포츠팬만큼 그들의 제품에 열정적인 고객을 가지기만을 오직 꿈꿀 수 있지만, 스포츠에 의해 유발된 정서는 또한 부정적인 영향을 미칠 수 있다. [6]스포츠의 정서적 강렬함은 조직이 향수와 구단 전통을 통해 과거에 대한 강한 애착을 가지고 있다는 것을 의미할 수 있다. [7]그 결과, 조직은 효율성, 생산성, 그리고 변화하는 시장 상황에 신속하게 대응할 필요성을 ④ 늘릴(→ 무시할) 수도 있다. [8]예를 들어, 더 매력적인 이미지를 투영하기 위해 구단 색깔을 바꾸자는 제안은 그것이 전통과의 관계를 끊기 때문에 ⑤ 무산될 수도 있다.

어휘

trigger 일으키다, 유발하다; (총을) 쏘다
bring forth ~을 야기하다
loyalty 충성(심), 충실
insurance 보험(료)
border on ~에 아주 가깝다, 거의 ~와 같다
addiction 중독
bind A to B A를 B에 결속시키다, A를 B에 묶다
on-field (스포츠) 구장 위[내]의
intensity 강렬함, 격렬함; 강도
attachment 애착; 부착, 부가(물)
nostalgia 향수(鄕愁)
club (프로 스포츠) 구단[클럽]
efficiency 효율(성)
productivity 생산성
proposal 제안, 제의
project 투영[투사]하다
defeat 무산시키다; 패배시키다

정답 가이드

스포츠는 팬에게 강렬한 정서적 반응을 일으켜 충성심을 유지하게 하는데, 이는 조직이 과거에 강한 애착을 가지게 해 변화에 신속히 대응하지 못하게 하는 부정적인 영향을 미칠 수 있다는 내용의 글이다. 스포츠와 관련된 조직은 전통을 고수하려 할 것이므로 효율성, 생산성, 그리고 변화하는 시장 상황에 신속하게 대응할 필요성을 무시할 것이다. 따라서 ④ 'increase(늘리다)'를 'ignore(무시하다)' 등으로 고쳐야 한다.

오답 클리닉

① identifying (3%) 동일시하는
스포츠와 달리 정서적 반응을 유발하지 않는 제품의 두 가지 예로 은행 고객이 기념품을 사서 충성심을 보여주려고 하지 않듯이 고객이 자동차 보험 회사와 '동일시해'서 회사 로고로 문신을 새기지는 않는다고 보는 것이 문맥상 자연스럽다.

② passionate (4%) 열정적인
일부 스포츠팬들이 매우 '열정적'이어서 그들의 스포츠에 대한 관심이 집착에 아주 가깝다는 연결은 자연스럽다.

③ failure (21%) 실패
일부 스포츠팬이 갖는 집착에 가까운 관심은 그들에게 정서적 접착제를 제공하여 어떤 부정적인 상황에서도 충성심을 유지하게 할 것이므로 '실패'는 문맥상 적절하다.

⑤ defeated (9%) 무산된
스포츠의 정서적 강렬함은 조직이 구단의 전통을 통해 과거에 대한 강한 애착을 갖는 것을 의미한다고 했다. 따라서 전통과의 관계를 끊어버리는 제안은 '무산될' 것이다.

02 ✦ 빈칸 추론 〈18학년도 9월 모평 32번 | 정답률 55%〉 ④

구문분석 & 직독직해

인지 개인의 주관에 따른 경험의 차이

[1] Let me spend a moment on the idea (of adjusting to another person's mental orientation).
생각에 관해 잠시 시간을 들여 보겠다 (다른 사람의 정신적 성향에 맞춘다는)

[2] What I mean / is this.
S(명사절) V C
내 말이 의미하는 것은 / 다음과 같다
↳ **도입:** '타인의 정신적 성향에 맞춘다는 것'에 대해 알아봄.

주제문
[3] At any moment, / a person has *a **particular take*** (**on what is happening**).
S V O on의 O(명사절)
어떤 순간에도 / 사람은 각자의 의견을 가지고 있다 (일어나고 있는 것에 대한)

★<A rather than B>: B라기보다는 A
[4] The person notices this rather than that, // and she has feelings and makes judgements / about one / rather than another aspect (of events).
S_1 V_1 O_1 S_2 V_{2-1} O_{2-1} V_{2-2} O_{2-2}
사람은 저것보다는 이것에 주목한다 // 그리고 감정을 가지고 판단을 한다 / 한 측면에 대해 / 또 다른 측면보다는 (사건의)
↳ 사람은 사건의 각기 다른 측면에 주목함.

[5] If she is hungry, / for example, // she may notice / that a shop is selling groceries; // her friend may notice only that it sells newspapers. ⊶ 감정에 따라 같은 것에 대해 주목하는 측면이 다름.
부사절 접속사(조건) S_1 V_1 O_1(명사절) S_2 V_2 O_2(명사절)
그 사람이 배고프다면 / 예를 들어 // 그 사람은 알아챌 수도 있다 / 한 상점이 식료품을 팔고 있다는 것을 //
그녀의 친구는 그 상점이 신문을 파는 것만을 알아챌 수도 있다
↳ **예 1:** 배고픈 사람과 그렇지 않은 사람은 각각 상점의 다른 상품에 주목함.

[6] If she is short of money, // she may resent / that the fruit is overpriced; // meanwhile her friend may feel tempted / by some juicy peaches. ⊶ 처한 상황에 따라 느끼는 감정이 다름.
부사절 접속사(조건) S_1 V_1 O(명사절) S_2 V_2 C(p.p.)
돈이 부족하다면 // 그 사람은 분개할지도 모른다 / 과일이 너무 비싸다고 //
한편 그녀의 친구는 마음이 끌릴지도 모른다 / 몇 개의 즙이 많은 복숭아에
↳ **예 2:** 돈이 부족한 사람과 그렇지 않은 사람은 과일을 보고 다른 감정을 느낌.

[7] In one sense / the two friends are experiencing the same shop and its contents, // but they are having quite different experiences (of that shop). ⊶ 같은 것을 서로 다르게 느끼고 겪음.
S_1 V_1 O_1 S_2 V_2 O_2
어떤 의미에서는 / 그 두 친구는 같은 상점과 그것의 내용물을 경험하고 있는 것이다 //
그러나 그들은 아주 다른 경험을 하고 있다 (그 상점에 대한)
↳ **결론:** 같은 경험이라도 개인이 각자 느끼고 겪는 것은 아주 다름.

해석

[1]다른 사람의 정신적 성향에 맞춘다는 생각에 관해 잠시 시간을 들여 보겠다. [2]내 말이 의미하는 것은 다음과 같다. [3]어떤 순간에도, 사람은 일어나고 있는 것에 대한 각자의 의견을 가지고 있다. [4]사람은 저것보다는 이것에 주목하며, 사건의 또 다른 측면보다는 한 측면에 대해 감정을 가지고 판단을 한다. [5]예를 들어, 그 사람이 배고프다면 한 상점이 식료품을 팔고 있다는 것을 알아챌 수도 있으며, 그녀의 친구는 그 상점이 신문을 파는 것만을 알아챌 수도 있다. [6]돈이 부족하다면, 그 사람은 과일이 너무 비싸다고 분개할지도 모르며, 한편 그녀의 친구는 몇 개의 즙이 많은 복숭아에 마음이 끌릴지도 모른다. [7]어떤 의미에서는 그 두 친구는 같은 상점과 그 내용물을 경험하고 있는 것이지만, 그들은 그 상점에 대한 아주 다른 경험을 하고 있다. [8]좀 더 극단적인 사례는 예를 들어 그 상점을 영화관으로 오인함에 있어서, 한 사람이 독특하고 개인적인 방식으로 사물을 이해할 때 발생한다.

어휘

adjust to A A에 맞추다[조절하다]
orientation 성향; 방향, 지향
particular 각자의; 개별적인; 특별한, 특수한
take 의견, 해석
notice 주목하다; 알아채다, 인지하다
judg(e)ment 판단(력); 판결, 심판
aspect 측면; 양상
grocery 식료품(점)
be short of ~가 부족하다
resent 분개하다, 화내다
overpriced 너무 비싼
meanwhile 한편; 그 동안에
tempt 마음을 끌다, 유혹하다
juicy 즙이 많은
in one sense 어떤 의미에서는
extreme 극단적인; 극심한

[8]A more extreme case arises // when one person comprehends things / in a peculiar and individual way, / for instance, / in mistaking the shop for a cinema.
S V 부사절 접속사(시간) S' V' O'
<in v-ing>: v함에 있어서
좀 더 극단적인 사례는 발생한다 // 한 사람이 사물을 이해할 때 / 독특하고 개인적인 방식으로 / 예를 들어 / 그 상점을 영화관으로 오인함에 있어서
↳ **부연 설명:** 개인이 특이한 방식으로 사물을 이해하는 경우에 아예 다른 것으로 이해할 수도 있음.

comprehend 이해하다
peculiar 독특한, 고유의; 특이한
[선택지] point of view 관점, 견해
preference 선호(도)
tendency 경향; 성향
stick to A A를 고수하다[지키다]

정답 가이드

사람이 '어떠한 것을' 가지고 있다는 것인지를 추론해야 한다. 빈칸 문장 바로 뒤의 문장에서 사람은 '다른 것이 아닌 어느 한 측면에 주목한다'고 했고, 이어지는 예에서도 사람들이 같은 것에 대해 서로 다르게 인식한다는 설명이 이어지고 있다. 따라서 빈칸에 들어갈 말로 가장 적절한 것은 ④ 'particular take on what is happening(일어나고 있는 것에 대한 각자의 의견)'이다.

오답 클리닉

① desire to make better choices (12%)
더 나은 선택을 하려는 욕구
더 나은 선택을 하려 한다는 내용은 없음.

② point of view similar to that of others (11%)
다른 사람들의 관점과 유사한 관점
같은 것이라도 각자가 가진 다른 관점에 따라 겪는 경험이 다르다는 글의 내용과 반대됨.

③ personal preference on where to shop (17%)
쇼핑할 장소에 관한 개인적 선호
같은 곳에서 서로 다른 경험을 한다는 것의 예로 상점이 등장하기는 했지만 개인별 선호하는 쇼핑 장소에 관한 내용이 아님.

⑤ tendency to stick to traditions (3%)
전통을 고수하려는 경향
전통을 지키려는 것에 관한 언급은 없음.

03 + 문장 넣기 (19학년도 대수능 38번 | 정답률 63%) ③

구문분석 & 직독직해 기술 정보 전파에 효과적인 인쇄기

주제문
[1]The printing press boosted / the power (of ideas to copy themselves).
S V O to-v의 의미상 주어
인쇄기는 신장시켰다 / 능력을 (생각이 스스로를 복제하는)
↳ 인쇄기는 생각이 스스로를 복제하는 능력을 신장시킴.

[2]Prior to low-cost printing, / ideas could and did spread / by word of mouth.
S V (→ 동사 강조)
저가 인쇄술 전에 / 생각은 퍼질 수 있었고 실제로 퍼졌다 / 구전으로
↳ **저가 인쇄술 이전 1:** 생각이 구전으로 전달되었음.

[3]While this was tremendously powerful, // it limited the complexity (of *the ideas* [that could be propagated]) / to *those* [that a single person could remember].
부사절 접속사(~하지만) (= 앞 문장) S V O 주격 관계대명사 (= ideas) 목적격 관계대명사
이것은 엄청나게 강력했지만 // 복잡성을 제한했다 (생각의 [전파될 수 있는]) / (~한) 것들(생각)로 [단 한 사람이 기억할 수 있는]

(①) [4]It also added / a certain amount of guaranteed error.
그것은 또한 더했다 / 일정량의 확실한 오류를

(②) [5]The spread (of ideas) (by word of mouth) / was equivalent / to a game of telephone (on a global scale).
S V C
전파는 (생각의) (구전에 의한) / 같았다 / 말 전달하기 놀이와 (전 세계적인 규모의)
↳ **부연 설명:** 구전으로 전해진 생각은 복잡성이 제한되고 오류가 있었으며, 말 전하기 놀이와 같았음.

🔑 손으로 쓴 두루마리와 책에는 강점이 있음.
(③ [6]The advent (of literacy) / and the creation (of handwritten scrolls and, eventually, handwritten books) / strengthened the ability (of large and complex ideas) to spread with high fidelity.)
S V O to-v의 의미상 주어
출현은 (글을 읽고 쓸 줄 아는 능력의) / 그리고 창안은 (손으로 쓴 두루마리와 마침내 손으로 쓴 책의) / 능력을 강화했다 (크고 복잡한 생각의) 높은 정확도로 퍼지는
↳ **저가 인쇄술 이전 2:** 손으로 쓴 두루마리와 책이 복잡한 생각을 정확하게 퍼지게 함.

해석

[1]인쇄기는 생각이 스스로를 복제하는 능력을 신장시켰다. [2]저가 인쇄술 전에, 생각은 구전으로 퍼질 수 있었고 실제로 퍼졌다. [3]이것은 엄청나게 강력했지만, 전파될 수 있는 생각의 복잡성을 단 한 사람이 기억할 수 있는 것들(생각)로 제한했다. (①) [4]그것은 또한 일정량의 확실한 오류를 더했다. (②) [5]구전에 의한 생각의 전파는 전 세계적인 규모의 말 전달하기 놀이와 같았다. (③ [6]글을 읽고 쓸 줄 아는 능력의 출현과 손으로 쓴 두루마리와 마침내 손으로 쓴 책의 창안은 높은 정확도로 퍼지는 크고 복잡한 생각의 능력을 강화했다.) [7]그러나 손으로 두루마리나 책을 복사하는 데 걸리는 엄청난 양의 시간은 이 방식으로 정보가 퍼질 수 있는 속도를 제한했다. (④) [8]잘 훈련된 수도승은 하루에 약 네 쪽의 문서를 필사할 수 있었다. (⑤) [9]인쇄기는 정보를 수천 배 더 빠르게 복사할 수 있었는데, 이는 지식이 이전 어느 때보다 최고의 정확도로 훨씬 더 빠르게 퍼질 수 있게 했다.

어휘

printing press 인쇄기
boost 신장시키다; 증가
prior to A A 이전에
spread 퍼지다; 펼치다; 전파, 확산
word of mouth 구전(口傳)
tremendously 엄청나게, 굉장히
guaranteed 확실한, 보장된
equivalent 같은, 동등한

⊶ 손으로 두루마리와 책을 복사하는 것의 한계가 역접 연결어 But으로 이어지므로 앞에는 그것의 강점이 제시되어야 함.

[7] But / *the incredible amount of time* (required to copy a scroll or book / by hand) / limited *the speed* [with which information could spread / this way].

S 과거분사구 V O / 전치사+관계대명사 S′ V′

그러나 / 엄청난 양의 시간은 (두루마리나 책을 복사하는 데 걸리는 / 손으로) / 속도를 제한했다 [정보가 퍼질 수 있는 / 이 방식으로]

(④) [8] A well-trained monk could transcribe / around four pages of text / per day.

S V O

잘 훈련된 수도승은 필사할 수 있었다 / 약 네 쪽의 문서를 / 하루에

↳ **단점:** 손으로 두루마리나 책을 복사하는 데에는 시간이 오래 걸림.

(⑤) [9] A printing press could copy information / thousands of times faster, /

S V O

인쇄기는 정보를 복사할 수 있었다 / 수천 배 더 빠르게 /

★<allow+O+to-v>: O가 v하는 것을 허락하다

allowing knowledge to spread far more quickly, / with full fidelity, / than ever before.

분사구문(= and it allowed ~) 비교급 강조 부사

이는 지식이 훨씬 더 빠르게 퍼질 수 있게 했다 / 최고의 정확도로 / 이전 어느 때보다

↳ **주제문 재진술:** 인쇄기는 지식이 정확하고 빠르게 퍼질 수 있게 함.

advent 출현, 도래
literacy 글을 읽고 쓸 줄 아는 능력
scroll 두루마리
strengthen 강화하다
require (시간 등이) 걸리다; 요구하다
monk 수도승
transcribe 필사하다; 기록하다

⊕ 말 전달하기 놀이(a game of telephone): 차례대로 여러 사람이 귓속말로 말을 전달한 다음, 처음 사람이 전한 내용과 마지막 사람이 들은 내용이 일치하는지를 비교하는 놀이.

정답 가이드

주어진 문장은 손으로 쓴 두루마리와 책이 크고 복잡한 생각을 정확하게 퍼져 나가게 했다는 내용이다. ③의 앞까지는 구전에 의한 생각의 전파와 그 한계에 관한 내용이 나오고, ③의 뒤에는 역접 연결어 But과 함께 손으로 두루마리나 책을 복사하는 것의 한계점이 제시된 것으로 보아 그와 상반되는 강점이 앞에 와야 함을 알 수 있다. 따라서 주어진 문장이 들어가기에 가장 적절한 곳은 ③이다.

오답 클리닉

① (3%) / ② (7%) 구전을 통한 생각의 전파에 관해 부연 설명하는 내용이다.
④ (17%) 손으로 책을 복사하는 데 많은 시간이 소요된다는 내용 뒤에, 잘 훈련된 수도승이 하루 필사할 수 있는 양을 예로 들어 보충 설명하는 것은 자연스럽다.
⑤ (9%) 앞서 언급된 방식들과 대조적으로 인쇄기는 지식이 더 정확하고 빠르게 퍼지게 한다고 재진술하는 내용이다.

01 ✦ 요약문 20학년도 9월 모평 40번 | 정답률 50% ②

구문분석 & 직독직해

건축 관습에서 벗어난 건축 접근법의 필요

[1] Over the past few decades, / architecture (as an idea and practice) / has increasingly limited its definition (of itself).
(S / 전치사(~로서) / V / O)

지난 수십 년 동안 / 건축은 (아이디어와 실행으로서의) / 점점 정의를 제한시켜 왔다 (그것 자신에 대한)

↳ **도입:** 건축은 스스로에 대한 정의를 제한해 옴.

주제문

[2] In the foreseeable future, / the instrumentality (of architecture) / in effecting actual change — / that is, / *change* [that challenges the dominance (of commercial institutions, their aims, and values)] — / will diminish.
(S / = / 주격 관계대명사 / V)

가까운 미래에 / 도움은 (건축의) / 실질적 변화에 영향을 미치는 데 있어서 / 즉 / 변화 [지배에 도전하는 (상업 기관과 그것들의 목표와 가치관의)] / 줄어들 것이다

↳ 건축은 실질적인 변화를 가져오는 데 별로 도움이 되지 않음.

🔑 (A) 오늘날이 혁신의 시대로 보이지만, 실제는 기존의 것을 답습함.

[3] While the present day seems / to be a time (of unparalleled innovation and freedom of choice), // the reality is // that architectural styles and forms are often the attractive packaging and repackaging (of the same proven, marketable concepts).
(부사절 접속사(~하지만) S′ / V′ / C′ / ↱ is의 C(명사절) / S / V / 명사절 접속사 / S′ / V′ / C′)

현대는 (~인 것처럼) 보이지만 / 시대인 것처럼 (비할 데 없는 혁신과 자유 선택의) //

현실은 ~이다 // 건축 방식과 형태는 매력적으로 포장하고 재포장하는 일이 흔하다는 것 (검증된, 시장성 있는 똑같은 컨셉을)

↳ **부연 설명:** 건축은 검증되고 시장성 있는 개념을 다르게 보이도록 포장할 뿐임.

[4] *The speed* [with which "radical" designs (by celebrity architects) / achieve acceptance and popularity] / demonstrates // that formal innovation has itself become an important commodity.
(S / 전치사+관계대명사 / ↱ demonstrates의 O(명사절) / V / 명사절 접속사 / S′ / V′)

속도는 ['급진적' 설계가 (유명 건축가들의) / 수용되고 인기를 얻는] / 증명한다 // 형태상의 혁신 그 자체가 중요한 상품이 되었다는 것을

*itself는 주어를 강조하는 재귀대명사로 생략 가능함.

🔑 (A) 기존 관습이 여전히 지배적이고 팔림.

[5] However, / beneath the cloak of radicalism, / the conventions (of existing building typologies and programs), / with all their comforting familiarity, / still rule — / and sell.
(S / = / V_1 / V_2)

그러나 / 급진주의라는 망토 이면에는 / 관습이 (기존의 건축 유형학과 건축 계획에 대한) / 편안함을 주는 익숙함 때문에 / 여전히 지배한다 / 그리고 팔린다

↳ **예:** '급진적인' 설계에서 형식적 혁신이 중요한 상품이 되었는데, 그 이면에는 편안하고 익숙한 건축 관습이 여전히 지배적임.

🔑 (B) 사고와 행동을 바꿀 건축의 잠재력을 풀어 줄 수 있는 접근법이 필요함.

[6] What is needed desperately today / are *approaches to architecture* [that can free *its potential* / (to transform our ways of thinking and acting)].
(S(명사절) / V / C / 주격 관계대명사)

*what 명사절은 단수 취급하지만 보어에 따라 복수 동사도 사용 가능함.

오늘날 절실하게 필요한 것은 / 건축 접근법들이다 [그것(건축)의 잠재력을 풀어 줄 수 있는 (우리의 사고와 행동에 변화를 주도록)]

↳ **결론:** 사고와 행동 방식을 바꾸는 건축의 잠재력을 풀어 줄 접근법이 필요함.

↓

[7] (Being) Seemingly innovative, / architecture has actually become **(A) trapped** / in its own convention and commercialized environment, // so efforts should be made / to **(B) activate** *its power* (to change us).
(being 생략 분사구문(= Though it is seemingly ~) / S_1 / V_1 / C / S_2 / V_2 / 목적(~하기 위해))

겉보기에는 혁신적이지만 / 건축은 사실 (A) 갇히게 되었다 / 그것 자체의 관습과 상업화된 환경에 //

그래서 노력이 이루어져야 한다 / 그것(건축)의 힘을 (B) 작동시키기 위해 (우리를 변화시킬 수 있는)

해석

[1]지난 수십 년 동안, 아이디어와 실행으로서의 건축은 그것 자신에 대한 정의를 점점 제한시켜왔다. [2]가까운 미래에 실질적 변화, 즉 상업 기관과 그것들의 목표와 가치관의 지배에 도전하는 변화에 영향을 미치는 데 있어서 건축의 도움은 줄어들 것이다. [3]현대는 비할 데 없는 혁신과 자유 선택의 시대인 것처럼 보이지만, 현실적으로 건축 양식과 형태는 검증된, 시장성 있는 똑같은 컨셉을 매력적으로 포장하고 재포장하는 일이 흔하다. [4]유명 건축가들의 '급진적' 설계가 수용되고 인기를 얻는 속도는 형태상의 혁신 그 자체가 중요한 상품이 되었다는 것을 증명한다. [5]그러나, 급진주의라는 망토 이면에는 기존의 건축 유형학과 (건축) 계획에 대한 관습이 편안함을 주는 익숙함 때문에 여전히 지배하고 팔린다.(▶ 급진적으로 보이는 많은 혁신적 건축 설계는 구매자들에게 익숙하고 어필하는 기존 건축 양식과 기능을 여전히 고수한다는 의미) [6]오늘날 절실하게 필요한 것은 우리의 사고와 행동을 바꾸는 건축의 잠재력을 풀어 줄 수 있는 건축 접근법들이다.

↓

[7]겉보기에는 혁신적이지만, 건축은 사실 그것 자체의 관습과 상업화된 환경에 (A) 갇히게 되었고, 그래서 우리를 변화시킬 수 있는 그것의 힘을 (B) 작동시키기 위해 노력이 이루어져야 한다.

어휘

architecture 건축(술)
in the foreseeable future 가까운 미래에
instrumentality 도움, 조력; 수단, 방편
effect (결과를) 가져오다; 결과, 효과
dominance 지배; 우세, 우위
commercial 상업의, 상업적인; 광고
cf. commercialize 상업화하다
diminish 줄어들다, 약해지다
unparalleled 비할[견줄] 데 없는
innovation 혁신
proven 검증을 거친, 입증[증명]된
marketable 시장성이 있는
radical 급진적인; 근본적인
cf. radicalism 급진주의
acceptance 수용, 받아들임; 승인
commodity 상품, 물품
convention 관습, 관례; 회의
transform (완전히) 바꾸다; 변형시키다
[요약문] seemingly 겉보기에는

정답 가이드

요약문을 통해 겉보기에는 혁신적인 건축의 실태와 변화를 위한 노력의 필요에 관한 글임을 알 수 있다. 오늘날이 혁신과 선택의 자유 시대인 것처럼 보이지만, 실제 건축은 이미 검증되고 시장성 있는 개념, 즉 기존의 관습에 '갇혀' 있기 때문에 우리는 우리의 사고를 바꾸는 건축의 잠재력을 '풀어 줄' 수 있는 접근법이 필요하다고 했다. 따라서 빈칸 (A)와 (B)에 각각 들어갈 말로 가장 적절한 것은 ② 'trapped(갇힌) - activate(작동시키다)'이다.

오답 클리닉

(A) (B)

① fixed - share (17%) 고정된 - 공유하다
(A)는 맞지만, (B)는 틀림.

③ standardized - control (10%) 표준화된 - 통제하다
(A)는 맞지만, (B)는 틀림.

④ localized - share (9%) 국지적인 - 공유하다
(A)는 맞지만, (B)는 틀림.

⑤ underestimated - activate (16%) 과소평가된 - 작동시키다
(A)는 틀리며, (B)는 맞음.

The 주의 건축이 겉보기에는 혁신적이나 사실 그렇지 않다는 내용에서 오히려 과대평가되었다고 볼 수 있다.

02~03 + 복합 유형 (21학년도 대수능 41~42번 | 정답률 02 66%, 03 74%)

02 ③ 03 ④

구문분석 & 직독직해

생물 동물 행동 복잡성의 요인

03-(a) 다른 종에 내적 복잡성이 있다는 생각은 잘못된 것이므로 복잡한 행동이 내적 복잡성의 '산물'이 아닐 것임.

[1]Our irresistible tendency (to see things in human terms) — // that we are often mistaken / in attributing complex human motives and processing abilities / to other species — //
(S, = , = , 동격 접속사)
*<attribute A to B>: A가 B에게 있다고 생각하다

우리의 억누를 수 없는 경향은 (인간의 견지에서 사물을 보는) // 우리가 흔히 잘못 생각하는 것 / 복잡한 인간의 동기와 처리 능력이 있다고 / 다른 종들에게 //

does not mean // that an animal's behavior is not, in fact, complex.
(V, O(명사절))

의미하지 않는다 // 동물의 행동이 사실 복잡하지 않다는 것을

주제문
(= our irresistible tendency ~ species)
[2]Rather, / it means // that the complexity (of the animal's behavior) / is not purely a **(a) product** (of its internal complexity).
(S V, O(명사절))

오히려 / 그것은 의미한다 // 복잡성이 (동물 행동의) / 순전히 산물이 아니라는 것을 (그것의 내적 복잡성의)
↳ 인간의 견지에서 동물의 행동을 복잡하게 보는 것은 동물이 내적으로 복잡하기 때문이 아님.

[3]Herbert Simon's "parable of the ant" / makes this point very clearly.
(S, V, O)

Herbert Simon의 '개미 우화'는 / 이 점을 매우 분명하게 한다
↳ 예: '개미 우화'를 예로 들어 설명함.

[4]Imagine an ant walking along a beach, / and (b) **visualize** tracking the trajectory of the ant // as it moves.
(V_1(명령문), O_1, C_1, V_2, O_2(동명사구), 부사절 접속사(~함에 따라))
03-(b) 개미가 해변을 따라 걷는 것을 상상하고 그 경로를 마음속에 '그려 봄'.

개미 한 마리가 해변을 따라 걷는 것을 상상해 보라 / 그리고 그 개미의 이동 경로를 추적하는 것을 마음속에 그려 보라 // 그것이 이동함에 따라

03-(e) 개미의 복잡한 이동 경로는 '관찰된' 행동임.

[5]The trajectory would show a lot of twists and turns, / and would be very irregular and complicated.
(S, V_1, O, V_2, C)

그 이동 경로는 많은 굴곡과 방향 전환을 보일 것이다 / 그리고 매우 불규칙하고 복잡할 것이다
↳ 해변을 따라 걷는 개미의 이동 경로는 불규칙하고 복잡함.

해석

[1]인간의 견지에서 사물을 보는 우리의 억누를 수 없는 경향, 즉 다른 종들에게 복잡한 인간의 동기와 처리 능력이 있다고 우리가 흔히 잘못 생각하는 것은 동물의 행동이 사실 복잡하지 않다는 것을 의미하지 않는다. [2]오히려 그것은 동물 행동의 복잡성이 순전히 그것의 내적 복잡성의 (a) 산물이 아니라는 것을 의미한다. [3]Herbert Simon의 '개미 우화'는 이 점을 매우 분명하게 한다. [4]개미 한 마리가 해변을 따라 걷는 것을 상상하며 그 개미가 이동함에 따라 그것의 이동 경로를 추적하는 것을 (b) 마음속에 그려 보라. [5]그 이동 경로는 많은 굴곡과 방향 전환을 보일 것이며, 매우 불규칙하고 복잡할 것이다. [6]그렇다면 그 개미가 (복잡한 이동 경로와) 동등하게 복잡한 (c) 내적 항행 능력을 가졌다고 가정하고, 그런 복잡한 항행 경로를 만들어 낼 수 있는 규칙과 기제를 추론하기 위해 그 이동 경로를 분석함으로써 이것(내적 항행 능력)이 무엇일 수 있는지를 알아낼 수 있을 것이다. [7]하지만 그 이동 경로의 복잡성은 '실제로 해변 지면의 복잡성이지 그 개미 안의 복잡성이 아니다'. [8]사실 그 개미는 일련의 매우 (d) 복잡한(→ 단순한) 규칙들을 사용하고 있을지도 모르는데, 그 복잡한 이동 경로를 실제로 만들어 내는 것은 그 개미 자체가 아니라 바로 이 규칙들과 환경의 상호 작용인 것이다. [9]개괄해서 말하자면, 개미 우화는 (e) 관찰된 행동의 복잡성과 그것을 만들어 내는 기제의 복잡성 사이에 필연적인 상관관계가 없음을 보여 준다.

[6]One could then suppose // that the ant had equally complicated **(c) internal** navigational abilities, //
S V₁ O₁(명사절)
그렇다면 가정할 수 있다 // 그 개미가 동등하게 복잡한 내적 항행 능력을 가졌다고 //
(= internal navigational abilities)
and work out // what these were likely to be / by analyzing the trajectory /
V₂ O₂(명사절) <by v-ing>: v함으로써
to infer *the rules and mechanisms* [that could produce / such a complex navigational path].
목적(~하기 위해) 주격 관계대명사
그리고 알아낼 수 있을 것이다 // 이것(내적 항행 능력)이 무엇일 수 있는지를 / 그 이동 경로를 분석함으로써 /
규칙과 기제를 추론하기 위해 [만들어 낼 수 있는 / 그런 복잡한 항행 경로를]

03-(c) 경로의 복잡성이 개미의 '내적' 복잡성이라고 가정한 앞 내용이 부정됨.

[7]The complexity (of the trajectory), / however, / "is really a complexity (in the surface of the beach), / not a complexity (in the ant)."
S V C₁ C₂

03-(d) 개미가 내적으로 복잡해서 이동 경로가 복잡한 것이 아니므로, 실제 개미의 내적 규칙은 복잡하지 않고 '간단할' 것임.

복잡성은 (그 이동 경로의) / 하지만 / '실제로 복잡성이다 (해변 지면의) /
복잡성이 아니라 (그 개미 안의)'
↳ 개미의 이동 경로의 복잡성은 복잡한 내적 항행 능력이 아니라 해변 지면(환경)의 복잡성 때문임.

[8]In reality, / the ant may be using / a set of very **(d) complex(→ simple)** rules: //
S V O
사실 / 그 개미는 사용하고 있을지도 모른다 / 일련의 매우 복잡한(→ 단순한) 규칙들을 //
it is the interaction (of these rules with the environment) // that actually produces the complex trajectory, / not the ant alone.
<it is ~ that ...> 강조구문: …인 것은 바로 ~이다
바로 상호 작용인 것이다 (이 규칙들과 환경의) // 그 복잡한 이동 경로를 실제로 만들어 내는 것은 / 그 개미 자체가 아니라

*<put more generally>: ((분사구문 관용 표현)) 개괄해서[더 일반적으로] 말하자면
[9]Put more generally, / the parable of the ant illustrates // that there is no necessary correlation (between the complexity (of an **(e) observed** behavior) / and the complexity (of *the mechanism* [that produces it])).
S V O(명사절)
주격 관계대명사 (= an observed behavior)
개괄해서 말하자면 / 개미 우화는 보여 준다 // 필연적인 상관관계가 없음을
(복잡성과 (관찰된 행동의) / 복잡성 사이에 (기제의 [그것을 만들어 내는]))
↳ **결론:** 개미의 복잡한 이동 경로는 개미의 내적 복잡성이 아니라 환경과 개미의 단순한 행동 규칙의 상호 작용의 산물임.
→ 개미 행동의 복잡성과 개미의 내적 복잡성은 관계가 없음.

어휘

irresistible 억누를[저항할] 수 없는
tendency 경향, 성향
in terms ~ 견지[측면]에서
motive 동기, 이유
complexity 복잡성
track 추적하다; 길; 자국
twist 굴곡, 꼬임
irregular 불규칙적인; 가지런하지 못한
navigational 항행의, 항해의
work out ~을 알아내다, 이해하다
analyze 분석하다
infer 추론하다
mechanism (특정한 기능을 수행하는 생물의) 기제, 구조
interaction 상호 작용
illustrate 보여 주다; 설명하다; 삽화를 넣다
correlation 상관관계, 연관성
[선택지] coexistence 공존

정답 가이드

02 동물 행동의 복잡성이 동물의 내적 복잡성의 산물이 아니라는 것을 '개미 우화'를 예로 들어 설명하는 글이다. 개미의 복잡한 이동 경로는 개미의 내적 복잡성이 아니라 개미가 사용하는 단순한 규칙과 환경의 상호 작용으로 만들어진다고 했다. 따라서 글의 제목으로 가장 적절한 것은 ③ 'What Makes the Complexity of Animal Behavior?(무엇이 동물 행동의 복잡성을 만드는가?)'이다.

03 문장 7에서 개미의 이동 경로의 복잡성은 해변 지면의 복잡성이지 개미의 내적 복잡성이 아니라고 했다. In reality로 시작하는 문장 8은 앞 내용과 반대되는 사실을 강조하므로 개미가 사용하는 내적 규칙은 실제로는 '복잡하지' 않고 '단순하다'는 내용이 되어야 한다. 따라서 ④ 'complex(복잡한)'를 'simple(단순한)' 등으로 바꾸어야 한다.

오답 클리닉

02 ① Open the Mysterious Door to Environmental Complexity! (17%)
환경의 복잡성(×)에 이르는 신비의 문을 열어라!
환경의 복잡성이 아닌 동물 행동의 복잡성에 관한 내용임.
② Peaceful Coexistence of Human Beings and Animals (5%)
인간과 동물의 평화로운 공존(×)
인간과 동물의 공존에 대한 내용은 언급되지 않음.
④ Animals' Dilemma: Finding Their Way in a Human World (6%)
동물의 딜레마(×) 즉 인간 세계에서 자신의 길을 찾아가는 것(×)
동물이 딜레마나 동물이 인간 세계에서 살아가는 방식에 대한 언급은 없음.
⑤ Environmental Influences on Human Behavior Complexity (7%)
인간 행동 복잡성(×)에 미치는 환경의 영향
인간이 아니라 동물 행동 복잡성에 관해 설명하고 있음.

03 ① product (2%) 산물
문장 1에서 다른 종에 내적 복잡성이 있다는 인간의 생각은 잘못된 것이라고 했으므로 동물의 복잡한 행동이 내적 복잡성으로 만들어지는 '산물'이 아니라는 내용이 되어야 한다.
② visualize (6%) 마음속에 그려보다, 상상하다
개미가 해변을 따라 걷는 것을 상상하며 그 이동 경로를 '마음속에 그려 보라'는 흐름은 적절하다. 문장 5의 많은 굴곡과 방향 전환이 보일 것이라는 내용과 연결도 자연스럽다.
③ internal (12%) 내적인
역접 연결어인 however가 포함된 문장 7에서 개미의 이동 경로의 복잡성은 개미의 '내적' 복잡성이 아니라고 부정하고 있으므로 문장 6에서 개미에게 복잡한 '내적' 항행 능력이 있을 것이라 가정한 것은 자연스럽다.
⑤ observed (6%) 관찰된
문장 5에서 개미의 이동 경로가 많은 굴곡과 방향 전환이 있어 복잡해 보일 것이라고 했으므로 동물의 복잡한 행동은 '관찰'로 알게 된 것이다.

01 + 빈칸 추론 (18학년도 9월 모평 31번 | 정답률 46%) ④

구문분석 & 직독직해

인지 창의성에 영향을 주는 생산성

주제문

(= creativity) ★<not A so much as B>: A라기보다는 B인

[1]One unspoken truth about creativity — // it isn't about wild talent so much // as it is about productivity.

창의성에 관한 무언의 사실 중 하나는 // 그것이 자연 그대로의(천부적인) 재능에 관한 것이라기보다는 // 생산성에 관한 것이라는 것이다

↳ 창의성은 생산성과 관련된 개념임.

[2]To find *a few ideas* [that work], / you need to try *a lot* [that don't (work)].

목적(~하기 위해) 주격 관계대명사 S V O(to-v구) 주격 관계대명사

몇몇 아이디어를 발견하기 위해서 [효과 있는] / 여러분은 많은 것들을 시도할 필요가 있다 [그렇지 않은]

↳ 상술: 효과 있는 아이디어를 발견하려면 효과 없는 많은 것들을 시도해 봐야 함.

(= creativity)

[3]It's a pure numbers game. ⊶ 숫자의 많고 적음이 승패를 결정함.

그것(창의성)은 순전한 숫자 놀음이다

↳ 비유: 창의성은 숫자 놀음임.

★<not necessarily>: ((부분 부정)) 반드시[꼭] ~한 것은 아닌

[4]Geniuses don't necessarily have a higher success rate / than other creators; //

S1 V1 O1

천재들이 반드시 더 높은 성공률을 갖는 것은 아니다 / 다른 창조자들보다 //

(= Geniuses)

they simply do more — // and they do a range of different things. ⊶ 천재들은 많이, 다양하게 시도함.

S2 V2 O2 S3 V3 O3

그들은 그저 더 많은 것을 한다 // 그리고 그들은 다양한 여러 가지의 것들을 한다

(= Geniuses)

[5]They have more successes and more failures.

S V O1 O2

그들은 더 많은 성공 '그리고' 더 많은 실패를 한다

↳ 예 1(천재): 천재들은 그저 더 많이, 다양한 것들을 해서 많은 성공과 실패를 겪음.

(= 앞 문장)

[6]That goes for teams and companies too.

S V

그것은 팀과 회사에도 해당된다

⊶ 나쁜 아이디어도 많이 만들어 내야 좋은 아이디어를 많이 만들어 낼 수 있음.

[7]It's impossible / to generate a lot of good ideas / without also generating a lot of bad ideas.

가주어 V C 진주어(to-v구) without의 O(동명사구)

(~은) 불가능하다 / 많은 좋은 아이디어를 만들어 내는 것은 / 많은 나쁜 아이디어를 만들어 내지도 않으면서

(is의 C(명사절))

[8]The thing about creativity is // that at the outset, / you can't tell // which ideas will succeed and which will fail. ★첫 번째 which는 의문형용사(어떤 ~)로, 두 번째 which는 의문대명사(어느 것)로 쓰임.

S V 명사절 접속사 S' V' O'1 O'2

창의성에 관해 중요한 것은 ~이다 // 처음에는 / 여러분이 알 수 없다는 것 // 어떤 아이디어가 성공하고 어느 것이 실패할 것인지를

[9]So *the only thing* [(which[that]) you can do] / is (to) try to fail faster //

S 목적격 관계대명사 생략 V C

so that you can move onto the next idea. ★주어를 수식하는 관계사절이 do로 끝나고 be동사가 이어지면 보어로 to를 생략한 원형부정사를 사용하는 경우가 많음.

부사절 접속사(~하도록)

그래서 유일한 것은 [여러분이 할 수 있는] / 더 빨리 실패하려고 하는 것이다 //

다음 아이디어로 넘어갈 수 있도록

↳ 예 2(팀과 회사): 여러 아이디어를 시도하고 실패를 겪어야 좋은 아이디어를 만들 수 있음.

해석

[1]창의성에 관한 무언의 사실 중 하나는 그것이 자연 그대로의(천부적인) 재능에 관한 것이라기보다는 생산성에 관한 것이라는 것이다. [2]효과 있는 몇몇 아이디어를 발견하기 위해서 여러분은 그렇지 않은 많은 것들을 시도할 필요가 있다. [3]그것은 순전한 숫자 놀음(▶ 숫자로 나타나는 수량적인 사항으로 어떤 일을 처리하는 것을 낮잡아 이르는 말. 여기서는 단순히 많은 수의 시도를 하면 창의적인 것이 나온다는 의미)이다. [4]천재들이 반드시 다른 창조자들보다 더 높은 성공률을 갖는 것은 아니고, 그들은 그저 더 많은 것을 하고, 다양한 여러 가지의 것들을 한다. [5]그들은 더 많은 성공 '그리고' 더 많은 실패를 한다. [6]그것은 팀과 회사에도 해당된다. [7]많은 나쁜 아이디어를 만들어 내지도 않으면서 많은 좋은 아이디어를 만들어 내는 것은 불가능하다. [8]창의성에 관해 중요한 것은, 처음에는 여러분이 어떤 아이디어가 성공하고 어떤 것이 실패할 것인지를 알 수 없다는 것이다. [9]그래서 여러분이 할 수 있는 유일한 것은 다음 아이디어로 넘어갈 수 있도록 더 빨리 실패하려고 하는 것이다.

어휘

unspoken 무언의; 입 밖에 내지 않은
wild 자연 그대로의, 야생의
productivity 생산성
work 효과가 있다; 작동되다; 일하다
pure 순전한; 순수한
rate -율, 비율; 속도
simply 그저, 단순히; 간단히
a range of 다양한
go for ~에 해당되다; ~을 좋아하다; ~에 찬성하다
generate 만들어 내다; 일으키다, 초래하다
at the outset 처음에
tell (정확히) 알다, 판단하다; 구별하다; 말하다

정답 가이드

빈칸 문장이 '창의성은 타고나는 재능이 아닌 '무엇'이다'라는 의미이므로 창의성이 '무엇'이라고 설명하는지를 파악해야 한다. 이어지는 설명에서 언급된 '효과 있는 몇몇 아이디어'는 곧 '창의성'을 달리 표현한 것이며, 이를 위해 효과 없는 '많은 것'을 시도할 필요가 있다고 했으므로 이를 다른 말로 표현하면 ④ 'productivity(생산성)'이다. 이어지는 구체적인 예에서도 더 많이 하는 것, 많은 아이디어를 만들어 내는 것이 중요하다고 설명하고 있는데 모두 productivity를 잘 뒷받침하는 것들이다.

오답 클리닉

① sensitivity (6%) 감성
창의성이 감성과 관련된다는 언급은 없음.
② superiority (11%) 우월성
얼마나 우월한지가 창의성을 결정짓는다는 내용이 아님.
③ imagination (8%) 상상력
핵심어인 creativity로 쉽게 연상되는 단어지만, 상상력에 대한 언급은 없음.
⑤ achievement (27%) 성취
유사한 의미의 success가 지문에 있긴 하지만, 천재들이 더 높은 성공률을 보이는 것은 아니라고 했으므로 창의성과 성취는 본문의 설명과 반대됨.

02 + 글의 순서 (19학년도 9월 모평 37번 | 정답률 57%) ⑤

구문분석 & 직독직해

정치 정치에 관한 무지와 불합리의 문제

[1]Ever since the first scientific opinion polls revealed // that most Americans are at best poorly informed / about politics, //
(Ever since: 부사절 접속사(~ 이후로), the first scientific opinion polls: S′, revealed: V′, that ~ informed: O′(명사절))
첫 번째 과학적 여론 조사가 밝힌 이후로 // 대부분의 미국인이 기껏해야 빈약하게 알고 있다는 것을 / 정치에 대해서 //

analysts have asked // whether citizens are equipped to play *the role* [(which[that]) democracy assigns them].
(analysts: S, have asked: V, whether ~: have asked의 O(명사절), whether: 명사절 접속사, citizens: S′, are equipped: V′, (which[that]): 목적격 관계대명사 생략, them = citizens)
★<assign+IO+DO(IO에게 DO를 부여하다)>의 구조에서 선행사 the role이 직접목적어임.
분석가들은 물었다 // 시민들이 역할을 할 능력이 있는지 [민주주의가 그들(시민들)에게 부여한]
↳ **도입:** 대부분의 미국인들은 정치에 대해서 잘 모름.

주제문 ⊶ 빈약하게 아는 것보다 잘못 아는 게 더 나쁘다는 내용이 이어짐.
(C) [2]However, / there is something worse / than an inadequately informed public, // and that's a misinformed public.
(is: V_1, something worse: S_1, that: S_2, 's: V_2, a misinformed public: C)
★-thing, -body, -one으로 끝나는 명사는 형용사가 뒤에서 수식함.
그러나 / 더 나쁜 것이 있다 / 불충분하게 알고 있는 대중보다 // 그리고 그것은 잘못 알고 있는 대중이다
↳ 정치를 모르는 것보다 잘못 아는 것이 더 나쁨.

[3]It's one thing // when citizens don't know something, and realize it, // which has always been a problem.
(It: 가주어, when ~ it: 진주어(명사절), when: 의문사, citizens: S′, don't know: V'_1, something: O'_1, realize: V'_2, it: O'_2, which: 관계대명사(앞 절 보충 설명))
★<A is one thing, B is another thing>: A와 B는 완전 별개이다
(~은) 하나의 경우이다 // 시민들이 어떤 것을 모르면서, 그것(모르는 것)을 인식하고 있는 경우는 // 그리고 그것은 늘 문제가 되어 왔다

[4]It's another thing // when citizens don't know something, but think // (that) they know it, // which is the new problem.
(It: 가주어, when ~ it: 진주어(명사절), when: 의문사, citizens: S′, don't know: V'_1, something: O'_1, think: V'_2, (that) they know it: O'_2(명사절), which: 관계대명사(앞 절 보충 설명))
(~은) 이와 별개이다 // 시민들이 어떤 것을 모르지만 생각하는 경우는 // 자신들이 알고 있다고 // 그리고 그것은 새로운 문제이다
↳ **부연 설명:** 정치를 모르는 것도 문제이지만, 모르면서 안다고 생각하는 것도 문제임.

(B) [5]It's the difference (between ignorance and irrationality).
(It: S, 's: V, the difference: C)
⊶ 정치에 대해 잘 모르는 것은 무지로, 잘못 아는 것을 불합리로 받음.
차이점이 있다 (무지와 불합리 사이에는)
↳ 이는 무지와 불합리 간의 차이임.

★여기서 whatever(어떤 것이 ~이라도)는 양보 부사절을 이끄는 접속사이면서 부사절의 목적어 역할도 하는 복합관계대명사임.
[6]Whatever else one might conclude / about self-government, //
(Whatever ~ conclude: 양보 부사절(= no matter what ~))
다른 어떤 것으로 결론을 내리더라도 / 자치 정부에 관해 //
it's at risk // when citizens don't know // what they're talking about.
(it: 가주어, when ~ about: 진주어(명사절), when: 의문사, citizens: S′, don't know: V′, what they're talking about: O′(명사절))
(~은) 위험하다 // 시민들이 알지 못하는 경우는 // 자신들이 무엇을 말하고 있는지
↳ **문제점:** 시민들이 잘 모르면서 정부에 대해 말하는 것은 위험함.

해석

[1]첫 번째 과학적 여론 조사가 대부분의 미국인이 정치에 대해서 기껏해야 빈약하게 알고 있다는 것을 밝힌 이후로, 분석가들은 시민들이 민주주의가 그들에게 부여한 역할을 할 능력이 있는지 물었다. (C) [2]그러나 불충분하게 알고 있는 대중보다 더 나쁜 것이 있는데, 그것은 잘못 알고 있는 대중이다. [3]시민들이 어떤 것을 모르면서, 그것(모르는 것)을 인식하고 있는 경우는 늘 문제가 되어 왔다. [4]이와 별개로, 시민들이 어떤 것을 모르지만 자신들이 알고 있다고 생각하는 경우는 새로운 문제이다. (B) [5]무지와 불합리 사이에는 차이점이 있다. [6]자치 정부에 관해 다른 어떤 것으로 결론을 내리더라도, 시민들이 자신들이 무엇을 말하고 있는지 알지 못하는 경우는 위험하다.(▶ 자치 정부에 대해 가지고 있는 의견과는 상관없이, 시민들이 제대로 알고 있지 못하면 민주주의가 부여한 역할(투표 등의 정치 참여 및 영향력 행사)을 제대로 수행할 수 없으므로 자치 정부가 위험해질 수 있다는 의미) [7]우리가 잘못 아는 것은 우리의 욕망에 맞는 방식으로 세상을 바라보는 우리의 경향을 포함하여, 부분적으로 심리적 요인들의 탓이다. (A) [8]하지만 그런 요인들은 늘 우리와 함께 있어 온 잘못된 정보만 설명할 수 있다. [9]최근에 잘못된 정보의 급격한 증가에는 다른 원인이 있는데, (그것은) 우리의 미디어이다. [10]"그것들(우리의 미디어)은 우리를 어리석게 만들고 있습니다."라고 한 논평자는 말한다. [11]사실이 허구에 굴복하면, 예견할 수 있는 결과는 정치적 불신과 대립이다.

어휘

reveal 밝히다, 드러내다
at best 기껏해야, 잘해야
poorly 빈약[불충분]하게; 형편없이
informed 알고 있는(↔ misinformed 잘못 알고 있는)
politics 정치(학)
analyst 분석가
be equipped to-v v할 능력이 있다
democracy 민주주의

[7]Our misinformation owes partly to psychological factors, / including our tendency (to see the world / in *ways* [that suit our desires]).
S V
전치사(~을 포함하여) = 주격 관계대명사
우리가 잘못 아는 것은 부분적으로 심리적 요인들의 탓이다 / 우리의 경향을 포함하여 (세상을 바라보는 / 방식으로 [우리의 욕망에 맞는])

(B)의 psychological factors를 가리킴.
(A) [8]Such factors, / however, / can explain only *the misinformation* [that has always been with us].
S V O 주격 관계대명사
그런 요인들은 / 하지만 / 잘못된 정보만 설명할 수 있다 [늘 우리와 함께 있어 온]
↳ **잘못 아는 것의 원인 1:** 편향된 심리적 요인

[9]The sharp rise (in misinformation) / in recent years / has a different source: / our media.
S(단수) V(단수) O =
급격한 증가에는 (잘못된 정보의) / 최근에 / 다른 원인이 있다 / 우리의 미디어
↳ **잘못 아는 것의 원인 2:** 미디어

(= Our media)
[10]"They are making us dumb," // says one observer.
S' V' O' C' V S
"그것들(우리의 미디어)은 우리를 어리석게 만들고 있습니다." // 한 논평자는 말한다

[11]When fact bends to fiction, // the predictable result is political distrust and polarization.
부사절 접속사(조건) S V C
사실이 허구에 굴복하면 // 예견할 수 있는 결과는 정치적 불신과 대립이다
↳ **부연 설명:** 미디어가 잘못된 정보를 퍼뜨려 정치적 불신과 대립을 초래함.

inadequately 불충분하게
ignorance 무지, 무식
irrationality 불합리
self-government 자치 정부
at risk 위험한
misinformation 잘못 아는 것; 잘못된 정보
owe to A A의 탓[책임]이다
tendency 성향; 경향
suit (목적·기호 등에) 맞다, 적합하다
sharp (변화가) 급격한; 날카로운
dumb 어리석은, 멍청한
observer 논평자; 관찰자, 관측자
bend 굴복[복종]하다; 구부러지다
fiction 허구; 소설
predictable 예견[예측]할 수 있는
distrust 불신(감)
polarization (의견의) 대립, 분열

정답 가이드

대부분의 미국인이 정치에 대해서 잘 모른다는 주어진 글 뒤에는 역접 연결어 however로 시작하여 잘 모르는 대중보다 잘못 아는 대중이 더 나쁘다고 대조하는 (C)가 이어져야 한다. (C)에서 언급한 모르는 것과 모르면서 알고 있다고 생각하는 경우를 각각 무지와 불합리로 받는 (B)가 그다음에 와야 한다. (B)의 마지막 문장에서 잘못 아는 것의 원인으로 psychological factors를 언급했고, 이를 Such factors로 받으며 또 다른 원인으로 미디어를 제시하는 (A)가 마지막에 오는 것이 적절하다.

오답 클리닉

① (A) - (C) - (B) (3%)
주어진 글에는 (A)의 Such factors가 지칭할 대상이 없으므로 주어진 글 뒤에 (A)가 바로 올 수 없다.
② (B) - (A) - (C) (12%) / ③ (B) - (C) - (A) (11%)
주어진 글에는 (B)의 무지(ignorance)에 해당하는 내용만 있고, 불합리(irrationality)에 해당하는 내용은 없으므로 (B)가 주어진 글 뒤에 올 수 없다.
④ (C) - (A) - (B) (16%)
(A)의 Such factors는 (B)의 psychological factors와 연결되므로 (B) 뒤에 와야 한다. 잘못 아는 것의 원인으로 (B)의 심리적 요인이 먼저 제시되고, (A)에서 미디어가 또 다른 원인으로 뒤에 제시되는 것이 흐름상 적절하다.

03 + 문장 넣기 〈19학년도 9월 모평 39번 | 정답률 37%〉 ⑤

구문분석 & 직독직해

심리 타인을 돌보고 가르치고자 하는 욕구

believes의 O(명사절)
[1]Erikson believes // that when we reach the adult years, // several physical, social, and psychological stimuli / trigger a sense (of *generativity*).
S V 명사절 접속사 부사절(시간) S' V' O'
Erikson은 믿는다 // 우리가 성년에 이를 때 // 몇 가지 신체적, 사회적, 그리고 심리적 자극이 / 인식을 유발한다고 ('생산성'에 대한)
↳ **성인기의 특징 1:** '생산성'에 대한 인식이 유발됨.

(= generativity)
[2]A central component (of this attitude) / is the desire (to care for others).
S V C =
한 가지 중심 구성 요소는 (이러한 태도(생산성)의) / 욕구이다 (다른 사람들을 돌보고자 하는)

(①) [3]For the majority of people, / parenthood is perhaps the most obvious and convenient opportunity (to fulfill this desire).
S V C =
대다수 사람들에게서 / 부모 되기는 아마 가장 분명하고 편리한 기회일 것이다 (이러한 욕구를 충족할)
↳ **부연 설명:** 생산성의 주요 요소는 타인을 돌보고자 하는 욕구로, 부모 되기가 해당됨.

해석

[1]Erikson은 우리가 성년에 이를 때, 몇 가지 신체적, 사회적, 그리고 심리적 자극이 '생산성'에 대한 인식을 유발한다고 믿는다. [2]이러한 태도(생산성)의 한 가지 중심 구성 요소는 다른 사람들을 돌보고자 하는 욕구이다. (①) [3]대다수 사람들에게서, 부모 되기는 아마 이러한 욕구를 충족할 가장 분명하고 편리한 기회일 것이다. (②) [4]Erikson은 성인기의 또 다른 독특한 특징이 가르치고자 하는 타고난 욕구의 출현이라고 믿는다. (③) [5]신체적으로 번식하는 것이 가능해지는 일이 헌신적인 관계, 성인 생활 패턴의 확립, 그리고 업무 책임 떠맡기에 참여하는 일들과 결합될 때 우리는 이 욕구(가르치고자 하는 타고난 욕구)를 인식하게 된다. (④) [6]Erikson에 따르면, 부모가 됨으로써, 우리는 우리의 지식, 보호, 그리고 지도에 의존하는 다른 사람들에게 필요해지

(②) [4]Erikson believes // that another distinguishing feature (of adulthood) / is the emergence (of an inborn desire (to teach)).

Erikson은 믿는다 // 또 다른 독특한 특징이 (성인기의) / 출현이라고 (타고난 욕구의 (가르치고자 하는))

↳ **성인기의 특징 2:** 누군가를 가르치고자 하는 타고난 욕구가 나타남.

(③) [5]We become aware of this desire // when the event (of being physically capable of reproducing) / is joined /

우리는 이 욕구(가르치고자 하는 타고난 욕구)를 인식하게 된다 // 일이 (~할) 때 (신체적으로 번식하는 것이 가능해지는) / 결합될 (때) /

with the events (of participating / in a committed relationship, the establishment of an adult pattern of living, and the assumption of job responsibilities).

일들과 (참여하는 / 헌신적인 관계, 성인 생활 패턴의 확립, 그리고 업무 책임 떠맡기에)

↳ **부연 설명(욕구의 인식 조건):** 신체적 번식 가능성과 사회적 책임이 결합될 때 우리는 가르치고자 하는 욕구를 인식하게 됨.

(④) [6]According to Erikson, / by becoming parents / we learn // that we have the need (to be needed / by *others* [who depend on our knowledge, protection, and guidance]).

자식에게 지식, 보호, 지도를 제공함으로써 필요한 존재가 되고자 하는 욕구가 있음.

Erikson에 따르면 / 부모가 됨으로써 / 우리는 알게 된다 // 우리가 욕구가 있음을 (필요해지고 싶은 / 다른 사람들에게 [우리의 지식, 보호, 그리고 지도에 의존하는])

자식에게 어떤 것을 가르치는지 구체적으로 설명함.

(⑤ [7]We become entrusted / to teach culturally appropriate behaviors, values, attitudes, skills, and information about the world.)

우리는 위임받게 된다 / 문화적으로 적절한 행동, 가치, 태도, 기술, 그리고 세상에 대한 정보를 가르치는 것을

↳ **예:** 부모가 됨으로써 타인에게 필요한 존재가 되고자 하는 욕구를 알게 되어 자식에게 세상에 대해 가르칠 책임을 지게 됨.

[8]By assuming the responsibilities (of being primary caregivers to children) / through their long years of physical and social growth, /

책임을 떠맡음으로써 (아이들에게 일차적인 보호자가 되는) / 신체적, 사회적으로 성장하는 긴 세월 동안 /

주어진 문장에서 설명한 부모의 가르침에 연결됨.

we concretely express // what Erikson believes / to be an inborn desire (to teach).

우리는 구체적으로 표현한다 // Erikson이 믿는 것을 / 타고난 욕구라고 (가르치고자 하는)

↳ **결론:** 아이들의 일차적인 보호자, 즉 부모가 됨으로써 가르치고자 하는 타고난 욕구를 표현함.

고 싶은 욕구가 있음을 알게 된다. (⑤ [7]우리는 문화적으로 적절한 행동, 가치, 태도, 기술, 그리고 세상에 대한 정보를 가르치는 것을 위임받게 된다.) [8]신체적, 사회적으로 성장하는 긴 세월 동안 아이들에게 일차적인 보호자가 되는 책임을 떠맡음으로써, 우리는 Erikson이 가르치고자 하는 타고난 욕구라고 믿는 것을 구체적으로 표현한다.

어휘

stimulus (*pl.* stimuli) 자극
trigger 유발하다, 촉발하다; 방아쇠
component (구성) 요소
care for ~을 돌보다; ~을 좋아하다
parenthood 부모임, 부모의 신분; 친자 관계
fulfill 충족시키다; 이행하다; 달성하다
distinguishing 독특한; 다른 것과 구별되는
feature 특징(으로 삼다); 특집(으로 다루다)
adulthood 성인(기)
emergence 출현; 발생
inborn 타고난, 선천적인
reproduce 번식하다; 복사[복제]하다
committed 헌신적인, 열성적인
establishment 확립, 확정; 설립
assumption 떠맡기; 추정
cf. assume (책임 등을) 떠맡다; 추정하다
guidance 지도[안내]
entrust 위임하다[맡기다]
primary 일차적인; 주요한; 초기의
caregiver 보호자
concretely 구체적으로

정답 가이드

주어진 문장은 우리가 여러 정보를 가르치는 것을 위임받게 된다는 것이다. 앞뒤 내용으로 예측되는 것이 없으므로 글을 처음부터 읽어야 한다. 우리가 성년에 이를 때 생산성에 대한 인식이 생기는데, 이는 '다른 사람들을 돌보고자 하는 욕구'이며 성인기에는 '가르치고자 하는 욕구' 또한 발현된다고 했다. 신체적 번식이 가능해지면 그 욕구를 인식하게 되며, 즉 부모가 됨으로써 우리는 자녀에게 필요한 존재가 되고자 하는 욕구를 알게 된다고 했다. 부모가 자녀에게 여러 정보를 가르치는 것을 위임받는다는 내용의 주어진 문장은 그다음인 ⑤ 앞에 들어가는 것이 가장 적절하다. 또한 주어진 문장 뒤에서는 보호자로서의 책임을 언급하는 흐름도 자연스럽다.

오답 클리닉

① (3%) this desire는 앞 문장의 다른 사람들을 돌보고자 하는 욕구를 받아 이 욕구가 부모가 되는 것으로 충족될 수 있다고 설명한다.

② (8%) 성인기에 나타나는 또 다른 특징으로 가르치고자 하는 욕구를 처음 언급하는 내용이다.

③ (28%) 앞서 언급한 가르치고자 하는 욕구를 this desire로 받으면서 그 욕구를 인식하게 되는 조건을 설명한다.

The 주의 주어진 문장은 부모가 자식에게 어떤 것을 가르치는지에 관한 내용이므로, 부모가 되는 것을 언급한 문장 6 이후에 오는 것이 적절하다.

④ (24%) 부모가 됨으로써 인식하는 바로 필요한 존재가 되고자 하는 욕구를 설명하는 내용이다.

01 ✦ 글의 주제 〈20학년도 6월 모평 23번 | 정답률 68%〉 ①

구문분석 & 직독직해 역사 식탁 예절에 의한 사회적 계층 분리

[1]In the twelfth to thirteenth centuries / there appeared *the first manuals* (teaching "table manners" / to the offspring of aristocrats).
V S 현재분사구

12세기부터 13세기에 / 최초의 안내서가 등장했다 ('식탁 예절'을 가르치는 / 귀족의 자녀들에게)

[2]It was *a genre* [that subsequently had a great success / in the early modern period / with *The Courtier* by Baldassare Castiglione, *The Galateo* by Monsignor Della Casa, and *many others* (produced in different European countries)].
S V C 주격 관계대명사 V′ O′ with의 O_1(명사구 병렬) with의 O_2(명사구 병렬) with의 O_3(명사구 병렬) 과거분사구

그것은 하나의 장르였다 [그 뒤에 큰 성공을 거둔 / 근대 초기에 / Baldassare Castiglione가 쓴 <The Courtier>, Monsignor Della Casa가 쓴 <The Galateo> 및 많은 다른 책들과 함께 (여러 유럽 국가에서 출판된)]

↳ **도입:** 식탁 예절 안내서는 근대 초기에 큰 성공을 거두어 하나의 장르가 됨.

🔑 안내서는 내부자와 외부자를 구분하도록 의도됨.

[3]In a variety of ways and meanings, / these are all *instruments* (intended to define or distinguish // who is *in* from who is *out*), / separating the participants / from the ostracized.
S V C 과거분사구 분사구문(= as they separate ~) ★<the+형용사>: ~한 사람들[것]

다양한 방식과 의미로 / 이 책들은 모두 수단들이다 (규정하거나 구별하도록 의도된 // 누가 '내부에' 있는지와 누가 '외부에' 있는지를) / (식탁) 참여자들을 분리하면서 / (식탁에서) 추방된 자들로부터

↳ **안내서의 목적:** 귀족과 귀족이 아닌 자를 구별하기 위함.

★<It ~ that ...>: …인 것은 바로 ~이다

[4]It is for this reason // that *manuals of "good manners"* (addressed to the aristocracy) / always have a negative reference / to *the peasant* [who behaves badly], // who "doesn't know" what the rules are, / and for this reason / is excluded from the lordly table.
강조구문 S′ 과거분사구 V′ O′ 주격 관계대명사 관계대명사(보충 설명) V'_1 O′(명사절) V'_2

바로 이런 이유에서이다 // '좋은 예절'의 안내서가 (귀족 계층에 초점이 맞춰진) / 항상 부정적으로 언급하는 것은 / 소작농에 대해 [(식탁) 예절이 좋지 않은] // 그런데 소작농은 규칙이 무엇인지를 '알지 못한다' / 그리고 이런 이유로 / 귀족의 식탁에서 배제된다

↳ 귀족 중심의 식탁 예절 안내서는 식탁 예절을 모르는 하층 계급을 나쁘게 묘사해서 배제시킴.

주제문

[5]Food etiquette had become a sign (of social barriers / and of the impossibility (of breaking them down)). 🔑 식사 예절을 아느냐 모르느냐로 계층이 구분됨.
S V C 전치사구 병렬 (= social barriers)

음식 예절은 표시가 되었다 (사회적 장벽에 대한 / 그리고 불가능성에 대한 (그 장벽을 허물어뜨리는 것의))

↳ **결과:** 음식 예절은 사회적 장벽의 표시가 됨.

해석

[1]12세기부터 13세기에 귀족의 자녀들에게 '식탁 예절'을 가르치는 최초의 안내서가 등장했다. [2]그것은 그 뒤에 Baldassare Castiglione가 쓴 <The Courtier>, Monsignor Della Casa가 쓴 <The Galateo> 및 여러 유럽 국가에서 출판된 많은 다른 책들과 함께 근대 초기에 큰 성공을 거둔 하나의 장르였다. [3]다양한 방식과 의미로, 이 책들은 모두 (식탁) 참여자들을 (식탁에서) 추방된 자들로부터 분리하면서, 누가 '내부에' 있는지와 누가 '외부에' 있는지를 규정하거나 구별하도록 의도된 수단들이다. [4]귀족 계층에 초점이 맞춰진 '좋은 예절'의 안내서가 (식탁) 예절이 좋지 않은 소작농에 대해 항상 부정적으로 언급하는 것은 바로 이런 이유에서인데, 소작농은 규칙이 무엇인지를 '알지 못하며', 이런 이유로 귀족의 식탁에서 배제된다. [5]음식 예절은 사회적 장벽, 그리고 그 장벽을 허물어뜨리는 것의 불가능성에 대한 표시가 되었다.

어휘

offspring 자녀, 자식; 자손
subsequently 그 뒤에, 나중에
instrument 수단; 도구, 기구
distinguish 구별하다
address 초점을 맞추다; (문제를) 다루다, 연설하다
aristocracy 귀족 (계층)
reference 언급; 참고, 참조
peasant 소작농; 농부
exclude 배제[제외]하다
lordly 귀족의, 귀족다운
barrier 장벽; 장애물
break A down A를 허물어뜨리다[부수다]
[선택지] distinction 구별, 차별
publication 출판물; 발표, 공개
bring about ~을 가져오다, ~을 유발하다
elaborate 정교하게 만들다; 자세히 설명하다
unite 통합[결속]시키다; 연합하다

정답 가이드

귀족 계층에 초점이 맞춰진 식탁 예절은 귀족과 소작농을 구별해서 분리하도록 의도된 것이었으며, 무너뜨릴 수 없는 사회적 장벽, 즉 계층 구분의 표시가 되었다고 했다. 따라서 글의 주제로 가장 적절한 것은 ① 'table manners as a marker for class distinction(계층 구별 표시로서의 식탁 예절)'이다.

오답 클리닉

② publications to bring about equality between classes (3%)
계층 간의 평등을 가져오기 위한(×) 출판물
식탁 예절 안내서는 계층 간의 분리를 가져왔으므로 글의 내용과 반대됨.

③ unintended effects of distinguishing insiders from outsiders (9%)
내부자와 외부자 구별의 의도되지 않은 결과(×)
식탁 예절의 의도가 내부자와 외부자를 구별하는 것이었다고 했으나, 그로 인한 의도되지 않은 결과는 언급되지 않음.

④ attempts to elaborate food etiquette for educational purposes (7%) 교육적 목적(×)을 위해 음식 예절을 정교하게 만들려는 시도
귀족들이 배운 음식 예절은 계층을 구분하기 위한 것이었으므로 교육적 목적이 있다고 볼 수 없음.

⑤ roles of manners in uniting people from different backgrounds (13%) 다른 배경 출신의 사람들을 통합시키는(×) 데 있어서 예절의 역할
식탁 예절이 다른 계층의 사람들을 분리하는 역할을 했다고 했으므로 글의 내용과 반대됨.

02 ✦ 빈칸 추론 〈18학년도 6월 모평 34번 | 정답률 40%〉 ①

구문분석 & 직독직해

생물 바다를 모방하는 담수 생명체

🔑 대부분의 생명체는 바다에 더 가까운 화학 성분을 가지고 있음.

[1]Since life began in the oceans, // most life, / (including freshwater life), / has a chemical composition (more like the ocean / than fresh water).
(부사절 접속사(~ 때문에) / S / 전치사구 삽입 / V / O)
생명체는 바다에서 시작되었기 때문에 // 대부분의 생명체는 / (담수 생명체를 포함한) / 화학 성분을 가지고 있다 (바다에 더 가까운 / 담수보다)
↳ 대부분의 생명체는 바다에 더 가까운 화학 성분을 지님.

[2]It appears // that most freshwater life did not originate / in fresh water, / but is secondarily adapted, / having passed / from ocean to land / and then back again to fresh water.
(S / V / 명사절 접속사 / S′ / V′₁ / V′₂; appears의 C(명사절); ★<not A but B>: A가 아니라 B; 분사구문(= as it had passed ~) ★부사절의 시제가 주절보다 앞서는 경우 완료 분사구문(having p.p.)을 사용함.)
~처럼 보인다 // 대부분의 담수 생명체는 시작된 것이 아니라 / 담수에서 / 이차적으로 적응된 (것처럼) / 건너가면서 / 바다에서 육지로 / 그런 다음 다시 담수로
↳ 담수 생명체는 바다에서 시작하여 담수로 이동하면서 적응한 것임.

★<(as+)형용사[부사/명사]+as+S′+V′>: 비록 ~이지만
🔑 수생 동물은 바다와 유사한 체액을 가짐.

[3]As improbable as this may seem, // the bodily fluids (of aquatic animals) / show a strong similarity to oceans, //
(부사절(양보) / S₁ / V₁ / O₁)
비록 이것이 있을 법하지 않은 것처럼 보이지만 // 체액은 (수생 동물의) / 바다와의 강한 유사성을 보여준다 //

and indeed, / most studies (of ion balance (in freshwater physiology)) / document *the complex regulatory mechanisms*
(S₂(복수) / V₂(복수) / O₂)
그리고 실제로 / 대부분의 연구는 (이온 균형에 관한 (담수 생리의)) / 복잡한 조절 기제를 기록하고 있다

[by which fish, amphibians and invertebrates attempt to **maintain an inner ocean** / **in spite of surrounding fresh water**].
(전치사+관계대명사 / S′ / V′ / 전치사(~에도 불구하고))
[어류, 양서류, 그리고 무척추동물이 내부의 바다 상태를 유지하려고 하는 / 주변의 담수에도 불구하고]
↳ 수생 동물의 체액은 바닷물과 유사하며 그 상태를 유지하려고 함.

[4]It is these sorts of unexpected complexities and apparent contradictions // that make ecology so interesting.
(<It is ~ that ...> 강조구문: ~인 것은 바로 …이다 / V′ / O′ / C′)
바로 이런 종류의 예기치 않은 복잡성과 명백한 모순이다 // 생태학을 매우 흥미롭게 만드는 것은
↳ 수생 동물의 이러한 복잡성과 모순적인 특징은 흥미로움.

🔑 담수에 사는 물고기는 바다를 모방하고자 몸속에 염분을 축적함.

[5]The idea (of a fish (in a freshwater lake) / struggling to accumulate salts inside its body / to mimic the ocean) / reminds one / of the other great contradiction (of the biosphere): //
(S₁ = 동명사의 의미상 주어 / of의 O(동명사구) / 목적(~하기 위해) / V₁ / O; ★<remind A of B>: A에게 B를 상기시키다)
생각은 (물고기가 (담수호에 있는) / 자기 몸속에 염분을 축적하려고 애쓴다는 / 바다를 흉내 내기 위해) / 사람에게 상기시킨다 / 또 다른 엄청난 모순을 (생물권의) //

해석

[1]생명체는 바다에서 시작되었기 때문에, 담수 생명체를 포함한 대부분의 생명체는 담수보다 바다에 더 가까운 화학 성분을 가지고 있다. [2]대부분의 담수 생명체는 담수에서 시작된 것이 아니라, 바다에서 육지로 그런 다음 다시 담수로 건너가면서 이차적으로 적응된 것처럼 보인다. [3]비록 이것이 있을 법하지 않은 것처럼 보이지만, 수생 동물의 체액은 바다와의 강한 유사성을 보여주며, 실제로 담수 생리의 이온 균형에 관한 대부분의 연구는 어류, 양서류, 그리고 무척추동물이 주변의 담수에도 불구하고 내부의 바다 상태를 유지하려고 하는 복잡한 조절 기제를 기록하고 있다. [4]생태학을 매우 흥미롭게 만드는 것은 바로 이런 종류의 예기치 않은 복잡성과 명백한 모순이다. [5]담수호에 있는 물고기가 바다를 흉내 내기 위해 자기 몸속에 염분을 축적하려고 애쓴다는 생각은 사람에게 생물권의 또 다른 엄청난 모순, 즉 식물은 대략 4분의 3의 질소로 구성된 대기에 뒤덮여 있지만 그것들의 성장은 질소 부족에 의해 흔히 제한된다는 것을 상기시킨다.

어휘

freshwater 담수[민물]의
composition 성분; 구성 (요소); 작곡; 작품
originate 시작되다, 비롯되다
secondarily 이차적으로
improbable 있을 법하지 않은
bodily fluid 체액
aquatic 수생의, 물속에 사는
physiology 생리 (기능); 생리학
document (상세한 내용을) 기록하다
regulatory 조절[조정]하는; 규정하는
attempt to-v v하려고 해보다
surrounding 주변의;
cf. surroundings (주위) 환경
contradiction 모순
ecology 생태학
struggle to-v v하려고 애쓰다[분투하다]

plants are bathed / in *an atmosphere* (composed of roughly three-quarters nitrogen), //
S2 V2 과거분사구
yet their growth is frequently restricted / by lack of nitrogen.
S3 V3
식물은 뒤덮여 있다 / 대기에 (대략 4분의 3의 질소로 구성된) //
그러나 그것들의 성장은 흔히 제한된다 / 질소 부족에 의해
↳ **모순적인 특징의 부연 설명:** 담수 물고기가 바닷물을 모방하고자 체내에 염분을 축적함.

accumulate 축적하다, 모으다
mimic 흉내 내다, 모방하다
biosphere 생물권
bathe 뒤덮다, 감싸다; 목욕시키다
nitrogen 《화학》 질소
[선택지] attain 이루다, 달성하다; 획득하다
natural enemy 천적
in accord with ~에 맞게, ~와 일치하여

정답 가이드

빈칸 문장이 매우 길고 복잡하므로 이를 요약해서 정리하면, 수생 동물의 체액이 바다와 유사한데, 수생 동물이 '무엇을' 하려 하는 복잡한 조절 기제를 갖고 있다는 것이다. 이어지는 설명에서 담수호에 사는 물고기가 바다를 흉내 내기 위해 체내에 염분을 축적하려고 애쓴다고 했으므로 이를 다른 말로 표현하면 ① 'maintain an inner ocean in spite of surrounding fresh water(주변의 담수에도 불구하고 내부의 바다 상태를 유지하다)'가 가장 적절하다.

오답 클리닉

② attain ion balance by removing salts from inside their body (21%)
자신의 몸 내부에서 염분을 제거함으로써 이온 균형을 이루다
마지막 문장에서 담수 물고기가 체내에 염분을 축적하려고 애쓴다고 했으므로 글의 내용과 반대됨.

The 주의 이온 균형을 이루기 위해 담수 생명체가 체내 염분을 제거할 것이라는 짐작으로 정답을 선택해서는 안 되며 본문 내용을 근거로 정답을 추론해야 한다.

③ return to the ocean to escape from their natural enemies (9%)
자신의 천적을 피하기 위해 바다로 되돌아가다
천적을 피하려고 한다는 언급은 없음.

④ rebuild their external environment to obtain resources (11%)
자원을 얻기 위해 자신의 외부 환경을 재건하다
담수 생물이 자원을 얻고자 외부 환경을 재건한다는 내용은 없음.

⑤ change their physiology in accord with their surroundings (16%)
자신의 환경에 맞게 생리를 바꾸다
담수 생물이 담수에 맞게 생리를 바꾸지 않고 반대로 바닷속 생리를 유지하려고 한다는 모순적 특징을 설명하는 내용임.

03 + 글의 순서 (19학년도 9월 모평 36번 | 정답률 59%) ②

구문분석 & 직독직해 생활 감정의 영향을 받는 식사

[1] Most of us have / a general, rational sense (of what to eat and when (to eat)) — //
S1 V1 O of의 O(명사구 병렬)
there is no shortage (of information / on the subject).
V2(단수) S2(단수)
우리 대부분은 가지고 있다 / 일반적이고 합리적인 관념을 (무엇을 먹을지 그리고 언제 먹을지에 대한) //
부족은 없다 (정보의 / 그 문제에 관한)
↳ 인간은 식사에 관한 일반적이고 합리적인 관념을 가짐.

주제문 역접 연결어 Yet 뒤에 주어진 글과 반대 내용이 이어짐.
(B) [2] Yet / there is often a disconnect (between what we know and what we do).
V S 명사절 병렬
하지만 / 종종 단절이 존재한다 (우리가 알고 있는 것과 우리가 행하는 것 사이에는)
↳ 아는 것과 행하는 것 사이의 단절이 있음.

[3] We may have the facts, // but decisions also involve our feelings.
S1 V1 O1 S2 V2 O2
우리가 진실을 알고 있을지도 모른다 // 그러나 결정은 우리의 감정도 수반한다

[4] *Many people* [who struggle with difficult emotions] / also struggle with eating problems.
S 주격 관계대명사 V
많은 사람들은 [힘겨운 감정과 씨름하는] / 또한 섭식 문제와 씨름한다
↳ 감정적으로 힘든 사람들이 섭식 문제도 겪음.

(B)의 eating problems를 설명함.
(A) [5] *Emotional eating* is *a popular term* (used to describe *eating* [that is influenced / by *emotions*, (both positive and negative)]).
S V C 과거분사구 주격 관계대명사
'감정적 식사'는 일반적인 용어이다 (식사를 말하는 데 사용되는 [영향받는 / 감정에 의해 (긍정적 그리고 부정적 모두)])
↳ **예:** 감정에 의해 영향을 받는 식사를 '감정적 식사'라고 함.

해석

[1]우리 대부분은 무엇을 먹을지, 그리고 언제 먹을지에 대한 일반적이고 합리적인 관념을 갖고 있는데, 그 문제에 관한 정보는 부족하지 않다. (B) [2]하지만 우리가 알고 있는 것과 우리가 행하는 것 사이에는 종종 단절이 존재한다. [3]우리가 진실을 알고 있을지도 모르지만, 결정은 우리의 감정도 수반한다. [4]힘겨운 감정과 씨름하는 많은 사람들은 또한 섭식 문제와 씨름한다. (A) [5]'감정적 식사'는 긍정적 감정과 부정적 감정 모두에 의해 영향받는 식사를 말하는데 사용되는 일반적인 용어이다. [6]여러분의 먹고자 하는 동기, 여러분의 음식 선택, 어디서 누구와 여러분이 식사할지, 그리고 여러분이 식사하는 속도를 포함하여, 감정은 여러분의 식사의 여러 측면에 영향을 미칠 수 있다. [7]대부분의 과식은 신체의 배고픔보다는 감정에 의해 유발된다. (C) [8]비만과 씨름하는 사람들은 감정에 반응하여 먹는 경향이 있다. [9]그러나 감정적인 이유로 먹는 사람이 반드시 과체중인 것은 아니다. [10]어떤 사이즈의 사람들이라도 스스로를 먹는 것에 몰두하게 하거나 자기 몸매와 몸무게에 대해 강박감을 가짐으로써 감정적 경험에서 벗어나려고 노력할지도 모른다.

[6]Feelings may affect / various aspects (of your eating), / including *your motivation* (to eat), your food choices, where and with whom you eat, and *the speed* [at which you eat].

S V O 전치사(~을 포함하여) 전치사+관계대명사

감정은 영향을 미칠 수 있다 / 여러 측면에 (여러분의 식사의) / 여러분의 동기 (먹고자 하는), 여러분의 음식 선택, 어디서 누구와 여러분이 식사할지, 그리고 속도를 포함하여 [여러분이 식사하는]

↳ 인간의 감정은 식사의 여러 측면에 영향을 미침.

[7]Most overeating is prompted / by feelings rather than physical hunger.

S V <A rather than B>: B라기보다는 A

대부분의 과식은 유발된다 / 신체의 배고픔보다는 감정에 의해

🔑 과식이 감정에 의해 유발된다는 (A)의 내용이 비만과 감정의 관계로 연결됨.

(C) [8]*Individuals* [who struggle with obesity] / tend to eat / in response to emotions.

S(복수) 주격 관계대명사 V(복수)

사람들은 [비만과 씨름하는] / 먹는 경향이 있다 / 감정에 반응하여

↳ 대부분의 과식은 감정에 의해 유발됨.

[9]However, / *people* [who eat for emotional reasons] are not necessarily overweight.

S 주격 관계대명사 V C ★<not necessarily>: ((부분 부정)) 반드시 ~은 아닌

그러나 / 사람들이 [감정적인 이유로 먹는] / 반드시 과체중인 것은 아니다

[10]People (of any size) / may try to escape an emotional experience / by preoccupying themselves with eating / or by obsessing over their shape and weight.

S V O <by v-ing>: v함으로써 전치사구 병렬

사람들 (어떤 사이즈의 ~라도) / 감정적인 경험에서 벗어나려고 노력할지도 모른다 / 스스로를 먹는 것에 몰두하게 함으로써 / 또는 자기 몸매와 몸무게에 대해 강박감을 가짐으로써

↳ 감정적인 이유로 먹는 사람이 모두 과체중인 것은 아닌 것은 감정적 경험에서 벗어나고자 노력하기 때문임.

어휘

rational 합리적인, 이성적인
shortage 부족, 결핍
subject 문제, 사안, 주제; 과목; (연구) 대상
disconnect 단절; 연결을 끊다
involve 수반[포함]하다; 관련시키다
struggle with ~와 씨름하다, ~로 고심하다
popular 일반적인; 인기 있는
term 용어; 학기; 기간
describe 말하다, 서술하다, 묘사하다
aspect 측면; 양상
motivation 동기 (부여); 자극
overeating 과식
prompt 유발하다; 자극하다; 즉각적인
physical 신체의; 물리적인
obesity 비만
in response to A A에 반응하여
overweight 과체중(의)
preoccupy 몰두하게 하다, ~의 마음을 빼앗다; 먼저 차지하다

⊕ 감정적 식사(emotional eating): 진짜 배고픔이 아니라 긍정적 또는 부정적 감정에 의한 가짜 배고픔을 채우기 위해 먹는 것. 즉 감정을 처리하기 위해 음식을 먹는 것을 말하며, 폭식으로 연결되거나 정신 건강상의 문제를 낳는 경우가 잦음.

정답 가이드

우리 대부분이 무엇을 언제 먹을지에 대한 합리적 관념을 갖고 있다는 주어진 글 뒤에는 역접 연결어 Yet과 함께 실제로는 우리가 알고 있는 것, 즉 합리적 관념과 우리가 실제로 행하는 것 사이에 단절이 존재한다는 (B)가 이어져야 한다. 감정 문제로 섭식 문제도 겪는다는 (B)의 마지막 내용 뒤에는 '감정적 식사'를 구체적으로 설명하는 (A)가 오는 것이 적절하다. 과식이 감정에 의해 유발된다는 (A)의 마지막 문장 뒤에는 비만인 사람들이 감정에 반응하여 식사하는 경향이 있다고 구체적으로 설명하는 (C)가 오는 것이 적절하다.

오답 클리닉

① (A) - (C) - (B) (5%)
주어진 글에는 감정이 식사에 영향을 미친다는 내용이 없으므로 (A)가 주어진 글 바로 뒤에 올 수 없다.
③ (B) - (C) - (A) (21%)
'감정적 식사'를 설명하는 (A)는 감정의 영향으로 인한 섭식 문제를 언급한 (B) 뒤에 예로 이어지는 것이 적절하다. 또한 (C)의 비만인 사람들이 감정에 반응해 먹는다는 내용 앞에는 과식이 감정에 의해 유발된다는 (A)의 일반적인 진술이 먼저 와야 한다.
④ (C) - (A) - (B) (9%) / ⑤ (C) - (B) - (A) (5%)
주어진 글에는 (C)에 나오는 비만과 감정의 관계에 관한 내용이 없으므로 (C)는 주어진 글 바로 뒤에 올 수 없다.

01 ✦ 글의 제목 (20학년도 6월 모평 24번 | 정답률 64%) ①

구문분석 & 직독직해

사회 미국 스포츠의 인종 및 민족적 문제 해결의 어려움

주제문

[1]Racial and ethnic relations in the United States / are better today / than in the past, //
(S_1 / V_1 / C)
미국의 인종 및 민족 관계는 / 오늘날 더 낫다 / 과거보다 //
★시간의 부사절에서 현재시제가 미래를 대신함.

but many changes are needed // before sports are a model (of inclusion and fairness).
(S_2 / V_2 / 부사절 접속사(시간) / S′ / V′ / C′)
하지만 많은 변화들이 요구된다 // 스포츠가 본보기가 되기까지 (포용과 공정의)
🔑 스포츠계의 인종·민족 관계는 여전히 개선이 필요함.
↳ **현재 상황:** 미국 스포츠계에 인종·민족 문제가 여전히 있음.

[2]The challenges today are different / from the ones (faced twenty years ago), //
(S_1 / V_1 / C / (= the challenges) / 과거분사구)
오늘날의 문제들은 다르다 / 것들과는 (20년 전에 직면했던) //

and experience shows // that / when current challenges are met, // a new social situation is created [in which new challenges emerge].
(↱ shows의 O(명사절) / S_2 / V_2 / 명사절 접속사 / 부사절 / S′ / V′ / 전치사+관계대명사 / S″ / V″)
🔑 한 문제가 해결되면 새로운 문제가 또 나옴.
★in which는 관계부사 where로 바꿔 쓸 수 있음. <주어+관계사절>에 비해 술어 부분(is created)이 짧아 관계사절이 술어 뒤에 위치함.
그리고 경험은 보여준다 // (~라는) 것을 / 현재의 문제들이 잘 처리되면 // 새로운 사회적 상황이 만들어진다는 (것을) [새로운 문제들이 생기는]
↳ **부연 설명:** 현재 직면한 문제는 과거의 것과 다르고, 한 문제가 해결되고 나면 새로운 문제 상황이 또 생김.

[3]For example, / once racial and ethnic segregation is eliminated // and people come together, //
(부사절 접속사(일단 ~하면) / S'_1 / V'_1 / S'_2 / V'_2)
예를 들어 / 일단 인종적, 민족적 차별이 제거되면 // 그리고 사람들이 함께하면 //

they must learn / to live, work, and play with each other / despite diverse experiences and cultural perspectives.
(S(= people) / V / O(to-v구) / 전치사(~에도 불구하고) / despite의 O(명사구))
그들은 배워야 한다 / 서로 함께 살고, 일하고, 노는 것을 / 다양한 경험과 문화적 관점에도 불구하고
↳ **예:** 인종·민족적 차별이 없어지고 나면(해결된 문제), 함께 지내는 법을 배워야 함(새로운 문제).

[4]Meeting this challenge / requires a commitment (to equal treatment), /
(S / V / O_1)
이 문제를 잘 처리하는 것은 / 헌신을 필요로 한다 (평등한 대우에 대한) /

plus / learning about the perspectives of others, / understanding how they define and give meaning to the world, / and then determining how to form and maintain relationships /
(O_3(동명사구) / 동명사 understanding의 O(명사절) / O_4(동명사구) / 동명사 determining의 O(명사구))
(~에) '덧붙여' / 다른 사람들의 관점에 대해 배우는 것 / 그들이 어떻게 세상을 규정하고 그것에 의미를 부여하는지를 이해하는 것 / 그런 다음 어떻게 관계를 형성하고 유지할지를 알아내는 것 /

while respecting differences, making compromises, and supporting one another / in the pursuit of goals [that may not always be shared].
(접속사를 생략하지 않은 분사구문(= while they respect ~, make ~, and support ~) / 주격 관계대명사)
★분사구문의 의미상 주어(they)가 '일반인'인 경우 생략 가능함.
차이를 존중하고, 타협하고, 서로를 지지하면서 / 목표를 위해 [항상 공유되지는 않을 수도 있는]
↳ **문제 해결 방법:** 인종·민족적 문제를 해결하려면 다양한 노력이 필요함.

🔑 문제는 한 번에 해결되지 않음.
[5]None of this is easy, // and challenges are never met / once and for all time.
(S_1 / V_1 / C / S_2 / V_2)
이것 중 어느 것도 쉽지 않다 // 그리고 문제는 절대 잘 처리되지 않는다 / 한 번에 영구히
↳ **결론:** 인종·민족적 문제는 해결되기 어렵고 단번에 해결될 수도 없음.

해석

[1]미국의 인종 및 민족 관계는 과거보다 오늘날 더 낫지만, 스포츠가 포용과 공정의 본보기가 되기까지 많은 변화들이 요구된다. [2]오늘날의 문제들은 20년 전에 직면했던 것들과는 다르며, 경험은 현재의 문제들이 잘 처리되면 새로운 문제들이 생기는 새로운 사회적 상황이 만들어진다는 것을 보여준다. [3]예를 들어, 일단 인종적, 민족적 차별이 제거되고 사람들이 함께하면, 그들은 다양한 경험과 문화적 관점에도 불구하고 서로 함께 살고, 일하고, 노는 것을 배워야 한다. [4]이 문제를 잘 처리하는 것은 평등한 대우에 대한 헌신에 '덧붙여' 다른 사람들의 관점에 대해 배우는 것, 그들이 어떻게 세상을 규정하고 그것에 의미를 부여하는지를 이해하는 것, 그런 다음 차이를 존중하고, 타협하고, 항상 공유되지는 않을 수도 있는 목표를 위해 서로를 지지하면서 어떻게 관계를 형성하고 유지할지를 알아내는 것을 필요로 한다. [5]이것 중 어느 것도 쉽지 않으며, 문제는 절대 한 번에 영구히 잘 처리되지 않는다.

어휘

racial 인종의, 종족의
ethnic 민족의
inclusion 포용; 포함, 함유
fairness 공정, 공평
challenge (큰 노력이 드는) 문제, 난제; 도전
face 직면하다; 마주보다
current 현재의, 지금의; 흐름
meet (문제를) 잘 처리하다; (요구를) 충족시키다
emerge (문제가) 생기다; 나타나다, 출현하다
eliminate 제거하다, 없애다
come together 함께하다, 모이다; (하나로) 합치다
perspective 관점, 시각
commitment 헌신, 전념
treatment 대우, 처우; 치료
determine 알아내다, 밝히다; 결정하다
compromise 타협(하다)
in pursuit of ~을 위해, ~을 추구하여
[선택지] ongoing 진행 중인, 계속하고 있는
injustice 불평등; 부당한 조치
cooperation 협력, 협동
lie (위치해) 있다; 누워 있다

정답 가이드

미국의 인종과 민족 문제는 과거보다는 나아지긴 했지만 스포츠에서는 여전히 많은 변화가 필요하며, 한 문제가 해결되어도 새로운 문제가 또 생겨나기 때문에 문제는 단번에 해결되기 어렵다고 했다. 따라서 제목으로 가장 적절한 것은 ① 'Ongoing Challenges in Sports: Racial and Ethnic Issues(스포츠에서 진행 중인 난제, 즉 인종 및 민족적 문제)'이다.

오답 클리닉

② Racial and Ethnic Injustice in Sports: Cause and Effect (12%)
스포츠에서의 인종 및 민족적 불평등, 원인과 결과(×)
스포츠계에서 인종 및 민족적 불평등이 있는 것은 맞지만, 그것의 원인과 결과에 대해서는 언급되지 않음.

③ The History of Racial and Ethnic Diversity in Sports (10%)
스포츠에서의 인종 및 민족적 다양성의 역사(×)
스포츠의 인종 및 민족적 다양성의 역사를 서술하는 내용이 아님.

④ All for One, One for All: The Power of Team Sports (9%)
하나를 위한 모두, 모두를 위한 하나, 즉 팀 스포츠의 힘(×)
팀 스포츠의 단결력에 대한 내용이 아님.

⑤ Cooperation Lies at the Heart of Sportsmanship (5%)
협력은 스포츠맨십(×)의 중심에 있다
인종 및 민족적 문제 해결을 위해 서로 존중하고 더불어 사는 것에 대해 언급하긴 했지만 스포츠맨십과는 관련이 없음.

02 ✦ 빈칸 추론 〈18학년도 6월 모평 33번 | 정답률 38%〉 ②

구문분석 & 직독직해

인지 모형을 변형시키는 인간의 능력

주제문

[1] To make plans for the future, / the brain must have / an ability (to take certain elements (of prior experiences) / and (to) reconfigure them / in *a way* [that does not copy / any actual past experience or present reality / exactly]).

(목적(~하기 위해) / S / V / O / them = certain ~ experiences / that: 주격 관계대명사)

미래에 대한 계획을 세우기 위해 / 뇌는 가지고 있어야 한다 / 능력을 (특정한 요소들을 받아들이는 (이전 경험의) / 그리고 그것들(이전 경험의 특정한 요소)을 바꿀 수 있는 / 방식으로 [모방하지 않는 / 어떤 실제 과거 경험이나 현실을 / 정확히])

🔑 과거 경험이나 현실을 그대로 모방하지 않고 바꿀 수 있는 능력이 있어야 함.

↳ 미래 계획을 세우기 위해서 뇌는 과거 경험이나 현실을 다르게 바꿀 수 있어야 함.

[2] To accomplish that, / the organism must go beyond / the mere ability (to form internal representations, / the models (of the world outside)).

(that = to take ~ and (to) reconfigure ~ / 목적(~하기 위해) / S / V)

그것을 성취하기 위해 / 유기체는 넘어서야 한다 / 단순한 능력을 (내적 표상을 만들어 내는 / 즉 모형 (외부 세계의))

[3] It must acquire the ability (to **manipulate and transform these models**).

(It = The organism / S / V / O)

그것(유기체)은 능력을 습득해야 한다 (이러한 모형을 조작하고 변형시키는)

↳ 내적 표상을 만드는 것을 넘어 그것을 조작하고 변형시킬 수 있어야 함.

[4] We can argue // that tool-making, / one (of the fundamental distinguishing features (of primate cognition)), / depends on this ability, // since a tool does not exist / in a ready-made form / in the natural environment / and has to be imagined / in order to be made.

(can argue의 O(명사절) / S / V / 명사절 접속사 / S' / V' / O' / 부사절 접속사(~ 때문에) / S' / V'₁ / V'₂ / 목적(~하기 위해))

우리는 주장할 수 있다 // 도구 제작이 / 하나인 (근본적인 독특한 특징 중의 (영장류 인지의)) / 이 능력에 의존한다고 // 왜냐하면 도구는 존재하지 않기 때문이다 / 이미 만들어져 있는 형태로 / 자연 환경 속에서 / 그래서 상상되어야 하기 때문이다 / 만들어지기 위해서는

🔑 도구 제작은 상상을 통해 모형을 변형시켜 없던 것을 만드는 것임.

↳ **예:** 처음부터 만들어진 형태로 존재하지 않는 것을 상상해서 만드는 도구 제작은 이 능력에 좌우됨.

[5] The neural machinery (for creating and holding 'images of the future') / was a necessary prerequisite (for tool-making, / and thus for launching human civilization).

(S / for의 O(동명사구) / V / C / 전치사구 병렬)

신경 기제는 ('미래의 이미지'를 만들어 내고 보유하는) / 필수적인 전제 조건이었다 (도구 제작을 위한 / 따라서 인간 문명을 시작하기 위한)

↳ 문명의 시작에는 '미래의 이미지'를 창조하고 기억하는 신경 기제가 필수적이었음.

해석

[1]미래에 대한 계획을 세우기 위해 뇌는 이전 경험의 특정한 요소들을 받아들이고 어떤 실제 과거 경험이나 현실을 정확히 모방하지 않는 방식으로 그것들(이전 경험의 특정한 요소)을 바꿀 수 있는 능력을 가지고 있어야 한다. [2]그것을 성취하기 위해 유기체는 내적 표상, 즉 외부 세계의 모형을 만들어 내는 단순한 능력을 넘어서야 한다. [3]그것(유기체)은 이러한 모형을 조작하고 변형시키는 능력을 습득해야 한다. [4]우리는 영장류 인지의 근본적인 독특한 특징 중의 하나인 도구 제작이 이 능력에 의존한다고 주장할 수 있는데, 왜냐하면 도구는 자연 환경 속에 이미 만들어져 있는 형태로 존재하지 않아서 만들어지기 위해서는 상상되어야 하기 때문이다. [5]'미래의 이미지'를 만들어 내고 보유하는 신경 기제는 도구 제작을 위한, 따라서 인간 문명을 시작하기 위한 필수적인 전제 조건이었다.

어휘

reconfigure 바꾸다, 변경하다
organism 유기체
go beyond ~을 넘어서다
mere 단순한, 순전한
internal representation 내적 표상
model 모형, 원형
acquire 습득하다, 얻다
manipulate 조작하다; 조종하다, 다루다
fundamental 근본[본질]적인
distinguishing 독특한, 특징적인
primate 영장류
cognition 인지, 인식
ready-made 이미 만들어져 있는, 기성품의
neural machinery 신경 기제
prerequisite 전제 조건
launch 시작하다; 출시하다; 개시
civilization 문명 (사회)
[선택지] mirror 반영하다; 반사하다, 비추다
faithfully (틀리지 않게) 정확히, 충실히

정답 가이드

빈칸 문장이 대명사 It을 포함하므로 무엇을 지칭하는지를 먼저 파악한 뒤 그것이 '어떤' 능력을 습득해야 하는지를 추론해야 한다. 앞에서 the organism(유기체)은 내적 표상을 만들어 내는 단순한 능력을 넘어서야 한다고 했고 빈칸 문장은 그것이 '어떤' 능력을 습득해야 한다고 했으므로 It은 '유기체'를 지칭한다. 빈칸 문장의 앞에서는 실제 과거 경험이나 현실을 모방하기보다는 이를 '바꿀' 수 있는 능력이 필요하다고 했으며, 뒤에서는 이것이 자연 속에 이미 만들어진 형태로 존재하지 않는 도구 제작에 필요한 능력이라고 설명했다. 즉, 이 능력은 외부 세계의 모형을 만들어 내는 것을 넘어서, 이를 변형하여 존재하지 않는 '미래의 이미지'를 만들어 내는 능력이다. 따라서 빈칸에 들어갈 말로 가장 적절한 것은 ② 'manipulate and transform these models(이러한 모형을 조작하고 변형시키다)'이다.

오답 클리닉

① mirror accurate images of the world outside (17%)
외부 세계의 정확한 이미지를 반영하다
문장 2에서 외부 세계의 모형을 만들어 내는 능력을 넘어서야 한다고 했으므로 글의 내용과 반대됨.

③ visualize the present reality as it is (18%)
현실을 있는 그대로 마음속에 떠올리다
문장 1에서 현실을 정확히 모방하지 않는 방식으로 바꿔야 한다고 했으므로 글의 내용과 반대됨.

④ bring the models back from memory (13%)
그 모형을 기억에서 다시 가져오다
외부 세계의 모형을 기억하는 것과는 관련이 없음.

⑤ identify and reproduce past experiences faithfully (11%)
과거 경험을 정확히 확인하고 재생하다
과거 경험을 정확히 모방하지 않아야 한다고 했음.

03 + 문장 넣기 (19학년도 9월 모평 38번 | 정답률 79%) ④

구문분석 & 직독직해

경제 연방 정부의 부채 증가와 요인

[1] Both the budget deficit and federal debt have soared / during the recent financial crisis and recession.
(the budget deficit and federal debt: S(복수) / have soared: V(복수))
재정 적자와 연방 정부의 부채가 모두 치솟았다 / 최근의 재정 위기와 경기 침체 동안에
↳ **도입:** 최근 재정 위기 및 경기 침체로 연방 정부의 재정 적자와 부채가 증가함.

★'부분'을 나타내는 표현에 이어지는 <of+명사>에서 명사의 수에 동사를 일치시킴.
(①) [2] During 2009—2010, / nearly 40 percent of federal expenditures were financed / by borrowing.
(percent of federal expenditures: S(복수) / were financed: V(복수))
2009년~2010년 동안에 / 연방 정부 지출의 거의 40퍼센트가 자금이 조달되었다 / 차입으로

(②) [3] The huge recent federal deficits have pushed the federal debt / to *levels* (not seen / since the years (immediately following World War II)).
(S / V / O / 과거분사구 / since: 전치사(~ 이후로))
최근의 막대한 연방 재정 적자는 연방 정부의 부채를 떠밀었다 / 수준까지 (보인 적이 없었던 / 기간 이후로 (제2차 세계 대전 바로 뒤에 이어진))
↳ **도입 부연 설명:** 연방 정부는 대출로 자금을 조달하고, 제2차 세계 대전 이후 수준까지 부채가 초래됨.

🔑 부채 증가의 요인으로 베이비붐 세대의 퇴직자 증가를 언급함.
(③) [4] The rapid growth (of baby-boomer retirees) / in the decade immediately ahead / will mean / higher spending levels and larger and larger deficits (for both Social Security and Medicare).
(S / V / O; ★<비교급 and 비교급>: 점점 더 ~한)
빠른 증가는 (베이비붐 세대 퇴직자의) / 임박한 향후 10년 동안 / 의미할 것이다 / 더 높은 지급 수준과 점점 더 커지는 적자를 (사회 보장 연금과 노인 의료 보험 제도 둘 다에 대한)
↳ **요인 1:** 베이비붐 세대 퇴직자의 증가로 연금 및 의료 보험의 부담이 커질 것임.

🔑 다른 부채 증가 요인을 Moreover로 추가함. ★<half of+N>: ((부분표현)) ~ 중 절반
(④ [5] Moreover, / more than half of Americans age 18 and older derive benefits / from various transfer programs, / while paying little or no personal income tax.)
(S / V(복수) / O; 접속사를 생략하지 않은 분사구문(= while they pay ~))
더욱이 / 18세 이상의 미국인들 중 절반이 넘는 사람들이 보조금을 얻는다 / 다양한 (소득) 이전 지출 프로그램으로부터 / 개인 소득세를 거의 혹은 전혀 내지 않으면서
↳ **요인 2:** 대부분의 미국 성인들이 개인 소득세를 내지 않고 보조금을 받음.

🔑 앞에 두 개 이상의 재정 위기 요인이 언급되어야 함.
[6] All of these factors are going to make it extremely difficult / to slow the growth (of federal spending) / and (to) keep the debt from ballooning out of control.
(S / V / 가목적어 / C / 진목적어₁(to-v구 병렬) / 진목적어₂(to-v구 병렬); ★<keep A from v-ing>: A가 v하지 못하게 막다)
이러한 모든 요인들은 (~을) 대단히 어렵게 만들 것이다 / 증가를 늦추는 것을 (연방 정부 지출의) / 그리고 부채가 통제할 수 없을 정도로 급증하지 못하게 막는 것을
↳ **결과:** 연방 정부의 지출 및 부채가 증가할 것임.

해석

[1]최근의 재정 위기와 경기 침체 동안에 재정 적자와 연방 정부의 부채가 모두 치솟았다. (①) [2]2009년~2010년 동안에 연방 정부 지출의 거의 40퍼센트가 차입으로 자금이 조달되었다. (②) [3]최근의 막대한 연방 재정 적자는 제2차 세계 대전 바로 뒤에 이어진 기간 이후로 보인 적이 없었던 수준까지 연방 정부의 부채를 떠밀었다. (③) [4]임박한 향후 10년 동안 베이비붐 세대 퇴직자의 빠른 증가는 사회 보장 연금과 노인 의료 보험 제도 둘 다에 대한 더 높은 지급 수준과 점점 더 커지는 적자를 의미할 것이다. (④ [5]더욱이, 18세 이상의 미국인들 중 절반이 넘는 사람들이 개인 소득세를 거의 혹은 전혀 내지 않으면서, 다양한 (소득) 이전 지출 프로그램으로부터 보조금을 얻는다.) [6]이러한 모든 요인들은 연방 정부 지출의 증가를 늦추는 것과 부채가 통제할 수 없을 정도로 급증하지 못하게 막는 것을 대단히 어렵게 만들 것이다. (⑤) [7]2019년쯤에는 연방 정부의 순부채가 국내 총생산의 90퍼센트까지 증가하리라는 것을 예측들이 보여주며, 많은 사람들은 곧 건설적인 조치가 취해지지 않는 한 그것(연방 정부의 순부채)이 훨씬 더 높아질 것이라고 생각한다.

어휘

recession 경기 침체, 불황; 후퇴
expenditure 지출; 비용; 소비
finance 자금(을 조달[공급]하다)
retiree 퇴직자, 은퇴자
Social Security 사회 보장 연금
Medicare 노인 의료 보험 제도
derive A from B B에서 A를 얻다
benefit (사회 보장 제도에 의한) 보조금; 혜택, 이득
income tax 소득세
balloon 급증하다; 부풀다; 풍선

(⑤) [7]Projections indicate // that the net federal debt will rise / to 90 percent of GDP / by 2019, //

(S1: Projections, V1: indicate, 명사절 접속사: that, S'1: the net federal debt, V'1: will rise, → indicate의 O(명사절))

예측들이 보여 준다 // 연방 정부의 순부채가 증가하리라는 것을 / 국내 총생산의 90퍼센트까지 / 2019년쯤에는 //

and many believe // (that) it will be even higher // unless constructive action is taken soon.

(S2: many, V2: believe, believe의 O(명사절), 부사절 접속사(조건): unless)

그리고 많은 사람들은 생각한다 // 그것(연방 정부의 순부채)이 훨씬 더 높아질 것이라고 // 곧 건설적인 조치가 취해지지 않는 한

↳ **결과 부연 설명:** 건설적인 조치가 취해지지 않는 한 연방 정부의 부채는 계속 늘어날 것임.

projection 예측[추정]; 투사(도)

net (돈의 액수에 대해) 순(純)-; 그물[망]

⊕ 이전 지출(transfer payments): 생산 활동과 무관하게 아무런 대가 없이 정부가 지급하는 소득의 이전으로, 실업 수당, 재해 보상금 등이 있음.

⊕ 재정 적자((government) budget deficit): 정부의 재정 지출이 재정 수입을 초과하면 발생함. 사회 보장 연금이나 노인 의료 보험 제도는 재정 지출에 해당하고, 재정 수입의 대부분은 세금으로 충당하므로, 세금을 내지 않으면서 정부 보조금을 받는 것은 재정 적자 악화의 요인이 됨.

정답 가이드

주어진 문장은 미국 성인의 절반이 넘는 사람들이 세금을 내지 않으면서 정부 보조금을 받는다는 것이고, 지문의 첫 문장은 연방 정부의 부채가 치솟았다는 것이므로, 주어진 문장은 부채 증가의 요인으로 제시된 것이다. 첨가를 나타내는 연결어 Moreover가 이끄는 것으로 보아 그 앞에는 또 다른 부채 증가 요인이 제시되어야 함을 알 수 있다. ④의 앞 문장은 베이비붐 세대의 퇴직자 증가로 인한 사회 보장 비용의 증가를 제시하고 있는데 이는 부채 증가의 요인이며, ④의 뒤 문장은 주어진 문장의 내용을 포함해 이 두 가지 요인을 All of these factors로 받아 이로 인한 결과를 전망하고 있으므로 주어진 문장이 들어가기에 가장 적절한 곳은 ④이다.

오답 클리닉

① (2%) 앞 문장에 언급된 재정 위기와 경기 침체를 부연 설명하는 내용이다.

② (5%) 최근의 재정 위기가 얼마나 심각한 수준인지를 부연 설명하는 내용이다.

③ (7%) 연방 정부의 재정 적자와 부채 증가의 첫 번째 요인으로 베이비붐 세대의 빠른 퇴직자 증가로 인한 사회 보장 비용의 증가를 제시하고 있다.

⑤ (8%) 연방 정부의 재정 문제가 더 어려워질 것이라는 전망에 대해 부채가 국내 총생산의 90퍼센트까지 증가할 것이라 예측하고, 건설적 조치의 필요성을 언급하며 글을 끝맺는다.

01 ✦ 함의 추론 〈19학년도 대수능 21번 | 정답률 52%〉 ①

구문분석 & 직독직해

과학 무지의 정제를 높이 평가하는 과학 정신

주제문

[1] Although (it is) not the explicit goal, // the best science can really be seen / as refining ignorance.
(it is: 주어+be동사 생략 / Although: 부사절 접속사(양보) / the best science: S / can really be seen: V / ★<see A as B(A를 B로 여기다)>의 수동형 / as: 전치사(~로(서)))
비록 명시적인 목표는 아니지만 // 최고의 과학은 실제로 여겨질 수 있다 / 무지를 정제하는 것으로
↳ 과학의 목표는 무지를 정제하는 것임.

[2] Scientists, (especially young ones), / can get too obsessed with results.
(Scientists: S / (especially young ones): 삽입어구 (= scientists) / can get: V / too obsessed with results: C)
과학자들, (특히 젊은 과학자들은) / 결과에 너무 집착하게 될 수 있다

[3] Society helps them along / in this mad chase.
(Society: S / helps ... along: V / them: O(= scientists))
사회는 그들(과학자들)을 도와서 하게 한다 / 이 어리석은 추구를
↳ **문제점:** 과학자들은 결과에 집착하고 사회가 이를 부추김.

[4] Big discoveries are covered in the press, / show up on the university's home page, / help get grants, / and make the case (for promotions).
(Big discoveries: S / are covered: V_1 / show up: V_2 / help: V_3 / get grants: O_3 / make: V_4 / the case: O_4)
큰 발견들이 언론에 보도된다 / 대학의 홈페이지에 등장한다 / 보조금을 받는 데 도움을 준다 / 그리고 근거를 만든다 (승진을 위한)
↳ **예:** 큰 발견은 대대적으로 인정받음.

[5] But it's wrong.
(it = being too obsessed with results)
그러나 그것(결과에 너무 집착하는 것)은 잘못된 것이다
↳ 결과 지향적인 과학은 옳지 않음.

[6] Great scientists, / *the pioneers* [that we admire], / are not concerned with results but (concerned) with the next questions.
(Great scientists: S / = the pioneers / that: 목적격 관계대명사 / are: V / concerned with results: C / ★<not A but B>: A가 아니라 B / (concerned): 반복어 생략)
🔑 위대한 과학자는 질문(모르는 것)에 관심 있음.
위대한 과학자들은 / 선구자들인 [우리가 존경하는] / 결과가 아니라 그다음 질문들에 관심이 있다
↳ **논거:** 결과가 아닌 다음 질문들에 관심을 가져야 함.

[7] The highly respected physicist Enrico Fermi told his students // that *an experiment* [that successfully proves a hypothesis] / is a measurement; // *one* [that doesn't (successfully prove a hypothesis)] / is discovery.
(The highly respected physicist Enrico Fermi: S / told: V / his students: IO / that: 명사절 접속사, told의 DO(명사절) / that successfully: 주격 관계대명사 / one: (= an experiment) / that doesn't: 수격 관계대명사 / (successfully prove a hypothesis): 반복어구 생략)
아주 존경받는 물리학자인 Enrico Fermi는 자신의 학생들에게 말했다 // 실험은 [가설을 성공적으로 입증하는] / 측정이라고 // 그리고 실험은 [그렇지 않은] / 발견이라고

[8] A discovery, an uncovering — / of new ignorance.
🔑 무지를 드러내는 발견을 해야 함.
발견, 즉 드러내는 것 / 새로운 무지를
↳ **예:** 가설을 입증하지 못하는 실험은 새로운 무지를 드러내는 발견임.

[9] The Nobel Prize, the pinnacle of scientific accomplishment, / is awarded, / not for a lifetime of scientific achievement, / but for a single discovery, a result.
(The Nobel Prize: S / = the pinnacle of scientific accomplishment / is awarded: V / not for ... / but for ...: 전치사구 병렬)
과학적 성취의 정점인 노벨상은 / 수여된다 / 평생의 과학적인 업적에 대해서가 아니라 / 하나의 발견, 즉 결과에 대해
↳ **비판:** 노벨상조차도 결과 중심적임.

해석

[1]비록 명시적인 목표는 아니지만, 최고의 과학은 실제로 무지를 정제하는 것(▶ 무지를 명료하게 하여 드러내는 것을 의미)으로 여겨질 수 있다. [2]과학자들, 특히 젊은 과학자들은 결과에 너무 집착하게 될 수 있다. [3]사회는 그들을 도와서 이 어리석은 추구를 하게 한다. [4]큰 발견들이 언론에 보도되고, 대학의 홈페이지에 등장하고, 보조금을 받는 데 도움을 주고, 승진을 위한 근거를 만든다. [5]그러나 그것은 잘못된 것이다. [6]우리가 존경하는 선구자들인 위대한 과학자들은 결과가 아니라 그다음 질문들에 관심이 있다. [7]아주 존경받는 물리학자인 Enrico Fermi는 자신의 학생들에게 가설을 성공적으로 입증하는 실험은 측정이며, 그렇지 않은 것은 발견이라고 말했다. [8]새로운 무지의 발견, 즉 (새로운 무지를) 드러내는 것이라고. [9]과학적 성취의 정점인 노벨상은 평생의 과학적인 업적에 대해서가 아니라 하나의 발견, 즉 결과에 대해 수여된다. [10]노벨상 위원회조차도 어떤 점에서는 이것이 실제로 과학의 진정한 의미 속에 있는 것이 아니라는 것을 인식하고 있으며, 그들의 상에 쓰인 문구들은 흔히 '한 분야를 연', '한 분야를 변화시킨', 혹은 '한 분야를 새롭고 예상치 못한 방향으로 이끈' 발견을 기린다.

어휘

explicit 명시적인, 명백한
refine 정제하다; 개선[개량]하다
ignorance 무지, 무식
obsessed with ~에 집착하는[사로잡힌]
help A along A를 도와서 나아가게 하다
chase 추구, 쫓음
cover 보도하다; 가리다, 덮다
grant 보조금; 승인[허락]하다; 수여하다
pioneer 선구자, 개척자
admire 존경하다
be concerned with ~에 관심이 있다
hypothesis 가설
measurement 측정, 측량; 치수
accomplishment 업적, 성취
committee 위원회
spirit 진정한 의미; 정신, 영혼
citation 인용(구)
[선택지] ultimate 궁극[최종]적인
account 설명; (예금) 계좌
existing 기존의, 현재의

[10]Even the Nobel committee realizes / in some way // that this is not really in the scientific spirit, //
S₁ V₁ 명사절 접속사 O₁(명사절)
노벨상 위원회조차도 인식하고 있다 / 어떤 점에서는 // 이것이 실제로 과학의 진정한 의미 속에 있는 것이 아니라는 것을 //
(= committee's) 노벨상은 무지를 드러낸 발견에 경의를 표함.
and their award citations commonly honor the discovery (for having "opened a field up," / "transformed a field," / or "taken a field in new and unexpected directions.")
S₂ V₂ O₂
그래서 그들(노벨상 위원회)의 상에 쓰인 문구들은 흔히 발견을 기린다 ('한 분야를 연,' / '한 분야를 변화시킨,' / 혹은 '한 분야를 새롭고 예상치 못한 방향으로 이끈')
*동명사의 완료형(having p.p.)을 써서 문장의 동사 honor보다 이전 일임을 나타냄.
↳ 이를 인식해 노벨상의 문구는 무지를 드러낸 발견을 기림.

objective 객관적인; 목적, 목표
inspire 고무시키다; 영감을 주다
publicize 발표하다; 홍보하다
significant 중요한, 의미 있는

정답 가이드

지나치게 결과 지향적인 과학을 비판하며 위대한 과학자들은 결과가 아닌 무지의 발견이 가져오는 그다음의 질문에 관심이 있다고 했다. 여기서 무지의 발견이란 가설을 성공적으로 입증하지 못한 실험이 드러내는 것이라고 했으므로, 밑줄 친 부분이 의미하는 바로 가장 적절한 것은 ① 'looking beyond what is known towards what is left unknown(알려진 것을 넘어서 알려지지 않은 채로 있는 것을 향해 보는 것)'임을 알 수 있다.

The 핵심 result가 what is known에, new ignorance가 what is left unknown에 대응되는 개념임을 파악할 수 있어야 한다.

오답 클리닉

② offering an ultimate account of what has been discovered (15%)
발견된 것에 대한(×) 궁극적인 설명을 제공하는 것
발견된 것, 즉 이미 아는 것이 아닌 모르는 것을 탐구해야 한다고 했으므로 글의 내용과 반대됨.

③ analyzing existing knowledge with an objective mindset (10%)
객관적인 사고방식(×)을 가지고 기존의 지식을 분석하는 것(×)
객관적인 사고방식에 대한 언급은 없으며 기존 지식을 분석하는 것은 새로운 무지를 드러내는 발견과 반대됨.

④ inspiring scientists to publicize significant discoveries (14%)
과학자들이 중요한 발견(×)을 발표하도록(×) 고무시키는 것
중요한 발견은 결과(result)에 해당하며 발표에 관한 내용도 아님.

⑤ informing students of a new field of science (9%)
과학의 새로운 분야에 대해 학생들에게 알려주는 것(×)
과학 분야를 학생들에게 알려준다는 내용은 언급되지 않음.

02 + 빈칸 추론 (18학년도 6월 모평 32번 | 정답률 43%) ②

구문분석 & 직독직해

정치 정치적 의견 차이의 필요성

[1]Politics cannot be suppressed, // whichever policy process is employed // and however sensitive and respectful of differences it might be.
S V(조동사+수동태) 양보 부사절 병렬 (= policy process)
*whichever(어느 쪽을 ~하더라도)는 복합관계형용사로 명사를 수식하며 양보의 부사절을 이끎.
정치적 견해는 억압될 수 없다 // 어떤 정책 과정이 사용되더라도 // 그리고 아무리 그 정책 과정이 세심하고 차이를 존중할지라도

[2]In other words, / there is no end / to politics.
V S
다시 말해 / 끝이 없다 / 정치적 견해에는
↳ **도입:** 정치적 견해는 억압될 수 없고 다양하게 존재함.

(→ to think의 O(명사절)) 의견 차이를 없앨 수 있다는 생각은 틀림.
[3]It is wrong to think // that proper institutions, knowledge, methods of consultation, or participatory mechanisms can make disagreement go away.
가주어 진주어(to-v구) 명사절 접속사 S′ V′ O′ C′
*<사역동사 make+O+원형부정사(v)>: O가 v하게 만들다
(~라고) 생각하는 것은 틀리다 // 적절한 제도, 지식, 협의 방법, 혹은 참여 기구가 의견 차이를 사라지게 할 수 있다고
↳ **세부 사항 1:** 어떤 방법으로도 정치적 의견 차이는 없앨 수 없음.

[4]Theories of all sorts promote the view // that there are *ways* [by which disagreement can be processed or managed / so as to make it disappear].
S V O (=) 동격 접속사 전치사+관계대명사
~하기 위해(= in order to) (= disagreement)
온갖 종류의 이론이 견해를 조장한다 // 방법들이 있다는 [의견 차이가 처리되거나 다뤄질 수 있는 / 그것(의견 차이)을 없애기 위해]

(→ is의 C(명사절))
[5]The assumption (behind those theories) / is // that disagreement is wrong // and consensus is the desirable state of things.
S(단수) V(단수) 명사절 접속사 S′₁ V′₁ C′₁ S′₂ V′₂ C′₂
전제는 (그런 이론들 뒤에 있는) / ~이다 // 의견 차이는 잘못된 것이라는 것 // 그리고 합의가 바람직한 상태라는 것

해석

[1]어떤 정책 과정이 사용되더라도, 그리고 아무리 그 정책 과정이 세심하고 차이를 존중할지라도, 정치적 견해는 억압될 수 없다. [2]다시 말해, 정치적 견해에는 끝이 없다. [3]적절한 제도, 지식, 협의 방법, 혹은 참여 기구가 의견 차이를 사라지게 할 수 있다고 생각하는 것은 틀리다. [4]온갖 종류의 이론이 의견 차이를 없애기 위해 그것이 처리되거나 다뤄질 수 있는 방법들이 있다는 견해를 조장한다. [5]그런 이론들 뒤에 있는 전제는 의견 차이는 잘못된 것이고 합의가 바람직한 상태라는 것이다. [6]사실, 몇몇 형태의 교묘한 강압 없이는 합의는 거의 일어나지 않으며, 의견 차이를 표현함에 있어서 두려움의 결여가 진정한 자유의 원천이다. [7]논쟁은 종종 더 나은 방향으로 의견 차이가 전개되게 하지만, 긍정적으로 전개되는 논쟁이 반드시 의견 차이의 감소와 같은 것은 아니다. [8]의견 차이의 억압은 결코 정치적 토의에서 목표가 되어서는 안 된다. [9]정치적 의견 차이가 정상적인 상태는 아니라는 어떠한 생각에도 맞서는 방어가 필요하다.

어휘

politics 정치적 견해; 정치(학)
suppress 억압하다; (감정을) 억누르다, 참다
cf. suppression 억압, 억제; 진압
policy 정책, 방침

🔑 '합의'는 강압 없이 발생하는 경우가 드묾 → 부정적 인식.

[6]In fact, / consensus rarely comes / without some forms of subtle coercion // and the absence (of fear) / in expressing a disagreement / is a source (of genuine freedom).

S1 V1 S2 V2 C2

사실 / 합의는 거의 일어나지 않는다 / 몇몇 형태의 교묘한 강압 없이는 //
그리고 결여가 (두려움의) / 의견 차이를 표현함에 있어 / 원천이다 (진정한 자유의)

↳ **세부 사항 2:** 의견 차이를 부정적으로, 합의를 긍정적으로 보는 시각과 달리 합의는 보통 강압 없이 이루어지지 않음.

★<cause+O+to-v>: O가 v하게 하다

[7]Debates cause disagreements to evolve, / often for the better, // but a positively evolving debate does not have to equal / a reduction (in disagreement).

S1 V1 O1 C1 S2 V2 O2

논쟁은 의견 차이가 전개되게 한다 / 종종 더 나은 방향으로 //
하지만 긍정적으로 전개되는 논쟁은 반드시 ~와 같지는 않다 / 감소 (의견 차이의)

↳ **세부 사항 3:** 의견 차이가 줄어든다고 반드시 좋은 논쟁은 아님.

주제문

🔑 '의견 차이'를 억압해서는 안 됨.

[8]The suppression (of disagreement) / should never be made into a goal / in political deliberation.

S V

억압은 (의견 차이의) / 결코 목표가 되어서는 안 된다 / 정치적 토의에서

[9]A defense is required / against any suggestion // that **political disagreement is not the normal state of things**.

S V 동격 접속사 S′ V′ C′

방어가 필요하다 / 어떠한 생각에도 맞서는 // 정치적 의견 차이가 정상적인 상태는 아니라는

↳ **결론:** 의견 차이는 억압되어서는 안 되며 의견 차이를 나쁘게 보는 것을 경계해야 함.

employ 사용하다; 고용하다
sensitive 세심한; 민감한, 예민한
respectful of ~을 존중하는
proper 적절한, 알맞은
institution 제도; 기관; 조직
consultation 협의, 상의; 회담
participatory 참여[참가]의
mechanism 기구, 조직; 기계 장치; 절차, 방법
disagreement 의견 차이[충돌]; 불일치
promote 조장하다; 홍보하다; 승진시키다
assumption 전제, 추정; 가정
state 상태, 형세
subtle 교묘한; 미묘한, 감지하기 힘든
genuine 진정한; 진짜의
evolve 전개[발전]되다; 진화하다
equal ~와 같다; 동일한; 동등한
deliberation 토의, 심의; 숙고
defense 방어, 수비
suggestion 생각, 계획; 제안
[선택지] freedom of speech 언론의 자유
restrict 제한[한정]하다
tolerance 관용, 용인

정답 가이드

필자가 맞서야 한다고 한 생각이 무엇인지를 추론해야 한다. 따라서 필자가 '긍정적으로 생각하는 것과 반대'이거나 또는 '부정적으로 생각하는 것'을 찾으면 된다. 앞에서부터 살펴보면, 정치적 견해는 억압될 수 없고, 의견 차이를 없앨 수 있다고 생각하는 것은 틀리며, 진정한 자유는 의견 차이를 두려움 없이 표현할 수 있는 것이라고 했다. 또한 빈칸 앞 문장에서 의견 차이의 억압이 정치적 토의의 목표가 되어서는 안 된다고 했다. 이들은 모두 '정치적 의견 차이를 억압하는 것'을 부정적으로 바라보는 것이므로, 빈칸에 들어갈 말로 가장 적절한 것은 ② 'political disagreement is not the normal state of things(정치적 의견 차이가 정상적인 상태는 아니다)'이다.

오답 클리닉

① political development results from the freedom of speech (13%)
정치적 발전은 언론의 자유에서 비롯된다
문장 6에서 이견 표현에 두려움이 없는 것이 진정한 자유라고 했지만, 언론의 자유에 대한 언급은 없음.

③ politics should not restrict any form of difference (16%)
정치는 어떤 형태의 차이도 제한해서는 안 된다
의견 차이의 형태는 언급되지 않았으며, 의견 차이를 제한하면 안 된다는 내용임.

④ freedom could be achieved only through tolerance (7%)
자유는 관용을 통해서만 성취될 수 있다
자유 성취에 관한 내용이 아니며 관용에 대한 언급도 없음.

⑤ suppression could never be a desirable tool in politics (18%)
억압은 정치에서 절대 바람직한 도구가 될 수 없다
빈칸에 들어갈 맞서야 하는 생각은 글의 주제와 반대되는 내용이어야 하는데, 정치적 억압을 부정적으로 보는 것은 필자의 주장과 같으므로 틀림.

03 + 무관 문장 〈20학년도 6월 모평 35번 | 정답률 60%〉 ④

구문분석 & 직독직해

생물 감정적 자극을 활용한 개의 훈련과 보상

↳ 부사절 접속사(시간) ★<train+O+to-v(O가 v하도록 훈련시키다)>의 수동형

[1]When a dog is trained / to detect drugs, explosives, contraband, or other items, // the trainer doesn't actually teach the dog / how to smell; // the dog already knows / how to discriminate one scent from another.

S′ V′ C′ S1 V1 IO1 DO1

개가 훈련받을 때 / 마약, 폭발물, 밀수품, 또는 다른 품목들을 탐지하도록 //
훈련사는 개에게 실제로 가르치지 않는다 / 냄새를 맡는 법을 //

★<discriminate A from B>: A와 B를 구별하다

S2 V2 O2

개는 이미 알고 있다 / 하나의 냄새를 다른 냄새와 구별하는 법을

↳ **도입:** 탐지견 훈련사는 개에게 냄새를 맡는 법을 가르치지 않음.

해석

[1]개가 마약, 폭발물, 밀수품, 또는 다른 품목들을 탐지하도록 훈련받을 때, 훈련사는 개에게 냄새를 맡는 법을 실제로 가르치지 않는데, 개는 이미 하나의 냄새를 다른 냄새와 구별하는 법을 알고 있기 때문이다. [2]오히려 개는 다른 냄새와 비교하여 한 냄새에 의해 감정적으로 자극받도록 훈련받는다. ① [3]단계적인 훈련 과정에서, 훈련사는 '감정적 자극'을 어느 특정한 냄새에 부여해서 개가 다른 어떤 냄새보다도 그 냄새에 끌리도록 한다. ② [4]그 다음에, 그 개는 훈련사가 (탐지) 행동을 통제하

주제문 ⊶ 감정적 자극을 이용한 탐지견 훈련에 관한 내용임.

[2] Rather, / the dog is trained to become emotionally aroused / by one smell / versus another.
S V C(to-v구)
오히려 / 개는 감정적으로 자극받도록 훈련받는다 / 한 냄새에 의해 / 다른 냄새와 비교하여
↳ 개는 한 냄새에 감정적으로 자극을 받도록 훈련됨.

*<attach A to B>: A를 B에 부여하다

① [3] In the step-by-step training process, / the trainer attaches an "emotional charge" to a particular scent // so that the dog is drawn to it / above all others.
S V O
부사절 접속사(~하도록) S′ V′ (= the particular scent)
단계적인 훈련 과정에서 / 훈련사는 '감정적 자극'을 어느 특정한 냄새에 부여한다 // 개가 그 냄새에 끌리도록 / 다른 어떤 냄새보다도

② [4] And then the dog is trained to search out the desired item / on cue, //
S V C
↱ 부사절 접속사(~하도록)
so that the trainer can control or release the behavior.
S′ V′ O′
그다음에 그 개는 (찾기를) 원하는 품목을 찾아내도록 훈련받는다 / 신호에 따라 //
훈련사가 (탐지) 행동을 통제하거나 그만두게 할 수 있도록
↳ **세부 사항 1(훈련):** 개가 특정한 냄새에 감정적 자극을 느끼게 만들어 신호에 따라 그 냄새를 찾도록 훈련함.

*why는 문장의 보어 역할을 하는 명사절을 이끎.

③ [5] This emotional arousal is also // (the reason) why playing tug with a dog is a more powerful emotional reward / in a training regime / than just giving a dog a food treat, //
S V 선행사 생략 관계부사 S′(동명사구) V′(단수) C′
이 감정적 자극은 또한 ~이다 // 개와 당기기 놀이를 하는 것이 더 강력한 감정적 보상인 이유
/ 훈련 체제에서 / 그저 개에게 특별한 먹이를 주는 것보다 //
↱ 부사절 접속사(~ 때문에)
since the trainer invests more emotion / into a game of tug.
S″ V″ O″
훈련사가 더 많은 감정을 투입하기 때문에 / 당기기 놀이에
↳ **세부 사항 2(보상):** 감정적 자극은 당기기 놀이로 감정적 보상을 주는 것이 먹이보다 더 좋은 이유임.

⊶ 감정적 자극이라는 글의 주제와 무관한 먹이 보상에 관한 내용임.

④ [6] As long as the trainer gives the dog a food reward regularly, // the dog can understand //
부사절 접속사(~하는 한) S′ V′ IO′ DO′ S V
↱ can understand의 O(명사절)
(that) its "good" behavior results in rewards.
명사절 접속사 생략 S′ V′ O′
훈련사가 개에게 규칙적으로 먹이 보상을 주는 한 // 개는 이해할 수 있다 // 자신의 '좋은' 행동이 보상을 야기한다는 것을
↳ 규칙적으로 먹이를 주면 개는 좋은 행동에 보상이 따름을 이해할 수 있음.

⑤ [7] From a dog's point of view, / the tug toy is compelling // because the trainer is "upset" / by the toy.
S V C(현재분사) 부사절 접속사(이유) S′ V′ C′
개의 관점에서 / 그 당기기 장난감은 흥미를 돋운다 // 훈련사가 '마음이 동요하기' 때문에 /
그 장난감에 의해
↳ **세부 사항 2의 부연 설명:** 당기기 놀이에는 훈련사의 감정이 담기기 때문에 개가 좋아함.

거나 그만두게 할 수 있도록 신호에 따라 원하는 품목을 찾아내도록 훈련받는다. ③ [5] 이 감정적 자극은 또한 개와 당기기 놀이를 하는 것이 그저 개에게 특별한 먹이를 주는 것보다 훈련 체제에서 더 강력한 감정적 보상인 이유인데, 훈련사가 당기기 놀이에 더 많은 감정을 투입하기 때문이다.(▶ 먹이보다 당기기 놀이가 더 큰 보상인 이유는 사람이 당기기 놀이에 감정을 투입하기 때문인데, 그러므로 개의 행동을 강화하기 위해 감정적 자극을 준다는 의미) ④ [6] 훈련사가 개에게 규칙적으로 먹이 보상을 주는 한, 개는 자신의 '좋은' 행동이 보상을 야기한다는 것을 이해할 수 있다. ⑤ [7] 개의 관점에서, 그 당기기 장난감은 훈련사가 그 장난감에 의해 '마음이 동요하기' 때문에 흥미를 돋운다.

어휘

detect 탐지하다, 찾다
explosive 폭발물; 폭발성의
scent 냄새, 향기
arouse 자극하다, 각성시키다
cf. arousal 자극, 흥분
step-by-step 단계적인
charge 자극, 흥분; 요금; 청구하다
draw 끌다, 당기다; 그리다
search out ~을 찾아내다
cue 신호, 단서
regime 체제, 제도; 정권
treat 특별한 것; 다루다
invest 투입하다, 투자하다
result in ~을 야기하다[낳다]
point of view 관점
compelling 흥미를 돋우는; 설득력 있는, 강력한

정답 가이드

도입 부분에서 개는 불법물을 탐지하도록 훈련받을 때 한 냄새에 감정적으로 자극받도록 훈련된다고 했으므로 이에 대한 구체적인 내용이 나올 것임을 예측할 수 있다. 이어서 훈련 내용에 대한 설명이 나오고, 감정적 자극을 주는 이유는 그것이 먹이보다 더 강력하게 개의 행동을 강화하기 때문이라고 했다. 그런데, ④는 규칙적인 먹이 보상으로 개의 좋은 행동을 강화한다는 내용이므로 ③과 논리적으로 연결되지 않는다. ③은 ⑤에서 개가 당기기 놀이를 흥미 있어 하는 이유와 더 잘 이어진다.

The 주의 ④의 a food reward는 ③의 a food treat에 연결되는 것처럼 보이기 위한 함정임에 주의한다. 먹이 보상은 감정적 보상을 주는 당기기 놀이와 비교하기 위해 언급된 것이다.

오답 클리닉

① (2%), ② (8%) 개가 한 냄새에 감정적으로 자극받도록 훈련된다는 앞 문장의 내용을 받아 그 과정을 상세히 설명하는 연결은 자연스럽다.
③ (14%) 훈련에서 보상으로 감정적 자극을 주는 것이 효과적임을 당기기 놀이를 예로 들어 설명한다.
⑤ (15%) 당기기 놀이는 감정적 자극이 있기 때문에 개가 좋아한다고 이유를 부연 설명한다.

01 ✦ 밑줄 어법 〈21학년도 대수능 29번 | 정답률 60%〉 ⑤

구문분석 & 직독직해

과학 과학자의 자기 실험의 위험성

[1] *Regulations* (covering scientific experiments on human subjects) / are strict.
S(복수) 현재분사구 V(복수) C
규정은 (인간 피험자에 관한 과학 실험을 다루는) / 엄격하다

[2] Subjects must give their informed, written consent, //
S₁ V₁ O₁
피험자는 충분한 설명에 입각한 서면으로 된 동의를 해야 한다 //

and experimenters must submit their proposed experiments / to thorough examination by overseeing bodies.
S₂ V₂ O₂
그리고 실험자는 자신들의 계획된 실험을 제출해야 한다 / 감독하는 단체에 의한 철저한 조사에

*조동사와 동사원형 사이에 부사절(functionally ~ legally)이 삽입됨.

[3] *Scientists* [who experiment on themselves] / can, (functionally if not legally), avoid *the restrictions* (① **associated** with experimenting on other people).
S 주격 관계대명사 V O 과거분사구
과학자들은 [자기 자신에게 실험하는] / (법률상으로는 아니라도 직무상으로는) 규제를 피할 수 있다 (다른 사람들에게 실험하는 것과 관련된)

(= Scientists ~ on themselves)
[4] They can also sidestep most of the ethical issues involved: //
S₁ V₁ O
그들(자기 자신에게 실험하는 과학자들)은 또한 관련된 윤리적 문제도 대부분 피할 수 있다 //

nobody, presumably, is more aware / of an experiment's potential hazards / than *the scientist* [who devised ② **it**].
S₂ V₂ C 주격 관계대명사
(= the experiment)
더 잘 알고 있는 사람은 짐작건대 아무도 없기 때문이다 / 실험의 잠재적인 위험을 / 과학자보다 [그것(실험)을 고안한]

주제문

[5] Nonetheless, / experimenting on oneself remains ③ **deeply** problematic.
S V C
그럼에도 불구하고 / 자신에게 실험하는 것은 여전히 매우 문제가 있다

[6] One obvious drawback is the danger involved; //
S₁ V₁ C
한 가지 분명한 문제점은 (실험에) 수반되는 위험이다 //

(= the danger)
knowing // that it exists / ④ **does** nothing / to reduce it.
S₂(단수) knowing의 O(명사절) V₂(단수) O 목적(~하기 위해)
아는 것은 // 위험이 존재한다는 것을 / 아무 것도 하지 않는다 / 위험을 줄이기 위해

[7] A less obvious drawback is / *the limited range of data* [that the experiment can generate].
S V C 목적격 관계대명사
덜 분명한 문제점은 ~이다 / 한정된 범위의 데이터 [실험이 초래할 수 있는]

[8] Human anatomy and physiology vary, / in small but significant ways, / according to gender, age, lifestyle, and other factors.
S V
인체의 해부학적 구조와 생리적 현상은 각기 다르다 / 사소하지만 중요한 방식으로 / 성별, 나이, 생활 방식, 그리고 기타 요인에 따라

[9] *Experimental results* (derived from a single subject) / are, therefore, of limited value; //
S₁(복수) 과거분사구 V₁(복수) C
실험 결과는 (단 한 명의 피험자로부터 나온) / 그러므로 가치가 제한적이다 //

to know의 O(명사절)
there is *no way* (to know // ⑤ **what**(→ **whether**) the subject's responses are typical or atypical / of the response of humans (as a group)).
V₂ S₂ 명사절 접속사 S' V' C'
방법이 없다 (알 // 그 피험자의 반응이 대표하는 것인지 아니면 이례적인 것인지를 / 인간 반응을 (집단으로서의))

해석

[1]인간 피험자에 관한 과학 실험을 다루는 규정은 엄격하다. [2]피험자는 충분한 설명에 입각한 서면으로 된 동의를 해야 하고, 실험자는 감독하는 단체에 의한 철저한 조사에 자신들의 계획된 실험을 제출해야 한다. [3]자기 자신에게 실험하는 과학자들은, 법률적으로는 아니라도 직무상으로는 다른 사람들에게 실험하는 것과 관련된 규제를 피할 수 있다. [4]그들은 또한 관련된 윤리적 문제도 대부분 피할 수 있는데, 실험을 고안한 과학자보다 실험의 잠재적인 위험을 더 잘 알고 있는 사람은 짐작건대 아무도 없기 때문이다. [5]그럼에도 불구하고, 자신에게 실험하는 것은 여전히 매우 문제가 있다. [6]한 가지 분명한 문제점은 (실험에) 수반되는 위험인데, 위험이 존재한다는 것을 아는 것은 위험을 줄이기 위해 아무것도 하지 않는다.(▶ 위험이 존재한다는 것을 아는 것만으로는 위험을 줄일 수 없다는 의미) [7]덜 분명한 문제점은 실험이 초래할 수 있는 한정된 범위의 데이터이다. [8]인체의 해부학적 구조와 생리적 현상은 성별, 나이, 생활 방식, 그리고 기타 요인에 따라 사소하지만 중요한 방식으로 각기 다르다. [9]그러므로, 단 한 명의 피험자로부터 나온 실험 결과는 가치가 제한적이며, 그 피험자의 반응이 집단으로서의 인간 반응을 대표하는 것인지 아니면 이례적인 것인지 알 방법이 없다.

어휘

regulation 규정, 규제
cover 다루다, 포함시키다; 덮다
subject 피험자, 실험 대상; 주제; 과목
propose 계획하다; 제안하다
thorough 철저한; 철두철미한
oversee 감독[감시]하다
functionally 직무상으로; 기능적으로
if not ~까지는 아니라 하더라도
restriction 규제, 제한
associated with ~와 관련된
sidestep 피하다; 회피하다
presumably 짐작건대, 아마
potential 잠재적인, 가능성이 있는; 가능성
hazard 위험 (요소)
devise 고안하다, 생각해 내다
drawback 문제점, 결점
generate 초래하다, 일으키다; 만들어 내다
typical 대표적인, 전형적인(↔ atypical 이례적인)

정답 가이드

⑤ **[what vs. 명사절 접속사 whether]**
뒤에 완전한 구조(SVC)의 절이 이어지고 있으므로 관계대명사(~하는 것)나 의문대명사(무엇) 역할을 하는 what은 쓸 수 없다. '~인지 (아닌지)'를 의미하면서 to know의 목적어 역할을 하는 명사절을 이끄는 접속사 whether로 고쳐야 한다.

오답 클리닉

① **[능동(v-ing) vs. 수동(p.p.)]** (3%)
문맥상 '관련된, 연관된'을 의미하므로 associated는 어법상 적절하다. associating with는 '(사람들)과 어울리는'의 의미로 쓰인다.

② **[대명사]** (15%)
과학자들이 고안한 것은 문맥상 potential hazards가 아니라 an experiment이므로, 이를 대신하는 단수 대명사 it은 어법상 적절하다.

③ **[형용사 vs. 부사]** (8%)
형용사 problematic을 수식하는 부사 deeply는 어법상 적절하다.

④ **[v-ing(동명사)구 주어+단수동사]** (14%)
동명사구 knowing that it(= the danger) exists가 아무 것도 하지 않는다는 의미이므로 주어에 해당한다. 동명사구 주어는 단수 취급하므로 단수동사 does는 어법상 적절하다. does 바로 앞의 that it exists는 knowing의 목적어절이다.

02 + 빈칸 추론 (18학년도 6월 모평 31번 | 정답률 59%) ①

구문분석 & 직독직해

과학 지질학에서 시간 척도의 중요성

🔑 아주 긴 시간에 관심을 둠.
★<set A apart from B>: A를 B와 구별하다

[1]Interest (in extremely long periods of time) / sets geology and astronomy / apart from other sciences.
(S / V / O)
관심은 (매우 긴 시간에 대한) / 지질학과 천문학을 구별한다 / 다른 과학들과
↳ 지질학과 천문학은 매우 긴 시간을 다룸.

🔑 지질학자들은 수십억 년의 시간에 대해 연구함.

[2]Geologists think / in terms of billions of years / for the age (of Earth and its oldest rocks) — / numbers [that, (like the national debt), / are not easily comprehended].
(S / V; 주격 관계대명사 that; 전치사구 삽입; V′)
★대시(—) 이하는 billions of years에 대한 부연 설명임.
지질학자들은 생각한다 / 수십억 년의 관점에서 / 나이에 대해 (지구와 가장 오래된 암석들의) / 숫자인 [(국가 부채처럼) / 쉽게 이해되지 않는]
↳ 지질학자들은 보통 사람들은 이해하기 어려운 수십억 년의 관점에서 연구함.

주제문

[3]Nevertheless, / the **time scales (of geological activity)** / are important / for environmental geologists //
(S(복수) / V(복수) / C)
그럼에도 불구하고 / 시간 척도는 (지질 활동의) / 중요하다 / 환경 지질학자들에게 //
🔑 '빈칸'은 자연계에 미친 인간의 영향을 측정하는 방법을 제공함.

because they provide / *a way* (to measure human impacts / on the natural world).
(부사절 접속사 / S′ (= the time ~ activity) / V′ / O′)
그것들(지질 활동의 시간 척도)이 제공하기 때문에 / 방법을 (인간의 영향을 측정하는 / 자연계에 미친)
↳ 지질 활동의 시간 척도는 자연계에 미친 인간의 영향을 측정하는 데 중요함.

🔑 인간의 영향을 알기 위해 토양 형성 속도를 연구함.

[4]For example, / we would like to know / the rate (of natural soil formation (from solid rock)) / to determine // whether topsoil erosion from agriculture is too great.
(S / V / O; 목적(~하기 위해); 명사절 접속사 → to determine의 O(명사절); S′ / V′ / C′)
예를 들어 / 우리는 알고 싶어 한다 / 속도를 (자연 토양 형성의 (단단한 암석으로부터의)) / 알아내기 위해 // 농업으로 인한 표토 침식이 너무 심한지를
↳ **예 1:** 농업에 의한 표토 침식 정도를 알기 위해 토양 형성의 속도를 알고자 함.

🔑 지구 온난화 추세를 가늠하기 위해 수백만 년의 기후 변화를 연구함.

[5]Likewise, / understanding // how climate has changed over millions of years / is vital / to properly assess current global warming trends.
(S(동명사구) / 동명사 understanding의 O(명사절) / V(단수) / C; 목적(~하기 위해))
마찬가지로 / 이해하는 것은 // 수백만 년에 걸쳐 기후가 어떻게 변해 왔는지를 / 매우 중요하다 / 현재의 지구 온난화 추세를 제대로 가늠하기 위해
↳ **예 2:** 지구 온난화 추세를 알기 위해 수백만 년에 걸친 기후의 변화를 이해해야 함.

해석

[1]매우 긴 시간에 대한 관심은 지질학과 천문학을 다른 과학들과 구별한다. [2]지질학자들은 지구와 가장 오래된 암석들의 나이에 대해, 국가 부채처럼 쉽게 이해되지 않는 숫자인 수십억 년의 관점에서 생각한다. [3]그럼에도 불구하고, 지질 활동의 시간 척도는 자연계에 미친 인간의 영향을 측정하는 방법을 제공하기 때문에 환경 지질학자들에게 중요하다. [4]예를 들어, 우리는 농업으로 인한 표토 침식이 너무 심한지를 알아내기 위해 단단한 암석으로부터의 자연 토양 형성의 속도를 알고 싶어 한다. [5]마찬가지로, 수백만 년에 걸쳐 기후가 어떻게 변해 왔는지를 이해하는 것은 현재의 지구 온난화 추세를 제대로 가늠하기 위해 매우 중요하다. [6]과거의 환경 변화에 대한 단서들은 서로 다른 많은 종류의 암석들에 잘 보존되어 있다.

어휘

geology 지질학
cf. geologist 지질학자
cf. geological 지질학의
astronomy 천문학
in terms of ~의 관점[면]에서
national debt 국가 부채
scale 척도, 기준; 규모; 등급
formation 형성, 구성; 대형, 진형
solid 단단한; 고체의
determine 알아내다, 밝히다; 결심하다
topsoil 표토, 겉흙
erosion 침식 (작용); 부식
agriculture 농업
vital 매우 중요한, 필수적인; 활력이 넘치는
assess 가늠하다[재다]; 평가하다
current 현재의; 흐름

[6]Clues (to past environmental change) / are well preserved / in many different kinds of rocks.
S(복수) V(복수)
단서들은 (과거의 환경 변화에 대한) / 잘 보존되어 있다 / 서로 다른 많은 종류의 암석들에
↳ **예 2의 부연 설명:** 과거의 환경 변화에 대한 단서들은 암석들에서 찾을 수 있음.

preserve 보존하다
[선택지] diversity 다양성
perception 인식; 지각
statistical 통계(학)상의
projection 예측, 예상; 투사, 투영
classification 분류

정답 가이드

'무엇'이 자연계에 미친 인간의 영향을 측정하는 방법인지를 추론해야 한다. 빈칸 문장 뒤에 이어지는 예에서 제시한 암석이 토양이 되는 속도를 알아내는 것과 과거의 기후 변화를 이해하는 것은 오랜 시간에 걸쳐 이루어진 지질 활동을 연구하여 자연계에 미친 인간의 영향을 측정할 수 있다는 의미로 귀결된다. 따라서 빈칸에 들어갈 말로 가장 적절한 것은 ① 'time scales of geological activity(지질 활동의 시간 척도)'이다.

오답 클리닉

② global patterns in species diversity (9%)
종 다양성의 전반적인 패턴
종 다양성에 관한 내용이 아님.

③ regional differences in time perception (10%)
시간 인식에서의 지역차
문장 1에 다른 과학과 달리 지질학이 긴 시간에 관심을 둔다는 내용은 있지만 이것을 지역적 차이로 볼 수 없음.

④ statistical methods for climate projections (13%)
기후 예측을 위한 통계학상의 방법
문장 5의 기후(climate)에 대한 예를 활용한 오답.

⑤ criticisms of geological period classifications (7%)
지질 시대 분류에 대한 비판
지질학과 관련된 내용이긴 하지만 지질 시대 분류에 대해 비판하는 글이 아님.

03 + 글의 순서 (19학년도 6월 모평 37번 | 정답률 50%) ②

구문분석 & 직독직해 사회 소프트 파워 창출 노력이 낳은 풍요의 역설

주제문
[1]Promoting attractive images of one's country is not new, // but the conditions (for trying to create soft power) / have changed dramatically / in recent years.
S1(동명사구) V1(단수) C S2(복수) V2(복수)
국가의 매력적인 이미지를 홍보하는 것이 새로운 것은 아니다 // 하지만 환경은 (소프트 파워를 창출하려는 노력을 위한) / 극적으로 바뀌었다 / 최근 몇 년 동안에
↳ **도입:** 소프트 파워 창출을 위한 환경이 최근에 많이 바뀜.

[2]For one thing, / nearly half the countries in the world are now democracies.
S(부분 표현) V(복수) C
한 예로 / 전 세계 국가의 거의 절반이 현재 민주 국가이다

In such circumstances는 주어진 글의 전 세계 국가의 거의 절반이 민주 국가인 상황을 가리킴.
(B) [3]In such circumstances, / *diplomacy* (aimed at public opinion) / can become as important to outcomes / as traditional classified diplomatic communications (among leaders).
★<A as 원급 as B>: A는 B만큼 ~한[하게] S 과거분사구 V C
그러한 상황에서 / 외교는 (대중의 의견을 목표로 하는) / 결과에 중요할 수 있다 / 전통적인 비밀 외교 소통만큼 (지도자들 사이의)
↳ **세부 사항 1:** 민주 국가에서 여론을 대상으로 하는 외교가 중요해짐.

[4]Information creates power, // and today a much larger part of the world's population has access to that power.
S1 V1 O1 비교급 강조 부사 S2 V2 O2
정보는 권력을 창출한다 // 그리고 오늘날 세계 인구의 훨씬 더 많은 부분이 그 권력에 접근할 수 있다
↳ **세부 사항 2:** 정보가 곧 권력이며 오늘날 세계 인구의 대부분이 정보에 접근할 수 있음.

(B)의 정보에 접근할 수 있는 사람이 많아졌다는 내용을 부연 설명함.
(A) [5]Technological advances have led / to a dramatic reduction (in the cost of processing and transmitting information).
S V of의 O(동명사구)
기술 발전은 이어졌다 / 극적인 감소로 (정보를 처리하고 전달하는 비용의)

(= an explosion of information)
[6]The result is an explosion (of information), // and that has produced a "paradox of plenty."
S1 V1 C S2 V2 O
그 결과는 폭발적 증가이다 (정보의) // 그리고 그것(정보의 폭발적 증가)은 '풍요의 역설'을 낳았다

해석

[1]국가의 매력적인 이미지를 홍보하는 것이 새로운 것은 아니지만, 소프트 파워를 창출하려는 노력을 위한 환경은 최근 몇 년 동안에 극적으로 바뀌었다. [2]한 예로 전 세계 국가의 거의 절반이 현재 민주 국가이다. (B) [3]그러한 상황에서 대중의 의견을 목표로 하는 외교는 지도자들 사이의 전통적인 비밀 외교 소통만큼 결과에 중요할 수 있다. [4]정보는 권력을 창출하며, 오늘날 세계 인구의 훨씬 더 많은 부분이 그 권력에 접근할 수 있다. (A) [5]기술 발전은 정보를 처리하고 전달하는 비용의 극적인 감소로 이어졌다. [6]그 결과는 정보의 폭발적 증가이고, 그것은 '풍요의 역설'을 낳았다. [7]풍부한 정보는 주의력 부족을 초래한다. (C) [8]사람들은 자신들이 직면해 있는 정보의 양에 압도될 때, 무엇에 집중해야 할지를 아는 데 어려움을 겪는다. [9]정보보다는 주의력이 부족한 자원이 되고, 가치 있는 정보를 배경의 혼란과 구별해 낼 수 있는 사람이 권력을 얻는다.

어휘

promote 홍보하다; 촉진하다; 승진시키다
condition ((*pl.*)) 환경, 상황; 조건
dramatically 극적으로
democracy 민주 국가; 민주주의
circumstance ((주로 *pl.*)) 상황, 환경
diplomacy 외교(술)
cf. diplomatic 외교의
aim at ~을 목표로 하다, 대상으로 하다
outcome 결과

[7]Plentiful information leads to scarcity of attention.
S V O
풍부한 정보는 주의력 부족을 초래한다
↳ **부연 설명:** 정보 처리 및 전달 비용의 감소로 정보가 폭발적으로 증가하여 주의력 부족이라는 역설을 초래함.

(A)의 마지막 문장을 자세히 설명함.
(C) [8]When people are overwhelmed / with *the volume of information* (confronting them), //
부사절 접속사(시간) ★<have difficulty (in) v-ing>: v하는 데 어려움을 겪다 현재분사구
they have difficulty (in) knowing / what to focus on.
S V O 동명사 knowing의 O(명사구)
사람들이 압도될 때 / 정보의 양에 (자신들이 직면해 있는) //
그들은 아는 데 어려움을 겪는다 / 무엇에 집중해야 할지를
↳ **예:** 정보가 많으면 사람들은 어떤 정보에 중점을 두어야 할지를 어려워함.

[9]Attention, / (rather than information), / becomes the scarce resource, //
S_1 ~보다는 V_1 C
and *those* [who can distinguish valuable information / from background clutter] / gain power.
S_2 주격 관계대명사 ★<distinguish A from B>: A를 B와 구별하다 V_2 O
주의력이 / (정보보다는) / 부족한 자원이 된다 //
그리고 사람이 [가치 있는 정보를 구별할 수 있는 / 배경의 혼란과] / 권력을 얻는다
↳ **결론:** 가치 있는 정보를 잘 선별하는 사람이 권력을 갖게 됨.

classified 비밀[기밀]의; 주제별로 분류된
access 접근(권); 입수, 이용
advance 발전; 전진
transmit 전달[전송]하다
explosion 폭발(적 증가)
paradox 역설
plenty 풍요; 풍부[충분]한 (양)
cf. plentiful 풍부한
scarcity 부족, 결핍
cf. scarce 부족한, 불충분한; 드문
overwhelm 압도하다, 제압하다
volume 양, 부피
confront 직면하다; 맞서다
⊕ 소프트 파워(soft power): 정보 과학이나 문화·예술 등이 행사하는 영향력. 군사력이나 경제 제재 등 물리적으로 표현되는 힘인 하드 파워(hard power)에 대응하는 개념으로 강제력보다는 매력을 통해, 명령이 아닌 자발적 동의에 의해 얻어지는 능력을 뜻함.

정답 가이드

주어진 글은 소프트 파워 창출을 위한 환경이 최근 크게 바뀌었으며, 그 예로 전 세계 절반이 민주 국가임을 드는 내용이다. 이 내용을 (B)에서 In such circumstances로 받아 그러한 상황에서 대중의 의견을 목표로 하는 외교가 중요할 수 있다고 설명한다. 이어서, 많은 사람들이 정보에서 나오는 권력에 접근할 수 있다는 (B)의 마지막 내용 뒤에는 기술 발전으로 정보가 폭발적으로 증가하게 되었다고 원인을 부연 설명하는 (A)가 오는 것이 자연스럽다. (A)에서는 그 결과로 풍부한 정보가 주의력 부족을 초래한다고 했는데, (C)에서 이 주의력 부족을 좀 더 구체적으로 설명하고 이로 인한 결과를 서술하므로 (C)가 마지막에 오는 것이 자연스럽다.

오답 클리닉

① (A) - (C) - (B) (12%)
전 세계 절반이 민주 국가라는 주어진 글 바로 뒤에 기술적 발전으로 정보가 증가했다는 내용의 (A)가 이어지는 것은 흐름상 자연스럽지 않다.
③ (B) - (C) - (A) (19%)
(C)는 풍부한 정보가 주의력의 부족을 초래한다는 (A)의 마지막 문장을 예를 들어 상세히 설명하고 결론을 내리고 있으므로 (A) 뒤에 와야 한다.
④ (C) - (A) - (B) (12%) / ⑤ (C) - (B) - (A) (8%)
(C)는 (A)에서 언급한 '풍요의 역설'을 구체적으로 설명하는 내용이므로 주어진 글 뒤에 이어질 수 없다.

01 + 낱말 쓰임 (21학년도 대수능 30번 | 정답률 73%) ⑤

구문분석 & 직독직해

인지 빛의 속도 측정에 영향을 미친 편승 효과

[1] How the bandwagon effect occurs is demonstrated / by the history (of measurements of the speed of light).
S(명사절) V(단수, 수동)
편승 효과가 어떻게 일어나는지는 입증된다 / 역사에 의해 (빛의 속도 측정의)

🔑 ① 빛의 속도는 측정된 '(물리적) 양'에 해당함.
[2] Because this speed is the basis (of the theory of relativity), //
부사절 접속사(이유) S′ V′ C′
이 속도는 기초이기 때문에 (상대성 이론의) //
↳ (= the speed of light) ★<one of the+최상급+복수명사>: 가장 ~한 것 중 하나
it's one (of the most frequently and carefully measured ① **quantities** / in science).
S V C
그것(빛의 속도)은 하나이다 (가장 빈번하고 주의 깊게 측정된 양 중 / 과학에서)

[3] As far as we know, // the speed hasn't changed / over time.
부사절 접속사(~하는 한)
우리가 아는 한 // (빛의) 속도는 변함이 없었다 / 시간이 흘러도

[4] However, / from 1870 to 1900, / all the experiments found *speeds* [that were too high].
주격 관계대명사
그러나 / 1870년부터 1900년까지 / 모든 실험은 속도를 발견했다 [너무 빠른]

[5] Then, / from 1900 to 1950, / the ② **opposite** happened — // all the experiments found *speeds* [that were too low]! 🔑 ② 너무 높은 속도와 너무 낮은 속도는 서로 '반대됨'.
주격 관계대명사
그러고 나서 / 1900년부터 1950년까지 / 정반대의 일이 일어났다 // 모든 실험이 속도를 발견했다 [너무 느린]

★<call+O+C(O를 C라고 부르다)>의 수동형
[6] *This kind of error*, // where results are always on one side (of the real value), / is called "bias."
S 관계부사(추상적 장소) V C
이런 종류의 오류는 // 거기서 결과가 항상 한쪽에 있기 때문에 (실제 값의) / '편향'이라고 불린다

[7] It probably happened // because over time, experimenters subconsciously adjusted their results / to ③ **match** what they expected to find.
S(= bias) V 부사절 접속사(이유) S′ V′ O′
목적(~하기 위해) to match의 O(명사절)
그것은 아마 생겼을 것이다 // 시간이 흐르면서 실험자들이 잠재의식적으로 그 결과를 조정했기 때문에 / 자신들이 발견할 거라 예상한 것과 일치하도록

↳ 부사절 접속사(조건)
[8] If a result fit what they expected, // they kept it.
S′ V′ O′(명사절) S V O
결과가 그들이 예상한 것에 들어맞으면 // 그들은 그것을 유지했다

🔑 ③ 실험자들은 실험 결과가 예상한 것과 일치하기를 바라므로 결과를 예상값과 '일치하도록' 조정했을 것임.

[9] If a result didn't fit, // they threw it out.
부사절 접속사(조건) S V O
결과가 들어맞지 않으면 // 그들은 그것을 버렸다

🔑 ④ 실험자들이 부정직한 것은 고의가 아니라고 했으므로 일반 통념에 '영향을 받았을' 것임.
[10] They weren't being intentionally dishonest, / just ④ **influenced** / by the conventional wisdom.
S V C 분사구문(= and they were just influenced ~)
그들은 고의로 부정직하게 군 것은 아니었다 / 단지 영향을 받았을 뿐 / 일반 통념에 의해

🔑 ⑤ 일반 통념을 따르는 패턴은 실제로 측정된 것을 보고할 용기가 '있었을' 때 변했을 것임.
[11] The pattern only changed // when someone ⑤ **lacked(→ had)** *the courage* (to report what was actually measured / instead of what was expected).
S V 부사절 접속사(시간) S′ V′ O′ =
전치사(~ 대신에) of의 O(명사절)
그 패턴은 오직 ~에만 바뀌었다 // 누군가가 용기가 없었을(→ 있었을) 때 (실제로 측정된 것을 보고할 / 예상된 것 대신에)

해석

[1]편승 효과가 어떻게 일어나는지는 빛의 속도 측정의 역사에 의해 입증된다. [2]이 (빛의) 속도는 상대성 이론의 기초이기 때문에, 그것은 과학에서 가장 빈번하고 주의 깊게 측정된 ① 양 중 하나이다. [3]우리가 아는 한, (빛의) 속도는 시간이 흘러도 변함이 없었다. [4]그러나 1870년부터 1900년까지, 모든 실험은 (빛의 실제 속도보다) 너무 빠른 (빛의) 속도를 발견했다. [5]그러고 나서 1900년부터 1950년까지, ② 정반대의 일이 일어났는데, 모든 실험이 (빛의 실제 속도보다) 너무 느린 (빛의) 속도를 발견했다! [6]이런 종류의 오류는, 거기서 결과가 항상 실제 값의 한쪽에 (치우쳐) 있기 때문에, '편향'이라고 불린다. [7]그것은 아마 시간이 흐르면서 실험자들이 자신들이 발견할 거라 예상한 것과 ③ 일치하도록 잠재의식적으로 그 결과를 조정했기 때문에 생겼을 것이다. [8]결과가 그들이 예상한 것에 들어맞으면, 그들은 그것을 유지했다. [9]결과가 들어맞지 않으면, 그들은 그것을 버렸다. [10]그들은 단지 일반 통념에 의해 ④ 영향을 받았을 뿐 고의로 부정직하게 군 것은 아니었다. [11]그 패턴은 오직 누군가가 예상된 것 대신에 실제로 측정된 것을 보고할 용기가 ⑤ 없었을(→ 있었을) 때에만 바뀌었다.

어휘

demonstrate 입증하다; 보여주다, 설명하다
measurement 측정, 측량
cf. measure 측정하다[재다]
theory of relativity 상대성 이론
experiment 실험(하다)
cf. experimenter 실험자
value 값; 가치
bias 편향, 편견
subconsciously 잠재의식적으로
adjust 조정[조절]하다; 적응하다
fit 들어맞다, 적절하다
intentionally 고의로, 의도적으로
conventional wisdom 일반 통념

⊕ 편승 효과(bandwagon effect): 개인적 판단이나 근거에 기반하지 않고, 인기 있거나 널리 받아들여지는 것을 따라 하는 현상을 의미. 이 지문에서 일반 통념에 영향받아 실험 결과를 조정한 것이 편승 효과에 영향받은 예임.

정답 가이드

과거에 있었던 빛의 속도 측정 실험에 편승 효과가 영향을 주었다는 내용의 글이다. 빛의 속도는 시간 흐름에 따라 변하지 않는 것인데도 역사적으로 더 빠르거나 느린 속도로 측정된 실험 결과들은 모두 일반 통념에 영향 받은 것이었다. 이런 잘못된 측정 결과를 발견하는 패턴은 누군가 '실제로 측정된 것', 즉 빛의 실제 속도라고 나온 결과를 (일반 통념에 따르지 않고) 보고할 용기가 있었을 때 바뀌었을 것이다. 따라서 ⑤ 'lacked(없었다)'를 'had(있었다)'로 바꿔 써야 한다.

오답 클리닉

① quantities (3%) 양
빛의 속도는 과학에서 측정되는 '(물리적) 양'에 해당한다.

② opposite (6%) 정반대의 일
문장 4와 5에서 너무 빠른 속도와 너무 느린 속도를 발견했다고 했으므로 둘은 서로 '정반대의 일'이 일어난 것이다.

③ match (9%) 일치하다
문장 8에서 결과가 실험자들이 예상한 것과 맞으면 취하고 아니면 버렸다고 했다. 따라서 실험자들은 그들이 발견할 거라고 예상한 것과 '일치하도록' 결과를 조정했을 것으로 추론할 수 있다.

④ influenced (9%) 영향을 받은
실험자들이 결과를 조정한 것은 의도적으로 부정직하게 행동한 것은 아니라고 했으므로 그들이 단지 일반 통념에 의해 '영향을 받은' 것으로 볼 수 있다.

02 ✦ 빈칸 추론 (17학년도 대수능 34번 | 정답률 53%) ②

구문분석 & 직독직해

건축 건물의 의미와 기능의 이해

주제문

[1]Over a period of time / *the buildings* [which housed social, legal, religious, and other rituals] /
(S, 주격 관계대명사)
일정한 시간을 지나면서 / 건물들은 [사회적인, 법적인, 종교적인, 그리고 다른 의식들의 장소를 제공한] /

evolved into *forms* [that we subsequently have come to recognize **and** (to) associate with / **those buildings' function**].
(V, 목적격 관계대명사, ★<come to-v>: v하게 되다)
형태로 발전했다 [우리가 나중에 인식하고 결부시키게 된 / 그러한 건물들의 기능을]
↳ 특정 건물들은 우리가 기능을 인식하고 결부시키는 형태로 발전해 왔음.

[2]This is a two-way process; // the building provides / the physical environment and setting (for a particular social ritual (such as traveling by train **or** going to the theater)), / **as well as** the symbolic setting.
(S_1 V_1 C_1 S_2 V_2 O_1, such as의 O(동명사구 병렬), O_2, ★<A as well as B>: B뿐만 아니라 A도)
이것은 양방향의 과정이다 // 즉 건물은 제공한다 / 물리적인 환경과 장소도 (특정한 사회적 의식을 위한 (기차로 여행을 한다거나 극장에 가는 것과 같은)) / 상징적인 장소뿐만 아니라
↳ **세부 사항 1:** 건물이 우리가 기능을 인식하고 결부시키는 형태로 발전한 것은 양방향의 과정임.

🔑 사람의 경험에 의해 건물의 의미가 발전하고 확립됨.

[3]The meaning (of buildings) / evolves **and** becomes established / by experience // **and** we in turn read our experience / into buildings.
(S_1(단수) V_{1-1}(단수) V_{1-2}(단수) C_{1-2}, S_2 V_2 O, ★<read A into B>: B에 A의 의미를 부여하다)
의미는 (건물의) / 발전하고 확립된다 / 경험에 의해서 // 그리고 우리는 그런 다음에 우리 경험의 의미를 부여한다 / 건물에
↳ **부연 설명 1:** 건물의 의미는 우리의 경험에 따라 발전하고 확립되며, 우리는 건물에 경험을 투영함.

🔑 투영된 경험을 통해 건물은 공감 반응을 일으킴.

[4]Buildings arouse / an empathetic reaction / in us / through these projected experiences, // **and** the strength (of these reactions) / is determined / by our culture, our beliefs, and our expectations.
(S_1 V_1 O_1, S_2(단수) V_2(단수))
건물은 불러일으킨다 / 공감할 수 있는 반응을 / 우리에게 / 이러한 투영된 경험을 통해서 // 그리고 강도는 (이러한 반응의) / 결정된다 / 우리의 문화, 우리의 믿음, 그리고 우리의 기대에 의해
↳ **부연 설명 2:** 투영된 경험을 통해 건물은 공감할 수 있는 반응을 일으킴.

해석

[1]일정한 시간을 지나면서 사회적인, 법적인, 종교적인, 그리고 다른 의식들의 장소를 제공한 건물들은 우리가 나중에 그러한 건물들의 기능을 인식하고 결부시키게 된 형태로 발전했다. [2]이것은 양방향의 과정인데, 건물은 상징적인 장소뿐만 아니라 기차로 여행을 한다거나 극장에 가는 것과 같은 특정한 사회적 의식을 위한 물리적인 환경과 장소도 제공한다. [3]건물의 의미는 경험에 의해서 발전하고 확립되며 우리는 그런 다음에 건물에 우리 경험의 의미를 부여한다. [4]건물은 이러한 투영된 경험을 통해서 우리에게 공감할 수 있는 반응을 불러일으키며, 이러한 반응의 강도는 우리의 문화, 믿음, 기대에 의해 결정된다. [5]그것들(건물)은 이야기를 들려주는데, 왜냐하면 그것들의 형태와 공간 구성이 그것들이 어떻게 사용되어야 하는지에 대한 힌트를 우리에게 주기 때문이다. [6]그것들(건물)의 물리적 구조는 어떤 사용을 권장하고 다른 사용은 저지하는데, 우리는 특별히 초대받지 않는 한 극장의 무대 뒤로 가지 않는다. [7]법정 안에서 법적 절차에 관련된 사람들의 정확한 위치는 설계의 필수적인 부분이며 법이 유지되는 것을 확실히 하는 꼭 필요한 부분이다.

어휘

house 장소를 제공하다; 집, 주택
ritual (종교적) 의식; 의식의[에 관한]
subsequently 나중에, 그 뒤에
associate A with B A를 B와 결부[연관]시키다
two-way 양방향의
in turn 다음에; 차례차례
arouse 불러일으키다; (잠에서) 깨우다
project 투영[투사]하다; 예상하다

🔑 건물의 형태와 공간 구성은 그 건물이 어떻게 사용되어야 하는지를 보여줌.

[5]They (= Buildings) tell stories, // for their form and spatial organization give us / hints (about how they (= Buildings) should be used).

S V O 부사절 접속사(이유) S′ V′ IO′ DO′ about의 O(명사절)

그것들(건물)은 이야기를 들려준다 // 왜냐하면 그것들의 형태와 공간 구성이 우리에게 주기 때문이다 / 힌트를 (그것들(건물)이 어떻게 사용되어야 하는지에 대한)

↳ **세부 사항 2:** 건물의 형태와 공간 구성으로 그 건물의 기능을 알 수 있음.

[6]Their (= Buildings') physical layout encourages some uses / and inhibits others (= other uses); //

S₁ V₁₋₁ O₁₋₁ V₁₋₂ O₁₋₂

그것들(건물들)의 물리적 구조는 어떤 사용을 권장한다 / 그리고 다른 사용은 저지한다 //

we do not go backstage in a theater // unless (we are) especially invited.

S₂ V₂ 부사절 접속사 주어+be동사 생략

우리는 극장의 무대 뒤로 가지 않는다 // 특별히 초대받지 않는 한

↳ **예 1:** 극장의 물리적 구조는 갈 수 있는 공간과 갈 수 없는 공간을 구별함.

[7]Inside a law court / the precise location (of *those* (involved in the legal process)) / is an integral part (of the design) / and an essential part (of ensuring // that the law is upheld).

S 과거분사구 V C₁ C₂ 동명사 ensuring의 O(명사절)

법정 안에서 / 정확한 위치는 (사람들의 (법적 절차에 관련된)) / 필수적인 부분이다 (설계의) / 그리고 꼭 필요한 부분 (확실히 하는 // 법이 유지되는 것을)

↳ **예 2:** 법정 내 자리의 위치가 법을 유지하는 중요한 역할을 함.

spatial 공간의, 공간적인
organization 구성; 조직, 단체
layout 구조; 배치, 레이아웃
inhibit 저지[억제]하다
law court 법정, 재판소
precise 정확한
integral 필수적인; 완전한, 빠진 것이 없는
uphold 유지시키다, 옹호하다
[선택지] architectural 건축(학)의
refine 세련되게 하다; 개선하다
cross-cultural 서로 다른 문화 간의
alter 변경하다, 바꾸다

정답 가이드

빈칸 문장으로 보아, 시간이 지나면서 특정 건물들이 우리가 나중에 '어떻게 하게' 된 형태로 발전했는지를 추론해야 한다. 건물의 '형태'에 대해 언급된 부분을 찾아보면, 문장 5에서 건물들의 '형태와 공간 구성'이 그것들이 '어떻게 사용되어야 하는지'를 알려준다고 했다. 이는 건물의 형태로 그 '기능'을 알 수 있음을 의미하는 것이므로, 빈칸에 들어갈 말로 가장 적절한 것은 ② 'to recognize and associate with those buildings' function(그러한 건물들의 기능을 인식하고 결부시키게)'이다.

오답 클리닉

① to identify and relate to a new architectural trend (6%)
확인하고 새로운 건축 동향과 관련짓게
새로운 건축 동향에 관한 언급은 없음.

③ to define and refine by reflecting cross-cultural interactions (15%)
규정하고 서로 다른 문화 간의 상호 작용을 반영함으로써 세련되게
문화 간 상호 작용에 관한 언급은 없음.

④ to use and change into an integral part of our environment (18%)
사용하고 우리 환경의 필수적인 부분으로 변화시키게
건물을 환경의 필수 부분으로 변화시킨다는 내용은 없음.

⑤ to alter and develop for the elimination of their meanings (8%)
변경하고 그것들의 의미를 없애기 위해서 발전시키게
건물의 의미가 경험에 의해서 발전하고 확립된다는 내용이므로, 그 의미를 없애는 것은 틀림.

03 ✦ 문장 넣기 〈19학년도 6월 모평 39번 | 정답률 34%〉 ⑤

구문분석 & 직독직해

신경과학 인간의 '두 얼굴'을 만드는 신경 체계

[1]Humans can tell lies / with their faces.

S V O

사람은 거짓말을 할 수 있다 / 자신의 얼굴로

[2]Although some are specifically trained / to detect lies / from facial expressions, //

부사절 접속사(양보) S′ V′ C′

어떤 사람들은 특별히 훈련되어 있지만 / 거짓말을 탐지하도록 / 얼굴 표정으로 //

the average person is often misled / into believing false and manipulated facial emotions.

S V into의 O(동명사구)

보통 사람은 흔히 현혹된다 / (그 결과) 거짓되고 조작된 얼굴에 나타난 감정을 믿는다

↳ 사람은 얼굴로 거짓말을 할 수 있는데, 보통 사람들은 그 얼굴에 나타난 거짓된 감정을 믿기 쉬움.

주제문

[3]One reason for this (= 앞 문장의 주절) is // that we are "two-faced."

S V C(명사절)

이것의 한 가지 이유는 ~이다 // 우리가 '두 얼굴'이기 때문

해석

[1]사람은 자신의 얼굴로 거짓말을 할 수 있다. [2]어떤 사람들은 얼굴 표정으로 거짓말을 탐지하도록 특별히 훈련되어 있지만, 보통 사람은 흔히 현혹되어 거짓되고 조작된 얼굴에 나타난 감정을 믿는다. [3]이것의 한 가지 이유는 우리가 '두 얼굴'이기 때문이다. [4]이 말로써 나는 우리가 얼굴 근육을 조종하는 두 가지 서로 다른 신경 체계를 가지고 있다는 것을 의미한다. (①) [5]하나의 신경 체계는 자발적인 통제하에 있고 다른 하나는 비자발적인 통제하에 작동한다. (②) [6]자발적인 표현을 통제하는 신경 체계가 손상된 사람들의 보고된 사례들이 있다. (③) [7]그들은 여전히 얼굴 표정이 있지만, 속이는 얼굴 표정을 지을 수는 없다. (④) [8]그들은 거짓된 얼굴

(= "two-faced")
[4]By this I mean // that we have *two different neural systems* [that manipulate our facial muscles].
S V mean의 O(명사절) 주격 관계대명사
이 말로써 나는 의미한다 // 우리가 두 가지 서로 다른 신경 체계를 가지고 있다는 것을 [얼굴 근육을 조종하는]

*<one ~ the other ...>: (둘 중) 한쪽은 ~ 다른 한쪽은 …
(①) [5]One neural system is under voluntary control // and the other (neural system) works under involuntary control.
S₁ V₁ S₂ V₂
하나의 신경 체계는 자발적인 통제하에 있다 // 그리고 다른 하나는 비자발적인 통제하에 작동한다
↳ **세부 사항(이유):** 우리는 얼굴 근육을 조종하는 두 가지 서로 다른 신경 체계(자발적인 것과 비자발적인 것)가 있음.

(②) [6]There are reported cases (of *individuals* [who have damaged *the neural system* [that controls voluntary expressions]]).
V S 주격 관계대명사 주격 관계대명사
보고된 사례들이 있다 (사람들의 [신경 체계가 손상된 [자발적인 표현을 통제하는]])
↳ **예 1:** 자발적인 표현을 통제하는 신경 체계가 손상된 경우가 있음.

(= individuals who ~ voluntary expressions)
(③) [7]They still have facial expressions, / but are incapable of producing deceitful ones.
S V₁ O V₂ C (= facial expressions)
그들은 여전히 얼굴 표정이 있다 / 그러나 속이는 것들(얼굴 표정)을 지을 수는 없다

(④) [8]*The emotion* [that you see] / is *the emotion* [(which[that]) they are feeling] //
S 목적격 관계대명사 V C 목적격 관계대명사 생략
감정은 [여러분이 보는] / 감정이다 [그들이 느끼고 있는] //
since they have lost *the needed voluntary control* (to produce false facial expressions).
부사절 접속사(~ 때문에)
그들은 필요한 자발적인 통제를 잃었기 때문에 (거짓 얼굴 표정을 짓기 위한)
↳ **부연 설명:** 이런 사람은 속이는 얼굴 표정을 지을 수 없으며, 느끼는 대로 감정이 얼굴에 드러남.

also로 앞 문장과 반대 사례를 제시함.
(⑤ [9]There are also *clinical cases* [that show the flip side of this coin].)
V S 주격 관계대명사
임상 사례도 있다 [이와는 다른 일면을 보여주는]
↳ **예 2:** 비자발적인 표현을 통제하는 신경 체계가 손상된 경우가 있음.

비자발적인 표현을 통제하는 체계가 손상된 경우를 설명함.
[10]These people have injured / *the system* [that controls their involuntary expressions], //
S V O 주격 관계대명사
이 사람들은 손상을 입었다 / 체계에 [자신의 비자발적인 표현을 통제하는] //
so that *the only changes* (in their demeanor) [(which[that]) you will see] / are actually willed expressions.
부사절 접속사(결과) S′(복수) 목적격 관계대명사 생략 V′(복수) C
그래서 유일한 변화는 (그들의 표정에서의) [여러분이 볼] / 실제로 자발적인 표정이다
↳ **부연 설명:** 이런 사람은 자발적인 표정 변화만 보임.

표정을 짓기 위해 필요한 자발적인 통제를 잃었기 때문에, 여러분이 보는 감정은 그들이 느끼고 있는 감정이다. (⑤ [9]이와는 다른 일면을 보여주는 임상 사례도 있다.) [10]이 사람들은 자신의 비자발적인 표현을 통제하는 체계에 손상을 입었으며, 그래서 여러분이 볼 그들의 유일한 표정에서의 변화는 실제로 자발적인 표정이다.

어휘

specifically 특별히; 분명히
detect 탐지하다; 알아내다
expression 표정; 표현
average 보통의; 평균(의)
mislead 현혹시키다; 잘못 이끌다
manipulate 조작하다; 조종하다
two-faced 두 얼굴의; 위선적인
neural 신경의
voluntary 자발적인 (↔ involuntary 비자발적인, 무의식의)
incapable of ~할 수 없는
deceitful 속이는, 기만하는
clinical 임상의
flip side of the coin (~와는) 다른 일면
willed 자발적인; (~의) 의지가 있는

정답 가이드

주어진 문장은 앞서 설명한 것과는 다른 일면을 보여주는 임상 사례도 있다는 내용이다. 따라서 어떤 설명이 끝나고 그와 다른 설명이 이어지기 전에 주어진 문장이 오는 것이 적절하다. 자발적 표현을 통제하는 신경 체계가 손상된 경우가 ⑤ 앞까지 설명되고, 그 뒤에는 비자발적인 표현을 통제하는 신경 체계가 손상된 경우가 나오므로 주어진 문장이 들어가기에 가장 적절한 곳은 ⑤이다.

오답 클리닉

① (5%) 앞에서 언급한 두 가지의 서로 다른 신경 체계가 무엇인지 설명하는 내용이다.
② (11%) 자발적인 표현을 통제하는 신경 체계가 손상된 경우에 대한 설명을 먼저 언급하고 있다.
③ (21%) They는 앞에서 언급한 자발적인 표현을 통제하는 신경 체계가 손상된 사람들을 지칭하며, 앞 내용을 부연 설명한다.
④ (30%) 앞 문장에 이어서 자발적인 통제를 잃은 사람들의 얼굴에 나타나는 감정에 대해 설명한다.

01 + 요약문 〈20학년도 6월 모평 40번 | 정답률 68%〉 ①

구문분석 & 직독직해

사회 '지속 가능성' 용어 사용자의 변화

[1] After the United Nations environmental conference (in Rio de Janeiro // in 1992) / made the term "sustainability" widely known around the world, //
(부사절 접속사(시간) / S' / V' / O' / C' / ★<make+O+C(형용사)>: O를 C하게 만들다)
국제 연합 환경 회의가 (~한) 후에 (리우데자네이루에서 열린 / 1992년에) / '지속 가능성'이라는 용어를 전 세계적으로 널리 알려지게 만든 //

the word became a popular buzzword / by *those* [who wanted to be seen as pro-environmental // but who did not really intend to change their behavior]. 🔑 (A) 친환경적으로 보이고 싶은 사람들이 사용함.
(S / V / O / 주격관계대명사 / to-v의 수동형 / 관계사절 병렬 / 주격 관계대명사)
그 단어는 인기 있는 유행어가 되었다 / 사람들에 의해 [친환경적으로 보이길 원하는 // 그러나 자신의 행동을 정말로 바꿀 의도는 아니었던]
↳ **대조 A:** '지속 가능성'이라는 용어는 친환경적으로 보이고 싶은 사람들에 의해 유행어가 됨.

(It = the term "sustainability")
[2] It became a public relations term, / *an attempt* (to be seen as (being) abreast / with the latest thinking (of what we must do) / to save our planet / from widespread harm).
(S / V / C / = / 전치사(~로(서)) / of의 O(명사절) / 목적(~하기 위해))
그것('지속 가능성'이라는 용어)은 홍보 용어가 되었다 / 즉 시도 (나란히 있는 것으로 보이려는 / 최신 생각과 (우리가 무엇을 해야 하는가에 관한) / 지구를 구하기 위해 / 널리 퍼진 위해로부터)
↳ **부연 설명:** '지속 가능성'은 지구를 위하는 것처럼 보이기 위한 홍보 용어가 됨.

[3] But then, / in a decade or so, / some governments, industries, educational institutions, and organizations / started to use the term / in a serious manner.
(S / V / O)
그러나 그런 다음 / 십여 년 후에 / 몇몇 정부, 산업, 교육 기관, 그리고 조직이 / 그 용어를 사용하기 시작했다 / 진지한 방식으로
↳ **대조 B:** 일부 단체들이 '지속 가능성'을 진지하게 사용하기 시작함.

[4] In the United States / a number of large corporations appointed a vice president for sustainability.
(★<a number of+복수명사>: 여러 ~ (= several) / S / V / O)
미국에서 / 여러 대기업이 지속 가능성 담당 부사장을 임명했다

[5] Not only were these officials interested in // how their companies could profit / by producing "green" products, // but they were often given the task (of making the company more efficient / by reducing wastes and pollution / and by reducing its carbon emissions).
(★부정어구가 문두에 나와 주어와 동사가 도치됨. / 🔑 (B) 실제로 환경을 보호하려는 사람들이 사용함. / 부정어 포함 어구 / V_1 / S_1 / C / in의 O(명사절) / <by v-ing>: v함으로써 / they = these officials / S_2 / V_2 / O / = / 전치사구 병렬)
이 임원들은 ~에 관심이 있었을 뿐만 아니라 // 자신들의 회사가 어떻게 이익을 낼 수 있을지 / '친환경' 제품을 만듦으로써 // 그들은 업무를 자주 받기도 했다 (회사를 더 효율적으로 만드는 / 쓰레기와 오염을 줄임으로써 / 그리고 회사의 탄소 배출을 줄임으로써)
↳ **부연 설명(예):** 여러 미국 대기업들이 '친환경' 제품을 만들고, 환경적으로 회사를 더 효율적으로 만들려고 함.

↓

[6] While the term "sustainability," / (in the initial phase), / was popular / among *those* [who **(A) pretended** to be eco-conscious], // it later came to be used / by *those* [who would **(B) actualize** their pro-environmental thoughts].
(부사절 접속사(~인 반면에) / 주격 관계대명사 / it = the term "sustainability" / S / V / 주격 관계대명사)
'지속 가능성'이라는 용어가 (~인 반면에) / (초기 단계에서) / 인기가 있었던 (반면에) / 사람들 사이에서 [친환경 의식이 있는 (A) 체했던] // 그것('지속 가능성'이라는 용어)은 나중에는 사용되게 되었다 / 사람들에 의해 [자신의 친환경주의적 생각을 (B) 실현하고자 하는]

해석

[1] 1992년에 리우데자네이루에서 열린 국제 연합 환경 회의가 '지속 가능성'이라는 용어를 전 세계적으로 널리 알려지게 만든 후에, 그 단어는 친환경적으로 보이길 원하지만 자신의 행동을 정말로 바꿀 의도는 아니었던 사람들에 의해 인기 있는 유행어가 되었다. [2] 그것은 홍보 용어, 즉 널리 퍼진 위해로부터 지구를 구하기 위해 우리가 무엇을 해야 하는가에 관한 최신 생각과 나란히 있는 것으로 보이려는 시도가 되었다. [3] 그러나 그런 다음 십여 년 후에, 몇몇 정부, 산업, 교육 기관, 그리고 조직이 그 용어를 진지한 방식으로 사용하기 시작했다. [4] 미국에서 여러 대기업이 지속 가능성 담당 부사장을 임명했다. [5] 이 임원들은 '친환경' 제품을 만듦으로써 자신들의 회사가 어떻게 이익을 낼 수 있을지에 관심이 있었을 뿐만 아니라, 쓰레기와 오염을 줄임으로써, 그리고 회사의 탄소 배출을 줄임으로써 회사를 더 효율적으로 만드는 업무를 자주 받기도 했다.

↓

[6] 초기 단계에서 '지속 가능성'이라는 용어가 친환경 의식이 있는 (A) 체했던 사람들 사이에서 인기가 있었던 반면에, 그것('지속 가능성'이라는 용어)은 나중에는 자신의 친환경주의적 생각을 (B) 실현하고자 하는 사람들에 의해 사용되게 되었다.

어휘

conference 회의; 회담
term 용어; 기간; 학기
sustainability 지속 가능성
pro-environmental 친환경적인
intend 의도하다, (~하려고) 생각하다
public relations 홍보
widespread 널리 퍼진, 광범위한
decade 10년
manner 방식; 태도; 예의
corporation 기업, 회사
appoint 임명[지명]하다
official 임원, 관리; 공식적인
profit 이익을 얻다; 이익, 이득
carbon emission 탄소 배출
[요약문] initial 초기의, 처음의
phase 단계, 국면
eco-conscious 환경 (보호) 의식이 강한, 환경에 관심이 큰

정답 가이드

요약문을 통해 '지속 가능성'이라는 용어를 초기에 사용한 사람들과 나중에 사용한 사람들을 대조하는 글임을 알 수 있다. '지속 가능성'은 처음에 행동은 바꾸지 않으면서 친환경적으로 '보이고' 싶어 하는 사람들의 유행어가 되었지만, 십여 년 후에는 친환경 제품을 생산하고 '실제로' 환경을 보호해 회사를 효율적으로 만들려는 사람들이 사용했다는 내용이다. 따라서 요약문의 빈칸 (A)와 (B)에 각각 들어갈 말로 가장 적절한 것은 ① 'pretended(~인 체했다) - actualize(실현하다)'이다.

오답 클리닉

(A) (B)

② pretended - disregard (12%) ~인 체했다 - 무시하다
(A)는 맞지만, (B)는 글의 내용과 반대됨.

③ refused - realize (10%) 거절했다 - 깨닫다
친환경적으로 보이고 싶어 하는 사람들이 '지속 가능성' 용어를 사용했으므로 (A)는 틀리며, (B)는 맞음.

④ refused - idealize (6%) 거절했다 - 이상화하다
(A)는 틀리며, (B)는 단순히 이상화하는 것이 아니라 실천하려는 움직임을 보인 것이므로 틀림.

⑤ attempted - mask (4%) 시도했다 - 가리다
(A)와 (B) 모두 틀림.

02~03 + 복합 유형 (21학년도 9월 모평 41~42번 | 정답률 02 62%, 03 56%)

02 ④ 03 ③

구문분석 & 직독직해

예술 글쓰기에서 충분한 문맥 제공의 중요성

03-(a) 잘 만들어진 텍스트는 전문 지식 없이도 이해할 수 있으므로 '최소한의' 노력으로 읽을 수 있음.

[1]To the extent that sufficient context has been provided, / the reader (S) can come (V1) to a well-crafted text / with no expert knowledge /
충분한 문맥이 제공된 경우에 / 독자는 잘 만들어진 텍스트를 읽을 수 있게 된다 / 전문적 지식 없이 /

and (can) come away with (V2) / a good approximation (of what has been intended by the author (of의 O(명사절))).
그리고 (~을) 가지고 읽기를 끝낼 수 있다 / 꽤 근접한 것을 (작가에 의해 의도된 것과)

↳ **대조 A:** 충분한 문맥이 제공되면 독자는 전문적 지식 없이도 작가의 의도를 파악할 수 있음.

[2]The text (S1) has become (V1) a public document (O1) // and the reader (S2) can read (V2) it (O2) / with a **(a) minimum** of effort and struggle; //
그 텍스트는 공문서가 되었다 // 그래서 독자는 그것을 읽을 수 있다 / 최소한의 노력과 분투로 //

*<describe A as B>: A를 B로 설명하다[묘사하다]

his experience (S3) comes close (V3) / to what Freud has described (to의 O(명사절)) / as (전치사(~로(서))) the deployment (of "evenly-hovering attention.")
독자의 경험이 가까워지기 때문이다 / Freud가 설명한 것과 / (전략적) 배치로 ('고르게 주의를 기울이는 것'의)

↳ **세부 사항:** 독자는 최소한의 노력으로 고르게 주의를 기울여 텍스트를 읽을 수 있음.

03-(b) 작가의 손에 자신을 맡겼으므로 데려가는 곳으로 '따라갈' 것임.

[3]He (S1, = The reader) puts (V1) himself (O1) in the author's hands / (some have had this experience / with great novelists (such as Dickens or Tolstoy)) // and he (S2) **(b) follows** (V2) // where the author leads (부사절).
독자는 작가의 손에 자신을 맡긴다 / (어떤 독자들이 이런 경험을 가졌다 / 위대한 소설가와 (Dickens나 Tolstoy와 같은)) // 그리고 그는 따라간다 // 작가가 이끄는 곳으로

[4]The real world (S1) has vanished (V1) // and the fictive world (S2) has taken (V2) its place (O).
현실 세계는 사라졌다 // 그리고 허구의 세계가 그것을 대신했다

↳ **부연 설명:** 독자는 작가가 이끄는 대로 글을 이해함.

[5]Now consider (V(명령문)) the other extreme (O).
이제 다른 쪽 극단을 생각해 보라

해석

[1]충분한 문맥이 제공된 경우에, 독자는 전문적 지식 없이 잘 만들어진 텍스트를 읽을 수 있게 되고 작가에 의해 의도된 것과 꽤 근접한 것을 가지고 읽기를 끝낼 수 있다. [2]그 텍스트는 공문서가 되어서(▶ 글이 대중을 위한 것이 되어 읽기 쉽고 이용 가능함을 의미) 독자는 (a) 최소한의 노력과 분투로 그것을 읽을 수 있는데, 독자의 경험이 Freud가 '고르게 주의를 기울이는 것'의 (전략적) 배치로 설명한 것과 가까워지기 때문이다.(▶ 문맥이 충분해서 어느 하나에 더 주의를 기울여야 할 필요 없이 글을 쉽게 이해할 수 있음을 의미) [3]독자는 작가의 손에 자신을 맡기고(어떤 독자들은 Dickens나 Tolstoy와 같은 위대한 소설가와 이런 경험을 가졌다) 작가가 이끄는 곳으로 (b) 따라간다. [4]현실 세계는 사라지고 허구의 세계가 그것을 대신했다. [5]이제 다른 쪽 극단을 생각해 보라. [6]문맥과 내용이 적절하게 결합되지 않은, 제대로 만들어지지 않은 텍스트를 우리가 읽을 때, 우리는 이해하려고 애써야 하고, 작가가 의도한 것에 대한 우리의 이해는 아마도 그의 본래 의도와 (c) 밀접한(→ 아주 적은) 관련성을 지닐 것이다. [7]시대에 뒤떨어진 번역은 우리에게 이런 경험을 줄 것인데, 우리가 읽으면서 언어를 최신의 것으로 해야 하고, 텍스트와 꽤 격렬한 분투를 하는 대가를 치러야만 이해가 이뤄지기 때문이다. [8]참조의 틀(문맥) 없이 잘못 제시된 내용도 (d) 같은 경험을 제공할 수 있는데, 우리는 단어를 보지만 그것들이 어떻게 받아들여져야 하는지를 이해하지 못하기 때문이다. [9]문맥을 제공하지 못하는 작가는 자신의 세계상이 그의 모든 독자에 의해 공유된다고 (e) 잘못 가정하고, 적절한 참조의 틀을 제공하는 것이 글쓰기라는 일의 중대한 부분임을 깨닫지 못한다.

03-(c) 문맥이 충분하지 않은 글은 이해하기가 어려워 작가의 의도와 우리의 이해는 관련성이 '아주 적을' 것임.

⁶When we come / to *a badly crafted text* **[in which context and content are not happily joined], //**
부사절 접속사(시간)　　　　　　전치사+관계대명사　S″　　　　　　　V″
우리가 읽을 때 / 제대로 만들어지지 않은 텍스트를 [문맥과 내용이 적절하게 결합되지 않은] //

we must struggle to understand, // and our sense (of what the author intended) / probably bears /
S₁　V₁　　　　　　　　　　　　　S₂　　of의 O(명사절)　　　　　　　V₂
(c) close(→ minimal) correspondence (to his original intention).
O
우리는 이해하려고 애써야 한다 // 그리고 우리의 이해는 (작가가 의도한 것에 대한) / 아마도 지닐 것이다 /
밀접한(→ 아주 적은) 관련성을 (그의 본래 의도와)

↳ **대조 B:** 문맥과 내용이 적절하게 결합되지 않은 텍스트는 독자가 작가의 의도를 거의 이해하지 못함.

03-(d) 시대에 뒤떨어진 번역과 참조의 틀이 없이 잘못 제시된 내용은 '같은' 이해의 어려움이 있음.

⁷An out-of-date translation will give us this experience; //
S₁　　　　　　　　　V₁　IO　DO
시대에 뒤떨어진 번역은 우리에게 이런 경험을 줄 것이다 //

as we read, // we must bring the language up to date, // and understanding comes /
부사절 접속사(~하면서) S₂　V₂　　　　　O　　　　　　　　　　　S₃　　V₃
only at the price (of a fairly intense struggle with the text).
우리가 읽으면서 // 우리는 언어를 최신의 것으로 해야 한다 // 그리고 이해가 이뤄진다 /
대가를 치러야만 (텍스트와 꽤 격렬한 분투를 하는)

↳ **예 1:** 시대에 뒤떨어진 번역은 이해하기 어려움.

⁸Badly presented content (with no frame of reference) / can provide (d) the same experience; //
S₁　　　　　　　　　　　　　　　　　　V₁　　　　　　　　O
잘못 제시된 내용도 (참조의 틀 없이) / 같은 경험을 제공할 수 있다//
★be to-v: ((의무)) v해야 한다
we see the words / but have no sense (of how they are to be taken).
S₂　V₂　　　　　V₃　　　　　　　　of의 O(명사절)
우리는 단어를 본다 / 하지만 이해하지 못한다 (그것들이 어떻게 받아들여져야 하는지를)

↳ **예 2:** 참조 틀 없는 잘못 제시된 내용도 이해하기 어려움.

⁹The author [who fails to provide the context] / has (e) mistakenly assumed //
S　　주격 관계대명사　　　　　　　　　　V₁
↦ has assumed의 O(명사절)
that his picture of the world is shared / by all his readers
명사절 접속사　　　S′　　　　　V′
작가는 [문맥을 제공하지 못하는] / 잘못 가정한다 // 자신의 세계상이 공유된다고 / 그의 모든 독자에 의해

03-(e) assumed 뒤에 문맥을 제공하지 못한 작가가 '잘못' 가정하는 내용이 나옴.

↦ to realize의 O(명사절)
and fails to realize // that supplying the right frame (of reference) /
V₂　O₂　　　　　명사절 접속사　　　S′(동명사구)
is a critical part (of the task of writing).
V′
그리고 깨닫지 못한다 // 적절한 틀을 제공하는 것이 (참조의) / 중대한 부분임을 (글쓰기라는 일의)

↳ 작가는 글에 자신의 세계상과 참조를 제공하는 것이 중요함.

[어휘]

to the extent that ~일 경우에; ~할 정도까지
sufficient 충분한
context 문맥, 맥락; 정황, 배경
come away with ~을 가지고 떠나다
approximation 근접한 것, 비슷한 것
intend 의도하다
struggle 분투[투쟁](하다)
vanish 사라지다
fictive 허구의, 상상의
extreme 극단; 극도의, 극심한
happily 적절하게; 만족스럽게; 기꺼이
sense 이해; 감각
bear 지니다; 가지다; 참다, 견디다; (아이를) 낳다
correspondence 관련성; 서신, 편지
out-of-date 시대에 뒤떨어진, 구식의
(↔ up to date 최신의, 현대식의)
translation 번역[통역]
at the price of ~의 대가로, ~을 희생하여
intense 격렬한, 강렬한
frame 틀, 뼈대, 구조
reference 참조; 언급
assume 가정[추측]하다
critical 중대한, 결정적인; 비판적인
[요약문] lighthouse 등대
trap 가두다; 덫, 함정
outlook 견해, 관점; 전망

정답 가이드

02 문맥이 충분히 제공된 텍스트와 그렇지 않은 텍스트를 읽는 경우 독자가 작가의 의도를 이해하는 데 차이가 있음을 대조하며 작가가 글을 쓸 때 적절한 문맥을 제공하는 것이 중요함을 설명하는 글이다. 따라서 글의 제목으로 가장 적절한 것은 ④ 'Context in Writing: A Lighthouse for Understanding Texts(글쓰기에서의 문맥은 텍스트 이해를 위한 등대)'이다.

03 문맥이 충분히 제공되면 독자는 전문 지식 없이도 작가의 의도를 파악할 수 있다는 앞부분의 내용과 대조되는 구조이므로 맥락과 내용이 적절하게 결합하지 않은 텍스트를 읽는 경우 독자는 작가의 의도를 거의 이해하지 못할 것이다. 따라서 ③의 'close(밀접한)'를 'minimal(아주 적은)' 등의 단어로 바꾸어야 한다.

오답 클리닉

02 ① Building a Wall Between Reality and the Fictive World (5%)
현실과 허구의 세계 사이에 벽 세우기(×)
문맥이 충분한 글을 읽을 때 현실과 허구의 세계의 벽이 허물어진다고 했으므로 글의 내용과 반대됨.
② Creative Reading: Going Beyond the Writer's Intentions (13%)
창의적(×) 독서는 작가의 의도를 넘어서는 것(×)
작가의 의도를 넘어서서 사고하는 독서에 대한 글이 아님.

③ Usefulness of Readers' Experiences for Effective Writing (11%)
효과적인 글쓰기를 위한(×) 독자 경험의 유용성(×)
글을 쓰는 데 독자의 경험이 유용하다는 내용이 아님.
⑤ Trapped in Their Own Words: The Narrow Outlook of Authors
(10%) 자기 자신의 말에 갇히는(×) 작가들의 좁은 견해(×)
작가들의 좁은 견해에 관한 내용이 아님.

03 ① minimum (6%) 최소한의
맥락이 충분히 제공된 텍스트는 전문 지식 없이도 이해할 수 있다는 것으로 보아 '최소한의' 노력으로 읽을 수 있을 것이다.
② follows (4%) 따라가다
텍스트를 잘 이해하는 경우를 설명하는 것이므로 작가가 이끄는 곳으로 '따라간다'는 것은 흐름상 자연스럽다.
④ the same (26%) 같은
시대에 뒤떨어진 번역을 이해하기 힘든 것처럼 참조의 틀이 없이 잘못 제시된 내용도 '같은' 어려움이 있다는 내용이므로 자연스럽다.
⑤ mistakenly (8%) 잘못
문맥을 제공하지 못하는 작가의 문제점으로 자신의 세계상을 독자들이 공유한다고 '잘못' 가정한다는 것을 지적하는 것은 적절하다.

01 + 빈칸 추론 17학년도 대수능 33번 | 정답률 32% ①

구문분석 & 직독직해

심리 부정적인 감정의 유용성

[1]Grief is unpleasant. // Would one(일반적인 사람) not then be better off / without it(= grief) altogether? // Why accept it(= grief) // even when(부사절 접속사(시간)) the loss is real?

슬픔은 불쾌하다 // 그렇다면 사람은 더 좋지 않을까 / 그것(슬픔)이 완전히 없으면 // 왜 그것(슬픔)을 받아들일까 // 손실이 실재할 때조차도

[2]Perhaps / we(S) should say(V) of it(= grief) // what Spinoza said of regret(O(명사절)): // that(동격 접속사) whoever feels it(= regret)(S′(명사절)) is(V′) "twice unhappy or twice helpless."(C′) *복합관계대명사 whoever가 이끄는 명사절 주어로, whoever는 anyone who로 바꿔 쓸 수 있음.

아마도 / 우리는 그것(슬픔)에 대해 말할 것이다 // Spinoza가 후회에 대해 했던 말을 // 즉 그것(후회)을 느끼는 누구든지 '두 배 불행하거나 두 배 무기력하다'는

↳ **도입(질문):** 왜 슬픔이 불쾌함에도 불구하고 받아들이는가?

주제문

[3]Laurence Thomas(S) has suggested(V) // that(명사절 접속사) the utility(S′(단수)) (of "negative sentiments") / (emotions (like grief, guilt, resentment, and anger), // which(관계대명사(보충 설명)) there is seemingly *a reason* (to believe // (that)(명사절 접속사 생략) we might be better off without)) / lies(V′(단수)) / in their(동명사의 의미상 주어) providing a kind of guarantee of authenticity(in의 O(동명사구)) (for such dispositional sentiments as love and respect). *<such A as B = A such as B>: B와 같은 A
(has suggested의 O(명사절); to believe의 O(명사절); their = negative sentiments)
🗝 부정적인 감정은 기질적 감정의 진실성을 보장해 준다는 점에서 유용함.

Laurence Thomas는 (~라고) 암시했다 // 유용성이 ('부정적인 감정'의) / (감정들 (슬픔, 죄책감, 분개, 분노와 같은) // 이유가 있어 보이는 (믿을 // 없으면 우리가 더 좋을 것이라고)) / 있다고 / 그것들(부정적인 감정)이 일종의 진실성을 보장해 주는 것에 (사랑과 존경과 같은 기질적인 감정에 대한)

↳ **답변:** 부정적인 감정은 (드러나지 않는) 기질적 감정의 진실성을 보장해 준다는 점에서 유용함.

🗝 사랑하거나 존경하는 감정은 그 감정이 사실인 내내 존재해야 하는 것은 아님.

[4]No occurrent feelings(S(복수)) (of love and respect) / need to(V(복수)) be present(O) / throughout(전치사(~동안 내내)) *the period* [in which(전치사+관계대명사) it(가주어) is true // that one loves or respects(진주어(명사절))].

그 어떤 현재 일어나고 있는 감정도 (사랑과 존경의) / 존재할 필요는 없다 / 그 기간 내내 [(~이) 사실인 // 누군가가 사랑하거나 존경하는 것이]

↳ **부연 설명(원인):** 현재 일어나는 사랑하거나 존경하는 감정이 사실인 내내 존재할 필요는 없음.

[5]One(S) might therefore sometimes suspect(V), / (in the absence of the positive occurrent feelings), // that one no longer loves(O(명사절)).

그러므로 사람은 때때로 의심할 수도 있다 / (현재 일어나고 있는 긍정적인 감정이 없는 상태에서) // 더 이상 사랑하지 않는다고

↳ **부연 설명(결과):** 현재 일어나고 있는 긍정적인 감정이 없으면 사랑하지 않는다고 의심할 수 있음.

🗝 부정적인 감정이 사랑과 존경의 진실성을 증명해 줌.

[6]At such times, / negative emotions(S(복수)) (like grief) / offer(V(복수)) / a kind of testimonial(O) (to the authenticity (of love or respect)).

그러한 때에 / 부정적인 감정이 (슬픔과 같은) / 제공한다 / 일종의 증거를 (진실성에 대한 (사랑이나 존경의))

↳ **결론:** 긍정적인 감정이 의심될 때, 부정적인 감정이 긍정적인 감정의 진실성을 증명해 줌.

해석

[1]슬픔은 불쾌하다. 그렇다면 그것이 완전히 없으면 더 좋지 않을까? 왜 손실이 실재할 때조차도 그것을 받아들일까? [2]아마도 우리는 그것(슬픔)에 대해 Spinoza가 후회에 대해 했던 말, 즉 그것(후회)을 느끼는 누구든지 '두 배 불행하거나 두 배 무기력하다'는 말을 할 것이다.(▶ 후회의 경우처럼 슬픔을 느끼는 누군가도 두 배 불행하거나 무기력함을 의미) [3]Laurence Thomas는 '부정적인 감정'(없으면 우리가 더 좋을 것이라고 믿을 이유가 있어 보이는 슬픔, 죄책감, 분개, 분노와 같은 감정들)의 유용성이 사랑과 존경과 같은 기질적인 감정에 대한 일종의 진실성을 보장해 주는 것에 있다고 암시했다. [4]그 어떤 현재 일어나고 있는 사랑과 존경의 감정도 누군가가 사랑하거나 존경하는 것이 사실인 그 기간 내내 존재할 필요는 없다. [5]그러므로 사람은 때때로 현재 일어나고 있는 긍정적인 감정이 없는 상태에서 더 이상 사랑하지 않는다고 의심할 수도 있다. [6]그러한 때에, 슬픔과 같은 부정적인 감정이 사랑이나 존경의 진실성에 대한 일종의 증거를 제공한다.(▶ 부정적 감정이 드러나지 않는 기질적 감정을 깨닫게 해줌을 의미. 예를 들어, 누군가를 상실하고 느끼는 슬픔으로 그 사람에 대한 사랑이 진짜였음을 알게 됨.)

어휘

grief (큰) 슬픔, 비탄
better off 더 좋은[나은]; 부유한
altogether 완전히
regret 후회(하다)
helpless 무(기)력한; 의지할 데 없는
suggest 암시[시사]하다; 제안하다
utility 유용(성), 효용
sentiment 감정, 정서
guilt 죄책감; 유죄
resentment 분개, 분함
seemingly 겉보기에는
guarantee 보장(하다); 보증(하다)
authenticity 진실성; 진짜임
occurrent 현재 일어나고 있는; 우연의
suspect 의심하다; 용의자
absence 없음; 결석
[선택지] hold 유지되다, 지속되다; 잡다

정답 가이드

긍정적인 감정이 일어나지 않는 상태에서 무엇을 의심할 수 있을지 추론해야 한다. 빈칸 문장에 therefore가 포함되므로, 앞 부분에 원인이 먼저 제시될 것임을 유추할 수 있다. 앞 문장에서 사랑과 존경의 감정은 그것이 진실인 기간 '내내' 존재할 필요는 없다고 했으므로, 이는 현재 일어나는 사랑과 존경의 감정이 없을 때도 있다는 것을 의미한다. 이런 원인으로 인해, 지금 그 감정이 일어나지 않고 있는 상태에서 사람들은 더는 그 감정을 느끼지 않는다고 의심할 수도 있다는 맥락이 되는 것이 자연스럽다. 따라서, 빈칸에 들어갈 말로 가장 적절한 것은 ① 'one no longer loves(더 이상 사랑하지 않는다)'이다.

오답 클리닉

② one is much happier (11%)
훨씬 더 행복하다
긍정적인 감정이 없는 상태에서 더 행복하다고 느끼면 긍정적 감정을 확인해주는 부정적 감정의 유용성은 없을 것임.

③ an emotional loss can never be real (14%)
감정적 손실은 결코 진짜일 수 없다
긍정적인 감정이 없을 때 감정적 손실이 진짜 있다고 의심할 것임.

④ respect for oneself can be guaranteed (21%)
자신에 대한 존경이 보장될 수 있다
존경의 감정이 사실인 기간 내내 일어나는 것은 아니므로 그 감정이 없는 상태에서는 존경이 보장될 수 없다고 의심할 것임.

⑤ negative sentiments do not hold any longer (21%)
부정적인 감정이 더 이상 유지되지 않는다
다음 문장에서 부정적인 감정이 긍정적인 감정의 증거를 제공한다고 했으므로, 부정적인 감정이 아닌 긍정적인 감정이 없다고 의심하는 것이 적절함.

02 ✦ 글의 순서 〈19학년도 6월 모평 36번 | 정답률 65%〉 ⑤

구문분석 & 직독직해

환경 지구의 주요 카본 싱크인 바다

[1]A carbon sink is *a natural feature* [that absorbs or stores / more carbon // than it releases].
(S: A carbon sink / V: is / C: a natural feature / that: 주격 관계대명사 / it: = a carbon sink)
카본 싱크는 자연적 특색이다 [흡수하거나 저장하는 / 더 많은 탄소를 // 그것이 방출하는 것보다]
↳ **도입(정의):** 카본 싱크는 탄소를 흡수하고 저장하는 자연의 특색 있는 요소임.

🔑 주어진 글의 정의에 이어 가치를 설명함.
(C) [2]The value (of carbon sinks) / is // that they can help create equilibrium (in the atmosphere) / by removing excess CO_2.
(S(단수): The value / V(단수): is / that절: is의 C(명사절) / they: = carbon sinks / <by v-ing>: v함으로써)
가치는 (카본 싱크의) / ~이다 // 그것들(카본 싱크)이 평형 상태를 만드는 데 도움을 줄 수 있다는 것 (대기 내의) / 과잉 이산화탄소를 제거함으로써
↳ **카본 싱크의 가치:** 대기 중의 과잉 이산화탄소를 제거해서 평형 상태를 만들어 줌.

[3]One example (of a carbon sink) / is a large forest.
(S: One example / V: is / C: a large forest)
한 예는 (카본 싱크의) / 거대한 숲이다

🔑 Its는 (C)의 a large forest를 지칭함.
(B) [4]Its mass of plants and other organic material / absorb and store tons of carbon.
(S: Its mass of plants and other organic material / V1: absorb / V2: store / O: tons of carbon)
그것(거대한 숲)의 수많은 식물 및 다른 유기 물질은 / 많은 탄소를 흡수하고 저장한다
↳ **예:** 거대한 숲의 식물과 유기 물질이 탄소를 흡수 및 저장함.

주제문
[5]However, / the planet's major carbon sink is its oceans.
(S: the planet's major carbon sink / V: is / C: its oceans)
하지만 / 지구의 주요 카본 싱크는 바다이다
↳ 지구의 주요 카본 싱크는 바다임.

[6]Since the Industrial Revolution began / in the eighteenth century, // *CO_2* (released during industrial processes) / has greatly increased / the proportion of carbon (in the atmosphere).
(Since: 부사절 접속사(~이후로) / S(단수): CO_2 / released during ...: 과거분사구 / V(단수): has greatly increased / O: the proportion of carbon)
산업 혁명이 시작된 이후로 / 18세기에 // 이산화탄소는 (산업 공정 중에 방출된) / 크게 증가시켰다 / 탄소 비율을 (대기의)

해석

[1]카본 싱크는 그것이 방출하는 것보다 더 많은 탄소를 흡수하거나 저장하는 자연적 특색이다. (C) [2]카본 싱크의 가치는 그것들이 과잉 이산화탄소를 제거함으로써 대기 내의 평형 상태를 만드는 데 도움을 줄 수 있다는 것이다. [3]카본 싱크의 한 예는 거대한 숲이다. (B) [4]그것(거대한 숲)의 수많은 식물 및 다른 유기 물질은 많은 탄소를 흡수하고 저장한다. [5]하지만, 지구의 주요 카본 싱크는 바다이다. [6]18세기에 산업 혁명이 시작된 이후로, 산업 공정 중에 방출된 이산화탄소는 대기의 탄소 비율을 크게 증가시켰다. (A) [7]카본 싱크는 이 과잉 이산화탄소 중 대략 절반을 흡수할 수 있었고 지구의 바다가 그 일의 주된 역할을 해왔다. [8]그것(지구의 바다)은 인간의 산업으로 인한 탄소 배출의 약 4분의 1을 흡수하며, 지구의 모든 카본 싱크가 하는 일을 합친 것의 절반을 한다.

어휘

feature 특색, 특징; 특집
absorb 흡수하다
carbon 탄소
release 방출하다; 발표, 개봉
atmosphere 대기; 분위기
excess 과잉의, 초과한; 과잉, 지나침
mass (양이) 많은; 대량의
organic 유기의; 유기농의
Industrial Revolution 산업 혁명
process 공정; 과정
greatly 크게, 대단히

(B)의 증가한 대기 중의 탄소 비율이 (A)의 this excess CO_2로 연결됨.

(A) [7]Carbon sinks have been able to absorb / about half of this excess CO_2, //
S1 V1 C
카본 싱크는 흡수할 수 있었다 / 이 과잉 이산화탄소 중 대략 절반을 //

and the world's oceans have done the major part of that job.
S2 V2 O
그리고 지구의 바다가 그 일의 주된 역할을 해왔다

↳ 논거: 산업 혁명 이후 증가한 이산화탄소를 흡수하는 데 바다가 큰 역할을 했음.

(= The world's oceans)
[8]They absorb / about one-fourth of humans' industrial carbon emissions, /
S V O
doing half the work (of *all Earth's carbon sinks* (combined)).
분사구문(= and they do ~) 과거분사
그것(지구의 바다)은 흡수한다 / 인간의 산업으로 인한 탄소 배출의 약 4분의 1을 /
일의 절반을 하며 (지구의 모든 카본 싱크의 (합쳐진))

↳ 부연 설명: 바다는 탄소 배출량의 약 1/4을 흡수하며 지구상의 모든 카본 싱크가 하는 일의 절반을 함.

proportion 비율, 부분; 균형
emission 배출(물)

⊕ 카본 싱크(carbon sink): 지구 온난화 방지를 도와 대기 중 온실가스를 흡수하는 곳으로 산림, 해양 등이 있음.

정답 가이드

카본 싱크를 정의하는 주어진 글 다음에는 그것의 가치를 설명하는 (C)가 오는 것이 자연스럽다. 이어서 (C)에서 카본 싱크의 예로 언급한 거대한 숲(a large forest)을 Its로 받아 설명하는 (B)가 나오고, 역접 연결어 However로 지구의 주요 카본 싱크는 바다라고 내용이 전환된다. (B)의 끝에 언급된 산업 혁명 이후 증가한 대기 중의 탄소 비율을 (A)의 this excess CO_2가 받아 주요 카본 싱크로서의 바다의 역할을 부연 설명하므로 (A)가 마지막에 오는 것이 흐름상 적절하다.

오답 클리닉

① (A) - (C) - (B) (7%)
주어진 글에서 (A)의 this excess CO_2가 가리키는 것을 찾을 수 없으므로 (A)는 주어진 글 바로 뒤에 올 수 없다.
② (B) - (A) - (C) (10%) / ③ (B) - (C) - (A) (9%)
(B)의 Its가 (C)의 a large forest를 가리키므로 (B)는 (C) 뒤에 와야 한다.
④ (C) - (A) - (B) (10%)
(C)의 a large forest가 (B)의 Its로 연결되고, (B)의 대기 중 증가한 탄소 비율이 (A)의 this excess CO_2로 이어져야 한다. (C)에서 카본 싱크의 예로 숲을 언급한 후, 카본 싱크로서 바다의 주요 역할을 설명하는 (A)가 오는 것은 흐름상 자연스럽지 않다.

03 + 문장 넣기 (19학년도 6월 모평 38번 | 정답률 39%) ①

구문분석 & 직독직해

관광 가상과 현실에서 동시에 일어나는 관광

주제문

(= the realm)
[1]Tourism takes place simultaneously / in the realm of the imagination / and that of the physical world.
S V in의 O(명사구 병렬)
관광은 동시에 일어난다 / 가상의 영역에서 / 그리고 물리적 세계의 영역에서

(= tourism)
[2]In contrast to literature or film, / it leads to 'real', tangible worlds, /
~와 대조적으로 S V O
문학 또는 영화와 대조적으로 / 그것(관광)은 '실제적인', 감지할 수 있는 세계로 이어진다 /
while nevertheless remaining tied / to the sphere (of fantasies, dreams, wishes — and myth).
접속사를 생략하지 않은 분사구문(= while nevertheless it remains ~)
반면에 그럼에도 불구하고 여전히 관련되어 있다 / 영역과 (환상, 꿈, 소망, 즉 허구의)

↳ 부연 설명: 관광은 문학이나 영화와 달리 상상과 현실에서 동시에 일어남.

[3]It thereby allows / the ritual enactment (of mythological ideas).
S(= Tourism) V O
그렇기 때문에 그것(관광)은 가능하게 한다 / 의식적 실행을 (허구적 생각의)

↳ 관광은 허구적 개념을 실행하는 의식임.

(→ as to의 O1(명사절))
(① [4]There is a considerable difference (as to whether people watch / a film (about the Himalayas)
V S 전치사(~에 관한) 명사절 접속사 S′ V′1 O′1
/ on television / and become excited / by the 'untouched nature' (of the majestic mountain peaks),
(→ as to의 O2(명사절)) V′2 C′
// or whether they get up and go on a trek / to Nepal).)
명사절 접속사 S′ V′1 V′2
상당한 차이가 있다 (사람들이 시청할지에 관해서는 / 영화를 (히말라야산맥에 대한) /
텔레비전에서 / 그리고 흥분하게 되는지에 관해서는 / '손대지 않은 자연'에 (장엄한 산봉우리의) //
또는 그들이 일어나서 길고 고된 여행을 하는지에 관해서는 / 네팔로)

↳ 예: 히말라야산맥을 영화로 보는 것과 네팔에 직접 가는 것은 상당한 차이가 있음.

해석

[1]관광은 가상의 영역 그리고 물리적 세계의 영역에서 동시에 일어난다. [2]문학 또는 영화와 대조적으로, 그것(관광)은 '실제적인', 감지할 수 있는 세계로 이어지는데, 반면에 그럼에도 불구하고 환상, 꿈, 소망, 즉 허구의 영역과 여전히 관련되어 있다. [3]그렇기 때문에 그것(관광)은 허구적 생각의 의식적 실행을 가능하게 한다.(▶ 관광은 사람들이 여행지에 대한 허구적 생각을 가지고 여행지를 직접 경험하는 의식이라는 의미) (① [4]사람들이 텔레비전에서 히말라야산맥에 대한 영화를 시청하고 장엄한 산봉우리의 '손대지 않은 자연'에 흥분하게 되는지, 또는 그들이 일어나서 네팔로 길고 고된 여행을 하는지에 관해서는 상당한 차이가 있다.) [5]심지어 후자의 경우에도, 사람들은 적어도 부분적으로는 가상의 세계에 머물러 있다. (②) [6]그들은 집에서 책, 안내 책자, 그리고 영화에서 이미 보았던 순간을 경험한다. (③) [7]손대지 않은 자연과 친절하고 순박한 토착민에 대한 그들의 (허구적) 관념은 아마도 더 분명해질 것이다. (④) [8]하지만 이제 이러한 (관념의) 확립은 물리적 경험에 단단히 기반을 두고 있다. (⑤) [9]따라서 허구는 텔레비전, 영화, 또는 책에 의한 것보다 훨씬 더 강력한 방식으로 전달된다.

⊶ 주어진 문장의 직접 네팔로 여행을 가는 경우를 지칭함.
[5]Even in the latter case, / they remain, / (at least partly), / in an imaginary world.
S(=people) V 부사구 삽입
심지어 후자의 경우에도 / 사람들은 머물러 있다 / (적어도 부분적으로는) / 가상의 세계에
↳ **예의 세부 내용:** 사람들은 실제 관광을 하는 동안에도 가상의 세계에 머물러 있음.

(②) [6]They experience / *moments* [that they have already seen at home / in books, brochures and films].
S(= people) V O 목적격 관계대명사
그들은 경험한다 / 순간을 [그들이 집에서 이미 보았던 / 책, 안내 책자 그리고 영화에서]

(③) [7]Their notions (of untouched nature and friendly, innocent indigenous people) / will probably be confirmed.
S V
그들의 관념은 (손대지 않은 자연과 친절하고 순박한 토착민에 대한) / 아마도 더 분명해질 것이다
↳ **부연 설명:** 책, 안내 책자, 영화를 통해 봤던 가상의 세상을 경험하며 상상하던 관념이 분명해짐.

(④) [8]But now / this confirmation is anchored / in a physical experience.
S V
하지만 이제 / 이러한 (관념의) 확립은 단단히 기반을 두고 있다 / 물리적 경험에

(⑤) [9]The myth is thus transmitted / in a much more powerful way / than by television, movies or books.
S V 비교급 강조 부사
따라서 허구는 전달된다 / 훨씬 더 강력한 방식으로 / 텔레비전, 영화, 또는 책에 의한 것보다
↳ **결론:** 경험에 기반한 여행지에 대한 관념의 확립은 다른 매체에 의한 것보다 훨씬 강력함.

어휘

take place 일어나다, 생기다
simultaneously 동시에
realm 영역; 왕국
tangible 감지할[만질] 수 있는
tie 관련시키다; 묶다
sphere 영역; 구(체)
myth 허구; 신화
cf. mythological 허구적인; 신화적인
ritual 의식상의; 의례적인
enactment 실행; 법률 제정, 입법
considerable 상당한, 많은
majestic 장엄한, 웅장한
trek 길고 고된 여행; 트레킹하다
brochure 안내 책자
notion 관념, 개념, 생각
confirm 더 분명히 하다; 확인하다
cf. confirmation 확립, 견고하게 함; 확인
anchor ~에 단단히 기반을 두다; 닻(을 내리다)
transmit 전달하다; 전송하다

정답 가이드

① 뒤 문장의 the latter case와 they가 지칭하는 내용을 ① 앞의 문장에서 찾을 수 없으므로, 그 사이에 주어진 문장이 빠져 있을 가능성을 생각해 볼 수 있다. 주어진 문장은 사람들이 히말라야산맥을 텔레비전에서 보고 느끼는 것과 네팔로 직접 여행을 가는 것에는 차이가 있다는 내용인데, ① 뒤 문장의 the latter case와 they가 각각 주어진 문장의 직접 여행을 가는 것과 사람들을 가리키므로 주어진 문장이 들어가기에 가장 적절한 곳은 ①이다.

The 주의 문장 넣기 유형에서 ①이 정답인 경우는 거의 없지만, 어느 선택지든 정답이 될 수 있음에 유의해야 한다.

오답 클리닉

② (13%) 앞 문장에 대한 부연 설명으로 사람들이 매체를 통해 봤던 가상의 세상을 직접 경험한다는 내용의 연결은 자연스럽다.
③ (25%) 사람들이 가상의 세상을 경험함으로써 상상했던 관념이 더 분명해진다는 내용이다.

The 핵심 손대지 않은 자연과 친절하고 순박한 토착민은 앞 문장에서 언급한 사람들이 매체를 통해 집에서 보았던 순간의 예로 볼 수 있다.

④ (13%) 앞에서 설명한 관념의 확립을 this confirmation으로 지칭해 그저 매체를 통해 보고 아는 것과 달리 이것은 물리적 경험에 기반을 두고 있다고 설명한다.
⑤ (10%) 허구가 관광을 통해 더 강력한 방식으로 전달된다고 결론을 내리고 있다.

01 ✦ 글의 주제 〈19학년도 대수능 23번 | 정답률 48%〉 ④

구문분석 & 직독직해

환경 빈민국 원조와 정책 개혁을 통한 기후 변화 대응

주제문

*주장·요구·제안·명령 등의 동사가 that절을 목적어로 취하고 그 내용이 당위성(~해야 한다)을 의미할 때 that절에 <(should +) 동사원형>을 씀.

[1]We argue // that the ethical principles of justice / (should) provide / an essential foundation (for policies (to protect unborn generations and the poorest countries / from climate change)).

S V 명사절 접속사 S′ V′ O′

🔑 기후 변화로부터 미래 세대와 빈민국을 보호하는 정책에 관한 내용임.

우리는 주장한다 // 정의의 윤리적 원칙이 / 제공해야 한다고 / 필수적 토대를 (정책에 (아직 태어나지 않은 세대와 가장 가난한 나라들을 보호하는 / 기후 변화로부터))

↳ 기후 변화로부터 미래 세대와 빈민국을 보호하기 위한 정책은 윤리적 원칙에 기초해야 함.

[2]Related issues arise / in connection with current and persistently inadequate aid (for these nations), / in the face of growing threats (to agriculture and water supply), / and the rules of international trade [that mainly benefit rich countries].

S V (= the poorest countries) of의 O(명사구 병렬) 주격 관계대명사 V′ O′

연계된 문제들이 발생한다 / 현재의 지속적으로 부족한 원조와 관련하여 (이 (가난한) 국가들에 대한) / 점점 증가하는 위협에 직면하여 (농업과 물 공급에 대한) / 그리고 국제 무역의 규칙에 (직면하여) [주로 부유한 국가들에 이득이 되는]

↳ 제기되는 문제점: 부족한 원조로 인해 빈민국들은 어려운 상황에 놓여 있음.

🔑 기후 변화 대응 방법 1: 빈민국 원조 개혁.

[3]Increasing aid (for the world's poorest peoples) / can be an essential part (of effective mitigation).

S V C

원조를 늘리는 것은 (세계의 가장 가난한 국민들을 위한) / 필수적인 부분일 수 있다 (효과적인 (빈곤과 탄소 배출) 완화의)

↳ 기후 변화 대응책 1: 빈민국 원조 증대하기.

*with가 '이유'를 나타내는 전치사구를 이끎.

[4]With 20 percent of carbon emissions / from (mostly tropical) deforestation, /

탄소 배출량의 20퍼센트가 오기 때문에 / (대개 열대 지역의) 벌채로부터 /

*<combine A with B>: A와 B를 결합하다

carbon credits (for forest preservation) / would combine aid (to poorer countries) / with one of the most cost-effective forms (of abatement).

S V O

탄소 크레디트는 (삼림 보존을 위한) / 원조와 결합시킬 것이다 (더 가난한 국가들에 대한) / 가장 비용 효율이 높은 형태 중의 하나를 ((탄소 배출) 감소의)

↳ 세부 정책(탄소 크레디트): 삼림 보존으로 빈민국은 탄소 크레디트(거래 가능한 재화)를 얻고 탄소 배출은 감소됨.

🔑 기후 변화를 막기 위한 방법 2: 보조금 정책 개혁.

[5]Perhaps / the most cost-effective but politically complicated policy reform would be / the removal of several hundred billions of dollars (of direct annual subsidies) / from the two biggest recipients (in the OECD) — / destructive industrial agriculture and fossil fuels.

S V(추측) C =

아마 / 비용 효율이 가장 높지만 정치적으로 복잡한 정책 개혁은 ~일 것이다 / 수천억 달러를 없애는 것 (직접적인 연간 보조금의) / 두 개의 가장 큰 수혜 분야로부터 / (OECD(경제 협력 개발 기구))에서 / 즉 파괴적인 산업화 농업과 화석 연료

↳ 기후 변화 대응책 2: 환경을 파괴하는 산업에 대한 보조금 없애기.

*조동사 would에 동사 accelerate와 encourage가 <A as well as B(B뿐만 아니라 A도)>로 연결됨.

[6]Even a small amount (of this money) / would accelerate the already rapid rate (of technical progress and investment / in renewable energy / in many areas), / as well as encourage the essential switch (to conservation agriculture).

S V_1 O_1 V_2 O_2

적은 양이라도 (이 돈의) / 이미 빠른 속도를 가속화할 것이다 (기술적 진보와 투자의 / 재생 가능한 에너지에 대한 / 많은 지역에서) / 근본적인 전환을 장려할 뿐만 아니라 (보존 농업으로의)

↳ 절감한 보조금은 환경 보호 사업에 유용하게 쓰일 수 있음.

해석

[1]우리는 정의의 윤리적 원칙이 아직 태어나지 않은 세대와 가장 가난한 나라들을 기후 변화로부터 보호하는 정책에 필수적 토대를 제공해야 한다고 주장한다. [2]농업과 물 공급에 대한 점점 증가하는 위협과 주로 부유한 국가들에 이득이 되는 국제 무역의 규칙에 직면하여, 이 (가난한) 국가들에 대한 현재의 지속적으로 부족한 원조와 관련하여 연계된 문제들이 발생한다. [3]세계의 가장 가난한 국민들을 위한 원조를 늘리는 것은 효과적인 (빈곤과 탄소 배출) 완화의 필수적인 부분일 수 있다. [4]탄소 배출량의 20퍼센트가 (대개 열대 지역의) 벌채로부터 오기 때문에, 삼림 보존을 위한 탄소 크레디트는 더 가난한 국가들에 대한 원조와 가장 비용 효율이 높은 (탄소 배출) 감소의 형태 중의 하나를 결합시킬 것이다. [5]아마 비용 효율이 가장 높지만 정치적으로 가장 복잡한 정책 개혁은 OECD(경제 협력 개발 기구)에서 두 개의 가장 큰 수혜 분야, 즉 파괴적인 산업화 농업과 화석 연료로부터 직접적인 연간 보조금 수천억 달러를 없애는 것일 것이다. [6]이 돈의 적은 양이라도 보존 농업으로의 근본적인 전환을 장려할 뿐만 아니라, 많은 지역에서 이미 빠른 재생 가능한 에너지에 대한 기술적 진보와 투자의 속도를 가속화할 것이다.

어휘

ethical 윤리적인
in connection with ~와 관련하여
persistently 지속적으로; 끈질기게
inadequate 부족한, 불충분한
in the face of ~에 직면하여
tropical 열대 지역의
deforestation (삼림) 벌채
reform 개혁(하다)
annual 연간의, 한 해의
recipient 수혜 분야; 받는 사람, 수령인
destructive 파괴적인
accelerate 가속화하다; 속도를 높이다
switch 전환, 변경
[선택지] diplomatic 외교의
cope with ~에 대처하다

⊕ 탄소 크레디트(carbon credit): 삼림 보호 등으로 온실가스를 줄였을 때 발행되는 탄소 배출권(일정량의 온실가스를 배출할 수 있는 권리)으로 거래소에서 자유롭게 사고팔 수 있음.

⊕ 탄소 배출(carbon emission): 온실 효과를 일으키는 주된 요인이며, 식물은 이산화탄소를 흡수하므로 삼림 보호는 기후 변화 완화를 도움.

⊕ 보존 농업(conservation agriculture): 지속 가능하고 친환경적인 방식의 농업.

정답 가이드

기후 변화 대응책으로 빈민국에 대한 원조를 늘리는 원조 개혁과, 환경 파괴적인 산업에 대한 보조금을 없애는 등의 정책 개혁을 언급하고 있다. 따라서 주제로 가장 적절한 것은 ④ 'coping with climate change by reforming aid and policies(원조와 정책 개혁으로 기후 변화에 대처하기)'이다.

오답 클리닉

① reforming diplomatic policies in poor countries (17%)
가난한 국가의 외교 정책(×) 개혁하기
외교 정책이 아닌 기후 변화 대응책에 관한 내용임.

② increasing global awareness of the environmental crisis (9%)
환경의 위기에 대한 세계적 인식 높이기(×)
기후 변화를 환경 위기로 볼 수 있으나 이에 대한 세계적 인식을 늘리는 내용은 없음.

③ reasons for restoring economic equality in poor countries (22%)
가난한 국가에서 경제적 평등을 복구하려는(×) 이유
가난한 국가에 원조를 늘리는 목적은 궁극적으로 기후 변화를 막기 위함임.

⑤ roles of the OECD in solving international conflicts (4%)
국제적 갈등(×) 을 해결하는 데 있어 OECD의 역할(×)
국제적 갈등이나 이에 대한 OECD의 역할에 대한 언급은 전혀 없음.

02 + 빈칸 추론 〈17학년도 대수능 32번 | 정답률 43%〉 ②

구문분석 & 직독직해

과학 연구에 따라 다양한 시간 해상도

[1]Temporal resolution (S) is (V) particularly interesting (C) / in the context of satellite remote sensing.
시간 해상도는 특히 흥미롭다 / 위성의 원격 감지의 맥락에서
↳ **도입:** 위성의 원격 감지에 있어 시간 해상도는 흥미로움.

[2]The temporal density (of remotely sensed imagery) (S) / is (V) large, impressive, and growing (C).
시간적인 밀도는 (원격으로 감지된 이미지의) / 크고, 인상적이고, 커지고 있다

[3]Satellites (S) are collecting (V) a great deal of imagery (O) // as (부사절 접속사(~할 때)) you read this sentence.
위성들은 많은 양의 이미지를 모으고 있다 // 여러분이 이 문장을 읽을 때에도
↳ **부연 설명:** 위성이 모으는 이미지의 시간 해상도는 미세해지고 있음.

[4]However, / most applications (in geography and environmental studies) (S) / do not require (V) extremely fine-grained temporal resolution (O).
그러나 / 대부분의 응용 프로그램들은 (지리학과 환경 연구에서의) / 극히 미세한 시간 해상도를 필요로 하지 않는다
↳ 지리학과 환경 연구의 대부분은 극히 미세한 시간 해상도가 필요하지 않음.

🔑 연구에 따라 요구하는 시간 해상도가 다름.

[5]Meteorologists (S_1) may require (V_1) / visible, infrared, and radar information (O_1) / at sub-hourly temporal resolution; //
기상학자들은 필요로 할 수도 있다 / 눈에 보이는, 적외선의, 레이더 정보를 / 한 시간 이내의 시간 해상도로 //
urban planners (S_2) might require (V_2) imagery (O_2) / at monthly or annual resolution; //
도시 계획자들은 이미지를 필요로 할지도 모른다 / 월간 혹은 연간 해상도로 //
and transportation planners (S_3) may not need (V_3) / any time series information (O_3) / at all / for some applications.
그리고 교통 계획자들은 필요로 하지 않을 수도 있다 / 어떠한 시계열(時系列) 정보도 / 전혀 / 어떤 응용 프로그램에 대해서는
↳ **예:** 연구 분야에 따라 필요로 하는 시간 해상도가 다름.

주제문
*used는 imagery를 수식하는 과거분사임.
[6]Again, / the temporal resolution (of *imagery* used) (S) / should **meet** (V) / **the requirements (of your inquiry)** (O).
다시 말해 / 시간 해상도는 (사용되는 사진의) / 충족시켜야 한다 / 필요조건을 (여러분의 연구의)
↳ 사용되는 사진의 시간 해상도는 연구의 필요 조건을 충족시켜야 함.

해석

[1]시간 해상도는 위성의 원격 감지의 맥락에서 특히 흥미롭다. [2]원격으로 감지된 이미지의 시간적인 밀도는 크고, 인상적이고, 커지고 있다.(▶ 위성이 사진을 찍는 빈도가 많아짐을 의미) [3]여러분이 이 문장을 읽을 때에도 위성들은 많은 양의 이미지를 모으고 있다. [4]그러나, 지리학과 환경 연구에서의 대부분의 응용 프로그램들은 극히 미세한 시간 해상도를 필요로 하지 않는다. [5]기상학자들은 눈에 보이는, 적외선의, 레이더 정보를 한 시간 이내의 시간 해상도로 필요로 할 수도 있으며, 도시 계획자들은 월간 혹은 연간 해상도로 이미지를 필요로 할지도 모르고, 교통 계획자들은 어떤 응용 프로그램에 대해서는 어떠한 시계열(時系列) 정보도 전혀 필요로 하지 않을 수도 있다. [6]다시 말해, 사용되는 사진의 시간 해상도는 여러분의 연구의 필요조건을 충족시켜야 한다. [7]때로 연구자들은 과거의 정보를 얻기 위해서 위성 이미지 모음보다 앞서는 항공 사진의 기록 보관소를 찾아봐야 한다.

어휘

satellite 위성 (장치); 위성의
remote 원격의; 외진; 먼
cf. remotely 원격으로; 멀리 (떨어져)
density 밀도; 농도
imagery 이미지; 심상
application 응용 프로그램; 지원[신청](서); 적용
cf. apply 적용하다; 지원[신청]하다
geography 지리(학)
fine-grained 미세한, 세밀한
visible (눈에) 보이는
sub- ~보다 적은; 아래
inquiry 연구, 탐구; 질문
archive 기록 보관소
aerial 항공(기)의; 공기[대기]의
pre-date ~보다 앞서다, 선행하다
collection 모음(집); 수집(품)
[선택지] occasion 경우, 때
exclusively 오직, 오로지; 배타적으로

[7]Sometimes / researchers have to search / *archives* (of aerial photographs) / to get information from that past / [that pre-date the collection of satellite imagery].

S V O 목적(~하기 위해) 주격 관계대명사

때로 / 연구자들은 찾아봐야 한다 / 기록 보관소를 (항공 사진의) / 과거의 정보를 얻기 위해서 / [위성 이미지 모음보다 앞서는]

↳ **부연 설명:** 연구에 필요한 경우 위성 이전의 사진 기록도 찾아봐야 함.

⊕ 시간[주기] 해상도(temporal resolution): 특정 지역에 대하여 얼마나 자주 영상 자료를 획득할 수 있는지를 나타냄. 동일 지역을 자주 방문할수록 시간[주기] 해상도가 높음.

⊕ 시계열(時系列)(time series information): 시간의 경과에 따라 변동하는 값을 관측값으로 기록한 것.

정답 가이드

빈칸 문장은 사용되는 사진의 시간 해상도가 '어떠해야' 하는지 설명하는 내용이다. 문장이 Again으로 이어지는 것으로 보아 앞 내용의 반복으로 볼 수 있는데, 앞에서는 기상학자, 도시 계획자, 교통 계획자들의 경우를 예로 들어 연구 분야에 따라 필요한 사진의 시간 해상도가 다르다고 설명하고 있다. 따라서 빈칸에 들어갈 말로 가장 적절한 것은 ② 'meet the requirements of your inquiry(여러분의 연구의 필요조건을 충족시키다)'이다.

오답 클리닉

① be selected for general purposes (18%)
일반적인 목적을 위해 선택되다
시간 해상도는 일반적인 목적이 아닌 연구에 따라 다르게 요구된다고 했으므로 틀림.

③ be as high as possible for any occasion (15%)
어떤 경우든 가능한 한 높다
대부분의 응용 프로그램이 극히 미세한 시간 해상도를 요구하지 않는다고 했으므로 어떤 경우든 높아야 하는 것은 아님.

④ be applied to new technology by experts (7%)
전문가에 의해 신기술에 적용되다
신기술에 적용되어야 한다는 언급은 없음.

⑤ rely exclusively upon satellite information (18%)
오직 위성의 정보에만 의존하다
과거 정보를 얻기 위해 위성 이전의 항공 사진을 찾아봐야 한다고 했으므로 틀림.

03 + 글의 순서 〈18학년도 대수능 37번 | 정답률 40%〉 ④

구문분석 & 직독직해

사회 원시 사회에서 질병의 의미

[1]To modern man / disease is *a biological phenomenon* [that concerns him / only as an individual] / and has no moral implications.

S V₁ C 주격 관계대명사 V₂ O

현대인에게 / 질병은 생물학적 현상이다 [그 자신과 관련 있는 / 오직 개인으로서] /
그리고 어떤 도덕적 함의도 지니지 않는다

↳ **대조 A(현대인):** 질병을 생물학적 현상으로 여김.

*<attribute A to B>: A를 B의 탓으로 보다

[2]When he contracts influenza, // he never attributes this event to his behavior (toward the tax collector or his mother-in-law).

부사절 접속사(시간) S V O

유행성 감기에 걸릴 때 // 그는 결코 이 일을 자신의 행동 탓으로 보지 않는다 (세금 징수원이나 자신의 장모에 대한)

↳ **예:** 감기에 걸린 것을 자신의 비난받을 만한 행동 탓으로 돌리지 않음.

🔑 주어진 글의 현대인과 대조되는 원시인이 질병에 대해 갖는 의미가 제시됨.

(C) [3]Among primitives, / because of their supernaturalistic theories, / the prevailing moral point of view gives a deeper meaning / to disease.

S V O

원시인들 사이에서는 / 그들의 초자연주의적인 생각 때문에 /
지배적인 도덕적 관점이 더 깊은 의미를 제공한다 / 질병에 대해

↳ **대조 B(원시인):** 질병을 도덕적 관점에서 생각함.

[4]*The gods* [who send disease] / are usually angered / by the moral offences of the individual.

S(복수) 주격 관계대명사 V(복수)

신들은 [질병을 주는] / 일반적으로 분노한다 / 개인의 도덕적 범죄에 의해

🔑 they는 (C)의 The gods who send disease를 가리킴.

<not A but B>: A가 아니라 B

(A) [5]Sometimes they may not strike the guilty person himself, / but rather (may strike) *one of his relatives or tribesmen*, // to whom responsibility is extended.

S V O₁ 재귀대명사(강조) O₂ 전치사+관계대명사(보충 설명)

때때로 그들(질병을 주는 신들)은 죄를 범한 사람 본인을 공격하는 것이 아니라 / 오히려 그의 친척이나 부족민 중의 한 명을 (공격할지도 모른다) // (죄의) 책임이 확장되어

해석

[1]현대인에게 질병은 오직 개인으로서 그 자신과 관련 있는 생물학적 현상이고 어떤 도덕적 함의도 지니지 않는다. [2]유행성 감기에 걸릴 때, 그는 결코 이 일을 세금 징수원이나 자신의 장모에 대한 자신의 행동 탓으로 보지 않는다. (C) [3]원시인들 사이에서는, 그들의 초자연주의적인 생각 때문에, 지배적인 도덕적 관점이 질병에 대해 더 깊은 의미를 제공한다. [4]질병을 주는 신들은 일반적으로 개인의 도덕적 범죄에 의해 분노한다. (A) [5]때때로 그들(질병을 주는 신들)은 죄를 범한 사람 본인이 아니라, 오히려 (죄의) 책임이 확장되어 그의 친척이나 부족민 중의 한 명을 공격할지도 모른다. [6]따라서 질병, 질병을 일으켰을지도 모르는 행동, 그리고 질병으로부터의 회복은 전체 원시 사회에 매우 중요한 관심사이다. (B) [7]사회적 부정행위에 대한 제재로서의 질병은 그러한 사회에서 질서의 가장 중요한 기본적인 부분 중의 하나가 된다. [8]많은 경우에 그것(질병)은 현대 사회에서 경찰관, 재판관, 그리고 사제에 의해 수행되는 역할을 떠맡는다.

어휘

biological 생물학적인
phenomenon 현상
concern 관련이 있다; 걱정시키다; 관심사; 중요성
moral 도덕적인
implication 함의; 암시; 영향

↱ 주격 관계대명사
[6]Disease, *action* [that might produce disease], and recovery (from disease) / are, therefore, of vital concern / to the whole primitive community.
S / V / C
*<of+추상명사>는 형용사로 해석함.
질병, 행동 [질병을 일으켰을지도 모르는], 그리고 회복은 (질병으로부터의) / 따라서 매우 중요한 관심사이다 / 전체 원시 사회에
↳ **부연 설명:** 원시인은 신이 죄에 대한 벌로 질병을 준다고 생각했음.

(B) [7]Disease, / (as a sanction against social misbehavior), / becomes one (of the most important pillars of order / in such societies).
S / 전치사구 삽입 / V / C
such societies가 (A)의 the whole primitive community를 받음.
질병은 / (사회적 부정행위에 대한 제재로서의) / 하나가 된다 (질서의 가장 중요한 기본적인 부분 중의 / 그러한 사회에서)

↱ (= Disease)
[8]It takes over, / in many cases, / *the role* (played by policemen, judges, and priests / in modern society).
S / V / O / 과거분사구
그것(질병)은 떠맡는다 / 많은 경우에 / 역할을 (경찰관, 재판관, 그리고 사제에 의해 수행되는 / 현대 사회에서)
↳ **결론(의의):** 원시 사회에서 질병은 사회적 부정행위에 대한 제재로 작용했음.

contract (병에) 걸리다; 계약(하다)
primitive 원시인; 원시의
supernaturalistic 초자연주의적인
theory 생각, 의견; 이론
prevailing 지배적인, 우세한
point of view 관점, 견해
offence 범죄; 모욕
strike 공격하다; 치다
guilty 죄를 범한, 유죄의; 죄책감이 드는
extend 확장[확대]하다; 연장하다
vital 매우 중요한, 필수적인
misbehavior 부정행위
pillar (시스템·조직 등의) 기본적인 부분[특징]
take over ~을 떠맡다, 인계받다
priest 사제; 성직자

정답 가이드

현대인은 질병을 생물학적 현상으로 여긴다는 주어진 글 다음에 그와 대조되는 원시인이 생각한 질병의 의미를 설명하는 (C)가 오는 것이 적절하다. 내용이 대조되더라도 역접 연결어가 명시되지 않기도 한다. (A)의 they는 (C)의 The gods who send disease를 받는 것으로, 죄를 지으면 신이 질병을 준다고 생각해서 원시 사회에서 질병은 매우 중요하게 여겨졌다고 설명한다. 마지막으로 (A)의 the whole primitive community가 (B)의 such societies로 연결되어 원시 사회에서 질병이 수행한 사회적 역할을 설명하는 내용이 이어지는 것이 자연스럽다.

오답 클리닉

① (A) - (C) - (B) (4%) / ⑤ (C) - (B) - (A) (12%)
(A)의 they는 (C)의 The gods who send disease를 가리키므로 (C) 바로 뒤에 와야 한다.
② (B) - (A) - (C) (28%) / ③ (B) - (C) - (A) (13%)
주어진 글 뒤에 (B)가 오면 such societies는 '현대 사회'를 의미하게 되는데, 주어진 글은 현대 사회에서 질병이 도덕적 함의를 지니지 않는다고 했으므로 질병이 사회적 부정행위를 막아주는 역할을 한다는 (B)의 내용과 모순된다.

The 주의 (B)의 마지막 문장에 in modern society가 있다고 해서 주어진 글과 같은 맥락의 내용일 것이라 섣부르게 판단하지 않도록 주의한다.

01 ✦ 글의 제목 〈19학년도 대수능 24번 | 정답률 66%〉 ①

구문분석 & 직독직해

심리 큰 숫자에 대한 사람들의 무감각

[1]A defining element (of catastrophes) / is the magnitude (of their harmful consequences).
S(단수) V(단수) C
정의하는 한 요소는 (큰 재해를) / 규모이다 (그 폐해의)
↳ **도입:** 재해는 피해 규모로 정의됨.

*<help+O+(to-)v>: O가 v하는 것을 돕다
[2]To help societies prevent [or] reduce damage from catastrophes, /
목적(~하기 위해) prevent와 reduce의 공통 O
사회가 큰 재해로 인한 피해를 예방하거나 줄이는 것을 돕기 위해서 /
a huge amount of effort and technological sophistication / are often employed /
S(복수) V(복수)
to assess and communicate the size and scope (of potential or actual losses).
목적(~하기 위해)
막대한 양의 노력과 기술적인 지식이 / 자주 사용된다 /
규모와 범위를 산정하고 전달하기 위해 (잠재적 혹은 실제적 손실의)
↳ 재해로 인한 피해 규모와 범위를 파악하는 데 많은 노력과 기술이 사용됨.

↱ assumes의 O(명사절)
[3]This effort assumes // that people can understand the resulting numbers /
S V 명사절 접속사 S′ V′₁ O′₁
[and] (can) act on them appropriately.
V′₂ O′₂(= the resulting numbers)
이 노력은 추정한다 // 사람들이 그 결과로서 생기는 수를 이해할 수 있다고 /
그리고 그것들에 따라 적절하게 행동할 수 있다고
↳ **노력과 기술 사용의 전제:** 사람들이 재난 피해의 수치를 이해하고 알맞게 대응할 수 있음.

🗝 앞 전제(수를 이해하고 대응 가능함)에 대한 의문을 제기함.
[4]However, / recent behavioral research casts doubt / on this fundamental assumption.
S V O (= 앞 문장의 that 명사절)
그러나 / 최근의 행동 연구는 (~에) 의문을 던진다 / 이 근본적인 추정에
↳ **반박:** 전제가 잘못됨.

주제문 🗝 사람들은 큰 숫자를 이해 못 함.
[5]Many people do not understand large numbers.
S V O
많은 사람들이 큰 수를 이해하지 못한다
↳ **논거:** 재난 피해로 산정된 큰 숫자를 많은 사람들이 이해하지 못함.

🗝 정서적 반응을 유발하지 않는 큰 숫자는 무의미함.
[6]Indeed, / large numbers have been found / to lack meaning / [and] to be underestimated /
S V C(to-v구 병렬)
in decisions // unless they convey affect (feeling).
부사절 접속사(~하지 않는 한)
실제로 / 큰 수는 확인되었다 / 의미가 없는 것으로 / 그리고 과소평가되는 것으로 /
결정에 // 그것들이 정서적 반응(감정)을 전달하지 않는 한
↳ **부연 설명:** 큰 숫자는 감정을 전달하지 않는 한 사람들이 제대로 이해할 수 없음.

↱ (= 앞 문장)
[7]This creates *a paradox* [that rational models (of decision making) / fail to represent].
S V O 목적격 관계대명사 S′ V′ O′
이것은 역설을 만들어 낸다 [합리적 모형이 (의사 결정의) / 나타내지 못하는]
↳ **결과:** 합리적 의사 결정 모형과 다른 역설이 생김.

[8]On the one hand, / we respond strongly / to aid a single individual (in need).
S V 목적(~하기 위해)
한편으로는 / 우리는 강하게 반응한다 / 한 개인을 돕기 위해 (어려움에 처한)

🗝 큰 규모의 피해를 예측해도 잘 대응하지 못함.
[9]On the other hand, / we often fail / to prevent mass tragedies / [or] (to) take *appropriate measures*
S V O(to-v구 병렬)
(to reduce potential losses from natural disasters).
다른 한편으로 / 우리는 자주 (~하지) 못한다 / 대규모의 비극을 막는 것을 / 또는 적절한 조치를 취하는 것을
(자연재해로 인한 잠재적인 손실을 줄일)
↳ **역설의 부연 설명:** 개인의 어려움에는 반응하는 반면, 대규모 비극에는 제대로 대응하지 못함.
→ 적은 수에는 크게 반응하지만 정작 큰 수에는 그렇지 않음.

해석

[1]큰 재해를 정의하는 한 요소는 그 폐해의 규모이다. [2]사회가 큰 재해로 인한 피해를 예방하거나 줄이는 것을 돕기 위해서, 막대한 양의 노력과 기술적인 지식이 잠재적 혹은 실제적 손실의 규모와 범위를 산정하고 전달하기 위해 자주 사용된다. [3]이 노력은 사람들이 그 결과로서 생기는 수를 이해할 수 있고 그것들에 따라 적절하게 행동할 수 있다고 추정한다. [4]그러나 최근의 행동 연구는 이 근본적인 추정에 의문을 던진다. [5]많은 사람들이 큰 수를 이해하지 못한다. [6]실제로 큰 수는 정서적 반응(감정)을 전달하지 않는 한 의미가 없고 결정에 과소평가되는 것으로 확인되었다. [7]이것은 합리적 의사 결정 모형이 나타내지 못하는 역설을 만들어 낸다. [8]한편으로는 우리는 어려움에 처한 한 개인을 돕기 위해 강하게 반응한다. [9]다른 한편으로, 우리는 자주 대규모의 비극을 막거나 자연재해로 인한 잠재적인 손실을 줄일 적절한 조치를 취하지 못한다.

어휘

magnitude 규모, 크기
sophistication (고도의) 지식, 소양; 세련; 정교함
employ 사용하다, 쓰다; 고용하다
assess (가치·양을) 산정[평가]하다
scope 범위
assume 추정[가정]하다
cf. assumption 가정, 전제
act on ~에 따라 행동하다
behavioral 행동의
cast doubt on ~에 의문을 던지다
fundamental 근본적인, 기본적인
underestimate 과소평가하다
affect 정서적 반응, 감정; 영향을 미치다
paradox 역설
rational 합리적인, 이성적인
in need 어려움에 처한
mass 대규모의, 대량의; 대중
[선택지] insensitivity 둔감, 무감각
classify 분류[구분]하다
desperate 간절히 필요로 하는; 극심한
magnify 과장[확대]하다

⊕ 합리적 (의사 결정) 모형(rational model (of decision making)): 사람들이 이익은 최대화하고 손실은 최소화하는 방향으로 의사 결정을 한다는 것. 직관(intuition)에 따르는 의사 결정 모형과 대비되며 좀 더 효과적인 것으로 설명됨. 이 지문에서는 이 합리적 모형과 역설적으로, 사람들이 한 개인의 어려움에 공감하고, 다수의 어려움에는 둔감한 것을 설명함.

정답 가이드

사람들이 재해 규모를 이해하고 적절하게 대응할 수 있다는 전제하에 그것을 측정하기 위한 많은 노력과 기술이 사용되는 것이라고 했는데, 역접 연결어 However 이후부터는 그러한 전제에 의문을 제기하며 사실 사람들은 큰 숫자를 이해하지 못한다고 했다. 이는 어려움에 처한 한 개인을 돕는 것에는 크게 반응하지만 큰 재해로 인한 큰 수의 피해 규모, 피해액에는 적절히 반응하지 못하는 역설을 야기한다고 했으므로 제목으로 가장 적절한 것은 ① 'Insensitivity to Mass Tragedy: We Are Lost in Large Numbers(대규모 비극에 대한 둔감, 즉 우리는 큰 수 앞에서 어떻게 할 줄을 모른다)'이다.

오답 클리닉

② Power of Numbers: A Way of Classifying Natural Disasters (15%)
수의 힘(×), 즉 자연재해를 분류하는 방법
도입에서 재해가 그 피해 규모에 따라 정의된다고 했으나 재해 분류는 중심 내용이 아니며, 사람들이 큰 수를 이해하지 못하므로 숫자가 힘을 가진다고 보기도 어려움.

③ How to Reach Out a Hand to People in Desperate Need (5%)
간절히 도움을 필요로 하는 사람들에게 손을 내미는 방법(×)
역설에 대한 예로 어려움에 처한 개인을 돕기 위해 반응한다는 내용은 있지만, 그들을 돕는 방법은 글의 내용과 관련이 없음.

④ Preventing Potential Losses Through Technology (7%)
기술을 통해 잠재적 손실을 방지하기(×)
도입부에서 기술적 지식으로 피해 규모를 파악한다고는 했으나, 사람들이 큰 숫자에 무감각하므로 실제로 손실을 방지한다고 볼 수 없음.

⑤ Be Careful, Numbers Magnify Feelings! (8%)
주의하라, 수는 감정을 과장한다(×)!
큰 숫자라도 감정을 전달하지 못하면 사람들은 무감각하게 반응한다는 내용이므로 수가 감정을 과장한다고 볼 수 없음.

02 ✦ 빈칸 추론 〈17학년도 대수능 31번 | 정답률 45%〉 ①

구문분석 & 직독직해

교육 창의력을 제한하는 과도하게 구조화된 환경

[1] *The creativity* [that children possess] / needs to be cultivated / throughout their development.
(S: The creativity / 목적격 관계대명사: that / V: needs to be cultivated / O)
창의력은 [아이들이 지닌] / 길러져야 한다 / 그들의 발달 내내
↳ **도입:** 아이들의 창의력은 성장하는 동안 길러져야 함.

주제문
[2] Research suggests // that overstructuring the child's environment / may actually limit / creative and academic development.
(S: Research / V: suggests / 명사절 접속사: that / → suggests의 O(명사절) / S′(동명사구): overstructuring the child's environment / V′: may actually limit / O′: creative and academic development)
연구는 시사한다 // 아이의 환경을 과도하게 구조화하는 것이 / 실제로 제한할지도 모른다는 것을 / 창의적 그리고 학문적 발달을

[3] This is a central problem / with much of science instruction.
(S: This / V: is / C: a central problem)
이것은 가장 중요한 문제이다 / 과학 교육의 많은 부분에서
↳ **연구 시사점:** 과학 교육에서 환경에 대한 과도한 구조화가 발달을 제한할 수 있음.

[4] The exercises or activities are devised / to eliminate different options / and to focus on predetermined results.
(S: The exercises or activities / V: are devised / 목적(~하도록): to-v구 병렬)
과제나 활동들은 고안된다 / 다양한 선택권을 없애도록 / 그리고 미리 결정된 결과에 집중하도록
↳ **부연 설명 1:** 과제 및 활동은 다양한 선택권을 없애고 정해진 결과에 집중하도록 고안됨.

[5] The answers are structured / to fit the course assessments, // and the wonder (of science) / is lost / along with cognitive intrigue.
(S_1: The answers / V_1: are structured / 목적(~하도록): to fit the course assessments / S_2: the wonder (of science) / V_2: is lost)
정답은 구조화된다 / 교과 과정 평가에 들어맞도록 //
그리고 경이감은 (과학에 대한) / 상실된다 / 인지적 흥미와 함께
↳ **부연 설명 2:** 정답은 평가에 맞춰 구조화되고 과학에 대한 아이들의 흥미와 경이감은 상실됨.

★<define A as B>: A를 B로 정의하다
[6] We define cognitive intrigue / as *the wonder* [that stimulates and intrinsically motivates / an individual to voluntarily engage in an activity].
(S: We / V: define / O: cognitive intrigue / 주격 관계대명사: that / V′: stimulates and intrinsically motivates / O′: an individual / C′: to voluntarily engage in an activity)
우리는 인지적 흥미를 정의한다 / 경이감으로 [자극하고 내재적으로 동기를 부여하는 / 한 개인이 어떤 활동에 자발적으로 참여하도록]

해석

[1]아이들이 지닌 창의력은 그들의 발달 내내 길러져야 한다. [2]연구는 아이의 환경을 과도하게 구조화하는 것이 실제로 창의적 발달과 학문적 발달을 제한할지도 모른다는 것을 시사한다. [3]이것은 과학 교육의 많은 부분에서 가장 중요한 문제이다. [4]과제나 활동들은 다양한 선택권을 없애고 미리 결정된 결과에 집중하도록 고안된다. [5]정답은 교과 과정 평가에 들어맞도록 구조화되고, 과학에 대한 경이감은 인지적 흥미와 함께 상실된다. [6]우리는 인지적 흥미를 한 개인이 어떤 활동에 자발적으로 참여하도록 자극하고 내재적으로 동기를 부여하는 경이감으로 정의한다. [7]인지적 흥미의 상실은 미리 정해진 결론을 가지고 놀잇감을 단 한 가지 방법으로 사용함으로 인해 시작되고, 학교에서의 기계적인 암기 교육에 의해 강화되는지도 모른다. [8]이것은 그 자체로 목적이 되어 계획된 목표를 숙달하는 것 이외에 개인에게 거의 요구하지 않는, 장난감, 게임, 그리고 수업에 의해 예증된다.

어휘

cultivate 기르다, 함양하다; 경작하다; 재배하다
overstructure 과도하게 구조화하다
academic 학문적인
devise 고안[창안]하다
eliminate 없애다, 제거하다
predetermine 미리 결정하다
fit ~에 들어맞다, 적합하다
assessment 평가
wonder 경이(감); 궁금해하다; 놀라다
along with ~와 함께
cognitive 인지적인

🔑 미리 정해진 결론으로 놀잇감을 한 가지 방법으로만 사용함으로써 인지적 흥미가 사라짐.

[7]The loss (of cognitive intrigue) / may be initiated / by the sole use of play items / with predetermined conclusions / and (may be) reinforced / by rote instruction (in school).

S / V1 / V2

상실은 (인지적 흥미의) / 시작되는지도 모른다 / 놀잇감을 단 한 가지 방법으로 사용함으로 인해 / 미리 정해진 결론을 가지고 / 그리고 강화되는지도 모른다 / 기계적인 암기 교육에 의해 (학교에서의)

↳ 학습에 대한 흥미는 미리 정해진 결론을 가지고 수업 용품을 단일한 방법으로만 사용하면 사라지고, 암기식 교육이 이를 악화시킴.

[8]This is exemplified / by *toys, games, and lessons* [that are an **end** in and of themselves / and require little of the individual / other than to master the planned objective].

S(= 앞 문장) / V / 주격 관계대명사 / V'1 / V'2 / *little: ((준부정어)) 거의 ~ 않는 / ~이외에 / other than의 O(to-v구)

이것은 예증된다 / 장난감, 게임, 그리고 수업에 의해 [그 자체로 목적이 되는 / 그리고 개인에게 거의 요구하지 않는 / 계획된 목표를 숙달하는 것 이외에]

🔑 장난감, 게임, 수업을 결론이 정해진 구조화된 활동의 예로 제시함.

↳ 예: 장난감, 게임, 수업은 그 자체로 목적이 되어 개인에게 계획된 목표를 숙달하는 것만 요구함.

intrigue 흥미, 호기심
stimulate 자극[고무]하다
intrinsically 내재적으로
voluntarily 자발적으로
engage in ~에 참여[관여]하다
initiate 시작하다, 개시하다
sole 단 하나의; 단독의
reinforce 강화하다
exemplify 예증하다, 예시하다
end 목적, 목표(= objective)
in and of itself 그 자체로
master 숙달[통달]하다

정답 가이드

빈칸 문장의 This는 앞에서 말한 인지적 흥미가 상실되는 원인을 지칭하며 이는 장난감, 게임, 수업에 의해 예증된다고 했다. 즉, 장난감, 게임, 수업은 미리 정해진, 계획된 목표를 숙달하는 것 외에는 개인에게 요구하는 것이 거의 없으므로 그 자체로 '목적'이 되고 있음을 추론할 수 있다. 따라서 빈칸에 들어갈 말로 가장 적절한 것은 ① 'end(목적)'이다.

오답 클리닉

② input (20%) 투입
장난감, 게임, 수업은 계획된 목표를 숙달하는 것이 요구된다고 했으므로 그 자체로 투입에 그친다고 볼 수 없음.

③ puzzle (11%) 어려운 문제
장난감, 게임, 수업이 어려운 문제인지는 유추할 수 없음.

④ interest (16%) 흥미
장난감, 게임, 수업은 결론이 정해진 구조화된 활동에 해당하므로 그 자체로 흥미가 된다는 내용은 글의 내용과 반대됨.

⑤ alternative (8%) 대안
장난감, 게임, 수업은 대안이 아니라 인지적 흥미의 상실이 시작되고 강화되는 활동의 예에 해당함.

03 + 문장 넣기 (18학년도 대수능 39번 | 정답률 51%) ④

구문분석 & 직독직해

환경 물고기 내 유기 수은 문제와 해결책

[1]An incident (in Japan / in the 1950s) / alerted the world / to the potential problems (of organic mercury in fish).

S / V / O / *<alert A to B>: A에게 B를 경고하다

한 사건이 (일본에서의 / 1950년대) / 전 세계에 경고했다 / 잠재적 문제를 (물고기에 들어 있는 유기 수은의)

[2]Factories were discharging mercury / into *the waters of Minamata Bay*, // which also harbored a commercial fishing industry.

S / V / O / 관계대명사(보충 설명)

공장들이 수은을 방출하고 있었다 / 미나마타만의 수역으로 // 그리고 그곳은 또한 상업적 어업의 거처가 되는 곳이었다

[3]Mercury was being bioaccumulated / in the fish tissue // and severe mercury poisoning occurred / in *many people* [who consumed the fish].

S1 / V1 / S2 / V2 / 주격 관계대명사

수은이 생체 내에 축적되고 있었다 / 물고기의 (세포) 조직 속 // 그리고 심한 수은 중독이 발생했다 / 많은 사람들에게 [그 물고기를 먹은]

(①) [4]The disabling neurological symptoms were subsequently called Minamata disease.

S / V / C / *<call+O+C(O를 C라고 부르다)>의 수동형

장애를 입히는 신경학적 증상은 그 뒤에 미나마타병으로 불렸다

↳ 도입: 공장에서 방출한 수은이 미나마타만 수역의 물고기 생체 내에 축적되어 그것을 먹은 사람들에게 수은 중독을 초래함.

(②) [5]Control (over direct discharge of mercury (from industrial operations)) / is clearly needed / for prevention.

S(단수) / V(단수)

통제가 (수은의 직접적 방출에 대한 (산업 활동으로부터 나오는)) / 확실히 필요하다 / 예방을 위해

↳ 산업 시설의 직접적인 수은 방출에 대한 통제가 필요함.

해석

[1]1950년대 일본에서의 한 사건이 물고기에 들어 있는 유기 수은의 잠재적 문제를 전 세계에 경고했다. [2]공장들이 미나마타만의 수역으로 수은을 방출하고 있었는데, 그곳은 또한 상업적 어업의 거처가 되는 곳이었다. [3]수은이 물고기의 (세포) 조직에 축적되고 있었으며 그 물고기를 먹은 많은 사람들에게 심한 수은 중독이 발생했다. (①) [4]장애를 입히는 신경학적 증상은 그 뒤에 미나마타병으로 불렸다. (②) [5]예방을 위해 산업 활동으로부터 나오는 수은의 직접적 방출에 대한 통제가 확실히 필요하다. (③) [6]하지만 이제는 그런 어떤 산업적 방출과는 동떨어진 호수에서도 소량의 수은이 나타날 수 있다고 알려져 있다. (④ [7]그러한 오염은 멀리 떨어진 발전소 혹은 지방 자치 단체의 소각로에서부터 공기를 통한 이동이 원인일 수 있다고 가정된다.) [8]이 문제를 최소화하기 위해서 그러한 근원(▶ 발전소와 소각로를 의미)에 대한 엄격하게 통제된 배출 기준이 요구된다. (⑤) [9]미국의 많은 호수들에 대해 물고기에 대한 권고안이 발표되었는데 이것들은 한 달에 특정한 종의 물고기가 섭취되어야 할 횟수에 관한 제한을 권고한다.

→ 진주어(명사절) 🔑 주어진 문장의 such contamination이 가리키는 내용.

(③) [6]However, / it is now recognized // that traces of mercury can appear / in *lakes* (far removed / from any such industrial discharge).

가주어 V 명사절 접속사 S′ V′ 과거분사구

하지만 / 이제는 (~라고) 알려져 있다 // 소량의 수은이 나타날 수 있다고 / 호수에서도 (동떨어진 / 그런 어떤 산업적 방출과는)

→ 진주어(명사절) 🔑 수은 방출 시설과 멀리 떨어진 호수에서 수은이 나오는 원인을 추정함.

(④) [7]It is postulated // that such contamination may result / from airborne transport (from remote power plants or municipal incinerators).)

가주어 V 명사절 접속사 S′ V′ 명사구 병렬

(~라고) 가정된다 // 그러한 오염은 원인일 수 있다고 / 공기를 통한 이동이 (멀리 떨어진 발전소 혹은 지방 자치 단체의 소각로에서부터)

↳ **문제점:** 공장에서 멀리 떨어진 호수에도 공기를 통해 수은이 유입될 수 있음.

→ (= remote power plants or municipal incinerators)

[8]Strictly controlled emission standards (for such sources) / are needed / to minimize this problem.

S V 목적(~하기 위해)

엄격하게 통제된 배출 기준이 (그러한 근원(멀리 떨어진 발전소 혹은 지방 자치 단체의 소각로)에 대한) / 요구된다 / 이 문제를 최소화하기 위해서

↳ **해결책 1:** 수은 배출 기준에 대한 엄격한 통제가 요구됨.

(⑤) [9]Fish advisories have been issued / for many lakes in the United States; //

S_1 V_1

물고기에 대한 권고안이 발표되었다 / 미국의 많은 호수들에 대해 //

these recommend / limits (on *the number of times per month* [(when) particular species of fish should be consumed]).

S_2(= fish advisories) V_2 O 관계부사 생략 S′ V′

이것들은 권고한다 / 제한을 (한 달에 횟수에 관한 [특정한 종의 물고기가 섭취되어야 할])

↳ **해결책 2:** 물고기 섭취 횟수를 제한하는 것이 권고됨.

어휘

organic mercury 유기 수은
discharge 방출[배출](하다); 해고하다
bay 만(灣) ((바다가 육지 쪽으로 들어와 있는 형태의 지형))
harbor ~의 거처가 되다; 항구
bioaccumulate 생체 내에 축적되다
tissue ((생물)) 조직
neurological 신경학(상)의
subsequently 그 뒤에, 나중에
trace 소량; 흔적; 추적하다
far removed from ~와 동떨어진
contamination 오염
result from ~이 원인이다, ~에서 기인하다
airborne 공기로 운반되는; 비행 중인
remote 멀리 떨어진; 외진
municipal 지방자치단체의
emission 배출(물)
advisory 권고; 자문의
issue 발표[공표]하다; 쟁점, 문제

⊕ 미나마타병(Minamata disease): 수은 중독으로 인해 발생하는 신경학적 증후군. 사지 마비, 진행성 보행 실조, 발음 장애 등이 발생할 수 있음.

정답 가이드

주어진 문장은 어떠한 오염의 원인으로 가정할 수 있는 것이 오염 시설들에서부터 공기를 통한 이동이라고 했다. 이는 수은 방출 산업 시설과 멀리 떨어진 호수에서도 수은이 나올 수 있다는 ④ 앞의 내용을 such contamination으로 받아 원인을 설명하는 것이며, 그 뒤 내용은 주어진 문장 내용에 대한 해결책에 해당하므로 주어진 문장이 들어가기에 가장 적절한 곳은 ④이다.

오답 클리닉

① (4%) 수은이 축적된 물고기를 먹은 사람들에게서 수은 중독이 발생했고 그것이 미나마타병으로 불렸다는 연결은 자연스럽다.
② (15%) 수은 중독 문제를 예방하기 위한 해결책으로 수은의 직접적 방출의 통제를 제시하는 것은 적절하다.
③ (23%) 산업 시설의 직접적인 수은 방출을 통제해야 한다는 앞 문장과 상반되는 산업적인 방출과는 멀리 떨어진 호수에서도 수은이 나올 수 있다는 문제점이 However로 이어지는 것은 적절하다.
⑤ (7%) 앞 문장의 해결책에 이어 물고기 섭취 횟수 제한이 또 다른 해결책임을 제시하고 있다.

01 ✦ 함의 추론 〈19학년도 9월 모평 21번 | 정답률 52%〉 ⑤

구문분석 & 직독직해

철학 개인의 창의적 업적과 환경의 상호 연관성

[1]Psychologist Mihaly Csikszentmihalyi suggests // that the common idea (of a creative individual coming up with great insights, discoveries, works, or inventions / in isolation) / is wrong.

(S: Psychologist Mihaly Csikszentmihalyi, V: suggests, that: 명사절 접속사 — suggests의 O(명사절), S′: the common idea, 동명사의 의미상 주어: a creative individual, of의 O(동명사구), V′: is, C′: wrong)

심리학자 Mihaly Csikszentmihalyi는 말한다 // 일반적인 생각은 (창의적인 개인이 위대한 통찰력, 발견물, 작품, 또는 발명품을 생각해 낸다는 / 홀로) / 잘못되었다고

↳ **도입(Myth):** 개인의 창의적인 업적은 홀로 이룬 것이 아님.

주제문 🔑 창의성은 한 개인과 환경 또는 문화 간의 상호 작용에서 비롯되며, 시기에 따라서도 달라짐.

[2]Creativity results / from a complex interaction (between a person and his or her environment or culture), / and also depends on timing.

(S: Creativity, V₁: results, V₂: depends on, O₂: timing)

창의성은 비롯된다 / 복잡한 상호 작용에서 (한 사람과 그의 환경 또는 문화 사이의) / 그리고 또한 시기에 달려 있다

↳ **사실(Truth):** 창의성은 사람과 환경 또는 문화의 상호 작용에서 비롯되며 시기에 따라 달라짐.

★가정법 과거완료 <if+S′+had p.p. ~, S+would have p.p. ...>: (과거에) ~했다면, …했을 텐데

[3]For instance, / if the great Renaissance artists (like Ghiberti or Michelangelo) had been born // only 50 years before they were (born), //

(if: 부사절 접속사(조건), S′: the great Renaissance artists, V′: had been born, before: 부사절 접속사(시간), S″: they, V″: were)

예를 들어 / 만약 위대한 르네상스 시대의 예술가들이 (Ghiberti나 Michelangelo와 같은) 태어났다면 // 그들이 태어나기 불과 50년 전에 //

the culture (of artistic patronage) / would not have been in place / (to fund or shape their great achievements).

(S: the culture, V: would not have been, C: in place, to fund와 (to) shape의 공통 O(명사구): their great achievements)

문화가 (예술 후원의) / 자리 잡지 않았을 것이다 / (그들의 위대한 업적에 자금을 제공하거나 구체화할)

↳ **예 1:** 예술 후원 문화가 있었기에 위대한 예술가가 나올 수 있었음.

[4]Consider also individual astronomers: //

(V₁(명령문): Consider, O: individual astronomers)

또한 독자적인 천문학자들을 생각해 보라 //

Their discoveries could not have happened // unless centuries of technological development of the telescope and evolving knowledge of the universe / had come before them.

(S₂: Their discoveries, V₂(가정법 과거완료): could not have happened, unless: 부사절 접속사(조건), S′₁: centuries of technological development of the telescope, S′₂: evolving knowledge of the universe, V′(가정법 과거완료): had come, them (= individual astronomers))

그들의 발견은 일어날 수 없었을 것이다 // 수세기에 걸친 망원경의 기술적인 발전과 우주에 관한 진화하는 지식이 ~이 아니라면 / 그들(독자적인 천문학자들) 이전에 이루어지(지 않았다면)

↳ **예 2:** 기술 발전과 지식이 뒷받침되었기에 천문학자들의 발견이 일어날 수 있었음.

★<A as 형용사/부사 as B>: A는 B만큼 ~한/하게

[5]Csikszentmihalyi's point is // that we should devote as much attention / to the development of a domain // as we do / to the people (working within it), //

(S: Csikszentmihalyi's point, V: is, that: 명사절 접속사 — is의 C(명사절), S′: we, V′: should devote, O′: much attention, do (= devote attention), working: 현재분사구, it (= the domain))

Csikszentmihalyi의 요점은 ~이다 // 우리가 많은 주의를 쏟아야 한다는 것 / 어떤 분야의 발전에 // 우리가 주의를 쏟는 것만큼 / 사람들에게 (그 분야에서 일하는) //

as only this can properly explain // how advances are made.

(as: 부사절 접속사(~ 때문에), S′: this (= 앞의 that절), V′: can properly explain, O′(명사절): how advances are made)

🔑 개인에게 주의를 쏟는 것만큼 그 분야의 발전에도 주의를 쏟아야 진보가 이루어짐.

이는 오직 이것만이 적절히 설명할 수 있기 때문이다 // 진보가 어떻게 이루어지는지를

[6]Individuals are only "**a link in a chain, a phase in a process**," // he notes.

(O(명사절): Individuals are only "a link in a chain, a phase in a process", a link in a chain = a phase in a process, S: he, V: notes)

개인은 단지 '사슬의 한 연결 고리, 과정의 한 단계'일 뿐이라고 // 그는 언급한다

↳ **결론:** 개인은 사슬의 한 연결 고리일 뿐이므로 개인뿐만 아니라 개인이 일하는 분야의 발전에도 주의를 쏟아야 함.

해석

[1]심리학자 Mihaly Csikszentmihalyi는 창의적인 개인이 홀로 위대한 통찰력, 발견물, 작품 또는 발명품을 생각해 낸다는 일반적인 생각은 잘못되었다고 말한다. [2]창의성은 한 사람과 그의 환경 또는 문화 사이의 복잡한 상호 작용에서 비롯되며, (그것은) 또한 시기에 달려 있다. [3]예를 들어, 만약 Ghiberti나 Michelangelo와 같은 위대한 르네상스 시대의 예술가들이 그들이 태어나기 불과 50년 전에 태어났다면, 그들의 위대한 업적에 자금을 제공하거나 구체화할 예술 후원의 문화가 자리 잡지 않았을 것이다. [4]또한 독자적인 천문학자들을 생각해 보라. 수세기에 걸친 망원경의 기술적인 발전과 우주에 관한 진화하는 지식이 그들(독자적인 천문학자들) 이전에 이루어지지 않았다면 그들의 발견은 일어날 수 없었을 것이다. [5]Csikszentmihalyi의 요점은 우리가 어떤 분야에서 일하는 사람들에게 주의를 쏟는 것만큼 그 분야의 발전에 많은 주의를 쏟아야 한다는 것인데, 이는 오직 이것만이 진보가 어떻게 이루어지는지를 적절히 설명할 수 있기 때문이다.(▶ 진보는 개인 혼자서 이룰 수 없고 그 개인이 일하는 분야의 발전이 뒷받침되어야 이룰 수 있다는 의미) [6]그는 개인은 단지 '사슬의 한 연결 고리, 과정의 한 단계'일 뿐이라고 언급한다.

어휘

individual 개인(의); 독자적인, 개성적인
come up with ~을 생각해 내다, 제안[제시]하다
in isolation 홀로; 고립된
result from ~에서 비롯되다
fund 자금(을 제공하다)
shape 구체화[구현]하다; 형성하다; 모양
astronomer 천문학자
telescope 망원경
devote A to B A를 B에 쏟다[바치다]
domain (지식·활동의) 분야[영역]; 영토
link (사슬의 연결) 고리; 연결(하다)
phase 단계, 국면
[선택지] breakthrough 획기적 발전; 돌파구
credit 인정; 신용(하다)
condition 조건; 상태; 상황

정답 가이드

밑줄 친 문장은 '개인'이 사슬의 '한 연결 고리', 과정의 '한 단계'일 뿐이라는 것이므로, 개인이 어떻게 서술되고 있는지를 찾아야 한다. 위대한 통찰력이나 발명품 등은 창의적인 개인이 홀로 이룬 것이 아니라 '한 개인과 환경 또는 문화 간의 상호 작용'에서 비롯된 것이며 '시기'에 따라서도 달라진다고 했다. 그에 대한 예들이 이어지고, 요점은 우리가 어떤 분야에서 일하는 사람만큼 그 분야의 발전에 주의를 쏟아야 한다는 것이라고 했다. 즉, 개인의 창의성이 발휘되기 위해서는 창의성이 발휘될 수 있는 주변 여건들이 선행되어야만 한다는 의미이므로, 밑줄 친 부분의 의미와 가장 가까운 것은 ⑤ 'Individual creativity emerges only in its necessary conditions.(개인의 창의성은 오직 필수 조건들이 갖춰져야만 나타난다.)'이다.

오답 클리닉

① Individuals' creativity results only from good fortune. (7%)
개인의 창의력은 오직 행운에서 비롯된다(×).
창의력이 행운에서 비롯된다는 내용은 언급되지 않음.

② Discoveries can be made only due to existing knowledge.(19%)
발견은 오직(×) 기존의 지식 덕분에 이루어질 수 있다.
발견은 기존 지식뿐만 아니라 기술적 발전 등 개인과 환경 또는 문화 간의 상호 작용에 의해 이루어짐.

③ One's genius is a key element of a series of breakthroughs. (8%)
사람의 천재성(×)은 일련의 획기적인 발전의 핵심 요소이다.
개인의 천재성으로만 발전을 이루는 것이 아니며 환경적 조건이 뒷받침되어야 함.

④ Individuals receive no credit for their creative achievements. (13%)
개인은 자신의 창의적인 업적에 대해 인정을 받지 못한다(×).
창의적인 업적을 개인이 홀로 이룬 것은 아니라고 했지만, 그 업적에 대해 인정을 받지 못한다는 내용은 없음.

02 + 빈칸 추론 〈17학년도 9월 모평 34번 | 정답률 55%〉

①

구문분석 & 직독직해

언어 구조적 유사성이 없는 언어와 생각

주제문

[1] Even if it is correct to say // that we *express* and *represent* / our thoughts / in language, //
(부사절 접속사(양보) / 가주어' / 진주어'(to-v구) / to say의 O(명사절))
말하는 것이 옳을지라도 // 우리가 '표현하고' '나타낸다'고 / 우리의 생각을 / 언어로 //

it may be a big mistake to suppose // that there are structural similarities (between what is doing the representing and what is represented).
(가주어 V C 진주어(to-v구) 명사절 접속사 V' S' / → to suppose의 O(명사절) / 명사절 병렬)
*<between A and B>: A와 B 사이의
⊶ 언어와 생각 사이에 구조적 유사성은 없음.
가정하는 것은 큰 실수일 수 있다 // 구조적 유사성이 있다고 (표현하고 있는 것과 표현되는 것 사이에)
↳ 생각을 언어로 표현한다고 해서 언어와 생각이 구조적으로 유사하다고 볼 수는 없음.

[2] Robert Stalnaker, (in his book *Inquiry*), suggests / an analogy / with the representation (of numbers): //
(S_1 전치사구 삽입 V_1 O)
Robert Stalnaker는 (자신의 책 <Inquiry>에서) 제시한다 / 한 가지 비유를 / 표현으로 ('숫자들'의) //

The number 9 can be *represented* / as '12 — 3' // but it does not follow // that 12, 3, or *subtraction* are *constituents* of the number 9.
(S_2 V_2 가주어 V_3 명사절 접속사 S' V' C' / → 진주어(명사절))
*<it does not follow that>: 결과적으로 ~라는 것은 아니다
즉 숫자 9는 '표현될' 수 있다 / '12-3'으로 // 하지만 결과적으로 (~라는 것은) 아니다 // 12, 3, 또는 '빼기'가 숫자 9의 '구성 요소들'이라는 것은
↳ 예 1: 숫자 9는 '12-3'으로 표현될 수 있으나 12, 3, '빼기'가 숫자 9의 구성 요소인 것은 아님.

*<compare A with B>: A를 B와 비교하다
[3] We could compare a thought and its verbal expression / with toothpaste and its 'expression' from a tube.
(S V O)
우리는 생각과 그것의 언어적 표현을 비교할 수 있다 / 치약과 튜브에서 그것을 '짜낸 것'과

[4] That the result of expressing toothpaste is a long, thin, cylinder / does not entail // that toothpaste itself is long, thin, or cylindrical.
(S(명사절) V(단수) / → does not entail의 O(명사절) 명사절 접속사 S' V' C')
*재귀대명사 itself는 강조 용법으로 쓰여 toothpaste를 강조함.
치약을 짜낸 것의 결과가 길고 가는 원통이라는 것이 / 의미하지는 않는다 //
치약 그 자체가 길거나, 가늘거나, 아니면 원통형이라는 것을
↳ 예 2: 치약을 짜낸 것(언어적 표현)이 길고 가는 원통이라고 해서 치약 자체(생각)가 그 형태인 것은 아님.

[5] Similarly, / a thought might get expressed out loud / in a statement (with a particular linguistic structure).
(S V)
마찬가지로 / 생각은 소리 내어 표현될 수 있다 / 진술로 (특정 언어적 구조를 지닌)

해석

[1] 우리가 우리의 생각을 언어로 '표현하고' '나타낸다'고 말하는 것이 옳을지라도, 표현하고 있는 것(언어)과 표현되는 것(생각) 사이에 구조적 유사성이 있다고 가정하는 것은 큰 실수일 수 있다. [2] Robert Stalnaker는 자신의 책 <Inquiry>에서 '숫자들'의 표현으로 한 가지 비유를 제시한다. 즉 숫자 9는 '12-3'으로 '표현될' 수 있지만, 결과적으로 12, 3, 또는 '빼기'가 숫자 9의 '구성 요소들'이라는 것은 아니다. [3] 우리는 생각과 그것의 언어적 표현을 치약과 튜브에서 그것을 '짜낸 것'과 비교할 수 있다. [4] 치약을 짜낸 것의 결과가 길고 가는 원통이라는 것이 치약 그 자체가 길거나, 가늘거나, 아니면 원통형이라는 것을 의미하지는 않는다. [5] 마찬가지로 생각은 특정 언어적 구조를 지닌 진술로 소리 내어 표현될 수 있다. [6] 결과적으로 생각 그 자체가 그러한 구조로 되어 있다는 것은 아니다. [7] 예를 들어 내가 과일 그릇을 보고 있으면서, 그 그릇 안에 사과와 오렌지가 들어 있다고 생각한다고 가정해 보라. [8] 내 눈앞에 있는 물체들은 과일 몇 개와 그릇을 포함하지만, '~와'라는 단어에 상응하는 어떤 물체도 세상이나 나의 시각 이미지에 존재하지 않는다.

어휘

express 표현하다; 짜내다
cf. expression 표현; 짜냄, 압착
represent 나타내다, 표현하다; 대표하다
cf. representation 표현, 묘사; 대표
structural 구조적인, 구조상의
similarity 유사성
analogy 비유; 유추
constituent 구성 요소
verbal 언어의; 구두의
cylinder 원통, 원기둥
cf. cylindrical 원통형의

⁶It does not follow // that **the thought itself has such a structure.**

(→ 진주어(명사절); 가주어 V / 명사절 접속사 S′ V′ O′)

결과적으로 (~라는 것은) 아니다 // 생각 그 자체가 그러한 구조로 되어 있다는 것은

↳ **주제문 재진술:** 생각이 특정 언어 구조로 표현될 수 있다고 해서 생각이 언어와 같은 구조를 가지는 것은 아님.

⁷Suppose, / for example, // that I look at a fruit bowl, / and think // that there is an apple and an orange / in that bowl.

(→ suppose의 O(명사절); V(명령문) / 명사절 접속사 S′ V′₁ O′₁ V′₂ O′₂(명사절))

가정해 보라 / 예를 들어 // 내가 과일 그릇을 보고 있다고 / 그리고 생각한다고 // 사과와 오렌지가 들어 있다고 / 그 그릇 안에

⁸The objects (in front of my eyes) / include some pieces of fruit and a bowl, //

(S₁ V₁ O)

물체들은 (내 눈앞에 있는) / 과일 몇 개와 그릇을 포함한다 //

but *no object* (corresponding to the word 'and') exists / either in the world or in my visual image.

(S₂ 현재분사구 V₂; ★<either A or B>: A와 B 둘 중 하나 — 전치사구 병렬)

🔑 단어 '~와(and)'에 상응하는 물체는 없음 → 생각와 언어 사이에 차이가 있음.

하지만 어떤 물체도 ('~와'라는 단어에 상응하는) 존재하지 않는다 / 세상이나 나의 시각 이미지에

↳ **예 3:** '과일 그릇에 사과와 오렌지가 들어 있다'고 생각한다고 할 때, 과일과 그릇은 있어도 '~와(and)'에 상응하는 물체는 없음.

out loud 소리 내어
statement 진술; 말함
linguistic 언어(학)의
object 물체, 물건; 반대하다
corresponding (~에) 상응[해당]하는
visual 시각의
[선택지] analysis 분석
unlikely 성공할 것 같지 않은; 있음직하지 않은
lack ~이 없다; 부족
logical 논리적인
distinct 별개의; 분명한

정답 가이드

빈칸 문장에 정보가 거의 없으므로 앞 문장과 함께 보면, (앞 내용과) 마찬가지로 생각은 특정한 구조의 언어로 표현될 수 있는데, 결과적으로 '~인' 것은 아니라는 내용이다. 이어지는 예에서 과일 그릇에 사과와 오렌지가 들어있다고 생각할 때 '~와(and)'라는 단어에 상응하는 물체는 없다고 했다. 이를 빈칸 앞 문장과 빈칸 문장에 대입하여 생각해보면, 생각이 어떤 언어 구조로 표현될 때 결과적으로 그 둘은 같지 않다는 것임을 추론할 수 있다. 따라서 빈칸에 들어갈 말로 가장 적절한 것은 ① 'the thought itself has such a structure(생각 그 자체가 그러한 구조로 되어 있다)'이다.

오답 클리닉

② linguistic analysis of a thought is unlikely (8%)
생각에 대한 언어적 분석은 성공할 것 같지 않다
생각을 언어적으로 분석하는 것에 관한 내용이 아님.

③ the language in mind lacks a logical structure (9%)
마음속의 언어는 논리적 구조가 없다
생각에 논리적 구조가 있는지 없는지를 밝히는 내용이 아님.

④ a thought and its verbal expression are distinct (18%)
생각과 그것의 언어적 표현은 별개다
언어와 생각은 구조적 유사성이 없다고 했으므로 글의 내용과 반대됨.

The 주의 빈칸 문장에 부정 표현(not, no, never, seldom, neither, little, rarely)이 있음에 주의한다.

⑤ the sentence structurally differs from the thought (8%)
문장은 구조적으로 생각과 다르다
생각과 언어는 구조적으로 다르다고 했으므로 글의 내용과 반대됨.

03 ✦ 무관 문장 〈19학년도 대수능 35번 | 정답률 71%〉 ④

구문분석 & 직독직해 — 예술 사진술의 등장과 회화의 변화

¹When photography came along in the nineteenth century, // painting was put in crisis.

(부사절 접속사 S′ V′ / S V)

사진술이 19세기에 나타났을 때 // 회화는 위기에 처했다 🔑 사진술의 등장으로 인한 회화의 위기에 관한 내용임.

²The photograph, / (it seemed), / did the work of imitating nature better // than the painter ever could (do the work of imitating nature).

(S 삽입절 V O / S′ V′ 반복어구 생략)

사진은 / (~인 것 같았다) / 자연을 모방하는 일을 더 잘했다 // 이제까지 화가가 할 수 있었던 것보다

↳ **도입:** 사진술의 등장으로 회화가 위기에 처함.

① ³Some painters made practical use of the invention.

(S V O(= photograph))

몇몇 화가들은 그 발명품(사진)을 실용적으로 이용했다

② ⁴There were *Impressionist painters* [who used a photograph / in place of *the model or landscape* [(which[that]) they were painting]].

(V S 주격 관계대명사 V′ O′ / 목적격 관계대명사 생략 S″ V″)

인상파 화가들이 있었다 [사진을 이용한 / 모델이나 풍경을 대신해서 [자신들이 그리고 있는]]

↳ **세부 사항 1:** 일부 화가는 사진을 실용적으로 이용함 → 모델이나 풍경 대신 사진을 보고 그림을 그림.

해석

¹사진술이 19세기에 나타났을 때, 회화는 위기에 처했다. ²사진은 이제까지 화가가 할 수 있었던 것보다 자연을 모방하는 일을 더 잘하는 것 같았다. ① ³몇몇 화가들은 그 발명품(사진)을 실용적으로 이용했다. ② ⁴자신들이 그리고 있는 모델이나 풍경을 대신해서 사진을 이용한 인상파 화가들이 있었다. ③ ⁵하지만 대체로, 사진은 회화에 대한 도전이었고 회화가 직접적인 묘사와 복제에서 20세기의 추상 회화로 옮겨간 하나의 원인이었다. ④ ⁶따라서 그 세기의 화가들은 자연, 사람, 그리고 도시를 현실에 있는 대로 표현하는 데 더 초점을 두었다. ⑤ ⁷사진은 사물이 세상에 존재하는 대로 표현하는 것을 아주 잘했기 때문에, 화가들은 화가의 그림에 고유한 색, 입체감, 선, 그리고 공간의 배치로 감정을 표현하면서 내면을 보고 자신들의 상상 속에서 있는 대로 사물을 표현하는 데 자유로워졌다.

주제문

③ [5]But by and large, / the photograph was a challenge (to painting) / and was one cause (of painting's moving away / from direct representation and reproduction / to the abstract painting of the twentieth century).

S V1 C1 V2 C2

동명사 moving의 의미상 주어 <from A to B>: A에서 B로

하지만 대체로 / 사진은 도전이었다 (회화에 대한) / 그리고 하나의 원인이었다 (회화가 옮겨간 / 직접적인 묘사와 복제에서 / 20세기의 추상 회화로)

↳ **세부 사항 2:** 20세기에 추상 회화로의 변화를 야기함.

회화가 사실적 표현에서 추상 회화로 변했다는 앞 문장의 내용과 반대됨.

④ [6]Therefore / the painters (of that century) / put more focus / on expressing nature, people, and cities // as they were in reality.

→ 부사절 접속사(~대로) S V O

(= nature, people, and cities)

따라서 / 화가들은 (그 세기의) / 더 초점을 두었다 / 자연, 사람, 그리고 도시를 표현하는 데 // 그것들이 현실에 있는 대로

↳ 화가들이 사실적 표현에 더 초점을 맞춤.

⑤ [7]Since photographs did such a good job (of representing things // as they existed in the world), //

부사절 접속사(~ 때문에) S′ V′ O′ → 부사절 접속사(~대로) S″(= things) V″

사진은 아주 잘했기 때문에 (사물을 표현하는 것을 // 그것들이 세상에 존재하는 대로) //

painters were freed / to look inward and (to) represent things // as they were in their imagination, / rendering emotion / in *the color, volume, line, and spatial configurations* (native to the painter's art).

S V C(to-v구 병렬) ★<free+O+to-v(O가 자유롭게 v하게 하다)>의 수동형 → 부사절 접속사(~대로) (= things)

분사구문(= and they rendered ~) 형용사구

화가들은 자유로워졌다 / 내면을 보고 사물을 표현하는 데 // 그것들(사물)이 자신들의 상상 속에서 있는 대로 / 감정을 표현하면서 / 색, 입체감, 선, 그리고 공간의 배치로 (화가의 그림에 고유한)

↳ **세부 사항 2의 부연 설명:** 사진이 실물 묘사를 잘했기 때문에 회화는 내면의 감정과 상상을 표현하는 것으로 변화함.

어휘

come along 나타나다; 동행하다
imitate 모방하다, 흉내 내다
make use of ~을 이용[활용]하다
practical 실용적인; 현실적인, 실제적인
in place of ~을 대신해서
by and large 대체로
reproduction 복제, 복사; 재현, 복원
abstract 추상적인
inward 내면; 내부, 안쪽
volume 《미술》 입체감; 용량; 양
spatial 공간의, 공간적인
native 고유한; 타고난, 선천적인

⊕ 인상파 화가(Impressionist painter): 19세기 실증주의와 사실주의의 영향으로 자연을 하나의 색채 현상으로 보고, 색채나 색조의 순간적 효과를 이용하여 눈에 보이는 세계를 정확하고 객관적으로 기록하려 함. 대표적 화가로는 모네, 드가, 고갱, 세잔 등이 있음.

정답 가이드

도입 부분을 통해, 사진술의 등장 이전에는 화가들이 자연을 모방하여 그렸음을 추론할 수 있고 사진이 자연을 더 잘 모방하기 때문에 회화가 처하게 된 상황에 대한 구체적 설명이 이어질 것임을 예측할 수 있다. 이어지는 내용에서 몇몇 화가들은 사진을 이용했지만 대체로 추상 회화로 옮겨갔다고 했다. 그런데 ④는 당시의 화가들이 세상을 있는 그대로 표현하는 것에 더 초점을 두었다는 내용으로 앞에서 말한 추상 회화로의 변화와 흐름상 반대되며, 이어지는 ⑤에서 화가들이 그림에 감정을 표현하고 상상하여 표현했다는 내용과도 연결되지 않으므로 글의 전체 흐름과 무관하다.

오답 클리닉

① (4%) 사진술이 등장하자 몇몇 화가들이 사진을 실용적으로 이용했다는 내용이다.
② (7%) 앞 문장의 예로 인상파 화가들이 사진을 실용적으로 이용한 것을 들었다.
③ (13%) 역접 연결어 But을 포함하여 앞의 인상파 화가들이 사진을 이용하기는 했지만, 대체로 사진은 20세기 추상 회화로의 변화를 야기했다는 내용으로 전환된다.
⑤ (4%) 화가들이 자유롭게 상상과 감정을 표현하게 된 추상 회화의 특징을 부연 설명하는 내용이다.

01 + 밑줄 어법 (21학년도 9월 모평 29번 | 정답률 42%) ①

구문분석 & 직독직해

생활 수행에 대한 건설적인 피드백

[1]Competitive activities can be / more than just *performance showcases* ① [**which**(→ **where**) the best is recognized and the rest are overlooked].
S V C 관계부사 S'1 V'1 S'2 V'2
경쟁을 하는 활동은 ~일 수 있다 / 단지 수행을 보여 주는 공개 행사를 넘어서는 것 [최고는 인정받고 나머지는 무시되는]

주제문
[2]The provision (of timely, constructive feedback / to participants / on performance) / ② **is** *an asset* [that some competitions and contests offer].
S(단수) V(단수) C 목적격 관계대명사
제공은 (시기적절하고 건설적인 피드백의 / 참가자에게 / 수행에 대한) / 자산이다 [일부 대회와 경연이 제공하는]

[3]In a sense, / all competitions give feedback.
S V O
어떤 의미에서 / 모든 대회가 피드백을 제공한다

[4]For many, / this is restricted to information (about whether the participant is an award- or prizewinner).
(this = feedback) S V (whether → about의 O(명사절)) 명사절 접속사 S' V' C'
많은 경우에 / 이것(피드백)은 정보에 제한된다 (참가자가 수상자인지에 관한)

[5]The provision (of that type of feedback) / can be interpreted / as shifting the emphasis / to demonstrating superior performance / but not ③ **necessarily** ((to) demonstrating) excellence.
S V 전치사(~로(서)) as의 O(동명사구) 전치사 to의 O(동명사구) <not necessarily>: 반드시 ~은 아닌 반복어구 생략
제공은 (그런 유형의 피드백의) / 해석될 수 있다 / 강조점을 이동하는 것으로 / 우월한 수행을 보여주는 것으로 / 반드시 탁월함(을 보여주는 것)이 아니라

[6]The best competitions promote excellence, / not just winning or "beating" others.
S V O
최고의 대회는 탁월함을 장려한다 / 단순히 승리하는 것이나 다른 사람을 '패배시키는 것'만이 아니라

[7]The emphasis on superiority is // what we typically see / as ④ **fostering** a detrimental effect of competition.
S V (what → is의 C(명사절)) 명사절 접속사 전치사(~로(서)) as의 O(동명사구)
우월성에 대한 강조는 ~이다 // 우리가 일반적으로 간주하는 것 / 유해한 경쟁 효과를 조장하는 것이라고

[8]Performance feedback requires // that the program (should) go beyond / the "win, place, or show" level of feedback.
S V (that → requires의 O(명사절)) 명사절 접속사 S' V' O'
*주장·요구·제안·명령 등의 동사가 that절을 목적어로 취하고 그 내용이 당위성(~해야 한다)을 의미할 때 that절에 <(should+)동사원형>을 씀.
수행에 대한 피드백은 요구한다 // 프로그램이 넘어설 것을 / '이기거나, 입상하거나, 또는 보여 주는' 수준의 피드백을

[9]Information (about performance) / can be very helpful, / not only to *the participant* [who does not win or place] / but also to *those* [who ⑤ **do**].
S V C (= the participants) 주격 관계대명사 주격 관계대명사 대동사(= win or place)
정보는 (수행에 관한) / 매우 도움이 될 수 있다 / 참가자에게뿐만 아니라 [이기지 못하거나 입상하지 못하는] / 참가자에게도 [이기거나 입상하는]

해석

[1]경쟁을 하는 활동은 최고는 인정받고 나머지는 무시되는, 단지 수행을 보여 주는 공개 행사를 넘어서는 것일 수 있다. [2]참가자에게 수행에 대한 시기적절하고 건설적인 피드백의 제공은 일부 대회와 경연이 제공하는 자산이다. [3]어떤 의미에서, 모든 대회가 피드백을 제공한다. [4]많은 경우에, 이것은 참가자가 수상자인지에 관한 정보에 제한된다. [5]그런 유형의 피드백의 제공은 반드시 탁월함이 아니라, 우월한 수행을 보여주는 것으로 강조점을 이동하는 것으로 해석될 수 있다. [6]최고의 대회는 단순히 승리하는 것이나 다른 사람을 '패배시키는 것'만이 아니라, 탁월함을 장려한다. [7]우월성에 대한 강조는 우리가 일반적으로 유해한 경쟁 효과를 조장하는 것이라고 간주하는 것이다. [8]수행에 대한 피드백은 프로그램이 '이기거나, 입상하거나, 또는 보여 주는' 수준의 피드백을 넘어설 것을 요구한다. [9]수행에 관한 정보는 이기지 못하거나 입상하지 못하는 참가자뿐만 아니라 이기거나 입상하는 참가자에게도 매우 도움이 될 수 있다.

어휘

competitive 경쟁을 하는, 경쟁적인
showcase (상품이나 퍼포먼스를 보여 주는) 공개 행사; 진열장
overlook 무시하다, 간과하다
provision 제공, 공급; 대비, 준비
timely 시기적절한
constructive 건설적인
asset 자산, 재산
restrict 제한하다, 한정하다
emphasis 강조(점), 주안점
demonstrate 보여 주다, 입증하다
superior 우월한, 우수한
cf. superiority 우월성
excellence 탁월함, 뛰어남
promote 장려하다, 증진하다
beat 패배시키다, 이기다
place 입상하다; 놓다, 두다

정답 가이드

① **[관계대명사 vs. 관계부사]** 뒤에 완전한 구조(SVO 수동태)의 절이 왔고, 절의 내용이 추상적 '장소'인 performance showcases를 수식하므로 관계부사 where로 고쳐야 한다.

오답 클리닉

② **[주어-동사의 수일치]** (3%)
주어는 The provision이고 of timely ~ performance가 수식어구이므로 동사는 단수 형태인 is가 어법상 적절하다. 주어를 수식하는 어구는 여러 개가 겹쳐 올 수 있으며, 수식어구 내의 명사와 동사를 수일치하지 않도록 주의해야 한다.

③ **[형용사 vs. 부사]** (20%)
not necessarily는 '반드시 ~은 아닌'이라는 부분 부정의 뜻으로, 문맥상 not necessarily와 excellence 사이에 (to) demonstrating이 생략된 것으로 볼 수 있다. 따라서 (to) demonstrating을 수식하는 부사 necessarily는 어법상 적절하다.

The 주의 단순히 뒤에 명사 excellence가 있다고 해서 형용사 자리로 판단하지 않도록 해야 한다. 병렬구조에서는 등위접속사 뒤에 반복되는 어구를 생략하는 경우가 많으므로 생략된 문장 성분을 잘 파악하여 판단하는 것이 중요하다.

④ **[전치사의 목적어]** (14%)
<see A as B(A를 B로 간주하다)>에서 전치사 as의 목적어 자리에 동명사 형태의 fostering을 쓴 것은 어법상 적절하다. 목적어 A는 앞의 what이 대신하고 있다.

⑤ **[대동사]** (20%)
반복을 피하기 위해 앞에 나온 win or place를 대신하는 대동사 do, does 중에 관계대명사절의 선행사 those의 수와 인칭, 시제에 맞는 do를 쓴 것은 어법상 적절하다. 대동사는 쓰이는 절의 주어와 시제에 맞추어야 하므로 앞에서 대신하는 동사와는 형태가 다를 수 있다는 점에 주의해야 한다.

02 ✦ 빈칸 추론 〈17학년도 6월 모평 34번 | 정답률 37%〉 ④

구문분석 & 직독직해

문화 원주민의 토테미즘

주제문 🔑 토테미즘에서 원주민들은 태어날 때 영혼과 정체성이 자연의 일부를 띤다고 여김.

[1]One remarkable aspect (of aboriginal culture) / is the concept of "*totemism*," // where the tribal member at birth assumes / the soul and identity (of a part of nature).
(S / V / C / 관계부사(보충 설명) S' / V' / O')

한 가지 주목할 만한 측면은 (원주민 문화의) / '토테미즘'의 개념이다 // 그리고 여기에서는 부족원이 태어날 때 띤다 / 영혼과 정체성을 (자연 일부의)

🔑 자신을 지구의 일부로 여겨 환경을 함부로 다루지 않음.

[2]This view (of the earth and its riches / as an intrinsic part of oneself) / clearly rules out / mistreatment (of the environment) //
(S / V / O)

이 견해는 (지구와 지구의 풍요를 보는 / 자신의 고유한 일부로) / 분명히 배제한다 / 함부로 다룸을 (환경을) //

because this would only constitute / a destruction (of self).
(this: = mistreatment of the environment; 부사절 접속사 S' / V' / O')

이것(환경을 함부로 다룸)은 ~가 될 뿐이기 때문이다 / 파괴 (자신에 대한)

↳ 토테미즘은 태어날 때부터 자연 일부의 영혼과 정체성을 띤다고 보고 환경을 함부로 다루지 않음.

[3]Totems are more than objects.
(S / V / C)

토템은 물체(자연물)를 넘어서는 것이다

[4]They include / spiritual rituals, oral histories, and the organization (of *ceremonial lodges*) [where records (of the past travel routes of the soul) / can be exchanged with others / and (can be) converted to mythology].
(They: = Totems; S / V / O_1 / O_2 / O_3 / 관계부사 S' / V')

그것들(토템)은 포함한다 / 영적 의식, 구전 역사, 그리고 구조를 (의식용 오두막의) [기록들이 (영혼의 과거 이동 경로에 대한) / 다른 사람들과 교환될 수 있는 / 그리고 신화로 전환될 수 있는]

↳ 토템은 숭배하는 자연물을 넘어 영적 의식, 구전 역사, 의식용 오두막의 구조 등을 포함함.

[5]The primary motivation is / the preservation (of tribal myths) / and a consolidation and sharing (of every individual's origins) / in nature.
(S / V / C(명사구 병렬))

그 주된 동기는 ~이다 / 보존 (부족 신화의) / 그리고 병합하고 공유하는 것 (모든 개인의 기원을) / 자연 속에서

↳ 위의 것들은 부족 신화를 보존하고 자연 속에서 개인의 기원을 병합하고 공유하기 위한 것임.

해석

[1]원주민 문화의 한 가지 주목할 만한 측면은 '토테미즘'의 개념인데, 여기에서는 부족원이 태어날 때 자연 일부의 영혼과 정체성을 띤다. [2]지구와 지구의 풍요를 자신의 고유한 일부로 보는 이 견해는 환경을 함부로 다룸을 분명히 배제하는데, 이것(환경을 함부로 다룸)은 자신에 대한 파괴가 될 뿐이기 때문이다. [3]토템은 물체(자연물)를 넘어서는 것이다. [4]그것들은 영적 의식, 구전 역사, 그리고 영혼의 과거 이동 경로에 대한 기록들이 다른 사람들과 교환되고 신화로 전환될 수 있는 의식용 오두막의 구조를 포함한다. [5]그 주된 동기는 부족 신화의 보존과 모든 개인의 기원을 자연 속에서 병합하고 공유하는 것이다. [6]원주민들은 자신들의 조상의 기원과 연결되는 토템들의 위계, 자신들을 지구와 하나로 두는 우주론, 그리고 생태계의 균형을 존중하는 행동 양식을 통해 환경과 자신들의 관계를 하나의 조화로운 연속체로 간주한다.

어휘

tribal 부족[종족]의
assume (성질·양상을) 띠다[취하다]; 추정하다; 맡다
identity 정체(성), 신원
intrinsic 고유한, 본질적인
rule out ~을 배제하다
mistreatment 학대, 혹사
constitute ~이 되다; 구성하다
ritual 의식(의); 전례
ceremonial 의식(용)의
lodge 오두막
convert 전환하다; 바꾸다
mythology 신화(= myth)
continuum 연속(체)
hierarchy 위계, 체계; 계급[계층]
ancestral 조상의

★<see A as B>: A를 B로 간주하다

[6]The aborigines see their relationship to the environment / as a single harmonious continuum, /
S V O 전치사(~로(서))
원주민들은 환경과 자신들의 관계를 간주한다 / 하나의 조화로운 연속체로 /

조상의 기원과 연결되고 지구와 동일시하며 생태계의 균형을 존중함.

through a hierarchy of *totems* [that connect to their ancestral origins], / *a cosmology* [that places them at one with the earth], / and *behavior patterns* [that respect ecological balance].
전치사(~을 통해) through의 O₁ 주격 관계대명사 through의 O₂ 주격 관계대명사 (= the aborigines) through의 O₃ 주격 관계대명사
토템들의 위계를 통해 [자신들의 조상의 기원과 연결되는] / 우주론(을 통해) [자신들을 지구와 하나로 두는] / 그리고 행동 양식(을 통해) [생태계의 균형을 존중하는]

↳ **결론:** 원주민들은 환경과 자신들의 관계를 하나의 조화로운 연속체로 간주함.

cosmology 우주론
(be) at one with ~와 하나가 되어
ecological 생태계[학]의; 환경의
[선택지] incompatible 양립할 수 없는
self-contained 독립된, 자립하는
communal 공동[공용]의
gateway 관문; 입구
⊕ 토테미즘(totemism): 원시 공동 사회의 종교의 한 형태로 어떤 동·식물을 자신이 속해 있는 집단과 공통의 기원을 갖거나 결합 관계에 있다고 믿으며 그 자연물을 토템이라 하여 상징으로 삼고 숭배하는 것이 특징임.

정답 가이드

빈칸 문장과 선택지로 보아, 원주민들이 자신들의 조상의 기원과 연결되는 토템의 위계, 자신들을 지구와 하나로 두는 우주론, 생태계의 균형을 존중하는 행동 양식을 통해 '무엇을 무엇으로' 간주하는지를 추론해야 한다. 토테미즘에서 원주민들은 태어날 때 자연 일부의 영혼과 정체성을 띤다고 여기며, 지구와 지구의 풍요를 자신의 고유한 일부로 간주해 환경을 함부로 다루지 않는다고 했다. 이를 통해 원주민들이 자신을 자연과 동일시하며 그것과의 연결을 중시함을 알 수 있으므로, 빈칸에 들어갈 말로 가장 적절한 것은 ④ 'their relationship to the environment as a single harmonious continuum(환경과 자신들의 관계를 하나의 조화로운 연속체로)'이다.

오답 클리닉

① themselves as incompatible with nature and her riches (10%)
자신들을 자연과 자연의 풍요와 양립할 수 없는 것으로
문장 2에서 지구와 지구의 풍요를 자신의 고유한 일부로 여긴다고 했으므로 글의 내용과 반대됨.

② their mythology as a primary motive toward individualism (13%)
자신들의 신화를 개인주의를 향한 주요한 동기로
원주민들이 개인주의를 지향한다는 내용이 아님.

③ their identity as being self-contained from surrounding nature (27%) 자신들의 정체성을 주변의 자연으로부터 독립된 것으로
원주민들은 태어날 때부터 자연 일부의 영혼과 정체성을 띤다고 여겼다고 했으므로 글의 내용과 반대됨.

⑤ their communal rituals as a gateway to distancing themselves from their origins (11%)
자신들의 공동 의식을 자신들의 기원으로부터 스스로를 멀리 떨어뜨리는 관문으로
토테미즘의 동기는 모든 개인의 기원을 자연 속에서 병합하고 공유하는 것이라고 했으므로 틀림.

03 ✦ 글의 순서 (18학년도 대수능 36번 | 정답률 74%) ③

구문분석 & 직독직해 미디어 소비자 잡지의 판매와 광고 방식

주제문

[1]Most consumer magazines depend on subscriptions and advertising.
S V O
대부분의 소비자 잡지는 구독과 광고에 의존한다
↳ 소비자 잡지는 구독과 광고에 의존함.

[2]Subscriptions account for / almost 90 percent (of total magazine circulation).
S V O
구독은 차지한다 / 거의 90퍼센트를 (전체 잡지 판매 부수의)

[3]Single-copy, or newsstand, sales account for the rest.
S (=) V O
낱권, 다시 말해 가판대 판매가 나머지를 차지한다
↳ **세부 사항 1(구독):** 잡지 판매 부수의 90퍼센트는 구독 판매이고, 10퍼센트는 낱권 판매임.

주어진 글 다음에 낱권 판매가 더 수익이 많아 중요하다는 반대 내용이 역접 연결어 however로 이어짐.

(B) [4]However, / single-copy sales are important: // they bring in more revenue / per magazine, //
S₁ V₁ C S₂ V₂ O
하지만 / 낱권 판매는 중요하다 // 그것(낱권 판매)이 더 많은 수익을 가져온다 / 잡지 한 권당 //

because subscription prices are typically at least 50 percent less / than the price (of buying single issues).
부사절 접속사(이유) S′ V′ C′
왜냐하면 구독 가격이 보통 최소 50퍼센트는 더 싸기 때문이다 / 가격보다 (낱권을 사는)
↳ **낱권 판매의 중요성 1:** 구독 판매보다 권당 수익률이 더 높음.

해석

[1]대부분의 소비자 잡지는 구독과 광고에 의존한다. [2]구독은 전체 잡지 판매 부수의 거의 90퍼센트를 차지한다. [3]낱권, 다시 말해 가판대 판매가 나머지를 차지한다. (B) [4]하지만, 낱권 판매는 중요한데, 왜냐하면 구독 가격이 낱권을 사는 가격보다 보통 최소 50퍼센트는 더 싸서, 그것이 잡지 한 권당 더 많은 수익을 가져오기 때문이다. (C) [5]게다가, 잠재적 독자들은 낱권을 구매함으로써 새로운 잡지를 탐색하는데, 구독 제안이 있는 그 모든 삽입 광고 카드는 여러분이 구독하도록 독려하기 위해 잡지에 포함되어 있다. [6]어떤 잡지는 오로지 구독에 의해서만 유통된다. [7]전문가용 잡지 또는 업계지는 전문화된 잡지이며 흔히 전문가 협회에 의해 출판된다. [8]그것들은 보통 매우 표적화된 광고를 특징으로 한다. (A) [9]예를 들어, <Columbia Journalism Review>는 전문 언론인들을 대상으로 판매되며 그 잡지의 몇 안 되는 광고는 언론사, 출판사 등이다. [10]<Consumer Reports>와 같은 몇몇 잡지는 객관성을 위해 노력하며, 따라서 어떠한 광고도 포함하지 않는다.

🔑 (B)에 이어 낱권 판매의 중요성을 추가로 제시함.

(C) [5]Further, / potential readers explore a new magazine / by buying a single issue; //
S1 V1 O <by v-ing>: v함으로써

게다가 / 잠재적 독자들은 새로운 잡지를 탐색한다 / 낱권을 구매함으로써 //

★<encourage+O+to-v>: O가 v하도록 독려하다

all those insert cards (with subscription offers) / are included in magazines / to encourage you to subscribe.
S2 V2 ~하기 위해(목적)

그 모든 삽입 광고 카드는 (구독 제안이 있는) / 잡지에 포함되어 있다 / 여러분이 구독하도록 독려하기 위해

↳ **낱권 판매의 중요성 2:** 잠재적 구독자를 유입시킴.

[6]Some magazines are distributed / only by subscription.
S V

어떤 잡지는 유통된다 / 오로지 구독에 의해서만

[7]Professional or trade magazines are specialized magazines / and are often published / by professional associations.
S V1 C V2

전문가용 잡지 또는 업계지는 전문화된 잡지이다 / 그리고 흔히 출판된다 / 전문가 협회에 의해

→ (= Professional or trade magazines)

[8]They usually feature / highly targeted advertising.
S V O

그것들(전문가용 잡지 또는 업계지)은 보통 특징으로 한다 / 매우 표적화된 광고를

↳ **세부 사항 2(광고):** 구독으로만 판매되는 전문화된 잡지는 표적화된 (맞춤) 광고를 실음.

🔑 (C)에서 언급한 전문화된 잡지의 표적화된 광고의 예를 제시함.

(A) [9]For example, / the *Columbia Journalism Review* is marketed / toward professional journalists //
S1 V1

예를 들어 / <Columbia Journalism Review>는 판매된다 / 전문 언론인들을 대상으로 //

and its few advertisements are news organizations, book publishers, and others.
S2 V2 C

그리고 그 잡지의 몇 안 되는 광고는 언론사, 출판사 등이다

↳ **예 1:** 전문 언론인들을 대상으로 한 잡지는 그 업계의 광고를 포함함.

[10]A few magazines, (like *Consumer Reports*), / work toward objectivity / and therefore contain no advertising.
S V1 V2 O2

몇몇 잡지는 (<Consumer Reports>와 같은) / 객관성을 위해 노력한다 / 그리고 따라서 어떠한 광고도 포함하지 않는다

↳ **예 2:** 객관성을 위해서 광고를 넣지 않기도 함.

어휘

subscription 구독(료)
cf. subscribe 구독하다
account for (비율을) 차지하다; 설명하다
circulation (신문·잡지의) 판매 부수; 순환; 유통
single-copy 낱권
newsstand (신문·잡지) 가판대
bring in (이익 등을) 가져오다; 도입하다
issue (정기 간행물의) 호; 쟁점, 문제
insert (책·신문·잡지에 끼워 넣은) 삽입 광고
distribute 유통시키다; 분배하다
trade magazine 업계지 ((특정 업계나 전문 직업인 상대의 잡지))
specialized 전문화된
association 협회; 연계; 연관
feature 특징(을 이루다); 특별히 포함하다
work toward(s) ~을 위해 노력하다
objectivity 객관성

정답 가이드

주어진 글은 소비자 잡지의 판매에서 구독이 90퍼센트, 낱권 판매가 나머지 10퍼센트를 차지한다는 내용이다. 그 뒤에는 역접 연결어 However로 연결되어 낱권 판매가 10퍼센트에 불과하지만 한 권당 수익이 더 많기 때문에 중요하다는 내용인 (B)가 이어지고, Further로 시작하여 낱권 판매의 또 다른 중요성을 설명하는 (C)가 그 다음에 오는 것이 자연스럽다. (C)의 전문화된 잡지의 광고가 표적화된 광고를 특징으로 한다는 내용 뒤에는 그에 대한 구체적인 예를 제시하는 (A)가 오는 것이 가장 적절하다.

오답 클리닉

① (A) - (C) - (B) (2%) / ② (B) - (A) - (C) (11%)
(A)는 (C)에서 언급한 전문화된 잡지의 표적화된 광고의 예에 해당하므로 (C) 뒤에 오는 것이 자연스럽다.
④ (C) - (A) - (B) (7%)
(C)는 Further로 이어져 낱권 판매의 중요성을 추가로 설명하므로 (B) 다음에 와야 한다.
⑤ (C) - (B) - (A) (6%)
(C)의 뒷부분에서는 전문화된 잡지의 표적화된 광고로 글의 초점이 이동하므로 낱권 판매의 중요성을 이야기하는 (B)가 그 뒤에 오는 것은 부적절하다.

01 + 낱말 쓰임 〈21학년도 9월 모평 30번 | 정답률 55%〉 ④

구문분석 & 직독직해

인지 반동 효과 현상이 일어나는 이유

[1]If I say to you, 'Don't think of a white bear,' // you will find it difficult / not to think of a white bear.
부사절 접속사(조건) S V 가목적어 C 진목적어(to-v구)
내가 당신에게 '백곰을 생각하지 마라'라고 한다면 // 당신은 (~이) 어렵다고 느낄 것이다 / 백곰을 생각하지 않는 것이

주제문 ① 사고 억제는 억제하고 싶은 생각을 '더 많이' 하게 함.
[2]In this way, / 'thought suppression can actually increase / the thoughts [(which[that]) one wishes to suppress] / instead of calming them.'
S V O 목적격 관계대명사 생략 (= the thoughts one wishes to suppress)
이런 식으로 / '사고 억제는 실제로 증가시킬 수 있다 / 생각을 [억제하고 싶은] / 그것(억제하고 싶은 생각)을 가라앉히는 대신에'

[3]One common example of this is // that people on a diet [who try not to think about food] / often begin to think much ① more / about food.
(= 앞 문장) is의 C(명사절) S V 명사절 접속사 주격 관계대명사 비교급 수식 부사
이것의 한 일반적인 예는 ~이다 // 다이어트를 하는 사람들이 [음식에 대해 생각하지 않으려고 애쓰는] / 흔히 훨씬 더 많이 생각하기 시작한다는 것 / 음식에 대해

★<be known as>: ~로 알려져 있다
[4]This process is therefore also known / as the rebound effect.
S V 전치사(~로(서))
따라서 이 과정은 또한 알려져 있다 / '반동 효과'로
② 생각을 억누를수록 더 하게 된다는 '반동 효과'가 '모순적인' 결과로 말바꿈 됨.

[5]The ② ironic effect seems to be caused / by the interplay (of two related cognitive processes).
S V C
그 모순적인 결과는 야기되는 것처럼 보인다 / 상호 작용에 의해 (두 개의 관련된 인지 과정의)

③ 의도적인 운영 과정은 의식적으로 억누르려는 생각과 '관련 없는' 생각을 하려고 할 것임.
[6]This dual-process system involves, / first, / an intentional operating process, // which consciously attempts to locate thoughts (③ unrelated to the suppressed ones).
S V O 관계대명사(보충 설명) V′ 과거분사구 (= thoughts)
이러한 이중 처리 시스템은 포함한다 / 우선 / 의도적인 운영 과정을 // 그리고 그것은 생각을 의식적으로 찾아내려고 시도한다 (억제된 생각과 관련 없는)

[7]Second, and simultaneously, / an unconscious monitoring process tests // whether the operating system is functioning effectively.
S V tests의 O(명사절) 명사절 접속사(~인지) S′ V′
두 번째로, 그리고 동시에 / 무의식적인 감시 과정은 검사한다 // 운영 체계가 효과적으로 기능하고 있는지

[8]If the monitoring system encounters thoughts (inconsistent with the intended ones), // it prompts the intentional operating process / to ensure // that these are replaced / by ④ inappropriate(→ appropriate) thoughts.
부사절 접속사(조건) S′ V′ O′ (= thoughts) S V O 목적(~하도록) to ensure의 O(명사절) (= thoughts inconsistent with the intended ones)
감시 체계가 생각과 마주친다면 (의도된 생각과 일치하지 않는) // 그것(감시 체계)은 의도적인 운영 과정을 자극한다 / 반드시 ~하도록 // 이것들(의도된 생각과 일치하지 않는 생각)이 대체되(도록) / 부적절한(→ 적절한) 생각에 의해
④ 의도된 생각과 일치하지 않는 생각, 즉 '부적절한' 생각을 대체하는 것은 '적절한' 생각이 되어야 함.

[9]However, / (it is argued), // the intentional operating system can fail / due to increased cognitive load (caused by fatigue, stress and emotional factors), // and so the monitoring process filters the inappropriate thoughts into consciousness, / making them highly ⑤ accessible.
삽입절 S_1 V_1 전치사(~로 인해) 과거분사구 S_2 V_2 O 분사구문(= and it makes ~)
그러나 / 주장되는 바로는 // 의도적인 운영 체계는 작동하지 않을 수 있다 / 증가된 인지 부하 때문에 (피로, 스트레스, 그리고 정서적 요인으로 인해 생긴) // 그래서 감시 과정이 부적절한 생각을 걸러내 의식으로 스며들게 한다 / 그리고 (그 결과) 그것(부적절한 생각)을 매우 접근하기 쉽게 만든다
⑤ 걸러져 나와 의식에 스며든 부적절한 생각은 '접근하기 쉬울' 것임.

해석

[1]내가 당신에게 '백곰을 생각하지 마라'라고 한다면, 당신은 백곰을 생각하지 않는 것이 어렵다고 느낄 것이다. [2]이런 식으로, '사고 억제는 억제하고 싶은 생각을 가라앉히는 대신에 실제로 그것을 증가시킬 수 있다.' [3]이것의 한 일반적인 예는 음식에 대해 생각하지 않으려고 애쓰는 다이어트를 하는 사람들이 흔히 음식에 대해 훨씬 ① 더 많이 생각하기 시작한다는 것이다. [4]따라서 이 과정은 '반동 효과'로 또한 알려져 있다. [5]그 ② 모순적인 결과는 두 개의 관련된 인지 과정의 상호 작용에 의해 야기되는 것처럼 보인다. [6]우선, 이러한 이중 처리 시스템은 의도적인 운영 과정을 포함하는데, 그것은 억제된 생각과 ③ 관련 없는 생각을 의식적으로 찾아내려고 시도한다. [7]두 번째로, 그리고 동시에, 무의식적인 감시 과정은 운영 체계가 효과적으로 기능하고 있는지 검사한다. [8]감시 체계가 의도된 생각과 일치하지 않는 생각과 마주친다면, 그것은 의도적인 운영 과정을 자극해서 반드시 이것들이 ④ 부적절한(→ 적절한) 생각에 의해 대체되도록 한다.(▶ 억제하려는 부적절한 생각과 관련 없는 생각을 의식적으로 하려고 하는데, 동시에 이것이 제대로 되고 있는지를 무의식적으로 감시하여 부적절한 생각이 발견되면 이를 적절한 생각으로 대체한다는 의미) [9]그러나 주장되는 바로는, 의도적인 운영 체계는 피로, 스트레스, 그리고 정서적 요인으로 인해 생긴 증가된 인지 부하로 인해 작동하지 않을 수 있고, 그래서 감시 과정이 부적절한 생각을 걸러내 의식으로 스며들게 하는데, (그 결과) 그것들(부적절한 생각)을 매우 ⑤ 접근하기 쉽게 만든다.(▶ 무의식은 피로 등의 요인으로 의식이 제대로 작동하지 않을 때도 계속해서 감시하므로 억제하려는 생각이 다시 의식으로 스며들어, 결과적으로 억제하려는 부적절한 생각을 하기 쉽게 만든다는 의미)

어휘

suppression 억제, 진압
cf. suppress 억제하다, 참다
rebound effect 반동 효과 ((어떤 일을 억제하면 할수록 그 반동으로 더 하게 되는 효과))
interplay 상호 작용
cognitive 인지[인식]의
dual 이중의, 두 부분으로 된
intentional 의도적인
locate 찾아내다; ~의 정확한 위치를 찾아내다
simultaneously 동시에
inconsistent with ~와 일치하지 않는
prompt 자극하다; 촉구하다
ensure 반드시 ~하게 하다, 보장하다
load 부하; 짐; 싣다
fatigue 피로

정답 가이드

반동 효과가 의도적인 운영 과정과 무의식적인 감시 과정의 상호 작용에 의해 생긴다는 내용의 글이다. 문장 8에서, 의식은 의도된 생각과 일치하지 않는 생각, 즉 억제하려는 생각과 마주치면 이를 적절한 생각(억제하려는 생각과 관련 없는 생각)으로 대체한다는 설명이 되어야 한다. 따라서, ④ 'inappropriate(부적절한)'을 'appropriate(적절한)'으로 바꿔 써야 한다.

오답 클리닉

① more (2%) 더 많이
사고 억제는 억제하려는 생각을 증가시킨다고 했으므로 음식 생각을 억제하려는 다이어트를 하는 사람들은 그 생각을 '더 많이' 하게 될 것이다.

② ironic (2%) 모순적인
생각을 억제할수록 더 하게 되는 것이 반동 효과로도 알려졌다고 했는데, 다음 문장에서 이를 '모순적인' 결과로 바꿔 말한 것은 의미상 적절하다.

③ unrelated (31%) 관련 없는
이중 처리 시스템에서 의도적인 운영 과정은 억제하려는 생각을 하지 않으려고 의식적으로 그와 '관련 없는' 다른 생각을 하려고 할 것이다.

The 주의 앞 문장의 the interplay of two related cognitive processes를 보고 같은 related가 와야 한다고 생각할 수 있다. 그러나 문장 6은 두 인지 과정 중 의도적인 운영 과정의 기능을 설명하는 내용이므로 이를 추론해 답을 판단해야 한다.

⑤ accessible (9%) 접근하기 쉬운
의도적인 운영 체계가 잘 작동하지 않으면 의도된 것과 다른 부적절한 생각이 걸러져 나와 의식에 스며든다고 했으므로 부적절한 생각에 매우 '접근하기 쉽게' 될 것이다.

02 ✦ 빈칸 추론 〈17학년도 6월 모평 33번 | 정답률 58%〉 ②

구문분석 & 직독직해

경제 사회적 장벽을 없애는 튼튼한 경제

주제문

[1]It is not hard to see // that *a strong economy*, // where opportunities are plentiful and jobs go begging, / **helps break down social barriers.**

(가주어 V, C, 진주어(to-v구), ↱ to see의 O(명사절), S'(단수), 관계부사(보충 설명), V'(단수), O')

(~라는 것을) 이해하기는 어렵지 않다 // 튼튼한 경제가 // 기회가 풍부하고 일자리를 원하는 사람이 없는 / 사회적 장벽을 부수는 데 도움이 된다는 것을

↳ 튼튼한 경제는 사회적 장벽을 부수는 데 도움이 됨.

[2]Biased employers may still dislike / hiring members (of one group or another), //

(S_1, V_1, O(동명사구))

편향된 고용주들은 여전히 싫어할 수도 있다 / 일원을 고용하기를 (이런저런 집단의) //

★<give way to A>: A로 대체되다

but when nobody else is available, // discrimination most often gives way / to the basic need (to get the work done). ★<get+O+p.p>: O가 ~되게 하다[만들다]

(부사절 접속사(시간), S', V', C', S_2, V_2, =)

그러나 다른 아무도 구할 수 없을 때는 // 차별은 아주 흔히 대체된다 / 기본적인 필요로 (일을 완수해야 하는)

[3]The same goes for / employees with prejudices (about whom they do and do not like working alongside).

(S, V, O, about의 O(명사절))

똑같은 것이 해당된다 / 편견을 가진 피고용자들에게도 (자신들이 정말 함께 일하고 싶어 하고 함께 일하고 싶어 하지 않는 사람들에 대한)

↳ **세부 사항:** 일할 사람을 구할 수 없을 때 고용주와 피고용자는 내키지 않는 사람들이라도 고용하고 함께 일할 수밖에 없음.

[4]In the American construction boom of the late 1990s, / for example, /
1990년대 후반 미국의 건설 호황기에 / 예를 들면 /

even *the carpenters' union* — / (long known / as a "traditional bastion (of white men), / *a world* [where a coveted union card was handed down / from father to son"]) — /

(S, 과거분사구, =, 관계부사)

목수 노동조합조차도 / (오랫동안 알려진 / '전통적 요새로 (백인 남성들의) / 즉 세계인 [부러움을 사는 (노동조합의) 조합원증이 물려졌던 / 아버지에게서 아들에게로'])) /

🔑 백인 남성의 요새로 알려진 목수 노동조합조차 건설 호황기에 여성, 흑인, 히스패닉을 고용하려 했음.

began openly encouraging / women, blacks, and Hispanics to join its internship program.

(V, O(동명사구), ★<encourage+O+to-v>: O가 v하도록 권장하다)

공개적으로 권장하기 시작했다 / 여성, 흑인 그리고 히스패닉계가 자기네 인턴 프로그램에 참가하도록

↳ **예:** 백인 남성들 위주였던 목수 노동조합도 건설 호황으로 일손이 부족해지자 성별, 인종에 상관없이 일꾼을 고용했음.

해석

[1]기회가 풍부하고 일자리를 원하는 사람이 없는 튼튼한 경제가 사회적 장벽을 부수는 데 도움이 된다는 것을 이해하기는 어렵지 않다. [2]편향된 고용주들은 이런저런 집단의 일원을 고용하기를 여전히 싫어할 수도 있지만, 다른 아무도 구할 수 없을 때는 차별은 아주 흔히 일을 완수해야 하는 기본적인 필요로 대체된다.(▶ 일할 사람을 구하기 힘든 경제 호황기에는 고용 차별이 사라짐을 의미) [3]자신들이 정말 함께 일하고 싶어 하고 함께 일하고 싶어하지 않는 사람들에 대한 편견을 가진 피고용자들에게도 똑같은 것이 해당된다. [4]예를 들면, 1990년대 후반 미국의 건설 호황기에 '백인 남성들의 전통적 요새, 즉 부러움을 사는 (노동조합의) 조합원증이 아버지에게서 아들에게로 물려졌던 세계'로 오랫동안 알려진 목수 노동조합조차도 여성과 흑인 그리고 히스패닉계가 자기네 인턴 프로그램에 참가하도록 공개적으로 권장하기 시작했다. [5]최소한 일터에서는 일자리가 사람을 쫓는 것이 사람이 일자리를 쫓는 것보다 유동적인 사회를 조성하기 위해 분명히 더 많은 것을 한다.(▶ 일사리가 많으면 사회 계층 간의 이동이 활발해짐을 의미)

어휘

plentiful 풍부한
go begging (물건 등을) 원하는 사람이 없다
break down ~을 부수다
barrier 장벽[장애물]
biased 편향된
available 구할[이용할] 수 있는
discrimination 차별
go for ~에 해당되다
prejudice 편견, 선입관
alongside ~와 함께

↱ 동명사의 의미상 주어 ⊶ 일자리가 사람을 쫓으면 유동적인 사회가 됨.

[5]At least in the workplace, / jobs chasing people obviously does more / to promote a fluid society / than people chasing jobs.

S(동명사구) V(단수) O 목적(~하기 위해) ↱ 동명사의 의미상 주어 than의 O(동명사구)

최소한 일터에서는 / 일자리가 사람을 쫓는 것이 분명히 더 많은 것을 한다 / 유동적인 사회를 조성하기 위해 / 사람이 일자리를 쫓는 것보다

↳ **주제문 재진술:** 많은 일자리는 보다 유동적인 사회를 촉진함.

boom 호황, 붐
carpenter 목수
union 노동조합; 연합
hand down ~을 물려주다
openly 공개적으로
promote 조성[조장]하다; 촉진하다
fluid 유동적인; 유(동)체
[선택지] wage 임금[급료]
productivity 생산성

정답 가이드

빈칸 문장은 (일을 할) 기회가 풍부하고 일자리를 원하는 사람이 없는 튼튼한 경제는 '~한다'는 것을 이해하기 어렵지 않다는 의미이므로, 튼튼한 경제가 '무엇을 하는지'를 파악해야 한다. 이어지는 세부 사항에서 일할 사람을 구할 수 없을 정도로 경제가 호황일 때 고용주나 피고용자들은 편견과 차별을 그만둔다고 한 뒤, 백인 남성들의 요새로 알려진 목수 노동조합조차 미국의 건설 호황기에는 여성, 흑인, 히스패닉계에게 함께 일하도록 권장했다는 예를 들고 있다. 따라서 빈칸에 들어갈 말로 가장 적절한 것은 ② 'helps break down social barriers(사회적 장벽을 부수는 데 도움이 된다)'이다.

오답 클리닉

① allows employees to earn more income (9%)
피고용인들이 더 많은 소득을 벌게 해 준다
피고용인들의 소득이 늘어난다는 내용은 언급되지 않음.

③ simplifies the hiring process (12%)
고용 과정을 단순화한다
고용 차별이 사라진다는 내용은 있으나, 고용 과정이 단순해진다는 언급은 없음.

④ increases wage discrimination (10%)
임금 차별을 증가시킨다
discrimination을 활용한 오답. 임금 차별이 늘어나는 것이 아닌 고용 차별이 없어진다는 내용임.

⑤ improves the productivity of a company (8%)
회사의 생산성을 향상시킨다
생산성에 관한 언급은 없음.

03 + 문장 넣기 (18학년도 대수능 38번 | 정답률 65%)

④

구문분석 & 직독직해 생물 단 음식 선호와 섭식 행동 조정

[1]Both humans and rats have evolved / taste preferences for *sweet foods*, // which provide rich sources of calories.

S V O 관계대명사(보충 설명)

사람과 쥐 모두 진화시켜 왔다 / '단' 음식에 대한 맛의 선호를 // 그리고 이것(단 음식)은 풍부한 열량의 원천을 제공한다

↳ **세부 사항 1:** 사람과 쥐는 열량이 높은 단 음식에 대한 선호를 진화시켜 옴.

[2]A study (of food preferences (among the Hadza hunter-gatherers of Tanzania)) / found // that honey was the most highly preferred food item, / *an item* [that has the highest caloric value].

S V O(명사절) = 주격 관계대명사

한 연구는 (음식 선호에 관한 (탄자니아의 Hadza 수렵 채집인 사이의)) / 발견했다 // 꿀이 가장 많이 선호되는 식품이었다는 것을 / 식품인 [가장 높은 열량값을 가진]

↳ **예 1:** 탄자니아의 Hadza 수렵 채집인들은 가장 높은 열량값을 가진 꿀을 가장 선호했음.

(①) [3]Human newborn infants also show / a strong preference for sweet liquids.

S V O

인간의 갓난아기 또한 보인다 / 단 액체에 대한 강한 선호를

↳ **예 2:** 갓난아기는 단 액체를 선호함.

(②) [4]Both humans and rats dislike *bitter and sour foods*, // which tend to contain toxins.

S V O 관계대명사(보충 설명)

사람과 쥐 모두 '쓰'고 '신' 음식을 싫어한다 / 이것들(쓰고 신 음식)은 독소를 포함하는 경향이 있다

↳ **세부 사항 1의 부연 설명:** 사람과 쥐는 쓰고 신 음식을 싫어함.

⊶ 물, 열량, 소금 부족에 대응한 섭식 행동을 조정함.

(③) [5]They also adaptively adjust their eating behavior / in response to deficits (in water, calories, and salt).

S(= Both humans and rats) V O ~에 대응하여

그들(사람과 쥐)은 또한 자신의 섭식 행동을 적응하도록 조정한다 / 부족에 대응하여 (물, 열량, 소금의)

↳ **세부 사항 2:** 사람과 쥐는 물, 열량, 소금 부족에 대응하여 섭식 행동을 조정함.

해석

[1]사람과 쥐 모두 '단' 음식에 대한 맛의 선호를 진화시켜 왔는데, 이것(단 음식)은 풍부한 열량의 원천을 제공한다. [2]탄자니아의 Hadza 수렵 채집인 사이의 음식 선호에 관한 한 연구는 가장 높은 열량값을 가진 식품인 꿀이 가장 많이 선호되는 식품이었다는 것을 발견했다. (①) [3]인간의 갓난아기 또한 단 액체에 대한 강한 선호를 보인다. (②) [4]사람과 쥐 모두 '쓰'고 '신' 음식을 싫어하는데, 이것들(쓰고 신 음식)은 독소를 포함하는 경향이 있다. (③) [5]그들(사람과 쥐)은 또한 자신의 섭식 행동을 물, 열량, 소금의 부족에 대응하여 적응하도록 조정한다. (④ [6]실험은 쥐가 소금 결핍을 처음 경험할 때 소금에 대한 즉각적인 기호를 보인다는 것을 보여준다.) [7]그것들(쥐)은 마찬가지로 에너지와 체액이 고갈된 경우에는 단것과 물 섭취를 늘린다. (⑤) [8]이것들은 음식 선택의 적응적 문제를 다루고 음식 섭취 패턴을 신체적 욕구와 조화시키도록 고안된, 특정한 진화된 기제처럼 보인다.

어휘

evolve 진화시키다[하다]; (서서히) 발전하다
preference 선호(도), 더 좋아함
calorie 열량, 칼로리
cf. caloric 열량의; 열의

부족에 대응한 섭식 행동 조정의 예.
(④) [6]Experiments show // that rats display an immediate liking for salt // the first time they experience a salt deficiency.)

S V O(명사절) 부사절 접속사(처음 ~할 때) S′ V′ O′

실험은 보여준다 // 쥐가 소금에 대한 즉각적인 기호를 보인다는 것을 // 소금 결핍을 처음 경험할 때

주어진 문장과 유사한 예가 이어짐.
[7]They likewise increase their intake (of sweets and water) // when their energy and fluids become depleted.

S(= Rats) V O 부사절 접속사(시간) S′ V′ C′

그것들(쥐)은 마찬가지로 섭취를 늘린다 (단것과 물의) // 에너지와 체액이 고갈된 경우에는

↳ **부연 설명:** 쥐는 소금, 열량, 물이 결핍되면 그것을 더 섭취하려고 함.

(= 문장 6, 7) *<appear to-v>: v인 것 같이 보이다
(⑤) [8]These appear to be *specific evolved mechanisms*, / (which are) designed / to deal with the adaptive problem of food selection, / and (to) coordinate consumption patterns / with physical needs.

S V C 주격 관계대명사+be동사 생략 부사구 병렬 부사구 병렬

이것들은 특정한 진화된 기제처럼 보인다 / 고안된 / 음식 선택의 적응적 문제를 다루도록 / 그리고 음식 섭취 패턴을 조화시키도록 / 신체적 욕구와

↳ **세부 사항 2의 결론:** 사람과 쥐는 신체적 욕구에 맞도록 음식 섭취 패턴을 조정하는 기제가 있음.

hunter-gatherer 수렵 채집인
newborn infant 갓난아기, 신생아
toxin 독소
adaptively 적응하도록, 적응하여
cf. adaptive 적응성의
adjust 조정[조절]하다
deficit 부족; 결손, 적자
experiment 실험(하다)
immediate 즉각적인
liking 기호, 좋아함
intake 섭취(량)
fluid (동물의) 체액; 유동체; 부드러운
mechanism 기제; 방법
design 고안하다; 설계하다
deal with ~을 다루다
coordinate 조화시키다
consumption (식품의) 섭취[소비](량)

정답 가이드

주어진 문장은 쥐가 소금 결핍을 처음 경험할 때, 소금에 대한 즉각적인 기호를 보인다는 실험 내용이다. 이는 사람과 쥐가 물, 열량, 소금 부족에 대응하여 자신의 섭식 행동을 조정한다는 내용의 ③ 뒤에서 이를 뒷받침하는 논거로 와야 하며, likewise로 주어진 문장과 유사한 논거를 첨가하는 ⑤ 앞의 문장과 자연스럽게 이어진다. 따라서 주어진 문장이 들어가기에 가장 적절한 곳은 ④이다.

오답 클리닉

① (3%) 사람과 쥐가 단 음식에 대한 맛의 선호를 진화시켜 왔다는 예로 탄자니아의 Hadza 수렵 채집인에 이어 갓난아기의 예가 이어지는 것은 자연스럽다.
② (4%) 단맛을 선호하는 예 뒤에 사람과 쥐가 쓰고 신 음식은 싫어한다는 부연 설명이 이어진다.
③ (18%) 앞 문장의 both humans and rats를 대명사 They로 받아 물, 열량, 소금 부족에 대응하여 섭식 행동을 조정한다는 세부 사항을 추가(also)로 제시하는 내용이다.
⑤ (10%) These는 문장 6, 7에서 쥐를 대상으로 한 실험 결과들을 가리키며, 결론을 도출하는 의견으로 글을 마무리 짓고 있다.

01 + 요약문 〈19학년도 대수능 40번 | 정답률 73%〉 ①

구문분석 & 직독직해

경제 화석 연료의 경쟁력

[1]Biological organisms, / (including human societies both with and without market systems), /
S / A와 B 모두 / 전치사구 삽입
생물학적 유기체들은 / (시장 체제가 있거나 없는 인간 사회를 비롯하여) /
discount distant outputs / over those available at the present time /
V / O / (= outputs)
🔑 (A) 바로 이용할 수 없는 생산물보다 현재 이용할 수 있는 생산물을 선호함.
based on *risks* (associated with an uncertain future).
과거분사구
(시간적으로) 멀리 있는 생산물을 낮게 평가한다 / 현재 이용할 수 있는 것들(생산물)보다 /
위험에 기초하여 (불확실한 미래와 관련된)
↳ **도입:** 인간은 현재 이용 가능한 생산물보다 나중에 이용 가능한 생산물을 낮게 평가함.

[2]As the timing of inputs and outputs varies greatly / depending on the type of energy, //
부사절 접속사(~ 때문에) S′ V′ ~에 따라
투입과 생산의 시기가 크게 다르기 때문에 / 에너지 유형에 따라 //
there is *a strong case* (to incorporate time) / when assessing energy alternatives.
V S O / 접속사를 생략하지 않은 분사구문(= when people assess ~)
강력한 주장이 있다 (시간을 포함해야 한다는) / 대체 에너지를 평가할 때
↳ **세부 사항:** 에너지 투입과 생산 시기가 달라서 대체 에너지를 평가할 때 시간을 포함해야 한다는 주장이 있음.

[3]For example, / *the energy output* (from solar panels or wind power engines), // where most investment happens / before they begin producing, /
S / 관계부사(보충 설명)
예를 들어 / 에너지 생산은 (태양 전지판이나 풍력 엔진으로부터의) // 대부분의 투자가 발생한다 / 그것들이 생산을 시작하기 전에 /
may need to be assessed differently / when compared to *most fossil fuel extraction technologies*, //
V / 접속사를 생략하지 않은 분사구문(= when it is compared ~)
다르게 평가될 필요가 있을 수 있다 / 대부분의 화석 연료 추출 기술과 비교될 때 //
🔑 (A) 화석 연료의 에너지 생산이 더 빠름.
where a large proportion (of the energy output) / comes much sooner, // and a larger (relative) proportion of inputs is applied / during the extraction process, / and (a larger (relative) proportion of inputs is) not upfront.
관계부사(보충 설명) S′₁ V′₁ S′₂(단수) V′₂(단수) 반복어구 생략
그것(화석 연료 추출 기술)에서는 많은 비율이 (에너지 생산의) / 훨씬 더 빨리 나온다 // 그리고 더 큰 투입의 (상대적) 비율이 적용된다 / 추출 과정 동안에 / 그리고 선행 투자되지 않는다
↳ **예:** 대체 에너지는 생산 전에 투자가 선행되지만, 화석 연료 에너지는 생산이 더 빨리되고 선행 투자되지 않음.

[4]Thus fossil fuels, / (particularly oil and natural gas), / in addition to having energy quality advantages (cost, storability, transportability, etc.) / over many renewable technologies), /
S / ~뿐 아니라 / in addition to의 O(동명사구)
따라서 화석 연료는 / (특히 석유와 천연가스) / 에너지 품질 이점(비용, 저장 가능성, 운송 가능성 등)을 가질 뿐만 아니라 / 많은 재생 가능한 기술보다 /
also have a "temporal advantage" / after accounting for human behavioral preference (for current consumption/return).
V O 전치사(~에 비추어)
🔑 (B) 투입하면 생산이 빨리 된다는 점에서 화석 연료는 시간적 이점이 있음.
또한 '시간적 이점'을 가진다 / 인간의 행동적 선호를 설명하는 것에 비추어 보면 (현재의 소비/수익에 대한)
↳ **결론:** 화석 연료는 재생 가능 에너지보다 품질과 시간의 면에서 이점이 있음.

↓

[5]Due to the fact // that people tend to favor more **(A) immediate** outputs, //
전치사(~ 때문에) = 동격 접속사
fossil fuels are more **(B) competitive** / than renewable energy alternatives /
S V C
in regards to the distance (between inputs and outputs).
~에 관해서
사실 때문에 // 사람들이 더 (A) 즉각적인 생산물을 선호하는 경향이 있다는 //
화석 연료는 더 (B) 경쟁력 있다 / 재생 가능한 대체 에너지보다 /
(시간적) 거리에 관해서는 (투입과 생산 간)

해석

[1]시장 체제가 있거나 없는 인간 사회를 비롯하여, 생물학적 유기체들은 불확실한 미래와 관련된 위험에 기초하여 현재 이용할 수 있는 것보다 (시간적으로) 멀리 있는 생산물을 낮게 평가한다.(▶ 미래는 불확실하므로 미래에 나올 생산물에는 가치를 덜 부여한다는 의미) [2]투입과 생산의 시기가 에너지 유형에 따라 크게 다르기 때문에, 대체 에너지를 평가할 때 시간을 포함해야 한다는 강력한 주장이 있다. [3]예를 들어, 태양 전지판이나 풍력 엔진으로부터의 에너지 생산은 대부분의 투자가 그것들이 생산을 시작하기 전에 발생하며, 대부분의 화석 연료 추출 기술과 비교될 때 다르게 평가될 필요가 있을 수 있는데, 그것(화석 연료 추출 기술)에서는 에너지 생산의 많은 비율이 훨씬 더 빨리 나오고, 더 큰 투입의 (상대적) 비율이 추출 과정 동안에 적용되며 선행 투자되지 않는다. [4]따라서 화석 연료, 특히 석유와 천연가스는 많은 재생 가능한 기술보다 에너지 품질 이점(비용, 저장 가능성, 운송 가능성 등)을 가질 뿐만 아니라 현재의 소비/수익에 대한 인간의 행동적 선호를 설명하는 것에 비추어 보면 '시간적 이점' 또한 가진다.

↓

[5]사람들이 더 (A) 즉각적인 생산물을 선호하는 경향이 있다는 사실 때문에, 화석 연료는 투입과 생산 간 (시간적) 거리에 관해서는 재생 가능한 대체 에너지보다 더 (B) 경쟁력 있다.

어휘

biological 생물학의, 생물체의
organism 유기체
discount 낮게 평가하다, 무시하다; 할인(하다)
output 생산(물); 산출(량) (↔ input 투입(량))
associated with ~와 관련된
vary 다르다, 달라지다
incorporate 포함하다; 합병하다
assess 평가하다
alternative 대체(의)
solar panel 태양 전지판
extraction 추출, 뽑아냄
proportion 비율, 부분
apply 적용하다; 신청하다
storability 저장 가능성
transportability 운송 가능성; 수송
renewable 재생 가능한
temporal 시간의; 현세적인; 일시적인
account for ~을 설명하다
consumption 소비(량)
return 수익; 돌아오다[가다]

정답 가이드

요약문을 통해 화석 연료와 재생 가능한 대체 에너지를 비교하는 글임을 알 수 있다. 사람들이 현재 이용할 수 있는 생산물보다 시간적으로 더 멀리 있는 생산물을 낮게 평가한다는 것에서 '즉각적인' 생산물을 선호한다는 것을 알 수 있고, 재생 에너지와 비교해 화석 연료의 에너지 생산이 더 빠르다는 점에서 시간적으로 더 '경쟁력 있다'고 볼 수 있다. 따라서 요약문의 빈칸 (A)와 (B)에는 각각 ① 'immediate(즉각적인) - competitive(경쟁력 있는)'가 들어가는 것이 가장 적절하다.

오답 클리닉

(A) (B)

② available - expensive (9%) 이용 가능한 - 비싼
(A)는 맞지만, 화석 연료는 '비용' 면에서도 재생 가능 에너지보다 이점이 있다고 했으므로 (B)는 틀림.

③ delayed - competitive (5%) 지체된 - 경쟁력 있는
(A)는 지문의 내용과 반대되며, (B)는 맞음.

④ convenient - expensive (4%) 편리한 - 비싼
(A)는 알 수 없는 내용이며, (B)는 틀림.

⑤ abundant - competitive (9%) 충분한 - 경쟁력 있는
(A)는 언급되지 않은 내용이며, (B)는 맞음.

02~03 + 복합 유형 (21학년도 6월 모평 41~42번 | 정답률 02 65%, 03 67%)

02 ① 03 ④

구문분석 & 직독직해

사회 토지로부터 분리된 물 이용 권리

03-(a) 물 이용 권리가 토지 소유와 연관되어, 즉 '결합되어' 있었음.

[1]In many mountain regions, / rights (of access to water) / are associated with the possession of land — //
(rights (of access to water): S1(복수), are associated: V1(복수))
많은 산악 지역에서 / 권리가 (물을 이용할) / 토지의 소유와 연관되어 있다 //

until recently in the Andes, / for example, / land and water rights were **(a) combined** // so water rights were transferred / with the land.
(land and water rights: S2, were combined: V2, so: 부사절 접속사(결과), water rights: S′, were transferred: V′)
최근까지 안데스 산맥에서는 / 예를 들어 / 토지와 물 권리가 결합되어 있었다 // 따라서 물 권리는 이전되었다 / 토지와 함께
↳ 산악 지역에서 물 이용 권리는 토지 소유와 결합되어 있었음.

주제문

03-(b) 물 권리가 경매될 수 있으면 비용을 지불할 수 있는 사람에게 '유리할' 것임.

[2]However, / through state land reforms [and] the development of additional sources of supply, / water rights have become separated from land, / [and] may be sold / at auction.
(state land reforms and the development of additional sources of supply: through의 O(명사구 병렬); water rights: S, have become: V1, separated: C, may be sold: V2)
그러나 / 국가 토지 개혁과 추가 공급원의 개발을 통해 /
물 권리는 토지와 분리되었다 / 그리고 팔릴지도 모른다 / 경매로

[3]This therefore **(b) favours** / *those* [who can pay], / rather than ensuring access / to all in the community.
(This: S(= 앞 문장), favours: V, those: O, who: 주격 관계대명사)
그러므로 이것은 유리하다 / 사람들에게 [비용을 지불할 수 있는] / 이용할 권리를 보장하기보다 / 지역 공동체의 모든 사람에게

[4]*The situation* arises, therefore, [where individuals may hold land / with no water.
(The situation: S, arises: V, where: 관계부사, individuals: S′, may hold: V′, land: O′)
따라서 상황이 발생한다 [개인이 땅을 보유할 수도 있는 / 물 (권리) 없이]
↳ 물 권리가 토지와 분리되어 따로 경매가 가능해지면서 물 권리 없이 땅만 보유하는 상황이 발생함.

[5]In Peru, / the government grants water to communities / separately from land, //
[and] it is up to the community / to allocate it. *<be up to ~>: ~에 달려 있다, ~가 할 일이다
(the government: S1, grants: V1, water: O1; it: 가주어, is: V2, to allocate it: 진주어, it (= water))
페루에서는 / 정부가 지역 공동체에 물을 준다 / 토지와는 별도로 //
그리고 (~은) 그 공동체에 달려 있다 / 그것(물)을 분배하는 것은
↳ **예 1(페루):** 정부가 토지와 별도로 물을 주고 지역 공동체에서 그것을 분배함.

[6]Likewise in Yemen, / the traditional allocation was / one measure (*tasah*) of water / to one hundred '*libnah*' of land.
(the traditional allocation: S, was: V, one measure ... of land: C)
예멘에서도 마찬가지로 / 전통적인 분배는 ~이었다 / 1척(타사)의 물 / 100'립나'의 토지에

해석

[1]많은 산악 지역에서 물을 이용할 권리가 토지의 소유와 연관되어 있는데, 예를 들어, 최근까지 안데스 산맥에서는 토지와 물 권리가 (a) 결합되어 있었고, 따라서 물 권리는 토지와 함께 이전되었다. [2]그러나 국가 토지 개혁과 추가 공급원의 개발을 통해 물 권리는 토지와 분리되었고, 경매로 팔릴지도 모른다. [3]그러므로 이것은 지역 공동체의 모든 사람에게 이용할 권리를 보장하기보다, 비용을 지불할 수 있는 사람에게 (b) 유리하다. [4]따라서 물 (권리) 없이 땅을 개인이 보유할 수도 있는 상황이 발생한다. [5]페루에서는 정부가 토지와는 별도로 지역 공동체에 물을 주며, 그것을 분배하는 것은 그 공동체에 달려 있다. [6]예멘에서도 마찬가지로, 전통적인 분배는 100'립나'의 토지에 1척(타사)의 물이었다. [7]이것은 유수(流水), 우물 등으로부터의 전통적인 관개(灌漑) 공급원들에만 적용되었는데, 그곳에서는 공급이 (c) 보장되었다. [8]갑자기 불어난 물을 받아둔 것에서 얻은 물은 불확실한 수원(水源)이 되는 것으로 여겨져서 이슬람 율법의 영향을 받지 않고, 따라서 그 물을 모아서 사용할 수 있는 사람들에게는 무료이다. [9]그러나 토지 단위에 의한 이 전통적인 분배는 부분적으로는 새로운 공급원들의 개발에 의해서 뿐만 아니라 경제적으로 상당히 중요한 작물의 재배 (d) 감소(→ 증가)에 의해서도 무시되었다. [10]이 작물은 일 년 내내 수확되고 따라서 그것의 적정한 몫의 물보다 더 많은 양을 필요로 한다. [11]그 작물의 경제적 지위는 생계형 작물로부터 물 권리가 구매되거나 매수될 수 있음을 (e) 보장한다.

어휘

region 지역, 지방
access 이용(할 권리); 접근
associated with ~와 관련된
possession 소유, 소지
transfer 이전[이동]하다
reform 개혁[개선](하다)

(= The traditional allocation)
[7] This applied only to *traditional irrigation supplies* — / from runoff, wells, etc., // where a supply was **(c) guaranteed.** 03-(c) 전통적 관개 공급은 '보장된' 공급임.
이것(전통적인 분배)은 전통적인 관개(灌漑) 공급원들에만 적용되었다 / 유수(流水), 우물 등으로부터의 // 그리고 그곳에서는 공급이 보장되었다

[8] *Water* (derived from the capture of flash floods) / is not subject to Islamic law // as this constitutes an uncertain source, / and is therefore free / for *those* (able to collect and use it).
물은 (갑자기 불어난 물을 받아둔 것에서 얻은) / 이슬람 율법의 영향을 받지 않는다 // 이것이 불확실한 수원(水源)이 되는 것으로 여겨져서 / 따라서 무료이다 / 사람들에게는 (그 물을 모아서 사용할 수 있는)
↳ **예 2(예멘):** 토지 단위별 일정량의 물을 분배했고, 수원이 불확실한 물은 스스로 모아 무료로 이용 가능함.

[9] However, / this traditional allocation (per unit of land) / has been bypassed, /
그러나 / 이 전통적인 분배는 (토지 단위에 의한) / 무시되었다 /
partly by the development (of new supplies), / but also by the **(d) decrease(→ increase)** in cultivation of a crop (of substantial economic importance). *<of+추상명사> = 형용사
부분적으로는 개발에 의해서 (새로운 공급원들의) / 작물의 재배 감소(→ 증가)에 의해서도 (경제적으로 상당히 중요한)
↳ 전통적 분배는 새로운 공급 개발과 경제적으로 중요한 작물 재배 증가에 의해 무시됨 → 물 권리가 토지와 분리되어 매매됨.

[10] This crop is harvested / throughout the year / and thus requires more / than its fair share of water. 03-(d) 경제적으로 중요한 작물이 일 년 내내 수확되므로 재배는 '증가'함.
이 작물은 수확된다 / 일 년 내내 / 그리고 따라서 더 많은 양을 필요로 한다 / 그것(그 작물)의 적정한 몫의 물보다

[11] The economic status (of the crop) / **(e) ensures** //
경제적 지위는 (그 작물의) / 보장한다 //
ensures의 O(명사절) 03-(e) 경제적으로 중요한 작물의 경제적 지위가 물 사용 권리를 '보장할' 것임.
that water rights can be bought or bribed / away from subsistence crops.
물 권리가 구매되거나 매수될 수 있음을 / 생계형 작물로부터
↳ **예:** 작물의 경제적 지위가 물 이용 권리의 매매를 보장함.

auction 경매
ensure 보장하다, 확실히 하다
grant 주다, 수여하다
allocate 분배하다, 할당하다
well 우물
flash flood 갑자기 불어난 물
be subject to A A의 영향을 받다
constitute ~이 되는 것으로 여겨지다; 구성하다
bypass 무시하다, 회피하다; 우회하다
cultivation 재배, 경작
crop 작물; 수확량
substantial 상당한
status 지위, 신분
[선택지] tie 얽매다, 구속하다; 묶다
stable 안정적인; 차분한
debate 토론(하다), 토의; 논쟁
⊕ 유수(流水)(runoff): 비나 녹은 눈은 땅속으로 흡수되지만 양이 과도할 때는 흡수되지 않고 땅 표면을 흐르는 유수가 되어 호수나 강을 이룸. 유수를 저장하여 관개에 사용하기도 함.

정답 가이드

02 산악 지역에서 많은 경우 물의 이용 권리가 토지 소유와 결합되어 있었다는 내용 다음에 역접 연결어 However로 내용이 전환되며 토지 개혁과 추가적인 공급원의 개발로 물 권리가 토지와 분리되어 매매가 가능해졌다고 했다. 이어지는 페루와 예멘의 예는, 페루에서는 토지와 별도로 지역 공동체가 물을 분배하며, 예멘에서는 토지에 따른 전통적 물 분배가 무시된다는 내용이므로 글의 제목으로 가장 적절한 것은 ① 'Water Rights No Longer Tied to Land(더는 토지에 얽매이지 않는 물 권리)'이다.

03 경제적으로 상당히 중요한 작물은 물을 많이 필요로 하는데, 그 작물의 재배가 '증가하여' 토지 단위에 의한 전통적 분배가 무시되었다는 맥락이 되어야 자연스럽다. 따라서 ④의 'decrease(감소)'를 'increase(증가)' 등으로 바꿔 써야 한다.

오답 클리닉

02 ② Strategies for Trading Water Rights (12%)
물 권리 매매 전략(×)
물 권리를 매매하는 전략을 알려주는 내용이 아님.
③ Water Storage Methods: Mountain vs. Desert (5%)
산 대(對) 사막(×)의 물 저장 방법(×)
사막 지역에 대한 언급은 없으며, 물 저장 방법에 관한 내용도 아님.
④ Water Supplies Not Stable in Mountain Regions (15%)
산악 지역에 안정적이지 않은 물 공급(×)
an uncertain source를 활용한 오답.
⑤ Unending Debates: Which Crop We Should Grow (3%)
끝없는 논쟁인 우리는 어떤 작물을 재배해야 하는가(×)
수익성이 높은 작물 재배는 토지 단위별 물 분배 방식에서 벗어난 이유로 언급된 것임.

03 ① combined (2%) 결합된
물을 이용할 권리가 토지 소유와 연관되어 있다고 했으므로, 토지 소유와 물 권리가 '결합된' 상태였다는 것은 흐름상 자연스럽다.
② favours (6%) 유리하다
문장 2에서 물 권리가 토지와 분리되어 경매될 수 있다고 했으므로, 돈을 지불할 수 있는 사람에게 '유리하다'고 볼 수 있다.
③ guaranteed (16%) 보장된
전통적 물 분배가 유일하게 적용되는 전통적 관개 공급원에서는 물 공급이 '보장된' 것으로 볼 수 있다.
⑤ ensures (8%) 보장하다
경제적으로 중요한 작물은 일 년 내내 재배되면서 많은 물을 필요로 하는데, 생계형 작물보다 경제적 지위가 높으므로 재배에 필요한 물 권리가 구매나 매수되는 것을 '보장할' 것이라는 문맥은 자연스럽다.

01 + 빈칸 추론 (17학년도 6월 모평 32번 | 정답률 35%) ①

구문분석 & 직독직해

생물 큰바다쇠오리의 멸종 이야기

주제문

[1]What story could be harsher / than that (of the Great Auk), / *the large black-and-white seabird* [that in northern oceans / took the ecological place (of a penguin)]?

S V C (= story) =

주격 관계대명사

어떤 이야기가 더 가혹할 수 있을까 / 그것(이야기)보다 (큰바다쇠오리의) / 흑백의 대형 바닷새인 [북쪽 대양에서 / 생태상 위치를 차지했던 (펭귄의)]

↳ **도입:** 큰바다쇠오리의 이야기는 가혹함.

*<with+O'+v-ing/p.p.>: O'가 ~하면서[되면서], O'가 ~한/된 채로

[2]Its tale rises and falls / like a Greek tragedy, / with island populations savagely destroyed / by humans // until almost all were gone.

S V 전치사(~처럼) 수동 관계 부사절 접속사(시간)

그것(큰바다쇠오리)의 이야기는 융성하고 쇠퇴한다 / 한 편의 그리스 비극처럼 / 섬의 개체군이 잔혹하게 죽임을 당하면서 / 인간에 의해 // 거의 모두가 사라질 때까지

[3]Then the very last colony found safety / on a special island, / *one* (protected from the destruction of humankind / by vicious and unpredictable ocean currents).

S V O = (= an island) 과거분사구

🔑 섬의 해류가 거칠어 인간이 접근할 수 없었음.

그 후에 정말 마지막 군집이 안전을 찾아냈다 / 한 특별한 섬에서 / 한 섬 (인간의 파괴로부터 보호받는 / 거칠고 예측할 수 없는 해류에 의해)

[4]These waters presented no problem / to perfectly adapted seagoing birds, //

S_1 V_1 O_1 (= the Great Auks)

이런 바다는 아무 문제도 일으키지 않았다 / 완벽하게 적응된 바다 여행에 알맞은 새에게는 //

but they prevented humans from making any kind of safe landing.

(= these waters) S_2 V_2 O_2 *<prevent A from v-ing>: A가 v하지 못하게 하다

🔑 거친 바다는 인간이 섬에 상륙하지 못하게 했음.

그러나 그것(이런 바다)은 사람들이 어떤 종류의 안전한 상륙도 하지 못하게 했다

↳ 인간에게 거의 모두가 죽임을 당한 큰바다쇠오리의 마지막 집단이 거친 해류 때문에 인간이 접근할 수 없는 섬을 찾아냄.

[5]After enjoying a few years of comparative safety, / disaster (of a different kind) / struck the Great Auk.

전치사(~ 뒤에) after의 O(동명사구) S V O

몇 년의 비교적 안전함을 누린 뒤에 / 재난이 (다른 종류의) / 큰바다쇠오리를 덮쳤다

[6]Volcanic activity caused the island refuge to sink / completely beneath the waves, //

S_1 V_1 O_1 C_1

화산 활동은 그 섬의 피난처가 가라앉게 했다 / 완전히 바다 밑에 //

*<force+O+to-v(O가 (어쩔 수 없이) v하게 만들다)>의 수동형

and surviving individuals were forced to find shelter elsewhere.

S_2 V_2 C_2

그리고 살아남은 개체들은 어딘가 다른 곳에서 피신처를 찾을 수밖에 없었다

↳ 몇 년 후, 섬에 화산 활동이 일어나 다른 피신처를 찾아야 했음.

[7]*The new island home* [(which[that]) they chose] / **lacked the benefits (of the old)** / in one terrible way.

S 목적격 관계대명사 생략 (= surviving individuals) V O

새로운 섬 서식지는 [그것들(살아남은 개체들)이 선택한] / 이점들이 없었다 (옛 것의) / 한 가지 끔찍한 면에서

[8]Humans could access it / with comparative ease, // and they did!

S_1 V_1 O(= the new island home) (= humans) S_2 V_2(= accessed it)

🔑 인간들이 새로운 서식지에 접근할 수 있었음.

인간들이 그것(새로운 섬 서식지)에 접근할 수 있었다 / 비교적 쉽게 // 그리고 그들(인간들)은 그렇게 했다

[9]Within just a few years / the last (of this once-plentiful species) / was entirely eliminated.

S(단수) V(단수)

단지 몇 년 이내에 / 마지막 개체가 (이 한때 풍부했던 종의) / 완전히 제거되었다

↳ 새로 찾은 섬은 인간이 접근할 수 있는 곳이어서 결국 큰바다쇠오리의 모든 개체가 멸종됨.

해석

[1]어떤 이야기가 북쪽 대양에서 생태상 펭귄의 위치를 차지했던 흑백의 대형 바닷새인 큰바다쇠오리의 것보다 더 가혹할 수 있을까? [2]섬의 개체군이 거의 모두가 사라질 때까지 인간에 의해 잔혹하게 죽임을 당하면서, 그것(큰바다쇠오리)의 이야기는 한 편의 그리스 비극처럼 융성하고 쇠퇴한다. [3]그 후에 정말 마지막 군집이 한 특별한 섬, 즉 거칠고 예측할 수 없는 해류에 의해 인간의 파괴로부터 보호받는 한 섬에서 안전을 찾아냈다. [4]이런 바다는 완벽하게 적응된 바다 여행에 알맞은 새에게는 아무 문제도 일으키지 않았지만, 그것(이런 바다)은 사람들이 어떤 종류의 안전한 상륙도 하지 못하게 했다. [5]몇 년의 비교적 안전함을 누린 뒤에 다른 종류의 재난이 큰바다쇠오리를 덮쳤다. [6]화산 활동은 그 섬의 피난처가 완전히 바다 밑에 가라앉게 했고, 살아남은 개체들은 어딘가 다른 곳에서 피신처를 찾을 수밖에 없었다. [7]그것들(살아남은 개체들)이 선택한 새로운 섬 서식지는 한 가지 끔찍한 면에서 옛 것의 이점들이 없었다. [8]인간들이 비교적 쉽게 그것(새로운 섬 서식지)에 접근할 수 있었고, 그들은 그렇게 했다! [9]단지 몇 년 이내에 이 한때 풍부했던 종의 마지막 개체가 완전히 제거되었다.

어휘

ecological 생태상의, 생태학의
tragedy 비극 (작품)
population 개체군; 인구
colony 군집, 집단; 식민지
humankind 인간, 인류
vicious 거친, 심한; 사악한
current 해류, 흐름; 현재의
present (문제 등을) 일으키다; 발표하다; 주다
adapt 적응하다; 조정하다
seagoing 바다 여행[항해]에 알맞은
landing 상륙, 착륙
comparative 비교적[상대적]인; 비교의
strike (재난 등이 갑자기) 덮치다, 발생하다
refuge 피난(처)
cf. refugee 피난자, 난민
shelter 피신처, 대피처; 주거지
lack ~이 없다, 부족하다
plentiful 풍부한, 많은
[선택지] deny A B A에게 B를 허락하지 않다

정답 가이드

빈칸 문장으로 보아, 살아남은 (큰바다쇠오리) 개체들이 선택한 새로운 서식지가 한 가지 끔찍한 면에서 '어떠했는지'를 추론해야 한다. 큰바다쇠오리의 마지막 군집이 안전을 찾아 이주한 섬은 거친 해류 때문에 인간이 접근할 수 없는 곳이었다고 했다. 그러나 화산 활동으로 그 섬이 가라앉게 되면서 인간이 비교적 쉽게 접근할 수 있는 섬으로 옮겨가게 된 큰바다쇠오리는 결국 멸종하게 되었다고 이야기한다. 다시 말해, 인간이 접근할 수 없었던 옛 서식지의 이점이 새로운 서식지에는 없어 큰바다쇠오리가 멸종하게 된 것이므로, 빈칸에 들어갈 말로 가장 적절한 것은 ① 'lacked the benefits of the old(옛 것의 이점들이 없었다)'이다.

오답 클리닉

② denied other colonies easy access (13%)
다른 군집들에게 쉬운 접근을 허락하지 않았다
인간이 쉽게 접근할 수 있었다고 했으므로 틀림.

③ faced unexpected natural disasters (27%)
예기치 못한 자연 재해에 직면했다
화산 활동이 발생한 섬은 인간이 접근할 수 없었던 이주하기 이전의 섬이므로 틀림.

④ caused conflicts among the refugees (7%)
피난 개체들 사이에 갈등을 유발했다
피난 개체들 사이의 갈등에 관한 언급은 없음.

⑤ had a similar disadvantage to the last island (14%)
마지막 섬과 비슷한 불이익이 있었다
새로운 섬으로 이주하기 전의 섬은 거친 해류 때문에 인간이 접근할 수 없다는 이점이 있었으므로 틀림.

02 + 글의 순서 (18학년도 9월 모평 37번 | 정답률 48%) ②

구문분석 & 직독직해

예술 예술가라는 용어의 원래 의미

★<be used to-v>: v하는 데 사용되다

[1]Today / the term artist(S) is used(V) / to refer to a broad range of creative individuals (across the globe) / from both past and present.
오늘날 / 예술가라는 용어는 사용된다 / 폭넓고 다양한 창의적인 개인들을 지칭하는 데 (전 세계의) / 과거와 현재 모두의
↳ 대조 A: 오늘날 예술가라는 용어는 넓은 범위의 창의적인 개인들을 지칭함.

[2]This rather general usage(S) erroneously suggests(V) // that(명사절 접속사; suggest의 O(명사절)) the concept or word "artist" existed / in original contexts.
이런 다소 일반적인 (용어의) 사용은 잘못 암시한다 // '예술가'라는 개념이나 말이 존재했음을 / 원래의 맥락 속에

⊶ 주어진 글의 '예술가'라는 용어의 광범위한 사용과 대조되는 정의가 제시됨.
(B) [3]In contrast to *the diversity* [(which[that]) it is applied to], / the meaning (of this term)(S) / continues to be mostly based(V) / on Western views and values(O).
(목적격 관계대명사 생략; it = the term artist)
다양성과는 대조적으로 [그것(예술가라는 용어)이 적용되는] / 의미는 (이 용어의) / 대체로 계속해서 기반을 두고 있다 / 서양의 관점과 가치에

[4]Since(전치사(~ 이래로)) the fifteenth century, / this tradition(S) has been concerned(V) / with recognizing individual achievements(with의 O(동명사구)).
15세기 이래로 / 이 전통은 관련이 있었다 / 개인의 업적을 인정하는 것과
↳ 대조 B: 예술가의 의미는 서양의 관점 및 가치에 기반을 두고 개인의 업적을 인정하는 데 쓰였음.

⊶ (B)에서 언급한 개인의 업적을 부연 설명함. ★<credit A to B(A를 B의 공으로 여기다)>의 수동형
(A) [5]Inventions, ideas, and discoveries(S) have been credited(V) / to *the persons* [who(주격 관계대명사) originated them(= inventions, ideas and discoveries)].
발명품, 아이디어, 그리고 발견은 공으로 여겨져 왔다 / 사람들의 [그것들을 만들어낸]
↳ 세부 사항 1: 발명품을 발명한 사람에게 공이 있다고 여김.

[6]This view is also / at the core (of the definition of an "artist.")
이 견해는 또한 있다 / 핵심에 ('예술가'라는 정의의)

[7]Artists(S) are perceived(V) to establish a strong bond(C) / with their art / to the point of(~라고 할 (수 있을) 정도로) combining into one "entity."(of의 O(동명사구))
예술가는 강한 유대를 확립한다고 인식된다 / 자신들의 예술 작품과 / 하나의 '실체'로 결합한다고 할 수 있을 정도로
↳ 세부 사항 2: 예술가는 자신의 예술 작품과 강한 유대감을 갖는다고 인식됨.

해석

[1]오늘날 예술가라는 용어는 과거와 현재 모두의 전 세계의 폭넓고 다양한 창의적인 개인들을 지칭하는 데 사용된다. [2]이런 다소 일반적인 (용어의) 사용은 '예술가'라는 개념이나 말이 원래의 맥락 속에 존재했음을 잘못 암시한다.(▶ '예술가'라는 용어가 최초로 생겨나 쓰였을 때는 지금의 일반적 개념이나 말이 아니었다는 의미) (B) [3]그것(예술가라는 용어)이 적용되는 다양성과는 대조적으로 이 용어의 의미는 대체로 서양의 관점과 가치에 계속해서 기반을 두고 있다. [4]15세기 이래로 이 전통은 개인의 업적을 인정하는 것과 관련이 있었다. (A) [5]발명품, 아이디어, 그리고 발견은 그것들을 만들어낸 사람들의 공으로 여겨져 왔다. [6]이 견해는 또한 '예술가'라는 정의의 핵심에 있다. [7]예술가는 하나의 '실체'로 결합한다고 할 수 있을 정도로 자신들의 예술 작품과 강한 유대를 확립한다고 인식된다. (C) [8]예술사는 이러한 일체감을 강화해 왔는데, Pablo Picasso가 그린 그림은 'a Picasso'라고 불린다. [9]예술가와 그들 작품 간의 이런 결합은 예술가의 필수 자질, 즉 독창성, 저작 작업, 그리고 진정성을 결정해 왔다.

어휘

term 용어; 기간; 학기
range 다양성; 범위
erroneously 잘못되게
context 맥락; 문맥
diversity 다양성
be concerned with ~와 관련이 있다
originate 만들어 내다, 발명하다
core 핵심
definition 정의

(A)의 예술가와 예술 작품이 하나의 실체로 결합되는 것을 지칭함.

(C) [8] Art history has reinforced this oneness: // A painting (by Pablo Picasso) / is called "a Picasso."
S1 V1 O S2 V2 C
예술사는 이러한 일체감을 강화해 왔다 // 그림은 (Pablo Picasso가 그린) / 'a Picasso'라고 불린다

[9] This union (between artists and their work) / has determined the essential qualities (of an artist): / originality, authorship, and authenticity.
S V O =
이런 결합은 (예술가와 그들 작품 간의) / 필수 자질을 결정해 왔다 (예술가의) / 즉 독창성, 저작 작업, 그리고 진정성
↳ **부연 설명:** 예술가와 작품 간의 일체감이 예술가의 필수 자질(독창성, 저작 작업, 진정성)을 결정함.

perceive 인식하다, 인지하다
establish 확립하다; 설립하다
bond 유대(감)
combine into ~로 결합하다
entity 실체
reinforce 강화하다
oneness 일체(감)
union 결합, 연합
originality 독창성
authorship 저작 (작업); 원작자(임)

정답 가이드

주어진 글은 오늘날 예술가라는 용어가 넓은 범위의 창의적인 개인들을 지칭하는 데 쓰인다는 내용이다. 이어서 이러한 다양한 적용과 대조를 이루어 과거에는 '예술가'라는 용어가 개인의 업적을 인정하는 데 쓰였다는 (B)가 뒤에 오는 것이 적절하다. 그 다음에 (A)의 발명품, 아이디어, 발견이 (B)의 개인의 업적을 부연 설명하며 예술가는 자신의 예술품과 하나의 '실체'로 결합한다는 내용이 이어지고, 이를 this oneness로 지칭하면서 Pablo Picasso와 그의 그림의 일체감을 예로 드는 (C)가 마지막에 오는 것이 적절하다.

오답 클리닉

① (A) - (C) - (B) (9%)
(A)의 Inventions, ideas, and discoveries는 (B)의 individual achievements를 설명하므로 (B) 앞에 올 수 없다.
③ (B) - (C) - (A) (16%)
(C)의 this oneness는 (A)의 예술가와 예술 작품이 하나의 실체로 결합하는 것을 지칭하므로 (A)의 뒤에 이어져야 한다.
④ (C) - (A) - (B) (13%) / ⑤ (C) - (B) - (A) (14%)
(C)의 this oneness가 지칭하는 내용을 주어진 글에서 찾을 수 없으므로 (C)가 주어진 글 바로 뒤에 올 수 없다.

03 + 문장 넣기 (18학년도 9월 모평 39번 | 정답률 43%) ⑤

구문분석 & 직독직해 예술 위대한 작곡가들의 빠른 작곡 속도

[1] There are many instances (of rapid work / on the part of the great composers); //
V1 S1
많은 예들이 있다 (빠른 작업의 / 위대한 작곡가들이 한) //
and their facility and quickness (of composition) / causes great wonder and admiration.
S2 V2 O
그리고 그들의 재능과 재빠름은 (작곡의) / 엄청난 경이감과 감탄을 불러일으킨다

주제문
(①) [2] But our admiration is often misdirected.
S V
그러나 우리의 감탄은 종종 잘못된 방향으로 보내진다
↳ **도입:** 우리가 감탄해야 할 것은 위대한 작곡가들의 빠른 작곡 능력이 아님.

(②) [3] When we hear / of some of the speedy writing (of great works / by Mozart or Mendelssohn), //
부사절 접속사(시간)
우리가 들을 때 / 일부 빠른 써 내림에 관해 (위대한 작품들의 / Mozart나 Mendelssohn에 의한) //
might think의 O(명사절) *<A as well as B>: B뿐만 아니라 A
we might think // that this speed was of the composing power as well as of pen, //
S1 V1 명사절 접속사 S′ V′ C′
우리는 생각할 수 있다 // 이 속도가 펜(으로 쓰는 것)뿐만 아니라 작곡하는 능력의 속도라고 //
but, in fact, / such was seldom the case.
S2 V2 C
그러나 실제로 / 그것은 거의 사실이 아니었다
↳ **통념:** 위대한 작곡가가 빠르게 곡을 써 내리는 것을 펜뿐만 아니라 작곡하는 능력의 빠른 속도라고 생각하지만 이는 사실이 아님.

(③) [4] These great musicians generally did their composition mentally / without reference to pen or piano, //
S V1 O1 ~와 관계없이
이 위대한 음악가들은 보통 마음속으로 작곡을 했다 / 펜이나 피아노와 관계없이 //
and simply postponed / the unpleasant manual labor (of committing their music to paper) //
V2 O2 =
부사절 접속사
until it became absolutely necessary.
S′ V′ C′
그리고 그저 미루었다 / 유쾌하지 않은 수작업을 (자신들의 음악을 종이에 적어 두는) //
그것이 절대적으로 필요할 때까지

해석

[1] 위대한 작곡가들이 한 빠른 작업의 많은 예들이 있는데, 그들의 작곡 재능과 재빠름은 엄청난 경이감과 감탄을 불러일으킨다. (①) [2] 그러나 우리의 감탄은 종종 잘못된 방향으로 보내진다. (②) [3] 우리가 Mozart나 Mendelssohn에 의한 위대한 작품들의 일부 빠른 써 내림에 관해 들을 때, 우리는 이 속도가 펜(으로 쓰는 것)뿐만 아니라 작곡하는 능력의 속도라고 생각할 수 있지만 실제로 그것은 거의 사실이 아니었다. (③) [4] 이 위대한 음악가들은 보통 펜이나 피아노와 관계없이 마음속으로 작곡을 했으며, 절대적으로 필요할 때까지 자신들의 음악을 종이에 적어 두는, 유쾌하지 않은 수작업을 그저 미루었다. (④) [5] 그렇게 하여 그들은 놀라운 작곡 속도로 명성을 얻게 되었다. (⑤ [6] 그러나 길고 복잡한 작품을 빠르고 정확하게 쓰는 것은 결코 쉬운 일이 아니다.) [7] 이것을 깨닫기 위해서는 누구나 한 곡의 음악을 그대로 옮겨 써보거나 전에 기억해둔 어떤 음악을 음표로 옮기려고 해보기만 하면 된다.

어휘

on the part of ~이 한[만든]
composer 작곡가
cf. composition 작곡; 작품
cf. compose 작곡하다
facility 재능; (편의) 시설
admiration 감탄; 존경
misdirect 잘못된 방향으로 보내다, 잘못 가리키다

(④) [5]Then / they got credit / for incredible rapidity of composition.

S V O

그렇게 하여 / 그들은 명성을 얻게 되었다 / 놀라운 작곡 속도로

↳ **사실:** 위대한 음악가들은 마음속으로 작곡을 하고, 종이에 옮기는 것을 미룬 것임.

앞과 상반되는 내용이 But으로 이어짐.

(⑤ [6]But / it is no light matter / to quickly and correctly pen / a long and complicated composition.)

가주어 V C 진주어(to-v구) to pen의 O

그러나 / (~은) 결코 쉬운 일이 아니다 / 빠르고 정확하게 쓰는 것은 / 길고 복잡한 작품을

[7]One has only to copy a piece of music / or (has only) to try to put into notes / *some piece of music* (previously memorized), / to realize this. this는 주어진 문장의 내용을 가리킴.

S V₁ O₁ V₂ O₂ 과거분사구 목적(~하기 위해) (= 앞 문장)

누구나 한 곡의 음악을 그대로 옮겨 써보기만 하면 된다 / 또는 음표로 옮기려고 해보기만 하면 된다 / 어떤 음악을 (전에 기억해둔) / 이것을 깨닫기 위해서는

↳ **부연 설명:** 마음속으로 작곡한 길고 복잡한 곡을 빠르고 정확하게 종이에 옮겨 쓰는 것은 쉬운 일이 아님.

mentally 마음속으로, 정신적으로
postpone 미루다, 연기하다
manual 손으로 하는, 수동의; 설명서
labor 노동; 노력; 힘든 일
commit 적어 두다; 저지르다; 전념하다
get credit 명성을 얻다
incredible 놀라운; 믿어지지 않는
rapidity 속도; 신속
piece (문학·예술·음악 등의) 작품, (작품) 한 점
note 음(표); 메모; 주목하다
previously 전에, 그에 앞서

정답 가이드

But으로 이어지는 주어진 문장은 길고 복잡한 곡을 빠르고 정확하게(quickly and correctly) 쓰는 것이 쉽지 않다는 내용이다. 이는 그러한 곡을 빠르고 정확하게 쓴다는 내용 뒤에 와야 적절할 것이고, 그 뒤에는 주어진 문장을 뒷받침하는 설명이 이어질 것이다. 글의 흐름을 보면 ⑤ 앞은 위대한 작곡가들이 '놀라운 작곡 속도(incredible rapidity)'로 명성을 얻었다는 내용이고, ⑤ 뒤의 this는 주어진 문장을 받아 이를 깨달을 수 있는 방법을 제시한 것이므로 주어진 문장이 들어가기에 가장 적절한 곳은 ⑤이다.

오답 클리닉

① (4%) '감탄을 불러일으킨다'는 앞 문장 뒤에 역접 연결어 But으로 '감탄의 방향이 잘못되었다'라는 내용이 연결되는 흐름은 자연스럽다.

② (5%) 감탄의 방향이 잘못되었다는 앞 내용을 어떤 생각이 잘못되었는지 부연 설명하는 내용이다.

③ (24%) 사실이 아니었다는 앞 내용에 이어 실제로는 마음속으로 작곡하고 종이에 쓰는 것을 미뤄둔 것이라고 사실을 밝히는 흐름은 적절하다. These great musicians는 앞 문장의 Mozart와 Mendelssohn을 지칭한다.

④ (25%) 위대한 작곡가들이 마음속으로 작곡한 것을 종이에 옮긴 것에서 빠른 작곡 속도로 명성을 얻게 되었다는 내용이 Then(그렇게 하여)으로 이어진다.

The 주의 위대한 음악가들이 놀라운 작곡 속도로 명성을 얻었다는 내용을 ⑤ 뒤에서 대명사 this로 받을 경우 내용이 자연스럽게 이어지지 않음을 파악해야 한다.

부록 | 초고난도 킬러 문항

p. 216

01 ②	02 ①	03 ⑤	04 ⑤	05 ②	06 ③	07 ④	08 ②
09 ②	10 ④	11 ①	12 ⑤	13 ⑤			

01 ✦ 함의 추론 〈22학년도 대수능 21번 | 정답률 34%〉 ②

구문분석 & 직독직해

생활 전문가들이 가진 전문 지식에 대한 신뢰

[1]Scientists have no special purchase / on moral or ethical decisions; //
S V O
과학자들은 특별한 권한이 없다 / 도덕적 혹은 윤리적 결정에 대해 //

a climate scientist is no more qualified / to comment on health care reform // than a physicist is (qualified) to judge the causes (of bee colony collapse).
형용사 qualified 수식 ★<A no more ~ than B>: A는 B와 마찬가지로 ~ 아니다, B가 아닌 것처럼 A도 ~ 아니다
반복어 생략 형용사 qualified 수식
기후 과학자가 자격이 있지 않은 것은 / 의료 개혁에 대해 견해를 밝힐 // 물리학자가 그렇지(자격이 있지) 않은 것과 같다 / 원인을 판단할 (꿀벌 군락 붕괴의) /
↳ 전문가들은 자기 분야를 벗어난 영역을 판단할 자격이 안 됨.

[2]*The very features* [that create expertise in a specialized domain] / lead to ignorance / in many others.
S 주격 관계대명사 V
(= other domains)
바로 그 특징이 [한 전문 영역에서의 전문 지식을 만들어내는] / 무지로 이어진다 / 많은 다른 영역에서의
↳ 한 분야의 전문가여도 다른 분야에는 무지함.

[3]In some cases / lay people — / farmers, fishermen, patients, native peoples — / may have *relevant experiences* [that scientists can learn from].
S V O
목적격 관계대명사
어떤 경우에는 / 전문가가 아닌 사람들 / 즉 농부, 어부, 환자, 토착민이 / 관련 경험을 가지고 있을 수 있다 [과학자들이 그것으로부터 배울 수 있는]
↳ 전문가가 비전문가의 경험으로부터 배울 수도 있음.

[4]Indeed, / in recent years, / scientists have begun to recognize this: // the Arctic Climate Impact Assessment includes / *observations* (gathered from local native groups).
S_1 V_1 O_1 (= 앞 문장) S_2 V_2 O_2 과거분사구
실제로 / 최근에 / 과학자들은 이를 인정하기 시작했다 // 북극 기후 영향 평가는 포함한다 / 관찰을 (지역 토착 집단에게서 수집된)
↳ 예: 과학자들이 비전문가(토착민)의 도움을 받음.

[5]So / our trust needs to be limited, and focused.
그러므로 / 우리의 신뢰는 한정되고 집중될 필요가 있다

[6]It needs to be very *particular*.
(= our trust)
그것(우리의 신뢰)은 매우 '특정할' 필요가 있다
↳ 주장: 전문가에 대한 신뢰는 한정되고 특정적이어야 함.

★<A as 원급 as B>: A는 B만큼 ~한[하게]
[7]Blind trust will get us into at least as much trouble / as no trust at all.
맹목적 신뢰는 적어도 우리를 많은 곤경에 빠뜨릴 것이다 / 전혀 신뢰가 없는 것만큼
↳ 근거: 전문가에 대한 맹목적인 신뢰는 문제를 유발함.

[8]But / without some degree of trust / in our designated experts — / *the men and women* [who have devoted their lives / to sorting out tough questions (about *the natural world* [(which[that]) we live in])] — / we are paralyzed, /
전치사(~이 없으면) 주격 관계대명사 전치사 목적격 관계대명사 생략 S V
⊶ 역접 연결어가 쓰여 전문가의 지식을 맹신하지 말아야 한다는 앞 내용과 반대되는 내용(전문 지식을 어느 정도는 믿어야 함)으로 전환됨.
하지만 / 어느 정도의 신뢰가 없으면 / 우리가 지명한 전문가들에게 / 즉 남녀들 [그들의 생애를 바친 / 어려운 문제들을 해결하는 데 (자연 세계에 관한 [우리가 사는])] / 우리는 마비된다 /

해석

[1]과학자들은 도덕적 혹은 윤리적 결정에 대해 특별한 권한이 없으며, 기후 과학자가 의료 개혁에 대해 견해를 밝힐 자격이 있지 않은 것은 물리학자가 꿀벌 군락 붕괴의 원인을 판단할 자격이 있지 않은 것과 같다. [2]한 전문 영역에서의 전문 지식을 만들어내는 바로 그 특징이 많은 다른 영역에서의 무지로 이어진다. [3]어떤 경우에는, 전문가가 아닌 사람들, 즉 농부, 어부, 환자, 토착민이, 과학자들이 그것으로부터 배울 수 있는 관련 경험을 가지고 있을 수 있다. [4]실제로, 최근에 과학자들은 이를 인정하기 시작했는데, 북극 기후 영향 평가는 지역 토착 집단에게서 수집된 관찰을 포함한다. [5]그러므로 우리의 신뢰는 한정되고 집중될 필요가 있다. [6]그것은 매우 '특정할' 필요가 있다. [7]맹목적 신뢰는 적어도 전혀 신뢰가 없는 것만큼 우리를 많은 곤경에 빠뜨릴 것이다. [8]하지만 우리가 지명한 전문가들, 즉 우리가 사는 자연 세계에 관한 어려운 문제들을 해결하는 데 그들의 생애를 바친 남녀들에게 어느 정도의 신뢰가 없으면, 우리는 마비되고, 사실상 아침 통근을 위해 준비해야 할지 말아야 할지를 알지 못할 것이다.(▶ 전문가들이 제공하는 정보를 믿지 못하면 아침 통근과 같은 기본적인 일상생활을 할지 말지도 결정하지 못할 정도로 마비된다는 의미)

어휘

purchase 권한, 권리; 구입(하다)
moral 도덕적인, 윤리적인(= ethical)
qualified 자격이 있는
comment 견해를 밝히다, 논평하다; 논평
reform 개혁(하다)
physicist 물리학자
colony 군락; 식민지
collapse 붕괴(하다); 쓰러지다
expertise 전문 지식
domain 영역, 분야
ignorance 무지, 무식
relevant 관련 있는, 적절한
arctic 북극의
assessment 평가
observation 관찰, 관측; 감시
particular 까다로운; 특정한
blind 맹목적인; 눈이 먼
get A into trouble A를 곤경에 빠뜨리다
designate 지명하다, 선정하다; 지정하다
devote A to B A를 B에 바치다

in effect / not knowing // **whether to make ready for the morning commute or not.**
분사구문(= and we don't know ~)
사실상 / 알지 못하며 // 아침 통근을 위해 준비해야 할지 말아야 할지를
↳ **반론:** 그럼에도 전문가의 정보를 어느 정도 신뢰할 필요가 있음.

sort out ~을 해결[처리]하다; 선별하다, 분류하다
[선택지] popularize 보급하다, 대중화하다
applicable 적용[응용]할 수 있는
practical 실용적인
biased 편향된, 선입견이 있는

정답 가이드

전문가는 자기 분야 밖의 영역에는 무지하고 전문 분야라도 경험이 많은 비전문가에게서 배우기도 하기 때문에 전문가의 지식을 맹목적으로 믿기보다는 신뢰를 한정할 필요가 있다고 했다. 그러나 역접 연결어 But 이후에 전문가의 지식을 어느 정도는 신뢰할 필요가 있다고 내용이 전환된다. 전문가들이 생애를 바쳐 연구한 지식을 믿지 못하면 우리는 마비된다고 했는데, 여기서 밑줄 친 '아침 통근을 위해 준비해야 할지 말아야 할지'를 알지 못하는 것은 아침 통근과 같은 아주 기본적인 일상생활을 위한 정보도 알지 못한다는 것을 의미한다. 따라서 밑줄 친 부분은 ② 'readily applicable information offered by specialized experts(전문적인 전문가들에 의해 제공된 쉽게 적용할 수 있는 정보)'를 의미한다.

The 핵심 전문 지식의 신뢰에 대한 글쓴이의 생각이 역접 연결어 But을 기준으로 앞 내용과 달라지는 것을 잘 파악해야 한다.

오답 클리닉

① questionable facts that have been popularized by non-experts (18%) 비전문가에 의해(×) 보급된 의심스러운 사실(×)
비전문가가 의심스러운 사실을 퍼뜨렸다는 내용은 없으며, 오히려 과학자들은 경험 있는 비전문가의 도움을 받기도 한다고 했음.

③ common knowledge that hardly influences crucial decisions (10%) 중대한 결정(×)에 거의 영향을 주지 않는 일반 지식(×)
일반 지식보다는 전문 지식에 관한 것이며, 출근 준비를 결정하는 것은 중대한 결정으로 보기 힘듦.

④ practical information produced by both specialists and lay people (28%) 전문가와 전문가가 아닌 사람들 모두(×)에 의해 생산된 실용적인 정보
문장 3~7의 비전문가의 실용적인 경험 지식에서 전문가가 배우기도 하기 때문에 전문가의 지식을 맹목적으로 신뢰하는 것은 위험하다는 내용을 이용한 오답. But 뒤에 나오는 내용은 전문가의 지식을 어느 정도 신뢰해야 한다는 것으로 비전문가와는 관련 없음.

The 주의 both, every와 같이 전체를 포괄하는 표현이 있는 경우 일부에 해당되는 내용이 아닌지 잘 확인해야 한다.

⑤ biased knowledge that is widespread in the local community (10%) 지역 공동체(×)에 널리 퍼져 있는 편향된 지식(×)
전문가의 지식이 편향되었다고 볼 수 없으며, 지역 공동체 또한 언급되지 않음.

02 + 빈칸 추론 〈24학년도 6월 모평 33번 | 정답률 33%〉 ①

구문분석 & 직독직해 학문 과학자와 예술가의 현실을 추구하는 방법의 차이

[1]Whatever their differences (are), / scientists and artists begin / with the same question: //
*whatever가 be동사의 보어인 경우 be동사는 생략 가능함. S V
그들의 차이점이 무엇이든 / 과학자와 예술가는 시작한다 / 똑같은 질문으로 //
can you and I see the same thing the same way? // If so, how?
즉 '당신과 내가 똑같은 것을 똑같은 방식으로 볼 수 있을까? // 만약 그렇다면 어떻게?'
↳ **도입:** 과학자와 예술가는 똑같은 사물을 똑같이 보는 방법에 대한 질문에서 시작함.

[2]The scientific thinker / looks for *features* (*of the thing* [that can be stripped of subjectivity]) — /
S V O 주격 관계대명사 *<strip A of B(A에게서 B를 박탈하다)>의 수동형
과학적 사고를 하는 사람은 / 특징들을 찾는다 (사물의 [주관성이 박탈될 수 있는]) /
ideally, *those aspects* [that can be quantified / and whose values will thus never change / from one observer to the next].
주격 관계대명사 소유격 관계대명사
즉 이상적으로 그런 측면들 [수량화될 수 있는 / 그래서 그것의 가치가 결코 바뀌지 않을 / 한 관찰자에서 다음 관찰자 사이에]

[3]In this way, / he arrives / at *a reality* (independent / of all observers).
(= the scientific thinker) S V 형용사구
이런 식으로 / 그(과학적 사고를 하는 사람)는 도달한다 / 현실에 (독립된 / 모든 관찰자로부터)
↳ **대조 A(과학자):** 사물에서 주관성이 박탈될 수 있는 특징을 찾아 관찰자의 영향을 받지 않는 독립된 현실에 도달함.

[4]The artist, / on the other hand, / relies on the strength (of her artistry) /
S V O
예술가는 / 반면에 / 힘에 의지한다 (자신의 예술성의) /

해석

[1]과학자와 예술가의 차이점이 무엇이든, 그들은 똑같은 질문, 즉 '당신과 내가 똑같은 것을 똑같은 방식으로 볼 수 있을까? 만약 그렇다면 어떻게?'라는 질문으로 시작한다. [2]과학적 사고를 하는 사람은 주관성이 박탈될 수 있는 사물의 특징들, 즉 이상적으로 수량화될 수 있고 그래서 그것의 가치가 한 관찰자에서 다음 관찰자 사이에 결코 바뀌지 않을 그런 측면들을 찾는다. [3]이런 식으로, 그는 모든 관찰자로부터 독립된 현실에 도달한다. [4]반면에, 예술가는 자기 자신의 주관성과 자기 독자의 주관성 간의 결합을 이루기 위해 자신의 예술성의 힘에 의지한다. [5]과학적 사고를 하는 사람에게, 이것은 틀림없이 마술적인 생각처럼 들릴 것인데, 즉 '당신이 뭔가를 아주 열심히 상상해서 당신이 그것을 마음속에 그리는 바로 그 방식으로 그것이 다른 누군가의 머릿속에 떠오를 것이라고 당신은 말하고 있는 것인가?' (▶ 예술가와 독자의 주관성 결합을 의미) [6]예술가는 과학자의 관찰자로부터 독립적인 현실과 정반대의 것을 추구해 왔다. [7]예술가는 관찰자에게 의존적인 현실, 사실상 그것(현실)이 조금이라도 존재하기

🔑 예술가는 자신의 주관성과 독자의 주관성의 결합을 이루려 함.

to effect a marriage (between her own subjectivity / and that of her readers).

목적(~하기 위해) <between A and B>: A와 B 사이의 (= subjectivity)

결합을 이루기 위해 (자기 자신의 주관성과 / 자기 독자의 그것(주관성) 간의)

↳ **대조 B(예술가):** 예술가 자신의 주관성과 독자의 주관성의 결합을 이루려 함.

(= 앞 문장)

[5]To a scientific thinker, / this must sound / like magical thinking: //

S V

과학적 사고를 하는 사람에게 / 이것은 틀림없이 들릴 것이다 / 마술적인 생각처럼 //

are saying의 O(명사절) *<so+형용사/부사(+that) ...>: 아주 ~해서 …하다

you're saying // (that) you will imagine something so hard // (that) it'll pop into someone else's head / exactly the way [(that) you envision it]?

(= an artist) 명사절 접속사 생략 부사절 접속사 생략 관계부사 생략

즉 '당신은 말하고 있는 것인가 // 당신이 뭔가를 아주 열심히 상상해서 // 그것이 다른 누군가의 머릿속에 떠오를 것이라고 / 바로 그 방식으로 [당신이 그것을 마음속에 그리는]'

🔑 예술가는 과학자가 추구하는 관찰자로부터 독립된 현실과 정반대의 것을 추구함.

[6]The artist has sought / the opposite (of the scientist's observer-independent reality).

S V O

예술가는 추구해 왔다 / 정반대의 것을 (과학자의 관찰자로부터 독립적인 현실과)

(= The artist) 형용사구 🔑 예술가는 관찰자에게 의존적인 현실을 만들어 냄.

[7]She creates *a reality* (dependent upon observers), / indeed *a reality* [in which **human beings must participate** / in order for it to exist at all].

S V O = 전치사+관계대명사 (= reality) *for it은 to exist의 의미상 주어임. 목적(~하기 위해)

예술가는 현실을 만들어 낸다 (관찰자에게 의존적인) / 사실상 현실인 [인간들이 참여해야만 하는 / 그것(현실)이 조금이라도 존재하기 위해서는]

↳ **부연 설명:** 예술가가 만들어내는 관찰자에 의존적인 현실이 존재하기 위해서는 관찰자가 참여해야 함.

위해서는 인간들이 참여해야만 하는 현실을 만들어 낸다.(▶ 예술은 인간과 별개로 존재할 수 없음을 의미)

어휘

feature 특징(으로 삼다); 특집 (기사로 다루다)
subjectivity 주관성(↔ objectivity 객관성)
ideally 이상적으로
quantify 수량화하다, 양을 나타내다
artistry 예술성; 예술적 기교
effect 이루다, 달성하다; (결과를) 가져오다; 영향
marriage (밀접한) 결합; 결혼
pop into one's head (생각 등이) 머릿속에 떠오르다
envision 마음속에 그리다[상상하다]
indeed 사실, 실은; 정말
participate 참여[참가]하다
[선택지] harmonize 조화를 이루다, 어울리다
disengage 분리하다, 떼어 내다; 해방시키다

정답 가이드

빈칸 문장과 앞 문장으로 보아, 그녀(예술가)는 과학자와 정반대의 것을 추구해왔으며, 그녀가 '어떤' 현실을 만들어 내는지를 추론해야 함을 알 수 있다. 도입부에서 과학자와 예술가는 모두, 어떤 방법으로 자신과 당신(일반 대중)이 똑같은 것을 똑같은 방식으로 볼 수 있는지를 질문한다고 했다. 그 방법으로, 과학자는 주관성이 박탈된 관찰자로부터 독립된 현실(수량화되고 객관적인 현실)을 찾고자 하고, 예술가는 자신과 독자의 주관성 간의 결합을 이루고자 한다고 했다. 즉 과학자와 달리, 예술가는 관찰자로부터 독립적이지 않고 그들의 주관성과 결합해야 하는 '의존적인' 현실을 만들어 낸다고 할 수 있다. 따라서 빈칸에 들어갈 말로 가장 적절한 것은 ① 'human beings must participate(인간들이 참여해야만 한다)'이다.

오답 클리닉

② objectivity should be maintained (26%)
객관성이 유지되어야 한다
관찰자로부터 독립적인 현실을 추구하는 과학자에 해당하는 내용이므로 틀림.

③ science and art need to harmonize (14%)
과학과 예술이 조화를 이룰 필요가 있다
과학과 예술이 조화를 이룰 필요성은 언급되지 않음.

④ readers remain distanced from the arts (9%)
독자가 예술로부터 거리를 둔다
문장 4에서 예술가는 자신의 주관성과 독자의 주관성을 결합하려 한다고 했으므로 거리를 두는 것은 틀림.

⑤ she is disengaged from her own subjectivity (18%)
그녀(예술가)가 자신의 주관성에서 분리된다
주관성에서 분리된 현실은 과학이 강조하는 현실이므로 틀림.

03 + 빈칸 추론 〈24학년도 6월 모평 34번 | 정답률 32%〉 ⑤

구문분석 & 직독직해

철학 감각적 지각과 구별되는 합리적 이성의 우월성

[1]One (of the common themes (of the Western philosophical tradition)) / is the distinction (between sensual perceptions and rational knowledge).

S V C <between A and B>: A와 B 사이의

하나는 (공통된 주제 중 (서양의 철학적 전통의)) / 구별이다 (감각적 지각과 합리적 지식 사이의)

↳ **도입:** 서양 철학은 감각적 지각과 합리적 지식을 구별함.

= (= rational reason)

[2]Since Plato, / the supremacy (of rational reason) / is based on the assertion // that it is able to extract true knowledge / from experience. 🔑 참된 지식을 끌어낼 수 있다는 점에서 합리적 이성이 감각적 지각보다 우월함.

전치사(~ 이후로) S V C 동격 접속사 S' V' C'

Plato(플라톤) 이후로 / 우월성은 (합리적 이성의) / 주장에 근거한다 // 그것(합리적 이성)이 참된 지식을 끌어낼 수 있다는 / 경험에서

해석

[1]서양의 철학적 전통의 공통된 주제 중 하나는 감각적 지각과 합리적 지식 사이의 구별이다. [2]Plato(플라톤) 이후로, 합리적 이성의 우월성은 그것(합리적 이성)이 경험에서 참된 지식을 끌어낼 수 있다는 주장에 근거한다. [3]<국가>에서의 논의가 설명하는 데 도움이 되듯이, 감각은 오류와 착각의 영향을 받기 쉽기 때문에 지각은 본질적으로 신뢰할 수 없고 오해의 소지가 있다. [4]오직 합리적 담론만이 착각을 극복하고 참된 지식을 가리키는 도구를 가지고 있다. [5]예를 들어, 지각은 멀리 있는 어떤 형체가 실제보다 더 작다는 것을 암시한다. [6]하지

[3]As the discussion (in the *Republic*) / helps to explain, // perceptions are inherently unreliable and misleading // because the senses are subject / to errors and illusions.

부사절 접속사(~듯이) S' V' O' S V C / 부사절 접속사(이유) S' V' C' ★<be subject to A>: A의 영향을 받기 쉽다

논의가 ~듯이 (<국가>에서의) / 설명하는 데 도움이 되(듯이) // 지각은 본질적으로 신뢰할 수 없고 오해의 소지가 있다 // 감각은 영향을 받기 쉽기 때문에 / 오류와 착각의

↳ **부연 설명:** 경험에서 참된 지식을 끌어내는 합리적 이성이 오류와 착각의 영향을 받기 쉬운 지각보다 우월함.

주제문

🔑 참된 지식을 가리키는 것은 합리적 담론임.

[4]Only the rational discourse has / *the tools* (to overcome illusions / and to point towards true knowledge).

S V O / to-v구 병렬

오직 합리적 담론만이 가지고 있다 / 도구를 (착각을 극복하는 / 그리고 참된 지식을 가리키는)

↳ 합리적 담론(합리적 이성)만이 착각을 극복하고 참된 지식을 가리키는 도구를 가짐.

[5]For instance, / perception suggests // that a figure (in the distance) / is smaller / than it really is.

S V 명사절 접속사 S' V' C' (suggests의 O(명사절))

예를 들어 / 지각은 암시한다 // 어떤 형체가 (멀리 있는) / 더 작다는 것을 / 실제보다

[6]Yet, / the application (of logical reasoning) / will reveal // that the figure only appears small // because it obeys the laws of geometrical perspective.

S V 명사절 접속사 S' V' C' (will reveal의 O(명사절)) / 부사절 접속사 (= the figure)

🔑 논리적 추론(합리적 이성)의 적용으로 형체의 진실을 밝힘.

하지만 / 적용은 (논리적 추론의) / 드러낼 것이다 // 그 형체는 작게 보일 뿐임을 // 그것이 기하학적 원근법을 따르기 때문에

↳ **예:** 지각은 멀리 있는 형체를 실제보다 더 작게 인식하지만, 논리적 추론은 기하학적 원근법으로 형체가 작게 보일 뿐임을 드러냄.

[7]Nevertheless, / even after the perspectival correction is applied / and reason concludes // that perception is misleading, // the figure still *appears* small, //

부사절 접속사(시간) S'₁ V'₁ S'₂ V'₂ / concludes의 O(명사절) / 명사절 접속사 S" V" C" / S V C

그럼에도 불구하고 / 원근법적인 보정이 적용된 후에도 / 그리고 이성이 결론을 내린 후에도 // 지각이 오해의 소지가 있다고 // 그 형체는 여전히 작게 '보인다' //

and the truth (of the matter) / is revealed / not **in the perception of the figure** but **in its rational representation**.

S V ★<not A but B>: A가 아니라 B / 전치사구 병렬 (its = the figure's)

그리고 진실은 (그 물체의) / 드러난다 / 형체의 지각에서가 아니라 / 그것(형체)의 합리적 재현에서

↳ **결론(주제문 재진술):** 감각적 지각의 오류를 인지해도 형체는 여전히 작게 보이며, 물체의 진실은 지각이 아닌 합리적 이성의 재현에 있음.

만, 논리적 추론의 적용은 그 형체는 기하학적 원근법을 따르기 때문에 작게 보일 뿐임을 드러낼 것이다. [7]그럼에도 불구하고, 원근법적인 보정이 적용되어 지각이 오해의 소지가 있다고 이성이 결론을 내린 후에도, 그 형체는 여전히 작게 '보인다', 그리고 그 물체의 진실은 형체의 지각에서가 아니라 그것의 합리적 재현에서 드러난다.

어휘

philosophical 철학적인
distinction 구별; 차이
sensual 감각적인
perception 지각; 인식
rational 합리적인; 이성적인
supremacy 우월(성)
reason 이성, 사고력; 추론하다
cf. reasoning 추론, 추리
assertion 주장; 단언
extract 끌어내다; 뽑다, 추출하다
inherently 본질적으로, 선천적으로
unreliable 신뢰할 수 없는
misleading 오해의 소지가 있는
illusion 착각, 오해; 환상, 환각
figure 형체, 형태; 수치; 인물
in the distance 멀리 있는
perspective 원근법; 관점
cf. perspectival 원근법적인
correction 보정; 수정
representation 재현; 표현, 묘사
[선택지] outcome 결과
blindly 맹목적으로, 무턱대고

정답 가이드

빈칸 문장으로 보아 물체의 진실이 '어떻게' 드러나는지를 추론해야 한다. 도입부에서 감각적 지각과 합리적 지식 사이의 구별이 나오고, 감각은 오해의 소지가 있지만 합리적 담론은 참된 지식을 가리키므로 우월성이 있다고 설명하고 있다. 이에 대한 예로, 지각은 멀리 있는 물체를 더 작게 느끼도록 하지만, 논리적 추론(합리적 지식)은 그것이 원근법에 따라 작아 보일 뿐임을 드러내준다고 했다. 이를 통해 물체의 진실은 감각적 지각이 아니라 합리적 이성을 통한 진실의 재현으로 드러남을 알 수 있다. 따라서 빈칸에 들어갈 말로 가장 적절한 것은 ⑤ 'not in the perception of the figure but in its rational representation(형체의 지각에서가 아닌 그것의 합리적 재현에서)'이다.

The 주의 빈칸 문장에 도달하기까지 역접 연결어(Yet, Nevertheless)가 두 번 나와서 의미 파악이 어려울 수 있다. '긍정-부정-부정'의 구조로 진행되는 글은 결국 '긍정'의 의미로 귀결된다는 것을 알아두자. 즉 A(긍정: 실제보다 더 작게 보임) - Yet B(부정: 실제로는 작은 것이 아니고 원근법 때문에 작게 보이는 것일 뿐임) - Nevertheless A(긍정: 원근법을 감안해도, 여전히 작게 보임)이므로 말하고자 하는 것은 A이다.

오답 클리닉

① as the outcome of blindly following sensual experience (19%)
감각적인 경험을 맹목적으로 따르는 것의 결과로
감각적 지각은 오류와 착각의 영향을 받기 쉬워 신뢰할 수 없다고 했으므로 물체의 진실을 드러내기 부적절함.

② by moving away from the idea of perfect representation (18%)
완벽한 재현이라는 생각에서 벗어남으로써
완벽한 재현에서 벗어나야 한다는 내용은 없음.

③ beyond the limit of where rational knowledge can approach (17%)
합리적 지식이 접근할 수 있는 곳의 한계 너머에서
진실은 합리적 지식을 뛰어넘는 곳이 아니라 합리적 지식으로 드러난다고 했음.

④ through a variety of experiences rather than logical reasoning (15%) 논리적 추론이 아닌 다양한 경험을 통해
참된 지식은 감각적 경험이 아닌 합리적 이성(논리적 추론)을 통해 얻을 수 있다고 했으므로 글의 내용과 반대됨.

⑤

구문분석 & 직독직해

인지 시간 분리가 기후 문제 인식에 미치는 영향

[1]We understand // that the segregation of our consciousness / into present, past, and future / is both a fiction and an oddly self-referential framework; //

(understand의 O(명사절); S₁ V₁ 명사절 접속사 S′ V′ C′₁ C′₂; A뿐만 아니라 B도)

우리는 이해한다 // 우리의 의식을 분리하는 것이 / 현재, 과거, 미래로 / 허구일 뿐만 아니라 이상하게 자기 지시적인 틀이기도 하다는 것을 //

your present was part (of your mother's future), // and your children's past will be / in part your present.

(S₂ V₂ C₂ S₃ V₃)

여러분의 현재는 일부였다 (여러분 어머니 미래의) // 그리고 여러분 자녀의 과거는 있을 것이다 / 여러분 현재의 일부에

[2]Nothing is generally wrong / with structuring our consciousness of time / in this conventional manner, // and it often works well enough.

(S₁ V₁ C₁ with의 O(동명사구); (= structuring ~ manner) S₂ V₂)

일반적으로 아무것도 잘못된 것은 없다 / 시간에 대한 우리의 의식을 구조화하는 것에는 / 이러한 전통적인 방식으로 // 그리고 그것은 흔히 충분히 효과적이다

↳ **도입:** 현재, 과거, 미래로 시간을 분리하는 것은 허상적이고 편협하긴 하나 잘못된 것은 아니며 오히려 효과적일 수 있음.

주제문

[3]In the case of climate change, / however, / the sharp division of time / into past, present, and future / has been desperately misleading / and has, most importantly, hidden / from view / the extent of the responsibility (of *those of us* (alive now)).

(S V₁ V₂ O₂)

기후 변화의 경우 / 그러나 / 시간을 분명하게 구분하는 것은 / 과거, 현재, 미래로 / 심하게 (사실을) 오도해왔다 / 그리고 가장 중요하게는 숨겨왔다 / 시야로부터 / 책임 범위를 (우리들의 (지금 살아 있는))

🔑 시간 구분이 현재 책임의 범위를 숨김.

↳ 그러나 시간 구분은 기후 변화에 관한 사실을 오도하고 우리가 책임 범위를 알지 못하게 함.

[4]The narrowing (of our consciousness of time) / smooths the way (to divorcing ourselves / from responsibility for developments / in *the past and the future* [with which our lives are in fact deeply intertwined]).

(S(동명사구) V(단수) O 전치사+관계대명사)

🔑 시간 분리가 현재의 우리를 과거와 미래에 대한 책임으로부터 단절시킴.

좁히는 것은 (시간에 대한 우리의 의식을) / 길을 닦는다 (우리를 단절시키는 것으로 가는 / 발전에 대한 책임으로부터 / 과거와 미래의 [사실 우리의 삶이 깊이 뒤얽혀 있는])

↳ **세부 사항:** 시간을 나눠 좁게 인식하는 것은 과거와 미래에 대한 책임으로부터 우리를 단절시킴.

[5]In the climate case, / it is not // that **we face the facts but then deny our responsibility**.

(is not의 C(명사절); S V 명사절 접속사 V′₁ O′₁ V′₂ O′₂)

기후의 경우 / ~이 아니다 // 우리가 사실을 직면하는데도 우리의 책임을 부인하는 것이

🔑 시간 분리가 현실을 제대로 보지 못하게 해 과거와 미래에 대한 책임이 있는지도 모름.

[6]It is // that the realities are obscured / from view / by the partitioning of time, / and so questions of responsibility (toward the past and future) do not arise naturally.

(is의 C(명사절); S V 명사절 접속사 S′₁ V′₁ S′₂ V′₂)

~이다 // 현실이 흐릿해지는 것 / 시야로부터 / 시간을 나눔으로써 / 그래서 책임에 관한 질문이 (과거와 미래를 향한) 자연스럽게 생기지 않는 것

↳ **부연 설명:** 우리는 기후 문제의 현실을 알면서도 책임을 부인하는 것이 아니라, 시간 분리가 현실을 가려 과거와 미래의 책임에 대한 질문이 생기지 않는 것임.

해석

[1]우리는 현재, 과거, 미래로 우리의 의식을 분리하는 것이 허구일 뿐만 아니라 이상하게 자기 지시적인 틀이기도 하다는 것을 이해하는데,(▶ 외부와의 시간의 연속적인 관계성을 보지 못한다는 의미) 여러분의 현재는 여러분 어머니 미래의 일부였고, 여러분 자녀의 과거는 여러분 현재의 일부에 있을 것이다. [2]시간에 대한 우리의 의식을 이러한 전통적인 방식으로 구조화하는 것에는 일반적으로 아무것도 잘못된 것은 없으며, 그것은 흔히 충분히 효과적이다. [3]그러나 기후 변화의 경우, 과거, 현재, 미래로 시간을 분명하게 구분하는 것은 심하게 (사실을) 오도해왔으며, 가장 중요하게는 지금 살아 있는 우리들의 책임 범위를 시야로부터 숨겨왔다. [4]시간에 대한 우리의 의식을 좁히는 것은 사실 우리의 삶이 깊이 뒤얽혀 있는 과거와 미래의 발전에 대한 책임으로부터 우리를 단절시키는 것으로 가는 길을 닦는다.(▶ 현재는 과거로 인한 것이고 현재로 인해 미래가 영향을 받으므로 과거, 현재, 미래는 서로 연관된 것이지만 이를 분리해서 보기 때문에 제대로 보지 못하고 책임지려 하지도 않는다는 의미) [5]기후의 경우, 우리가 (기후 변화) 사실을 직면하는데도 우리의 책임을 부인하는 것이 아니다. [6]시간을 나눔으로써 현실이 시야로부터 흐릿해지고 그래서 과거와 미래를 향한 책임에 관한 질문이 자연스럽게 생기지 않는 것이다.(▶ 시간을 분리하여 연속적인 관점에서 현실을 제대로 파악할 수 없으므로 과거와 미래에 대한 책임도 알지 못하게 된다는 의미)

어휘

consciousness 의식
oddly 이상하게
self-referential 자기 지시적인; 자신에게 언급하는
framework 틀; 뼈대; 체제
structure 구조화[조직화]하다; 구조(물); 체계
conventional 전통적인
division 구분; 분할
desperately 심하게, 극도로; 필사적으로
misleading 오도하는, 오해의 소지가 있는
extent 범위, 정도
smooth the way (발전을 돕는) 길을 닦다
divorce 단절(시키다), 분리(하다); 이혼(하다)
partition 나누다, 분할(하다)
arise 생기다, 발생하다
[선택지] sufficient 충분한
urgent 긴급한

정답 가이드

빈칸이 it is not that 뒤에 있고, 다음 문장은 It is that으로 시작한다. 즉 기후의 경우, 빈칸 'A'가 아니라 다음 문장에서 말하는 'B'라는 의미이다. B를 보면 '시간을 나눠서 보기 때문에 현실을 제대로 보지 못하고 과거와 미래의 책임에 관한 질문이 생기지 않는다는 내용이다. A를 추론하기 위해 앞 내용부터 읽어보면, 시간을 현재, 과거, 미래로 나누는 것은 효과적이지만 기후 변화의 경우에는 그렇지 않고 과거와 미래 발전에 대한 책임을 숨겨서 그로부터 단절시킨다고 했다. 이는 책임을 제대로 지고 있지 않다는 것을 의미한다. 즉 기후 (변화)의 경우, A라는 문제 때문이 아니라 B(현실을 제대로 보지 못하여 과거나 미래의 책임도 인식하지 못해서)라는 문제 때문에 책임을 제대로 지고 있지 않다는 맥락이 되어야 한다. 따라서 빈칸에 들어갈 말로 가장 적절한 것은 ⑤ 'we face the facts but then deny our responsibility(우리가 사실을 직면하는데도 우리의 책임을 부인한다)'이다.

오답 클리닉

① all our efforts prove to be effective and are thus encouraged (20%)
우리의 모든 노력이 효과적이라고 밝혀지고 따라서 장려된다
기후 변화에 대해 노력을 했다거나 효과가 있었다는 언급은 없음.

② sufficient scientific evidence has been provided to us (27%)
충분한 과학적인 증거가 우리에게 제공되어 왔다
과학적 증거에 대한 언급은 없음.

③ future concerns are more urgent than present needs (17%)
미래의 우려가 현재의 필요보다 더욱 긴급하다
기후 변화에 있어 현재와 미래의 중요성을 비교하는 내용은 없음.

④ our ancestors maintained a different frame of time (15%)
우리의 조상들이 다른 시간적 틀을 유지했다
지문에 언급된 framework를 이용한 오답. 조상들의 다른 시간적 틀은 언급되지 않음.

05 + 빈칸 추론 (22학년도 대수능 34번 | 정답률 30%) ②

구문분석 & 직독직해

역사 과학과 대조되는 역사적 통찰의 특징과 목표

[1]Precision and determinacy(S1) are(V1) a necessary requirement(C1) (for all meaningful scientific debate), //
정확성과 확정성은 필요조건이다 (모든 의미 있는 과학적 토론을 위한) //
[and] progress in the sciences(S2(단수)) is(V2(단수)), / to a large extent, / the ongoing process (of achieving ever greater precision)(C2).
그리고 과학에서의 발전은 ~이다 / 대부분 / 진행 중인 과정 (그 어느 때보다 더 높은 정확성을 달성하는)
↳ 대조 A(과학): 정확성과 확정성을 중시함.

주제문
[2]But / historical representation(S) puts a premium on(V) / a proliferation (of representations)(O), /
그러나 / 역사적 진술은 ~을 중시한다 / 증식 (진술의) /
hence [not] on the refinement (of one representation) / [but] on the production (of an ever more varied set of representations).
*<not A but B>: A가 아니라 B — 전치사구 병렬
🔑 역사는 한 가지 진술이 아닌 다양한 진술을 생성하는 과정임.
그러니까 정제가 아니라 (한 가지 진술의) / 생성을 (훨씬 더 다양한 진술 집합의)
↳ 대조 B(역사): 진술의 다양성을 중시함.

[3]Historical insight(S) is(V1) [not] a matter (of a continuous "narrowing down" of previous options)(C1-1), / [not] (a matter) (of an approximation of the truth)(C1-2), //
역사적 통찰은 문제가 아니다 (이전의 선택들을 계속해서 '좁혀 가는 것'의) / 즉 (문제가) 아니다 (진리에 근접함의) //
[but], on the contrary, / is(V2) an "explosion" (of possible points of view)(C2).
반대로 / '폭발적 증가'이다 (가능한 관점들의)
↳ 역사적 통찰의 정의: 진리에 다다르는 것이 아니라 관점이 다양해지는 것을 말함.

🔑 역사적 통찰은 확정성과 정확성을 환상으로 보고 드러내려 함.
[4]It(S) (= Historical insight) therefore aims(V) / at the unmasking of previous illusions (of determinacy and precision) / by the production of new and alternative representations, /
전치사구 병렬
그러므로 그것(역사적 통찰)은 목표로 한다 / 이전 환상의 정체를 드러내는 것을 (확정성과 정확성에 대한) /
새롭고 대안적인 진술의 생성에 의해 /
[rather than] at achieving truth / by a careful analysis (of what was right and wrong / in those previous representations).
*<A rather than B>: B라기보다는 A — 전치사구 병렬 — 전치사 of의 O(명사절)
진리를 획득하는 것보다는 / 신중한 분석으로 (무엇이 옳고 틀렸는지에 대한 / 이전의 진술에서)
↳ 역사적 통찰의 목표: 확정성과 정확성의 환상을 드러냄.

해석

[1]정확성과 확정성은 모든 의미 있는 과학적 토론을 위한 필요조건이며, 과학에서의 발전은 대부분 그 어느 때보다 더 높은 정확성을 달성하는 진행 중인 과정이다. [2]그러나 역사적 진술은 진술의 증식을, 그러니까 한 가지 진술의 정제가 아니라 훨씬 더 다양한 진술 집합의 생성을 중시한다. [3]역사적 통찰은 이전의 선택들을 계속해서 '좁혀 가는 것'의 문제, 즉 진리에 근접함의 문제가 아니라, 반대로 가능한 관점들의 '폭발적 증가'이다. [4]그러므로 그것(역사적 통찰)은 이전의 진술에서 무엇이 옳고 틀렸는지에 대한 신중한 분석으로 진리를 획득하는 것보다는, 새롭고 대안적인 진술의 생성에 의해 확정성과 정확성에 대한 이전 환상의 정체를 드러내는 것을 목표로 한다. [5]그리고 이러한 관점에서 보면, 외부인에 의해 역사적 통찰의 발전은 과학에서처럼 진리에 훨씬 더 많이 근접함보다는, 훨씬 더 많은 혼란을 만들어 내는 과정, 즉 이미 획득한 것처럼 보이는 확실성과 정확성에 대한 계속적인 의문 제기로 진정 여겨질 수도 있다.

어휘

precision 정확성; 신중함
determinacy 확정성, 결정성
necessary requirement 필요조건
progress 발전, 진보; 진행, 진척
to a large extent 대부분은, 크게
ongoing 진행 중인
representation 진술, 설명; 표현, 묘사
put a premium on ~을 중시하다
refinement 정제, 개선; 세련, 고상
insight 통찰(력)
matter 문제, 일; 중요하다
approximation 근접, 근사
explosion 폭발(적 증가)
unmask 정체를 드러내다, 가면을 벗기다

★<regard A as B(A를 B로 여기다)>의 수동형

[5]And / from this perspective, / the development of historical insight may indeed be regarded / by the outsider / 🗝 계속 의문을 제기하는 것이 외부인에게는 혼란을 만들어 내는 과정으로 여겨질 수 있음.

S V

그리고 / 이러한 관점에서 보면 / 역사적 통찰의 발전은 진정 여겨질 수도 있다 / 외부인에 의해 /

as a process (of creating ever more confusion), / a continuous questioning (of ***certainty and precision*** (seemingly achieved already)), /

전치사구 병렬 = 과거분사구

과정으로 (훨씬 더 많은 혼란을 만들어 내는) / 즉 계속적인 의문 제기 (확실성과 정확성에 대한 (이미 획득한 것처럼 보이는)) /

rather than, as in the sciences, / an ever greater approximation to the truth.

전치사구 병렬

과학에서처럼 / 진리에 훨씬 더 많이 근접함보다는

↳ **외부인의 인식:** 확실성과 정확성에 의문을 제기하는 역사적 통찰이 혼란을 만드는 것처럼 보일 수 있음.

illusion 환상, 착각
alternative 대안적인, 대체의
analysis 분석
perspective 관점, 시각
questioning 의문 제기, 탐구
seemingly ~인 것처럼 보이는; 겉보기에는
[선택지] criterion (*pl.* criteria) 기준, 표준
interpretation 해석, 이해
coexistence 공존
reliability 신뢰도, 확실성

정답 가이드

빈칸 문장으로 보아, 역사적 통찰의 발전은 과학처럼 진리에 근접하는 것이 아니라 혼란을 만들어 내는, 즉 '무엇'에 대한 계속적인 의문 제기인지를 추론해야 한다. 앞부분부터 살펴보면, 과학이 정확성과 확정성을 중시하는 반면, 역사적 진술은 다양한 진술의 생성을 중시한다고 했다. 역사적 통찰은 이전의 진술에서 진리를 획득하는 것이 아니라 새로운 진술을 만들어 내서 '이전 환상의 정체'를 드러내는 것이 목표인데, 이는 외부인이 보기에 혼란을 만들어 내는 것으로 여겨질 수 있을 것이다. 따라서 빈칸에 들어갈 말로 가장 적절한 것은 ② 'certainty and precision seemingly achieved already(이미 획득한 것처럼 보이는 확실성과 정확성)'이다.

오답 클리닉

① criteria for evaluating historical representations (26%)
역사적 진술을 평가하는 기준
역사적 진술을 평가한다는 언급은 없음.

③ possibilities of alternative interpretations of an event (27%)
어떤 사건에 대한 대안적 해석의 가능성
역사적 통찰은 다양한 진술을 만들어 내는 것을 목표로 하기 때문에 대안적 해석의 가능성에 의문을 제기하지 않을 것임.

The 주의 빈칸 앞에 의문을 제기한다는 말이 있으므로 역사적 통찰이 반대하는 내용을 골라야 한다.

④ coexistence of multiple viewpoints in historical writing (9%)
역사 저술에서 다양한 관점의 공존
역사적 통찰은 다양한 관점을 중시하므로 이에 의문을 제기하지 않을 것임.

⑤ correctness and reliability of historical evidence collected (8%)
수집된 역사적 증거의 정확성과 신뢰도
역사적 증거의 정확성과 신뢰성이 아니라 진리로 생각하는 정확성과 확실성에 의문을 제기하는 것임.

06 + 빈칸 추론 〈22학년도 6월 모평 31번 | 정답률 24%〉 ③

구문분석 & 직독직해 학문 지적 활동으로서의 지위를 상실한 수집

[1]The growth (of academic disciplines and sub-disciplines, (such as art history or palaeontology)), / and (of particular figures (such as the art critic)), /

S 전치사구 병렬 전치사구 병렬

성장은 (학문 분야와 하위 학문 분야의 (미술사학이나 고생물학과 같은)) / 그리고 (특정 인물의 (미술 비평가와 같은)) /

helped produce principles and practices (for selecting and organizing / what was worthy of keeping), // though it remained a struggle.

V O 동명사 selecting과 organizing의 공통 O (명사절) 부사절 접속사(양보) ↳(= selecting ~ keeping)

원칙과 관행을 만들어 내는 것을 도왔다 (선택하고 정리하기 위한 / 보존할 가치가 있는 것을) //
비록 그것(보존할 가치가 있는 것을 선택하고 정리하는 것)이 많은 노력이 필요한 일로 남긴 했지만

↳ **도입:** 학문 분야와 관련 인물의 성장으로 보존의 원칙과 관행이 생김.

주제문

[2]Moreover, / as museums and universities drew further apart / toward the end of the nineteenth century, // and as the idea / of objects (as a highly valued route (to knowing the world)) / went into decline, //

부사절 접속사(~하면서) S'1 V'1 부사절 접속사(~하면서) S'2 = 전치사(~로(서)) V'2

게다가 / 박물관과 대학이 서서히 더욱 멀어지면서 / 19세기 말경에 //
그리고 개념이 ~하면서 / 사물이라는 (매우 가치 있는 수단으로서의 (세상을 이해하는)) / 쇠퇴(하면서)

collecting began to lose its status (as a worthy intellectual pursuit), / especially in the sciences.

S V O 전치사(~로(서))

수집은 지위를 잃기 시작했다 (가치 있는 지적 활동으로서의) / 특히 과학에서 🗝 수집은 지적 활동으로서의 지위를 잃게 됨.

↳ 특히 과학에서 수집은 지적 활동으로서의 가치를 잃음.

해석

[1]학문 분야와 미술사학이나 고생물학과 같은 하위 학문 분야의 성장, 그리고 미술 비평가와 같은 특정 인물의 성장은 비록 많은 노력이 필요한 일로 남긴 했지만, 보존할 가치가 있는 것을 선택하고 정리하기 위한 원칙과 관행을 만들어 내는 것을 도왔다. [2]게다가, 19세기 말경에 박물관과 대학이 서서히 더욱 멀어지면서, 그리고 세상을 이해하는 매우 가치 있는 수단으로서의 사물이라는 개념이 쇠퇴하면서, 수집은 특히 과학에서 가치 있는 지적 활동으로서의 지위를 잃기 시작했다. [3]과학의 정말로 흥미롭고 중요한 측면은 점점 더 육안으로는 볼 수 없는 것들이었고, 수집된 것들에 대한 분류는 더 이상 최첨단의 지식을 생산할 것 같지 않았다. [4]'나비 수집'이라는 말은 부차적인 학문적 지위의 수행을 나타내기 위해 형용사 '(한낱) ~에 불과한'과 함께 사용되게 될 수 있다.

어휘

discipline 학문 분야[부문]
sub- ((접두사)) 하위; 아래
figure 인물; 수치; 계산(하다)
critic 비평가, 평론가

[3]The really interesting and important aspects (of science) / were increasingly *those* (invisible to the naked eye), //

S1(복수) V1(복수) C1(= the aspects)

정말로 흥미롭고 중요한 측면은 (과학의) / 점점 더 (~한) 것들이었다 (육안으로는 볼 수 없는) //

and the classification (of *things* (collected)) / no longer promised to produce cutting-edge knowledge. 🔑 수집의 가치가 없어짐.

S2 과거분사 V2 O2

그리고 분류는 ((~한) 것들에 대한 (수집된)) / 더 이상 최첨단의 지식을 생산할 것 같지 않았다

↳ **논거:** 과학에서 눈에 보이지 않는 것들이 중요해지고, 수집품은 지식을 생산할 것 같지 않게 됨.

★<come to-v>: v하게 되다

[4]The term "butterfly collecting" could come to be used / with the adjective "mere" / to indicate a pursuit (of **secondary** academic status). 🔑 별로 중요하지 않다는 mere와 쓰여 수집이 주된 것이 아님을 의미함.

S V C 목적(~하기 위해)

'나비 수집'이라는 말은 사용되게 될 수 있다 / 형용사 '(한낱) ~에 불과한'과 함께 / 수행을 나타내기 위해 (부차적인 학문적 지위의)

↳ **예:** 나비 수집은 '(한낱) ~에 불과한'이라는 말과 같이 쓰일 정도로 학문적 지위를 잃음.

principle 원칙; 주의, 신조
practice 관행; 실행(하다); 연습(하다)
worthy 가치 있는, 훌륭한
struggle 많은 노력이 필요한 일; 투쟁(하다)
draw apart 서서히 멀어지다
route 수단, 방법; 경로
decline 쇠퇴(하다); 경사(지다); 거절하다
status 지위, 신분; 상황
pursuit 수행, 실행; 활동[일]; 추구
invisible 볼 수 없는, 보이지 않는
naked eye ((안경 등을 쓰지 않은)) 육안
classification 분류, 구분
promise ~일 것 같다; 약속(하다); 가능성
cutting-edge 최첨단의
mere (한낱) ~에 불과한; 단지 ~만의
secondary 부차적인, 이차적인

정답 가이드

'나비 수집'과 같은 말이 '어떤' 학문적 지위의 수행인지를 나타내기 위해 형용사 'mere'와 함께 사용될 것인지를 추론해야 한다. 학문 분야와 관련 인물의 성장은 보존할 가치가 있는 것을 선택하고 정리하는 원칙과 관행을 만들어냈는데, 세상을 이해하는 수단으로서의 사물의 개념이 쇠퇴하였다고 했다. 눈으로 볼 수 있는 사물의 수집이 가치 있는 지적 활동으로서의 지위를 잃고 눈으로 볼 수 없는 것이 중요하게 된 것이다. 이를 통해 '나비 수집'이 '(한낱) ~에 불과한'이라는 말과 함께 쓰일 만큼 수집의 학문적 지위가 '낮아졌음'을 알 수 있으므로, 빈칸에 들어갈 말로 가장 적절한 것은 ③ 'secondary(부차적인)'이다.

오답 클리닉

① competitive (16%) 경쟁력 있는
수집이 과학에서 경쟁력을 잃었다는 글의 내용과 반대됨.
② novel (22%) 새로운
수집은 새로운 지적 수행으로 볼 수 없음.
④ reliable (18%) 신뢰할 수 있는
수집의 신뢰도가 높다는 내용이 아님.
⑤ unconditional (20%) 절대적인
수집이 절대적인 학문적 지위를 갖는다는 내용은 없음.

07 + 빈칸 추론 (20학년도 6월 모평 34번 | 정답률 27%) ④

구문분석 & 직독직해

인문 적극적 버전과 소극적 버전의 황금률

주제문 ★<not all>: ((부분 부정)) 모두 ~인 것은 아닌

[1]Not all Golden Rules are alike; // two kinds emerged / over time.

S1 V1 C1 S2 V2

모든 황금률이 서로 같은 것은 아니다 // 두 종류가 생겨났다 / 시간이 지나면서

[2]The negative version instructs restraint; // the positive encourages intervention.

S1 V1 O1 S2 V2 O2

소극적인 버전은 자제를 지시한다 // 적극적인 버전은 개입을 장려한다

↱ (= The negative version)

[3]One sets / a baseline (of at least not causing harm); //

S1 V1 O1

하나는 설정한다 / 기준선을 (최소한 해를 끼치지 않는) //

↱ (= the positive version)

the other points toward / aspirational or idealized beneficent behavior.

S2 V2 O2

다른 하나는 가리킨다 / 열망하거나 이상화된 선을 베푸는 행위를

↳ **황금률의 두 종류:** 1. 소극적 버전: 해를 끼치지 않는 기준선을 설정해 자제시킴. / 2. 적극적 버전: 선을 베푸는 개입을 장려함.

[4]While examples of these rules abound, / too many to list exhaustively, //

부사절 접속사(~이긴 하지만) S' V' ★<too ~ to-v>: 너무 ~해서 v할 수 없는

let these versions suffice / for our purpose / here: //

V1 O1(= 콜론(:) 뒤의 내용) C1

이러한 규칙의 예는 아주 많지만 / 너무 많아서 남김없이 열거할 수 없이 //

다음의 버전으로 충분하다고 하자 / 우리의 목적을 위해 / 여기서는 //

해석

[1]모든 황금률이 서로 같은 것은 아니며 시간이 지나면서 두 종류가 생겨났다. [2]소극적인 버전은 자제를 지시하고, 적극적인 버전은 개입을 장려한다. [3]하나는 최소한 해를 끼치지 않는 기준선을 설정하고, 다른 하나는 열망하거나 이상화된 선을 베푸는 행위를 가리킨다. [4]이러한 규칙의 예는 너무 많아서 남김없이 열거할 수 없이 아주 많지만, 여기서는 우리의 목적을 위해 다음의 버전, 즉 "자신이 싫은 것은 다른 사람에게 행하지 말라."와 "타인을 자신처럼 사랑하라."로 충분하다고 하자. [5]해치지 않는 것과 같은 부작위를 통해서든, 아니면 적극적으로 개입함에 의한 작위를 통해서든, 두 버전 모두 다른 사람을 배려할 것을 주장한다. [6]그러나 이러한 황금률이 행위자에게 타자를 배려하도록 장려하는 반면, 그것들은 자신에 대한 이기적인 관심을 완전히 버리기를 요구하지 않는다. [7]자아로부터 멀어지는 의도적인 관심의 이동(▶ 타인을 배려하기 위해 자아가 아닌 타인에게로 향하는 관심의 이동을 의미)은 그럼에도 불구하고 부분적으로는 자신을 가리키는 상태로 남아 있다. [8]소극적인 버전과 적극적인 버전

"What is hateful to you do not do to another" / and "Love another as yourself."

O₂ V₂(명령문) V₃(명령문) O₃

즉 "자신이 싫은 것을 다른 사람에게 행하지 말라." / 그리고 "타인을 자신처럼 사랑하라."

↳ **예:** 소극적 황금률은 '하지 않는 것'이고 적극적 황금률은 '하는 것'임.

★<whether A or B>: A이든 B이든

[5] Both versions insist on caring for others, / whether through acts of omission, / such as not injuring, / or through acts of commission, / by actively intervening.

S V O 전치사구 병렬 전치사구 병렬

두 버전 모두 다른 사람을 배려할 것을 주장한다 / 부작위를 통해서든 / 해치지 않는 것과 같은 / 아니면 작위를 통해서든 / 적극적으로 개입함에 의한

↳ **공통점:** 두 버전 모두 타인을 배려할 것을 주장함.

[6] Yet / while these Golden Rules encourage / an agent to care for an other, //

부사절 접속사(반면에) S′ V′ O′ C′

그러나 / 이러한 황금률이 장려하는 반면 / 행위자가 타자를 배려하도록

↱ (= these golden rules)

they **do not require** / **abandoning self-concern** / **altogether**.

S V O

그것들은 요구하지 않는다 / 자신에 대한 이기적인 관심을 버리기를 / 완전히

↳ 타인을 배려한다고 자신에게 관심을 두지 말라는 것이 아님.

[7] The purposeful displacement (of concern) / away from the ego / nonetheless remains partly self-referential. 🔑 자신에게도 관심이 남아 있음.

S V C

의도적인 이동은 (관심의) / 자아로부터 멀어지는 / 그럼에도 불구하고 부분적으로는 자신을 가리키는 상태로 남아 있다

[8] Both the negative and the positive versions / invoke the ego / as *the fundamental measure* [against which behaviors are to be evaluated]. 🔑 두 버전 모두 자아를 행동 평가의 척도로 중시함.

S V O 선치사(~로(서)) 전치사+관계대명사 S′ V′ C′

소극적인 버전과 적극적인 버전은 둘 다 / 자아를 언급한다 / 본질적인 척도로서 [행동이 평가되는]

↳ **부연 설명:** 두 버전 모두 자아에 관심을 두고 행동 평가의 기준으로 삼음.

은 둘 다 행동이 평가되는 본질적인 척도로서 자아를 언급한다.

어휘

emerge 생겨나다; 나타나다
negative 소극적인; 부정적인(↔ positive 적극적인; 긍정적인)
instruct 지시하다; 가르치다
restraint 자제; 규제; 통제
intervention 개입, 간섭
cf. intervene 개입하다; 방해하다
aspirational 열망하는; 야심적인
idealize 이상화하다
beneficent 선을 베푸는, 도움을 주는
abound 아주 많다, 풍부하다
exhaustively 남김없이, 철저하게
suffice 충분하다
agent 행위자; 대리인, 중개상
self-concern 자신에 대한 이기적인 관심
purposeful 의도적인; 목적이 있는
displacement 이동
self-referential 자신을 가리키는, 자기 지시적인
invoke 언급하다; (법을) 적용하다; 불러일으키다
[선택지] contradiction 모순

⊕ 작위(commission) 의무: 일정한 행위를 해야만 하는 의무

⊕ 부작위(omission) 의무: 일정한 행위를 하지 아니하는 의무(예. 남의 재산을 침범하지 않는 의무)

정답 가이드

빈칸 문장으로 보아, 황금률이 행위자에게 다른 사람을 배려하도록 권장하는 반면, '무엇을 한다'는 것인지를 추론해야 한다. 빈칸 문장이 역접 연결어 Yet으로 시작하므로 앞과는 역접 관계이고 이 문장에 대한 구체적 설명은 뒤에 이어질 가능성이 크다. 이어지는 문장을 보면, 타인을 배려하기 위해 자아로부터 멀어지는 의도적 관심의 이동에도 불구하고 부분적으로는 자신을 가리키는 상태로 남아있다고 했고, 황금률의 두 가지 버전 모두 본질적 척도는 자아라고 했다. 따라서 두 황금률은 다른 사람을 배려하는 동시에 '자신도 배려한다'라는 내용이 되어야 하므로 빈칸에 들어갈 말로 가장 적절한 것은 ④ 'do not require abandoning self-concern altogether(자신에 대한 이기적인 관심을 완전히 버리기를 요구하지 않는다)'이다.

오답 클리닉

① do not lead the self to act on concerns for others (24%)
자신이 다른 사람들을 염려하여 행동하도록 하지 않는다
황금률은 타인을 배려하도록 권장한다고 했으므로 글의 내용과 반대됨.

② reveal inner contradiction between the two versions (26%)
두 버전 사이의 내적 모순을 드러낸다
황금률의 두 버전 사이의 모순에 대해서는 언급되지 않음.

③ fail to serve as a guide when faced with a moral dilemma (15%)
도덕적 딜레마에 직면했을 때 지침으로서의 역할을 하지 못한다
도덕적 딜레마 상황은 언급되지 않았으며, 황금률은 타인을 배려하는 행동 지침의 역할을 한다고 볼 수 있음.

⑤ hardly consider the benefits of social interactions (8%)
사회적 상호 작용의 이점을 거의 고려하지 않는다
사회적 상호 작용에 대해서는 언급되지 않음.

08 + 빈칸 추론 〈19학년도 대수능 34번 | 정답률 30%〉 ②

구문분석 & 직독직해

인지 문화적 재활용을 통한 인간의 기능성 확장

[1]The human species is unique / in its ability (to expand its functionality / by inventing new cultural tools).
S V C / = / <by v-ing>: v함으로써

인간은 유일무이하다 / 능력에 있어서 (자신의 기능성을 확장하는 / 새로운 문화적 도구를 발명함으로써)

[2]Writing, arithmetic, science — // all are recent inventions.

쓰기, 산수, 과학 // 이 모든 것은 최근의 발명들이다

↳ **도입:** 인간은 문화적 도구를 발명해 자신의 기능성을 확장해 나감.

[3]Our brains did not have *enough time* (to evolve for them), //
S_1 V_1 O_1 (them → recent inventions =)

우리의 뇌는 충분한 시간이 없었다 (그것들(최근의 발명들)을 위해 진화할) //

주제문

but I reason // that they were made possible // because **we can mobilize our old areas / in novel ways.**
S_2 V_2 명사절 접속사 S′ V′ C′ 부사절 접속사(이유)
(that → reason의 O(명사절)) *SVOC 문형의 수동형: <be p.p.+C>

그러나 나는 추론한다 // 그것들이 가능하게 되었다고 // 우리가 우리의 오래된 영역들을 동원할 수 있기 때문에 / 새로운 방식들로

↳ 뇌의 오래된 영역들을 새로운 방식으로 이용해 기능성을 확장함.

🔑 시각 영역을 재활용하여 읽는 법을 배움.

[4]When we learn to read, // we recycle *a specific region of our visual system* (known as the visual word-form area), /
부사절 접속사(시간) S V O 과거분사구

우리가 읽는 것을 배울 때 // 우리는 우리의 시각 시스템의 특정 영역을 재활용한다 (시각적인 단어-형태 영역이라고 알려진) /

*<enable+O+to-v(O가 v할 수 있게 하다)>에서 목적격보어인 to recognize와 (to) connect가 and로 연결됨.

enabling us to recognize strings of letters / and (to) connect them to language areas.
분사구문(= and it enables ~) (= strings of letters)

이것이 우리가 일련의 글자를 인식할 수 있게 한다 / 그리고 그것들(일련의 글자)을 언어 영역에 연결(할 수 있게 한다)

↳ **예 1(읽기 학습):** 시각 시스템의 특정 영역을 재활용해 인식한 글자를 언어 영역에 연결함.

🔑 시각 영역(숫자 모양)을 수량 영역으로 연결해 아라비아 숫자를 배움.

[5]Likewise, / when we learn Arabic numerals // we build *a circuit* (to quickly convert those shapes into quantities) — / a fast connection (from bilateral visual areas / to the parietal quantity area).
부사절 접속사(시간) S V O / <from A to B>: A에서 B로

*대시(—)는 앞의 어구(a circuit ~ quantities)에 대한 설명을 이끎.

마찬가지로 / 우리가 아라비아 숫자를 배울 때 // 우리는 회로를 만들어 낸다 (그 모양들을 수량으로 빠르게 전환시키는) / 빠른 연결 ((뇌) 양측의 시각 영역에서 / 정수리 부분의 수량 영역으로의)

↳ **예 2(숫자 학습):** 시각 영역을 수량 영역과 연결하는 회로를 만듦.

*<A as 원급(형용사/부사) as B>:A는 B만큼 ~한/하게

[6]Even *an invention* (as elementary as finger-counting) / changes our cognitive abilities dramatically.
S 형용사구 V O

발명조차도 (손가락으로 숫자 세기만큼 단순한) / 우리의 인지 능력을 극적으로 변화시킨다

↳ **부연 설명:** 단순한 손가락으로 숫자 세기도 인지 능력을 변화시킴.

[7]*Amazonian people* [who have not invented counting] / are unable to make exact calculations (as simple as, say, 6–2).
S 주격 관계대명사 V C

아마존 사람들은 [수를 세는 것을 발명하지 않은] / 정확한 계산을 할 수 없다 (가령 6 빼기 2만큼 간단한)

↳ **반례:** 아마존 사람들은 간단한 계산을 위한 문화적 도구(인지 능력)가 없음.

🔑 기존 영역을 활용해 문화적 도구를 발명하는 것을 '문화적 재활용'으로 지칭함.

[8]This "cultural recycling" implies // that the functional architecture (of the human brain) / results from a complex mixture (of biological and cultural constraints).
S V 명사절 접속사 S′ V′ O′ (that → implies의 O(명사절))

이러한 '문화적 재활용'은 시사한다 // 기능적 구조가 (인간 두뇌의) / 복잡한 혼합물에서 비롯된다는 것을 (생물학적 및 문화적 제약의)

↳ **시사점:** '문화적 재활용'은 생물학적 제약(뇌가 진화할 시간이 부족함)과 문화적 제약(이용할 문화적 도구가 없음) 때문에 기존 영역을 활용해서 기능성을 확장해나가는 것을 의미함.

해석

[1]인간은 새로운 문화적 도구를 발명함으로써 자신의 기능성을 확장하는 능력에 있어서 유일무이하다. [2]쓰기, 산수, 과학, 이 모든 것은 최근의 발명들이다. [3]우리의 뇌는 그것들을 위해 진화할 충분한 시간이 없었으나, 나는 우리가 우리의 오래된 영역들을 새로운 방식들로 동원할 수 있기 때문에 그것들이 가능하게 되었다고 추론한다. [4]우리가 읽는 것을 배울 때, 우리는 시각적인 단어-형태 영역이라고 알려진 우리의 시각 시스템의 특정 영역을 재활용하는데, 이것이 우리가 일련의 글자를 인식할 수 있게 하고, 그것들을 언어 영역에 연결할 수 있게 한다. [5]마찬가지로, 우리가 아라비아 숫자를 배울 때 우리는 그 모양들을 수량으로 빠르게 전환시키는 회로를 만들어 내는데, 이것은 (뇌) 양측의 시각 영역에서 정수리 부분의 수량 영역으로의 빠른 연결이다. [6]손가락으로 숫자 세기만큼 단순한 발명조차도 우리의 인지 능력을 극적으로 변화시킨다. [7]수를 세는 것을 발명하지 않은 아마존 사람들은, 가령, 6 빼기 2만큼 간단한 것을 정확하게 계산할 수 없다. [8]이러한 '문화적 재활용'은 인간 두뇌의 기능적 구조가 생물학적 및 문화적 제약의 복잡한 혼합물로부터 비롯된다는 것을 시사한다.

어휘

expand 확장[확대]하다
functionality 기능(성)
cf. functional 기능적인
arithmetic 산수, 셈
evolve 진화하다; 발달시키다
mobilize 동원하다
novel 새로운, 참신한; 소설
a string of 일련의
Arabic numeral 아라비아 숫자
circuit 회로
convert A into B A를 B로 전환시키다
quantity 수량, 양
elementary 단순한, 간단한; 기본적인
cognitive 인지[인식]의
dramatically 극적으로
calculation 계산; 추정
imply 시사[암시]하다
architecture 구조; 건축(학)
result from ~에서 비롯되다
mixture 혼합물
biological 생물학적인
[선택지] diversity 다양성
stabilize 안정시키다
operate 작동하다; 운용하다
isolated 분리된; 고립된
manner 방식
adapt 적응하다; 조정하다

정답 가이드

뇌가 진화할 시간이 충분하지 않았음에도 문화적 도구(쓰기, 산수, 과학)의 발명이 가능했던 이유를 추론해야 한다. 빈칸 문장 뒤에서 읽기와 아라비아 숫자 학습을 예로 들며, 우리가 시각 시스템의 특정 영역을 활용해 인식한 형태를 각각 언어 영역과 수량 영역으로 연결시킨다고 했다. 문장 8에서 이 학습을 '문화적 재활용'이라고 했는데, 이는 기존 인지 영역을 언어와 수학 영역에 연결해 활용하는 방식으로 볼 수 있으므로, 빈칸에 들어갈 말로 가장 적절한 것은 ② 'we can mobilize our old areas in novel ways(우리가 우리의 오래된 영역들을 새로운 방식들로 동원할 수 있다)'이다.

오답 클리닉

① our brains put a limit on cultural diversity (21%)
우리의 뇌가 문화적 다양성에 제한을 가한다
인간이 문화적 도구를 발명해 기능성을 확장한다고 했으므로 제한을 한다고 볼 수 없음.

③ cultural tools stabilize our brain functionality (38%)
문화적 도구가 우리의 뇌 기능성을 안정시킨다
cultural tools와 functionality를 활용한 오답. 문화적 도구를 발명해 기능성을 확장하는 인간의 능력에 관한 글이므로, 뇌 기능성을 안정시킨다는 것은 적절하지 않음.

④ our brain regions operate in an isolated manner (6%)
우리의 뇌 영역이 분리된 방식으로 작동한다
문장 4와 5의 예에서 뇌의 영역들이 서로 연결된다고 했으므로 틀림.

⑤ we cannot adapt ourselves to natural challenges (3%)
우리는 우리 자신을 자연의 도전에 적응시킬 수 없다
자연의 도전에 대한 인간의 적응 여부는 언급되지 않음.

09 ✦ 빈칸 추론 〈19학년도 6월 모평 34번 | 정답률 28%〉 ②

구문분석 & 직독직해

스포츠 스포츠 규칙의 특징과 의의

*<think of A as B: A를 B로 생각하다>의 수동형

[1] Rules can be thought of / as formal types (of game cues).
규칙은 생각될 수 있다 / 공식적인 유형으로 (경기 신호의)

(= Rules) 🔑 규칙이 시험의 구조(문제와 해결 방법)를 정함.

[2] They(S) tell(V) us(IO) / the structure (of the test)(DO), / that is, what should be accomplished / and how we should accomplish it. (= / 명사절(간접의문문) 병렬)
규칙은 우리에게 알려준다 / 구조를 (그 시험의) / 즉, 무엇이 성취되어야 하는지 / 그리고 그것을 어떻게 성취해야 하는지
↳ **도입:** 경기 규칙은 무엇을 어떻게 성취해야 하는지를 알려줌.

주제문

[3] In this sense, / **rules(S) create(V) *a problem*(O) [that(주격 관계대명사) is artificial yet intelligible]**.
이런 의미에서 / 규칙은 문제를 만들어 낸다 [인위적이지만 이해할 수 있는]
↳ 규칙이 만드는 문제는 인위적이지만 이해할 수 있는 것임.

*부정어구가 문두에 위치하면서 <조동사+S+V> 어순으로 도치됨. 🔑 해당 종목의 규칙 내에서만 특정 행위가 의미를 가짐 → 인위적 성격

[4] Only within the rules of the game (of, say, basketball or baseball) (only(준부정어) 포함 어구) / do(조동사) the activities(S) (of jump shooting and fielding ground balls) / make sense(V1) and take on value(V2).
경기의 규칙 내에서만 (예를 들면, 농구나 야구의) / 행위가 (점프 슈팅과 땅볼을 처리하는) / 의미가 통하고 가치를 띤다
↳ **예:** 점프 슈팅과 땅볼을 잡는 것(규칙이 만든 인위적 문제)은 농구나 야구에서만 의미 있음(이해 가능함).

*<It is ~ that ...> 강조구문으로, 주어(the artificiality ~ the rules)가 강조됨.

[5] It is precisely *the artificiality*(S′) (created by the rules)(과거분사구), / *the distinctive problem* (to be solved), / that gives(V′) sport(IO′) its special meaning(DO′). 🔑 규칙이 정한 인위성이 스포츠에 의미를 부여해 이해 가능하도록 함
바로 인위성이다 (규칙에 의해 만들어진) / 즉 독특한 문제 (해결되어야 하는) / 스포츠에 특별한 의미를 부여하는 것은
↳ 규칙이 만든 인위성이 스포츠에 의미를 부여함.

[6] That(S) is(V) // (*the reason*)(선행사 생략) why(관계부사) getting a basketball through a hoop // while not using a ladder /(S′1(동명사구)) or pitching a baseball across home plate(S′2(동명사구)) // while standing a certain distance away / becomes(V′(단수)) an important human project(C′). (→ is의 C(명사절))
그것이 ~한 이유이다 // 농구공을 링으로 통과시키는 것이 // 사다리를 사용하지 않으면서 / 또는 본루쪽으로 야구공을 던지는 것이 // 일정한 거리를 두고 선 채로 / 인간의 중요한 활동이 되는
↳ 농구와 야구 규칙이 만드는 인위성이 스포츠의 중요 활동이 됨.

해석

[1]규칙은 경기 신호의 공식적인 유형으로 생각될 수 있다. [2]규칙은 그 시험의 구조, 즉 무엇이 성취되어야 하고, 그것을 어떻게 성취해야 하는지를 우리에게 알려준다. [3]이런 의미에서 규칙은 인위적이지만 이해할 수 있는 문제를 만들어 낸다. [4]예를 들면, 농구나 야구 경기의 규칙 내에서만 점프 슈팅과 땅볼을 처리하는 행위가 의미가 통하고 가치를 띤다. [5]스포츠에 특별한 의미를 부여하는 것은 바로 규칙에 의해 만들어진 인위성, 즉 해결되어야 하는 독특한 문제이다. [6]그것이 사다리를 사용하지 않으면서 농구공을 링으로 통과시키거나 일정한 거리를 두고 선 채로 본루쪽으로 야구공을 던지는 것이 인간의 중요한 활동이 되는 이유이다. [7]규칙을 존중하는 것은 스포츠를 보존할 뿐만 아니라 탁월성 창출과 의미 발생의 여지도 만들어 내는 것처럼 보인다. [8]일상적인 삶에서 중요하지 않다고 여겨질 수 있는 행위에 관여하는 것은 또한 우리를 약간 해방시켜서, 보호된 환경에서 우리의 능력을 탐구하는 것을 가능하게 한다.

어휘

formal 공식적인; 형식적인
cue 신호, 단서
artificial 인위적인
cf. artificiality 인위(성)
intelligible 이해할 수 있는, 알기 쉬운
field (공을) 처리하다[잡아서 던지다]
ground ball (야구의) 땅볼
make sense 의미가 통하다; 말이 되다
take on (양상 등을) 띠다, 나타내다
precisely 바로, 정확히
distinctive 독특한, 특수한
hoop (농구의) 링
pitch 던지다; 음조

⁷It appears // that respecting the rules not only preserves sport / but also makes room (for the creation of excellence and the emergence of meaning).

(진주어(명사절); ★<not only A but also B>: A뿐만 아니라 B도; 가주어 V 명사절 접속사 S'(동명사구) V'₁(단수) O' V'₂(단수) O')

~처럼 보인다 // 규칙을 존중하는 것은 스포츠를 보존할 뿐만 아니라 / 여지도 만들어 내는 것(처럼) (탁월성 창출과 의미 발생의)

↳ **의의 1:** 스포츠 규칙에 대한 존중은 스포츠를 보존하며, 탁월성을 창출하고 의미를 발생시킴.

⁸Engaging in *acts* [that would be considered inconsequential / in ordinary life] / also liberates us a bit, / making it possible to explore our capabilities / in a protected environment.

(주격 관계대명사; S(동명사구); 가목적어; V(단수) O 분사구문(= and it makes ~) 진목적어)

행위에 관여하는 것은 [중요하지 않다고 여겨질 수 있는 / 일상적인 삶에서] / 또한 우리를 약간 해방시킨다 / 그리하여 우리의 능력을 탐구하는 것을 가능하게 한다 / 보호된 환경에서

↳ **의의 2:** 스포츠 활동으로 우리는 능력을 탐구하며 해방감을 느낌.

home plate (야구의) 본루
project 활동, 목표; 계획
preserve 보존하다, 유지하다
room 여지; 공간
emergence 발생, 출현
engage in ~에 관여[참여]하다
ordinary 일상적인, 보통의; 평범한
liberate 해방시키다
[선택지] apply to A A에 적용되다
spectator 관중, 관람자

정답 가이드

빈칸 문장 이전의 내용은 경기 규칙에 따라 (경기에서) 성취해야 할 것과 성취 방법이 정해진다는 것이다. 빈칸은 이런 의미에서 할 수 있는 말인데, 이어지는 예와 설명에서, 규칙이 (스포츠 경기에서) 해결해야 할 독특한 문제인 인위성을 만들어낸다고 했고, 스포츠 활동이 인간의 중요한 활동이 되는 이유라고 했다. 따라서, 빈칸에 들어갈 말로 가장 적절한 것은 ② 'rules create a problem that is artificial yet intelligible(규칙은 인위적이지만 이해할 수 있는 문제를 만들어 낸다)'이다.

오답 클리닉

① rules prevent sports from developing a special meaning (22%)
규칙은 스포츠가 특별한 의미를 발전시키는 것을 막는다
문장 5에서 규칙이 만든 인위성이 스포츠에 특별한 의미를 부여한다고 했으므로, 글의 내용과 반대됨.

③ game structures can apply to other areas (16%)
게임 구조는 다른 분야에 적용될 수 있다
점프 슈팅과 땅볼을 처리하는 행위는 농구나 야구에서만 의미가 통한다고 했으므로 틀림.

④ sports become similar to real life due to rules (26%)
스포츠는 규칙 때문에 실제 생활과 비슷하게 된다
문장 8에서 일상에서는 중요하지 않은 행위가 스포츠에서는 규칙에 의해 의미가 있는 행위가 되기도 한다고 했으므로 비슷하게 된다고 볼 수 없음.

⑤ game cues are provided by player and spectator interaction (9%)
경기 신호는 선수와 관중의 상호 작용에 의해 제공된다
선수와 관중 간의 상호 작용에 관한 언급은 없음.

10 ✦ 글의 순서 〈23학년도 대수능 37번 | 정답률 34%〉 ④

구문분석 & 직독직해 법 성공 보수 책정의 방식과 특징

주제문

¹The most commonly known form (of results-based pricing) / is *a practice* (called *contingency pricing*, / (used by lawyers)).

(S V C 과거분사구 과거분사구)

가장 일반적으로 알려진 형태는 (결과에 기반한 가격 책정의) / 관행이다 ('성공 보수 책정'이라고 불리는 / (변호사에 의해 사용되는))

↳ '성공 보수 책정'은 결과에 기반한 가격 책정 방식임.

🔑 주어진 글에 언급된 성공 보수 책정을 구체적으로 설명함.

(C) ²Contingency pricing is *the major way* [that personal injury and certain consumer cases are billed].

(S V C 관계부사)

성공 보수 책정은 주요 방식이다 [개인 상해와 특정 소비자 소송에 비용이 청구되는]

³In this approach, / lawyers do not receive fees or payment // until *the case is settled*, // when they are paid / a percentage of *the money* [that the client receives].

(S V O 부사절 접속사(시간) 관계부사절(보충 설명) 목적격 관계대명사)

이 접근법에서 / 변호사는 수수료나 보수를 받지 않는다 // 소송이 해결될 때까지 // 그리고 그때 그들(변호사들)은 받는다 / 돈의 일정 비율을 [의뢰인이 받는]

↳ **부연 설명:** 성공 보수 책정 방식에 따라 변호사는 소송이 해결된 후 합의금의 일정 비율을 받음.

해석

¹결과에 기반한 가격 책정의 가장 일반적으로 알려진 형태는 변호사에 의해 사용되는 '성공 보수 책정'이라고 불리는 관행이다. (C) ²성공 보수 책정은 개인 상해와 특정 소비자 소송에 비용이 청구되는 주요 방식이다. ³이 접근법에서 변호사는 소송이 해결될 때까지 수수료나 보수를 받지 않는데, 소송이 해결될 때 그들은 의뢰인이 받는 돈의 일정 비율을 받는다. (A) ⁴따라서 의뢰인에게 유리한 결과만이 보수가 지불된다. ⁵의뢰인의 관점에서, 이런 소송들의 의뢰인 대부분이 법률 회사에 익숙하지 않고 어쩌면 겁을 먹기 때문에 그 가격 책정은 부분적으로 타당하다. ⁶그들의 가장 큰 두려움은 해결하는 데 수년이 걸릴지도 모르는 소송에 대한 높은 변호사 수임료이다. (B) ⁷성공 보수 책정을 사용함으로써 의뢰인은 합의금을 받을 때까지 어떤 수임료도 내지 않는 것을 보장받는다. ⁸성공 보수 책정의 이러한 그리고 다른 사례에서 서비스의 경제적 가치는 서비스 전에 결정하기 어렵고, (서비스) 공급자는 구매자에게 금액에 대한 대가를 제공하는 데 있어서의 위험과 보상을 자신들이 (구매자와) 분담하게 하는 가격을 형성한다.

(C)의 마지막 문장에 대한 결과를 설명함.
(A) 4 Therefore, / only an outcome (in the client's favor) / is compensated.
S V
따라서 / 결과만이 (의뢰인에게 유리한) / 보수가 지불된다
↳ **결과:** 의뢰인의 소송이 성공해야만 보수를 받을 수 있음.

(C)에서 언급된 소송들을 지칭함.
5 From the client's point of view, / the pricing makes sense in part // because *most clients* (in these cases) / are unfamiliar with [and] (are) possibly intimidated by law firms.
S V 부사절 접속사(이유) S′ V′1 V′2 with와 by의 공통 O
의뢰인의 관점에서 / 그 가격 책정은 부분적으로 타당하다 // 의뢰인 대부분이 (이런 소송들의) (~하기) 때문에 / 법률 회사에 익숙하지 않고 어쩌면 겁을 먹기

★<take+시간+to-v>: v하는 데 시간이 걸리다
6 Their biggest fears are high fees (for *a case* [that may take years to settle]).
S V C 주격 관계대명사
그들(대부분의 의뢰인들)의 가장 큰 두려움은 높은 변호사 수임료이다 (소송에 대한 [해결하는 데 수년이 걸릴지도 모르는])

(B) 7 By using contingency pricing, / clients are ensured // that they pay no fees // until they receive a settlement.
<by+v-ing>: v함으로써 S V O(명사절)
(A)에서 언급한 의뢰인의 두려움이 성공 보수 책정으로 해결됨.
성공 보수 책정을 사용함으로써 / 의뢰인은 보장받는다 // 그들이 어떤 수임료도 내지 않는 것을 // 합의금을 받을 때까지
↳ **부연 설명(성공 보수 책정의 타당성):** 의뢰인은 특히 높은 수임료를 두려워하는데 성공 보수 책정이 이를 해결해줌.

8 In these and other instances (of contingency pricing), / the economic value (of the service) / is hard to determine / before the service, //
S_1 V_1 C 형용사 hard 수식
이러한 그리고 다른 사례에서 (성공 보수 책정의) / 경제적 가치는 (서비스의) / 결정하기 어렵다 / 서비스 전에 //
[and] providers develop / *a price* [that allows them to share / the risks and rewards (of delivering value to the buyer)].
(= providers)
S_2 V_2 O 주격 관계대명사 ★<allow+O+to-v>: O가 v하게 하다
서비스로 사례를 확장시켜 공급자의 입장에서 성공 보수 책정의 타당성을 설명함.
그리고 (서비스) 공급자는 형성한다 / 가격을 [자신들이 (구매자와) 분담하게 하는 / 위험과 보상을 (구매자에게 금액에 대한 대가를 제공하는 데 있어서의)]
↳ **공급자의 입장:** 서비스의 경제적 가치를 미리 결정하기 어려운 경우 성공 보수 책정을 사용함.

어휘

commonly 일반적으로, 보통
practice 관행; 연습(하다); 실행(하다)
injury 상해, 부상
case 소송 (사건); 경우; 사실
bill 비용을 청구하다; 지폐; 법안
settle 해결하다, 합의를 보다; 정착하다
cf. settlement 합의(금), 해결; 정착
in one's favor ~에게 유리한
compensate 보수[급여]를 지불하다
make sense 타당하다, 말이 되다; 이해가 되다
be unfamiliar with ~에 익숙하지 않다
possibly 어쩌면, 아마
⊕ 성공 보수 책정(contingency pricing): 주로 민사 재판에 승소했을 때 변호사에게 지급하는 보수. 성공 보수를 '승소로 인한 경제적 이익분의 3%'로 책정한다고 하면, 10억 원 반환 소송에 승소하면 의뢰인이 3천만 원을 변호사에게 지급해야 하는 것. 이러한 성공 보수는 긴 재판 과정에서 의뢰인이 경제적 부담을 더는 장점이 있고, 변호사가 승소를 위해 최선을 다하는 강력한 동력이기도 함.

정답 가이드

일반적으로 변호사가 사용하는 성공 보수 책정을 언급한 주어진 글 뒤에는 이에 대해 구체적으로 설명하는 (C)가 와야 한다. 변호사는 소송이 해결될 때 의뢰인이 받는 돈의 일정 비율을 받는다는 (C)의 마지막 내용은 (A)의 Therefore로 연결된 결과(의뢰인에게 유리한 결과만 보수가 지불됨)로 이어지므로 (A)는 (C) 뒤에 와야 한다. 의뢰인들이 높은 변호사 수임료를 두려워한다는 (A)에서 언급된 문제가 성공 보수 책정을 사용해 해결된다고 설명한 후, 다른 서비스로 사례를 확장시켜 서비스 공급자 입장에서 성공 보수 책정을 설명하는 (B)가 마지막에 오는 것이 자연스럽다.

오답 클리닉

① (A) - (C) - (B) (1%)
(A)는 의뢰인에게 유리한 결과만이 보수가 지불된다는 결과이므로 앞에 그 결과를 이끌만한 원인이 서술되어야 하는데 주어진 글은 내용상 (A)의 원인이 될 수 없다.
② (B) - (A) - (C) (13%) / ③ (B) - (C) - (A) (11%)
주어진 글의 contingency pricing이 (B)의 By using contingency pricing으로 연결된다고 생각할 수 있으나, (A)에서 언급된 의뢰인이 높은 수임료를 두려워한다는 문제가 (B)에서 성공 보수 책정을 사용해 해결되는 흐름이 적절하므로 (B)는 (A) 뒤에 와야 한다.
⑤ (C) - (B) - (A) (42%)
서비스의 가치를 미리 책정하기 어렵다는 (B)의 마지막 문장의 내용에서 (A)의 의뢰인에게 유리한 결과만이 보수가 지불된다는 결과를 이끌어 낼 수 없으므로 오답이다.

The 주의 (A)의 Therefore를 보고 글 전체를 결론 짓는 마무리 단락으로 속단하지 않도록 주의해야 한다.

구문분석 & 직독직해

인지 그 자체보다 크게 여겨지는 공간 기준점

주제문

[1]Spatial reference points are larger / than themselves.
S V C
공간 기준점은 더 크다 / 그것들 자체보다

(= 앞 문장)
[2]This isn't really a paradox: // landmarks are themselves, // but they also define / neighborhoods (around themselves).
S1 V1 C1 S2 V2 C2 S3 V3 O3
이것은 사실 역설이 아니다 // 랜드마크는 그 자체이다 // 하지만 그것들은 범위로 정하기도 한다 / 구역을 (그것 주위의)
↳ 공간 기준점인 랜드마크는 주변 구역을 그 범위로 정하므로 그것 자체보다 더 큼.

주어진 글을 구체적으로 설명하는 캠퍼스 랜드마크에 대한 연구 내용이 이어짐.
(A) [3]In *a paradigm* [that has been repeated / on many campuses], / researchers first collect / a list (of campus landmarks) / from students.
주격 관계대명사 S V O
한 전형적인 예에서 [반복되어 온 / 많은 대학 캠퍼스에서] / 연구원들은 먼저 수집한다 / 목록을 (캠퍼스 랜드마크의) / 학생들에게서

★<ask+O+to-v>: O가 v하도록 요청하다
[4]Then they ask another group of students / to estimate the distances (between pairs of locations), / some to landmarks, / some to ordinary buildings (on campus).
S V O C
그런 다음 그들은 다른 학생 집단에게 요청한다 / 거리를 추정하도록 (쌍으로 이루어진 장소들 사이의) / 즉 어떤 장소에서 랜드마크까지 / 어떤 장소에서 평범한 건물까지의 (캠퍼스에 있는)
↳ **연구 내용:** 학생들에게서 캠퍼스 랜드마크 목록을 수집한 후, 쌍으로 이루어진 장소 사이의 거리를 추정하게 함.

is의 C(명사절) (A)의 연구에 대한 결과가 이어짐.
(C) [5]The remarkable finding is // that distances (from an ordinary location to a landmark) / are judged shorter / than distances (from a landmark to an ordinary location).
S V S'(복수) V'(복수) C'
주목할 만한 결과는 ~이다 // 거리가 (평범한 장소에서 랜드마크까지의) / 더 짧게 추정된다는 것 / 거리보다 (랜드마크에서 평범한 장소까지의)
↳ **연구 결과:** 평범한 장소에서 랜드마크까지의 거리가 랜드마크에서 평범한 장소까지의 거리보다 더 짧다고 여김.

[6]So, / people would judge / the distance (from Pierre's house to the Eiffel Tower) / to be shorter / than the distance (from the Eiffel Tower to Pierre's house).
S V O C
그래서 / 사람들은 추정할 것이다 / 거리가 (Pierre의 집에서 에펠탑까지의) / 더 짧다고 / 거리보다 (에펠탑에서 Pierre의 집까지의)
↳ **예:** 사람들은 Pierre의 집에서 에펠탑까지의 거리가 그 반대의 경우보다 더 짧다고 추정함.

★<seem to-v>: v인 것 같다
[7]Like black holes, / landmarks seem to pull ordinary locations / toward themselves, // but ordinary places do not (seem to pull landmarks toward themselves).
전치사(~처럼) S1 V1 C1 S2 V2 반복어구 생략
블랙홀처럼 / 랜드마크는 평범한 장소를 끌어들이는 것처럼 보인다 / 자기 자신 쪽으로 // 하지만 평범한 장소들은 그렇지 않다
↳ **부연 설명:** 랜드마크는 평범한 장소를 자신 쪽으로 끌어들여 가는 거리가 더 짧게 느껴짐.

평범한 장소와 랜드마크 사이의 거리가 다르게 추정되는 (C)의 결과를 가리킴.
(B) [8]This asymmetry (of distance estimates) / violates the most elementary principles (of Euclidean distance), // that the distance (from A to B) / must be the same / as the distance (from B to A).
S(단수) V(단수) O = 동격 접속사 S' V' C'
이 비대칭은 (거리 추정에 관한) / 가장 기본적인 원칙을 위반한다 (유클리드 거리의) // 거리는 (A에서부터 B까지의) / 같아야 한다는 / 거리와 (B에서부터 A까지의)
↳ 거리 추정에 관한 비대칭은 유클리드 거리의 기본 원칙에 위배됨.

★<not necessarily>: ((부분 부정)) 반드시[꼭] ~은 아닌
[9]Judgments (of distance), / then, / are not necessarily coherent.
S(복수) V(복수) C
추정은 (거리에 관한) / 그렇다면 / 반드시 일관성 있는 것은 아니다
↳ **결론:** 거리에 관한 추정이 항상 일관된 것은 아님.

해석

[1]공간 기준점은 그것들 자체보다 더 크다. [2]이것은 사실 역설이 아닌데, 랜드마크는 그 자체이지만, 그것 주위의 구역을 범위로 정하기도 한다. (A) [3]많은 대학 캠퍼스에서 반복되어 온 한 전형적인 예에서, 연구원들은 먼저 학생들에게서 캠퍼스 랜드마크의 목록을 수집한다. [4]그런 다음 그들은 다른 학생 집단에게 쌍으로 이루어진 장소들 사이의 거리, 즉 캠퍼스에 있는 어떤 장소에서 랜드마크까지, 어떤 장소에서 평범한 건물까지의 거리를 추정하도록 요청한다. (C) [5]주목할 만한 결과는 평범한 장소에서 랜드마크까지의 거리가 랜드마크에서 평범한 장소까지의 거리보다 더 짧게 추정된다는 것이다. [6]그래서 사람들은 Pierre의 집(평범한 장소)에서 에펠탑까지의 거리가 에펠탑에서 Pierre의 집까지의 거리보다 더 짧다고 추정할 것이다. [7]블랙홀처럼, 랜드마크는 평범한 장소를 자기 자신 쪽으로 끌어들이는 것처럼 보이지만, 평범한 장소들은 그렇지 않다.(▶ 예를 들어, 에펠탑은 그 주변까지도 범위에 포함하므로 근처에만 가도 다 왔다는 느낌이 듦) (B) [8]거리 추정에 관한 이 비대칭은 A에서부터 B까지의 거리는 B에서부터 A까지의 거리와 같아야 한다는 유클리드 거리의 가장 기본적인 원칙을 위반한다. [9]그렇다면, 거리에 관한 추정은 반드시 일관성 있는 것은 아니다.

어휘

spatial 공간의, 공간적인
reference point 기준(점)
paradox 역설(적인 것)
landmark 랜드마크, 주요 지형지물
define (범위·경계를) 정하다; 정의하다; 규정하다
neighborhood 구역, 장소; 이웃 (사람들)
paradigm 전형적인 예; 패러다임
estimate 추정(하다); 평가(하다)
ordinary 평범한; 보통의
remarkable 주목할[놀랄] 만한
finding (연구) 결과
judge 추정하다; 판단하다
cf. judgment 추정; 판단; 재판
elementary 기본적인; 초보[초급]의
coherent 일관성 있는
⊕ 유클리드 거리(Euclidean distance): 두 점 사이의 거리를 계산할 때 흔히 쓰이는 방법으로 피타고라스의 정리와 비슷함.

정답 가이드

공간 기준점인 랜드마크는 주변 구역을 범위로 정하기 때문에 그것 자체보다 크다는 주어진 글 다음에는 이에 대한 설명으로 캠퍼스의 랜드마크에 관한 연구 내용을 예로 든 (A)가 이어져야 한다. 그 뒤에는 연구 결과인 (C)가 와야 하며, (C)에서 설명한 연구 결과를 This asymmetry of distance estimates로 받아 설명하고 결론적으로 거리 추정이 반드시 일관성 있지는 않다고 끝맺는 (B)가 마지막에 오는 것이 적절하다.

오답 클리닉

② (B) - (A) - (C) (20%) / ③ (B) - (C) - (A) (9%)

(B)의 This asymmetry of distance estimates가 가리킬 내용이 주어진 글에 없으므로 (B)는 주어진 글 뒤에 올 수 없다.

④ (C) - (A) - (B) (22%) / ⑤ (C) - (B) - (A) (20%)

(C)가 The remarkable findings으로 시작한 것으로 보아 앞에는 관련된 연구 내용이 먼저 와야 함을 알 수 있으므로 (C)는 (A) 뒤에 와야 한다.

The 핵심 (A)의 a paradigm에서 부정관사 a가 쓰였으므로 처음 제시되는 내용이고 (B)의 The remarkable findings은 그 결과임을 알 수 있다.

12 + 문장 넣기 〈22학년도 대수능 38번 | 정답률 31%〉 ⑤

구문분석 & 직독직해

경영 로봇 도입으로 인한 노동자의 두려움 완화 방안

[1]Introduction (of robots) / into factories, // while employment (of human workers) / is being reduced, / creates worry and fear.

S(단수) / 부사절 접속사(~하는 사이에) / S′(단수) / V′(단수) / V(단수) / O

도입은 (로봇의) / 공장으로의 // 고용이 (인간 노동자의) / 줄어드는 사이에 / 걱정과 두려움을 불러일으킨다

↳ **도입:** 로봇 도입으로 인한 고용 감소는 걱정을 야기함.

주제문

(①) [2]It is the responsibility (of management) / to prevent [or], at least, to ease these fears.

가주어 V / C / 진주어(to-v구)

(~은) 책임이다 (경영진의) / 이러한 두려움을 예방하거나 최소한 완화하는 것은

↳ 경영진은 로봇으로 인한 고용 감소의 두려움을 예방하고 완화하는 조치를 취해야 함.

(②) [3]For example, / robots could be introduced / only in new plants / rather than replacing humans / in existing assembly lines.

S / V / ~대신에 / than의 O(동명사구)

예를 들어 / 로봇은 도입될 수 있다 / 새로운 공장에만 / 인간을 대체하는 대신에 / 기존 조립 라인에서

↳ **방안 1:** 로봇을 새로운 공장에만 도입할 수 있음.

(③) [4]Workers should be included / in the planning (for new factories / [or] the introduction of robots into existing plants), // so they can participate in the process.

S_1 / V_1 / for의 O(명사구 병렬) / S_2(= workers) / V_2

노동자들은 포함되어야 한다 / 계획에 (새로운 공장에 대한 / 또는 기존 공장으로의 로봇의 도입(에 대한) // 그들(노동자들)이 그 (계획) 과정에 참여할 수 있도록

↳ **방안 1의 부연 설명 1:** 노동자들을 계획 과정에 참여시켜야 함.

(④) [5]It may be // that robots are needed / to reduce manufacturing costs // so that the company remains competitive, // [but] planning (for such cost reductions) / should be done jointly / by labor and management.

may be의 C(명사절) / S_1 V_1 / 명사절 접속사 S′ / V′ / 목적(~하기 위해) / 부사절 접속사(목적) / S″ / V″ / C″ / S_2 / V_2

~일 수도 있다 // 로봇이 필요한 것 / 제조 원가를 낮추기 위해 // 회사가 경쟁력을 유지하도록 // 그러나 계획은 (그러한 원가 절감을 위한) / 함께 행해져야 한다 / 노사에 의해

↳ **방안 1의 부연 설명 2:** 원가 절감을 위한 계획은 노동자와 경영진이 함께 참여해야 함.

직원의 두려움을 완화하는 다른 방안이 also로 추가됨.

(⑤ [6]Retraining current employees / for new positions (within the company) / will also greatly reduce / their fear (of being laid off).)

S(동명사구) / V / O / of의 O(동명사구)

현재 직원을 재교육하는 것은 / 새로운 직책을 위해 (회사 내의) / 또한 크게 줄일 것이다 / 그들의 두려움을 (해고되는 것에 대한)

↳ **방안 2:** 현재 직원들을 새로운 직책을 위해 재교육함.

해석

[1]공장으로 로봇을 도입하는 것은 인간 노동자의 고용이 줄어드는 사이에 걱정과 두려움을 불러일으킨다. (①) [2]이러한 두려움을 예방하거나 최소한 완화하는 것은 경영진의 책임이다. (②) [3]예를 들어 로봇은 기존 조립 라인에서 인간을 대체하는 대신에 새로운 공장에만 도입될 수 있다. (③) [4]노동자들이 그 (계획) 과정에 참여할 수 있도록 새로운 공장에 대한 또는 기존 공장으로 로봇을 도입하는 것에 대한 계획에 포함되어야 한다. (④) [5]회사가 경쟁력을 유지하도록 제조 원가를 낮추기 위해 로봇이 필요한 것일 수도 있지만, 그러한 원가 절감을 위한 계획은 노사에 의해 함께 행해져야 한다. (⑤ [6]회사 내의 새로운 직책을 위해 현재 직원을 재교육하는 것은 해고되는 것에 대한 그들의 두려움을 또한 크게 줄일 것이다.) [7]로봇은 특히 매우 반복적인 단순 동작을 잘하기 때문에, 대체된 인간 노동자는 로봇의 능력을 넘어선 판단과 결정이 요구되는 직책으로 옮겨져야 한다.

어휘

introduction 도입; 소개
cf. introduce 도입하다; 소개하다
employment 고용; 사용
management 경영(진); 관리
ease 완화[진정]시키다; 편하게 하다
plant (제조) 공장; 식물; 심다
replace 대체[대신]하다
existing 기존의, 현재 사용되는
assembly line 조립 라인
manufacturing 제조(업)(의)
jointly 함께, 공동으로
retrain 재교육을 하다[받다]
lay off ~을 해고하다
repetitive 반복적인

[7]Since robots are particularly good at / highly repetitive simple motions, //

부사절 접속사(~ 때문에) ★<be good at>: ~을 잘하다

로봇은 특히 잘하기 때문에 / 매우 반복적인 단순 동작을 //

주어진 문장을 부연 설명하는 내용임.

the replaced human workers should be moved / to *positions* [where judgment and decisions (beyond the abilities of robots) / are required].

S V 관계부사 S′ V′

대체된 인간 노동자는 옮겨져야 한다 / 직책으로 [판단과 결정이 (로봇의 능력을 넘어선) / 요구되는]

↳ **방안 2의 부연 설명:** 노동자를 로봇이 할 수 없는 판단과 결정이 요구되는 직책으로 옮겨야 함.

정답 가이드

주어진 문장은 로봇 도입으로 인한 직원의 해고에 대한 두려움을 완화하는 방안으로 새로운 직책을 위해 현재 직원을 재교육하는 것을 제시하는 내용이다. 첨가를 나타내는 also가 쓰인 것으로 보아, 앞에는 그들의 두려움을 완화하는 다른 구체적인 방안에 대한 설명이 먼저 나와야 한다. ② 뒤에 그 첫 번째 방안이 제시되고 이에 대한 부연 설명이 문장 4, 5에서 이어진다. 그런데, ⑤ 뒤에 나오는 마지막 문장은 주어진 문장의 'current employees for new positions'를 'the replaced human workers'로 받아, 구체적으로 어떤 직책으로 옮겨져야 하는지를 부연 설명하고 있다. 즉, 주어진 문장은 첫 번째 방안에 이어지는 두 번째 방안이고, 마지막 문장에 의해서 부연 설명되므로 ⑤에 들어가는 것이 가장 적절하다.

오답 클리닉

① (4%) 앞 문장의 로봇 도입으로 인해 노동자의 고용이 줄어들면서 야기되는 두려움을 these fears로 받으며 경영진의 책임을 강조한다.

② (12%) 앞에서 노동자의 두려움을 완화하는 것은 경영진의 책임이라고 한 뒤, 해결 방안을 제시하는 내용이다.

③ (22%) 노동자들이 계획 과정에 포함되어야 한다고 앞에서 언급한 방안을 부연 설명하는 내용이다.

④ (31%) ④ 앞 문장에서 언급한 방안을 부연 설명하는 내용으로, 계획 과정에 노동자가 같이 참여해야 한다는 내용이 이어지는 것은 자연스럽다.

The 주의 주어진 문장이 ④에 들어갈 경우, 직책을 옮기는 것에 대해 부연 설명하는 마지막 문장과의 연결이 어색해짐에 주의한다.

13 + 문장 넣기 (22학년도 9월 모평 39번 | 정답률 30%)

⑤

구문분석 & 직독직해

경제 개인의 선호와 더 큰 관심사가 결합된 소비자 집단

주제문

[1]The growing complexity (of *the social dynamics* (determining food choices)) / makes / the job (of marketers and advertisers) / increasingly more difficult.

S(단수) 현재분사구 V(단수) O C

증가하는 복잡성은 (사회적 역학의 (식품 선택을 결정하는)) / 만든다 /

업무를 (마케팅 담당자와 광고주의) / 점점 더 어렵게

↳ 식품 선택에 미치는 사회적 역학이 복잡해짐에 따라 마케팅이 어려워짐.

(①) [2]In the past, / mass production allowed / for accessibility and affordability of products, / as well as their wide distribution, / and was accepted / as a sign of progress.

★<A as well as B>: B뿐만 아니라 A도 S V_1 O_{1-1}(명사구 병렬) O_{1-2}(명사구 병렬) V_2 전치사(~로(서))

과거에 / 대량 생산은 가능하게 했다 / 제품에 대한 접근과 감당할 수 있는 비용을 /

그것들(제품)의 광범위한 유통뿐만 아니라 / 그리고 받아들여졌다 / 발전의 신호로

↳ **대조 A(과거):** 대량 생산은 상품에 대한 접근성을 높이고, 비용 부담을 낮추고, 광범위한 유통을 가능하게 했음.

(②) [3]Nowadays / it is increasingly replaced / by the fragmentation of consumers / among *smaller and smaller segments* [that are supposed to reflect personal preferences].

(= mass production) S V 전치사(~의 사이에서) 주격 관계대명사 ★<be supposed to-v>: v해야만 한다

요즘 / 그것(대량 생산)은 점점 더 대체된다 / 소비자의 파편화에 의해 /

점점 더 작은 부분들의 사이에서 [개인의 선호를 반영해야만 하는]

↳ **대조 B(현재):** 대량 생산이 개인의 선호를 반영하는 작은 부분에서 소비자 파편화로 대체되고 있음.

(③) [4]Everybody feels different and special / and expects *products* (serving his or her inclinations).

S(단수) V_1(단수) C V_2(단수) O 현재분사구

모든 사람은 각기 다르고 특별하다고 느낀다 / 그리고 제품을 기대한다 (자신의 기호를 만족시키는)

↳ **부연 설명:** 오늘날 사람들은 각기 다른 기호를 반영한 제품을 선호함.

(④) [5]In reality, / these supposedly individual preferences end up overlapping /

★<end up v-ing>: 결국 v하게 되다 S V

현실에서 / 개인적 선호라고 생각되는 이런 것들은 결국 겹치게 된다 /

해석

[1]식품 선택을 결정하는 사회적 역학의 증가하는 복잡성은 마케팅 담당자와 광고주의 업무를 점점 더 어렵게 만든다. (①) [2]과거에 대량 생산은 제품의 광범위한 유통뿐만 아니라 그것들(제품)에 대한 접근과 감당할 수 있는 비용을 가능하게 했으며, 발전의 신호로 받아들여졌다. (②) [3]요즘 그것(대량 생산)은 개인의 선호를 반영해야만 하는 점점 더 작은 부분들의 사이에서 소비자 파편화에 의해 점점 더 대체된다. (③) [4]모든 사람은 각기 다르고 특별하다고 느끼며, 자신의 기호를 만족시키는 제품을 기대한다. (④) [5]현실에서, 개인적 선호라고 생각되는 이런 것들은 결국 문화적 감성, 사회적 일체감, 정치적 감성, 그리고 식이 요법과 건강에 관한 관심을 중심으로 확고해지는, 최근에 생겨나고, 일시적이며, 항상 바뀌고, 거의 부족적인 형성물들과 겹치게 된다.(▶ 개인적 선호는 문화, 사회, 정치 등의 여러 관심사를 중심으로 만들어진 부족적인 형성물, 즉 작은 사회적 집단의 선호와 일치한다는 의미) (⑤ [6]개인의 이야기는 더 큰 이야기와 연결되어, 결국 새로운 정체성을 만들어 낸다.) [7]이들 소비자 집단은 국경을 넘어 개념, 이미지, 관습의 전 세계의 널리 공유된 저장소 때문에 더 강해진다.(▶ 개인은 더 큰 이야기에 자신의 이야기(선호)를 더해 새로운 정체성(소비자 집단)을 만들어 내고, 자원을 공유하며 국경을 넘어 번창한다는 의미. 예를 들어 채식주의자들은 전 세계에 있으며, 채식에 대한 다양한 정보를 공유함.)

🔑 주어진 문장의 개인적 이야기와 더 큰 이야기가 언급됨.

with *emerging, temporary, always changing, almost tribal formations* (solidifying / around cultural sensibilities, social identifications, political sensibilities, and dietary and health concerns).

현재분사구 / around의 O(명사구)

최근에 생겨나고, 일시적이며, 항상 바뀌고, 거의 부족적인 형성물들과 (확고해지는 / 문화적 감성, 사회적 일체감, 정치적 감성, 그리고 식이 요법과 건강에 관한 관심을 중심으로)

↳ 개인적 선호(개인의 이야기)는 결국 문화적 감성, 사회적 일체감, 정치적 감성 등(더 큰 이야기)과 겹쳐짐.

🔑 개인적 이야기가 더 큰 이야기와 연결됨.

(⑤ [6]Personal stories connect / with larger narratives / to generate new identities.)

S V 결과(~해서 (결국) v하다)

개인의 이야기는 연결된다 / 더 큰 이야기와 / 결국 새로운 정체성을 만들어 낸다

↳ 더 큰 이야기에 개인의 이야기를 더해 새로운 정체성을 만들어 냄.

🔑 주어진 문장의 new identities를 가리킴.

[7]These consumer communities go beyond national boundaries, / feeding on global and widely shared repositories (of ideas, images, and practices).

S V O 분사구문(= and they feed on ~)

이들 소비자 집단은 국경을 넘는다 / 그리고 전 세계의 널리 공유된 저장소 때문에 더 강해진다 (개념, 이미지, 관습의)

↳ **결론:** 개인의 선호가 더해진 소비자 집단은 개념, 이미지, 관습을 공유하며 국경을 넘어 존재함.

어휘

dynamics 역학; 원동력; 활력
accessibility 접근 (가능성); 입수 가능함
affordability 감당할 수 있는 비용
distribution 유통; 분배
segment 부분, 단편, 조각
serve 만족시키다; 제공하다
inclination 기호; 경향; 경사
overlap 겹쳐지다
tribal 부족의, 종족의
solidify 확고해지다, 굳어지다
sensibility 감성, 감수성
identification 일체감; 신원 확인
dietary 식이 요법의
narrative 이야기
go beyond ~을 넘다
boundary 경계(선)
feed on ~ 때문에 더 강해지다; ~을 먹다
practice 관습, 관례; 실행; 연습

정답 가이드

주어진 문장은 개인의 이야기가 더 큰 이야기와 연결되어 새로운 정체성을 만들어 낸다는 내용이다. 이는 개인적 선호라고 생각되는 것들(개인의 이야기)이 결국 문화적 감성, 사회적 일체감, 정치적 감성 등(더 큰 이야기)과 겹치게 된다는 ⑤ 앞의 문장을 함축해 요약하는 내용이다. 또한 주어진 문장의 new identities를 ⑤ 뒤에서 These consumer communities로 받아 설명하고 있으므로, 주어진 문장이 들어가기에 가장 적절한 곳은 ⑤이다.

오답 클리닉

① (2%) / ② (7%) 과거의 대량 생산과 오늘날 소비자 파편화를 대조해 오늘날 식품 선택을 결정하는 복잡한 사회적 역학을 설명하는 내용이다. ②는 앞 문장의 mass production을 it으로 받아 연결된다.

③ (24%) 앞 문장의 소비자 파편화를 부연 설명하는 내용이다.

④ (38%) 앞 문장의 his or her inclinations를 these supposedly individual preferences로 받아 개인적 선호는 결국 여러 관심사들을 중심으로 굳어진 부족적 형성물들과 겹쳐진다는 내용이다.